*The work of science is to substitute facts for appearances
and demonstrations for impressions.*—Ruskin.

ACTUARIAL MATHEMATICS

By
NEWTON L. BOWERS, JR.
HANS U. GERBER
JAMES C. HICKMAN
DONALD A. JONES
CECIL J. NESBITT

Published by
THE SOCIETY OF ACTUARIES
1997

Library of Congress Cataloging-in-Publication Data

Actuarial mathematics / by Newton L. Bowers . . . [et al.].
    p.   cm.
   Includes bibliographical references and index.
   ISBN 0–938959–46–8 (alk. paper)
   1. Insurance—Mathematics. I. Bowers, Newton L., 1933–
HG8781.A26 1997
368'.01—dc21   97-8528
                                                 CIP

Second Edition

Printed in the United States of America
12 11 10 09 08   10 9 8 7 6

Edited by David Anderson
Society of Actuaries Liaisons:
   Judy F. Anderson, F.S.A., Staff Fellow, Actuarial Education
   Jill Arce, Managing Editor
Cover and interior design by Word Management, Highland Park, Ill., and Stet Graphics Incorporated,
   Schaumburg, Ill.
Typeset by Sally A. Groft at Pro-Image Corporation, York, Pa.
Printed by Edwards Brothers, Inc., Ann Arbor, Mich.

Preface for the Society of Actuaries

The first edition of *Actuarial Mathematics*, published in 1986, has served the profession well by presenting the modern mathematical foundations underlying actuarial science and developing powerful tools for the actuary of the future. The text not only introduced a stochastic approach to complement the deterministic approach of earlier texts but also integrated contingency theory with risk theory and population theory. As a result, actuaries now have the methods and skills to quantify the variance of random events as well as the expected value.

Since the publication of the first edition, the technology available to actuaries has changed rapidly and the practice has advanced. To reflect these changes, three of the original five authors agreed to update and revise the text.

The Education and Examination Committee of the Society has directed the project. Richard S. Mattison helped to define the specifications and establish the needed funding. Robert C. Campbell, Warren Luckner, Robert A. Conover, and Sandra L. Rosen have all made major contributions to the project.

Richard Lambert organized the peer review process for the text. He was ably assisted by Bonnie Averback, Jeffrey Beckley, Keith Chun, Janis Cole, Nancy Davis, Roy Goldman, Jeff Groves, Curtis Huntington, Andre L'Esperance, Graham Lord, Esther Portnoy, David Promislow, Elias Shiu, McKenzie Smith, and Judy Strachan.

The Education and Examination Committee, the Peer Review Team, and all others involved in the revision of this text are most appreciative of the efforts of Professors Bowers, Hickman and Jones toward the education of actuaries.

DAVID M. HOLLAND
President

ALAN D. FORD
General Chairperson
Education and Examination
Steering and Coordinating Committee

Table of Contents

AUTHORS' BIOGRAPHIES

NEWTON L. BOWERS, JR., Ph.D., F.S.A., M.A.A.A., received a B.S. from Yale University and a Ph.D. from the University of Minnesota. After his graduate studies, he joined the faculty at the University of Michigan and later moved to Drake University. He held the position of Ellis and Nelle Levitt Professor of Actuarial Science until his retirement in 1996.

HANS U. GERBER, Ph.D., A.S.A., received the Ph.D. degree from the Swiss Federal Institute of Technology. He has been a member of the faculty at the Universities of Michigan and Rochester. Since 1981 he has been on the faculty at the Business School, University of Lausanne, where he is currently head of the Institute of Actuarial Science.*

JAMES C. HICKMAN, Ph.D., F.S.A., A.C.A.S., M.A.A.A., received a B.A. from Simpson College and a Ph.D. from the University of Iowa. He was a member of the faculty at the University of Iowa and at the University of Wisconsin, Madison, until his retirement in 1993. For five years he was Dean of the School of Business at Wisconsin.

DONALD A. JONES, Ph.D., F.S.A., E.A., M.A.A.A., received a B.S. from Iowa State University and M.S. and Ph.D. degrees from the University of Iowa. He was a member of the actuarial faculty at the University of Michigan and a working partner of Ann Arbor Actuaries until 1990 when he became Director of the Actuarial Science Program at Oregon State University.

CECIL J. NESBITT, Ph.D., F.S.A., M.A.A.A., received his mathematical education at the University of Toronto and the Institute for Advanced Study in Princeton. He taught actuarial mathematics at the University of Michigan from 1938 to 1980. He served the Society of Actuaries from 1985 to 1987 as Vice-President for Research and Studies. Professor Nesbitt died in 2001.*

*Professors Gerber and Nesbitt were involved as consultants with the revisions incorporated in the second edition.

AUTHORS' INTRODUCTIONS AND GUIDE TO STUDY

Introduction to First Edition*

This text represents a first step in communicating the revolution in the actuarial profession that is taking place in this age of high-speed computers. During the short period of time since the invention of the microchip, actuaries have been freed from numerous constraints of primitive computing devices in designing and managing insurance systems. They are now able to focus more of their attention on creative solutions to society's demands for financial security.

To provide an educational basis for this focus, the major objectives of this work are to integrate life contingencies into a full risk theory framework and to demonstrate the wide variety of constructs that are then possible to build from basic models at the foundation of actuarial science. Actuarial science is ever evolving, and the procedures for model building in risk theory are at its forefront. Therefore, we examine the nature of models before proceeding with a more detailed discussion of the text.

Intellectual and physical models are constructed either to organize observations into a comprehensive and coherent theory or to enable us to simulate, in a laboratory or a computer system, the operation of the corresponding full-scale entity. Models are absolutely essential in science, engineering, and the management of large organizations. One must, however, always keep in mind the sharp distinction between a model and the reality it represents. A satisfactory model captures enough of reality to give insights into the successful operation of the system it represents.

The insurance models developed in this text have proved useful and have deepened our insights about insurance systems. Nevertheless, we need to always keep

---

*Chapter references and nomenclature have been changed to be in accord with the second edition. These changes are indicated by italics.

before us the idea that real insurance systems operate in an environment that is more complex and dynamic than the models studied here. Because models are only approximations of reality, the work of model building is never done; approximations can be improved and reality may shift. It is a continuing endeavor of any scientific discipline to revise and update its basic models. Actuarial science is no exception.

Actuarial science developed at a time when mathematical tools (probability and calculus, in particular), the necessary data (especially mortality data in the form of life tables), and the socially perceived need (to protect families and businesses from the financial consequences of untimely death) coexisted. The models constructed at the genesis of actuarial science are still useful. However, the general environment in which actuarial science exists continues to change, and it is necessary to periodically restate the fundamentals of actuarial science in response to these changes.

We illustrate this with three examples:
1. The insurance needs of modern societies are evolving, and, in response, new systems of employee benefits and social insurance have developed. New models for these systems have been needed and constructed.
2. Mathematics has also evolved, and some concepts that were not available for use in building the original foundations of actuarial science are now part of a general mathematics education. If actuarial science is to remain in the mainstream of the applied sciences, it is necessary to recast basic models in the language of contemporary mathematics.
3. Finally, as previously stated, the development of high-speed computing equipment has greatly increased the ability to manipulate complex models. This has far-reaching consequences for the degree of completeness that can be incorporated into actuarial models.

This work features models that are fundamental to the current practice of actuarial science. They are explored with tools acquired in the study of mathematics, in particular, undergraduate level calculus and probability. The proposition guiding Chapters 1–14 is that there is a set of basic models at the heart of actuarial science that should be studied by all students aspiring to practice within any of the various actuarial specialities. These models are constructed using only a limited number of ideas. We will find many relationships among those models that lead to a unity in the foundations of actuarial science. These basic models are followed, in Chapters 15–21, by some more elaborate models particularly appropriate to life insurance and pensions.

While this book is intended to be comprehensive, it is not meant to be exhaustive. In order to avoid any misunderstanding, we will indicate the limitations of the text:
- Mathematical ideas that could unify and, in some cases, simplify the ideas presented, but which are not included in typical undergraduate courses, are not used. For example, moment generating functions, but not characteristic functions, are used in developments regarding probability distributions. Stieltjes integrals, which could be used in some cases to unify the presentation

of discrete and continuous cases, are not used because of this basic decision on mathematical prerequisites.

- The chapters devoted to life insurance stress the randomness of the time at which a claim payment must be made. In the same chapters, the interest rates used to convert future payments to a present value are considered deterministic and are usually taken as constants. In view of the high volatility possible in interest rates, it is natural to ask why probability models for interest rates were not incorporated. Our answer is that the mathematics of life contingencies on a probabilistic foundation (except for interest) does not involve ideas beyond those covered in an undergraduate program. On the other hand, the modeling of interest rates requires ideas from economics and statistics that are not included in the prerequisites of this volume. In addition, there are some technical problems in building models to combine random interest and random time of claim that are in the process of being solved.
- Methods for estimating the parameters of basic actuarial models from observations are not covered. For example, the construction of life tables is not discussed.
- This is not a text on computing. The issues involved in optimizing the organization of input data and computation in actuarial models are not discussed. This is a rapidly changing area, seemingly best left for readers to resolve as they choose in light of their own resources.
- Many important actuarial problems created by long-term practice and insurance regulation are not discussed. This is true in sections treating topics such as premiums actually charged for life insurance policies, costs reported for pensions, restrictions on benefit provisions, and financial reporting as required by regulators.
- Ideas that lead to interesting puzzles, but which do not appear in basic actuarial models, are avoided. Average age at death problems for a stationary population do not appear for this reason.

This text has a number of features that distinguish it from previous fine textbooks on life contingencies. A number of these features represent decisions by the authors on material to be included and will be discussed under headings suggestive of the topics involved.

Probability Approach

As indicated earlier, the sharpest break between the approach taken here and that taken in earlier English language textbooks on actuarial mathematics is the much fuller use of a probabilistic approach in the treatment of the mathematics of life contingencies. Actuaries have usually written and spoken of applying probabilities in their models, but their results could be, and often were, obtained by a deterministic rate approach. In this work, the treatment of life contingencies is based on the assumption that time-until-death is a continuous-type random variable. This admits a rich field of random variable concepts such as distribution function, probability density function, expected value, variance, and moment generating function. This approach is timely, based on the availability of high-speed computers, and is called for, based on the observation that the economic role of life insurance and pensions can be best seen when the random value of time-until-death is stressed. Also, these probability ideas are now part of general education in mathematics, and a fuller realization thereof relates life contingencies to other fields of applied probability, for example, reliability theory in engineering.

Additionally, the deterministic rate approach is described for completeness and is a tool in some developments. However, the results obtained from using a deterministic model usually can be obtained as expected values in a probabilistic model.

Integration with Risk Theory

Risk theory is defined as the study of deviations of financial results from those expected and methods of avoiding inconvenient consequences from such deviations. The probabilistic approach to life contingencies makes it easy to incorporate long-term contracts into risk theory models and, in fact, makes life contingencies only a part, but a very important one, of risk theory. Ruin theory, another important part of risk theory, is included as it provides insight into one source, the insurance claims, of adverse long-term financial deviations. This source is the most unique aspect of models for insurance enterprises.

Utility Theory

This text contains topics on the economics of insurance. The goal is to provide a motivation, based on a normative theory of individual behavior in the face of uncertainty, for the study of insurance models. Although the models used are highly simplified, they lead to insights into the economic role of insurance, and to an appreciation of some of the issues that arise in making insurance decisions.

Consistent Assumptions

The assumption of a uniform distribution of deaths in each year of age is consistently used to evaluate actuarial functions at nonintegral ages. This eliminates some of the anomalies that have been observed when inconsistent assumptions are applied in situations involving high interest rates.

Newton L. Bowers
Hans U. Gerber
James C. Hickman
Donald A. Jones
Cecil J. Nesbitt

Introduction to Second Edition

Actuarial science is not static. In the time since the publication of the first edition of *Actuarial Mathematics*, actuarial science has absorbed additional ideas from economics and the mathematical sciences. At the same time, computing and communications have become cheaper and faster, and this has helped to make feasible more complex actuarial models. During this period the financial risks that modern societies seek to manage have also altered as a result of the globalization of business, technological advances, and political shifts that have changed public policies.

It would be impossible to capture the full effect of all these changes in the revision of a basic textbook. Our objective is more modest, but we hope that it is realistic. This edition is a step in an ongoing process of adaptation designed to keep the fundamentals of actuarial science current with changing realities.

In the second edition, changes in notation and nomenclature appear in almost every section. There are also basic changes from the first edition that should be listed.

1. Commutation functions, a classic tool in actuarial calculations, are not used. This is in response to the declining advantages of these functions in an age when interest rates are often viewed as random variables, or as varying deterministically, and the probability distribution of time until decrement may depend on variables other than attained age. Starting in Chapter 3, exercises that illustrate actuarial calculations using recursion formulas that can be implemented with current software are introduced. It is logically necessary that the challenge of implementing tomorrow's software is left to the reader.

2. Utility theory is no longer confined to the first chapter. Examples are given that illustrate how utility theory can be employed to construct consistent models for premiums and reserves that differ from the conventional model that implicitly depends on linear utility of wealth.

3. In the first edition readers were seldom asked to consider more than the first and second moments of loss random variables. In this edition, following the intellectual path used earlier in physics and statistics, the distribution functions and probability density functions of loss variables are illustrated.

4. The basic material on reserves is now presented in two chapters. This facilitates a more complete development of the theory of reserves for general life insurances with varying premiums and benefits.

5. In recent years considerable actuarial research has been done on joint distributions for several future lifetime random variables where mutual independence is not assumed. This work influences the chapters on multiple life actuarial functions and multiple decrement theory.

6. There are potentially serious estimation and interpretation problems in multiple decrement theory when the random times until decrement for competing causes of decrement are not independent. Those problems are illustrated in the second edition.

7. The applications of multiple decrement theory have been consolidated. No attempt is made to illustrate in this basic textbook the variations in benefit formulas driven by rapid changes in pension practice and regulation.

8. The confluence of new research and computing capabilities has increased the use of recursive formulas in calculating the distribution of total losses derived from risk theory models. This development has influenced Chapter 12.

9. The material on pricing life insurance with death and withdrawal benefits and accounting for life insurance operations has been reorganized. Business and regulatory considerations have been concentrated in one chapter, and the foundations of accounting and provisions for expenses in an earlier chapter. The discussion of regulation has been limited to general issues and options for addressing these issues. No attempt has been made to present a definitive interpretation of regulation for any nation, province, or state.

10. The models for some insurance products that are no longer important in the market have been deleted. Models for new products, such as accelerated benefits for terminal illness or long-term care, are introduced.

11. The final chapter contains a brief introduction to simple models in which interest rates are random variables. In addition, ideas for managing interest rate risk are discussed. It is hoped that this chapter will provide a bridge to recent developments within the intersection of actuarial mathematics and financial economics.

As the project of writing this second edition ends, it is clear that a significant new development is under way. This new endeavor is centered on the creation of general models for managing the risks to individuals and organizations created by uncertain future cash flows when the uncertainty derives from any source. This blending of the actuarial/statistical approach to building models for financial security systems with the approach taken in financial economics is a worthy assignment for the next cohort of actuarial students.

Newton L. Bowers
James C. Hickman
Donald A. Jones

Guide to Study

The reader can consider this text as covering the two branches of risk theory. Individual risk theory views each policy as a unit and allows construction of a model for a group of policies by adding the financial results for the separate policies in the group. Collective risk theory uses a probabilistic model for total claims that avoids the step of adding the results for individual policies. This distinction is sometimes difficult to maintain in practice. The chapters, however, can be classified as illustrated below.

Chapters Classified by Branch of Risk Theory

Individual Risk Theory	Collective Risk Theory
1, 2, 3, 4, 5, 6, 7, 8, 9, 10, 11, 15, 16, 17, 18, 21	12, 13, 14, 19, 20

It is also possible to divide insurance models into those appropriate for short-term insurance, where investment income is not a significant factor, and long-term insurance, where investment income is important. The following classification scheme provides this division of chapters along with an additional division of long-term models between those for life insurance and those for pensions.

Chapters Classified by Term of Insurance and Field of Application

	Long-Term Insurances	
Short-Term Insurances	Life Insurance	Pensions
1, 2, 12, 13, 14	3, 4, 5, 6, 7, 8, 9, 10, 11, 15, 16, 17, 18, 21	9, 10, 11, 19, 20, 21

The selection of topics and their organization do not follow a traditional pattern. As stated previously, the new organization arose from the goal to first cover material considered basic for all actuarial students (Chapters 1–14) and then to include a more in-depth treatment of selected topics for students specializing in life insurance and pensions (Chapters 15–21).

The discussion in Chapter 1 is devoted to two ideas: that random events can disrupt the plans of decision makers and that insurance systems are designed to reduce the adverse financial effects of these events. To illustrate the latter, single insurance policies are discussed and convenient, if not necessarily realistic, distributions of the loss random variable are used. In subsequent chapters, more detailed models are constructed for use with insurance systems.

In Chapter 2, the individual risk model is developed, first in regard to single policies, then in regard to a portfolio of policies. In this model, a random variable, S, the total claims in a single period, is the sum of a fixed number of independent random variables, each of which is associated with a single policy. Each component of the sum S can take either the value 0 or a random claim amount in the course of a single period.

From the viewpoint of risk theory, the ideas developed in Chapters 3 through 11 can be seen as extending the ideas of Chapter 2. Instead of considering the potential claims in a short period from an individual policy, we consider loss variables that take into account the financial results of several periods. Since such random variables are no longer restricted to a short time period, they reflect the time value of money. For groups of individuals, we can then proceed, as in

Chapter 2, to use an approximation, such as the normal approximation, to make probability statements about the sum of the random variables that are associated with the individual members.

In Chapter 3, time-of-death is treated as a continuous random variable, and, after defining the probability density function, several features of the probability distribution are introduced and explored. In Chapters 4 and 5, life insurances and annuities are introduced, and the present values of the benefits are expressed as functions of the time-of-death. Several characteristics of the distributions of the present value of future benefits are examined. In Chapter 6, the equivalence principle is introduced and used to define and evaluate periodic benefit premiums. In Chapters 7 and 8, the prospective future loss on a contract already in force is investigated. The distribution of future loss is examined, and the benefit reserve is defined as the expected value of this loss. In Chapter 9, annuity and insurance contracts involving two lives are studied. (Discussion of more advanced multiple life theory is deferred until Chapter 18.) The discussion in Chapters 10 and 11 investigates a more realistic model in which several causes of decrement are possible. In Chapter 10, basic theory is examined, whereas in Chapter 11 the theory is applied to calculating actuarial present values for a variety of insurance and pension benefits.

In Chapter 12, the collective risk model is developed with respect to single-period considerations of a portfolio of policies. The distribution of total claims for the period is developed by postulating the characteristics of the portfolio in the aggregate rather than as a sum of individual policies. In Chapter 13, these ideas are extended to a continuous-time model that can be used to study solvency requirements over a long time period. Applications of risk theory to insurance models are given an overview in Chapter 14.

Elaboration of the individual model to incorporate operational constraints such as acquisition and administrative expenses, accounting requirements, and the effects of contract terminations is treated in Chapters 15 and 16. In Chapter 17, individual risk theory models are used to obtain actuarial present values, benefit and contract premiums, and benefit reserves for selected special plans including life annuities with certain periods that depend on the contract premium, variable and flexible products, and accelerated benefits. In Chapter 18, the elementary models for plans involving two lives are extended to incorporate contingencies based on a larger number of lives and more complicated benefits.

In Chapter 19, concepts of population theory are introduced. These concepts are then applied to tracing the progress of life insurance benefits provided on a group, or population, basis. The tools from population theory are applied to tracing the progress of retirement income benefits provided on a group basis in Chapter 20.

Chapter 21 is a step into the future. Interest rates are assumed to be random variables. Several stochastic models are introduced and then integrated into models for basic insurance and annuity contracts.

The following diagram illustrates the prerequisite structure of the chapters. The arrows indicate the direction of the flow. For any chapter, the chapters that are upstream are prerequisite. For example, Chapter 6 has as prerequisites Chapters 1, 2, 3, 4, and 5.

Interrelationships of Chapters

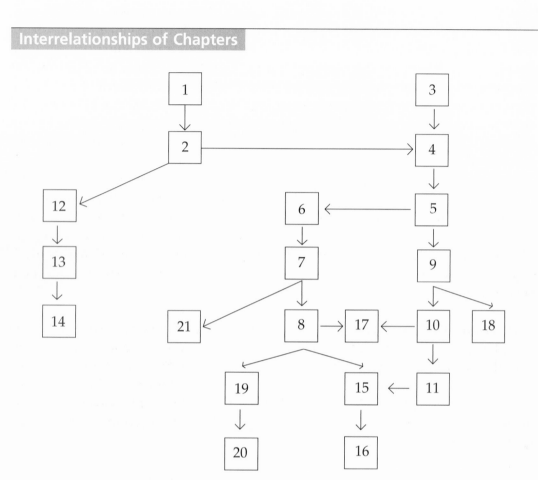

We have a couple of hints for the reader, particularly for one for whom the material is new. The exercises are an important part of the text and include material not covered in the main discussion. In some cases, hints will be offered to aid in the solution. Answers to all exercises are provided except where the answer is given in the formulation of the problem. Writing computer programs and using electronic spreadsheets or mathematical software for the evaluation of basic formulas are excellent ways of enhancing the level of understanding of the material. The student is encouraged to use these tools to work through the computing exercises.

We conclude these introductory comments with some miscellaneous information on the format of the text. First, each chapter concludes with a reference section that provides guidance to those who wish to pursue further study of the topics covered in the chapter. These sections also contain comments that relate the ideas used in insurance models to those used in other areas.

Second, Chapters 1, 12, 13, 14, and 18 contain some theorems with their proofs included as chapter appendices. These proofs are included for completeness, but are not essential to an understanding of the material. They may be excluded from study at the reader's discretion. Exercises associated with these appendices should also be considered optional.

Third, general appendices appear at the end of the text. Included here are numerical tables for computations for examples and exercises, an index to notation, a discussion of general rules for writing actuarial symbols, reference citations, answers to exercises, a subject index, and supplemental mathematical formulas that are not assumed to be a part of the mathematical prerequisites.

Fourth, we observe two notational conventions. A referenced random variable, X, for example, is designated with a capital letter. This notational convention is not used in older texts on probability theory. It will be our practice, in order to indicate the correspondence, to use the appropriate random variable symbol as a subscript on functions and operators that depend on the random variable. We will use the general abbreviation *log* to refer to natural (base e) logarithms, because a distinction between natural and common logarithms is unnecessary in the examples and exercises. We assume the natural logarithm in our computations.

Fifth, currencies such as dollar, pound, lira, or yen are not specified in the examples and exercises due to the international character of the required computations.

Finally, since we have discussed prerequisites to this work, some major theorems from undergraduate calculus and probability theory will be used without review or restatement in the discussions and exercises.

THE ECONOMICS OF INSURANCE

1.1   Introduction

Each of us makes plans and has expectations about the path his or her life will follow. However, experience teaches that plans will not unfold with certainty and sometimes expectations will not be realized. Occasionally plans are frustrated because they are built on unrealistic assumptions. In other situations, fortuitous circumstances interfere. Insurance is designed to protect against serious financial reversals that result from random events intruding on the plans of individuals.

We should understand certain basic limitations on insurance protection. First, it is restricted to reducing those consequences of random events that can be measured in monetary terms. Other types of losses may be important, but not amenable to reduction through insurance.

For example, pain and suffering may be caused by a random event. However, insurance coverages designed to compensate for pain and suffering often have been troubled by the difficulty of measuring the loss in monetary units. On the other hand, economic losses can be caused by events such as property set on fire by its owner. Whereas the monetary terms of such losses may be easy to define, the events are not insurable because of the nonrandom nature of creating the losses.

A second basic limitation is that insurance does not directly reduce the probability of loss. The existence of windstorm insurance will not alter the probability of a destructive storm. However, a well-designed insurance system often provides financial incentives for loss prevention activities. An insurance product that encouraged the destruction of property or the withdrawal of a productive person from the labor force would affect the probability of these economically adverse events. Such insurance would not be in the public interest.

Several examples of situations where random events may cause financial losses are the following:
- The destruction of property by fire or storm is usually considered a random event in which the loss can be measured in monetary terms.

- A damage award imposed by a court as a result of a negligent act is often considered a random event with resulting monetary loss.
- Prolonged illness may strike at an unexpected time and result in financial losses. These losses will be due to extra health care expenses and reduced earned income.
- The death of a young adult may occur while long-term commitments to family or business remain unfulfilled. Or, if the individual survives to an advanced age, resources for meeting the costs of living may be depleted.

These examples are designed to illustrate the definition:

An *insurance system* is a mechanism for reducing the adverse financial impact of random events that prevent the fulfillment of reasonable expectations.

It is helpful to make certain distinctions between insurance and related systems. Banking institutions were developed for the purpose of receiving, investing, and dispensing the savings of individuals and corporations. The cash flows in and out of a savings institution do not follow deterministic paths. However, unlike insurance systems, savings institutions do not make payments based on the size of a financial loss occurring from an event outside the control of the person suffering the loss.

Another system that does make payments based on the occurrence of random events is gambling. Gambling or wagering, however, stands in contrast to an insurance system in that an insurance system is designed to protect against the economic impact of risks that exist independently of, and are largely beyond the control of, the insured. The typical gambling arrangement is established by defining payoff rules about the occurrence of a contrived event, and the risk is voluntarily sought by the participants. Like insurance, a gambling arrangement typically redistributes wealth, but it is there that the similarity ends.

Our definition of an insurance system is purposefully broad. It encompasses systems that cover losses in both property and human-life values. It is intended to cover insurance systems based on individual decisions to participate as well as systems where participation is a condition of employment or residence. These ideas are discussed in Section 1.4.

The economic justification for an insurance system is that it contributes to general welfare by improving the prospect that plans will not be frustrated by random events. Such systems may also increase total production by encouraging individuals and corporations to embark on ventures where the possibility of large losses would inhibit such projects in the absence of insurance. The development of marine insurance, for reducing the financial impact of the perils of the sea, is an example of this point. Foreign trade permitted specialization and more efficient production, yet mutually advantageous trading activity might be too hazardous for some potential trading partners without an insurance system to cover possible losses at sea.

1.2 Utility Theory

If people could foretell the consequences of their decisions, their lives would be simpler but less interesting. We would all make decisions on the basis of preferences for certain consequences. However, we do not possess perfect foresight. At best, we can select an action that will lead to one set of uncertainties rather than another. An elaborate theory has been developed that provides insights into decision making in the face of uncertainty. This body of knowledge is called *utility theory.* Because of its relevance to insurance systems, its main points will be outlined here.

One solution to the problem of decision making in the face of uncertainty is to define the value of an economic project with a random outcome to be its expected value. By this *expected value principle* the distribution of possible outcomes may be replaced for decision purposes by a single number, the expected value of the random monetary outcomes. By this principle, a decision maker would be indifferent between assuming the random loss X and paying amount E[X] in order to be relieved of the possible loss. Similarly, a decision maker would be willing to pay up to E[Y] to participate in a gamble with random payoff Y. In economics the expected value of random prospects with monetary payments is frequently called the *fair* or *actuarial value* of the prospect.

Many decision makers do not adopt the expected value principle. For them, their wealth level and other aspects of the distribution of outcomes influence their decisions.

Below is an illustration designed to show the inadequacy of the expected value principle for a decision maker considering the value of accident insurance. In all cases, it is assumed that the probability of an accident is 0.01 and the probability of no accident is 0.99. Three cases are considered according to the amount of loss arising from an accident; the expected loss is tabulated for each.

Case	Possible Losses		Expected Loss
1	0	1	0.01
2	0	1 000	10.00
3	0	1 000 000	10 000.00

A loss of 1 might be of little concern to the decision maker who then might be unwilling to pay more than the expected loss to obtain insurance. However, the loss of 1,000,000, which may exceed his net worth, could be catastrophic. In this case, the decision maker might well be willing to pay more than the expected loss of 10,000 in order to obtain insurance. The fact that the amount a decision maker would pay for protection against a random loss may differ from the expected value suggests that the expected value principle is inadequate to model behavior.

We now study another approach to explain why a decision maker may be willing to pay more than the expected value. At first we simply assume that the value or utility that a particular decision maker attaches to wealth of amount w, measured in monetary units, can be specified in the form of a function $u(w)$, called a **utility function.** We demonstrate a procedure by which a few values of such a function can be determined. For this we assume that our decision maker has wealth equal to 20,000. A linear transformation,

$$u^*(w) = a\, u(w) + b \qquad a > 0,$$

yields a function $u^*(w)$, which is essentially equivalent to $u(w)$. It then follows by choice of a and b that we can determine arbitrarily the 0 point and one additional point of an individual's utility function. Therefore, we fix $u(0) = -1$ and $u(20{,}000) = 0$. These values are plotted on the solid line in Figure 1.2.1.

FIGURE 1.2.1

Determination of a Utility Function

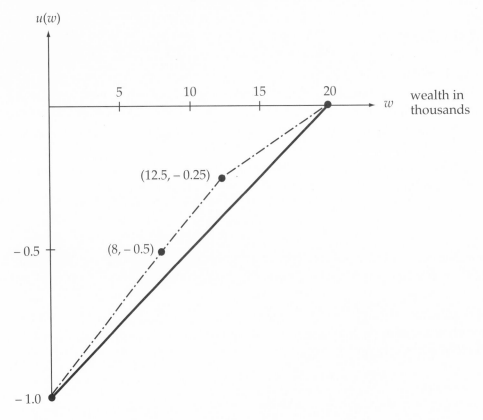

We now ask a question of our decision maker: Suppose you face a loss of 20,000 with probability 0.5, and will remain at your current level of wealth with probability 0.5. What is the maximum amount* G you would be willing to pay for

---

*Premium quantities, by convention in insurance literature, are capitalized although they are not random variables.

---

complete insurance protection against this random loss? We can express this question in the following way: For what value of G does

$$u(20{,}000 - G) = 0.5\, u(20{,}000) + 0.5\, u(0)$$

$$= (0.5)(0) + (0.5)(-1) = -0.5?$$

If he pays amount G, his wealth will certainly remain at $20{,}000 - G$. The equal sign indicates that the decision maker is indifferent between paying G with certainty and accepting the expected utility of wealth expressed on the right-hand side.

Suppose the decision maker's answer is $G = 12{,}000$. Therefore,

$$u(20{,}000 - 12{,}000) = u(8{,}000) = -0.5.$$

This result is plotted on the dashed line in Figure 1.2.1. Perhaps the most important aspect of the decision maker's response is that he is willing to pay an amount for insurance that is greater than

$$(0.5)(0) + (0.5)(20{,}000) = 10{,}000,$$

the expected value of the loss.

This procedure can be used to add as many points $[w, u(w)]$, for $0 \le w \le 20{,}000$, as needed to obtain a satisfactory approximation to the decision maker's utility of wealth function. Once a utility value has been assigned to wealth levels w_1 and w_2, where $0 \le w_1 < w_2 \le 20{,}000$, we can determine an additional point by asking the decision maker the following question: What is the maximum amount you would pay for complete insurance against a situation that could leave you with wealth w_2 with specified probability p, or at reduced wealth level w_1 with probability $1 - p$? We are asking the decision maker to fix a value G such that

$$u(w_2 - G) = (1 - p)u(w_1) + p\, u(w_2). \qquad (1.2.1)$$

Once the value $w_2 - G = w_3$ is available, the point $[w_3, (1 - p)u(w_1) + p\, u(w_2)]$ is determined as another point of the utility function. Such a process has been used to assign a fourth point $(12{,}500, -0.25)$ in Figure 1.2.1. Such solicitation of preferences leads to a set of points on the decision maker's utility function. A smooth function with a second derivative may be fitted to these points to provide for a utility function everywhere.

After a decision maker has determined his utility of wealth function by the method outlined, the function can be used to compare two random economic prospects. The prospects are denoted by the random variables X and Y. We seek a decision rule that is consistent with the preferences already elicited in the determination of the utility of wealth function. Thus, if the decision maker has wealth w, and must compare the random prospects X and Y, the decision maker selects X if

$$E[u(w + X)] > E[u(w + Y)],$$

and the decision maker is indifferent between X and Y if

$$E[u(w + X)] = E[u(w + Y)].$$

Although the method of eliciting and using a utility function may seem plausible, it is clear that our informal development must be augmented by a more rigorous chain of reasoning if utility theory is to provide a coherent and comprehensive framework for decision making in the face of uncertainty. If we are to understand the economic role of insurance, such a framework is needed. An outline of this more rigorous theory follows.

The theory starts with the assumption that a rational decision maker, when faced with two distributions of outcomes affecting wealth, is able to express a preference for one of the distributions or indifference between them. Furthermore, the preferences must satisfy certain consistency requirements. The theory culminates in a theorem stating that if preferences satisfy the consistency requirements, there is a utility function $u(w)$ such that if the distribution of X is preferred to the distribution of Y, $E[u(X)] > E[u(Y)]$, and if the decision maker is indifferent between the two distributions, $E[u(X)] = E[u(Y)]$. That is, the qualitative preference or indifference relation may be replaced by a consistent numerical comparison. In Section 1.6, references are given for the detailed development of this theory.

Before turning to applications of utility theory for insights into insurance, we record some observations about utility.

Observations:

1. Utility theory is built on the assumed existence and consistency of preferences for probability distributions of outcomes. A utility function should reveal no surprises. It is a numerical description of existing preferences.
2. A utility function need not, in fact, cannot, be determined uniquely. For example, if

$$u^*(w) = a\, u(w) + b \qquad a > 0,$$

then

$$E[u(X)] > E[u(Y)]$$

is equivalent to

$$E[u^*(X)] > E[u^*(Y)].$$

That is, preferences are preserved when the utility function is an increasing linear transformation of the original form. This fact was used in the Figure 1.2.1 illustration where two points were chosen arbitrarily.
3. Suppose the utility function is linear with a positive slope; that is,

$$u(w) = a\,w + b \qquad a > 0.$$

Then, if $E[X] = \mu_X$ and $E[Y] = \mu_Y$, we have

$$E[u(X)] = a\,\mu_X + b > E[u(Y)] = a\,\mu_Y + b$$

if and only if $\mu_X > \mu_Y$. That is, for increasing linear utility functions, preferences for distributions of outcomes are in the same order as the expected values of the distributions being compared. Therefore, the expected value principle for rational economic behavior in the face of uncertainty is consistent with the expected utility rule when the utility function is an increasing linear one.

1.3 Insurance and Utility

In Section 1.2 we outlined utility theory for the purpose of gaining insights into the economic role of insurance. To examine this role we start with an illustration. Suppose a decision maker owns a property that may be damaged or destroyed in the next accounting period. The amount of the loss, which may be 0, is a random variable denoted by X. We assume that the distribution of X is known. Then E[X], the expected loss in the next period, may be interpreted as the long-term average loss if the experiment of exposing the property to damage may be observed under identical conditions a great many times. It is clear that this long-term set of trials could not be performed by an individual decision maker.

Suppose that an insurance organization (*insurer*) was established to help reduce the financial consequences of the damage or destruction of property. The insurer would issue contracts (*policies*) that would promise to pay the owner of a property a defined amount equal to or less than the financial loss if the property were damaged or destroyed during the period of the policy. The contingent payment linked to the amount of the loss is called a *claim* payment. In return for the promise contained in the policy, the owner of the property (*insured*) pays a consideration (*premium*).

The amount of the premium payment is determined after an economic decision principle has been adopted by each of the insurer and insured. An opportunity exists for a mutually advantageous insurance policy when the premium for the policy set by the insurer is less than the maximum amount that the property owner is willing to pay for insurance.

Within the range of financial outcomes for an individual insurance policy, the insurer's utility function might be approximated by a straight line. In this case, the insurer would adopt the expected value principle in setting its premium, as indicated in Section 1.2, Observation 3; that is, the insurer would set its basic price for full insurance coverage as the expected loss, $E[X] = \mu$. In this context μ is called the *pure* or *net premium* for the 1-period insurance policy. To provide for expenses, taxes, and profit and for some security against adverse loss experience, the insurance system would decide to set the premium for the policy by *loading,* adding to, the pure premium. For instance, the loaded premium, denoted by H, might be given by

$$H = (1 + a)\mu + c \qquad a > 0, \qquad c > 0.$$

In this expression the quantity $a\mu$ can be viewed as being associated with expenses that vary with expected losses and with the risk that claims experience will deviate from expected. The constant c provides for expected expenses that do not vary with losses. Later, we will illustrate other economic principles for determining premiums that might be adopted by the insurer.

We now apply utility theory to the decision problems faced by the owner of the property subject to loss. The property owner has a utility of wealth function $u(w)$ where wealth w is measured in monetary terms. The owner faces a possible loss due to random events that may damage the property. The distribution of the random loss X is assumed to be known. Much as in (1.2.1), the owner will be indifferent between paying an amount G to the insurer, who will assume the random financial loss, and assuming the risk himself. This situation can be stated as

$$u(w - G) = E[u(w - X)]. \tag{1.3.1}$$

The right-hand side of (1.3.1) represents the expected utility of not buying insurance when the owner's current wealth is w. The left-hand side of (1.3.1) represents the expected utility of paying G for complete financial protection.

If the owner has an increasing linear utility function, that is, $u(w) = bw + d$ with $b > 0$, the owner will be adopting the expected value principle. In this case the owner prefers, or is indifferent to, the insurance when

$$u(w - G) = b(w - G) + d \geq E[u(w - X)] = E[b(w - X) + d],$$

$$b(w - G) + d \geq b(w - \mu) + d,$$

$$G \leq \mu.$$

That is, if the owner has an increasing linear utility function, the premium payments that will make the owner prefer, or be indifferent to, complete insurance are less than or equal to the expected loss. In the absence of a subsidy, an insurer, over the long term, must charge more than its expected losses. Therefore, in this case, there seems to be little opportunity for a mutually advantageous insurance contract. If an insurance contract is to result, the insurer must charge a premium in excess of expected losses and expenses to avoid a bias toward insufficient income. The property owner then cannot use a linear utility function.

In Section 1.2 we mention that the preferences of a decision maker must satisfy certain consistency requirements to ensure the existence of a utility function. Although these requirements were not listed, they do not include any specifications that would force a utility function to be linear, quadratic, exponential, logarithmic, or any other particular form. In fact, each of these named functions might serve as a utility function for some decision maker or they might be spliced together to reflect some other decision maker's preferences.

Nevertheless, it seems natural to assume that $u(w)$ is an increasing function, "more is better." In addition, it has been observed that for many decision makers, each additional equal increment of wealth results in a smaller increment of associated utility. This is the idea of decreasing marginal utility in economics.

The approximate utility function of Figure 1.2.1 consists of straight line segments with positive slopes. It is such that $\Delta^2 u(w) \leq 0$. If these ideas are extended to smoother functions, the two properties suggested by observation are $u'(w) > 0$ and $u''(w) < 0$. The second inequality indicates that $u(w)$ is a strictly concave downward function.

In discussing insurance decisions using strictly concave downward utility functions, we will make use of one form of *Jensen's inequalities.* These inequalities state that for a random variable X and function $u(w)$,

$$\text{if } u''(w) < 0, \text{ then } E[u(X)] \leq u(E[X]), \qquad (1.3.2)$$

$$\text{if } u''(w) > 0, \text{ then } E[u(X)] \geq u(E[X]). \qquad (1.3.3)$$

Jensen's inequalities require the existence of the two expected values. Proofs of the inequalities are required by Exercise 1.3. A second proof of (1.3.2) is almost immediate from consideration of Figure 1.3.1 as follows.

FIGURE 1.3.1

**Proof of Jensen's Inequalities
for the Case $u'(w) > 0$
and $u''(w) < 0$**

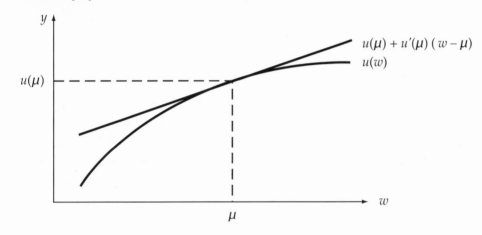

If $E[X] = \mu$ exists, one considers the line tangent to $u(w)$,

$$y = u(\mu) + u'(\mu)(w - \mu),$$

at the point $(\mu, u(\mu))$. Because of the strictly concave characteristic of $u(w)$, the graph of $u(w)$ will be below the tangent line; that is,

$$u(w) \leq u(\mu) + u'(\mu)(w - \mu) \qquad (1.3.4)$$

for all values of w. If w is replaced by the random variable X, and the expectation is taken on each side of the inequality (1.3.4), we have $E[u(X)] \leq u(\mu)$.

This basic inequality has several applications in actuarial mathematics. Let us apply Jensen's inequality (1.3.2) to the decision maker's insurance problem as formulated in (1.3.1). We will assume that the decision maker's preferences are such that $u'(w) > 0$ and $u''(w) < 0$. Applying Jensen's inequality to (1.3.1), we have

$$u(w - G) = E[u(w - X)] \leq u(w - \mu). \qquad (1.3.5)$$

Because $u'(w) > 0$, $u(w)$ is an increasing function. Therefore, (1.3.5) implies that $w - G \leq w - \mu$, or $G \geq \mu$ with $G > \mu$ unless X is a constant. In economic terms, we have found that if $u'(w) > 0$ and $u''(w) < 0$, the decision maker will pay an amount greater than the expected loss for insurance. If G is at least equal to the premium set by the insurer, there is an opportunity for a mutually advantageous insurance policy.

Formally we say a decision maker with utility function $u(w)$ is **risk averse** if, and only if, $u''(w) < 0$.

We now employ a general utility function for the insurer. We let $u_I(w)$ denote the utility of wealth function of the insurer and w_I denote the current wealth of the insurer measured in monetary terms. Then the minimum acceptable premium H for assuming random loss X, from the viewpoint of the insurer, may be determined from (1.3.6):

$$u_I(w_I) = \text{E}[u_I(w_I + H - X)].\qquad(1.3.6)$$

The left-hand side of (1.3.6) is the utility attached to the insurer's current position. The right-hand side is the expected utility associated with collecting premium H and paying random loss X. In other words, the insurer is indifferent between the current position and providing insurance for X at premium H. If the insurer's utility function is such that $u_I'(w) > 0$, $u_I''(w) < 0$, we can use Jensen's inequality (1.3.2) along with (1.3.6) to obtain

$$u_I(w_I) = \text{E}[u_I(w_I + H - X)] \leq u_I(w_I + H - \mu).$$

Following the same line of reasoning displayed in connection with (1.3.5), we can conclude that $H \geq \mu$. If G, as determined by the decision maker by solving (1.3.5), is such that $G \geq H \geq \mu$, an insurance contract is possible. That is, the expected utility of neither party to the contract is decreased.

A utility function is based on the decision maker's preferences for various distributions of outcomes. An insurer need not be an individual. It may be a partnership, corporation, or government agency. In this situation the determination of $u_I(w)$, the insurer's utility function, may be a rather complicated matter. For example, if the insurer is a corporation, one of management's responsibilities is the formulation of a coherent set of preferences for various risky insurance ventures. These preferences may involve compromises between conflicting attitudes toward risk among the groups of stockholders.

Several elementary functions are used to illustrate properties of utility functions. Here we examine exponential, fractional power, and quadratic functions. Exercises 1.6, 1.8, 1.9, 1.10(b), and 1.13 cover the logarithmic utility function.

An **exponential utility function** is of the form

$$u(w) = -e^{-\alpha w} \qquad \text{for all } w \text{ and for a fixed } \alpha > 0$$

and has several attractive features. First,

$$u'(w) = \alpha e^{-\alpha w} > 0.$$

Second,

$$u''(w) = -\alpha^2 e^{-\alpha w} < 0.$$

Therefore, $u(w)$ may serve as the utility function of a risk-averse individual. Third, finding

$$E[-e^{-\alpha X}] = -E[e^{-\alpha X}] = -M_X(-\alpha)$$

is essentially the same as finding the moment generating function (m.g.f.) of X. In this expression,

$$M_X(t) = E[e^{tX}]$$

denotes the m.g.f. of X. Fourth, insurance premiums do not depend on the wealth of the decision maker. This statement is verified for the insured by substituting the exponential utility function into (1.3.1). That is,

$$-e^{-\alpha(w-G)} = E[-e^{-\alpha(w-X)}],$$

$$e^{\alpha G} = M_X(\alpha),$$

$$G = \frac{\log M_X(\alpha)}{\alpha}$$

and G does not depend on w.

The verification for the insurer is done by substituting the exponential utility function with parameter α_I into (1.3.6):

$$-e^{-\alpha_I w_I} = E[-e^{-\alpha_I(w_I + H - X)}],$$

$$-e^{-\alpha_I w_I} = -e^{-\alpha_I(w_I + H)} M_X(\alpha_I),$$

$$H = \frac{\log M_X(\alpha_I)}{\alpha_I}.$$

Example 1.3.1

A decision maker's utility function is given by $u(w) = -e^{-5w}$. The decision maker has two random economic prospects (gains) available. The outcome of the first, denoted by X, has a normal distribution with mean 5 and variance 2. Henceforth, a statement about a normal distribution with mean μ and variance σ^2 will be abbreviated as $N(\mu, \sigma^2)$. The second prospect, denoted by Y, is distributed as $N(6, 2.5)$. Which prospect will be preferred?

Solution:
We have

$$E[u(X)] = E[-e^{-5X}]$$

$$= -M_X(-5) = -e^{[-5(5) + (5^2)(2)/2]}$$

$$= -1,$$

and

$$E[u(Y)] = E[-e^{-5Y}]$$

$$= -M_Y(-5) = -e^{[-5(6)+(5^2)(2.5)/2]}$$

$$= -e^{1.25}.$$

Therefore,

$$E[u(X)] = -1 > E[u(Y)] = -e^{1.25},$$

and the distribution of X is preferred to the distribution of Y. ▼

In Example 1.3.1 prospect X is preferred to Y despite the fact that $\mu_X = 5 < \mu_Y = 6$. Since the decision maker is risk averse, the fact that the distribution of Y is more diffuse than the distribution of X is weighted heavily against the distribution of Y in assessing its desirability. If Y had a $N(6, 2.4)$ distribution, $E[u(Y)] = -1$ and the decision maker would be indifferent between the distributions of X and Y.

The family of *fractional power utility* functions is given by

$$u(w) = w^\gamma \qquad w > 0, 0 < \gamma < 1.$$

A member of this family might represent the preferences of a risk-averse decision maker since

$$u'(w) = \gamma w^{\gamma-1} > 0$$

and

$$u''(w) = \gamma(\gamma - 1)w^{\gamma-2} < 0.$$

In this family, premiums depend on the wealth of the decision maker in a manner that may be sufficiently realistic in many situations.

Example 1.3.2

A decision maker's utility function is given by $u(w) = \sqrt{w}$. The decision maker has wealth of $w = 10$ and faces a random loss X with a uniform distribution on $(0, 10)$. What is the maximum amount this decision maker will pay for complete insurance against the random loss?

Solution:
Substituting into (1.3.1) we have

$$\sqrt{10 - G} = E[\sqrt{10 - X}]$$

$$= \int_0^{10} \sqrt{10 - x}\ 10^{-1}\ dx$$

$$= \left. \frac{-2(10 - x)^{3/2}}{3(10)} \right|_0^{10}$$

$$= \frac{2}{3} \sqrt{10},$$

$$G = 5.5556.$$

The decision maker is risk averse and has $u'(w) > 0$. Following the discussion of (1.3.5), we would expect $G > E[X]$, and in this example $G = 5.5556 > E[X] = 5$. ▼

The family of *quadratic utility* functions is given by

$$u(w) = w - \alpha w^2 \qquad w < (2\alpha)^{-1}, \qquad \alpha > 0.$$

A member of this family might represent the preferences of a risk-averse decision maker since $u''(w) = -2\alpha$. While a quadratic utility function is convenient because decisions depend only on the first two moments of the distributions of outcomes under consideration, there are certain consequences of its use that strike some people as being unreasonable. Example 1.3.3 illustrates one of these consequences.

Example 1.3.3

A decision maker's utility of wealth function is given by

$$u(w) = w - 0.01w^2 \qquad w < 50.$$

The decision maker will retain wealth of amount w with probability p and suffer a financial loss of amount c with probability $1 - p$. For the values of w, c, and p exhibited in the table below, find the maximum insurance premium that the decision maker will pay for complete insurance. Assume $c \leq w < 50$.

Solution:
For the facts stated, (1.3.1) becomes

$$u(w - G) = pu(w) + (1 - p)u(w - c),$$

$$(w - G) - 0.01(w - G)^2 = p(w - 0.01w^2)$$
$$+ (1 - p)[(w - c) - 0.01(w - c)^2].$$

For given values of w, p, and c this expression becomes a quadratic equation. Two solutions are shown.

Wealth w	Loss c	Probability p	Insurance Premium G
10	10	0.5	5.28
20	10	0.5	5.37

▼

In Example 1.3.3, as anticipated, G is greater than the expected loss of 5. However, the maximum insurance premium for exactly the same loss distribution increases with the wealth of the decision maker. This result seems unreasonable to some who anticipate that more typical behavior would be a decrease in the amount a decision maker would pay for insurance when an increase in wealth would permit the decision maker to absorb more of a random loss. Unfortunately, a maximum insurance premium that increases with wealth is a property of quadratic utility functions. Consequently, these utility functions should not be selected by a decision maker who perceives that his ability to absorb random losses goes up with increases in wealth.

If we rework Example 1.3.3 using an exponential utility function, we know that the premium G will not depend on w, the amount of wealth. In fact, if $u(w) = -e^{-0.01w}$, it can be shown that $G = 5.12$ for both $w = 10$ and $w = 20$.

Example 1.3.4

The probability that a property will not be damaged in the next period is 0.75. The probability density function (p.d.f.) of a positive loss is given by

$$f(x) = 0.25(0.01e^{-0.01x}) \qquad x > 0.$$

The owner of the property has a utility function given by

$$u(w) = -e^{-0.005w}.$$

Calculate the expected loss and the maximum insurance premium the property owner will pay for complete insurance.

Solution:

The expected loss is given by

$$E[X] = 0.75(0) + 0.25 \int_0^\infty x(0.01e^{-0.01x})dx$$

$$= 25.$$

We apply (1.3.1) to determine the maximum premium that the owner will pay for complete insurance. This premium will be consistent with the property owner's preferences as summarized in the utility function:

$$u(w - G) = 0.75u(w) + \int_0^\infty u(w - x)f(x)dx,$$

$$-e^{-0.005(w-G)} = -0.75e^{-0.005w} - 0.25 \int_0^\infty e^{-0.005(w-x)}(0.01e^{-0.01x})dx,$$

$$e^{0.005G} = 0.75 + (0.25)(2)$$

$$= 1.25,$$

$$G = 200 \log 1.25$$

$$= 44.63.$$

Therefore, in accord with the property owner's preferences, he will pay up to $44.63 - 25 = 19.63$ in excess of the expected loss to purchase insurance covering all losses in the next period. ▼

In Example 1.3.5 the notion of insurance that covers something less than the complete loss is introduced. A modification is made in (1.3.1) to accommodate the fact that losses are shared by the decision maker and the insurance system.

Example 1.3.5

The property owner in Example 1.3.4 is offered an insurance policy that will pay 1/2 of any loss during the next period. The expected value of the partial loss payment is $E[X/2] = 12.50$. Calculate the maximum premium that the property owner will pay for this insurance.

Solution:

Consistent with his attitude toward risk, as summarized in his utility function, the premium is determined from

$$0.75u(w - G) + \int_0^\infty u\left(w - G - \frac{x}{2}\right) f(x)dx$$

$$= 0.75u(w) + \int_0^\infty u(w - x)f(x)dx.$$

The left-hand side of this equation represents the expected utility with the partial insurance coverage. The right-hand side represents the expected utility with no insurance. For the exponential utility function and p.d.f. of losses specified in Example 1.3.4, it can be shown that $G = 28.62$. The property owner is willing to pay up to $G - \mu = 28.62 - 12.50 = 16.12$ more than the expected partial loss for the partial insurance coverage. ▼

1.4 Elements of Insurance

Individuals and organizations face the threat of financial loss due to random events. In Section 1.3 we saw how insurance can increase the expected utility of a decision maker facing such random losses. Insurance systems are unique in that the alleviation of financial losses in which the number, size, or time of occurrence is random is the primary reason for their existence. In this section we review some of the factors influencing the organization and management of an insurance system.

An insurance system can be organized only after the identification of a class of situations where random losses may occur. The word random is taken to mean, along with other attributes, that the frequency, size, or time of loss is not under the control of the prospective insured. If such control exists, or if a claim payment exceeds the actual financial loss, an incentive to incur a loss will exist. In such a situation, the assumptions under which the insurance system was organized will become invalid. The actual conditions under which premiums are collected and claims paid will be different from those assumed in organizing the system. The system will not achieve its intended objective of not decreasing the expected utilities of both the insured and the insurer.

Once a class of insurable situations is identified, information on the expected utilities and the loss-generating process can be obtained. Market research in insurance can be viewed as an effort to learn about the utility functions, that is, the risk preferences of consumers.

The processes generating size and time of loss may be sufficiently stable over time so that past information can be used to plan the system. When a new insurance system is organized, directly relevant statistics are not often available. However, enough ancillary information from similar risk situations may be obtained to

---

identify the risks and to provide preliminary estimates of the probability distributions needed to determine premiums. Because most insurance systems operate under dynamic conditions, it is important that a plan exist for collecting and analyzing insurance operating data so that the insurance system can adapt. Adaptation in this case may mean changing premiums, paying an experience-based dividend or premium refund, or modifying future policies.

In a competitive economy, market forces encourage insurers to price short-term policies so that deviations of experience from expected value behave as independent random variables. Deviations should exhibit no pattern that might be exploited by the insured or insurer to produce consistent gains. Such consistent deviations would indicate inefficiencies in the insurance market.

As a result, the classification of risks into homogeneous groups is an important function within a market-based insurance system. Experience deviations that are random indicate efficiency or equity in classification. In a competitive insurance market, the continual interaction of numerous buyers and sellers forces experimentation with classification systems as the market participants attempt to take advantage of perceived patterns of deviations. Because insurance losses may be relatively rare events, it is often difficult to identify nonrandom patterns. The cost of classification information for a refined classification system also places a bound on experimentation in this area.

For insurance systems organized to serve groups rather than individuals, the issue is no longer whether deviations in insurance experience are random for each individual. Instead, the question is whether deviations in group experience are random. Consistent deviations in experience from that expected would indicate the need for a revision in the system.

Group insurance decisions do not rest on individual expected utility comparisons. Instead, group insurance plans are based on a collective decision on whether the system increases the total welfare of the group. Group health insurance providing benefits for the employees of a firm is an example.

1.5 Optimal Insurance

The ideas outlined in Sections 1.2, 1.3, and 1.4 have been used as the foundation of an elaborate theory for guiding insurance decision makers to actions consistent with their preferences. In this section we present one of the main results from this theory and review many of the ideas introduced so far.

A decision maker has wealth of amount w and faces a loss in the next period. This loss is a random variable X. The decision maker can buy an insurance contract that will pay $I(x)$ of the loss x. To avoid an incentive to incur the loss, we assume that all *feasible* insurance contracts are such that $0 \leq I(x) \leq x$. We make the simplifying assumption that all feasible insurance contracts with $E[I(X)] = \beta$ can be purchased for the same amount P.

The decision maker has formulated a utility function $u(w)$ that is consistent with his preferences for distributions of outcomes. We assume that the decision maker is risk averse, $u''(w) < 0$. We further assume that the decision maker has decided on the amount, denoted by P, to be paid for insurance. The question is: which of the insurance contracts from the class of feasible contracts with expected claims, β, and premium, P, should be purchased to maximize the expected utility of the decision maker?

One subclass of the class of feasible insurance contracts is defined as follows:

$$I_d(x) = \begin{cases} 0 & x < d \\ x - d & x \geq d. \end{cases} \tag{1.5.1}$$

This class of contracts is characterized by the fact that claim payments do not start until the loss exceeds the **deductible** amount d. For losses above the deductible amount, the excess is paid under the terms of the contract. This type of contract is sometimes called **stop-loss** or **excess-of-loss insurance**, the choice depending on the application.

In the problem discussed in this section the expected claims are denoted by β. In (1.5.2) the symbol $f(x)$ denotes the p.d.f. and the symbol $F(x)$ denotes the distribution function (d.f.) associated with the random loss X:

$$\beta = \int_d^\infty (x - d)f(x)dx \tag{1.5.2A}$$

or

$$\beta = \int_d^\infty [1 - F(x)]dx. \tag{1.5.2B}$$

Equation (1.5.2B) is obtained from (1.5.2A) by integration by parts. When β is given, then (1.5.2) provides explicit equations for the corresponding deductible, denoted by d^*. In Exercise 1.17, it is shown that d^* exists and is unique.

The main result of this section can be stated as a theorem.

Theorem 1.5.1

If a decision maker
- has wealth of amount w
- is risk averse, in other words, has utility of wealth function $u(w)$ such that $u''(w) < 0$
- faces a random loss X
- will spend amount P on insurance

and the insurance market offers for a payment of P all feasible insurance contracts of the form $I(x)$, $0 \leq I(x) \leq x$, with $E[I(X)] = \beta$, then the decision maker's expected utility will be maximized by purchasing an insurance policy

$$I_{d^*}(x) = \begin{cases} 0 & x < d^* \\ x - d^* & x \geq d^* \end{cases}$$

where d^* is the solution of

$$\beta - \int_d^\infty (x - d)f(x)dx = 0.$$

The theorem is proved in the Appendix to this chapter.

Theorem 1.5.1 is an important result and illustrates many of the ideas developed in this chapter. However, it is instructive to consider certain limitations on its applicability. First, the ratio of premium to expected claims is the same for all available contracts. In fact, the distributions of the random variables $I(X)$ can be very different, and the provision for risk in the premium usually depends on the characteristics of the distribution of $I(X)$. Second, in Theorem 1.5.1, it is assumed that the premium P is fixed by a budget constraint. Alternatives to amount P are not considered. In Exercise 1.22, relaxation of the budget constraint is considered. Third, while the theorem indicates the form of insurance, it does not help to determine the amount P to spend. In the theorem, P is fixed.

1.6   Notes and References

Definitions and principles of actuarial science can be found in "Principles of Actuarial Science" (SOA Committee on Actuarial Principles 1992).

The role of risk in business was developed in a pioneering thesis by Willett (1951). Borch (1974) has published a series of papers applying utility theory to insurance questions. DeGroot (1970) gives a complete development of utility theory starting from basic axioms for consistency among preferences for various distributions of outcomes. DeGroot and Borch both discuss the historically important St. Petersburg paradox, outlined in Exercise 1.2. A paper by Friedman and Savage (1948) provides many insights into utility theory and human behavior.

Pratt (1964) has studied (1.3.1) and derived several theorems about premiums and utility functions. Exercise 1.10, which uses two rough approximations, is related to one of Pratt's results.

Theorem 1.5.1 on optimal insurance was proved by Arrow (1963) in the context of health insurance. The theorem in Exercise 1.21, in which the goal of insurance is to minimize the variance of retained losses, was the subject of papers by Borch (1960) and Kahn (1961). The use of the variance of losses as a measure of stability is discussed by Beard, Pentikäinen, and Pesonen (1984). Exercise 1.23 is based on their discussion.

Appendix

Lemma:
If $u''(w) < 0$ for all w in $[a, b]$, then for w and z in $[a, b]$,

$$u(w) - u(z) \leq (w - z)u'(z). \qquad (1.A.1)$$

Proof:
The lemma may be established with the aid of Figure 1.3.1. Using the point slope form, a line tangent to $u(w)$ at the point $(z, u(z))$ has the equation $y - u(z) = u'(z)(w - z)$ and is above the graph of the function $u(w)$ except at the point $(z, u(z))$. Therefore,

$$u(w) - u(z) \leq u'(z)(w - z). \qquad ■$$

Figure 1.3.1 shows the case $u'(w) > 0$. The same argument holds for $u'(w) < 0$.

In Exercise 1.20 an alternative proof is required.

Proof of Theorem 1.5.1:

Let $I(x)$ be associated with an insurance policy satisfying the hypothesis of the theorem. Then from the lemma,

$$u(w - x + I(x) - P) - u(w - x + I_{d^*}(x) - P)$$

$$\leq [I(x) - I_{d^*}(x)]u'(w - x + I_{d^*}(x) - P). \qquad (1.A.2)$$

In addition, we claim

$$[I(x) - I_{d^*}(x)]u'(w - x + I_{d^*}(x) - P)$$

$$\leq [I(x) - I_{d^*}(x)]u'(w - d^* - P). \qquad (1.A.3)$$

To establish inequality (1.A.3), we must consider three cases:

Case I. $I_{d^*}(x) = I(x)$
          In this case equality holds, (1.A.3) is 0 on both sides.

Case II. $I_{d^*}(x) > I(x)$
          In this case $I_{d^*}(x) > 0$ and from (1.5.1), $x - I_{d^*}(x) = d^*$. Therefore, equality holds with each side of (1.A.3) equal to $[I(x) - I_{d^*}(x)]u'(w - d^* - P)$.

Case III. $I_{d^*}(x) < I(x)$
          In this case $I(x) - I_{d^*}(x) > 0$. From (1.5.1) we obtain $I_{d^*}(x) - x \geq -d^*$ and $I_{d^*}(x) - x - P \geq -d^* - P$. Therefore,

$$u'(w - x + I_{d^*}(x) - P) \leq u'(w - d^* - P)$$

          since the second derivative of $u(x)$ is negative and $u'(x)$ is a decreasing function.

Therefore, in each case

$$[I(x) - I_{d^*}(x)]u'(w - x + I_{d^*}(x) - P) \leq [I(x) - I_{d^*}(x)]u'(w - P - d^*),$$

establishing inequality (1.A.3).

Now, combining inequalities (1.A.2) and (1.A.3) and taking expectations, we have

$$E[u(w - X + I(X) - P)] - E[u(w - X + I_{d^*}(X) - P)]$$

$$\leq E[I(X) - I_{d^*}(X)]u'(w - d^* - P) = (\beta - \beta)u'(w - d^* - P) = 0.$$

Therefore,

$$E[u(w - X + I(X) - P)] \leq E[u(w - X + I_{d^*}(X) - P)]$$

and the expected utility will be maximized by selecting $I_{d^*}(x)$, the stop-loss policy.

∎

Exercises

Section 1.2

1.1. Assume that a decision maker's current wealth is 10,000. Assign $u(0) = -1$ and $u(10,000) = 0$.

   a. When facing a loss of X with probability 0.5 and remaining at current wealth with probability 0.5, the decision maker would be willing to pay up to G for complete insurance. The values for X and G in three situations are given below.

X	G
10 000	6 000
6 000	3 300
3 300	1 700

   Determine three values on the decision maker's utility of wealth function u.

   b. Calculate the slopes of the four line segments joining the five points determined on the graph $u(w)$. Determine the rates of change of the slopes from segment to segment.

   c. Put yourself in the role of a decision maker with wealth 10,000. In addition to the given values of $u(0)$ and $u(10,000)$, elicit three additional values on your utility of wealth function u.

   d. On the basis of the five values of your utility function, calculate the slopes and the rates of change of the slopes as done in part (b).

1.2. **St. Petersburg paradox:** Consider a game of chance that consists of tossing a coin until a head appears. The probability of a head is 0.5 and the repeated trials are independent. Let the random variable N be the number of the trial on which the first head occurs.

a. Show that the probability function (p.f.) of N is given by

$$f(n) = \left(\frac{1}{2}\right)^n \qquad n = 1, 2, 3, \ldots .$$

b. Find $E[N]$ and $Var(N)$.

c. If a reward of $X = 2^N$ is paid, prove that the expectation of the reward does not exist.

d. If this reward has utility $u(w) = \log w$, find $E[u(X)]$.

Section 1.3

1.3. **Jensen's inequalities:**

a. Assume $u''(w) < 0$, $E[X] = \mu$, and $E[u(X)]$ exist; prove that $E[u(X)] \leq u(\mu)$. [Hint: Express $u(w)$ as a series around the point $w = \mu$ and terminate the expansion with an error term involving the second derivative. Note that Jensen's inequalities do not require that $u'(w) > 0$.]

b. If $u''(w) > 0$, prove that $E[u(X)] \geq u(\mu)$.

c. Discuss Jensen's inequalities for the special case $u(w) = w^2$. What is

$$E[u(X)] - u(E[X])?$$

1.4. If a utility function is such that $u'(w) > 0$ and $u''(w) > 0$, use (1.3.1) to show $G \leq \mu$. A decision maker with preferences consistent with $u''(w) > 0$ is a *risk lover.*

1.5. Construct a geometric argument, based on a graph like that displayed in Figure 1.3.1, that if $u'(w) < 0$ and $u''(w) < 0$, then (1.3.4) follows.

1.6. Confirm that the utility function $u(w) = \log w$, $w > 0$, is the utility function of a decision maker who is risk averse for $w > 0$.

1.7. A utility function is given by

$$u(w) = \begin{cases} e^{-(w-100)^2/200} & w < 100 \\ 2 - e^{-(w-100)^2/200} & w \geq 100. \end{cases}$$

a. Is $u'(w) \geq 0$?

b. For what range of w is $u''(w) < 0$?

1.8. If one assumes, as did D. Bernoulli in his comments on the St. Petersburg paradox, that utility of wealth satisfies the differential equation

$$\frac{du(w)}{dw} = \frac{k}{w} \qquad w > 0, k > 0,$$

confirm that $u(w) = k \log w + c$.

1.9. A decision maker has utility function $u(w) = k \log w$. The decision maker has wealth w, $w > 1$, and faces a random loss X, which has a uniform distribution on the interval $(0, 1)$. Use (1.3.1) to show that the maximum insurance premium that the decision maker will pay for complete insurance is

$$G = w - \frac{w^w}{e(w-1)^{w-1}}.$$

1.10. a. In (1.3.1) use the approximations

$$u(w - G) \cong u(w - \mu) + (\mu - G)u'(w - \mu),$$

$$u(w - x) \cong u(w - \mu) + (\mu - x)u'(w - \mu) + \frac{1}{2}(\mu - x)^2 u''(w - \mu)$$

and derive the following approximation for G:

$$G \cong \mu - \frac{1}{2}\frac{u''(w - \mu)}{u'(w - \mu)}\sigma^2.$$

b. If $u(w) = k \log w$, use the approximation developed in part (a) to obtain

$$G \cong \mu + \frac{1}{2}\frac{\sigma^2}{(w - \mu)}.$$

1.11. The decision maker has a utility function $u(w) = -e^{-\alpha w}$ and is faced with a random loss that has a chi-square distribution with n degrees of freedom. If $0 < \alpha < 1/2$, use (1.3.1) to obtain an expression for G, the maximum insurance premium the decision maker will pay, and prove that $G > n = \mu$.

1.12. Rework Example 1.3.4 for
   a. $u(w) = -e^{-w/400}$
   b. $u(w) = -e^{-w/150}$.

1.13. a. An insurer with net worth 100 has accepted (and collected the premium for) a risk X with the following probability distribution:

$$Pr(X = 0) = Pr(X = 51) = \frac{1}{2}.$$

What is the maximum amount G it should pay another insurer to accept 100% of this loss? Assume the first insurer's utility function of wealth is $u(w) = \log w$.

   b. An insurer, with wealth 650 and the same utility function, $u(w) = \log w$, is considering accepting the above risk. What is the minimum amount H this insurer would accept as a premium to cover 100% of the loss?

1.14. If the complete insurance of Example 1.3.4 can be purchased for 40 and the 50% coinsurance of Example 1.3.5 can be purchased for 25, the purchase of which insurance maximizes the property owner's expected utility?

Section 1.4

1.15. A hospital expense policy is issued to a group consisting of n individuals. The policy pays B dollars each time a member of the group enters a hospital.

The group is not homogeneous with respect to the expected number of hospital admissions each year. The group may be divided into r subgroups. There are n_i individuals in subgroup i and $\sum_1^r n_i = n$. For subgroup i the number of annual hospital admissions for each member has a Poisson distribution with parameter λ_i, $i = 1, 2, \ldots, r$. The number of annual hospital admissions for members of the group are mutually independent.

a. Show that the expected claims payment in one year is

$$B \sum_1^r n_i \lambda_i = Bn\bar{\lambda}$$

where

$$\bar{\lambda} = \frac{\sum_1^r n_i \lambda_i}{n}.$$

b. Show that the number of hospital admissions in 1 year for the group has a Poisson distribution with parameter $n\,\bar{\lambda}$.

Section 1.5

1.16. Perform the integration by parts indicated in (1.5.2). Use the fact that if $E[X]$ exists, if and only if, $\lim_{x \to \infty} x[1 - F(x)] = 0$.

1.17. a. Differentiate the right-hand side of (1.5.2B) with respect to d.
   b. Let β be a number such that $0 < \beta < E[X]$. Show that (1.5.2) has a unique solution d^*.

1.18. Let the loss random variable X have a p.d.f. given by

$$f(x) = 0.1e^{-0.1x} \qquad x > 0.$$

a. Calculate $E[X]$ and $\text{Var}(X)$.
b. If $P = 5$ is to be spent for insurance to be purchased by the payment of the pure premium, show that

$$I(x) = \frac{x}{2}$$

and

$$I_d(x) = \begin{cases} 0 & x < d \\ x - d & x \geq d, \text{ where } d = 10 \log 2, \end{cases}$$

both represent feasible insurance policies with pure premium $P = 5$. $I(x)$ is called **proportional insurance.**

1.19. The loss random variable X has a p.d.f. given by

$$f(x) = \frac{1}{100} \qquad 0 < x < 100.$$

a. Calculate $E[X]$ and $Var(X)$.

b. Consider a proportional policy where

$$I(x) = kx \qquad 0 < k < 1,$$

and a stop-loss policy where

$$I_d(x) = \begin{cases} 0 & x < d \\ x - d & x \geq d. \end{cases}$$

Determine k and d such that the pure premium in each case is $P = 12.5$.

c. Show that $Var[X - I(X)] > Var[X - I_d(X)]$.

Appendix

1.20. Establish the lemma by using an analytic rather than a geometric argument. [Hint: Expand $u(w)$ in a series as far as a second derivative remainder around the point z and subtract $u(z)$.]

1.21. Adopt the hypotheses of Theorem 1.5.1 with respect to β and insurance contracts $I(x)$ and assume $E[X] = \mu$. Prove that

$$Var[X - I(X)] = E[(X - I(X) - \mu + \beta)^2]$$

is a minimum when $I(x) = I_{d^*}(x)$. You will be proving that for a fixed pure premium, a stop-loss insurance contract will minimize the variance of retained claims. [Hint: we may follow the proof of Theorem 1.5.1 by first proving that $x^2 - z^2 \geq (x - z)(2z)$ and then establishing that

$$[x - I(x)]^2 - [x - I_{d^*}(x)]^2 \geq [I_{d^*}(x) - I(x)][2x - 2I_{d^*}(x)]$$

$$\geq 2[I_{d^*}(x) - I(x)]d^*.$$

The final inequality may be established by breaking the proof into three cases. Alternatively, by proper choice of wealth level and utility function, the result of this exercise is a special case of Theorem 1.5.1.]

1.22. Adopt the hypotheses of Theorem 1.5.1, except remove the budget constraint; that is, assume that the decision maker will pay premium P, $0 < P \leq E[X] = \mu$, that will maximize expected utility. In addition, assume that any feasible insurance can be purchased for its expected value. Prove that the optimal insurance is $I_0(x)$. This result can be summarized by stating that full coverage is optimal in the absence of a budget constraint if insurance can be purchased for its pure premium. [Hint: Use the lemma with the role of w played by $w - x + I(x) - P$ and that of z played by $w - x + I_0(x) - E[X] = w - \mu$. Take expectations and establish that $E[u(w - X) + I(X) - P] \leq u(w - \mu).$]

1.23. Optimality properties of stop-loss insurance were established in Theorem 1.5.1 and Exercise 1.21. These results depended on the decision criteria, the constraints, and the insurance alternatives available. In each of these developments, there was a budget constraint. Consider the situation where there is a risk constraint and the price of insurance depends on the insurance risk as measured by the variance.

  (i) The insurance premium is $E[I(X)] + f(\text{Var}[I(X)])$, where $f(w)$ is an increasing function. The amount of $f(\text{Var}[I(X)])$ can be interpreted as a *security loading.*

 (ii) The decision maker elects to retain loss $X - I(X)$ such that $\text{Var}[X - I(X)] = V \geq 0$. This requirement imposes a risk rather than a budget constraint. The constant is determined by the degree of risk aversion of the decision maker. Fixing the accepted variance, and then optimizing expected results, is a decision criterion in investment portfolio theory.

(iii) The decision maker selects $I(x)$ to minimize $f(\text{Var}[I(X)])$. The objective is to minimize the security loading, the premium paid less the expected insurance payments. Confirm the following steps:

   a. $\text{Var}[I(X)] = V + \text{Var}(X) - 2\,\text{Cov}[X, X - I(X)]$.

   b. The $I(x)$ that minimizes $\text{Var}[I(X)]$ and thereby $f(\text{Var}[I(X)])$ is such that the correlation coefficient between X and $X - I(x)$ is 1.

   c. It is known that if two random variables W and Z have correlation coefficient 1, then $\Pr\{W = aZ + b, \text{ where } a > 0\} = 1$. In words, the probability of their joint distribution is concentrated on a line of positive slope. In part (b), the correlation coefficient of X and $X - I(X)$ was found to be 1. Thus, $X - I(X) = aX + b$, which implies that $I(X) = (1 - a)X - b$. To be a feasible insurance, $0 \leq I(x) \leq x$ or $0 \leq (1 - a)x - b \leq x$. These inequalities imply that $b = 0$ and $0 \leq 1 - a \leq 1$ and $0 \leq a \leq 1$.

   d. To determine a, set the correlation coefficient of X and $X - I(X)$ equal to 1, or equivalently, their covariance equal to the product of their standard deviations. Thus, show that $a = \sqrt{V/\text{Var}(X)}$ and thus that the insurance that minimizes $f(\text{Var}[X])$ is $I(X) = [1 - \sqrt{V/\text{Var}(X)}]X$.

INDIVIDUAL RISK MODELS FOR A SHORT TERM

2.1 Introduction

In Chapter 1 we examined how a decision maker can use insurance to reduce the adverse financial impact of some types of random events. That examination was quite general. The decision maker could have been an individual seeking protection against the loss of property, savings, or income. The decision maker could have been an organization seeking protection against those same types of losses. In fact, the organization could have been an insurance company seeking protection against the loss of funds due to excess claims either by an individual or by its portfolio of insureds. Such protection is called *reinsurance* and is introduced in this chapter.

The theory in Chapter 1 requires a probabilistic model for the potential losses. Here we examine one of two models commonly used in insurance pricing, reserving, and reinsurance applications.

For an insuring organization, let the random loss of a segment of its risks be denoted by S. Then S is the random variable for which we seek a probability distribution. Historically, there have been two sets of postulates for distributions of S. The *individual risk model* defines

$$S = X_1 + X_2 + \cdots + X_n \qquad (2.1.1)$$

where X_i is the loss on insured unit i and n is the number of risk units insured. Usually the X_i's are postulated to be independent random variables, because the mathematics is easier and no historical data on the dependence relationship are needed. The other model is the collective risk model described in Chapter 12.

The individual risk model in this chapter does not recognize the time value of money. This is for simplicity and is why the title refers to short terms. Chapters 4–11 cover models for long terms.

In this chapter we discuss only *closed models;* that is, the number of insured units n in (2.1.1) is known and fixed at the beginning of the period. If we postulate about migration in and out of the insurance system, we have an *open model.*

2.2 Models for Individual Claim Random Variables

First, we review basic concepts with a life insurance product. In a *one-year term life insurance* the insurer agrees to pay an amount b if the insured dies within a year of policy issue and to pay nothing if the insured survives the year. The probability of a claim during the year is denoted by q. The claim random variable, X, has a distribution that can be described by either its probability function, p.f., or its distribution function, d.f. The p.f. is

$$f_X(x) = \Pr(X = x) = \begin{cases} 1 - q & x = 0 \\ q & x = b \\ 0 & \text{elsewhere,} \end{cases} \qquad (2.2.1)$$

and the d.f. is

$$F_X(x) = \Pr(X \le x) = \begin{cases} 0 & x < 0 \\ 1 - q & 0 \le x < b \\ 1 & x \ge b. \end{cases} \qquad (2.2.2)$$

From the p.f. and the definition of moments,

$$E[X] = bq,$$

$$E[X^2] = b^2 q, \qquad (2.2.3)$$

and

$$\text{Var}(X) = b^2 q(1 - q). \qquad (2.2.4)$$

These formulas can also be obtained by writing

$$X = Ib \qquad (2.2.5)$$

where b is the constant amount payable in the event of death and I is the random variable that is 1 for the event of death and 0 otherwise. Thus, $\Pr(I = 0) = 1 - q$ and $\Pr(I = 1) = q$, the mean and variance of I are q and $q(1 - q)$, respectively, and the mean and variance of X are bq and $b^2 q(1 - q)$ as above.

The random variable I with its $\{0, 1\}$ range is widely applicable in actuarial models. In probability textbooks it is called an *indicator, Bernoulli random variable,* or *binomial random variable* for a single trial. We refer to it as an indicator for the sake of brevity and because it indicates the occurrence, $I = 1$, or nonoccurrence, $I = 0$, of a given event.

We now seek more general models in which the amount of claim is also a random variable and several claims can occur in a period. Health, automobile, and other property and liability coverages provide immediate examples. Extending (2.2.5), we postulate that

$$X = IB \qquad (2.2.6)$$

where X is the claim random variable for the period, B gives the total claim amount incurred during the period, and I is the indicator for the event that at least one claim has occurred. As the indicator for this event, I reports the occurrence ($I = 1$) or nonoccurrence ($I = 0$) of claims in this period and not the number of claims in the period. $\Pr(I = 1)$ is still denoted by q.

Let us look at several situations and determine the distributions of I and B for a model. First, consider a 1-year term life insurance paying an extra benefit in case of accidental death. To be specific, if death is accidental, the benefit amount is 50,000. For other causes of death, the benefit amount is 25,000. Assume that for the age, health, and occupation of a specific individual, the probability of an accidental death within the year is 0.0005, while the probability of a nonaccidental death is 0.0020. More succinctly,

$$\Pr(I = 1 \text{ and } B = 50{,}000) = 0.0005$$

and

$$\Pr(I = 1 \text{ and } B = 25{,}000) = 0.0020.$$

Summing over the possible values of B, we have

$$\Pr(I = 1) = 0.0025,$$

and then

$$\Pr(I = 0) = 1 - \Pr(I = 1) = 0.9975.$$

The conditional distribution of B, given $I = 1$, is

$$\Pr(B = 25{,}000 | I = 1) = \frac{\Pr(B = 25{,}000 \text{ and } I = 1)}{\Pr(I = 1)} = \frac{0.0020}{0.0025} = 0.8,$$

$$\Pr(B = 50{,}000 | I = 1) = \frac{\Pr(B = 50{,}000 \text{ and } I = 1)}{\Pr(I = 1)} = \frac{0.0005}{0.0025} = 0.2.$$

Let us now consider an automobile insurance providing collision coverage (this indemnifies the owner for collision damage to his car) above a 250 deductible up to a maximum claim of 2,000. For illustrative purposes, assume that for a particular individual the probability of one claim in a period is 0.15 and the chance of more than one claim is 0:

$$\Pr(I = 0) = 0.85,$$

$$\Pr(I = 1) = 0.15.$$

This unrealistic assumption of no more than one claim per period is made to simplify the distribution of B. We remove that assumption in a later section after we discuss the distribution of the sum of a number of claims. Since B is the claim incurred by the insurer, rather than the amount of damage to the car, we can infer two characteristics of I and B. First, the event $I = 0$ includes those collisions in which the damage is less than the 250 deductible. The other inference is that B's distribution has a probability mass at the maximum claim size of 2,000. Assume this probability mass is 0.1. Furthermore, assume that claim amounts between 0 and 2,000 can be modeled by a continuous distribution with a p.d.f. proportional to $1 - x/2{,}000$ for $0 < x < 2{,}000$. (In practice the continuous curve chosen to represent the distribution of claims is the result of a study of claims by size over a recent period.) Summarizing these assumptions about the conditional distribution of B, given $I = 1$, we have a mixed distribution with positive density from 0 to 2,000 and a mass at 2,000. This is illustrated in Figure 2.2.1. The d.f. of this conditional distribution is

$$\Pr(B \leq x | I = 1) = \begin{cases} 0 & x \leq 0 \\ 0.9 \left[1 - \left(1 - \dfrac{x}{2{,}000} \right)^2 \right] & 0 < x < 2{,}000 \\ 1 & x \geq 2{,}000. \end{cases}$$

FIGURE 2.2.1

Distribution Function for *B*, given *I* = 1

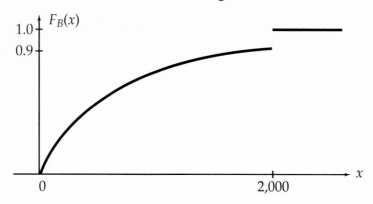

We see in Section 2.4 that the moments of the claim random variable, X, in particular the mean and variance, are extensively used. For this automobile insurance, we shall calculate the mean and the variance by two methods. First, we derive the distribution of X and use it to calculate $E[X]$ and $\text{Var}(X)$. Letting $F_X(x)$ be the d.f. of X, we have

$$F_X(x) = \Pr(X \leq x) = \Pr(IB \leq x)$$

$$= \Pr(IB \leq x | I = 0)\, \Pr(I = 0) \tag{2.2.7}$$

$$+ \Pr(IB \leq x | I = 1)\, \Pr(I = 1).$$

For $x < 0$,

$$F_X(x) = 0(0.85) + 0(0.15) = 0.$$

For $0 \leq x < 2{,}000$,

$$F_X(x) = 1(0.85) + 0.9 \left[1 - \left(1 - \frac{x}{2{,}000} \right)^2 \right] (0.15).$$

For $x \geq 2{,}000$,

$$F_X(x) = 1(0.85) + 1(0.15) = 1.$$

This is a mixed distribution. It has both probability masses and a continuous part as can be seen in its graph in Figure 2.2.2.

FIGURE 2.2.2

Distribution Function of $X = IB$

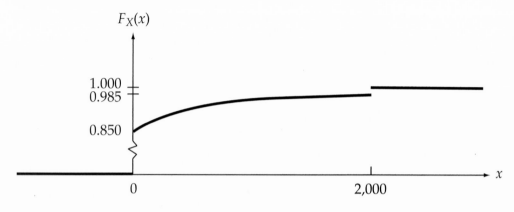

Corresponding to this d.f. is a combination p.f. and p.d.f. given by

$$\Pr(X = 0) = 0.85,$$

$$\Pr(X = 2{,}000) = 0.015 \qquad (2.2.8)$$

with p.d.f.

$$f_X(x) = \begin{cases} F'_X(x) = 0.000135 \left(1 - \dfrac{x}{2{,}000}\right) & 0 < x < 2{,}000 \\ 0 & \text{elsewhere.} \end{cases}$$

Moments of X can then be calculated by

$$E[X^k] = 0 \times \Pr(X = 0) + (2{,}000)^k \times \Pr(X = 2{,}000) + \int_0^{2{,}000} x^k f_X(x)\, dx, \quad (2.2.9)$$

specifically,

$$E[X] = 120$$

and

$$E[X^2] = 150{,}000.$$

Thus,

$$\text{Var}(X) = 135{,}600.$$

There are some formulas relating the moments of random variables to certain conditional expectations. General versions of these formulas for the mean and variance are

$$E[W] = E[E[W|V]] \qquad (2.2.10)$$

---

and
$$\text{Var}(W) = \text{Var}(\text{E}[W|V]) + \text{E}[\text{Var}(W|V)]. \qquad (2.2.11)$$

In these equations we think of calculating the terms of the left-hand sides by direct use of W's distribution. In the terms on the right-hand sides, $\text{E}[W|V]$ and $\text{Var}(W|V)$ are calculated by use of W's conditional distribution for a given value of V. These components are then functions of the random variable V, and we can calculate their moments by use of V's distribution.

In many actuarial models conditional distributions are used. This makes the formulas above directly applicable. In our model, $X = IB$, we can substitute X for W and I for V to obtain

$$\text{E}[X] = \text{E}[\text{E}[X|I]] \qquad (2.2.12)$$

and

$$\text{Var}(X) = \text{Var}(\text{E}[X|I]) + \text{E}[\text{Var}(X|I)]. \qquad (2.2.13)$$

Now let us write

$$\mu = \text{E}[B|I = 1], \qquad (2.2.14)$$

$$\sigma^2 = \text{Var}(B|I = 1), \qquad (2.2.15)$$

and look at the conditional means

$$\text{E}[X|I = 0] = 0 \qquad (2.2.16)$$

and

$$\text{E}[X|I = 1] = \text{E}[B|I = 1] = \mu. \qquad (2.2.17)$$

Formulas (2.2.16) and (2.2.17) define $\text{E}[X|I]$ as a function of I, which can be written by the formula

$$\text{E}[X|I] = \mu I. \qquad (2.2.18)$$

Hence,

$$\text{E}[\text{E}[X|I]] = \mu \text{E}[I] = \mu q \qquad (2.2.19)$$

and

$$\text{Var}(\text{E}[X|I]) = \mu^2 \,\text{Var}(I) = \mu^2 q(1 - q). \qquad (2.2.20)$$

Since $X = 0$ for $I = 0$, we have

$$\text{Var}(X|I = 0) = 0. \qquad (2.2.21)$$

For $I = 1$, we have $X = B$ and

$$\text{Var}(X|I = 1) = \text{Var}(B|I = 1) = \sigma^2. \qquad (2.2.22)$$

Formulas (2.2.21) and (2.2.22) can be combined as

$$\text{Var}(X|I) = \sigma^2 I. \qquad (2.2.23)$$

Then

$$E[\text{Var}(X|I)] = \sigma^2 E[I] = \sigma^2 q. \qquad (2.2.24)$$

Substituting (2.2.19), (2.2.20), and (2.2.24) into (2.2.12) and (2.2.13), we have

$$E[X] = \mu q \qquad (2.2.25)$$

and

$$\text{Var}(X) = \mu^2 q(1 - q) + \sigma^2 q. \qquad (2.2.26)$$

Let us now apply these formulas to calculate $E[X]$ and $\text{Var}(X)$ for the automobile insurance in Figure 2.2.2. Since the p.d.f. for B, given $I = 1$, is

$$f_{B|I}(x|1) = \begin{cases} 0.0009 \left(1 - \dfrac{x}{2{,}000}\right) & 0 < x < 2{,}000 \\ 0 & \text{elsewhere,} \end{cases}$$

with $\Pr(B = 2{,}000|I = 1) = 0.1$, we have

$$\mu = \int_0^{2{,}000} 0.0009\, x \left(1 - \frac{x}{2{,}000}\right) dx + (0.1)(2{,}000) = 800,$$

$$E[B^2|I = 1] = \int_0^{2{,}000} 0.0009\, x^2 \left(1 - \frac{x}{2{,}000}\right) dx + (0.1)(2{,}000)^2 = 1{,}000{,}000,$$

and

$$\sigma^2 = 1{,}000{,}000 - (800)^2 = 360{,}000.$$

Finally, with $q = 0.15$ we obtain the following from (2.2.25) and (2.2.26):

$$E[X] = 800(0.15) = 120$$

and

$$\text{Var}(X) = (800)^2(0.15)(0.85) + (360{,}000)(0.15)$$

$$= 135{,}600.$$

There are other possible models for B in different insurance situations. As an example, let us consider a model for the number of deaths due to crashes during an airline's year of operation. We can start with a random variable for the number of deaths, X, on a single flight and then add up a set of such random variables over the set of flights for the year. For a single flight, the event $I = 1$ will be the event of an accident during the flight. The number of deaths in the accident, B, will be modeled as the product of two random variables, L and Q, where L is the load factor, the number of persons on board at the time of the crash, and Q is the fraction of deaths among persons on board. The number of deaths B is modeled in this way since separate statistical data for the distributions of L and Q may be more readily available than are total data for B. We have $X = ILQ$. While the fraction of passengers killed in a crash and the fraction of seats occupied are probably related, L and Q might be assumed to be independent as a first approximation.

2.3 Sums of Independent Random Variables

In the individual risk model, claims of an insuring organization are modeled as the sum of the claims of many insured individuals.

The claims for the individuals are assumed to be independent in most applications. In this section we review two methods for determining the distribution of the sum of independent random variables. First, let us consider the sum of two random variables, $S = X + Y$, with the sample space shown in Figure 2.3.1.

FIGURE 2.3.1

Event $\{X + Y \le s\}$

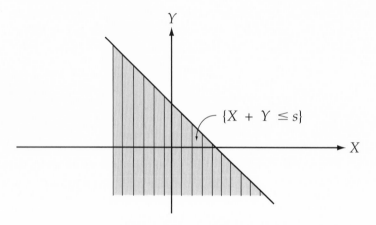

The line $X + Y = s$ and the region below the line represent the event

$$[S = X + Y \le s].$$

Hence the d.f. of S is

$$F_S(s) = \Pr(S \le s) = \Pr(X + Y \le s). \tag{2.3.1}$$

For two discrete, non-negative random variables, we can use the law of total probability to write (2.3.1) as

$$F_S(s) = \sum_{\text{all } y \le s} \Pr(X + Y \le s | Y = y) \Pr(Y = y)$$

$$= \sum_{\text{all } y \le s} \Pr(X \le s - y | Y = y) \Pr(Y = y). \tag{2.3.2}$$

When X and Y are independent, this last sum can be written

$$F_S(s) = \sum_{\text{all } y \le s} F_X(s - y) f_Y(y). \tag{2.3.3}$$

The p.f. corresponding to this d.f. can be calculated by

$$f_S(s) = \sum_{\text{all } y \le s} f_X(s - y) f_Y(y). \tag{2.3.4}$$

For continuous, non-negative random variables the formulas corresponding to (2.3.2), (2.3.3), and (2.3.4) are

---

$$F_S(s) = \int_0^s \Pr(X \le s - y | Y = y) f_Y(y) \, dy, \qquad (2.3.5)$$

$$F_S(s) = \int_0^s F_X(s - y) f_Y(y) \, dy, \qquad (2.3.6)$$

$$f_S(s) = \int_0^s f_X(s - y) f_Y(y) \, dy. \qquad (2.3.7)$$

When either one, or both, of X and Y have a mixed-type distribution (typical in individual risk model applications), the formulas are analogous but more complex. For random variables that may also take on negative values, the sums and integrals in the formulas above are over all y values from $-\infty$ to $+\infty$.

In probability, the operation in (2.3.3) and (2.3.6) is called the **convolution** of the pair of distribution functions $F_X(x)$ and $F_Y(y)$ and is denoted by $F_X * F_Y$. Convolutions can also be defined for a pair of probability functions or probability density functions as in (2.3.4) and (2.3.7).

To determine the distribution of the sum of more than two random variables, we can use the convolution process iteratively. For $S = X_1 + X_2 + \cdots + X_n$ where the X_i's are independent random variables, F_i is the d.f. of X_i, and $F^{(k)}$ is the d.f. of $X_1 + X_2 + \cdots + X_k$, we proceed thus:

$$F^{(2)} = F_2 * F^{(1)} = F_2 * F_1$$

$$F^{(3)} = F_3 * F^{(2)}$$

$$F^{(4)} = F_4 * F^{(3)}$$

$$\vdots$$

$$F^{(n)} = F_n * F^{(n-1)}.$$

Example 2.3.1 illustrates the procedure using probability functions for three discrete random variables.

Example 2.3.1

The random variables X_1, X_2, and X_3 are independent with distributions defined by columns (1), (2), and (3) of the table below. Derive the p.f. and d.f. of

$$S = X_1 + X_2 + X_3.$$

Solution:
The notation of the previous paragraph is used in the table:
- Columns (1)–(3) are given information.
- Column (4) is derived from columns (1) and (2) by use of (2.3.4).
- Column (5) is derived from columns (3) and (4) by use of (2.3.4).

The determination of column (5) completes the determination of the distribution of S. Its d.f. in column (8) is the set of partial sums of column (5) from the top.

---

x	(1) $f_1(x)$	(2) $f_2(x)$	(3) $f_3(x)$	(4) $f^{(2)}(x)$	(5) $f^{(3)}(x)$	(6) $F_1(x)$	(7) $F^{(2)}(x)$	(8) $F^{(3)}(x)$
0	0.4	0.5	0.6	0.20	0.120	0.4	0.20	0.120
1	0.3	0.2	0.0	0.23	0.138	0.7	0.43	0.258
2	0.2	0.1	0.1	0.20	0.140	0.9	0.63	0.398
3	0.1	0.1	0.1	0.16	0.139	1.0	0.79	0.537
4		0.1	0.1	0.11	0.129	1.0	0.90	0.666
5			0.1	0.06	0.115	1.0	0.96	0.781
6				0.03	0.088	1.0	0.99	0.869
7				0.01	0.059	1.0	1.00	0.928
8					0.036	1.0	1.00	0.964
9					0.021	1.0	1.00	0.985
10					0.010	1.0	1.00	0.995
11					0.004	1.0	1.00	0.999
12					0.001	1.0	1.00	1.000

For illustrative purposes we include column (6), the d.f. for column (1), column (7) which can be derived directly from columns (2) and (6) by use of (2.3.3), and column (8), derived similarly from columns (3) and (7). Column (5) can then be obtained by differencing column (8). ▼

We follow with two examples involving continuous random variables.

Example 2.3.2

Let X have a uniform distribution on $(0, 2)$ and let Y be independent of X with a uniform distribution over $(0, 3)$. Determine the d.f. of $S = X + Y$.

Solution:

Since X and Y are continuous, we use (2.3.6):

$$F_X(x) = \begin{cases} 0 & x < 0 \\ \dfrac{x}{2} & 0 \le x < 2 \\ 1 & x \ge 2 \end{cases}$$

and

$$f_Y(y) = \begin{cases} \dfrac{1}{3} & 0 < y < 3 \\ 0 & \text{elsewhere.} \end{cases}$$

Then

$$F_S(s) = \int_0^s F_X(s - y) f_Y(y)\, dy.$$

The X, Y sample space is illustrated in Figure 2.3.2. The rectangular region contains all of the probability for X and Y. The event of interest, $X + Y \le s$, has been

FIGURE 2.3.2

Convolution of Two Uniform Distributions

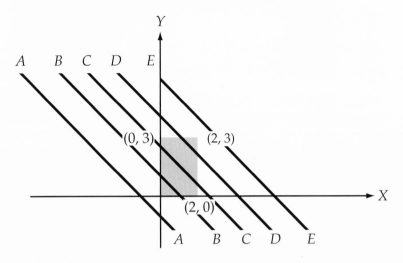

illustrated in the figure for five values of s. For each value, the line intersects the y-axis at s and the line $x = 2$ at $s - 2$. The values of F_S for these five cases are

$$
F_S(s) = \begin{cases}
0 & s < 0 & \text{line } A \\[2mm]
\displaystyle\int_0^s \frac{s-y}{2}\,\frac{1}{3}\,dy = \frac{s^2}{12} & 0 \le s < 2 & \text{line } B \\[2mm]
\displaystyle\int_0^{s-2} 1\,\frac{1}{3}\,dy + \int_{s-2}^s \frac{s-y}{2}\,\frac{1}{3}\,dy = \frac{s-1}{3} & 2 \le s < 3 & \text{line } C \\[2mm]
\displaystyle\int_0^{s-2} 1\,\frac{1}{3}\,dy + \int_{s-2}^3 \frac{s-y}{2}\,\frac{1}{3}\,dy = 1 - \frac{(5-s)^2}{12} & 3 \le s < 5 & \text{line } D \\[2mm]
1 & s \ge 5 & \text{line } E.
\end{cases}
$$

▼

Example 2.3.3

Consider three independent random variables X_1, X_2, X_3. For $i = 1, 2, 3$, X_i has an exponential distribution and $E[X_i] = 1/i$. Derive the p.d.f. of $S = X_1 + X_2 + X_3$ by the convolution process.

Solution:

$$f_1(x) = e^{-x} \qquad x > 0,$$

$$f_2(x) = 2e^{-2x} \qquad x > 0,$$

$$f_3(x) = 3e^{-3x} \qquad x > 0.$$

Using (2.3.7) twice, we have

$$f^{(2)}(x) = \int_0^x f_1(x - y) f_2(y)\, dy = \int_0^x e^{-(x-y)}\, 2e^{-2y}\, dy$$

$$= 2e^{-x} \int_0^x e^{-y}\, dy$$

$$= 2e^{-x} - 2e^{-2x} \qquad x > 0,$$

$$f_s(x) = f^{(3)}(x) = \int_0^x f^{(2)}(x - y) f_3(y)\, dy$$

$$= \int_0^x (2e^{-(x-y)} - 2e^{-2(x-y)})3e^{-3y}\, dy$$

$$= 6e^{-x} \int_0^x e^{-2y}\, dy - 6e^{-2x} \int_0^x e^{-y}\, dy$$

$$= (3e^{-x} - 3e^{-3x}) - (6e^{-2x} - 6e^{-3x})$$

$$= 3e^{-x} - 6e^{-2x} + 3e^{-3x} \qquad x > 0. \qquad \blacktriangledown$$

Another method to determine the distribution of the sum of random variables is based on the uniqueness of the ***moment generating function*** (m.g.f.), which, for the random variable X, is defined by $M_X(t) = \mathrm{E}[e^{tX}]$. If this expectation is finite for all t in an open interval about the origin, then $M_X(t)$ is the only m.g.f. of the distribution of X, and it is not the m.g.f. of any other distribution. This uniqueness can be used as follows. For the sum $S = X_1 + X_2 + \cdots + X_n$,

$$M_S(t) = \mathrm{E}[e^{tS}] = \mathrm{E}[e^{t(X_1 + X_2 + \cdots + X_n)}]$$

$$= \mathrm{E}[e^{tX_1} e^{tX_2} \cdots e^{tX_n}]. \tag{2.3.8}$$

If $X_1, X_2, \ldots, X_n$ are independent, then the expectation of the product in (2.3.8) is equal to

$$\mathrm{E}[e^{tX_1}]\, \mathrm{E}[e^{tX_2}] \cdots \mathrm{E}[e^{tX_n}]$$

so that

$$M_S(t) = M_{X_1}(t)\, M_{X_2}(t) \cdots M_{X_n}(t). \tag{2.3.9}$$

Recognition of the unique distribution corresponding to (2.3.9) would complete the determination of S's distribution. If inversion by recognition is not possible, then inversion by numerical methods may be used. (See Section 2.6.)

Example 2.3.4

Consider the random variables of Example 2.3.3. Derive the p.d.f. of $S = X_1 + X_2 + X_3$ by recognition of the m.g.f. of S.

Solution:

By (2.3.9), $M_S(t) = \left(\dfrac{1}{1 - t}\right)\left(\dfrac{2}{2 - t}\right)\left(\dfrac{3}{3 - t}\right)$, which we write, by the method of partial fractions, as

$$M_s(t) = \frac{A}{1-t} + \frac{2B}{2-t} + \frac{3C}{3-t}.$$

The solution for this is $A = 3$, $B = -3$, $C = 1$. But $\beta/(\beta - t)$ is the moment generating function of an exponential distribution with parameter β, so the p.d.f. for S is

$$f_S(x) = 3(e^{-x}) - 3(2e^{-2x}) + (3e^{-3x}). \qquad \blacktriangledown$$

Example 2.3.5

The *inverse Gaussian distribution* was developed in the study of stochastic processes. Here it is used as the distribution of B, the claim amount. It will have a similar role in risk theory in Chapters 12–14. The p.d.f. and m.g.f. associated with the inverse Gaussian distribution are given by

$$f_X(x) = \frac{\alpha}{\sqrt{2\pi\beta}}\, x^{-3/2} \exp\left[-\frac{(\beta x - \alpha)^2}{2\beta x} \right] \qquad x > 0,$$

$$M_X(t) = \exp\left[\alpha \left(1 - \sqrt{1 - \frac{2t}{\beta}} \right) \right].$$

Find the distribution of $S = X_1 + X_2 + X_3 + \cdots + X_n$ where the random variables $X_1, X_2, \ldots, X_n$ are independent and have identical inverse Gaussian distributions.

Solution:

Using (2.3.9), the m.g.f. of S is given by

$$M_S(t) = [M_X(t)]^n = \exp\left[n\alpha \left(1 - \sqrt{1 - \frac{2t}{\beta}} \right) \right].$$

The m.g.f. $M_S(t)$ can be recognized and shows that S has an inverse Gaussian distribution with parameters $n\alpha$ and β. $\qquad \blacktriangledown$

2.4   Approximations for the Distribution of the Sum

The *central limit theorem* suggests a method to obtain numerical values for the distribution of the sum of independent random variables. The usual statement of the theorem is for a sequence of independent and identically distributed random variables, $X_1, X_2, \ldots,$ with $E[X_i] = \mu$ and $Var(X_i) = \sigma^2$. For each n, the distribution of $\sqrt{n}\,(\bar{X}_n - \mu)/\sigma$, where $\bar{X}_n = (X_1 + X_2 + \cdots + X_n)/n$, has mean 0 and variance 1. The sequence of distributions ($n = 1, 2, \ldots$) is known to approach the standard normal distribution. When n is large the theorem is applied to approximate the distribution of $\bar{X}_n$ by a normal distribution with mean μ and variance σ^2/n. Equivalently, the distribution of the sum of the n random variables is approximated by a normal distribution with mean $n\mu$ and variance $n\sigma^2$. The effectiveness of these approximations depends not only on the number of variables but also on the departure of the distribution of the summands from normality. Many elementary statistics textbooks recommend that n be at least 30 for the approximations to be reasonable. One routine used to generate normally distributed random variables for simulation is based on the average of only 12 independent random variables uniformly distributed over (0, 1).

In many individual risk models the random variables in the sum are not identically distributed. This is illustrated by examples in the next section. The central limit theorem extends to sequences of nonidentically distributed random variables.

To illustrate some applications of the individual risk model, we use a normal approximation to the distribution of the sum of independent random variables to obtain numerical answers. If

$$S = X_1 + X_2 + \cdots + X_n,$$

then

$$E[S] = \sum_{k=1}^{n} E[X_k],$$

and, further, under the assumption of independence,

$$Var(S) = \sum_{k=1}^{n} Var(X_k).$$

For an application we need only
- Evaluate the means and variances of the individual loss random variables
- Sum them to obtain the mean and variance for the loss of the insuring organization as a whole
- Apply the normal approximation.

Illustrations of this process follow.

2.5 Applications to Insurance

In this section four examples illustrate the results of Section 2.2 and use of the normal approximation.

Example 2.5.1

A life insurance company issues 1-year term life contracts for benefit amounts of 1 and 2 units to individuals with probabilities of death of 0.02 or 0.10. The following table gives the number of individuals n_k in each of the four classes created by a benefit amount b_k and a probability of claim q_k.

k	q_k	b_k	n_k
1	0.02	1	500
2	0.02	2	500
3	0.10	1	300
4	0.10	2	500

The company wants to collect, from this population of 1,800 individuals, an amount equal to the 95th percentile of the distribution of total claims. Moreover, it wants each individual's share of this amount to be proportional to that individual's expected claim. The share for individual j with mean $E[X_j]$ would be $(1 + \theta)E[X_j]$. The 95th percentile requirement suggests that $\theta > 0$. This extra amount, $\theta E[X_j]$, is the *security loading* and θ is the *relative security loading.* Calculate θ.

Solution:

The criterion for θ is $\Pr(S \leq (1 + \theta)E[S]) = 0.95$ where $S = X_1 + X_2 + \cdots + X_{1,800}$. This probability statement is equivalent to

$$\Pr\left[\frac{S - E[S]}{\sqrt{\text{Var}(S)}} \leq \frac{\theta E[S]}{\sqrt{\text{Var}(S)}}\right] = 0.95.$$

Following the discussion of the central limit theorem in Section 2.4, we approximate the distribution of $(S - E[S])/\sqrt{\text{Var}(S)}$ by the standard normal distribution and use its 95th percentile to obtain

$$\frac{\theta E[S]}{\sqrt{\text{Var}(S)}} = 1.645.$$

It remains to calculate the mean and variance of S and to calculate θ by this equation.

For the four classes of insured individuals, we have the results given below.

k	q_k	b_k	Mean $b_k q_k$	Variance $b_k^2 q_k(1 - q_k)$	n_k
1	0.02	1	0.02	0.0196	500
2	0.02	2	0.04	0.0784	500
3	0.10	1	0.10	0.0900	300
4	0.10	2	0.20	0.3600	500

Then

$$E[S] = \sum_{j=1}^{1,800} E[X_j] = \sum_{k=1}^{4} n_k b_k q_k = 160$$

and

$$\text{Var}(S) = \sum_{j=1}^{1,800} \text{Var}(X_j) = \sum_{k=1}^{4} n_k b_k^2 q_k(1 - q_k) = 256.$$

Thus, the relative security loading is

$$\theta = 1.645 \frac{\sqrt{\text{Var}(S)}}{E[S]} = 1.645 \frac{16}{160} = 0.1645.$$

▼

Example 2.5.2

The policyholders of an automobile insurance company fall into two classes.

Class k	Number in Class n_k	Claim Probability q_k	Distribution of Claim Amount, B_k, Parameters of Truncated Exponential	
			λ	L
1	500	0.10	1	2.5
2	2 000	0.05	2	5.0

A truncated exponential distribution is defined by the d.f.

$$F(x) = \begin{cases} 0 & x < 0 \\ 1 - e^{-\lambda x} & 0 \le x < L \\ 1 & x \ge L. \end{cases}$$

This is a mixed distribution with p.d.f. $f(x) = \lambda e^{-\lambda x}$, $0 < x < L$, and a probability mass $e^{-\lambda L}$ at L. A graph of the d.f. appears in Figure 2.5.1.

FIGURE 2.5.1
Truncated Exponential Distribution

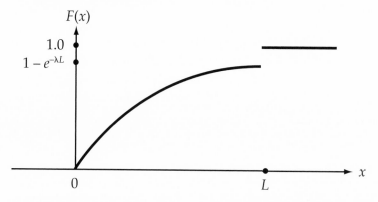

Again, the probability that total claims exceed the amount collected from policyholders is 0.05. We assume that the relative security loading, θ, is the same for the two classes. Calculate θ.

Solution:

This example is much like the previous one. It differs in that the claim amounts are random variables. First, we obtain formulas for the moments of the truncated exponential distribution in preparation for applying (2.2.25) and (2.2.26):

$$\mu = E[B|I = 1] = \int_0^L x\lambda e^{-\lambda x}\, dx + Le^{-\lambda L} = \frac{1 - e^{-\lambda L}}{\lambda},$$

$$E[B^2|I = 1] = \int_0^L x^2\lambda e^{-\lambda x}\, dx + L^2 e^{-\lambda L} = \frac{2}{\lambda^2}(1 - e^{-\lambda L}) - \frac{2L}{\lambda}e^{-\lambda L},$$

$$\sigma^2 = E[B^2|I = 1] - (E[B|I = 1])^2 = \frac{1 - 2\lambda L e^{-\lambda L} - e^{-2\lambda L}}{\lambda^2}.$$

Using the parameter values given and applying (2.2.25) and (2.2.26), we obtain the following results.

k	q_k	μ_k	σ_k^2	Mean $q_k\mu_k$	Variance $\mu_k^2 q_k(1 - q_k) + \sigma_k^2 q_k$	n_k
1	0.10	0.9179	0.5828	0.09179	0.13411	500
2	0.05	0.5000	0.2498	0.02500	0.02436	2 000

Then S, the sum of the claims, has moments

$$E[S] = 500\,(0.09179) + 2{,}000\,(0.02500) = 95.89,$$

$$\mathrm{Var}(S) = 500\,(0.13411) + 2{,}000\,(0.02436) = 115.78.$$

The criterion for θ is the same as in Example 2.5.1,

$$\Pr(S \le (1 + \theta)E[S]) = 0.95.$$

Again by the normal approximation,

$$\frac{\theta E[S]}{\sqrt{\mathrm{Var}(S)}} = 1.645$$

and

$$\theta = \frac{1.645\sqrt{115.78}}{95.89} = 0.1846.$$

▼

Example 2.5.3

A life insurance company covers 16,000 lives for 1-year term life insurance in amounts shown below.

Benefit Amount	Number Covered
10 000	8 000
20 000	3 500
30 000	2 500
50 000	1 500
100 000	500

The probability of a claim q for each of the 16,000 lives, assumed to be mutually independent, is 0.02. The company wants to set a **retention limit**. For each life, the retention limit is the amount below which this (the **ceding**) company will retain the insurance and above which it will purchase *reinsurance* coverage from another (the *reinsuring*) company. For example, assume the retention limit is 20,000. The company will retain up to 20,000 on each life and purchase reinsurance for the difference between the benefit amount and 20,000 for each of the 4,500 individuals with benefit amounts in excess of 20,000. As a decision criterion, the company wants to minimize the probability that retained claims plus the amount that it pays for reinsurance will exceed 8,250,000. Reinsurance is available at a cost of 0.025 per unit of coverage (i.e., at 125% of the expected claim amount per unit, 0.02). We will consider the block of business as closed. New policies sold during the year are not to enter this decision process. Calculate the retention limit that minimizes the probability that the company's retained claims plus cost of reinsurance exceeds 8,250,000.

Partial Solution:

First, do all calculations in benefit units of 10,000. As an illustrative step, let S be the amount of retained claims paid when the retention limit is 2 (20,000). Our portfolio of retained business is given by

k	Retained Amount b_k	Number Covered n_k
1	1	8 000
2	2	8 000

and

$$E[S] = \sum_{k=1}^{2} n_k b_k q_k = 8{,}000\ (1)(0.02) + 8{,}000\ (2)(0.02) = 480$$

and

$$\text{Var}(S) = \sum_{k=1}^{2} n_k b_k^2 q_k (1 - q_k)$$

$$= 8{,}000\ (1)(0.02)(0.98) + 8{,}000\ (4)(0.02)(0.98) = 784.$$

In addition to the retained claims, S, there is the cost of reinsurance premiums. The total coverage in the plan is

$$8{,}000\ (1) + 3{,}500\ (2) + 2{,}500\ (3) + 1{,}500\ (5) + 500\ (10) = 35{,}000.$$

The retained coverage for the plan is

$$8{,}000\ (1) + 8{,}000\ (2) = 24{,}000.$$

Therefore, the total amount reinsured is $35{,}000 - 24{,}000 = 11{,}000$ and the reinsurance cost is $11{,}000(0.025) = 275$. Thus, at retention limit 2, the retained claims plus reinsurance cost is $S + 275$. The decision criterion is based on the probability that this total cost will exceed 825,

$$\Pr(S + 275 > 825) = \Pr(S > 550)$$

$$= \Pr\left[\frac{S - E[S]}{\sqrt{Var(S)}} > \frac{550 - E[S]}{\sqrt{Var(S)}}\right]$$

$$= \Pr\left[\frac{S - E[S]}{\sqrt{Var(S)}} > 2.5\right].$$

Using the normal distribution, this is approximately 0.0062. The solution is completed in Exercises 2.13 and 2.14. ▼

In Section 1.5 stop-loss insurance, which is available as a reinsurance coverage, was discussed. The expected value of the claims paid under the stop-loss reinsurance coverage can be approximated by using the normal distribution as the distribution of total claims.

Let total claims, X, have a normal distribution with mean μ and variance σ^2 and let d be the deductible of the stop-loss insurance. Then, by (1.5.2A), the expected reinsurance claims equal

$$E[I_d(X)] = \frac{1}{\sqrt{2\pi}\sigma} \int_d^\infty (x - d) \exp\left[\frac{-(x - \mu)^2}{2\sigma^2}\right] dx. \qquad (2.5.1)$$

Changing the variable of integration to $z = (x - \mu)/\sigma$ and defining β by $d = \mu + \beta\sigma$, we obtain the following general expression for the expected value of stop-loss claims under a normal distribution assumption:

$$E[I_d(X)] = \sigma \left\{\frac{\exp(-\beta^2/2)}{(2\pi)^{0.5}} - \beta[1 - \Phi(\beta)]\right\} \qquad (2.5.2)$$

where $\Phi(x)$ is the distribution function for the standard normal distribution.

Example 2.5.4

Consider the portfolio of insurance contracts in Example 2.5.3. Calculate the expected value of the claims provided by a stop-loss reinsurance coverage where
a. There is no individual reinsurance and the deductible amount is 7,500,000
b. There is a retention amount of 20,000 on individual policies and the deductible amount on the business retained is 5,300,000.

Solution:

a. With no individual reinsurance and the use of 10,000 as the unit,

$$E[S] = 0.02[8,000(1) + 3,500(2) + 2,500(3) + 1,500(5) + 500(10)] = 700$$

and

$$Var(S) = (0.02)(0.98)[8,000(1) + 3,500(4) + 2,500(9) + 1,500(25) + 500(100)]$$

$$= 2,587.2$$

so
$$\sigma(S) = 50.86.$$

Then, with

$$\beta = \frac{(d - \mu)}{\sigma} = \frac{(750 - 700)}{50.86} = 0.983$$

the application of (2.5.2) gives us

$$P = 50.86[0.24608 - (0.983)(0.16280)] = 4.377.$$

This is equivalent to 43,770 in the example as posed.

b. In Example 2.5.3 we determined the mean and the variance of the aggregate claims, after imposing a 20,000 retention limit per individual, to be 480 and 784, respectively, in units of 10,000. Thus $\sigma(S) = 28$.

Then, with

$$\beta = \frac{d - \mu}{\sigma} = \frac{530 - 480}{28} = 1.786$$

the application of (2.5.2) gives us

$$P = 28[0.08100 - (1.786)(0.03707)] = 0.414.$$

This is equivalent to 4,140 in the example as posed.   ▼

2.6   Notes and References

The basis of the material in Sections 2.2, 2.3, and 2.4 can be found in a number of post-calculus probability and statistics texts. Mood et al. (1974) prove the theorems given in (2.2.10) and (2.2.11). They also provide an extensive discussion of properties of the moment generating function. For a discussion of the advanced mathematical methods for deriving the distribution function that corresponds to a given moment generating function, see Bellman et al. (1966). Methods are also available to obtain the p.f. of a discrete distribution from its *probability generating function;* see Kornya (1983).

DeGroot (1986) provides a discussion of several conditions under which the central limit theorem holds. Kendall and Stuart (1977) give material on *normal power expansions* that may be viewed as modifications of the normal approximation to improve numerical results. Bowers (1967) also describes the use of normal power expansions and gives an application to approximate the distribution of present values for an annuity portfolio.

Exercises

Section 2.2

2.1. Use (2.2.3) and (2.2.4) to obtain the mean and variance of the claim random variable X where $q = 0.05$ and the claim amount is fixed at 10.

2.2. Obtain the mean and variance of the claim random variable X where $q = 0.05$ and the claim amount random variable B is uniformly distributed between 0 and 20.

2.3. Let X be the number of heads observed in five tosses of a true coin. Then, X true dice are thrown. Let Y be the sum of the numbers showing on the dice. Determine the mean and variance of Y. [Hint: Apply (2.2.10) and (2.2.11).]

2.4. Let X be the number showing when one true die is thrown. Let Y be the number of heads obtained when X true coins are then tossed. Calculate $E[Y]$ and $Var(Y)$.

2.5. Let X be the number obtained when one true die is tossed. Let Y be the sum of the numbers obtained when X true dice are then thrown. Calculate $E[Y]$ and $Var(Y)$.

2.6. The probability of a fire in a certain structure in a given time period is 0.02. If a fire occurs, the damage to the structure is uniformly distributed over the interval $(0, a)$ where a is its total value. Calculate the mean and variance of fire damage to the structure within the time period.

Section 2.3

2.7. Independent random variables X_k for four lives have the discrete probability functions given below.

x	$Pr(X_1 = x)$	$Pr(X_2 = x)$	$Pr(X_3 = x)$	$Pr(X_4 = x)$
0	0.6	0.7	0.6	0.9
1	0.0	0.2	0.0	0.0
2	0.3	0.1	0.0	0.0
3	0.0	0.0	0.4	0.0
4	0.1	0.0	0.0	0.1

Use a convolution process on the non-negative integer values of x to obtain $F_S(x)$ for $x = 0, 1, 2, \ldots , 13$ where $S = X_1 + X_2 + X_3 + X_4$.

2.8. Let X_i for $i = 1, 2, 3$ be independent and identically distributed with the d.f.

$$F(x) = \begin{cases} 0 & x < 0 \\ x & 0 \le x < 1 \\ 1 & x \ge 1. \end{cases}$$

Let $S = X_1 + X_2 + X_3$.

a. Show that $F_S(x)$ is given by

$$F_S(x) = \begin{cases} 0 & x < 0 \\[2mm] \dfrac{x^3}{6} & 0 \le x < 1 \\[3mm] \dfrac{x^3 - 3(x-1)^3}{6} & 1 \le x < 2 \\[3mm] \dfrac{x^3 - 3(x-1)^3 + 3(x-2)^3}{6} & 2 \le x < 3 \\[3mm] 1 & x \ge 3. \end{cases}$$

b. Show that $E[S] = 1.5$ and $\mathrm{Var}(S) = 0.25$.

c. Evaluate the following probabilities using the d.f. of part (a):

(i) $\Pr(S \le 0.5)$
(ii) $\Pr(S \le 1.0)$
(iii) $\Pr(S \le 1.5)$.

2.9. Find the mean and variance of the inverse Gaussian distribution by using its m.g.f. as given in Example 2.3.5.

Section 2.4

2.10. Calculate the mean and variance of X and Y in Example 2.3.2. Use a normal distribution to approximate $\Pr(X + Y > 4)$. Compare this with the exact answer.

2.11. a. Use the central limit theorem to calculate b, c, and d, for given a, in the statement

$$\Pr\left(\sum_1^n X_i \ge n\mu + a\sqrt{n}\,\sigma\right) \cong c + b\Phi(d)$$

where the X_i's are independent and identically distributed with mean μ and variance σ^2 and $\Phi(z)$ is the d.f. of the standard normal distribution.

b. Evaluate the probabilities in Exercise 2.8(c) by use of the normal approximation developed in part (a).

2.12. A random variable U has m.g.f.

$$M_U(t) = (1 - 2t)^{-9} \qquad t < \frac{1}{2}.$$

a. Use the m.g.f. to calculate the mean and variance of U.

b. Use a normal approximation to calculate points $y_{0.05}$ and $y_{0.01}$ such that $\Pr(U > y_\epsilon) = \epsilon$.

Note the random variable U has a gamma distribution with parameters $\alpha = 9$ and $\beta = 1/2$. Gamma distributions with $\alpha = n/2$ and $\beta = 1/2$ are chi-square distributions with n degrees of freedom. Thus U has a chi-square distribution with 18 degrees of freedom. From tables of d.f.'s of chi-square distributions, we obtain $y_{0.05} = 28.869$ and $y_{0.01} = 34.805$.

Section 2.5

2.13. Calculate the probability that the total cost in Example 2.5.3 will exceed 8,250,000 if the retention limit is
      a. 30,000   b. 50,000.

2.14. Calculate the retention limit that minimizes the probability of the total cost in Example 2.5.3 exceeding 8,250,000. Assume that the limit is between 30,000 and 50,000.

2.15. A fire insurance company covers 160 structures against fire damage up to an amount stated in the contract. The numbers of contracts at the different contract amounts are given below.

Contract Amount	Number of Contracts
10 000	80
20 000	35
30 000	25
50 000	15
100 000	5

Assume that for each of the structures, the probability of one claim within a year is 0.04, and the probability of more than one claim is 0. Assume that fires in the structures are mutually independent events. Furthermore, assume that the conditional distribution of the claim size, given that a claim has occurred, is uniformly distributed over the interval from 0 to the contract amount. Let N be the number of claims and let S be the amount of claims in a 1-year period.
    a. Calculate the mean and variance of N.
    b. Calculate the mean and variance of S.
    c. What relative security loading, θ, should be used so the company can collect an amount equal to the 99th percentile of the distribution of total claims? (Use a normal approximation.)

2.16. Consider a portfolio of 32 policies. For each policy, the probability q of a claim is $1/6$ and B, the benefit amount given that there is a claim, has p.d.f.

$$f(y) = \begin{cases} 2(1 - y) & 0 < y < 1 \\ 0 & \text{elsewhere.} \end{cases}$$

Let S be the total claims for the portfolio. Using a normal approximation, estimate $\Pr(S > 4)$.

SURVIVAL DISTRIBUTIONS AND LIFE TABLES

3.1 Introduction

Chapter 1 was dedicated to showing how insurance can increase the expected utility of individuals facing random losses. In Chapter 2 simple models for single-period insurance policies were developed. The foundations of these models were Bernoulli random variables associated with the occurrence or nonoccurrence of a loss. The occurrence of a loss, in some examples, resulted in a second random process generating the amount of the loss. Chapters 4 through 8 deal primarily with models for insurance systems designed to manage random losses where the randomness is related to how long an individual will survive. In these chapters the *time-until-death* random variable, $T(x)$, is the basic building block. This chapter develops a set of ideas for describing and using the distribution of time-until-death and the distribution of the corresponding *age-at-death*, X.

We show how a distribution of the age-at-death random variable can be summarized by a *life table.* Such tables are useful in many fields of science. Consequently a profusion of notation and nomenclature has developed among the various professions using life tables. For example, engineers use life tables to study the reliability of complex mechanical and electronic systems. Biostatisticians use life tables to compare the effectiveness of alternative treatments of serious diseases. Demographers use life tables as tools in population projections. In this text, life tables are used to build models for insurance systems designed to assist individuals facing uncertainty about the times of their deaths. This application determines the viewpoint adopted. However, when it provides a bridge to other disciplines, notes relating the discussion to alternative applications of life tables are added.

A life table is an indispensable component of many models in actuarial science. In fact, some scholars fix the date of the beginning of actuarial science as 1693. In that year, Edmund Halley published "An Estimate of the Degrees of the Mortality of Mankind, Drawn from Various Tables of Births and Funerals at the City of

Breslau." The life table, called the Breslau Table, contained in Halley's paper remains of interest because of its surprisingly modern notation and ideas.

3.2 Probability for the Age-at-Death

In this section we formulate the uncertainty of age-at-death in probability concepts.

3.2.1 The Survival Function

Let us consider a newborn child. This newborn's age-at-death, X, is a continuous-type random variable. Let $F_X(x)$ denote the distribution function (d.f.) of X,

$$F_X(x) = \Pr(X \le x) \qquad x \ge 0, \tag{3.2.1}$$

and set

$$s(x) = 1 - F_X(x) = \Pr(X > x) \qquad x \ge 0. \tag{3.2.2}$$

We always assume that $F_X(0) = 0$, which implies $s(0) = 1$. The function $s(x)$ is called the *survival function* (s.f.). For any positive x, $s(x)$ is the probability a newborn will attain age x. The distribution of X can be defined by specifying either the function $F_X(x)$ or the function $s(x)$. Within actuarial science and demography, the survival function has traditionally been used as a starting point for further developments. Within probability and statistics, the d.f. usually plays this role. However, from the properties of the d.f., we can deduce corresponding properties of the survival function.

Using the laws of probability, we can make probability statements about the age-at-death in terms of either the survival function or the distribution function. For example, the probability that a newborn dies between ages x and z ($x < z$) is

$$\Pr(x < X \le z) = F_X(z) - F_X(x)$$

$$= s(x) - s(z).$$

3.2.2 Time-until-Death for a Person Age x

The conditional probability that a newborn will die between the ages x and z, given survival to age x, is

$$\Pr(x < X \le z | X > x) = \frac{F_X(z) - F_X(x)}{1 - F_X(x)}$$

$$= \frac{s(x) - s(z)}{s(x)}. \tag{3.2.3}$$

The symbol (x) is used to denote a *life-age-x*. The future lifetime of (x), $X - x$, is denoted by $T(x)$.

Within actuarial science, it is frequently necessary to make probability statements about $T(x)$. For this purpose, and to promote research and communication, a set of symbols, part of the International Actuarial Notation, was originally adopted by the 1898 International Actuarial Congress. Symbols for common actuarial functions and principles to guide the adoption of new symbols were established. This system has been subject to constant review and is revised or extended as necessary by the International Actuarial Association's Permanent Committee on Notation. These notational conventions are followed in this book whenever possible.

These symbols differ from those used for probability notation, and the reader may be unfamiliar with them. For example, a single-variate function that would be written $q(x)$ in probability notation is written q_x in this system. Likewise, a multivariate function is written in actuarial notation using combinations of subscripts, superscripts, and other symbols. The general rules for defining a function in actuarial notation are given in Appendix 4. The reader may want to study these forms before continuing the discussion of the future-lifetime random variable.

To make probability statements about $T(x)$, we use the notations

$$_t q_x = \Pr[T(x) \le t] \qquad t \ge 0, \tag{3.2.4}$$

$$_t p_x = 1 - _t q_x = \Pr[T(x) > t] \qquad t \ge 0. \tag{3.2.5}$$

The symbol $_t q_x$ can be interpreted as the probability that (x) will die within t years; that is, $_t q_x$ is the d.f. of $T(x)$. On the other hand, $_t p_x$ can be interpreted as the probability that (x) will attain age $x + t$; that is, $_t p_x$ is the s.f. for (x). In the special case of a life-age-0, we have $T(0) = X$ and

$$_x p_0 = s(x) \qquad x \ge 0. \tag{3.2.6}$$

If $t = 1$, convention permits us to omit the prefix in the symbols defined in (3.2.4) and (3.2.5), and we have

$$q_x = \Pr[(x) \text{ will die within 1 year}],$$

$$p_x = \Pr[(x) \text{ will attain age } x + 1].$$

There is a special symbol for the more general event that (x) will survive t years and die within the following u years; that is, (x) will die between ages $x + t$ and $x + t + u$. This special symbol is given by

$$_{t|u} q_x = \Pr[t < T(x) \le t + u]$$

$$= _{t+u} q_x - _t q_x$$

$$= _t p_x - _{t+u} p_x. \tag{3.2.7}$$

As before, if $u = 1$, the prefix is deleted in $_{t|u} q_x$, and we have $_{t|} q_x$.

At this point it appears there are two expressions for the probability that (x) will die between ages x and $x + u$. Formula (3.2.7) with $t = 0$ is one such expression; (3.2.3) with $z = x + u$ is a second expression. Are these two probabilities different? Formula (3.2.3) can be interpreted as the conditional probability that a newborn will die between ages x and $z = x + u$, given survival to age x. The only information on the newborn, now at age x, is its survival to that age. Hence, the probability statement is based on a conditional distribution of survival for newborns.

On the other hand, (3.2.7) with $t = 0$ defines a probability that a life observed at age x will die between ages x and $x + u$. The observation on the life at age x might include information other than simply survival. Such information might be that the life has just passed a physical examination for insurance, or it might be that the life has commenced treatment for a serious illness. Life tables for situations where the observation of a life at age x implies more than simply survival of a newborn to age x are discussed in Section 3.8, where additional notation for those life tables is introduced. We will continue development of the theory without further reference to the distinction between (3.2.3) and (3.2.7), and we assume that until that section, observation of survival at age x will yield the same conditional distribution of survival as the hypothesis that a newborn has survived to age x; that is,

$$
{}_tp_x = \frac{{}_{x+t}p_0}{{}_xp_0} = \frac{s(x + t)}{s(x)}, \tag{3.2.8}
$$

$$
{}_tq_x = 1 - \frac{s(x + t)}{s(x)}. \tag{3.2.9}
$$

Under this approach, (3.2.7), and its many special cases, can be expressed as

$$
\begin{aligned}
{}_{t|u}q_x &= \frac{s(x + t) - s(x + t + u)}{s(x)} \\
&= \left[\frac{s(x + t)}{s(x)} \right]\left[\frac{s(x + t) - s(x + t + u)}{s(x + t)} \right] \\
&= {}_tp_x \; {}_uq_{x+t}.
\end{aligned} \tag{3.2.10}
$$

3.2.3   Curtate-Future-Lifetime

A discrete random variable associated with the future lifetime is the number of future years completed by (x) prior to death. It is called the *curtate-future-lifetime* of (x) and is denoted by $K(x)$. Because $K(x)$ is the greatest integer in $T(x)$, its p.f. is

$$
\begin{aligned}
\Pr[K(x) = k] &= \Pr[k \le T(x) < k + 1] \\
&= \Pr[k < T(x) \le k + 1] \\
&= {}_kp_x - {}_{k+1}p_x \\
&= {}_kp_x \, q_{x+k} = {}_{k|}q_x \qquad k = 0, 1, 2, \ldots . \tag{3.2.11}
\end{aligned}
$$

The switching of inequalities is possible since, under our assumption that $T(x)$ is a continuous-type random variable, $\Pr[T(x) = k] = \Pr[T(x) = k + 1] = 0$. Expression (3.2.11) is a special case of (3.2.7) where $u = 1$ and k is a non-negative integer. From (3.2.11) we can see that the d.f. of $K(x)$ is the step function

$$
F_{K(x)}(y) = \sum_{h=0}^{k} {}_{h|}q_x = {}_{k+1}q_x, \qquad y \ge 0 \text{ and } k \text{ is the greatest integer in } y.
$$

It often follows from the context that $T(x)$ is the future lifetime of (x), in which case we may write T instead of $T(x)$. Likewise, we may write K instead of $K(x)$.

3.2.4 Force of Mortality

Formula (3.2.3) expresses, in terms of the d.f. and in terms of the survival function, the conditional probability that (0) will die between ages x and z, given survival to x. With $z - x$ held constant, say, at c, then considered as a function of x, this conditional probability describes the distribution of the probability of death in the near future (between time 0 and c) for a life of attained age x. An analogue of this function for instantaneous death can be obtained by using the density of probability of death at attained age x, that is, using (3.2.3) with $z = x + \Delta x$,

$$\Pr(x < X \le x + \Delta x \,|\, X > x) = \frac{F_X(x + \Delta x) - F_X(x)}{1 - F_X(x)}$$

$$\cong \frac{f_X(x)\Delta x}{1 - F_X(x)}. \tag{3.2.12}$$

In this expression $F'_X(x) = f_X(x)$ is the p.d.f. of the continuous age-at-death random variable. The function

$$\frac{f_X(x)}{1 - F_X(x)}$$

in (3.2.12) has a conditional probability density interpretation. For each age x, it gives the value of the conditional p.d.f. of X at exact age x, given survival to that age, and is denoted by $\mu(x)$.

We have

$$\mu(x) = \frac{f_X(x)}{1 - F_X(x)}$$

$$= \frac{-s'(x)}{s(x)}. \tag{3.2.13}$$

The properties of $f_X(x)$ and $1 - F_X(x)$ imply that $\mu(x) \ge 0$.

In actuarial science and demography $\mu(x)$ is called the *force of mortality.* In reliability theory, the study of the survival probabilities of manufactured parts and systems, $\mu(x)$ is called the *failure rate* or *hazard rate* or, more fully, the *hazard rate function.*

As is true for the s.f., the force of mortality can be used to specify the distribution of X. To obtain this result, we start with (3.2.13), change x to y, and rearrange to obtain

$$-\mu(y)\, dy = d \log s(y).$$

Integrating this expression from x to $x + n$, we have

$$-\int_x^{x+n} \mu(y)\,dy = \log\left[\frac{s(x+n)}{s(x)}\right]$$

$$= \log\ {}_np_x,$$

and on taking exponentials obtain

$${}_np_x = \exp[-\int_x^{x+n} \mu(y)\,dy]. \tag{3.2.14}$$

Sometimes it is convenient to rewrite (3.2.14), with $s = y - x$, as

$${}_np_x = \exp[-\int_0^n \mu(x + s)\,ds]. \tag{3.2.15}$$

In particular, we will change the notation to conform with that used in (3.2.6) by setting the age already lived to 0 and denoting the time of survival by x. We then have

$${}_xp_0 = s(x) = \exp[-\int_0^x \mu(s)\,ds]. \tag{3.2.16}$$

In addition,

$$F_X(x) = 1 - s(x) = 1 - \exp[-\int_0^x \mu(s)\,ds] \tag{3.2.17}$$

and

$$F_X'(x) = f_X(x) = \exp[-\int_0^x \mu(s)\,ds]\ \mu(x)$$

$$= {}_xp_0\ \mu(x). \tag{3.2.18}$$

Let $F_{T(x)}(t)$ and $f_{T(x)}(t)$ denote, respectively, the d.f. and p.d.f. of $T(x)$, the future lifetime of (x). From (3.2.4) we note that $F_{T(x)}(t) = {}_tq_x$; therefore,

$$f_{T(x)}(t) = \frac{d}{dt}\ {}_tq_x$$

$$= \frac{d}{dt}\left[1 - \frac{s(x+t)}{s(x)}\right]$$

$$= \frac{s(x+t)}{s(x)}\left[-\frac{s'(x+t)}{s(x+t)}\right]$$

$$= {}_tp_x\ \mu(x+t) \qquad t \geq 0. \tag{3.2.19}$$

Thus ${}_tp_x\ \mu(x + t)\ dt$ is the probability that (x) dies between t and $t + dt$, and

$$\int_0^\infty {}_tp_x\ \mu(x+t)\,dt = 1$$

where the upper limit on the integral is written as positive infinity (an abbreviation for integrating over all positive probability density).

It follows from (3.2.19) that

$$\frac{d}{dt}(1 - {}_tp_x) = -\frac{d}{dt}\ {}_tp_x = {}_tp_x\ \mu(x+t). \tag{3.2.20}$$

This equivalent form is useful in several developments in actuarial mathematics.

Since

$$\lim_{n \to \infty} {}_n p_x = 0,$$

we have

$$\lim_{n \to \infty} (-\log {}_n p_x) = \infty;$$

that is,

$$\lim_{n \to \infty} \int_x^{x+n} \mu(y) \, dy = \infty.$$

The developments of this section are summarized in Table 3.2.1.

The lower half of Table 3.2.1 summarizes some of the relationships among functions of general probability theory and those specific to age-at-death applications. There are many other examples where age-at-death questions can be formed in the more general probability setting. The following will illustrate this point.

TABLE 3.2.1
Probability Theory Functions for Age-at-Death, X

	d.f. $F_X(x)$	Survival Function $s(x)$		p.d.f. $f_X(x)$	Force of Mortality $\mu(x)$
For		Requirements	For		Requirements
$x < 0$	$F_X(x) = 0$	$s(x) = 1$	$x < 0$ $\quad f_X(x) = 0$		$\mu(x) = 0$
$x = 0$	$F_X(0) = 0$	$s(0) = 1$	$x = 0$ $\quad$ undefined		undefined
$x \geq 0$	nondecreasing	nonincreasing	$x > 0$ $\quad f_X(x) \geq 0$		$\mu(x) \geq 0$
$\lim\limits_{x \to \infty}$	$F_X(\infty) = 1$	$s(\infty) = 0$	$\lim\limits_{x \to \infty}$ $\quad \int_0^\infty f_X(x) \, dt = 1$		$\int_0^\infty \mu(x) dx = \infty$
Functions in Terms of			Relationships		
$F_X(x)$	$F_X(x)$	$1 - F_X(x)$	$F_X'(x)$		$F_X'(x) / [1 - F_X(x)]$
$s(x)$	$1 - s(x)$	$s(x)$	$-s'(x)$		$-s'(x) / s(x)$
$f_X(x)$	$\int_0^x f_X(u) du$	$\int_x^\infty f_X(u) du$	$f_X(x)$		$f_X(x) / \int_x^\infty f_X(u) du$
$\mu(x)$	$1 - \exp[-\int_0^x \mu(t) \, dt]$	$\exp[-\int_0^x \mu(t) \, dt]$	$\mu(x)\exp[-\int_0^x \mu(t) \, dt]$		$\mu(x)$

Example 3.2.1

If $\bar{A}$ refers to the complement of the event A within the sample space and $\Pr(\bar{A}) \neq 0$, the following expresses an identity in probability theory:

$$\Pr(A \cup B) = \Pr(A) + \Pr(\bar{A}) \, \Pr(B|\bar{A}).$$

Rewrite this identity in actuarial notation for the events $A = [T(x) \leq t]$ and $B = [t < T(x) \leq 1]$, $0 < t < 1$.

Solution:

$\Pr(A \cup B)$ becomes $\Pr[T(x) \le 1] = q_x$, $\Pr(A)$ is ${}_t q_x$, and $\Pr(B|\bar{A})$ is ${}_{1-t}q_{x+t}$; hence

$$q_x = {}_t q_x + {}_t p_x \, {}_{1-t}q_{x+t}.$$

▼

3.3 Life Tables

A published life table usually contains tabulations, by individual ages, of the basic functions q_x, l_x, d_x, and, possibly, additional derived functions. Before presenting such a table, we consider an interpretation of these functions that is directly related to the probability functions discussed in the preceding section.

3.3.1 Relation of Life Table Functions to the Survival Function

In (3.2.9) we expressed the conditional probability that (x) will die within t years by

$$_t q_x = 1 - \frac{s(x + t)}{s(x)},$$

and, in particular, we have

$$q_x = 1 - \frac{s(x + 1)}{s(x)}.$$

We now consider a group of l_0 newborns, $l_0 = 100{,}000$, for instance. Each newborn's age-at-death has a distribution specified by s.f. $s(x)$. In addition, we let $\mathscr{L}(x)$ denote the group's number of survivors to age x. We index these lives by $j = 1, 2, \ldots, l_0$ and observe that

$$\mathscr{L}(x) = \sum_{j=1}^{l_0} I_j$$

where I_j is an indicator for the survival of life j; that is,

$$I_j = \begin{cases} 1 & \text{if life } j \text{ survives to age } x \\ 0 & \text{otherwise.} \end{cases}$$

Since $\mathrm{E}[I_j] = s(x)$,

$$\mathrm{E}[\mathscr{L}(x)] = \sum_{j=1}^{l_0} \mathrm{E}[I_j] = l_0 \, s(x).$$

We denote $\mathrm{E}[\mathscr{L}(x)]$ by l_x; that is, l_x represents the expected number of survivors to age x from the l_0 newborns, and we have

$$l_x = l_0 \, s(x). \tag{3.3.1}$$

Moreover, under the assumption that the indicators I_j are mutually independent, $\mathscr{L}(x)$ has a binomial distribution with parameters $n = l_0$ and $p = s(x)$. Note, however, that (3.3.1) does not require the independence assumption.

In a similar fashion, $_n\mathcal{D}_x$ denotes the number of deaths between ages x and $x + n$ from among the initial l_0 lives. We denote $E[_n\mathcal{D}_x]$ by $_nd_x$. Since a newborn has probability $s(x) - s(x + n)$ of death between ages x and $x + n$ we can, by an argument similar to that for l_x, express

$$_nd_x = E[_n\mathcal{D}_x] = l_0[s(x) - s(x + n)]$$

$$= l_x - l_{x+n}. \qquad (3.3.2)$$

When $n = 1$, we omit the prefixes on $_n\mathcal{D}_x$ and $_nd_x$.

From (3.3.1), we see that

$$-\frac{1}{l_x}\frac{dl_x}{dx} = -\frac{1}{s(x)}\frac{ds(x)}{dx} = \mu(x) \qquad (3.3.3)$$

and

$$-dl_x = l_x \,\mu(x)\,dx. \qquad (3.3.4)$$

Since

$$l_x \,\mu(x) = l_0 \,_xp_0\, \mu(x) = l_0 \,f_X(x),$$

the factor $l_x \,\mu(x)$ in (3.3.4) can be interpreted as the expected density of deaths in the age interval $(x, x + dx)$. We note further that

$$l_x = l_0 \exp[-\int_0^x \mu(y)\,dy], \qquad (3.3.5)$$

$$l_{x+n} = l_x \exp[-\int_x^{x+n} \mu(y)\,dy], \qquad (3.3.6)$$

$$l_x - l_{x+n} = \int_x^{x+n} l_y \,\mu(y)\,dy. \qquad (3.3.7)$$

For convenience of reference, we call this concept of l_0 newborns, each with survival function $s(x)$, a ***random survivorship group***.

3.3.2   Life Table Example

In "Life Table for the Total Population: United States, 1979–81" (Table 3.3.1), the functions $_tq_x$, l_x, and $_td_x$ are presented with $l_0 = 100,000$. Except for the first year of life, the value of t in the tabulated functions $_tq_x$ and $_td_x$ is 1. The other functions appearing in the table are discussed in Section 3.5.

The 1979–81 U.S. Life Table was not constructed by observing 100,000 newborns until the last survivor died. Instead, it was based on estimates of probabilities of death, given survival to various ages, derived from the experience of the entire U.S. population in the years around the 1980 census. In using the random survivorship group concept with this table, we must make the assumption that the probabilities derived from the table will be appropriate for the lifetimes of those who belong to the survivorship group.

TABLE 3.3.1

Life Table for the Total Population: United States, 1979–81

(1)	(2)	(3)	(4)	(5)	(6)	(7)
	Proportion Dying	**Of 100,000 Born Alive**		**Stationary Population***		**Average Remaining Lifetime**
Age Interval	**Proportion of Persons Alive at Beginning of Age Interval Dying during Interval**	**Number Living at Beginning of Age Interval**	**Number Dying during Age Interval**	**Years Lived in the Age Interval**	**Years Lived in This and All Subsequent Age Intervals**	**Average Number of Years of Life Remaining at Beginning of Age Interval**
Period of Life between Two Ages x to $x + t$	$_tq_x$	l_x	$_td_x$	$_tL_x$	T_x	$\overset{\circ}{e}_x$
Days						
0–1	0.00463	100 000	463	273	7 387 758	73.88
1–7	0.00246	99 537	245	1 635	7 387 485	74.22
7–28	0.00139	99 292	138	5 708	7 385 850	74.38
28–365	0.00418	99 154	414	91 357	7 380 142	74.43
Years						
0–1	0.01260	100 000	1 260	98 973	7 387 758	73.88
1–2	0.00093	98 740	92	98 694	7 288 785	73.82
2–3	0.00065	98 648	64	98 617	7 190 091	72.89
3–4	0.00050	98 584	49	98 560	7 091 474	71.93
4–5	0.00040	98 535	40	98 515	6 992 914	70.97
5–6	0.00037	98 495	36	98 477	6 894 399	70.00
6–7	0.00033	98 459	33	98 442	6 795 922	69.02
7–8	0.00030	98 426	30	98 412	6 697 480	68.05
8–9	0.00027	98 396	26	98 383	6 599 068	67.07
9–10	0.00023	98 370	23	98 358	6 500 685	66.08
10–11	0.00020	98 347	19	98 338	6 402 327	65.10
11–12	0.00019	98 328	19	98 319	6 303 989	64.11
12–13	0.00025	98 309	24	98 297	6 205 670	63.12
13–14	0.00037	98 285	37	98 266	6 107 373	62.14
14–15	0.00053	98 248	52	98 222	6 009 107	61.16
15–16	0.00069	98 196	67	98 163	5 910 885	60.19
16–17	0.00083	98 129	82	98 087	5 812 722	59.24
17–18	0.00095	98 047	94	98 000	5 714 635	58.28
18–19	0.00105	97 953	102	97 902	5 616 635	57.34
19–20	0.00112	97 851	110	97 796	5 518 733	56.40
20–21	0.00120	97 741	118	97 682	5 420 937	55.46
21–22	0.00127	97 623	124	97 561	5 323 255	54.53
22–23	0.00132	97 499	129	97 435	5 225 694	53.60
23–24	0.00134	97 370	130	97 306	5 128 259	52.67
24–25	0.00133	97 240	130	97 175	5 030 953	51.74
25–26	0.00132	97 110	128	97 046	4 933 778	50.81
26–27	0.00131	96 982	126	96 919	4 836 732	49.87
27–28	0.00130	96 856	126	96 793	4 739 813	48.94
28–29	0.00130	96 730	126	96 667	4 643 020	48.00
29–30	0.00131	96 604	127	96 541	4 546 353	47.06

*Stationary population is a demographic concept treated in Chapter 19.

TABLE 3.3.1—Continued

Life Table for the Total Population: United States, 1979–81

(1) Age Interval Period of Life between Two Ages x to $x + t$	(2) Proportion Dying Proportion of Persons Alive at Beginning of Age Interval Dying during Interval ${}_tq_x$	(3) Of 100,000 Born Alive Number Living at Beginning of Age Interval l_x	(4) Number Dying during Age Interval ${}_td_x$	(5) Stationary Population* Years Lived in the Age Interval ${}_tL_x$	(6) Years Lived in This and All Subsequent Age Intervals T_x	(7) Average Remaining Lifetime Average Number of Years of Life Remaining at Beginning of Age Interval $\overset{\circ}{e}_x$
Years						
30–31	0.00133	96 477	127	96 414	4 449 812	46.12
31–32	0.00134	96 350	130	96 284	4 353 398	45.18
32–33	0.00137	96 220	132	96 155	4 257 114	44.24
33–34	0.00142	96 088	137	96 019	4 160 959	43.30
34–35	0.00150	95 951	143	95 880	4 064 940	42.36
35–36	0.00159	95 808	153	95 731	3 969 060	41.43
36–37	0.00170	95 655	163	95 574	3 873 329	40.49
37–38	0.00183	95 492	175	95 404	3 777 755	39.56
38–39	0.00197	95 317	188	95 224	3 682 351	38.63
39–40	0.00213	95 129	203	95 027	3 587 127	37.71
40–41	0.00232	94 926	220	94 817	3 492 100	36.79
41–42	0.00254	94 706	241	94 585	3 397 283	35.87
42–43	0.00279	94 465	264	94 334	3 302 698	34.96
43–44	0.00306	94 201	288	94 057	3 208 364	34.06
44–45	0.00335	93 913	314	93 756	3 114 307	33.16
45–46	0.00366	93 599	343	93 427	3 020 551	32.27
46–47	0.00401	93 256	374	93 069	2 927 124	31.39
47–48	0.00442	92 882	410	92 677	2 834 055	30.51
48–49	0.00488	92 472	451	92 246	2 741 378	29.65
49–50	0.00538	92 021	495	91 773	2 649 132	28.79
50–51	0.00589	91 526	540	91 256	2 557 359	27.94
51–52	0.00642	90 986	584	90 695	2 466 103	27.10
52–53	0.00699	90 402	631	90 086	2 375 408	26.28
53–54	0.00761	89 771	684	89 430	2 285 322	25.46
54–55	0.00830	89 087	739	88 717	2 195 892	24.65
55–56	0.00902	88 348	797	87 950	2 107 175	23.85
56–57	0.00978	87 551	856	87 122	2 019 225	23.06
57–58	0.01059	86 695	919	86 236	1 932 103	22.29
58–59	0.01151	85 776	987	85 283	1 845 867	21.52
59–60	0.01254	84 789	1 063	84 258	1 760 584	20.76
60–61	0.01368	83 726	1 145	83 153	1 676 326	20.02
61–62	0.01493	82 581	1 233	81 965	1 593 173	19.29
62–63	0.01628	81 348	1 324	80 686	1 511 208	18.58
63–64	0.01767	80 024	1 415	79 316	1 430 522	17.88
64–65	0.01911	78 609	1 502	77 859	1 351 206	17.19

*Stationary population is a demographic concept treated in Chapter 19.

TABLE 3.3.1—Continued

Life Table for the Total Population: United States, 1979–81

(1) Age Interval Period of Life between Two Ages x to $x + t$	(2) Proportion Dying Proportion of Persons Alive at Beginning of Age Interval Dying during Interval $_tq_x$	(3) Of 100,000 Born Alive Number Living at Beginning of Age Interval l_x	(4) Number Dying during Age Interval $_td_x$	(5) Stationary Population* Years Lived in the Age Interval $_tL_x$	(6) Years Lived in This and All Subsequent Age Intervals T_x	(7) Average Remaining Lifetime Average Number of Years of Life Remaining at Beginning of Age Interval $\overset{\circ}{e}_x$
Years						
65–66	0.02059	77 107	1 587	76 314	1 273 347	16.51
66–67	0.02216	75 520	1 674	74 683	1 197 033	15.85
67–68	0.02389	73 846	1 764	72 964	1 122 350	15.20
68–69	0.02585	72 082	1 864	71 150	1 049 386	14.56
69–70	0.02806	70 218	1 970	69 233	978 236	13.93
70–71	0.03052	68 248	2 083	67 206	909 003	13.32
71–72	0.03315	66 165	2 193	65 069	841 797	12.72
72–73	0.03593	63 972	2 299	62 823	776 728	12.14
73–74	0.03882	61 673	2 394	60 476	713 905	11.58
74–75	0.04184	59 279	2 480	58 039	653 429	11.02
75–76	0.04507	56 799	2 560	55 520	595 390	10.48
76–77	0.04867	54 239	2 640	52 919	539 870	9.95
77–78	0.05274	51 599	2 721	50 238	486 951	9.44
78–79	0.05742	48 878	2 807	47 475	436 713	8.93
79–80	0.06277	46 071	2 891	44 626	389 238	8.45
80–81	0.06882	43 180	2 972	41 694	344 612	7.98
81–82	0.07552	40 208	3 036	38 689	302 918	7.53
82–83	0.08278	37 172	3 077	35 634	264 229	7.11
83–84	0.09041	34 095	3 083	32 553	228 595	6.70
84–85	0.09842	31 012	3 052	29 486	196 042	6.32
85–86	0.10725	27 960	2 999	26 461	166 556	5.96
86–87	0.11712	24 961	2 923	23 500	140 095	5.61
87–88	0.12717	22 038	2 803	20 636	116 595	5.29
88–89	0.13708	19 235	2 637	17 917	95 959	4.99
89–90	0.14728	16 598	2 444	15 376	78 042	4.70
90–91	0.15868	14 154	2 246	13 031	62 666	4.43
91–92	0.17169	11 908	2 045	10 886	49 635	4.17
92–93	0.18570	9 863	1 831	8 948	38 749	3.93
93–94	0.20023	8 032	1 608	7 228	29 801	3.71
94–95	0.21495	6 424	1 381	5 733	22 573	3.51
95–96	0.22976	5 043	1 159	4 463	16 840	3.34
96–97	0.24338	3 884	945	3 412	12 377	3.19
97–98	0.25637	2 939	754	2 562	8 965	3.05
98–99	0.26868	2 185	587	1 892	6 403	2.93
99–100	0.28030	1 598	448	1 374	4 511	2.82

*Stationary population is a demographic concept treated in Chapter 19.

TABLE 3.3.1—Continued
Life Table for the Total Population: United States, 1979–81

(1)	(2)	(3)	(4)	(5)	(6)	(7)
	Proportion Dying					Average Remaining Lifetime
	Proportion of Persons Alive at Beginning of Age Interval Dying during Interval	Of 100,000 Born Alive			Stationary Population*	Average Number of Years of Life Remaining at Beginning of Age Interval
Age Interval		Number Living at Beginning of Age Interval	Number Dying during Age Interval	Years Lived in the Age Interval	Years Lived in This and All Subsequent Age Intervals	
Period of Life between Two Ages x to $x + t$	$_tq_x$	l_x	$_td_x$	$_tL_x$	T_x	$\overset{\circ}{e}_x$
Years						
100–101	0.29120	1 150	335	983	3 137	2.73
101–102	0.30139	815	245	692	2 154	2.64
102–103	0.31089	570	177	481	1 462	2.57
103–104	0.31970	393	126	330	981	2.50
104–105	0.32786	267	88	223	651	2.44
105–106	0.33539	179	60	150	428	2.38
106–107	0.34233	119	41	99	278	2.33
107–108	0.34870	78	27	64	179	2.29
108–109	0.35453	51	18	42	115	2.24
109–110	0.35988	33	12	27	73	2.20

*Stationary population is a demographic concept treated in Chapter 19.

Several observations about the 1979–81 U.S. Life Table are instructive.

Observations:

1. Approximately 1% of a survivorship group of newborns would be expected to die in the first year of life.
2. It would be expected that about 77% of a group of newborns would survive to age 65.
3. The maximum number of deaths within a group would be expected to occur between ages 83 and 84.
4. For human lives, there have been few observations of age-at-death beyond 110. Consequently, it is often assumed that there is an age ω such that $s(x) > 0$ for $x < \omega$, and $s(x) = 0$ for $x \geq \omega$. The age ω, if assumed, is called the *limiting age.* The limiting age for this table is not defined. It is clear that there is a positive probability of survival to age 110, but the table does not indicate the age ω.
5. Local minimums in the expected number of deaths occur around ages 11 and 27 and a local maximum around age 24.
6. Although the values of l_x have been rounded to integers, there is no compelling reason, according to (3.3.1), to do so.

A display such as Table 3.3.1 is the conventional method for describing the distribution of age-at-death. Alternatively, an s.f. can be described in analytic form such as $s(x) = e^{-cx}$, $c > 0$, $x \geq 0$. However, most studies of human mortality for insurance purposes use the representation $s(x) = l_x/l_0$, as illustrated in Table 3.3.1. Since 100,000 $s(x)$ is displayed for only integer values of x, there is a need to interpolate in evaluating $s(x)$ for noninteger values. This is the subject of Section 3.6.

Example 3.3.1

On the basis of Table 3.3.1, evaluate the probability that (20) will
a. Live to 100
b. Die before 70
c. Die in the tenth decade of life.

Solution:

a. $\dfrac{s(100)}{s(20)} = \dfrac{l_{100}}{l_{20}} = \dfrac{1{,}150}{97{,}741} = 0.0118$

b. $\dfrac{[s(20) - s(70)]}{s(20)} = 1 - \dfrac{l_{70}}{l_{20}} = 1 - \dfrac{68{,}248}{97{,}741} = 0.3017$

c. $\dfrac{[s(90) - s(100)]}{s(20)} = \dfrac{(l_{90} - l_{100})}{l_{20}} = \dfrac{(14{,}154 - 1{,}150)}{97{,}741} = 0.1330.$ ▼

Insight into life table functions can be obtained by studying Figures 3.3.1, 3.3.2, and 3.3.3. These are drawn to be representative of current human mortality and are not taken directly from Table 3.3.1.

FIGURE 3.3.1

Graph of $\mu(x)$

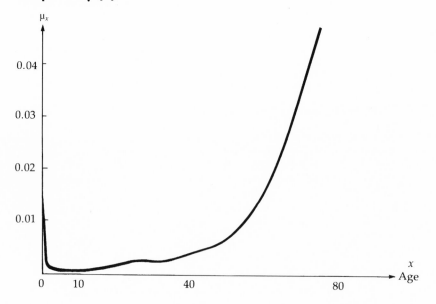

In Figure 3.3.1 note two features:
- The force of mortality is positive and the requirement

$$\int_0^\infty \mu(x)\, dx = \infty$$

appears satisfied. (See Table 3.2.1.)
- The force of mortality starts out rather large and then drops to a minimum around age 10.

FIGURE 3.3.2

Graph of $l_x\, \mu(x)$

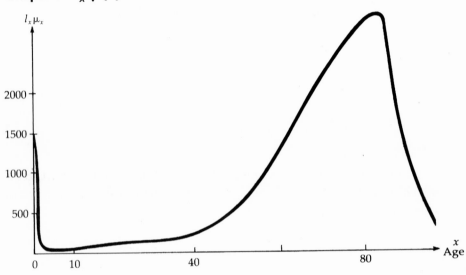

FIGURE 3.3.3

Graph of l_x

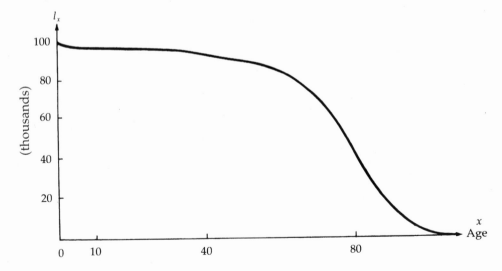

In Figures 3.3.2 and 3.3.3 note the following:

- The function $l_x \, \mu(x)$ is proportional to the p.d.f. of the age-at-death of a new-born. Since $l_x \, \mu(x)$ is the expected density of deaths at age x, under the random survivorship group idea, the graph of $l_x \, \mu(x)$ is called *the curve of deaths.*
- There is a local minimum of $l_x \, \mu(x)$ at about age 10. The mode of the distribution of deaths—the age at which the maximum of the curve of deaths occurs—is around age 80.
- The function l_x is proportional to the survival function $s(x)$. It can also be interpreted as the expected number living at age x out of an initial group of size l_0.
- Local extreme points of $l_x \, \mu(x)$ correspond to points of inflection of l_x since

$$\frac{d}{dx} \, l_x \, \mu(x) = \frac{d}{dx}\left(-\frac{d}{dx} \, l_x\right) = -\frac{d^2}{dx^2} \, l_x.$$

3.4   The Deterministic Survivorship Group

We proceed now to a second, and nonprobabilistic, interpretation of the life table. This is rooted mathematically in the concept of decrement (negative growth) rates. As such, it is related to growth-rate applications in biology and economics. It is deterministic in nature and leads to the concept of a *deterministic survivorship group* or *cohort.*

A deterministic survivorship group, as represented by a life table, has the following characteristics:

- The group initially consists of l_0 lives age 0.
- The members of the group are subject, at each age of their lives, to effective annual rates of mortality (decrement) specified by the values of q_x in the life table.
- The group is closed. No further entrants are allowed beyond the initial l_0. The only decreases come as a result of the effective annual rates of mortality (decrement).

From these characteristics it follows that the progress of the group is determined by

$$l_1 = l_0(1 - q_0) = l_0 - d_0,$$

$$l_2 = l_1(1 - q_1) = l_1 - d_1 = l_0 - (d_0 + d_1),$$

$$\vdots \quad \vdots \qquad \vdots \quad \vdots$$

$$l_x = l_{x-1}(1 - q_{x-1}) = l_{x-1} - d_{x-1} = l_0 - \sum_{y=0}^{x-1} d_y$$

$$= l_0\left(1 - \frac{\sum_{y=0}^{x-1} d_y}{l_0}\right) = l_0(1 - {}_x q_0) \tag{3.4.1}$$

where l_x is the number of lives attaining age x in the survivorship group. This chain of equalities, generated by a value l_0 called the **radix** and a set of q_x values, can be rewritten as

$$l_1 = l_0\, p_0,$$

$$l_2 = l_1\, p_1 = (l_0\, p_0)\, p_1,$$

$$\vdots \quad \vdots \qquad \vdots$$

$$l_x = l_{x-1}\, p_{x-1} = l_0 \left(\prod_{y=0}^{x-1} p_y \right) = l_0\; {}_x p_0. \tag{3.4.2}$$

There is an analogy between the deterministic survivorship group and the model for compound interest. Table 3.4.1 is designed to summarize some of this parallelism.

TABLE 3.4.1

Related Concepts of the Mathematics of Compound Interest and of Deterministic Survivorship Groups

Compound Interest	Survivorship Group
$A(t)$ = Size of fund at time t, time measured in years	l_x = Size of group at age x, age measured in years
Effective annual rate of interest (increment)	Effective annual rate of mortality (decrement)
$i_t = \dfrac{A(t+1) - A(t)}{A(t)}$	$q_x = \dfrac{l_x - l_{x+1}}{l_x}$
Effective n-year rate of interest, starting at time t	Effective n-year rate of mortality, starting at age x
${}_n i_t^* = \dfrac{A(t+n) - A(t)}{A(t)}$	${}_n q_x = \dfrac{l_x - l_{x+n}}{l_x}$
Force of interest at time t	Force of mortality at age x
$\delta_t = \lim\limits_{\Delta t \to 0} \left[\dfrac{A(t + \Delta t) - A(t)}{A(t)\, \Delta t} \right]$	$\mu(x) = \lim\limits_{\Delta x \to 0} \left(\dfrac{l_x - l_{x+\Delta x}}{l_x\, \Delta x} \right)$
$= \dfrac{1}{A(t)} \dfrac{dA(t)}{dt}$	$= -\dfrac{1}{l_x} \dfrac{dl_x}{dx}$

*There is no universally accepted symbol for an effective n-year rate of interest.

The headings of the ${}_t q_x$, l_x, and ${}_t d_x$ columns in Table 3.3.1 refer to the deterministic survivorship group interpretation. Although the mathematical foundations of the random survivorship group and the deterministic survivorship group are different, the resulting functions q_x, l_x, and d_x have the same mathematical properties and subsequent analysis. The random survivorship group concept has the advantage of allowing for the full use of probability theory. The deterministic survivorship group

---

is conceptually simple and easy to apply but does not take account of random variation in the number of survivors.

3.5 Other Life Table Characteristics

In this section we derive expressions for some commonly used characteristics of the distributions of $T(x)$ and $K(x)$ and introduce a general method for computing several of these characteristics.

3.5.1 Characteristics

The expected value of $T(x)$, denoted by $\overset{\circ}{e}_x$, is called the ***complete-expectation-of-life.*** By definition and an integration by parts, we have

$$\overset{\circ}{e}_x = \mathrm{E}[T(x)] = \int_0^\infty t \,_t p_x \,\mu(x + t) \, dt$$

$$= \int_0^\infty t \, d_t(-\,_t p_x)$$

$$= t(-\,_t p_x)\big|_0^\infty + \int_0^\infty \,_t p_x \, dt. \tag{3.5.1}$$

The existence of $\mathrm{E}[T(x)]$ implies the $\lim_{t \to \infty} t(-\,_t p_x) = 0$. Thus

$$\overset{\circ}{e}_x = \int_0^\infty \,_t p_x dt. \tag{3.5.2}$$

The complete-expectation-of-life at various ages is often used to compare levels of public health among different populations.

A similar integration by parts yields equivalent expressions for $\mathrm{E}[T(x)^2]$:

$$\mathrm{E}[T(x)^2] = \int_0^\infty t^2 \,_t p_x \,\mu(x + t) \, dt$$

$$= 2 \int_0^\infty t \,_t p_x \, dt. \tag{3.5.3}$$

This result is useful in the calculation of Var $[T(x)]$ by

$$\mathrm{Var}[T(x)] = \mathrm{E}[T(x)^2] - \mathrm{E}[T(x)]^2$$

$$= 2 \int_0^\infty t \,_t p_x \, dt - \overset{\circ}{e}_x^2. \tag{3.5.4}$$

In these developments, we assume that $\mathrm{E}[T(x)]$ and $\mathrm{E}[T(x)^2]$ exist. One can construct s.f.'s such as $s(x) = (1 + x)^{-1}$ where this would not be true.

Other characteristics of the distribution of $T(x)$ can be determined. The ***median future lifetime*** of (x), to be denoted by $m(x)$, can be found by solving

$$\Pr[T(x) > m(x)] = \frac{1}{2}$$

or

$$\frac{s[x + m(x)]}{s(x)} = \frac{1}{2} \tag{3.5.5}$$

for $m(x)$. In particular, $m(0)$ is given by solving $s[m(0)] = 1/2$. We can also find the **mode** of the distribution of $T(x)$ by locating the value of t that yields a maximum value of $_tp_x\, \mu(x + t)$.

The expected value of $K(x)$ is denoted by e_x and is called the ***curtate-expectation-of-life.*** By definition and use of summation by parts as described in Appendix 5, we have

$$e_x = E[K] = \sum_{k=0}^{\infty} k\; _kp_x\; q_{x+k}$$

$$= \sum_{k=0}^{\infty} k\; \Delta(-\,_kp_x)$$

$$= k(-\,_kp_x)\big|_0^{\infty} + \sum_{k=0}^{\infty} {}_{k+1}p_x. \tag{3.5.6}$$

Again, the existence of $E[K(x)]$ implies the $\lim_{k\to\infty} k(-\,_kp_x) = 0$. Thus, with a change of the summation variable,

$$e_x = \sum_{k=1}^{\infty} {}_kp_x. \tag{3.5.7}$$

Following the outline used for the continuous model and using summation by parts, we have

$$E[K(x)^2] = \sum_{k=0}^{\infty} k^2\; _kp_x\; q_{x+k}$$

$$= \sum_{k=0}^{\infty} k^2\; \Delta(-\,_kp_x)$$

$$= k^2(-\,_kp_x)\big|_0^{\infty} + \sum_{k=0}^{\infty} (\Delta k^2)(_{k+1}p_x). \tag{3.5.8}$$

The existence of $E[K(x)^2]$ implies $\lim_{k\to\infty} k^2(-\,_kp_x) = 0$. With a change of the summation variable,

$$E[K(x)^2] = \sum_{k=0}^{\infty} (2k + 1)\; _{k+1}p_x = \sum_{k=1}^{\infty} (2k - 1)\; _kp_x \tag{3.5.9}$$

Now,

$$\mathrm{Var}(K) = E[K^2] - E[K]^2$$

$$= \sum_{k=1}^{\infty} (2k - 1)\; _kp_x - e_x^2. \tag{3.5.10}$$

To complete the discussion of some of the entries in Table 3.3.1, we must define additional functions. The symbol L_x denotes the total expected number of years lived between ages x and $x + 1$ by survivors of the initial group of l_0 lives. We have

$$L_x = \int_0^1 t \, l_{x+t} \, \mu(x + t) \, dt + l_{x+1} \qquad (3.5.11)$$

where the integral counts the years lived of those who die between ages x and $x + 1$, and the term l_{x+1} counts the years lived between ages x and $x + 1$ by those who survive to age $x + 1$. Integration by parts yields

$$L_x = -\int_0^1 t \, dl_{x+t} + l_{x+1}$$

$$= -t \, l_{x+t}\big|_0^1 + \int_0^1 l_{x+t} \, dt + l_{x+1}$$

$$= \int_0^1 l_{x+t} \, dt. \qquad (3.5.12)$$

The function L_x is also used in defining the **central-death-rate** over the interval from x to $x + 1$, denoted by m_x where

$$m_x = \frac{\int_0^1 l_{x+t} \, \mu(x + t) \, dt}{\int_0^1 l_{x+t} \, dt} = \frac{l_x - l_{x+1}}{L_x}. \qquad (3.5.13)$$

An application of this function is found in Chapter 10.

The definitions for m_x and L_x can be extended to age intervals of length other than one:

$$_nL_x = \int_0^n t \, l_{x+t} \, \mu(x + t) \, dt + n l_{x+n}$$

$$= \int_0^n l_{x+t} \, dt, \qquad (3.5.14)$$

$$_nm_x = \frac{\int_0^n l_{x+t} \, \mu(x + t) \, dt}{\int_0^n l_{x+t} \, dt} = \frac{l_x - l_{x+n}}{_nL_x}. \qquad (3.5.15)$$

For the random survivorship group, $_nL_x$ is the total expected number of years lived between ages x and $x + n$ by the survivors of the initial group of l_0 lives and $_nm_x$ is the average death rate experienced by this group over the interval $(x, x + n)$.

The symbol T_x denotes the total number of years lived beyond age x by the survivorship group with l_0 initial members. We have

$$T_x = \int_0^\infty t \, l_{x+t} \, \mu(x+t) \, dt$$

$$= -\int_0^\infty t \, d_t \, l_{x+t}$$

$$= \int_0^\infty l_{x+t} \, dt. \tag{3.5.16}$$

The final expression can be interpreted as the integral of the total time lived between ages $x+t$ and $x+t+dt$ by the l_{x+t} lives who survive to that age interval. We also recognize T_x as the limit of $_nL_x$ as n goes to infinity.

The average number of years of future lifetime of the l_x survivors of the group at age x is given by

$$\frac{T_x}{l_x} = \frac{\int_0^\infty l_{x+t} \, dt}{l_x}$$

$$= \int_0^\infty {}_tp_x \, dt$$

$$= \overset{\circ}{e}_x,$$

as determined in (3.5.1) and (3.5.2).

We can express the average number of years lived between x and $x+n$ by the l_x survivors at age x as

$$\frac{_nL_x}{l_x} = \frac{\int_0^n l_{x+t} \, dt}{l_x}$$

$$= \frac{T_x - T_{x+n}}{l_x}$$

$$= \int_0^n {}_tp_x \, dt. \tag{3.5.17}$$

This function is the *n-year temporary complete life expectancy* of (x) and is denoted by $\overset{\circ}{e}_{x:\overline{n}|}$. (See Exercise 3.16.)

A final function, related to the interpretation of the life table developed in this section, is the average number of years lived between ages x and $x+1$ by those of the survivorship group who die between those ages. This function is denoted by $a(x)$ and is defined by

$$a(x) = \frac{\int_0^1 t \, l_{x+t} \, \mu(x + t) \, dt}{\int_0^1 l_{x+t} \, \mu(x + t) \, dt}. \tag{3.5.18}$$

For the probabilistic view of the life table, we would have

$$a(x) = \frac{\int_0^1 t \, {}_t p_x \, \mu(x + t) \, dt}{\int_0^1 {}_t p_x \, \mu(x + t) \, dt} = E[T|T < 1].$$

If we assume that

$$l_{x+t} \, \mu(x + t) \, dt = d_x \, dt \qquad 0 \le t \le 1,$$

that is, if deaths are uniformly distributed in the year of age, we have

$$a(x) = \int_0^1 t \, dt = \frac{1}{2}.$$

This is the usual approximation for $a(x)$, except for young and old years of age where Figure 3.3.2 shows that the assumption may be inappropriate.

Example 3.5.1

Show that

$$L_x = a(x) \, l_x + [1 - a(x)] \, l_{x+1}$$

and

$$L_x \cong \frac{l_x + l_{x+1}}{2}.$$

Solution:

From (3.5.11), (3.5.12), and (3.5.18), we have

$$a(x) = \frac{L_x - l_{x+1}}{l_x - l_{x+1}}$$

or

$$L_x = a(x) \, l_x + [1 - a(x)] \, l_{x+1}.$$

The formula

$$L_x \cong \frac{l_x + l_{x+1}}{2}$$

can be justified by using the trapezoidal rule for approximate integration on (3.5.12). ▼

Key life table terminology, defined in Sections 3.3–3.5, is summarized as part of Table 3.9.1 in Section 3.9.

3.5.2 Recursion Formulas

Example 3.5.1 illustrates the use of a numerical analysis technique to evaluate a life table characteristic. The trapezoidal rule for approximate integration is used. The calculation of complete and curtate expectations-of-life can be used to illustrate another computational tool called *recursion formulas*. The application of recursion formulas in this book typically involves one of two forms:

Backward Recursion Formula

$$u(x) = c(x) + d(x)\, u(x + 1) \tag{3.5.19}$$

or

Forward Recursion Formula

$$u(x + 1) = -\frac{c(x)}{d(x)} + \frac{1}{d(x)}\, u(x). \tag{3.5.20}$$

The variable x is usually a non-negative integer.

To evaluate a function $u(x)$, for a domain of non-negative integer values of x, we need to have available values of $c(x)$ and $d(x)$ and a starting value of $u(x)$. This procedure is used in subsequent chapters and is illustrated in Table 3.5.1 where backward recursion formulas are developed to compute e_x and $\overset{\circ}{e}_x$.

TABLE 3.5.1

Backward Recursion Formulas for e_x and $\overset{\circ}{e}_x$

Step	e_x	$\overset{\circ}{e}_x$
1. Basic equation	$e_x = \sum_{k=1}^{\infty} {}_k p_x$	$\overset{\circ}{e}_x = \int_0^{\infty} {}_s p_x\, ds$
2. Separate the operation	$e_x = p_x + \sum_{k=2}^{\infty} {}_k p_x$	$\overset{\circ}{e}_x = \int_0^1 {}_s p_x\, ds + \int_1^{\infty} {}_s p_x\, ds$
3. Factor p_x and change variable in the operation	$e_x = p_x + p_x \sum_{k=1}^{\infty} {}_k p_{x+1}$ $= p_x + p_x\, e_{x+1}$	$\overset{\circ}{e}_x = \int_0^1 {}_s p_x\, ds + p_x \int_0^{\infty} {}_t p_{x+1}\, dt$ $= \int_0^1 {}_s p_x\, ds + p_x\, \overset{\circ}{e}_{x+1}$
4. Recursion formula[a]	$u(x) = e_x,\ c(x) = p_x$ $d(x) = p_x$	$u(x) = \overset{\circ}{e}_x,\ c(x) = \int_0^1 {}_s p_x ds$ $d(x) = p_x$
5. Starting value[b]	$e_{\omega} = u(\omega) = 0$	$\overset{\circ}{e}_{\omega} = u(x) = 0$

[a] The integral $c(x) = \int_0^1 {}_s p_x ds$ can be evaluated using the trapezoidal rule as $c(x) = (1 + p_x)/2$.
[b] From Section 3.3.1 we have $s(x) = 0,\ x \geq \omega$, and $s(x) > 0,\ x < \omega$. In this development we will assume that ω is an integer.

3.6 Assumptions for Fractional Ages

In this chapter we have discussed the continuous random variable remaining lifetime, T, and the discrete random variable curtate-future-lifetime, K. The life table developed in Section 3.3 specifies the probability distribution of K completely. To specify the distribution of T, we must postulate an analytic form or adopt a life table and an assumption about the distribution between integers.

We will examine three assumptions that are widely used in actuarial science. These will be stated in terms of the s.f. and in a form to show the nature of interpolation over the interval $(x, x + 1)$ implied by each assumption. In each statement, x is an integer and $0 \leq t \leq 1$. The assumptions are the following:

- *Linear interpolation:* $s(x + t) = (1 - t) s(x) + t \, s(x + 1)$. This is known as the **uniform distribution** or, perhaps more properly, a uniform distribution of deaths assumption within each year of age. Under this assumption $_tp_x$ is a linear function.
- *Exponential interpolation,* or linear interpolation on $\log s(x + t)$: $\log s(x + t) = (1 - t) \log s(x) + t \log s(x + 1)$. This is consistent with the assumption of a **constant force** of mortality within each year of age. Under this assumption $_tp_x$ is exponential.
- *Harmonic interpolation:* $1 / s(x + t) = (1 - t) / s(x) + t / s(x + 1)$. This is what is known as the **hyperbolic** (historically **Balducci***) assumption, for under it $_tp_x$ is a hyperbolic curve.

With these basic definitions, formulas can be derived for other standard probability functions in terms of life table probabilities. These results are presented in Table 3.6.1. Note that we just as well could have elected to propose equivalent definitions in terms of the p.d.f., the d.f., or the force of mortality.

The derivations of the entries in Table 3.6.1 are exercises in substituting the stated assumption about $s(x + t)$ into the appropriate formulas of Sections 3.2 and 3.3. We will illustrate the process for the uniform distribution of deaths, an assumption that is used extensively throughout this text.

To derive the first entry in the uniform distribution column, we start with

$$_tq_x = \frac{s(x) - s(x + t)}{s(x)} \qquad 0 \leq t \leq 1,$$

then substitute for $s(x + t)$,

$$_tq_x = \frac{s(x) - [(1 - t) s(x) + t \, s(x + 1)]}{s(x)} = \frac{t \, [s(x) - s(x + 1)]}{s(x)} = t q_x.$$

For the second entry, we use (3.2.13) and

$$\mu(x + t) = - \frac{s'(x + t)}{s(x + t)};$$

---

*This assumption is named after G. Balducci, an Italian actuary, who pointed out its role in the traditional actuarial method of constructing life tables.

TABLE 3.6.1

Probability Theory Functions for Fractional Ages

| Function | Assumption | | |
	Uniform Distribution	Constant Force	Hyperbolic
$_tq_x$	tq_x	$1 - p_x^t$	$\dfrac{tq_x}{1 - (1 - t)q_x}$
$\mu(x + t)$	$\dfrac{q_x}{1 - tq_x}$	$-\log p_x$	$\dfrac{q_x}{1 - (1 - t)q_x}$
$_{1-t}q_{x+t}$	$\dfrac{(1 - t)\, q_x}{1 - tq_x}$	$1 - p_x^{1-t}$	$(1 - t)q_x$
$_yq_{x+t}$	$\dfrac{yq_x}{1 - tq_x}$	$1 - p_x^y$	$\dfrac{yq_x}{1 - (1 - y - t)q_x}$
$_tp_x$	$1 - tq_x$	p_x^t	$\dfrac{p_x}{1 - (1 - t)q_x}$
$_tp_x\mu(x + t)$	q_x	$-p_x^t \log p_x$	$\dfrac{q_x\, p_x}{[1 - (1 - t)q_x]^2}$

Note that, in this table, x is an integer, $0 < t < 1$, $0 \le y \le 1$, $y + t \le 1$. For rows one, three, four, and five, the relationships also hold for $t = 0$ and $t = 1$.

then, substituting for $s(x + t)$, we have

$$\mu(x + t) = \frac{[s(x) - s(x + 1)]}{[(1 - t)\, s(x) + t\, s(x + 1)]}.$$

Dividing both numerator and denominator of the right-hand side by $s(x)$ yields

$$\mu(x + t) = \frac{q_x}{(1 - tq_x)}.$$

The third entry is the special case of the fourth entry with $y = 1 - t$.

For the fourth entry we start with

$$_yq_{x+t} = \frac{s(x + t) - s(x + t + y)}{s(x + t)},$$

then substitute for $s(x + t)$ and $s(x + t + y)$ to obtain

$$_yq_{x+t} = \frac{[(1 - t)\, s(x) + t\, s(x + 1)] - [(1 - t - y)\, s(x) + (t + y)\, s(x + 1)]}{(1 - t)\, s(x) + t\, s(x + 1)}$$

$$= \frac{y[s(x) - s(x + 1)]\, /\, s(x)}{\{s(x) - t[s(x) - s(x + 1)]\}\, /\, s(x)}$$

$$= \frac{yq_x}{1 - tq_x}.$$

The fifth entry is the complement of the first, and the final entry for the uniform distribution column is the product of the second and fifth entries.

If, as before, x is an integer, insight can be obtained by defining a random variable $S = S(x)$ by

$$T = K + S \tag{3.6.1}$$

where T is time-until-death, K is the curtate-future-lifetime, and S is the random variable representing the fractional part of a year lived in the year of death. Since K is a non-negative integer random variable and S is a continuous-type random variable with all of its probability mass on the interval $(0, 1)$, we can examine their joint distribution by writing

$$\Pr[(K = k) \cap (S \leq s)] = \Pr(k < T \leq k + s)$$

$$= {}_{k}p_x \; {}_{s}q_{x+k}.$$

Now, using the expression for ${}_{s}q_{x+k}$ under the uniform distribution assumption as shown in Table 3.6.1, we have

$$\Pr[(K = k) \cap (S \leq s)] = {}_{k}p_x \; s \; q_{x+k}$$

$$= {}_{k|}q_x \; s$$

$$= \Pr(K = k) \Pr(S \leq s). \tag{3.6.2}$$

Therefore, the joint probability involving K and S can be factored into separate probabilities of K and S. It follows that, under the uniform distribution of deaths assumption, the random variables K and S are independent. Since $\Pr(S \leq s) = s$ is the d.f. of a uniform distribution on $(0, 1)$, S has such a uniform distribution.

Example 3.6.1

Under the constant force of mortality assumption, are the random variables K and S independent?

Solution:

Using entries from Table 3.6.1 for the constant force assumption, we obtain

$$\Pr[(K = k) \cap (S \leq s)] = {}_{k}p_x \; {}_{s}q_{x+k}$$

$$= {}_{k}p_x \left[1 - (p_{x+k})^s\right].$$

To discuss this result, we distinguish two cases:

- If p_{x+k} is not independent of k, we cannot factor the joint probability of K and S into separate probabilities. We conclude that K and S are not independent.
- In the special case where $p_{x+k} = p_x$, a constant,

$$\Pr[(K = k) \cap (S \leq s)] = p_x^k(1 - p_x^s) = \frac{(1 - p_x)p_x^k(1 - p_x^s)}{(1 - p_x)}$$

$$= \Pr(K = k) \Pr(S \leq s).$$

For this special case we conclude that K and S are independent under the constant force assumption. ▼

Example 3.6.2

Under the assumption of uniform distribution of deaths, show that

a. $\overset{\circ}{e}_x = e_x + \dfrac{1}{2}$

b. $\text{Var}(T) = \text{Var}(K) + \dfrac{1}{12}$.

Solution:

a. $\overset{\circ}{e}_x = E[T] = E[K + S]$

$= E[K] + E[S]$

$= e_x + \dfrac{1}{2}$.

b. $\text{Var}(T) = \text{Var}(K + S)$.

From the independence of K and S, under the uniform distribution assumption, it follows that

$$\text{Var}(T) = \text{Var}(K) + \text{Var}(S).$$

Further, since S is uniformly distributed over $(0, 1)$,

$$\text{Var}(T) = \text{Var}(K) + \dfrac{1}{12}. \qquad \blacktriangledown$$

3.7 Some Analytical Laws of Mortality

There are three principal justifications for postulating an analytic form for mortality or survival functions. The first is philosophical. Many phenomena studied in physics can be explained efficiently by simple formulas. Therefore, using biological arguments, some authors have suggested that human survival is governed by an equally simple law. The second justification is practical. It is easier to communicate a function with a few parameters than it is to communicate a life table with perhaps 100 parameters or mortality probabilities. In addition, some of the analytic forms have elegant properties that are convenient in evaluating probability statements that involve more than one life. The third justification for a simple analytic survival function is the ease of estimating a few parameters of the function from mortality data.

The support for simple analytic survival functions has declined in recent years. Many feel that the belief in universal laws of mortality is naive. With the increasing speed and storage capacity of computers, the advantages of some analytic forms in computations involving more than one life are no longer of great importance. Nevertheless, some interesting research has recently reiterated the biological arguments for analytic laws of mortality.

In Table 3.7.1, several families of simple analytic mortality and survival functions, corresponding to various postulated laws, are displayed. The names of the originators of the laws and the dates of publication are included for identification purposes.

TABLE 3.7.1
Mortality and Survival Functions under Various Laws

Originator	$\mu(x)$	$s(x)$	Restrictions
De Moivre (1729)	$(\omega - x)^{-1}$	$1 - \dfrac{x}{\omega}$	$0 \leq x < \omega$
Gompertz (1825)	Bc^x	$\exp[-m(c^x - 1)]$	$B > 0, c > 1, x \geq 0$
Makeham (1860)	$A + Bc^x$	$\exp[-Ax - m(c^x - 1)]$	$B > 0, A \geq -B, c > 1, x \geq 0$
Weibull (1939)	kx^n	$\exp(-ux^{n+1})$	$k > 0, n > 0, x \geq 0$

Note:
- The special symbols are defined as

$$m = \frac{B}{\log c}, \qquad u = \frac{k}{(n + 1)}.$$

- Gompertz's law is a special case of Makeham's law with $A = 0$.
- If $c = 1$ in Gompertz's and Makeham's laws, the exponential (constant force) distribution results.
- In connection with Makeham's law, the constant A has been interpreted as capturing the accident hazard, and the term Bc^x as capturing the hazard of aging.

The entries in the $s(x)$ column of Table 3.7.1 were obtained by substituting into (3.2.16). For example, for Makeham's law, we have

$$s(x) = \exp[-\int_0^x (A + Bc^s)ds]$$

$$= \exp\left[-Ax - B\frac{(c^x - 1)}{\log c}\right]$$

$$= \exp[-Ax - m(c^x - 1)]$$

where $m = B / \log c$.

Two objectives governed the development of a mortality table for computational purposes in the examples and exercises of this book. One objective was to have mortality rates in the middle of the range of variation for groups, such variation caused by factors such as residence, gender, insured status, annuity status, marital status, and occupation. The second objective was to have a Makeham law at most ages to illustrate how calculations for multiple lives can be performed.

The Illustrative Life Table in Appendix 2A is based on the Makeham law for ages 13 and greater,

$$1,000 \ \mu(x) = 0.7 + 0.05 \ (10^{0.04})^x. \tag{3.7.1}$$

The calculations of the basic functions q_x, l_x, and d_x from (3.7.1) were all done directly from (3.7.1) instead of calculating l_x and d_x from the truncated values of q_x.

It was found that the latter choice would make little difference in the applications. It should be kept in mind that the Illustrative Life Table, as its name implies, is for illustrative purposes only.

3.8 Select and Ultimate Tables

In Section 3.2 we discussed how $_tp_x$ [the probability that (x) will survive to age $x + t$] might be interpreted in two ways. The first interpretation was that the probability can be evaluated by a survival function appropriate for newborns, under the single hypothesis that the newborn has survived to age x. This interpretation has been the basis of the notation and development of the formulas. The second interpretation was that additional knowledge available about the life at age x might make the original survival function inappropriate for evaluating probability statements about the future lifetime of (x). For example, the life might have been underwritten and accepted for life insurance at age x. This information would lead us to believe that (x)'s future-lifetime distribution is different from what we might otherwise assume for lives age x. As a second example, the life might have become disabled at age x. This information would lead us to believe that the future-lifetime distribution for (x) is different from that of those not disabled at age x. In these two illustrations, a special force of mortality that incorporates the particular information available at age x would be preferred. Without this particular information for (x), the form of mortality at duration t would be a function of only the attained age $x + t$, denoted in the previous sections by $\mu(x + t)$. Given the additional information at x, the force of mortality at $x + t$ is a function of this information at x and duration t. Its notation will be $\mu_x(t)$, showing separately the age, x, at which the additional information was available, and the duration, t. The additional information is usually not explicit in the notation but is conveyed by the context. In other words, the complete model for such lives is a set of survival functions including one for each age at which information is available on issue of insurance, disability, and so on. This set of survival functions can be thought of as a function of two variables. One variable is the age at *selection* (e.g., at policy issue or the onset of disability), $[x]$, and the second variable is the duration since policy issue or duration since selection, t. Then each of the usual life table functions associated with this bivariate survival function is a two-dimensional array on $[x]$ and t. Note the bracket notation to indicate which variable identifies the age of selection. When the select status can be inferred from the force of mortality, the bracket notation will be suppressed to reduce the clutter of the symbols.

The schematic diagram in Figure 3.8.1 illustrates these ideas. For instance, suppose some special information is available about a group of lives age 30. Perhaps they have been accepted for life insurance or perhaps they have become disabled. A special life table can be built for these lives. The conditional probability of death in each year of duration would be denoted by $q_{[30]+i}$, $i = 0, 1, 2, \ldots$, and would be entered on the first row of Figure 3.8.1. The subscript reflects the bivariate nature of this function with the bracketed thirty, [30], denoting that the survival function in the first row is conditional on special information available at age 30. The second row of Figure 3.8.1 would contain the probabilities of death for lives on which the

FIGURE 3.8.1

Select, Ultimate, and Aggregate Mortality, 15-Year Select Period

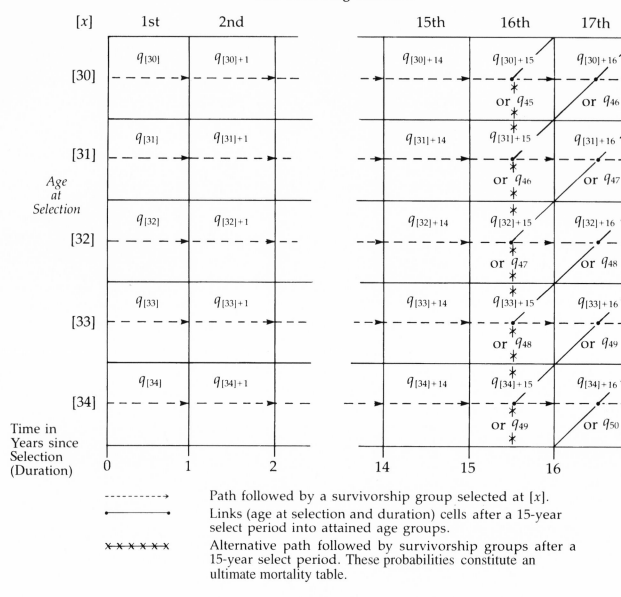

Year Following Selection

Path followed by a survivorship group selected at [x].

Links (age at selection and duration) cells after a 15-year select period into attained age groups.

✕✕✕✕✕✕   Alternative path followed by survivorship groups after a 15-year select period. These probabilities constitute an ultimate mortality table.

Notes:

1. In biostatistics the select table index [x] may not be age. For example, in cancer research, [x] could be a classification index that depends on the size and location of the tumor, and time following selection would be measured from the time of diagnosis.

2. Ultimate mortality, following a 15-year select period, for age [x] + 15, would be estimated by using observations from all cells identified by [x − j] + 15 + j, for j = 0, 1, 2, ... Therefore, $q_{[x]+15} = q_{x+15}$ is estimated by a weighted average of mortality estimates from several different selection groups. If the effect of selection is not small, the resulting estimate will be influenced by the amount of data from the various cells.

special information became available at age 31. In actuarial science such a two-dimensional life table is called a *select life* table.

The impact of selection on the distribution of time-until-death, T, may diminish following selection. Beyond this time period the q's at equal attained ages would be essentially equal regardless of the ages at selection. More precisely, if there is a smallest integer r such that $|q_{[x]+r} - q_{[x-j]+r+j}|$ is less than some small positive constant for all ages of selection $[x]$ and for all $j > 0$, it would be economical to construct a set of *select-and-ultimate* tables by truncation of the two-dimensional array after the $(r + 1)$ column. For durations beyond r we would use

$$q_{[x-j]+r+j} \cong q_{[x]+r} \qquad j > 0.$$

The first r years of duration comprise the *select period.*

The resulting array remains a set of life tables, one for each age at selection. For a single age at selection, the life table entries are horizontal during the select period and then vertical during the ultimate period. This is shown in Figure 3.8.1 by the arrows.

The Society of Actuaries mortality studies of lives who were issued individual life insurance on a standard basis use a 15-year select period as illustrated in Figure 3.8.1; that is, it is accepted that

$$q_{[x-j]+15+j} \cong q_{[x]+15} \qquad j > 0.$$

Beyond the select period, the probabilities of death are subscripted by attained age only; that is, $q_{[x-j]+r+j}$ is written as q_{x+r}. For instance, with $r = 15$, $q_{[30]+15}$ and $q_{[25]+20}$ would both be written as q_{45}.

A life table in which the functions are given only for attained ages is called an *aggregate table*, Table 3.3.1, for instance. The last column in a select-and-ultimate table is a special aggregate table that is usually referred to as an *ultimate table*, to reflect the select table setting.

Table 3.8.1 contains mortality probabilities and corresponding values of the $l_{[x]+k}$ function, as given in the Permanent Assurances, Females, 1979–82, Table, published by the Institute of Actuaries and the Faculty of Actuaries; it is denoted as the

TABLE 3.8.1

Excerpt from the AF80 Select-and-Ultimate Table

[x]	(1)\n1,000 $q_{[x]}$	(2)\n1,000 $q_{[x]+1}$	(3)\n1,000 q_{x+2}	(4)\n$l_{[x]}$	(5)\n$l_{[x]+1}$	(6)\n$l_{x+2}$	(7)\nx + 2
30	0.222	0.330	0.422	9 906.7380	9 904.5387	9 901.2702	32
31	0.234	0.352	0.459	9 902.8941	9 900.5769	9 897.0919	33
32	0.250	0.377	0.500	9 898.7547	9 896.2800	9 892.5491	34
33	0.269	0.407	0.545	9 894.2903	9 891.6287	9 887.6028	35
34	0.291	0.441	0.596	9 889.4519	9 886.5741	9 882.2141	36

AF80 Table. This table has a 2-year select period and is easier to use for illustrative purposes than tables with a 15-year select period such as the Basic Tables, published by the Society of Actuaries.

In Table 3.8.1 we observe three mortality probabilities for age 32, namely,

$$q_{[32]} = 0.000250 < q_{[31]+1} = 0.000352 < q_{32} = 0.000422.$$

The order among these probabilities is plausible since mortality should be lower for lives immediately after acceptance for life insurance. Column (3) can be viewed as providing ultimate mortality probabilities.

Given the 1-year mortality rates of a select-and-ultimate table, the construction of the corresponding select-and-ultimate life table (survival functions) is started with the ultimate portion. Formulas such as (3.4.1) can be used, which would yield a set of values of $l_{x+r} = l_{[x]+r}$ where r is the length of the select period. We would then complete the select segments by using the relation

$$l_{[x]+r-k-1} = \frac{l_{[x]+r-k}}{p_{[x]+r-k-1}} \qquad k = 0, 1, 2, \ldots, r-1,$$

working from duration $r - 1$ down to 0.

Example 3.8.1

Use Table 3.8.1 to evaluate

a. $_2p_{[30]}$ b. $_5p_{[30]}$

c. $_{1|}q_{[31]}$ d. $_3q_{[31]+1}$.

Solution:

Formulas developed earlier in this chapter can be adapted to select-and-ultimate tables yielding

a. $_2p_{[30]} = \dfrac{l_{[30]+2}}{l_{[30]}} = \dfrac{l_{32}}{l_{[30]}} = \dfrac{9{,}901.2702}{9{,}906.7380} = 0.99945$

b. $_5p_{[30]} = \dfrac{l_{35}}{l_{[30]}} = \dfrac{9{,}887.6028}{9{,}906.7380} = 0.99807$

c. $_{1|}q_{[31]} = \dfrac{l_{[31]+1} - l_{33}}{l_{[31]}} = \dfrac{9{,}900.5769 - 9{,}897.0919}{9{,}902.8941} = 0.00035$

d. $_3q_{[31]+1} = \dfrac{l_{[31]+1} - l_{35}}{l_{[31]+1}} = \dfrac{9{,}900.5769 - 9{,}887.6028}{9{,}900.5769} = 0.00131.$ ▼

TABLE 3.9.1

Chapter 3 Concepts

Symbol	Name or Description of the Concept
(x)	Notation for a life age x
$[x]$	Age, or other status, at selection
X	Age at death, a random variable
$T(x)$	Future lifetime of (x), equals $X - x$
$K(x)$	Curtate-future-lifetime of (x), equals the integer part of $T(x)$
$S(x)$	Future lifetime of (x) within the year of death, equals $T(x) - K(x)$
$s(x)$	Survival function, equal to the probability that a newborn will live to at least x
$\mu(x)$	Force of mortality at age x in an aggregate life table
$\mu_x(t)$	Force of mortality at attained age $x + t$ given selection at age x
$_tq_x$	Probability that (x) dies within t years
$_tp_x$	Probability that (x) survives at least t years
$_{t|u}q_x$	Probability that (x) dies between t and $t + u$ years
$\overset{\circ}{e}_x$	Complete expectation of life for (x), equals $E[T(x)]$
e_x	Curtate expectation of life for (x), equals $E[K(x)]$
$\mathcal{L}(x)$	Cohort's number of survivors to age x, a random variable
$_n\mathcal{D}_x$	Cohort's number of deaths between ages x and $x + n$
l_x	Expected number of survivors at age x, equals $E[\mathcal{L}(x)]$
$_nd_x$	Expected number of deaths between ages x and $x + n$, equals $E[_n\mathcal{D}_x]$
$_nL_x$	Expected number of years lived between ages x and $x + n$ by survivors to age x of the initial group of l_0 lives
T_x	Expected number of years lived beyond age x by the survivors to age x of the initial group of l_0 lives
m_x	Central death rate over the interval $(x, x + 1)$
ω	Omega, the limiting age of a life table

3.9 Notes and References

Table 3.9.1 summarizes this chapter's new concepts with their names, symbols, and descriptions. Life tables are a cornerstone of actuarial science. Consequently they are extensively discussed in several English-language textbooks on life contingencies:

- King (1902)
- Spurgeon (1932)
- Jordan (1967)
- Hooker and Longley-Cook (1953)
- Neill (1977).

These have been used in actuarial education. In addition, life tables are used by biostatisticians. An exposition of this latter approach is given by Chiang (1968) and Elandt-Johnson and Johnson (1980). The deterministic rate function interpretation is discussed by Allen (1907). London (1988) summarizes several methods for estimating life tables from data.

The historically important analytic forms for survival functions are referred to in Table 3.6. Brillinger (1961) provides an argument for certain analytic forms from the viewpoint of statistical life testing. Tenenbein and Vanderhoof (1980) restate the case for analytic laws of mortality and develop formulas for select mortality. Balducci's (1921) contribution was preceded by a remarkable set of papers by Wittstein (1873). Wittstein's papers were published first in German and translated into English by T. B. Sprague. Some of the methods for evaluating probabilities for fractional ages are reviewed by Mereu (1961) and in Batten's textbook on mortality estimation (1978) (see also Seal's 1977 historical review). Discussions of the length of the select period for various types of insurance selection procedures have a long history, for example, Williamson (1942), Thompson (1934), and Jenkins (1943). The Society of Actuaries 1975–80 Basic Tables use a 15-year select period and are published in *TSA Reports 1982*. International Actuarial Notation is outlined in *TASA 48* (1947).

We planned to use the 1989–91 U.S. Life Table for illustrative purposes in Table 3.2.1, but this plan was not realized because the life tables based on the 1990 U.S. Census were not completed when this chapter was revised.

Exercises

Section 3.2

3.1. Using the ideas summarized in Table 3.2.1, complete the entries below.

$s(x)$	$F_X(x)$	$f_X(x)$	$\mu(x)$
			$\tan x,\ 0 \leq x \leq \dfrac{\pi}{2}$
$e^{-x},\ x \geq 0$			
	$1 - \dfrac{1}{1+x},\ x \geq 0$		

3.2. Confirm that each of the following functions can serve as a force of mortality. Show the corresponding survival function. In each case $x \geq 0$.
   a. $B\,c^x$ $B > 0$ $c > 1$ (Gompertz)
   b. $k\,x^n$ $n > 0$ $k > 0$ (Weibull)
   c. $a\,(b+x)^{-1}$ $a > 0$ $b > 0$ (Pareto)

3.3. Confirm that the following can serve as a survival function. Show the corresponding $\mu(x)$, $f_X(x)$, and $F_X(x)$.
$$s(x) = e^{-x^3/12} \qquad x \geq 0.$$

3.4. State why each of the following functions cannot serve in the role indicated by the symbol:
   a. $\mu(x) = (1 + x)^{-3} \qquad x \geq 0$

b. $s(x) = 1 - \dfrac{22x}{12} + \dfrac{11x^2}{8} - \dfrac{7x^3}{24}$ $0 \le x \le 3$

c. $f_X(x) = x^{n-1}\,e^{-x/2}$ $x \ge 0,\ n \ge 1$.

3.5. If $s(x) = 1 - x/100,\ 0 \le x \le 100$, calculate
a. $\mu(x)$ b. $F_X(x)$
c. $f_X(x)$ d. $\Pr(10 < X < 40)$.

3.6. Given the survival function of Exercise 3.5, determine the survival function, force of mortality, and p.d.f. of the future lifetime of (40).

3.7. If $s(x) = [1 - (x/100)]^{1/2},\ 0 \le x \le 100$, evaluate

a. $_{17}p_{19}$ b. $_{15}q_{36}$ c. $_{15|13}q_{36}$
d. $\mu(36)$ e. $E[T(36)]$.

3.8. Confirm that $_{k|}q_0 = -\Delta s(k)$, and that $\displaystyle\sum_{k=0}^{\infty} {}_{k|}q_0 = 1$.

3.9. If $\mu(x) = 0.001$ for $20 \le x \le 25$, evaluate $_{2|2}q_{20}$.

Sections 3.3, 3.4

3.10. If the survival times of 10 lives in a survivorship group are independent with survival defined in Table 3.3.1, exhibit the p.f. of $\mathcal{L}(65)$ and the mean and variance of $\mathcal{L}(65)$.

3.11. If $s(x) = 1 - x/12,\ 0 \le x \le 12,\ l_0 = 9$, and the survival times are independent, then $(_3\mathcal{D}_0,\ _3\mathcal{D}_3,\ _3\mathcal{D}_6,\ _3\mathcal{D}_9)$ is known to have a multinomial distribution. Calculate
a. The expected value of each random variable
b. The variance of each random variable
c. The coefficient of correlation between each pair of random variables.

3.12. On the basis of Table 3.3.1,
a. Compare the values of $_5q_0$ and $_5q_5$
b. Evaluate the probability that (25) will die between ages 80 and 85.

3.13. Given that l_{x+t} is strictly decreasing in the interval $0 \le t \le 1$, show that
a. If l_{x+t} is concave down, then $q_x > \mu(x)$
b. If l_{x+t} is concave up, then $q_x < \mu(x)$.

3.14. Show that

a. $\dfrac{d}{dx} l_x\,\mu(x) < 0$ when $\dfrac{d}{dx}\mu(x) < \mu^2(x)$

b. $\dfrac{d}{dx} l_x\,\mu(x) = 0$ when $\dfrac{d}{dx}\mu(x) = \mu^2(x)$

c. $\dfrac{d}{dx} l_x\,\mu(x) > 0$ when $\dfrac{d}{dx}\mu(x) > \mu^2(x)$.

3.15. Consider a random survivorship group consisting of two subgroups: (1) the survivors of 1,600 persons joining at birth; (2) the survivors of 540 persons joining at age 10. An excerpt from the appropriate mortality table for both subgroups follows:

x	l_x
0	40
10	39
70	26

If Y_1 and Y_2 are the numbers of survivors to age 70 out of subgroups (1) and (2), respectively, estimate a number c such that $\Pr(Y_1 + Y_2 > c) = 0.05$. Assume the lives are independent and ignore half-unit corrections.

Section 3.5

3.16. Let the random variable

$$T^*(x) = T(x) \qquad 0 < T(x) \le n$$

$$= n \qquad n < T(x)$$

and denote $E[T^*(x)]$ by $\overset{\circ}{e}_{x:\overline{n}|}$. This expectation is called a ***temporary complete life expectancy.*** It is used in public health planning; the same expectation, under the name ***limited expected value function,*** is used in the analysis of loss amount distributions. Show that

a. $\overset{\circ}{e}_{x:\overline{n}|} = \displaystyle\int_0^n t \; {}_tp_x \; \mu(x + t) \; dt + n \; {}_np_x$

$\qquad = \displaystyle\int_0^n {}_tp_x \; dt = \dfrac{T_x - T_{x+n}}{l_x}$

b. $\mathrm{Var}[T^*(x)] = \displaystyle\int_0^n t^2 \; {}_tp_x \; \mu(x + t) \; dt + n^2 \; {}_np_x - (\overset{\circ}{e}_{x:\overline{n}|})^2$

$\qquad = 2 \displaystyle\int_0^n t \; {}_tp_x \; dt - \overset{\circ}{e}_{x:\overline{n}|}{}^2.$

3.17. Let the random variable

$$K^*(x) = K(x) \qquad K(x) = 0, 1, 2, \dots, n - 1$$

$$= n \qquad K(x) = n, n + 1, \dots$$

and denote $E[K^*(x)]$ by $e_{x:\overline{n}|}$. This expectation is called a ***temporary curtate life expectancy.*** Show that

a. $e_{x:\overline{n}|} = \displaystyle\sum_0^{n-1} k \; {}_{k|}q_x + n \; {}_np_x$

$\qquad = \displaystyle\sum_1^n {}_kp_x$

b. $\text{Var}[K^*(x)] = \sum_{0}^{n-1} k^2 \; {}_{k|}q_x + n^2 \; {}_n p_x - (e_{x:\overline{n}|})^2$

$$= \sum_{1}^{n} (2k - 1) \; {}_k p_x - (e_{x:\overline{n}|})^2.$$

3.18. If the random variable T has p.d.f. given by $f_T(t) = ce^{-ct}$ for $t \geq 0$, $c > 0$, calculate

a. $\overset{\circ}{e}_x = \text{E}[T]$ b. $\text{Var}(T)$ c. median (T)
d. The mode of the distribution of T.

3.19. If $\mu(x + t) = t, t \geq 0$, calculate

a. ${}_t p_x \, \mu(x + t)$ b. $\overset{\circ}{e}_x$.
[Hint: Recall, from the study of probability, that $(1/\sqrt{2\pi}) \, e^{-t^2/2}$ is the p.d.f. for the standard normal distribution.]

3.20. If the random variable $T(x)$ has d.f. given by

$$F_{T(x)}(t) = \begin{cases} \dfrac{t}{(100 - x)} & 0 \leq t < 100 - x \\ 1 & t \geq 100 - x, \end{cases}$$

calculate

a. $\overset{\circ}{e}_x$ b. $\text{Var}[T(x)]$ c. median $[T(x)]$.

3.21. Show that

a. $\dfrac{\partial}{\partial x} \, {}_t p_x = {}_t p_x \, [\mu(x) - \mu(x + t)]$

b. $\dfrac{d}{dx} \, \overset{\circ}{e}_x = \overset{\circ}{e}_x \, \mu(x) - 1$

c. $\Delta e_x = q_x \, e_{x+1} - p_x$.

3.22. Confirm the following statements:

a. $a(x) \, d_x = L_x - l_{x+1}$
b. The approximation developed in Example 3.5.1 was not used to calculate L_0 in Table 3.3.1, but was used to calculate L_1

c. $T_x = \displaystyle\sum_{k=0}^{\infty} L_{x+k}$.

3.23. The survival function is given by

$$s(x) = 1 - \frac{x}{10} \qquad 0 \leq x \leq 10$$

$$= 0 \qquad\qquad \text{elsewhere.}$$

Calculate values of $\overset{\circ}{e}_x$ and e_x, $x = 0, 1, 2, \ldots, 9$
a. Using formulas (3.5.2) and (3.5.7)
b. Using the formulas developed in Table 3.5.1.

3.24. Find $u(0)$, $-c(x)/d(x)$, and $d(x)$ if $u(x) = \Pr[X = x]$ where (3.5.20) is to be used to produce a table of the p.f. of the random variable X when it has a
  a. A Poisson distribution with parameter λ
  b. A binomial distribution with parameters n and p.

3.25. Formula (3.5.20) is to be used to produce tables of compound interest functions. Find $u(1)$, $-c(x)/d(x)$, and $1/d(x)$ when
  a. $u(x) = \ddot{a}_{\overline{x}|}$
  b. $u(x) = \ddot{s}_{\overline{x}|}$.

Section 3.6

3.26. Verify the entries for the constant force of mortality and the hyperbolic assumption in Table 3.6.1. Note that the entry for $_s p_x$ in the hyperbolic column provides justification for the hyperbolic name.

3.27. Graph $\mu(x + t)$, $0 < t < 1$, for each of the three assumptions in Table 3.6.1. Also graph the survival function for each assumption.

3.28. Using the l_x column of Table 3.3.1, compute $_{1/2}p_{65}$ for each of the three assumptions in Table 3.6.1.

3.29. Use Table 3.3.1 and an assumption of uniform distribution of deaths in each year of age to find the median of the future lifetime of a person
  a. Age 0   b. Age 50.

3.30. If $q_{70} = 0.04$ and $q_{71} = 0.05$, calculate the probability that (70) will die between ages 70½ and 71½ under
  a. The assumption that deaths are uniformly distributed within each year of age
  b. The hyperbolic assumption for each year of age.

3.31. Using the l_x column in Table 3.3.1 and each of the assumptions in Table 3.6.1, compute
  a. $\lim_{h\to 0^-} \mu(60 + h)$
  b. $\lim_{h\to 0^+} \mu(60 + h)$
  c. $\mu(60 + \tfrac{1}{2})$.

3.32. If the constant force assumption is adopted, show that
  a. $a(x) = \dfrac{[(1 - e^{-\mu})/\mu] - e^{-\mu}}{1 - e^{-\mu}}$ b. $a(x) \cong \dfrac{1}{2} - \dfrac{q_x}{12}$.

3.33. If the hyperbolic assumption is adopted, show
  a. $a(x) = -\dfrac{p_x}{q_x^2}(q_x + \log p_x)$ b. $a(x) \cong \dfrac{1}{2} - \dfrac{q_x}{6}$.

3.34. Verify the entries in Table 3.7.1 for De Moivre's law and Weibull's law.

3.35. Consider a modification of De Moivre's law given by

$$s(x) = \left(1 - \frac{x}{\omega}\right)^{\alpha} \qquad 0 \le x < \omega, \qquad \alpha > 0.$$

Calculate

a. $\mu(x)$ b. $\overset{\circ}{e}_x$.

Section 3.8

3.36. Using Table 3.8.1, calculate

a. $_2q_{[32]+1}$ b. $_2p_{[31]+1}$.

3.37. The quantity

$$1 - \frac{q_{[x]+k}}{q_{x+k}} = I(x, k)$$

has been called the **index of selection.** When it is close to 0, the indication is that selection has worn off. From Table 3.8.1, calculate the index for $x = 32$, $k = 0, 1$.

3.38. The force of mortality for a life selected at age (x) is given by $\mu_{\mathbf{x}}(t) = \Psi(\mathbf{x})\mu(t)$, $t > 0$. In this formula $\mu(t)$ is the standard force of mortality. The symbol $\mathbf{x}$ denotes a vector of numerical information about the life at the time of selection. This information would include the age and other classification information. It is required that $\Psi(\mathbf{x}) > 0$ and $\Psi(\mathbf{x}_0) = 1$, where $\mathbf{x}_0$ denotes standard information. Show that the select survival function is

$$_tp_{[\mathbf{x}]} = \left(_tp_{[\mathbf{x}_0]}\right)^{\Psi(\mathbf{x})}$$

and the p.d.f. of $T(\mathbf{x})$, the random variable time-until-death given the information $\mathbf{x}$, is $-\Psi(\mathbf{x}) \; _tp'_{[\mathbf{x}_0]}(_tp_{[\mathbf{x}_0]})^{\Psi(\mathbf{x})-1}$, where $_tp'_{[\mathbf{x}_0]}$ is the derivative with respect to t of $_tp_{[\mathbf{x}_0]}$. This is called a **proportional hazard model.**

Miscellaneous

3.39. A life at age 50 is subject to an extra hazard during the year of age 50 to 51. If the standard probability of death from age 50 to 51 is 0.006, and if the extra risk may be expressed by an addition to the standard force of mortality that decreases uniformly from 0.03 at the beginning of year to 0 at the end of the year, calculate the probability that the life will survive to age 51.

3.40. If the force of mortality $\mu_x(t)$, $0 \le t \le 1$, changes to $\mu_x(t) - c$ where c is a positive constant, find the value of c for which the probability that (x) will die within a year will be halved. Express the answer in terms of $q_{[x]}$.

3.41. From a standard mortality table, a second table is prepared by doubling the force of mortality of the standard table. Is the rate of mortality, q'_x, at any

---

given age under the new table, more than double, exactly double, or less than double the mortality rate, q_x, of the standard table?

3.42. If $\mu(x) = B\,c^x$, $c > 1$, show that the function $l_x\,\mu(x)$ has its maximum at age x_0 where $\mu(x_0) = \log c$. [Hint: This exercise makes use of Exercise 3.14.]

3.43. Assume $\mu(x) = \dfrac{A\,c^x}{1 + B\,c^x}$ for $x > 0$.

    a. Calculate the survival function, $s(x)$.

    b. Verify that the mode of the distribution of X, the age-at-death, is given by

$$x_0 = \frac{\log(\log c) - \log A}{\log c}.$$

3.44. If $\mu(x) = \dfrac{3}{100 - x} - \dfrac{10}{250 - x}$ for $40 < x < 100$, calculate

    a. $_{40}p_{50}$

    b. The mode of the distribution of X, the age-at-death.

3.45. a. Show that, under the uniform distribution of deaths assumption,

$$m_x = \frac{q_x}{1 - (1/2)q_x} \quad \text{and} \quad q_x = \frac{m_x}{1 + (1/2)m_x}.$$

    b. Calculate m_x in terms of q_x under the constant force assumption.

    c. Calculate m_x in terms of q_x under the hyperbolic assumption.

    d. If $l_x = 100 - x$ for $0 \le x \le 100$, calculate $_{10}m_{50}$ where

$$_{n}m_x = \frac{\displaystyle\int_0^n l_{x+t}\,\mu(x + t)\,dt}{\displaystyle\int_0^n l_{x+t}\,dt}.$$

3.46. Show that K and S are independent if and only if the expression

$$\frac{_s q_{[x]+k}}{q_{[x]+k}}$$

does not depend on k for $0 \le s \le 1$.

Computing Exercises:

These are the first in a series of exercises that involve sufficient computation to make it worthwhile to use a computer. The series will continue in the following chapters, and in each exercise it is assumed that the results of previous exercises are available. For example, in Exercise 3.47, you are asked to set up a life table that will then be used in risk analysis in Chapters 4 and 5.

3.47. Using spreadsheet or other mathematical software, set up an object that will accept input values for the Makeham law parameters and then calculate and display the values of p_x and q_x for ages 0 to 140. As a check on your output, input the parameter values given in (3.7.1) and compare your q_x values with those for $x = 13, 14, \ldots$ in the Illustrative Life Table in Appendix 2A. We will refer to this computing object as your Illustrative Life Table. When the Makeham parameter values are not stated, those of (3.7.1) are implied. [Remark: With a Makeham Table, $s(x) > 0$ for all $x > 0$, so ω does not exist as defined in Section 3.3.1. For the parameter values of the Illustrative Life Table, q_{140} is zero to eight decimal places; thus we choose $\omega = 140$ for our Illustrative Life Table, that is, Table 2A.]

3.48. In your Illustrative Life Table use the forward recursion formula $l_{x+1} = (p_x)(l_x)$ and initial value $l_{13} = 96,807.88$ to calculate the l_x values of Table 2A. [Remark: The Makeham law was not realistic for ages less than 13, so the Illustrative Life Table is a blend of some ad hoc values from 0 through 12 and the Makeham law table from age 13 up.]

3.49. Illustrate the result of Exercise 3.41 by doubling the A and B parameter values in your Illustrative Life Table.

3.50. Use the backward recursion formula of Table 3.5.1 to calculate values of e_x in your Illustrative Life Table for ages 13 to 140.

3.51. Compare the values of e_x at $x = 20, 40, 60, 80,$ and 100 in your Illustrative Life Table with those found when the force of mortality is doubled.

3.52. Use the backward recursion formula of Table 3.5.1 and the trapezoidal rule to calculate values of $\overset{\circ}{e}_x$ in your Illustrative Life Table for ages 13 to 110.

3.53. Verify the following backward recursion formula for the temporary curtate life expectancy to age y:

$$e_{x:\overline{y-x}|} = p_x + p_x\, e_{x+1:\overline{y-(x+1)}|} \quad \text{for } x = 0, 1, \ldots, y - 1.$$

Determine an appropriate starting value for use with this formula. For your Illustrative Life Table calculate the curtate temporary life expectancy up to age 45 for ages 13 to 44.

3.54. Verify the following backward recursion formula for the n-year temporary curtate life expectancy:

$$e_{x:\overline{n}|} = p_x\,(1 - {}_np_{x+1}) + p_x\, e_{x+1:\overline{n}|} \quad \text{for } x = 0, 1, \ldots, \omega - 1.$$

Determine an appropriate starting value for use with this formula. For your Illustrative Life Table calculate the 10-year temporary curtate life expectancy for ages 13 to 139.

3.55. "Look up" $e_{15:\overline{25}|}$ in your Illustrative Life Table. [Hint: Since the $c(x)$ term in the relation in Exercise 3.53 does not depend on n, it may be more efficient to view $e_{15:\overline{25}|}$ as a curtate temporary life expectancy to age 40 for (15).]

LIFE INSURANCE

4.1 Introduction

We have stated that insurance systems are established to reduce the adverse financial impact of some types of random events. Within these systems individuals and organizations adopt utility models to represent preferences, stochastic models to represent uncertain financial impact, and economic principles to guide pricing. Agreements are reached after analyses of these models.

In Chapter 2 we developed an elementary model for the financial impact of random events in which the occurrence and the size of impact are both uncertain. In that model, the policy term is assumed to be sufficiently short so the uncertainty of investment income from a random payment time could be ignored.

In this chapter we develop models for life insurances designed to reduce the financial impact of the random event of untimely death. Due to the long-term nature of these insurances, the amount of investment earnings, up to the time of payment, provides a significant element of uncertainty. This uncertainty has two causes: the unknown rate of earnings over, and the unknown length of, the investment period. A probability distribution is used to model the uncertainty in regards to the investment period throughout this book. In this chapter a deterministic model is used for the unknown investment earnings, and in Chapter 21 stochastic models for this uncertainty are discussed. In other words, our model will be built in terms of functions of T, the insured's future-lifetime random variable.

While everything in this chapter will be stated as insurances on human lives, the ideas would be the same for other objects such as equipment, machines, loans, and business ventures. In fact, the general model is useful in any situation where the size and time of a financial impact can be expressed solely in terms of the time of the random event.

4.2 Insurances Payable at the Moment of Death

In this chapter, the amount and the time of payment of a life insurance benefit depend only on the length of the interval from the issue of the insurance to the death of the insured. Our model will be developed with a **benefit function,** b_t, and a **discount function,** v_t. In our model, v_t is the interest discount factor from the time of payment back to the time of policy issue, and t is the length of the interval from issue to death. In the case of endowments, covered in this section, t can be greater than or equal to the length of the interval from issue to payment.

For the discount function we assume that the underlying force of interest is deterministic; that is, the model does not include a probability distribution for the force of interest. Moreover, we usually show the simple formulas resulting from the assumption of a constant, as well as a deterministic, force of interest.

We define the **present-value function,** z_t, by

$$z_t = b_t v_t. \tag{4.2.1}$$

Thus, z_t is the present value, at policy issue, of the benefit payment. The elapsed time from policy issue to the death of the insured is the insured's future-lifetime random variable, $T = T(x)$, defined in Section 3.2.2. Thus, the present value, at policy issue, of the benefit payment is the random variable z_T. Unless the context requires a more elaborate symbol, we denote this random variable by Z and base the model for the insurance on the equation

$$Z = b_T v_T. \tag{4.2.2}$$

The random variable Z is an example of a claim random variable and, as such, of an X_i term in the sum of the individual risk model, as defined by (2.1.1). This model is used in later sections when we consider applications involving portfolios. We now turn to the development of the probability model for Z.

The first step in our analysis of a life insurance will be to define b_t and v_t. The next step is to determine some characteristics of the probability distribution of Z that are consequences of an assumed distribution for T, and we work through these steps for several conventional insurances. A summary is provided in Table 4.2.1 on page 109.

4.2.1 Level Benefit Insurance

An **n-year term life insurance** provides for a payment only if the insured dies within the n-year term of an insurance commencing at issue. If a unit is payable at the moment of death of (x), then

$$b_t = \begin{cases} 1 & t \leq n \\ 0 & t > n, \end{cases}$$

$$v_t = v^t \qquad t \geq 0,$$

$$Z = \begin{cases} v^T & T \leq n \\ 0 & T > n. \end{cases}$$

These definitions use three conventions. First, since the future lifetime is a non-negative variable, we define b_t, v_t, and Z only on non-negative values. Second, for a t value where b_t is 0, the value of v_t is irrelevant. At these values of t, we adopt definitions of v_t by convenience. Third, unless stated otherwise, the force of interest is assumed to be constant.

The expectation of the present-value random variable, Z, is called the *actuarial present value* of the insurance. The reader will find that the expectation of the present value of a set of payments contingent on the occurrence of a set of events is referred to by different terms in different actuarial contexts. In Chapter 1, the expected loss was called the pure premium. This vocabulary is commonly used in property-liability insurance. A more exact term, but more cumbersome, would be *expectation of the present value of the payments.* We denote actuarial present values by their symbols according to the International Actuarial Notation (see Appendix 4).

The principal symbol for the actuarial present value of an insurance paying a unit benefit is A. The subscript includes the age of the insured life at the time of the calculation. How this age is displayed depends upon the form of the mortality assumption. For the actuarial present value of an insurance on (40), the age might be displayed as [40], 40, or [20] + 20, for example. As in Section 3.8, the bracket indicates selection at that age and hence the use of a select table commencing at that age. The unbracketed age indicates the use of an aggregate or ultimate table. Thus [20] + 20 indicates the calculation for a 40-year-old on the basis of a select table commencing at age 20.

The actuarial present value for the n-year term insurance with a unit payable at the moment of death of (x), $E[Z]$, is denoted by $\bar{A}^1_{x:\overline{n}|}$. This can be calculated by recognizing Z as a function of T so that $E[Z] = E[z_T]$. Then we use the p.d.f. of T to obtain

$$\bar{A}^1_{x:\overline{n}|} = E[Z] = E[z_T] = \int_0^\infty z_t \, f_T(t) \, dt = \int_0^n v^t \, {}_tp_x \, \mu_x(t) \, dt. \qquad (4.2.3)$$

The j-th moment of the distribution of Z can be found by

$$E[Z^j] = \int_0^n (v^t)^j \, {}_tp_x \, \mu_x(t) \, dt$$

$$= \int_0^n e^{-(\delta j)t} \, {}_tp_x \, \mu_x(t) \, dt.$$

The second integral shows that the j-th moment of Z is equal to the actuarial present value for an n-year term insurance for a unit amount payable at the moment of death of (x), calculated at a force of interest equal to j times the given force of interest, or $j\delta$.

This property, which we call the **rule of moments**, holds generally for insurances paying only a unit amount when the force of interest is deterministic, constant or not. More precisely,

$$E[Z^j] \,@\, \delta_t = E[Z] \,@\, j\delta_t. \tag{4.2.4}$$

In addition to the existence of the moments, the sufficient condition for the rule of moments is $b_t^j = b_t$ for all $t \geq 0$, that is, for each t the benefit amount is 0 or 1. Demonstration that this is sufficient is left to Exercise 4.30.

It follows from the rule of moments that

$$\text{Var}(Z) = {}^2\bar{A}^1_{x:\overline{n}|} - (\bar{A}^1_{x:\overline{n}|})^2 \tag{4.2.5}$$

where ${}^2\bar{A}^1_{x:\overline{n}|}$ is the actuarial present value for an n-year term insurance for a unit amount calculated at force of interest 2δ.

Whole life insurance provides for a payment following the death of the insured at any time in the future. If the payment is to be a unit amount at the moment of death of (x), then

$$b_t = 1 \qquad t \geq 0,$$
$$v_t = v^t \qquad t \geq 0,$$
$$Z = v^T \qquad T \geq 0.$$

The actuarial present value is

$$\bar{A}_x = E[Z] = \int_0^\infty v^t \,{}_tp_x\, \mu_x(t)\, dt. \tag{4.2.6}$$

For a life selected at x and now age $x + h$, the expression would be

$$\bar{A}_{[x]+h} = \int_0^\infty v^t \,{}_tp_{[x]+h}\, \mu_x(h + t)\, dt.$$

Whole life insurance is the limiting case of n-year term insurance as $n \to \infty$.

Example 4.2.1

The p.d.f. of the future lifetime, T, for (x) is assumed to be

$$f_T(t) = \begin{cases} 1/80 & 0 \leq t \leq 80 \\ 0 & \text{elsewhere.} \end{cases}$$

At a force of interest, δ, calculate for Z, the present-value random variable for a whole life insurance of unit amount issued to (x):

a. The actuarial present value

b. The variance

c. The 90th percentile, $\xi_Z^{0.9}$.

Solution:

a. $\bar{A}_x = E[Z] = \displaystyle\int_0^\infty v^t\, f_T(t)\, dt = \int_0^{80} e^{-\delta t}\, \frac{1}{80}\, dt = \frac{1 - e^{-80\delta}}{80\,\delta} \qquad \delta \neq 0.$

b. By the rule of moments,

$$\text{Var}(Z) = \frac{1 - e^{-160\delta}}{160\,\delta} - \left(\frac{1 - e^{-80\delta}}{80\,\delta}\right)^2 \qquad \delta \neq 0.$$

c. For the continuous random variable, Z, we have $\Pr(Z \leq \xi_Z^{0.9}) = 0.9$.

Since we have the p.d.f. for T and not for Z, we proceed by finding the event for T which corresponds to $Z \leq \xi_Z^{0.9}$. From Figure 4.2.1, which shows the general relationship between the sample space of T (on the horizontal axis) and the sample space of Z (on the vertical axis), we see that $\xi_Z^{0.9} = v^{\xi_T^{0.1}}$. Because Z is a strictly decreasing function of T for whole life insurance, the percentile from T's distribution that is related to 90th percentile of Z's distribution is at the complementary probability level, 0.1. In this example T is uniformly distributed over the interval $(0, 80)$, so $\xi_T^{0.1} = 8.0$ and thus $\xi_Z^{0.9} = v^{8.0}$. $\qquad\blacktriangledown$

The graph in Figure 4.2.1 can be used to establish relationships between the d.f. and p.d.f. of Z and those of T:

FIGURE 4.2.1

Relationship of *Z* to *T* for Whole Life Insurance

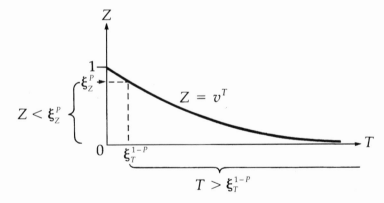

For $z \leq 0$, $\{Z \leq z\}$ is the null event

For $0 < z < 1$, $\{Z \leq z\} = \{T \geq \log z / \log v\}$, and

For $z \geq 1$, $\{Z \leq z\}$ is the certain event.

Therefore,

$$F_Z(z) = \begin{cases} 0 & z \leq 0 \\ 1 - F_T(\log z / \log v) & 0 < z < 1 \\ 1 & 1 \leq z. \end{cases} \qquad (4.2.7)$$

By differentiation of (4.2.7),

$$f_Z(z) = \begin{cases} f_T[(\log z)/(\log v)][1/(\delta z)] & 0 < z < 1 \\ 0 & \text{elsewhere.} \end{cases} \qquad (4.2.8)$$

Example 4.2.2

For the assumptions in Example 4.2.1, determine
a. Z's d.f.
b. Z's p.d.f.

Solution:

a.

$$\text{From } F_T(t) = \begin{cases} t/80 & 0 \leq t \leq 80 \\ 1 & t \geq 80, \end{cases}$$

we see that $\Pr\{T > 80\} = 0.0$, so $\Pr\{0 < Z < v^{80}\} = 0.0$. Therefore, from (4.2.7)

$$F_Z(z) = \begin{cases} 0 & z < v^{80} \\ 1 - [(\log z)/(\log v)]/80 & v^{80} < z < 1 \\ 1 & z \geq 1. \end{cases}$$

b. By differentiation of the d.f. in part (a),

$$f_Z(z) = \begin{cases} (1/80)(1/\delta z) & v^{80} < z < 1 \\ 0 & \text{elsewhere.} \end{cases} \qquad \blacktriangledown$$

We now turn our attention to a common application involving portfolios of risk: determining an initial investment fund for a segment of insurances in the total portfolio. The individual risk model and the normal approximation (as discussed in Section 2.4) are used.

Example 4.2.3

Assume that each of 100 independent lives
- Is age x
- Is subject to a constant force of mortality, $\mu = 0.04$, and
- Is insured for a death benefit amount of 10 units, payable at the moment of death.

The benefit payments are to be withdrawn from an investment fund earning $\delta = 0.06$. Calculate the minimum amount at $t = 0$ so that the probability is approximately 0.95 that sufficient funds will be on hand to withdraw the benefit payment at the death of each individual.

Solution:

For each life,

$$b_t = 10 \qquad t \geq 0,$$
$$v_t = v^t \qquad t \geq 0,$$
$$Z = 10v^T \qquad T \geq 0.$$

If we think of the lives as numbered, perhaps by the order of issuing policies, then at $t = 0$ the present value of all payments to be made is

$$S = \sum_1^{100} Z_j$$

where Z_j is the present value at $t = 0$ for the payment to be made at the death of the life numbered j.

We can use the fact that Z is 10 times the present-value random variable for the unit amount whole life insurance to calculate the mean and variance. For constant forces of interest, δ, and mortality, μ, the actuarial present value for the unit amount whole life insurance is

$$\bar{A}_x = \int_0^\infty e^{-\delta t}\, e^{-\mu t}\, \mu\, dt = \frac{\mu}{\mu + \delta}.$$

Then, for this example,

$$E[Z] = 10\bar{A}_x = 10\,\frac{0.04}{0.1} = 4,$$

$$E[Z^2] = 10^2\,{}^2\bar{A}_x = 100\,\frac{0.04}{0.04 + 2(0.06)} = 25$$

and $\mathrm{Var}(Z) = 9$.

Using these values for the mean and the variance of each term in the sum for S, we have

$$E[S] = 100(4) = 400,$$
$$\mathrm{Var}(S) = 100(9) = 900.$$

Analytically, the required minimum amount is a number, h, such that

$$\Pr(S \leq h) = 0.95,$$

or equivalently

$$\Pr\left[\frac{S - E[S]}{\sqrt{\mathrm{Var}(S)}} \leq \frac{h - 400}{30}\right] \doteq 0.95.$$

By use of a normal approximation, we obtain

$$\frac{h - 400}{30} = 1.645,$$

$$h = 449.35.$$ ▼

Observations:

1. The 49.35 difference between this initial fund of 449.35 and the expectation of the present value of all payments, 400, is the risk loading of Chapter 1. The loading is 0.4935 per life, or 4.935% per unit payment, or 12.34% of the actuarial present value.
2. This example, like Examples 2.5.2 and 2.5.3, used the individual risk model and a normal approximation to the probability distribution of S. In the short-period examples, the collected income, equal to expected claims plus a risk loading, was determined to have a high probability of being in excess of claims. In this long-period life insurance example, the collected income plus interest income on it at the assumed interest rate is determined to be sufficient to cover the benefit payments. The initial fund of 449.35 will cover less than 45% of the eventual certain payout of 1,000.
3. A graph of the amount in the fund during the first 2 years for a payout pattern when one death occurs at each of times 1/8, 7/8, 9/8, 13/8, and 15/8, and two deaths occur at time 10/8 is shown in Figure 4.2.2. Between the benefit payments, represented by the discontinuities, are exponential arcs representing the growth of the fund at $\delta = 0.06$.

FIGURE 4.2.2

Graph of an Outcome for the Fund

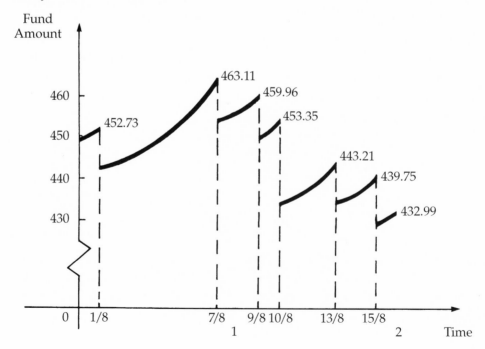

4. There are infinitely many payout patterns, each with its own graph. Both the number of claims and the times of those claims affect the fund. For example, had the seven claims all occurred within the first instant, instead of the payout pattern of Figure 4.2.2, the fund would have dropped immediately to 379.35 and then grown to 427.72 by the end of the second year.

These examples illustrate the different roles of the three random elements in risk model building, that is, whether or not a claim will occur, the size, and the time of payment if one occurs. In Example 2.5.2 there was uncertainty about only the occurrence of the claim. In Example 4.2.2 there was uncertainty about only the time of claim payment. Other uncertainties have been ignored in these models. In Examples 4.2.1, 4.2.2, and 4.2.3 we have ignored the possibility of the fund earning interest at rates different from the deterministic rates assumed.

4.2.2   Endowment Insurance

An *n-year pure endowment* provides for a payment at the end of the n years if and only if the insured survives at least n years from the time of policy issue. If the amount payable is a unit, then

$$b_t = \begin{cases} 0 & t \le n \\ 1 & t > n, \end{cases}$$

$$v_t = v^n \qquad t \ge 0,$$

$$Z = \begin{cases} 0 & T \le n \\ v^n & T > n. \end{cases}$$

The only element of uncertainty in the pure endowment is whether or not a claim will occur. The size and time of payment, if a claim occurs, are predetermined. In the expression $Z = v^n Y$, Y is the indicator of the event of survival to age $x + n$. This Y has the value 1 if the insured survives to age $x + n$ and has the value 0 otherwise. The n-year pure endowment's actuarial present value has two symbols. In an insurance context it is $A_{x:\overline{n}|}^{\ 1}$. We see in the next chapter that it is denoted by $_nE_x$ in an annuity context. This distinction is not strict; the reader will have to be ready for either:

$$A_{x:\overline{n}|}^{\ 1} = E[Z] = v^n\, E[Y] = v^n\, _np_x,$$

and

$$Var(Z) = v^{2n}\, Var(Y) = v^{2n}\, _np_x\, _nq_x$$

$$= {}^2A_{x:\overline{n}|}^{\ 1} - (A_{x:\overline{n}|}^{\ 1})^2. \tag{4.2.9}$$

An *n-year endowment insurance* provides for an amount to be payable either following the death of the insured or upon the survival of the insured to the end of the n-year term, whichever occurs first. If the insurance is for a unit amount and the death benefit is payable at the moment of death, then

$$b_t = 1 \qquad t \geq 0,$$

$$v_t = \begin{cases} v^t & t \leq n \\ v^n & t > n, \end{cases}$$

$$Z = \begin{cases} v^T & T \leq n \\ v^n & T > n. \end{cases}$$

The actuarial present value is denoted by $\bar{A}_{x:\overline{n}|}$. Since $b_t = 1$ for the endowment insurance, we have by the rule of moments

$$E[Z^j] @ \delta = E[Z] @ j\delta.$$

Moreover,

$$\mathrm{Var}(Z) = {}^2\bar{A}_{x:\overline{n}|} - (\bar{A}_{x:\overline{n}|})^2. \qquad (4.2.10)$$

This insurance can be viewed as the combination of an n-year term insurance and an n-year pure endowment—each for a unit amount. Let Z_1, Z_2, and Z_3 denote the present-value random variables of the term, the pure endowment, and the endowment insurances, respectively, with death benefits payable at the moment of death of (x). From the preceding definitions we have

$$Z_1 = \begin{cases} v^T & T \leq n \\ 0 & T > n, \end{cases}$$

$$Z_2 = \begin{cases} 0 & T \leq n \\ v^n & T > n, \end{cases}$$

$$Z_3 = \begin{cases} v^T & T \leq n \\ v^n & T > n. \end{cases}$$

It follows that

$$Z_3 = Z_1 + Z_2, \qquad (4.2.11)$$

and by taking expectations of both sides

$$\bar{A}_{x:\overline{n}|} = \bar{A}^1_{x:\overline{n}|} + A_{x:\overline{n}|}{}^{\;1}. \qquad (4.2.12)$$

We can also find the $\mathrm{Var}(Z_3)$ by using (4.2.11),

$$\mathrm{Var}(Z_3) = \mathrm{Var}(Z_1) + \mathrm{Var}(Z_2) + 2\,\mathrm{Cov}(Z_1, Z_2). \qquad (4.2.13)$$

By use of the formula

$$\mathrm{Cov}(Z_1, Z_2) = E[Z_1 Z_2] - E[Z_1]\,E[Z_2] \qquad (4.2.14)$$

and the observation that

$$Z_1 Z_2 = 0$$

for all T, we have

$$\mathrm{Cov}(Z_1, Z_2) = -E[Z_1]\,E[Z_2] = -\bar{A}^1_{x:\overline{n}|} A_{x:\overline{n}|}{}^{\;1}. \qquad (4.2.15)$$

Substituting (4.2.5), (4.2.9), and (4.2.15) into (4.2.13) produces a formula for $\mathrm{Var}(Z_3)$ in terms of actuarial present values for an n-year term insurance and a pure endowment.

Since the actuarial present values are positive, the $\text{Cov}(Z_1, Z_2)$ is negative. This is to be anticipated since, of the pair Z_1 and Z_2, one is always zero and the other positive. On the other hand, the correlation coefficient of Z_1 and Z_2 is not -1 since they are not linear functions of each other; recall Exercise 1.23(c).

4.2.3 Deferred Insurance

An *m-year deferred insurance* provides for a benefit following the death of the insured only if the insured dies at least m years following policy issue. The benefit payable and the term of the insurance may be any of those discussed above. For example, an m-year deferred whole life insurance with a unit amount payable at the moment of death has

$$b_t = \begin{cases} 1 & t > m \\ 0 & t \le m, \end{cases}$$

$$v_t = v^t \qquad t > 0,$$

$$Z = \begin{cases} v^T & T > m \\ 0 & T \le m. \end{cases}$$

The actuarial present value is denoted by $_{m|}\bar{A}_x$ and is equal to

$$\int_m^\infty v^t \,_t p_x \, \mu_x(t) \, dt. \tag{4.2.16}$$

Example 4.2.4

Consider a 5-year deferred whole life insurance payable at the moment of the death of (x). The individual is subject to a constant force of mortality $\mu = 0.04$. For the distribution of the present value of the benefit payment, at $\delta = 0.10$:
a. Calculate the expectation
b. Calculate the variance
c. Display the distribution function
d. Calculate the median $\xi_Z^{0.5}$.

Solution:

a. For arbitrary forces μ and δ,

$$_{5|}\bar{A}_x = \int_5^\infty e^{-\delta t} \, e^{-\mu t} \, \mu \, dt = \frac{\mu}{\mu + \delta} \, e^{-5(\mu+\delta)};$$

thus for $\mu = 0.04$ and $\delta = 0.10$,

$$_{5|}\bar{A}_x = \frac{2}{7} e^{-0.7} = 0.1419.$$

b. By the rule of moments,

$$\text{Var}(Z) = \frac{0.04}{0.04 + 0.20} e^{-5(0.04+0.20)} - \frac{4}{49} e^{-1.4} = 0.0301.$$

---

c. As for the case of whole life insurance, a graph of the relation between Z and T provides an outline for the solution. For the general m-year deferred whole life insurance, the graph is given in Figure 4.2.3.

FIGURE 4.2.3
Relationship of *Z* to *T* for Deferred Whole Life Insurance

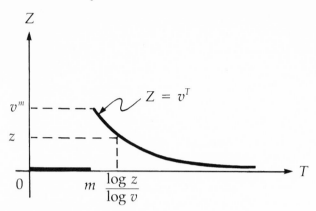

Although T is a continuous random variable, Z is mixed with a probability mass at 0 because $Z = 0$ corresponds to $T \leq m$.

For general mortality assumptions and a constant force of interest, we have for $Z = 0$,

$$F_Z(0) = \Pr(T \leq m) = F_T(m); \qquad (4.2.17)$$

for $0 < z < v^m$,

$$
\begin{aligned}
F_Z(z) = \Pr(Z \leq z) &= \Pr(Z = 0) + \Pr(0 < Z \leq z) \\
&= \Pr(T \leq m) + \Pr(0 < v^T \leq z) \\
&= \Pr(T \leq m) + \Pr\left(T > \frac{\log z}{\log v}\right) \\
&= F_T(m) + 1 - F_T\left(\frac{\log z}{\log v}\right); \qquad (4.2.18)
\end{aligned}
$$

for $z > v^m$,

$$F_Z(z) = 1. \qquad (4.2.19)$$

In this example of 5-year deferred whole life insurance where $\mu = 0.04$ and $\delta = 0.10$, we have

from (4.2.17),

$$F_Z(0) = F_T(5) = 1 - e^{-0.2} = 0.1813;$$

from (4.2.18) for $0 < z < v^5$,

$$F_Z(z) = F_T(5) + 1 - F_T \frac{\log z}{-0.1}$$

$$= 1 - e^{-0.2} + z^{0.04/0.10} = 0.1813 + z^{0.4}; \qquad (4.2.20)$$

from (4.2.19) for $z > v^5$,

$$F_Z(z) = 1.$$

The graph of this d.f. is shown in Figure 4.2.4.

FIGURE 4.2.4
Distribution Function of Z

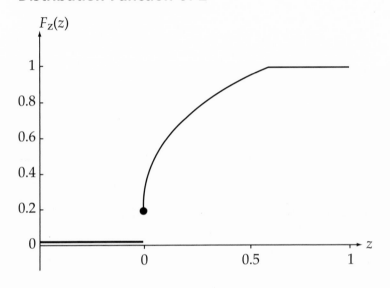

d. From Figure 4.2.4 or (4.2.20), we see that the median is the solution of

$$0.5 = 0.1813 + z^{0.4}.$$

Thus, $\xi_Z^{0.5} = 0.0573$.   ▼

Observations:

1. The largest value of Z with nonzero probability density in this example is $e^{-0.1(5)} = 0.6065$, corresponding to $T = 5$.
2. The distribution of Z in this example is highly skewed to the right. While its total mass is in the interval [0, 0.6065] and its mean is 0.1419, its median is only 0.0573. This skewness in the direction of large positive values is characteristic of many claim distributions in all fields of insurance.

4.2.4   Varying Benefit Insurance

The general model given by (4.2.1) can be used for analysis in most applications. We have used it with level benefit life insurances. It can also be applied to insurances where the level of the death benefit either increases or decreases in arithmetic

---

progression over all or a part of the term of the insurance. Such insurances are often sold as an additional benefit when a basic insurance provides for the return of periodic premiums at death or when an annuity contract contains a guarantee of sufficient payments to match its initial premium.

An ***annually increasing whole life insurance*** providing 1 at the moment of death during the first year, 2 at the moment of death in the second year, and so on, is characterized by the following functions:

$$b_t = \lfloor t + 1 \rfloor \qquad t \geq 0,$$
$$v_t = v^t \qquad t \geq 0,$$
$$Z = \lfloor T + 1 \rfloor v^T \qquad T \geq 0,$$

where the $\lfloor \ \rfloor$ denote the greatest integer function.

The actuarial present value for such an insurance is

$$(I\bar{A})_x = \text{E}[Z] = \int_0^\infty \lfloor t + 1 \rfloor \, v^t \, {}_t p_x \, \mu_x(t) \, dt.$$

The higher order moments are not equal to the actuarial present value at an adjusted force of interest as was the case for insurances with benefit payments equal to 0 or 1. These moments can be calculated directly from their definitions.

The increases in the benefit of the insurance can occur more, or less, frequently than once per year. For an m-thly increasing whole life insurance the benefit would be $1/m$ at the moment of death during the first m-th of a year of the term of the insurance, $2/m$ at the moment of death during the second m-th of a year during the term of the insurance, and so on, increasing by $1/m$ at m-thly intervals throughout the term of the insurance. For such a whole life insurance the functions are

$$b_t = \frac{\lfloor tm + 1 \rfloor}{m} \qquad t \geq 0,$$

$$v_t = v^t \qquad t \geq 0,$$

$$Z = \frac{v^T \lfloor Tm + 1 \rfloor}{m} \qquad T \geq 0.$$

The actuarial present value is

$$(I^{(m)} \bar{A})_x = \text{E}[Z].$$

The limiting case, as $m \to \infty$ in the m-thly increasing whole life insurance, is an insurance paying t at the time of death, t. Its functions are

$$b_t = t \qquad t \geq 0,$$
$$v_t = v^t \qquad t \geq 0,$$
$$Z = Tv^T \qquad T \geq 0.$$

Its actuarial present-value symbol is $(\bar{I}\bar{A})_x$.

This continuously increasing whole life insurance is equivalent to a set of deferred level whole life insurances. This equivalence is shown graphically in Figure 4.2.5 where the region between the line $b_t = t$ and the t-axis represents the insurance over the future lifetime. If the infinitesimal regions are joined in the vertical direction for a fixed t, the total benefit payable at t is obtained. If they are joined in the horizontal direction for a fixed s, an s-year deferred whole life insurance for the level amount ds is obtained.

FIGURE 4.2.5
Continuously Increasing Insurance

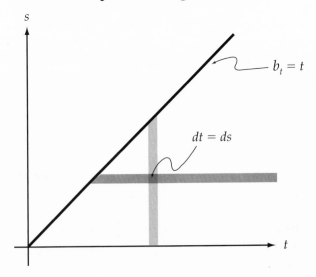

This equivalence implies that the actuarial present values for the coverages are equal. The equality can be established as follows.

By definition,

$$(\bar{I}\bar{A})_x = \int_0^\infty t \, v^t \, {}_tp_x \, \mu_x(t) \, dt,$$

and interpreting t in the integrand as the integral from zero to t in Figure 4.2.5 we have

$$(\bar{I}\bar{A})_x = \int_0^\infty \left(\int_0^t ds \right) v^t \, {}_tp_x \, \mu_x(t) \, dt.$$

If we interchange the order of integration and, for each s value, integrate on t from s to x, we have

$$(\bar{I}\bar{A})_x = \int_0^\infty \int_s^\infty v^t \, {}_tp_x \, \mu_x(t) \, dt \, ds$$

$$= \int_0^\infty {}_{s|}\bar{A}_x \, ds$$

by (4.2.16).

If, for any of these m-thly increasing life insurances, the benefit is payable only if death occurs within a term of n years, the insurance is an **m-*thly increasing* n-*year term life insurance*.**

Complementary to the anually increasing n-year term life insurance is the ***anually decreasing n-year term life insurance*** providing n at the moment of death during the first year, $n - 1$ at the moment of death during the second year, and so on, with coverage terminating at the end of the n-th year. Such an insurance has the following functions:

$$b_t = \begin{cases} n - \lfloor t \rfloor & t \le n \\ 0 & t > n, \end{cases}$$

$$v_t = v^t \qquad\qquad t > 0,$$

$$Z = \begin{cases} v^T(n - \lfloor T \rfloor) & T \le n \\ 0 & T > n. \end{cases}$$

The actuarial present value for this insurance is

$$(D\bar{A})^1_{x:\overline{n}|} = \int_0^n v^t \, (n - \lfloor t \rfloor) \; {}_tp_x \; \mu_x(t) \, dt.$$

This insurance is complementary to the anually increasing n-year term insurance in the sense that the sum of their benefit functions is the constant $n + 1$ for the n-year term.

Table 4.2.1 is a summary of the models in this section. The insurance plan name appears in the first column followed by the benefit and discount functions that define it in terms of the future lifetime of the insured at policy issue. The present-value function, which is always derived as the product of the previous two functions, is shown next. In the fifth column the International Actuarial Notation for the actuarial present value is shown. In the last column, a reference is given to a footnote stating whether or not the rule of moments can be used in the calculation of higher order moments.

4.3   Insurances Payable at the End of the Year of Death

In the previous section we developed models for life insurances with death benefits payable at the moment of death. In practice, most benefits are considered payable at the moment of death and then earn interest until the payment is actually made. The models were built in terms of T, the future lifetime of the insured at policy issue. In most life insurance applications, the best information available on the probability distribution of T is in the form of a discrete life table. This is the probability distribution of K, the curtate-future-lifetime of the insured at policy issue, a function of T. In this and the following section we bridge this gap by building models for life insurances in which the size and time of payment of the death benefits depend only on the number of complete years lived by the insured from policy issue up to the time of death. We refer to these insurances simply as *payable at the end of the year of death.*

TABLE 4.2.1

Summary of Insurances Payable Immediately on Death

(1) Insurance Name	(2) Benefit Function b_t	(3) Discount Function v_t	(4) Present-Value Function z_t	(5) Actuarial Present Value	(6) Higher Moments
Whole life	1	v^t	v^t	$\bar{A}_x$	*
n-Year term	$\begin{array}{ll}1 & t \le n \\ 0 & t > n\end{array}$	v^t	$\begin{array}{ll}v^t & t \le n \\ 0 & t > n\end{array}$	$\bar{A}^1_{x:\overline{n}|}$	*
n-Year pure endowment	$\begin{array}{ll}0 & t \le n \\ 1 & t > n\end{array}$	v^n	$\begin{array}{ll}0 & t \le n \\ v^n & t > n\end{array}$	$A_{x:\overline{n}|}^{\;\;1}$, $_nE_x$	*
n-Year endowment	1	$\begin{array}{ll}v^t & t \le n \\ v^n & t > n\end{array}$	$\begin{array}{ll}v^t & t \le n \\ v^n & t > n\end{array}$	$\bar{A}_{x:\overline{n}|}$	*
m-Year deferred n-Year term	$\begin{array}{ll}1 & m < t \le n + m \\ 0 & t \le m, t > n + m\end{array}$	v^t	$\begin{array}{ll}v^t & m < t \le n + m \\ 0 & t \le m, t > n + m\end{array}$	$_{m|n}\bar{A}_x$	*
n-Year term increasing annually	$\begin{array}{ll}\lfloor t + 1\rfloor & t \le n \\ 0 & t > n\end{array}$	v^t	$\begin{array}{ll}\lfloor t + 1\rfloor v^t & t \le n \\ 0 & t > n\end{array}$	$(I\bar{A})^1_{x:\overline{n}|}$	†
n-Year term decreasing annually	$\begin{array}{ll}n - \lfloor t\rfloor & t \le n \\ 0 & t > n\end{array}$	v^t	$\begin{array}{ll}(n - \lfloor t\rfloor)v^t & t \le n \\ 0 & t > n\end{array}$	$(D\bar{A})^1_{x:\overline{n}|}$	†
Whole life increasing m-thly	$\lfloor tm + 1\rfloor/m$	v^t	$v^t\lfloor tm + 1\rfloor/m$	$(I^{(m)}\bar{A})_x$	†

Note: b_t, v_t, and z_t are defined only for $t \ge 0$.

*The j-th moment is equal to the actuarial present value at j times the given force of interest, denoted by ^jA for $j > 1$. Then the variance is $^2A - A^2$, symbolically.

†Calculated directly from the definition, $E[Z^j]$.

Our model is in terms of functions of the curtate-future-lifetime of the insured. The benefit function, b_{k+1}, and the discount function, v_{k+1}, are, respectively, the benefit amount payable and the discount factor required for the period from the time of payment back to the time of policy issue when the insured's curtate-future-lifetime is k, that is, when the insured dies in year $k + 1$ of insurance. The present value, at policy issue, of this benefit payment, denoted by z_{k+1}, is

$$z_{k+1} = b_{k+1}v_{k+1}. \tag{4.3.1}$$

Measured from the time of policy issue, the insurance year of death is 1 plus the curtate-future-lifetime random variable, K, defined in Section 3.2.3. As in the previous section, we denote the present-value random variable z_{K+1}, by Z.

For an n-year term insurance providing a unit amount at the end of the year of death, we have

$$b_{k+1} = \begin{cases} 1 & k = 0, 1, \ldots, n - 1 \\ 0 & \text{elsewhere,} \end{cases}$$

$$v_{k+1} = v^{k+1},$$

$$Z = \begin{cases} v^{K+1} & K = 0, 1, \ldots, n - 1 \\ 0 & \text{elsewhere.} \end{cases}$$

The actuarial present value for this insurance is given by

$$A^1_{x:\overline{n}|} = \mathrm{E}[Z] = \sum_{k=0}^{n-1} v^{k+1} \, {}_kp_x \, q_{x+k}. \tag{4.3.2}$$

Note that the International Actuarial Notation symbol for the actuarial present value of an insurance payable at the end of the year of death is the symbol for the corresponding insurance payable at the moment of death with the bar removed.

The rule of moments, with the appropriate changes in notation, also holds for insurances payable at the end of the year of death. For example, for the n-year term insurance above,

$$\mathrm{Var}(Z) = {}^2A^1_{x:\overline{n}|} - (A^1_{x:\overline{n}|})^2$$

where

$${}^2A^1_{x:\overline{n}|} = \sum_{k=0}^{n-1} e^{-2\delta(k+1)} \, {}_kp_x \, q_{x+k}.$$

In Section 3.5 recursion relations for life expectancies are derived and used to determine their values. Recursion relations for the term insurance actuarial present values can be derived algebraically from (4.3.2):

$$A^1_{x:\overline{n|}} = \sum_{k=0}^{n-1} v^{k+1} \, {}_kp_x \, q_{x+k} = vq_x + \sum_{k=1}^{n-1} v^{k+1} \, {}_kp_x \, q_{x+k}$$

$$= vq_x + vp_x \sum_{k=1}^{n-1} v^k \, {}_{k-1}p_{x+1} \, q_{x+k}$$

$$= vq_x + vp_x \sum_{j=0}^{n-2} v^{j+1} \, {}_jp_{x+1} \, q_{x+1+j} = vq_x + vp_x \, A^1_{x+1:\overline{n-1|}}. \qquad (4.3.3)$$

For (4.3.3) to be true at $n = 1$, we define $A^1_{x:\overline{0|}} = 0.0$ for all x.

Note: On a select table basis, all x's in the subscripts in (4.3.3) would be enclosed in brackets.

Example 4.3.1

On the basis of the Illustrative Life Table and $i = 0.04$, determine the mean and variance of the present-value random variable for a 10-year term insurance with a unit benefit payable at the end of the year of death issued on (30).

Solution:
Starting with the initial value $A^1_{40:\overline{0|}} = 0.0$ and using (4.3.3) adapted to this insurance,

$$A^1_{30+k:\overline{10-k|}} = vq_{30+k} + vp_{30+k} \, A^1_{30+k+1:\overline{10-(k+1)|}} \quad k = 0, 1, \ldots, 8, 9,$$

we have by working from age 40 to age 30,

$$A^1_{30:\overline{10|}} = 0.01577285$$

and

$$\text{Var}(Z) = 0.01271978 - (0.01577285)^2 = 0.01247099.$$

These values were determined by the spreadsheet constructed in the Computing Exercises. ▼

For a whole life insurance issued to (x), the model may be obtained by letting $n \to \infty$ in the n-year term insurance model. For the actuarial present value we have

$$A_x = \sum_{k=0}^{\infty} v^{k+1} \, {}_kp_x \, q_{x+k}. \qquad (4.3.4)$$

Multiplication of both sides of (4.3.4) by l_x yields

$$l_x A_x = \sum_{k=0}^{\infty} v^{k+1} \, d_{x+k}. \qquad (4.3.5)$$

Formula (4.3.5) shows the balance, at the time of policy issue, between the aggregate fund of actuarial present values for l_x lives insured at age x and the outflow of funds in accordance with the expected deaths of the l_x lives. It is a compound interest equation of value that is stated on an expected value basis.

The expression

$$\sum_{k=r}^{\infty} v^{k+1}\, d_{x+k} \qquad (4.3.6)$$

is that part of the fund at issue that, together with interest at the assumed rate, will provide the payments for the expected deaths after the r-th insurance year.

Accumulation of (4.3.6) at the assumed interest rate for r years yields

$$\sum_{k=r}^{\infty} v^{k-r+1}\, d_{x+k}, \qquad (4.3.7)$$

the expected amount in the fund after r insurance years. A comparison of expression (4.3.7) with (4.3.5) shows it to be $l_{x+r} A_{x+r}$. The difference between this amount and an actual fund is due to deviations of the actual deaths from the expected deaths (according to the life table adopted), and deviations of the actual interest income from the interest income at the assumed rate.

Example 4.3.2

A group of 100 lives age 30 set up a fund to pay 1,000 at the end of the year of death of each member to a designated survivor. Their mutual agreement is to pay into the fund an amount equal to the whole life insurance actuarial present value calculated on the basis of the Illustrative Life Table at 6% interest. The members, not selected by an insurance company, decided to use this population table as the basis of their plan. The actual experience of the fund is one death in each of the second and fifth years; interest income is at 6% in the first year, 6-1/2% in the second and third years, 7% in the fourth and fifth years. What is the difference, at the end of the first 5 years, between the expected size of the fund as determined at the inception of the plan and the actual fund?

Solution:

On the agreed bases, $1{,}000\, A_{30} = 102.4835$, so, for the 100 lives, the fund starts at 10,248.35. Also, $A_{35} = 0.1287194$ and $l_{35}/l_{30} = 0.9915040$.

For 100 lives age 30, the expected size of the fund after 5 years will be

$$(1{,}000)(100)\, \frac{l_{35}}{l_{30}}\, A_{35} = 12{,}762.58.$$

The development of the actual fund would be as follows, where F_k denotes its size at the end of insurance year k:

$$F_0 = 10,248.35$$

$$F_1 = (10,248.35)(1.06) = 10,863.25$$

$$F_2 = (10,863.25)(1.065) - 1,000 = 10,569.36$$

$$F_3 = (10,569.36)(1.065) = 11,256.37$$

$$F_4 = (11,256.37)(1.07) = 12,044.32$$

$$F_5 = (12,044.32)(1.07) - 1,000 = 11,887.42.$$

Thus the required difference is $12,762.58 - 11,887.42 = 875.16$. This result combines the investment experience and the mortality experience for the 5-year period. There were gains from the investment earnings in excess of the assumed rate of 6%. On the other hand, there were losses on the mortality experience of two deaths as compared to the expected number of 0.8496. The interpretation of such results in terms of the various sources such as investment earnings and mortality is an actuarial responsibility. ▼

We derived the recursion relations for n-year term insurance actuarial present values (4.3.3) algebraically. Whereas the relationship will hold for whole life insurance actuarial present values as the limiting case of n-year term insurance, as n goes to ∞, we will establish the whole life insurance relationship independently to illustrate a probabilistic derivation.

Consider A_x from its definition $E[Z] = E[v^{K(x)+1}]$. For emphasis we now write this as

$$A_x = E[Z] = E[v^{K(x)+1}|K(x) \geq 0],$$

which is redundant since all of $K(x)$'s probability is on the non-negative integers.

$E[Z]$ can be calculated by considering the event that (x) dies in the first year, that is, $K(x) = 0$, and its complement, that (x) survives the first year, that is, $K(x) \geq 1$. We can write

$$E[Z] = E[v^{K(x)+1}|K(x) = 0] \Pr[K(x) = 0]$$
$$+ E[v^{K(x)+1}|K(x) \geq 1] \Pr[K(x) \geq 1]. \qquad (4.3.8)$$

In this expression we can readily substitute

$$E[v^{K(x)+1}|K(x) = 0] = v,$$
$$\Pr[K(x) = 0] = q_x,$$

and

$$\Pr[K(x) \geq 1] = p_x.$$

To find an expression for the remaining factor, we rewrite it as

$$E[v^{K(x)+1}|K(x) \geq 1] = v\,E[v^{(K(x)-1)+1}|K(x) - 1 \geq 0].$$

Since $K(x)$ is the curtate-future-lifetime of (x), given $K(x) \geq 1$, $K(x) - 1$ must be the curtate-future-lifetime of $(x + 1)$.

If we are willing to use the same probabilities for the conditional distribution of $K(x) - 1$ given $K(x) \geq 1$, as we would for a newly considered life age $x + 1$, then we may write

$$E[v^{(K(x)-1)+1}|K(x) - 1 \geq 0] = A_{x+1} \qquad (4.3.9)$$

and substitute it into (4.3.8) to obtain

$$A_x = vq_x + vA_{x+1}p_x. \qquad (4.3.10)$$

The assumed equality,

(the distribution of the future lifetime
of a newly insured life aged $x + 1$)

= (the distribution of the future lifetime of a life
now age $x + 1$ who was insured 1 year ago),

was discussed in Section 3.8. In terms of select tables, the right-hand side of (4.3.9) would be $A_{[x]+1}$. In (4.3.10) every x would be $[x]$.

Note that (4.3.10) is the same backward recursion formula as (4.3.3). That is,

$$u(x) = vq_x + vp_x \, u(x +1).$$

It is the starting value that makes the solution the actuarial present value of whole life insurance or of n-year term insurance. We see this same recursion formula for the actuarial present values of n-year endowment insurance where the starting values are the endowment maturity value.

Analysis of relationship (4.3.10) can give more insight into the nature of A_x. After replacement of p_x by $1 - q_x$ and multiplication of both sides by $(1 + i)l_x$, (4.3.10) can be rearranged as

$$l_x (1 + i)A_x = l_xA_{x+1} + d_x(1 - A_{x+1}). \qquad (4.3.11)$$

For the random survivorship group, this equation has the following interpretation. Together with 1 year's interest, A_x will provide A_{x+1} for all l_x lives and an additional $1 - A_{x+1}$ for those expected to die within the year. This latter amount for each expected death, that is, $q_x(1 - A_{x+1})$, is considered the *annual cost of insurance.* The A_{x+1} is set aside for survivors and deaths, the $1 - A_{x+1}$ is required only for a death.

Dividing by l_x and then subtracting $A_x + q_x(1 - A_{x+1})$ from both sides of (4.3.11), we have

$$A_{x+1} - A_x = iA_x - q_x(1 - A_{x+1}). \qquad (4.3.12)$$

In words, the difference between the actuarial present values at age x and one later at age $x + 1$ is equal to the interest on the actuarial present value at x less the annual cost of insurance for the year.

Another expression for A_x can be obtained from (4.3.10) by replacing p_x by $1 - q_x$, multiplying both sides by v^x, and rearranging the terms to get

$$v^{x+1}A_{x+1} - v^x A_x = -v^{x+1}q_x(1 - A_{x+1}),$$

or

$$\Delta v^x A_x = -v^{x+1}q_x(1 - A_{x+1}).$$

Summing from $x = y$ to ∞ (see Appendix 5), we obtain

$$-v^y A_y = -\sum_{x=y}^{\infty} v^{x+1}q_x(1 - A_{x+1})$$

and thus

$$A_y = \sum_{x=y}^{\infty} v^{x+1-y}q_x(1 - A_{x+1}).$$

This expression shows that the actuarial present value at y is the present value at y of the annual costs of insurance over the remaining lifetime of the insured.

The n-year endowment insurance with a unit amount payable at the end of the year of death is a combination of the n-year term insurance of this section and the n-year pure endowment for a unit amount that was discussed in the previous section. Thus the functions for it are

$$b_{k+1} = 1 \qquad k = 0, 1, \ldots,$$

$$v_{k+1} = \begin{cases} v^{k+1} & k = 0, 1, \ldots, n-1 \\ v^n & k = n, n+1, \ldots, \end{cases}$$

$$Z = \begin{cases} v^{K+1} & K = 0, 1, \ldots, n-1 \\ v^n & K = n, n+1, \ldots. \end{cases}$$

The actuarial present value is

$$A_{x:\overline{n}|} = \sum_{k=0}^{n-1} v^{k+1} {}_kp_x\, q_{x+k} + v^n\, {}_np_x. \tag{4.3.13}$$

The annually increasing whole life insurance, paying $k + 1$ units at the end of insurance year $k + 1$ provided the insured dies in that insurance year, has the benefit and discount functions and present-value random variable as follows:

$$b_{k+1} = k + 1 \qquad k = 0, 1, 2, \ldots,$$

$$v_{k+1} = v^{k+1} \qquad k = 0, 1, 2, \ldots,$$

$$Z = (K + 1)\, v^{K+1} \qquad K = 0, 1, 2, \ldots.$$

The actuarial present value is denoted by $(IA)_x$.

The annually decreasing n-year term insurance, during the n-year period, provides a benefit at the end of the year of death in an amount equal to $n - k$ where

k is the number of complete years lived by the insured since issue. Its functions are

$$b_{k+1} = \begin{cases} n - k & k = 0, 1, \ldots, n - 1 \\ 0 & k = n, n + 1, \ldots, \end{cases}$$

$$v_{k+1} = v^{k+1} \qquad\qquad k = 0, 1, \ldots,$$

$$Z = \begin{cases} (n - K)v^{K+1} & K = 0, 1, \ldots, n - 1 \\ 0 & K = n, n + 1, \ldots. \end{cases}$$

The actuarial present-value symbol for this insurance is $(DA)^1_{x:\overline{n}|}$.

As illustrated by Figure 4.2.5 for insurances payable at the moment of death, annually increasing insurances payable at the end of the year of death are equivalent to a combination of deferred level insurances each for a unit amount. Similarly, annually decreasing term insurances are equivalent to a combination of level term insurances of various term lengths. Figure 4.3.1 illustrates this for an annually decreasing 8-year term insurance.

Figure 4.3.1 shows the graph of the benefit function b_{k+1}. Each unit square region between the horizontal steps and the k-axis represents a deferred 1-year term insurance. When these are summed vertically, the deferred 1-year term insurances

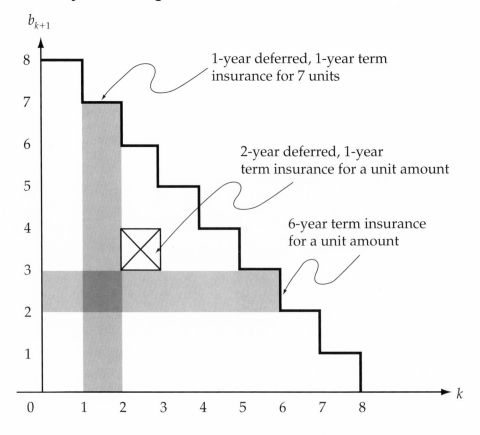

FIGURE 4.3.1

Annually Decreasing 8-Year Term Insurance

for the decreasing amounts are obtained. When the squares are summed horizontally, the level amount term insurances of varying duration are obtained. These vertical and horizontal sums are also indicated in Figure 4.3.1.

The equality of the actuarial present values for the combination of level term insurances and the combination of deferred term insurances can be demonstrated analytically. Thus, by definition

$$(DA)^1_{x:\overline{n}|} = \sum_{k=0}^{n-1} (n-k)\, v^{k+1}\, {}_kp_x\, q_{x+k}$$

$$= \sum_{k=0}^{n-1} (n-k)\, (v^k\, {}_kp_x)\, (vq_{x+k})$$

$$= \sum_{k=0}^{n-1} (n-k)\, {}_{k|1}A_x, \qquad\qquad (4.3.14)$$

the total of the column sums.

In (4.3.14) we can substitute

$$n-k = \sum_{j=0}^{n-k-1} (1)$$

to obtain

$$(DA)^1_{x:\overline{n}|} = \sum_{k=0}^{n-1} \sum_{j=0}^{n-k-1} (1)\, v^{k+1}\, {}_kp_x\, q_{x+k}.$$

By interchanging the order of summation we obtain

$$\sum_{j=0}^{n-1} \sum_{k=0}^{n-j-1} (1)\, v^{k+1}\, {}_kp_x\, q_{x+k},$$

and then by comparing the inner summation to (4.3.2), we can write

$$(DA)^1_{x:\overline{n}|} = \sum_{j=0}^{n-1} A^1_{x:\overline{n-j}|}.$$

Table 4.3.1 provides a summary of functions and symbols for the elementary insurances payable at the end of the year of death.

We close this section with a summary of the recursion relations for the actuarial present values of the insurances payable at the end of the year of death. Consider the list on page 119 arranged in the order of the entries of Table 4.3.1. Each entry is arranged across its line as the recursion relation, the domain for the relation, and the initial condition. Values for the actuarial present value would be generated from the lowest age of the mortality table to age y or ω.

TABLE 4.3.1
Summary of Insurances Payable at End of Year of Death

(1) Insurance Name	(2) Benefit Function b_{k+1}	(3) Discount Function v_{k+1}	(4) Present-Value Function z_{k+1}	(5) Actuarial Present Value	(6) Higher Moments
(a) Whole life	1	v^{k+1}	v^{k+1}	A_x	*
(b) n-Year term	1 $k = 0, 1, \ldots, n-1$ 0 $k = n, n+1, \ldots$	v^{k+1}	v^{k+1} $k = 0, 1, \ldots, n-1$ 0 $k = n, n+1, \ldots$	$A^1_{x:\overline{n}|}$	*
(c) n-Year endowment	1	v^{k+1} $k = 0, 1, \ldots, n-1$ v^n $k = n, n+1, \ldots$	v^{k+1} $k = 0, 1, \ldots, n-1$ v^n $k = n, n+1, \ldots$	$A_{x:\overline{n}|}$	*

(d) m-Year deferred n-year term	1 $k = m, m+1, \ldots, m+n-1$
	 0 $k = 0, \ldots, m-1,$
	      $k = m+n, \ldots$
		v^{k+1}	v^{k+1} $k = m, m+1, \ldots, m+n-1$
			 0 $k = 0, \ldots, m-1,$
			      $k = m+n, \ldots$
				$_{m|n}A_x$	*

(e) n-Year term increasing annually	$k+1$ $k = 0, 1, \ldots, n-1$ 0 $k = n, n+1, \ldots$	v^{k+1}	$(k+1)v^{k+1}$ $k = 0, 1, \ldots, n-1$ 0 $k = n, n+1, \ldots$	$(IA)^1_{x:\overline{n}|}$	†
(f) n-Year term decreasing annually	$n-k$ $k = 0, 1, \ldots, n-1$ 0 $k = n, n+1, \ldots$	v^{k+1}	$(n-k)v^{k+1}$ $k = 0, 1, \ldots, n-1$ 0 $k = n, n+1, \ldots$	$(DA)^1_{x:\overline{n}|}$	†
(g) Whole life increasing annually	$k+1$ $k = 0, 1, \ldots$	v^{k+1}	$(k+1)v^{k+1}$ $k = 0, 1, \ldots$	$(IA)_x$	†

b_{k+1}, v_{k+1}, and z_{k+1} are defined only for non-negative integral values of k.
*Rule of moments holds, thus $\text{Var}(Z) = {}^2A - A^2$ symbolically.
†Rule of moments does not hold.

(a) $\quad A_x = vq_x + vp_x\, A_{x+1} \qquad x = 0, 1, \ldots, \omega - 1,$

$\qquad$ and $A_\omega = 0.$

(b) $\quad A^1_{x:\overline{y-x}|} = vq_x + vp_x\, A^1_{x+1:\overline{y-(x+1)}|} \qquad x = 0, 1, \ldots, y - 1,$

$\qquad$ and $A^1_{y:\overline{0}|} = 0.$

(c) $\quad A_{x:\overline{y-x}|} = vq_x + vp_x\, A_{x+1:\overline{y-(x+1)}|} \qquad x = 0, 1, \ldots, y - 1,$

$\qquad$ and $A_{y:\overline{0}|} = 1.$

(d) $\quad _{y-x|n}A_x = 0 + vp_x\ _{y-(x+1)|n}A_{x+1} \qquad x = 0, 1, \ldots, y - 1,$

$\qquad$ and $_{0|n}A_y = A^1_{y:\overline{n}|}.$

(e) $\quad (IA)^1_{x:\overline{y-x}|} = [vq_x + vp_x\, A^1_{x+1:\overline{y-(x+1)}|}] + vp_x\, (IA)^1_{x+1:\overline{y-(x+1)}|}$

$\qquad x = 0, 1, \ldots, y - 1,$ and $(IA)^1_{y:\overline{0}|} = 0.$

(f) $\quad (DA)^1_{x:\overline{y-x}|} = (y - x)vq_x + vp_x\, (DA)^1_{x+1:\overline{y-(x+1)}|}$

$\qquad x = 0, 1, \ldots, y - 1,$ and $(DA)^1_{y:\overline{0}|} = 0.$

(g) $\quad (IA)_x = [vq_x + vp_x\, A_{x+1}] + vp_x\, (IA)_{x+1} \qquad x = 0, 1, \ldots, \omega - 1,$

$\qquad$ and $(IA)_\omega = 0.$

Observations:

1. Only (a) and (b) have been justified in this section. Arguments for (c) through (g) are similar to those for (a) and (b).
2. All seven equations are of the form

$$u(x) = c(x) + vp_x\, u(x + 1),$$

   where $c(x)$ is a given function defined for the domain of the relation. In the language of difference equations, all seven equations have the same corresponding homogeneous equation, $u(x) = vp_x\, u(x + 1)$. It is linear but does not have constant coefficients.
3. Since $c(x) = vq_x$ for (a), (b), and (c), those actuarial present values are all solutions of the same recursion formula and are distinguished only by their starting values.

4.4 Relationships between Insurances Payable at the Moment of Death and the End of the Year of Death

We begin the study of these relationships with an analysis of the actuarial present value for whole life insurance paying a unit benefit at the moment of death. From (4.2.6) we have

$$\bar{A}_x = \int_0^\infty v^t\ _tp_x\ \mu_x(t)\ dt = \int_0^1 v^t\ _tp_x\ \mu_x(t)\ dt + \int_1^\infty v^t\ _tp_x\ \mu_x(t)\ dt.$$

The change of variables $s = t - 1$ in the second integral gives

$$\bar{A}_x = \int_0^1 v^t\ _tp_x\ \mu_x(t)\ dt + v \int_0^\infty v^s\ _{s+1}p_x\ \mu_x(s+1)\ ds. \qquad (4.4.1)$$

On an aggregate mortality basis

$$_{s+1}p_x\ \mu_x(s+1) = p_x\ _sp_{x+1}\ \mu(x+s+1)$$

so the second term of (4.4.1) would be $vp_x\bar{A}_{x+1}$. On a select mortality basis the second term would be $vp_{[x]}\bar{A}_{[x]+1}$. Returning to (4.4.1) and using aggregate notation, we have

$$\bar{A}_x = \int_0^1 v^t\ _tp_x\ \mu_x(t)\ dt + vp_x\ \bar{A}_{x+1} = \bar{A}^1_{x:\overline{1}|} + vp_x\ \bar{A}_{x+1}. \qquad (4.4.2)$$

The integral in (4.4.2) can be expressed in discrete life table functions by adopting one of the assumptions about the form of the mortality function between integers as discussed in Section 3.6.

Under the assumption of a uniform distribution of deaths over each year of age,

$$_tp_y\ \mu_y(t) = q_y \qquad 0 \le t \le 1,\ \text{and}\ y = 0, 1, \ldots$$

which can be placed in (4.4.2) to obtain

$$\bar{A}_x = q_x \int_0^1 v^t\ dt + vp_x\bar{A}_{x+1},$$

$$= \frac{i}{\delta}\ vq_x + vp_x\ \bar{A}_{x+1}. \qquad (4.4.3)$$

The domain for this relationship is $x = 0, 1, \ldots, \omega - 1$, and the starting value is $\bar{A}_\omega = 0$.

If we multiply both sides of recursion formula (a) by i/δ, we have

$$\frac{i}{\delta}\ A_x = \frac{i}{\delta}\ vq_x + vp_x \left(\frac{i}{\delta}\ A_{x+1}\right).$$

Since (a) and (4.4.3) embody the same recursion formula and have the same domain and the same initial value of 0 at ω, $(i/\delta)A_x$ is the solution for (4.4.3), and

$$\bar{A}_x = \frac{i}{\delta}\ A_x. \qquad (4.4.4)$$

Formula (4.4.4) might have been anticipated under the assumption of a uniform distribution of deaths between integral ages. The effect of the assumption is to make the unit payable at the moment of death equivalent to a unit payable continuously throughout the year of death. With respect to interest, a unit payable continuously over the year is equivalent to i/δ at the end of the year.

The identity in (4.4.4) can be reached using the properties of the future-lifetime random variable under the assumption of a uniform distribution of deaths in each year of age as developed in Section 3.6. From (3.6.1) we write $T = K + S$. We observed there that, under the assumption of a uniform distribution of deaths in each year of age, K and S are independent and S has a uniform distribution over the unit interval. As corollaries to these observations, $K + 1$ and $1 - S$ are also independent, and $1 - S$ has a uniform distribution over the unit interval. In the identity

$$\bar{A}_x = E[v^T] = E[v^{K+1}(1 + i)^{1-S}],$$

we can use the independence of $K + 1$ and $1 - S$ to calculate the expectation of the product as the product of the expectations,

$$E[v^{K+1}(1 + i)^{1-S}] = E[v^{K+1}]\,E[(1 + i)^{1-S}]. \qquad (4.4.5)$$

The first factor on the right-hand side is A_x. Since $1 - S$ has the uniform distribution over the unit interval, the second factor is

$$E[(1 + i)^{1-S}] = \int_0^1 (1 + i)^t\, 1\, dt = \frac{i}{\delta}.$$

Hence, again we have $\bar{A}_x = (i/\delta)A_x$ under the assumption of uniform distribution of deaths in each year of age.

A similar argument, again based on the assumption of a uniform distribution of deaths in each year of age, can be used to show that the actuarial present value of a whole life insurance which pays a unit at the end of the m-th of a year of death is equal to

$$A_x^{(m)} = \frac{i}{i^{(m)}}\, A_x. \qquad (4.4.6)$$

This argument is outlined in Exercise 4.19.

In Section 3.6 we also discussed the assumption that the force of mortality is constant between integral ages. The relationship between the actuarial present values for whole life insurances payable at the moment of death and at the end of the year of death under this assumption is developed in Exercise 4.19. Since the hyperbolic assumption implies that the force of mortality decreases over the year of age (see Exercise 3.27), it is seldom realistic for human lives. Moreover, it leads to more complicated relationships that we will not develop here.

Next we turn to an analysis of the annually increasing n-year term insurance payable at the moment of death. For this insurance, the present-value random variable is

$$Z = \begin{cases} \lfloor T + 1 \rfloor v^T & T < n \\ 0 & T \geq n. \end{cases}$$

Since $\lfloor T + 1 \rfloor = K + 1$, we can use the relation $T = K + S$ to obtain

$$Z = \begin{cases} (K + 1)v^{K+1}v^{S-1} & T < n \\ 0 & T \geq n. \end{cases}$$

If we let W be the present-value random variable for the annually increasing n-year term insurance payable at the end of the year of death,

$$W = \begin{cases} (K + 1)v^{K+1} & K = 0, 1, \ldots, n - 1 \\ 0 & K = n, n + 1, \ldots . \end{cases}$$

Then

$$Z = W(1 + i)^{1-S}$$

and

$$E[Z] = E[W(1 + i)^{1-S}].$$

Since W is a function of $K + 1$ alone and $K + 1$ and $1 - S$ are independent,

$$E[Z] = E[W]\, E[(1 + i)^{1-S}]$$

$$= (IA)^1_{x:\overline{n}|}\, \frac{i}{\delta}.$$

These results for the whole life and the increasing term insurances payable at the moment of death, under the assumption of a uniform distribution of deaths over each year of age, are very similar,

$$\bar{A}_x = \frac{i}{\delta}\, A_x$$

and

$$(I\bar{A})^1_{x:\overline{n}|} = \frac{i}{\delta}\, (IA)^1_{x:\overline{n}|}.$$

Let us look at the general model to find the basis of the similarities. From (4.2.2),

$$Z = b_T v_T. \tag{4.4.7}$$

For the two continuous insurances above, the conditions used were
- $v_T = v^T$, and
- b_T was a function of only the integral part of T, the curtate-future-lifetime, K.

Writing this latter property as $b_T = b^*_{K+1}$ we can write (4.4.7) for these insurances as

$$Z = b^*_{K+1}v^T$$

$$= b^*_{K+1}v^{K+1}(1 + i)^{1-S}$$

and

$$E[Z] = E[b^*_{K+1}v^{K+1}(1 + i)^{1-S}]. \tag{4.4.8}$$

Under the assumption of a uniform distribution of deaths over each year of age, we can infer the independence of K and S and that $1 - S$ also has a uniform distribution. Then we can write (4.4.8) as

$$E[Z] = E[b_{K+1}^* v^{K+1}] \, E[(1 + i)^{1-S}]$$

$$= E[b_{K+1}^* v^{K+1}] \, \frac{i}{\delta}. \qquad\qquad (4.4.9)$$

Example 4.4.1

Calculate the actuarial present value and the variance for a 10,000 benefit, 30-year endowment insurance providing the death benefit at the moment of death of a male age 35 at issue of the policy. Use the Illustrative Life Table, the uniform distribution of deaths over each year of age assumption, and $i = 0.06$.

Solution:

For endowment insurance, $v_T \neq v^T$. Therefore, we cannot apply (4.4.9) directly. Recalling (4.2.11), which showed the endowment insurance as the sum of a term insurance and pure endowment, we can apply (4.4.9) to the term insurance component and then calculate the pure endowment insurance part. Thus, using (4.2.12) and (4.2.10), we can calculate the actuarial present value as follows:

$$\bar{A}_{35:\overline{30}|} = \frac{i}{\delta} \, A^1_{35:\overline{30}|} + A_{35:\overline{30}|}^{\;\;1}$$

$$= (1.0297087)[0.06748179] + 0.1392408$$

$$= 0.208727,$$

and the variance as

$$Var(Z) = {}^2\bar{A}_{35:\overline{30}|} - (\bar{A}_{35:\overline{30}|})^2$$

$$= 0.0309294 + 0.0242432 - (0.208727)^2$$

$$= 0.011606.$$

For the 10,000 sum insured, $10,000 \, \bar{A}_{35:\overline{30}|} = 2{,}087.27$ and $(10{,}000)^2 \, Var(Z) = 1{,}160{,}600$. ▼

Example 4.4.2

Calculate, for a life age 50, the actuarial present value for an annually decreasing 5-year term insurance paying 5,000 at the moment of death in the first year, 4,000 in the second year, and so on. Use the Illustrative Life Table, uniform distribution of deaths over each year of age assumption, and $i = 0.06$.

Solution:

Referring to Table 4.2.1, we see that

$$b_t = \begin{cases} 5 - \lfloor t \rfloor & t \leq 5 \\ 0 & t > 5 \end{cases}$$

is a function of only k, the integral part of t, and hence we may write it as

$$b_t = \begin{cases} 5 - k & k = 0, 1, 2, 3, 4 \\ 0 & k > 4. \end{cases}$$

The discount function is v^t, so we have

$$(D\bar{A})^1_{50:\overline{5}|} = \frac{i}{\delta} (DA)^1_{50:\overline{5}|}$$

$$= (1.0297087) \sum_{k=0}^{4} (5 - k)\, v^{k+1}\, {}_kp_{50}\, q_{50+k}$$

$$= (1.0297087) \frac{\sum_{k=0}^{4} (5 - k)\, v^{k+1}\, d_{50+k}}{l_{50}}$$

$$= 0.088307.$$

Then, $1{,}000\, (D\bar{A})^1_{50:\overline{5}|} = 88.307.$ ▼

For an insurance providing a death benefit at the moment of death that is not a function of K, further analysis is required to express its values in terms of those for an insurance payable at the end of the year of death. Consider the continuously increasing whole life insurance payable at the moment of death. This insurance is discussed extensively in Section 4.2, and its benefit function analyzed in Figure 4.2.5. Its functions are

$$b_t = t \qquad t > 0,$$

$$v_t = v^t \qquad t > 0,$$

$$z_t = t v^t \qquad t > 0.$$

To find $(\bar{I}\bar{A})_x$ we rewrite

$$Z = (K + S)v^{K+S}$$

$$= (K + 1)v^{K+S} - (1 - S)v^{K+1}(1 + i)^{1-S}$$

$$= (K + 1)v^{K+1}(1 + i)^{1-S} - v^{K+1}(1 - S)(1 + i)^{1-S}.$$

Now taking expectations, under the assumption of a uniform distribution of deaths over each year of age, we have

$$E[Z] = E[(K + 1)v^{K+1}]\, E[(1 + i)^{1-S}] - E[v^{K+1}]\, E[(1 - S)(1 + i)^{1-S}]$$

$$= (IA)_x \frac{i}{\delta} - A_x\, E[(1 - S)(1 + i)^{1-S}].$$

We can simplify the last factor directly since $1 - S$ has a uniform distribution,

$$E[(1 - S)(1 + i)^{1-S}] = \int_0^1 u(1 + i)^u\, du = (\bar{D}\bar{s})_{\overline{1}|} = \frac{1 + i}{\delta} - \frac{i}{\delta^2}.$$

Thus, we can write

$$(\bar{I}\bar{A})_x = \frac{i}{\delta}\left[(IA)_x - \left(\frac{1}{d} - \frac{1}{\delta}\right) A_x \right].$$

4.5 Differential Equations for Insurances Payable at the Moment of Death

Recursive-type expressions can be established for insurances payable at the moment of death. These are developed using calculus and lead to differential equations.

For a whole life insurance on (x),

$$\frac{d}{dx}\bar{A}_x = -\mu(x) + \bar{A}_x[\delta + \mu(x)] = \delta\bar{A}_x - \mu(x)(1 - \bar{A}_x), \tag{4.5.1}$$

which are the continuous analogues of (4.3.12). The notation used here is for an aggregate mortality basis. Verification of these expressions has been left to Exercise 4.21.

On the other hand, (4.5.1) can be developed from the definition of $\bar{A}_x$ by using conditional expectation as we did for A_x:

$$\bar{A}_x = E[v^T]$$

$$= E[v^T|T \leq h]\Pr(T \leq h) + E[v^T|T > h]\Pr(T > h). \tag{4.5.2}$$

Now,

$$\Pr(T \leq h) = {}_hq_x \quad \text{and} \quad \Pr(T > h) = {}_hp_x, \tag{4.5.3}$$

and the conditional p.d.f. of T given $T \leq h$ is

$$f_T(t|T \leq h) = \begin{cases} \dfrac{f_T(t)}{F_T(h)} = \dfrac{{}_tp_x\,\mu(x + t)}{{}_hq_x} & 0 \leq t \leq h \\ 0 & \text{elsewhere.} \end{cases}$$

Thus,

$$E[v^T|T \leq h] = \int_0^h v^t\,\frac{{}_tp_x\,\mu(x + t)}{{}_hq_x}\,dt. \tag{4.5.4}$$

As we did in the expression for A_x, we will write

$$E[v^T|T > h] = v^h E[v^{T-h}|(T - h) > 0]$$

$$= v^h \bar{A}_{x+h}. \tag{4.5.5}$$

Substitution of (4.5.3), (4.5.4), and (4.5.5) into (4.5.2) yields

$$\bar{A}_x = \int_0^h v^t\,\frac{{}_tp_x\,\mu(x + t)}{{}_hq_x}\,dt\,{}_hq_x + v^h\,\bar{A}_{x+h}\,{}_hp_x. \tag{4.5.6}$$

Then, on both sides of (4.5.6), we multiply by -1, add $\bar{A}_{x+h}$, and divide by h to obtain

$$\frac{\bar{A}_{x+h} - \bar{A}_x}{h} = \frac{-1}{h} \int_0^h v^t \, _tp_x \, \mu(x + t) \, dt + \bar{A}_{x+h} \frac{1 - v^h \, _hp_x}{h}. \qquad (4.5.7)$$

Next,

$$\lim_{h \to 0} \frac{1}{h} \int_0^h v^t \, _tp_x \, \mu(x + t) \, dt = \frac{d}{ds} \int_0^s v^t \, _tp_x \, \mu(x + t) \, dt \Big|_{s=0} = \mu(x)$$

and

$$\lim_{h \to 0} \frac{1 - v^h \, _hp_x}{h} = -\frac{d}{dt}(v^t \, _tp_x)\Big|_{t=0} = \mu(x) + \delta.$$

Using these two limits as $h \to 0$ in (4.5.7) we obtain (4.5.1),

$$\frac{d}{dx} \bar{A}_x = -\mu(x) + \bar{A}_x[\mu(x) + \delta].$$

Solutions of this differential equation are outlined in Exercise 4.22.

4.6 Notes and References

The life contingencies textbooks listed in Appendix 6 give other developments of formulas for life insurance actuarial present values. Commutation functions, which were fundamental to actuarial calculations until this quarter century, are employed extensively in Jordan (1967).

There is little material in these textbooks on the concept of the time-until-death of an insured as a random variable. Until recently, research and exposition on this concept has been called *individual risk theory.* Cramér (1930) gives a detailed exposition of the ideas up to that time. Kahn (1962) and Seal (1969) give concise bibliographical information on both research and expository papers over a 100-year span.

Since 1970 there has been interest in actuarial models that consider both the time-until-death and the investment-rate-of-return as random variables. This combination is discussed in Chapter 21.

Exercises

Assume, unless otherwise stated, that insurances are payable at the moment of death, and that the force of interest is a constant δ with i and d as the equivalent rates of interest and discount.

Section 4.2

4.1. If $\mu(x) = \mu$, a positive constant, for all $x > 0$, show that $\bar{A}_x = \mu/(\mu + \delta)$.

4.2. Let $\mu(x) = 1/(1 + x)$, for all $x > 0$.

a. Integrate by parts to show that

$$\bar{A}_x = 1 - \delta \int_0^\infty e^{-\delta t} \frac{1 + x}{1 + x + t} \, dt.$$

b. Use the expression in (a) to show that $d\bar{A}_x/dx < 0$ for all $x > 0$.

4.3. Show that $d\bar{A}_x/di = -v(\bar{I}\bar{A})_x$.

4.4. Show that the expressions for the variance of the present value of an n-year endowment insurance paying a unit benefit, as given by (4.2.10) and (4.2.13), are identical.

4.5. Let Z_1 and Z_2 be as defined for equation (4.2.11).
   a. Show that $\lim_{n \to 0} \text{Cov}(Z_1, Z_2) = \lim_{n \to \infty} \text{Cov}(Z_1, Z_2) = 0$.
   b. Develop an implicit equation for the term of the endowment for which $\text{Cov}(Z_1, Z_2)$ is minimized.
   c. Develop a formula for the minimum in (b).
   d. Simplify the formulas in (b) and (c) for the case when the force of mortality is a constant μ.

4.6. Assume mortality is described by $l_x = 100 - x$ for $0 \le x \le 100$ and that the force of interest is $\delta = 0.05$.
   a. Calculate $\bar{A}^1_{40:\overline{25}|}$.
   b. Determine the actuarial present value for a 25-year term insurance with benefit amount for death at time t, $b_t = e^{0.05t}$, for a person age 40 at policy issue.

4.7. Assuming De Moivre's survival function with $\omega = 100$ and $i = 0.10$, calculate
   a. $\bar{A}^1_{30:\overline{10}|}$
   b. The variance of the present value, at policy issue, of the benefit of the insurance in (a).

4.8. If $\delta_t = 0.2/(1 + 0.05t)$ and $l_x = 100 - x$ for $0 \le x \le 100$, calculate
   a. For a whole life insurance issued at age x, the actuarial present value and the variance of the present value of the benefits
   b. $(\bar{I}\bar{A})_x$.

4.9. a. Show that $\bar{A}_x$ is the moment generating function of T, the future lifetime of (x), evaluated at $-\delta$.
   b. Show that if T has a gamma distribution with parameters α and β, then $\bar{A}_x = (1 + \delta/\beta)^{-\alpha}$.

4.10. Given $b_t = t$, $\mu_x(t) = \mu$, and $\delta_t = \delta$ for all $t > 0$, derive expressions for
   a. $(\bar{I}\bar{A})_x = E[b_T v^T]$ b. $\text{Var}(b_T v^T)$.

4.11. The random variable Z is the present-value random variable for a whole life insurance of unit amount payable at the moment of death and issued to (x). If $\delta = 0.05$ and $\mu_x(t) = 0.01$:
   a. Display the formula for the p.d.f. of Z.
   b. Graph the p.d.f. of Z.
   c. Calculate $\bar{A}_x = E[Z]$ and $Var(Z)$.

4.12. The random variable Z is the present-value random variable for an n-year endowment insurance as defined in Section 4.2.2. Exhibit the d.f. of Z in terms of the d.f. of T.

4.13. The random variable Z is defined as in Exercise 4.12. If $\delta = 0.05$, $\mu_x(t) = 0.01$, and $n = 20$:
   a. Display the d.f. of Z.
   b. Graph the d.f. of Z.
   c. Calculate $\bar{A}_{x:\overline{n}|} = E[Z]$ using the distribution of Z. [Hint: Consider using the complement of the d.f.]

Section 4.3

4.14. If $l_x = 100 - x$ for $0 \le x \le 100$ and $i = 0.05$, evaluate
   a. $A_{40:\overline{25}|}$ b. $(IA)_{40}$.

4.15. Show that $A_{x:\overline{n}|} = A^1_{x:\overline{m}|} + v^m \; {}_mp_x \; A_{x+m:\overline{n-m}|}$ for $m < n$ and interpret the result in words.

4.16. If $A_x = 0.25$, $A_{x+20} = 0.40$, and $A_{x:\overline{20}|} = 0.55$, calculate
   a. $A^1_{x:\overline{20}|}$ b. $A^1_{x:\overline{20}|}$.

4.17. a. Describe the benefits of the insurance with actuarial present value given by the symbol $(IA)_{x:\overline{m}|}$.
   b. Express the actuarial present value of (a) in terms of the symbols given in Tables 4.2.1 and 4.3.1.

4.18. In Example 4.3.2, let the expected size of the fund k years after the agreement, and immediately after the payment of death claims, be denoted by E_k, where $E_0 = (100)(1,000 \, A_{30}) = 10,248.35$.
   a. Start with (4.3.10) and develop the forward recursion formula
   $$E_k = 1.06E_{k-1} - 100,000_{k-1|}q_{30}.$$
   b. Use the recursion formula developed in (a) to confirm that $E_5 = 12,762.58$.

Section 4.4

4.19. Consider the timescale measured in intervals of length $1/m$ where the unit is a year. Let a whole life insurance for a unit amount be payable at the end of the m-thly interval in which death occurs. Let k be the number of complete insurance years lived prior to death and let j be the number of complete m-ths of a year lived in the year of death.

a. What is the present-value function for this insurance?

b. Set up a formula analogous to (4.4.2) for the actuarial present value, $A_x^{(m)}$, for this insurance.

c. Show algebraically that, under the assumption of a uniform distribution of deaths over the insurance year of age,

$$A_x^{(m)} = \frac{i}{i^{(m)}} A_x.$$

4.20. Show, under the assumption of a constant force of mortality between integral ages, that

$$\bar{A}_x = \sum_{k=0}^{\infty} v^{k+1} \, {}_kp_x \, \mu_x(k) \, \frac{i + q_{x+k}}{\delta + \mu_x(k)}$$

where $\mu_x(k) = -\log p_{x+k}$.

Section 4.5

4.21. a. Show that (4.2.6), for an aggregate mortality basis, can be rewritten as

$$\bar{A}_x = \frac{1}{{}_xp_0 \, v^x} \int_x^{\infty} v^y \, {}_yp_0 \, \mu(y) \, dy \qquad x \ge 0.$$

b. Differentiate the formula of (a) to establish (4.5.1),

$$\frac{d\bar{A}_x}{dx} = [\mu(x) + \delta]\bar{A}_x - \mu(x) \qquad x \ge 0.$$

c. Use the same technique to show

$$\frac{d\bar{A}^1_{x:\overline{n}|}}{dx} = [\mu(x) + \delta]\bar{A}^1_{x:\overline{n}|} + \mu(x + n)A^{\;1}_{x:\overline{n}|} - \mu(x) \qquad x \ge 0.$$

4.22. Solve the differential equation (4.5.1) as follows:

a. Use the integrating factor

$$\exp\left\{ -\int_y^x [\delta + \mu(z)] \, dz \right\}$$

to obtain

$$\bar{A}_y = \int_y^{\infty} \mu(x) \, \exp\left\{ -\int_y^x [\delta + \mu(z)] \, dz \right\} dx.$$

b. Use the integrating factor $e^{-\delta x}$ to obtain

$$\bar{A}_y = \int_y^{\infty} \mu(x) \, v^{x-y}(1 - \bar{A}_x) \, dx.$$

Miscellaneous

4.23. Display the actuarial present value of a Double Protection to Age 65 policy that provides a benefit of 2 in the event of death prior to age 65 and a benefit of 1 after age 65 in symbols of Table 4.3.1. Assume benefits are paid at the end of the year of death.

4.24. A policy is issued at age 20 with the following graded scale of death benefits payable at the moment of death.

Age	Death Benefits
20	1 000
21	2 000
22	4 000
23	6 000
24	8 000
25–40	10 000
41 and over	50 000

Calculate the actuarial present value on the basis of the Illustrative Life Table with uniform distribution of deaths over each year of age and $i = 0.05$. [Hint: A backward recursion formula for the actuarial present value will include a function $c(x)$ that incorporates the death benefit scale.]

4.25. a. Determine whether or not a constant increase in the force of mortality has the same effect on A_x as the same increase in the force interest.
   b. Show that if the single probability of death q_{x+n} is increased to $q_{x+n} + c$, then A_x will be increased by

$$c v^{n+1} \, _np_x \, (1 - \dot{A}_{x+n+1}).$$

4.26. The actuarial present value for a modified pure endowment of 1,000 issued at age x for n years is 700 with a death benefit equal to the actuarial present value in event of death during the n-year period and is 650 with no death benefit.
   a. Calculate the actuarial present value for a modified pure endowment of 1,000 issued at age x for n years if $100k\%$ of the actuarial present value is to be paid at death during the period.
   b. For the modified pure endowment in (a), express the variance of the present value at policy issue in terms of actuarial present values for pure endowments and term insurances.

4.27. An appliance manufacturer sells his product with a 5-year warranty promising the return of cash equal to the pro rata share of the initial purchase price for failure within 5 years. For example, if failure is reported 3-3/4 years following purchase, 25% of the purchase price will be returned. From statistical studies, the probability of failure of a new product during the first year is estimated to be 0.2, in each of the second, third, and fourth years 0.1, and in the fifth year 0.2.
   a. Assuming that failures are reported uniformly within each year since purchase, determine the fraction of the purchase price that equals the actuarial present value for this warranty. Assume $i = 0.10$.

b. If the warranted return is the reduction on the purchase price of a new product with a 5-year warranty, would the answer to (a) change?

4.28. Assume that $T(x)$ has a p.d.f. given by

$$f_{T(x)}(t) = \frac{2}{10\sqrt{2\pi}}\, e^{-t^2/200} \qquad t > 0$$

and $\delta = 0.05$.
Show:
a. $\bar{A}_x = 2e^{0.125}[1 - \Phi(0.5)] = 0.6992$
b. $^2\bar{A}_x = 2e^{-0.5}[1 - \Phi(1)] = 0.5232$
c. $\text{Var}(Z) = 0.0343$, where $Z = v^T$
d. $\xi_Z^{0.5} = 0.7076$ [Hint: Use Figure 4.2.1]
e. $v^{\mathring{e}_x} = 0.6710 < 0.6992 = \bar{A}_x$.

4.29. Generalize Exercise 4.28(e) by showing that if $\delta > 0$, then

$$v^{\mathring{e}_x} \leq \bar{A}_x.$$

[Hint: Use Jensen's Inequality in Section 1.3 when $u''(x) > 0$.]

4.30. For a whole life insurance the benefit amount, b_t, is 0 or 1 for each $t \geq 0$. For calculations at force of interest δ_t:
a. Express the discount function in terms of δ_t.
b. Express the present-value random variable, Z, in terms of T.
c. Show that Z^j@force of interest δ_t equals Z@force of interest $j\delta_t$.

Computing Exercises

4.31. Augment your Illustrative Life Table to include input of a constant interest rate, i, and a payment frequency, m. It will be helpful for the equivalent rates δ, $d^{(m)}$, $i^{(m)}$, d, and v to be shown in your Illustrative Life Table output.

4.32. Develop a set of values of $\ddot{a}_{\overline{n}|}$, $n = 1, 2, \ldots, 100$ at $i = 0.06$ by using the forward recursion formula (3.5.20). [Hint: Review Exercise 3.25 or use $\ddot{a}_{\overline{n+1}|} = 1 + v\ddot{a}_{\overline{n}|}$.]

4.33. a. Using the backward recursion formula of (4.3.10) in your Illustrative Life Table and the appropriate starting value, calculate $1,000A_x$ for $x = 13$ to 140 for an interest rate of 0.06.
b. Compare your values to those in Appendix 2A.

4.34. a. Use (4.3.3) and your Illustrative Life to determine $A^1_{20:\overline{20}|}$ and $^2A^1_{20:\overline{20}|}$ at $i = 0.05$.
b. What is the variance for the present-value random variable for a 20-year term insurance with benefit amount 100,000 issued to (20)?

4.35. a. By an algebraic or probabilistic argument, verify the following backward recursion formula of an n-year term insurance with a unit benefit:

$$A^1_{x:\overline{n}|} = vq_x - v^{n+1}{}_np_x\, q_{x+n} + vp_x\, A^1_{x+1:\overline{n}|}.$$

b. Determine an appropriate starting value for use with this formula.

c. Use your Illustrative Life Table with $i = 0.06$ to calculate the actuarial present value of a 10-year term insurance issued at ages $x = 13, \ldots, 130$.

4.36. a. Use recursion relation (g) at the end of Section 4.3 and your Illustrative Life Table to calculate $(IA)_{28}$ at $i = 0.06$.

b. Modify the recursion relation of part (a) to obtain one for $(I\bar{A})_x$ and determine a starting value for it.

c. Modify the recursion relation of part (b) to obtain one for $(\bar{I}\bar{A})_x$ and determine a starting value for it.

d. Make the recursion relations of parts (b) and (c) specific to the assumption of a uniform distribution of deaths over each year of age.

4.37. Use your Illustrative Life Table to verify the numerical solutions to parts (a) and (b) of Example 4.2.4. [Hint: Set $B = 0.00$ and $A = 0.04$ in your Makeham law parameters, $i = e^{0.10} - 1$, and use recursion formula (d) at the end of Section 4.3. Remember that the insurance in Example 4.2.4 is payable at the moment of death.]

4.38. a. By an algebraic or probabilistic argument, verify the following backward recursion formula for the actuarial present value of a unit benefit endowment insurance to age y with the death benefit payable at the moment of death:

$$\bar{A}_{x:\overline{y-x}|} = \bar{A}^1_{x:\overline{1}|} + vp_x\, \bar{A}_{x+1:\overline{y-(x+1)}|} \qquad x = 0, 1, \ldots, y - 1.$$

b. Determine an appropriate starting value for use with this formula.

c. Use your Illustrative Life Table with the assumption of uniform distribution of deaths over each year of age and $i = 0.06$ to calculate the actuarial present value of a unit benefit endowment insurance to age 65 with the death benefit payable at the moment of death for issue ages $x = 13, \ldots, 64$.

d. By an algebraic or probabilistic argument, verify the following backward recursion formula for the actuarial present value of a unit benefit n-year endowment insurance with the death benefit payable at the moment of death:

$$\bar{A}_{x:\overline{n}|} = \bar{A}^1_{x:\overline{1}|} + v^n\,{}_np_x\,(1 - \bar{A}_{x+n:\overline{1}|}) + vp_x\, \bar{A}_{x+1:\overline{n}|} \qquad x = 0, 1, \ldots, \omega - 1.$$

4.39. Let Z be the present-value random variable for a 100,000 unit 20-year endowment insurance with the death benefit payable at the moment of death. Use your Illustrative Life Table to calculate the mean and the variance of Z on the basis of a Makeham law with $A = 0.001$, $B = 0.00001$, $c = 1.10$, and $\delta = 0.05$. Use issue age 45.

LIFE ANNUITIES

5.1 Introduction

In the preceding chapter we studied payments contingent on death, as provided by various forms of life insurances. In this chapter we study payments contingent on survival, as provided by various forms of life annuities. A *life annuity* is a series of payments made continuously or at equal intervals (such as months, quarters, years) while a given life survives. It may be temporary, that is, limited to a given term of years, or it may be payable for the whole of life. The payment intervals may commence immediately or, alternatively, the annuity may be deferred. Payments may be due at the beginnings of the payment intervals (*annuities-due*) or at the ends of such intervals (*annuities-immediate*).

Through the study of *annuities-certain* in the theory of interest, the reader already has a knowledge of annuity terminology, notation, and theory. Life annuity theory is analogous but brings in survival as a condition for payment. This condition has been encountered in Chapter 4 in connection with pure endowments and the maturity payments under endowment insurances.

Life annuities play a major role in life insurance operations. As we see in the next chapter, life insurances are usually purchased by a life annuity of premiums rather than by a single premium. The amount payable at the time of claim may be converted through a settlement option into some form of life annuity for the beneficiary. Some types of life insurance carry this concept even further and, instead of featuring a lump sum payable on death, provide stated forms of income benefits. Thus, for example, there may be a monthly income payable to a surviving spouse or to a retired insured.

Annuities are even more central in pension systems. In fact, a retirement plan can be regarded as a system for purchasing deferred life annuities (payable during retirement) by some form of temporary annuity of contributions during active service. The temporary annuity may consist of varying contributions, and valuation of it may take into account not only interest and mortality, but other factors such as salary increases and the termination of participation for reasons other than death.

Life annuities also have a role in disability and workers' compensation insurances. In the case of disability insurance, termination of the annuity benefit by reason of recovery of the disabled insured may need to be considered. For surviving spouse benefits under workers' compensation, remarriage may terminate the annuity.

We proceed in this chapter as we did in Chapter 4 and express the present value of benefits to be received by the annuitant as a function of T, the annuitant's future-lifetime random variable. It then will be possible to study properties of the distribution of this financial value random variable. The expectation, still called the actuarial present value, can be evaluated in an alternative way using either integration by parts or summation by parts depending, respectively, on whether a continuous or discrete set of payments is being evaluated. The results of this process have a useful interpretation and lead to an alternative method of obtaining actuarial present values called the *current payment technique.*

As in the preceding chapter on life insurance, unless otherwise stated we assume a constant effective annual rate of interest i (or the equivalent constant force of interest δ). We also assume aggregate mortality for most of the development in this chapter and indicate those situations where a select mortality assumption makes a major difference.

In most applications of the theory developed in this chapter, annuity payments continue while a human life remains in a particular status. However, the possible applications of the theory are much wider. It may be applied to any set of periodic payments where the payments are not made with certainty. Examples of some of these applications are seen in later chapters dealing with multiple lives or multiple causes of decrement.

5.2 Continuous Life Annuities

We start with annuities payable continuously at the rate of 1 per year. This is of course an abstraction but makes use of familiar mathematical tools and as a practical matter closely approximates annuities payable on a monthly basis. A *whole life annuity* provides for payments until death. Hence, the present value of payments to be made is $Y = \bar{a}_{\overline{T}|}$ for all $T \geq 0$ where T is the future lifetime of (x). The distribution function of Y can be obtained from that for T as follows:

$$F_Y(y) = \Pr(Y \leq y) = \Pr(\bar{a}_{\overline{T}|} \leq y) = \Pr(1 - v^T \leq \delta y)$$

$$= \Pr(v^T \geq 1 - \delta y) = \Pr\left[T \leq \frac{-\log(1 - \delta y)}{\delta}\right]$$

$$= F_T\left(\frac{-\log(1 - \delta y)}{\delta}\right) \quad \text{for } 0 < y < \frac{1}{\delta}. \tag{5.2.1}$$

From this we obtain the probability density function for Y as

$$f_Y(y) = \frac{d}{dy} F_Y(y) = \frac{d}{dy} F_T\left(\frac{-\log(1 - \delta y)}{\delta}\right)$$

$$= \frac{f_T([-\log(1 - \delta y)]/\delta)}{1 - \delta y} \quad \text{for } 0 < y < \frac{1}{\delta}. \tag{5.2.2}$$

The distribution function for Y depends on the distribution of T but would resemble that shown at the end of this section in Figure 5.2.1(a).

The actuarial present value for a continuous whole life annuity is denoted by $\bar{a}_x$ where the post fixed subscript, x, indicates that the annuity ceases at the death of (x) and that the distribution of $T(x)$ may depend on information available at age x. Under aggregate mortality the p.d.f. of T is $_tp_x\,\mu(x + t)$, and the actuarial present value can be calculated by

$$\bar{a}_x = \mathrm{E}[Y] = \int_0^\infty \bar{a}_{\overline{t}|}\,_tp_x\,\mu(x + t)\,dt. \tag{5.2.3}$$

Using integration-by-parts with $f(t) = \bar{a}_{\overline{t}|}$, $dg(t) = _tp_x\,\mu(x + t)\,dt$, $g(t) = -_tp_x$, and $df(t) = v^t\,dt$, we obtain

$$\bar{a}_x = \int_0^\infty v^t\,_tp_x\,dt = \int_0^\infty {}_tE_x\,dt. \tag{5.2.4}$$

This integral can be considered as involving a momentary payment of $1\,dt$ made at time t, discounted at interest back to time zero by multiplying by v^t and further multiplied by $_tp_x$ to reflect the probability that a payment is made at time t. This is the current payment form of the actuarial present value for the whole life annuity. In general, the current payment technique for determining an actuarial present value for an annuity gives

$$\mathrm{APV} = \int_0^\infty v^t\,\Pr[\text{payments are being made at time } t]$$

$$\times\,[\text{Payment rate at time } t]\,dt. \tag{5.2.5}$$

Let us rewrite (5.2.4) by splitting off that portion of the integral involving t values from 0 to 1. Thus

$$\bar{a}_x = \int_0^1 v^t\,_tp_x\,dt + \int_1^\infty v^t\,_tp_x\,dt$$

$$= \bar{a}_{x:\overline{1}|} + v\,p_x \int_0^\infty v^s\,_sp_{x+1}\,ds$$

$$= \bar{a}_{x:\overline{1}|} + v\,p_x\,\bar{a}_{x+1}. \tag{5.2.6}$$

The actuarial present-value symbol, $\bar{a}_{x:\overline{1}|}$, used above is introduced below in (5.2.11). Expression (5.2.6) is an example of the backward recursion formula first observed in Section 3.5 and explored more fully in Section 4.3. Here $u(x) = \bar{a}_x$, $c(x) = \bar{a}_{x:\overline{1}|}$, and $d(x) = v\,p_x$. The initial value to use for the whole life annuity is $\bar{a}_\omega = 0$. There are several ways to evaluate the $c(x)$ term. A simple approach is to use a trapezoid approximation for the integral

$$\bar{a}_{x:\overline{1}|} = \int_0^1 v^t \, _tp_x \, dt = \frac{1 + v \, p_x}{2}.$$

Another approach, based on the assumption of a uniform distribution of deaths within each year of age, is examined in Section 5.4.

A relationship, familiar from compound interest theory, is that

$$1 = \delta \, \bar{a}_{\overline{t}|} + v^t.$$

This can be interpreted as indicating that a unit invested now will produce annual interest of δ payable continuously for t years at which point interest ceases and the investment is repaid. This relationship holds for all values of t and thus is true for the random variable T:

$$1 = \delta \, \bar{a}_{\overline{T}|} + v^T. \tag{5.2.7}$$

Then, taking expectations, we obtain

$$1 = \delta \, \bar{a}_x + \bar{A}_x. \tag{5.2.8}$$

This is subject to the same kind of interpretation as above. A unit invested now will produce annual interest of δ payable continuously for as long as (x) survives, and, at the time of death, interest ceases and the investment of 1 is repaid.

To measure, on the basis of the assumptions in our model, the mortality risk in a continuous life annuity, we are interested in $\text{Var}(\bar{a}_{\overline{T}|})$. We determine

$$\text{Var}(\bar{a}_{\overline{T}|}) = \text{Var}\left(\frac{1 - v^T}{\delta}\right)$$

$$= \frac{\text{Var}(v^T)}{\delta^2}$$

$$= \frac{{}^2\bar{A}_x - (\bar{A}_x)^2}{\delta^2}. \tag{5.2.9}$$

Further, we can observe that since $1 = \delta \, \bar{a}_{\overline{T}|} + v^T$, $\text{Var}(\delta \, \bar{a}_{\overline{T}|} + v^T) = 0$. Thus there is no mortality risk for the combination of a continuous life annuity of δ per year and a life insurance of 1 payable at the moment of death.

Example 5.2.1

Under the assumptions of a constant force of mortality, μ, and of a constant force of interest, δ, evaluate
a. $\bar{a}_x = \text{E}[\bar{a}_{\overline{T}|}]$
b. $\text{Var}(\bar{a}_{\overline{T}|})$
c. The probability that $\bar{a}_{\overline{T}|}$ will exceed $\bar{a}_x$.

Solution:

a. $\bar{a}_x = \int_0^\infty v^t \, _tp_x \, dt = \int_0^\infty e^{-\delta t} \, e^{-\mu t} \, dt = \frac{1}{\delta + \mu}.$

b. $\bar{A}_x = 1 - \delta\, \bar{a}_x = \dfrac{\mu}{\delta + \mu}$

$${}^{2}\bar{A}_x = \dfrac{\mu}{2\delta + \mu} \quad \text{by the rule of moments}$$

$$\mathrm{Var}(\bar{a}_{\overline{T}|}) = \dfrac{1}{\delta^2}\left[\dfrac{\mu}{2\delta + \mu} - \left(\dfrac{\mu}{\delta + \mu}\right)^2\right] = \dfrac{\mu}{(2\delta + \mu)(\delta + \mu)^2}.$$

c. $\Pr(\bar{a}_{\overline{T}|} > \bar{a}_x) = \Pr\left(\dfrac{1 - v^{T}}{\delta} > \bar{a}_x\right) = \Pr\left[T > -\dfrac{1}{\delta}\log\left(\dfrac{\mu}{\delta + \mu}\right)\right]$

$$= {}_{t_0}p_x \qquad \text{where } t_0 = -\dfrac{1}{\delta}\log\left(\dfrac{\mu}{\delta + \mu}\right)$$

$$= \left(\dfrac{\mu}{\delta + \mu}\right)^{\mu/\delta}.$$

▼

We now turn to temporary and deferred life annuities. The present value of a benefits random variable for an **n-*year temporary life annuity*** of 1 per year, payable continuously while (x) survives during the next n years, is

$$Y = \begin{cases} \bar{a}_{\overline{T}|} & 0 \le T < n \\ \bar{a}_{\overline{n}|} & T \ge n. \end{cases} \tag{5.2.10}$$

The distribution of Y in this case is a mixed distribution. In particular, the maximum value of Y is limited to $\bar{a}_{\overline{n}|}$, and there is a positive probability associated with $\bar{a}_{\overline{n}|}$ of $\Pr(T \ge n) = {}_np_x$. A typical distribution function for this random variable is illustrated in Figure 5.2.1(b).

The actuarial present value of an n-year temporary life annuity is denoted by $\bar{a}_{x:\overline{n}|}$ and equals

$$\bar{a}_{x:\overline{n}|} = \mathrm{E}[Y] = \int_0^n \bar{a}_{\overline{t}|}\, {}_tp_x\, \mu(x + t)\, dt + \bar{a}_{\overline{n}|}\, {}_np_x. \tag{5.2.11}$$

Integration by parts gives

$$\bar{a}_{x:\overline{n}|} = \int_0^n v^t\, {}_tp_x\, dt. \tag{5.2.12}$$

This is the current payment integral for the actuarial present value for the n-year temporary annuity. It can be considered as involving a momentary payment $1\, dt$ made at time t, discounted at interest back to time 0 by multiplying by v^t and further multiplied by ${}_tp_x$ to reflect the probability that a payment is made at time t for times up to time n. No payments are to be made after time n so the probability of such payments is 0.

The same recursion formula as indicated for (5.2.6) applies here with $u(x) = \bar{a}_{x:\overline{y-x}|}$ and the same $c(x)$ function which we now recognize as $\bar{a}_{x:\overline{1}|}$. We use here $n = y - x$. The only thing that needs to be changed is the initial value, for which we use $u(y) = \bar{a}_{y:\overline{0}|} = 0$. Another form of a recursion formula for a temporary annuity with the n-year period fixed is examined in Exercise 5.7.

Returning to (5.2.10) we note that

$$Y = \begin{cases} \bar{a}_{\overline{T}|} = \dfrac{1 - Z}{\delta} & 0 \leq T < n \\[2ex] \bar{a}_{\overline{n}|} = \dfrac{1 - Z}{\delta} & T \geq n \end{cases} \tag{5.2.13}$$

where

$$Z = \begin{cases} v^T & 0 \leq T < n \\ v^n & T \geq n. \end{cases} \tag{5.2.14}$$

In (5.2.14), Z is the present-value random variable for an n-year endowment insurance. Hence

$$\mathrm{E}[Y] = \bar{a}_{x:\overline{n}|} = \mathrm{E}\left[\frac{1 - Z}{\delta}\right] = \frac{1 - \bar{A}_{x:\overline{n}|}}{\delta} \tag{5.2.15}$$

and

$$\mathrm{Var}(Y) = \frac{\mathrm{Var}(Z)}{\delta^2} = \frac{{}^2\bar{A}_{x:\overline{n}|} - (\bar{A}_{x:\overline{n}|})^2}{\delta^2}. \tag{5.2.16}$$

In terms of annuity values, (5.2.16) becomes

$$\mathrm{Var}(Y) = \frac{1 - 2\delta\,{}^2\bar{a}_{x:\overline{n}|} - (1 - \delta\,\bar{a}_{x:\overline{n}|})^2}{\delta^2}$$

$$= \frac{2}{\delta}\left(\bar{a}_{x:\overline{n}|} - {}^2\bar{a}_{x:\overline{n}|}\right) - (\bar{a}_{x:\overline{n}|})^2.$$

The analysis for an **n-*year deferred whole life annuity*** is similar. The present-value random variable Y is defined as

$$Y = \begin{cases} 0 & = \bar{a}_{\overline{T}|} - \bar{a}_{\overline{T}|} & 0 \leq T < n \\ v^n\,\bar{a}_{\overline{T-n}|} = \bar{a}_{\overline{T}|} - \bar{a}_{\overline{n}|} & T \geq n. \end{cases} \tag{5.2.17}$$

Here the random variable Y can take on a value no larger than $(1/\delta) - \bar{a}_{\overline{n}|} = v^n/\delta$, and the probability that it takes on a zero value is $\Pr(T \leq n) = {}_nq_x$. A typical distribution function is illustrated in Figure 5.2.1(c).

Then,

$$_{n|}\bar{a}_x = \mathrm{E}[Y] = \int_n^\infty v^n\,\bar{a}_{\overline{t-n}|}\,{}_tp_x\,\mu(x + t)\,dt$$

$$= \int_0^\infty v^n\,\bar{a}_{\overline{s}|}\,{}_{n+s}p_x\,\mu(x + n + s)\,ds$$

$$= v^n\,{}_np_x \int_0^\infty \bar{a}_{\overline{s}|}\,{}_sp_{x+n}\,\mu(x + n + s)\,ds$$

which shows that

$$_{n|}\bar{a}_x = {}_nE_x\,\bar{a}_{x+n}. \tag{5.2.18}$$

An alternative development would be to note that, from the definitions of Y,

    (Y for an n-year deferred = (Y for a whole life annuity)
      whole life annuity)

                              $- $ (Y for an n-year temporary
                                          life annuity).

Taking expectations gives

$$_{n|}\bar{a}_x = \bar{a}_x - \bar{a}_{x:\overline{n}|}. \tag{5.2.19}$$

Integration by parts can be employed to verify the result given by the current payment technique. Since the annuity will be paying after time n if x survives, the actuarial present value can be written as

$$_{n|}\bar{a}_x = \int_n^\infty v^t \; {}_tp_x \; dt = \int_n^\infty {}_tE_x \; dt. \tag{5.2.20}$$

To develop the backward recursion formula for deferred annuities with $n = y - x > 1$, we note that we have no term corresponding to the integral for t values between 0 and 1. Thus, for $u(x) = {}_{y-x|}\bar{a}_x$ at ages less than y, $c(x) = 0$, and $d(x) = v \; p_x$. For a starting value we would use $u(y) = \bar{a}_y$.

One way to calculate the variance of Y for the deferred annuity is the following:

$$\mathrm{Var}(Y) = \int_n^\infty v^{2n} \, (\bar{a}_{\overline{t-n}|})^2 \; {}_tp_x \; \mu(x + t) \; dt - (_{n|}\bar{a}_x)^2$$

$$= v^{2n} \; {}_np_x \int_0^\infty (\bar{a}_{\overline{s}|})^2 \; {}_sp_{x+n} \; \mu(x + n + s) \; ds - (_{n|}\bar{a}_x)^2,$$

and using integration by parts,

$$= v^{2n} \; {}_np_x \int_0^\infty 2\bar{a}_{\overline{s}|} \; v^s \; {}_sp_{x+n} \; ds - (_{n|}\bar{a}_x)^2$$

$$= \frac{2}{\delta} v^{2n} \; {}_np_x \int_0^\infty (v^s - v^{2s}) \; {}_sp_{x+n} \; ds - (_{n|}\bar{a}_x)^2$$

$$= \frac{2}{\delta} v^{2n} \; {}_np_x \, (\bar{a}_{x+n} - {}^2\bar{a}_{x+n}) - (_{n|}\bar{a}_x)^2. \tag{5.2.21}$$

For an alternative development of this formula, see Exercise 5.37.

We now turn to analysis of an **n-year certain and life annuity.** This is a whole life annuity with a guarantee of payments for the first n years. The present value of annuity payments is

$$Y = \begin{cases} \bar{a}_{\overline{n}|} & T \le n \\ \bar{a}_{\overline{T}|} & T > n. \end{cases} \tag{5.2.22}$$

A typical distribution function is shown in Figure 5.2.1(d), which reflects the mixed nature of the distribution and the minimum value and upper bound of Y, which are $\bar{a}_{\overline{n}|}$ and $1/\delta$, respectively.

The actuarial present value is denoted by $\bar{a}_{\overline{x:\overline{n}|}}$. This symbol is adopted to indicate that payments continue until $\max[T(x), n]$:

$$\bar{a}_{\overline{x:\overline{n}|}} = \mathrm{E}[Y] = \int_0^n \bar{a}_{\overline{n}|}\,{}_tp_x\,\mu(x+t)\,dt$$

$$+ \int_n^\infty \bar{a}_{\overline{t}|}\,{}_tp_x\,\mu(x+t)\,dt$$

$$= {}_nq_x\,\bar{a}_{\overline{n}|} + \int_n^\infty \bar{a}_{\overline{t}|}\,{}_tp_x\,\mu(x+t)\,dt. \qquad (5.2.23)$$

Integration by parts can be used to obtain

$$\bar{a}_{\overline{x:\overline{n}|}} = \bar{a}_{\overline{n}|} + \int_n^\infty v^t\,{}_tp_x\,dt. \qquad (5.2.24)$$

This is the current payment form for the actuarial present value, since at times 0 to n payment is certain, whereas for times greater than n payment is made if (x) survives.

Further insight can be obtained by rewriting Y as

$$Y = \begin{cases} \bar{a}_{\overline{n}|} + 0 & T \le n \\ \bar{a}_{\overline{n}|} + (\bar{a}_{\overline{T}|} - \bar{a}_{\overline{n}|}) & T > n. \end{cases}$$

Here Y is the sum of a constant $\bar{a}_{\overline{n}|}$ and the random variable for the n-year deferred annuity. Thus,

$$\bar{a}_{\overline{x:\overline{n}|}} = \bar{a}_{\overline{n}|} + {}_{n|}\bar{a}_x$$

$$= \bar{a}_{\overline{n}|} + {}_nE_x\,\bar{a}_{x+n} \qquad \text{by (5.2.18)}$$

$$= \bar{a}_{\overline{n}|} + (\bar{a}_x - \bar{a}_{x:\overline{n}|}) \qquad \text{by (5.2.19).} \qquad (5.2.25)$$

Furthermore, since $\mathrm{Var}(Y - \bar{a}_{\overline{n}|}) = \mathrm{Var}(Y)$, the variance for the n-year certain and life annuity is the same as that of the n-year deferred annuity given by (5.2.21).

A backward recursion for $\bar{a}_{\overline{x:\overline{n}|}}$ with a fixed n-year certain period is examined in Exercise 5.9.

Analogous to the function

$$\bar{s}_{\overline{n}|} = \int_0^n (1+i)^{n-t}\,dt$$

in the theory of interest, we have for life annuities

$$\bar{s}_{x:\overline{n}|} = \frac{\bar{a}_{x:\overline{n}|}}{{}_nE_x} = \int_0^n \frac{1}{{}_{n-t}E_{x+t}}\,dt, \qquad (5.2.26)$$

representing the actuarial accumulated value at the end of the term of an n-year temporary life annuity of 1 per year payable continuously while (x) survives.

Such accumulated value, which is often said to have been accumulated under (or with the benefit of) interest and survivorship, is available at age $x + n$ if (x) survives.

We obtain an expression for $d\bar{a}_x/dx$ by differentiating the integral in (5.2.4), assuming that the probabilities are derived from an aggregate table:

$$\frac{d}{dx}\bar{a}_x = \int_0^\infty v^t \left(\frac{\partial}{\partial x}\, _tp_x\right) dt = \int_0^\infty v^t\, _tp_x\, [\mu(x) - \mu(x + t)]\, dt$$

$$= \mu(x)\, \bar{a}_x - \bar{A}_x = \mu(x)\, \bar{a}_x - (1 - \delta\, \bar{a}_x).$$

Therefore,

$$\frac{d}{dx}\bar{a}_x = [\mu(x) + \delta]\, \bar{a}_x - 1. \tag{5.2.27}$$

The interpretation of (5.2.27) is that the actuarial present value changes at a rate that is the sum of the rate of interest income $\delta\, \bar{a}_x$ and the rate of survivorship benefit $\mu(x)\, \bar{a}_x$, less the rate of payment outgo.

Example 5.2.2

Assuming that probabilities come from an aggregate table, obtain formulas for

$$\text{a.} \quad \frac{\partial}{\partial x}\bar{a}_{x:\overline{n}|} \qquad \text{b.} \quad \frac{\partial}{\partial n}\, _{n|}\bar{a}_x.$$

Solution:

a. Proceeding as in the development of (5.2.27), we obtain

$$\frac{\partial}{\partial x}\bar{a}_{x:\overline{n}|} = \mu(x)\, \bar{a}_{x:\overline{n}|} - \bar{A}^1_{x:\overline{n}|}$$

$$= \mu(x)\, \bar{a}_{x:\overline{n}|} - (1 - \delta\, \bar{a}_{x:\overline{n}|} - _nE_x)$$

$$= [\mu(x) + \delta]\, \bar{a}_{x:\overline{n}|} - (1 - _nE_x).$$

b. $\dfrac{\partial}{\partial n}\, _{n|}\bar{a}_x = \dfrac{\partial}{\partial n}\displaystyle\int_n^\infty v^t\, _tp_x\, dt = -v^n\, _np_x.$ ▼

Table 5.2.1 summarizes concepts for continuous life annuities.

Figure 5.2.1 shows typical distribution functions for the several types of continuous life annuities studied in this section. Limiting values and points of discontinuities are indicated on one or both axes.

When $F_Y(0) = 0$, $E[Y] = \int_0^\infty [1 - F_Y(y)]\, dy$, the actuarial present value of Y can be visualized as the area above the graph of $z = F_Y(y)$, below $z = 1$, and to the right of the line $y = 0$. This interpretation can provide a bridge between the actuarial

TABLE 5.2.1

Summary of Continuous Life Annuities (Annuity of 1 per Annum Payable Continuously)

Annuity Name	Present-Value Random Variable Y	Actuarial Present Value $E[Y]$ Equal to
Whole Life Annuity	$\bar{a}_{\overline{T}\mid} \qquad T \geq 0$	$\bar{a}_x = \displaystyle\int_0^\infty v^t \,_t p_x \, dt$
n-Year Temporary Life Annuity	$\begin{cases} \bar{a}_{\overline{T}\mid} & 0 \leq T < n \\ \bar{a}_{\overline{n}\mid} & T \geq n \end{cases}$	$\bar{a}_{x:\overline{n}\mid} = \displaystyle\int_0^n v^t \,_t p_x \, dt$
n-Year Deferred Whole Life Annuity	$\begin{cases} 0 & 0 \leq T < n \\ \bar{a}_{\overline{T}\mid} - \bar{a}_{\overline{n}\mid} & T \geq n \end{cases}$	$_{n\mid}\bar{a}_x = \displaystyle\int_n^\infty v^t \,_t p_x \, dt$
n-Year Certain and Life Annuity	$\begin{cases} \bar{a}_{\overline{n}\mid} & 0 \leq T < n \\ \bar{a}_{\overline{T}\mid} & T \geq n \end{cases}$	$\bar{a}_{\overline{x:\overline{n}\mid}} = \bar{a}_{\overline{n}\mid} + \displaystyle\int_n^\infty v^t \,_t p_x \, dt$

Additional relations are

- $1 = \delta\,\bar{a}_x + \bar{A}_x$

- $1 = \delta\,\bar{a}_{x:\overline{n}\mid} + \bar{A}_{x:\overline{n}\mid}$

- $_{n\mid}\bar{a}_x = \bar{a}_x - \bar{a}_{x:\overline{n}\mid}$

- $\bar{s}_{x:\overline{n}\mid} = \dfrac{\bar{a}_{x:\overline{n}\mid}}{_nE_x} = \displaystyle\int_0^n (1 + i)^{n-t} \dfrac{l_{x+t}}{l_{x+n}} \, dt.$

FIGURE 5.2.1

Typical Distribution Functions for the Present-Value Random Variables, Y

(a) Whole life annuity   (b) n-year temporary life annuity

(c) n-year deferred life annuity   (d) n-year certain and life annuity

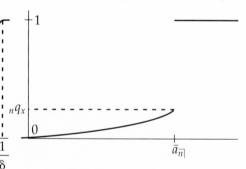

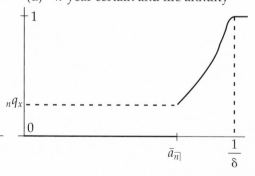

present value as evaluated from the definition of the random variable and the current payment form for the actuarial present value.

5.3 Discrete Life Annuities

The theory of discrete life annuities is analogous, step-by-step, to the theory of continuous life annuities, with integrals replaced by sums, integrands by summands, and differentials by differences. For continuous annuities there was no distinction between payments at the beginning of payment intervals or at the ends, that is, between annuities-due and annuities-immediate. For discrete annuities, the distinction is meaningful, and we start with annuities-due as they have a more prominent role in actuarial applications. For example, most individual life insurances are purchased by an annuity-due of periodic premiums.

We consider an annuity that pays a unit amount at the beginning of each year that the annuitant (x) survives. In the nomenclature this is called a *whole life annuity-due.* The present-value random variable, Y, for such an annuity, is given by $Y = \ddot{a}_{\overline{K+1}|}$ where the random variable K is the curtate-future-lifetime of (x). The possible values of this random variable are a discrete set of values ranging from $\ddot{a}_{\overline{1}|} = 1$ to $\ddot{a}_{\overline{\omega-x}|}$, a value which is less than $1/d$. The probability associated with the value $\ddot{a}_{\overline{k+1}|}$ is $\Pr(K = k) = {}_k p_x\, q_{x+k}$.

Let us now consider $\ddot{a}_x$, the actuarial present value of the annuity:

$$\ddot{a}_x = E[Y] = E[\ddot{a}_{\overline{K+1}|}]$$

$$= \sum_{k=0}^{\infty} \ddot{a}_{\overline{k+1}|}\, {}_k p_x\, q_{x+k}, \qquad (5.3.1)$$

since $\Pr(K = k) = {}_k p_x\, q_{x+k}$. By summation-by-parts (see Appendix 5) with $\Delta f(k) = {}_k p_x\, q_{x+k} = {}_k p_x - {}_{k+1} p_x$ and $g(k) = \ddot{a}_{\overline{k+1}|}$ and use of the relations

$$\Delta\, g(k) = \Delta\, \ddot{a}_{\overline{k+1}|} = v^{k+1} \text{ and } f(k) = -{}_k p_x,$$

(5.3.1) converts to

$$\ddot{a}_x = 1 + \sum_{k=0}^{\infty} v^{k+1}\, {}_{k+1} p_x \qquad (5.3.2)$$

$$= \sum_{k=0}^{\infty} v^k\, {}_k p_x. \qquad (5.3.3)$$

The expression (5.3.3) is the current payment form of the actuarial present value for a whole life annuity-due where the ${}_k p_x$ term is the probability of a payment of size 1 being made at time k.

Starting with the sum in (5.3.2) above we have

$$\ddot{a}_x = 1 + \sum_{k=0}^{\infty} v^{k+1} {}_{k+1}p_x = 1 + v\, p_x \sum_{k=0}^{\infty} v^k {}_k p_{x+1}$$

$$= 1 + v\, p_x\, \ddot{a}_{x+1}. \tag{5.3.4}$$

This expression is an example of the backward recursion formula first observed in Section 3.5 and explored more fully in Sections 4.3 and 5.2. Here $u(x) = \ddot{a}_x$, $c(x) = 1$, and $d(x) = v\, p_x$. The initial value to use for the whole life annuity is $\ddot{a}_\omega = 0$.

From (5.3.1) we obtain in succession

$$\ddot{a}_x = \mathrm{E}\left[\frac{1 - v^{K+1}}{d}\right]$$

$$= \frac{1 - A_x}{d}, \tag{5.3.5}$$

and

$$\ddot{a}_x = \ddot{a}_{\overline{\infty}} - \ddot{a}_{\overline{\infty}}\, A_x, \tag{5.3.6}$$

$$1 = d\ddot{a}_x + A_x. \tag{5.3.7}$$

This should be compared with its continuous counterpart (5.2.8). Formula (5.3.7) indicates that a unit invested now will produce interest-in-advance of d per year while (x) survives plus repayment of the unit at the end of the year of death of (x).

The variance formula is

$$\mathrm{Var}(\ddot{a}_{\overline{K+1}}) = \mathrm{Var}\left(\frac{1 - v^{K+1}}{d}\right) = \frac{\mathrm{Var}(v^{K+1})}{d^2}$$

$$= \frac{{}^2 A_x - (A_x)^2}{d^2}; \tag{5.3.8}$$

see (5.2.9).

The present-value random variable of an **n-*year temporary life annuity-due*** of 1 per year is

$$Y = \begin{cases} \ddot{a}_{\overline{K+1}} & 0 \le K < n \\ \ddot{a}_{\overline{n}} & K \ge n, \end{cases}$$

and its actuarial present value is

$$\ddot{a}_{x:\overline{n}} = \mathrm{E}[Y] = \sum_{k=0}^{n-1} \ddot{a}_{\overline{k+1}} {}_k p_x\, q_{x+k} + \ddot{a}_{\overline{n}} {}_n p_x. \tag{5.3.9}$$

Summation by parts can be used to transform (5.3.9) into

$$\ddot{a}_{x:\overline{n}} = \sum_{k=0}^{n-1} v^k {}_k p_x, \tag{5.3.10}$$

which is the actuarial present value in the current payment form.

Again separating out the first term and factoring out vp_x, we obtain the backward recursion formula for a temporary annuity-due payable to age $y = x + n$:

$$\ddot{a}_{x:\overline{y-x}|} = 1 + vp_x\,\ddot{a}_{x+1:\overline{y-(x+1)}|}. \tag{5.3.11}$$

This recursive formula for the actuarial present values is the same as (5.3.4) but differs in that here we use an initial value of $\ddot{a}_{y:\overline{0}|} = 0$.

Since $Y = (1 - Z)/d$, where

$$Z = \begin{cases} v^{K+1} & 0 \le K < n \\ v^n & K \ge n \end{cases}$$

is the present-value random variable for a unit of endowment insurance, payable at the end of the year of death or at maturity, we have

$$\ddot{a}_{x:\overline{n}|} = \frac{1 - E[Z]}{d} = \frac{1 - A_{x:\overline{n}|}}{d}; \tag{5.3.12}$$

see (5.2.15).

Rearrangement of (5.3.12) yields

$$1 = d\ddot{a}_{x:\overline{n}|} + A_{x:\overline{n}|}. \tag{5.3.13}$$

To calculate the variance, we can use

$$\mathrm{Var}(Y) = \frac{\mathrm{Var}(Z)}{d^2} = \frac{{}^2A_{x:\overline{n}|} - (A_{x:\overline{n}|})^2}{d^2}. \tag{5.3.14}$$

For an **n-*year deferred whole life annuity-due*** of 1 payable at the beginning of each year while (x) survives from age $x + n$ onward, the present-value random variable is

$$Y = \begin{cases} 0 & 0 \le K < n \\ {}_{n|}\ddot{a}_{\overline{K+1-n}|} & K \ge n, \end{cases}$$

and its actuarial present value is

$$E[Y] = {}_{n|}\ddot{a}_x = {}_nE_x\,\ddot{a}_{x+n} \tag{5.3.15}$$

$$= \ddot{a}_x - \ddot{a}_{x:\overline{n}|} \tag{5.3.16}$$

$$= \sum_{k=n}^{\infty} v^k\,{}_kp_x; \tag{5.3.17}$$

see (5.2.18)–(5.2.20).

The backward recursion formula for a deferred annuity-due with $n = y - x > 1$ is identical to that for the continuous version in that it uses $c(x) = 0$ and $d(x) = vp_x$. The change is that we use the actuarial present value for an annuity-due, $u(y) = \ddot{a}_y$, for the starting value.

The variance of Y can be developed in a manner completely analogous to that used in formula (5.2.21) and leads to the expression

$$\text{Var}(Y) = \frac{2}{d} v^{2n} \, {}_n p_x \, (\ddot{a}_{x+n} - {}^2 \ddot{a}_{x+n}) + {}_{n|}^2 \ddot{a}_x - ({}_{n|} \ddot{a}_x)^2. \tag{5.3.18}$$

We turn now to analysis of an **n-*year certain and life annuity-due.*** This is a life annuity with a guarantee of payments for at least n years. The present value of the annuity payments is

$$Y = \begin{matrix} \ddot{a}_{\overline{n}|} & 0 \le K < n \\ \ddot{a}_{\overline{K+1}|} & K \ge n. \end{matrix} \tag{5.3.19}$$

Then

$$\ddot{a}_{\overline{x:\overline{n}|}} = \text{E}[Y] = \ddot{a}_{\overline{n}|} \, {}_n q_x + \sum_{k=n}^{\infty} \ddot{a}_{\overline{k+1}|} \, {}_k p_x \, q_{x+k}, \tag{5.3.20}$$

and this can be transformed by summation by parts into the current payment version of the actuarial present value

$$\ddot{a}_{\overline{x:\overline{n}|}} = \ddot{a}_{\overline{n}|} + \sum_{k=n}^{\infty} v^k \, {}_k p_x. \tag{5.3.21}$$

This can be written as

$$\ddot{a}_{\overline{x:\overline{n}|}} = \ddot{a}_{\overline{n}|} + \ddot{a}_x - \ddot{a}_{x:\overline{n}|}.$$

The actuarial accumulated value at the end of the term of an n-year temporary life annuity-due of 1 per year, payable while (x) survives, is denoted by $\ddot{s}_{x:\overline{n}|}$. Formulas for this function are

$$\ddot{s}_{x:\overline{n}|} = \frac{\ddot{a}_{x:\overline{n}|}}{{}_n E_x} = \sum_{k=0}^{n-1} \frac{1}{{}_{n-k} E_{x+k}}, \tag{5.3.22}$$

which are analogous to formulas for $\ddot{s}_{\overline{n}|}$ in the theory of interest.

The procedures used above for annuities-due can be adapted for annuities-immediate where payments are made at the ends of the payment periods. For instance, for a *whole life annuity-immediate,* the present-value random variable is $Y = a_{\overline{K}|}$. Then,

$$a_x = \text{E}[Y] = \sum_{k=0}^{\infty} {}_k p_x \, q_{x+k} \, a_{\overline{k}|}, \tag{5.3.23}$$

and a summation by parts will give the current payment form of the actuarial present value as

$$a_x = \sum_{k=1}^{\infty} v^k \, {}_k p_x. \tag{5.3.24}$$

Since Y equals $(1 - v^K)/i = [1 - (1 + i) v^{K+1}]/i$, we have, taking expectations,

$$a_x = \text{E}[Y] = \frac{1 - (1 + i) A_x}{i}. \tag{5.3.25}$$

This formula can be rewritten as $1 = i a_x + (1 + i) A_x$. A comparison of this formula with (5.3.7) shows that an interest payment of i is made at the end of each year while (x) remains alive and that at the end of the year of death an interest payment of i along with the principal amount of 1 must be paid. This formula has significance for estate taxation. For each unit of an estate, define ia_x as the *life estate* and $(1 + i) A_x = 1 - ia_x$ as the *remainder,* which, if designated for a qualified charitable organization, is exempt from estate taxation.

The analysis for the other forms of the annuity-immediate is similar. The present-value random variable can be formed in a manner analogous to that for the annuity-due. Formulas for the actuarial present value from the definition and by summation by parts can be obtained. Formulas for the variances of the annuities-immediate in this section can also be obtained.

Example 5.3.1

Find formulas for the expectation and variance of the present-value random variable for the temporary life annuity-immediate.

Solution:

We start with the present-value random variable for an n-year temporary annuity-immediate:

$$Y = \begin{cases} a_{\overline{K}|} = \dfrac{1 - v^K}{i} & 0 \leq K < n \\ a_{\overline{n}|} = \dfrac{1 - v^n}{i} & K \geq n. \end{cases}$$

We now introduce two new random variables

$$Z_1 = \begin{cases} (1 + i)v^{K+1} & 0 \leq K < n \\ 0 & K \geq n \end{cases}$$

and

$$Z_2 = \begin{cases} 0 & 0 \leq K < n \\ v^n & K \geq n \end{cases}$$

so that $Y = (1 - Z_1 - Z_2)/i$ for all K. Now taking expectations, we have

$$E[Y] = a_{x:\overline{n}|} = \frac{1 - (1 + i) A^1_{x:\overline{n}|} - A_{x:\overline{n}|}^{\ 1}}{i}.$$

This can be rewritten, following (5.3.13),

$$1 = i\, a_{x:\overline{n}|} + i\, A^1_{x:\overline{n}|} + A_{x:\overline{n}|}.$$

The variance calculation is as follows:

$$\text{Var}(Y) = \frac{\text{Var}(Z_1 + Z_2)}{i^2} = \frac{\text{Var}(Z_1) + 2\,\text{Cov}(Z_1, Z_2) + \text{Var}(Z_2)}{i^2}.$$

Recall $\text{Var}(Z_1) = (1 + i)^2 \, [^2A^{\,1}_{x:\overline{n}|} - (A^{\,1}_{x:\overline{n}|})^2]$ and $\text{Var}(Z_2) = v^{2n}\,{}_np_x\,(1 - {}_np_x)$. Since $Z_1 Z_2 = 0$ for all K, we have $\text{Cov}(Z_1, Z_2) = -(1 + i)\,A^{\,1}_{x:\overline{n}|}\,v^n\,{}_np_x$. Combining, we obtain

$$\text{Var}(Y) = \frac{(1 + i)^2 \, [^2A^{\,1}_{x:\overline{n}|} - (A^{\,1}_{x:\overline{n}|})^2] - 2(1 + i)\,A^{\,1}_{x:\overline{n}|}\,v^n\,{}_np_x + v^{2n}\,{}_np_x\,(1 - {}_np_x)}{i^2}.$$

▼

TABLE 5.3.1

Summary of Discrete Life Annuities [Annuity of 1 Per Annum Payable at the Beginning of Each Year (Annuity-Due) or at the End of Each Year (Annuity-Immediate)]

Annuity Name	Present-Value Random Variable Y	Actuarial Present Value $E[Y]$ Equal to
Whole Life Annuity		
• Due	$\ddot{a}_{\overline{K+1}|} \qquad K \geq 0$	$\ddot{a}_x = \sum_{k=0}^{\infty} v^k \,{}_kp_x$
• Immediate	$a_{\overline{K}|} \qquad K \geq 0$	$a_x = \sum_{k=1}^{\infty} v^k \,{}_kp_x$
n-Year Temporary Life Annuity		
• Due	$\begin{cases} \ddot{a}_{\overline{K+1}|} & 0 \leq K < n \\ \ddot{a}_{\overline{n}|} & K \geq n \end{cases}$	$\ddot{a}_{x:\overline{n}|} = \sum_{k=0}^{n-1} v^k \,{}_kp_x$
• Immediate	$\begin{cases} a_{\overline{K}|} & 0 \leq K < n \\ a_{\overline{n}|} & K \geq n \end{cases}$	$a_{x:\overline{n}|} = \sum_{k=1}^{n} v^k \,{}_kp_x$
n-Year Deferred Whole Life Annuity		
• Due	$\begin{cases} 0 & 0 \leq K < n \\ \ddot{a}_{\overline{K+1}|} - \ddot{a}_{\overline{n}|} & K \geq n \end{cases}$	${}_{n|}\ddot{a}_x = \sum_{k=n}^{\infty} v^k \,{}_kp_x$
• Immediate	$\begin{cases} 0 & 0 \leq K < n \\ a_{\overline{K}|} - a_{\overline{n}|} & K \geq n \end{cases}$	${}_{n|}a_x = \sum_{k=n+1}^{\infty} v^k \,{}_kp_x$
n-Year Certain and Whole Life Annuity		
• Due	$\begin{cases} \ddot{a}_{\overline{n}|} & 0 \leq K < n \\ \ddot{a}_{\overline{K+1}|} & K \geq n \end{cases}$	$\ddot{a}_{\overline{x:\overline{n}|}} = \ddot{a}_{\overline{n}|} + \sum_{k=n}^{\infty} v^k \,{}_kp_x$
• Immediate	$\begin{cases} a_{\overline{n}|} & 0 \leq K < n \\ a_{\overline{K}|} & K \geq n \end{cases}$	$a_{\overline{x:\overline{n}|}} = a_{\overline{n}|} + \sum_{k=n+1}^{\infty} v^k \,{}_kp_x$

Additional relations are
- $1 = d\,\ddot{a}_x + A_x$
- $A_x = v\,\ddot{a}_x - a_x$
- $1 = d\,\ddot{a}_{x:\overline{n}|} + A_{x:\overline{n}|}$
- $\ddot{a}_{x:\overline{n}|} = 1 + a_{x:\overline{n-1}|}$
- $A^{\,1}_{x:\overline{n}|} = v\,\ddot{a}_{x:\overline{n}|} - a_{x:\overline{n}|}$

- $A_{x:\overline{n}|} = v\,\ddot{a}_{x:\overline{n}|} - a_{x:\overline{n-1}|}$
- ${}_{n|}\ddot{a}_x = \ddot{a}_x - \ddot{a}_{x:\overline{n}|}$
- $\ddot{a}_{\overline{x:\overline{n}|}} = \ddot{a}_{\overline{n}|} + \ddot{a}_x - \ddot{a}_{x:\overline{n}|}$
- $\ddot{s}_{x:\overline{n}|} = \dfrac{\ddot{a}_{x:\overline{n}|}}{{}_nE_x}$

$$= \sum_{k=0}^{n-1} (1 + i)^{n-k}\,\frac{l_{x+k}}{l_{x+n}}.$$

5.4 Life Annuities with *m*-thly Payments

In practice, life annuities are often payable on a monthly, quarterly, or semi-annual basis. In International Actuarial Notation, the actuarial present value of a life annuity of 1 per year, payable in installments of $1/m$ at the beginning of each m-th of the year while (x) survives, is denoted by $\ddot{a}_x^{(m)}$.

We start the analysis of the distribution of Y, the present value of the life annuity-due, with payments made on an m-thly basis, by expressing Y in terms of the interest rate and the random variables, K and $J = \lfloor (T - K)m \rfloor$. The "$\lfloor \ \rfloor$" in the expression for J denote the greatest integer function so that J is the number of complete m-ths of a year lived in the year of death. For an annuity-due there would be m payments for each of the K complete years and then $J + 1$ payments of $1/m$ in the year of death; thus,

$$Y = \sum_{j=0}^{mK+J} \frac{1}{m} v^{j/m} = \ddot{a}_{\overline{K+(J+1)/m|}}^{(m)} = \frac{1 - v^{K+(J+1)/m}}{d^{(m)}}. \tag{5.4.1}$$

The actuarial present value, $E[Y]$, which can be determined using Exercise 4.19, is

$$E[Y] = \ddot{a}_x^{(m)} = \frac{1 - A_x^{(m)}}{d^{(m)}}. \tag{5.4.2}$$

The current payment form, which is the sum of the actuarial present value of the set of payments, is

$$\ddot{a}_x^{(m)} = \frac{1}{m} \sum_{h=0}^{\infty} v^{h/m} \ {}_{h/m}p_x. \tag{5.4.3}$$

Again using (5.4.1), we obtain

$$\text{Var}(Y) = \frac{\text{Var}(v^{K+(J+1)/m})}{(d^{(m)})^2} = \frac{{}^2A_x^{(m)} - (A_x^{(m)})^2}{(d^{(m)})^2}. \tag{5.4.4}$$

It is convenient to use (5.3.7) and (5.4.2) to obtain various relationships between the actuarial present values for m-thly annuities and those with annual payments:

$$1 = d\,\ddot{a}_x + A_x = d^{(m)}\,\ddot{a}_x^{(m)} + A_x^{(m)}. \tag{5.4.5}$$

These show that an investment of 1 will produce interest-in-advance at the beginning of each interest period and repayment of the unit at the end of the period in which death occurs.

From the right two members of (5.4.5) we obtain

$$\ddot{a}_x^{(m)} = \frac{d}{d^{(m)}}\,\ddot{a}_x - \frac{1}{d^{(m)}}\,(A_x^{(m)} - A_x)$$

$$= \ddot{a}_{\overline{1|}}^{(m)}\,\ddot{a}_x - \ddot{a}_{\overline{\infty|}}^{(m)}\,(A_x^{(m)} - A_x). \tag{5.4.6}$$

This can be interpreted as follows: The m-thly payment life annuity is equivalent to a series of 1-year annuities-certain in each year that (x) begins, with cancellation in the year of death of installments payable beyond the m-th (month, quarter, half-year) of death. The cancellation is accomplished by an m-thly payment perpetuity beginning at the end of the m-th of death less a similar perpetuity beginning at the end of the year of death. Alternatively, from (5.4.2), we can write

$$\ddot{a}_x^{(m)} = \frac{1 - A_x^{(m)}}{d^{(m)}} = \ddot{a}_{\overline{\infty}|}^{(m)} - \ddot{a}_{\overline{\infty}|}^{(m)} A_x^{(m)}, \tag{5.4.7}$$

which is left to the reader to interpret.

Remark:

In the study of interest theory the calculation of the present value of an annuity with payment periods and effective interest periods of different lengths was reduced to the calculation of the present value of an annuity with payment periods and interest periods of equal length in one of two ways. The first was to replace the payments corresponding to an interest period by a single equivalent payment (at the given interest rate) at one end or the other of the interest period. The expression for the m-thly whole life annuity in (5.4.6) is an extension of this method to a set of contingent payments. When calculators with exponentiation keys replaced interest tables, the second method, using the equivalent effective interest rate per payment period, became the preferred way to match payment period and interest period lengths. The extension of this second method to m-thly whole life annuities would be to use an m-thly mortality table along with the equivalent effective interest rate per m-th of a year. Using this, the recursion relations of Section 5.3 could be used to obtain the actuarial present value of the m-thly whole life annuity. An advantage of this second approach is that it frees us to use other assumptions about the distribution of deaths within each year of age, like constant force or Makeham's, in place of the uniform distribution that is central in the discussion below.

Now let us assume that deaths have a uniform distribution in each year of age. This means that S has a uniform distribution on $(0, 1)$ so that J is uniformly distributed on the integers $\{0, 1, \ldots, m-1\}$. Exercise 4.19 shows that this implies

$$A_x^{(m)} = \frac{i}{i^{(m)}} A_x = s_{\overline{1}|}^{(m)} A_x,$$

and from (5.4.6) we have

$$\ddot{a}_x^{(m)} = \ddot{a}_{\overline{1}|}^{(m)} \ddot{a}_x - \frac{s_{\overline{1}|}^{(m)} - 1}{d^{(m)}} A_x. \tag{5.4.8}$$

Formula (5.4.8) shows that the value of the m-thly life annuity-due is the difference between
a. The value of an annual life annuity-due with each annual payment sufficient to pay a 1-year annuity certain of $1/m$ at the beginning of each m-th; and

b. The value of an insurance payable at the end of the year of death with the benefit equal to the coefficient of A_x. It can be shown that, under the assumption of uniform distribution of deaths in each year of age, this coefficient is the actuarial accumulated value of those payments of $1/m$ for the m-ths after death. See the bracketed expression in Exercise 5.15.

By substituting $1 - d\, \ddot{a}_x$ for A_x, in (5.4.8) and noting that $d^{(m)}\, \ddot{a}_{\overline{1}|}^{(m)} = d$, we obtain a formula involving only annuity functions, namely,

$$\ddot{a}_x^{(m)} = \frac{1 - s_{\overline{1}|}^{(m)}\,(1 - d\,\ddot{a}_x)}{d^{(m)}}$$

$$= s_{\overline{1}|}^{(m)}\, \ddot{a}_{\overline{1}|}^{(m)}\, \ddot{a}_x - \frac{(s_{\overline{1}|}^{(m)} - 1)}{d^{(m)}}. \tag{5.4.9}$$

An alternative, widely used, formula is

$$\ddot{a}_x^{(m)} = \ddot{a}_x - \frac{m-1}{2m}. \tag{5.4.10}$$

This result can be obtained by assuming that the function $v^{k+(j/m)}\, _{k+(j/m)}p_x$ is linear in j for $j = 0, 1, 2, \ldots, m - 1$. In that case,

$$\sum_{j=0}^{m-1} \frac{1}{m}\, v^{k+(j/m)}\, _{k+(j/m)}p_x = \sum_{j=0}^{m-1} \frac{1}{m} \left[\left(1 - \frac{j}{m}\right) v^k\, _kp_x + \frac{j}{m}\, v^{k+1}\, _{k+1}p_x \right]$$

$$= v^k\, _kp_x - (v^k\, _kp_x - v^{k+1}\, _{k+1}p_x) \sum_{j=0}^{m-1} \frac{j}{m^2}$$

$$= v^k\, _kp_x - \frac{m-1}{2m}\, (v^k\, _kp_x - v^{k+1}\, _{k+1}p_x).$$

Thus

$$\ddot{a}_x^{(m)} = \sum_{k=0}^{\infty} \sum_{j=0}^{m-1} \frac{1}{m}\, v^{k+(j/m)}\, _{k+(j/m)}p_x$$

$$= \sum_{k=0}^{\infty} v^k\, _kp_x - \frac{m-1}{2m} \sum_{k=0}^{\infty} (v^k\, _kp_x - v^{k+1}\, _{k+1}p_x)$$

$$= \ddot{a}_x - \frac{m-1}{2m}.$$

Note that this is not the same assumption as that of linearity of $_tp_x$, which would follow if a uniform distribution of deaths within each year of age is assumed. Consistent use of the assumption of a uniform distribution of deaths in each year of age assures that relations such as (5.4.5) are satisfied exactly. It has also been observed that formulas derived from (5.4.10) can, for high rates of interest and low rates of mortality, produce distorted annuity values, such as $a_{x:\overline{1}|}^{(m)} > a_{\overline{1}|}^{(m)}$; see Exercise 5.50. For these reasons, (5.4.8) and equivalently (5.4.9) are presented as replacements for the widely used formula (5.4.10).

It is convenient for writing purposes to express (5.4.9) in the form

$$\ddot{a}_x^{(m)} = \alpha(m)\, \ddot{a}_x - \beta(m), \tag{5.4.11}$$

where

$$\alpha(m) = s_{\overline{1}|}^{(m)} \ddot{a}_{\overline{1}|}^{(m)} = \frac{id}{i^{(m)} d^{(m)}}, \qquad (5.4.12)$$

and

$$\beta(m) = \frac{s_{\overline{1}|}^{(m)} - 1}{d^{(m)}} = \frac{i - i^{(m)}}{i^{(m)} d^{(m)}}. \qquad (5.4.13)$$

We note that $\alpha(m)$ and $\beta(m)$ depend only on m and the rate of interest and are independent of the year of age. Further, for $m = 1$, (5.4.11) is an identity where $\alpha(1) = 1$ and $\beta(1) = 0$. Also, $\beta(m)$ is the coefficient of the cancellation term in (5.4.8); that is, (5.4.8) can be written as

$$\ddot{a}_x^{(m)} = \ddot{a}_{\overline{1}|}^{(m)} \ddot{a}_x - \beta(m)A_x. \qquad (5.4.14)$$

For series expansions of $\alpha(m)$ and $\beta(m)$, see Exercise 5.41.

Example 5.4.1

On the basis of the Illustrative Life Table, with interest at the effective annual rate of 6%, calculate the actuarial present value of a whole life annuity-due of 1,000 per month for a retiree age 65 by (5.4.9) and (5.4.10) and its standard deviation by (5.4.4).

Solution:

Here

$$\alpha(12) = s_{\overline{1}|}^{(12)} \ddot{a}_{\overline{1}|}^{(12)} = (1.02721070)(0.97378368) = 1.0002810,$$

$$\beta(12) = \frac{s_{\overline{1}|}^{(12)} - 1}{d^{(12)}} = 0.46811951,$$

$$\frac{11}{24} = 0.45833333.$$

Observe that $\alpha(12) \cong 1$, and $\beta(12)$ is fairly close to the $11/24$ that appears in the traditional approximation.

By the Illustrative Life Table, as defined by (3.7.1), with interest at 6%,

$$\ddot{a}_{65} = 9.89693,$$

$$A_{65} = 1 - d\,\ddot{a}_{65} = 0.4397965.$$

Then, $12{,}000\ddot{a}_{65}^{(12)}$ can be calculated as follows:

by (5.4.11) $12{,}000[\alpha(12)\ddot{a}_{65} - \beta(12)]$

$$= 12{,}000[(1.0002810)(9.89693) - 0.46811951]$$

$$= 113{,}179 \text{ and}$$

by (5.4.10) $12{,}000\left(\ddot{a}_{65} - \dfrac{11}{24}\right) = 113{,}263.$

The variance of $12{,}000Y = 12{,}000(1 - v^{K+(J+1)/12})/d^{(12)}$ is equal to

$$\left(\frac{12{,}000}{d^{(12)}}\right)^2 \mathrm{Var}[v^{K+1}(1+i)^{1-(J+1)/12}]$$

$$= \left(\frac{12{,}000}{d^{(12)}}\right)^2 \{E[v^{2(K+1)}(1+i)^{2(1-(J+1)/12)}] - (E[v^{(K+1)}(1+i)^{(1-(J+1)/12)}])^2\}$$

$$= \left(\frac{12{,}000}{d^{(12)}}\right)^2 \left\{{}^2A_{65}\,E[(1+i)^{2(1-(J+1)/12)}] - \left(\frac{A_{65}\,i}{i^{(12)}}\right)^2\right\}$$

$$= (206{,}442.14)^2\,[(0.2360299 \times 1.055458268) - (0.4397965 \times 1.02721069)^2]$$

$$= 1{,}919{,}074{,}762.$$

This means that the standard deviation for the present value for the payments to an individual is 43,807 as compared to the actuarial present value of 113,179. ▼

The development starting with random variables can be followed for m-thly temporary and deferred annuities-due. However, if all we seek is formulas for their actuarial present values, we can proceed by starting with (5.4.14). Thus

$$\ddot{a}^{(m)}_{x:\overline{n}|} = \ddot{a}^{(m)}_x - {}_nE_x\,\ddot{a}^{(m)}_{x+n}$$

$$= \ddot{a}^{(m)}_{\overline{1}|}\ddot{a}_x - \beta(m)A_x - {}_nE_x[\ddot{a}^{(m)}_{\overline{1}|}\ddot{a}_{x+n} - \beta(m)A_{x+n}]$$

$$= \ddot{a}^{(m)}_{\overline{1}|}\ddot{a}_{x:\overline{n}|} - \beta(m)A^{1}_{x:\overline{n}|}; \qquad (5.4.15)$$

and similarly,

$$_{n|}\ddot{a}^{(m)}_x = \ddot{a}^{(m)}_{\overline{1}|}\,{}_{n|}\ddot{a}_x - \beta(m)\,{}_{n|}A_x. \qquad (5.4.16)$$

Alternately from (5.4.11),

$$\ddot{a}^{(m)}_{x:\overline{n}|} = \alpha(m)\ddot{a}_{x:\overline{n}|} - \beta(m)(1 - {}_nE_x), \qquad (5.4.17)$$

$$_{n|}\ddot{a}^{(m)}_x = \alpha(m)\,{}_{n|}\ddot{a}_x - \beta(m)\,{}_nE_x. \qquad (5.4.18)$$

Backward recursion formulas can be developed directly for m-thly life annuities, and the reader is asked to do this in Exercise 5.16 for an m-thly annuity-due. A more direct approach, however, would be to use the recursions of Section 5.3 and then adjust from annual to m-thly life annuities by means of (5.4.11), (5.4.17), and (5.4.18) or the equivalent formulas (5.4.14), (5.4.15), and (5.4.16).

The distribution of the present value of the payments of a life annuity-immediate with m-thly payments can be explored in steps analogous with those for the annuity-due. For example, the present-value random variable, Y, would be

$$Y = a^{(m)}_{\overline{K+(J/m)|}} = \frac{1 - v^{K+(J/m)}}{i^{(m)}} \qquad (5.4.19)$$

for the whole life annuity-immediate with m-thly payments. This exploration leads to the following formula analogous to (5.4.5):

$$1 = i\,a_x + (1+i)A_x = i^{(m)}a^{(m)}_x + \left(1 + \frac{i^{(m)}}{m}\right)A^{(m)}_x. \qquad (5.4.20)$$

The meaning here is that an investment of 1 will produce interest at the end of each interest period plus the repayment of the unit together with interest then due at the end of the interest period in which death occurs.

The actuarial present values for the annuities-immediate can also be obtained by adjusting the actuarial present values of the corresponding life annuities-due. For instance,

$$a_x^{(m)} = \ddot{a}_x^{(m)} - \frac{1}{m},$$

$$a_{x:\overline{n}|}^{(m)} = \ddot{a}_{x:\overline{n}|}^{(m)} - \frac{1}{m}(1 - {}_nE_x). \tag{5.4.21}$$

5.5 Apportionable Annuities-Due and Complete Annuities-Immediate

With discrete annuities each payment is made either for the following period (an annuity-due) or for the preceding period (an annuity-immediate). A question may arise about having an adjustment for the payment period of death. For instance, suppose that a life insurance contract is purchased by annual payments payable at the beginning of each contract year. If the insured dies 1 month after making an annual payment, a refund of premium for the 11 months the insured did not complete in the policy year of death might seem appropriate. As another example, if a retirement income life annuity-immediate provides annual payments and the annuitant dies 1 month before the due date of the next payment, there might be a final payment for the 11-month period that the annuitant has survived since the last full payment. Consider first the appropriate size for the adjustment payment in such cases.

Let us examine the first case above. The insured dies at time T after paying a full yearly premium of 1 at time K. Assume that the premium is earned or accrued at a uniform rate over the year following the payment. In this case the rate of accrual, c, is given by $c\,\bar{a}_{\overline{1}|} = 1$. If accrual ceases at death, then $c\,\bar{s}_{\overline{T-K}|}$ has been earned to that date, while

$$(1 + i)^{T-K} - c\,\bar{s}_{\overline{T-K}|} = 1 \times (1 + i)^{T-K} - \frac{\bar{s}_{\overline{T-K}|}}{\bar{a}_{\overline{1}|}} = \frac{\bar{a}_{\overline{K+1-T}|}}{\bar{a}_{\overline{1}|}}$$

is unearned and is the amount to be refunded. The present-value random variable, at time 0, of all the payments less the refund is

$$Y = \ddot{a}_{\overline{K+1}|} - v^T \frac{\bar{a}_{\overline{K+1-T}|}}{\bar{a}_{\overline{1}|}}$$

$$= \ddot{a}_{\overline{K+1}|} - \frac{v^T - v^{K+1}}{d}$$

$$= \frac{1 - v^T}{d} = \ddot{a}_{\overline{T}|}. \tag{5.5.1}$$

When the annual rate of payments is 1, the actuarial present value at time 0 of the payments is denoted by $\ddot{a}_x^{\{1\}}$:

$$\ddot{a}_x^{\{1\}} = E[\ddot{a}_{\overline{T}|}] = E\left[\frac{\delta}{d}\,\bar{a}_{\overline{T}|}\right] = \frac{\delta}{d}\,\bar{a}_x. \tag{5.5.2}$$

This type of life annuity-due, one with a refund for the period between the time of death and the end of the period represented by the last full regular payment, is called an *apportionable annuity-due.*

We can extend this idea to annuities that are paid more frequently than once a year. As in Section 5.4, we define $J = \lfloor (T - K)m \rfloor$ to be the number of m-ths of a year completed in the year of death, so $K + (J + 1)/m - T$ is the length of the period to be compensated for by the refund. The accrual rate is given by $c\,\bar{a}_{\overline{1/m}|} = 1/m$. Then, proceeding as above,

$$\begin{aligned}
Y &= \ddot{a}^{(m)}_{\overline{K+(J+1)/m}|} - v^T\left(\frac{\bar{a}_{\overline{K+(J+1)/m-T}|}}{m\bar{a}_{\overline{1/m}|}}\right) \\[2mm]
&= \ddot{a}^{(m)}_{\overline{K+(J+1)/m}|} - \frac{v^T - v^{K+(J+1)/m}}{d^{(m)}} \\[2mm]
&= \frac{1 - v^T}{d^{(m)}} = \ddot{a}^{(m)}_{\overline{T}|}. \tag{5.5.3}
\end{aligned}$$

When the annual rate of payments is 1, the actuarial present value of payments, less the refund, is $\ddot{a}_x^{\{m\}}$:

$$\ddot{a}_x^{\{m\}} = E\left[\frac{1 - v^T}{d^{(m)}}\right] = \frac{\delta}{d^{(m)}}\,\bar{a}_x. \tag{5.5.4}$$

Alternatively, using the second line of (5.5.3),

$$\begin{aligned}
\ddot{a}_x^{\{m\}} &= E\left[\frac{1 - v^{K+(J+1)/m}}{d^{(m)}}\right] - E\left[\frac{v^T - v^{K+(J+1)/m}}{d^{(m)}}\right] \\[2mm]
&= \ddot{a}_x^{(m)} - E\left[\frac{v^T - v^{K+(J+1)/m}}{d^{(m)}}\right]. \tag{5.5.5}
\end{aligned}$$

The second term on the right-hand side of (5.5.5) is the actuarial present value of the refund. Using the ideas developed in Exercise 4.19 we have

$$E\left[\frac{v^T - v^{K+(J+1)/m}}{d^{(m)}}\right] = \frac{\bar{A}_x - A_x^{(m)}}{d^{(m)}}. \tag{5.5.6}$$

Under the uniform distribution of death assumption for each year of age, this becomes

$$\frac{i}{d^{(m)}}\left(\frac{1}{\delta} - \frac{1}{i^{(m)}}\right)A_x$$

and

$$\ddot{a}_x^{\{m\}} = \ddot{a}_x^{(m)} - \frac{i}{d^{(m)}}\left(\frac{1}{\delta} - \frac{1}{i^{(m)}}\right)A_x. \tag{5.5.7}$$

Let us now develop a parallel theory for annuities-immediate. Assume the annuitant dies at time T after receiving a last regular payment of size $1/m$ at time $K + J/m$, where $J = \lfloor (T - K)m \rfloor$. Now $T - K - (J/m)$ is the length of the period to be compensated for by an additional payment. Assume that each payment is accrued at a uniform rate over the m-th of the year preceding its payment. In this case the rate of accrual, c, is given by $c\,\bar{s}_{\overline{1/m}|} = 1/m$. If accrual ceases at death, an appropriate payment at death is that portion of the next payment that has been accrued to date and is given by $c\,\bar{s}_{\overline{T-K-(J/m)}|} = \bar{s}_{\overline{T-K-(J/m)}|}/(m\bar{s}_{\overline{1/m}|})$. The present value, at time 0, of all of the payments is

$$
Y = a^{(m)}_{\overline{K+J/m}|} + v^T \left(\frac{\bar{s}_{\overline{T-K-(J/m)}|}}{m\bar{s}_{\overline{1/m}|}} \right)
$$

$$
= a^{(m)}_{\overline{K+J/m}|} + \frac{v^{K+J/m} - v^T}{i^{(m)}}
$$

$$
= \frac{1 - v^T}{i^{(m)}} = a^{(m)}_{\overline{T}|}. \tag{5.5.8}
$$

When the annual rate of payments is 1, the actuarial present value at 0 of the payments is denoted by $\overset{\circ}{a}^{(m)}_x$. When $m = 1$, the (1) in the notation is omitted for this annuity:

$$
\overset{\circ}{a}^{(m)}_x = \mathrm{E}\left[\frac{1 - v^T}{i^{(m)}} \right] = \frac{\delta}{i^{(m)}}\,\bar{a}_x. \tag{5.5.9}
$$

Alternatively, using the second line of (5.5.8),

$$
\overset{\circ}{a}^{(m)}_x = \mathrm{E}[a^{(m)}_{\overline{K+J/m}|}] + \mathrm{E}\left[\frac{v^{K+J/m} - v^T}{i^{(m)}} \right]
$$

$$
= a^{(m)}_x + \mathrm{E}\left[\frac{v^{K+J/m} - v^T}{i^{(m)}} \right]. \tag{5.5.10}
$$

The second term on the right-hand side of (5.5.10) is the actuarial present value of the final partial payment. Using the ideas developed in Exercise 4.19, we have

$$
\mathrm{E}\left[\frac{v^{K+J/m} - v^T}{i^{(m)}} \right] = \frac{(1 + i)^{1/m} A^{(m)}_x - \bar{A}_x}{i^{(m)}}. \tag{5.5.11}
$$

Under the uniform distribution of death assumption for each year of age, this becomes

$$
\frac{i}{i^{(m)}} \left(\frac{1}{d^{(m)}} - \frac{1}{\delta} \right) A_x
$$

and

$$
\overset{\circ}{a}^{(m)}_x = a^{(m)}_x + \frac{i}{i^{(m)}} \left(\frac{1}{d^{(m)}} - \frac{1}{\delta} \right) A_x. \tag{5.5.12}
$$

This type of life annuity-immediate, one with a partial payment for the period between the last full payment and the time of death, is called a **complete annuity-immediate**.

For use in subsequent material, (5.5.3) and (5.5.8) seem to be most useful. We illustrate this in the following example.

Example 5.5.1

Compare the variances of the present-value random variables for the complete annuity-immediate and apportionable annuity-due.

Solution:

For the apportionable annuity-due, we have

$$\text{Var}(\ddot{a}_{\overline{T}|}^{(m)}) = \text{Var}\left(\frac{1 - v^T}{d^{(m)}}\right) \qquad \text{from (5.5.3)}$$

$$= \frac{\text{Var}(v^T)}{(d^{(m)})^2}$$

$$= \frac{{}^2\bar{A}_x - (\bar{A}_x)^2}{(d^{(m)})^2}.$$

For the complete annuity-immediate, we have

$$\text{Var}(a_{\overline{T}|}^{(m)}) = \text{Var}\left(\frac{1 - v^T}{i^{(m)}}\right) \qquad \text{from (5.5.8)}$$

$$= \frac{\text{Var}(v^T)}{(i^{(m)})^2}$$

$$= \frac{{}^2\bar{A}_x - (\bar{A}_x)^2}{(i^{(m)})^2}.$$

Since $i^{(m)}$ is larger than $d^{(m)}$, and in fact $i^{(m)} = d^{(m)} (1 + i)^{1/m}$, the variance of the complete annuity-immediate is the smaller. ▼

5.6 Notes and References

Taylor (1952) presents new formulas analogous to (5.4.6). Various inquiries into the probability distribution of annuity costs are made by Boermeester (1956), Fretwell and Hickman (1964), and Bowers (1967). This work is summarized by McCrory (1984). Mereu (1962) gives a means of calculating annuity values directly from Makeham constants. The use of the floor function, $\lfloor t \rfloor$, in actuarial science, in particular with respect to actuarial present values of life annuities, is found in Shiu (1982) and in the discussions to that paper. Complete and apportionable annuities are involved, explicitly or implicitly, in papers by Rasor and Greville (1952), Lauer (1967), and Scher (1974) and in the discussions thereto.

Exercises

Section 5.2

5.1. Using the assumption of a uniform distribution of deaths in each year of age and the Illustrative Life Table with interest at the effective annual rate of 6%, calculate

   a. $\bar{a}_{20}$, $\bar{a}_{50}$, $\bar{a}_{80}$
   b. $\text{Var}(\bar{a}_{\overline{T}|})$ for $x = 20, 50, 80$.
   [Hint: Use (5.2.8), (5.2.9), and (4.4.4).]

5.2. Using the values obtained in Exercise 5.1, calculate the standard deviation and the coefficient of variation, σ/μ, of the following present-value random variables.

   a. Individual annuities issued at ages 20, 50, 80 with life incomes of 1,000 per year payable continuously.
   b. A group of 100 annuities, each issued at age 50, with life income of 1,000 per year payable continuously.

5.3. Show that $\text{Var}(\bar{a}_{\overline{T}|})$ can be expressed as

$$\frac{2}{\delta}\left(\bar{a}_x - {}^2\bar{a}_x\right) - \bar{a}_x^2,$$

where ${}^2\bar{a}_x$ is based on the force of interest 2δ.

5.4. Calculate $\text{Cov}(\delta\,\bar{a}_{\overline{T}|},\, v^T)$.

5.5. If a deterministic (rate function) approach is adopted, (5.2.27) could be taken as the starting point for the development of a theory of continuous life annuities. For this, we would begin with

$$\frac{d\bar{a}_y}{dy} = [\mu(y) + \delta]\bar{a}_y - 1 \qquad x \le y < \omega,$$

$$\bar{a}_y = 0 \qquad \omega \le y.$$

   a. Use the integrating factor $\exp\{-\int_0^y[\mu(z) + \delta]dz\}$ to solve the differential equation to obtain (5.2.3).
   b. Use the integrating factor $e^{-\delta y}$ to obtain

$$\bar{a}_x = \bar{a}_{\overline{\omega-x}|} - \int_x^\omega e^{-\delta(y-x)}\,\bar{a}_y\,\mu(y)\,dy$$

   and give an interpretation of it in words.

5.6. Assume that $\mu(x + t) = \mu$ and the force of interest is δ for all $t \ge 0$.
   a. If $Y = \bar{a}_{\overline{T}|}$, $0 \le T$, display the formula for the distribution function of Y.

b. If

$$Y = \begin{cases} \bar{a}_{\overline{T}|} & 0 \leq T < n \\ \bar{a}_{\overline{n}|} & T \geq n, \end{cases}$$

display the formula for the distribution function of Y.

c. If

$$Y = \begin{cases} 0 & 0 \leq T < n \\ \bar{a}_{\overline{T}|} - \bar{a}_{\overline{n}|} & T \geq n, \end{cases}$$

display the formula for the distribution function of Y.

d. If

$$Y = \begin{cases} \bar{a}_{\overline{n}|} & 0 \leq T < n \\ \bar{a}_{\overline{T}|} & T \geq n, \end{cases}$$

display the formula for the distribution function of Y.

5.7. By considering the integral $\int_0^{n+1} v^t {}_t p_x \, dt$ and breaking it in two different ways into subintervals (first, from 0 to 1 and 1 to $n + 1$ and then 0 to n and n to $n + 1$), establish a backward recursion formula for the n-year temporary life annuity based on a fixed n-year temporary period. What starting value is appropriate for this recursion formula?

5.8. By considering the integral $\int_n^\infty v^t {}_t p_x \, dt$ and breaking it into subintervals from n to $n + 1$ and $n + 1$ to ∞, establish a backward recursion formula for the n-year deferred whole life annuity based on a fixed n-year deferral period. What starting value is appropriate for this recursion formula?

5.9. Combine the result from Exercise 5.8 with the first line of (5.2.25) to establish a backward recursion formula for $u(x) = \bar{a}_{x:\overline{n}|}$. What starting value is appropriate for this recursion formula?

5.10. If the probabilities come from an aggregate table, establish (5.2.6) by a probabilistic derivation starting with a rewrite of (5.2.3) as

$$\bar{a}_x = \mathrm{E}[\bar{a}_{\overline{T}|}] = \mathrm{E}[\bar{a}_{\overline{T}|} \,|\, 0 \leq T < 1] \, \mathrm{Pr}(0 \leq T < 1) + \mathrm{E}[\bar{a}_{\overline{T}|} \,|\, 1 \leq T] \, \mathrm{Pr}(1 \leq T).$$

Section 5.3

5.11. Show that

$$\mathrm{Var}(a_{\overline{K}|}) = \mathrm{Var}(\ddot{a}_{\overline{K+1}|}) = \frac{\mathrm{Var}(v^{K+1})}{d^2}.$$

5.12. Prove and interpret the given relations:

a. $a_{x:\overline{n}|} = {}_1 E_x \, \ddot{a}_{x+1:\overline{n}|}$

b. ${}_{n|}a_x = \dfrac{A_{x:\overline{n}|} - A_x}{d} - {}_n E_x.$

5.13. Using (5.3.13), prove and interpret the following relation in words:

$$A_{x:\overline{n}|} = v\,\ddot{a}_{x:\overline{n}|} - a_{x:\overline{n-1}|}.$$

5.14. Obtain an alternative expression for the variance given in Example 5.3.1 by starting with

$$Y^2 = \begin{cases} \dfrac{1 - 2v^K + v^{2K}}{i^2} = \dfrac{2(1 - v^K) - (1 - v^{2K})}{i^2} & K = 0, 1, n - 1 \\[2ex] (a_{\overline{n}|})^2 & K = n, n + 1 \ldots. \end{cases}$$

Section 5.4

5.15. Assume a uniform distribution of deaths over each year of age. Simplify

$$\sum_{k=0}^{\infty} {}_kp_x\, v^{k+1} \left[\sum_{j=0}^{m-1} \left({}_{j/m}p_{x+k}\; {}_{1/m}q_{x+k+j/m} \right) \ddot{s}^{(m)}_{1-(j+1)/m|} \right]$$

for use in interpretation of (5.4.8).

5.16. Consider an m-thly temporary life annuity-due that pays 1 per annum to an annuitant age x for $y - x$ years.
   a. Express the current payment form of the actuarial present value of the above annuity as a sum of that for payments in the first year and for the remaining $y - x - 1$ years.
   b. Express the actuarial present value of payments in the first year in terms of $\alpha(m)$ and $\beta(m)$ under an assumption of the uniform distribution of deaths within each year of age.
   c. Find the form of the $c(x)$ and $d(x)$ expressions for a recursion relation for such an annuity and indicate a starting value.

5.17. Using (5.4.10), derive alternative formulas to (5.4.17) and (5.4.18).

5.18. Show that the annuity-immediate analogue for (5.4.6) is

$$a_x^{(m)} = s_{\overline{1}|}^{(m)}\, a_x + \frac{1}{i^{(m)}} \left[(1 + i)A_x - \left(1 + \frac{i^{(m)}}{m} \right) A_x^{(m)} \right],$$

and that under the assumption of a uniform distribution of deaths in each year of age, this becomes

$$a_x^{(m)} = s_{\overline{1}|}^{(m)}\, a_x + (1 + i)\, \frac{1 - \ddot{a}_{\overline{1}|}^{(m)}}{i^{(m)}}\, A_x.$$

5.19. Show that the annuity-immediate analogues for (5.4.7) are

$$a_x^{(m)} = \frac{1 - (1 + i^{(m)}/m)A_x^{(m)}}{i^{(m)}} = a_{\overline{\infty}|}^{(m)} - \ddot{a}_{\overline{\infty}|}^{(m)}\, A_x^{(m)}$$

and that under the assumption of a uniform distribution of deaths in each year of age these become

$$a_x^{(m)} = \alpha(m)a_x + \frac{1 - \ddot{a}_{\overline{1}|}^{(m)}}{i^{(m)}}.$$

5.20. a. Use (5.4.3) as a starting point to verify that

$$\lim_{m \to \infty} \ddot{a}_x^{(m)} = \bar{a}_x.$$

b. Use (5.4.10) and the result in (a) to show

$$\bar{a}_x \cong a_x + \frac{1}{2}.$$

5.21. Using the traditional approximation given in (5.4.10), establish the following:

a. $a_x^{(m)} \cong a_x + \dfrac{m - 1}{2m}$

b. $a_{x:\overline{n}|}^{(m)} \cong a_{x:\overline{n}|} + \dfrac{m - 1}{2m}(1 - {}_nE_x)$

c. ${}_{n|}a_x^{(m)} \cong {}_{n|}a_x + \dfrac{m - 1}{2m}{}_nE_x.$

5.22. a. Develop a formula for $\ddot{s}_{25:\overline{40}|}^{(m)}$ in terms of $\ddot{s}_{25:\overline{40}|}$.

b. On the basis of the Illustrative Life Table with interest at the effective annual rate of 6%, calculate the values of

(i) $\ddot{a}_{25:\overline{40}|}^{(12)}$ (ii) $\ddot{s}_{25:\overline{40}|}^{(12)}$.

5.23. The actuarial present value of a standard increasing temporary life annuity with respect to (x) with

- Yearly income of 1 in the first year, 2 in the second year, and so on, ending with n in the n-th year,

- Payments made m-thly on a due basis

is denoted by $(I\ddot{a})_{x:\overline{n}|}^{(m)}$.

a. Display the present-value random variable, Y, for this annuity as a function of the K and J random variables.

b. Show that the actuarial present value can be expressed as

$$\sum_{k=0}^{n-1} {}_{k|}\ddot{a}_{x:\overline{n-k}|}^{(m)}.$$

5.24. The actuarial present value of a standard decreasing temporary life annuity with respect to (x) with

- Yearly income of n in the first year, $n - 1$ in the second year, and so on, ending with 1 in the n-th year,

- Payments, made m-thly on a due basis

is denoted by $(D\ddot{a})_{x:\overline{n}|}^{(m)}$.

a. Display the present-value random variable, Y, for this annuity as a function of the K and J random variables.

b. Show that the actuarial present value can be expressed as

$$\sum_{k=1}^{n} \ddot{a}_{x:\overline{k}|}^{(m)}.$$

5.25. If in Exercise 5.23 the yearly income does not cease at age $x + n$ but continues at the level n while (x) survives therafter, the actuarial present value is denoted by $(I_{\overline{n}|}\ddot{a})_{x}^{(m)}$.
   a. Display the present-value random variable, Y, for this annuity as a function of the K and J random variables.
   b. Show that the actuarial present value can be expressed as

$$\sum_{k=0}^{n-1} {}_{k|}\ddot{a}_{x}^{(m)}.$$

5.26. Verify the formula

$$\delta(\bar{I}\bar{a})_{\overline{T}|} + T\, v^{T} = \bar{a}_{\overline{T}|},$$

where T represents the future lifetime of (x). Use it to prove that

$$\delta(\bar{I}\bar{a})_{x} + (\bar{I}\bar{A})_{x} = \bar{a}_{x},$$

where $(\bar{I}\bar{a})_{x}$ is the actuarial present value of a life annuity to (x) under which payments are being made continuously at the rate of t per annum at time t.

5.27. From $a_{x:\overline{n}|}^{(m)} = a_{x}^{(m)} + a_{\overline{n}|}^{(m)} - a_{x:\overline{n}|}^{(m)}$, show that the assumption of uniform distribution of deaths in each year of age leads to

$$a_{x:\overline{n}|}^{(m)} = \frac{i}{i^{(m)}}\left[a_{\overline{n}|} + v^{n}\,{}_{n}p_{x}\,a_{x+n} + \left(\frac{1}{d} - \frac{1}{d^{(m)}} \right) v^{n}\,{}_{n}p_{x}\,A_{x+n} \right].$$

Section 5.5

5.28. Establish and interpret the following formulas:
   a. $1 = i^{(m)}\,\mathring{a}_{x}^{(m)} + \bar{A}_{x}$
   b. $1 = d^{(m)}\,\ddot{a}_{x}^{\{m\}} + \bar{A}_{x}$
   c. $\mathring{a}_{x:\overline{n}|}^{(m)} = (\delta/i^{(m)})\,\bar{a}_{x:\overline{n}|}$
   d. $\ddot{a}_{x:\overline{n}|}^{\{m\}} = (\delta/d^{(m)})\,\bar{a}_{x:\overline{n}|}$
   e. $\ddot{a}_{x:\overline{n}|}^{\{m\}} = (1 + i)^{1/m}\,\mathring{a}_{x:\overline{n}|}^{(m)}.$

5.29. Let $H(m) = \ddot{a}_{x}^{\{m\}} - \mathring{a}_{x}^{(m)}$. Prove that $H(m) \geq 0$ and $\lim_{m \to \infty} H(m) = 0$.

Miscellaneous

5.30. For $0 \leq t \leq 1$ and the assumption of a uniform distribution of deaths in each year of age, show that
   a. $\ddot{a}_{x+t} = \dfrac{(1 + it)\ddot{a}_{x} - t(1 + i)}{1 - t\, q_{x}}$
   b. ${}_{t|}\ddot{a}_{x} = v^{t}[(1 + it)\ddot{a}_{x} - t(1 + i)]$

c. $_{1-t|}\ddot{a}_{x+t} = \dfrac{(1 + i)^t}{1 - tq_x}(\ddot{a}_x - 1)$

d. $A_{x+t} = \dfrac{1 + it}{1 - tq_x}A_x - \dfrac{t\,q_x}{1 - t\,q_x}.$

5.31. Obtain formulas for the evaluation of a life annuity-due to (x) with an initial payment of 1 and with annual payments increasing thereafter by
a. 3% of the initial annual payment
b. 3% of the previous year's annual payment.

5.32. Express $(\bar{D}\bar{a})_{x:\overline{n}|}$ as an integral and prove the formula

$$\frac{\partial}{\partial n}(\bar{D}\bar{a})_{x:\overline{n}|} = \bar{a}_{x:\overline{n}|}.$$

5.33. Give an expression for the actuarial accumulated value at age 70 of an annuity with the following monthly payments:
- 100 at the end of each month from age 30 to 40
- 200 at the end of each month from age 40 to 50
- 500 at the end of each month from age 50 to 60
- 1,000 at the end of each month from age 60 to 70.

5.34. Derive a simplified expression for the actuarial present value for a 25-year term insurance payable immediately on the death of (35), under which the death benefit in case of death at age $35 + t$ is $\bar{s}_{\overline{t}|}$, $0 \le t \le 25$. Interpret your result.

5.35. Derive a simplified expression for the actuarial present value for an n-year term insurance payable at the end of the year of death of (x), under which the death benefit in case of death in year $k + 1$ is $\ddot{s}_{\overline{k+1}|}$, $0 \le k < n$. Interpret your result.

5.36. Obtain a simplified expression for

$$(I\ddot{a})_{x:\overline{25}|}^{(12)} - (Ia)_{x:\overline{25}|}^{(12)}.$$

5.37. Consider an n-year deferred continuous life annuity of 1 per year as an insurance with probability of claim, $_np_x$, and random amount of claim, $v^n\,\bar{a}_{\overline{T}|}$. Here T has p.d.f., $_tp_{x+n}\,\mu_x(n + t)$. Apply (2.2.13) to show that the variance of the insurance equals

$$v^{2n}\,_np_x\,(1 - {_np_x})\,\bar{a}_{x+n}^2 + v^{2n}\,_np_x\,\frac{^2\bar{A}_{x+n} - (\bar{A}_{x+n})^2}{\delta^2}$$

and verify that this reduces to (5.2.21).

5.38. Write the discrete analogue of the variance formula in Exercise 5.37.

5.39. Consider the indicator random variable, I_k, defined by

$$I_k = \begin{cases} 1 & T(x) \geq k \\ 0 & T(x) < k. \end{cases}$$

Show the following:

a. The present value of a life annuity to (x), with annual payment b_k on survival to age $x + k$, $k = 0, 1, 2, \ldots$, can be written as

$$\sum_{k=0}^{\infty} v^k \, b_k \, I_k.$$

b. $E[I_j I_k] = {}_k p_x \qquad j \leq k$
   $\mathrm{Cov}(I_j, I_k) = {}_k p_x \, {}_j q_x \qquad j \leq k.$

c. $\mathrm{Var}\left(\sum_{k=0}^{\infty} v^k \, b_k \, I_k \right) = \sum_{k=0}^{\infty} v^{2k} \, b_k^2 \, {}_k p_x \, {}_k q_x + 2 \sum_{k=0}^{\infty} \sum_{j<k} v^{j+k} \, b_j \, b_k \, {}_k p_x \, {}_j q_x.$

5.40. If a left superscript 2 indicates that interest is at force 2δ, show that
   a. ${}^2 A_x = 1 - (2d - d^2) \, {}^2 \ddot{a}_x$
   b. $\mathrm{Var}\,(v^{K+1}) = 2d(\ddot{a}_x - {}^2\ddot{a}_x) - d^2\,(\ddot{a}_x^2 - {}^2\ddot{a}_x)$
   c. $\mathrm{Var}(\ddot{a}_{\overline{K+1}|}) = \dfrac{2}{d}\,(\ddot{a}_x - {}^2\ddot{a}_x) - (\ddot{a}_x^2 - {}^2\ddot{a}_x).$

5.41. a. Expand, in terms of powers of δ, the annuity coefficients $\alpha(m)$ and $\beta(m)$.
   b. What do the expansions in (a) become for $m = \infty$?

5.42. Use Jensen's inequality to show, for $\delta > 0$, that
   a. $\bar{a}_x < \bar{a}_{\overline{\mathring{e}_x}|}$ b. $a_x < a_{\overline{\mathring{e}_x}|}$ $x < \omega - 1$.

5.43. If $g(x)$ is a non-negative function and X is a random variable with p.d.f. $f(x)$, justify the inequality

$$E[g(X)] = \int_{-\infty}^{\infty} g(x)\, f(x)\, dx \geq k \, \mathrm{Pr}[g(X) \geq k] \qquad k > 0$$

and use it to show that

$$\bar{a}_x \geq \bar{a}_{\overline{\mathring{e}_x}|}\, \mathrm{Pr}(\bar{a}_{\overline{T}|} \geq \bar{a}_{\overline{\mathring{e}_x}|}) = \bar{a}_{\overline{\mathring{e}_x}|}\, \mathrm{Pr}(T \geq \mathring{e}_x).$$

5.44. A unit is to be used to purchase a combination benefit consisting of a life income of I per year payable continuously while (x) survives and an insurance of J payable immediately on the death of (x). Write the present-value random variable for this combination and give its mean and variance.

5.45. Using the assumption of a uniform distribution of deaths in each year of age and the Illustrative Life Table with interest at the effective annual rate of 6%, calculate
   a. $\ddot{a}_{40}^{(12)}$ b. $\ddot{a}_{40:\overline{30}|}^{(12)}$ c. ${}_{30|}\ddot{a}_{40}^{(12)}.$

5.46. If $A''_{x:\overline{m}|}$ and $\ddot{a}''_{x:\overline{m}|}$ are actuarial present values calculated using
- An interest rate of i for the first n years, $n < m$, and
- An interest rate i' for the remaining $m - n$ years,

show algebraically and interpret

a. $A''_{x:\overline{m}|} = 1 - d\,\ddot{a}_{x:\overline{n}|} - v^n\,{}_np_x\,d'\,\ddot{a}'_{x+n:\overline{m-n}|}$

b. $A''_{x:\overline{m}|} = 1 - d'\,\ddot{a}''_{x:\overline{m}|} + (d' - d)\,\ddot{a}_{x:\overline{n}|}$.

5.47. Show that

$$\frac{d\ddot{a}_x}{di} = -v(Ia)_x,$$

where

$$(Ia)_x = \sum_{t=1}^{\infty} t\,v^t\,{}_tp_x,$$

and interpret the relation.

5.48. Show that a constant increase in the force of mortality has the same effect on $\ddot{a}_x$ as a constant increase in the force of interest, but that this is not the case for $\ddot{a}_x^{(m)}$ evaluated by $\alpha(m)\,\ddot{a}_x - \beta(m)$.

5.49. Show that

$$\alpha(m) - \beta(m)d = \ddot{a}_{\overline{1}|}^{(m)}.$$

5.50. Show that, if $q_x < (i^{(2)}/2)^2$, the approximation

$$\ddot{a}_{x:\overline{n}|}^{(m)} = \ddot{a}_{x:\overline{n}|} - \frac{m-1}{2m}(1 - {}_nE_x),$$

in the special case with $n = 1$, $m = 2$, leads to

$$\ddot{a}_{x:\overline{1}|}^{(2)} > \ddot{a}_{\overline{1}|}^{(2)}.$$

5.51. Consider the following portfolio of annuities-due currently being paid from the assets of a pension fund.

Age	Number of Annuitants
65	30
75	20
85	10

Each annuity has an annual payment of 1 as long as the annuitant survives. Assume an earned interest rate of 6% and a mortality as given in the Illustrative Life Table. For the present value of these obligations of the pension fund, calculate
a. The expectation
b. The variance

c. The 95th percentile of its distribution.

For parts (b) and (c), assume the lives are mutually independent.

Computing Exercises

5.52. a. For your Illustrative Life Table with $i = 0.06$, calculate the actuarial present value of a life annuity-due of 1 per annum for ages 13 to 140.

b. Compare your values to those given in Table 2A.

5.53. For your Illustrative Life Table with $i = 0.06$, calculate the actuarial present value of a temporary life annuity-due of 1 per annum payable to age 65 for ages 13 to 64.

5.54. Using your Illustrative Life Table with the assumption of a uniform distribution of deaths within each year of age and $i = 0.06$, calculate the actuarial present value of a 10-year temporary life annuity of 1 per annum payable continuously and issued at ages 13 to 99 using the results of Exercise 5.7.

5.55. a. Add $\alpha(m)$ and $\beta(m)$ to the interest functions calculated and stored in your Illustrative Life Table. Refer to Exercise 4.31.

b. Determine $\alpha(12)$ and $\beta(12)$ at $i = 0.06$ and compare your results to those given in Example 5.4.1.

[Remark: We suggest using the series derived in Exercise 5.41 for accurate results with small interest rates.]

5.56. Using your Illustrative Life Table with $i = 0.06$ and the assumption of uniform distribution of deaths over each year of age, calculate the actuarial present value of a temporary life annuity of 1 per annum payable continuously to age 65 for ages 13 to 64.

5.57. Let Y be the present-value random variable for a continuous 10-year temporary life annuity of 1 per annum commencing at age 60. On the basis of your Illustrative Life Table with uniform distribution of deaths over each year of age and $i = 0.08$, calculate the mean and variance of Y.

5.58. Let Y be the present-value random variable for a life annuity-due of 1 per annum, payable monthly to (65). On the basis of your Illustrative Life Table with uniform distribution of deaths over each year of age and $i = 0.05$, calculate the mean and variance of Y.

5.59. Use the Illustrative Life Table with uniform distribution of deaths over each year of age and $i = 0.07$ to determine $\mathring{a}_{30:\overline{20}|}$.

BENEFIT PREMIUMS

6.1 Introduction

In Chapters 4 and 5 we discussed actuarial present values of the payments of various life insurances and annuities. These ideas are combined in this chapter to determine the level of life annuity payments necessary to buy, or fund, the benefits of an insurance or annuity contract. In practice individual life insurance is usually purchased by a life annuity of *contract premiums*—the insurance contract specifies the premium to be paid. Contract premiums provide for benefits, expenses of initiating and maintaining the insurance, and margins for profit and for offsetting possible unfavorable experience. The premiums studied in this chapter are determined only by the pattern of benefits and premiums and do not consider expenses, profit, or contingency margins.

In Chapter 1 we discussed the idea that determination of the insurance premium requires the adoption of a *premium principle*. Example 6.1.1 illustrates the application of three such premium principles. All three principles are based on the impact of the insurance on the wealth of the insuring organization. The random variable that gives the present value at issue of the insurer's loss, if the insurance is contracted at a certain premium level, is the key in the model for the principles. Principle I requires that the loss random variable be positive with no more than a specified probability. Principles II and III are based on the expected utility of the insurer's wealth as discussed in Section 1.3. We will see that Principle II, which uses a linear utility function, could also be characterized as requiring that the loss random variable have zero expected value.

Example 6.1.1

An insurer is planning to issue a policy to a life age 0 whose curtate-future-lifetime, K, is governed by the p.f.

$$_{k|}q_0 = 0.2 \qquad k = 0, 1, 2, 3, 4.$$

The policy will pay 1 unit at the end of the year of death in exchange for the payment of a premium P at the beginning of each year, provided the life survives. Find the annual premium, P, as determined by:

---

a. Principle I: P will be the least annual premium such that the insurer has probability of a positive financial loss of at most 0.25.
b. Principle II: P will be the annual premium such that the insurer, using a utility of wealth function $u(x) = x$, will be indifferent between accepting and not accepting the risk.
c. Principle III: P will be the annual premium such that the insurer, using a utility of wealth function $u(x) = -e^{-0.1x}$, will be indifferent between accepting and not accepting the risk.

For all three parts assume the insurer will use an annual effective interest rate of $i = 0.06$.

Solution:

For $K = k$ and an arbitrary premium, P, the present value of the financial loss at policy issue is $l(k) = v^{k+1} - P\ddot{a}_{\overline{k+1}|} = (1 + P/d) v^{k+1} - P/d$, $k = 0, 1, 2, 3, 4$. The corresponding loss random variable is $L = v^{K+1} - P\ddot{a}_{\overline{K+1}|}$.

a. Since $l(k)$ decreases as k increases, the requirement of Principle I will hold if P is such that $v^2 - P \ddot{a}_{\overline{2}|} = 0$. Then the financial loss is positive for only $K = 0$, which has probability $0.2 < 0.25$. Thus, for this principle, $P = 1/\ddot{s}_{\overline{2}|} = 0.45796$.

b. By an extension of (1.3.6), we seek the premium P such that $u(w) = \text{E}[u(w - L)]$. By Principle II $u(x) = x$ so we have

$$w = \text{E}[w - L] = w - \text{E}[L].$$

Thus, Principle II is equivalent to requiring that P be chosen so that $\text{E}[L] = 0$. For this example, we require

$$\sum_{k=0}^{4} (v^{k+1} - P \ddot{a}_{\overline{k+1}|}) \Pr(K = k) = 0 \qquad (6.1.1)$$

which gives $P = 0.30272$.

c. Again by (1.3.6) and now using the utility function in Principle III, we have

$$-e^{-0.1w} = \text{E}[-e^{-0.1(w-L)}] = -e^{-0.1w} \text{E}[e^{0.1L}].$$

Thus, Principle III is equivalent to requiring that P be chosen so that $\text{E}[e^{0.1L}] = 1$. Here, we require

$$\sum_{k=0}^{4} \exp[0.1 (v^{k+1} - P \ddot{a}_{\overline{k+1}|})] \Pr(K = k) = 1, \qquad (6.1.2)$$

which gives $P = 0.30628$.

These three results are summarized below.

Outcome k	Probability $_{k\mid}q_0$	General Formula	Present Value of Financial Loss When Premium Is by Principle			$\exp(0.1L)$
			I	II	III	III
0	0.2	$v^1 - P\,\ddot{a}_{\overline{1}\rvert}$	0.48544	0.64067	0.63712	1.06579
1	0.2	$v^2 - P\,\ddot{a}_{\overline{2}\rvert}$	0	0.30169	0.29477	1.02992
2	0.2	$v^3 - P\,\ddot{a}_{\overline{3}\rvert}$	-0.45796	-0.01811	-0.02819	0.99718
3	0.2	$v^4 - P\,\ddot{a}_{\overline{4}\rvert}$	-0.89000	-0.31981	-0.33287	0.96726
4	0.2	$v^5 - P\,\ddot{a}_{\overline{5}\rvert}$	-1.29758	-0.60443	-0.62031	0.93985
	Premium		0.45796	0.30272	0.30628	
	Expected Value		-0.43202	0.00000	-0.00990	1.00000

The table shows that for this example the decision makers adopting principles I and III reduce their risk in the sense that they are demanding an expected present value of loss to be negative. ▼

Premiums defined by Principle I are known as *percentile premiums.* Although the principle is attractive on the surface, it is easy to show that it can lead to quite unsatisfactory premiums. Such cases are examined in Example 6.2.3.

Principle II has many applications in practice. To formalize its concepts, we define the insurer's loss, L, as the random variable of the present value of benefits to be paid by the insurer less the annuity of premiums to be paid by the insured. Principle II is called the *equivalence principle* and has the requirement that

$$E[L] = 0. \qquad (6.1.3)$$

We will speak of *benefit premiums* as those satisfying (6.1.3). Equivalently, benefit premiums will be such that

E[present value of benefits] = E[present value of benefit premiums].

Methods developed in Chapters 4 and 5 for calculating these actuarial present values can be used to reduce this equality to a form that can be solved for the premiums. For instance, in Example 6.1.1, which has constant benefit premiums and constant benefits of 1, equation (6.1.1) can be rewritten as $A_0 = P\ddot{a}_0$, and $\ddot{a}_0$ can be calculated as

$$\sum_{k=0}^{4} v^k {}_k p_0.$$

When the equivalence principle is used to determine a single premium at policy issue for a life insurance or a life annuity, the premium is equal to the actuarial present value of benefit payments and is called the *single benefit premium.*

Premiums based on Principle III, using an exponential utility function, are known as *exponential premiums.* Exponential premiums are nonproportional in the sense that the premium for the policy with a benefit level of 10 is more than 10 times the premium for a policy with a benefit level of 1 (see Exercise 6.2). This is consistent for a risk averse utility function.

6.2 Fully Continuous Premiums

The basic concepts involved in the determination of annual benefit premiums using the equivalence principle will be illustrated first for the case of the fully continuous level annual benefit premium for a unit whole life insurance payable immediately on the death of (x). For any continuously paid premium, $\bar{P}$, consider

$$l(t) = v^t - \bar{P}\bar{a}_{\overline{t}|}, \tag{6.2.1}$$

the present value of the loss to the insurer if death occurs at time t.

We note that $l(t)$ is a decreasing function of t with $l(0) = 1$ and $l(t)$ approaching $-\bar{P}/\delta$ as $t \to \infty$. If t_0 is the time when $l(t_0) = 0$, death before t_0 results in a positive loss, whereas death after t_0 produces a negative loss, that is, a gain. Figure 6.2.1 later in this section illustrates these ideas.

We now consider the loss random variable,

$$L = l(T) = v^T - \bar{P}\,\bar{a}_{\overline{T}|}, \tag{6.2.2}$$

corresponding to the loss function $l(t)$. If the insurer determines his premium by the equivalence principle, the premium is denoted by $\bar{P}(\bar{A}_x)$ and is such that

$$E[L] = 0. \tag{6.2.3}$$

It follows from (4.2.6) and (5.2.3) that

$$\bar{A}_x - \bar{P}(\bar{A}_x)\bar{a}_x = 0,$$

or

$$\bar{P}(\bar{A}_x) = \frac{\bar{A}_x}{\bar{a}_x}. \tag{6.2.4}$$

Remark:
In this chapter we continue to suppress the select notation except in situations in which it is necessary or helpful to eliminate ambiguity.

The variance of L can be used as a measure of the variability of losses on an individual whole life insurance due to the random nature of time-until-death. When $E[L] = 0$,

$$\text{Var}(L) = E[L^2]. \tag{6.2.5}$$

For the loss in (6.2.2), we have

$$\text{Var}(v^T - \bar{P}\,\bar{a}_{\overline{T}|}) = \text{Var}\left[v^T - \frac{\bar{P}(1 - v^T)}{\delta} \right]$$

$$= \text{Var}\left[v^T \left(1 + \frac{\bar{P}}{\delta} \right) - \frac{\bar{P}}{\delta} \right]$$

$$= \mathrm{Var}\left[v^T\left(1 + \frac{\bar{P}}{\delta}\right)\right]$$

$$= \mathrm{Var}\,(v^T)\left(1 + \frac{\bar{P}}{\delta}\right)^2$$

$$= [^2\bar{A}_x - (\bar{A}_x)^2]\left(1 + \frac{\bar{P}}{\delta}\right)^2. \qquad (6.2.6)$$

For the premium determined by the equivalence principle, we can use (6.2.4) and (5.2.8), $\delta\bar{a}_x + \bar{A}_x = 1$, to rewrite (6.2.6) as

$$\mathrm{Var}(L) = \frac{{}^2\bar{A}_x - (\bar{A}_x)^2}{(\delta\bar{a}_x)^2}. \qquad (6.2.7)$$

Example 6.2.1

Calculate $\bar{P}(\bar{A}_x)$ and $\mathrm{Var}(L)$ with the assumptions that the force of mortality is a constant $\mu = 0.04$ and the force of interest $\delta = 0.06$.

Solution:

These assumptions yield $\bar{a}_x = 10, \bar{A}_x = 0.4$, and ${}^2\bar{A}_x = 0.25$. Using (6.2.4), we obtain

$$\bar{P}(\bar{A}_x) = \frac{\bar{A}_x}{\bar{a}_x} = 0.04,$$

and from (6.2.7)

$$\mathrm{Var}(L) = \frac{0.25 - 0.16}{(0.6)^2} = 0.25. \qquad \blacktriangledown$$

By reference to (6.2.7) we can see that the numerator of this last expression can be interpreted as the variance of the loss, $v^T - \bar{A}_x$, associated with a single-premium whole life insurance. This latter variance is 0.09, and hence the standard deviation of the loss associated with this annual premium insurance is $\sqrt{0.25/0.09} = 5/3$ times the standard deviation of the loss in the single-premium case. Additional uncertainty about the present value of the premium income increases the variability of losses due to the random nature of time-until-death.

In Example 6.2.1, $\bar{P}(\bar{A}_x) = 0.04$, the constant force of mortality. We can confirm this as a general result by using parts of Examples 4.2.3 and 5.2.1. Under the constant force of mortality assumption,

$$\bar{A}_x = \frac{\mu}{\mu + \delta}$$

and

$$\bar{a}_x = \frac{1}{\mu + \delta},$$

thus

$$\bar{P}(\bar{A}_x) = \frac{\mu(\mu + \delta)^{-1}}{(\mu + \delta)^{-1}} = \mu,$$

which does not depend on the force of interest or the age at issue.

Using the equivalence principle, as in (6.1.3), we can determine formulas for annual premiums of a variety of fully continuous life insurances. Our general loss is

$$b_T v_T - \bar{P} Y = Z - \bar{P} Y \qquad (6.2.8)$$

where

- b_t and v_t are, respectively, the benefit amount and discount factor defined in connection with (4.2.1)
- $\bar{P}$ is a general symbol for a fully continuous net annual premium
- Y is a continuous annuity random variable as defined, for example, in (5.2.13), and
- Z is defined by (4.2.2).

Application of the equivalence principle yields

$$E[b_T v_T - \bar{P} Y] = 0$$

or

$$\bar{P} = \frac{E[b_T v_T]}{E[Y]}.$$

These ideas are used to display annual premium formulas in Table 6.2.1.

It is of interest to note how these steps can be used for an n-year deferred whole life annuity of 1 per year payable continuously. In this case $b_T v_T = 0$, $T \leq n$ and $b_T v_T = \bar{a}_{\overline{T-n}|} v^n$, $T > n$. Then,

$$E[b_T v_T] = {}_n p_x \, E[\bar{a}_{\overline{T-n}|} v^n | T > n]$$

$$= v^n \, {}_n p_x \, \bar{a}_{x+n} = A_{x:\overline{n}|}^{\;1} \, \bar{a}_{x+n}.$$

In practice, however, deferred life annuities usually provide some type of death benefit during the period of deferment. One contract of this type is examined in Example 6.6.2.

Example 6.2.2

Express the variance of the loss, L, associated with an n-year endowment insurance, in terms of actuarial present values (see the third row of Table 6.2.1).

TABLE 6.2.1

Fully Continuous Benefit Premiums

Plan	Loss Components		Premium Formula $\bar{P} = \dfrac{E[b_T v_T]}{E[Y]}$
	$b_T v_T$	$\bar{P}\, Y$ Where Y Is	
Whole life insurance	$1\, v^T$	$\bar{a}_{\overline{T}\|}$	$\bar{P}(\bar{A}_x) = \dfrac{\bar{A}_x}{\bar{a}_x}$
n-Year term insurance	$1\, v^T$ 0	$\bar{a}_{\overline{T}\|},\ T \leq n$ $\bar{a}_{\overline{n}\|},\ T > n$	$\bar{P}(\bar{A}^{\,1}_{x:\overline{n}\|}) = \dfrac{\bar{A}^{\,1}_{x:\overline{n}\|}}{\bar{a}_{x:\overline{n}\|}}$
n-Year endowment insurance	$1\, v^T$ $1\, v^n$	$\bar{a}_{\overline{T}\|},\ T \leq n$ $\bar{a}_{\overline{n}\|},\ T > n$	$\bar{P}(\bar{A}_{x:\overline{n}\|}) = \dfrac{\bar{A}_{x:\overline{n}\|}}{\bar{a}_{x:\overline{n}\|}}$
h-Payment years* whole life insurance	$1\, v^T$ $1\, v^T$	$\bar{a}_{\overline{T}\|},\ T \leq h$ $\bar{a}_{\overline{h}\|},\ T > h$	$_h\bar{P}(\bar{A}_x) = \dfrac{\bar{A}_x}{\bar{a}_{x:\overline{h}\|}}$
h-Payment years,* n-year endowment insurance	$1\, v^T$ $1\, v^T$ $1\, v^n$	$\bar{a}_{\overline{T}\|},\ T \leq h$ $\bar{a}_{\overline{h}\|},\ h < T \leq n$ $\bar{a}_{\overline{h}\|},\ T > n$	$_h\bar{P}(\bar{A}_{x:\overline{n}\|}) = \dfrac{\bar{A}_{x:\overline{n}\|}}{\bar{a}_{x:\overline{h}\|}}$
n-Year pure endowment	0 $1\, v^n$	$\bar{a}_{\overline{T}\|},\ T \leq n$ $\bar{a}_{\overline{n}\|},\ T > n$	$\bar{P}^{\ 1}_{x:\overline{n}\|} = \dfrac{A^{\ 1}_{x:\overline{n}\|}}{\bar{a}_{x:\overline{n}\|}}$
n-Year † deferred whole life annuity	0 $\bar{a}_{\overline{T-n}\|}\, v^n$	$\bar{a}_{\overline{T}\|},\ T \leq n$ $\bar{a}_{\overline{n}\|},\ T > n$	$\bar{P}(_n\|\bar{a}_x) = \dfrac{A^{\,1}_{x:\overline{n}\|}\,\bar{a}_{x+n}}{\bar{a}_{x:\overline{n}\|}}$

*The insurances described in the fourth and fifth rows provide for a premium paying period that is shorter than the period over which death benefits are paid.

†The annuity product described above provides no death benefits and has a level premium with premiums payable for n years. A different, perhaps more realistic, design for an n-year level premium-deferred annuity is given in Example 6.6.2.

Solution:

Using the notation of (4.2.11), we have

$$\text{Var}(L) = \text{Var}\left\{ Z_3 \left[1 + \frac{\bar{P}(\bar{A}_{x:\overline{n}\|})}{\delta} \right] - \frac{\bar{P}(\bar{A}_{x:\overline{n}\|})}{\delta} \right\}.$$

We now use (4.2.10) to obtain

$$\text{Var}(L) = \left[1 + \frac{\bar{P}(\bar{A}_{x:\overline{n}\|})}{\delta} \right]^2 [^2\bar{A}_{x:\overline{n}\|} - (\bar{A}_{x:\overline{n}\|})^2].$$

From the second additional relation given in Table 5.2.1, we have

$$(\delta\, \bar{a}_{x:\overline{n}\|})^{-1} = 1 + \frac{\bar{P}(\bar{A}_{x:\overline{n}\|})}{\delta},$$

which implies that

$$\text{Var}(L) = \frac{{}^{2}\bar{A}_{x:\overline{n}|} - (\bar{A}_{x:\overline{n}|})^{2}}{(\delta\,\bar{a}_{x:\overline{n}|})^{2}}.$$

▼

The two identities, (5.2.8) and (5.2.15), can be used to derive relationships among continuous benefit premiums. For example, starting with (5.2.8),

$$\delta\,\bar{a}_{x} + \bar{A}_{x} = 1,$$

$$\delta + \bar{P}(\bar{A}_{x}) = \frac{1}{\bar{a}_{x}},$$

$$\bar{P}(\bar{A}_{x}) = \frac{1}{\bar{a}_{x}} - \delta$$

$$= \frac{1 - \delta\,\bar{a}_{x}}{\bar{a}_{x}}$$

$$= \frac{\delta\,\bar{A}_{x}}{1 - \bar{A}_{x}}. \tag{6.2.9}$$

Starting with (5.2.14) we obtain

$$\delta\,\bar{a}_{x:\overline{n}|} + \bar{A}_{x:\overline{n}|} = 1,$$

$$\delta + \bar{P}(\bar{A}_{x:\overline{n}|}) = \frac{1}{\bar{a}_{x:\overline{n}|}},$$

$$\bar{P}(\bar{A}_{x:\overline{n}|}) = \frac{1}{\bar{a}_{x:\overline{n}|}} - \delta$$

$$= \frac{1 - \delta\,\bar{a}_{x:\overline{n}|}}{\bar{a}_{x:\overline{n}|}}$$

$$= \frac{\delta\,\bar{A}_{x:\overline{n}|}}{1 - \bar{A}_{x:\overline{n}|}}. \tag{6.2.10}$$

Verbal interpretations of the discrete analogues of (6.2.9) and (6.2.10) are given in Example 6.3.4.

The premiums discussed so far in this section are benefit premiums, those derived from the equivalence principle. We now turn to an example that describes two ways that percentile premiums give unsatisfactory results.

Example 6.2.3

Find the 25th percentile premium for an insured age 55 for the following plans of insurance:
a. 20-year endowment
b. 20-year term
c. 10-year term.

Assume a fully continuous basis with a force of interest, $\delta = 0.06$ and mortality following the Illustrative Life Table.

Solution:

a. The loss function for 20-year endowment insurance is

$$L = v^T - \bar{P}\bar{a}_{\overline{T}|} \qquad T < 20$$

$$= v^{20} - \bar{P}\bar{a}_{\overline{20}|} \qquad T \geq 20$$

and is a nonincreasing function of T. Thus the values of T for which the loss L is to be positive, which are to have probability of 0.25, are those values below $\xi_T^{0.25}$. Since $l_{55} = 86{,}408.60$ and $l_{70.617} = 64{,}806.45$ (by linear interpolation), $\Pr(T < 15.617) = 0.25$. Thus, the premium required by the 25th percentile principle is that which sets the loss at $T = 15.617$ equal to zero and is $v^{15.617}/\bar{a}_{\overline{15.617}|}$ $= 0.03865$.

b. The loss function for 20-year term insurance is

$$L = v^T - \bar{P}\bar{a}_{\overline{T}|} \qquad T < 20$$

$$= \qquad - \bar{P}\bar{a}_{\overline{20}|} \qquad T \geq 20.$$

This is still a nonincreasing function of T, and since $\Pr(T < 15.617) = 0.25$, the premium required by the 25th percentile principle is again $v^{15.617}/\bar{a}_{\overline{15.617}|} = 0.03865$. It is, of course, unsatisfactory that the same premium is generated for two different plans of insurance, particularly since the benefit premium at this age for 20-year endowment is almost two times that for 20-year term.

c. The loss function for a 10-year term insurance is

$$L = v^T - \bar{P}\bar{a}_{\overline{T}|} \qquad T < 10$$

$$= - \bar{P}\bar{a}_{\overline{10}|} \qquad T \geq 10.$$

If the premium is set at zero, then $\Pr(L > 0) = \Pr(T < 10)$, and this probability equals, by the Illustrative Life Table,

$$\frac{(l_{55} - l_{65})}{l_{55}} = 0.1281.$$

Thus, zero is the least non-negative annual premium such that the insurer's probability of financial loss is at most 0.25. In this case $\Pr(L > 0) = 0.1281$, and $\bar{P} = 0$ the 25th percentile premium. The benefit premium in this case is 70% of that for 20-year term insurance. ▼

The conclusion from this example is that the percentile premium principle yields conflicting results for insurances on a single individual. Its use will be minimal in what follows.

For a whole life insurance, as defined in the first row of Table 6.2.1,

$$L = v^T - \bar{P}\bar{a}_{\overline{T}|} \qquad T \geq 0.$$

The d.f. of L can be developed as follows:

$$F_L(u) = \Pr(L \le u)$$

$$= \Pr\left[v^T - \bar{P}\left(\frac{1 - v^T}{\delta}\right) \le u\right]$$

$$= \Pr\left(v^T \le \frac{\delta u + \bar{P}}{\delta + \bar{P}}\right)$$

$$= \Pr\left[T \ge -\frac{1}{\delta}\log\left(\frac{\delta u + \bar{P}}{\delta + \bar{P}}\right)\right]$$

$$= 1 - F_T\left(-\frac{1}{\delta}\log\left[\frac{\delta u + \bar{P}}{\delta + \bar{P}}\right]\right) \qquad -\frac{\bar{P}}{\delta} < u. \qquad (6.2.11)$$

The p.d.f. of L is

$$\frac{d}{du}F_L(u) = f_L(u) = f_T\left(-\frac{1}{\delta}\log\left[\frac{\delta u + \bar{P}}{\delta + \bar{P}}\right]\right)\left(\frac{1}{\delta u + \bar{P}}\right) \qquad -\frac{\bar{P}}{\delta} < u. \qquad (6.2.12)$$

Using the language of decision analysis, we can say that the determination of the premium $\bar{P}$ is equivalent to selecting the distribution of L, given by (6.2.11), that is optimal from the viewpoint of the premium principle adopted by the decision maker. This principle reflects the preferences of the decision maker.

Schematic diagrams of $l(t)$, the p.d.f. of $T(x)$, and the induced p.d.f. of L are combined in Figure 6.2.1.

The set of d.f.'s of L is indexed by the parameter $\bar{P}$. The value of $\bar{P}$ is selected by the premium principle adopted. For illustration, use Figure 6.2.1 where $\Pr(T \le c) = \Pr(L > 0)$ and this probability is taken as 0.25. We assume that the

FIGURE 6.2.1
Schematic Diagrams of $l(t)$ and the p.d.f.'s of $T(x)$ and L

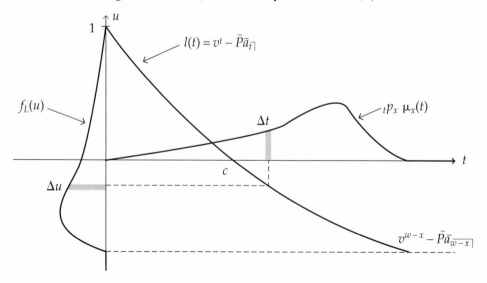

value of $\bar{P}$ will be obtained by solving $F_L(0) = 1 - 0.25 = 0.75$. This illustration uses a percentile premium principle with the probability for a positive value of L set at 0.25.

It is evident from Figure 6.2.1 that the events $(T \le c)$ and $(L > 0)$ are equivalent in the sense that the occurrence of one of the two events implies the occurrence of the other. To continue our illustration, if the decision maker has adopted the percentile premium principle with $\Pr(L > 0) = p$, then $\Pr(T \le c) = p$, where $c = \xi^p_T$, the $100p$-th percentile of the distribution of T. Furthermore, because of the equivalence of these two events, the premium can be determined from an equation involving the loss function, that is, from

$$v^{\xi^p_T} - \bar{P}\bar{a}_{\overline{\xi^p_T}|} = 0,$$

or

$$\bar{P} = \frac{v^{\xi^p_T}}{\bar{a}_{\overline{\xi^p_T}|}} = \frac{1}{\bar{s}_{\overline{\xi^p_T}|}}. \tag{6.2.13}$$

Because $\bar{P}$ is the rate of payment into a fund that will provide a unit payment at time ξ^p_T, there is intuitive support for the result. The accumulation $\bar{s}_{\overline{T}|}/\bar{s}_{\overline{\xi^p_T}|}$ will be less than 1 with probability p and greater than 1 with probability $1 - p$.

Example 6.2.4

This example builds on Example 6.2.3, except that $T(55)$ has a De Moivre distribution, with p.d.f.

$$_tp_{55}\,\mu_{55}(t) = 1/45 \qquad 0 < t < 45.$$

For the three loss variables, display the d.f. of L and determine the parameter $\bar{P}$ as the smallest non-negative number such that $\Pr(L > 0) \le 0.25$.

Solution:

a. Adapting (6.2.11), with recognition of the jump in the d.f. at $u = v^{20} - \bar{P}\bar{a}_{\overline{20}|}$ induced by the constraint on L if $T \ge 20$, we have the following set of d.f.'s indexed by $\bar{P}$:

$$F_L(u) = 0 \qquad\qquad\qquad\qquad\qquad u < v^{20} - \bar{P}\bar{a}_{\overline{20}|}$$

$$= 1 + \frac{1}{0.06} \frac{\log\,[(0.06u + \bar{P})/(0.06 + \bar{P})]}{45} \qquad v^{20} - \bar{P}\bar{a}_{\overline{20}|} \le u \le 1$$

$$= 1 \qquad\qquad\qquad\qquad\qquad\qquad 1 < u.$$

Figure 6.2.2a is a diagram of the d.f. associated with a 20-year endowment insurance. This figure provides a graphical way of thinking of premium determination using the percentile principle. The d.f. within the set of d.f.'s indexed by $\bar{P}$ that crosses the vertical axis at 0.75 is sought. Analytically this means that the premium is determined by solving, for $\bar{P}$,

---

$$F_L(0) = 0.75$$

$$= 1 + \frac{1}{0.06} \frac{\log[\bar{P}/(0.06 + \bar{P})]}{45} = 0.75,$$

or

$$\log\left(\frac{\bar{P}}{0.06 + \bar{P}}\right) = -0.675,$$

and

$$\bar{P} = \frac{0.06e^{-0.675}}{(1 - e^{-0.675})}$$

$$= \frac{1}{\bar{s}_{\overline{11.25}|}}$$

$$= 0.06224.$$

In view of the discussion about (6.2.11), this is not surprising. The 25th percentile of the De Moivre distribution of T in this example is $\xi_T^{0.25} = 11.25$.

FIGURE 6.2.2

Distribution Functions of L Developed in Example 6.2.4

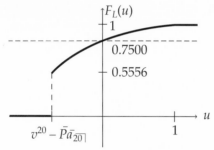

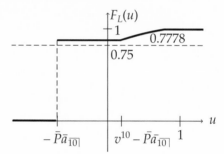

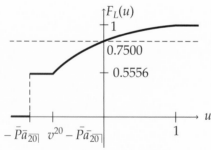

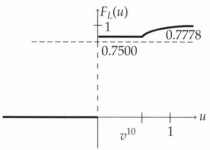

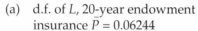

(a) d.f. of L, 20-year endowment insurance $\bar{P} = 0.06244$

(b) d.f. of L, 20-year term insurance $\bar{P} = 0.06244$

(c) d.f. of 10-year term insurance $\bar{P} = 0.06244$

(d) d.f. of 10-year term insurance $\bar{P} = 0$

For comparison, the benefit, or equivalence principle, premium is

$$\bar{P}(\bar{A}_{55:\overline{20|}}) = \frac{\int_0^{20} (v^t/45)\, dt + (25/45)\, v^{20}}{\int_0^{20} v^t\, [1 - (t/45)]\, dt} = 0.04456.$$

b. Adapting (6.2.11) with recognition of the jump in the d.f. of L at $u = -\bar{P}\bar{a}_{\overline{20|}}$, induced by the constraint on the 20-year term insurance loss variable, we have the following set of d.f.'s indexed by $\bar{P}$:

$$F_L(u) = 0 \qquad\qquad\qquad\qquad\qquad u < -\bar{P}\bar{a}_{\overline{20|}}$$

$$= \frac{25}{45} \qquad\qquad\qquad\qquad -\bar{P}\bar{a}_{\overline{20|}} \le u \le v^{20} - \bar{P}\bar{a}_{\overline{20|}}$$

$$= 1 + \frac{1}{0.06}\, \frac{\log\,[(0.06u + \bar{P})/(0.06 + \bar{P})]}{45} \qquad v^{20} - \bar{P}\bar{a}_{\overline{20|}} < u \le 1$$

$$= 1 \qquad\qquad\qquad\qquad\qquad\qquad 1 < u.$$

A diagram of the d.f. associated with a 20-year term insurance is shown in Figure 6.2.2b. The premium is determined by solving $F_L(0) = 0.75$ for $\bar{P}$. Using part (a) we find, once more, that $\bar{P} = 0.06224$.

c. Adapting (6.2.11), with recognition of the jump in the d.f. at $u = -\bar{P}\bar{a}_{\overline{10|}}$ induced by the constraint on L for 10-year term insurance, we have the family of d.f.'s indexed by $\bar{P}$:

$$F_L(u) = 0 \qquad\qquad\qquad\qquad\qquad u < -\bar{P}\bar{a}_{\overline{10|}}$$

$$= \frac{35}{45} \qquad\qquad\qquad\qquad -\bar{P}\bar{a}_{\overline{10|}} \le u \le v^{10} - \bar{P}\bar{a}_{\overline{10|}}$$

$$= 1 + \frac{1}{0.06}\, \frac{\log\,[(0.06u + \bar{P})/(0.06 + \bar{P})]}{45} \qquad v^{10} - \bar{P}\bar{a}_{\overline{10|}} < u \le 1$$

$$= 1 \qquad\qquad\qquad\qquad\qquad\qquad 1 < u.$$

It is tempting to conjecture that $\bar{P} = 0.06224$, as it was in parts (a) and (b), when we observe that the only nonconstant values of the d.f. have the same formula as in the earlier parts of this example. When we observe that for any u in the interval $(-\bar{P}\bar{a}_{\overline{10|}}, v^{10} - \bar{P}\bar{a}_{\overline{10|}})$, $F_L(u) = 35/45 > 0.75$, it appears that the conjecture is wrong. Figure 6.2.2c displays the d.f. of L when $\bar{P} = 0.06224$ and confirms this judgment. As in Example 6.2.3, try $\bar{P} = 0$. The corresponding d.f. of L is

$$F_L(u) = 0 \qquad\qquad\qquad u < 0$$

$$= \frac{35}{45} \qquad\qquad\qquad 0 \le u \le v^{10}$$

$$= 1 + \frac{1}{0.06}\, \frac{\log u}{45} \qquad v^{10} < u \le 1$$

$$= 1 \qquad\qquad\qquad\qquad 1 < u$$

and the probability of a positive value of L is

$$\Pr(L > 0) = \frac{10}{45} < 0.25.$$

This is illustrated in Figure 6.2.2d.

As in Example 6.2.3c, the specifications for applying the percentile premium principle leads to $\bar{P} = 0$, an anomalous result from a business perspective. ▼

6.3 Fully Discrete Premiums

In Section 6.2 we have discussed the theory of fully continuous benefit premiums. In this section we consider annual premium insurances like the one that appeared in Example 6.1.1; that is, the sum insured is payable at the end of the policy year in which death occurs, and the first premium is payable when the insurance is issued. Subsequent premiums are payable on anniversaries of the policy issue date while the insured survives during the contractual premium payment period. The set of annual premiums form a life annuity-due. This model does not conform to practice but is of historic importance in the development of actuarial theory.

Under these circumstances, the level annual benefit premium for a unit whole life insurance is denoted by P_x, where the absence of $(\bar{A}_x)$ means that the insurance is payable at the end of the policy year of death. The loss for this insurance is

$$L = v^{K+1} - P_x \ddot{a}_{\overline{K+1}|} \qquad K = 0, 1, 2, \ldots . \qquad (6.3.1)$$

The equivalence principle requires that $E[L] = 0$, or

$$E[v^{K+1}] - P_x E[\ddot{a}_{\overline{K+1}|}] = 0,$$

which yields

$$P_x = \frac{A_x}{\ddot{a}_x}. \qquad (6.3.2)$$

This is the discrete analogue of (6.2.4).

Using (5.3.7) in place of (5.2.8) in steps parallel to those taken in obtaining (6.2.7), we obtain

$$\text{Var}(L) = \frac{{}^2A_x - (A_x)^2}{(d\,\ddot{a}_x)^2}. \qquad (6.3.3)$$

Example 6.3.1

If

$$_{k|}q_x = c(0.96)^{k+1} \qquad k = 0, 1, 2, \ldots$$

where $c = 0.04/0.96$ and $i = 0.06$, calculate P_x and $\text{Var}(L)$.

Solution:

First we exhibit the components of (6.3.2),

$$A_x = c \sum_{k=0}^{\infty} (1.06)^{-k-1} (0.96)^{k+1} = 0.40,$$

$$\ddot{a}_x = \frac{1 - A_x}{d} = 10.60.$$

Then using (6.3.2) we obtain

$$P_x = \frac{A_x}{\ddot{a}_x} = 0.0377.$$

For $\text{Var}(L)$, we calculate

$$^2A_x = c \sum_{k=0}^{\infty} [(1.06)^2]^{-k-1} (0.96)^{k+1} = 0.2445.$$

Therefore,

$$\text{Var}(L) = \frac{0.2445 - 0.1600}{[(0.06)(10.60)/(1.06)]^2}$$

$$= 0.2347. \qquad\qquad \blacktriangledown$$

There is a connection between Examples 6.2.1 and 6.3.1. Since

$$_{k|}q_x = \int_k^{k+1} {}_tp_x \, \mu_x(t) \, dt \qquad k = 0, 1, 2, \ldots \qquad\qquad (6.3.4)$$

for the situation described in Example 6.3.1, we have

$$\frac{0.04}{0.96} (0.96)^{k+1} = \int_k^{k+1} {}_tp_x \, \mu_x(t) \, dt.$$

If the force of mortality is a constant, μ, it follows that

$$\frac{0.04}{0.96} (0.96)^{k+1} = e^{-(k+1)\mu} (e^\mu - 1),$$

and then $e^{-\mu} = 0.96$ and $\mu = 0.0408$. The geometric distribution, with p.f.

$$_{k|}q_x = \frac{0.04}{0.96} (0.96)^{k+1},$$

is a discrete version of the exponential distribution with $\mu = 0.0408$. Formula (6.3.4) provides the bridge between the discrete and continuous versions. The fully continuous annual benefit premium corresponding to $P_x = 0.0377$ in Example 6.3.1 would be $\bar{P}(\bar{A}_x) = \mu = 0.0408$.

Continuing to use the equivalence principle, we can determine formulas for annual benefit premiums for a variety of fully discrete life insurances. Our general loss will be

$$ b_{K+1} v^{K+1} - P Y $$

where

- b_{k+1} and v_{k+1} are, respectively, the benefit and discount functions defined in (4.3.1)
- P is a general symbol for an annual premium paid at the beginning of each policy year during the premium paying period while the insured survives and
- Y is a discrete annuity random variable as defined, for example, in connection with (5.3.9).

Application of the equivalence principle yields

$$ E[b_{K+1} v_{K+1} - P Y] = 0, $$

or

$$ P = \frac{E[b_{K+1} v_{K+1}]}{E[Y]}. $$

These ideas are used in Table 6.3.1 to display premium formulas for fully discrete insurances.

Example 6.3.2

Express the variance of the loss, L, associated with an n-year endowment insurance, in terms of actuarial present values (see the third row of Table 6.3.1).

Solution:
We start with the notation of Table 6.3.1. Let

$$ Z = \begin{cases} v^{K+1} & K = 0, 1, \ldots, n - 1 \\ v^n & K = n, n + 1, \ldots. \end{cases} $$

Then we can write, by reference to the third row of Table 6.3.1,

$$ L = Z - P_{x:\overline{n}|} \frac{1 - Z}{d}; $$

therefore we have

$$ \mathrm{Var}(L) = \mathrm{Var}\left[Z \left(1 + \frac{P_{x:\overline{n}|}}{d} \right) - \frac{P_{x:\overline{n}|}}{d} \right]. $$

We can use the rule of moments to find $\mathrm{Var}(Z)$, as indicated in Table 4.3.1, and then obtain

TABLE 6.3.1

Fully Discrete Annual Benefit Premiums

Plan	Loss Components		Premium Formula $P = \dfrac{E[b_{K+1}v_{K+1}]}{E[Y]}$
	$b_{K+1}v_{K+1}$	$P\,Y$ Where Y Is	
Whole life insurance	$1\,v^{K+1}$	$\ddot{a}_{\overline{K+1}},\ K = 0, 1, 2, \ldots$	$P_x = \dfrac{A_x}{\ddot{a}_x}$.
n-Year term insurance	$1\,v^{K+1}$ 0	$\ddot{a}_{\overline{K+1}},\ K = 0, 1, \ldots, n-1$ $\ddot{a}_{\overline{n}},\ K = n, n+1, \ldots$	$P^1_{x:\overline{n}} = \dfrac{A^1_{x:\overline{n}}}{\ddot{a}_{x:\overline{n}}}$
n-Year endowment insurance	$1\,v^{K+1}$ $1\,v^n$	$\ddot{a}_{\overline{K+1}},\ K = 0, 1, \ldots, n-1$ $\ddot{a}_{\overline{n}},\ K = n, n+1, \ldots$	$P_{x:\overline{n}} = \dfrac{A_{x:\overline{n}}}{\ddot{a}_{x:\overline{n}}}$
h-Payment whole life insurance	$1\,v^{K+1}$ $1\,v^{K+1}$	$\ddot{a}_{\overline{K+1}},\ K = 0, 1, \ldots, h-1$ $\ddot{a}_{\overline{h}},\ K = h, h+1, \ldots$	$_hP_x = \dfrac{A_x}{\ddot{a}_{x:\overline{h}}}$
h-Payment, n-year endowment insurance	$1\,v^{K+1}$ $1\,v^{K+1}$ $1\,v^n$	$\ddot{a}_{\overline{K+1}},\ K = 0, 1, \ldots, h-1$ $\ddot{a}_{\overline{h}},\ K = h, \ldots, n-1$ $\ddot{a}_{\overline{h}},\ K = n, n+1, \ldots$	$_hP_{x:\overline{n}} = \dfrac{A_{x:\overline{n}}}{\ddot{a}_{x:\overline{h}}}$
n-Year pure endowment	0 $1\,v^n$	$\ddot{a}_{\overline{K+1}},\ K = 0, 1, \ldots, n-1$ $\ddot{a}_{\overline{n}},\ K = n, n+1, \ldots$	$P^{\ 1}_{x:\overline{n}} = \dfrac{A^{\ 1}_{x:\overline{n}}}{\ddot{a}_{x:\overline{n}}}$
n-Year deferred whole life annuity	0 $\ddot{a}_{\overline{K+1-n}}v^n$	$\ddot{a}_{\overline{K+1}},\ K = 0, 1, \ldots, n-1$ $\ddot{a}_{\overline{n}},\ K = n, n+1, \ldots$	$P(_n|\ddot{a}_x) = \dfrac{A^{\ 1}_{x:\overline{n}}\,\ddot{a}_{x+n}}{\ddot{a}_{x:\overline{n}}}$

$$\text{Var}(L) = \left(1 + \frac{P_{x:\overline{n}}}{d}\right)^2 [^2A_{x:\overline{n}} - (A_{x:\overline{n}})^2].$$

Formula (5.3.13) and the entry from the third row of Table 6.3.1 can be combined as follows:

$$d\,\ddot{a}_{x:\overline{n}} + A_{x:\overline{n}} = 1,$$

$$1 + \frac{P_{x:\overline{n}}}{d} = \frac{1}{d\,\ddot{a}_{x:\overline{n}}}.$$

Therefore, the variance we seek is

$$\frac{^2A_{x:\overline{n}} - (A_{x:\overline{n}})^2}{(d\,\ddot{a}_{x:\overline{n}})^2}. \tag{6.3.5}$$

▼

Example 6.3.3

Consider a 10,000 fully discrete whole life insurance. Let π denote an annual premium for this policy and $L(\pi)$ denote the loss-at-issue random variable for one such policy on the basis of the Illustrative Life Table, 6% interest and issue age 35.

a. Determine the premium, π_a, such that the distribution of $L(\pi_a)$ has mean 0. Calculate the variance of $L(\pi_a)$.

b. Approximate the smallest non-negative premium, π_b, such that the probability is less than 0.5 that the loss $L(\pi_b)$ is positive. Find the variance of $L(\pi_b)$.

c. Determine the premium, π_c, such that the probability of a positive total loss on 100 such independent policies is 0.05 by the normal approximation.

Solution:

a. By the equivalence principle, (6.1.3),

$$\pi_a = 10{,}000\ P_{35} = 10{,}000\ \frac{A_{35}}{\ddot{a}_{35}}$$

$$= \frac{1287.194}{15.39262}$$

$$= 83.62.$$

From (6.3.3)

$$\text{Var}[L(\pi_a)] = (10{,}000)^2\ \frac{{}^2A_{35} - (A_{35})^2}{(d\,\ddot{a}_{35})^2}$$

$$= 10^8\ \frac{0.0348843 - (0.1287194)^2}{[(0.06/1.06)(15.39262)]^2}$$

$$= \frac{1{,}831{,}562}{0.7591295}$$

$$= 2{,}412{,}713.$$

b. We want π_b such that

$$\Pr[L(\pi_b) > 0] < 0.5,$$

or in terms of curtate-future-lifetime, K,

$$\Pr(10{,}000 v^{K+1} - \pi_b\,\ddot{a}_{\overline{K+1}|} > 0) < 0.5.$$

From the Illustrative Life Table, $_{42}p_{35} = 0.5125101$ and $_{43}p_{35} = 0.4808964$. Therefore, if π_b is chosen so that

$$10{,}000 v^{43} - \pi_b\,\ddot{a}_{\overline{43}|} = 0,$$

then $\Pr[L(\pi_b) > 0)] = \Pr(K < 42) < 0.5$. Thus,

$$\pi_b = \frac{10{,}000}{\ddot{s}_{\overline{43}|}} = 50.31.$$

Using the fully discrete analogue of (6.2.6) we can write

$$\text{Var}[L(\pi_b)] = (10{,}000)^2[^2A_{35} - (A_{35})^2]\left(1 + \frac{\pi_b}{10{,}000}\frac{1}{d}\right)^2$$

$$= (1{,}831{,}562)(1.18567)$$

$$= 2{,}171{,}630.$$

c. With a premium π_c, the loss on one policy is

$$L(\pi_c) = 10{,}000v^{K+1} - \pi_c\ddot{a}_{\overline{K+1}|} = \left(10{,}000 + \frac{\pi_c}{d}\right)v^{K+1} - \frac{\pi_c}{d},$$

and its expectation and variance are as follows:

$$E[L(\pi_c)] = \left(10{,}000 + \frac{\pi_c}{d}\right)A_{35} - \frac{\pi_c}{d}$$

$$= (0.1287194)\left(10{,}000 + \frac{\pi_c}{d}\right) - \frac{\pi_c}{d}$$

and

$$\text{Var}[L(\pi_c)] = \left(10{,}000 + \frac{\pi_c}{d}\right)^2[^2A_{35} - (A_{35})^2]$$

$$= \left(10{,}000 + \frac{\pi_c}{d}\right)^2(0.01831562).$$

For each of 100 such policies each loss $L_i(\pi_c)$ is distributed like $L(\pi_c)$, $i = 1$, 2, ..., 100 and

$$S = \sum_{i=1}^{100} L_i(\pi_c)$$

for the total loss on the portfolio. Then

$$E[S] = 100\ E[L(\pi_c)],$$

and, using the assumption of independent policies,

$$\text{Var}(S) = 100\ \text{Var}[L(\pi_c)].$$

To determine π_c so that $\Pr(S > 0) = 0.05$ by the normal approximation, we want

$$\frac{0 - E[S]}{\sqrt{\text{Var}(S)}} = 1.645,$$

$$10\left\{\frac{-E[L(\pi_c)]}{\sqrt{\text{Var}[L(\pi_c)]}}\right\} = 1.645,$$

$$10\left[\frac{-A_{35}[10{,}000 + (\pi_c/d)] + (\pi_c/d)}{[10{,}000 + (\pi_c/d)]\sqrt{^2A_{35} - (A_{35})^2}}\right] = 1.645.$$

Thus

$$\pi_c = 10{,}000\,d\left[\frac{(0.1645)\;\sqrt{^2A_{35} - (A_{35})^2} + A_{35}}{1 - (A_{35} + 0.1645\;\sqrt{^2A_{35} - (A_{35})^2})}\right]$$

$$= 100.66. \qquad \blacktriangledown$$

The two identities, (5.3.7) and (5.3.13), can be used to derive relationships among discrete premiums. For example, starting with (5.3.7), we have for whole life insurances

$$d\,\ddot{a}_x + A_x = 1,$$

$$d + P_x = \frac{1}{\ddot{a}_x},$$

$$P_x = \frac{1}{\ddot{a}_x} - d$$

$$= \frac{1 - d\,\ddot{a}_x}{\ddot{a}_x}$$

$$= \frac{d\,A_x}{1 - A_x}. \qquad (6.3.6)$$

Starting with (5.3.13) we obtain a similar chain of equalities for n-year endowment insurances:

$$d\,\ddot{a}_{x:\overline{n}|} + A_{x:\overline{n}|} = 1,$$

$$d + P_{x:\overline{n}|} = \frac{1}{\ddot{a}_{x:\overline{n}|}},$$

$$P_{x:\overline{n}|} = \frac{1}{\ddot{a}_{x:\overline{n}|}} - d$$

$$= \frac{1 - d\,\ddot{a}_{x:\overline{n}|}}{\ddot{a}_{x:\overline{n}|}}$$

$$= \frac{d\,A_{x:\overline{n}|}}{1 - A_{x:\overline{n}|}}. \qquad (6.3.7)$$

Example 6.3.4

Give interpretations in words of the following equations from the (6.3.6) set:

$$\frac{1}{\ddot{a}_x} = P_x + d \qquad (6.3.8)$$

and

$$P_x = \frac{d\,A_x}{1 - A_x}. \qquad (6.3.9)$$

Solution:

We will use the word equivalent to mean equal in terms of actuarial present value. For (6.3.8), first note that a unit now is equivalent to a life annuity of $\ddot{a}_x^{-1}$ payable at the beginning of each year while (x) survives. A unit now is also equivalent to interest-in-advance of d at the beginning of each year while (x) survives with the repayment of the unit at the end of the year of (x)'s death; that is, $1 = \ddot{a}_x/\ddot{a}_x = d\ddot{a}_x + A_x$. The repayment of the unit at the end of the year of death is, in turn, equivalent to a life annuity-due of P_x while (x) survives. Therefore, the unit now is equivalent to $P_x + d$ at the beginning of each year during the lifetime of (x). Then $\ddot{a}_x^{-1} = P_x + d$, for each side of the equality, represents the annual payment of a life annuity produced by a unit available now.

For (6.3.9), we consider an insured (x) who borrows the single benefit premium A_x for the purchase of a single-premium unit whole life insurance. The insured agrees to pay interest-in-advance in the amount of $d\,A_x$ on the loan at the beginning of each year during survival and to repay the A_x from the unit death benefit at the end of the year of death. In essence, the insured is paying an annual benefit premium of $d\,A_x$ for an insurance of amount $1 - A_x$. Then for a full unit of insurance, the annual benefit premium must be $d\,A_x/(1 - A_x)$. ▼

Similar interpretations exist for corresponding relationships involving endowment insurances as given in the second and fifth equalities in the (6.3.7) set. There is an analogy between (6.3.8), the corresponding formula involving endowment insurances,

$$\ddot{a}_{x:\overline{n}|}^{-1} = P_{x:\overline{n}|} + d,$$

and the interest-only formula

$$\ddot{a}_{\overline{n}|}^{-1} = \ddot{s}_{\overline{n}|}^{-1} + d.$$

Example 6.3.5

Prove and interpret the formula

$$P_{x:\overline{n}|} = {}_nP_x + P_{x:\overline{n}|}^{1}(1 - A_{x+n}). \tag{6.3.10}$$

Solution:

The proof is completed using entries from Table 6.3.1:

$$P_{x:\overline{n}|}\ddot{a}_{x:\overline{n}|} = A_{x:\overline{n}|} = A_{x:\overline{n}|}^{1} + A_{x:\overline{n}|}^{1},$$

$${}_nP_x\ddot{a}_{x:\overline{n}|} = A_x = A_{x:\overline{n}|}^{1} + A_{x:\overline{n}|}^{1} A_{x+n}.$$

By subtraction,

$$(P_{x:\overline{n}|} - {}_nP_x)\ddot{a}_{x:\overline{n}|} = A_{x:\overline{n}|}^{1}(1 - A_{x+n}),$$

from which (6.3.10) follows.

The interpretation is that both $P_{x:\overline{n}|}$ and $_nP_x$ are payable during the survival of (x) to a maximum of n years. During these years, both insurances provide a death benefit of 1 payable at the end of the year of the death of (x). If (x) survives the n years, $P_{x:\overline{n}|}$ provides a maturity benefit of 1, while $_nP_x$ provides whole life insurance without further premiums, that is, an insurance with an actuarial present value of A_{x+n}. Hence, the difference $P_{x:\overline{n}|} - _nP_x$ is the level annual premium for a pure endowment of $1 - A_{x+n}$.   ▼

In practice, life insurances are payable soon after death rather than at the end of the policy year of death, so there is a need for annual payment, semicontinuous benefit premiums. Such premiums, following the same order used in Tables 6.2.1 and 6.3.1, are denoted by $P(\bar{A}_x)$, $P(\bar{A}^1_{x:\overline{n}|})$, $P(\bar{A}_{x:\overline{n}|})$, $_nP(\bar{A}_x)$, and $_nP(\bar{A}_{x:\overline{n}|})$. There is no need for a semicontinuous annual premium n-year pure endowment since no death benefit is involved. The equivalence principle can be applied to produce formulas like those in Table 6.3.1, but with the general symbol A replaced by $\bar{A}$. For example,

$$P(\bar{A}_x) = \frac{\bar{A}_x}{\ddot{a}_x}. \qquad (6.3.11)$$

We observe that the notation for this premium is not $\bar{P}_x$, the annual premium payable continuously for a unit whole life insurance benefit payable at the end of the year of death and equal to $A_x / \bar{a}_x$. If a uniform distribution of deaths is assumed over each year of age, we can use the notations of Section 4.4 to write

$$P(\bar{A}_x) = \frac{i}{\delta} \frac{A_x}{\ddot{a}_x} = \frac{i}{\delta} P_x,$$

$$P(\bar{A}^1_{x:\overline{n}|}) = \frac{i}{\delta} P^1_{x:\overline{n}|},$$

and

$$P(\bar{A}_{x:\overline{n}|}) = \frac{i}{\delta} P^1_{x:\overline{n}|} + P_{x:\overline{n}|}. \qquad (6.3.12)$$

6.4 True *m*-thly Payment Premiums

If premiums are payable m times a policy year, rather than annually, with no adjustment in the death benefit, the resulting premiums are called *true fractional premiums*. Thus $P^{(m)}_x$ denotes the *true level annual benefit premium*, payable in m-thly installments at the beginning of each m-thly period, for a unit whole life insurance payable at the end of the year of death. The symbol $P^{(m)}(\bar{A}_x)$ would have the same interpretation except that the insurance is payable at the moment of death. Typically, m is 2, 4, or 12.

The development in this section stresses the payment of insurance benefits at the end of the policy year of death. Table 6.4.1 specifies the symbols and formulas for true fractional premiums for common life insurances. The premium formulas can be obtained by applying the equivalence principle.

TABLE 6.4.1

True Fractional Benefit Premiums*

Plan	Payment of Benefits	
	At End of Policy Year	At Moment of Death
Whole life insurance	$P_x^{(m)} = \dfrac{A_x}{\ddot{a}_x^{(m)}}$	$P^{(m)}(\bar{A}_x) = \dfrac{\bar{A}_x}{\ddot{a}_x^{(m)}}$
n-Year term insurance	$P_{x:\overline{n}|}^{1\,(m)} = \dfrac{A_{x:\overline{n}|}^1}{\ddot{a}_{x:\overline{n}|}^{(m)}}$	$P^{(m)}(\bar{A}_{x:\overline{n}|}^1) = \dfrac{\bar{A}_{x:\overline{n}|}^1}{\ddot{a}_{x:\overline{n}|}^{(m)}}$
n-Year endowment insurance	$P_{x:\overline{n}|}^{(m)} = \dfrac{A_{x:\overline{n}|}}{\ddot{a}_{x:\overline{n}|}^{(m)}}$	$P^{(m)}(\bar{A}_{x:\overline{n}|}) = \dfrac{\bar{A}_{x:\overline{n}|}}{\ddot{a}_{x:\overline{n}|}^{(m)}}$
h-Payment years, whole life insurance	$_hP_x^{(m)} = \dfrac{A_x}{\ddot{a}_{x:\overline{h}|}^{(m)}}$	$_hP^{(m)}(\bar{A}_x) = \dfrac{\bar{A}_x}{\ddot{a}_{x:\overline{h}|}^{(m)}}$
h-Payment years, n-year endowment insurance	$_hP_{x:\overline{n}|}^{(m)} = \dfrac{A_{x:\overline{n}|}}{\ddot{a}_{x:\overline{h}|}^{(m)}}$	$_hP^{(m)}(\bar{A}_{x:\overline{n}|}) = \dfrac{\bar{A}_{x:\overline{n}|}}{\ddot{a}_{x:\overline{h}|}^{(m)}}$

*The actual amount of each fractional premium, payable m times each policy year, during the premium paying period and the survival of (x), is $P^{(m)}/m$. Note that here h refers to the number of payment years, not to the number of payments.

In some applications it is useful to write the m-thly payment premium as a multiple of the annual premium. This will be illustrated for $_hP_{x:\overline{n}|}^{(m)}$, the premium for a rather general insurance. The resulting formula can be modified to produce premium formulas for other common insurances. From the last row of Table 6.4.1 we have

$$_hP_{x:\overline{n}|}^{(m)} = \frac{A_{x:\overline{n}|}}{\ddot{a}_{x:\overline{h}|}^{(m)}}. \tag{6.4.1}$$

Since

$$A_{x:\overline{n}|} = {}_hP_{x:\overline{n}|}\,\ddot{a}_{x:\overline{h}|},$$

(6.4.1) can be rearranged as

$$_hP_{x:\overline{n}|}^{(m)} = \frac{{}_hP_{x:\overline{n}|}\,\ddot{a}_{x:\overline{h}|}}{\ddot{a}_{x:\overline{h}|}^{(m)}}. \tag{6.4.2}$$

Formula (6.4.2) is used in the next chapter; it expresses the m-thly payment premium as equal to the corresponding annual payment premium times a ratio of annuity values. This ratio can be arranged in various ways each corresponding to a different formula used to express the relationship between $\ddot{a}_{x:\overline{h}|}^{(m)}$ and $\ddot{a}_{x:\overline{h}|}$ (see Exercise 6.14).

Example 6.4.1

a. Calculate the level annual benefit premium payable in semiannual installments for a 10,000, 20-year endowment insurance with proceeds paid at the end of the policy year of death (discrete) issued to (50), on the basis of the Illustrative Life Table with interest at the effective annual rate of 6%.

b. Determine the corresponding premium with proceeds paid at the moment of death (semicontinuous).

For both parts, assume a uniform distribution of deaths in each year of age.

Solution:

a. We require $10,000\, P^{(2)}_{50:\overline{20}|}$. As preliminary steps we calculate

$$d = 0.056603774,$$

$$i^{(2)} = 0.059126028,$$

$$d^{(2)} = 0.057428275,$$

$$\ddot{a}^{(2)}_{\overline{1}|} = 0.98564294,$$

$$s^{(2)}_{\overline{1}|} = 1.01478151,$$

$$\alpha(2) = s^{(2)}_{\overline{1}|}\ddot{a}^{(2)}_{\overline{1}|} = 1.0002122,$$

$$\beta(2) = \frac{s^{(2)}_{\overline{1}|} - 1}{d^{(2)}} = 0.25739081,$$

and the following actuarial present values:

$$\ddot{a}_{50:\overline{20}|} = 11.291832,$$

$$A^{1}_{50:\overline{20}|} = 0.13036536,$$

$$P^{1}_{50:\overline{20}|} = 0.01154510,$$

$$_{20}E_{50} = 0.23047353,$$

$$A_{50:\overline{20}|} = 0.36083889,$$

$$P_{50:\overline{20}|} = 0.03195574.$$

Then, under the assumption of a uniform distribution of deaths for each year of age, the required premium can be calculated by use of (6.4.1), with $x = 50$, $n = 20$, $h = 20$, and $m = 2$. For this purpose, we calculate

$$\ddot{a}^{(2)}_{50:\overline{20}|} = \alpha(2)\ddot{a}_{50:\overline{20}|} - \beta(2)(1 - {}_{20}E_{50}) = 11.096159,$$

and then

$$10,000\, P^{(2)}_{50:\overline{20}|} = 325.19.$$

b. The corresponding semicontinuous premium can be obtained by multiplying the values in (a) by the ratio

$$\frac{P(\bar{A}_{50:\overline{20}|})}{P_{50:\overline{20}|}} = \frac{\bar{A}_{50:\overline{20}|}}{A_{50:\overline{20}|}}.$$

Under the uniform distribution of deaths assumption this ratio is

$$\frac{(i/\delta)\,P_{50:\overline{20}|}^{1} + P_{50:\overline{20}|}^{1}}{P_{50:\overline{20}|}}, \tag{6.4.3}$$

and the result is

$$10{,}000\,P^{(2)}(\bar{A}_{50:\overline{20}|}) = 328.68. \qquad\qquad \blacktriangledown$$

6.5 Apportionable Premiums

A second type of fractional premium is the **apportionable premium.** Here, at death, a refund is made of a portion of the premium related to the length of time between the time of death and the time of the next scheduled premium payment. In practice this may be on a pro rata basis without interest. In this section we consider interest and view the sequence of m-thly premiums as an apportionable life annuity-due in the sense of Section 5.5. The symbols used to denote these level apportionable annual benefit premiums payable m-thly are like the symbols for true fractional premiums on the semicontinuous basis. They differ in that the superscript m is enclosed in braces rather than parentheses, for example, $P^{\{m\}}(\bar{A}_x)$. In view of the premium refund feature, it is natural to assume that the death benefit is payable at the moment of death.

Again, we use an h-payment years, n-year endowment insurance to illustrate the development of formulas for apportionable premiums paid m-thly. The equivalence principle leads to the formulas

$$_hP^{\{m\}}(\bar{A}_{x:\overline{n}|})\,\ddot{a}_{x:\overline{h}|}^{\{m\}} = \bar{A}_{x:\overline{n}|}$$

and

$$_hP^{\{m\}}(\bar{A}_{x:\overline{n}|}) = \frac{\bar{A}_{x:\overline{n}|}}{\ddot{a}_{x:\overline{h}|}^{\{m\}}}. \tag{6.5.1}$$

Utilizing the temporary annuity version of (5.5.4), we obtain

$$_hP^{\{m\}}(\bar{A}_{x:\overline{n}|}) = \frac{\bar{A}_{x:\overline{n}|}}{(\delta/d^{(m)})\bar{a}_{x:\overline{h}|}} = \frac{d^{(m)}}{\delta}\,_h\bar{P}(\bar{A}_{x:\overline{n}|}). \tag{6.5.2}$$

This implies that the m-thly installment is

$$\frac{1}{m}\,_hP^{\{m\}}(\bar{A}_{x:\overline{n}|}) = {}_h\bar{P}(\bar{A}_{x:\overline{n}|})\frac{1 - v^{1/m}}{\delta} = {}_h\bar{P}(\bar{A}_{x:\overline{n}|})\,\bar{a}_{\overline{1/m}|}, \tag{6.5.3}$$

and in particular, for $m = 1$,

$$_hP^{\{1\}}(\bar{A}_{x:\overline{n}|}) = {}_h\bar{P}(\bar{A}_{x:\overline{n}|})\bar{a}_{\overline{1}|}. \tag{6.5.4}$$

Formulas (6.5.3) and (6.5.4) demonstrate that these apportionable premiums are equivalent to fully continuous premiums, discounted for interest to the start of each payment period. Similar formulas exist for other types of insurance. For example, by letting h and $n \to \infty$, (6.5.4) becomes

$$P^{\{1\}}(\bar{A}_x) = \bar{P}(\bar{A}_x)\, \ddot{a}_{\overline{1}|}. \tag{6.5.5}$$

The apportionable benefit premium $P^{\{1\}}(\bar{A}_x)$ and the semicontinuous benefit premium $P(\bar{A}_x)$ are both payable annually at the beginning of each year while (x) survives. Each insurance provides a unit at the death of (x). The two insurances differ only in respect to the refund provided by $P^{\{1\}}(\bar{A}_x)$. Thus, the difference

$$P^{\{1\}}(\bar{A}_x) - P(\bar{A}_x) \tag{6.5.6}$$

is a level annual benefit premium paid at the beginning of each year for the refund-of-premium feature. We verify this assertion about the expression in (6.5.6) in the following analysis.

From (5.5.1), we note that the random variable for the present value of the refund-of-premium feature is

$$\frac{P^{\{1\}}(\bar{A}_x)\, v^T\, \bar{a}_{\overline{K+1-T}|}}{\bar{a}_{\overline{1}|}}$$

where K and T are defined as in Chapter 3. The actuarial present value for this feature is

$$\bar{A}_x^{PR} = P^{\{1\}}(\bar{A}_x)\, \mathrm{E}\!\left[v^T\, \frac{\bar{a}_{\overline{K+1-T}|}}{\bar{a}_{\overline{1}|}} \right].$$

Using (6.5.5) we obtain

$$\bar{A}_x^{PR} = \bar{P}(\bar{A}_x)\, \mathrm{E}\!\left[\frac{v^T - v^{K+1}}{\delta} \right]$$

$$= \bar{P}(\bar{A}_x)\left(\frac{\bar{A}_x - A_x}{\delta} \right). \tag{6.5.7}$$

The level annual benefit premium is then, by the equivalence principle,

$$P(\bar{A}_x^{PR}) = \frac{\bar{P}(\bar{A}_x)(\bar{A}_x - A_x)}{\delta \ddot{a}_x}. \tag{6.5.8}$$

Formula (6.5.7) has the following interpretation: The actuarial present value of the refund feature is the difference between the value of a continuous perpetuity of $\bar{P}(\bar{A}_x)$ per year beginning at the death of (x), and the value of a continuous perpetuity of $\bar{P}(\bar{A}_x)$ payable from the end of the year of death of (x).

We return now to (6.5.6) where, by (6.5.5), we have

$$P^{\{1\}}(\bar{A}_x) - P(\bar{A}_x) = \bar{P}(\bar{A}_x) \frac{d}{\delta} - \frac{\bar{A}_x}{\ddot{a}_x}$$

$$= \bar{P}(\bar{A}_x) \left(\frac{d}{\delta} - \frac{\bar{a}_x}{\ddot{a}_x} \right)$$

$$= \bar{P}(\bar{A}_x) \frac{d\,\ddot{a}_x - \delta\,\bar{a}_x}{\delta\,\ddot{a}_x}$$

$$= \bar{P}(\bar{A}_x) \frac{\bar{A}_x - A_x}{\delta\,\ddot{a}_x}$$

$$= P(\bar{A}_x^{PR}), \qquad\qquad (6.5.9)$$

as obtained in (6.5.8). This confirms our assertion about (6.5.6).

This analysis can be extended to m-thly payment premiums and to other life insurance in addition to whole life. In general,

$$P^{\{m\}}(\bar{A}) - P^{(m)}(\bar{A})$$

is an m-thly payment premium for the refund feature.

Example 6.5.1

If the policy of Example 6.4.1(b) is to have apportionable premiums, what increase occurs in the annual benefit premium?

Solution:

The apportionable annual benefit premium per unit of insurance is given by (6.5.2),

$$P^{\{2\}}(\bar{A}_{50:\overline{20}|}) = \bar{P}(\bar{A}_{50:\overline{20}|}) \frac{d^{(2)}}{\delta} = \frac{\bar{A}_{50:\overline{20}|}}{\bar{a}_{50:\overline{20}|}} \frac{d^{(2)}}{\delta}.$$

Under the assumption of a uniform distribution of deaths in each age interval, this becomes

$$= \frac{(i/\delta)A^{\,1}_{50:\overline{20}|} + A_{50:\overline{20}|}^{\;\;1}}{\alpha(\infty)\ddot{a}_{50:\overline{20}|} - \beta(\infty)(1 - {}_{20}E_{50})} \frac{d^{(2)}}{\delta}$$

$$= \frac{(i/\delta)\,P^{\,1}_{50:\overline{20}|} + P_{50:\overline{20}|}^{\;\;1}}{\alpha(\infty) - \beta(\infty)(P^{\,1}_{50:\overline{20}|} + d)} \frac{d^{(2)}}{\delta}.$$

Here $\alpha(\infty) = \bar{s}_{\overline{1}|}\bar{a}_{\overline{1}|} = i\,d/\delta^2 = 1.00028$, $\beta(\infty) = (\bar{s}_{\overline{1}|} - 1)/\delta = 0.50985$. Using other values available in Example 6.4.1 we find

$$10{,}000\, P^{\{2\}}(\bar{A}_{50:\overline{20}|}) = 329.69.$$

Then the increase in annual premium is

$$10{,}000[P^{(2)}(\bar{A}_{50:\overline{20}|}) - P^{(2)}(\bar{A}_{50:\overline{20}|})] = 1.01,$$

which is the annual benefit premium payable semiannually for the refund feature.

▼

6.6 Accumulation-Type Benefits

The analysis in this section is in terms of annual premiums for insurances payable at the end of the year of death. An analogous development is possible for fully continuous premiums and, with some adjustment, for semicontinuous premiums. We first seek the actuarial present value for an n-year term insurance on (x) for which the sum insured, in case death occurs in year $k + 1$, is $\ddot{s}_{\overline{k+1}|j}$. The present-value random variable of this benefit, at policy issue, is

$$W = \begin{cases} v^{K+1}\ddot{s}_{\overline{K+1}|j} = \dfrac{1}{d_{(j)}}[v^{K+1}(1 + j)^{K+1} - v^{K+1}] & 0 \le K < n \\ 0 & K \ge n \end{cases}$$

where the insurer's present values are computed at interest rate i and $d_{(j)}$ is the discount rate equivalent to interest rate j. The actuarial present value is

$$E[W] = \frac{A'^{1}_{x:\overline{n}|} - A^{1}_{x:\overline{n}|}}{d_{(j)}} \tag{6.6.1}$$

where $A'^{1}_{x:\overline{n}|}$ is calculated at the rate of interest $i' = (i - j)/(1 + j)$.

If $i = j$, then $i' = 0$, and the actuarial present value is

$$\frac{{}_{n}q_x - A^{1}_{x:\overline{n}|}}{d} = \frac{1 - {}_{n}p_x - A_{x:\overline{n}|} + v^{n}\,{}_{n}p_x}{d}$$

$$= \ddot{a}_{x:\overline{n}|} - {}_{n}p_x\,\ddot{a}_{\overline{n}|}$$

$$= \ddot{a}_{x:\overline{n}|} - {}_{n}E_x\,\ddot{s}_{\overline{n}|}. \tag{6.6.2}$$

Formula (6.6.2) indicates that, when $j = i$, this special term insurance is equivalent to an n-year life annuity-due except for the event that (x) survives the n years. Then the term insurance would provide a benefit of zero, whereas the life annuity payments, given survival for n years, would have value $\ddot{s}_{\overline{n}|}$ at time n.

Now let us consider the situation where (x) has the choice of purchasing an n-year unit endowment insurance with an annual premium of $P_{x:\overline{n}|}$ or of establishing a savings fund with deposits of $1/\ddot{s}_{\overline{n}|}$ at the beginning of each of n years and purchasing a special decreasing term insurance. The special insurance will provide, in the event of death in year $k + 1$, the difference,

$$1 - \frac{\ddot{s}_{\overline{k+1}|}}{\ddot{s}_{\overline{n}|}} \qquad k = 0, 1, 2, \ldots, n - 1,$$

between the unit benefit under the endowment insurance and the accumulation in the savings fund. We suppose further that the same interest rate i is applicable in valuing all these transactions. The same benefits are provided by the endowment insurance and by the combination of the special term insurance and the savings fund. Therefore one would anticipate that

(the annual benefit premium $P_{x:\overline{n}|}$ = (the annual benefit premium
   for the endowment insurance)   for the special term insurance)

        + (the annual savings fund deposit $1/\ddot{s}_{\overline{n}|}$).

To verify this conjecture, we consider the present-value random variable for the special decreasing term insurance,

$$\tilde{W} = \begin{cases} v^{K+1}\left(1 - \dfrac{\ddot{s}_{\overline{K+1}|}}{\ddot{s}_{\overline{n}|}}\right) = v^{K+1} - \dfrac{\ddot{a}_{\overline{K+1}|}}{\ddot{s}_{\overline{n}|}} & 0 \le K < n \\ 0 & K \ge n. \end{cases} \qquad (6.6.3)$$

The actuarial present value of $\tilde{W}$ is denoted by $\tilde{A}^1_{x:\overline{n}|}$ and given by

$$\tilde{A}^1_{x:\overline{n}|} = E[\tilde{W}]$$

$$= A^1_{x:\overline{n}|} - \frac{\ddot{a}_{x:\overline{n}|} - {_n}p_x\,\ddot{a}_{\overline{n}|}}{\ddot{s}_{\overline{n}|}}$$

$$= A^1_{x:\overline{n}|} - \frac{\ddot{a}_{x:\overline{n}|} - {_n}E_x\,\ddot{s}_{\overline{n}|}}{\ddot{s}_{\overline{n}|}}$$

[see (6.6.2)].

The annual benefit premium for the special term insurance is therefore

$$\tilde{P}^1_{x:\overline{n}|} = \frac{\tilde{A}^1_{x:\overline{n}|}}{\ddot{a}_{x:\overline{n}|}} = P^1_{x:\overline{n}|} - \frac{1}{\ddot{s}_{\overline{n}|}} + P_{x:\overline{n}|}^{1}$$

$$= P_{x:\overline{n}|} - \frac{1}{\ddot{s}_{\overline{n}|}},$$

and then

$$P_{x:\overline{n}|} = \tilde{P}^1_{x:\overline{n}|} + \frac{1}{\ddot{s}_{\overline{n}|}}. \qquad (6.6.4)$$

We have already seen that

$$P_{x:\overline{n}|} = P^1_{x:\overline{n}|} + P_{x:\overline{n}|}^{1},$$

and now (6.6.4) provides an alternative decomposition of $P_{x:\overline{n}|}$. The components are the annual premium for the special term insurance and the annual savings fund deposits, $1/\ddot{s}_{\overline{n}|}$, which accumulate to one at the end of n years.

Example 6.6.1

Derive formulas for the annual benefit premium for a 5,000, 20-year term insurance on (x) providing, in case of death within the 20 years, the return of the annual benefit premiums paid:

a. Without interest

b. Accumulated at the interest rate used in the determination of premiums.

In each case, the return of premiums is in addition to the 5,000 sum insured and benefit payments are made at the end of the year of death.

Solution:

a. Let π_a be the benefit premium. Then

$$\pi_a \, \ddot{a}_{x:\overline{20|}} = 5{,}000 \, A^1_{x:\overline{20|}} + \pi_a (IA)^1_{x:\overline{20|}}$$

and

$$\pi_a = 5{,}000 \, \frac{A^1_{x:\overline{20|}}}{\ddot{a}_{x:\overline{20|}} - (IA)^1_{x:\overline{20|}}}.$$

b. Let π_b be the benefit premium. We use (6.6.2) to obtain

$$\pi_b \, \ddot{a}_{x:\overline{20|}} = 5{,}000 \, A^1_{x:\overline{20|}} + \pi_b (\ddot{a}_{x:\overline{20|}} - {}_{20}E_x \, \ddot{s}_{\overline{20|}}),$$

$$\pi_b \, {}_{20}E_x \ddot{s}_{\overline{20|}} = 5{,}000 \, A^1_{x:\overline{20|}},$$

$$\pi_b = 5{,}000 \, \frac{A^1_{x:\overline{20|}}}{{}_{20}E_x \, \ddot{s}_{\overline{20|}}}$$

$$= 5{,}000 \, \frac{A^1_{x:\overline{20|}}}{{}_{20}p_x \, \ddot{a}_{\overline{20|}}}.$$

In practice, annual contract premiums would be refunded, and the formulas would take this into account. ▼

Example 6.6.2

A deferred annuity issued to (x) for an annual income of 1 commencing at age $x + n$ is to be paid for by level annual benefit premiums during the deferral period. The benefit for death during the premium paying period is the return of annual benefit premiums accumulated with interest at the rate used for the premium. Assuming the death benefit is paid at the end of the year of death, determine the annual benefit premium.

Solution:

Equating the actuarial present value of the annual benefit premiums, π, to the actuarial present value of the benefits, we have

$$\pi \ddot{a}_{x:\overline{n|}} = {}_nE_x \, \ddot{a}_{x+n} + \pi(\ddot{a}_{x:\overline{n|}} - {}_nE_x \, \ddot{s}_{\overline{n|}})$$

where the second term on the right-hand side comes from (6.6.2). Solving for π yields

$$\pi = \frac{\ddot{a}_{x+n}}{\ddot{s}_{\overline{n|}}}.$$

▼

6.7 Notes and References

Lukacs (1948) provides a survey of the development of the equivalence principle. Premiums derived by an application of the equivalence principle are often called actuarial premiums in the literature of the economics of uncertainty. Gerber (1976, 1979) discussed exponential premiums and reserves; these were illustrated in Example 6.1.1 under Principle III. Fractional premiums of various types are important in practice. Scher (1974) has discussed developments in this area, namely, the relations among fully continuous, apportionable, and semicontinuous premiums. The decomposition of an endowment insurance premium appeared in a paper by Linton (1919).

Exercises

Section 6.1

6.1. Calculate the expectation and the variance of the present value of the financial loss for the insurance in Example 6.1.1, when the premium is determined by Principle I.

6.2. Verify that the exponential premium (with $\alpha = 0.1$) for the insurance in Example 6.1.1, modified so that the benefit amount is 10, is 3.45917. (Note that this is roughly 11.3 times as large as the exponential premium for a benefit amount of 1 found in Example 6.1.1.)

6.3. Using the assumptions of Example 6.1.1, determine the annual premium that maximizes the expected utility of an insurer with initial wealth $w = 10$ and utility function $u(x) = x - 0.01x^2$, $x < 50$. [Hint: Use (1.3.6), $w - 0.01w^2 = E[(w - L) - 0.01(w - L)^2]$.]

Section 6.2

6.4. A fully continuous whole life insurance with unit benefit has a level premium. The time-until-death random variable, $T(x)$, has an exponential distribution with $E[T(x)] = 50$ and the force of interest is $\delta = 0.06$.
   a. If the principle of equivalence is used, find the benefit premium rate.
   b. Find the premium rate if it is to be such that $\Pr(L > 0) = 0.50$.
   c. Repeat part (b) if the force of interest, δ, equals 0.

6.5. If the force of mortality strictly increases with age, show that $\bar{P}(\bar{A}_x) > \mu_x(0)$. [Hint: Show that $\bar{P}(\bar{A}_x)$ is a weighted average of $\mu_x(t)$, $t > 0$.]

6.6. Following Example 6.2.1, derive a general expression for

$$\frac{{}^2\bar{A}_x - (\bar{A}_x)^2}{(\delta \bar{a}_x)^2}$$

where $\mu_x(t) = \mu$ and δ is the force of interest for $t > 0$.

6.7. If $\delta = 0$, show that

$$\bar{P}(\bar{A}_x) = \frac{1}{\overset{\circ}{e}_x}.$$

6.8. Prove that the variance of the loss associated with a single premium whole life insurance is less than the variance of the loss associated with an annual premium whole life insurance. Assume immediate payment of claims on death and continuous payment of benefit premiums.

6.9. Show that

$$\left(1 + \frac{d\bar{a}_x}{dx}\right) \bar{P}(\bar{A}_x) - \frac{d\bar{A}_x}{dx} = \mu(x).$$

Section 6.3

6.10. On the basis of the Illustrative Life Table and an interest rate of 6%, calculate values for the annual premiums in the following table. Note any patterns of inequalities that appear in the matrix of results.

Fully Continuous	Semicontinuous	Fully Discrete
$\bar{P}(\bar{A}_{35:\overline{10|}})$	$P(\bar{A}_{35:\overline{10|}})$	$P_{35:\overline{10|}}$
$\bar{P}(\bar{A}_{35:\overline{30|}})$	$P(\bar{A}_{35:\overline{30|}})$	$P_{35:\overline{30|}}$
$\bar{P}(\bar{A}_{35:\overline{60|}})$	$P(\bar{A}_{35:\overline{60|}})$	$P_{35:\overline{60|}}$
$\bar{P}(\bar{A}_{35})$	$P(\bar{A}_{35})$	P_{35}
$\bar{P}(\bar{A}^{1}_{35:\overline{30|}})$	$P(\bar{A}^{1}_{35:\overline{30|}})$	$P^{1}_{35:\overline{30|}}$
$\bar{P}(\bar{A}^{1}_{35:\overline{10|}})$	$P(\bar{A}^{1}_{35:\overline{10|}})$	$P^{1}_{35:\overline{10|}}$

6.11. Show that

$$_{20}P^{1}_{x:\overline{30|}} - P^{1}_{x:\overline{20|}} = {}_{20}P(_{20|10}A_x).$$

6.12. Generalize Example 6.3.1 where

$$_{k|}q_x = (1 - r)r^k \qquad k = 0, 1, 2, \ldots;$$

that is, derive expressions in terms of r and i for A_x, $\ddot{a}_x$, P_x, and $[^2A_x - (A_x)^2]/(d\,\ddot{a}_x)^2$.

Section 6.4

6.13. Using the information given in Example 6.4.1, calculate the value $P^{(2)}_{50}$.

6.14. Using various formulas for $\ddot{a}^{(m)}_{x:\overline{n|}}$, first under the assumption of a uniform distribution of deaths in each year of age, show that the ratio

$$\frac{\ddot{a}_{x:\overline{h|}}}{\ddot{a}^{(m)}_{x:\overline{h|}}}$$

in (6.4.2) can be expressed as the reciprocal of each of (a) and (b). As an alternative, if the development of (5.4.10) is followed show that the ratio is the reciprocal of (c).

a. $\ddot{a}_{\overline{1}|}^{(m)} - \beta(m)P_{x:\overline{h}|}^1$

b. $\alpha(m) - \beta(m)(P_{x:\overline{h}|}^1 + d)$

c. $1 - \dfrac{m-1}{2m}(P_{x:\overline{h}|}^1 + d)$.

6.15. Refer to Example 6.4.1(b) and directly calculate

$$P^{(2)}(\bar{A}_{50:\overline{20}|}) = \frac{\bar{A}_{50:\overline{20}|}}{\ddot{a}_{50:\overline{20}|}^{(2)}}$$

using the Illustrative Life Table for the actuarial present values in the numerator and the denominator.

6.16. If

$$\frac{P_{x:\overline{20}|}^{1\,(12)}}{P_{x:\overline{20}|}^1} = 1.032$$

and $P_{x:\overline{20}|} = 0.040$, what is the value of $P_{x:\overline{20}|}^{(12)}$?

Section 6.5

6.17. Arrange in order of magnitude and indicate your reasoning:
$P^{(2)}(\bar{A}_{40:\overline{25}|})$, $\bar{P}(\bar{A}_{40:\overline{25}|})$, $P^{\{4\}}(\bar{A}_{40:\overline{25}|})$, $P(\bar{A}_{40:\overline{25}|})$, $P^{\{12\}}(\bar{A}_{40:\overline{25}|})$.

6.18. Given that

$$\frac{d}{d^{(12)}} = \frac{99}{100},$$

evaluate

$$\frac{P^{\{12\}}(\bar{A}_x)}{P^{\{1\}}(\bar{A}_x)}.$$

6.19. If $\bar{P}(\bar{A}_x) = 0.03$, and if interest is at the effective annual rate of 5%, calculate the semiannual benefit premium for a 50,000 whole life insurance on (x) where premiums are apportionable.

6.20. Show that

$$P^{\{m\}}(\bar{A}_{x:\overline{n}|}) - P^{(m)}(\bar{A}_{x:\overline{n}|}) = \bar{P}(\bar{A}_{x:\overline{n}|})\left(\frac{\bar{A}_{x:\overline{n}|} - A_{x:\overline{n}|}^{(m)}}{\delta\,\ddot{a}_{x:\overline{n}|}^{(m)}}\right)$$

$$= \bar{P}(\bar{A}_{x:\overline{n}|})\left(\frac{\bar{A}_{x:\overline{n}|}^1 - A_{x:\overline{n}|}^{1\,(m)}}{\delta\,\ddot{a}_{x:\overline{n}|}^{(m)}}\right).$$

6.21. Express

$$1 - \frac{\ddot{s}_{\overline{20}|}}{\ddot{s}_{45:\overline{20}|}}$$

as an annual premium. Interpret your result.

6.22. On the basis of the Illustrative Life Table and an interest rate of 6%, calculate the components of the two decompositions

a. $1,000 \, P_{50:\overline{20}|} = 1,000(P^1_{50:\overline{20}|} + P_{50:\overline{20}|}^{1})$

b. $1,000 \, P_{50:\overline{20}|} = 1,000 \left(\tilde{P}^1_{50:\overline{20}|} + \frac{1}{\ddot{s}_{\overline{20}|}} \right).$

6.23. Consider the continuous random variable analogue of (6.6.3),

$$\tilde{\tilde{W}} = \begin{cases} v^T \left(1 - \dfrac{\bar{s}_{\overline{T}|}}{\bar{s}_{\overline{n}|}} \right) & 0 \le T < n \\[2ex] 0 & T \ge n. \end{cases}$$

The loss,

$$L = \tilde{\tilde{W}} - \tilde{\bar{A}}^1_{x:\overline{n}|},$$

can be used with the equivalence principle to determine $\tilde{\bar{A}}^1_{x:\overline{n}|}$, the single benefit premium for this special policy. Show that

a. $\tilde{\bar{A}}^1_{x:\overline{n}|} = \bar{A}^1_{x:\overline{n}|} - \dfrac{\bar{a}_{x:\overline{n}|} - {}_np_x \, \bar{a}_{\overline{n}|}}{\bar{s}_{\overline{n}|}}$

b. $E[\tilde{\tilde{W}}^2] = \dfrac{(1 + i)^{2n} \, {}^2\bar{A}^1_{x:\overline{n}|} - 2(1 + i)^n \, \bar{A}^1_{x:\overline{n}|} + (1 - {}_np_x)}{[(1 + i)^n - 1]^2}.$

Miscellaneous

6.24. Express

$$A_{40} \, P_{40:\overline{25}|} + (1 - A_{40})P_{40}$$

as an annual benefit premium.

6.25. a. Show that

$$\frac{1}{\ddot{a}_{65:\overline{10}|}} - \frac{1}{\ddot{s}_{65:\overline{10}|}} = P^1_{65:\overline{10}|} + d.$$

b. What is the corresponding formula for

$$\frac{1}{\ddot{a}^{(12)}_{65:\overline{10}|}} - \frac{1}{\ddot{s}^{(12)}_{65:\overline{10}|}}?$$

c. Show that the amount of annual income provided by a single benefit premium of 100,000 where
   - The income is payable at the beginning of each month while (65) survives during the next 10 years, and

- The single premium is returned at the end of 10 years if (65) reaches age 75,

is given by

$$100,000 \left(\frac{1}{\ddot{a}_{65:\overline{10}|}^{(12)}} - \frac{1}{\ddot{s}_{65:\overline{10}|}^{(12)}} \right) = 100,000(\beta)$$

where (β) denotes the answer to part (b) of this exercise.

6.26. An insurance issued to (35) with level premiums to age 65 provides
- 100,000 in case the insured survives to age 65, and
- The return of the annual contract premiums with interest at the valuation rate to the end of the year of death if the insured dies before age 65.
If the annual contract premium G is 1.1π where π is the annual benefit premium, write an expression for π.

6.27. If $_{15}P_{45} = 0.038$, $P_{45:\overline{15}|} = 0.056$, and $A_{60} = 0.625$, calculate $P^1_{45:\overline{15}|}$.

6.28. A 20-payment life policy is designed to return, in the event of death, 10,000 plus all contract premiums without interest. The return-of-premium feature applies both during the premium paying period and after. Premiums are annual and death claims are paid at the end of the year of death. For a policy issued to (x), the annual contract premium is to be 110% of the benefit premium plus 25. Express in terms of actuarial present-value symbols the annual contract premium.

6.29. Express in terms of actuarial present-value symbols the initial annual benefit premium for a whole life insurance issued to (25), subject to the following provisions:
- The face amount is to be one for the first 10 years and two thereafter.
- Each premium during the first 10 years is 1/2 of each premium payable thereafter.
- Premiums are payable annually to age 65.
- Claims are paid at the end of the year of death.

6.30. Let L_1 be the insurer's loss on a unit of whole life insurance, issued to (x) on a fully continuous basis. Let L_2 be the loss to (x) on a continuous life annuity purchased for a single premium of one. Show that $L_1 \equiv L_2$ and give an explanation in words.

6.31. An ordinary life contract for a unit amount on a fully discrete basis is issued to a person age x with an annual premium of 0.048. Assume $d = 0.06$, $A_x = 0.4$, and $^2A_x = 0.2$. Let L be the insurer's loss function at issue of this policy.
   a. Calculate E[L].
   b. Calculate Var(L).

c. Consider a portfolio of 100 policies of this type with face amounts given below.

Face Amount	Number of Policies
1	80
4	20

Assume the losses are independent and use a normal approximation to calculate the probability that the present value of gains for the portfolio will exceed 20.

6.32. Express, in terms of actuarial present-value symbols, the initial annual benefit premium for a unit of whole life insurance for (x) if after 5 years the annual benefit premium is double that payable during the first 5 years. Assume that death claims are made at the moment of death.

6.33. Repeat Exercise 6.20 for h-payment whole life insurance.

6.34. The function $l(t)$ is given by (6.2.1).
   a. Establish that $l''(t) \geq 0$.
   b. Adapt Jensen's inequality from Section 1.3 to establish that if $\bar{P} = \bar{P}(\bar{A}_x)$, then $\bar{P}(\bar{A}_x) \geq v^{\overset{\circ}{e}_x}/\bar{a}_{\overline{\overset{\circ}{e}_x}|}$.

6.35. If $T(x)$ has an exponential distribution with parameter μ,
   a. Exhibit the p.d.f. of L as shown in (6.2.12)
   b. Show that $E[L] = (\mu - \bar{P})/(\mu + \delta)$.
   c. Use part (b) to confirm that $E[L] = 0$ when $\bar{P} = \bar{P}(\bar{A}_x)$.

6.36. Use the assumptions of Exercise 6.35, with $\mu = 0.03$ and $\delta = 0.06$.
   a. Evaluate $\Pr(L \leq 0)$ when $\bar{P} = \bar{P}(\bar{A}_x)$.
   b. Determine $\bar{P}$ so that $\Pr(L > 0) = 0.5$.

BENEFIT RESERVES

7.1 Introduction

In Chapter 6 we introduced several principles that can be used for the determination of benefit premiums. The equivalence principle was used extensively in our discussion in Chapter 6. By it, an equivalence relation is established on the date a long-term contract is entered into by two parties who agree to exchange a set of payments. For example, under an amortized loan, a borrower may pay a series of equal monthly payments equivalent to the single payment by a lender at the date of the loan. An insured may pay a series of benefit premiums to an insurer equivalent, at the date of policy issue, to the sum to be paid on the death of the insured, or on survival of the insured to the maturity date. An individual may purchase a deferred life annuity by means of level premiums payable to an annuity organization equivalent, at the date of contract agreement, to monthly payments by the annuity organization to the individual when that person survives beyond a specified age. Equivalence in the loan example is in terms of present value, whereas in the insurance and annuity examples it is an equivalence between two actuarial present values.

After a period of time, however, there will no longer be an equivalence between the future financial obligations of the two parties. A borrower may have payments remaining to be made, whereas the lending organization has already performed its responsibilities. In other settings both parties may still have obligations. The insured may still be required to pay further benefit premiums, whereas the insurer has the duty to pay the face amount on maturity or the death of the insured. In our deferred annuity example, the individual may have completed the payments, whereas the annuity organization still has monthly remunerations to make.

In this chapter we study payments in time periods beyond the date of initiation. For this, a balancing item is required, and this item is a liability for one of the parties and an asset for the other. In the loan case, the balancing item is the outstanding principal, an asset for the lender and a liability for the borrower. In the other two cases, if the individual continues to survive, the balancing item is called a reserve. This is typically a liability that should be recognized in any financial statement of an insurer or annuity organization, as the case may be. It is also typically an asset for the insured or individual purchasing the annuity.

We illustrate the determination of the balancing item spoken of above by continuation of Example 6.1.1 in the two cases where a utility function was used to define the premium principle.

Example 7.1.1

An insurer has issued a policy paying 1 unit at the end of the year of death in exchange for the payment of a premium P at the beginning of each year, provided the life survives. Assume that the insured is still alive 1 year after entering into the contract. Further, assume that the insurer continues to use $i = 0.06$ and the following mortality assumption for K:

$$_{k|}q_0 = 0.2 \qquad k = 0, 1, 2, 3, 4.$$

Find the reserve, $_1V$, as determined by the following:

a. Principle II: The insurer, using a utility of wealth function $u(x) = x$, will be indifferent between continuing with the risk while receiving premiums of 0.30272 (from Example 6.1.1) and paying the amount $_1V$ to a reinsurer to assume the risk.

b. Principle III: The insurer, using a utility of wealth function $u(x) = -e^{-0.1x}$, will be indifferent between continuing with the risk while receiving premiums of 0.30628 (from Example 6.1.1) and paying the amount $_1V$ to a reinsurer to assume the risk.

Solution:

The conditional probability function for K, the curtate-future-lifetime, given that $K \geq 1$, is

$$\Pr(K = k | K \geq 1) = \frac{\Pr(K = k)}{\Pr(K \geq 1)} = \frac{0.2}{0.8} = 0.25 \qquad k = 1, 2, 3, 4.$$

The present value at duration 1 of the insurer's future financial loss is $_1L = v^{(K-1)+1} - P\,\ddot{a}_{\overline{(K-1)+1}|}$, where P is the premium determined in Example 6.1.1.

a. According to (1.3.1), we seek the amount $_1V$ such that $u(w - {_1V}) = E[u(w - {_1L})|K \geq 1]$. By Principle II $u(x) = x$, so we have

$$w - {_1V} = E[w - {_1L}|K \geq 1] = w - E[{_1L}|K \geq 1].$$

Thus, Principle II is equivalent to requiring that $_1V$ be chosen so that $_1V = E[{_1L}|K \geq 1]$. For this example, this requirement is

$$_1V = \sum_{k=1}^{4} (v^{(k-1)+1} - 0.30272\,\ddot{a}_{\overline{(k-1)+1}|}) \times \Pr(K = k|K \geq 1)$$

$$= \sum_{k=1}^{4} v^{(k-1)+1}\,\Pr(K = k|K \geq 1) - 0.30272\sum_{k=1}^{4} \ddot{a}_{\overline{(k-1)+1}|} \times \Pr(K = k|K \geq 1),$$

$$(7.1.1)$$

which gives $_1V = 0.15111$ as shown in the following calculation.

| Outcome k | Conditional Probability | Present Value (1 Year after Issue) of Future Obligations of | | Insurer's Prospective Loss |
		Insurer	Insured	
1	0.25	$v = 0.94340$	$P\,\ddot{a}_{\overline{1}|} = 0.30272$	0.64067
2	0.25	$v^2 = 0.89000$	$P\,\ddot{a}_{\overline{2}|} = 0.58831$	0.30169
3	0.25	$v^3 = 0.83962$	$P\,\ddot{a}_{\overline{3}|} = 0.85773$	-0.01811
4	0.25	$v^4 = 0.79209$	$P\,\ddot{a}_{\overline{4}|} = 1.11191$	-0.31981
Expected Value		0.86628	0.71517	0.15111

The actuarial present value of the insurer's prospective loss is

$$0.86628 - 0.71517 = 0.15111.$$

b. Again by (1.3.1) and now using the utility function in Principle III, we have

$$-e^{-0.1(w - _1V)} = \mathrm{E}[-e^{-0.1(w - _1L)}|K \geq 1] = -e^{-0.1w}\,\mathrm{E}[e^{0.1_1L}|K \geq 1].$$

Thus, Principle III is equivalent to requiring that $_1V$ be chosen so that $e^{0.1\,_1V} = \mathrm{E}[e^{0.1\,_1L}|K \geq 1]$ or that $_1V = 10\log\mathrm{E}[e^{0.1\,_1L}|K \geq 1]$.

The following table summarizes the calculation of $_1V$ using the premium (0.30628) from part (c) of Example 6.1.1.

Outcome k	Conditional Probability	Insurer's Prospective Loss, $_1L$	$e^{(0.1_1L)}$
1	0.25	0.63712	1.06579
2	0.25	0.29477	1.02992
3	0.25	-0.02819	0.99718
4	0.25	-0.33287	0.96726

Thus, $\mathrm{E}[e^{0.1\,_1L}|K \geq 1] = (1.06579 + 1.02992 + 0.99718 + 0.96726)(0.25) = 1.01504$ and $_1V = (\log 1.01504)/0.1 = 0.14925$. ▼

Henceforth, benefit reserves will be based on benefit premiums as determined by the equivalence principle in part (a) of Example 7.1.1. Thus, the *benefit reserve at time t* is the conditional expectation of the difference between the present value of future benefits and the present value of future benefit premiums, the conditioning event being survivorship of the insured to time t. The type of reserve found in part (b) of Example 7.1.1 is called an *exponential reserve.*

The sections in Chapter 7 parallel sections of Chapter 6 on benefit premiums. We assume, as we do in Example 7.1.1, that the mortality and interest rates adopted at policy issue for the determination of benefit premiums continue to be appropriate and are used in the determination of benefit reserves.

7.2 Fully Continuous Benefit Reserves

We now develop the benefit reserves related to the fully continuous benefit premiums developed in Section 6.2 by application of the equivalence principle.

Let us consider reserves for a whole life insurance of 1 issued to (x) on a fully continuous basis with an annual benefit premium rate of $\bar{P}(\bar{A}_{[x]})$. The corresponding reserve for an insured surviving t years later is defined under the equivalence principle as the conditional expected value of the prospective loss at time t, given that (x) has survived to t. More formally, for $T(x) > t$ the prospective loss is

$$_tL = v^{T(x)-t} - \bar{P}(\bar{A}_{[x]})\,\bar{a}_{\overline{T(x)-t}|}. \tag{7.2.1}$$

The reserve, as a conditional expectation, is calculated using the conditional distribution of the future lifetime at t for a life selected at x, given it has survived to t. In International Actuarial Notation symbols this is

$$_t\bar{V}(\bar{A}_{[x]}) = \mathrm{E}[_tL|T(x) > t]$$

$$= \mathrm{E}[v^{T(x)-t}|T(x) > t] - \bar{P}(\bar{A}_{[x]})\,\mathrm{E}[\bar{a}_{\overline{T(x)-t}|}|T(x) > t]$$

$$= \bar{A}_{[x]+t} - \bar{P}(\bar{A}_{[x]})\,\bar{a}_{[x]+t}. \tag{7.2.2}$$

If the attained age was the only given information at issue of the insurance at age x, or for some other reason an aggregate mortality table is used for the distribution of the future lifetime, then the conditional distribution of $T(x) - t$ is the same as the distribution of $T(x + t)$, and (7.2.2) in symbols is

$$_t\bar{V}(\bar{A}_x) = \bar{A}_{x+t} - \bar{P}(\bar{A}_x)\bar{a}_{x+t}. \tag{7.2.3}$$

Formulas (7.2.2) and (7.2.3) state that

(the benefit reserve) = (the actuarial present value for the
     whole life insurance from age $x + t$)

     − (the actuarial present value of future
     benefit premiums payable after age $x + t$ at an annual rate
     of $\bar{P}(\bar{A}_x)$).

The formulations of $\bar{P}(\bar{A}_x)$ and $_t\bar{V}(\bar{A}_x)$ are related. When $t = 0$, (7.2.3) yields $_0\bar{V}(\bar{A}_x) = 0$. This is a consequence of applying the equivalence principle as of the time the contract was established.

Remark on Notation (Restated):

In this book, we will simplify the appearance of the formulas by suppressing the select notation unless its use is necessary or helpful in the particular situation. The symbol $\mu_x(t)$ will be used for the force of mortality in the development of benefit reserves to reinforce the idea that the conditional distributions used in reserve calculations are derived from the distribution of $T(x)$.

Benefit reserves are defined in Section 7.1 as the conditional expectation of loss variables. In evaluating these conditional expected values in this section, the distribution of $T(x) - t$, given $T(x) > t$, was used. The interest rate and the distribution of $T(x)$ used with the equivalence principle at time $t = 0$ to determine the benefit premium were used again. The survival of the life (x) to time t was the only new information incorporated into the expected value calculation. A comprehensive reserve principle would require that all new information relevant to the loss variables and their distributions be incorporated into the reserve calculation. The objective of this requirement would be to estimate liabilities appropriate for the time that the valuation is made. In Chapters 7 and 8 the process of learning from experience to modify the assumptions under which benefit reserves are estimated are not studied.

By steps analogous to those used to obtain (6.2.6), we can determine the variance of $_tL$ as follows:

$$_tL = v^{T(x)-t}\left[1 + \frac{\bar{P}(\bar{A}_x)}{\delta}\right] - \frac{\bar{P}(\bar{A}_x)}{\delta},\tag{7.2.4}$$

thus

$$\text{Var}[_tL|T(x) > t] = \left[1 + \frac{\bar{P}(\bar{A}_x)}{\delta}\right]^2 \text{Var}[v^{T(x)-t}|T(x) > t]$$

$$= \left[1 + \frac{\bar{P}(\bar{A}_x)}{\delta}\right]^2 [^2\bar{A}_{x+t} - (\bar{A}_{x+t})^2].\tag{7.2.5}$$

Note the relation to (6.2.6) and that the development holds for all premium levels. It is not dependent on the equivalence principle.

Example 7.2.1

Follow up Example 6.2.1 by calculating $_t\bar{V}(\bar{A}_x)$ and Var $[_tL|T(x) > t]$.

Solution:
Since $\bar{A}_x$, $\bar{a}_x$, and $\bar{P}(\bar{A}_x)$ are independent of age x, (7.2.3) becomes

$$_t\bar{V}(\bar{A}_x) = \bar{A}_x - \bar{P}(\bar{A}_x)\,\bar{a}_x = 0 \qquad t \geq 0.$$

In this case, future premiums are always equivalent to future benefits, and no reserve is needed.

Also, in this case, (7.2.5) reduces to

$$\text{Var}[_tL|T(x) > t] = \left[1 + \frac{\bar{P}(\bar{A}_x)}{\delta}\right]^2 [^2\bar{A}_x - (\bar{A}_x)^2] = \text{Var}(L) = 0.25,$$

as in Example 6.2.1. Here the variance of $_tL$ depends on neither the age x nor the duration t. ▼

Example 7.2.2

On the basis of De Moivre's law with $l_x = 100 - x$ and the interest rate of 6%, calculate

a. $\bar{P}(\bar{A}_{35})$

b. $_t\bar{V}(\bar{A}_{35})$ and $\text{Var}[_tL | T(x) > t]$ for $t = 0, 10, 20, \ldots, 60$.

Solution:

a. From $l_x = 100 - x$, we obtain $_tp_{35} = 1 - t/65$ and $_tp_{35}\,\mu(35 + t) = 1/65$ for $0 \le t < 65$. It follows that

$$\bar{A}_{35} = \int_0^{65} v^t \frac{1}{65}\, dt = \frac{\bar{a}_{\overline{65}|0.06}}{65} = 0.258047.$$

Then

$$\bar{P}(\bar{A}_{35}) = \frac{\delta\, \bar{A}_{35}}{1 - \bar{A}_{35}} = 0.020266.$$

b. At age $35 + t$, we have $\bar{A}_{35+t} = \bar{a}_{\overline{65-t}|}/(65 - t)$ and

$$_t\bar{V}(\bar{A}_{35}) = \bar{A}_{35+t} - 0.020266\, \frac{1 - \bar{A}_{35+t}}{\log(1.06)}.$$

Further,

$$^2\bar{A}_{35+t} = \int_0^{65-t} v^{2u} \frac{1}{65 - t}\, du = \frac{^2\bar{a}_{\overline{65-t}|}}{65 - t}$$

and, from (7.2.5),

$$\text{Var}[_tL | T(x) > t] = \left[1 + \frac{0.020266}{\log(1.06)}\right]^2 [^2\bar{A}_{35+t} - (\bar{A}_{35+t})^2].$$

Applying these formulas, we obtain the following results.

t	$_t\bar{V}(\bar{A}_{35})$	$\text{Var}[_tL | T(35) > t]$
0	0.0000	0.1187
10	0.0557	0.1201
20	0.1289	0.1173
30	0.2271	0.1073
40	0.3619	0.0861
50	0.5508	0.0508
60	0.8214	0.0097

Note the convergence of $\text{Var}[_tL | T(35) > t]$ toward zero. There is a rendezvous with certainty. ▼

The table in Example 7.2.2 provides the mean and the variance of the conditional distributions of $_tL$ for selected values of t. To gain more insight into the nature of reserves, let us explore these distributions of $_tL$ in more depth. We previously studied the case for $t = 0$ at (6.2.11) following Example 6.2.3. From (7.2.1),

$$_tL = v^{T(x)-t} - \bar{P}(\bar{A}_x)\,\bar{a}_{\overline{T(x)-t|}}$$

$$= v^{T(x)-t}\left[\frac{\delta + \bar{P}(\bar{A}_x)}{\delta}\right] - \frac{\bar{P}(\bar{A}_x)}{\delta}.\qquad(7.2.6)$$

If $\delta > 0$, $_tL$ is a decreasing function of $T(x) - t$ and lies in the interval

$$-\frac{\bar{P}(\bar{A}_x)}{\delta} < {_tL} \le 1.\qquad(7.2.7)$$

Using Figure 6.2.1 as a guide we can repeat the steps of (6.2.11) to establish the following relationship between $F_{T(x)}(u)$ and the d.f. of the conditional distribution of $_tL$, given $T(x) > t$, which we denote by $F_{_tL}(y)$. For a y in the interval given by (7.2.7),

$$F_{_tL}(y) = \Pr[_tL \le y | T(x) > t]$$

$$= \Pr\left[v^{T(x)-t}\left[\frac{\delta + \bar{P}(\bar{A}_x)}{\delta}\right] - \frac{\bar{P}(\bar{A}_x)}{\delta} \le y \,\Big|\, T(x) > t\right]$$

$$= \Pr\left[v^{T(x)-t} \le \frac{\delta y + \bar{P}(\bar{A}_x)}{\delta + \bar{P}(\bar{A}_x)} \,\Big|\, T(x) > t\right]$$

$$= \Pr\left[T(x) \ge t - \frac{1}{\delta}\log\left[\frac{\delta y + \bar{P}(\bar{A}_x)}{\delta + \bar{P}(\bar{A}_x)}\right] \,\Big|\, T(x) > t\right]$$

$$= \frac{\Pr[T(x) \ge t - (1/\delta)\,\{\log\,[\delta y + \bar{P}(\bar{A}_x)]/[\delta + \bar{P}(\bar{A}_x)]\}]}{\Pr[T(x) > t]}\qquad(7.2.8)$$

$$= \frac{1 - F_{T(x)}(t - (1/\delta)\log\,\{[\delta y + \bar{P}(\bar{A}_x)]/[\delta + \bar{P}(\bar{A}_x)]\})}{1 - F_{T(x)}(t)}.\qquad(7.2.9)$$

Differentiation of (7.2.9) with respect to y derives the p.d.f. for the conditional distribution of $_tL$, given $T(x) > t$:

$$f_{_tL}(y) = \left\{\frac{1}{[\delta y + \bar{P}(\bar{A}_x)][1 - F_{T(x)}(t)]}\right\} f_{T(x)}\left(t - \frac{1}{\delta}\log\left[\frac{\delta y + \bar{P}(\bar{A}_x)}{\delta + \bar{P}(\bar{A}_x)}\right]\right).\qquad(7.2.10)$$

For an aggregate mortality law the conditional distribution of $T(x) - t$, given $T(x) > t$, is the same as the distribution of $T(x + t)$, so (7.2.8), (7.2.9), and (7.2.10) reduce to

$$F_{_tL}(y) = \Pr\left[T(x + t) \ge -\frac{1}{\delta}\log\left[\frac{\delta y + \bar{P}(\bar{A}_x)}{\delta + \bar{P}(\bar{A}_x)}\right]\right]\qquad(7.2.11)$$

$$= 1 - F_{T(x+t)}\left(-\frac{1}{\delta}\log\left[\frac{\delta y + \bar{P}(\bar{A}_x)}{\delta + \bar{P}(\bar{A}_x)}\right]\right),\qquad(7.2.12)$$

$$f_{_tL}(y) = \frac{1}{[\delta y + \bar{P}(\bar{A}_x)]} f_{T(x+t)}\left(-\frac{1}{\delta}\log\left[\frac{\delta y + \bar{P}(\bar{A}_x)}{\delta + \bar{P}(\bar{A}_x)}\right]\right).\qquad(7.2.13)$$

To illustrate these concepts we will extend Example 7.2.2.

Example 7.2.3

For the insurance contract and assumptions in Example 7.2.2:

a. Exhibit the formulas for the d.f. and the p.d.f. of the conditional distribution for $_tL$, given $T(x) > t$.

b. Display graphs of these conditional p.d.f.'s for $t = 0, 20, 40,$ and 60.

Solution:

a. Since Example 7.2.2 specifies an aggregate mortality law, we use formulas (7.2.12) and (7.2.13). In Example 7.2.2,

$$F_{T(35+t)}(u) = \frac{u}{65 - t} \qquad \text{for } 0 \le u \le 65 - t$$

$$= 1 \qquad \text{for } 65 - t < u,$$

$$f_{T(35+t)}(u) = \frac{1}{65 - t} \qquad \text{for } 0 \le u \le 65 - t$$

$$= 0 \qquad \text{elsewhere.}$$

Figure 7.2.1 shows Figure 6.2.1 as it applies to this example. In this figure the outcome space of $T(35 + t)$ is on the u-axis, and the outcome space of the loss random variable, $_tL$, is on the y-axis. The relationship between the outcomes of $T(35 + t)$ and the outcomes of $_tL$ is given by the loss function $y = l_t(u)$ and is indicated by the dashed line connecting u and y in the figure. The p.d.f. $f_{T(35+t)}(u)$ has its domain on the u-axis and its range on the y-axis. The domain of the p.d.f. $f_{tL}(y)$ is on the y-axis, and its range is to be imagined on an axis perpendicular to the u-y plane, but for the sketch it has been laid perpendicular to the y-axis in the u-y plane.

FIGURE 7.2.1

Schematic Diagrams of $l_t(u)$, $f_{T(35+t)}(u)$, and $f_{tL}(y)$

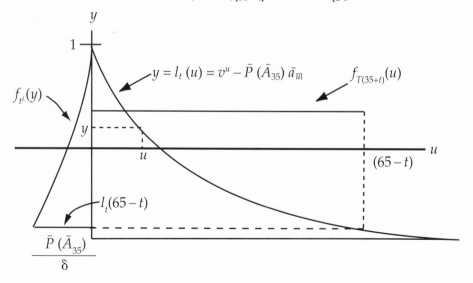

To determine the d.f. by $_tL$ we start with a value of y corresponding to a value of u in the interval $(0, 65 - t)$. For such a y we have, by (7.2.12),

$$F_{_tL}(y) = 1 - \frac{(-1/\delta) \log \{[\delta y + \bar{P}(\bar{A}_{35})]/[\delta + \bar{P}(\bar{A}_{35})]\}}{65 - t} \qquad 0 \le y \le 1.$$

For a $y > 1$, $F_{_tL}(y) = 1$.

Again, for a value of y corresponding to a value of u in the interval $(0, 65 - t)$, and using (7.2.13), we have

$$f_{_tL}(y) = \begin{cases} \left(\dfrac{1}{65 - t}\right)\left[\dfrac{1}{\delta y + \bar{P}(\bar{A}_{35})}\right] & -\dfrac{\bar{P}(\bar{A}_{35})}{\delta} \le y \le 1 \\ 0 & \text{elsewhere.} \end{cases}$$

b. Figure 7.2.2 is the composite of the required graphs of the p.d.f.'s $f_{_tL}(y)$, for $t = 0, 20, 40,$ and 60. Figure 7.2.1 is a graph for one value of t. Compare Figures 7.2.1 and 7.2.2 as follows: The vertical y-axis of Figure 7.2.1 is the horizontal axis in Figure 7.2.2. The axis that was imagined to be perpendicular to the u-y plane in Figure 7.2.1 is the vertical axis in Figure 7.2.2. Note the curves in the y-t plane that indicate the minimum and maximum possible losses, the expected loss (benefit reserve), and the expected loss plus one standard deviation of the loss. ▼

FIGURE 7.2.2

$f_{_tL}(y)$ for $t = 0, 20, 40,$ and 60

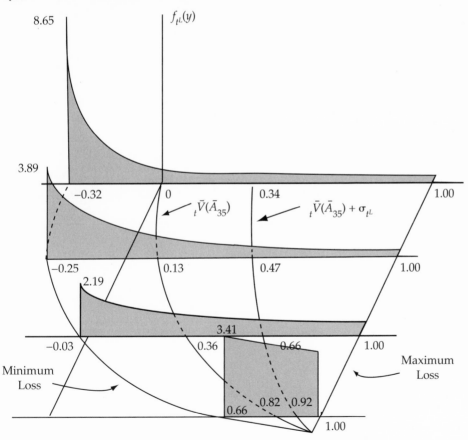

Corresponding to Table 6.2.1, Table 7.2.1 for benefit reserves is presented. We have not tabulated details of the prospective loss, $_tL$, and explicit formulas for $\text{Var}[_tL|T(x) > t]$, corresponding to the several benefit reserves, are not displayed.

TABLE 7.2.1

Fully Continuous Benefit Reserves; Age at Issue x, Duration t, Unit Benefit

Plan	International Actuarial Notation	Prospective Formula	
Whole life insurance	$_t\bar{V}(\bar{A}_x)$	$\bar{A}_{x+t} - \bar{P}(\bar{A}_x)\,\bar{a}_{x+t}$	
n-Year term insurance	$_t\bar{V}(\bar{A}^1_{x:\overline{n}\rvert})$	$\begin{cases}\bar{A}^1_{x+t:\overline{n-t}\rvert} - \bar{P}(\bar{A}^1_{x:\overline{n}\rvert})\,\bar{a}_{x+t:\overline{n-t}\rvert} \\ 0\end{cases}$	$\begin{aligned} t<n \\ t=n\end{aligned}$
n-Year endowment insurance	$_t\bar{V}(\bar{A}_{x:\overline{n}\rvert})$	$\begin{cases}\bar{A}_{x+t:\overline{n-t}\rvert} - \bar{P}(\bar{A}_{x:\overline{n}\rvert})\,\bar{a}_{x+t:\overline{n-t}\rvert} \\ 1\end{cases}$	$\begin{aligned} t<n \\ t=n\end{aligned}$
h-Payment years, whole life insurance	$_t^h\bar{V}(\bar{A}_x)$	$\begin{cases}\bar{A}_{x+t} - {_h\bar{P}(\bar{A}_x)}\,\bar{a}_{x+t:\overline{h-t}\rvert} \\ \bar{A}_{x+t}\end{cases}$	$\begin{aligned} t\le h \\ t>h\end{aligned}$
h-Payment years, n-year endowment insurance	$_t^h\bar{V}(\bar{A}_{x:\overline{n}\rvert})$	$\begin{cases}\bar{A}_{x+t:\overline{n-t}\rvert} - {_h\bar{P}(\bar{A}_{x:\overline{n}\rvert})}\,\bar{a}_{x+t:\overline{h-t}\rvert} \\ \bar{A}_{x+t:\overline{n-t}\rvert} \\ 1\end{cases}$	$\begin{aligned} t\le h<n \\ h<t<n \\ t=n\end{aligned}$
n-Year pure endowment	$_t\bar{V}^{\,1}_{x:\overline{n}\rvert}$	$\begin{cases}A_{x+t:\overline{n-t}\rvert}^{\;\;\;1} - \bar{P}^{\,1}_{x:\overline{n}\rvert}\,\bar{a}_{x+t:\overline{n-t}\rvert} \\ 1\end{cases}$	$\begin{aligned} t<n \\ t=n\end{aligned}$
Whole life annuity	$_t\bar{V}(_{n\rvert}\bar{a}_x)$	$\begin{cases}_{n-t\rvert}\bar{a}_{x+t} - \bar{P}(_{n\rvert}\bar{a}_x)\,\bar{a}_{x+t:\overline{n-t}\rvert} \\ \bar{a}_{x+t}\end{cases}$	$\begin{aligned} t\le n \\ t>n\end{aligned}$

7.3 Other Formulas for Fully Continuous Benefit Reserves

So far we have defined the benefit reserve as the conditional expectation of the prospective loss random variable and developed only one method to write formulas for fully continuous benefit reserves, namely, the ***prospective method***, stating that the benefit reserve is the difference between the actuarial present values of future benefits and of future benefit premiums. From the prospective method, we can easily develop three other general formulas for policies with level benefits and level benefit premium rates. We illustrate these for the case of n-year endowment insurances.

The ***premium-difference formula*** for $_t\bar{V}(\bar{A}_{x:\overline{n}\rvert})$ is obtained by factoring $\bar{a}_{x+t:\overline{n-t}\rvert}$ out of the prospective formula for $_t\bar{V}(\bar{A}_{x:\overline{n}\rvert})$:

$$_t\bar{V}(\bar{A}_{x:\overline{n}\rvert}) = \left[\frac{\bar{A}_{x+t:\overline{n-t}\rvert}}{\bar{a}_{x+t:\overline{n-t}\rvert}} - \bar{P}(\bar{A}_{x:\overline{n}\rvert})\right]\bar{a}_{x+t:\overline{n-t}\rvert}$$

$$= \left[\bar{P}(\bar{A}_{x+t:\overline{n-t}\rvert}) - \bar{P}(\bar{A}_{x:\overline{n}\rvert})\right]\bar{a}_{x+t:\overline{n-t}\rvert}. \tag{7.3.1}$$

Formula (7.3.1) exhibits the benefit reserve as the actuarial present value of a premium difference payable over the remaining premium-payment term. The premium difference is obtained by subtracting the original annual benefit premium from the benefit premium for an insurance issued at the attained age $x + t$ for the remaining benefits.

A second formula is obtained by factoring the actuarial present value of future benefits out of the prospective formula. Thus, for ${}_t\bar{V}(\bar{A}_{x:\overline{n}|})$ we have

$$
{}_t\bar{V}(\bar{A}_{x:\overline{n}|}) = \left[1 - \bar{P}(\bar{A}_{x:\overline{n}|}) \frac{\bar{a}_{x+t:\overline{n-t}|}}{\bar{A}_{x+t:\overline{n-t}|}} \right] \bar{A}_{x+t:\overline{n-t}|}
$$

$$
= \left[1 - \frac{\bar{P}(\bar{A}_{x:\overline{n}|})}{\bar{P}(\bar{A}_{x+t:\overline{n-t}|})} \right] \bar{A}_{x+t:\overline{n-t}|}. \tag{7.3.2}
$$

This exhibits the benefit reserve as the actuarial present value of a portion of the remaining future benefits, that portion which is not funded by the future benefit premiums still to be collected. Note that $\bar{P}(\bar{A}_{x+t:\overline{n-t}|})$ is the benefit premium required if the future benefits were to be funded from only the future benefit premiums, but $\bar{P}(\bar{A}_{x:\overline{n}|})$ is the benefit premium actually payable. Thus, $\bar{P}(\bar{A}_{x:\overline{n}|}) / \bar{P}(\bar{A}_{x+t:\overline{n-t}|})$ is the portion of future benefits funded by future benefit premiums. This is called a *paid-up insurance formula,* named from the paid-up insurance nonforfeiture benefit to be discussed in Chapter 16. Formulas analogous to (7.3.1) and (7.3.2) exist for a wide variety of benefit reserves.

A third expression is the *retrospective formula.* We develop this from a more general relationship. We have, from Exercise 4.12 and from formulas (5.2.18) and (5.2.19), for $t < n - s$,

$$
\bar{A}_{x+s:\overline{n-s}|} = \bar{A}^1_{x+s:\overline{t}|} + {}_tE_{x+s}\, \bar{A}_{x+s+t:\overline{n-s-t}|}
$$

and

$$
\bar{a}_{x+s:\overline{n-s}|} = \bar{a}_{x+s:\overline{t}|} + {}_tE_{x+s}\, \bar{a}_{x+s+t:\overline{n-s-t}|}.
$$

Substituting these expressions into the prospective formula for ${}_s\bar{V}(\bar{A}_{x:\overline{n}|})$, we obtain

$$
{}_s\bar{V}(\bar{A}_{x:\overline{n}|}) = \bar{A}^1_{x+s:\overline{t}|} - \bar{P}(\bar{A}_{x:\overline{n}|})\, \bar{a}_{x+s:\overline{t}|}
$$

$$
+ {}_tE_{x+s}\, [\bar{A}_{x+s+t:\overline{n-t-s}|} - \bar{P}(\bar{A}_{x:\overline{n}|})\, \bar{a}_{x+s+t:\overline{n-s-t}|}]
$$

$$
= \bar{A}^1_{x+s:\overline{t}|} + {}_tE_{x+s}\, {}_{s+t}\bar{V}(\bar{A}_{x:\overline{n}|}) - \bar{P}(\bar{A}_{x:\overline{n}|})\, \bar{a}_{x+s:\overline{t}|}. \tag{7.3.3}
$$

Thus the benefit reserves at the beginning and end of a t-year interval are connected by the following argument:

(the benefit reserve at the beginning of the interval) = (the actuarial present value at the beginning of the interval of benefits payable during the interval)

+ (the actuarial present value at the beginning of the interval of a pure endowment for the amount of the benefit reserve at the end of the interval)

− (the actuarial present value of benefit premiums payable during the interval).

The rearranged symbolic form,

$$_s\bar{V}(\bar{A}_{x:\overline{n}|}) + \bar{P}(\bar{A}_{x:\overline{n}|})\,\bar{a}_{x+s:\overline{n-t}|}$$

$$= \bar{A}_{x+s:\overline{t}|} + {}_t E_{x+s}\,{}_{s+t}\bar{V}(\bar{A}_{x:\overline{n}|}), \tag{7.3.4}$$

shows that the actuarial present values of the insurer's resources and obligations are equal.

The retrospective formula is obtained from (7.3.4) by setting $s = 0$, noting that $_0\bar{V}(\bar{A}_{x:\overline{n}|}) = 0$ by the equivalence principle, and solving for $_t\bar{V}(\bar{A}_{x:\overline{n}|})$. Thus,

$$_t\bar{V}(\bar{A}_{x:\overline{n}|}) = \frac{1}{_t E_x}\left[\bar{P}(\bar{A}_{x:\overline{n}|})\,\bar{a}_{x:\overline{t}|} - \bar{A}^1_{x:\overline{t}|}\right].$$

Further, $\bar{s}_{x:\overline{t}|} = \bar{a}_{x:\overline{t}|}/{_t E_x}$ so the formula reduces to

$$_t\bar{V}(\bar{A}_{x:\overline{n}|}) = \bar{P}(\bar{A}_{x:\overline{n}|})\,\bar{s}_{x:\overline{t}|} - {_t\bar{k}_x}. \tag{7.3.5}$$

Here

$$_t\bar{k}_x = \frac{\bar{A}^1_{x:\overline{t}|}}{_t E_x} \tag{7.3.6}$$

is called the **accumulated cost of insurance.** One notes that

$$_t\bar{k}_x = \int_0^t \frac{v^s\,{_s p_x}\,\mu_x(s)\,ds}{v^t\,{_t p_x}}$$

$$= \int_0^t \frac{(1+i)^{t-s}\,l_{x+s}\,\mu_x(s)\,ds}{l_{x+t}}. \tag{7.3.7}$$

This can be interpreted as the assessment against each of the l_{x+t} survivors to provide for the accumulated value of the death claims in the survivorship group between ages x and $x + t$. Thus, the reserve can be viewed as the difference between the benefit premiums, accumulated with interest and shared among only the survivors at age $x + t$, and the accumulated cost of insurance.

We conclude this section with some special formulas that express the whole life insurance benefit reserves in terms of a single actuarial function. Analogous formulas hold for n-year endowment insurance benefit reserves when benefit premiums are payable continuously for the n years. Because we used (5.2.8) to express $\bar{P}(\bar{A}_x)$ in terms of δ and either $\bar{a}_x$ or $\bar{A}_x$, we can use those ideas here to express $_t\bar{V}(\bar{A}_x)$ in terms of one of the actuarial functions $\bar{a}_x$, $\bar{A}_x$, or $\bar{P}(\bar{A}_x)$ and δ.

For an annuity function formula, substitute (6.2.9) and (5.2.8) into the prospective formula (7.2.3) to obtain

$$_t\bar{V}(\bar{A}_x) = 1 - \delta\bar{a}_{x+t} - \left(\frac{1}{\bar{a}_x} - \delta\right)\bar{a}_{x+t}$$

$$= 1 - \frac{\bar{a}_{x+t}}{\bar{a}_x}. \tag{7.3.8}$$

Further, substituting (6.2.9) into the premium-difference formula, we have

$$_t\bar{V}(\bar{A}_x) = [\bar{P}(\bar{A}_{x+t}) - \bar{P}(\bar{A}_x)]\,\bar{a}_{x+t}$$

$$= \frac{\bar{P}(\bar{A}_{x+t}) - \bar{P}(\bar{A}_x)}{\bar{P}(\bar{A}_{x+t}) + \delta}. \qquad (7.3.9)$$

Finally, we can rewrite (7.3.8) using $\bar{A}_{x+t} = 1 - \delta\bar{a}_{x+t}$ to obtain

$$_t\bar{V}(\bar{A}_x) = 1 - \frac{1 - \bar{A}_{x+t}}{1 - \bar{A}_x} = \frac{\bar{A}_{x+t} - \bar{A}_x}{1 - \bar{A}_x}. \qquad (7.3.10)$$

These last three formulas depend on relationship (5.2.8) between the annuity for the premium paying period and the insurance for the benefit period. Thus they are available only for whole life and endowment insurances where the premium-paying period and the benefit period are the same. Moreover, the frequency of premium payment must be the same as the "frequency" of benefit payment. We will see that apportionable premiums satisfy these requirements in their own way.

Remark:

Although benefit reserves are non-negative in most applications, there is no mathematical theorem that guarantees this property. Indeed, the reader can combine Exercise 4.2 and formula (7.3.10) for a quick verification that negative benefit reserves are a real possibility.

7.4   Fully Discrete Benefit Reserves

The benefit reserves of this section are for the insurances of Section 6.3 which have annual premium payments and payment of the benefit at the end of the year of death. As in Section 7.2 the underlying mortality assumption can be on a select or aggregate basis. We will display the formulas for the aggregate case, which has simpler notation. Let us consider a whole life insurance with benefit issued to (x) with benefit premium P_x. Following the development in Section 7.2, for an insured surviving k years later, we define the benefit reserve, denoted by $_kV_x$, as the conditional expectation of the prospective loss, $_kL$, at duration k. More precisely,

$$_kL = v^{(K(x)-k)+1} - P_x\,\ddot{a}_{\overline{(K(x)-k)+1|}} \qquad (7.4.1)$$

$$_kV_x = \mathrm{E}[_kL|K(x) = k, k+1, \ldots]. \qquad (7.4.2)$$

The prospective formula for the benefit reserve is

$$_kV_x = A_{x+k} - P_x\,\ddot{a}_{x+k}. \qquad (7.4.3)$$

As in Section 7.2 this formula is the actuarial present value of future benefits less the actuarial present value of future benefit premiums.

Analogous to (7.2.4), we have

$$\mathrm{Var}[_kL|K(x) = k, k + 1, \ldots]$$

$$= \mathrm{Var}\left[v^{[K(x)-k]+1}\left(1 + \frac{P_x}{d}\right)\Big| K(x) = k, k + 1, \ldots\right]$$

$$= \left(1 + \frac{P_x}{d}\right)^2 \mathrm{Var}[v^{[K(x)-k]+1}|K(x) = k, k + 1, \ldots]$$

$$= \left(1 + \frac{P_x}{d}\right)^2 [^2A_{x+k} - (A_{x+k})^2]. \qquad (7.4.4)$$

Example 7.4.1

Follow up Example 6.3.1 by calculating $_kV_x$ and $\mathrm{Var}[_kL|K(x) = k, k + 1, \ldots]$.

Solution:

Here A_x, $\ddot{a}_x$, and P_x are independent of age x so that $A_{x+k} = A_x$ and

$$_kV_x = A_x - P_x\ddot{a}_x = 0 \qquad k = 0, 1, 2, \ldots.$$

Also, from (7.4.4), $\mathrm{Var}[_kL|K(x) = k, k + 1, \ldots] = \mathrm{Var}(L) = 0.2347.$ ▼

The benefit reserve formulas tabulated in Table 7.4.1 correspond to the benefit premiums in Table 6.3.1 and are analogous to the benefit reserves in Table 7.2.1.

TABLE 7.4.1

Fully Discrete Benefit Reserves; Age at Issue x, Duration k, Unit Benefit

Plan	International Actuarial Notation	Prospective Formula	
Whole life insurance	$_kV_x$	$A_{x+k} - P_x\ddot{a}_{x+k}$	
n-Year term insurance	$_kV^1_{x:\overline{n}\|}$	$\begin{cases} A^1_{x+k:\overline{n-k}\|} - P^1_{x:\overline{n}\|}\ddot{a}_{x+k:\overline{n-k}\|} \\ 0 \end{cases}$	$\begin{matrix} k < n \\ k = n \end{matrix}$
n-Year endowment insurance	$_kV_{x:\overline{n}\|}$	$\begin{cases} A_{x+k:\overline{n-k}\|} - P_{x:\overline{n}\|}\ddot{a}_{x+k:\overline{n-k}\|} \\ 1 \end{cases}$	$\begin{matrix} k < n \\ k = n \end{matrix}$
h-Payment years, whole life insurance	$^h_kV_x$	$\begin{cases} A_{x+k} - {}_hP_x\ddot{a}_{x+k:\overline{h-k}\|} \\ A_{x+k} \end{cases}$	$\begin{matrix} k < h \\ k \geq h \end{matrix}$
h-Payment years, n-year endowment insurance	$^h_kV_{x:\overline{n}\|}$	$\begin{cases} A_{x+k:\overline{n-k}\|} - {}_hP_{x:\overline{n}\|}\ddot{a}_{x+k:\overline{h-k}\|} \\ A_{x+k:\overline{n-k}\|} \\ 1 \end{cases}$	$\begin{matrix} k < h < n \\ h \leq k < n \\ k = n \end{matrix}$
n-Year pure endowment	$_kV^{\ 1}_{x:\overline{n}\|}$	$\begin{cases} A_{x+k:\overline{n-k}\|}^{\ \ 1} - P^{\ 1}_{x:\overline{n}\|}\ddot{a}_{x+k:\overline{n-k}\|} \\ 1 \end{cases}$	$\begin{matrix} k < n \\ k = n \end{matrix}$
Whole life annuity	$_kV(_n|\ddot{a}_x)$	$\begin{cases} {}_{n-k\|}\ddot{a}_{x+k} - P(_n|\ddot{a}_x)\ddot{a}_{x+k:\overline{n-k}\|} \\ \ddot{a}_{x+k} \end{cases}$	$\begin{matrix} k < n \\ k \geq n \end{matrix}$

Example 7.4.2

Determine an expression in actuarial present values and benefit premiums for the $\text{Var}[_kL|K(x) = k, k + 1, \ldots]$ for a fully discrete n-year endowment insurance with a unit benefit.

Solution:

$$_kL = v^{K(x)-k+1}\left(1 + \frac{P_{x:\overline{n}|}}{d}\right) - \frac{P_{x:\overline{n}|}}{d} \qquad K(x) = k, k + 1, \ldots, n - 1$$

$$= v^{n-k}\left(1 + \frac{P_{x:\overline{n}|}}{d}\right) - \frac{P_{x:\overline{n}|}}{d} \qquad K(x) = n, n + 1, \ldots,$$

$$\text{Var}[_kL|K(x) = k, k + 1, \ldots]$$

$$= \left(1 + \frac{P_{x:\overline{n}|}}{d}\right)^2 [^2A_{x+k:\overline{n-k}|} - (A_{x+k:\overline{n-k}|})^2].\qquad \blacktriangledown$$

In cases other than whole life or endowment insurances with premiums payable throughout the insurance term, the expressions for the variance of the loss may be difficult to summarize in convenient notation.

Formulas similar to those of Section 7.3 can be developed for fully discrete benefit reserves. We illustrate these by writing the formulas for $_kV_{x:\overline{n}|}$ with a minimum of discussion. Verbal interpretations and algebraic developments closely parallel those for fully continuous benefit reserves.

The premium difference formula is

$$_kV_{x:\overline{n}|} = (P_{x+k:\overline{n-k}|} - P_{x:\overline{n}|})\,\ddot{a}_{x+k:\overline{n-k}|}. \tag{7.4.5}$$

The paid-up insurance formula is

$$_kV_{x:\overline{n}|} = \left(1 - \frac{P_{x:\overline{n}|}}{P_{x+k:\overline{n-k}|}}\right)A_{x+k:\overline{n-k}|}. \tag{7.4.6}$$

For the retrospective formula, we first establish a result analogous to (7.3.3), namely, for $h < n - j$,

$$_jV_{x:\overline{n}|} = A^1_{x+j:\overline{h}|} - P_{x:\overline{n}|}\,\ddot{a}_{x+j:\overline{h}|} + _hE_{x+j}\,_{j+h}V_{x:\overline{n}|}. \tag{7.4.7}$$

Then, if $j = 0$, we have, since $_0V_{x:\overline{n}|} = 0$,

$$_hV_{x:\overline{n}|} = \frac{1}{_hE_x}\,(P_{x:\overline{n}|}\,\ddot{a}_{x:\overline{h}|} - A^1_{x:\overline{h}|})$$

$$= P_{x:\overline{n}|}\,\ddot{s}_{x:\overline{h}|} - _hk_x. \tag{7.4.8}$$

Here the accumulated cost of insurance is $_hk_x = A^1_{x:\overline{h}|}/_hE_x$, and a survivorship group interpretation is possible.

An interesting observation follows from the retrospective formula for the benefit reserve. Let us consider two different policies issued to (x), each for a unit of

---

insurance during the first h years. Here, h is less than or equal to the shorter of the two premium-payment periods. The retrospective formula for the benefit reserve on policy one is

$$_hV_{(1)} = P_{(1)}\,\ddot{s}_{x:\overline{h}|} - {}_hk_x$$

and that for the benefit reserve on policy two is

$$_hV_{(2)} = P_{(2)}\,\ddot{s}_{x:\overline{h}|} - {}_hk_x.$$

It follows that

$$_hV_{(1)} - {}_hV_{(2)} = (P_{(1)} - P_{(2)})\,\ddot{s}_{x:\overline{h}|}, \tag{7.4.9}$$

which shows that the difference in the two benefit reserves equals the actuarial accumulated value of the difference in the benefit premiums $P_{(1)} - P_{(2)}$. Since $1/\ddot{s}_{x:\overline{h}|} = P^{\;1}_{x:\overline{h}|}$, formula (7.4.9) can be rearranged as

$$P_{(1)} - P_{(2)} = P^{\;1}_{x:\overline{h}|}\,({}_hV_{(1)} - {}_hV_{(2)}). \tag{7.4.10}$$

The difference in the benefit premiums is expressed as the benefit premium for an h-year pure endowment of the difference in the benefit reserves at the end of h years. Formula (6.3.10) is a special case of (7.4.10) with $_nV_{x:\overline{n}|} = 1$ and $_n^nV_x = A_{x+n}$. Another illustration of (7.4.10) is

$$P_x = P^1_{x:\overline{n}|} + P^{\;1}_{x:\overline{n}|}\,{}_nV_x \tag{7.4.11}$$

since $_nV^1_{x:\overline{n}|} = 0$.

As in the fully continuous case, there are special formulas for whole life and endowment insurance benefit reserves in the fully discrete case. Parallel to (7.3.8)–(7.3.10), we have, by use of the relations $A_y = 1 - d\,\ddot{a}_y$ and $1/\ddot{a}_y = P_y + d$,

$$_kV_x = 1 - d\,\ddot{a}_{x+k} - \left(\frac{1}{\ddot{a}_x} - d\right)\ddot{a}_{x+k}$$

$$= 1 - \frac{\ddot{a}_{x+k}}{\ddot{a}_x}, \tag{7.4.12}$$

$$_kV_x = 1 - \frac{P_x + d}{P_{x+k} + d} = \frac{P_{x+k} - P_x}{P_{x+k} + d}, \tag{7.4.13}$$

and

$$_kV_x = 1 - \frac{1 - A_{x+k}}{1 - A_x} = \frac{A_{x+k} - A_x}{1 - A_x}. \tag{7.4.14}$$

Similar special formulas also hold for fully discrete n-year endowment insurance benefit reserves, but not for insurance benefit reserves in general.

Fully discrete insurances provide instructive examples for the deterministic, or expected cash flow, model of the operations of benefit reserves. This is displayed in Examples 7.4.3 and 7.4.4.

Example 7.4.3

Assume that a 5-year term life insurance of 1,000 is issued on a fully discrete basis to each member of a group of l_{50} persons at age 50. Trace the cash flow expected for this group on the basis of the Illustrative Life Table with interest at 6%, and, as a by-product, obtain the benefit reserves.

Solution:

We first calculate the annual benefit premium $\pi = 1,000\, P^1_{50:\overline{5}|} = 6.55692$. Then the expected accumulation of funds for the group through the collection of benefit premiums, the crediting of interest, and the payment of claims is as stated in the following:

(1)	(2)	(3)	(4)	(5)	(6)	(7)	(8)
	Expected Benefit Premiums at Beginning of Year	Expected Fund at Beginning of Year	Expected Interest	Expected Death Claims	Expected Fund at End of Year	Expected Number of Survivors at End of Year	$1,000\, {}_hV^1_{50:\overline{5}|}$
Year h	$l_{50+h-1}\,\pi$	$(2)_h + (6)_{h-1}$	$(0.06)\,(3)_h$	$1,000\, d_{50+h-1}$	$(3)_h + (4)_h - (5)_h$	l_{50+h}	$(6)_h/(7)_h$
1	586 903	586 903	35 214	529 884	92 233	88 979.11	1.04
2	583 429	675 662	40 540	571 432	144 770	88 407.68	1.64
3	579 682	724 452	43 467	616 416	151 503	87 791.26	1.73
4	575 640	727 143	43 629	665 065	105 707	87 126.20	1.21
5	571 280	676 987	40 619	717 606	0	86 408.60	0.00

Note that the benefit reserves derived in the table match those calculated by formula. For example, at duration 2 we have

$$1,000\, A^1_{52:\overline{3}|} = 20.09 \quad \text{and} \quad \ddot{a}_{52:\overline{3}|} = 2.81391.$$

Then

$$1,000\, {}_2V^1_{50:\overline{5}|} = 20.09 - (6.55692)(2.81391) = 1.54. \qquad \blacktriangledown$$

Example 7.4.4

Assume that a 5-year endowment insurance of 1,000 is issued on a fully discrete basis to each member of a group of l_{50} persons at age 50. Trace the cash flow expected for this group on the basis of the Illustrative Life Table with interest at 6%, and as a by-product obtain the benefit reserves.

Solution:

Here the annual benefit premium is $\pi = 1,000\, P_{50:\overline{5}|} = 170.083$. The expected cash flow is displayed in the following table:

(1)	(2)	(3)	(4)	(5)	(6)	(7)	(8)
Year h	Expected Benefit Premiums at Beginning of Year $l_{50+h-1}\,\pi$	Expected Fund at Beginning of Year $(2)_h + (6)_{h-1}$	Expected Interest $(0.06)\,(3)_h$	Expected Death Claims $1{,}000\,d_{50+h-1}$	Expected Fund at End of Year $(3)_h + (4)_h - (5)_h$	Expected Number of Survivors at End of Year l_{50+h}	$1{,}000\,_hV^{\,1}_{50:\overline{5}|}$ $(6)_h \div (7)_h$
1	15 223 954	15 223 954	913 437	529 884	15 607 507	88 979.11	175.14
2	15 133 829	30 741 336	1 844 480	571 432	32 014 384	88 407.68	362.12
3	15 036 638	47 051 022	2 823 061	616 416	49 257 667	87 791.26	561.08
4	14 931 796	64 189 463	3 851 368	665 065	67 375 766	87 126.20	773.31
5	14 818 680	82 194 446	4 931 667	717 606	86 408 507	86 408.60	1 000.00

▼

Figures 7.4.1 and 7.4.2 display the expected benefit premiums and expected death claims for the preceding two examples. In Example 7.4.3, expected benefit premiums exceed expected death claims for 2 years, but thereafter are less than expected claims. The excess benefit premiums accumulate a fund in the early years to be drawn on in the later years when expected claims are higher. At the end of 5 years, the fund is expected to be exhausted.

FIGURE 7.4.1

Expected Benefit Premiums and Expected Death Claims for Example 7.4.3

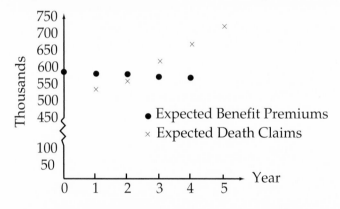

FIGURE 7.4.2

Expected Benefit Premiums and Expected Death Claims for Example 7.4.4

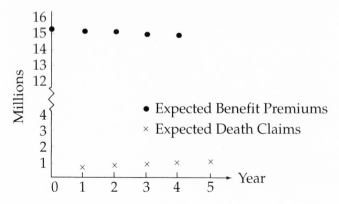

For the 5-year endowment case of Example 7.4.4, the picture is much different. As shown in Figure 7.4.2, the expected benefit premiums remain far in excess of expected death claims throughout. The expected fund at the end of 5 years is sufficient to provide 1,000 in maturity payments to each of the expected survivors.

The 5-year term insurance exemplifies a low-premium, low-accumulation life insurance, whereas the 5-year endowment insurance exemplifies a high-premium, high-accumulation form. Most life insurances would fall between these two extremes.

7.5 Benefit Reserves on a Semicontinuous Basis

We noted at the end of Section 6.3 that, in practice, there is a need for semicontinuous annual benefit premiums $P(\bar{A}_x)$, $P(\bar{A}_{x:\overline{n}|})$, $P(\bar{A}^1_{x:\overline{n}|})$, $_hP(\bar{A}_x)$, and $_hP(\bar{A}_{x:\overline{n}|})$ to take account of immediate payment of death claims. In such cases, the benefit reserve formulas in Table 7.4.1 need to be revised by replacement of A by $\bar{A}$ and of P by $P(\bar{A})$. Moreover, the principal symbol for the benefit reserve is now $V(\bar{A})$ with a subscript on the $\bar{A}$ to indicate the type of insurance as in the benefit premium symbol. For example, for an h-payment years, n-year endowment insurance

$$_k^h V(\bar{A}_{x:\overline{n}|}) = \begin{cases} \bar{A}_{x+k:\overline{n-k}|} - {}_hP(\bar{A}_{x:\overline{n}|})\,\ddot{a}_{x+k:\overline{h-k}|} & k < h < n \\ \bar{A}_{x+k:\overline{n-k}|} & h \le k < n \\ 1 & k = n. \end{cases} \tag{7.5.1}$$

If a uniform distribution of deaths over each year of age is assumed, we have, from (4.4.2) and (6.3.12),

$$_k^h V(\bar{A}_{x:\overline{n}|}) = \frac{i}{\delta}\,{}_k^h V^1_{x:\overline{n}|} + {}_k^h V_{x:\overline{n}|}^{\ 1}. \tag{7.5.2}$$

Under this circumstance benefit reserves on a semicontinuous basis are easily calculated from the corresponding fully discrete benefit reserves.

7.6 Benefit Reserves Based on True m-thly Benefit Premiums

In this section we examine the benefit reserve formulas corresponding to the formulas for true m-thly benefit premiums discussed in Section 6.4. By the prospective method, one can write a direct formula for $_k^h V^{(m)}_{x:\overline{n}|}$, namely,

$$_k^h V^{(m)}_{x:\overline{n}|} = A_{x+k:\overline{n-k}|} - {}_hP^{(m)}_{x:\overline{n}|}\,\ddot{a}^{(m)}_{x+k:\overline{h-k}|} \qquad k < h. \tag{7.6.1}$$

This can be evaluated after obtaining $_hP^{(m)}_{x:\overline{n}|}$ by means of (6.4.1) or (6.4.2), and $\ddot{a}^{(m)}_{x+k:\overline{h-k}|}$ by means of (5.4.15) or (5.4.17).

We now consider the difference between $_k^h V^{(m)}_{x:\overline{n}|}$ and $_k^h V_{x:\overline{n}|}$ in the general case of a limited payment endowment insurance. We have, for $k < h$,

$$\small {}_{k}^{h}V_{x:\overline{n}|}^{(m)} - {}_{k}^{h}V_{x:\overline{n}|} = {}_{h}P_{x:\overline{n}|} \, \ddot{a}_{x+k:\overline{h-k}|} - {}_{h}P_{x:\overline{n}|}^{(m)} \, \ddot{a}_{x+k:\overline{h-k}|}^{(m)}$$

$$= {}_{h}P_{x:\overline{n}|}^{(m)} \frac{\ddot{a}_{x:\overline{h}|}^{(m)}}{\ddot{a}_{x:\overline{h}|}} \, \ddot{a}_{x+k:\overline{h-k}|} - {}_{h}P_{x:\overline{n}|}^{(m)} \, \ddot{a}_{x+k:\overline{h-k}|}^{(m)}. \qquad (7.6.2)$$

Under the assumption of a uniform distribution of deaths in each year of age, (7.6.2) becomes

$$\small {}_{k}^{h}V_{x:\overline{n}|}^{(m)} - {}_{k}^{h}V_{x:\overline{n}|} = {}_{h}P_{x:\overline{n}|}^{(m)} \left\{ \frac{\ddot{a}_{\overline{1}|}^{(m)} \, \ddot{a}_{x:\overline{h}|} - \beta(m) \, A_{x:\overline{h}|}^{1}}{\ddot{a}_{x:\overline{h}|}} \, \ddot{a}_{x+k:\overline{h-k}|} \right.$$

$$\left. - \left[\ddot{a}_{\overline{1}|}^{(m)} \, \ddot{a}_{x+k:\overline{n-k}|} - \beta(m) \, A_{x+k:\overline{h-k}|}^{1} \right] \right\}.$$

The terms involving $\ddot{a}_{\overline{1}|}^{(m)}$ cancel to yield

$$\small {}_{k}^{h}V_{x:\overline{n}|}^{(m)} - {}_{k}^{h}V_{x:\overline{n}|} = \beta(m) \, {}_{h}P_{x:\overline{n}|}^{(m)} \, {}_{k}V_{x:\overline{h}|}^{1}. \qquad (7.6.3)$$

Thus,

(the benefit reserve for an insurance = (the corresponding fully
with true m-thly benefit premiums)   discrete benefit reserve)

$$+ \left(\begin{array}{l} \text{a fully discrete benefit reserve for term insurance over} \\ \text{the premium paying period for a fraction, } \beta(m), \text{ of the} \\ \text{true } m\text{-thly benefit premium for the plan of insurance} \end{array} \right).$$

A similar result holds for benefit reserves on a semicontinuous basis with true m-thly benefit premiums under the assumption of uniform distribution of deaths in each year of age. By the prospective method, we have for $k < h$,

$$\small {}_{k}^{h}V^{(m)}(\bar{A}_{x:\overline{n}|}) = \bar{A}_{x+k:\overline{n-k}|} - {}_{h}P^{(m)}(\bar{A}_{x:\overline{n}|}) \, \ddot{a}_{x+k:\overline{h-k}|}^{(m)}. \qquad (7.6.4)$$

By steps analogous to those connecting (7.6.1) and (7.6.3), we obtain

$$\small {}_{k}^{h}V^{(m)}(\bar{A}_{x:\overline{n}|}) = {}_{k}^{h}V(\bar{A}_{x:\overline{n}|}) + \beta(m) \, {}_{h}P^{(m)}(\bar{A}_{x:\overline{n}|}) \, {}_{k}V_{x:\overline{h}|}^{1}. \qquad (7.6.5)$$

Further, by letting $m \to \infty$ above, we obtain for a fully continuous basis

$$\small {}_{k}^{h}\bar{V}(\bar{A}_{x:\overline{n}|}) = {}_{k}^{h}V(\bar{A}_{x:\overline{n}|}) + \beta(\infty) \, {}_{h}\bar{P}(\bar{A}_{x:\overline{n}|}) \, {}_{k}V_{x:\overline{h}|}^{1}. \qquad (7.6.6)$$

Note again that the term insurance benefit reserve is on a fully discrete basis.

Example 7.6.1

On the basis of the Illustrative Life Table with the assumption of uniform distribution of deaths over each year of age and $i = 0.06$ calculate the following for a 20-year endowment insurance issued to (50) with a unit benefit and true semiannual benefit premiums:

a. The benefit reserve at the end of the tenth year if the benefit is payable at the end of the year of death.

b. The benefit reserve at the end of the tenth year if the benefit is payable at the moment of death.

Also verify (7.6.5) in relation to the benefit reserve in part (b).

Solution:

a. In addition to the values calculated in Example 6.4.1, we require

$$A^1_{60:\overline{10}|} = 0.13678852$$

$$A_{60:\overline{10}|} = 0.58798425$$

$$\ddot{a}_{60:\overline{10}|} = 7.2789425$$

$$_{10}V^1_{50:\overline{20}|} = A^1_{60:\overline{10}|} - P^1_{50:\overline{20}|}\ddot{a}_{60:\overline{10}|} = 0.052752$$

$$_{10}V_{50:\overline{20}|} = A_{60:\overline{10}|} - P_{50:\overline{20}|}\ddot{a}_{60:\overline{10}|} = 0.355380.$$

Then, under the assumption of a uniform distribution of deaths over each year of age, we have

$$\ddot{a}^{(2)}_{60:\overline{10}|} = \alpha(2)\,\ddot{a}_{60:\overline{10}|} - \beta(2)\,(1 - {_{10}E_{60}}) = 7.1392299.$$

The benefit reserve, $_{10}V^{(2)}_{50:\overline{20}|}$, can be calculated using either

(7.6.1): $$A_{60:\overline{10}|} - P^{(2)}_{50:\overline{20}|}\ddot{a}^{(2)}_{60:\overline{10}|} = 0.355822$$

or

(7.6.3): $$_{10}V_{50:\overline{20}|} + \beta(2)\,P^{(2)}_{50:\overline{20}|}\,{_{10}V^1_{50:\overline{20}|}} = 0.355822.$$

b. We need additional calculated values:

$$\frac{i}{\delta}\,A^1_{50:\overline{20}|} = 0.13423835$$

$$P^{(2)}(\bar{A}_{50:\overline{20}|}) = \frac{\bar{A}_{50:\overline{20}|}}{\ddot{a}^{(2)}_{50:\overline{20}|}} = 0.03286830$$

$$\frac{i}{\delta}\,A^1_{60:\overline{10}|} = 0.14085233$$

$$\bar{A}_{50:\overline{20}|} = 0.36471188$$

$$P(\bar{A}_{50:\overline{20}|}) = \frac{\bar{A}_{50:\overline{20}|}}{\ddot{a}_{50:\overline{20}|}} = 0.03229873$$

$$\bar{A}_{60:\overline{10}|} = 0.59204806$$

$$_{10}V(\bar{A}_{50:\overline{20}|}) = \bar{A}_{60:\overline{10}|} - P(\bar{A}_{50:\overline{20}|})\,\ddot{a}_{60:\overline{10}|} = 0.3569475$$

$$_{10}V^{(2)}(\bar{A}_{50:\overline{20}|}) = \bar{A}_{60:\overline{10}|} - P^{(2)}(\bar{A}_{50:\overline{20}|})\,\ddot{a}^{(2)}_{60:\overline{10}|} = 0.3573937$$

$$\beta(2)\,P^{(2)}(\bar{A}_{50:\overline{20}|})\,{_{10}V^1_{50:\overline{20}|}} = 0.000446.$$

This last value is the difference between the two directly above it, as shown in (7.6.5). ▼

7.7 Benefit Reserves on an Apportionable or Discounted Continuous Basis

In Section 6.5 we discussed apportionable, or discounted continuous, benefit premiums, and we now consider the corresponding benefit reserves. For integer k, we have by the prospective method

$$_k^h V^{\{m\}}(\bar{A}_{x:\overline{n}|}) = \bar{A}_{x+k:\overline{n-k}|} - {}_h P^{\{m\}}(\bar{A}_{x:\overline{n}|})\, \ddot{a}^{\{m\}}_{x+k:\overline{h-k}|} \qquad k < h. \tag{7.7.1}$$

But by (6.5.2),

$$_h P^{\{m\}}(\bar{A}_{x:\overline{n}|}) = \frac{d^{(m)}}{\delta}\, {}_h \bar{P}(\bar{A}_{x:\overline{n}|}),$$

and by (5.5.4),

$$\ddot{a}^{\{m\}}_{x+k:\overline{h-k}|} = \frac{\delta}{d^{(m)}}\, \bar{a}_{x+k:\overline{h-k}|}.$$

Substitution into (7.7.1) yields, for an integer k,

$$_k^h V^{\{m\}}(\bar{A}_{x:\overline{n}|}) = \bar{A}_{x+k:\overline{n-k}|} - {}_h \bar{P}(\bar{A}_{x:\overline{n}|})\, \bar{a}_{x+k:\overline{h-k}|} = {}_k^h \bar{V}(\bar{A}_{x:\overline{n}|}). \tag{7.7.2}$$

This means that, on anniversaries of the issue date, fully continuous benefit reserves can be used for all apportionable cases, independent of the premium-paying mode. The condition that k be an integer can be relaxed to being at the end of an m-th for m-thly premiums.

In Section 6.5, it was noted that the apportionable benefit premium could be decomposed as

$$P^{\{1\}}(\bar{A}_x) = P(\bar{A}_x) + P(\bar{A}_x^{\mathrm{PR}}) \tag{7.7.3}$$

where the superscript PR is used to denote an insurance for the benefit premium refund feature. A similar decomposition for the benefit reserves can be verified by use of the prospective method and (6.5.7). The steps are:

$$_k V(\bar{A}_x^{\mathrm{PR}}) = \bar{P}(\bar{A}_x)\, \frac{\bar{A}_{x+k} - A_{x+k}}{\delta} - P(\bar{A}_x^{\mathrm{PR}})\, \ddot{a}_{x+k}$$

$$= \bar{P}(\bar{A}_x)\, \frac{d\ddot{a}_{x+k} - \delta\bar{a}_{x+k}}{\delta} - [P^{\{1\}}(\bar{A}_x) - P(\bar{A}_x)]\, \ddot{a}_{x+k}.$$

Since

$$\frac{d}{\delta}\, \bar{P}(\bar{A}_x) = P^{\{1\}}(\bar{A}_x),$$

the expression can be reduced to

$$_k V(\bar{A}_x^{\mathrm{PR}}) = -\bar{P}(\bar{A}_x)\, \bar{a}_{x+k} + P(\bar{A}_x)\, \ddot{a}_{x+k}$$

$$= \bar{A}_{x+k} - \bar{P}(\bar{A}_x)\, \bar{a}_{x+k} - [\bar{A}_{x+k} - P(\bar{A}_x)\, \ddot{a}_{x+k}]$$

$$= {}_k\bar{V}(\bar{A}_x) - {}_kV(\bar{A}_x)$$

$$= {}_kV^{\{1\}}(\bar{A}_x) - {}_kV(\bar{A}_x).$$

Thus we have

$$_kV^{\{1\}}(\bar{A}_x) = {}_kV(\bar{A}_k) + {}_kV(\bar{A}_x^{\mathrm{PR}}). \qquad (7.7.4)$$

7.8   Notes and References

This chapter has developed the idea of a reserve in parallel to the development of premiums in Chapter 6. Discussion of recursion formulas for reserves is deferred to Chapter 8. Reserve principles based on the utility functions used in Chapter 6 were first applied. Gerber (1976, 1979) develops these reserves in a more abstract setting. Benefit reserves, which followed from a linear utility function, were studied extensively. Scher (1974) explored the apportionable benefit premium reserves as discounted fully continuous benefit reserves.

Exercises

Section 7.1

7.1.   Determine the benefit reserve for $t = 2, 3, 4,$ and 5 for the insurance in Example 6.1.1.

7.2.   Determine the exponential reserve for $t = 2, 3, 4,$ and 5 for the insurance in Example 6.1.1.

7.3.   Determine the exponential reserve for $t = 1, 2, 3, 4,$ and 5 for the insurance in Exercise 6.2.

7.4.   Consider the insurance in Example 7.1.1 and the insurer of Exercise 6.3 with utility function $u(x) = x - 0.01\, x^2, 0 < x < 50$. Determine the reserve, $_kV$, for $k = 1, 2, 3,$ and 4 such that the insurer, with wealth 10 at each duration, will be indifferent between continuing the risk while receiving premiums of 0.30360 (from Exercise 6.3) and paying the amount $_kV$ to a reinsurer to assume the risk.

7.5.   Consider a unit insurance issued to (0) on a fully continuous basis using the following assumptions:
   i. De Moivre's law with $\omega = 5$
   ii. $i = 0.06$
   iii. Principle III of Example 6.1.1 with $\alpha = 0.1$.
   a. Display equations which can be solved for the exponential premium and the exponential reserve at $t = 1$.

b. Solve the equations of (a) for the numerical values for the exponential premium and exponential reserve. Numerical methods must be used to obtain these required solutions.

Section 7.2

7.6. For an n-year unit endowment insurance issued on a fully continuous basis to (x), define $_tL$, the prospective loss after duration t. Confirm that

$$\text{Var}(_tL|T > t) = \frac{^2\bar{A}_{x+t:\overline{n-t}|} - (\bar{A}_{x+t:\overline{n-t}|})^2}{(\delta\bar{a}_{x:\overline{n}|})^2}.$$

7.7. The prospective loss, after duration t, for a single benefit premium n-year continuous temporary life annuity of 1 per annum issued to (x) is given by

$$_tL = \begin{cases} \bar{a}_{\overline{T-t}|} & t \le T < n \\ \bar{a}_{\overline{n-t}|} & T \ge n. \end{cases}$$

Express $E[_tL|T > t]$ and $\text{Var}(_tL|T > t)$ in symbols of actuarial present values.

7.8. Write prospective formulas for
   a. $_{10}^{20}\bar{V}(\bar{A}_{35:\overline{30}|})$
   b. the benefit reserve at the end of 5 years for a unit benefit 10-year term insurance issued to (45) on a single premium basis.

7.9. a. For the fully continuous whole life insurance with the benefit premium determined by the equivalence principle, determine the outcome $u_0 = T(x) - t$ such that the loss is zero. [Caution: For large values of t, a solution may not exist.]
   b. Determine the value of u_0 for $t = 20$ in Example 7.2.3 and compare it to Figure 7.2.1 for reasonableness.

7.10. The assumptions of Example 7.2.3 are repeated. Find the value of t such that the minimum loss is zero. Check your result by examining Figure 7.2.2.

7.11. a. Repeat the development leading to (7.2.9) to obtain the d.f. for the loss variable associated with an n-year fully continuous endowment insurance.
   b. Draw the sketch that corresponds to Figure 7.2.1 for this endowment insurance.

7.12. Repeat Exercise 7.11 for an n-year fully continuous term insurance.

7.13. Confirm that (7.2.10) satisfies the conditions for a p.d.f.

Section 7.3

7.14. Write four formulas for $_{10}^{20}\bar{V}(\bar{A}_{40})$.

7.15. Write seven formulas for $_{10}\bar{V}(\bar{A}_{40:\overline{20}|})$.

7.16. Give the retrospective formula for $_{20}^{30}\bar{V}(_{30|}\bar{a}_{35})$.

7.17. For $0 < t \le m$, show

a. $\bar{P}(\bar{A}_{x:\overline{m+n}|}) = \bar{P}(\bar{A}^1_{x:\overline{m}|}) + \bar{P}^1_{x:\overline{m}|}\ _m\bar{V}(\bar{A}_{x:\overline{m+n}|})$

b. $_t\bar{V}(\bar{A}_{x:\overline{m+n}|}) = \ _t\bar{V}(\bar{A}^1_{x:\overline{m}|}) + \ _t\bar{V}^1_{x:\overline{m}|}\ _m\bar{V}(\bar{A}_{x:\overline{m+n}|})$

and give an interpretation in words.

7.18. State what formula in Section 7.3 the following equation is related to, and give an interpretation in words:

$$^{20}_{10}\bar{V}(\bar{A}_{30}) = \bar{A}^1_{40:\overline{5}|} + \ _5E_{40}\ ^{20}_{15}\bar{V}(\bar{A}_{30}) - \ _{20}\bar{P}(\bar{A}_{30})\ \bar{a}_{40:\overline{5}|}.$$

Section 7.4

7.19. Write four formulas for $^{20}_{10}V_{40}$.

7.20. Write seven formulas for $_{10}V_{40:\overline{20}|}$.

7.21. For $0 < k \le m$, show

$$_kV_{x:\overline{m+n}|} = \ _kV^1_{x:\overline{m}|} + \ _kV^1_{x:\overline{m}|}\ _mV_{x:\overline{m+n}|}.$$

7.22. If $k < n/2$, $_kV_{x:\overline{n}|} = 1/6$, and $\ddot{a}_{x:\overline{n}|} + \ddot{a}_{x+2k:\overline{n-2k}|} = 2\ \ddot{a}_{x+k:\overline{n-k}|}$, calculate $_kV_{x+k:\overline{n-k}|}$.

Section 7.5

7.23. On the basis of the Illustrative Life Table and interest of 6%, calculate values for the benefit reserves in the following table. (See Exercise 6.10.)

Fully Continuous	Semicontinuous	Fully Discrete
$_{10}\bar{V}(\bar{A}_{35:\overline{30}|})$	$_{10}V(\bar{A}_{35:\overline{30}|})$	$_{10}V_{35:\overline{30}|}$
$_{10}\bar{V}(\bar{A}_{35})$	$_{10}V(\bar{A}_{35})$	$_{10}V_{35}$
$_{10}\bar{V}(\bar{A}^1_{35:\overline{30}|})$	$_{10}V(\bar{A}^1_{35:\overline{30}|})$	$_{10}V^1_{35:\overline{30}|}$

7.24. Under the assumption of a uniform distribution of deaths in each year of age, which of the following are correct?

a. $_kV(\bar{A}_{x:\overline{n}|}) = \dfrac{i}{\delta}\ _kV_{x:\overline{n}|}$

b. $_kV(\bar{A}_x) = \dfrac{i}{\delta}\ _kV_x$

c. $_kV(\bar{A}^1_{x:\overline{n}|}) = \dfrac{i}{\delta}\ _kV^1_{x:\overline{n}|}$

Section 7.6

7.25. Show that, under the assumption of a uniform distribution of deaths in each year of age,

$$\dfrac{_5V^{(4)}_{30:\overline{20}|} - \ _5V_{30:\overline{20}|}}{^{20}_5V^{(4)}_{30} - \ ^{20}_5V_{30}} = \dfrac{A_{30:\overline{20}|}}{A_{30}}.$$

(The assumption is sufficient but not necessary.)

7.26. Which of the following are correct formulas for $_{15}V_{40}^{(m)}$?

    a. $(P_{55}^{(m)} - P_{40}^{(m)})\, \ddot{a}_{55}^{(m)}$
                    b. $\left(1 - \dfrac{P_{40}^{(m)}}{P_{55}^{(m)}}\right) A_{55}$

    c. $P_{40}^{(m)}\, \ddot{s}_{40:\overline{15}|}^{(m)} - {}_{15}k_{40}$
                d. $1 - \dfrac{\ddot{a}_{55}^{(m)}}{\ddot{a}_{40}^{(m)}}$

Section 7.7

7.27. Which of the following are correct formulas for $_{15}V^{(4)}(\bar{A}_{40})$?

    a. $_{15}\bar{V}(\bar{A}_{40})$
                  b. $[P^{(4)}(\bar{A}_{55}) - P^{(4)}(\bar{A}_{40})]\ddot{a}_{55}^{(4)}$

    c. $[\bar{P}(\bar{A}_{55}) - \bar{P}(\bar{A}_{40})]\bar{a}_{55}$
            d. $\left[1 - \dfrac{\bar{P}(\bar{A}_{40})}{\bar{P}(\bar{A}_{55})}\right]\bar{A}_{55}$

    e. $1 - \dfrac{\bar{a}_{55}}{\bar{a}_{40}}$
                f. $\bar{P}(\bar{A}_{40})\, \bar{s}_{40:\overline{15}|} - {}_{15}\bar{k}_{40}$

7.28. Show that
    a. $P^{(m)}(\bar{A}_{x:\overline{n}|}) = {}_nP^{(m)}(\bar{A}_x) + (1 - \bar{A}_{x+n})P_{\frac{1}{x:\overline{n}|}}^{(m)}$
    b. $_kV^{(m)}(\bar{A}_{x:\overline{n}|}) = {}_k^nV^{(m)}(\bar{A}_x) + (1 - \bar{A}_{x+n})_kV_{\frac{1}{x:\overline{n}|}}^{(m)}$.

Give an interpretation in words.

Miscellaneous

7.29. Calculate the value of $P_{x:\overline{n}|}^1$ if $_nV_x = 0.080$, $P_x = 0.024$, and $P_{x:\overline{n}|}^{\;1} = 0.2$.

7.30. If $_{10}V_{35} = 0.150$ and $_{20}V_{35} = 0.354$, calculate $_{10}V_{45}$.

7.31. A whole life insurance issued to (25) pays a unit benefit at the end of the year of death. Premiums are payable annually to age 65. The benefit premium for the first 10 years is P_{25} followed by an increased level annual benefit premium for the next 30 years. Use your Illustrative Life Table and $i = 0.06$ to find the following.
    a. The annual benefit premium payable at ages 35 through 64.
    b. The tenth-year benefit reserve.
    c. At the end of 10 years the policyholder has the option to continue with the benefit premium P_{25} until age 65 in return for reducing the death benefit to B for death after age 35. Calculate B.
    d. If the option in (c) is selected, calculate the twentieth-year benefit reserve.

7.32. Assuming $\delta = 0.05$, $q_x = 0.05$, and a uniform distribution of deaths in each year of age, calculate
    a. $(\bar{I}\bar{A})_{x:\overline{1}|}^1$
        b. $_{1/2}V((\bar{I}\bar{A})_{x:\overline{1}|}^1)$.

ANALYSIS OF BENEFIT RESERVES

8.1 Introduction

In Chapter 3 probability distributions for future lifetime random variables were developed. Chapters 4 and 5 studied the present-value random variables for insurances and annuities. The funding of insurance and annuities with a system of periodic payments was explored in Chapter 6, and in Chapter 7 the evolution of the liabilities under the periodic payments to fund an insurance or annuity was discussed. In these last two chapters the emphasis was on *level* benefits funded by *level* periodic payments that are usually determined by an application of the equivalence principle.

Why was the emphasis on level payments? First, traditional insurance products are purchased with level contract premiums. It is natural to think of a constant portion of each premium being for the benefit, hence a level benefit premium. Second, the single equation of the equivalence principle yields a solution for only one parameter. It is natural to think of this parameter as the benefit premium. Third, until the incidence of expenses is discussed in Chapter 15, one of the motivations of nonlevel benefit premiums is not present. Fourth, historically some regulatory standards have been specified in terms of benefit reserves defined by level benefit premiums.

In this chapter we define benefit reserves as we did in Chapter 7, but the definition is applied to general contracts with possibly nonlevel benefits and premiums. Of course, level premiums are a special case of nonlevel premiums, so the ideas here apply to the examples of Chapter 7. However, the reverse is not true. The special technique and relationships of Chapter 7 may not apply to the more general contracts of this chapter.

We start with definitions of general fully continuous and fully discrete insurances, and recursion relations are developed for these general models. The general discrete model is used to obtain formulas for benefit reserves at durations other than a contract anniversary, something that was not obtained in Chapter 7. An

---

allocation of loss and of risk of the contract to the various periods of the contract duration is obtained by use of the general fully discrete model. Again, these ideas apply to the contracts of Chapter 7, and the reader is encouraged to exercise this application.

8.2   Benefit Reserves for General Insurances

Consider a general fully discrete insurance on (x) in which
- The death benefit is payable at the end of the policy year of death
- Premiums are payable annually, at the beginning of the policy year
- The death benefit in the j-th policy year is b_j, $j = 1, 2, \ldots$
- The benefit premium payment in the j-th policy year is π_{j-1}, $j = 1, 2, \ldots$

Note that the subscripts of b and π are the times of payment.

For a non-negative integer, h, the prospective loss, $_hL$, is the present value at h of the future benefits less the present value at h of the future benefit premiums. Expressed as a function of $K(x)$, it is

$$_hL = \begin{cases} 0 & K(x) = 0, 1, \ldots h - 1 \\ b_{K(x)+1}\, v^{K(x)+1-h} - \displaystyle\sum_{j=h}^{K(x)} \pi_j\, v^{j-h} & K(x) = h, h + 1, \ldots . \end{cases} \tag{8.2.1}$$

Note: This definition extends the one given in (7.4.1) by including values (zeros) of $_hL$ for $K(x)$ less than h. Of course, this extension will not change the value of the benefit reserve because it is the conditional expectation given $K(x) \geq h$. The extension will be used in the development of recursion relations.

The benefit reserve at h, which we will denote by $_hV$, is defined as

$$_hV = \mathrm{E}[_hL | K(x) \geq h]$$

$$= \mathrm{E}\left[b_{K(x)+1}\, v^{K(x)+1-h} - \sum_{j=h}^{K(x)} \pi_j\, v^{j-h} \Big| K(x) \geq h \right]$$

$$= \mathrm{E}\left[b_{(K(x)-h)+h+1}\, v^{(K(x)-h)+1} - \sum_{j=0}^{K(x)-h} \pi_{h+j}\, v^j \Big| K(x) \geq h \right]. \tag{8.2.2}$$

Under the assumption that the conditional distribution of $K(x) - h$, given $K(x) = h, h + 1, \ldots$, is equal to the distribution of $K(x + h)$, this last expression can be rewritten as

$$_hV = \mathrm{E}\left[b_{K(x+h)+h+1}\, v^{K(x+h)+1} - \sum_{j=0}^{K(x+h)} \pi_{h+j}\, v^j \right]$$

$$= \sum_{j=0}^{\infty} \left(b_{h+j+1}\, v^{j+1} - \sum_{k=0}^{j} \pi_{h+k}\, v^k \right) {}_jp_{x+h}\, q_{x+h+j}. \tag{8.2.3}$$

Note that if this assumption fails, we are in the select mortality mode. By applying summation by parts (see Appendix 5) or reversing the order of summation, (8.2.3) can be rewritten as

$$_hV = \sum_{j=0}^{\infty} b_{h+j+1} \, v^{j+1} \, {}_jp_{x+h} \, q_{x+h+j} - \sum_{j=0}^{\infty} \pi_{h+j} \, v^j {}_jp_{x+h}. \tag{8.2.4}$$

Thus, $_hV$ as defined by (8.2.2) converts readily to the prospective formula: the actuarial present value of future benefits less the actuarial present value of future benefit premiums.

In Chapter 7 we discussed four types of formulas for the benefit reserve: prospective, retrospective, premium-difference, and paid-up insurance. These were applicable to benefit reserves for contracts with level benefit premiums and level benefits. Only the prospective and retrospective forms extend naturally to the general fully discrete insurance. The retrospective formula will be developed in the next section.

Example 8.2.1

A fully discrete whole life insurance with a unit benefit issued to (x) has its first year's benefit premium equal to the actuarial present value of the first year's benefit, and the remaining benefit premiums are level and determined by the equivalence principle. Determine formulas for (a) the first year's benefit premium, (b) the level benefit premium after the first year, and (c) the benefit reserve at the first duration.

Solution:

a. From Chapter 4, $\pi_0 = A^1_{x:\overline{1}|}$.
b. By the equivalence principle $A^1_{x:\overline{1}|} + \pi a_x = A_x$, so $\pi = (A_x - A^1_{x:\overline{1}|})/a_x = A_{x+1}/\ddot{a}_{x+1} = P_{x+1}$.
c. By the prospective formula, $_1V = A_{x+1} - \pi\ddot{a}_{x+1} = 0$. ▼

Example 8.2.1 illustrates one approach to nonlevel premiums. Another approach would be to set a premium pattern in the loss variable $_0L$ as defined in (8.2.1) by a set of weights, w_j, for $j = 0, 1, 2, \ldots$. Applying the equivalence principle, we have in a special case of (8.2.1)

$$E[_0L] = 0,$$

or

$$\sum_{j=0}^{\infty} b_{j+1} \, v^{j+1} \, {}_jp_x \, q_{x+j} = \pi \sum_{j=0}^{\infty} w_j \, v^j \, {}_jp_x \tag{8.2.5}$$

and

$$\pi = \frac{\displaystyle\sum_{j=0}^{\infty} b_{j+1} \, v^{j+1} \, {}_jp_x \, q_{x+j}}{\displaystyle\sum_{j=0}^{\infty} w_j \, v^j \, {}_jp_x}. \tag{8.2.6}$$

By different selections of sequences $\{b_{j+1}; j = 0, 1, 2, \ldots\}$ and $\{w_j; j = 0, 1, 2, \ldots\}$, the various benefit premium formulas can be obtained.

If we consider the sequence $\{b_{j+1}; j = 0, 1, 2, \ldots\}$ to be fixed, there remains great flexibility in selecting the sequence $\{w_j; j = 0, 1, 2, \ldots\}$, which in turn determines the sequence $\{\pi_j; j = 0, 1, 2, \ldots\}$. There may be commercial considerations to require that $w_j \geq 0$ for all j, but the equivalence principle does not impose this condition. In Example 8.2.1, $b_{j+1} = 1$ for all j, but $\pi w_0 = A^1_{x:\overline{1}|}$ and $\pi w_j = (A_x - A^1_{x:\overline{1}|})/a_x$, $j = 1, 2, \ldots$, and (8.2.6) is satisfied. A different application is found in Example 8.2.2.

<hr>

Example 8.2.2

The annual benefit premiums for a fully discrete whole life insurance with a unit benefit issued to (x) are $\pi_j = \pi w_j$, where $w_j = (1 + r)^j$. The rate r might be selected to estimate the expected growth rate in the insured's income.

Develop formulas for
a. π
b. $_hV$ and
c. $_hV$ when $r = i$.

Solution:

a. Using (8.2.5), $\pi = A_x / \ddot{a}^*_x$, where $\ddot{a}^*_x$ is valued at the rate of interest $i^* = (i - r)/(1 + r)$. When $r = i$, $\pi = A_x / (e_x + 1)$.
b. Using (8.2.4),

$$_hV = A_{x+h} - \sum_{j=0}^{\infty} \pi_{j+h}\, v^j\, {}_jp_{x+h}$$

$$= A_{x+h} - \frac{A_x}{\ddot{a}^*_x} (1 + r)^h \sum_{j=0}^{\infty} \left(\frac{1 + r}{1 + i}\right)^j {}_jp_{x+h}$$

$$= A_{x+h} - \frac{A_x}{\ddot{a}^*_x} (1 + r)^h \ddot{a}^*_{x+h}.$$

c. $_hV = A_{x+h} - [A_x/(e_x + 1)](1 + r)^h(e_{x+h} + 1)$. ▼

In Example 8.2.2, negative benefit reserves are possible with higher values of r. See Exercise 8.32 for a variation of this policy.

Now consider a general fully continuous insurance on (x) under which
• The death benefit payable at the moment of death, t, is b_t, and
• Benefit premiums are payable continuously at t at the annual rate, π_t.
The prospective loss for a life insured at x and surviving at t is the present value at t of the future benefits less the present value at t of the future benefit premiums:

$$_tL = \begin{cases} 0 & T(x) \le t \\ b_{T(x)} \, v^{T(x)-t} - \displaystyle\int_t^{T(x)} \pi_u \, v^{u-t} \, du & T(x) > t. \end{cases} \tag{8.2.7}$$

The benefit reserve for this general case, which we will denote by $_t\bar{V}$, is then

$$_t\bar{V} = \mathrm{E}[_tL | T(x) > t]$$

$$= \mathrm{E}\left[b_{T(x)} \, v^{T(x)-t} - \int_t^{T(x)} \pi_u \, v^{u-t} \, du \Big| T(x) > t \right]$$

$$= \mathrm{E}\left[b_{(T(x)-t)+t} \, v^{T(x)-t} - \int_0^{T(x)-t} \pi_{t+r} \, v^r \, dr \Big| T(x) > t \right]. \tag{8.2.8}$$

As assumed to obtain (8.2.3) for the fully discrete insurance, we assume here that the conditional distribution of $T(x) - t$, given $T(x) > t$, is the same as the distribution of $T(x + t)$ and proceed to

$$_t\bar{V} = \mathrm{E}\left[b_{T(x+t)+t} \, v^{T(x+t)} - \int_0^{T(x+t)} \pi_{t+r} \, v^r \, dr \right]$$

$$= \int_0^{\infty} \left(b_{t+u} \, v^u - \int_0^u \pi_{t+r} \, v^r \, dr \right) \, _up_{x+t} \, \mu_x(t + u) \, du$$

$$= \int_0^{\infty} b_{t+u} \, v^u \, _up_{x+t} \, \mu_x(t + u) \, du - \int_0^{\infty} \pi_{t+r} \, v^r \, _rp_{x+t} \, dr. \tag{8.2.9}$$

The second integral in (8.2.9) is obtained by integration by parts, or, alternatively, by reversing the order of integration. In other words, $_t\bar{V}$ can be expressed as the actuarial present value of future benefits less the actuarial present value of future benefit premiums. If the assumption about the conditional distribution of $T(x) - t$, given $T(x) > t$, does not hold, we are in the select mortality mode.

8.3 Recursion Relations for Fully Discrete Benefit Reserves

One objective of this chapter is to explore recursion relations among the loss random variables, their expected values, and variances. We start with a definition for the insurer's net cash loss (negative cash flow) within each insurance year for the fully discrete model as defined for (8.2.1). Figure 8.3.1 is a time diagram that shows the annual cash income and cash outgo.

FIGURE 8.3.1

Insurer's Cash Income and Outgo for General Fully Discrete Insurance

Outgo	0	0	0		0	0	$b_{K(x)+1}$	0	0	
Income	π_0	π_1	π_2	π_3	$\pi_{K(x)-1}$	$\pi_{K(x)}$	0	0	0	etc.
	0	1	2	3	$K(x)-1$	$K(x)$	$K(x)+1$	$K(x)+2$	$K(x)+3$	

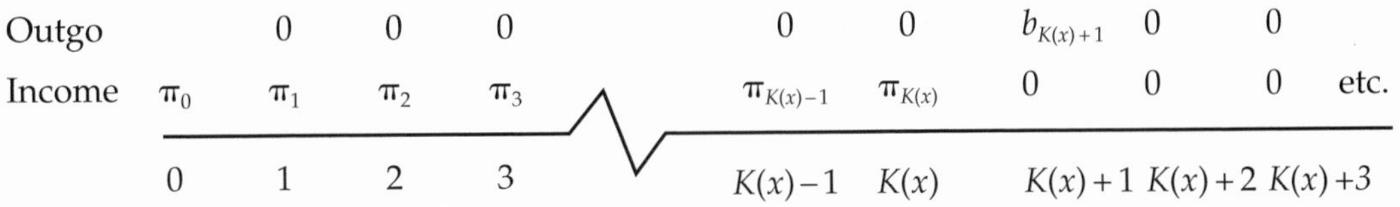

Let C_h denote the present value at h of the net cash loss during the year $(h, h + 1)$. If $(h, h + 1)$ is before the year of death $[h < K(x)]$, then $C_h = -\pi_h$. If $(h, h + 1)$ is the year of death $[h = K(x)]$, then $C_h = v\, b_{h+1} - \pi_h$. And if $(h, h + 1)$ is after the year of death, of course, $C_h = 0$. Restating this definition as an explicit function of $K(x)$,

$$C_h = \begin{cases} 0 & K(x) = 0, 1, \ldots, h - 1 \\ v\, b_{h+1} - \pi_h & K(x) = h \\ -\pi_h & K(x) = h + 1, h + 2, \ldots. \end{cases} \tag{8.3.1}$$

For the conditional distribution of C_h, given $K(x) \geq h$, we observe that

$$C_h = vb_{h+1}\, I - \pi_h,$$

where

$$I = \begin{cases} 1 & \text{with probability } q_{x+h} \\ 0 & \text{with probability } p_{x+h}. \end{cases}$$

Therefore,

$$E[C_h | K(x) \geq h] = v\, b_{h+1}\, q_{x+h} - \pi_h \tag{8.3.2}$$

and

$$\text{Var}[C_h | K(x) \geq h] = (v\, b_{h+1})^2\, q_{x+h}\, p_{x+h}. \tag{8.3.3}$$

Moreover, using (2.2.10) and (2.2.11) along with (8.3.1)–(8.3.3),

$$E[C_h] = (v\, b_{h+1}\, q_{x+h} - \pi_h)\, {}_hp_x \tag{8.3.4}$$

and

$$\text{Var}(C_h) = (v\, b_{h+1}\, q_{x+h} - \pi_h)^2\, {}_hp_x\, {}_hq_x + (v\, b_{h+1})^2 q_{x+h}\, p_{x+h}\, {}_hp_x. \tag{8.3.5}$$

Finally, for $j > h$, C_j and C_h are correlated, an assertion that is left for the student to verify in Exercises 8.5 and 8.6.

As previously defined in (8.2.1), ${}_hL$ is the present value at h of the insurer's future cash outflow less the present value at h of the insurer's future cash income. By rearranging the terms in this definition, an equivalent one that states ${}_hL$ as the sum of the present values at h of the insurer's future net annual cash losses is obtained. This is

$$_hL = \sum_{j=h}^{\infty} v^{j-h}\, C_j. \tag{8.3.6}$$

For $h < K(x)$, we have from (8.3.1),

$$_hL = \sum_{j=h}^{K(x)} v^{j-h}\, C_j = v^{K(x)-h} \left(v\, b_{K(x)+1} - \pi_{K(x)} \right) - \sum_{j=h}^{K(x)-1} v^{j-h}\pi_j$$

$$= v^{K(x)+1-h}\, b_{K(x)+1} - \sum_{j=h}^{K(x)} v^{j-h}\, \pi_j$$

as before. For $h = K(x)$, ${}_hL = C_{K(x)} = (v\, b_{K(x)+1} - \pi_{K(x)})$. And for $h > K(x)$, both sides of (8.3.6) are zero.

A recursion relation for the loss variables follows from (8.3.6):

$$_hL = C_h + v \sum_{j=h+1}^{\infty} v^{j-(h+1)} C_j = C_h + v\ _{h+1}L. \tag{8.3.7}$$

A recursion relation for the benefit reserves can be obtained from (8.3.7) by

$$_hV = \mathrm{E}[_hL|K(x) \geq h]$$

$$= \mathrm{E}[C_h + v\ _{h+1}L|K(x) \geq h]$$

$$= v\ b_{h+1}\ q_{x+h} - \pi_h + v\ \mathrm{E}[_{h+1}L|K(x) \geq h]. \tag{8.3.8}$$

Since $_{h+1}L$ is zero when $K(x)$ is h, we have

$$_hV = v\ b_{h+1}\ q_{x+h} - \pi_h + v\ \mathrm{E}[_{h+1}L|K(x) \geq h + 1]\ p_{x+h}$$

$$= v\ b_{h+1}\ q_{x+h} - \pi_h + v\ _{h+1}V\ p_{x+h}. \tag{8.3.9}$$

Formula (8.3.9) is a backward recursion formula $[u(h) = c(h) + d(h) \times u(h + 1)]$ for the general fully discrete benefit reserve. Note that $d(h) = vp_{x+h}$ again and $c(h) = vb_{h+1}q_{x+h} - \pi_h$. A forward recursion formula can be obtained by solving (8.3.9) for $_{h+1}V$. (See Exercise 8.7.) This forward formula was used in Examples 7.4.3 and 7.4.4 in an aggregate mode; that is, the mortality functions were in life table form.

Further insight to the progress of benefit reserves can be gained by rearrangements of (8.3.9). First, add π_h to both sides, to see

$$_hV + \pi_h = b_{h+1}\ v\ q_{x+h} + _{h+1}V\ v\ p_{x+h}. \tag{8.3.10}$$

In words, the resources required at the beginning of insurance year $h + 1$ equal the actuarial present value of the year-end requirements. The sum $_hV + \pi_h$ is called the ***initial benefit reserve*** for the policy year $h + 1$. In contrast, $_hV$ and $_{h+1}V$ are called the ***terminal benefit reserves*** for insurance years h and $h + 1$ to indicate that they are year-end benefit reserves.

Formula (8.3.10) can be rearranged to separate the benefit premium π_h into components for insurance year $h + 1$, namely,

$$\pi_h = b_{h+1}\ v\ q_{x+h} + (_{h+1}V\ v\ p_{x+h} - _hV). \tag{8.3.11}$$

The first component on the right-hand side of (8.3.11) is the 1-year term insurance benefit premium for the sum insured b_{h+1}. The second component, $_{h+1}V\ v\ p_{x+h} - _hV$, represents the amount which, if added to $_hV$ at the beginning of the year, would accumulate under interest and survivorship to $_{h+1}V$ at the end of the year.

For the purpose of subsequent comparison with formulas for a fully continuous insurance, we multiply both sides of (8.3.11) by $1 + i$ and rearrange the formula to

$$\pi_h + (_hV + \pi_h)i + _{h+1}Vq_{x+h} = b_{h+1}\ q_{x+h} + \Delta(_hV). \tag{8.3.12}$$

The left-hand side of (8.3.12) indicates resources for insurance year $h + 1$, namely, the benefit premium, interest for the year on the initial benefit reserve, and the expected release by death of the terminal benefit reserve. The right-hand side consists of the expected payment of the death benefit at the end of the year and the increment $_{h+1}V - _hV$ in the benefit reserve.

An analysis different than (8.3.10)–(8.3.12) results if one considers that the benefit reserve $_{h+1}V$ is to be available to offset the death benefit b_{h+1}, and that only the *net amount at risk*, $b_{h+1} - _{h+1}V$, needs to be covered by 1-year term insurance. For this analysis we have, on substituting $1 - q_{x+h}$ for p_{x+h} in (8.3.10) and multiplying through by $1 + i$,

$$_{h+1}V = (_hV + \pi_h)(1 + i) - (b_{h+1} - _{h+1}V)q_{x+h}. \tag{8.3.13}$$

Corresponding to (8.3.11), we now have

$$\pi_h = (b_{h+1} - _{h+1}V)v\, q_{x+h} + (v\, _{h+1}V - _hV). \tag{8.3.14}$$

The first component on the right-hand side of (8.3.14) is the 1-year term insurance benefit premium for the net amount of risk. The second component, $v\, _{h+1}V - _hV$, is the amount which, if added to $_hV$ at the beginning of the year, would accumulate under interest to $_{h+1}V$ at the end of the year. In this formulation $_{h+1}V$ is used, in case of death, to offset the death benefit. Consequently, the benefit reserve accumulates as a savings fund. This is shown again by the formula corresponding to (8.3.12), namely,

$$\pi_h + (_hV + \pi_h)i = (b_{h+1} - _{h+1}V)q_{x+h} + \Delta(_hV), \tag{8.3.15}$$

which is left for the reader to interpret.

The analysis by (8.3.11) does not use the benefit reserve to offset the death benefit, and consequently the benefit reserve accumulates under interest and survivorship. Both components of the right-hand side of (8.3.11) involve mortality risk, whereas in (8.3.14) only the first component does. We see in Section 8.5 that (8.3.14) is related to a flexible means for calculating the variance of loss attributable to the random nature of time until death.

Formulas (8.3.10)–(8.3.15) are all recursion relations for the benefit reserve at integral durations. None of the six is written in the form of an explicit backward or forward formula; rather, each is written to give an insight. In Example 8.3.1, recursion relation (8.3.14) is used to obtain an explicit formula for the benefit premium and benefit reserve.

Example 8.3.1

A deferred whole life annuity-due issued to (x) for an annual income of 1 commencing at age $x + n$ is to be paid for by level annual benefit premiums during the deferral period. The benefit for death prior to age $x + n$ is the benefit reserve. Assuming the death benefit is paid at the end of the year of death, determine the annual benefit premium and the benefit reserve at the end of year k for $k \le n$.

Solution:

Using the fact that $b_{h+1} = {}_{h+1}V$ for $h = 0, 1, 2, \ldots, n-1$, in (8.3.14), we have

$$\pi = v \,{}_{h+1}V - {}_hV.$$

On multiplication by v^h, we have

$$\pi v^h = v^{h+1}\,{}_{h+1}V - v^h\,{}_hV = \Delta(v^h\,{}_hV). \qquad (8.3.16)$$

Summing over $h = 0, 1, 2, \ldots, n-1$, we obtain

$$v^n\,{}_nV - v^0\,{}_0V = \pi \sum_{h=0}^{n-1} v^h = \pi\ddot{a}_{\overline{n}|},$$

and, since ${}_0V = 0$ and ${}_nV = \ddot{a}_{x+n}$, it follows that

$$\pi = v^n \frac{\ddot{a}_{x+n}}{\ddot{a}_{\overline{n}|}} = \frac{\ddot{a}_{x+n}}{\ddot{s}_{\overline{n}|}}.$$

Thus, this annuity is identical to that described in Example 6.6.2. The benefit reserve at the end of k years can be found by summing (8.3.16) over $h = 0, 1, 2, \ldots, k-1$ to give

$$v^k\,{}_kV = \pi\ddot{a}_{\overline{k}|},$$

from which

$$_kV = \pi\ddot{s}_{\overline{k}|}. \qquad \blacktriangledown$$

Example 8.3.2

A fully discrete n-year endowment insurance on (x) provides, in case of death within n years, a payment of 1 plus the benefit reserve. Obtain formulas for the level benefit premium and the benefit reserve at the end of k years, given that the maturity value is 1.

Solution:

In this case $b_h = 1 + {}_hV$, and the net amount at risk has constant value 1. Denoting the annual benefit premium by π and using (8.3.14), we have

$$v\,{}_{h+1}V - {}_hV = \pi - v\,q_{x+h} \qquad h = 0, 1, \ldots, n-1.$$

On multiplication by v^h, this becomes

$$\Delta(v^h\,{}_hV) = \pi\,v^h - v^{h+1}\,q_{x+h}. \qquad (8.3.17)$$

Summing this over $h = 0, 1, 2, \ldots, n-1$, we obtain

$$v^n\,{}_nV = \pi\,\ddot{a}_{\overline{n}|} - \sum_{h=0}^{n-1} v^{h+1}q_{x+h}$$

so that, with ${}_nV = 1$ (the maturity value is 1),

$$\pi = \frac{v^n + \displaystyle\sum_{h=0}^{n-1} v^{h+1}q_{x+h}}{\ddot{a}_{\overline{n}|}}.$$

By summing (8.3.17) over $h = 0, 1, 2, \ldots, k - 1$, and solving for $_kV$, we have

$$_kV = \pi\ddot{s}_{\overline{k}|} - \sum_{h=0}^{k-1} (1 + i)^{k-h-1} q_{x+h}. \qquad \blacktriangledown$$

Just before Example 8.2.1 we promised to develop a retrospective formula for the benefit reserve of the general fully discrete insurance in this section. We start by rewriting recursion relation (8.3.11) in the form

$$\pi_h - b_{h+1}\, v\, q_{x+h} = {}_{h+1}V\, v\, p_{x+h} - {}_hV$$

and then multiplying both sides by $v^h\, {}_hp_x$ to obtain

$$\pi_h\, v^h\, {}_hp_x - b_{h+1}\, v^{h+1}\, {}_hp_x\, q_{x+h} = {}_{h+1}V\, v^{h+1}\, {}_{h+1}p_x - {}_hV\, v^h\, {}_hp_x$$

$$= \Delta({}_hV\, v^h\, {}_hp_x), \qquad (8.3.18)$$

which holds for $h = 0, 1, 2, \ldots$. When we sum both sides of (8.3.18) over the values from 0 to $k - 1$, we have

$$\sum_{h=0}^{k-1} (\pi_h\, v^h\, {}_hp_x - b_{h+1}\, v^{h+1}\, {}_hp_x\, q_{x+h}) = {}_kV\, v^k\, {}_kp_x - {}_0V.$$

With equivalence principle premiums, $_0V = 0$, so we can rewrite this last equation for the terminal benefit reserve of the general fully discrete insurance as

$$_kV = \sum_{h=0}^{k-1} \frac{\pi_h\, v^h\, {}_hp_x - b_{h+1}\, v^{h+1}\, {}_hp_x\, q_{x+h}}{v^k\, {}_kp_x}$$

and then as

$$_kV = \sum_{h=0}^{k-1} (\pi_h - vb_{h+1}\, q_{x+h}) \frac{(1 + i)^{k-h}}{{}_{k-h}p_{x+h}}. \qquad (8.3.19)$$

Formula (8.3.19) shows the benefit reserve at k as the sum over the first k years of each year's premium less its expected death benefit accumulated with respect to interest and mortality to k.

8.4 Benefit Reserves at Fractional Durations

We consider again the general fully discrete insurance of (8.2.1) on (x) for a death benefit of b_{j+1} at the end of insurance year $j + 1$, purchased by annual benefit premiums of π_j, $j = 0, 1, \ldots$, payable at the beginning of the insurance year. We seek a formula for, and an approximation to, the **interim benefit reserve**, that is, $_{h+s}V$ for $h = 0, 1, 2, \ldots$ and $0 < s < 1$. Extending the earlier definition of the benefit reserve as stated in (8.2.1) and (8.2.2), we have for the interim case

$$_{h+s}L = \begin{cases} 0 & K(x) = 0, 1, \ldots, h - 1 \\ v^{1-s}\, b_{K(x)+1} & K(x) = h \\ v^{K(x)+1-(h+s)}\, b_{K(x)+1} - \displaystyle\sum_{j=h+1}^{K(x)} v^{j-(h+s)}\, \pi_j & K(x) = h + 1, h + 2, \ldots \end{cases}$$

$$(8.4.1)$$

and

$$_{h+s}V = E[_{h+s}L|T(x) > h + s]. \tag{8.4.2}$$

From (8.4.2),

$$_{h+s}V = v^{1-s}\, b_{h+1}\,_{1-s}q_{x+h+s} + v^{1-s}\,_{h+1}V\,_{1-s}p_{x+h+s}. \tag{8.4.3}$$

Now multiply both sides of (8.4.3) by $v^s\,_sp_{x+h}$ to obtain

$$v^s\,_sp_{x+h}\,_{h+s}V = v\, b_{h+1}(_{s|1-s}q_{x+h}) + v(_{h+1}V)\, p_{x+h}. \tag{8.4.4}$$

Equation (8.3.9) provides an expression for $vb_{h+1}\,q_{x+h}$, which can be substituted into (8.4.4) to obtain

$$v^s\,_sp_{x+h}\,_{h+s}V = (_hV + \pi_h -\,_{h+1}V\, v\, p_{x+h})\frac{_{s|1-s}q_{x+h}}{q_{x+h}} + v\,_{h+1}V\, p_{x+h},$$

which can be rearranged to

$$v^s\,_sp_{x+h}\,_{h+s}V = (_hV + \pi_h)\frac{_{s|1-s}q_{x+h}}{q_{x+h}} + (_{h+1}V\, v\, p_{x+h})\left(1 - \frac{_{s|1-s}q_{x+h}}{q_{x+h}}\right). \tag{8.4.5}$$

This exact expression shows that when the interim benefit reserve at $h + s$ is discounted with respect to interest and mortality to h, the result is equal to an interpolated value between the initial benefit reserve at h and the value of the terminal benefit reserve at $h + 1$ discounted to h.

We emphasize that the interpolation is, in general, not linear; however, under the assumption of uniform distribution of deaths over the age interval the interpolation weights are linear and (8.4.5) is

$$v^s\,_sp_{x+h}\,_{h+s}V = (_hV + \pi_h)(1 - s) + (_{h+1}V\, v\, p_{x+h})(s). \tag{8.4.6}$$

By replacing i and q_{x+h} with zeros in (8.4.6), as an approximation, the result is linear interpolation between the initial benefit reserve at h and the terminal benefit reserve. The approximate result is

$$_{h+s}V = (1 - s)(_hV + \pi_h) + s(_{h+1}V), \tag{8.4.7}$$

which is often written in the form

$$_{h+s}V = (1 - s)(_hV) + s(_{h+1}V) + (1 - s)\pi_h. \tag{8.4.8}$$

Here the interim benefit reserve is the sum of the value obtained by linear interpolation between the terminal benefit reserves,

$$(1 - s)(_hV) + s(_{h+1}V),$$

and the **unearned benefit premium** $(1 - s)\pi_h$. In general,

(the unearned benefit premium   = (the benefit premium
  at a given time during the year)   for the year)

                        × (the difference between the time
                           through which the premium
                           has been paid and the given time).

Thus, on an annual premium basis, the benefit premium has been paid to the end of the year so at time s the unearned benefit premium is $(1 - s)\pi_h$. This notion of an unearned benefit premium will be used in discussing approximations to benefit reserves when the premiums are collected by installments more frequent than an annual basis.

We consider now one such case, that of true semiannual premiums with claims paid at the end of the insurance year of death. For $0 < s \le 1/2$ we could start with the random variable giving the present value of prospective losses as of time $h + s$ and then calculate its conditional expectation given that (x) has survived to $h + s$. This is a bit more complex than it was for (8.4.4), so we start with the equation corresponding to (8.4.3) by noting that it is the prospective formula

$$_{h+s}V^{(2)} = v^{1-s}\,b_{h+1}\big(_{1-s}q_{x+h+s}\big) + v^{1-s}\big(_{h+1}V^{(2)}\big)\,_{1-s}p_{x+h+s}$$

$$- \frac{\pi_h^{(2)}}{2}\,(v^{0.5-s})\big(_{0.5-s}p_{x+h+s}\big). \tag{8.4.9}$$

The first two terms of (8.4.9) can be viewed as the actuarial present value of the death benefit and an endowment benefit of amount equal to the reserve, and the third term is the actuarial present value of the future benefit premium for the $1 - s$ year endowment insurance. Multiplying both sides of (8.4.9) by $_{s}p_{x+h}\,v^{s}$, we have

$$_{s}p_{x+h}\,v^{s}\,_{h+s}V^{(2)} = vb_{h+1}\big(_{s|1-s}q_{x+h}\big) + v\big(_{h+1}V^{(2)}\big)\,p_{x+h}$$

$$- \frac{\pi_h^{(2)}}{2}\,(v^{0.5})\big(_{0.5}p_{x+h}\big). \tag{8.4.10}$$

For the semiannual premium policy the equation corresponding to (8.3.10) is also a prospective benefit reserve formula:

$$_{h}V^{(2)} = b_{h+1}vq_{x+h} + {}_{h+1}V^{(2)}vp_{x+h} - \frac{\pi_h^{(2)}}{2}\big(1 + v^{0.5}\,_{0.5}p_{x+h}\big). \tag{8.4.11}$$

Equation (8.4.11) provides an expression for vb_{h+1} to substitute in (8.4.10), which yields

$$_{s}p_{x+h}\,v^{s}\,_{h+s}V^{(2)} = \left(_{h}V^{(2)} + \frac{\pi_h^{(2)}}{2}\right)\frac{_{s|1-s}q_{x+h}}{q_{x+h}}$$

$$+ \left[v\big(_{h+1}V^{(2)}\big)\,p_{x+h} - \frac{\pi_h^{(2)}}{2}\,(v^{0.5})\big(_{0.5}p_{x+h}\big)\right]$$

$$\times \left(1 - \frac{_{s|1-s}q_{x+h}}{q_{x+h}}\right). \tag{8.4.12}$$

Formula (8.4.12) corresponds to (8.4.5), which showed that the interim benefit reserve at $h + s$, discounted with respect to interest and mortality to h, is equal to a nonlinear interpolated value between the initial benefit reserve at h and the discounted value to h of the terminal benefit reserve at $h + 1$. For the semiannual premium case, this terminal reserve has been reduced by the amount of the discounted value of the midyear benefit premium. Under the assumption of a uniform distribution of deaths over the age interval, we have linear interpolation on the right-hand side:

$$_s p_{x+h} \, v^s \, {}_{h+s}V^{(2)} = \left({}_h V^{(2)} + \frac{\pi_h^{(2)}}{2} \right)(1 - s)$$

$$+ \left[v\left({}_{h+1}V^{(2)} \right) p_{x+h} - \frac{\pi_h^{(2)}}{2} \left(v^{0.5} \right) \left({}_{0.5}p_{x+h} \right) \right](s). \qquad (8.4.13)$$

Again setting i and q_{x+h} equal to zero, as an approximation, we obtain simple linear interpolation between the initial benefit reserve and the terminal benefit reserve reduced by the benefit premium due at midyear:

$$_{h+s}V^{(2)} = \left({}_h V^{(2)} + \frac{\pi_h^{(2)}}{2} \right)(1 - s) + \left({}_{h+1}V^{(2)} - \frac{\pi_h^{(2)}}{2} \right)(s).$$

This formula can be rearranged as the interpolated value between the terminal benefit reserves plus the unearned benefit premium $(\pi_h^{(2)})(1/2 - s)$:

$$_{h+s}V^{(2)} = \left[(1 - s){}_h V^{(2)} + s \, {}_{h+1}V^{(2)} \right] + \left(\frac{1}{2} - s \right) \pi_h^{(2)}. \qquad (8.4.14)$$

For the last half of the year when $1/2 < s \le 1$, we can proceed as above to obtain the following exact formula for the benefit reserve at $h + s$ discounted with respect to interest and mortality to h:

$$_s p_{x+h} \, v^s \, {}_{h+s}V^{(2)} = \left[{}_h V^{(2)} + \frac{\pi_h^{(2)}}{2} \left(1 + v^{0.5}{}_{0.5}p_{x+h} \right) \right] \frac{_{s|1-s}q_{x+h}}{q_{x+h}}$$

$$+ \left[v\left({}_{h+1}V^{(2)} \right) p_{x+h} \right] \left(1 - \frac{_{s|1-s}q_{x+h}}{q_{x+h}} \right). \qquad (8.4.15)$$

Again under uniform distribution of death in the year of age, we have the linear interpolation

$$_s p_{x+h} \, v^s \, {}_{h+s}V^{(2)} = (1 - s) \left[{}_h V^{(2)} + \frac{\pi_h^{(2)}}{2} \left(1 + v^{0.5}{}_{0.5}p_{x+h} \right) \right]$$

$$+ s \left[v\left({}_{h+1}V^{(2)} \right) p_{x+h} \right], \qquad (8.4.16)$$

and with i and q_{x+h} set equal to zero, as an approximation, we have the simple linear interpolation plus the unearned benefit premium

$$_{h+s}V^{(2)} = {}_h V^{(2)}(1 - s) + {}_{h+1}V^{(2)}(s) + \pi_h^{(2)}(1 - s). \qquad (8.4.17)$$

(For the general result for m-thly reserves see Exercise 8.12.)

8.5 Allocation of the Risk to Insurance Years

In Section 8.3 recursion relations for benefit reserves are developed by an analysis of the insurer's annual cash income and cash outflow. Now we extend this analysis to an accrual or incurred basis and develop allocations of the risk, as measured by the variance of the loss variables, to the insurance years. Figure 8.5.1 shows in a time diagram the insurer's annual cash incomes, cash outflows, and changes in liability for the general fully discrete insurance of (8.2.1). The random variable C_h is related to the cash flows of the policy year $(h, h + 1)$. We now define a random variable related to the total change in liability, cash flow, and reserves.

Insurer's Cash Incomes, Outflows, and Changes in Liability for Fully Discrete General Insurance

Outflow		0	0		0	$b_{K(x)+1}$	0	
Income	π_0	π_1	π_2		$\pi_{K(x)}$	0	0	
ΔLiability		$_1V$	$_2V - (1+i)\,_1V$		$_{K(x)}V - (1+i)_{K(x)-1}V$	$-(1+i)_{K(x)}V$	0	etc.
	0	1	2		$K(x)$	$K(x)+1$	$K(x)+2$	

Let Λ_h denote the present value at h (a non-negative integer) of the insurer's cash loss plus change in liability during the year $(h, h + 1)$. If $(h, h + 1)$ is before the year of death $[h < K(x)]$, then

$$\Lambda_h = C_h + v\,\Delta\text{Liability} = -\pi_h + v\,_{h+1}V - {_h}V.$$

If $(h, h + 1)$ is the year of death $[h = K(x)]$, then

$$\Lambda_h = C_h + v\Delta\text{Liability} = v\,b_{h+1} - \pi_h - {_h}V.$$

And if $(h, h + 1)$ is after the year of death, of course $\Lambda_h = 0$. Restating this definition as a function of $K(x)$, and rearranging the terms,

$$\Lambda_h = \begin{cases} 0 & K(x) = 0, 1, \ldots, h - 1 \\ (v\,b_{h+1} - \pi_h) + \quad\quad\quad (-{_h}V) & K(x) = h \\ (-\pi_h) \quad\quad + (v\,_{h+1}V - {_h}V) & K(x) = h + 1, h + 2, \ldots. \end{cases} \tag{8.5.1}$$

The definition of Λ_h in (8.5.1) can be rewritten to display Λ_h as the loss variable for a 1-year term insurance with a benefit equal to the amount at risk on the basic policy. See Exercise 8.31.

It follows that

$$E[\Lambda_h|K(x) \geq h] = v\,b_{h+1}\,q_{x+h} + v\,_{h+1}V\,p_{x+h} - (\pi_h + {_h}V), \tag{8.5.2}$$

which is zero by (8.3.10).

Since the conditional distribution of Λ_h, given $K(x) = h, h + 1, \ldots,$ is a two-point distribution, then

$$\text{Var}[\Lambda_h|K(x) \geq h] = [v(b_{h+1} - {_{h+1}}V)]^2\,p_{x+h}\,q_{x+h}. \tag{8.5.3}$$

With $j \leq h$ we can use (2.2.10) and (2.2.11) to obtain

$$E[\Lambda_h|K(x) \geq j] = 0 \tag{8.5.4}$$

and

$$\mathrm{Var}[\Lambda_h | K(x) \geq j] = \mathrm{Var}[\Lambda_h | K(x) \geq h] \,_{h-j}p_{x+j}. \qquad (8.5.5)$$

Unlike the C_h's of Section 8.3, the Λ_h's are uncorrelated, an assertion that is proved in the following lemma. This fact conveys some sense of the role of reserves in stabilizing financial reporting of insurance operations.

Lemma 8.5.1:

For non-negative integers satisfying $g \leq h < j$,

$$\mathrm{Cov}[\Lambda_h, \Lambda_j | K(x) \geq g] = 0. \qquad (8.5.6)$$

Proof:

From (8.5.4), $\mathrm{E}[\Lambda_h | K(x) \geq g] = 0$; therefore,

$$\mathrm{Cov}[\Lambda_h, \Lambda_j | K(x) \geq g] = \mathrm{E}[\Lambda_h \Lambda_j | K(x) \geq g].$$

From (8.5.1) we see that Λ_h is equal to the constant $(v \,_{h+1}V - \,_h V - \pi_h)$ where Λ_j is nonzero. Thus,

$$\Lambda_h \Lambda_j = (v \,_{h+1}V - \,_h V - \pi_h)\Lambda_j \qquad \text{for all } K(x), \qquad (8.5.7)$$

$$\mathrm{E}[\Lambda_h \Lambda_j | K(x) \geq g] = (v \,_{h+1}V - \,_h V - \pi_h)\mathrm{E}[\Lambda_j | K(x) \geq g] = 0,$$

and

$$\mathrm{Cov}[\Lambda_k \Lambda_j | K(x) \geq g] = 0. \qquad \blacksquare$$

We now express the loss variables $_h L$ in terms of the Λ_h's. From the definition of the Λ_h's and formula (8.3.6),

$$\sum_{j=h}^{\infty} v^{j-h} \Lambda_j = \sum_{j=h}^{\infty} v^{j-h}[C_j + v\Delta\mathrm{Liability}\,(j, j + 1)]$$

$$= \,_h L + \sum_{j=h}^{\infty} v^{j-h+1} \Delta\mathrm{Liability}\,(j, j + 1). \qquad (8.5.8)$$

Conceptually the last term will be the present value of the final liability minus the liability at h, that is, $0 - \,_h V$. Thus we have the relationship

$$_h L = \begin{cases} 0 & K(x) < h \\ \displaystyle\sum_{j=h}^{\infty} v^{j-h} \Lambda_j + \,_h V & K(x) \geq h, \end{cases} \qquad (8.5.9)$$

which can be rewritten as

$$_h L = \begin{cases} 0 & K(x) < h \\ \displaystyle\sum_{j=h}^{h+i-1} v^{j-h} \Lambda_j + \sum_{j=h+i}^{\infty} v^{j-h} \Lambda_j + \,_h V & K(x) \geq h. \end{cases} \qquad (8.5.10)$$

These relationships can be interpreted as stating that the present value of future losses, measured at time h following issue, is equal to the present value of future cash flows, adjusted for changes in reserves, plus the reserve at h.

Using the representation of $_h L$ shown in (8.5.9), we have

$$\text{Var}[_hL|K(x) \geq h] = \sum_{j=h}^{\infty} v^{2(j-h)} \, \text{Var}[\Lambda_j|K(x) \geq h]$$

$$= \sum_{j=h}^{\infty} v^{2(j-h)} \, _{j-h}p_{x+h} \, \text{Var}[\Lambda_j|K(x) \geq j]$$

$$= \sum_{j=h}^{\infty} v^{2(j-h)} \, _{j-h}p_{x+h}\{[v(b_{j+1} - \, _{j+i}V)]^2 \, p_{x+j}q_{x+j}\}. \qquad (8.5.11)$$

In this development the first line makes use of Lemma 8.5.1, the second (8.5.5), and the third (8.5.3).

Starting with (8.5.10) we can follow identical steps to obtain

$$\text{Var}[_hL|K(x) \geq h] = \sum_{j=h}^{h+i-1} v^{2(j-h)} \, \text{Var}[\Lambda_j|K(x) \geq h]$$

$$+ \sum_{j=h+i}^{\infty} v^{2(j-h)} \, \text{Var}[\Lambda_j|K(x) \geq h]$$

$$= \sum_{j=h}^{h+i-1} v^{2(j-h)} \, _{j-h}p_{x+h}\{[v(b_{j+1} - \, _{j+1}V)]^2 \, p_{x+j}q_{x+j}\}$$

$$+ \sum_{j=h+i}^{\infty} v^{2(j-h)} \, _{j-h}p_{x+h}\{[v(b_{j+1} - \, _{j+1}V)]^2 \, p_{x+j}q_{x+j}\}. \qquad (8.5.12)$$

The second summation can be rewritten by replacing the summation variable j by $l + h$ to obtain

$$\sum_{l=i}^{\infty} v^{2l} \, _lp_{x+h}\{[v(b_{h+l+1} - \, _{h+l+1}V)]^2 \, p_{x+h+l}q_{x+h+l}\}$$

$$= v^{2i} \, _ip_{x+h} \sum_{l=i}^{\infty} v^{2(l-i)} \, _{l-i}p_{x+h+i} \, \{[v(b_{h+l+1} - \, _{h+l+1}V)]^2 \, p_{x+h+l}q_{x+h+l}\}$$

$$= v^{2i} \, _ip_{x+h} \, \text{Var}[_{h+i}L|K(x) \geq h + i]. \qquad (8.5.13)$$

The main results of these developments will be summarized as a theorem.

Theorem 8.5.1

$$\text{Var}(_hL|K(x) \geq h)$$

$$\text{a.} = \sum_{j=h}^{\infty} v^{2(j-h)} \, \text{Var}[\Lambda_j|K(x) \geq h] \qquad (8.5.14)$$

$$\text{b.} = \sum_{j=h}^{\infty} v^{2(j-h)} \, _{j-h}p_{x+h} \, \{[v(b_{j+1} - \, _{j+1}V)]^2 \, p_{x+j}q_{x+j}\} \qquad (8.5.15)$$

$$\text{c.} = \sum_{j=h}^{h+i-1} v^{2(j-h)} \, _{j-h}p_{x+h}\{[v(b_{j+1} - \, _{j+1}V)]^2 \, p_{x+j}q_{x+j}\}$$

$$+ v^{2i} \, _ip_{x+h} \, \text{Var}[_{h+i}L|K(x) \geq h + i]. \qquad (8.5.16)$$

Proof:

(a) follows from (8.5.11), first line
(b) follows from (8.5.11), third line
(c) follows from (8.5.12) and (8.5.13).

We refer to this theorem as the Hattendorf theorem, and we illustrate its application in the following two examples. Items (b) and (c) of the theorem can be used as backward recursion formulas that are useful for understanding the duration allocation of risk and, perhaps, for computing.

Just as the random variables C, introduced in (8.3.1), allocate each loss to insurance years, and the random variables Λ, introduced in (8.5.1), allocate cash loss and liability adjustment to insurance years, the Hattendorf theorem facilitates the allocation of mortality risk, as measured by $\mathrm{Var}[_hL|K(x) \geq h]$, to insurance years. This allocation facilitates risk management planning for a limited number of future insurance years rather than for the entire insurance period. This option permits sequential risk management decisions.

The formula $\mathrm{Var}[\Lambda_h|K(x) \geq h] = [v(b_{h+1} - {}_{h+1}V)]^2 p_{x+h}q_{x+h}$ confirms that the amount at risk $(b_{h+1} - {}_{h+1}V)$ is a major determinate of mortality risk, as measured by the variance. In fact if $b_{h+1} = {}_{h+1}V$ for all non-negative integer values of h, mortality risk drops to zero.

Example 8.5.1

Consider an insured from Example 7.4.3 who has survived to the end of the second policy year. For this insured, evaluate
a. $\mathrm{Var}[_2L|K(50) \geq 2]$ directly
b. $\mathrm{Var}[_2L|K(50) \geq 2]$ by means of the Hattendorf theorem
c. $\mathrm{Var}[_3L|K(50) \geq 3]$
d. $\mathrm{Var}[_4L|K(50) \geq 4]$.

Solution:

a. For the direct calculation, we need a table of values for $_2L$.

Outcome of $K(50) - 2 = j$	$_2L$	Conditional Probability of Outcome
0	$1{,}000v - 6.55692\,\ddot{a}_{\overline{1}} = 936.84$	$_{0|}q_{52} = 0.0069724$
1	$1{,}000v^2 - 6.55692\,\ddot{a}_{\overline{2}} = 877.25$	$_{1|}q_{52} = 0.0075227$
2	$1{,}000v^3 - 6.55692\,\ddot{a}_{\overline{3}} = 821.04$	$_{2|}q_{52} = 0.0081170$
≥ 3	$0 - 6.55692\,\ddot{a}_{\overline{3}} = -18.58$	$_3p_{52} = 0.9773879$

Then $\mathrm{E}[_2L|K(50) \geq 2] = 1.64$, in agreement with the value shown in Example 7.4.3 and

---

$$\text{Var}[_2L|K(50) \geq 2] = \text{E}[_2L^2|K(50) \geq 2] - (\text{E}[_2L|K(50) \geq 2])^2$$

$$= 17{,}717.82 - (1.64)^2$$

$$= 17{,}715.1.$$

b. To apply the Hattendorf theorem, we can use the benefit reserves from Example 7.4.3 to calculate the variances of the losses associated with the 1-year term insurances.

j	q_{52+j}	$v^2 \, (1{,}000 - 1{,}000 \, _{2+j+1}V^1_{50:\overline{5}|})^2 \, p_{52+j} \, q_{52+j}$
0	0.0069724	6 140.842
1	0.0075755	6 674.910
2	0.0082364	7 269.991

Then by (8.5.15),

$$\text{Var}[_2L|K(50) \geq 2] = 6{,}140.842 + (1.06)^{-2}(6{,}674.910)p_{52}$$

$$+ (1.06)^{-4}(7{,}269.991)_2p_{52} = 17{,}715.1,$$

which agrees with the value found by the direct calculation in part (a).

Note that in the direct method it was necessary to consider the gain in the event of survival to age 55; but for the Hattendorf theorem, we need to consider only the losses associated with the 1-year term insurances for the net amounts at risk in the remaining policy years. Thereafter, the net amount at risk is 0, and the corresponding terms in (8.5.15) vanish.

Also note that the standard deviation, $\sqrt{17{,}751.1} = 133.1$, for a single policy is more than 80 times the benefit reserve, $\text{E}[_2L|K(50)=2, 3, \ldots] = 1.64$.

Similarly, we use (8.5.15) to calculate

c. $\text{Var}[_3L|K(50) \geq 3] = 6{,}674.910 + (1.06)^{-2}(7{,}269.991) \, p_{53} = 13{,}096.2$

d. $\text{Var}[_4L|K(50) \geq 4] = 7{,}269.991$, or after rounding, 7,270.0. ▼

Example 8.5.2

Consider a portfolio of 1,500 policies of the type described in Example 7.4.3 and discussed in Example 8.5.1. Assume all policies have annual premiums due immediately. Further, assume 750 policies are at duration 2, 500 are at duration 3, and 250 are at duration 4, and that the policies in each group are evenly divided between those with 1,000 face amount and those with 3,000 face amount.

a. Calculate the aggregate benefit reserve.

b. Calculate the variance of the prospective losses over the remaining periods of coverage of the policies assuming such losses are independent. Also, calculate the amount which, on the basis of the normal approximation, will give the insurer a probability of 0.95 of meeting the future obligations to this block of business.

c. Calculate the variance of the losses associated with the 1-year term insurances for the net amounts at risk under the policies and the amount of supplement to the aggregate benefit reserve that, on the basis of the normal approximation, will give the insurer a probability of 0.95 of meeting the obligations to this block of business for the 1-year period.

d. Redo (b) and (c) with each set of policies increased 100-fold in number.

Solution:

a. Let Z be the sum of the prospective losses on the 1,500 policies. The symbols $E[Z]$ and $Var(Z)$ used below for the mean and variance of the portfolio of 1,500 policies are abridged, for in both cases the expectations are to be computed with respect to the set of conditions given above for the insureds. Using the results of Example 7.4.3, we have for the aggregate benefit reserve

$$E[Z] = [375(1) + 375(3)](1.64) + [250(1) + 250(3)](1.73)$$

$$+ [125(1) + 125(3)](1.21)$$

$$= 4,795.$$

b. From Example 8.5.1, we have

$$Var(Z) = [375(1) + 375(9)](17,715.1)$$

$$+ [250(1) + 250(9)](13,096.2)$$

$$+ [125(1) + 125(9)](7,270.0)$$

$$= (1.0825962) \times 10^8$$

and $\sigma_Z = 10,404.8$.

Then, if

$$0.05 = Pr(Z > c) = Pr\left(\frac{Z - 4,795.0}{10,404.8} > \frac{c - 4,795.0}{10,404.8}\right),$$

the normal approximation would imply

$$\frac{c - 4,795.0}{10,404.8} = 1.645,$$

or

$$c = 21,911,$$

which is 4.6 times the aggregate benefit reserve, $E[Z]$.

c. Here we take account of only the next year's risk. For each policy, we consider a variable equal to the loss associated with a 1-year term insurance for the net amount at risk. Let Z_1 be the sum of these loss variables. The expected loss for each of the 1-year term insurances is 0, hence $E[Z_1] = 0$.

From the table in part (b) of Example 8.5.1 we can obtain the variances of the losses in regard to the 1-year term insurances, and hence

$$\text{Var}(Z_1) = [375(1) + 375(9)](6{,}140.8) + [250(1) + 250(9)](6{,}674.9)$$

$$+ [125(1) + 125(9)](7{,}270.0)$$

$$= (4.880275) \times 10^7$$

and $\sigma_{Z_1} = 6985.9$.

If c_1 is the required supplement to the aggregate benefit reserve, then

$$0.05 = \text{Pr}(Z_1 > c_1) = \text{Pr}\left(\frac{Z_1 - 0}{6{,}985.9} > \frac{c_1 - 0}{6{,}985.9}\right),$$

and we determine, again by the normal approximation,

$$c_1 = (1.645)(6{,}985.9) = 11{,}492,$$

which is 2.4 times the aggregate benefit reserve 4,795.

d. In this case, $\text{E}[Z] = 479{,}500$ and $\text{Var}(Z) = (1.0825962) \times 10^{10}$. By the normal approximation the amount c required to provide a probability of 0.95 that all future obligations will be met is

$$479{,}500 + 1.645 \sqrt{1.0825962} \times 10^5 = 650{,}659,$$

which is 1.36 times the aggregate benefit reserve $\text{E}[Z]$.

Also, $\text{Var}(Z_1)$ is now $(4.880275) \times 10^9$. The amount c_1 of supplement to the aggregate benefit reserve required to give a 0.95 probability that the insurer can meet policy obligations for the next year is $1.645 \sqrt{4.880275} \times 10^{4.5} = 114{,}918$, or 24% of the aggregate benefit reserve. ▼

8.6 Differential Equations for Fully Continuous Benefit Reserves

In Section 8.2 a general fully discrete insurance and a general fully continuous model is developed. Section 8.3 contains the recursion relations for the fully discrete model. The parallel results for the fully continuous model are developed in this section.

The expression for the benefit reserve at t, $_t\bar{V}$, is given in (8.2.9) and is restated here:

$$_t\bar{V} = \int_0^\infty b_{t+u}\, v^u\, {}_u p_{x+t}\, \mu_x(t + u)\, du - \int_0^\infty \pi_{t+u}\, v^u\, {}_u p_{x+t}\, du.$$

To simplify the calculation of the derivative with respect to t of $_t\bar{V}$, we combine the two integrals, replace the variable of integration by the substitution $s = t + u$, and then multiply inside and divide outside by the factor $v^t\, {}_t p_x$ to obtain

$$\,_t\bar{V} = \frac{\int_t^\infty [b_s\,\mu_x(s) - \pi_s]v^s\,{}_sp_x\,ds}{v^t\,{}_tp_x}.$$

(8.6.1)

Now

$$\frac{d_t\bar{V}}{dt} = (-1)[b_t\,\mu_x(t) - \pi_t] + \frac{\mu_x(t) + \delta}{v^t\,{}_tp_x}\int_t^\infty [b_s\,\mu_x(s) - \pi_s]v^s\,{}_sp_x ds,$$

$$\frac{d_t\bar{V}}{dt} = \pi_t + [\delta + \mu_x(t)]_t\bar{V} - b_t\,\mu_x(t).$$

(8.6.2)

Here the rate of change of the benefit reserve is made up of three components: the benefit premium rate, the rate of increase of the benefit reserve under interest and survivorship, and the rate of benefit outgo. A rearrangement of formula (8.6.2) provides a formula corresponding to (8.3.12):

$$\pi_t + \delta\,_t\bar{V} + \,_t\bar{V}\,\mu_x(t) = b_t\,\mu_x(t) + \frac{d_t\bar{V}}{dt}.$$

(8.6.3)

This balances the sum of income rates to the sum of the rate of benefit outgo and the rate of change in the benefit reserve.

If the benefit reserve is treated as a savings fund available to offset the death benefit, we have

$$\pi_t + \delta\,_t\bar{V} = (b_t - \,_t\bar{V})\,\mu_x(t) + \frac{d_t\bar{V}}{dt}.$$

(8.6.4)

Here the income rates are in respect to benefit premiums and to interest on the benefit reserve, and these balance with the outgo rate, $(b_t - \,_t\bar{V})\,\mu_x(t)$, based on the net amount at risk and the rate of change in the benefit reserve. Formula (8.6.4) corresponds to (8.3.15). Again, the left side represents the resources available, benefit premiums, and investment income, and the right side represents their allocation to benefits and benefit resources.

Example 8.6.1

Use (8.6.2) to develop a retrospective formula for the benefit reserve for the general fully continuous insurance.

Solution:
We start by moving all of the benefit reserve terms of (8.6.2) to the left-hand side and then multiplying both sides by the integrating factor $\exp\{-\int_0^t[\delta + \mu_x(s)]\,ds\}$. Thus,

$$v^t\,{}_tp_x\left\{\frac{d_t\bar{V}}{dt} - [\delta + \mu_x(t)]\,_t\bar{V}\right\} = [\pi_t - b_t\,\mu_x(t)]\,v^t\,{}_tp_x,$$

or

$$\frac{d}{dt}\left(v^t \,_tp_x \,_t\bar{V}\right) = [\pi_t - b_t \,\mu_x(t)]\, v^t \,_tp_x.$$

Integration of both sides of this last equation over the interval $(0, r)$ yields

$$v^r \,_rp_x \,_r\bar{V} - {}_0\bar{V} = \int_0^r [\pi_t - b_t \,\mu_x(t)]\, v^t \,_tp_x \, dt.$$

For equivalence principle benefit premium rates, ${}_0V = 0$, so

$$_r\bar{V} = \frac{\displaystyle\int_0^r [\pi_t - b_t \,\mu_x(t)]\, v^t \,_tp_x \, dt}{v^r \,_rp_x}. \tag{8.6.5}$$

▼

8.7 Notes and References

Recursive formulas and differential equations for the loss variables as functions of duration and the expectations and variances of these loss variables provide basic insight into long-term insurance and annuity processes. In particular, one of these recursive formulas is applied to develop Hattendorf's theorem (1868); for references, see Steffensen (1929), Hickman (1964), and Gerber (1976). This formula allocates the variance of the loss to the separate insurance years. This discussion of reserves can be easily extended to more general insurances using martingales of probability theory; see, for example, Gerber (1979). Another application of the recursion relations is to the formulation of the interim reserves at fractional durations, which is discussed for the fully discrete case in Section 8.4.

Exercises

Section 8.2

8.1. Assume that $_jp_x = r^j$, $b_{j+1} = 1$, $j = 0, 1, 2, 3, \ldots$, and $0 < r < 1$.
   a. If $w_0 = w_1 = w_2 = \ldots = 1$, use (8.2.6) to calculate π at the interest rate i.
   b. If $w_j = (-1)^j$, $j = 0, 1, 2, \ldots$, use (8.2.6) to calculate π at the interest rate i.

8.2. Develop a continuous analogue of (8.2.6) by applying the equivalence principle to the loss variable of (8.2.7) with $t = 0$ and $\pi_t = \pi w(t)$, where $w(t)$ is given.

8.3. If $_0L = T(x)\, v^{T(x)} - \pi \bar{a}_{\overline{T(x)}}$ and the forces of mortality and interest are constant, express (a) π and (b) $_t\bar{V}$ in terms of μ and δ.

8.4. For the general fully discrete insurance of Section 8.2, show that for $j < h$,
$$\text{Cov}(C_j, C_h) = (\pi_h - vb_{h+1}\, q_{x+h})\, _hp_x(\pi_j \,_jq_x + vb_{j+1} \,_jp_x \, q_{x+j}).$$

8.5. Consider the life insurance policy described in Example 8.2.1. Display, for $0 < j < h$:

a. The covariance of C_0 and C_h.

b. Repeat part (a) for C_j and C_h.

c. Give a rule for determining h such that the covariance of C_j and C_h is negative.

8.6. Consider the deferred annuity described in Example 8.3.1. Find $\text{Cov}(C_j, C_h)$, $j < h \leq n$ and, for a fixed j, determine a condition on h such that $\text{Cov}(C_j, C_h) < 0$. [Note that this condition on h does not depend on j.]

8.7. Show that (8.3.9), with h replaced by $h + 1$, can be rearranged as

$$_{h+1}V = (_hV + \pi_h)\frac{1+i}{p_{x+h}} - b_{h+1}\frac{q_{x+h}}{p_{x+h}}.$$

Give an interpretation in words. (This is called the **Fackler reserve** accumulation formula, after the American actuary David Parks Fackler.)

8.8. For a fully discrete whole life insurance of 1 issued to (x), use recursion relations [(8.3.11) in (a) and (8.3.14 in (b)] to prove that

a. $_kV_x = \sum_{h=0}^{k-1} \frac{P_x - vq_{x+h}}{_{k-h}E_{x+h}}$

b. $_kV_x = \sum_{h=0}^{k-1} [P_x - vq_{x+h}(1 - _{h+1}V_x)](1+i)^{k-h}.$

Give an interpretation of the formulas in words.

8.9. If $b_{h+1} = _{h+1}V$, $_0V = 0$, and $\pi_h = \pi$, for $h = 0, 1, \ldots, k - 1$, prove that $_kV = \pi\ddot{s}_{\overline{k}|}$. [Hint: Use (8.3.14).]

8.10. Show that if π is the level annual benefit premium for an n-year term insurance with $b_h = \ddot{a}_{\overline{n+1-h}|}$, $h = 1, 2, \ldots, n$, $_0V = _nV = 0$, then

a. $\pi = \dfrac{a_{\overline{n}|} - a_{x:\overline{n}|}}{\ddot{a}_{x:\overline{n}|}}$

b. $_kV = a_{\overline{n-k}|} - a_{x+k:\overline{n-k}|} - \pi\ddot{a}_{x+k:\overline{n-k}|}.$

[Hint: This can be shown directly or by use of (8.3.10).]

Section 8.4

8.11. Starting with (8.4.3), establish the equation

$$_sp_{x+h} \, _{h+s}V + v^{1-s} \, _sq_{x+h} \, b_{h+1} = (1+i)^s(_hV + \pi_h) \qquad 0 < s < 1.$$

Explain the result by general reasoning.

8.12. Interpret the formulas

a. $_{k+(h/m)+r}V^{(m)} \cong \left(1 - \dfrac{h}{m} - r\right) {}_kV^{(m)}$

$$+ \left(\dfrac{h}{m} + r\right) {}_{k+1}V^{(m)} + \left(\dfrac{1}{m} - r\right) P^{(m)}$$

b. $_{k+(h/m)+r}V^{\{m\}} \cong \left(1 - \dfrac{h}{m} - r\right) {}_kV^{\{m\}}$

$$+ \left(\dfrac{h}{m} + r\right) {}_{k+1}V^{\{m\}} + \left(\dfrac{1}{m} - r\right) P^{\{m\}},$$

where $0 < r < 1/m$.

8.13. For each of the following benefit reserves, develop formulas similar to one or more of (8.4.8), (8.4.14), and (8.4.18).

a. $_{20^1/_2}V(\bar{A}_{x:\overline{40|}})$ b. $_{20^1/_2}\bar{V}(\bar{A}_{x:\overline{40|}})$

c. $_{20^1/_2}V^{(2)}(\bar{A}_{x:\overline{40|}})$ d. $_{20^2/_3}V^{(2)}(\bar{A}_{x:\overline{40|}})$

e. $_{20^1/_2}V^{\{2\}}(\bar{A}_{x:\overline{40|}})$ f. $_{20^2/_3}V^{\{2\}}(\bar{A}_{x:\overline{40|}})$

8.14. On the basis of the Illustrative Life Table and interest of 6%, approximate

$_{10^1/_6}V^{\{4\}}(\bar{A}_{25})$.

Section 8.5

8.15. For a fully discrete whole life insurance of amount 1 issued to (x) with premiums payable for life, show that

a. $\mathrm{Var}[L] = \displaystyle\sum_{h=0}^{\infty} \left(\dfrac{\ddot{a}_{x+h+1}}{\ddot{a}_x}\right)^2 v^{2(h+1)} \, {}_hp_x \, p_{x+h} \, q_{x+h}$

b. $\mathrm{Var}[_kL|K(x) \geq k] = \displaystyle\sum_{h=0}^{\infty} \left(\dfrac{\ddot{a}_{x+k+h+1}}{\ddot{a}_x}\right)^2 v^{2(h+1)} \, {}_hp_{x+k} \, p_{x+k+h} \, q_{x+k+h} \, .$

8.16. For a life annuity-due of 1 per annum payable while (x) survives, consider the whole life loss

$$L = \ddot{a}_{\overline{K+1|}} - \ddot{a}_x \qquad K = 0, 1, 2, \ldots$$

and the loss Λ_h, valued at time h, that is allocated to annuity year h, namely,

$$\Lambda_h = \begin{cases} 0 & K \leq h - 1 \\ -(\ddot{a}_{x+h} - 1) \qquad\qquad = -vp_{x+h}\,\ddot{a}_{x+h+1} & K = h \\ v\ddot{a}_{x+h+1} - (\ddot{a}_{x+h} - 1) = vq_{x+h}\,\ddot{a}_{x+h+1} & K \geq h + 1. \end{cases}$$

a. Interpret the formulas for Λ_h.

b. Show that

$$\text{(i) } L = \sum_{h=0}^{\infty} v^h \, \Lambda_h$$

$$\text{(ii) } \mathrm{E}[\Lambda_h] = 0$$

$$\text{(iii) } \mathrm{Var}(\Lambda_h) = v^2 \, (\ddot{a}_{x+h+1})^2 \, {}_hp_x \, p_{x+h} \, q_{x+h}.$$

8.17. a. For the insurance of Example 8.3.2, establish that

$$\text{Var}(L) = \sum_{h=0}^{n-1} v^{2(h+1)} \, {}_hp_x \, p_{x+h} \, q_{x+h}.$$

b. If $\delta = 0.05$, $n = 20$, and $\mu_x(t) = 0.01$, $t \geq 0$, calculate $\text{Var}(L)$ for the insurance in (a).

8.18. A 20-payment whole life policy with unit face amount was issued on a fully discrete basis to a person age 25. On the basis of your Illustrative Life Table and interest of 6%, calculate

a. ${}_{20}P_{25}$
b. ${}_{19}^{20}V_{25}$
c. ${}_{20}^{20}V_{25}$
d. $\text{Var}[{}_{20}L|K(25) \geq 20]$
e. $\text{Var}[{}_{18}L|K(25) \geq 18]$, using Theorem 8.5.1.

Section 8.6

8.19. Interpret the differential equations

a. $\dfrac{d}{dt} \, {}_t\bar{V} = \pi_t + [\delta + \mu_x(t)] \, {}_t\bar{V} - b_t \, \mu_x(t)$

b. $\dfrac{d}{dt} \, {}_t\bar{V} = \pi_t + \delta \, {}_t\bar{V} - (b_t - {}_t\bar{V}) \, \mu_x(t).$

8.20. If $b_t = {}_t\bar{V}$, ${}_0\bar{V} = 0$, and $\pi_t = \pi$, $t \geq 0$, show that ${}_t\bar{V} = \pi\bar{s}_{\overline{t}|}$.

8.21. Evaluate $(d/dt) \{[1 - {}_t\bar{V}(\bar{A}_x)] \, {}_tp_x\}$.

8.22. Use (8.6.2) to write expressions for

a. $\dfrac{d}{dt} \, ({}_tp_x \, {}_t\bar{V})$
b. $\dfrac{d}{dt} \, (v^t \, {}_t\bar{V})$
c. $\dfrac{d}{dt} \, (v^t \, {}_tp_x \, {}_t\bar{V})$

and interpret the results.

Miscellaneous

8.23. Show that the formula equivalent to (8.4.6) under the hyperbolic assumption for mortality within the year of age is

$$_{k+s}V = v^{1-s}[(1 - s)({}_kV + \pi_k)(1 + i) + s \, {}_{k+1}V].$$

8.24. Prove that

$$\int_0^\infty [v^t - \bar{P}(\bar{A}_x)\bar{a}_{\overline{t}|}]^2 \, {}_tp_x \, \mu_x(t) \, dt = \int_0^\infty [1 - {}_t\bar{V}(\bar{A}_x)]^2 \, v^{2t} \, {}_tp_x \, \mu_x(t) \, dt$$

and interpret the result.

8.25. For a different form of the Hattendorf theorem, consider the following:

$$_{k,m}L = \begin{cases} b_{K+1} \, v^{(K-k)+1} - {}_kV - \displaystyle\sum_{h=0}^{(K-k)} \pi_{k+h} \, v^h & K(x) = k, \, k+1, \ldots, k+m-1 \\[2em] _{k+m}V \, v^m - {}_kV - \displaystyle\sum_{h=0}^{m-1} \pi_{k+h} \, v^h & K(x) = k+m, \, k+m+1, \ldots, \end{cases}$$

and, for $h = 0, 1, \ldots, m-1$,

$$\Lambda_{k+h} = \begin{cases} 0 & K(x) = k, k+1, \ldots, k+h-1 \\ vb_{k+h+1} - (_{k+h}V + \pi_{k+h}) & K(x) = k+h \\ v \, _{k+h+1}V - (_{k+h}V + \pi_{k+h}) & K(x) = k+h+1, k+h+2, \ldots. \end{cases}$$

Show that

a. $_{k,m}L = \sum_{h=0}^{m-1} v^h \Lambda_{k+h}$

b. $\text{Var}[_{k,m}L|K(x) \geq k] = \sum_{h=0}^{m-1} v^{2h} \text{Var}[\Lambda_{k+h}|K(x) \geq k].$

8.26. Repeat Example 8.5.1 in terms of an insured from Example 7.4.4 who has survived to the end of the second policy year.

8.27. Repeat Example 8.5.2 in terms of a portfolio of 1,500 policies of the type described in Example 7.4.4 and discussed in Exercise 8.26.

8.28. In Exercise 8.27 there is no uncertainty about the amount or time of payment for the insureds who have survived to the end of the fourth policy year. Redo Exercise 8.27 for just those insureds at durations 2 and 3.

8.29. Write a formula, in terms of benefit premium and terminal benefit reserve symbols, for the benefit reserve at the middle of the eleventh policy year for a 10,000 whole life insurance with apportionable premiums payable annually issued to (30).

8.30. A 3-year endowment policy for a face amount of 3 has the death benefit payable at the end of the year of death and a benefit premium of 0.94 payable annually. Using an interest rate of 20%, the following benefit reserves are generated:

End of Year	Benefit Reserve
1	0.66
2	1.56
3	3.00

Calculate

a. q_x

b. q_{x+1}

c. The variance of the loss at policy issue, $_0L$

d. The conditional variance, given that the insured has survived through the first year, of the loss at the end of the first year, $_1L$.

8.31. a. Use (8.3.10) to transform (8.5.1) to

$$\Lambda_h = \begin{cases} 0 & K(x) \le h - 1 \\ (b_{h+1} - {}_{h+1}V) \, v - (b_{h+1} - {}_{h+1}V) \, v \, q_{x+h} & K(x) = h \\ 0 \quad - (b_{h+1} - {}_{h+1}V) \, v \, q_{x+h} & K(x) \ge h + 1. \end{cases}$$

In this interpretation Λ_h is the loss on the 1-year term insurance for the amount at risk in the year $(h, h + 1)$.

b. Use the display in (a) to verify $E[\Lambda_h] = 0$.

c. Use parts (a) and (b) to obtain $\mathrm{Var}(\Lambda_h)$.

Computing Exercises

8.32. Consider a variation of the insurance of Example 8.2.2 which provides a unit benefit whole life insurance to (20) with geometrically increasing benefit premiums payable to age 65. On the basis of your Illustrative Life Table and $i = 0.06$, determine the maximum value of r such that the benefit reserve is non-negative at all durations.

8.33. Use the backward recursion formula (8.3.9) to calculate the benefit reserves of

a. Example 7.4.3 [Hint: ${}_5V = 0.0.$]

b. Example 7.4.4. [Hint ${}_5V = 1.0.$]

8.34. A decreasing term insurance to age 65 with immediate payment of death claims is issued to (30) with the following benefits:

For Death between Ages	Benefit
30–50	100,000
50–55	90,000
55–60	80,000
60–65	60,000

On the basis of your Illustrative Life Table with uniform distribution of deaths within each year of age and $i = 0.06$, determine

a. The annual apportionable benefit premium, payable semiannually and

b. The reserve at the end of 30 years, if benefit premiums are as in (a).

8.35. A single premium insurance contract issued to (35) provides 100,000 in case the insured survives to age 65, and it returns (at the end of the year of death) the single benefit premium without interest if the insured dies before age 65. If the single benefit premium is denoted by S, write expressions, in terms of actuarial functions, for

a. S

b. The prospective formula for the benefit reserve at the end of k years

c. The retrospective formula for the benefit reserve at the end of k years

d. On the basis of your Illustrative Life Table and $d = 0.05$, calculate S and the benefit reserve ${}_{20}V$.

8.36. In terms of $P = {}_{20}P^{(12)}(\bar{A}_{30:\overline{35}|})$ and actuarial functions, write prospective and retrospective formulas for the following:

a. ${}_{10}^{20}V^{(12)}(\bar{A}_{30:\overline{35}|})$

b. ${}_{25}^{20}V^{(12)}(\bar{A}_{30:\overline{35}|})$

c. On the basis of your Illustrative Life Table with uniform distribution of deaths within each year of age and $\delta = 0.05$, calculate P and the benefit reserves of parts (a) and (b).

MULTIPLE LIFE FUNCTIONS

9.1 Introduction

In Chapters 3 through 8 we developed a theory for the analysis of financial benefits contingent on the time of death of a single life. We can extend this theory to benefits involving several lives. An application of this extension commonly found in pension plans is the joint-and-survivor annuity option. Other applications of multiple life actuarial calculations are common. In estate and gift taxation, for example, the investment income from a trust can be paid to a group of heirs as long as at least one of the group survives. Upon the last death, the principal from the trust is to be donated to a qualified charitable institution. The amount of the charitable deduction allowed for estate tax purposes is determined by an actuarial calculation. There are family policies in which benefits differ due to the order of the deaths of the insured and the spouse, and there are insurance policies with benefits payable on the first or last death providing cash in accordance with an estate plan.

In this chapter we discuss models involving two lives. Actuarial present values for basic benefits are derived by applying the concepts and techniques developed in Chapters 3 through 5. Models built on the assumption that the two future life-time random variables are independent constitute most of the chapter. Section 9.6 introduces special models in which the two future lifetime random variables are dependent. Annual benefit premiums, reserves, and models involving three or more lives are covered in Chapter 18.

A useful abstraction in the theory of life contingencies, particularly as it is applied to several lives, is that of *status* for which there are definitions of survival and failure. Two elements are necessary for a status to be defined. The general term *entities* is used in the definition because of the broad range of application of the concept:
- There must be a finite set of entities, and for each member it must be possible to define a future lifetime random variable.
- There must be a rule by which the survival of the status can be determined at any future time.

To compute probabilities or actuarial present values associated with the survival of a status, the joint distribution of the future lifetime random variables must be available. Some of these random variables may have a marginal distribution such that all the probability is at one point.

Several illustrations of the status concept may be helpful. A single life age x defines a status that survives while (x) lives. Thus, the random variable $T(x)$, used in Chapter 3 to denote the future lifetime of (x), can be interpreted as the period of survival of the status and also as the time-until-failure of the status. A term certain, $\overline{n|}$, defines a status surviving for exactly n years and then failing. More complex statuses can be defined in terms of several lives in various ways. Survival can mean that all members survive or, alternatively, that at least one member survives. Still more complicated statuses can be in regard to two men and two women with the status considered to survive only as long as at least one man and at least one woman survive.

After a status and its survival have been defined, we can apply the definition to develop models for annuities and insurances. An annuity is payable as long as the status survives, whereas an insurance is payable upon the failure of the status. Insurances also can be restricted so they are payable only if the individuals die in a specific order.

9.2 Joint Distributions of Future Lifetimes

The time-until-failure of a status is a function of the future lifetimes of the lives involved. In theory these future lifetimes will be dependent random variables. We will explore the consequences of that dependence. For convenience, or because of the lack of data on dependent lives, in practice, an assumption of independence among the future lifetimes has traditionally been made. With the independence assumption numerical values from the marginal distributions (life tables) for single lives can be used.

Example 9.2.1

While the distribution in this example is not realistic, it is offered as a vehicle to explore a joint distribution for two dependent future lifetimes. For two lives (x) and (y), the joint p.d.f. of their future lifetimes, $T(x)$ and $T(y)$, is

$$f_{T(x)T(y)}(s, t) = \begin{cases} 0.0006(t - s)^2 & 0 < s < 10, 0 < t < 10 \\ 0 & \text{elsewhere.} \end{cases}$$

Determine the following:
a. The joint d.f. of $T(x)$ and $T(y)$
b. The p.d.f., d.f., $_sp_x$, and $\mu(x + s)$ for the marginal distribution of $T(x)$. Note the symmetry of the distribution in s and t, which implies that $T(x)$ and $T(y)$ are identically distributed.
c. The correlation coefficient of $T(x)$ and $T(y)$.

Solution:

a. Before calculating, we look at the sample space of $T(x)$ and $T(y)$ in Figure 9.2.1 and observe the region where the joint p.d.f. is positive. At points outside the first quadrant, the d.f. will be 0. In the first quadrant we start by calculating the d.f. at a point in Region I where both s and t are between 0 and 10:

$$F_{T(x)T(y)}(s, t) = \Pr[T(x) \le s \text{ and } T(y) \le t]$$

$$= \int_{-\infty}^{s} \int_{-\infty}^{t} f_{T(x)T(y)}(u, v)\, dv\, du$$

$$= \int_{0}^{s} \int_{0}^{t} 0.0006(v - u)^2\, dv\, du$$

$$= 0.00005[s^4 + t^4 - (t - s)^4]$$

$$0 < s \le 10, \ 0 < t \le 10.$$

Figure 9.2.1

Sample Space of $T(x)$ and $T(y)$

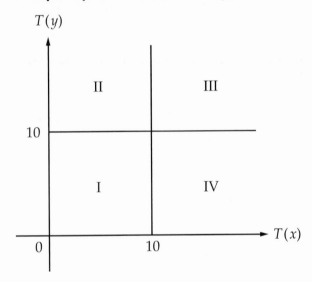

Sample Space of $T(x)$ and $T(y)$

Since the joint p.d.f. is 0 in regions II, III, and IV, we have

$$\left.\begin{aligned} F_{T(x)T(y)}(s, t) &= F_{T(x)T(y)}(s, 10) = F_{T(x)}(s) \\ &= \frac{1}{2} + 0.00005[s^4 - (10 - s)^4] \end{aligned}\right\} \text{ in Region II}$$

$$\left.\begin{aligned} &= F_{T(x)T(y)}(10, t) = F_{T(y)}(t) \\ &= \frac{1}{2} + 0.00005[t^4 - (10 - t)^4] \end{aligned}\right\} \text{ in Region IV}$$

$$= 1 \qquad\qquad\qquad\qquad\qquad \text{ in Region III.}$$

---

b. Using the d.f. obtained in part (a), we have

$$F_{T(x)T(y)}(s, 10) = F_{T(x)}(s)$$

$$= 0 \qquad\qquad s \le 0$$

$$= \frac{1}{2} + 0.00005[s^4 - (10 - s)^4] \qquad 0 < s \le 10$$

$$= 1 \qquad\qquad s > 10$$

and

$$f_{T(x)}(s) = F'_{T(x)}(s) = \begin{cases} 0.0002[s^3 + (10 - s)^3] & 0 < s \le 10 \\ 0 & \text{elsewhere.} \end{cases}$$

The survival probability and force of mortality are given by

$$_s p_x = 1 - F_{T(x)}(s)$$

$$= \frac{1}{2} + 0.00005[(10 - s)^4 - s^4] \qquad 0 < s \le 10$$

$$= 0 \qquad\qquad s > 10,$$

and
$$\mu(x + t) = \frac{f_{T(x)}(t)}{1 - F_{T(x)}(t)}$$

$$= \frac{0.0002[s^3 + (10 - s)^3]}{1/2 + 0.00005[(10 - s)^4 - s^4]} \qquad 0 < s \le 10.$$

c.
$$E[T(x)] = \int_0^{10} s(0.0002)[s^3 + (10 - s)^3] \, ds = 5 = E[T(y)],$$

$$E[T(x)^2] = \int_0^{10} s^2(0.0002)[s^3 + (10 - s)^3] \, ds = \frac{110}{3} = E[T(y)^2],$$

$$\text{Var}[T(x)] = \frac{35}{3} = \text{Var}[T(y)],$$

$$E[T(x)T(y)] = \int_0^{10} \int_0^{10} st(0.0006)(t - s)^2 \, ds \, dt = \frac{50}{3},$$

$$\text{Cov}[T(x), T(y)] = E[T(x)T(y)] - E[T(x)]E[T(y)] = -\frac{25}{3},$$

$$\rho_{T(x)T(y)} = \frac{\text{Cov}[T(x), T(y)]}{\sigma_{T(x)}\sigma_{T(y)}} = \frac{-25/3}{35/3} = -\frac{5}{7}.$$ ▼

For the joint life distribution, we define the *joint survival function* as

$$s_{T(x)T(y)}(s, t) = \Pr[T(x) > s \text{ and } T(y) > t]. \qquad (9.2.1)$$

Unlike the single life distribution, the d.f. and survival function do not necessarily add up to 1. Their relationship for the joint life distribution can be illustrated by a graph of their joint sample space as shown in Figure 9.2.2. The d.f. $F_{T(x)\,T(y)}\,(s, t)$ gives the probability of Region A, "southwest" of the point (s, t), and $s_{T(x)\,T(y)}(s, t)$ gives the probability of Region B, "northeast" of (s, t).

Figure 9.2.2

Sample Space of Future Lifetime Random Variables $T(x)$ and $T(y)$

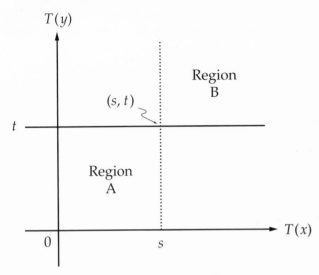

Sample Space of Future Lifetime
Random Variables $T(x)$ and $T(y)$

Example 9.2.2

For the distribution of $T(x)$ and $T(y)$ in Example 9.2.1 determine the joint survival function.

Solution:

For $0 < s < 10$ and $0 < t < 10$,

$$s_{T(x)T(y)}(s, t) = \Pr[T(x) > s \cap T(y) > t]$$

$$= \int_s^\infty \int_t^\infty f_{T(x)T(y)}(u, v)\,dv\,du$$

$$= \int_s^{10} \int_t^{10} 0.0006(v - u)^2\,dv\,du$$

$$= 0.00005[(10 - t)^4 + (10 - s)^4 - (t - s)^4].$$

For other points in the first quadrant, $s_{T(x)\,T(y)}(s, t)$ will be 0 and for all points in the third quadrant it will be 1. In the second quadrant, where $s < 0$ and $t > 0$,

$$s_{T(x)\,T(y)}(s, t) = s_{T(y)}(t) = {}_tp_y.$$

In the fourth quadrant, where $s > 0$ and $t < 0$,

$$s_{T(x)\,T(y)}(s, t) = s_{T(x)}(s) = {}_tp_x.$$

▼

In Example 9.2.1 we were given the joint distribution of two dependent future lifetimes and then determined their marginal distributions and their correlation coefficient, which indicated their degree of dependence. In applications, the dependence of the time-until-death random variables may be difficult to quantify. Consequently, the future lifetimes are usually assumed to be independent, and then their joint distribution is obtained from their marginal single life distributions that we discussed in Chapter 3. This is illustrated in the next example.

Example 9.2.3

The future lifetimes $T(x)$ and $T(y)$ are independent, and each has the distribution defined by the p.d.f.

$$f(t) = \begin{cases} 0.02\,(10 - t) & 0 < t < 10 \\ 0 & \text{elsewhere.} \end{cases}$$

a. Determine the d.f., survival function, and force of mortality of this distribution.
b. Determine the joint p.d.f., d.f., and survival function for $T(x)$ and $T(y)$.

Solution:

a.
$$F_{T(x)}(t) = \int_{-\infty}^{t} f_{T(x)}(s)\,ds$$

$$= \begin{cases} 0 & t \le 0 \\ 1 - 0.01(10 - t)^2 = 0.2t - 0.01t^2 & 0 < t \le 10 \\ 1 & t > 10, \end{cases}$$

$$s_{T(x)}(t) = 1 - F_{T(x)}(t) = \begin{cases} 1 & t < 0 \\ 0.01(10 - t)^2 & 0 \le t < 10 \\ 0 & t \ge 10, \end{cases}$$

$$\mu(x + t) = \frac{f_{T(x)}(t)}{s_{T(x)}(t)} = \frac{2}{10 - t} \qquad 0 < t < 10.$$

b. $f_{T(x)T(y)}(s, t) = f_{T(x)}(s)f_{T(y)}(t)$

$$= \begin{cases} (0.02)^2(10 - s)(10 - t) & 0 < s < 10,\ 0 < t < 10 \\ 0 & \text{elsewhere,} \end{cases}$$

$$F_{T(x)T(y)}(s, t) = F_{T(x)}(s)F_{T(y)}(t)$$

$$= (0.2)^2(t - 0.05t^2)(s - 0.05s^2) \qquad 0 < s \le 10,\ 0 < t \le 10$$
$$= F_{T(x)}(s) = (0.2)(s - 0.05s^2) \qquad 0 < s \le 10,\ t > 10$$
$$= F_{T(y)}(t) = (0.2)(t - 0.05t^2) \qquad s > 10,\ 0 < t \le 10,$$

$$s_{T(x)T(y)}(s, t) = s_{T(x)}(s)s_{T(y)}(t)$$

$$= (0.01)^2(10 - s)^2(10 - t)^2 \qquad 0 \le s < 10,\ 0 \le t < 10$$
$$= s_{T(x)}(s) = (0.01)(10 - s)^2 \qquad 0 \le s < 10,\ t < 0$$
$$= s_{T(y)}(t) = (0.01)(10 - t)^2 \qquad s < 0,\ 0 \le t < 10$$
$$= 0 \qquad s \ge 10,\ t \ge 10. \qquad \blacktriangledown$$

9.3 The Joint-Life Status

A status that survives as long as all members of a set of lives survive and fails upon the first death is called a *joint-life status.* It is denoted by $(x_1, x_2, \ldots, x_m)$, where x_i represents the age of member i of the set and m represents the number of members. Notation introduced in Chapters 3 through 5 is used here with the subscript listing several ages rather than a single age. For example, A_{xy} and $_tp_{xy}$ have the same meaning for the joint-life status (xy) as A_x and $_tp_x$ have for the single life (x).

A joint-life status is an example of what we call a *survival status,* that is, a status for which there is a future lifetime random variable, and, therefore, a survival function can be defined. For the future lifetime of a survival status, the concepts and relationships established in Sections 3.2.2 through 3.5 (excluding the life table example in Section 3.3.2) apply to the distribution of the survival status. These concepts will be used here without new proofs.

We now consider the distribution of the time-until-failure of a joint-life status. For m lives, $T(x_1, x_2, \ldots, x_m) = \min[T(x_1), T(x_2), \ldots, T(x_m)]$, where $T(x_i)$ is the time of death of individual i. For the special case of two lives, (x) and (y), we have $T(xy) = \min[T(x), T(y)]$. When clear by context, we denote the future lifetime of the joint-life status by simply T. The student can interpret the time-until-failure of the joint-life status as the *smallest order statistic* of the m lifetimes in the set. In previous studies of order statistics, the random variables in the sample have usually been independent and identically distributed. Here the random variables are typically independent by assumption but are rarely identically distributed.

We begin by expressing the distribution function of T, for $t > 0$, in terms of the joint distribution of $T(x)$ and $T(y)$ for the general (dependent) case:

$$F_T(t) = {}_tq_{xy} = \Pr(T \le t)$$

$$= \Pr\{\min[T(x), T(y)] \le t\}$$

$$= 1 - \Pr\{\min[T(x), T(y)] > t\}$$

$$= 1 - \Pr\{T(x) > t \text{ and } T(y) > t\}$$

$$= 1 - s_{T(x)\ T(y)}(t, t). \tag{9.3.1}$$

Another equation can be obtained from the second line by recognizing that the event $\{\min[T(x), T(y)] \le t\}$ is the union of $\{T(x) \le t\}$ and $\{T(y) \le t\}$. Then,

$$F_T(t) = \Pr\{\min[T(x), T(y)] \le t\},$$

and using a basic result in probability, we have

$$F_T(t) = \Pr[T(x) \le t] + \Pr[T(y) \le t] - \Pr[T(x) \le t \cap T(y) \le t]$$

$$= {}_tq_x + {}_tq_y - F_{T(x)\ T(y)}(t, t). \tag{9.3.2}$$

The mixture of IAN and standard probability/statistics notation in (9.3.2) demonstrates that although the IAN system may accommodate survival statuses, it does not provide for the joint distribution of several statuses except in the independent case which can be expressed in single survival status symbols.

When $T(x)$ and $T(y)$ are independent, the two expressions for the d.f. of T can be written in terms of single life functions as:

$$F_T(t) = \Pr\{\min[T(x), T(y)] \leq t\}$$

$$= 1 - s_{T(x)\ T(y)}(t, t) = 1 - {}_tp_x\ {}_tp_y, \tag{9.3.3}$$

and

$$F_T(t) = {}_tq_x + {}_tq_y - F_{T(x)\ T(y)}(t, t) = {}_tq_x + {}_tq_y - {}_tq_x\ {}_tq_y. \tag{9.3.4}$$

The survival function for the joint-life status, ${}_tp_{xy}$, is obtained by subtracting the d.f. from 1.

For the general case, ${}_tp_{xy} = s_{T(x)\ T(y)}(t, t)$ using (9.3.1). In the independent case, we have by (9.3.3)

$$_tp_{xy} = {}_tp_x\ {}_tp_y. \tag{9.3.5}$$

Expression (9.3.5) is the convenient starting point for the independent case since the joint-life status survives to t if, and only if, both (x) and (y) survive to t.

Example 9.3.1

Determine the d.f., survival function, and complete expectation for the joint-life status, $T(xy)$, for the lives of Example 9.2.1.

Solution:

For $t \leq 0$ and $t > 10$, the value of $F_{T(xy)}(t)$ would be 0 and 1, respectively. For $0 < t \leq 10$, we have by the results of Example 9.2.1(a) and (b) and (9.3.2)

$$F_{T(xy)}(t) = 2\{0.5 + 0.00005[t^4 - (10 - t)^4]\} - 0.0001\ t^4$$

$$= 1 - 0.0001\ (10 - t)^4$$

for $0 < t \leq 10$.

Now,

$$_tp_{xy} = 1 - F_{T(xy)}(t) = 0.0001(10 - t)^4 \qquad 0 \leq t < 10.$$

From (3.5.2),

$$\overset{\circ}{e}_{xy} = E[T(xy)] = \int_0^\infty {}_tp_{xy}\ dt = \int_0^{10} 0.0001(10 - t)^4\ dt = 2. \qquad \blacktriangledown$$

Example 9.3.2

Determine the d.f. and survival function and the complete expectation for the joint-life status, $T(xy)$, for the distribution of Example 9.2.3.

Solution:

For independent lives we use (9.3.5) and the results of Example 9.2.3 to obtain

$$_t p_{xy} = [0.01(10 - t)^2]^2 = 0.0001(10 - t)^4 \qquad \text{for } 0 \le t < 10.$$

Then

$$F_{T(xy)}(t) = 1 - (0.0001)(10 - t)^4 \qquad \text{for } 0 < t \le 10$$

and

$$\overset{\circ}{e}_{xy} = \int_0^{10} 0.0001(10 - t)^4 \, dt = 2. \qquad \blacktriangledown$$

An insight can be gained from the two previous examples. Although the joint distributions of the two underlying future lifetime random variables of the two examples are not the same, the distributions of their joint-life statuses are the same. This is a important point in practice when only the first-to-die can be observed. In such case the underlying joint distribution is not uniquely determined. In statistics this is called **nonidentifiability** because of the difficulty in distinguishing among two or more models for the same observed data.

The p.d.f. for T can be obtained by differentiating its d.f. as displayed in either (9.3.1) or (9.3.2). For (9.3.1) we will need the derivative, with respect to t, of

$$s_{T(x) \, T(y)}(t, t) = \int_t^\infty \int_t^\infty f_{T(x)T(y)}(u, v) \, du \, dv.$$

Using the formula from calculus in Appendix 5, we have

$$\frac{d}{dt} s_{T(x) \, T(y)}(t, t) = -\left[\int_t^\infty f_{T(x)T(y)}(t, v) \, dv + \int_t^\infty f_{T(x)T(y)}(u, t) \, du \right].$$

Hence,

$$f_{T(xy)}(t) = \int_t^\infty f_{T(x)T(y)}(t, v) \, dv + \int_t^\infty f_{T(x)T(y)}(u, t) \, du. \qquad (9.3.6)$$

Using (9.3.2), the reader can show that the p.d.f. of T can also be written as

$$f_{T(xy)}(t) = f_{T(x)}(t) + f_{T(y)}(t) - \left[\int_0^t f_{T(x)T(y)}(t, v) \, dv + \int_0^t f_{T(x)T(y)}(u, t) \, du \right],$$

or with actuarial notation as

$$f_{T(xy)}(t) = {}_t p_x \, \mu(x + t) + {}_t p_y \, \mu(y + t)$$

$$- \left[\int_0^t f_{T(x)T(y)}(t, v) \, dv + \int_0^t f_{T(x)T(y)}(u, t) \, du \right]. \qquad (9.3.7)$$

When $T(x)$ and $T(y)$ are independent, $f_{T(x)T(y)}(u, v) = {}_u p_x \, \mu(x + u) \, {}_v p_y \, \mu(y + v)$, and (9.3.6) reduces directly to

$$= {}_t p_y \, {}_t p_x \, [\mu(x + t) + \mu(y + t)]. \qquad (9.3.8)$$

Example 9.3.3

By use of (9.3.6) determine the p.d.f. of $T(xy)$ for Example 9.2.1. Verify your result by examination of the d.f. in Example 9.3.1.

Solution:

Using (9.3.6) we obtain

$$f_T(t) = \begin{cases} \displaystyle\int_t^{10} 0.0006\,(t-v)^2\,dv + \int_t^{10} 0.0006\,(u-t)^2\,du \\ \qquad\qquad = 0.0004(10-t)^3 \qquad \text{for } 0 < t < 10, \\[1em] 0 \qquad\qquad\qquad\qquad\qquad\qquad\qquad \text{elsewhere.} \end{cases}$$

This is the derivative of the d.f. in Example 9.3.1. ▼

We saw that $T(xy)$ has the same distribution in Examples 9.3.1 and 9.3.2. If we use (9.3.8) to obtain the p.d.f. of $T(xy)$ for Example 9.2.3, we will see this again. This is left as Exercise 9.8.

As explained in Chapter 3, the distribution of $T = T(xy)$ can also be specified by the force of "mortality," or more generally, the force of "failure." First we consider a notation for the force of failure of the status at time t. The traditional notation for this force is $\mu_{x+t:y+t}$ (in analogy with μ_{x+t}), but, in preparation for discussing other statuses where duration must be recognized, and in accordance with the notational convention adopted in Chapter 3, we use the notation $\mu_{xy}(t)$. The notation $\mu_{xy}(t)$ does not necessarily mean that (x) and (y) or the survival status (xy) were subject to a selection process, but the status did come into existence at these ages.

By analogy with the first formula of (3.2.12) and with $f_{T(x)}(x)$ and $F_{T(x)}(x)$ replaced by $f_{T(xy)}(t)$ and $F_{T(xy)}(t)$, we have

$$\mu_{xy}(t) = \frac{f_{T(xy)}(t)}{1 - F_{T(xy)}(t)}. \tag{9.3.9}$$

For dependent $T(x)$, $T(y)$, this expression does not simplify beyond the general form. However, using (9.3.3) and (9.3.8) for the independent case, we have $\mu_{xy}(t) = \mu(x+t) + \mu(y+t)$.

In words, if the future lifetimes are independent, the force of failure for their joint-life status is the sum of the forces of mortality for the individuals. As in Chapter 3 with the single life case, we can characterize the distribution of $T(xy)$ by the p.d.f., the d.f., the survival function, or the force of failure.

Example 9.3.4

Determine the force of failure for the joint-life statuses of (x) and (y) in Examples 9.2.1 and 9.2.3.

Solution:

Since the joint distributions of the two examples produce the same distribution for $T(xy)$, we will use the independent case. From the results of part (a) of Example 9.2.3 and (9.3.9),

$$\mu_{xy}(t) = \frac{4}{10 - t} \qquad 0 < t < 10.$$

▼

We now turn to the curtate future lifetime of the joint-life status.

The probability that the joint-life status fails during the time k to $k + 1$ is determined by

$$\Pr(k < T \le k + 1) = \Pr(T \le k + 1) - \Pr(T \le k)$$

$$= {}_kp_{xy} - {}_{k+1}p_{xy}$$

$$= {}_kp_{xy}\, q_{x+k:y+k}. \tag{9.3.10}$$

When the future lifetimes of (x) and (y) are independent, the probability of the joint-life status $(x + k : y + k)$ failing within the next year can be written in terms of the probabilities of independent failure of the individual lives as follows:

$$q_{x+k:y+k} = 1 - p_{x+k:y+k}$$

$$= 1 - p_{x+k}\, p_{y+k}$$

$$= 1 - (1 - q_{x+k})(1 - q_{y+k})$$

$$= q_{x+k} + q_{y+k} - q_{x+k}\, q_{y+k}$$

$$= q_{x+k} + (1 - q_{x+k})\, q_{y+k}. \tag{9.3.11}$$

From the discussion of curtate-future-lifetime of (x) in Section 3.2.3, we see that (9.3.10) also provides the p.f. of the random variable K, the number of years completed prior to failure of the joint-life status; that is, for $k = 0, 1, 2, \ldots$,

$$\Pr(K = k) = \Pr(k \le T < k + 1)$$

$$= \Pr(k < T \le k + 1)$$

$$= {}_kp_{xy}\, q_{x+k:y+k}$$

$$= {}_{k|}q_{xy}. \tag{9.3.12}$$

Example 9.3.5

Determine the p.f. and curtate expectation of $K(xy)$ using the common d.f. of Examples 9.3.1 and 9.3.2.

Solution:

From Example 9.3.2,

$${}_kp_{xy} = 0.0001(10 - k)^4.$$

Hence

$$\Pr[K(xy) = k] = 0.0001[(10 - k)^4 - (9 - k)^4],$$
$$k = 0, 1, 2, 3, \ldots, 9.$$

From (3.5.5),

$$e_{xy} = \mathrm{E}[K(xy)] = \sum_{k=0}^{\infty} {}_{k+1}p_{xy} = \sum_{k=0}^{9} 0.0001(9 - k)^4 = 1.5333.$$

▼

9.4 The Last-Survivor Status

In addition to benefits defined in terms of the time of the first death, there are those defined in terms of the time of the last death. In this section we will examine situations in which the random variable is the time of the last death.

A survival status that exists as long as at least one member of a set of lives is alive and fails upon the last death is called the **last-survivor status**. It is denoted by $\overline{(x_1 \, x_2 \cdots x_m)}$, where x_i represents the age of member i and m represents the number of members of the set. We consider the distribution of the time-until-failure of the last-survivor status, the random variable $T = \max[T(x_1), T(x_2), \ldots, T(x_m)]$, where $T(x_i)$ is the time-until-death of individual i. The random variable T can be interpreted as the **largest order statistic** associated with $[T(x_1), T(x_2), \ldots, T(x_m)]$. Unlike the typical situation in the study of inferential statistics, the m random variables here are not necessarily independent and identically distributed.

For the case of two lives (x) and (y), $T(\overline{xy}) = \max[T(x), T(y)]$. General relationships exist among $T(xy)$, $T(\overline{xy})$, $T(x)$, and $T(y)$. For each outcome, $T(xy)$ equals either $T(x)$ or $T(y)$ and $T(\overline{xy})$ equals the other. Thus, for all joint distributions of $T(x)$ and $T(y)$, the following relationships hold:

$$T(xy) + T(\overline{xy}) = T(x) + T(y), \tag{9.4.1}$$

$$T(xy) \, T(\overline{xy}) = T(x) \, T(y), \tag{9.4.2}$$

$$a^{T(xy)} + a^{T(\overline{xy})} = a^{T(x)} + a^{T(y)} \qquad \text{for } a > 0. \tag{9.4.3}$$

There are also some general relationships among the distributions of these four random variables that come from the method of inclusion-exclusion of probability; that is,

$$\Pr(A \cup B) + \Pr(A \cap B) = \Pr(A) + \Pr(B). \tag{9.4.4}$$

Defining A as $\{T(x) \le t\}$ and B as $\{T(y) \le t\}$, we have $A \cap B = \{T(\overline{xy}) \le t\}$ and $A \cup B = \{T(xy) \le t\}$, which lead to

$$F_{T(xy)}(t) + F_{T(\overline{xy})}(t) = F_{T(x)}(t) + F_{T(y)}(t). \tag{9.4.5}$$

From this it follows that

$$_t p_{xy} + {}_t p_{\overline{xy}} = {}_t p_x + {}_t p_y \tag{9.4.6}$$

and

$$f_{T(xy)}(t) + f_{T(\overline{xy})}(t) = f_{T(x)}(t) + f_{T(y)}(t). \tag{9.4.7}$$

The relationships developed above allow the distribution of the last-survivor status to be explored by use of the distribution of the joint-life status that is developed in the previous section. An illustration of this fact is provided by substituting (9.3.2) into (9.4.5) to obtain

$$F_{T(\overline{xy})}(t) = F_{T(x)}(t) + F_{T(y)}(t) - F_{T(xy)}(t) = F_{T(x)T(y)}(t, t),$$

a relationship that also follows from $F_{T(\overline{xy})}(t) = \Pr[T(x) \le t \cap T(y) \le t]$.

Example 9.4.1

Determine the d.f., survival function and p.d.f. of $T(\overline{xy})$ for the lives in Example 9.2.1.

Solution:

From (9.4.5) and the solutions to part (b) of Example 9.2.1 and Example 9.3.1,

$$F_{T(\overline{xy})}(t) = 2\{0.5 + 0.00005[t^4 - (10 - t)^4]\} - [1 - 0.0001(10 - t)^4]$$

$$= 0.0001t^4 = F_{T(x)T(y)}(t, t) \qquad 0 \le t < 10,$$

$$_tp_{\overline{xy}} = 1 - F_{T(\overline{xy})}(t) = 1 - 0.0001t^4 \qquad 0 < t \le 10.$$

By differentiation,

$$f_{T(\overline{xy})}(t) = 0.0004\, t^3 \qquad 0 < t < 10. \qquad \blacktriangledown$$

Example 9.4.2

Determine the d.f., survival function and p.d.f. of $T(\overline{xy})$ for the lives in Example 9.2.3.

Solution:

From (9.4.5) and the solutions to Examples 9.2.3 and 9.3.2 for $0 < t \le 10$,

$$F_{T(\overline{xy})}(t) = 2[1 - 0.01(10 - t)^2] - [1 - 0.0001(10 - t)^4]$$

$$= [1 - 0.01(10 - t)^2]^2$$

$$= t^2(0.2 - 0.01t)^2 = F_{T(x)T(y)}(t, t),$$

$$_tp_{\overline{xy}} = 1 - F_{T(\overline{xy})}(t) = 1 - t^2(0.2 - 0.01t)^2,$$

$$f_{T(\overline{xy})}(t) = 0.04t(2 - 0.1t)(1 - 0.1t) \qquad 0 < t < 10. \qquad \blacktriangledown$$

An observation derived by comparing Examples 9.3.1 and 9.3.2 with Examples 9.4.1 and 9.4.2 is that two different joint distributions may produce the same distribution for the joint-life status but different distributions for the last-survivor status. This possibility could have been anticipated by the general nature of (9.4.5).

For applications it is preferable to rearrange and to restate (9.4.5) and (9.4.7) in actuarial notation:

$$_tq_{\overline{xy}} = {}_tq_x + {}_tq_y - {}_tq_{xy}, \qquad\qquad \text{(9.4.5) restated}$$

$$_tp_{\overline{xy}}\, \mu_{\overline{xy}}(t) = {}_tp_x\, \mu(x+t) + {}_tp_y\, \mu(y+t) - {}_tp_{xy}\, \mu_{xy}(t). \qquad \text{(9.4.7) restated}$$

The force of failure for the last-survivor status is implicitly defined in this restatement of (9.4.7) as

$$\mu_{\overline{xy}}(t) = \frac{f_{T(\overline{xy})}(t)}{1 - F_{T(\overline{xy})}(t)}$$

$$= \frac{{}_tp_x\, \mu(x+t) + {}_tp_y\, \mu(y+t) - {}_tp_{xy}\, \mu_{xy}(t)}{{}_tp_{\overline{xy}}}. \qquad (9.4.8)$$

When $T(x)$ and $T(y)$ are independent $\mu_{xy}(t)$ can be replaced by $\mu_x(t) + \mu_y(t)$ in (9.4.7) and (9.4.8), and they can be rewritten as

$$_tp_{\overline{xy}}\, \mu_{\overline{xy}}(t) = {}_tq_y\, {}_tp_x\, \mu(x+t) + {}_tq_x\, {}_tp_y\, \mu(y+t) \qquad (9.4.9)$$

and

$$\mu_{\overline{xy}}(t) = \frac{{}_tq_y\, {}_tp_x\, \mu(x+t) + {}_tq_x\, {}_tp_y\, \mu(y+t)}{{}_tq_y\, {}_tp_x + {}_tq_x\, {}_tp_y + {}_tp_x\, {}_tp_y}. \qquad (9.4.10)$$

In this form the force of failure of the last-survivor status is a weighted average of forces of mortality. Forces of mortality are conditional p.d.f.'s, and the probability density that (x) and (y) will die at t is 0. As a result, the force associated with ${}_tp_x\, {}_tp_y$ in the weighted average is 0.

Example 9.4.3

Determine the force of failure for the last survivor of the two lives in
a. Example 9.2.1, and
b. Example 9.2.3.

Solution:
a. Using the results of Example 9.4.1,

$$\mu_{\overline{xy}}(t) = \frac{0.0004t^3}{1 - 0.0001t^4} = \frac{4t^3}{10,000 - t^4}.$$

b. Using the results of Example 9.4.2,

$$\mu_{\overline{xy}}(t) = \frac{0.04t(2 - 0.1t)(1 - 0.1t)}{1 - t^2(0.2 - 0.01t)^2} = \frac{4t(20 - t)(10 - t)}{10,000 - t^2(20 - t)^2}. \qquad \blacktriangledown$$

Discrete analogues of relationships (9.4.1)–(9.4.3) and (9.4.5)–(9.4.7) exist for the curtate-future-lifetimes. These are

$$K(xy) + K(\overline{xy}) = K(x) + K(y), \qquad (9.4.11)$$

$$K(xy)\, K(\overline{xy}) = K(x)\, K(y), \qquad (9.4.12)$$

$$a^{K(xy)} + a^{K(\overline{xy})} = a^{K(x)} + a^{K(y)} \qquad \text{for } a > 0, \tag{9.4.13}$$

$$F_{K(xy)}(k) + F_{K(\overline{xy})}(k) = F_{K(x)}(k) + F_{K(y)}(k). \tag{9.4.14}$$

From (9.4.14) it follows that

$$f_{K(xy)}(k) + f_{K(\overline{xy})}(k) = f_{K(x)}(k) + f_{K(y)}(k). \tag{9.4.15}$$

The distribution of $K(\overline{xy})$, the number of years completed prior to failure of the last-survivor status, that is, the number of years completed prior to the last death, can now be determined from these relationships and the results for the curtate-future-lifetime of the joint-life survivor status. From (9.4.15),

$$\Pr[K(\overline{xy}) = k] = f_{K(\overline{xy})}(k) = {}_kp_x \, q_{x+k} + {}_kp_y \, q_{y+k} - {}_kp_{xy} \, q_{x+k:y+k}. \tag{9.4.16}$$

For independent lives, (9.3.5) and (9.3.12) allow us to write (9.4.16) as

$$\Pr[K(\overline{xy}) = k] = {}_kp_x \, q_{x+k} + {}_kp_y \, q_{y+k} - {}_kp_x \, {}_kp_y \, (q_{x+k} + q_{y+k} - q_{x+k}q_{y+k})$$

$$= (1 - {}_kp_y) \, {}_kp_x \, q_{x+k} + (1 - {}_kp_x) \, {}_kp_y \, q_{y+k} + {}_kp_x \, {}_kp_y \, q_{x+k} \, q_{y+k}.$$

In this last form, the first two terms are the probability that only the second death occurs between times k and $k + 1$. The third term is the probability that both deaths occur during that year. This expression for $\Pr[K(\overline{xy}) = k]$ is analogous to (9.4.9) for the p.d.f. of $T(\overline{xy})$ where, since the probability that two deaths occur in the same instant is 0, there are only two terms.

9.5 More Probabilities and Expectations

In Sections 9.3 and 9.4 we express the p.d.f.'s and the d.f.'s of the future lifetimes of the joint-life status and the last-survivor status in terms of the functions of the probability distributions for the single lives. In this section we use these expressions to solve probability problems and to obtain expectations, variances, and, for independent individual future lifetimes, the covariance of the joint-life and last-survivor future lifetimes.

Example 9.5.1

Assuming the future lifetimes of (80) and (85) are independent, obtain an expression, in single life table functions, for the probability that their
a. First death occurs after 5 and before 10 years from now, and
b. Last death occurs after 5 and before 10 years from now.

Solution:

a. With $T = T(80:85)$ we obtain

$$\Pr(5 < T \le 10) = \Pr(T > 5) - \Pr(T > 10)$$

$$= {}_5p_{80:85} - {}_{10}p_{80:85}$$

$$= {}_5p_{80} \, {}_5p_{85} - {}_{10}p_{80} \, {}_{10}p_{85}.$$

Note that the independence assumption is used only in the last step.

b. With $T = T(\overline{80:85})$

$$\Pr(5 < T \leq 10) = \Pr(T > 5) - \Pr(T > 10)$$

$$= {}_5p_{\overline{80:85}} - {}_{10}p_{\overline{80:85}},$$

and from (9.4.6) we obtain

$$= {}_5p_{80} - {}_{10}p_{80} + {}_5p_{85} - {}_{10}p_{85} - ({}_5p_{80:85} - {}_{10}p_{80:85}).$$

Using the independence assumption, we can substitute ${}_5p_{80}\,{}_5p_{85}$ for ${}_5p_{80:85}$ and ${}_{10}p_{80}\,{}_{10}p_{85}$ for ${}_{10}p_{80:85}$. ▼

The results of Section 3.5 concerning expected values of the distribution of T, the time-until-the death of (x), are also valid if $T = T(u)$ the time-until-failure of a survival status (u). We used some of these ideas in the previous two sections; now we will state them explicitly.

From (3.5.2) we have that $\overset{\circ}{e}_u = \mathrm{E}[T(u)]$, which for a survival status (u) can be obtained from the formula

$$\overset{\circ}{e}_u = \int_0^\infty {}_tp_u \, dt. \tag{9.5.1}$$

If (u) is the joint-life status (xy), then

$$\overset{\circ}{e}_{xy} = \int_0^\infty {}_tp_{xy} \, dt, \tag{9.5.2}$$

and for the last-survivor status $(\overline{xy})$ we have

$$\overset{\circ}{e}_{\overline{xy}} = \int_0^\infty {}_tp_{\overline{xy}} \, dt. \tag{9.5.3}$$

Upon taking expectation of both sides of (9.4.1), we see that

$$\overset{\circ}{e}_{\overline{xy}} = \overset{\circ}{e}_x + \overset{\circ}{e}_y - \overset{\circ}{e}_{xy}. \tag{9.5.4}$$

From (3.5.5), the expected value of $K = K(u)$ is

$$e_u = \sum_1^\infty {}_kp_u$$

for a survival status, (u). Special cases include

$$e_{xy} = \sum_1^\infty {}_kp_{xy}$$

and

$$e_{\overline{xy}} = \sum_1^\infty {}_kp_{\overline{xy}}.$$

It follows from (9.4.11) that

$$e_{\overline{xy}} = e_x + e_y - e_{xy}. \tag{9.5.5}$$

The variance formulas derived in Section 3.5 can be used to calculate the variance of the future lifetime, or curtate-future-lifetime, of any survival status, (u). Thus,

$$\text{Var}[T(xy)] = 2 \int_0^\infty t \, {}_t p_{xy} \, dt - (\mathring{e}_{xy})^2 \qquad (9.5.6)$$

and

$$\text{Var}[T(\overline{xy})] = 2 \int_0^\infty t \, {}_t p_{\overline{xy}} \, dt - (\mathring{e}_{\overline{xy}})^2. \qquad (9.5.7)$$

In Example 9.2.1 we calculated the covariance of $T(x)$ and $T(y)$ for dependent future lifetimes. For the moment, we return to dependent future lifetimes to explore the covariance of $T(xy)$ and $T(\overline{xy})$ in the general case:

$$\text{Cov}[T(xy), T(\overline{xy})] = E[T(xy) \, T(\overline{xy})] - E[T(xy)] \, E[T(\overline{xy})]. \qquad (9.5.8)$$

On the basis of (9.4.2),

$$E[T(xy) \, T(\overline{xy})] = E[T(x) \, T(y)].$$

Using this result and (9.5.4), we can write

$$\text{Cov}[T(xy), T(\overline{xy})] = E[T(x) \, T(y)] - E[T(xy)] \, \{E[T(x)] + E[T(y)] - E[T(xy)]\},$$

which can be rewritten as

$$= \text{Cov}[T(x), T(y)] + \{E[T(x)] - E[T(xy)]\} \, \{E[T(y)] - E[T(xy)]\}. \qquad (9.5.9)$$

If $T(x)$ and $T(y)$ are uncorrelated, then

$$\text{Cov}[T(xy), T(\overline{xy})] = (\mathring{e}_x - \mathring{e}_{xy})(\mathring{e}_y - \mathring{e}_{xy}). \qquad (9.5.10)$$

Since both factors of (9.5.10) must be non-negative, we can see that when $T(x)$ and $T(y)$ are uncorrelated, $T(xy)$ and $T(\overline{xy})$ are positively correlated, except in the trivial case where $\mathring{e}_x$ or $\mathring{e}_y$ equals $\mathring{e}_{xy}$.

Example 9.5.2

For $T(x)$ and $T(y)$ of Examples 9.2.1 and 9.2.3 determine (a) $\text{Cov}[T(xy), T(\overline{xy})]$, and (b) the correlation coefficient of $T(xy)$ and $T(\overline{xy})$.

Solution:

Most of the required calculations have been done in previous examples. The remaining calculations can be done readily with the p.d.f.'s that were determined there. We will complete the calculations by displaying intermediate results in tabular form along with the number of the formula being illustrated.

	Distribution	
Item	Examples 9.2.1, 9.3.1, 9.4.1	Examples 9.2.3, 9.3.2, 9.4.2
a. $\overset{\circ}{e}_x = \overset{\circ}{e}_y = E[T(x)] = E[T(y)]$	5	10/3
$\overset{\circ}{e}_{xy} = E[T(xy)]$	2	2
$\text{Cov}[T(x), T(y)]$	$-25/3$	0
$\text{Cov}[T(xy), T(\overline{xy})]$	2/3	16/9
b. $E[T(xy)^2]$	20/3	20/3
$\text{Var}[T(xy)]$	8/3	8/3
$E[T(\overline{xy})]$	8	14/3
$E[T(\overline{xy})^2]$	200/3	80/3
$\text{Var}[T(\overline{xy})]$	8/3	44/9
$\rho_{T(xy)\ T(\overline{xy})}$	1/4	$\sqrt{8/33}$

▼

9.6 Dependent Lifetime Models

In Section 9.2 the concept of the joint distribution of $[T(x), T(y)]$ was introduced. Two examples, which did not appear plausible as models for the joint distribution of $[T(x), T(y)]$ for human lives, were used to illustrate the ideas. Example 9.2.1 illustrated the ideas when $T(x)$ and $T(y)$ are dependent, and Example 9.2.3 provided similar illustrations for independent random variables.

In this section, two general approaches to specifying the joint distribution of $[T(x), T(y)]$ will be studied. The convenient independent case is included within each model.

9.6.1 Common Shock

Let $T^*(x)$ and $T^*(y)$ denote two future lifetime random variables that, in the absence of the possibility of a common shock, are independent; that is,

$$s_{T^*(x)\ T^*(y)}(s, t) = \Pr[T^*(x) > s \cap T^*(y) > t]$$

$$= s_{T^*(x)}(s)\ s_{T^*(y)}(t). \qquad (9.6.1)$$

In addition, there is a **common shock** random variable, to be denoted by Z, that can affect the joint distribution of the time-until-death of lives (x) and (y). This common shock random variable is independent of $[T^*(x), T^*(y)]$ and has an exponential distribution; that is,

$$s_Z(z) = e^{-\lambda z} \quad z > 0, \lambda \geq 0.$$

We can picture the random variable Z as being associated with the time of a catastrophe such as an earthquake or aircraft crash. The random variables of interest in building models for life insurance or annuities to (x) and (y) are $T(x) = \min[T^*(x), Z]$ and $T(y) = \min[T^*(y), Z]$. The joint survival function of $[T(x), T(y)]$ is

$$s_{T(x)T(y)}(s, t) = \Pr\{\min[T^*(x), Z] > s \cap \min[T^*(y), Z] > t\}$$

$$= \Pr\{[T^*(x) > s \cap Z > s] \cap [T^*(y) > t \cap Z > t]\}$$

$$= \Pr[T^*(x) > s \cap T^*(y) > t \cap Z > \max(s, t)]$$

$$= s_{T^*(x)}(s)\, s_{T^*(y)}(t)\, e^{-\lambda[\max(s,t)]}. \tag{9.6.2}$$

The final line of (9.6.2) follows from the independence of $[T^*(x), T^*(y), Z]$.

Using the joint survival function displayed in (9.6.2), we can determine the joint p.d.f. of $[T(x), T(y)]$. Except when $s = t$, the p.d.f. can be found by partial differentiation. We have

$$f_{T(x)T(y)}(s, t) = \frac{\partial^2}{\partial s \partial t}\, s_{T^*(x)}(s)\, s_{T^*(y)}(t)\, e^{-\lambda[\max(s,t)]}$$

$$= [s'_{T^*(x)}(s)\, s'_{T^*(y)}(t) - \lambda s_{T^*(x)}(s)\, s'_{T^*(y)}(t)]\, e^{-\lambda s} \quad 0 < t < s \tag{9.6.3a}$$

$$= [s'_{T^*(x)}(s)\, s'_{T^*(y)}(t) - \lambda s'_{T^*(x)}(s)\, s_{T^*(y)}(t)]\, e^{-\lambda t} \quad 0 < s < t. \tag{9.6.3b}$$

This display does not complete the definition of the p.d.f. When $s = t$, the common shock contribution to the p.d.f. is

$$f_{T(x)T(y)}(t, t) = \lambda e^{-\lambda t}\, s_{T^*(x)}(t)\, s_{T^*(y)}(t) \qquad t \geq 0. \tag{9.6.3c}$$

The domain of this mixed p.d.f., with a ridge of density along the line $s = t$, is shown in Figure 9.6.1.

Figure 9.6.1

Domain of Common Shock p.d.f.

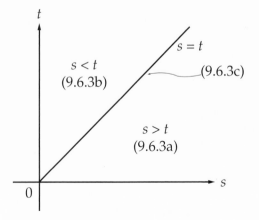

Remark:

The interpretation of the p.d.f. given in (9.6.3.a), (9.6.3.b), and (9.6.3c) requires a careful analysis of the distribution of $[T^*(x), T^*(y)]$ and the derived distribution of $\{T(x) = \min[T^*(x),Z], T(y) = \min[T^*(y), Z]\}$. Table 9.6.1 facilitates this analysis. Because of the intervention of the common shock, realizations of $T^*(x)$ and $T^*(y)$ may not be observed because of the prior realization of Z. The common shock random variable can mask or censor observations of $T^*(x)$ and $T^*(y)$. In addition, events such as $T^*(x) < Z < T^*(y)$ and $T^*(y) < Z < T^*(x)$ can contribute to the p.d.f.

The marginal survival functions are given by

$$s_{T(x)}(s) = \Pr\{[T(x) > s] \cap [T(y) > 0]\}$$

$$= s_{T^*(x)}(s)e^{-\lambda s} \tag{9.6.4a}$$

and

$$s_{T(y)}(t) = \Pr\{[T(x) > 0] \cap [T(y) > t]\}$$

$$= s_{T^*(y)}(t)e^{-\lambda t}. \tag{9.6.4b}$$

Table 9.6.1

Interpretation of p.d.f. of $(T(x), T(y))$, Common Shock Model

Formula	Interpretation	Domain
9.6.3a	$\Pr\{[(s < T^*(x) \le s + \Delta s) \cap (t < T^*(y) \le t + \Delta t) \cap (Z > s)] \cup [(T^*(x) > s) \cap (t < T^*(y) \le t + \Delta t) \cap (s < Z \le s + \Delta s)]\} \approx$ $[f_{T^*(x)}(s) f_{T^*(y)}(t) s_Z(s) + s_{T^*(x)}(s) f_{T^*(y)}(t) f_Z(s)]\Delta s \Delta t$	$0 < t < s$
9.6.3b	$\Pr\{[(s < T^*(x) \le s + \Delta s) \cap (t < T^*(y) \le t + \Delta t) \cap (Z > t)] \cup [(s < T^*(x) \le s + \Delta s) \cap (T^*(y) > t) \cap (t < Z \le t + \Delta t)]\} \approx$ $[f_{T^*(x)}(s) f_{T^*(y)}(t) s_Z(t) + f_{T^*(x)}(s) s_{T^*(y)}(t) f_Z(t)]\Delta s \Delta t$	$0 < s < t$
9.6.3c	$\Pr\{(T^*(x) > t) \cap (T^*(y) > t) \cap (t < Z \le t + \Delta t)\} \approx$ $s_{T^*(x)}(t) s_{T^*(y)}(t) f_Z(t) \Delta t$	$s = t$

If we are interested in the distribution of $T(xy) = \min[T(x), T(y)]$, the joint-life status in the common shock model, the survival function can be obtained using (9.3.1) and (9.6.3):

$$s_{T(xy)}(t) = s_{T^*(x)}(t)\, s_{T^*(y)}(t)\, e^{-\lambda t} \quad 0 < t. \tag{9.6.5}$$

The distribution of $T(\overline{xy}) = \max[T(x), T(y)]$, the last-survivor status in the common shock model, can be derived by using (9.4.5), (9.6.5), (9.6.4a), and (9.6.4b):

$$s_{T(\overline{xy})}(t) = [s_{T^*(x)}(t) + s_{T^*(y)}(t) - s_{T^*(x)T^*(y)}(t, t)]\, e^{-\lambda t} \quad 0 < t. \tag{9.6.6}$$

If the common shock parameter $\lambda = 0$, formulas (9.6.5) and (9.6.6) revert to the form where $T(x)$ and $T(y)$ are independent. When $\lambda > 0$ the joint-life and last-survivor survival functions are each less than the corresponding survival function when $\lambda = 0$.

Example 9.6.1

Exhibit $\mu_{xy}(t)$ as derived from (9.6.5).

Solution:

$$\mu_{xy}(t) = -\frac{d}{dt} \log \left[s_{T^*(x)}(t) \, s_{T^*(y)}(t) e^{-\lambda t} \right]$$

$$= \mu(x + t) + \mu(y + t) + \lambda.$$ ▼

Example 9.6.2

The random variables $T^*(x)$, $T^*(y)$, and Z are independent and have exponential distributions with, respectively, parameter μ_1, μ_2, and λ. These three random variables are components of a common shock model.

a. Exhibit the marginal p.d.f. of $T(y)$ by evaluating

$$f_{T(y)}(t) = \int_0^t f_{T(x)T(y)}(s, t) \, ds + f_{T(x)T(y)}(t, t) + \int_t^\infty f_{T(x)T(y)}(s, t) \, ds.$$

b. Exhibit the marginal survival function of $T(y)$ by evaluating

$$s_{T(y)}(t) = \int_t^\infty f_{T(y)}(u) \, du.$$

c. Evaluate

$$\Pr[T(x) = T(y)] = \int_0^\infty f_{T(x)T(y)}(t, t) \, dt.$$

Solution:

a. We use the three elements of (9.6.3), adapted for exponential distributions, to obtain

$$f_{T(y)}(t) = \int_0^t \mu_1(\mu_2 + \lambda) e^{-\mu_1 s - (\mu_2 + \lambda)t} \, ds + \lambda e^{-(\mu_1 + \mu_2 + \lambda)t}$$

$$+ \int_t^\infty \mu_2(\mu_1 + \lambda) e^{-(\mu_1 + \lambda)s - \mu_2 t} \, ds$$

$$= (\mu_2 + \lambda) e^{-(\mu_2 + \lambda)t} (1 - e^{-\mu_1 t}) + \lambda e^{-(\mu_1 + \mu_2 + \lambda)t} + \mu_2 e^{-(\mu_1 + \mu_2 + \lambda)t}$$

$$= (\mu_2 + \lambda) e^{-(\mu_2 + \lambda)t} \quad 0 < t.$$

b. $s_{T(y)}(t) = \int_t^\infty f_{T(y)}(u) \, du = e^{-(\mu_2 + \lambda)t} = s_{T^*(y)}(t) e^{-\lambda t}$, which agrees with (9.6.4.b).

c. $\Pr[T(x) = T(y)] = \int_0^\infty \lambda e^{-(\mu_1 + \mu_2 + \lambda)t} \, dt = \dfrac{\lambda}{\lambda + \mu_1 + \mu_2}.$ ▼

9.6.2   Copulas

The word *copula* means something that connects or joins together. Copula is used in multivariate statistical analysis to define a class of bivariate distributions with specified marginal distributions.

In this section we will illustrate actuarial applications of Frank's copula. The notation will be that used in Section 9.2. It is claimed that

$$F_{T(x)T(y)}(s, t) = \frac{1}{\alpha} \log \left[1 + \frac{(e^{\alpha F_{T(x)}(s)} - 1)(e^{\alpha F_{T(y)}(t)} - 1)}{e^{\alpha} - 1} \right] \qquad (9.6.7)$$

when $\alpha \neq 0$ is a joint d.f. with marginal distribution $F_{T(x)}(s)$ and $F_{T(y)}(t)$. This claim can be verified by confirming that

$$F_{T(x)T(y)}(0, 0) = 0, \qquad (9.6.8)$$

$$F_{T(x)T(y)}(\infty, \infty) = 1, \qquad (9.6.9)$$

$$\frac{\partial^2}{\partial s \partial t} F_{T(x)T(y)}(s, t) = f_{T(x)T(y)}(s, t)$$

$$= \frac{\alpha f_{T(x)}(s) f_{T(y)}(t) [e^{\alpha[F_{T(x)}(s) + F_{T(y)}(t)]}]}{[(e^{\alpha} - 1) + (e^{\alpha F_{T(x)}(s)} - 1)(e^{\alpha F_{T(y)}(t)} - 1)]^2} (e^{\alpha} - 1) \geq 0, \quad (9.6.10)$$

and

$$F_{T(x)T(y)}(s, \infty) = F_{T(x)}(s),$$

$$F_{T(x)T(y)}(\infty, t) = F_{T(y)}(t).$$

Statements (9.6.8) and (9.6.9) are necessary for $F_{T(x)T(y)}(s, t)$ to be a d.f. of two future lifetime random variables. Statement (9.6.10) exhibits the joint p.d.f. and shows that it is non-negative.

The parameter α in the d.f. displayed in (9.6.7) and the p.d.f. displayed in (9.6.10) controls the dependence of $T(x)$ and $T(y)$. This can be appreciated by finding

$$\lim_{\alpha \to 0} f_{T(x)T(y)}(s, t) = f_{T(x)}(s) f_{T(y)}(t) \left\{ \lim_{\alpha \to 0} [A(\alpha) B(\alpha) C(\alpha)] \right\},$$

where

$$A(\alpha) = e^{\alpha[F_{T(x)}(s) + F_{T(y)}(t)]},$$

$$B(\alpha) = \frac{(e^{\alpha} - 1)\alpha}{(e^{\alpha} - 1)^2},$$

and

$$C(\alpha) = \frac{1}{\{1 + [(e^{\alpha F_{T(x)}(s)} - 1)(e^{\alpha F_{T(y)}(t)} - 1)/(e^{\alpha} - 1)]\}^2}.$$

We have

$$\lim_{\alpha \to 0} A(\alpha) = 1,$$

$$\lim_{\alpha \to 0} B(\alpha) = 1,$$

and $\lim\limits_{\alpha \to 0} C(\alpha)$ depends on the term in the denominator

$$\lim_{\alpha \to 0} \left[\frac{(e^{\alpha F_{T(x)}(s)} - 1)(e^{\alpha F_{T(y)}(t)} - 1)}{e^{\alpha} - 1} \right]$$

$$= \lim_{\alpha \to 0} \left\{ \frac{F_{T(x)}(s)\, e^{\alpha F_{T(x)}(s)}(e^{\alpha F_{T(y)}(t)} - 1) + F_{T(y)}(t) e^{\alpha F_{T(y)}(t)}(e^{\alpha F_{T(x)}(s)} - 1)}{e^{\alpha}} \right\}$$

$$= 0.$$

Therefore, $\lim\limits_{\alpha \to 0} C(\alpha) = 1$, and $\lim\limits_{\alpha \to 0} f_{T(x)T(y)}(s, t) = f_{T(x)}(s)\, f_{T(y)}(t)$. This means that $T(x)$ and $T(y)$ are independent in the limit as $\alpha \to 0$. We interpret the joint p.d.f. in this fashion when $\alpha = 0$.

Example 9.6.3

Let $F_{T(x)}(s) = s$, $0 < s \le 1$, and $F_{T(y)}(t) = t$, $0 < t \le 1$, in (9.6.7) and $T(xy) = \min[T(x), T(y)]$.

a. Find the d.f. of $T(xy)$.
b. Find the p.d.f. of $T(xy)$.

Solution:

a. Using (9.3.2),

$$F_{T(xy)}(t) = F_{T(x)}(t) + F_{T(y)}(t) - F_{T(x)T(y)}(t, t)$$

$$= 2t - \frac{1}{\alpha} \log \left[1 + \frac{(e^{\alpha t} - 1)^2}{e^{\alpha} - 1} \right] \qquad 0 < t < 1.$$

b.
$$f_{T(xy)}(t) = \frac{d}{dt} F_{T(xy)}(t)$$

$$= 2 - \frac{2\alpha(e^{\alpha t} - 1)e^{\alpha t}/(e^{\alpha} - 1)}{\alpha\{1 + [(e^{\alpha t} - 1)^2/(e^{\alpha} - 1)]\}}$$

$$= 2 - \left[\frac{2(e^{\alpha t} - 1)e^{\alpha t}}{(e^{\alpha} - 1) + (e^{\alpha t} - 1)^2} \right] \qquad 0 < t < 1. \qquad \blacktriangledown$$

9.7   Insurance and Annuity Benefits

Insurances and annuities, previously discussed for an individual life, can be defined for the survival status, (u), and are discussed in this section. We also investigate more complicated examples in which an annuity, payable to a survival status, (u), is deferred until another status, (v), has failed.

9.7.1   Survival Statuses

With the single-life status, (x), replaced by the survival status, (u), the models and formulas of Chapters 4 and 5 are applicable here. Expressions for the actuarial

---

present values, variances, and percentiles in terms of the distribution of (u) are immediately available. The relationships of Sections 9.3 and 9.4 can then be used to be these expressions in terms of functions for the individual lives of the survival status.

For an insurance of unit amount payable at the end of the year in which the "survival" status fails, the model and formulas of Section 4.3 apply. Thus if K denotes the curtate-future-lifetime of (u), then the
- Time of payment is $K + 1$,
- Present value at issue of the payment is $Z = v^{K+1}$,
- Actuarial present value, A_u, is $E[Z] = \sum_0^\infty v^{k+1} \Pr(K = k)$, $\qquad$ (9.7.1)
- $\text{Var}(Z) = {}^2A_u - (A_u)^2$. $\qquad$ (9.7.2)

As an illustration, consider a unit sum insured payable at the end of the year in which the last survivor of (x) and (y) dies. From (9.4.16) and (9.7.1) we have

$$A_{\overline{xy}} = \sum_0^\infty v^{k+1} \left({}_kp_x\, q_{x+k} + {}_kp_y\, q_{y+k} - {}_kp_{xy}\, q_{x+k:y+k} \right),$$

which can be used at forces of interest δ and 2δ to obtain the variance by (9.7.2).

The numerous formulas for discrete annuities in Section 5.3 are valid when the annuity payments are contingent on the survival of a survival status. For example, if we replace x with u to emphasize that K is the curtate-future-lifetime of the survival status, (u), we can restate the following formulas for an n-year temporary life annuity in regard to (u):

$$Y = \begin{cases} \ddot{a}_{\overline{K+1}|} & K = 0, 1, \ldots, n-1 \\ \ddot{a}_{\overline{n}|} & K = n, n+1, \ldots, \end{cases} \qquad \text{(5.3.9) restated}$$

$$\ddot{a}_{u:\overline{n}|} = E[Y] = \sum_0^{n-1} \ddot{a}_{\overline{K+1}|}\, {}_{k|}q_u + \ddot{a}_{\overline{n}|}\, {}_np_u, \qquad \text{(9.7.3)}$$

$$\ddot{a}_{u:\overline{n}|} = \sum_0^{n-1} {}_kE_u = \sum_0^{n-1} v^k\, {}_kp_u, \qquad \text{(5.3.9) restated}$$

$$\ddot{a}_{u:\overline{n}|} = \frac{1}{d}\left(1 - A_{u:\overline{n}|}\right), \qquad \text{(5.3.12) restated}$$

$$\text{Var}(Y) = \frac{1}{d^2}\left[{}^2A_{u:\overline{n}|} - (A_{u:\overline{n}|})^2\right]. \qquad \text{(5.3.14) restated}$$

As an illustration, consider an annuity of 1, payable at the beginning of each year to which both (x) and (y) survive during the next n years. This is an annuity to the joint-life status (xy). By substituting ${}_tp_{xy}$, or ${}_tp_x\, {}_tp_y$ if the lifetimes are independent, for ${}_tp_u$ in the above formulas, we can obtain the actuarial present value of the annuity. For the variance as given in (5.3.14), we can use

$$A_{xy:\overline{n}|} = 1 - d\ddot{a}_{xy:\overline{n}|}$$

and

$$^2A_{xy:\overline{n}|} = 1 - (2d - d^2)\,^2\ddot{a}_{xy:\overline{n}|},$$

or we can calculate the actuarial present values directly.

In addition, we can establish relationships among the present-value random variables for annuities and insurances on the last-survivor status and the joint-life status. From relationship (9.4.13), we have

$$v^{K(\overline{xy})+1} + v^{K(xy)+1} = v^{K(x)+1} + v^{K(y)+1}, \tag{9.7.4}$$

$$\ddot{a}_{\overline{K(\overline{xy})+1}|} + \ddot{a}_{\overline{K(xy)+1}|} = \ddot{a}_{\overline{K(x)+1}|} + \ddot{a}_{\overline{K(y)+1}|}. \tag{9.7.5}$$

By taking the expectations of both sides of (9.7.4) and (9.7.5), we have

$$A_{\overline{xy}} + A_{xy} = A_x + A_y$$

and

$$\ddot{a}_{\overline{xy}} + \ddot{a}_{xy} = \ddot{a}_x + \ddot{a}_y.$$

These formulas allow us to express the actuarial present values of last-survivor annuities and insurances in terms of those for the individual lives and the joint-life status. Note that these formulas hold for all joint distributions; independence is not required.

We now consider continuous insurances and annuities. If T, the future-lifetime random variable in Sections 4.2 and 5.2, is reinterpreted as $T(u)$, the time-until-failure of the survival status, (u), the formulas of those sections for present values, actuarial present values, percentiles, and variances hold for insurances and annuities for the status (u).

For an insurance paying a unit amount at the moment of failure of (u), the present value at policy issue, the actuarial present value and the variance are given by

$$Z = v^T,$$

$$\bar{A}_u = \int_0^\infty v^t \, _tp_u \, \mu_u(t) \, dt, \tag{4.2.6} \text{ restated}$$

$$\text{Var}(Z) = {}^2\bar{A}_u - (\bar{A}_u)^2.$$

As an illustration, the restated (4.2.6) for the last survivor of (x) and (y) would be

$$\bar{A}_{\overline{xy}} = \int_0^\infty v^t \, _tp_{\overline{xy}} \, \mu_{\overline{xy}}(t) \, dt.$$

From (9.4.7), this is

$$\bar{A}_{\overline{xy}} = \int_0^\infty v^t \, [_tp_x \, \mu(x + t) + {}_tp_y \, \mu(y + t) - {}_tp_{xy} \, \mu_{xy}(t)] \, dt.$$

For an annuity payable continuously at the rate of 1 per annum until the time-of-failure of (u), we have

$$Y = \bar{a}_{\overline{T}|},$$

$$\bar{a}_u = \int_0^\infty \bar{a}_{\overline{t}|} \; {}_tp_u \; \mu_u(t) \; dt \qquad \text{(5.2.3) restated}$$

$$= \int_0^\infty v^t \; {}_tp_u \; dt, \qquad \text{(5.2.4) restated}$$

$$\text{Var}(Y) = \frac{{}^2\bar{A}_u - (\bar{A}_u)^2}{\delta^2}. \qquad \text{(5.2.9) restated}$$

The interest identity,

$$\delta \, \bar{a}_{\overline{T}|} + v^T = 1, \qquad \text{(5.2.7) restated}$$

is also available for $T = T(u)$ and provides the connection between the models for insurances and annuities.

As an application, consider an annuity payable continuously at the rate of 1 per year as long as at least one of (x) or (y) survives. This is an annuity in respect to $(\overline{xy})$, so we have from the above formulas with $T = T(\overline{xy})$

$$Y = \bar{a}_{\overline{T}|},$$

$$\bar{a}_{\overline{xy}} = \int_0^\infty \bar{a}_{\overline{t}|} \left[{}_tp_x \, \mu(x + t) + {}_tp_y \, \mu(y + t) - {}_tp_{xy} \, \mu_{xy}(t) \right] dt$$

$$= \int_0^\infty v^t \; {}_tp_{\overline{xy}} \; dt,$$

$$\text{Var}(Y) = \frac{{}^2\bar{A}_{\overline{xy}} - (\bar{A}_{\overline{xy}})^2}{\delta^2}.$$

Formula (9.4.3) implies that

$$v^{T(\overline{xy})} + v^{T(xy)} = v^{T(x)} + v^{T(y)} \qquad (9.7.6)$$

and

$$\bar{a}_{\overline{T(\overline{xy})}|} + \bar{a}_{\overline{T(xy)}|} = \bar{a}_{\overline{T(x)}|} + \bar{a}_{\overline{T(y)}|}, \qquad (9.7.7)$$

and (9.4.1) implies that

$$v^{T(\overline{xy})} \, v^{T(xy)} = v^{T(x)} \, v^{T(y)}. \qquad (9.7.8)$$

These identities can be used to obtain the relations among the actuarial present values, variances, and covariances of insurances and annuities for the various statuses. For example, taking the expectations of both sides of (9.7.6) and (9.7.7), we obtain

$$\bar{A}_{\overline{xy}} + \bar{A}_{xy} = \bar{A}_x + \bar{A}_y, \qquad (9.7.9)$$

$$\bar{a}_{\overline{xy}} + \bar{a}_{xy} = \bar{a}_x + \bar{a}_y. \qquad (9.7.10)$$

In the same way that $\text{Cov}[T(\overline{xy}), T(xy)]$ was expressed as

$$\text{Cov}[T(\overline{xy}), T(xy)] = \text{Cov}[T(x), T(y)] + (\bar{e}_x - \bar{e}_{xy})(\bar{e}_y - \bar{e}_{xy}),$$

it can be shown that

$$\text{Cov}(v^{T(\overline{xy})}, v^{T(xy)}) = \text{Cov}(v^{T(x)}, v^{T(y)}) + (\bar{A}_x - \bar{A}_{xy})(\bar{A}_y - \bar{A}_{xy}). \qquad (9.7.11)$$

Both factors in the second term of (9.7.11) are nonpositive, so it will be non-negative and will be zero only in the trivial case where either $\bar{A}_x$ or $\bar{A}_y$ equals $\bar{A}_{xy}$.

The actuarial present value of a continuous annuity paid with respect to $(\overline{xy})$ where, because (x) and (y) are subject to common shock, the joint survival function is given by (9.6.5) can be written in current payment form as

$$\bar{a}_{\overline{xy}} = \int_0^\infty e^{-(\delta+\lambda)t} s_{T^*(x)}(t) \, dt + \int_0^\infty e^{-(\delta+\lambda)t} s_{T^*(y)}(t) \, dt$$

$$- \int_0^\infty e^{-(\delta+\lambda)t} s_{T^*(x)}(t) s_{T^*(y)}(t) \, dt. \qquad (9.7.12)$$

Formula (9.7.12) illustrates how the common shock parameter λ can be combined with the force of interest in some calculations.

Example 9.7.1

a. Extend (9.7.9) to the actuarial present value of an n-year term insurance paying a death benefit of 1 at the moment of the last death of (x) and (y) if this death occurs before time n. If at least one individual survives to time n, no payment is made.
b. Use the formula to calculate the actuarial present value, on the basis of $\delta = 0.05$, of a 5-year term insurance payable on the death of the last survivor of the two lives in Example 9.2.1.

Solution:

a. By restating (9.7.6) for n-year term insurance random variables and then taking expectation of both sides, we have

$$\bar{A}^{\,1}_{\overline{xy}:\overline{n}|} = \bar{A}^{\,1}_{x:\overline{n}|} + \bar{A}^{\,1}_{y:\overline{n}|} - \bar{A}^{\,1}_{\overline{xy}\backslash:\overline{n}|}.$$

The symbol $\bar{A}^{\,1}_{\overline{xy}\backslash:\overline{n}|}$ represents the actuarial present value of an n-year term insurance payable at the failure of the joint-life status if it occurs prior to n.
b. From Example 9.2.1, $T(x)$ and $T(y)$ each has p.d.f. $f_T(t) = 0.0002 \, [t^3 + (10 - t)^3]$, $0 \le t < 10$. Therefore,

$$\bar{A}^{\,1}_{x:\overline{5}|} = \bar{A}^{\,1}_{y:\overline{5}|} = \int_0^5 e^{-0.05t}\{0.0002[t^3 + (10 - t)^3]\} \, dt$$

$$= 0.4563.$$

From Example 9.3.3, we have that $f_{T(xy)}(t) = 0.0004(10 - t)^3$, $0 < t < 10$, so

$$\bar{A}^{\,1}_{\overline{xy}\backslash:\overline{5}|} = \int_0^5 e^{-0.05t}[0.0004(10 - t)^3] \, dt = 0.8614.$$

Using the result from part (a),

$$\bar{A}^1_{\overline{xy}:\overline{5}|} = 2(0.4563) - 0.8614 = 0.0512.$$

▼

9.7.2 Special Two-Life Annuities

In this section we illustrate by an example special annuities in which the payment rate depends on the survival of two lives.

Example 9.7.2

An annuity is payable continuously at the rate of
- 1 per year while both (x) and (y) are alive,
- 2/3 per year while one of (x) or (y) is alive and the other is dead.

Derive expressions for

a. The annuity's present-value random variable
b. The annuity's actuarial present value
c. The variance of the random variable in (a), under the assumption that $T(x)$ and $T(y)$ are independent.

Solution:

a. The annuity is a combination of one that is payable at the rate of 2/3 per year while at least one of (x) and (y) is alive—until time $T(\overline{xy})$]—and one that is payable at the rate of 1/3 per year while both individuals are alive—until time $T(xy)$. The present value of the payments is

$$Z = \frac{2}{3}\,\bar{a}_{\overline{T(\overline{xy})}|} + \frac{1}{3}\,\bar{a}_{\overline{T(xy)}|}.$$

b. The actuarial present value is

$$E[Z] = \frac{2}{3}\,\bar{a}_{\overline{xy}} + \frac{1}{3}\,\bar{a}_{xy}.$$

Using (9.7.10) to substitute for $\bar{a}_{\overline{xy}}$, we have

$$E[Z] = \frac{2}{3}\,\bar{a}_x + \frac{2}{3}\,\bar{a}_y - \frac{1}{3}\,\bar{a}_{xy}.$$

Alternatively, from (5.3.2B) restated, we have

$$E[Z] = \frac{2}{3}\int_0^\infty v^t\,{}_tp_{\overline{xy}}\,dt + \frac{1}{3}\int_0^\infty v^t\,{}_tp_{xy}\,dt.$$

Then, by considering the three mutually exclusive cases as to which of the lives may be surviving when $(\overline{xy})$ is surviving at time t, we can write

$${}_tp_{\overline{xy}} = {}_tp_{xy} + ({}_tp_x - {}_tp_{xy}) + ({}_tp_y - {}_tp_{xy}).$$

Substitution of this expression into the first integral and combining the results with the second give

$$E[Z] = \int_0^\infty v^t \, {}_tp_{xy} \, dt + \frac{2}{3} \int_0^\infty v^t \, ({}_tp_x - {}_tp_{xy}) \, dt$$

$$+ \frac{2}{3} \int_0^\infty v^t \, ({}_tp_y - {}_tp_{xy}) \, dt.$$

This expression of E[Z] can be directly obtained by considering the three cases. The first term is the actuarial present value of the payments at the rate of 1 per year while both (x) and (y) survive. The second term is the actuarial present value of the payments at the rate of 2/3 per year at those times t when (x) is alive (with probability ${}_tp_x$) but not both of (x) and (y) are alive (with probability ${}_tp_{xy}$). The third term has a similar interpretation with x and y interchanged.

c.
$$\text{Var}(Z) = \text{Var}\left(\frac{2}{3} \bar{a}_{\overline{T(\overline{xy})}|} + \frac{1}{3} \bar{a}_{\overline{T(xy)}|}\right)$$

$$= \frac{4}{9} \text{Var}(\bar{a}_{\overline{T(\overline{xy})}|}) + \frac{1}{9} \text{Var}(\bar{a}_{\overline{T(xy)}|}) + \frac{4}{9} \text{Cov}(\bar{a}_{\overline{T(\overline{xy})}|}, \bar{a}_{\overline{T(xy)}|}).$$

But, by Exercise 9.23, for independent $T(x)$ and $T(y)$,

$$\text{Cov}(\bar{a}_{\overline{T(\overline{xy})}|}, \bar{a}_{\overline{T(xy)}|}) = \frac{\text{Cov}(v^{T(\overline{xy})}, v^{T(xy)})}{\delta^2}$$

$$= \frac{(\bar{A}_x - \bar{A}_{xy})(\bar{A}_y - \bar{A}_{xy})}{\delta^2}.$$

Hence

$$\text{Var}(Z) = \left\{\frac{4/9 \, [{}^2\bar{A}_{\overline{xy}} - (\bar{A}_{\overline{xy}})^2] + 1/9 \, [{}^2\bar{A}_{xy} - (\bar{A}_{xy})^2] + 4/9 \, (\bar{A}_x - \bar{A}_{xy})(\bar{A}_y - \bar{A}_{xy})}{\delta^2}\right\}.$$ ▼

9.7.3   Reversionary Annuities

A *reversionary annuity* is payable during the existence of a status (u), but only after the failure of a second status (v). Conceptually, this is a deferred life annuity with a random deferment period equal to the time until failure of the second status. In fact, it is a generalization of the deferred life annuity, for if (v) is an n-year term certain, then reversionary annuity reduces to an n-year deferred annuity. If (u) is a term certain, the reversionary annuity reduces to a form of insurance, family income insurance, studied in Chapter 17. The basic notation for the actuarial present value of this annuity is $a_{v|u}$ with adornments to indicate frequency and timing of payments. The concept has been useful to obtain expressions for the more complex annuity arrangements in terms of single and joint status annuities (see Example 9.7.3). Here we will study the present-value random variables for reversionary annuities.

We start with an annuity of 1 per year payable continuously to (y) after the death of (x). The present value at 0, denoted by Z, is

$$Z = \begin{cases} {}_{T(x)|}\bar{a}_{\overline{T(y)-T(x)|}} & T(x) \leq T(y) \\ 0 & T(x) > T(y). \end{cases} \tag{9.7.13}$$

This can be written as

$$Z = \begin{cases} \bar{a}_{\overline{T(y)|}} - \bar{a}_{\overline{T(x)|}} & T(x) \leq T(y) \\ 0 & T(x) > T(y), \end{cases} \tag{9.7.14}$$

or as

$$Z = \begin{cases} \bar{a}_{\overline{T(y)|}} - \bar{a}_{\overline{T(x)|}} & T(x) \leq T(y) \\ \bar{a}_{\overline{T(y)|}} - \bar{a}_{\overline{T(y)|}} & T(x) > T(y), \end{cases} \tag{9.7.15}$$

which is the same as

$$Z = \bar{a}_{\overline{T(y)|}} - \bar{a}_{\overline{T(xy)|}}. \tag{9.7.16}$$

Thus,

$$\bar{a}_{x|y} = \mathrm{E}[Z] = \mathrm{E}[\bar{a}_{\overline{T(y)|}}] - \mathrm{E}[\bar{a}_{\overline{T(xy)|}}] = \bar{a}_y - \bar{a}_{xy}. \tag{9.7.17}$$

Formulas (9.7.16) and (9.7.17) hold for survival statuses (u) and (v). For example,

$$\bar{a}_{x:\overline{n}|y} = \bar{a}_y - \bar{a}_{xy:\overline{n}|},$$

$$\bar{a}_{x|y:\overline{n}|} = \bar{a}_{y:\overline{n}|} - \bar{a}_{xy:\overline{n}|}.$$

We note that (9.7.17) holds for dependent future lifetimes.

Example 9.7.3

Calculate the actuarial present value of an annuity payable continuously at the rates shown in the following display.

Case, Rate, and Condition
1. 1 per year with certainty until time n,
2. 1 per year after time n if both (x) and (y) are alive,
3. 3/4 per year after time n if (x) is alive and (y) is dead, and
4. 1/2 per year after time n if (y) is alive and (x) is dead.

Solution:
We use the reversionary annuity idea to write the actuarial present value of this arrangement in terms of single-life and joint-life annuities.
- Case 1: This is an n-year annuity-certain: $\bar{a}_{\overline{n}|}$.
- Case 2: This is n-year deferred joint life annuity to (xy):
$$_{n|}\bar{a}_{xy} = \bar{a}_{xy} - \bar{a}_{xy:\overline{n}|}.$$
- Case 3: This is a reversionary annuity of 3/4 per annum to x after $\overline{y:\overline{n}|}$:
$$\frac{3}{4}\,\bar{a}_{\overline{y:\overline{n}|}|x} = \frac{3}{4}\left(\bar{a}_x - \bar{a}_{x:(\overline{y:\overline{n}|})}\right) = \frac{3}{4}\left(\bar{a}_x - \bar{a}_{xy} - \bar{a}_{x:\overline{n}|} + \bar{a}_{xy:\overline{n}|}\right).$$

- Case 4: This is a reversionary annuity of 1/2 per annum to y after $\overline{x:\overline{n}}$:

$$\frac{1}{2}\,\bar{a}_{\overline{x:\overline{n}}|y} = \frac{1}{2}\,(\bar{a}_y - \bar{a}_{xy} - \bar{a}_{y:\overline{n}} + \bar{a}_{xy:\overline{n}}).$$

Adding the results for the four cases together, we obtain the required actuarial present value,

$$\bar{a}_{\overline{n}|} + \frac{3}{4}\,\bar{a}_x + \frac{1}{2}\,\bar{a}_y - \frac{1}{4}\,\bar{a}_{xy} - \frac{3}{4}\,\bar{a}_{x:\overline{n}} - \frac{1}{2}\,\bar{a}_{y:\overline{n}} + \frac{1}{4}\,\bar{a}_{xy:\overline{n}}. \qquad \blacktriangledown$$

9.8   Evaluation—Special Mortality Assumptions

In Section 9.7 the actuarial present values of a variety of insurance and annuity benefits that involve two lifetime random variables were developed. These developments typically culminated in an integral or summation. In this section we study several assumptions about the distribution of $T(u)$ that will simplify the evaluation of these integrals and summations.

9.8.1   Gompertz and Makeham Laws

Here we examine the assumption that mortality follows Makeham's law, or its important special case, Gompertz's law, and the implications for the computations of actuarial present values with respect to multiple life statuses. Independent future lifetime random variables will be assumed.

We begin with the assumption that mortality for each life follows Gompertz's law, $\mu(x) = Bc^x$. We seek to substitute a single-life survival status (w) that has a force of failure equal to the force of failure of the joint-life status (xy) for all $t \geq 0$. Consider

$$\mu_{xy}(s) = \mu(w + s) \qquad s \geq 0; \qquad (9.8.1)$$

that is,

$$Bc^{x+s} + Bc^{y+s} = Bc^{w+s},$$

or

$$c^x + c^y = c^w, \qquad (9.8.2)$$

which defines the desired w. It follows that for $t > 0$,

$$_tp_w = \exp\left[-\int_0^t \mu(w + s)\,ds\right]$$

$$= \exp\left[-\int_0^t \mu_{xy}(s)\,ds\right]$$

$$= {}_tp_{xy}. \qquad (9.8.3)$$

Thus for w defined in (9.8.2), all probabilities, expected values, and variances for the joint-life status (xy) equal those for the single life (w). For tabled values, the need for a two-dimensional array has been replaced by the need for a one-dimensional array, but typically w is nonintegral, and therefore the determination of its values requires interpolation in the single array.

The assumption that mortality for each life follows Makeham's law (see Table 3.6) makes the search more complex. The force of mortality for the joint-life status is

$$\mu_{xy}(s) = \mu(x + s) + \mu(y + s) = 2A + Bc^s (c^x + c^y). \tag{9.8.4}$$

We cannot substitute a single life for the two lives because of the $2A$. Instead, we replace (xy) with another joint-life status (ww), and then

$$\mu_{ww}(s) = 2\mu(w + s) = 2(A + Bc^s c^w), \tag{9.8.5}$$

and we choose w such that

$$2c^w = c^x + c^y. \tag{9.8.6}$$

Unlike the Gompertz case where the one-dimensional array is based on functions from a single life table, this one-dimensional array is based on functions for a joint-life status (ww) involving equal-age lives.

Example 9.8.1

Use (3.7.1) and the $\ddot{a}_{xx}$ values based on the Illustrative Life Table (Appendix 2A) with interest at 6% to calculate the value of $\ddot{a}_{60:70}$. Compare your result with the values of $\ddot{a}_{60:70}$ in the table of $\ddot{a}_{x:x+10}$.

Solution:

From $c = 10^{0.04}$ and $c^{60} + c^{70} = 2c^w$, we obtain $w = 66.11276$. Then using linear interpolation, $\ddot{a}_{60:70} = 0.88724\ddot{a}_{66:66} + 0.11276\ddot{a}_{67:67} = 7.55637$. The value by the $\ddot{a}_{x:x+10}$ table is 7.55633. ▼

9.8.2 Uniform Distribution

We retain the independence assumption, and in addition we assume a uniform distribution of deaths in each year of age for each individual in the joint-life status. With this additional assumption, we can evaluate the actuarial present values of annuities payable more frequently than once a year and insurance benefits payable at the moment of death.

We recall from Table 3.6 that, under the assumption of a uniform distribution of deaths for each year of age, $_tp_x = 1 - tq_x$ and

$$_tp_x\, \mu(x + t) = \frac{d}{dt} (1 - {_tp_x}) = q_x. \tag{9.8.7}$$

When we apply this assumption to a joint-life status (xy), with independent $T(x)$ and $T(y)$, we obtain, for $0 \le t \le 1$,

$$_tp_{xy}\,\mu_{xy}(t) = {_tp_x}\,{_tp_y}\,[\mu(x + t) + \mu(y + t)]$$

$$= {_tp_y}\,{_tp_x}\,\mu(x + t) + {_tp_x}\,{_tp_y}\,\mu(y + t)$$

$$= (1 - tq_y)q_x + (1 - tq_x)q_y$$

$$= q_x + q_y - q_xq_y + (1 - 2t)q_xq_y$$

$$= q_{xy} + (1 - 2t)q_xq_y. \tag{9.8.8}$$

On the basis of (4.4.1), the actuarial present value for an insurance benefit in regard to a survival status, (u), can be written as

$$\bar{A}_u = \sum_{k=0}^{\infty} v^{k+1}\,{_kp_u}\int_0^1 (1 + i)^{1-s}\,\frac{_{k+s}p_u}{_kp_u}\,\mu_u(k + s)\,ds.$$

Using (9.8.8), we can rewrite this for the joint-life status, (xy), as

$$\bar{A}_{xy} = \sum_{k=0}^{\infty} v^{k+1}\,{_kp_{xy}}\left[q_{x+k:y+k}\int_0^1 (1 + i)^{1-s}\,ds \right.$$

$$\left. + q_{x+k}\,q_{y+k}\int_0^1 (1 + i)^{1-s}\,(1 - 2s)\,ds \right]$$

$$= \frac{i}{\delta}A_{xy} + \frac{i}{\delta}\left(1 - \frac{2}{\delta} + \frac{2}{i}\right)\sum_{k=0}^{\infty} v^{k+1}\,{_kp_{xy}}\,q_{x+k}\,q_{y+k}. \tag{9.8.9}$$

To interpret the right-hand side of (9.8.9), we see from (4.4.2) that the first term is equal to $\bar{A}_{xy}$ if $T(xy)$, the time-until-failure of (xy), is uniformly distributed in each year of future lifetime. Such is not the case for $T(xy) = \{\min[T(x), T(y)]\}$ when $T(x)$ and $T(y)$ are distributed independently and uniformly over such years. Under this latter assumption, the conditional distribution of $T(xy)$, given that $T(x)$ and $T(y)$ are in different yearly intervals, is also uniform over each year of future lifetime. However, given that $T(x)$ and $T(y)$ are within the same interval, the distribution of their minimum is shifted toward the beginning of the interval (see Exercise 9.38). A consequence of this shift is to require the second term in (9.8.9) to cover the additional expected costs of the earlier claims in those years. The second term, which is the product of an interest term that is close to $i/6$ (see Exercise 9.39) and a actuarial present value for an insurance payable if both individuals die in the same future year, is very small. The actuarial present value $\bar{A}_{xy}$ is often approximated by ignoring the small correction term, thereby simplifying (9.8.9) to

$$\bar{A}_{xy} \cong \frac{i}{\delta}A_{xy}, \tag{9.8.10}$$

which is exact, as noted previously, if $T(xy)$ is uniformly distributed in each year of future lifetime.

To evaluate $\bar{a}_{xy}$, we have from (5.2.8), with survival status (x) replaced by (xy),

$$\bar{a}_{xy} = \frac{1}{\delta}(1 - \bar{A}_{xy}),$$

and, on substitution from (9.8.9), obtain

$$\bar{a}_{xy} = \frac{1}{\delta}\left\{1 - \frac{i}{\delta}\left[A_{xy} + \left(1 - \frac{2}{\delta} + \frac{2}{i}\right)\sum_{k=0}^{\infty} v^{k+1}\,_kp_{xy}\,q_{x+k}\,q_{y+k}\right]\right\}.$$

Now, on the basis of (5.3.7) for the status (xy), we substitute $1 - d\ddot{a}_{xy}$ for A_{xy} and use (5.4.12) and (5.4.13) to write

$$\bar{a}_{xy} = [\alpha(\infty)\ddot{a}_{xy} - \beta(\infty)]$$

$$- \frac{i}{\delta^2}\left(1 - \frac{2}{\delta} + \frac{2}{i}\right)\sum_{k=0}^{\infty} v^{k+1}\,_kp_{xy}\,q_{x+k}\,q_{y+k}. \tag{9.8.11}$$

Formula (9.8.11) follows from the assumption that $T(x)$ and $T(y)$ are distributed independently and uniformly over future years. If we assume that $T(xy)$ itself is uniformly distributed over each future year, then from the continuous case of (5.4.11), $m = \infty$, we would have immediately

$$\bar{a}_{xy} = \alpha(\infty)\ddot{a}_{xy} - \beta(\infty). \tag{9.8.12}$$

Formula (9.8.12) differs from (9.8.11) by a small amount, which approximates the product of $i/(6\delta)$ and the actuarial present value for an insurance payable if both individuals die in the same future year.

To use the same approach to evaluate the actuarial present value of an annuity-due payable m-thly, we need an expression for $A_{xy}^{(m)}$ under the assumption of a uniform distribution of deaths for each of the individuals in each year of age. In analogy to the continuous case, we start with

$$A_{xy}^{(m)} = \sum_{k=0}^{\infty} v^k\,_kp_{xy}\sum_{j=1}^{m} v^{j/m}\left(_{(j-1)/m}p_{x+k:y+k} - \,_{j/m}p_{x+k:y+k}\right). \tag{9.8.13}$$

In Exercise 9.40 this expression, under the assumption that $T(x)$ and $T(y)$ are independently and uniformly distributed over each year of age, is reduced to

$$A_{xy}^{(m)} = \frac{i}{i^{(m)}} A_{xy} + \frac{i}{i^{(m)}}\left(1 + \frac{1}{m} - \frac{2}{d^{(m)}} + \frac{2}{i}\right)\sum_{k=0}^{\infty} v^{k+1}\,_kp_{xy}\,q_{x+k}\,q_{y+k}. \tag{9.8.14}$$

As $m \to \infty$, the expression in (9.8.14) approach their counterparts in (9.8.9). To interpret the right-hand side of (9.8.14), we see by analogy to (9.8.9) that the first term is the usual approximation for $A_{xy}^{(m)}$ and is exact if $T(xy)$ is uniformly distributed in each year. Then,

$$\frac{i}{i^{(m)}}\left(1 + \frac{1}{m} - \frac{2}{d^{(m)}} + \frac{2}{i}\right) \cong \frac{m^2 - 1}{6m^2}\,i,$$

which is less than $i/6$.

By substituting (9.8.14) into (5.4.4) restated for (xy), and replacing A_{xy} by $1 - d\ddot{a}_{xy}$, we obtain the formula for $\ddot{a}_{xy}^{(m)}$ that is analogous to (9.8.11). If the second term of (9.8.14) is ignored, the formula for $\ddot{a}_{xy}^{(m)}$ reduces to

$$\ddot{a}_{xy}^{(m)} = \alpha(m)\ddot{a}_{xy} - \beta(m). \tag{9.8.15}$$

Again by (5.4.11), this is exact under the assumption that the distribution of $T(xy)$ is uniform over each year of future lifetime.

9.9   Simple Contingent Functions

In this section we study insurances that, in addition to being dependent on the time of failure of the status, are contingent on the order of the deaths of the individuals in the group. In this section we will assume that $T(x)$ and $T(y)$ have a continuous joint d.f. This is done to exclude the common shock model of Section 9.6.1.

We begin with an evaluation of the probability that (x) dies before (y) and before n years from now. In IAN this probability is denoted by ${}_nq^1_{xy}$, where the 1 over the x indicates the probability is for an event in which (x) dies before (y), and n indicates that the event occurs within n years. Then ${}_nq^1_{xy}$ equals the double integral of the joint p.d.f. of $T(x)$ and $T(y)$ over the set of outcomes such that $T(x) \le T(y)$ and $T(x) \le n$:

$$
{}_nq^1_{xy} = \int_0^n \int_s^\infty f_{T(x)T(y)}(s, t) \, dt \, ds
$$

$$
= \int_0^n \int_s^\infty f_{T(y)|T(x)}(t|s) \, dt \, f_{T(x)}(s) \, ds
$$

$$
= \int_0^n \Pr[T(y) > s|T(x) = s] \, f_{T(x)}(s) \, ds
$$

$$
= \int_0^n \Pr[T(y) > s|T(x) = s] \, {}_sp_x \, \mu(x + s) \, ds. \qquad (9.9.1)
$$

For the independent case, $\Pr[T(y) \ge s|T(x) = s] = {}_sp_y$, so

$$
{}_nq^1_{xy} = \int_0^n {}_sp_y \, {}_sp_x \, \mu(x + s) \, ds. \qquad (9.9.2)
$$

An interpretation of (9.9.2) involves three elements. First, because s is the time of death of (x), the probability ${}_sp_x \, {}_sp_y$ indicates that both (x) and (y) survive to time s. Second, $\mu(x + s) \, ds$ is the probability that (x), now age $x + s$, will die in the interval $(s, s + ds)$. Third, the probabilities are summed for all times s between 0 and n.

Example 9.9.1

Calculate ${}_5q^1_{xy}$ for the lives in Example 9.2.1.

Solution:
From (9.9.1),

$$
{}_5q^1_{xy} = \int_0^5 \int_s^{10} 0.0006(t - s)^2 \, dt \, ds
$$

$$
= \int_0^5 0.0002(10 - s)^3 \, ds = 0.46875. \qquad \blacktriangledown
$$

We can also evaluate the probability that (y) dies after (x) and before n years from now. This probability is denoted by ${}_nq_{\overline{xy}}^{\,2}$, the 2 above the y indicating that (y) dies second and n requiring that this occurs within n years. To evaluate ${}_nq_{\overline{xy}}^{\,2}$, we integrate the joint p.d.f. of $T(x)$ and $T(y)$ over the event $[0 \leq T(x) \leq T(y) \leq n]$:

$$
{}_nq_{\overline{xy}}^{\,2} = \int_0^n \int_0^t f_{T(x)T(y)}(s,\,t)\ ds\ dt
$$

$$
= \int_0^n \int_0^t f_{T(x)|T(y)}(s|t)\ ds\ f_{T(y)}(t)\ dt
$$

$$
= \int_0^n \Pr[T(x) \leq t|T(y) = t]\ f_{T(y)}(t)\ dt
$$

$$
= \int_0^n \Pr[T(x) \leq t|T(y) = t]\ {}_tp_y\ \mu(y+t)\ dt. \tag{9.9.3}
$$

Again in the independent case, we have

$$
{}_nq_{\overline{xy}}^{\,2} = \int_0^n {}_tq_x\ {}_tp_y\ \mu(y+t)\ dt
$$

$$
= {}_nq_y - {}_nq_{\overline{xy}}^{\,1}. \tag{9.9.4}
$$

If the integration of (9.9.3) is set up in the reverse order, we have

$$
{}_nq_{\overline{xy}}^{\,2} = \int_0^n \int_s^n f_{T(x)T(y)}(s,\,t)\ dt\ ds
$$

$$
= \int_0^n \int_s^n f_{T(y)|T(x)}(t|s)\ dt\ f_{T(x)}(s)\ ds
$$

$$
= \int_0^n \Pr[s < T(y) \leq n|T(x) = s]\ {}_sp_x\ \mu(x+s)\ ds.
$$

Making the assumption of independence for $T(x)$ and $T(y)$, we can rewrite this as

$$
{}_nq_{\overline{xy}}^{\,2} = \int_0^n ({}_sp_y - {}_np_y)\ {}_sp_x\ \mu(x+s)\ ds
$$

$$
= {}_nq_{\overline{xy}}^{\,1} - {}_np_y\ {}_nq_x. \tag{9.9.5}
$$

In (9.9.5) the integrand is interpreted as the probability that (x) dies at time s, with $0 < s < n$, and (y) survives to time s but not to time n. Moreover, we now have that

$$
{}_nq_{\overline{xy}}^{\,1} = {}_nq_{\overline{xy}}^{\,2} + {}_np_y\ {}_nq_x.
$$

This implies

$$
{}_nq_{\overline{xy}}^{\,1} \geq {}_nq_{\overline{xy}}^{\,2}.
$$

Similar integrals can be written for the actuarial present values of contingent insurances, but some do not simplify to the same extent. Consider the actuarial present value of an insurance of 1 payable at the moment of death of (x) provided that (y) is still alive. This actuarial present value, denoted by $\bar{A}_{\overline{xy}}^{1}$, is $E[Z]$ where

$$Z = \begin{cases} v^{T(x)} & T(x) \le T(y) \\ 0 & T(x) > T(y). \end{cases}$$

Since Z is a function of $T(x)$ and $T(y)$, the expectation of Z can be obtained by using the joint p.d.f. of $T(x)$ and $T(y)$:

$$\bar{A}^1_{xy} = \int_0^\infty \int_s^\infty v^s f_{T(x)T(y)}(s, t) \, dt \, ds$$

$$= \int_0^\infty \int_s^\infty v^s f_{T(y)|T(x)}(t|s) \, dt \, f_{T(x)}(s) \, ds$$

$$= \int_0^\infty \left[\int_s^\infty f_{T(y)|T(x)}(t|s) \, dt \right] v^s \, {}_sp_x \, \mu(x + s) \, ds. \tag{9.9.6}$$

In the case of independent future lifetimes, $T(x)$ and $T(y)$, we can simplify (9.9.6) and express it in IAN as

$$\bar{A}^1_{xy} = \int_0^\infty \left[\int_s^\infty {}_tp_y \, \mu(y + t) \, dt \right] v^s \, {}_sp_x \, \mu(x + s) \, ds$$

$$= \int_0^\infty v^s \, {}_sp_y \, {}_sp_x \, \mu(x + s) \, ds. \tag{9.9.7}$$

The final expression can be interpreted as follows: If (x) dies at any future time s and (y) is still surviving, then a payment of 1, with present value v^s, is made. When $\delta = 0$, $\bar{A}^1_{xy} = {}_\infty q^1_{xy}$.

Example 9.9.2

Determine the actuarial present value of a payment of 1,000 at the moment of death of (x) providing that (y) is still alive for (x) and (y) in Example 9.2.3 and on the basis of $\delta = 0.04$.

Solution:

Since $T(x)$ and $T(y)$ are independent in Example 9.2.3, we can use the results of that example in (9.9.7) to have

$$1{,}000 \, \bar{A}^1_{xy} = 1{,}000 \int_0^\infty e^{-0.04s} \, {}_sp_y \, {}_sp_x \, \mu(x + s) \, ds$$

$$= 1{,}000 \int_0^{10} e^{-0.04s} \, 0.01(10 - s)^2 \, 0.02(10 - s) \, ds$$

$$= 0.2 \int_0^{10} e^{-0.04s} \, (10 - s)^3 \, ds = 462.52.$$

▼

Example 9.9.3

a. Derive the single integral expression for the actuarial present value of an insurance of 1 payable at the time of death of (y) if predeceased by (x).

b. Simplify the integral under the assumption of independent future lifetimes.

---

c. Obtain a second answer for part (b) by reversing the order of integration in the part (b) double integral.

Solution:

a. The actuarial present value, denoted by $\bar{A}_{xy}^{2}$, is $E[Z]$ where

$$Z = \begin{cases} v^{T(y)} & T(x) \le T(y) \\ 0 & T(x) > T(y). \end{cases}$$

Again, Z is a function of $T(x)$ and $T(y)$, so we write an integral for the expectation of Z by using the joint p.d.f. of $T(x)$ and $T(y)$,

$$\bar{A}_{xy}^{2} = \int_{0}^{\infty} \int_{0}^{t} v^{t} f_{T(x)T(y)}(s, t) \, ds \, dt$$

$$= \int_{0}^{\infty} v^{t} \int_{0}^{t} f_{T(x)|T(y)}(s|t) \, ds \, f_{T(y)}(t) \, dt$$

$$= \int_{0}^{\infty} v^{t} \Pr[T(x) \le t | T(y) = t] \, f_{T(y)}(t) \, dt.$$

b. Invoking the independence assumption and writing in IAN we have

$$\bar{A}_{xy}^{2} = \int_{0}^{\infty} v^{t} \, _{t}q_{x} \, _{t}p_{y} \, \mu(y + t) \, dt$$

$$= \int_{0}^{\infty} v^{t}(1 - \, _{t}p_{x}) \, _{t}p_{y} \, \mu(y + t) \, dt$$

$$= \bar{A}_{y} - \bar{A}_{xy}^{1}.$$

We note for the independent case that we can express the actuarial present value for a simple contingent insurance, payable on a death other than the first death, in terms of the actuarial present values for insurances payable on the first death. This is the initial step in the numerical evaluation of simple contingent insurances for independent lives.

c. We have

$$\bar{A}_{xy}^{2} = \int_{0}^{\infty} \int_{s}^{\infty} v^{t} \, _{s}p_{x} \, \mu(x + s) \, _{t}p_{y} \, \mu(y + t) \, dt \, ds.$$

To simplify we replace t with $r + s$ in the inner integral and rewrite the expression

$$\bar{A}_{xy}^{2} = \int_{0}^{\infty} \int_{0}^{\infty} v^{r+s} \, _{r+s}p_{y} \, \mu(y + r + s) \, _{s}p_{x} \, \mu(x + s) \, dr \, ds$$

$$= \int_{0}^{\infty} v^{s} \, _{s}p_{y} \, _{s}p_{x} \, \mu(x + s) \left[\int_{0}^{\infty} v^{r} \, _{r}p_{y+s} \, \mu(y + s + r) \, dr \right] ds$$

$$= \int_{0}^{\infty} v^{s} \, \bar{A}_{y+s} \, _{s}p_{y} \, _{s}p_{x} \, \mu(x + s) \, ds.$$

This last integral is an application of the general result given in (2.2.10), $E[W] = E[E[W|V]]$. Here $V = T(x)$, $W = Z$, and we see that the conditional expectation of Z, given $T(x) = s$, is the actuarial present value, $v^s {}_s p_y \bar{A}_{y+s}$, of the pure endowment for an amount A_{y+s} sufficient to fund a unit insurance on $(y + s)$.

▼

9.10 Evaluation—Simple Contingent Functions

We now turn to the evaluation of simple contingent probabilities and actuarial present values, noting the effects of assuming Gompertz's law, Makeham's law, and a uniform distribution of deaths. The ubiquitous assumption of independence will be made.

___

Example 9.10.1

Assuming Gompertz's law for the forces of mortality, calculate
a. The actuarial present value for an n-year term contingent insurance paying a unit amount at the moment of death of (x) only if (x) dies before (y)
b. The probability that (x) dies within n years and predeceases (y).

Solution:

a.
$$\bar{A}^1_{xy:\overline{n}|} = \int_0^n v^t \, {}_t p_{xy} \, \mu(x + t) \, dt.$$

Under Gompertz's law,

$$\bar{A}^1_{xy:\overline{n}|} = \int_0^n v^t \, {}_t p_{xy} \, Bc^x \, c^t \, dt$$

$$= \frac{c^x}{c^x + c^y} \int_0^n v^t \, {}_t p_{xy} \, B(c^x + c^y)c^t \, dt$$

$$= \frac{c^x}{c^x + c^y} \int_0^n v^t \, {}_t p_{xy} \, \mu_{xy}(t) \, dt$$

$$= \frac{c^x}{c^x + c^y} \bar{A}^1_{\overline{xy}\backslash :\overline{n}|}. \tag{9.10.1}$$

Furthermore, if (9.8.2) holds, then

$$\bar{A}^1_{\overline{xy}\backslash :\overline{n}|} = \bar{A}^1_{w:\overline{n}|},$$

and

$$\bar{A}^1_{xy:\overline{n}|} = \frac{c^x}{c^w} \bar{A}^1_{w:\overline{n}|}. \tag{9.10.2}$$

b. Referring to (9.9.2) we see that ${}_n q^1_{xy}$ is $\bar{A}^1_{xy:\overline{n}|}$ with $v = 1$. Thus, it follows from (9.10.2) that, under Gompertz's law,

$${}_n q^1_{xy} = \frac{c^x}{c^w} \, {}_n q_w, \tag{9.10.3}$$

where $c^w = c^x + c^y$.

▼

___

Example 9.10.2

Assuming Makeham's law for the forces of mortality, repeat Example 9.10.1.

Solution:

a.
$$\bar{A}^1_{xy:\overline{n}} = \int_0^n v^t\, {}_tp_{xy}\, (A + Bc^xc^t)\, dt$$

$$= A \int_0^n v^t\, {}_tp_{xy}\, dt + \frac{c^x}{c^x + c^y} \int_0^n v^t\, {}_tp_{xy}\, B(c^x + c^y)c^t\, dt$$

$$= A\left(1 - \frac{2c^x}{c^x + c^y}\right) \int_0^n v^t\, {}_tp_{xy}\, dt$$

$$+ \frac{c^x}{c^x + c^y} \int_0^n v^t\, {}_tp_{xy}\, [2A + B(c^x + c^y)c^t]\, dt$$

$$= A\left(1 - \frac{2c^x}{c^x + c^y}\right) \bar{a}_{xy:\overline{n}} + \frac{c^x}{c^x + c^y}\, \bar{A}^{\ 1}_{\overline{xy}:\overline{n}}.$$

Then by using (9.8.6), we obtain

$$\bar{A}^1_{xy:\overline{n}} = A\left(1 - \frac{c^x}{c^w}\right) \bar{a}_{ww:\overline{n}} + \frac{c^x}{2c^w}\, \bar{A}^{\ 1}_{\overline{ww}:\overline{n}}. \tag{9.10.4}$$

b. Again, we set $v = 1$ in the result of part (a) to have

$${}_nq^1_{xy} = A\left(1 - \frac{c^x}{c^w}\right) \mathring{e}_{ww:\overline{n}} + \frac{c^x}{2c^w}\, {}_nq_{ww}. \tag{9.10.5}$$

▼

The actuarial present value for a contingent insurance payable at the end of the year of death is

$$A^1_{xy} = \sum_{k=0}^{\infty} v^{k+1}\, {}_kp_{xy}\, q^{\ 1}_{x+k:y+k}. \tag{9.10.6}$$

Under the assumption of a uniform distribution of deaths for each individual and independence between the pair of future lifetime random variables, we have

$$q^{\ 1}_{x+k:y+k} = \int_0^1 {}_sp_{x+k:y+k}\, \mu(x + k + s)\, ds$$

$$= \int_0^1 q_{x+k}(1 - sq_{y+k})\, ds$$

$$= q_{x+k}\left(1 - \frac{1}{2}\, q_{y+k}\right). \tag{9.10.7}$$

We can now rewrite ${}_sp_{x+k:y+k}\, \mu(x + k + s)$ in terms of $q^{\ 1}_{x+k:y+k}$,

$$_s p_{x+k:y+k}\, \mu(x + k + s) = q_{x+k}(1 - s q_{y+k})$$

$$= q_{x+k}\left(1 - \frac{1}{2}\, q_{y+k}\right)$$

$$+ \left(\frac{1}{2} - s\right) q_{x+k} q_{y+k}$$

$$= q_{\frac{1}{x+k:y+k}} + \left(\frac{1}{2} - s\right) q_{x+k} q_{y+k}. \qquad (9.10.8)$$

When the benefit is payable at the moment of death, the actuarial present value is

$$\bar{A}_{xy}^1 = \sum_{k=0}^{\infty} v^k\, {}_k p_{xy} \int_0^1 v^s\, {}_s p_{x+k:y+k}\, \mu(x + k + s)\, ds$$

$$= \sum_{k=0}^{\infty} v^{k+1}\, {}_k p_{xy} \left[q_{\frac{1}{x+k:y+k}} \int_0^1 (1 + i)^{1-s}\, ds \right.$$

$$\left. + q_{x+k}\, q_{y+k} \int_0^1 (1 + i)^{1-s} \left(\frac{1}{2} - s\right) ds \right]$$

$$= \frac{i}{\delta}\, A_{xy}^1 + \frac{1}{2}\frac{i}{\delta}\left(1 - \frac{2}{\delta} + \frac{2}{i}\right) \sum_{k=0}^{\infty} v^{k+1}\, {}_k p_{xy}\, q_{x+k}\, q_{y+k}. \qquad (9.10.9)$$

The second term (9.10.9) is very small relative to the total amount. It is 1/2 of the second term in (9.8.9).

9.11 Notes and References

The concept of the future-lifetime random variable, developed for a single life in previous chapters, has been extended to a survival status, particular cases of which are statuses defined by several lives. Probability distributions, actuarial present values, variances, and covariances based on these new random variables were obtained for statuses defined by two lives by adaptation of the single life theory. These concepts are developed for more than two lives in Chapter 18.

Discussions of the ideas of this chapter without the use of random variables can be found in Chapters 9–13 of Jordan (1967) and Chapters 7–8 of Neill (1977). A general analysis of laws of mortality, which simplify the formulas for actuarial functions based on more than one life, is given by Greville (1956). Exercise 9.36 illustrates Greville's analysis.

Marshall and Olkin (1967, 1988) contributed to the literature on families of bivariate distributions. In particular, they wrote about the common shock model. Frank's family of bivariate distributions is named for M. J. Frank, who developed it. This family is reviewed by Genest (1987).

Frees, Carriere, and Valdez (1996) used Frank's copula to analyze data from last-survivor annuity experience. They assumed that the marginal distributions belong to the Gompertz family. The estimation process yielded an estimate of α of approximately -3.4. Comparing this estimate with the approximate standard error of the estimate leads to the conclusion that $T(x)$ and $T(y)$ were dependent in that experience.

The parameter α is not a conventional measure of association. The value -3.4 is associated with a positive correlation between $T(x)$ and $T(y)$. This might have been expected because in practice lives receiving payments until the last survivor dies live in the same environment.

Frees et al. also found that the assumption of independence between $T(x)$ and $T(y)$ resulted in higher estimated last-survivor annuity actuarial present values than those estimated using a model that permits dependence. The difference was in the range of 3% to 5%.

Exercises

Unless otherwise indicated, all lives in question are subject to the same table of mortality rates, and their times-until-death are independent random variables.

Section 9.2

9.1. The joint p.d.f. of $T(x)$ and $T(y)$ is given by

$$f_{T(x)T(y)}(s, t) = \frac{(n - 1)(n - 2)}{(1 + s + t)^n} \qquad 0 < s, 0 < t, n > 2.$$

Find:
a. The joint d.f. of $T(x)$ and $T(y)$.
b. The p.d.f., d.f., and $\mu(x + s)$ for the marginal distribution of $T(x)$. Note the symmetry in s and t which implies that $T(x)$ and $T(y)$ are identically distributed.
c. The covariance and correlation coefficient of $T(x)$ and $T(y)$, given that $n > 4$.

9.2. Display the joint survival function of $[T(x), T(y)]$ where the distribution is defined in Exercise 9.1.

9.3. The future lifetime random variables $T(x)$ and $T(y)$ are independent and identically distributed with p.d.f.

$$f(t) = \frac{n - 2}{(1 + t)^{n-1}} \qquad n > 3, t > 0.$$

Determine the joint d.f. and the joint survival function.

9.4. In terms of the single life probabilities $_np_x$ and $_np_y$, express
    a. The probability that (xy) will survive n years
    b. The probability that exactly one of the lives (x) and (y) will survive n years
    c. The probability that at least one of the lives (x) and (y) will survive n years
    d. The probability that (xy) will fail within n years
    e. The probability that at least one of the lives will die within n years
    f. The probability that both lives will die within n years.

9.5. Show that the probability that (x) survives n years and (y) survives $n-1$ years may be expressed either as

$$\frac{_np_{x:y-1}}{p_{y-1}}$$

or as

$$p_x \; _{n-1}p_{x+1:y}.$$

9.6. Evaluate

$$\int_0^n \; _tp_{xx}\, \mu_{xx}(t)\, dt.$$

9.7. Using the distribution of $T(x)$ and $T(y)$ shown in Exercise 9.1 display (a) the d.f., (b) the survival function, and (c) $E[T(xy)]$ for $T(xy)$. Assume $n > 3$.

9.8. Use (9.3.8) to obtain the p.d.f. of $T(xy)$ for the joint distribution of $T(x)$ and $T(y)$ given in Example 9.2.3.

Section 9.4

9.9. Show

$$_tp_{\overline{xy}} = \; _tp_{xy} + \; _tp_x\,(1 - \; _tp_y) + \; _tp_y\,(1 - \; _tp_x)$$

algebraically and by general reasoning.

9.10. Find the probability that at least one of two lives (x) and (y) will die in the year $(n + 1)$. Is this the same as $_n|q_{\overline{xy}}$? Explain.

9.11. The random variables $T(x)$ and $T(y)$ have the joint p.d.f. displayed in Exercise 9.1. Find (a) the d.f. and the p.d.f. of $T(\overline{xy})$, (b) $E[T(\overline{xy})]$ for $n > 3$, and (c) $\mu_{\overline{xy}}(t)$.

Section 9.5

9.12. Given that $_{25}p_{25:50} = 0.2$ and $_{15}p_{25} = 0.9$, calculate the probability that a person age 40 will survive to age 75.

9.13. If $\mu(x) = 1/(100 - x)$ for $0 \leq x < 100$, calculate

a. $_{10}p_{40:50}$

b. $_{10}p_{\overline{40:50}}$

c. $\overset{\circ}{e}_{40:50}$

d. $\overset{\circ}{e}_{\overline{40:50}}$

e. $\mathrm{Var}[T(40:50)]$

f. $\mathrm{Var}[T(\overline{40:50})]$

g. $\mathrm{Cov}[T(40:50), T(\overline{40:50})]$

h. The correlation between $T(40:50)$ and $T(\overline{40:50})$.

9.14. Evaluate $\dfrac{d\overset{\circ}{e}_{xx}}{dx}$.

9.15. Show that the probability of two lives (30) and (40) dying in the same year can be expressed as

$$1 + e_{30:40} - p_{30}(1 + e_{31:40}) - p_{40}(1 + e_{30:41}) + p_{30:40}(1 + e_{31:41}).$$

9.16. Show that the probability of two lives (30) and (40) dying at the same age last birthday can be expressed as

$$_{10}p_{30}(1 + e_{40:40}) - 2 \, _{11}p_{30} \, (1 + e_{40:41}) + p_{40} \, _{11}p_{30} \, (1 + e_{41:41}).$$

9.17. Assume that the forces of mortality that apply to individuals I and II, respectively, are

$$\mu^{\mathrm{I}}(x) = \log \frac{10}{9} \quad \text{for all } x$$

and

$$\mu^{\mathrm{II}}(x) = (10 - x)^{-1} \quad \text{for } 0 \leq x < 10.$$

Evaluate the probability that, if both individuals are of exact age 1, the first death will occur between exact ages 3 and 5.

Section 9.6

9.18. This is a continuation of Example 9.6.3. Exhibit (a) the d.f. and (b) the p.d.f. of $T(\overline{xy})$.

9.19. If $_5q_x = 0.05$ and $_5q_y = 0.03$, calculate the corresponding value of $F_{T(x)T(y)}$ (5, 5) using (9.6.7). Your answer will depend on the parameter α.

9.20. Use the result of Exercise 9.19 to evaluate $_5q_{\overline{xy}}$ for (a) $\alpha = 0$, (b) $\alpha = 3$, and (c) $\alpha = -3$. [Hint: Recall (9.4.5) and (9.3.2).]

Section 9.7

9.21. Show that

$$a_{\overline{/xy\backslash\,:\overline{n}|}} = a_{\overline{n}|} + {}_{n|}\bar{a}_x.$$

Describe the underlying benefit.

9.22. For an actuarial present value denoted by $\bar{A}_{\overline{x:n|}}$, describe the benefit. Show that

$$\bar{A}_{\overline{x:n|}} = \bar{A}_x - \bar{A}_{x:\overline{n|}} + v^n.$$

9.23. For independent lifetimes $T(x)$ and $T(y)$, show that

$$\text{Cov}(v^{T(\overline{xy})}, v^{T(xy)}) = (\bar{A}_x - \bar{A}_{xy})(\bar{A}_y - \bar{A}_{xy}).$$

9.24. Express, in terms of single- and joint-life annuity values, the actuarial present value of an annuity payable continuously at a rate of 1 per year while at least one of (25) and (30) survives and is below age 50.

9.25. Express, in terms of single- and joint-life annuity values, the actuarial present value of a deferred annuity of 1 payable at the end of any year as long as either (25) or (30) is living after age 50.

9.26. Express, in terms of single- and joint-life annuity values, the actuarial present value of an n-year temporary annuity-due, payable in respect to $(\overline{xy})$, providing annual payments of 1 while both lives survive, reducing to $1/2$ on the death of (x) and to $1/3$ on the death of (y).

9.27. An annuity-immediate of 1 is payable to (x) as long as he lives jointly with (y) and for n years after the death of (y), except that in no event will payments be made after m years from the present time, $m > n$. Show that the actuarial present value is

$$a_{x:\overline{n|}} + {}_nE_x\, a_{x+n:y:\overline{m-n|}}.$$

9.28. Obtain an expression for the actuarial present value of a continuous annuity of 1 per annum payable while at least one of two lives (40) and (55) is living and is over age 60, but not if (40) is alive and under age 55.

9.29. A joint-and-survivor annuity to (x) and (y) is payable at an initial rate per year while (x) lives, and, if (y) survives (x), is continued at the fraction p, $1/2 \le p \le 1$, of the initial rate per year during the lifetime of (y) following the death of (x).

a. Express the actuarial present value of such an annuity-due with an initial rate of 1 per year, payable in m-thly installments, in terms of the actuarial present values of single-life and joint-life annuities.

b. A joint-and-survivor annuity to (x) and (y) and a life annuity to (x) are said to be actuarially equivalent on the basis of stated assumptions if they have equal actuarial present values on such basis. Derive an expression for the ratio of the initial payment of the joint-and-survivor annuity to the payment rate of the actuarially equivalent life annuity to (x).

9.30. Show that

a. $\bar{A}^2_{xy} = \bar{A}^1_{xy} - \delta \bar{a}^1_{y|x}$ [This exercise depends on material in Section 9.9.]

b. $\dfrac{\partial}{\partial x}\, \bar{a}_{y|x} = \mu(x)\, \bar{a}_{y|x} - \bar{A}^2_{xy}.$

9.31. When, under Makeham's law, the status (xy) is replaced by the status (ww), show that

$$w - y = \frac{\log(c^\Delta + 1) - \log 2}{\log c}$$

where $\Delta = x - y \geq 0$. (This indicates that w can be obtained from the younger age y by adding an amount that is a function of $\Delta = x - y$. Such a property is referred to as a *law of uniform seniority*.)

9.32. On the basis of your Illustrative Life Table with interest of 6% calculate $\ddot{a}_{50:60:\overline{10|}}$. In your solution, use
   a. Values interpolated in the $\ddot{a}_{xx}$ table
   b. Values from the $\ddot{a}_{x:x+10}$ table.

9.33. Given a mortality table that follows Makeham's law and ages x and y for which (ww) is the equivalent equal-age status, show that
   a. $_tp_w$ is the geometric mean of $_tp_x$ and $_tp_y$
   b. $_tp_x + _tp_y > 2\,_tp_w$ for $x \neq y$
   c. $a_{\overline{xy}} > a_{\overline{ww}}$ for $x \neq y$.

9.34. Given a mortality table that follows Makeham's law, show that $\bar{a}_{xy}$ is equal to the actuarial present value of an annuity with a single life (w) where $c^w = c^x + c^y$ and force of interest $\delta' = \delta + A$. Further, show that

$$\bar{A}_{xy} = \bar{A}'_w + A\bar{a}'_w$$

where the primed functions are evaluated at force of interest δ'.

9.35. Consider two mortality tables, one for males, M, and one for females, F, with

$$\mu^M(z) = 3a + \frac{3bz}{2} \quad \text{and} \quad \mu^F(z) = a + bz.$$

We wish to use a table of actuarial present values for two lives, one male and one female, each of age w, to evaluate the actuarial present value of a joint-life annuity for a male age x and a female age y. Express w in terms of x and y.

9.36. From Section 9.5 we know that if $T(x)$ and $T(y)$ are independent,

$$\bar{a}_{xy} = \int_0^\infty e^{-\int_0^t [\delta + \mu(x+s) + \mu(y+s)] ds}\, dt.$$

If we could find δ', k, and w such that

$$\delta + \mu(x + t) + \mu(y + t) = \delta' + k\mu(w + t) \qquad (*)$$

we would have

$$\bar{a}_{xy} = \int_0^\infty v^t ({}_t p_w)^k \, dt$$

$$= \bar{a}'_{w(k)},$$

where the prime on the discount factor indicates that it is valued at force of interest δ' and $w(k)$ indicates a joint-life status with k "lives" (k is not necessarily an integer).

If $\mu(x + t) = a + b(x + t) + c(x + t)^2$, confirm that (*) is satisfied if

$$k = 2,$$

$$w = \frac{x + y}{2},$$

$$\delta' = \delta + c(x^2 + y^2 - 2w^2).$$

9.37. Find $\overset{\circ}{e}_{xy}$ if $q_x = q_y = 1$ and the deaths are uniformly distributed over the year of age for each of (x) and (y).

9.38. Let $T(x)$ and $T(y)$ be independent and uniformly distributed in the next year of age. Given that both (x) and (y) die within the next year, demonstrate that the time-of-failure of (xy) is not uniformly distributed over the year. [Hint: Show that $\Pr[T(xy) \le t | (T(x) \le 1) \cap (T(y) \le 1)] = 2t - t^2$.]

9.39. Show

$$\frac{1}{\delta} = \frac{1}{i[1 - (i/2 - i^2/3 + i^2/4 - i^4/5 + \cdots)]}$$

$$= \frac{1}{i}\left(1 + \frac{i}{2} - \frac{i^2}{12} + \frac{i^3}{24} - \frac{19i^4}{720} + \cdots\right).$$

Hence, show

$$\frac{i}{\delta}\left(1 - \frac{2}{\delta} + \frac{2}{i}\right) \cong \frac{i}{6} - \frac{i^3}{360} + \cdots.$$

9.40. Show that if deaths are uniformly distributed over each year of age, then

$$_{(j-1)/m}p_{xy} - {}_{j/m}p_{xy} = \frac{1}{m} q_{xy} + \frac{m + 1 - 2j}{m^2} q_x \, q_y$$

for any x and y and $j = 1, 2, 3, \ldots, m$. Hence, verify (9.8.14).

Section 9.9

9.41. Show by general reasoning that

$$_n q^1_{xy} = {}_n q^2_{xy} + {}_n q_x \, {}_n p_y.$$

When $n \to \infty$, what does the equation become?

9.42. Show that the actuarial present value for an insurance of 1 payable at the end of the year of death of (x), provided that (y) survives to the time of payment, can be expressed as $v p_y \ddot{a}_{x:y+1} - a_{xy}$.

9.43. Show that $A^1_{xy} - A^2_{xy} = A_{xy} - A_y$.

9.44. Express, in terms of actuarial present values for single life and first death contingent insurances, the net single premium for an insurance of 1 payable at the moment of death of (50), provided that (20), at that time, has died or attained age 40.

9.45. Express, in terms of actuarial present values for pure endowment and first death contingent insurances, the actuarial present value for an insurance of 1 payable at the time of the death of (x) provided (y) dies during the n years preceding the death of (x).

9.46. If $\mu(x) = 1/(100 - x)$ for $0 \le x < 100$, calculate $_{25}q^2_{25:\overline{50}}$.

Section 9.10

9.47. In a mortality table known to follow Makeham's law, you are given that $A = 0.003$ and $c^{10} = 3$.
 a. If $\overset{\circ}{e}_{40:50} = 17$, calculate $_\infty q^1_{40:50}$.
 b. Express $\bar{A}^1_{40:50}$ in terms of $\bar{A}_{40:50}$ and $\bar{a}_{40:50}$.

9.48. Given that mortality follows Gompertz's law with $\mu(x) = 10^{-4} \times 2^{x/8}$ for $x > 35$ and that by (9.10.2)

$$\bar{A}^1_{40:48:\overline{10}|} = f \bar{A}^1_{w:\overline{10}|},$$

calculate f and w.

Miscellaneous

9.49. The survival status $(\overline{n}|)$ is one that exists for exactly n years. It has been used in conjunction with life statuses, for example, in $\bar{A}_{x:\overline{n}|}$, $\bar{A}^1_{x:\overline{n}|}$, $\bar{A}^{\,1}_{x:\overline{n}|}$, $\ddot{a}_{x:\overline{n}|}$, $A_{xy:\overline{n}|}$. Simplify and interpret the following:
 a. $\bar{a}_{\overline{x:n}|}$
 b. $\bar{A}^2_{x:\overline{n}|}$.

9.50. Use the probability rule $\Pr(A \cup B) = \Pr(A) + \Pr(B) - \Pr(A \cap B)$ to obtain (9.4.6).

9.51. Evaluate $\dfrac{\partial}{\partial x} \overset{\circ}{e}_{xy}$.

9.52. The random variables $T^*(x)$, $T^*(y)$, and Z are independent and have exponential distributions with, respectively, parameters μ_1, μ_2, and λ. These three random variable are components of a common shock model.

a. Exhibit the marginal p.d.f. of $T(y)$ by evaluating

$$f_{T(y)}(t) = \int_0^t f_{T(x)T(y)}(s, t)\, ds + f_{T(x)T(y)}(t, t) + \int_t^\infty f_{T(x)T(y)}(s, t)\, ds.$$

b. Exhibit the marginal survival function of $T(y)$ by evaluating

$$s_{T(y)}(t) = \int_t^\infty f_{T(y)}(u)\, du.$$

Compare the result with (9.6.4b).

c. Evaluate

$$\Pr[T(x) = T(y)] = \int_0^\infty f_{T(x)T(y)}(t, t)\, dt.$$

MULTIPLE DECREMENT MODELS

10.1 Introduction

In Chapter 9 we extended the theory of Chapters 3 through 8 from an individual life to multiple lives, subject to a single contingency of death. We now return to the case of a single life, but here subject to multiple contingencies. As an application of this extension, we observe that the number of workers for an employer is reduced when an employee withdraws, becomes disabled, dies, or retires. In manpower planning, it might be necessary to estimate only the numbers of those presently at work who will remain active to various years into the future. For this task, the model for survivorship developed in Chapter 3 is adequate, with time-until-termination of employment rather than time-until-death as the interpretation of the basic random variable. Employee benefit plans, however, provide benefits paid on termination of employment that may depend on the cause of termination. For example, the benefits on retirement often differ from those payable on death or disability. Therefore, survivorship models for employee benefit systems include random variables for both time-of-termination and cause of termination. Also, the benefit structure often depends on earnings, which is another and different kind of uncertainty that is discussed in Chapter 11.

As another application, most individual life insurances provide payment of a nonforfeiture benefit if premiums stop before the end of the specified premium payment term. A comprehensive model for such insurances incorporates both time-until-termination and cause of termination as random variables.

Disability income insurance provides periodic payments to insureds who satisfy the definition of disability contained in the policy. In some cases, the amount of the periodic payments may depend on whether the disability was caused by illness or accident. A person may cease to be an active insured by dying, withdrawing, becoming disabled, or reaching the end of the coverage period. A complete model for disability insurance incorporates a random variable for time-until-termination, when the insured ceases to be a member of the active insureds, as well as a random variable for the cause of termination.

Public health planners are interested in the analysis of mortality and survivorship by cause of death. Public health goals may be set by a study of the joint distribution of time-until-death and cause of death. Priorities in cardiovascular and cancer research were established by this type of analysis.

The main purpose of this chapter is to build a theory for studying the distribution of two random variables in regard to a single life: time-until-termination from a given status and cause of the termination. The resulting model is used in each of the applications described in this section. Within actuarial science, the termination from a given status is called *decrement*, and the subject of this chapter is called *multiple decrement theory*. Within biostatistics it is referred to as the *theory of competing risks*.

It is also possible to develop multiple decrement theory in terms of deterministic rates and rate functions. There is some recapitulation of the theory from this point of view in Section 10.4.

10.2 Two Random Variables

Chapter 3 was devoted in part to methods for specifying and using the distribution of the continuous random variable $T(x)$, the time-until-death of (x). The same methods can be used to study time-until-termination from a status, such as employment with a particular employer, with only minor changes in vocabulary. In fact, we use the same notation $T(x)$, or T, to denote the time random variable in this new setting.

In this section we expand the basic model by introducing a second random variable, cause of decrement, to be denoted by $J(x) = J$. We assume that J is a discrete random variable.

The applications in Section 10.1 provide examples of these random variables. For employee benefit plan applications, the random variable J could be assigned the values 1, 2, 3, or 4 depending on whether termination is due to withdrawal, disability, death, or retirement, respectively. In the life insurance application, J could be assigned the values 1 or 2, depending on whether the insured dies or chooses to terminate payment of premiums. For the disability insurance application, J could be assigned the values 1, 2, 3, or 4 depending on whether the insured dies, withdraws, becomes disabled, or reaches the end of the coverage period. Finally, in the public health application, there are many possibilities for causes of decrement. For example, in a given study, J could be assigned the values 1, 2, 3, or 4 depending on whether death was caused by cardiovascular disease, cancer, accident, or all other causes.

Our purpose is to describe the joint distribution of T and J and the related marginal and conditional distributions. We denote the joint p.d.f. of T and J by $f_{T,J}(t, j)$, the marginal p.f. of J by $f_J(j)$, and the marginal p.d.f. of T by $f_T(t)$. Figure

10.2.1 illustrates these distributions. They may seem strange at first because J is a discrete random variable and T is continuous.

FIGURE 10.2.1

Graph of $f_{T,J}(t, j)$

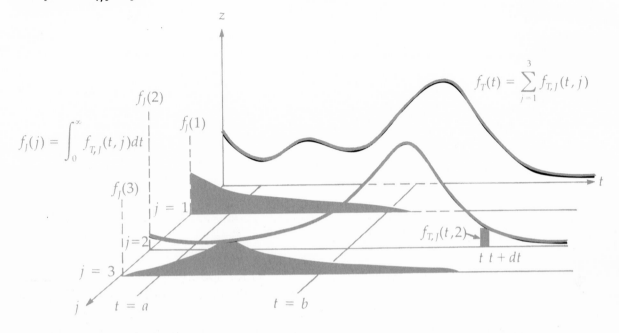

The joint p.d.f. of T and J, $f_{T,J}(t, j)$, can be pictured as falling on m parallel sheets, as illustrated in Figure 10.2.1 for three causes of decrement ($m = 3$). There is a separate sheet for each of the m causes of decrement recognized in the model. In Figure 10.2.1 the following relations hold:

$$\sum_{j=1}^{3} f_J(j) = 1$$

and

$$\int_0^{\infty} f_T(t) \, dt = 1.$$

The p.d.f. $f_{T,J}(t, j)$ can be used in the usual ways to calculate the probabilities of events defined by T and J. For example,

$$f_{T,J}(t, j) \, dt = \Pr\{(t < T \leq t + dt) \cap (J = j)\} \tag{10.2.1}$$

expresses the probability of decrement due to cause j between t and $t + dt$,

$$\int_0^t f_{T,J}(s, j) \, ds = \Pr\{(0 < T \leq t) \cap (J = j)\} \tag{10.2.2}$$

expresses the probability of decrement due to cause j before time t, and

---

$$\sum_{j=1}^{m} \int_{a}^{b} f_{T,J}(t, j) \, dt = \Pr\{a < T \le b\}$$

expresses the probability of decrement due to all causes between a and b.

The probability of decrement before time t due to cause j given in (10.2.2) has the special symbol

$$_tq_x^{(j)} = \int_0^t f_{T,J}(s, j) \, ds \qquad t \ge 0, \ j = 1, 2, \dots, m, \qquad (10.2.3)$$

which is illustrative of the use of the superscript to denote the cause of decrement in multiple decrement theory.

The use of information given at age x to select a distribution is similar to the concepts in Chapter 3. If being in the survival status at age x is the only information available, then an aggregate distribution would be used. On the other hand, if there is additional information, then the distribution would be a select distribution and the age of selection would be enclosed in brackets.

By the definition of the marginal distribution for J, appearing as $f_J(j)$ in the (j, z) plane of Figure 10.2.1, we have the probability of decrement due to cause j at any time in the future to be

$$f_J(j) = \int_0^\infty f_{T,J}(s, j) \, ds = {}_\infty q_x^{(j)} \qquad j = 1, 2, \dots, m. \qquad (10.2.4)$$

This is new and without a counterpart in Chapter 3, unlike the marginal p.d.f. for $T, f_T(t)$ in the (t, z) plane of Figure 10.2.1. For $f_T(t)$, and the d.f., $F_T(t)$, we have for $t \ge 0$

$$f_T(t) = \sum_{j=1}^{m} f_{T,J}(t, j) \qquad (10.2.5)$$

and

$$F_T(t) = \int_0^t f_T(s) \, ds.$$

The notations introduced in Chapter 3 for the functions of the distribution of the future-lifetime random variable, T, can be extended to accommodate those of the time-until-decrement random variable of the multiple decrement model. Using the superscript (τ) to indicate that a function refers to all causes, or total force, of decrement, we obtain

$$_tq_x^{(\tau)} = \Pr\{T \le t\} = F_T(t) = \int_0^t f_T(s) \, ds, \qquad (10.2.6)$$

$$_tp_x^{(\tau)} = \Pr\{T > t\} = 1 - {}_tq_x^{(\tau)}, \qquad (10.2.7)$$

$$\mu_x^{(\tau)}(t) = \frac{f_T(t)}{1 - F_T(t)} = \frac{1}{{}_tp_x^{(\tau)}} \frac{d}{dt} {}_tq_x^{(\tau)}$$

$$= -\frac{1}{{}_tp_x^{(\tau)}} \frac{d}{dt} {}_tp_x^{(\tau)}$$

$$= -\frac{d}{dt} \log {}_tp_x^{(\tau)}, \tag{10.2.8}$$

and

$$_tp_x^{(\tau)} = e^{-\int_0^t \mu_x^{(\tau)}(s) \, ds}. \tag{10.2.9}$$

Mathematically, these functions for the random variable T of this chapter are identical to those for the T of Chapter 3; the difference is in their interpretation in the applications. The choice of the symbol $\mu_x^{(\tau)}(t)$ for the force of total decrement is influenced by these applications. For example, in pension applications (x) is an age of entry into the pension plan, and although no special selection information may be available, subsequent causes of decrement may depend on this age.

As with the applications in previous chapters, the statement in (10.2.1) can be analyzed by conditioning on survival in the given status to time t. In this way, we have

$$f_{T,J}(t, j) \, dt = \Pr\{T > t\} \Pr\{[(t < T \le t + dt) \cap (J = j)]|T > t\}. \tag{10.2.10}$$

By analogy with (3.2.12) this suggests the definition of the **force of decrement due to cause j** as

$$\mu_x^{(j)}(t) = \frac{f_{T,J}(t, j)}{1 - F_T(t)} = \frac{f_{T,J}(t, j)}{{}_tp_x^{(\tau)}}. \tag{10.2.11}$$

The force of decrement at age $x + t$ due to cause j has a conditional probability interpretation. It is the value of the joint conditional p.d.f. of T and J at $x + t$ and j, given survival to $x + t$. Then (10.2.10) can be rewritten as

$$f_{T,J}(t, j) \, dt = {}_tp_x^{(\tau)} \mu_x^{(j)}(t) \, dt \qquad j = 1, 2, \ldots, m, t \ge 0. \tag{10.2.10 restated}$$

Restated in words,

(the probability of decrement between t and $t + dt$ due to cause j) $=$ (the probability, ${}_tp_x^{(\tau)}$, that (x) remains in the given status until time t)

$\times$ (the conditional probability, $\mu_x^{(j)}(t) \, dt$, that decrement occurs between t and $t + dt$ due to cause j, given that decrement has not occurred before time t).

It follows, from differentiation of (10.2.3) and use of (10.2.11), that

$$\mu_x^{(j)}(t) = \frac{1}{{}_tp_x^{(\tau)}} \frac{d}{dt} {}_tq_x^{(j)}. \tag{10.2.12}$$

Now, from (10.2.6), (10.2.5), and (10.2.3),

$$_tq_x^{(\tau)} = \int_0^t f_T(s)\, ds = \int_0^t \sum_{j=1}^m f_{T,J}(s,j)\, ds$$

$$= \sum_{j=1}^m \int_0^t f_{T,J}(s,j)\, ds = \sum_{j=1}^m {}_tq_x^{(j)}. \qquad (10.2.13)$$

That the first and last members of (10.2.13) are equal is immediately interpretable. Combining (10.2.8), (10.2.13), and (10.2.12), we have

$$\mu_x^{(\tau)}(t) = \sum_{j=1}^m \mu_x^{(j)}(t); \qquad (10.2.14)$$

that is, the force of total decrement is the sum of the forces of decrement due to the m causes.

We can summarize the definitions here by expressing the joint, marginal, and conditional p.d.f.'s in actuarial notation and repeating the defining equation numbers:

$$f_{T,J}(t,j) = {}_tp_x^{(\tau)}\, \mu_x^{(j)}(t), \qquad (10.2.11)\text{ restated}$$

$$f_J(j) = {}_\infty q_x^{(j)}, \qquad (10.2.4)\text{ restated}$$

$$f_T(t) = {}_tp_x^{(\tau)}\, \mu_x^{(\tau)}(t). \qquad (10.2.8)\text{ restated}$$

The conditional p.f. of J, given decrement at time t, is

$$f_{J|T}(j|t) = \frac{f_{T,J}(t,j)}{f_T(t)} = \frac{{}_tp_x^{(\tau)}\, \mu_x^{(j)}(t)}{{}_tp_x^{(\tau)}\, \mu_x^{(\tau)}(t)}$$

$$= \frac{\mu_x^{(j)}(t)}{\mu_x^{(\tau)}(t)}. \qquad (10.2.15)$$

Finally, we note that the probability in (10.2.3) can be rewritten as

$$_tq_x^{(j)} = \int_0^t {}_sp_x^{(\tau)}\, \mu_x^{(j)}(s)\, ds. \qquad (10.2.16)$$

Example 10.2.1

Consider a multiple decrement model with two causes of decrement; the forces of decrement are given by

$$\mu_x^{(1)}(t) = \frac{t}{100} \qquad t \geq 0,$$

$$\mu_x^{(2)}(t) = \frac{1}{100} \qquad t \geq 0.$$

For this model, calculate the p.f. (or p.d.f.) for the joint, marginal, and conditional distributions.

Solution:

Since

$$\mu_x^{(\tau)}(s) = \mu_x^{(1)}(s) + \mu_x^{(2)}(s) = \frac{s+1}{100},$$

the survival probability $_tp_x^{(\tau)}$ is

$$_tp_x^{(\tau)} = \exp\left(-\int_0^t \frac{s+1}{100} ds\right)$$

$$= \exp\left(\frac{-(t^2 + 2t)}{200}\right) \quad t \geq 0,$$

and the joint p.d.f. of T and J is

$$f_{T,J}(t, j) = \begin{cases} \dfrac{t}{100} \exp\left[\dfrac{-(t^2 + 2t)}{200}\right] & t \geq 0, j = 1 \\ \\ \dfrac{1}{100} \exp\left[\dfrac{-(t^2 + 2t)}{200}\right] & t \geq 0, j = 2. \end{cases}$$

The marginal p.d.f. of T is

$$f_T(t) = \sum_{j=1}^2 f_{T,J}(t, j) = \frac{t+1}{100} \exp\left[\frac{-(t^2 + 2t)}{200}\right] \quad t \geq 0,$$

and the marginal p.f. of J is

$$f_J(j) = \begin{cases} \displaystyle\int_0^\infty f_{T,J}(t, 1) \, dt & j = 1 \\ \\ \displaystyle\int_0^\infty f_{T,J}(t, 2) \, dt & j = 2. \end{cases}$$

It is somewhat easier to evaluate $f_J(2)$. In the following development, $\Phi(x)$ is the d.f. for the standard normal distribution $N(0, 1)$. By completing the square we have

$$f_J(2) = \frac{1}{100} e^{0.005} \int_0^\infty \exp\left[\frac{-(t+1)^2}{200}\right] dt$$

$$= \frac{1}{100} e^{0.005} \sqrt{2\pi} \, 10 \int_0^\infty \frac{1}{\sqrt{2\pi}\,10} \exp\left[\frac{-(t+1)^2}{200}\right] dt.$$

We now make the change of variable $z = (t+1)/10$ and obtain

$$f_J(2) = \frac{1}{10} e^{0.005} \sqrt{2\pi} \int_{0.1}^\infty \frac{1}{\sqrt{2\pi}} \exp\left(\frac{-z^2}{2}\right) dz$$

$$= \frac{1}{10} e^{0.005} \sqrt{2\pi} \, [1 - \Phi(0.1)]$$

$$= 0.1159.$$

Therefore $f_J(1) = 0.8841$. Finally, the conditional p.f. of J, given decrement at t, is derived from (10.2.15) as

$$f_{J|T}(1|t) = \frac{t}{t+1}$$

and

$$f_{J|T}(2|t) = \frac{1}{t+1}.$$

▼

Example 10.2.2

For the joint distribution of T and J specified in Example 10.2.1, calculate $E[T]$ and $E[T|J = 2]$.

Solution:

Using the marginal p.d.f. $f_T(t)$, we have

$$E[T] = \int_0^\infty t \left\{ \frac{t+1}{100} \exp\left[\frac{-(t^2 + 2t)}{200} \right] \right\} dt.$$

Integration by parts, as in (3.5.1), yields

$$E[T] = -t \exp\left[\frac{-(t^2 + 2t)}{200} \right] \Bigg|_0^\infty$$

$$+ \int_0^\infty \exp\left[\frac{-(t^2 + 2t)}{200} \right] dt$$

$$= 0 + 100 f_J(2),$$

hence

$$E[T] = 11.59.$$

Using the conditional p.d.f. $f_{T,J}(t, 2)/f_J(2)$, we have

$$E[T|J = 2] = \int_0^\infty t \left\{ 100^{-1} \exp\left[\frac{-(t^2 + 2t)}{200} \right] \right\} (0.1159)^{-1}\, dt.$$

This integral may be evaluated as follows:

$$E[T|J = 2] = E[(T + 1) - 1|J = 2]$$

$$= (0.1159)^{-1} \int_0^\infty \frac{t+1}{100} \exp\left[\frac{-(t^2 + 2t)}{200} \right] dt - 1$$

$$= -(0.1159)^{-1} \exp\left[\frac{-(t^2 + 2t)}{200} \right] \Bigg|_0^\infty - 1$$

$$= 7.63.$$

The point of Examples 10.2.1 and 10.2.2 is that once the joint distribution of T and J is specified, marginal and conditional distributions can be derived, and the moments of these distributions determined.

▼

In some instances, a particular application may require a modification of the above model. A continuous distribution for time-until-termination, T, is inadequate

---

in applications where there is a time at which there is a positive probability of decrement. One example of this is a pension plan with a mandatory retirement age, an age at which all remaining active employees must retire. A second example is term life insurance in which there is typically no benefit paid on withdrawal. Thus, after a premium is paid, none of the remaining insureds withdraw until the next premium due date. Here we do not attempt to extend the notation to cover such situations. However, in Section 11.2 we describe extended models for each of these examples.

The random variable K, the curtate-future-years before decrement of (x), is defined as in Chapter 3 to be the greatest integer less than T. Using (10.2.1) and (10.2.11), we can write the joint p.f. K and J as

$$\Pr\{(K = k) \cap (J = j)\} = \Pr\{(k < T \le k + 1) \cap (J = j)\}$$

$$= \int_k^{k+1} {}_t p_x^{(\tau)}\, \mu_x^{(j)}(t)\, dt. \tag{10.2.17}$$

Rewriting ${}_t p_x^{(\tau)}$ of the integrand in the exponential form of (10.2.9) and factoring it into two factors changes (10.2.17) to

$$= {}_k p_x^{(\tau)} \int_k^{k+1} e^{-\int_k^t \mu_x^{(\tau)}(u)\, du}\, \mu_x^{(j)}(t)\, dt.$$

Changing the variables of the integrations by $r = u - k$ and $s = t - k$ yields

$$= {}_k p_x^{(\tau)} \int_0^1 e^{-\int_0^s \mu_x^{(\tau)}(k+r)\, dr}\, \mu_x^{(j)}(k + s)\, ds.$$

Thus far we have done manipulations that hold in all tables. If we are using an aggregate or ultimate (a nonselect) table where the forces of decrement depend on an initial age and the duration only through their sum, that is, the **attained age**, then for τ and all j,

$$\mu_x(k + s) = \mu_{x+k}(s) \qquad \text{for all } x, k, \text{ and } s \ge 0,$$

and (10.2.17) may be written

$$_k p_x^{(\tau)} \int_0^1 {}_s p_{x+k}^{(\tau)}\, \mu_{x+k}^{(j)}(s)\, ds = {}_k p_x^{(\tau)}\, q_{x+k}^{(j)}. \tag{10.2.18}$$

The probability of decrement from all causes between ages $x + k$ and $x + k + 1$, given survival to age $x + k$, is denoted by $q_{x+k}^{(\tau)}$, and it follows that

$$q_{x+k}^{(\tau)} = \int_0^1 {}_s p_{x+k}^{(\tau)}\, \mu_{x+k}^{(\tau)}(s)\, ds$$

$$= \int_0^1 {}_s p_{x+k}^{(\tau)} \sum_{j=1}^m \mu_{x+k}^{(j)}(s)\, ds$$

$$= \sum_{j=1}^m q_{x+k}^{(j)}. \tag{10.2.19}$$

An examination of (10.2.18) and (10.2.19) discloses why multiple decrement theory is also called the theory of competing risks. The probability of decrement between ages $x + k$ and $x + k + 1$ due to cause j depends on ${}_s p_{x+k}^{(\tau)}$, $0 \le s \le 1$, and thus on all the component forces. When the forces for other decrements are increased, ${}_s p_{x+k}^{(\tau)}$ is reduced, and then $q_{x+k}^{(j)}$ is also decreased.

10.3 Random Survivorship Group

Let us consider a group of $l_a^{(\tau)}$ lives age a years. Each life is assumed to have a distribution of time-until-decrement and cause of decrement specified by the p.d.f.

$$f_{T,J}(t, j) = {}_t p_a^{(\tau)} \, \mu_a^{(j)}(t) \qquad t \ge 0, j = 1, 2, \ldots, m.$$

We denote by ${}_n \mathcal{D}_x^{(j)}$ the random variable equal to the number of lives who leave the group between ages x and $x + n$, $x \ge a$, from cause j. We denote $E[{}_n \mathcal{D}_x^{(j)}]$ by ${}_n d_x^{(j)}$ and obtain

$$ {}_n d_x^{(j)} = E[{}_n \mathcal{D}_x^{(j)}] \tag{10.3.1a}$$

$$= l_a^{(\tau)} \int_{x-a}^{x+n-a} {}_t p_a^{(\tau)} \, \mu_a^{(j)}(t) \, dt.$$

As usual, if $n = 1$, we delete the prefixes on ${}_n \mathcal{D}_x^{(j)}$ and ${}_n d_x^{(j)}$. We note that

$$ {}_n \mathcal{D}_x^{(\tau)} = \sum_{j=1}^{m} {}_n \mathcal{D}_x^{(j)}$$

and define

$$ {}_n d_x^{(\tau)} = E[{}_n \mathcal{D}_x^{(\tau)}] = \sum_{j=1}^{m} {}_n d_x^{(j)}. \tag{10.3.1b}$$

Then, using (10.3.1a), we have

$$ {}_n d_x^{(\tau)} = l_a^{(\tau)} \sum_{j=1}^{m} \int_{x-a}^{x+n-a} {}_t p_a^{(\tau)} \, \mu_a^{(j)}(t) \, dt$$

$$= l_a^{(\tau)} \int_{x-a}^{x+n-a} {}_t p_a^{(\tau)} \, \mu_a^{(\tau)}(t) \, dt. \tag{10.3.2}$$

If $\mathcal{L}^{(\tau)}(x)$ is defined as the random variable equal to the number of survivors at age x out of the $l_a^{(\tau)}$ lives in the original group at age a, then by analogy with (3.3.1) we can write

$$ l_x^{(\tau)} = E[\mathcal{L}^{(\tau)}(x)]$$

$$= l_a^{(\tau)} \, {}_{x-a} p_a^{(\tau)}. \tag{10.3.3}$$

We recognize the integral of (10.3.1a) with $n = 1$ as the integral of (10.2.17) with $x = a$ and $k = x - a$. Thus for a nonselect table, we have from (10.2.18)

$$ d_x^{(j)} = l_a^{(\tau)} \, {}_{x-a} p_a^{(\tau)} \, q_x^{(j)} = l_x^{(\tau)} \, q_x^{(j)}. \tag{10.3.4}$$

This result lets us display a table of $p_x^{(\tau)}$ and $q_x^{(j)}$ values in a corresponding table of $l_x^{(\tau)}$ and $d_x^{(j)}$ values. Either table is called a ***multiple decrement table.***

Example 10.3.1

Construct a table of $l_x^{(\tau)}$ and $d_x^{(j)}$ values corresponding to the probabilities of decrement given below.

x	$q_x^{(1)}$	$q_x^{(2)}$
65	0.02	0.05
66	0.03	0.06
67	0.04	0.07
68	0.05	0.08
69	0.06	0.09
70	0.00	1.00

Although this display is designed for computational ease, it may be roughly suggestive of a double decrement situation with cause 1 related to death and cause 2 to retirement. It appears that, in this case, 70 is the mandatory retirement age.

Solution:

We assume the arbitrary value of $l_{65}^{(\tau)} = 1,000$ and use (10.3.4) as indicated below.

x	$q_x^{(1)}$	$q_x^{(2)}$	$q_x^{(\tau)}$	$p_x^{(\tau)}$	$l_x^{(\tau)} = l_{x-1}^{(\tau)}\, p_{x-1}^{(\tau)}$	$d_x^{(1)} = l_x^{(\tau)}\, q_x^{(1)}$	$d_x^{(2)} = l_x^{(\tau)}\, q_x^{(2)}$
65	0.02	0.05	0.07	0.93	1 000.00	20.00	50.00
66	0.03	0.06	0.09	0.91	930.00	27.90	55.80
67	0.04	0.07	0.11	0.89	846.30	33.85	59.24
68	0.05	0.08	0.13	0.87	753.21	37.66	60.26
69	0.06	0.09	0.15	0.85	655.29	39.32	58.98
70	0.00	1.00	1.00	0.00	557.00	0.00	557.00

Note, as a check on the calculations, that $l_{x+1}^{(\tau)} = l_x^{(\tau)} - d_x^{(1)} - d_x^{(2)}$, except for rounding error.

We continue this example with the evaluation, from first principles, of several probabilities:

$$_2 p_{65}^{(\tau)} = p_{65}^{(\tau)}\, p_{66}^{(\tau)} = (0.93)(0.91) = 0.8463,$$

$$_{2|}q_{66}^{(1)} = p_{66}^{(\tau)}\, p_{67}^{(\tau)}\, q_{68}^{(1)} = (0.91)(0.89)(0.05) = 0.0405,$$

$$_2 q_{67}^{(2)} = q_{67}^{(2)} + p_{67}^{(\tau)}\, q_{68}^{(2)} = 0.07 + (0.89)(0.08) = 0.1412.$$

The last three columns of the above table may be used to obtain the same probabilities. The answers agree to four decimal places:

$$2p_{65}^{(\tau)} = \frac{l_{67}^{(\tau)}}{l_{65}^{(\tau)}} = \frac{846.30}{1{,}000.00} = 0.8463,$$

$$2|q_{66}^{(1)} = \frac{d_{68}^{(1)}}{l_{66}^{(\tau)}} = \frac{37.66}{930.00} = 0.0405,$$

$$2q_{67}^{(2)} = \frac{d_{67}^{(2)} + d_{68}^{(2)}}{l_{67}^{(\tau)}} = \frac{59.24 + 60.26}{846.30} = 0.1412. \qquad \blacktriangledown$$

10.4 Deterministic Survivorship Group

The total force of decrement can also be viewed as a total (nominal annual) rate of decrement rather than as a conditional probability density. In this view, where we assume a continuous model, a group of $l_a^{(\tau)}$ lives advance through age subject to deterministic forces of decrement $\mu_a^{(\tau)}(y - a)$, $y \geq a$. The number of survivors to age x from the original group of $l_a^{(\tau)}$ lives at age a is given by

$$l_x^{(\tau)} = l_a^{(\tau)} \exp\left[-\int_a^x \mu_a^{(\tau)}(y - a) \, dy \right], \qquad (10.4.1)$$

and the total decrement between ages x and $x + 1$ is

$$
\begin{aligned}
d_x^{(\tau)} &= l_x^{(\tau)} - l_{x+1}^{(\tau)} \\[1mm]
&= l_x^{(\tau)} \left(1 - \frac{l_{x+1}^{(\tau)}}{l_x^{(\tau)}} \right) \\[1mm]
&= l_x^{(\tau)} \left\{ 1 - \exp\left[-\int_x^{x+1} \mu_a^{(\tau)}(y - a) \, dy \right] \right\} \\[1mm]
&= l_x^{(\tau)}(1 - p_x^{(\tau)}) \\[1mm]
&= l_x^{(\tau)} q_x^{(\tau)}. \qquad (10.4.2)
\end{aligned}
$$

Further, by definition or from differentiating (10.4.1), we have

$$\mu_a^{(\tau)}(x - a) = -\frac{1}{l_x^{(\tau)}} \frac{dl_x^{(\tau)}}{dx}. \qquad (10.4.3)$$

These formulas are analogous to those for life tables in Section 3.4. Here $q_x^{(\tau)}$ is the effective annual total rate of decrement for the year of age x to $x + 1$ equivalent to the forces $\mu_a^{(\tau)}(y - a)$, $x \leq y < x + 1$.

Consider next m causes of decrement and assume that the $l_x^{(\tau)}$ survivors to age x will, at future ages, be fully depleted by these m forms of decrement. Then the $l_x^{(\tau)}$ survivors can be visualized as falling into distinct subgroups $l_x^{(j)}$, $j = 1, 2, \ldots, m$, where $l_x^{(j)}$ denotes the number from the $l_x^{(\tau)}$ survivors who will terminate at future ages due to cause j, so that

$$l_x^{(\tau)} = \sum_{j=1}^m l_x^{(j)}. \qquad (10.4.4)$$

We define the force of decrement at age x due to cause j by

$$\mu_a^{(j)}(x - a) = \lim_{h \to 0} \frac{l_x^{(j)} - l_{x+h}^{(j)}}{h l_x^{(\tau)}}$$

where $l_x^{(\tau)}$, not $l_x^{(j)}$, appears in the denominator. This yields

$$\mu_a^{(j)}(x - a) = -\frac{1}{l_x^{(\tau)}} \frac{dl_x^{(j)}}{dx}. \tag{10.4.5}$$

From (10.4.3)–(10.4.5) it follows that

$$\mu_a^{(\tau)}(x - a) = -\frac{1}{l_x^{(\tau)}} \frac{d}{dx} \sum_{j=1}^{m} l_x^{(j)} = \sum_{j=1}^{m} \mu_a^{(j)}(x - a). \tag{10.4.6}$$

Formula (10.4.5), substituting y for x, can be written as

$$-dl_y^{(j)} = l_y^{(\tau)} \, \mu_a^{(j)}(y - a) \, dy,$$

and integration from $y = x$ to $y = x + 1$ gives

$$l_x^{(j)} - l_{x+1}^{(j)} = d_x^{(j)} = \int_x^{x+1} l_y^{(\tau)} \, \mu_a^{(j)}(y - a) \, dy. \tag{10.4.7}$$

Summation over $j = 1, 2, \ldots, m$ yields

$$l_x^{(\tau)} - l_{x+1}^{(\tau)} = d_x^{(\tau)} = \int_x^{x+1} l_y^{(\tau)} \, \mu_a^{(\tau)}(y - a) \, dy. \tag{10.4.8}$$

Further, from division of formula (10.4.7) by $l_x^{(\tau)}$, we have

$$\frac{d_x^{(j)}}{l_x^{(\tau)}} = \int_x^{x+1} {}_{y-x}p_x^{(\tau)} \, \mu_a^{(j)}(y - a) \, dy = q_x^{(j)}. \tag{10.4.9}$$

Here $q_x^{(j)}$ is defined as the proportion of the $l_x^{(\tau)}$ survivors to age x who terminate due to cause j before age $x + 1$ when all m causes of decrement are operating.

As was the case for life tables, the deterministic model provides an alternative language and conceptual framework for multiple decrement theory.

10.5 Associated Single Decrement Tables

For each of the causes of decrement recognized in a multiple decrement model, it is possible to define a single decrement model that depends only on the particular cause of decrement. We define the *associated single decrement model* functions as follows:

$${}_tp_x'^{(j)} = \exp\left[-\int_0^t \mu_x^{(j)}(s) \, ds \right],$$

$${}_tq_x'^{(j)} = 1 - {}_tp_x'^{(j)}. \tag{10.5.1}$$

Quantities such as ${}_tq_x'^{(j)}$ are called *net probabilities of decrement* in biostatistics because they are net of other causes of decrement. However, many other names have been given to the same quantity. One is *independent rate of decrement,* chosen because cause j does not compete with other causes in determining $_tq_x'^{(j)}$. The term we use for $_tq_x'^{(j)}$ is **absolute rate of decrement.** The use of the word **rate** in describing $_tq_x'^{(j)}$ stems from a desire to distinguish between q and q'. The symbol $_tq_x^{(j)}$ denotes a probability of decrement for cause j between ages x and $x + t$, and we will show that it differs from $_tq_x'^{(j)}$. In addition, $_tp_x'^{(j)}$, unlike $_tp_x^{(\tau)}$, is not necessarily a survivorship function, because it is not required that $\lim_{t\to\infty} {_tp_x'^{(j)}} = 0$.

While

$$\int_0^\infty \mu_x^{(\tau)}(t)\, dt = \infty,$$

we can conclude from (10.2.14) only that

$$\int_0^\infty \mu_x^{(j)}(t)\, dt = \infty$$

for at least one j. There may be causes of decrement for which this integral is finite.

We seldom have an opportunity to observe the operation of a random survival system in which a single cause of decrement operates. In an employee benefit plan, retirement, disabilities, and voluntary terminations make it impossible to directly observe the operation of a single decrement model for mortality during active service. In biostatistical applications random withdrawals from observation and arbitrary ending of the period of study may prevent the observation of mortality alone operating on a group of lives.

As we see in Section 10.6, a usual first step in constructing a multiple decrement model is to select absolute rates of decrement and to make assumptions concerning the incidence of the decrements within any single year of age to obtain probabilities $q_x^{(j)}$. The converse problem of obtaining absolute rates from the probabilities also involves assumptions about the incidence of the decrements. These assumptions are implicit in statistical methods for estimating absolute rates and will be discussed in Section 10.5.5.

In the next subsection we examine a number of relationships between a multiple decrement table and its associated single decrement tables. Then we examine a number of special assumptions about incidence of decrement over the year of age and note some implied relationships. In Section 10.5.5 some of the statistical issues in estimating a multiple decrement distribution are examined.

10.5.1 Basic Relationships

First, note that since

$$_tp_x^{(\tau)} = \exp\left\{-\int_0^t [\mu_x^{(1)}(s) + \mu_x^{(2)}(s) + \cdots + \mu_x^{(m)}(s)]\, ds\right\},$$

we have

$$iP_x^{(\tau)} = \prod_{i=1}^{m} iP_x'^{(i)}. \tag{10.5.2}$$

This result does not involve any approximation. It is based on the definition of an associated single decrement table where the sole force of decrement is equal to the force for that decrement in the multiple decrement model. We require that it hold for any method used to construct a multiple decrement table from a set of absolute rates of decrement.

Now compare the size of the absolute rates and the probabilities. From (10.5.2) we see, if some cause other than j is operating, that

$$iP_x'^{(j)} \geq iP_x^{(\tau)}.$$

This implies

$$iP_x'^{(j)} \, \mu_x^{(j)}(t) \geq iP_x^{(\tau)} \, \mu_x^{(j)}(t),$$

and if these functions are integrated with respect to t over the interval $(0, 1)$, we obtain

$$q_x'^{(j)} = \int_0^1 iP_x'^{(j)} \, \mu_x^{(j)}(t) \, dt \geq \int_0^1 iP_x^{(\tau)} \, \mu_x^{(j)}(t) \, dt = q_x^{(j)}. \tag{10.5.3}$$

The magnitude of other forces of decrement can cause $iP_x'^{(j)}$ to be considerably greater than $iP_x^{(\tau)}$, and thus there can be corresponding differences between the absolute rates and the probabilities.

10.5.2 Central Rates of Multiple Decrement

There is one function of the multiple decrement model that is quite close to the corresponding function for an associated single decrement model. To introduce this function, we return to a mortality table and recall the central rate of mortality, or central-death-rate at age x, denoted by m_x and defined in (3.5.13) by

$$m_x = \frac{\int_0^1 iP_x \, \mu_x(t) \, dt}{\int_0^1 iP_x \, dt} = \frac{\int_0^1 l_{x+t} \, \mu_x(t) \, dt}{\int_0^1 l_{x+t} \, dt} = \frac{d_x}{L_x}. \tag{10.5.4}$$

Thus, m_x is a weighted average of the force of mortality between ages x and $x + 1$, and this justifies the term *central rate*.

Such central rates can be defined in a multiple decrement context. The *central rate of decrement from all causes* is defined by

$$m_x^{(\tau)} = \frac{\int_0^1 iP_x^{(\tau)} \, \mu_x^{(\tau)}(t) \, dt}{\int_0^1 iP_x^{(\tau)} \, dt} \tag{10.5.5}$$

and is a weighted average of $\mu_x^{(\tau)}(t)$, $0 \leq t < 1$. Similarly, the *central rate of decrement from cause j* is

$$m_x^{(j)} = \frac{\int_0^1 {}_tp_x^{(\tau)}\, \mu_x^{(j)}(t)\, dt}{\int_0^1 {}_tp_x^{(\tau)}\, dt} \tag{10.5.6}$$

and is a weighted average of $\mu_x^{(j)}(t)$, $0 \leq t < 1$. Clearly,

$$m_x^{(\tau)} = \sum_{j=1}^{m} m_x^{(j)}.$$

The corresponding central rate for the associated single decrement table is given by

$$m_x'^{(j)} = \frac{\int_0^1 {}_tp_x'^{(j)}\, \mu_x^{(j)}(t)\, dt}{\int_0^1 {}_tp_x'^{(j)}\, dt}. \tag{10.5.7}$$

This is again a weighted average of $\mu_x^{(j)}(t)$ over the same age range, the weight function now ${}_tp_x'^{(j)}$ rather than ${}_tp_x^{(\tau)}$. If the force $\mu_x^{(j)}(t)$ is constant for $0 \leq t < 1$, we have $m_x^{(j)} = m_x'^{(j)} = \mu_x^{(j)}(0)$. If $\mu_x^{(j)}(t)$ is an increasing function of t, then ${}_tp_x'^{(j)}$ gives more weight to higher values than does ${}_tp_x^{(\tau)}$, and $m_x'^{(j)} > m_x^{(j)}$. If $\mu_x^{(j)}(t)$ is a decreasing function of t, then $m_x'^{(j)} < m_x^{(j)}$. See Exercise 10.33 for a more formal treatment of these statements.

Central rates provide a convenient but approximate means of proceeding from the $q_x'^{(j)}$ to the $q_x^{(j)}$, $j = 1, 2, \ldots, m$, and vice versa. This is illustrated in Exercise 10.18.

10.5.3 Constant Force Assumption for Multiple Decrements

Let us examine specific assumptions concerning the incidence of decrements. First, let us use an assumption of a constant force for decrement j and for the total decrement over the interval $(x, x + 1)$. This implies

$$\mu_x^{(j)}(t) = \mu_x^{(j)}(0)$$

and

$$\mu_x^{(\tau)}(t) = \mu_x^{(\tau)}(0) \qquad 0 \leq t < 1.$$

Then, for $0 \leq s \leq 1$, we have

$${}_sq_x^{(j)} = \int_0^s {}_tp_x^{(\tau)}\, \mu_x^{(j)}(t)\, dt$$

$$= \frac{\mu_x^{(j)}(0)}{\mu_x^{(\tau)}(0)} \int_0^s {}_tp_x^{(\tau)}\, \mu_x^{(\tau)}(t)\, dt = \frac{\mu_x^{(j)}(0)}{\mu_x^{(\tau)}(0)}\, {}_sq_x^{(\tau)}. \tag{10.5.8}$$

But also for any r in $(0, 1)$, under the constant force assumption,

$$r\mu_x^{(\tau)}(0) = -\log {}_rp_x^{(\tau)}$$

and

$$r\mu_x^{(j)}(0) = -\log {}_rp_x'^{(j)},$$

so that from (10.5.8),

$${}_sq_x^{(j)} = \frac{\log {}_rp_x'^{(j)}}{\log {}_rp_x^{(\tau)}} {}_sq_x^{(\tau)}. \tag{10.5.9}$$

Equation (10.5.9) can be rearranged as
$${}_rp_x'^{(j)} = ({}_rp_x^{(\tau)})^{{}_sq_x^{(j)}/{}_sq_x^{(\tau)}}$$

and then in the limit as r goes to 1 can be solved for $q_x'^{(j)}$ to give

$$q_x'^{(j)} = 1 - (p_x^{(\tau)})^{{}_sq_x^{(j)}/{}_sq_x^{(\tau)}}. \tag{10.5.10}$$

If the constant force assumption holds for all decrements (and then automatically for the total decrement), (10.5.9), as r and s approach 1, together with (10.5.2), can be used for calculating $q_x^{(j)}$ from given values of $q_x'^{(j)}$, $j = 1, 2, \ldots, m$. Also, (10.5.10) is useful for obtaining absolute rates from a set of probabilities of decrement. Note that for (10.5.9) and (10.5.10) special treatment is required if $p_x'^{(j)}$ or $p_x^{(\tau)}$ equals 0.

10.5.4 Uniform Distribution Assumption for Multiple Decrements

Formula (10.5.10) holds under alternative assumptions. One of these is that both decrement j and total decrement, in the multiple decrement context, have a uniform distribution of decrement over the interval $(x, x + 1)$. Thus we assume that

$${}_tq_x^{(j)} = t\ q_x^{(j)}$$

and

$${}_tq_x^{(\tau)} = t\ q_x^{(\tau)}.$$

Also under the given assumption, we see from (10.2.12) that

$${}_tp_x^{(\tau)}\ \mu_x^{(j)}(t) = q_x^{(j)} \tag{10.5.11}$$

and

$$\mu_x^{(j)}(t) = \frac{q_x^{(j)}}{{}_tp_x^{(\tau)}} = \frac{q_x^{(j)}}{1 - t\ q_x^{(\tau)}}.$$

Then

$$\begin{aligned}
{}_sp_x'^{(j)} &= \exp\left[-\int_0^s \mu_x^{(j)}(t)\ dt\right] \\
&= \exp\left(-\int_0^s \frac{q_x^{(j)}}{1 - t\ q_x^{(\tau)}}\ dt\right) \\
&= \exp\left[\frac{q_x^{(j)}}{q_x^{(\tau)}} \log\left(1 - sq_x^{(\tau)}\right)\right] \\
&= ({}_sp_x'^{(\tau)})^{q_x^{(j)}/q_x^{(\tau)}}. \tag{10.5.12}
\end{aligned}$$

At $s = 1$, (10.5.10) and (10.5.12) yield the same equation relating $q_x'^{(j)}$ with $q_x^{(j)}$ and $q_x^{(\tau)}$. As a result, (10.5.9) with $r = 1$ can be used to obtain $q_x^{(j)}$. Exercise 10.22 provides additional insights into the connection between the developments in Sections 10.5.3 and 10.5.4.

Example 10.5.1

Continue Example 10.3.1 evaluating $q_x'^{(1)}$ and $q_x'^{(2)}$ by (10.5.10).

Solution:

By (10.5.10), the following results are obtained.

x	$q_x^{(1)}$	$q_x^{(2)}$	$q_x'^{(1)}$	$q_x'^{(2)}$
65	0.02	0.05	0.02052	0.05052
66	0.03	0.06	0.03095	0.06094
67	0.04	0.07	0.04149	0.07147
68	0.05	0.08	0.05215	0.08213
69	0.06	0.09	0.06294	0.09291
70	0.00	1.00	—	—

At age 70, the rates depend on mandatory retirement, and there is no particular need for $q_{70}'^{(1)}$, $q_{70}'^{(2)}$ although they could be identified, respectively, using $q_{70}^{(1)}$ and $q_{70}^{(2)}$. ▼

10.5.5 Estimation Issues

The definition of the absolute rate of decrement given in (10.5.1) depends on the force of decrement in multiple decrement theory as defined in (10.2.11). From definition (10.5.1), the developments in this section and their application in constructing multiple decrement distributions from assumed absolute rates of decrement follow. Questions remain, however, about the interpretation and estimation of $_t p_x'^{(j)}$.

If the joint p.d.f. $f_{T,J}(t, j)$ is known, then the survival function and forces of decrement are determined using the formulas of Section 10.2. For example, (10.2.13) follows as a consequence of the assumption that decrements occur from m mutually exclusive causes. The issue is, under what conditions can information obtained in a single decrement environment be used to construct the distribution of (T, J)?

We will illustrate this issue by considering two causes of decrement. Each associated single decrement environment has its time-until-decrement random variable $T_j(x)$ and its survival function $s_{T_j}(t) = \Pr\{T_j(x) > t\}$, $j = 1, 2$. The joint survival function of $T_1(x)$ and $T_2(x)$ is given by

$$s_{T_1, T_2}(t_1, t_2) = \Pr\{(T_1(x) > t_1) \cap (T_2(x) > t_2)\}.$$

In this context, the time-until-decrement random variable T equals the minimum of $T_1(x)$ and $T_2(x)$ and, in accordance with Section 9.3, (9.3.1), its survival function is

$$s_T(t) = s_{T_1, T_2}(t, t).$$

If $T_1(x)$ and $T_2(x)$ are independent,

$$s_T(t) = s_{T_1}(t)s_{T_2}(t) = s_{T_1, T_2}(t, 0)s_{T_1, T_2}(0, t),$$

and

$$\mu_x^{(\tau)}(t) = -\frac{d}{dt} \log s_{T_1}(t)s_{T_2}(t)$$

$$= \mu_x^{(1)}(t) + \mu_x^{(2)}(t). \qquad (10.5.13)$$

On the other hand, if $T_1(x)$ and $T_2(x)$ are dependent,

$$\mu_x^{(\tau)}(t) = -\frac{d}{dt} \log s_{T_1, T_2}(t, t)$$

$$\neq -\frac{d}{dt} \log s_{T_1, T_2}(t, 0) - \frac{d}{dt} \log s_{T_1, T_2}(0, t). \qquad (10.5.14)$$

The two terms on the right-hand side of (10.5.13) are called **marginal forces of decrement** associated, in order, with $T_1(x)$ and $T_2(x)$.

If $T_1(x)$ and $T_2(x)$ are independent, then the marginal forces of decrement from a single decrement environment can be used with (10.5.2) to determine $_t p_x^{(\tau)}$. If $T_1(x)$ and $T_2(x)$ are dependent, we have no assurance that assuming (10.5.2) yields the survival function of time-until-decrement in a multiple decrement environment.

Example 10.5.2

This example builds on Examples 9.2.1, 9.2.2, and 9.3.1. The dependent random variables $T_1(x)$ and $T_2(x)$ have a joint p.d.f. given by

$$f_{T_1, T_2}(s, t) = 0.0006(s - t)^2 \qquad 0 < s < 10, 0 < t < 10$$

$$= 0 \qquad \text{elsewhere.}$$

The joint survival function is exhibited in Example 9.2.2, and the survival function of $T = \min[T_1, T_2]$ is exhibited in Example 9.3.1.

Show that

$$-\frac{d}{dt} \log s_T(t) \neq -\frac{d}{dt} \log s_{T_1, T_2}(t, 0) - \frac{d}{dt} \log s_{T_1, T_2}(0, t).$$

Solution:

$$-\frac{d}{dt} \log s_T(t) = \frac{4}{(10 - t)} \qquad 0 < t < 10,$$

and

$$-\frac{d}{dt}\log s_{T_1,T_2}(t, 0) = \frac{4{,}000 - 1{,}200t + 120t^2}{20{,}000 - 4{,}000t + 600t^2 - 40t^3}$$

$$= \frac{100 - 30t + 3t^2}{500 - 100t + 15t^2 - t^3}$$

$$= \frac{100 - 30t + 3t^2}{(10 - t)(50 - 5t + t^2)},$$

which by symmetry is also equal to $-\dfrac{d}{dt}\log s_{T_1,T_2}(0, t)$. Therefore

$$-\frac{d}{dt}\log s_T(t) = \frac{4}{10 - t} \neq \frac{1}{10 - t}\left(\frac{200 - 60t + 6t^2}{50 - 5t + t^2}\right). \qquad \blacktriangledown$$

Example 10.5.3

This example builds on Examples 9.2.3 and 9.3.2. The independent random variables $T_1(x)$ and $T_2(x)$ have a joint p.d.f. given by

$$f_{T_1,T_2}(s, t) = [0.02(10 - s)][0.02(10 - t)] \qquad \begin{array}{l} 0 < s < 10 \\ 0 < t < 10. \end{array}$$

Show that

$$-\frac{d}{dt}\log s_T(t) = -\frac{d}{dt}\log s_{T_1,T_2}(t, 0) - \frac{d}{dt}\log s_{T_1,T_2}(0, t).$$

Solution:

The survival function of $T = \min[T_1(x), T_2(x)]$ is displayed in Example 9.3.2. Therefore,

$$-\frac{d}{dt}\log s_T(t) = \frac{4}{10 - t} \qquad 0 < t < 10,$$

$$-\frac{d}{dt}\log s_{T_1,T_2}(t, 0) = \frac{2}{10 - t} \qquad 0 < t < 10,$$

and by symmetry

$$-\frac{d}{dt}\log s_{T_1,T_2}(0, t) = \frac{2}{10 - t} \qquad 0 < t < 10.$$

As a result,

$$-\frac{d}{dt}\log s_T(t) = -\frac{d}{dt}\log s_{T_1 T_2}(t, 0) - \frac{d}{dt}\log s_{T_1 T_2}(0, t). \qquad \blacktriangledown$$

An interesting but distressing aspect of Examples 10.5.2 and 10.5.3 is that two dependent time-until-decrement random variables and two independent time-until-decrement random variables yield the same distribution of $T = \min[T_1(x), T_2(x)]$. Values of T can be observed, but without additional information it is impossible to select between the two models that may be generating the data. This, as in Section 9.3, is an example of nonidentifiability. Henceforth, in this chapter when constructing multiple decrement distributions from associated single decrement distributions, we assume that the component random variables are independent.

Remark:

The correspondence between the theory for the joint life model and the theory for the multiple decrement model can provide insights, but it is not complete. The difference between the two models centers on two facts that were identified in the discussion of (10.5.2) and Example 10.5.2. Realizations of both $T(x)$ and $T(y)$ can, at least in theory, be observed, while only the minimum of $T_1(x)$ and $T_2(x)$ and which one is the minimum can be observed. The corresponding problem in estimating joint life models was mentioned in Section 9.3. In addition, $\lim_{t\to\infty} {}_t p_x = \lim_{t\to\infty} {}_t p_y = 0$, whereas there is no assurance that

$$\lim_{t\to\infty} {}_t p_x'^{(j)} = 0 \qquad j = 1, 2.$$

10.6   Construction of a Multiple Decrement Table

In building a multiple decrement model it is best if data, including that on age and cause of decrement for the population under study, can be used to estimate directly the probabilities $q_x^{(j)}$. Large, well-established employee benefit plans may have such data. For other plans, such data are frequently not available. An alternative is to construct the model from associated single decrement rates assumed appropriate for the population under study. The adequacy of the model should then be tested by reviewing data as they become available.

Once satisfactory associated single decrement tables are selected, the results of Section 10.5 can be used to complete the construction of the multiple decrement table. The availability of a set of $p_x'^{(j)}$, for $j = 1, 2, \ldots, m$ and all values of x, will permit the computation of $p_x^{(\tau)}$ by (10.5.2) and of $q_x^{(\tau)}$ by $q_x^{(\tau)} = 1 - p_x^{(\tau)}$. The remaining step is to break $q_x^{(\tau)}$ into its components $q_x^{(j)}$ for $j = 1, 2, \ldots, m$. If either the constant force or the uniform distribution of decrement assumption is adopted in the model, (10.5.9) can be used for the calculation of the $q_x^{(j)}$.

Example 10.6.1

Use (10.5.2) and (10.5.9) to obtain the multiple decrement table corresponding to absolute rates of decrement given below. Presumably the actuary has examined the characteristics of the participant group and has decided that associated single decrement tables yielding these rates are appropriate for the group under study. It is also assumed that cause 3 is retirement that can occur between ages 65 and 70 and is mandatory at 70.

---

x	$q_x^{\prime(1)}$	$q_x^{\prime(2)}$	$q_x^{\prime(3)}$
65	0.020	0.02	0.04
66	0.025	0.02	0.06
67	0.030	0.02	0.08
68	0.035	0.02	0.10
69	0.040	0.02	0.12

Solution:

The table below contains the results of the calculation of the probabilities of decrement. Formula (10.5.2) can be rewritten as

$$q_x^{(\tau)} = 1 - \prod_{j=1}^{3} (1 - q_x^{\prime(j)}).$$

In this equation the assumed independence among the three causes of decrement is apparent. Formula (10.5.9), and the mandatory retirement condition, yield the multiple decrement probabilities. The multiple decrement table is constructed as in Example 10.3.1.

x	$q_x^{(\tau)}$	$q_x^{(1)}$	$q_x^{(2)}$	$q_x^{(3)}$	$l_x^{(\tau)}$	$d_x^{(1)}$	$d_x^{(2)}$	$d_x^{(3)}$
65	0.07802	0.01940	0.01940	0.03921	1 000.00	19.40	19.40	39.21
66	0.10183	0.02401	0.01916	0.05867	921.99	22.14	17.67	54.09
67	0.12545	0.02851	0.01891	0.07803	828.09	23.61	15.66	64.62
68	0.14887	0.03290	0.01866	0.09731	724.20	23.83	13.51	70.47
69	0.17210	0.03720	0.01841	0.11649	616.39	22.93	11.35	71.80
70	1.00000	0.00000	0.00000	1.00000	510.31	0.00	0.00	510.31

▼

It has been noted that (10.5.9) and (10.5.10) will not be used if $p_x^{\prime(j)}$ or $p_x^{(\tau)} = 0$; some alternative device will be necessary. One such method, which handles this indeterminacy and lends itself to special adjustments, is based on assumed distributions of decrement in the associated single decrement tables rather than on assumptions about multiple decrement probabilities as in Section 10.5. We first examine an assumption of uniform distribution of decrement (in each year of age) in the associated single decrement tables. We restrict our attention to situations with three decrements, but the method and formulas easily extend for $m > 3$. Under the stated assumption,

$$_t p_x^{\prime(j)} = 1 - t\, q_x^{\prime(j)} \qquad j = 1, 2, 3; 0 \le t \le 1 \tag{10.6.1}$$

and

$$_t p_x^{\prime(j)}\, \mu_x^{(j)}(t) = \frac{d}{dt}\left(-_t p_x^{\prime(j)}\right) = q_x^{\prime(j)}. \tag{10.6.2}$$

It follows that

$$q_x^{(1)} = \int_0^1 {}_tp_x^{(\tau)} \, \mu_x^{(1)}(t) \, dt$$

$$= \int_0^1 {}_tp_x'^{(1)} \, \mu_x^{(1)}(t) \, {}_tp_x'^{(2)} \, {}_tp_x'^{(3)} \, dt$$

$$= q_x'^{(1)} \int_0^1 (1 - t \, q_x'^{(2)})(1 - t \, q_x'^{(3)}) \, dt$$

$$= q_x'^{(1)} \left[1 - \frac{1}{2} (q_x'^{(2)} + q_x'^{(3)}) + \frac{1}{3} q_x'^{(2)}q_x'^{(3)} \right]. \tag{10.6.3}$$

Similar formulas hold for $q_x^{(2)}$, $q_x^{(3)}$, and it can be verified that

$$q_x^{(1)} + q_x^{(2)} + q_x^{(3)} = q_x'^{(1)} + q_x'^{(2)} + q_x'^{(3)}$$

$$- (q_x'^{(1)}q_x'^{(2)} + q_x'^{(1)}q_x'^{(3)} + q_x'^{(2)}q_x'^{(3)})$$

$$+ q_x'^{(1)}q_x'^{(2)}q_x'^{(3)}$$

$$= 1 - (1 - q_x'^{(1)})(1 - q_x'^{(2)})(1 - q_x'^{(3)}) = q_x^{(\tau)}. \tag{10.6.4}$$

Example 10.6.2

Obtain the probabilities of decrement for ages 65–69 from the data in Example 10.6.1, under the assumption of a uniform distribution of decrement in each year of age in each of the associated single decrement tables.

Solution:

This is an application of (10.6.3).

x	$q_x'^{(1)}$	$q_x'^{(2)}$	$q_x'^{(3)}$	$q_x^{(1)}$	$q_x^{(2)}$	$q_x^{(3)}$
65	0.020	0.02	0.04	0.01941	0.01941	0.03921
66	0.025	0.02	0.06	0.02401	0.01916	0.05866
67	0.030	0.02	0.08	0.02852	0.01892	0.07802
68	0.035	0.02	0.10	0.03292	0.01867	0.09727
69	0.040	0.02	0.12	0.03723	0.01843	0.11643

These probabilities are close to those obtained by (10.5.9), displayed in Example 10.6.1. ▼

We conclude this section with another example illustrating the use of a special distribution for one of the decrements. Special distributions are sometimes required by the facts of the situation being modeled.

Example 10.6.3

Consider a situation with three causes of decrement: mortality, disability, and withdrawal. Assume mortality and disability are uniformly distributed in each year of age in the associated single decrement tables with absolute rates of $q_x'^{(1)}$ and

$q_x'^{(2)}$, respectively. Also assume that withdrawals occur only at the end of the year with an absolute rate of $q_x'^{(3)}$.

a. Give formulas for the probabilities of decrement in the year of age x to $x + 1$ for the three causes.

b. Reformulate the probabilities under the assumptions that

   (i) In the associated single decrement model, withdrawals occur only at the age's midyear or year end, and

   (ii) Equal proportions, namely $(1 / 2)$, $q_x'^{(3)}$, of those beginning the year withdraw at the midyear and at the year end.

Remark:

Until now our multiple decrement models have been fully continuous, except possibly to recognize a mandatory retirement age. Moreover, our theory began with a multiple decrement model and after defining the forces $\mu_x^{(j)}(t)$, $j = 1, 2, \ldots, m$ proceeded to the associated single decrement tables. In this example we start with the single decrement tables, and in one of these tables the decrement takes place discretely at the ends of stated intervals. We do not attempt to define a force of decrement for this discrete case but proceed by direct methods to build, from the single decrement tables, a multiple decrement model possessing the relationships (10.2.19) and (10.5.2) established in our prior theory.

Solution:

a. Figure 10.6.1 displays survival factors for the given single decrement tables and for a multiple decrement table where

$$_tp_x^{(\tau)} = {}_tp_x'^{(1)} \; {}_tp_x'^{(2)} \; {}_tp_x'^{(3)}$$

for nonintegral $t \geq 0$. At $t = 1$, $_tp_x'^{(3)}$ and $_tp_x^{(\tau)}$ are discontinuous, so we consider

$$\lim_{t \to 1-} {}_tp_x^{(\tau)} = {}_tp_x'^{(1)} \; {}_tp_x'^{(2)} \; 1$$

and

$$p_x^{(\tau)} = p_x'^{(1)}p_x'^{(2)}(1 - q_x'^{(3)}).$$

We also require that, for our multiple decrement table,

$$q_x^{(\tau)} = q_x^{(1)} + q_x^{(2)} + q_x^{(3)} = 1 - p_x^{(\tau)} = 1 - p_x'^{(1)}p_x'^{(2)}(1 - q_x'^{(3)}).$$

We set

$$q_x^{(1)} = \int_0^1 {}_tp_x^{(\tau)} \; \mu_x^{(1)}(t) \; dt$$

$$= \int_0^1 {}_tp_x'^{(1)}{}_tp_x'^{(2)}(1)\mu_x^{(1)}(t) \; dt$$

$$= q_x'^{(1)} \int_0^1 (1 - tq_x'^{(2)}) \; dt$$

$$= q_x'^{(1)} \left(1 - \frac{1}{2} q_x'^{(2)}\right).$$

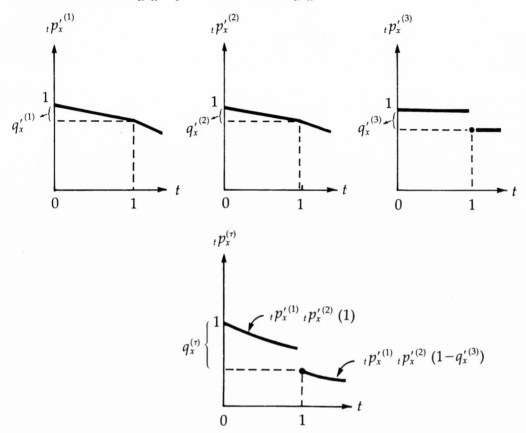

Similarly, we set

$$q_x^{(2)} = q_x'^{(2)} \left(1 - \frac{1}{2}\, q_x'^{(1)} \right).$$

Then

$$q_x^{(3)} = q_x^{(\tau)} - (q_x^{(1)} + q_x^{(2)})$$

$$= 1 - p_x'^{(1)}p_x'^{(2)}(1 - q_x'^{(3)}) - q_x'^{(1)} - q_x'^{(2)} + q_x'^{(1)}q_x'^{(2)},$$

and, since

$$1 - q_x'^{(1)} - q_x'^{(2)} + q_x'^{(1)}q_x'^{(2)} = p_x'^{(1)}p_x'^{(2)},$$

$$q_x^{(3)} = p_x'^{(1)}p_x'^{(2)}q_x'^{(3)}.$$

Note that

$$\lim_{t \to 1-} {}_tp_x^{(\tau)} - \lim_{t \to 1+} {}_tp_x^{(\tau)} = p_x'^{(1)}p_x'^{(2)}q_x'^{(3)} = q_x^{(3)} \ ;$$

that is, the discontinuity at $t = 1$ equals $q_x^{(3)}$.

b. Here $_tp_x'^{(1)}$ and $_tp_x'^{(2)}$ are as in Figure 10.6.1, but $_tp_x'^{(3)}$ and $_tp_x^{(\tau)}$ now have discontinuities at $t = 1/2$ and $t = 1$, as shown in Figure 10.6.2.

FIGURE 10.6.2

Survival Factors, $_tp_x'^{(3)}$ and $_tp_x^{(\tau)}$

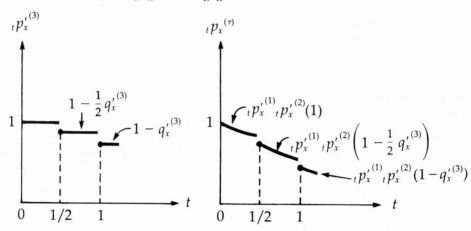

Proceeding as in (a), but taking account of the intervals $[0, 1/2)$ and $[1/2, 1)$, we set

$$q_x^{(1)} = q_x'^{(1)} \int_0^{1/2} (1 - t\, q_x'^{(2)})\, dt$$

$$+ q_x'^{(1)} \left(1 - \frac{1}{2} q_x'^{(3)}\right) \int_{1/2}^1 (1 - t\, q_x'^{(2)})\, dt$$

$$= q_x'^{(1)} \left(1 - \frac{1}{2} q_x'^{(2)} - \frac{1}{4} q_x'^{(3)} + \frac{3}{16} q_x'^{(2)} q_x'^{(3)}\right).$$

Similarly, we set

$$q_x^{(2)} = q_x'^{(2)} \left(1 - \frac{1}{2} q_x'^{(1)} - \frac{1}{4} q_x'^{(3)} + \frac{3}{16} q_x'^{(1)} q_x'^{(3)}\right).$$

Then,

$$q_x^{(3)} = 1 - p_x^{(\tau)} - q_x^{(1)} - q_x^{(2)}$$

$$= 1 - p_x'^{(1)} p_x'^{(2)} (1 - q_x'^{(3)}) - q_x^{(1)} - q_x^{(2)},$$

which reduces to

$$q_x^{(3)} = q_x'^{(3)} \left(1 - \frac{3}{4} q_x'^{(1)} - \frac{3}{4} q_x'^{(2)} + \frac{5}{8} q_x'^{(1)} q_x'^{(2)}\right). \qquad \blacktriangledown$$

10.7   Notes and References

The history of multiple decrement theory was reviewed by Seal (1977). Chiang (1968) developed the theory using the language of competing risks. The foundation for the actuarial theory of multiple decrement models was built by Makeham (1874). Menge (1932) and Nesbitt and Van Eenam (1948) provided insight into the deterministic interpretation of forces of decrement and of increment. Bicknell and

Nesbitt (1956) developed a very general theory for individual insurances using a deterministic multiple decrement model. Hickman (1964) redeveloped this theory using the language of the stochastic model, and this redevelopment is the basis for much of this chapter. The analysis of life tables by cause of death is the subject of papers by Greville (1948) and Preston, Keyfitz, and Schoen (1973).

The perplexing estimation issues that arise when the times-until-decrement are not independent are discussed by Elandt-Johnson and Johnson (1980). Promislow (1991b) makes the excellent point that in practice multiple decrement models should be select in the sense of Chapter 3. He developed a theory and associated notation for select multiple decrement models. Exercises 10.3 and 10.24 are built on a discussion by Robinson (1984).

Carriere (1994) applied copulas, discussed in Section 9.6.2, to create multiple decrement distributions that incorporate dependent component random variables. Carriere also discusses the problem of identifiability and reviews the conditions under which it is possible to identify a unique joint survival function $s_{T_1(x)\ T_2(x)}(t, t)$.

Exercises

Section 10.2

10.1. Let $\mu_x^{(j)}(t) = \mu_x^{(j)}(0)$, $j = 1, 2, \ldots, m$, $t \geq 0$. Obtain expressions for
  a. $f_{T,J}(t, j)$ b. $f_J(j)$ c. $f_T(t)$.
  The functions called for in (a) and (c) are p.d.f.'s, and the function in (b) is a p.f. Show that T and J are independent random variables.

10.2. A multiple decrement model with two causes of decrement has forces of decrement given by

$$\mu_x^{(1)}(t) = \frac{1}{100 - (x + t)}$$

and

$$\mu_x^{(2)}(t) = \frac{2}{100 - (x + t)} \qquad t < 100 - x.$$

  If $x = 50$, obtain expressions for
  a. $f_{T,J}(t, j)$ b. $f_T(t)$ c. $f_J(j)$ d. $f_{J|T}(j|t)$.

10.3. Given the joint p.d.f.

$$f_{T,J}(t, j) = pu_1\, e^{-(u_1+v_1)t} + (1 - p)u_2\, e^{-(u_2+v_2)t} \qquad 0 \leq t, j = 1$$

$$= pv_1\, e^{-(u_1+v_1)t} + (1 - p)v_2\, e^{-(u_2+v_2)t} \qquad 0 \leq t, j = 2$$

  where $0 < p < 1$ and $0 < u_1, u_2, v_1, v_2$,

---

find

    a. The marginal p.d.f.s $f_T(t)$ and $f_J(j)$

    b. The survival function $s_T(t)$.

Section 10.3

10.4. Using the multiple decrement probabilities given in Example 10.3.1, evaluate the following:

    a. $_3p_{65}^{(\tau)}$ b. $_{3|}q_{65}^{(1)}$ c. $_3q_{65}^{(2)}$.

10.5. The following multiple decrement probabilities apply to students entering a 4-year college.

Curtate Duration, at Beginning of Academic Year	Probability of		
	Academic Failure, $j = 1$	Withdrawal for All Other Reasons, $j = 2$	Survival through the Academic Year
0	0.15	0.25	0.60
1	0.10	0.20	0.70
2	0.05	0.15	0.80
3	0.00	0.10	0.90

An entering class has 1,000 members.

    a. What is the expectation of the number of graduates? What is the variance?

    b. What is the expected number of those who will fail sometime during the 4-year program? What is the variance of the number of students who will fail?

10.6. Construct a multiple decrement table on the basis of the data in Exercise 10.5 and use it to exhibit

    a. The marginal distribution of the random variable J (mode of exit), which takes on values for academic failure, withdrawal, and graduation

    b. The conditional distribution of the mode of termination, given that a student has terminated in the third year.

Section 10.4

10.7. Given that $\mu^{(1)}(x) = 1/(a - x)$, $0 \le x < a$, and $\mu^{(2)}(x) = 1$, derive expressions for

    a. $l_x^{(\tau)}$ b. $d_x^{(1)}$ c. $d_x^{(2)}$.

    Assume $l_0^{(\tau)} = a$.

10.8. Given $\mu^{(1)}(x) = 2x/(a - x^2)$, $0 \le x \le \sqrt{a}$, and $\mu^{(2)}(x) = c$, $c > 0$, and $l_0^{(\tau)} = 1{,}000$, derive an expression for $l_x^{(\tau)}$.

10.9. For a deterministic survivorship group with $a < x$, derive expressions for:

    a. $\dfrac{d}{dx}\,_tq_x^{(\tau)}$ b. $\dfrac{d}{dx}\,_tq_x^{(j)}$ c. $\dfrac{d}{dt}\,_tq_x^{(j)}$.

10.10. Using the data in Exercise 10.5, and assuming a uniform distribution of all decrements in the multiple decrement model, calculate a table of $q_k^{(j)}$, $j = 1, 2$, $k = 0, 1, 2, 3$ (where k is the curtate duration).

10.11. If $\mu_x^{(1)}(t)$ is a constant c for $0 \leq t \leq 1$, derive expressions in terms of c and $_t p_x^{(\tau)}$ for
   a. $q_x'^{(1)}$ b. $m_x^{(1)}$ c. $q_x^{(1)}$.

10.12. Show that under appropriate assumptions of a uniform distribution of decrements

a. $m_x^{(\tau)} = \dfrac{q_x^{(\tau)}}{1 - (1/2)\, q_x^{(\tau)}}$ b. $m_x^{(j)} = \dfrac{q_x^{(j)}}{1 - (1/2)\, q_x^{(\tau)}}$ c. $m_x'^{(j)} = \dfrac{q_x'^{(j)}}{1 - (1/2)\, q_x'^{(j)}}$

and, conversely,

d. $q_x^{(\tau)} = \dfrac{m_x^{(\tau)}}{1 + (1/2)\, m_x^{(\tau)}}$ e. $q_x^{(j)} = \dfrac{m_x^{(j)}}{1 + (1/2)\, m_x^{(\tau)}}$ f. $q_x'^{(j)} = \dfrac{m_x'^{(j)}}{1 + (1/2)\, m_x'^{(j)}}$.

10.13. Order the following in terms of magnitude and state your reasons:
$$q_x'^{(j)}, \quad q_x^{(j)}, \quad m_x'^{(j)}.$$

10.14. Given, for a double decrement table, that $q_{40}'^{(1)} = 0.02$ and $q_{40}'^{(2)} = 0.04$, calculate $q_{40}^{(\tau)}$ to four decimal places.

10.15. For a double decrement table you are given that $m_{40}^{(\tau)} = 0.2$ and $q_{40}'^{(1)} = 0.1$. Calculate $q_{40}'^{(2)}$ to four decimal places assuming
   a. Uniform distribution of decrements in the multiple decrement model
   b. Uniform distribution of decrements in the associated single decrement tables.

10.16. Using the data in Exercise 10.5 and assuming a uniform distribution of decrements in the multiple decrement model, construct a table of $m_k^{(j)}$, $j = 1, 2$, $k = 0, 1, 2, 3$ (where k is the curtate duration). Calculate each result to five decimal places.

10.17. Given that decrement may be due to death, 1, disability, 2, or retirement, 3, use (10.5.9) to construct a multiple decrement table based on the following absolute rates.

Age x	$q_x'^{(1)}$	$q_x'^{(2)}$	$q_x'^{(3)}$
62	0.020	0.030	0.200
63	0.022	0.034	0.100
64	0.028	0.040	0.120

10.18. Recalculate the multiple decrement table from the absolute rates of decrement in Exercise 10.17 by means of the **central rate bridge.** [Hint: To use the central rate bridge, first calculate $m_x^{\prime(j)}$ by the formula

$$m_x^{\prime(j)} \cong \frac{q_x^{\prime(j)}}{1 - (1/2)\, q_x^{\prime(j)}} \qquad j = 1, 2, 3,$$

which holds if there is a uniform distribution of decrement in the associated single decrement tables. Next, assume $m_x^{(j)} \cong m_x^{\prime(j)}$, $j = 1, 2, 3$, and proceed to $q_x^{(j)}$ by

$$q_x^{(j)} = \frac{d_x^{(j)}}{l_x^{(\tau)}} = \frac{d_x^{(j)}}{l_x^{(\tau)} - (1/2)\, d_x^{(\tau)} + (1/2)\, d_x^{(\tau)}} = \frac{m_x^{(j)}}{1 + (1/2)\, m_x^{(\tau)}}.$$

This second relation holds if there is a uniform distribution of total decrement in the multiple decrement table. But then

$$_tp_x^{(\tau)} = 1 - {}_tq_x^{(\tau)} \neq {}_tp_x^{\prime(1)}\, {}_tp_x^{\prime(2)}\, {}_tp_x^{\prime(3)}$$

$$= (1 - {}_tq_x^{\prime(1)})(1 - {}_tq_x^{\prime(2)})(1 - {}_tq_x^{\prime(3)})$$

under the condition of a uniform distribution in the associated single decrement tables. Thus there is an inconsistency in the stated conditions, but the calculations may be accurate enough for this purpose.]

10.19. Indicate arguments for the following relations:

a. $m_x^{\prime(j)} \cong m_x^{(j)}$

b. $\dfrac{q_x^{\prime(j)}}{1 - (1/2)\, q_x^{\prime(j)}} \cong \dfrac{q_x^{(j)}}{1 - (1/2)\, q_x^{(\tau)}}$.

Show that these lead to

c. $q_x^{(j)} \cong \dfrac{q_x^{\prime(j)}\, [1 - (1/2)\, q_x^{(\tau)}]}{1 - (1/2)\, q_x^{\prime(j)}}$

d. $q_x^{\prime(j)} \cong \dfrac{q_x^{(j)}}{1 - (1/2)\, (q_x^{(\tau)} - q_x^{(j)})}$.

Compare (c) and (d) to (10.5.9) and (10.5.10).

10.20. Use the values of $q_x^{(j)}$, $q_x^{\prime(j)}$ from Example 10.5.1 to calculate values of $m_x^{(j)}$, $m_x^{\prime(j)}$, $j = 1, 2$, $x = 65, \ldots, 69$, under appropriate assumptions of uniform distribution of decrements (see Exercise 10.12).

10.21. Which of the following statements would you accept? Revise where necessary.

a. $q_x^{(j)} \cong \dfrac{m_x^{(j)}}{1 + (1/2)\, m_x^{(j)}}$

b. $\displaystyle\int_0^1 l_{x+t}^{(\tau)}\, dt \cong \dfrac{l_x^{(\tau)}}{1 + (1/2)\, m_x^{(\tau)}}$

c. $q_x^{(1)} = q_x^{\prime(1)}[1 - (1/2)q_x^{\prime(2)}]$ in a double decrement table where there is a uniform distribution of decrement for the year of age x to $x + 1$ in each of the associated single decrement tables.

10.22. a. For a certain age x, particular cause of decrement j, and constant K_j, show that the following conditions are equivalent:

(i) $_t q_x^{(j)} = K_j \, _t q_x^{(\tau)}$ $\quad 0 \leq t \leq 1$

(ii) $\mu_x^{(j)}(t) = K_j \, \mu_x^{(\tau)}(t)$ $\quad 0 \leq t \leq 1$

(iii) $1 - \, _t q_x'^{(j)} = (1 - \, _t q_x^{(\tau)})^{K_j}$ $\quad 0 \leq t \leq 1$.

[Hint: Show (i) $\Rightarrow$ (ii) $\Rightarrow$ (iii) $\Rightarrow$ (ii) $\Rightarrow$ (i).]

b. Verify that, in a multiple decrement table, where either

$$\mu_x^{(j)}(t) = \mu_x^{(j)}(0) \quad 0 \leq t \leq 1, j = 1, 2, \ldots, m$$

(the constant force assumption for each cause of decrement) or

$$_t q_x^{(j)} = t \, q_x^{(j)} \quad 0 \leq t \leq 1, j = 1, 2, \ldots, m$$

(the uniform distribution for each cause of decrement), then

$$_t q_x^{(j)} = K_j \, _t q_x^{(\tau)} \quad 0 \leq t \leq 1, j = 1, 2, \ldots, m.$$

c. Assume that in part (a), condition (ii), $\mu_x^{(\tau)}(t)$, $0 \leq t \leq 1$, is given by

(i) kt^n $\quad k > 0, n > 0$ (Weibull)

(ii) Bc^t $\quad B > 0, c > 1$ (Gompertz)

and for each example find the corresponding expressions for $_t q_x^{(j)}$ and $1 - \, _t q_x'^{(j)}$.

10.23. a. Prove that

$$\mu_x^{(j)}(t) = K_j \, \mu_x^{(\tau)}(t) \quad 0 \leq t, j = 1, 2$$

where

$$K_j = \int_0^\infty \, _t p_x^{(\tau)} \, \mu_x^{(j)}(t) \, dt \quad j = 1, 2,$$

if and only if the random variables T and J are independent.

b. If $T_1(x)$ and $T_2(x)$ are independent and J and T are independent, show that

$$_t p_x'^{(j)} = (_t p_x^{(\tau)})^{K_j} \quad j = 1, 2.$$

[Remark: Note that $K_j = f_J(j)$.]

10.24. This exercise is a continuation of Exercise 10.3 and uses the notation of Section 10.5.5. The joint survival function is given by

$$s_{T_1, T_2}(t_1, t_2) = p e^{-u_1 t_1 - v_1 t_2} + (1 - p) e^{-u_2 t_1 - v_2 t_2}$$

$$0 \leq t_1, t_2, u_1, u_2, v_1, v_2$$

$$0 < p < 1.$$

Confirm that

$$s_{T_1, T_2}(t, t) \neq s_{T_1, T_2}(t, 0) \, s_{T_1, T_2}(0, t)$$

and

$$-\left.\frac{\partial \log s_{T_1, T_2}(t_1, t_2)}{\partial t_1}\right|_{t_1=t_2=t} \neq -\frac{d \log s_{T_1, T_2}(t, 0)}{dt}.$$

Section 10.6

10.25. Redo Exercise 10.10 by use of the formula for $q_x'^{(j)}$ in Exercise 10.19.

10.26. Show that $\mu_x^{(j)}(1/2) = m_x^{(j)}$, under the assumption of a uniform distribution of each decrement in each year of age in a multiple decrement context.

10.27. How would you proceed to construct the multiple decrement table if the given rates were those given below?
   a. $q_x'^{(1)}$, $q_x'^{(2)}$, $q_x^{(3)}$
   b. $q_x'^{(1)}$, $q_x^{(2)}$, $q_x^{(3)}$

10.28. In Example 10.6.2 suppose that decrement 3 at age 69 is not uniformly distributed but follows the pattern

$$_{t}p_{69}'^{(3)} = \begin{cases} 1 - 0.12t & 0 < t < 1 \\ 0 & t = 1. \end{cases}$$

In words, the cause 3 absolute rate is 0.12 during the year. Then, just before age 70, all remaining survivors terminate due to cause 3. This is consistent with an assumption that $q_{69}'^{(3)} = 1$. What then is the value of $q_{69}^{(3)}$?

10.29. In a double decrement table where cause 1 is death and cause 2 is withdrawal, it is assumed that
   • Deaths in the year from age h to $h + 1$ are uniformly distributed,
   • Withdrawals in the year from age h to age $h + 1$ occur immediately after the attainment of age h.
   From this table it is noted that, at age 50, $l_{50}^{(\tau)} = 1,000$, $q_{50}^{(2)} = 0.2$, and $d_{50}^{(1)} = 0.06\ d_{50}^{(2)}$. Determine $q_{50}'^{(1)}$.

Miscellaneous

10.30. On the basis of a triple decrement table, display an expression for the probability that (20) will not terminate before age 65 for cause 2.

10.31. a. You are given $q_x'^{(1)}$, $q_x'^{(2)}$, $m_x^{(3)}$, $m_x^{(4)}$. How would you proceed to construct a multiple decrement table where active service of an employee group is subject to decrement from death, 1, withdrawal, 2, disability, 3, and retirement, 4?
   b. On the basis of the table in (a), give an expression for the probability that, in the future, an active member age y will not retire but will terminate from service for some other cause.

10.32. Prove and interpret the relation

$$q_x^{(j)} = q_x'^{(j)} - \sum_{k \neq j} \int_0^1 {}_t p_x^{(\tau)}\ \mu_x^{(k)}(t)\ {}_{1-t}q_{x+t}'^{(j)}\ dt.$$

10.33. Let

$$w^{(\tau)}(t) = \frac{{}_tp_x^{(\tau)}}{\int_0^1 {}_tp_x^{(\tau)}\,dt}$$

and

$$w^{(j)}(t) = \frac{{}_tp_x'^{(j)}}{\int_0^1 {}_tp_x'^{(j)}\,dt} \qquad 0 \le t \le 1.$$

Assume that j and at least one other cause have positive forces of decrement on the interval $0 \le t \le 1$.

a. Show that
  (i) $w^{(\tau)}(0) > w^{(j)}(0)$
  (ii) $w^{(\tau)}(1) < w^{(j)}(1)$
  (iii) There exists a unique number r, $0 < r < 1$, such that $w^{(\tau)}(r) = w^{(j)}(r)$.

b. Let

$$-I = \int_0^r [w^{(j)}(t) - w^{(\tau)}(t)]\,dt.$$

Show that

$$I = \int_r^1 [w^{(j)}(t) - w^{(\tau)}(t)]\,dt.$$

c. Assume that $\mu_x^{(j)}(t)$ is an increasing function on the interval $0 \le t \le 1$. Use the mean value theorem for integrals to establish the following inequalities:

$$m_x'^{(j)} - m_x^{(j)} = \int_0^1 [w^{(j)}(t) - w^{(\tau)}(t)]\mu_x^{(j)}(t)\,dt$$

$$= \int_0^r [w^{(j)}(t) - w^{(\tau)}(t)]\mu_x^{(j)}(t)\,dt$$

$$+ \int_r^1 [w^{(j)}(t) - w^{(\tau)}(t)]\mu_x^{(j)}(t)\,dt$$

$$= -\mu_x^{(j)}(t_0)\,I + \mu_x^{(j)}(t_1)\,I \qquad 0 < t_0 < r < t_1 < 1$$

$$= I\,[\mu_x^{(j)}(t_1) - \mu_x^{(j)}(t_0)] > 0.$$

10.34. The joint distribution of T and J is specified by

$$\left.\begin{array}{c}
\mu_x^{(1)}(t) = \dfrac{\theta t^{\alpha-1} e^{-\beta t}}{\displaystyle\int_t^\infty s^{\alpha-1} e^{-\beta s}ds} \\[2em]
\mu_x^{(2)}(t) = \dfrac{(1-\theta)t^{\alpha-1} e^{-\beta t}}{\displaystyle\int_t^\infty s^{\alpha-1} e^{-\beta s}\,ds}
\end{array}\right\}
\begin{array}{l}
0 < \theta < 1 \\[0.5em]
\alpha > 0 \\[0.5em]
\beta > 0 \\[0.5em]
t \ge 0.
\end{array}$$

a. Obtain expressions for $f_{T,J}(t, j)$, $f_J(j)$, and $f_T(t)$.
b. Express $E[T]$ and $\mathrm{Var}(T)$ in terms of α and β.
c. Confirm that J and T are independent.

APPLICATIONS OF MULTIPLE DECREMENT THEORY

11.1 Introduction

The multiple decrement model developed in Chapter 10 provides a framework for studying many financial security systems. For example, life insurance policies frequently provide for special benefits if death occurs by accidental means or if the insured becomes disabled. The single decrement model, the subject of Chapters 3 through 9, does not provide a mathematical model for policies with such multiple benefits. In addition, there may be nonforfeiture benefits that are paid when the insured withdraws from the set of premium-paying policyholders. The determination of the amount of these nonforfeiture benefits, and related public policy issues, are discussed in Chapter 16. The basic models associated with these multiple benefits are developed in this chapter.

Another major application of multiple decrement models is in pension plans. In this chapter we consider basic methods used in calculating the actuarial present values of benefits and contributions for a participant in a pension plan. The participants of a plan may be a group of employees of a single employer, or they may be the employees of a group of employers engaged in similar activities. A plan, upon a participant's retirement, typically provides pensions for age and service or for disability. In case of withdrawal from employment, there can be a return of accumulated participant contributions or a deferred pension. For death occurring before the other contingencies, there can be a lump sum or income payable to a beneficiary. Payments to meet the costs of the benefits are referred to as contributions, not premiums as for insurance, and are payable in various proportions by the participants and the plan sponsor.

A pension plan can be regarded as a system for purchasing deferred life annuities (payable during retirement) and certain ancillary benefits with a temporary annuity of contributions during active service. The balancing of the actuarial present values of benefits and contributions may be on an individual basis, but frequently it is on some aggregate basis for the whole group of participants. Methods to accomplish this balance comprise the theory of pension funding. Here we are concerned with only the separate valuation of the pension plan's actuarial present value of benefits and contributions with respect to a typical participant. Aggregate values can then be obtained by summation over all the participants. The basic tools for valuing the benefits of, and the contributions to, a pension plan are presented here, but their application to the possible funding methods for a plan is deferred to Chapter 20.

In Section 11.6 we study disability benefits commonly found in conjunction with individual life insurance. The benefits include those for waiver of premium and for disability income. There is a discussion of a widely used single decrement approximation for calculating benefit premiums and benefit reserves for these disability coverages.

11.2 Actuarial Present Values and Their Numerical Evaluation

Actuarial applications of multiple decrement models arise when the amount of benefit payment depends on the mode of exit from the group of active lives. We let $B_{x+t}^{(j)}$ denote the value of a benefit at age $x + t$ incurred by a decrement at that age by cause j. Then the actuarial present value of the benefits, denoted in general by $\bar{A}$, will be given by

$$\bar{A} = \sum_{j=1}^{m} \int_{0}^{\infty} B_{x+t}^{(j)} \, v^t \, {}_tp_x^{(\tau)} \, \mu_x^{(j)}(t) \, dt. \tag{11.2.1}$$

If $m = 1$ and $B_{x+t}^{(1)} = 1$, $\bar{A}$ reduces to $\bar{A}_x$, the actuarial present value for a unit of whole life insurance with immediate payment of claims.

More appropriate for this chapter is the example of a ***double indemnity provision***, which provides for the death benefit to be doubled when death is caused by accidental means. Let $J = 1$ for death by accidental means and $J = 2$ for death by other means, and take $B_{x+t}^{(1)} = 2$ and $B_{x+t}^{(2)} = 1$. The actuarial present value for an n-year term insurance is given by

$$\bar{A} = 2 \int_{0}^{n} v^t \, {}_tp_x^{(\tau)} \mu_x^{(1)}(t) \, dt + \int_{0}^{n} v^t \, {}_tp_x^{(\tau)} \, \mu_x^{(2)}(t) \, dt. \tag{11.2.2}$$

For numerical evaluation, the first step is to break the expression into a set of integrals, one for each of the years involved. For the first integral,

$$2 \int_{0}^{n} v^t \, {}_tp_x^{(\tau)} \, \mu_x^{(1)}(t) \, dt = 2 \sum_{k=0}^{n-1} v^k \, {}_kp_x^{(\tau)} \int_{0}^{1} v^s \, {}_sp_{x+k}^{(\tau)} \, \mu_x^{(1)}(k + s) \, ds.$$

If now we assume, as for (10.5.11), that each decrement in the multiple decrement context has a uniform distribution in each year of age, we have

$$2 \int_0^n v^t \, _tp_x^{(\tau)} \, \mu_x^{(1)}(t) \, dt = 2 \sum_{k=0}^{n-1} v^{k+1} \, _kp_x^{(\tau)} \, q_{x+k}^{(1)} \int_0^1 (1 + i)^{1-s} \, ds$$

$$= \frac{2i}{\delta} \sum_{k=0}^{n-1} v^{k+1} \, _kp_x^{(\tau)} \, q_{x+k}^{(1)}.$$

Applying a similar argument for the second integral and combining, we get

$$\bar{A} = \frac{i}{\delta} \left[\sum_{k=0}^{n-1} v^{k+1} \, _kp_x^{(\tau)}(\, (2q_{x+k}^{(1)} + q_{x+k}^{(2)}) \right]$$

$$= \frac{i}{\delta} \sum_{k=0}^{n-1} v^{k+1} \, _kp_x^{(\tau)} \, (q_{x+k}^{(1)} + q_{x+k}^{(\tau)})$$

$$= \bar{A}_{x:\overline{n}|}^{1\,(1)} + \bar{A}_{x:\overline{n}|}^1, \tag{11.2.3}$$

where $\bar{A}_{x:\overline{n}|}^{1\,(1)}$ is the actuarial present value of term insurance benefits of 1 covering death from accidental means and $\bar{A}_{x:\overline{n}|}^1$ is the actuarial present value for term insurance benefits of 1 covering death from all causes. Here $_kp_x^{(\tau)}$ could be taken as the survival function from a mortality table. If values of $q_{x+k}^{(1)}$ are available, it would be unnecessary to develop the full double decrement table in order to calculate (11.2.3) under the assumption that each decrement has a uniform distribution in each year of age.

This example is simple because the benefit amount does not change as a function of age at decrement, and, in particular, it does not change within a year of age. For a contrasting example, we take $B_{x+t}^{(1)} = t$ and $B_{x+t}^{(2)} = 0$ for $t > 0$. In this case,

$$\bar{A} = \int_0^\infty t \, v^t \, _tp_x^{(\tau)} \, \mu_x^{(1)}(t) \, dt = \sum_{k=0}^\infty v^k \, _kp_x^{(\tau)} \int_0^1 (k + s)v^s \, _sp_{x+k}^{(\tau)} \, \mu_x^{(1)}(k + s) \, ds.$$

We again make the assumption that each decrement in the multiple decrement context has a uniform distribution in each year of age, and we obtain

$$\bar{A} = \sum_{k=0}^\infty v^{k+1} \, _kp_x^{(\tau)} \, q_{x+k}^{(1)} \int_0^1 (k + s)(1 + i)^{1-s} \, ds$$

$$= \sum_{k=0}^\infty v^{k+1} \, _kp_x^{(\tau)} \, q_{x+k}^{(1)} \frac{i}{\delta} \left(k + \frac{1}{\delta} - \frac{1}{i} \right). \tag{11.2.4}$$

In practice, $B_{x+t}^{(j)}$ is often a complicated function, possibly requiring some degree of approximation. For such a case, if we apply the uniform distribution assumption to the j-th integral in (11.2.1), we obtain

$$\sum_{k=0}^\infty v^{k+1} \, _kp_x^{(\tau)} \, q_{x+k}^{(j)} \int_0^1 B_{x+k+s}^{(j)} (1 + i)^{1-s} \, ds.$$

Then, use of the midpoint integration rule yields

$$\sum_{k=0}^\infty v^{k+1/2} \, _kp_x^{(\tau)} \, q_{x+k}^{(j)} \, B_{x+k+1/2}^{(j)} \tag{11.2.5}$$

as a practical formula for the evaluation of the integral.

As an example, we return to (11.2.4) where the quantity

$$k + \frac{1}{\delta} - \frac{1}{i}$$

can be viewed as an effective mean benefit amount for the year $k + 1$, and the familiar i/δ term can be viewed as the correction needed to provide immediate payment of claims. The value given by (11.2.4) is closely approximated by

$$\sum_{k=0}^{\infty} v^{k+1/2} \, {}_k p_x^{(\tau)} \, q_{x+k}^{(j)} \left(k + \frac{1}{2} \right), \qquad (11.2.6)$$

which makes use of the midpoint rule for approximate integration to evaluate

$$\int_0^1 (k + s)(1 + i)^{1-s} \, ds.$$

In Section 10.6 we discussed situations where a uniform distribution of decrement assumption was not appropriate. For such situations, special adjustments to the actuarial present value should be made. We reexamine Example 10.6.3 where, in the associated single decrement model for decrement (3), one-half the expected withdrawals occur at midyear and the other half occur at year end. The actuarial present value for withdrawal benefits is given by

$$\bar{A} = \sum_{k=0}^{\infty} v^k \, {}_k p_x^{(\tau)} \left[\frac{1}{2} q_{x+k}'^{(3)} \, v^{1/2} \, B_{x+k+1/2}^{(3)} \left(1 - \frac{1}{2} q_{x+k}'^{(1)} \right) \left(1 - \frac{1}{2} q_{x+k}'^{(2)} \right) \right.$$

$$\left. + \frac{1}{2} q_{x+k}'^{(3)} \, v \, B_{x+k+1}^{(3)} (1 - q_{x+k}'^{(1)})(1 - q_{x+k}'^{(2)}) \right].$$

Here we are dealing with the distribution of decrement in the context of the associated single decrement tables, rather than in the multiple decrement context. A possible approximation would be to use a geometric average value of the interest factor in the year of withdrawal, such as $v^{3/4}$, and the arithmetic average value of the withdrawal benefit, such as

$$\hat{B}_{x+k}^{(3)} = \frac{1}{2} \left(B_{x+k+1/2}^{(3)} + B_{x+k+1}^{(3)} \right).$$

Thus,

$$\bar{A} \cong \sum_{k=0}^{\infty} v^{k+3/4} \, {}_k p_x^{(\tau)} \, \hat{B}_{x+k}^{(3)} \left[\frac{1}{2} q_{x+k}'^{(3)} \left(1 - \frac{1}{2} q_{x+k}'^{(1)} \right) \left(1 - \frac{1}{2} q_{x+k}'^{(2)} \right) \right.$$

$$\left. + \frac{1}{2} q_{x+k}'^{(3)} (1 - q_{x+k}'^{(1)})(1 - q_{x+k}'^{(2)}) \right]$$

$$= \sum_{k=0}^{\infty} v^{k+3/4} \, {}_k p_x^{(\tau)} \, q_{x+k}^{(3)} \, \hat{B}_{x+k}^{(3)}.$$

Remark:

In this section we have not used the format employed in Chapter 6 to state premium determination problems. This was done to achieve brevity. The premium problems of this section could have been approached by formulating a loss function and invoking the equivalence principle or some other premium principle.

Assume, for example, an insurance to (x) paying

a. $2B$ upon death due to an accident before age r
b. B upon death due to all other causes before age r, and
c. B upon death after age r.

Two causes of decrement are recognized, $J = 1$, the accidental cause, and $J = 2$, the nonaccidental cause. The loss function is

$$ L = \begin{cases} 2Bv^T - \pi & J = 1 & 0 < T \le r - x \\ Bv^T - \pi & J = 2 & 0 < T \le r - x \\ Bv^T - \pi & J = 1, 2 & T > r - x. \end{cases} $$

The equivalence principle requires that $E[L] = 0$, or

$$ \pi = B \left[\int_0^{r-x} v^t \, {}_tp_x^{(\tau)} \, \mu_x^{(1)}(t) \, dt + \int_0^\infty v^t \, {}_tp_x^{(\tau)} \, \mu_x^{(\tau)}(t) \, dt \right]. $$

A measure of the dispersion due to the random natures of time and cause of death is provided by $\text{Var}(L) = E[L^2]$. One can verify that, for this case,

$$ \text{Var}(L) = B^2 \left[3 \int_0^{r-x} v^{2t} \, {}_tp_x^{(\tau)} \, \mu_x^{(1)}(t) \, dt + \int_0^\infty v^{2t} \, {}_tp_x^{(\tau)} \, \mu_x^{(\tau)}(t) \, dt \right] - \pi^2. $$

In the general case, with actuarial present value given by (11.2.1), we have

$$ \text{Var}(L) = E[L^2] = \sum_{j=1}^m \int_0^\infty (B_{x+t}^{(j)} \, v^t - \bar{A})^2 \, {}_tp_x^{(\tau)} \, \mu_x^{(j)}(t) \, dt, $$

which can be reduced to

$$ \text{Var}(L) = \sum_{j=1}^m \int_0^\infty (B_{x+t}^{(j)} \, v^t)^2 \, {}_tp_x^{(\tau)} \, \mu_{x(t)}^{(j)} \, dt - (\bar{A})^2. \tag{11.2.7} $$

11.3 Benefit Premiums and Reserves

We examine, in this section, a method of paying for benefits included in a life insurance policy in a multiple decrement setting. Often these extra benefits are included in life insurance contracts on a policy rider basis; that is, a specified extra premium is charged for the extra benefit, and a separate reserve is held for this benefit. The extra premium is payable only for as long as the benefit has value. In the case of double indemnity it is common to pay the extra amount only for death from accidental means before a specific age, such as 65, and thus the specified extra premiums would be payable only until that age.

We henceforth consider the double indemnity benefit as such a benefit. The model is not complete because the possibility of withdrawal, with a corresponding withdrawal benefit, is not included. We consider withdrawal benefits in Section 11.4, but most of this subject is discussed in Chapters 15 and 16.

Consider the fully discrete model for a whole life policy to a person age 30 with a double indemnity rider. The benefit amount is one for nonaccidental death, decrement $J = 1$, and is two for death by accidental means, decrement $J = 2$. The principle of equivalence is now applied twice, once for the premium payable for life for the policy without the rider and once for the premium payable to age 65 for the extra benefit payable on accidental death before age 65.

For the policy without the rider the benefit level is one under either decrement 1 or 2 and the premium is payable for life. Thus

$$P_{30}^{(\tau)} = \frac{\sum_{k=0}^{\infty} v^{k+1} \, {}_k p_{30}^{(\tau)} \, q_{30+k}^{(\tau)}}{\sum_{k=0}^{\infty} v^k \, {}_k p_{30}^{(\tau)}}. \tag{11.3.1}$$

The benefit premium for the rider reflects that the premium is payable through age 64, and its benefit amount, payable under decrement 2 only, is unity. It is given by

$$_{35}P_{30}^{(2)} = \frac{\sum_{k=0}^{34} v^{k+1} \, {}_k p_{30}^{(\tau)} \, q_{30+k}^{(2)}}{\sum_{k=0}^{34} v^k \, {}_k p_{30}^{(\tau)}}. \tag{11.3.2}$$

We now display the benefit reserve for the policy with the rider for years prior to attaining age 65:

$$_kV = \sum_{h=0}^{\infty} v^{h+1} \, {}_h p_{30+k}^{(\tau)} \, q_{30+k+h}^{(\tau)} + \sum_{h=0}^{34-k} v^{h+1} \, {}_h p_{30+k}^{(\tau)} \, q_{30+k+h}^{(2)}$$

$$- \left(P_{30}^{(\tau)} \sum_{h=0}^{\infty} v^h \, {}_h p_{30+k}^{(\tau)} + {}_{35}P_{30}^{(2)} \sum_{h=0}^{34-k} v^h \, {}_h p_{30+k}^{(\tau)} \right).$$

This reserve is the sum of a reserve on the base policy plus a reserve on a policy that pays only on failure through decrement 2. The reserve on the base policy is a Chapter 7 benefit reserve for a fully discrete whole life insurance with $q_x = q_x^{(\tau)} = q_x^{(1)} + q_x^{(2)}$.

11.4 Withdrawal Benefit Patterns That Can Be Ignored in Evaluating Premiums and Reserves

A single decrement model for an individual life insurance benefit with annual premiums and reserves was built in Chapters 6 through 8. In that model the timing and, perhaps, the amount of benefit payments are determined by the time of death of the insured, and premiums are paid until death or the end of the premium period as specified in the policy. In practice, there is no way to prevent the cessation of premium payments by the policyholder before death or the end of the premium period. In this situation an issue arises about how to reconcile the interests of the parties to the policy for which a model derived from multiple decrement theory is appropriate. Public policy considerations that should guide the reconciliation of the interests of the insurance system and the terminating insured have been subject to discussion since the early days of insurance.

Before premiums and reserves can be determined, a guiding principle must be adopted. A guiding principle is required as well in the determination of *nonforfeiture benefits,* those benefits that will not be lost because of the premature cessation of premium payments. In this section we adopt a simple operational principle, one that is, in effect, close to that adopted in U.S. insurance regulation. The principle is that the withdrawing insured receives a value such that the benefit, premium, and reserve structure, built using the single decrement model, remains appropriate in the multiple decrement context.

This principle is motivated by a particular concept of equity about the treatment of the two classes of policyholders, those who terminate before the basic insurance contract is fulfilled and those who continue. Clearly several concepts of what constitutes equity are possible, ranging from the view that terminating policyholders have not fulfilled the contract, and are therefore not entitled to nonforfeiture benefits, to the view that a terminating policyholder should be returned to his original position by the return of the accumulated value of all premiums, perhaps less an insurance charge. The concept of equity, which is the foundation of the principle adopted in the United States, is an intermediate one; that is, withdrawing life insurance policyholders are entitled to nonforfeiture benefits, but these benefits should not force a change in the price-benefit structure for continuing policyholders.

To illustrate some of the implications of this principle, we will develop a model for a whole life policy on a fully continuous payment basis with death and withdrawal benefits. The force of withdrawal is denoted by $\mu_x^{(2)}(t)$ with $\mu_x^{(\tau)}(t) = \mu_x^{(1)}(t) + \mu_x^{(2)}(t)$. For multiple decrement models, it is required that

$$\int_0^\infty \mu_{x+t}^{(\tau)}\, dt = \infty$$

so that

$$\lim_{t\to\infty} {}_tp_x^{(\tau)} = 0,$$

but it is not necessary for $\mu_x^{(2)}(t)$ and the derived ${}_tp_x'^{(2)}$ to have these properties.

We assume that the introduction of withdrawals into the model does not change the force of mortality, which is labeled for this development $\mu_x^{(1)}(t)$ in both the single and double decrement models. In other words, time-until-death and time-until-withdrawal will be assumed to be independent, but this assumption may not be realized in practice. This issue was discussed in Chapter 10.

We start our model by specializing (8.6.4) to the case of a whole life insurance and single decrement premiums and reserves:

$$\frac{d}{dt} \, {}_t\bar{V}(\bar{A}_x) = \bar{P}(\bar{A}_x) + \delta \, {}_t\bar{V}(\bar{A}_x) - \mu_x^{(1)}(t) \, [1 - {}_t\bar{V}(\bar{A}_x)]. \tag{11.4.1}$$

Recalling from Section 10.2 that

$$\frac{d}{dt} \, {}_tp_x^{(\tau)} = -{}_tp_x^{(\tau)}[\mu_x^{(1)}(t) + \mu_x^{(2)}(t)],$$

we can express the following derivative as

$$\frac{d}{dt} \, [v^t \, {}_tp_x^{(\tau)} \, {}_t\bar{V}(\bar{A}_x)] = v^t \, {}_tp_x^{(\tau)}\{\bar{P}(\bar{A}_x) + \delta \, {}_t\bar{V}(\bar{A}_x) - \mu_x^{(1)}(t)[1 - {}_t\bar{V}(\bar{A}_x)]\}$$

$$- v^t \, {}_tp_x^{(\tau)} \, {}_t\bar{V}(\bar{A}_x)[\delta + \mu_x^{(1)}(t) + \mu_x^{(2)}(t)]$$

$$= v^t \, {}_tp_x^{(\tau)}[\bar{P}(\bar{A}_x) - \mu_x^{(1)}(t) - \mu_x^{(2)}(t) \, {}_t\bar{V}(\bar{A}_x)]. \tag{11.4.2}$$

The progress of the reserves for a whole life insurance that includes withdrawal benefit ${}_t\bar{V}(\bar{A}_x)$ using premiums and reserves derived from a double decrement model is analogous to (11.4.1) and is shown in (11.4.3). In this expression, the superscript ^{2} denotes premiums and reserves based on the double decrement model:

$$\frac{d}{dt} \, [{}_t\bar{V}(\bar{A}_x)^{\underline{2}}] = \bar{P}(\bar{A}_x)^{\underline{2}} + \delta \, {}_t\bar{V}(\bar{A}_x)^{\underline{2}}$$

$$- \mu_x^{(1)}(t)[1 - {}_t\bar{V}(\bar{A}_x)^{\underline{2}}] - \mu_x^{(2)}(t)[{}_t\bar{V}(\bar{A}_x) - {}_t\bar{V}(\bar{A}_x)^{\underline{2}}]. \tag{11.4.3}$$

The last term in (11.4.3) is the net cost of withdrawal when the reserve ${}_t\bar{V}(\bar{A}_x)^{\underline{2}}$ is treated as a savings fund available to offset benefits [see (8.4.5)]. Thus,

$$\frac{d}{dt} \, [v^t \, {}_tp_x^{(\tau)} \, {}_t\bar{V}(\bar{A}_x)^{\underline{2}}] = v^t \, {}_tp_x^{(\tau)} \{\bar{P}(\bar{A}_x)^{\underline{2}} + \delta \, {}_t\bar{V}(\bar{A}_x)^{\underline{2}} - \mu_x^{(1)}(t)[1 - {}_t\bar{V}(\bar{A}_x)^{\underline{2}}]$$

$$- \mu_{x+t}^{(2)}[{}_t\bar{V}(\bar{A}_x) - {}_t\bar{V}(\bar{A}_x)^{\underline{2}}]\}$$

$$- v^t \, {}_tp_x^{(\tau)} \, {}_t\bar{V}(\bar{A}_x)^{\underline{2}} [\delta + \mu_x^{(1)}(t) + \mu_x^{(2)}(t)]$$

$$= v^t \, {}_tp_x^{(\tau)}[\bar{P}(\bar{A}_x)^{\underline{2}} - \mu_x^{(1)}(t) - \mu_x^{(2)}(t) \, {}_t\bar{V}(\bar{A}_x)]. \tag{11.4.4}$$

Combining (11.4.2) and (11.4.4), we obtain

$$\frac{d}{dt} \, \{v^t \, {}_tp_x^{(\tau)}[{}_t\bar{V}(\bar{A}_x)^{\underline{2}} - {}_t\bar{V}(\bar{A}_x)]\} = v^t \, {}_tp_x^{(\tau)}[\bar{P}(\bar{A}_x)^{\underline{2}} - \bar{P}(\bar{A}_x)]. \tag{11.4.5}$$

We now integrate (11.4.5) from $t = 0$ to $t = \infty$ to obtain

$$0 = \bar{a}_x^{(\tau)}[\bar{P}(\bar{A}_x)^{\underline{2}} - \bar{P}(\bar{A}_x)], \tag{11.4.6}$$

which implies that

$$\bar{P}(\bar{A}_x)^2 = \bar{P}(\bar{A}_x).$$

Thus (11.4.5) reduces to

$$\frac{d}{dt}\{v^t \, {}_tp_x^{(\tau)}[{}_t\bar{V}(\bar{A}_x)^2 - {}_t\bar{V}(\bar{A}_x)]\} = 0,$$

which, with the initial condition that

$${}_0\bar{V}(\bar{A}_x)^2 = {}_0\bar{V}(\bar{A}_x),$$

implies that

$${}_t\bar{V}(\bar{A}_x)^2 = {}_t\bar{V}(\bar{A}_x) \qquad \text{for all } t \geq 0. \tag{11.4.7}$$

Therefore, if the withdrawal benefit in a double decrement model whole life insurance, fully continuous payment basis, is equal to the reserve under the single decrement model, the premium and reserves under the double decrement model are equal to the premium and reserves under the single decrement model. This result is not directly applied to the practical problem of defining nonforfeiture benefits. However, it does suggest the basic idea of how to minimize the impact of withdrawal or nonforfeiture benefits on premiums and reserves (determined under a single decrement model). These ideas are developed further in Chapter 16.

The ideas of this section are closely related to Example 6.6.2, where it was demonstrated that if the death benefit during the premium-paying period for a deferred life annuity is the accumulated value of the premiums, then the premium does not depend on the mortality assumption during the deferral period. This idea is elaborated in Example 11.4.1.

Example 11.4.1

A continuously paid life annuity issued on (x) provides an income benefit commencing at age $x + n$ at an annual rate of 1. The benefit for death (decrement $J = 1$) or withdrawal (decrement $J = 2$) during the n-year deferral period, paid at the moment of death, will be the accumulated benefit premiums with interest at the rate used in the premium calculation. Premiums are paid continuously from age x to $x + n$ or to the age of decrement, if less than $x + n$. Assume that there are no withdrawals after the commencement of the annuity payments.
a. Formulate a loss variable.
b. Determine the annual benefit premium rate π using the principle of equivalence.
c. Determine the benefit reserve at time t, $0 \leq t \leq n$.

Solution:

a.
$$L = \begin{cases} \pi \, v^T \, \bar{s}_{\overline{T}|} - \pi \, \bar{a}_{\overline{T}|} & 0 \leq T \leq n, \quad J = 1, 2 \\ v^n \, \bar{a}_{\overline{T-n}|} - \pi \, \bar{a}_{\overline{n}|} & T > n, \qquad J = 1. \end{cases}$$

b. Applying the principle of equivalence, we obtain

$$\text{E}[L] = \int_n^\infty (v^n \, \bar{a}_{\overline{T-n}|} - \pi \, \bar{a}_{\overline{n}|}) \, {}_tp_x^{(\tau)} \, \mu_x^{(1)}(t) \, dt.$$

This yields

$$v^n \; _np_x^{(\tau)} \; \bar{a}_{x+n} = \pi \; \bar{a}_{\overline{n}|} \; _np_x^{(\tau)} \quad \text{and} \quad \pi = \frac{v^n \; \bar{a}_{x+n}}{\bar{a}_{\overline{n}|}} = \frac{\bar{a}_{x+n}}{\bar{s}_{\overline{n}|}}.$$

c. The reserve at time t, $t \leq n$, viewed prospectively, is given by

$$\int_0^{n-t} (\pi \; v^s \; \bar{s}_{\overline{t+s}|} - \pi \; \bar{a}_{\overline{s}|}) \; _sp_{x+t}^{(\tau)} \; \mu_x^{(\tau)}(t+s) \; ds$$

$$+ \int_{n-t}^{\infty} (v^{n-t} \; \bar{a}_{\overline{s-(n-t)}|} - \pi \; \bar{a}_{\overline{n-t}|}) \; _sp_{x+t}^{(\tau)} \; \mu_x^{(1)}(t+s) \; ds$$

$$= \pi \; \bar{s}_{\overline{t}|}(1 - \; _{n-t}p_{x+t}^{(\tau)}) + \; _{n-t}|\bar{a}_{x+t} - \pi \; \bar{a}_{\overline{n-t}|} \; _{n-t}p_{x+t}^{(\tau)}$$

$$= \pi \; \bar{s}_{\overline{t}|}.$$

The simplification of the last term comes from the definition of π in part (b). The benefit premium and reserve during the deferred period can be viewed as derived from a zero decrement model. ▼

11.5 Valuation of Pension Plans

Two sets of assumptions are needed to determine the actuarial present values of pension plan benefits and of contributions to support these benefits. These sets can be identified as demographic (the service table and survival functions for retired lives, disabled lives, and perhaps lives who have withdrawn) and economic (investment return and salary scale) assumptions.

11.5.1 Demographic Assumptions

A starting point for the valuation of pension plan benefits is a multiple decrement (service) table constructed to represent a survivorship group of participants subject, in the various years of active service, to given probabilities of
- Withdrawal from service
- Death in service
- Retirement for disability, and
- Retirement for age-service.

The notations for these probabilities for the year of age x to $x + 1$ are $q_x^{(w)}$, $q_x^{(d)}$, $q_x^{(i)}$, and $q_x^{(r)}$, respectively. These are consistent with the notations developed in Chapter 10. Also, we use the survivorship function $l_x^{(\tau)}$ from Chapter 10, which satisfies

$$l_{x+1}^{(\tau)} = l_x^{(\tau)}[1 - (q_x^{(w)} + q_x^{(d)} + q_x^{(i)} + q_x^{(r)})] = l_x^{(\tau)} \; p_x^{(\tau)}.$$

This function can be used to evaluate such expression as $_kp_x^{(\tau)}$, thus,

$$_kp_x^{(\tau)} = \frac{l_{x+k}^{(\tau)}}{l_x^{(\tau)}}.$$

One can also proceed by direct recursion, namely,

$$_kp_x^{(\tau)} = {}_{k-1}p_x^{(\tau)}\ p_{x+k-1}^{(\tau)}.$$

The forces of decrement related to a service table will be continuous at most ages. They will be denoted by $\mu_x^{(w)}(t)$, $\mu_x^{(d)}(t)$, $\mu_x^{(i)}(t)$, and $\mu_x^{(r)}(t)$. At some ages, discontinuities may occur. This occurs most frequently at age α, the first eligible age for retirement. We generally assume that decrements are spread across each year of age.

In the early years of service, withdrawal rates tend to be high, and the benefit for withdrawal may be only the participant's contributions, if any, possibly accumulated with interest. After a period of time, for example, 5 years, withdrawal rates will be somewhat lower, and the withdrawing participant may be eligible for a deferred pension. If these conditions hold, it may be necessary to use select rates of withdrawal for an appropriate number of years. Conditions for disability retirement may also indicate a need for a select basis. The mathematical modifications to a select basis are relatively easy to make, and the theory is more adaptable if select functions are used. In this chapter we denote the age of entry by x, but we do not otherwise indicate whether an aggregate table, select table, or select-and-ultimate table is intended.

The Illustrative Service Table in Appendix 2B illustrates a service table for entry age 30, earliest age for retirement $\alpha = 60$, and with no probability of active service beyond age 71. Here $l_{71}^{(\tau)} = 0$.

As noted earlier, the principal benefits under a pension plan are annuities to eligible beneficiaries. For the valuation of such annuity benefits, it is necessary to adopt appropriate mortality tables that will differ if retirement is for disability, for age-service, or perhaps withdrawal. The corresponding annuity values will be indicated by post-fixed superscripts. The continuous annuity value is used as a convenient means of approximating the actual form of pension payment that usually is monthly, but may have particular conditions as to initial and final payments.

11.5.2 Projecting Benefit Payment and Contribution Rates

A common form of pension plan is one that defines the rate of retirement income by formula. These plans are called ***defined benefit plans.*** Some pension plans define benefit income rates as a function of the level of compensation at or near retirement. In these cases, it is necessary to estimate future salaries to value the benefits. Sponsor contributions are also often expressed as a percentage of salary, so here too estimation of future salaries is important. To accomplish these estimations, we define the following salary functions:

$(AS)_{x+h}$ is the actual annual salary rate at age $x + h$, for a participant who entered at age x and is now at attained age $x + h$,

$(ES)_{x+h+t}$ is the projected (estimated) annual salary rate at age $x + h + t$.

Further, we assume that we have a salary scale function S_y to use for these projections, such that

$$(ES)_{x+h+t} = (AS)_{x+h} \frac{S_{x+h+t}}{S_{x+h}}. \tag{11.5.1}$$

The salary functions S_y may reflect merit and seniority increases in salary as well as those caused by inflation. For example, in the Illustrative Service Table, $S_y = (1.06)^{y-30} s_y$, where the s_y factor represents the progression of salary due to individual merit and experience increases, and the 6% accumulation factor is to allow for long-term effects of inflation and of increases in productivity of all members of the plan. As was the case of the $l_x^{(\tau)}$ function, one of the values of S_y can be chosen arbitrarily. For instance, in the Illustrative Service Table, S_{30} is taken as unity. The S_y function is usually assumed to be a step function, with constant level throughout any given year of age.

We now move to the problem of estimating the benefit level for a pension plan. For this purpose, we introduce the function $R(x, h, t)$ to denote the projected annual income benefit rate to commence at age $x + h + t$ for a participant, who entered h years ago at age x. Both x and h are assumed to be integers. We assume that the income benefit rate remains level during payout so that when we come to expressing the actuarial present value of the benefit at time of retirement, it will simply be $R(x, h, t)\bar{a}_{x+h+t}^r$. As stated in the previous section, the post-fixed superscript r indicates that a mortality table appropriate for retired lives should be used.

We now consider several common types of income benefit rate functions $R(x, h, t)$. The estimation procedure falls into two groups. First, there are functions that do not depend on salary levels. For other types of benefit formulas, which depend on future salaries, the projected annual income rate must be estimated. There are those that depend on either the final salary rate or on an average salary rate over the last several years prior to retirement. There are also formulas that depend on the average salary over the career with the plan sponsor. The following are examples of the more common types of benefit formula together with their estimation.

a. Consider an income benefit rate that is a fraction d of the final salary rate. Thus $R(x, h, t) = d(ES)_{x+h+t}$. Here we estimate the final salary from the current salary at age $x + h$ by $(ES)_{x+h+t} = (AS)_{x+h}(S_{x+h+t}/S_{x+h})$ so that $R(x, h, t) = d(AS)_{x+h}(S_{x+h+t}/S_{x+h})$.

b. A *final m-year average salary benefit* rate is a fraction d of the average salary rate over the last m years prior to retirement. We illustrate this in the common case where $m = 5$. In this case, if $t > 5$, an estimate of the average salary over the last 5 years is given as

$$(AS)_{x+h} \frac{0.5\, S_{x+h+k-5} + S_{x+h+k-4} + S_{x+h+k-3} + S_{x+h+k-2} + S_{x+h+k-1} + 0.5\, S_{x+h+k}}{5\, S_{x+h}}$$

where k is the greatest integer in t.

The thinking behind this expression is that if retirement occurs at midyear, the current year's salary is earned only for the last half year of service. A notation in common usage for the above average is $_5Z_{x+h+k}/S_{x+h}$. If the participant is within 5 years of possible retirement, account could be taken of actual rather than projected salaries.

The above formulas do not reflect the amount of service of the participant at retirement. We now look at three formulas where the benefits are proportional to the number of years of service at retirement.

c. Consider an income benefit that is d times the total number of years of service, including any fraction in the final year of employment. In this case $R(x, h, t) = d(h + t)$. If only whole years of service are to be counted, then $R(x, h, t) = d(h + k)$, where k is the greatest integer in t.

d. Consider an income benefit rate that is the product of a fraction d of the final 5-year average salary and the number of years of service at retirement. A typical formula would be, where d is a designated fraction,

$$= d(h + t)(AS)_{x+h} \frac{_5Z_{x+h+k}}{S_{x+h}}.$$

Again, if the participant is within 5 years of possible retirement, account could be taken of actual rather than projected salaries.

e. Consider an income benefit rate that is d times the number of years of service times the average salary over the entire career. Such a benefit formula is called a *career average benefit.* This formula is equivalent to a benefit rate of a fraction d of the entire career earnings of the retiree.

The analysis of career average retirement benefits breaks naturally into two parts, one for past service for which the salary information is known and one for future service where salaries must be estimated. Here past salaries enter into the valuation of benefits for all participants and not just for those participants very near to retirement age. If the total of past salaries for a participant at age $x + h$ is denoted by $(TPS)_{x+h}$, the benefit rate attributed to past service is $d(TPS)_{x+h}$. The retirement income benefit rate based on future service is given by

$$d(AS)_{x+h} \frac{S_{x+h} + S_{x+h+1} + \cdots + S_{x+h+k-1} + 0.5\ S_{x+h+k}}{S_{x+h}},$$

where k is the greatest integer in t and retirements are assumed to occur at midyear.

Finally, we display one benefit formula where the service component for participants with a large number of years of service at retirement is modified.

f. Consider an income benefit rate that is the product of the 3-year final average salary and 0.02 times the number of years of service at retirement for the first 30 years of service with an additional 0.01 per year of service above 30 years. Following (d),

$$= 0.02\ (h + t)\ (AS)_{x+h} \frac{_3Z_{x+h+k}}{S_{x+h}} \qquad h + t \le 30$$

$$= [0.30 + 0.01\ (h + t)]\ (AS)_{x+h} \frac{_3Z_{x+h+k}}{S_{x+h}} \quad h + t > 30.$$

11.5.3 Defined-Benefit Plans

We now seek to develop formulas for actuarial present values of such benefits and of the contributions expected to be used to fund the promised benefits. We do so first for a general case of a defined-benefit plan and then examine a specific example that includes a typical pattern of defined benefits.

Let us first look at the evaluation of, and approximation to, the actuarial present value for an age-retirement benefit. Assume that the benefit rate function has been found as $R(x, h, t)$ and that the benefit involves life annuities with no certain period. We can then write an integral expression for the actuarial present value of the retirement benefit as

$$\text{APV} = \int_{\alpha-x-h}^{\infty} v^t \, {}_tp_{x+h}^{(\tau)} \, \mu_x^{(r)}(h + t) \, R(x, h, t) \, \bar{a}_{x+h+t}^r \, dt. \qquad (11.5.2)$$

As in Section 11.2, we approximate the integral for practical calculation of the actuarial present value. To do so, we write

$$\text{APV} = \sum_{k=\alpha-x-h}^{\infty} v^k \, {}_kp_{x+h}^{(\tau)} \int_0^1 v^s \, {}_sp_{x+h+k}^{(\tau)} \, \mu_x^{(r)}(h + k + s) \, R(x, h, k + s) \, \bar{a}_{x+h+k+s}^r \, ds.$$

By assuming a uniform distribution of retirements in each year of age, we can rewrite this as

$$\text{APV} = \sum_{k=\alpha-x-h}^{\infty} v^k \, {}_kp_{x+h}^{(\tau)} \, q_{x+h+k}^{(r)} \int_0^1 v^s \, R(x, h, k + s) \, \bar{a}_{x+h+k+s}^r \, ds.$$

Using the midpoint approximation for the remaining integrals gives

$$\text{APV} = \sum_{k=\alpha-x-h}^{\infty} v^{k+1/2} \, {}_kp_{x+h}^{(\tau)} \, q_{x+h+k}^{(r)} \, R(x, h, k + 1/2) \, \bar{a}_{x+h+k+1/2}^r. \qquad (11.5.3)$$

Formula (11.5.3) is the general means by which we calculate the actuarial present value of retirement and, by extension, other benefits of a pension plan.

We now present an example that shows the types of calculations that might be used for the valuation of the several benefits of a hypothetical defined-benefit pension plan.

Example 11.5.1

Find the actuarial present values of the following benefits for a participant who was hired 3 years ago at age 30 and who currently has a salary of $45,000.

a. Retirement income for any participant of at least age 65 or whenever the sum of the attained age and the number of years of service exceeds a total of 90. The benefit is in the form of a 10-year certain and life annuity, payable monthly, at an annual rate of 0.02 times the final 5-year average salary times the total number of years of service, including any final fraction.

b. Retirement income for any participant with at least 5 years of service upon withdrawal. The benefit and income benefit rate formula is as for age retirement. However, the initial payment of the annuity is deferred until the earliest possible date of age retirement had the participant continued in the active status.

c. Retirement income for those disabled participants too young for age retirement. The income benefit rate is the larger of 50% or the percentage based on years of service, uses the average salary over the preceding 5 years, and is for a 10-year certain and life annuity.

d. Lump sum benefit for those participants who die while still in active status. The benefit amount is two times the salary rate at the time of death.

Solution:

The participant was hired at age 30 and so is eligible for retirement at age 60 $[60 + (60 - 30) = 90]$. Assuming midyear retirements, the income benefit rate is given by

$$= 0.02 \ (h \ + \ t) \ (AS)_{x+h} \ \frac{_5Z_{x+h+k}}{S_{x+h}}$$

$$= 0.02 \ (3 \ + \ k \ + \ 0.5) \ (45{,}000) \ \frac{_5Z_{30+3+k}}{S_{30+3}}$$

for retirements starting in the year following age $33 + k$. The actuarial present value of age-retirement benefits is approximated by

$$\text{APV} = 900 \ \sum_{k=27}^{\infty} v^{k+1/2} \ {}_kp^{(\tau)}_{30+3} \ q^{(r)}_{30+3+k}$$

$$\times \ (3.5 \ + \ k) \ \frac{_5Z_{30+3+k}}{S_{30+3}} \ \ddot{a}^r_{33+k+1/2:\overline{10}|}.$$

Benefits are paid for those withdrawing from active status between ages 35 and 60. After attaining age 60, the withdrawals are classified as retirements. The income benefit rate is again given by

$$= 0.02 \ (h \ + \ t) \ (AS)_{x+h} \ \frac{_5Z_{x+h+k}}{S_{x+h}}$$

$$= 0.02 \ (3 \ + \ k \ + \ 0.5) \ (45{,}000) \ \frac{_5Z_{30+3+k}}{S_{30+3}}.$$

For withdrawals at ages 35 through 37, adjustments using actual wage data rather than the Z function could be made. The actuarial present value of the withdrawal benefits is approximated by

$$\text{APV} = 900 \ \sum_{k=2}^{26} v^{k+1/2} \ {}_kp^{(\tau)}_{30+3} \ q^{(w)}_{30+3+k}$$

$$\times \ (3.5 \ + \ k) \ \frac{_5Z_{30+3+k}}{S_{30+3}} \ {}_{27-k-1/2|}\ddot{a}^w_{33+k+1/2:\overline{10}|}.$$

For the disability benefit the income benefit rate function makes a distinction between disabilities starting before and after the participant has worked for 25 years. Thus the income benefit rate is

$$= 0.5 \, (AS)_{x+h} \frac{_5 Z_{x+h+k}}{S_{x+h}} = 0.5 \, (45{,}000) \frac{_5 Z_{30+3+k}}{S_{30+3}} \qquad \text{for } 0 \le k \le 21$$

$$= 0.02 \, (h+t) \, (AS)_{x+h} \frac{_5 Z_{x+h+k}}{S_{x+h}} = 0.02 \, (3+k+0.5) \, (45{,}000) \frac{_5 Z_{30+3+k}}{S_{30+3}}$$

$$\text{for } 22 \le k \le 26.$$

Thus, the actuarial present value of the disability benefits is approximated by

$$\text{APV} = 22{,}500 \sum_{k=0}^{21} v^{k+1/2} \; _k p_{30+3}^{(\tau)} \; q_{30+3+k}^{(i)} \frac{_5 Z_{30+3+k}}{S_{30+3}} \, \bar{a}^{\,i}_{33+k+1/2:\overline{10|}}$$

$$+ 900 \sum_{k=22}^{26} v^{k+1/2} \; _k p_{30+3}^{(\tau)} \; q_{30+3+k}^{(i)} \frac{_5 Z_{30+3+k}}{S_{30+3}} \, (3.5+k) \, \bar{a}^{\,i}_{33+k+1/2:\overline{10|}}.$$

For the death benefit, the projected lump sum benefit amount is

$$= 2 \, (AS)_{x+h} \frac{S_{x+h+k}}{S_{x+h}}$$

$$= 2 \, (45{,}000) \frac{S_{30+3+k}}{S_{30+3}}.$$

Thus, the actuarial present value of the death benefits is approximated by

$$\text{APV} = 90{,}000 \sum_{k=0}^{\infty} v^{k+1/2} \; _k p_{30+3}^{(\tau)} \; q_{30+3+k}^{(d)} \frac{S_{30+3+k}}{S_{30+3}}. \qquad \blacktriangledown$$

There are many funding or budgeting methods available to assure that contributions are made to the plan in an orderly and appropriate manner. An overview of these methods is presented in Chapter 20.

11.5.4   Defined-Contribution Plans

The principal benefit under a pension plan is normally the deferred annuity for age-service retirement. In *defined-contribution plans,* the actuarial present value is simply the accumulation under interest of contributions made by or for the participant, and the benefit is an annuity that can be purchased by such accumulation. The accumulated amount is typically available upon death and, under certain conditions, upon withdrawal before retirement. We examine the interplay between the rate of contribution and the rate of income provided to the participant in the following example. The defined-contribution rate can be determined with a retirement income goal. The risk that the goal will not be achieved is held by the participant of the plan, not the sponsor. Budget constraints on the sponsor may, of course, restrict the amount of the contributions.

Example 11.5.2

Find the contribution level for the sponsor to provide for age-retirement at age 65 that has as its objective a 10-year certain and life annuity with an initial benefit rate of 50% of the average salary over the 5 years between ages 60 and 65. The contribution rate, which is to be applied as a proportion of salary, is calculated for a new participant at age 30. Assume that there are no withdrawal benefits for the first 5 years but after that the contributions accumulated with interest are vested, that is, become the property of the withdrawing participant, and will be applied toward an annuity to start no earlier than age 60. (An active participant who becomes disabled is treated as a withdrawal and is covered by a separate disability income coverage for the period between the date of disability and age 65 at which time a regular age retirement commences.) Upon death after the end of the 5-year vesting period but before retirement income has commenced, the accumulated contributions are paid out.

Solution:

We start by calculating the actuarial present value of a contribution rate of c times the annual salary rate, assumed for convenience to be 1, at age 30:

$$\text{APV} = c \left\{ \sum_{k=0}^{34} {}_k p_{30}^{(\tau)} \left(q_{30+k}^{(d)} + q_{30+k}^{(w)} \right) \left[\sum_{j=0}^{k} v^{j+1/2} \frac{S_{30+j}}{S_{30}} - \frac{v^{k+1/2} S_{30+k}}{2 S_{30}} \right] \right.$$

$$\left. + {}_{35} p_{30}^{(\tau)} \sum_{k=0}^{34} v^{k+1/2} \frac{S_{30+k}}{S_{30}} \right\}. \tag{11.5.4}$$

In (11.5.4) contributions are assumed to occur at midyear, and the projected salary rate at age $30 + k$ is (S_{30+k} / S_{30}) times 1, the initial salary at age 30.

We now estimate the desired benefit payment rate at age 65 as the first step in estimating the actuarial present value of the target benefits. The average salary projected to be earned between the ages of 60 and 65 is $(S_{60} + S_{61} + S_{62} + S_{63} + S_{64})/(5 S_{30})$. The desired benefit rate is one-half of this, and the actuarial present value of the target benefit is given by

$$\text{APV} = {}_{35} p_{30}^{(\tau)} v^{35} (0.5) \frac{S_{60} + S_{61} + S_{62} + S_{63} + S_{64}}{5 S_{30}} \bar{a}_{\overline{65:\overline{10}|}}^{r}. \tag{11.5.5}$$

This expression is the actuarial present value at age 30 of the new participant's target income benefit.

The actuarial present value of the vested benefit is given by

$$\text{APV} = c \left\{ \sum_{k=5}^{34} v^{k+1/2} {}_k p_{30}^{(\tau)} \left(q_{30+k}^{(d)} + q_{30+k}^{(w)} \right) \left[\sum_{j=0}^{k} (1+i)^{k-j} \frac{S_{30+j}}{S_{30}} - \frac{1}{2} \frac{S_{30+k}}{S_{30}} \right] \right\}. \tag{11.5.6}$$

The expression for the actuarial present value of contributions, (11.5.4), less the expression for the actuarial present value of vested benefits, (11.5.6), is

$$c \left\{ \sum_{k=0}^{4} {}_k p_{30}^{(\tau)} \left(q_{30+k}^{(d)} + q_{30+k}^{(w)} \right) \left[\sum_{j=0}^{k} v^{j+1/2} \frac{S_{30+j}}{S_{30}} - v^{k+1/2} \frac{S_{30+k}}{2S_{30}} \right] \right.$$

$$\left. + {}_{35} p_{30}^{(\tau)} \sum_{k=0}^{34} v^{k+1/2} \frac{S_{30+k}}{S_{30}} \right\}. \tag{11.5.7}$$

The benefits in this plan, after the 5 years when vesting occurs, are similar to those discussed in Example 11.4.1.

We now equate the two actuarial present values from (11.5.4) and (11.5.7) to solve for c, the sponsor's contribution rate, which will be applied to all future salary payment in accordance with the plan to achieve the stated retirement income goal. ▼

Some plans of this type have both sponsor and participant contributions. It is common here for some kind of matching between the size of the sponsor contribution and the size of the participant contribution.

11.6   Disability Benefits with Individual Life Insurance

In Section 11.5.3 we discuss disability benefits included in pension plans. We now turn to disability benefits commonly found with individual life insurance. Provision can be made for the waiver of life insurance premiums during periods of disability. Alternatively, policies can contain a provision for a monthly income, sometimes related to the face amount, if disability occurs. The multiple decrement model is appropriate for studying these provisions.

The usual disability clause provides a benefit for total disability. Total disability can require a disability severe enough to prevent engaging in any gainful occupation, or it can require only the inability to engage in one's own occupation. Total disability that has been continuous for a period of time specified in the policy, called the *waiting or elimination period,* qualifies the policyholder to receive benefit payments. The waiting period can be 1, 3, 6, or 12 months. In policies with waiver of premium, it is common to make the benefits *retroactive,* that is, to refund any premiums paid by the insured during the waiting periods. Coverage is only for disabilities that occur prior to a disability benefit expiry age, typically 60 or 65. However, benefits in the form of an annuity, either as disability income or as waiver or premiums, will often continue to a higher age, typically the maturity date or paid-up date of the life insurance policy.

11.6.1   Disability Income Benefits

Let us start by expressing the actuarial present value of a disability income benefit of 1,000 per month issued to (x) under coverage expiring at age y and with income running to age u. We assume that the waiting period is m months. Using notation from Chapter 10 and earlier sections of Chapter 11, we can express the actuarial present value as a definite integral as

$$\bar{A} = \int_0^{y-x} v^t \, {}_tp_x^{(\tau)} \, \mu_x^{(i)}(t) \, v^{m/12} \, {}_{m/12}p_{[x+t]}^i \left(12{,}000 \, \ddot{a}_{[x+t]+m/12:\overline{u-x-t-m/12}}^{(12)i}\right) dt. \quad (11.6.1)$$

The i superscript on ${}_{m/12}p_{[x+t]}^i$ indicates a survival probability for a disabled life. We now break up the integral into separate integrals for each year. Upon making the assumption of uniform distribution for the disability decrement within each year of age and replacing t by $k + s$, we obtain an expression for the actuarial present value much like (11.2.5):

$$\bar{A} = 12{,}000 \sum_{k=0}^{y-x-1} v^k \, {}_kp_x^{(\tau)} \, q_{x+k}^{(i)} \, v^{m/12}$$

$$\times \int_0^1 v^s \, {}_{m/12}p_{[x+k+s]}^i \, \ddot{a}_{[x+k+s]+m/12:\ \overline{u-x-k-s-m/12}}^{(12)i} \, ds. \quad (11.6.2)$$

A simplification of this formula occurs when the decrement i (disability) is defined to occur only if the person who is disabled survives to the end of the waiting period of m months. If death occurs during the waiting period, the decrement is regarded as death. This means that the disabled life survivorship factor, ${}_{m/12}p_{[x+k+s]}^i$, is unnecessary as it has been taken into account in the definition of $q_{x+k}^{(i)}$. We note that it also means that the attained age at entry into the disabled life state is reached at the completion of the waiting period and is so indicated in the select age of the disabled life annuity function.

By the midpoint method the integrals in (11.6.2) are evaluated as

$$\int_0^1 v^s \, \ddot{a}_{[x+k+s+m/12]:\overline{u-x-k-s-m/12}}^{(12)i} \, ds = v^{1/2} \, \ddot{a}_{[x+k+1/2+m/12]:\overline{u-x-k-1/2-m/12}}^{(12)i}. \quad (11.6.3)$$

With these two changes (11.6.2) can be written as

$$A = 12{,}000 \sum_{k=0}^{y-x-1} v^{k+1/2} \, {}_kp_x^{(\tau)} q_{x+k}^{(i)} v^{m/12} \ddot{a}_{[x+k+1/2+m/12]:\overline{u-x-k-1/2-m/12}}^{(12)i}. \quad (11.6.4)$$

11.6.2 Waiver-of-Premium Benefits

Let us go through the same process for a waiver of premium benefit. We assume that the premium, P, to be waived is payable g times per year for life. The primary difference between this and the disability income benefit is that the waiver benefit is a g-thly payment annuity starting at the first premium due date after the end of the waiting period.

We start with a special case with its actuarial present value written with the definite integrals already broken down to individual years of time of disablement. The case chosen is the waiver of semiannual premiums, payable for life, in the event of a disability occurring prior to age y and continuing through a 4-month waiting period. We further assume that the benefits are retroactive by which we mean that for a premium paid to the insurer on a due date during the waiting period, reimbursement with interest at the valuation rate will be made. This will increase the number of integrals within each year of age because disabilities that start within the first 2 months of each half year do not have premiums due during the waiting period:

$$
\bar{A} = P \sum_{k=0}^{y-x-1} v^k \, {}_k p_x^{(\tau)} \left[\int_0^{1/6} v^s \, {}_s p_{x+k}^{(\tau)} \, \mu_x^{(i)}(k+s) \, {}_{1/2-s|}\ddot{a}_{[x+k+s]}^{(2)i} \, ds \right.
$$

$$
+ \int_{1/6}^{1/2} v^s \, {}_s p_{x+k}^{(\tau)} \, \mu_x^{(i)}(k+s) \left({}_{1-s|}\ddot{a}_{[x+k+s]}^{(2)i} + {}_{4/12}p_{[x+k+s]}^i \, v^{1/2-s} \frac{1}{2} \right) ds
$$

$$
+ \int_{1/2}^{2/3} v^s \, {}_s p_{x+k}^{(\tau)} \, \mu_x^{(i)}(k+s) \, {}_{1-s|}\ddot{a}_{[x+k+s]}^{(2)i} \, ds
$$

$$
+ \left. \int_{2/3}^{1} v^s \, {}_s p_{x+k}^{(\tau)} \, \mu_x^{(i)}(k+s) \left({}_{3/2-s|}\ddot{a}_{[x+k+s]}^{(2)i} + {}_{4/12}p_{[x+k+s]}^i \, v^{1-s} \frac{1}{2} \right) ds \right]. \quad (11.6.5)
$$

If we incorporate the assumption of a uniform distribution of disability within each year of age and include only those disabilities that survive the waiting period as disabilities, (11.6.5) becomes

$$
\bar{A} = P \sum_{k=0}^{y-x-1} v^k \, {}_k p_x^{(\tau)} q_{x+k}^{(i)} \left[\int_0^{1/6} v^{s+4/12} \, {}_{1/2-s-4/12|}\ddot{a}_{[x+k+s+4/12]}^{(2)i} \, ds \right.
$$

$$
+ \int_{1/6}^{1/2} v^{s+4/12} \, {}_{1-s-4/12|}\ddot{a}_{[x+k+s+4/12]}^{(2)i} + v^{1/2} \frac{1}{2} \, ds
$$

$$
+ \int_{1/2}^{2/3} v^{s+4/12} \, {}_{1-s-4/12|}\ddot{a}_{[x+k+s+4/12]}^{(2)i} \, ds
$$

$$
+ \left. \int_{2/3}^{1} v^{s+4/12} \, {}_{3/2-s-4/12|}\ddot{a}_{[x+k+s+4/12]}^{(2)i} + v \frac{1}{2} \, ds \right]. \quad (11.6.6)
$$

We now use the midpoint approximate integration method for each of the several integrals within each year of age to obtain

$$
\bar{A} = P \sum_{k=0}^{y-x-1} v^k \, {}_k p_x^{(\tau)} \, q_{x+k}^{(i)} \left[\frac{1}{6} v^{5/12} \, {}_{1/12|}\ddot{a}_{[x+k+5/12]}^{(2)i} \right.
$$

$$
+ \frac{1}{3} \left(v^{2/3} \, {}_{1/3|}\ddot{a}_{[x+k+2/3]}^{(2)i} + v^{1/2} \frac{1}{2} \right) + \frac{1}{6} v^{11/12} \, {}_{1/12|}\ddot{a}_{[x+k+11/12]}^{(2)i}
$$

$$
+ \left. \frac{1}{3} \left(v^{7/6} \, {}_{1/3|}\ddot{a}_{[x+k+7/6]}^{(2)i} + v \frac{1}{2} \right) \right]. \quad (11.6.7)
$$

11.6.3   Benefit Premiums and Reserves

Equivalence principle benefit premiums for disability income and waiver of premium benefits are found by equating the actuarial present value of benefits to the actuarial present value of premiums. For the waiver benefit discussed in Section 11.6.2, the annual benefit premium, $_{y-x}\Pi_x$, equals $\bar{A}$ of (11.6.7) divided by $\ddot{a}_{x:\overline{y-x}|}^{(\tau)}$.

Active life benefit reserves, that is, the reserve when premiums are not being waived, are most conveniently expressed by a premium difference formula:

$$_kV = \left(_{y-x-k}\Pi_{x+k} - {}_{y-x}\Pi_x \right) \ddot{a}^{(\tau)}_{x+k:\overline{y-x-k}}. \qquad (11.6.8)$$

The terminal reserve for a disabled life is the actuarial present value of future disability benefits, calculated on the assumption that the insured has incurred a disability. The amount of premium waived, or disability income rate, is multiplied by the actuarial present value of an appropriate disabled life annuity. This value takes into account the age at disablement, the duration since disablement, and the terminal age for benefits.

11.7   Notes and References

We have not defined insurer's losses and studied their variances in this chapter. Formula (11.2.7) gave a means of doing so if we consider the total benefits for all causes of decrements. If we consider only a single benefit, such as the retirement benefit, there is more than one way of defining losses. The usual concept is that premiums and reserves, for a benefit in regard to a particular cause of decrement, apply only to that decrement. Thus, if decrement due to a second cause occurs, then, with respect to the first cause, there is zero benefit and a gain emerges. An insurer's loss based on this concept would lead, for example, to (11.4.3). However, losses defined in this way may have nonzero covariances, so that the loss variance for all benefits is not the sum of the loss variances for the individual benefits.

Alternatively, one may consider that when a particular cause of decrement occurs, the reserves accumulated for the benefits in regard to all the other causes are released to offset the benefit outgo for the given cause. In this case, the loss random variables defined for the benefits for the several causes of decrement have zero-valued covariances, and the loss variance for all benefits is the sum of the loss variances for the individual benefits. However, the premiums and reserves for the individual benefits are more difficult to compute on this second basis and individually differ significantly from those on the usual basis. For insights into these matters, see Hickman (1964).

The result stated in Section 11.4 concerning the neutral impact on premiums and reserves when a withdrawal benefit equals the reserve on the death benefit does not hold for fully discrete insurances. This was pointed out by Nesbitt (1964), who reported on work by Schuette. The problem results from the fact that, in the discrete model, the probability of withdrawal

$$q^{(w)}_{x+k} = \int_0^1 \exp\left[-\int_0^t \mu^{(\tau)}_x(k+s)\, ds \right] \mu^{(w)}_x(k+t)\, dt$$

depends on the force of mortality.

While there are many papers and a number of books dealing with pension fund mathematics, it seems useful for the purposes of this introductory treatment to refer only to other actuarial texts with similar chapters; see, for example, Hooker and Longley-Cooke (1957), Jordan (1967), and Neill (1977). These authors stress the formulation of actuarial present values in terms of pension commutation functions and the use of tables of such functions to carry out computations.

In contrast, a major portion of our presentation has been in terms of integrals and approximating sums, with the integrands or summands expressed in terms of basic functions. These approximating sums can be computed by various processes that may or may not make use of commutation functions. For pension benefits determined by complex eligibility or income conditions, it can be more flexible and efficient to calculate by processes not requiring extensive formulation by commutation functions. An opposing view, indicating the power of commutation functions for expressing actuarial present values and controlling their computation, is given by Chamberlain (1982).

There is an alternative foundation for constructing a model for disability insurance. In Section 11.6 we used a multiple decrement model that did not explicitly provide for recovery from disability. Models with several states of disability, with provision for transition from state to state, have been developed. These models are frequently the foundation of long-term care insurance. Hoem (1988) provides an introduction with valuable references to these ideas.

The multiple decrement model developed in Chapter 10 and applied in this chapter can be viewed as being made up of $m + 1$ states; m are called absorbing states in that it is impossible to return from them to the active state. These m states are associated with the m causes of decrement, and the remaining state is associated with continuing survival. If some of the m decrements are not absorbing, but are such that transition to the active state or one of the other nonabsorbing states is possible, a more complex but possibly more realistic model results. Estimation of the probabilities of transition among the states can be difficult because the probabilities can depend on the path followed to the current state.

Exercises

Section 11.2

11.1. Employees enter a benefit plan at age 30. If an employee remains in service until retirement, the employee receives an annual pension of 300 times years of service. If the employee dies in service before retirement, the beneficiary is paid 20,000 immediately. If the employee withdraws before age 70 for any reason except death, the member receives a deferred (to age 70) life annuity of 300 times years of service. Give an expression, in terms of integrals and continuous annuities, for the actuarial present value of these benefits at age 30.

11.2. Let $J = 1$ represent death by accidental means and $J = 2$ represent death by other means. You are given that

(i) $\delta = 0.05$

(ii) $\mu_x^{(1)}(t) = 0.005$ for $t \geq 0$ where $\mu_x^{(1)}(t)$ is the force of decrement for death by accidental means.

(iii) $\mu_x^{(2)}(t) = 0.020$ for $t \geq 0$.

A 20-year term insurance policy, payable at the moment of death, is issued to a life age (x) providing a benefit of 2 if death is by accidental means and providing a benefit of 1 for other deaths. Find the expectation and variance of the present value of benefits random variable.

Section 11.4

11.3. A double decrement model is defined by $\mu_x^{(1)}(t) = \mu_x^{(2)}(t) = 1/(a - t)$, $0 \leq t < a$.

a. In the single decrement model with decrement (1) only, the prospective loss variable at duration t is given by

$$_t L^1_- = v^{T(x)-t} \qquad 0 < t \leq T(x), J = 1.$$

Confirm that

$$_t V^1_- = \frac{1 - e^{-\delta(a-t)}}{\delta(a - t)} = A^1_{x+t}.$$

b. In the double decrement model, the prospective loss variable at duration t is given by

$$_t L^2_- = v^{T(x)-t} \qquad 0 < t \leq T(x), J = 1$$

$$= v^{T(x)-t} \, _{T(x)} V^1_- \quad 0 < t \leq T(x), J = 2.$$

Confirm that $E[_t L^2_- | T \geq t] = {}_t V^1_-$.

Section 11.5

11.4. A pension plan valuation assumes a linear salary scale function satisfying $S_{20} = 1$. If $(ES)_{45} = 2(AS)_{25}$, find S_x for $x \geq 20$.

11.5. A new pension plan with two participants, (35) and (40), provides annual income at retirement equal to 2% of salary at the final rate times the number of years of service, including any fraction of a year. If
   (i) Salary increases occur continuously,
   (ii) For (40), $(AS)_{40} = 50,000$ and $S_{40+t} = 1 + 0.06t$, and
   (iii) For (35), $(AS)_{35} = 35,000$ and $S_{35+t} = 1 + 0.10t$,
   calculate the maximum value of $[R(40, 0, t) - R(35, 0, t)]$ for $t \geq 0$.

11.6. It is assumed that, for a new participant entering at age 30, there will be annual increases in salary at the rate of 5% per year to take care of the effects of inflation and increases in productivity. In addition, it is assumed that promotion raises of 10% of the existing salary will occur at ages 40, 50, and 60.

a. Construct a salary scale function, S_{30+k}, to express these assumptions.

b. Write an expression for the actuarial present value of contributions of 10% of future salary for a new entrant with annual salary 24,000 and with increases in salary according to the scale constructed in (a).

11.7. Every year, a plan sponsor contributes 10% of that portion of each participant's salary in excess of a certain amount. That amount is 15,000 this year and will increase by 5% annually. Express the actuarial present value of the sponsor's contribution for a participant entering now at age 35 with a salary of 40,000.

11.8. A plan provides for an income benefit rate, payable from retirement to age 65, of 2% of the final 3-year average salary for each year of service. After age 65 the income benefit rate is 1-1/3% of the final 3-year average salary for each year of service.
   a. For a participant age 50, who entered service at age 30 and currently has a salary of 48,000, express the actuarial present value of the participant's benefit if the earliest retirement age is 55 and there is no mandatory retirement age.
   b. If the maximum number of years to be credited in the plan is 35, express the actuarial present value of the benefit for the above participant.
   c. Give an expression for the actuarial present value of the income benefit associated with past service for the above participant.

11.9. A career average plan provides a retirement income of 2% of aggregate salary during a participant's years of service. The earliest age of retirement is 58, and all retirements are completed by age 68. For a participant age 50 who entered service at age 30 and has 450,000 total of past salaries with a current salary of 42,000, write expressions for
   a. The participant's total income benefit rate in case of retirement at exact age 65
   b. The participant's midyear total income benefit rate in case of retirement between ages 65 and 66
   c. The actuarial present value of this participant's retirement benefit for past service
   d. The actuarial present value of this participant's retirement benefit for future service.

11.10. A new participant in a pension plan, age 45, has a choice of two benefit options:
   (1) A defined-contribution plan with contributions of 20% of salary each year. Contributions are made at the beginning of each year and earn 5% per year. Accumulated contributions are used to purchase a monthly life annuity-due.
   (2) A defined-benefit plan with an annual benefit, payable monthly, of 40% of the final 2-year average salary.
   You are given that (a) $\ddot{a}_{65}^{(12)} = 10$ and (b) $S_{45+k} = (1.05)^k$ for $k \geq 0$ where S_y is a step function, constant over each year of age. Assuming that retirement

occurs at exact age 65 and that the participant survives to retirement, calculate the ratio of the expected monthly payment under the defined-contribution plan to that under the defined-benefit plan.

11.11. Display definite integrals for the actuarial present values of the following possible benefits of an employee benefit package. Assume that the employee is currently age 40 and earning 40,000 annually. This employee was hired at age 25 and has received a total of 320,000 in salary since hire. Retirement benefits are available only after age 55, and withdrawal benefits are only available before age 55 in the form of an annuity with payments deferred until the employee reaches age 55.

a. A retirement benefit at the annual benefit rate of 50% of the final salary.
b. A retirement benefit at the rate of 0.015 times the product of the final salary rate multiplied by the exact number of years (including fractions) of service at the moment of retirement.
c. A withdrawal benefit using the benefit income formula in (b).
d. A retirement benefit at the rate of 0.025 times the total salary paid over the whole career to the employee.
e. A withdrawal benefit using the benefit income formula in (d).

11.12. A retirement benefit consisting of a continuous annuity, payable for life, is part of an employer's benefit package. The annual benefit income rate is 60% of the salary rate applicable at the moment of retirement for retirements between ages 60 and 70. For retirements after attaining age 70, the benefit rate is 60% of the salary rate applicable between ages 69 and 70. Give an approximating sum for the actuarial present value of this benefit for a person age 30 who has just been hired at a salary of 35,000.

Section 11.6

11.13. a. Give an expression for the annual benefit premium, payable to age 60, for a disability income insurance issued to (35) of 2,000 per month payable to age 65 in case (35) becomes disabled before age 60 and survives a waiting period of 6 months.
b. Give an expression for the active life benefit reserve at the end of 10 years for the insurance in (a).

Miscellaneous

11.14. The Hattendorf theorem for the fully continuous model as stated in Exercise 8.24 can be restated in the definitions and notation of this chapter for the fully continuous multiple decrement model:

$$\text{Var}({}_0L^{\underline{m}}) = \sum_{j=1}^{m} \int_0^\infty [v^t \, (B^{(j)}_{x+t} - {}_t\bar{V}^{\underline{m}})]^2 \; {}_tp^{(\tau)}_x \, \mu^{(j)}_x(t) \; dt.$$

Confirm that this result holds for the fully continuous whole life insurance discussed in Section 11.4.

Outline of solution:

a. Confirm that the loss random variable for this insurance is

$$
_0L_-^2 = \begin{cases} v^T - \bar{P}(\bar{A}_x)^2\,\bar{a}_{\overline{T}\rvert} & 0 \le T, J = 1 \\ v^T\,_T\bar{V}(\bar{A}_x) - \bar{P}(\bar{A}_x)^2\,\bar{a}_{\overline{T}\rvert} & 0 \le T, J = 2. \end{cases}
$$

b. Use (11.4.6) and (11.4.7) to rewrite the differential equation (11.4.3) and then employ the integrating factor $e^{-\delta t}$ to obtain the solution

$$
v^t\,_t\bar{V}(\bar{A}_x) = \bar{P}(\bar{A}_x)\,\bar{a}_{\overline{t}\rvert} - \int_0^t e^{-\delta s}\,\mu_x^{(1)}(s)\,[1 - {}_s\bar{V}(\bar{A}_x)]\,ds.
$$

c. Use the result of part (b) to modify both lines of the definition of $_0L_-^2$ in part (a) and then show that

$$
\mathrm{Var}(_0L_-^2) = \int_0^\infty \left\{ v^t[1 - {}_t\bar{V}(\bar{A}_x)] \right.
$$

$$
\left. - \int_0^t v^s\,\mu_x^{(1)}(s)\,[1 - {}_s\bar{V}(\bar{A}_x)]\,ds \right\}^2 {}_tp_x^{(\tau)}\mu_x^{(1)}(t)\,dt
$$

$$
+ \int_0^\infty \left\{ \int_0^t v^s\,\mu_x^{(1)}(s)\,[1 - {}_s\bar{V}(\bar{A}_x)]\,ds \right\}^2 {}_tp_x^{(\tau)}\,\mu_x^{(2)}(t)\,dt.
$$

d. Perform the indicated squaring operation on the factor in the integrand of the first integral in part (c) and combine the two integrals that include $\{\int_0^t v^s\,\mu_x^{(1)}(s)\,[1 - {}_s\bar{V}(\bar{A}_x)]\,ds\}^2$ as a component of the integrand. Then use integration by parts to obtain

$$
\mathrm{Var}(_0L_-^2) = \int_0^\infty \{v^t\,[1 - {}_t\bar{V}(\bar{A}_x)]\}^2\,{}_tp_x^{(\tau)}\,\mu_x^{(1)}(t)\,dt.
$$

This result provides a reduction of variance argument for establishing the withdrawal benefit as $_t\bar{V}(\bar{A}_x)$.

COLLECTIVE RISK MODELS FOR A SINGLE PERIOD

12.1 Introduction

In Chapters 3 through 11 we considered models for long-term insurances. The inclusion of interest in these models was essential. In this chapter we return to a topic introduced in Chapter 2, namely, short-term insurance policies. Consequently interest will be ignored. The purpose of this chapter is to present an alternative to the individual policy model discussed in Chapter 2.

The individual risk model of Chapter 2 considers individual policies and the claims produced by each policy. Then aggregate claims are obtained by summing over all the policies in the portfolio.

For the *collective risk model* we assume a random process that generates claims for a portfolio of policies. This process is characterized in terms of the portfolio as a whole rather than in terms of the individual policies comprising the portfolio. The mathematical formulation is as follows: Let N denote the number of claims produced by a portfolio of policies in a given time period. Let X_1 denote the amount of the first claim, X_2 the amount of the second claim, and so on. Then,

$$S = X_1 + X_2 + \cdots + X_N \qquad (12.1.1)$$

represents the aggregate claims generated by the portfolio for the period under study. The number of claims, N, is a random variable and is associated with the frequency of claim. The individual claim amounts $X_1, X_2, \ldots$ are also random variables and are said to measure the severity of claims.

In order to make the model tractable, we usually make two fundamental assumptions:
1. $X_1, X_2, \ldots$ are identically distributed random variables.
2. The random variables $N, X_1, X_2, \ldots$ are mutually independent.
Expression (12.1.1) will be called a random sum, and unless stated otherwise, assumptions (1) and (2) will be made concerning its components.

A principal tool for developing the theory of this chapter is the moment generating function (m.g.f.). These functions provide a simple but powerful means for the reader to gain a working knowledge of the collective theory of risk. A reader who has not worked with them recently would do well to review the m.g.f.'s, means, and variances of the widely used probability distributions summarized in Appendix 5.

12.2   The Distribution of Aggregate Claims

In this section we see how the distribution of aggregate claims in a fixed time period can be obtained from the distribution of the number of claims and the distribution of individual claim amounts.

Let $P(x)$ denote the common d.f. of the independent and identically distributed X_i's. Let X be a random variable with this d.f. Then let

$$p_k = E[X^k] \tag{12.2.1}$$

denote the k-th moment about the origin, and

$$M_X(t) = E[e^{tX}] \tag{12.2.2}$$

denote the m.g.f. of X. In addition, let

$$M_N(t) = E[e^{tN}] \tag{12.2.3}$$

denote the m.g.f. of the number of claims, and let

$$M_S(t) = E[e^{tS}] \tag{12.2.4}$$

denote the m.g.f. of aggregate claims. The d.f. of aggregate claims will be denoted by $F_S(s)$.

Using (2.2.10) and (2.2.11), in conjunction with assumptions (1) and (2) of Section 12.1, we obtain

$$E[S] = E[E[S|N]] = E[p_1 N] = p_1 E[N] \tag{12.2.5}$$

and

$$\begin{aligned} Var(S) &= E[Var(S|N)] + Var(E[S|N]) \\ &= E[N \, Var(X)] + Var(p_1 N) \\ &= E[N] \, Var(X) + p_1^2 \, Var(N) \end{aligned} \tag{12.2.6}$$

where $Var(X) = p_2 - p_1^2$.

The result stated in (12.2.5), that the expected value of aggregate claims is the product of the expected individual claim amount and the expected number of claims, is not surprising. Expression (12.2.6) for the variance of aggregate claims also has a natural interpretation. The variance of aggregate claims is the sum of two components where the first is attributed to the variability of individual claim amounts and the second to the variability of the number of claims.

In a similar fashion we derive an expression for the m.g.f. of S:

$$M_S(t) = E[e^{tS}] = E[E[e^{tS}|N]]$$

$$= E[M_X(t)^N] = E[e^{N \log M_X(t)}]$$

$$= M_N[\log M_X(t)]. \qquad (12.2.7)$$

Example 12.2.1

Assume that N has a geometric distribution; that is, the p.f. of N is given by

$$\Pr(N = n) = pq^n \qquad n = 0, 1, 2, \ldots \qquad (12.2.8)$$

where $0 < q < 1$ and $p = 1 - q$. Determine $M_S(t)$ in terms of $M_X(t)$.

Solution:
Since

$$M_N(t) = E[e^{tN}] = \sum_{n=0}^{\infty} p(qe^t)^n = \frac{p}{1 - qe^t},$$

(12.2.7) tells us that

$$M_S(t) = \frac{p}{1 - qM_X(t)}. \qquad (12.2.9)$$

▼

To derive the d.f. of S, we distinguish according to how many claims occur and use the law of total probability,

$$F_S(x) = \Pr(S \le x) = \sum_{n=0}^{\infty} \Pr(S \le x|N = n) \Pr(N = n)$$

$$= \sum_{n=0}^{\infty} \Pr(X_1 + X_2 + \cdots + X_n \le x) \Pr(N = n). \qquad (12.2.10)$$

In terms of the convolution defined in Section 2.3, we can write

$$\Pr(X_1 + X_2 + \cdots + X_n \le x) = P * P * P * \cdots * P(x)$$

$$= P^{*n}(x), \qquad (12.2.11)$$

which is the n-th convolution of P defined in Chapter 2. Recall that

$$P^{*0}(x) = \begin{cases} 1 & x \ge 0 \\ 0 & x < 0. \end{cases}$$

Thus (12.2.10) becomes

$$F_S(x) = \sum_{n=0}^{\infty} P^{*n}(x) \Pr(N = n). \qquad (12.2.12)$$

If the individual claim amount distribution is discrete with p.f. $p(x) = \Pr(X = x)$, the distribution of aggregate claims is also discrete. By analogy with the above derivation, the p.f. of S can be obtained directly as

---

$$f_S(x) = \sum_{n=0}^{\infty} p^{*n}(x)\, \Pr(N = n) \tag{12.2.13}$$

where

$$p^{*n}(x) = p*p* \cdots * p(x) = \Pr(X_1 + X_2 + \cdots + X_n = x) \tag{12.2.11A}$$

$$\text{and } p^{*0}(x) = \begin{cases} 0 & x \neq 0 \\ 1 & x = 0. \end{cases}$$

Here the inequality sign in the probability symbol in (12.2.11) has been replaced by the equal sign.

Example 12.2.2

Consider an insurance portfolio that will produce zero, one, two, or three claims in a fixed time period with probabilities 0.1, 0.3, 0.4, and 0.2, respectively. An individual claim will be of amount 1, 2, or 3 with probabilities 0.5, 0.4, and 0.1, respectively. Calculate the p.f. and d.f. of the aggregate claims.

Solution:

The calculations are summarized below. Only nonzero entries are exhibited.

(1) x	(2) $p^{*0}(x)$	(3) $p^{*1}(x) = p(x)$	(4) $p^{*2}(x)$	(5) $p^{*3}(x)$	(6) $f_S(x)$	(7) $F_S(x)$
0	1.0	—	—	—	0.1000	0.1000
1	—	0.5	—	—	0.1500	0.2500
2	—	0.4	0.25	—	0.2200	0.4700
3	—	0.1	0.40	0.125	0.2150	0.6850
4	—	—	0.26	0.300	0.1640	0.8490
5	—	—	0.08	0.315	0.0950	0.9440
6	—	—	0.01	0.184	0.0408	0.9848
7	—	—	—	0.063	0.0126	0.9974
8	—	—	—	0.012	0.0024	0.9998
9	—	—	—	0.001	0.0002	1.0000
n	0	1	2	3	—	—
$\Pr(N = n)$	0.1	0.3	0.4	0.2	—	—

Since there are at most three claims and each produces a claim amount of at most 3, we can limit the calculations to $x = 0, 1, 2, \ldots, 9$.

Column (2) lists the p.f. of a degenerate distribution with all the probability mass at 0. Column (3) lists the p.f. of the individual claim amount random variable. Columns (4) and (5) are obtained recursively by applying

$$p^{*(n+1)}(x) = \Pr(X_1 + X_2 + \cdots + X_{n+1} = x)$$

$$= \sum_y \Pr(X_{n+1} = y)\, \Pr(X_1 + X_2 + \cdots + X_n = x - y)$$

$$= \sum_y p(y)\, p^{*n}(x - y). \tag{12.2.14}$$

Since only three different claim amounts are possible, the evaluation of (12.2.14) will involve a sum of three or fewer terms. Next, (12.2.13) is used to compute the p.f. displayed in column (6). For this step, it is convenient to record the p.f. of N in the last row of the results. Finally, the elements of column (7) are obtained as partial sums of column (6). An alternative approach, not illustrated here, would be to perform the convolutions in terms of the d.f.'s, obtain $F_S(x)$ from (12.2.12), and calculate $f_S(x) = F_S(x) - F_S(x - 1)$. ▼

If the claim amount distribution is continuous, it cannot be concluded that the distribution of S is continuous. If $\Pr(N = 0) > 0$, the distribution of S will be of the mixed type; that is, it will have a mass of probability at 0 and be continuous elsewhere. This idea is illustrated in the following example.

Example 12.2.3

In Example 12.2.1, add the assumption that

$$P(x) = 1 - e^{-x} \qquad x > 0;$$

that is, the individual claim amount distribution is exponential with mean 1. Then show that

$$M_S(t) = p + q\,\frac{p}{p - t} \tag{12.2.15}$$

and interpret the formula.

Solution:

First, we rewrite (12.2.9) as follows:

$$M_S(t) = p + q\,\frac{pM_X(t)}{1 - qM_X(t)}.$$

Then we substitute

$$M_X(t) = \int_0^\infty e^{tx}\, e^{-x}\, dx = (1 - t)^{-1}$$

to obtain (12.2.15).

Since 1 is the m.g.f. of the constant 0 and $p/(p - t)$ is the m.g.f. of the exponential distribution with d.f. $1 - e^{-px}$, $x > 0$, (12.2.15) can be interpreted as a weighted average (with weights p and q, respectively). It follows that the d.f. of S is the corresponding weighted average of distributions. Thus, for $x > 0$

$$F_S(x) = p(1) + q(1 - e^{-px}) = 1 - qe^{-px}. \tag{12.2.16}$$

This distribution is of the mixed type. Its d.f. is shown in Figure 12.2.1. ▼

FIGURE 12.2.1
Graph of $F_S(x)$

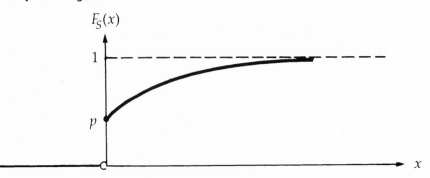

12.3 Selection of Basic Distributions

In this section we discuss some issues in selecting the distribution of the number of claims N and the common distribution of the X_i's. As different considerations apply to these two selections, a separate subsection will be devoted to each.

12.3.1 The Distribution of N

One choice for the distribution of N is the Poisson with p.f. given by

$$\Pr(N = n) = \frac{\lambda^n e^{-\lambda}}{n!} \qquad n = 0, 1, 2, \ldots \tag{12.3.1}$$

where $\lambda > 0$. For the Poisson distribution, $E[N] = \text{Var}(N) = \lambda$. With this choice for the distribution of N, the distribution of S is called a ***compound Poisson distribution.*** Using (12.2.5) and (12.2.6), we have that

$$E[S] = \lambda\, p_1 \tag{12.3.2}$$

and

$$\text{Var}(S) = \lambda\, p_2 . \tag{12.3.3}$$

Substituting the m.g.f. of the Poisson distribution

$$M_N(t) = e^{\lambda(e^t - 1)} \tag{12.3.4}$$

into (12.2.7), we obtain the m.g.f. of the compound Poisson distribution,

$$M_S(t) = e^{\lambda[M_X(t) - 1]} . \tag{12.3.5}$$

The compound Poisson distribution has many attractive features, some of which are discussed in Section 12.4.

When the variance of the number of claims exceeds its mean, the Poisson distribution is not appropriate. In this situation, use of the negative binomial distribution has been suggested. The negative binomial distribution has a p.f. given by

$$\Pr(N = n) = \binom{r + n - 1}{n} p^r q^n \qquad n = 0, 1, 2, \ldots . \tag{12.3.6}$$

This distribution has two parameters: $r > 0$ and $0 < p < 1$; $q = 1 - p$. For this distribution, we have

$$M_N(t) = \left(\frac{p}{1 - q e^t}\right)^r, \tag{12.3.7}$$

$$E[N] = \frac{rq}{p}, \tag{12.3.8}$$

and

$$\mathrm{Var}(N) = \frac{rq}{p^2} . \tag{12.3.9}$$

When a negative binomial distribution is chosen for N, the distribution of S is called a *compound negative binomial distribution.* Substituting from (12.3.8) and (12.3.9) into (12.2.5) and (12.2.6), we have

$$E[S] = \frac{rq}{p} p_1 \tag{12.3.10}$$

and

$$\mathrm{Var}(S) = \frac{rq}{p} p_2 + \frac{rq^2}{p^2} \cdot p_1^2 . \tag{12.3.11}$$

Substituting from (12.3.7) into (12.2.7), we obtain

$$M_S(t) = \left[\frac{p}{1 - q M_X(t)}\right]^r . \tag{12.3.12}$$

We observe that the family of geometric distributions used in Examples 12.2.1 and 12.2.3 is contained as a special case ($r = 1$) of the two-parameter family of negative binomial distributions.

A family of distributions for the number of claims can be generated by assuming that the Poisson parameter Λ is a random variable with p.d.f. $u(\lambda)$, $\lambda > 0$, and that the conditional distribution of N, given $\Lambda = \lambda$, is Poisson with parameter λ. There are several situations in which this might be a useful way to consider the distribution of N. For example, consider a population of insureds where various classes of insureds within the population generate numbers of claims according to Poisson distributions with different values of λ for the various classes. If the relative frequency of the values of λ is denoted by $u(\lambda)$, we can use the law of total probability to obtain

$$\Pr(N = n) = \int_0^\infty \Pr(N = n | \Lambda = \lambda) \, u(\lambda) d\lambda$$

$$= \int_0^\infty \frac{e^{-\lambda} \lambda^n}{n!} \, u(\lambda) d\lambda. \tag{12.3.13}$$

Furthermore, using (2.2.10) and (2.2.11), we have

$$E[N] = E[E[N|\Lambda]] = E[\Lambda] \tag{12.3.14}$$

and

$$Var(N) = E[Var(N|\Lambda)] + Var(E[N|\Lambda])$$
$$= E[\Lambda] + Var(\Lambda). \tag{12.3.15}$$

Also,

$$M_N(t) = E[e^{tN}] = E[E[e^{tN}|\Lambda]] = E[e^{\Lambda(e^t-1)}] = M_\Lambda(e^t - 1). \tag{12.3.16}$$

The equality,

$$E[e^{tN}|\Lambda] = e^{\Lambda(e^t-1)},$$

follows from the hypothesis that the conditional distribution of N, given Λ, is Poisson with parameter Λ.

A comparison of (12.3.14) and (12.3.15) shows that, as in the case of the negative binomial distribution, $E[N] < Var(N)$. In fact, the negative binomial distribution can be derived in this fashion, which will be shown in the following example.

Example 12.3.1

Assume that $u(\lambda)$ is the gamma p.d.f. with parameters α and β,

$$u(\lambda) = \frac{\beta^\alpha}{\Gamma(\alpha)} \lambda^{\alpha-1} e^{-\beta\lambda} \qquad \lambda > 0 \tag{12.3.17}$$

where

$$\Gamma(\alpha) = \int_0^\infty y^{\alpha-1} e^{-y} \, dy.$$

a. Show that the marginal distribution of N is negative binomial with parameters

$$r = \alpha, \qquad p = \frac{\beta}{1 + \beta}. \tag{12.3.18}$$

b. By substituting $E[\Lambda] = \alpha/\beta$ and $Var(\Lambda) = \alpha/\beta^2$ into (12.3.14) and (12.3.15), verify (12.3.8) and (12.3.9).

Solution:

a. Substituting

$$M_\Lambda(t) = \left(\frac{\beta}{\beta - t} \right)^\alpha \tag{12.3.19}$$

into (12.3.16), we have

$$M_N(t) = M_\Lambda(e^t - 1) = \left[\frac{\beta}{\beta - (e^t - 1)} \right]^\alpha$$

$$= \left\{ \frac{\beta/(\beta + 1)}{1 - [1 - \beta/(\beta + 1)]e^t} \right\}^\alpha. \tag{12.3.20}$$

Comparison of (12.3.20) with (12.3.7) confirms that this distribution for N is negative binomial with parameters $r = \alpha$,

$$p = \frac{\beta}{1 + \beta}, \qquad (12.3.21)$$

$$q = 1 - p = \frac{1}{1 + \beta}.$$

b. The suggested substitutions into (12.3.14) and (12.3.15) yield

$$E[N] = \frac{\alpha}{\beta} = \frac{rq}{p}$$

as in (12.3.8) and

$$\text{Var}(N) = \frac{\alpha}{\beta} + \frac{\alpha}{\beta^2} = \frac{rq}{p}\left(1 + \frac{q}{p}\right) = \frac{rq}{p^2}$$

as in (12.3.9). ▼

The following is another example of a distribution for N that is obtained by mixing Poisson distributions.

Example 12.3.2

Assume that $u(\lambda)$ is the inverse Gaussian p.d.f. with parameters α and β. Exhibit the moment generating function of N, $E[N]$, and $\text{Var}(N)$.

Solution:

Example 2.3.5 contains the basic facts about the inverse Gaussian distribution.

Applying (12.3.16) yields

$$M_N(t) = M_\Lambda(e^t - 1) = e^{\alpha\{1 - [1 - 2(e^t - 1)/\beta]^{1/2}\}},$$

and from (12.3.14) and (12.3.15) we obtain

$$E[N] = E[\Lambda] = \frac{\alpha}{\beta}$$

and

$$\text{Var}(N) = E[\Lambda] + \text{Var}(\Lambda)$$

$$= \frac{\alpha}{\beta} + \frac{\alpha}{\beta^2} = \frac{\alpha(\beta + 1)}{\beta^2}.$$

This distribution is called the *Poisson inverse Gaussian distribution*. ▼

Table 12.3.1 summarizes pertinent information on the compound distributions resulting from the selections for N discussed here.

TABLE 12.3.1

Compound Distributions of S

$$S = \sum_{j=1}^{N} X_j$$

$N, X_1, X_2, \ldots$ are
independent random variables.
Each X_j has d.f. $P(x)$,
m.g.f. $M_X(t)$, and
$p_k = E[X^k]$ $k = 1, 2, \ldots$

$$P^{*0}(x) = \begin{bmatrix} 1 & x \geq 0 \\ 0 & \text{elsewhere} \end{bmatrix}$$

$$P^{*n}(x) = \begin{cases} \sum_{j=0}^{x} p(x-j)P^{*(n-1)}(j), \text{ or} \\ \int_0^x p(x-y)P^{*(n-1)}(y)dy \end{cases}$$

Definitions	Distribution Function, $F_S(x)$	Restrictions on Parameters	Moment Generating Function, $M_S(t)$	Mean	Variance
General	$\sum_{n=0}^{\infty} \Pr(N=n)P^{*n}(x)$	—	$M_N[\log M_X(t)]$	$p_1 E[N]$	$E[N](p_2 - p_1^2) + p_1^2 \operatorname{Var}(N)$
Compound Poisson	$\sum_{n=0}^{\infty} \dfrac{e^{-\lambda}\lambda^n}{n!} P^{*n}(x)$	$\lambda > 0$	$e^{\lambda[M_X(t)-1]}$	λp_1	λp_2
Compound Negative Binomial	$\sum_{n=0}^{\infty} \binom{r+n-1}{n} p^r q^n P^{*n}(x)$	$0 < p < 1$ $q = 1-p$ $r > 0$	$\left[\dfrac{p}{1-qM_X(t)}\right]^r$ $qM_X(t) < 1$	$\dfrac{rqp_1}{p}$	$\dfrac{rqp_2}{p} + \dfrac{rq^2p_1^2}{p^2}$
Compound Poisson Inverse Gaussian	no known closed form	$\alpha > 0$ $\beta > 0$	$\exp\left\{ \alpha \left[1 - \left\{ 1 - \dfrac{2[M_X(t)-1]}{\beta} \right\}^{1/2} \right] \right\}$	$\dfrac{\alpha}{\beta} p_1$	$\dfrac{\alpha}{\beta}\left(p_2 + \dfrac{p_1^2}{\beta}\right)$

12.3.2   The Individual Claim Amount Distribution

On the basis of (12.2.12) we see that convolutions of the individual claim amount distribution may be required. Thus, when possible, it is convenient to select that distribution from a family of distributions for which convolutions can be calculated easily either by formula or numerically. For example, if the claim amount has the normal distribution with mean μ and variance σ^2, then its n-th convolution is the normal distribution with mean $n\mu$ and variance $n\sigma^2$. For many types of insurance, the claim amount random variable is only positive, and its distribution is skewed to the right. For these insurances we might choose a gamma distribution that also has these properties. The n-th convolution of a gamma distribution with parameters α and β is also a gamma distribution but with parameters $n\alpha$ and β. This can be confirmed by noting from (12.3.19) that $M_X(t) = [\beta/(\beta - t)]^\alpha$, and hence the m.g.f. associated with $P^{*n}(x)$ is

$$M_X(t)^n = \left(\frac{\beta}{\beta - t}\right)^{n\alpha} \qquad t < \beta. \tag{12.3.22}$$

If the claim amounts have an exponential distribution with parameter 1, the p.d.f. is given by

$$p(x) = e^{-x} \qquad x > 0.$$

This is a gamma distribution with $\alpha = \beta = 1$. Then, by using (12.3.19), we conclude that the n-th convolution is a gamma distribution with parameters $\alpha = n$, $\beta = 1$; that is,

$$p^{*n}(x) = \frac{x^{n-1} e^{-x}}{(n - 1)!} \qquad x > 0. \tag{12.3.23}$$

To obtain an expression for $P^{*n}(x)$, we perform integration by parts n times as follows:

$$
\begin{aligned}
1 - P^{*n}(x) &= \int_x^\infty \frac{y^{n-1} e^{-y}}{(n - 1)!} \, dy \\
&= -\frac{y^{n-1}}{(n - 1)!} e^{-y} \Big|_x^\infty + \int_x^\infty \frac{y^{n-2} e^{-y}}{(n - 2)!} \, dy \\
&= \frac{x^{n-1}}{(n - 1)!} e^{-x} + [1 - P^{*(n-1)}(x)] \\
&= e^{-x} \sum_{i=0}^{n-1} \frac{x^i}{i!}. \tag{12.3.24}
\end{aligned}
$$

Then, using (12.2.12), we have

$$1 - F_S(x) = \sum_{n=1}^\infty \Pr(N = n) e^{-x} \sum_{i=0}^{n-1} \frac{x^i}{i!} \qquad x > 0. \tag{12.3.25}$$

This exponential distribution case shows that even with simple assumed distributions, the distribution of aggregate claims may not have a simple form. Therefore, it may be more practical to select a discrete claim amount distribution and calculate the required convolutions numerically. For compound Poisson distributions it has been established that the convolution method can be shortened or, alternatively, that it can be bypassed by use of a recursive formula for directly calculating the distribution function of S. These computational shortcuts are discussed in the following section.

12.4 Properties of Certain Compound Distributions

In this section we discuss some mathematical properties of certain compound distributions. Two theorems concerning the compound Poisson are presented.

The first shows that the sum of independent random variables, each having a compound Poisson distribution, also has a compound Poisson distribution.

Theorem 12.4.1

If $S_1, S_2, \ldots, S_m$ are mutually independent random variables such that S_i has a compound Poisson distribution with parameter λ_i and d.f. of claim amount $P_i(x)$, $i = 1, 2, \ldots, m$, then $S = S_1 + S_2 + \cdots + S_m$ has a compound Poisson distribution with

$$\lambda = \sum_{i=1}^{m} \lambda_i \qquad (12.4.1)$$

and

$$P(x) = \sum_{i=1}^{m} \frac{\lambda_i}{\lambda} P_i(x). \qquad (12.4.2)$$

Proof:

We let $M_i(t)$ denote the m.g.f. of $P_i(x)$. According to (12.3.5), the m.g.f. of S_i is

$$M_{S_i}(t) = \exp\{\lambda_i[M_i(t) - 1]\}.$$

By the assumed independence of $S_1, \ldots, S_m$, the m.g.f. of their sum is

$$M_S(t) = \prod_{i=1}^{m} M_{S_i}(t) = \exp\left\{\sum_{i=1}^{m} \lambda_i[M_i(t) - 1]\right\}.$$

Finally, we rewrite the exponent to obtain

$$M_S(t) = \exp\left\{\lambda\left[\sum_{i=1}^{m} \frac{\lambda_i}{\lambda} M_i(t) - 1\right]\right\}. \qquad (12.4.3)$$

Since this is the m.g.f. of the compound Poisson distribution, specified by (12.4.1) and (12.4.2), the theorem follows. ∎

This result has two important consequences for building insurance models. First, if we combine m insurance portfolios, where the aggregate claims of each of the portfolios have compound Poisson distributions and are mutually independent, then the aggregate claims for the combined portfolio will also have a compound Poisson distribution. Second, we can consider a single insurance portfolio for a period of m years. Here we assume independence among the annual aggregate claims for the m years and that the aggregate claims for each year have a compound Poisson distribution. It is not necessary that the annual aggregate claims distributions be identical. Then it follows from Theorem 12.4.1 that the total claims for the m-year period will have a compound Poisson distribution.

Example 12.4.1

Let $x_1, x_2, \ldots, x_m$ be m different numbers and suppose that $N_1, N_2, \ldots, N_m$ are mutually independent random variables. Further, suppose that N_i $(i = 1, 2, \ldots, m)$ has a Poisson distribution with parameter λ_i. What is the distribution of

$$x_1 N_1 + x_2 N_2 + \cdots + x_m N_m? \qquad (12.4.4)$$

Solution:

By interpreting $x_i N_i$ to have a compound Poisson distribution with Poisson parameter λ_i and a degenerate claim amount distribution at x_i, we can apply Theorem 12.4.1 to establish that the sum in (12.4.4) has a compound Poisson distribution with

$$\lambda = \sum_{i=1}^{m} \lambda_i$$

and p.f. of claim amount $p(x)$ where

$$p(x) = \begin{cases} \dfrac{\lambda_i}{\lambda} & x = x_i, \quad i = 1, 2, \ldots, m \\ 0 & \text{elsewhere.} \end{cases} \qquad (12.4.5)$$

▼

We show in Theorem 12.4.2 that the construction in Example 12.4.1 is reversible: that is, every compound Poisson distribution with a discrete claim amount distribution can be represented as a sum of the form (12.4.4). We let $x_1, x_2, \ldots, x_m$ denote the discrete values for individual claim amounts and let

$$\pi_i = p(x_i) \qquad i = 1, 2, \ldots, m \qquad (12.4.6)$$

denote their respective probabilities. Let N_i be the number of terms in (12.1.1) that are equal to x_i. Then, by collecting terms, we see that

$$S = x_1 N_1 + x_2 N_2 + \cdots + x_m N_m . \qquad (12.4.7)$$

In general, the N_i's of (12.4.7) are dependent random variables. However, in the special case of a compound Poisson distribution for S, they are independent, as is shown in Theorem 12.4.2.

Before stating Theorem 12.4.2, we cite some properties of the *multinomial distribution* that are used in the proof. For the multinomial, each of n independent

---

trials result in one of m different outcomes. The probability that a trial ends in outcome i is denoted by π_i. We denote the random variable that counts the number of outcomes i in n trials by N_i. Then

$$1 = \sum_{i=1}^{m} \pi_i, \qquad n = \sum_{i=1}^{m} N_i,$$

and the joint p.f. of $N_1, N_2, \ldots, N_m$ is given by

$$\Pr(N_1 = n_1, N_2 = n_2, \ldots, N_m = n_m) = \frac{n!}{n_1!\, n_2! \cdots n_m!}\, \pi_1^{n_1}\, \pi_2^{n_2} \cdots \pi_m^{n_m}. \qquad (12.4.8)$$

By using (12.4.8) we obtain

$$\mathrm{E}\left[\exp\left(\sum_{i=1}^{m} t_i N_i\right)\right] = (\pi_1 e^{t_1} + \pi_2 e^{t_2} + \cdots + \pi_m e^{t_m})^n. \qquad (12.4.9)$$

The multivariate discrete distribution with p.f. given by (12.4.8) and m.g.f. given by (12.4.9) is called a multinomial distribution with parameters $n, \pi_1, \ldots, \pi_m$.

Theorem 12.4.2

If S, as given in (12.4.7), has a compound Poisson distribution with parameter λ and p.f. of claim amounts given by the discrete p.f. exhibited in (12.4.6), then
a. $N_1, N_2, \ldots, N_m$ are mutually independent.
b. N_i has a Poisson distribution with parameter $\lambda_i = \lambda \pi_i$, $i = 1, 2, \ldots, m$.

Proof:

We start by defining the m.g.f. of the joint distribution of $N_1, N_2, \ldots, N_m$ by use of (2.2.10) for conditional expectations. Note that for a fixed number of independent claims (trials) where each claim results in one of m claim amounts, the numbers of claims of each amount have a multinomial distribution with parameters $n, \pi_1, \pi_2, \ldots, \pi_m$. Hence, given

$$N = \sum_{i=1}^{m} N_i = n,$$

the conditional distribution of $N_1, N_2, \ldots, N_m$ is this multinomial distribution. For this case, we use (12.4.9) to obtain

$$\mathrm{E}\left[\exp\left(\sum_{i=1}^{m} t_i N_i\right)\right] = \sum_{n=0}^{\infty} \mathrm{E}\left[\exp\left(\sum_{i=1}^{m} t_i N_i\right)\,\bigg|\, N = n\right]\Pr(N = n)$$

$$= \sum_{n=0}^{\infty} (\pi_1 e^{t_1} + \cdots + \pi_m e^{t_m})^n \frac{e^{-\lambda}\lambda^n}{n!}. \qquad (12.4.10)$$

We now perform the required summation by recognizing (12.4.10) as a Taylor series expansion of an exponential function. We obtain

$$E\left[\exp\left(\sum_{i=1}^{m} t_i\, N_i\right)\right] = \exp(-\lambda)\, \exp\left(\lambda \sum_{i=1}^{m} \pi_i\, e^{t_i}\right)$$

$$= \prod_{i=1}^{m} \exp[\lambda\, \pi_i(e^{t_i} - 1)]. \tag{12.4.11}$$

Since this is the product of m functions each of a single variable t_i, (12.4.11) shows the mutual independence of the N_i's. Furthermore, if we set $t_i = t$, and $t_j = 0$ for $j \neq i$ in (12.4.11), we obtain

$$E[\exp(tN_i)] = \exp[\lambda\, \pi_i(e^t - 1)], \tag{12.4.12}$$

which is the m.g.f. of the Poisson distribution with parameter $\lambda\, \pi_i$. This proves statement (b). ∎

Formula (12.4.7) and Theorem 12.4.2 provide an alternative method for tabulating a compound Poisson distribution with a discrete claim amount distribution. First, we compute the p.f.'s of $x_1 N_1, x_2 N_2, \ldots, x_m N_m$. Since the nonzero entries for the p.f. of $x_i N_i$ are at multiples of x_i and are Poisson probabilities, this is an easy task. Then the convolution of these m distributions is calculated to obtain the p.f. of S. This method is particularly convenient if m, the number of different claim amounts, is small. Even if a continuous distribution has been selected for the individual claim amounts, a discrete approximation can sometimes be used with this alternative method to produce a satisfactory approximation to the distribution of S. The basic and the alternative methods for tabulating the distribution of S are compared in the following example.

Example 12.4.2

Suppose that S has a compound Poisson distribution with $\lambda = 0.8$ and individual claim amounts that are 1, 2, or 3 with probabilities 0.25, 0.375, and 0.375, respectively. Compute $f_S(x) = \Pr(S = x)$ for $x = 0, 1, \ldots, 6$.

Solution:

For the basic method, the calculations parallel those in Example 12.2.2 and are summarized below.

Basic Method Calculations

(1) x	(2) $p^{*0}(x)$	(3) $p(x)$	(4) $p^{*2}(x)$	(5) $p^{*3}(x)$	(6) $p^{*4}(x)$	(7) $p^{*5}(x)$	(8) $p^{*6}(x)$	(9) $f_S(x)$
0	1	—	—	—	—	—	—	0.449329
1	—	0.250000	—	—	—	—	—	0.089866
2	—	0.375000	0.062500	—	—	—	—	0.143785
3	—	0.375000	0.187500	0.015625	—	—	—	0.162358
4	—	—	0.328125	0.070313	0.003906	—	—	0.049905
5	—	—	0.281250	0.175781	0.023438	0.000977	—	0.047360
6	—	—	0.140625	0.263672	0.076172	0.007324	0.000244	0.030923

	n	0	1	2	3	4	5	6
$e^{-0.8}\dfrac{(0.8)^n}{n!}$		0.449329	0.359463	0.143785	0.038343	0.007669	0.001227	0.000164

For the alternative method outlined in this section, the calculations are displayed below.

Alternative Method Calculations

(1) (x)	(2) $\Pr(1N_1 = x)$	(3) $\Pr(2N_2 = x)$	(4) $\Pr(3N_3 = x)$	(5) $\Pr(N_1 + 2N_2 = x)$ $= (2)*(3)$	(6) $\Pr(N_1 + 2N_2 + 3N_3 = x)$ $= (4)*(5) = f_S(x)$
0	0.818731	0.740818	0.740818	0.606531	0.449329
1	0.163746	—	—	0.121306	0.089866
2	0.016375	0.222245	—	0.194090	0.143785
3	0.001092	—	0.222245	0.037201	0.162358
4	0.000055	0.033337	—	0.030973	0.049905
5	0.000002	—	—	0.005703	0.047360
6	0.000000	0.003334	0.033337	0.003287	0.030923
i	1	2	3		
λ_i	0.2	0.3	0.3		
	$\dfrac{e^{-0.2}(0.2)^x}{x!}$	$\dfrac{e^{-0.3}(0.3)^{x/2}}{(x/2)!}$	$\dfrac{e^{-0.3}(0.3)^{x/3}}{(x/3)!}$		

For the application of the formulas of this section, we note that $m = 3$, $x_1 = 1$, $x_2 = 2$, $x_3 = 3$, $\lambda_1 = \lambda\, p(1) = 0.2$, $\lambda_2 = \lambda\, p(2) = 0.3$, and $\lambda_3 = \lambda\, p(3) = 0.3$. First, we compute columns (2), (3), and (4). The nonzero entries are Poisson probabilities. Then we obtain the convolution of the p.f.'s in columns (2) and (3) and record the result in column (5). Finally, we convolute the p.f.'s displayed in columns (4) and (5) and record the result in column (6).

Remember that the complete p.f. is not displayed in either set of calculations. The example required probabilities for only $x = 0, 1, \ldots, 6$. However, $\Pr(S \leq 6)$ $= f_S(0) + f_S(1) + \cdots + f_S(6) = 0.973526$. ▼

Formula (12.4.7) and Theorem 12.4.2 have another implication. Instead of defining a compound Poisson distribution of S by specifying the parameter λ and the d.f. $P(x)$ of the discrete individual claim amounts, we can define the distribution in terms of the possible individual claim amounts $x_1, x_2, \ldots, x_m$ and the parameters $\lambda_1, \lambda_2, \ldots, \lambda_m$ of the associated Poisson distributions described in part (b) of Theorem 12.4.2. Thus for x_i there is an associated Poisson distribution of N_i with parameter λ_i. In terms of this new definition of the distribution of S, we have from $E[N_i] = \text{Var}(N_i) = \lambda_i$ and the independence of the N_i's that

$$E[S] = E\left[\sum_{i=1}^{m} x_i N_i\right] = \sum_{i=1}^{m} x_i \lambda_i \qquad (12.4.13)$$

and

$$\text{Var}(S) = \text{Var}\left(\sum_{i=1}^{m} x_i N_i\right) = \sum_{i=1}^{m} x_i^2 \lambda_i. \qquad (12.4.14)$$

Formula (12.4.13) could be obtained by starting from (12.3.2) and noting that

$$\lambda\,p_1 = \lambda \sum_{i=1}^{m} x_i \pi_i = \sum_{i=1}^{m} x_i \lambda_i.$$

Similarly we can obtain (12.4.14) from (12.3.3).

In some cases it is useful, as in Example 12.4.1, to regard S as a sum of mutually independent random variables $x_i N_i$, $i = 1, 2, \ldots, m$, where $x_i N_i$ has a compound Poisson distribution with parameter λ_i and degenerate claim amount distribution at x_i. This interpretation follows from Theorem 12.4.2 and underlies the alternative method illustrated in Example 12.4.2.

There is a third way, the ***recursive method,*** for evaluating certain compound distributions for which the only possible claim amounts are positive integers. It is based on the recursive formula of the following theorem.

Theorem 12.4.3

For compound distributions where the probability distribution for N, the number of claims, satisfies the condition $\Pr(N = n) / \Pr(N = n - 1) = a + (b/n)$ for $n = 1, 2, \ldots$, and where the distribution of claim amounts is restricted to the positive integers,

$$f_S(x) = \sum_{i=1}^{x} \left[a + \left(\frac{bi}{x} \right) \right] p(i)\, f_S(x - i) \qquad x = 1, 2, \ldots, \qquad (12.4.15)$$

with the starting value given by $f_S(0) = \Pr(N = 0)$.

We establish the following lemma to be used in the proof of the theorem.

Lemma

For $X_1, X_2, X_3, \ldots, X_n$ which are independent and identically distributed random variables taking on values restricted to the positive integers, we have, for positive integer values of x,

(i)
$$p^{*n}(x) = \sum_{i=1}^{x} p(i)\, p^{*(n-1)}(x - i)$$

(ii)
$$p^{*n}(x) = \frac{n}{x} \sum_{i=1}^{x} i\, p(i)\, p^{*(n-1)}(x - i).$$

Proof of the Lemma:

For $n = 1$, both (i) and (ii) reduce to $p^{*1}(x) = p(x) \times p^{*0}(0)$. For $n > 1$ we establish (i) by using the Law of Total Probability to evaluate $\Pr(X_1 + X_2 + \cdots + X_n = x)$ by conditioning on the value taken by X_1 as

$$\sum_{i=1}^{x} \Pr(X_1 = i)\, \Pr(X_2 + X_3 + \cdots + X_n = x - i).$$

We then note that $\Pr(X_2+X_3+ \cdots +X_n = x - i)$ and $\Pr(X_1+X_2+ \cdots +X_n = x)$ can be evaluated by using $(n - 1)$-fold and n-fold convolutions, respectively, of $p(i)$; see (2.3.4).

For $n > 1$, we establish (ii) by considering the conditional expectations $E[X_k|X_1+X_2+X_3+ \cdots +X_n = x]$ for $k = 1, 2, 3, \ldots , n$. From reasons of symmetry, these quantities are the same for all such k. Since their sum is x, each is equal to x/n. The conditional expectation $E[X_1|X_1+X_2+X_3+ \cdots +X_n = x]$ is evaluated as

$$\sum_{i=1}^{x} i \Pr(X_1 = i) \Pr(X_2+X_3+ \cdots +X_n = x - i)/\Pr(X_1 + X_2 + X_3+ \cdots +X_n = x).$$

We then note that $\Pr(X_2+X_3+ \cdots +X_n = x - i)$ and that $\Pr(X_1+X_2+ \cdots +X_n = x)$ can be evaluated by using $(n - 1)$-fold and n-fold convolutions, respectively, of $p(i)$. Solving for $p^{*n}(x)$ completes the proof. ∎

Proof of the Theorem:

First,

$$f_S(x) = \sum_{n=1}^{\infty} \Pr(N = n) \, p^{*n}(x).$$

With $\Pr(N = n) = [a + (b/n)] \Pr(N = n - 1)$, we have

$$f_S(x) = a \sum_{n=1}^{\infty} \Pr(N = n - 1) \, p^{*n}(x) + \sum_{n=1}^{\infty} \frac{b}{n} \Pr(N = n - 1) \, p^{*n}(x),$$

and by the two parts of the lemma

$$f_S(x) = a \sum_{n=1}^{\infty} \Pr(N = n - 1) \sum_{i=1}^{x} p(i) \, p^{*(n-1)}(x - i)$$

$$+ \sum_{n=1}^{\infty} \frac{b}{n} \Pr(N = n - 1) \frac{n}{x} \sum_{i=1}^{x} i \, p(i) \, p^{*(n-1)}(x - i).$$

Interchanging the order of summation, we get

$$f_S(x) = a \sum_{i=1}^{x} p(i) \sum_{n=1}^{\infty} \Pr(N = n - 1) \, p^{*(n-1)}(x - i)$$

$$+ \frac{b}{x} \sum_{i=1}^{x} i p(i) \sum_{n=1}^{\infty} \Pr(N = n - 1) \, p^{*(n-1)}(x - i)$$

$$= a \sum_{i=1}^{x} p(i) f_S(x - i) + \frac{b}{x} \sum_{i=1}^{x} i \, p(i) f_S(x - i)$$

$$= \sum_{i=1}^{x} \left(a + \frac{b\,i}{x} \right) p(i) f_S(x - i).$$
∎

We now examine the only three distributions that satisfy the required relationship between successive values of $\Pr(N = n)$.

a. Poisson: $[\Pr(N = n)/\Pr(N = n - 1)] = \lambda/n$. The recursion formula for the compound Poisson is

$$f_S(x) = \frac{\lambda}{x} \sum_{i=1}^{x} i p(i) f_S(x - i) \quad \text{with} \quad f_S(0) = e^{-\lambda}. \qquad (12.4.16)$$

b. Negative binomial: $[\Pr(N = n) / \Pr(N = n - 1)] = (1 - p)[(n + r - 1)/n]$ so that $a = (1 - p)$ and $b = (1 - p)(r - 1)$. The recursion formula for the compound negative binomial is

$$f_S(x) = (1 - p) \sum_{i=1}^{x} \left[(r - 1) \frac{i}{x} + 1 \right] p(i) f_S(x - i) \qquad (12.4.17)$$

with $f_S(0) = p^r$.

c. Binomial with parameters m and p:

$$\frac{\Pr(N = n)}{\Pr(N = n - 1)} = \frac{m + 1 - n}{n} \frac{p}{1 - p}$$

so that $a = -[p/(1 - p)]$ and $b = (m + 1)[p/(1 - p)]$. The recursion formula in this case is

$$f_S(x) = \left(\frac{p}{1 - p} \right) \sum_{i=1}^{x} \left[(m + 1) \frac{i}{x} - 1 \right] p(i) f_S(x - i) \qquad (12.4.18)$$

with $f_S(0) = (1 - p)^m$.

Example 12.4.2
(recomputed)

For the compound Poisson distribution of this example, compute $f_S(x) = \Pr(S = x)$ by the recursive method.

Solution:

Substituting the values used for the alternative method of calculation into (12.4.16) yields

$$f_S(x) = \frac{1}{x} [0.2 f_S(x - 1) + 0.6 f_S(x - 2) + 0.9 f_S(x - 3)] \qquad x = 1, 2, \ldots.$$

Recalling that $f_S(x) = 0$, $x < 0$, and $f_S(0) = e^{-\lambda} = 0.449329$, we readily reproduce the values of $f_S(x)$ given in the basic method calculations. ▼

12.5 Approximations to the Distribution of Aggregate Claims

In Section 2.4 the normal distribution was employed as an approximation to the distribution of aggregate claims in the individual model. The normal approximation is the first developed here for use with the collective model.

For the compound Poisson distribution, the two parameters of the normal approximation are given by (12.3.2) and (12.3.3). For the compound negative binomial distribution the parameters are given by (12.3.10) and (12.3.11). In each of the two cases the approximation is better when the expected number of claims is large, or, in other words, when λ is large for the compound Poisson case and when r is large

---

for the negative binomial. These two results are contained in Theorem 12.5.1, which may be interpreted as a version of the central limit theorem.

Theorem 12.5.1

a. If S has a compound Poisson distribution, specified by λ and $P(x)$, then the distribution of

$$Z = \frac{S - \lambda\, p_1}{\sqrt{\lambda\, p_2}} \qquad (12.5.1)$$

converges to the standard normal distribution as $\lambda \to \infty$.

b. If S has a compound negative binomial distribution, specified by r, p, and $P(x)$, then the distribution of

$$Z = \frac{S - r(q/p)p_1}{\sqrt{r(q/p)p_2 + r(q^2/p^2)p_1^2}} \qquad (12.5.2)$$

converges to the standard normal distribution as $r \to \infty$.

Proof:

We shall prove statement (a) by showing that

$$\lim_{\lambda \to \infty} M_Z(t) = e^{t^2/2}.$$

Statement (b) can be proved using a similar strategy, but the proof involves additional steps.

From (12.5.1), it follows that

$$M_Z(t) = M_S\left(\frac{t}{\sqrt{\lambda p_2}}\right) \exp\left(-\frac{\lambda p_1\, t}{\sqrt{\lambda p_2}}\right).$$

Now we use (12.3.5) to obtain

$$M_Z(t) = \exp\left\{\lambda\left[M_X\left(\frac{t}{\sqrt{\lambda p_2}}\right) - 1\right] - \frac{\lambda p_1\, t}{\sqrt{\lambda p_2}}\right\}, \qquad (12.5.3)$$

and then substitute the expansion

$$M_X(t) = 1 + \frac{p_1 t}{1!} + \frac{p_2 t^2}{2!} + \cdots, \qquad (12.5.4)$$

with $t/\sqrt{\lambda p_2}$ in place of t, into (12.5.3) to obtain

$$M_Z(t) = \exp\left(\frac{1}{2}t^2 + \frac{1}{6}\frac{1}{\sqrt{\lambda}}\frac{p_3}{p_2^{3/2}}t^3 + \cdots\right). \qquad (12.5.5)$$

Then as $\lambda \to \infty$, $M_Z(t)$ approaches $e^{t^2/2}$, the m.g.f. of the standard normal distribution. ∎

A normal distribution may not be the best approximation to the aggregate claim distribution because the normal distribution is symmetric and the distribution of aggregate claims is often skewed. This skewness is evident in Table 12.5.1, which shows that the third central moment of S under each of the compound Poisson and compound negative binomial distributions is not 0. For positive claim amount distributions, $P(0) = 0$, and the third central moment of S is positive in each case.

TABLE 12.5.1

Calculation of Third Central Moment of S

	Distribution of S	
Step	**Compound Poisson**	**Compound Negative Binomial**
$M_S(t)$	$\exp\{\lambda[M_X(t) - 1]\}$	$\left[\dfrac{p}{1 - qM_X(t)}\right]^r$
$\log M_S(t)$	$\lambda[M_X(t) - 1]$	$r \log p - r \log[1 - qM_X(t)]$
$\dfrac{d^3}{dt^3} \log M_S(t)$	$\lambda M_X'''(t)$	$\dfrac{rqM_X'''(t)}{1 - qM_X(t)} + \dfrac{3rq^2M_X'(t)M_X''(t)}{[1 - qM_X(t)]^2} + \dfrac{2rq^3M_X'(t)^3}{[1 - qM_X(t)]^3}$
$\begin{aligned}&E[(S - E[S])^3] \\ &= \dfrac{d^3}{dt^3} \log M_S(t)\Big|_{t=0}\end{aligned}$ *	λp_3	$\dfrac{rqp_3}{p} + \dfrac{3rq^2p_1p_2}{p^2} + \dfrac{2rq^3p_1^3}{p^3}$

*For $k \geq 4$, $\dfrac{d^k}{dt^k} \log M(t)\Big|_{t=0}$ is not the k-th central moment.

In completing Table 12.5.1 we use properties of the logarithm of a m.g.f., for example,

$$\frac{d}{dt} \log M_X(t)\Big|_{t=0} = \frac{M_X'(0)}{M_X(0)} = \mu$$

and

$$\frac{d^2}{dt^2} \log M_X(t)\Big|_{t=0} = \frac{M_X''(0)M_X(0) - M_X'(0)^2}{M_X(0)^2} = \sigma^2.$$

In Exercise 12.23(a), the reader is asked to confirm the relation used in the last row of Table 12.5.1.

Because of this skewness we seek a more general approximation to the distribution of aggregate claims, one that accommodates skewness. For this second approximation, we begin with a gamma distribution. This choice is motivated by the fact that the gamma distribution has a positive third central moment as do the compound Poisson and compound negative binomial distributions with positive claim amounts. We let $G(x:\alpha, \beta)$ denote the d.f. of the gamma distribution with parameters α and β; that is,

$$G(x:\alpha, \beta) = \int_0^x \frac{\beta^\alpha}{\Gamma(\alpha)} t^{\alpha-1} e^{-\beta t} \, dt. \tag{12.5.6}$$

Then for any x_0 we define a new d.f., denoted by $H(x:\alpha, \beta, x_0)$, as

$$H(x{:}\alpha,\ \beta,\ x_0) = G(x - x_0{:}\alpha,\ \beta). \tag{12.5.7}$$

This amounts to a translation of the distribution $G(x{:}\alpha,\ \beta)$ by x_0. Figure 12.5.1 illustrates this for the case $x_0 > 0$ where $g(x)$, $x \geq 0$, and $h(x)$, $x \geq x_0$, denote, respectively, the p.d.f.'s associated with $G(x{:}\alpha,\ \beta)$ and $H(x{:}\alpha,\ \beta,\ x_0)$.

FIGURE 12.5.1
Translated Gamma Distribution

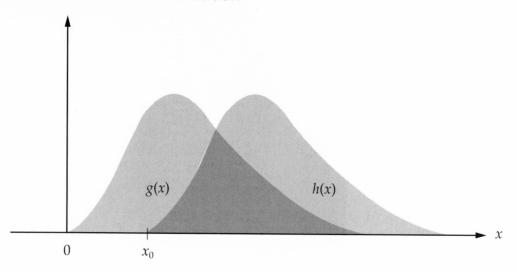

We approximate the distribution of aggregate claims S by a translated gamma distribution where the parameters α, β, and x_0 are selected by equating the first moment and second and third central moments of S with the corresponding characteristics of the translated gamma distribution. Since central moments of the translated gamma are the same as for the basic gamma distribution, this procedure imposes the requirements

$$E[S] = x_0 + \frac{\alpha}{\beta}, \tag{12.5.8}$$

$$\mathrm{Var}(S) = \frac{\alpha}{\beta^2}, \tag{12.5.9}$$

$$E[(S - E[S])^3] = \frac{2\alpha}{\beta^3}. \tag{12.5.10}$$

From these we obtain

$$\beta = 2\,\frac{\mathrm{Var}(S)}{E[(S - E[S])^3]}, \tag{12.5.11}$$

$$\alpha = 4\,\frac{[\mathrm{Var}(S)]^3}{E[(S - E[S])^3]^2}, \tag{12.5.12}$$

$$x_0 = E[S] - 2\,\frac{[\mathrm{Var}(S)]^2}{E[(S - E[S])^3]}. \tag{12.5.13}$$

For a compound Poisson distribution this procedure leads to

$$\alpha = 4\lambda \frac{p_2^3}{p_3^2}, \qquad (12.5.14)$$

$$\beta = 2 \frac{p_2}{p_3}, \qquad (12.5.15)$$

$$x_0 = \lambda\, p_1 - 2\lambda \frac{p_2^2}{p_3}. \qquad (12.5.16)$$

Remark:

We can show that if $\alpha \to \infty$, $\beta \to \infty$, and $x_0 \to -\infty$ such that

$$x_0 + \frac{\alpha}{\beta} = \mu \text{ (constant)}, \qquad (12.5.17)$$

$$\frac{\alpha}{\beta^2} = \sigma^2 \text{ (constant)},$$

the distribution $H(x{:}\alpha, \beta, x_0)$ converges to the $N(\mu, \sigma^2)$ distribution. Therefore, the family of normal distributions is contained, as limiting distributions, within this family of three-parameter gamma distributions. In this sense, this approximation is a generalization of the normal approximation.

Example 12.5.1

Consider the Poisson distribution with parameter $\lambda = 16$. This is the same as the compound Poisson distribution with $\lambda = 16$ and a degenerate claim amount distribution at 1. Compare this distribution with approximations by
a. A translated gamma distribution
b. A normal distribution.

Solution:

a. Here $p_k = 1$, $k = 1, 2, 3$, and from (12.5.14)–(12.5.16), we have $\alpha = 64$, $\beta = 2$, $x_0 = -16$. Note that, unlike the case in Figure 12.5.1, x_0 is negative.
b. For the normal approximation, we use $\mu = 16$ and $\sigma = 4$.

The results given below compare the three distributions. In the approximations, the half-integer discontinuity correction was used to approximate $F_S(x)$ for $x = 5$, $10, \ldots, 40$.

	Exact	Approximations	
x	$\sum_{y=0}^{x} \frac{e^{-16}\,(16)^y}{y!}$	$G(x+16.5 : 64, 2)$	$\Phi\left(\dfrac{x + 0.5 - 16}{4}\right)$
5	0.001384	0.001636	0.004332
10	0.077396	0.077739	0.084566
15	0.466745	0.466560	0.450262
20	0.868168	0.868093	0.869705
25	0.986881	0.986604	0.991226
30	0.999433	0.999378	0.999856
35	0.999988	0.999985	0.999999
40	1.000000	1.000000	1.000000

▼

In the case of the compound negative binomial distribution there is an additional argument that supports the use of a gamma approximation. The argument is outlined in the Appendix to this chapter.

12.6 Notes and References

Chapter 2 of Seal (1969) contains an extensive survey of the literature on collective risk models, including the pioneering work of Lundberg on the compound Poisson distribution. Several authors, for example, Dropkin (1959) and Simon (1960), have used the negative binomial distribution to model the number of automobile accidents by a collection of policyholders in a fixed period.

In Example 12.3.1 we derived the negative binomial distribution by assuming that the unknown Poisson parameter has a gamma distribution. This idea goes back at least as far as Greenwood and Yule's work on accident proneness (1920). An alternative derivation in terms of a contagion model is due to Polya and Eggenberger and may be found in Chapter 2 of Bühlmann (1970). In the special case where r is an integer, the negative binomial can be obtained as the distribution of the number of Bernoulli trials that end in failure prior to the r-th success. This development may be found in most probability texts, but has little relevance to the subject of this chapter.

Theorem 12.4.2 has been known for some time and can be studied in Section 2, Chapter 2 of Feller (1968). The alternative method for computing probabilities for a compound Poisson distribution, which is based on Theorem 12.4.2, was suggested by Pesonen (1967) and implemented by Halmstad (1976) in the calculation of stop-loss premiums. Theorem 12.4.2 has a converse, which was not stated in Section 12.4. Renyi (1962) shows that the mutual independence of $N_1, N_2, \ldots, N_m$ implies that N has a Poisson distribution. Hence the alternative method of computing will work only for the compound Poisson distribution.

The alternative method of computation may also be adopted to build a simulation model for aggregate claims. Instead of determining the individual claim amounts, one simulates $N_1, N_2, \ldots, N_m$ and obtains a realization of S directly from (12.4.7). For one determination of S, the expected number of random numbers required is $1 + \lambda$ under the basic method. If the alternative method is used, exactly m random numbers are required for each determination of a value of S.

There are several more elaborate methods of approximating the distribution of aggregate claims. The normal power and Esscher approximations are described in Beard, Pesonen, and Pentikäinen (1984). Several of the approximation methods have been compared by Bohman and Esscher (1963, 1964). Seal (1978a) presents the case for the translated gamma approximation and illustrates its excellent performance. Bowers (1966) approximated the distribution of aggregate claims by a sum of orthogonal functions, the first term of which is the gamma distribution. The result, stated in the Appendix to this chapter, that the gamma distribution can be obtained as a limit from the compound negative binomial is due to Lundberg (1940).

Sometimes the distribution of aggregate claims can be obtained from a numerical inversion of its m.g.f.; this is developed in Chapter 3 of Seal (1978).

A monograph by Panjer and Willmot (1992) develops more completely the ideas of this chapter with particular emphasis on recursive calculation and discrete approximations.

Appendix

Theorem 12.A.1

If the random variables S_k, $k = 0, 1, 2, \ldots$, have compound negative binomial distributions with parameters r and $p(k)$ and claim amount d.f. $P(x)$, and if the parameters of the negative binomial distributions are such that

$$\frac{q(k)}{p(k)} = k \frac{q}{p}$$

for $k = 1, 2, 3, \ldots$, where $q = 1 - p$ is a constant, then the distribution of

$$\frac{S_k}{\mathrm{E}[S_k]}$$

approaches $G(x{:}r, r)$ as $k \to \infty$.

Proof:

Using (12.3.12), we find the m.g.f. of $S_k / \mathrm{E}[S_k]$ to be

$$\left[\frac{p(k)}{1 - q(k)M_X(t / \mathrm{E}[S_k])} \right]^r. \tag{12.A.1}$$

We also have

$$M_X\left(\frac{t}{\mathrm{E}[S_k]} \right) = 1 + \frac{p_1}{\mathrm{E}[S_k]} t + \frac{p_2}{2\mathrm{E}[S_k]^2} t^2 + \cdots. \tag{12.A.2}$$

If (12.A.2) is substituted into (12.A.1), we obtain

$$\left\{ \frac{p(k)}{1 - q(k) - [q(k)p_1 / \mathrm{E}[S_k]]t - [q(k)p_2 / 2\mathrm{E}[S_k]^2]t^2 - \cdots} \right\}^r. \tag{12.A.3}$$

Now, since

$$\mathrm{E}[S_k] = r \frac{q(k)p_1}{p(k)} = r \frac{kqp_1}{p},$$

we see that the m.g.f. of $S_k / \mathrm{E}[S_k]$ is

$$\left[1 - \frac{1}{r}t - \frac{p_2}{2r^2p_1^2(q/p)k}t^2 - \cdots\right]^{-r} = \left[1 - \frac{1}{r}t - R(k)\right]^{-r}$$

where the remainder term $R(k)$ is such that $\lim_{k\to\infty} R(k) = 0$. Therefore,

$$\lim_{k\to\infty} \mathrm{E}\left[\exp\left(t\,\frac{S_k}{\mathrm{E}[S_k]}\right)\right] = \left(\frac{r}{r-t}\right)^r, \tag{12.A.4}$$

which is the m.g.f. of a $G(x{:}r, r)$ distribution. ∎

It follows from (12.A.4) that the m.g.f. of S_k itself is approximately

$$\left(\frac{r}{r - \mathrm{E}[S_k]t}\right)^r = \left\{\frac{r}{r - [rq(k)/p(k)]p_1 t}\right\}^r = \left\{\frac{p(k)/[q(k)p_1]}{p(k)/[q(k)p_1] - t}\right\}^r,$$

which is the m.g.f. of $G\{x{:}r, [p(k)/q(k)p_1]\}$. Thus, when k is large, which under the hypothesis of Theorem 12.A.1 implies that the expected number of claims, $rq(k)/p(k) = rk(q/p)$, is large, the distribution of aggregate claims is approximately a gamma distribution.

Theorem 12.A.1 is presented to provide an argument supporting the use of gamma distributions to approximate the distribution of aggregate claims. Comparison of the main ideas in Theorem 12.5.1(b) and Theorem 12.A.1 leads to insights. Theorem 12.5.1(b) follows closely the pattern of the central limit theorem. If in (12.5.2) one writes

$$Z = \frac{S/r - (q/p)p_1}{\sqrt{(q/p)p_2 + (q^2/p^2)p_1^2}/\sqrt{r}},$$

the correspondence is clear, with the parameter r playing the role of n in the central limit theorem.

In Theorem 12.A.1 the parameter r of the negative binomial distribution remains fixed. The expected number of claims changes in proportion to a size parameter k, by compensating changes in $q(k)$ and $p(k) = 1 - q(k)$. Under the hypothesis of Theorem 12.A.1,

$$\mathrm{Var}(S_k) = \frac{rkq}{p}p_2 + r\frac{k^2q^2}{p^2}p_1^2$$

and

$$\mathrm{Var}\left(\frac{S_k}{\mathrm{E}[S_k]}\right) = \frac{p}{rkqp_1^2}p_2 + \frac{1}{r}.$$

As the size parameter $k \to \infty$,

$$\mathrm{Var}\left(\frac{S_k}{\mathrm{E}[S_k]}\right) \to \frac{1}{r},$$

as indicated by Theorem 12.A.1. Thus the gamma approximation may be considered in the negative binomial case when the expected number of claims is large and the claim amount distribution has relatively small dispersion.

Exercises

12.1. Let S denote the number of people crossing a certain intersection by car in a given hour. How would you model S as a random sum?

12.2. Let S denote the total amount of rain that falls at a weather station in a given month. How would you model S as a random sum?

Section 12.2

12.3. Suppose N has a binomial distribution with parameters n and p. Express each of the following in terms of n, p, p_1, p_2, and $M_X(t)$:
a. E[S]   b. Var(S)   c. $M_S(t)$.

12.4. For the distribution specified in Example 12.2.2, calculate
a. E[N]   b. Var(N)   c. E[X]
d. Var(X)   e. E[S]   f. Var(S).

Section 12.3

12.5. Suppose that the claim amount distribution is the same as in Example 12.2.2, but that N has a Poisson distribution with E[N] = 1.7. Calculate
a. E[S]   b. Var(S).

12.6. Suppose that S has a compound Poisson distribution with $\lambda = 2$ and $p(x) = 0.1x$, $x = 1, 2, 3, 4$. Calculate probabilities that aggregate claims equal 0, 1, 2, 3, and 4.

12.7. Consider the family of negative binomial distributions with parameters r and p. Let $r \to \infty$ and $p \to 1$ such that $r(1 - p) = \lambda$ remains constant. Show that the limit obtained is the Poisson distribution with parameter λ. [Hint: Note that $p^r = [1 - (\lambda / r)]^r \to e^{-\lambda}$ as $r \to \infty$, and consider the convergence of the m.g.f.]

12.8. Suppose that S has a compound Poisson distribution with Poisson parameter λ and claim amount p.f.

$$p(x) = [-\log(1 - c)]^{-1} \frac{c^x}{x} \qquad x = 1, 2, 3, \ldots, \qquad 0 < c < 1.$$

Consider the m.g.f. of S and show that S has a negative binomial distribution with parameters p and r. Express p and r in terms of c and λ.

12.9. Let

$$g(x) = 3^{18} \, x^{17} \frac{e^{-3x}}{17!}$$

and

$$h(x) = 3^6 \, x^5 \frac{e^{-3x}}{5!} \qquad x > 0$$

be two p.d.f.'s. Write the convolution of these two distributions, that is, exhibit $g*h(x)$. [Hint: Proceed directly from the definition of convolution in Section 2.3, or make use of (12.3.19).]

12.10. Suppose that the number of accidents incurred by an insured driver in a single year has a Poisson distribution with parameter λ. If an accident happens, the probability is p that the damage amount will exceed a deductible amount. On the assumption that the number of accidents is independent of the severity of the accidents, derive the distribution of the number of accidents that result in a claim payment.

12.11. The m.g.f. of the Poisson inverse Gaussian distribution is given in the solution to Example 12.3.2. Replace the α parameter by $\lambda\beta$ so that the mean is now λ and the variance is $\lambda + \lambda/\beta$. Show that

$$\lim_{\beta\to\infty} M_N(t) = e^{\lambda(e^t-1)}.$$

This confirms that the Poisson inverse Gaussian distribution approaches the Poisson distribution as $\beta \to \infty$ and the mean remains constant.

Section 12.4

12.12. Suppose that S_1 has a compound Poisson distribution with Poisson parameter $\lambda = 2$ and claim amounts that are 1, 2, or 3 with probabilities 0.2, 0.6, and 0.2, respectively. In addition, S_2 has a compound Poisson distribution with Poisson parameter $\lambda = 6$ and claim amounts that are either 3 or 4 with probability 0.5 for each. If S_1 and S_2 are independent, what is the distribution of $S_1 + S_2$?

12.13. Suppose that N_1, N_2, N_3 are mutually independent and that N_i has a Poisson distribution with $E[N_i] = i^2$, $i = 1, 2, 3$. What is the distribution of $S = -2N_1 + N_2 + 3N_3$?

12.14. If N has a Poisson distribution with parameter λ, express $\Pr(N = n + 1)$ in terms of $\Pr(N = n)$.

Note that this recursive formula may be useful in calculations such as those for successive entries in columns (2), (3), and (4) of the alternate method calculations of Example 12.4.2.

12.15. Suppose that S has a compound Poisson distribution with parameter λ and discrete p.f. $p(x)$, $x > 0$. Let $0 < \alpha < 1$.

Consider $\tilde{S}$ with a distribution that is compound Poisson with Poisson parameter $\tilde{\lambda} = \lambda/\alpha$ and claim amount p.f. $\tilde{p}(x)$ where

$$\tilde{p}(x) = \begin{cases} \alpha p(x) & x > 0 \\ 1 - \alpha & x = 0. \end{cases}$$

This means we are allowing for claim amounts of 0 (as could happen if there is a deductible) and are modifying the distributions accordingly. Show that S and $\tilde{S}$ have the same distribution by

a. Comparing the m.g.f.'s of S and $\tilde{S}$

b. Comparing the definition of the distribution of S and $\tilde{S}$ in terms of possible claim amounts and the Poisson parameters of the distributions of their frequencies.

12.16. In Example 12.2.2, let N_1 be the random number of claims of amount 1 and N_2 the random number of claims of amount 2. Compute

    a. $\Pr(N_1 = 1)$ b. $\Pr(N_2 = 1)$ c. $\Pr(N_1 = 1, N_2 = 1)$.

Are N_1 and N_2 independent?

12.17. Compute $f_S(x)$ for $x = 0, 1, 2, \ldots, 5$ for the following three compound distributions, each with claim amount distribution given by $p(1) = 0.7$ and $p(2) = 0.3$:

    a. Poisson with $\lambda = 4.5$

    b. Negative binomial with $r = 4.5$ and $p = 0.5$

    c. Binomial with $m = 9$ and $p = 0.5$

    d. For each of the distributions of (a), (b), and (c) calculate the mean and variance of the number of claims.

12.18. Let S, as given in (12.4.7), have a compound negative binomial distribution with parameters r and p and p.f. of claim amounts given by the discrete p.f. exhibited in (12.4.6).

    a. Show that N_i has a negative binomial distribution with parameters r and $p/(p + q\pi_i)$.

    b. Show that, in general, N_1 and N_2 are not independent.

    [Hint: Use the joint m.g.f. of $N_1, N_2, \ldots, N_m$ as in the proof of Theorem 12.4.2.]

12.19. Show that the compound distribution of Example 12.2.2 does not satisfy the hypotheses of Theorem 12.4.3.

Section 12.5

12.20. Show that if N has a Poisson distribution with parameter λ, the distribution of

$$Z = \frac{N - \lambda}{\sqrt{\lambda}}$$

approaches a $N(0, 1)$ distribution as $\lambda \to \infty$.

12.21. Use log $M_S(t)$ as given in Table 12.5.1 to verify (12.3.3) and (12.3.11).

12.22. Suppose that the d.f. of S is $G(x{:}\alpha, \beta)$. Use the m.g.f. [see (12.3.19)] to show that

$$E[S^h] = \frac{\alpha(\alpha + 1)(\alpha + 2) \cdots (\alpha + h - 1)}{\beta^h} \qquad h = 1, 2, 3, \ldots.$$

12.23. a. Verify that

$$\left.\frac{d^3}{dt^3} \log M_X(t)\right|_{t=0} = E[(X - E[X])^3].$$

b. Use (a) to show that if S has a $G(x{:}\alpha, \beta)$ distribution, then

$$E[(S - E[S])^3] = \frac{2\alpha}{\beta^3}.$$

12.24. a. For a given α, determine β and x_0 so that $H(x{:}\alpha, \beta, x_0)$ has mean 0 and variance 1.
b. What is the limit of $H(x{:}\alpha, \sqrt{\alpha}, -\sqrt{\alpha})$ as $\alpha \to \infty$?

12.25. Suppose that S has a compound Poisson distribution with $\lambda = 12$ and claim amounts that are uniformly distributed between 0 and 1. Approximate $\Pr(S < 10)$ using
a. The normal approximation
b. The translated gamma approximation.

Miscellaneous

12.26. The loss ratio for a collection of insurance policies over a single premium period is defined as $R = S/G$ where S is aggregate claims and G is aggregate premiums. Assume that $G = p_1 E[N](1 + \theta)$, $\theta > 0$.
a. Show that

$$E[R] = (1 + \theta)^{-1}$$

and that

$$\mathrm{Var}(R) = \frac{E[N] \; \mathrm{Var}(X) + p_1^2 \; \mathrm{Var}(N)}{[p_1 \; E[N](1 + \theta)]^2}.$$

b. Develop an expression for $\mathrm{Var}(R)$ if
  (i) N has a Poisson distribution
  (ii) N has a negative binomial distribution.

12.27. Suppose that the distribution of S_1 is compound Poisson, given by λ and $P_1(x)$, and that the distribution of S_2 is compound negative binomial, given by r, p with $q = 1 - p$, and $P_2(x)$. Show that S_1 and S_2 have the same distribution provided that $\lambda = -r \log p$ and

$$P_1(x) = \frac{\displaystyle\sum_{k=1}^{\infty} (q^k / k) \; P_2^{*k}(x)}{-\log p}.$$

[Hint: Show equality of the m.g.f.'s.]

Note that, in the sense of this exercise, every compound negative binomial distribution can be considered as compound Poisson.

12.28. Let S, as given in (12.4.7), have a compound Poisson inverse Gaussian distribution with parameters α and β and p.f. of claim amounts given by the discrete p.f. exhibited in (12.4.6).

    a. Show that N_i has a Poisson inverse Gaussian distribution and determine its parameter values.

    b. Show that, in general, N_1 and N_2 are not independent.

12.29. Follow the steps displayed in Table 12.5.1 to show that the third central moment of S, when it has a compound Poisson inverse Gaussian distribution, can be expressed in the parameters of its distribution as

$$\frac{\alpha}{\beta} p_3 + \frac{3\alpha}{\beta^2} p_1 p_2 + \frac{3\alpha}{\beta^3} p_1^3.$$

12.30. a. Verify that the extension of (2.2.10) for the mean and (2.2.11) for the variance to the third central moment, $\mu_3(W) = E[\{W - E[W]\}^3]$, is $E[\mu_3(W|V)] + 3\,\text{Cov}(\text{Var}(W|V), E[W|V]) + \mu_3(E[W|V])$.

[Hint: Write $W - E[W] = (W - E[W|V]) + (E[W|V] - E[W])$, expand to the third power, and take expectations termwise.]

    b. Apply the result of (a) to S of (12.1.1) to express its third central moment in terms of the parameters of its distribution in the style of (12.2.6).

    c. Apply the formula of (b) to the compound distributions of Table 12.5.1 to confirm the third central moments shown there.

    d. Apply the formula of (b) to the compound Poisson inverse Gaussian distribution to confirm the formula of the previous exercise.

COLLECTIVE RISK MODELS OVER AN EXTENDED PERIOD

13.1 Introduction

The purpose of this chapter is to present mathematical models for the variations in the amount of an insurer's *surplus* over an extended period of time. By surplus we mean the excess of the initial fund plus premiums collected over claims paid. This is a convenient mathematical, but not accounting, definition of surplus.

Let $U(t)$ denote the surplus at time t, $c(t)$ denote premiums collected through time t, and $S(t)$ denote aggregate claims paid through time t. If u is the surplus on hand at time 0, perhaps as a result of past operations, then $U(t)$ is given by

$$U(t) = u + c(t) - S(t) \qquad t \geq 0. \tag{13.1.1}$$

Now motivated by the question of exhausting surplus at least once in a period of time, we want to explore probability questions about $U(t)$ for many—indeed, infinitely many—values of t simultaneously. Since the questions involve more than a finite number of random variables, consistent with the language of probability, we call $U(t)$ the **surplus process** and $S(t)$ the **aggregate claims process.** The premiums collected, $c(t)$, will be deterministic, not a stochastic process.

In this setting the models in the previous chapter can be viewed as being concerned with the distribution of the random variable, $U(t)$, for a single value of t. The monitoring for a negative value of the surplus, $U(t)$, can be on a period-to-period basis or on an ongoing basis. In the latter case we would look at the continuous time surplus process

$$\{U(t): t \geq 0\}.$$

A typical outcome of this surplus process, $\{U(t), t \geq 0\}$, is shown in Figure 13.1.1. We assume a constant premium rate, c, $c > 0$, and set $c(t) = ct$ throughout this chapter. Then the surplus increases linearly (with slope c) except at those times when a claim occurs. At that time the surplus drops by the amount of the claim. If the initial surplus u were increased or decreased by the amount h, the graph of

FIGURE 13.1.1

A Typical Outcome of the Continuous Time Surplus Process

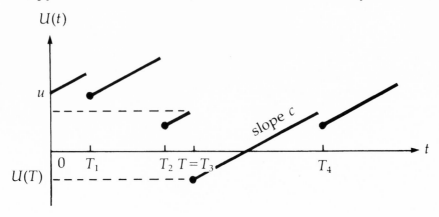

$U(t)$ would be raised or lowered h units of height but would be unchanged otherwise.

As illustrated in Figure 13.1.1, the surplus might become negative at certain times. When this first happens, we speak of **ruin** having occurred. This term has its roots in the gambler's ruin problem of probability theory. It is not equivalent to **insolvency** of an insurer. The typical application of the ideas of this chapter is to a project or line of business of an insurer. However, a useful measure of the financial risk in an insurance organization can be obtained by calculating the probability of ruin as a consequence of variations in the amount and timing of claims.

Let

$$T = \min \{t : t \geq 0 \text{ and } U(t) < 0\} \tag{13.1.2}$$

denote the time of ruin with the understanding that $T = \infty$ if $U(t) \geq 0$ for all t. Let

$$\psi(u) = \Pr(T < \infty) \tag{13.1.3}$$

denote the probability of ruin considered as a function of the initial surplus u. We are also interested in $U(T)$, the negative surplus at the time of ruin.

Because of changes in the world of applications, the useful lifetime of a model is limited so that a realistic planning horizon might be a long—but finite—period. More precisely, consideration would be limited to

$$\psi(u, t) = \Pr(T < t), \tag{13.1.4}$$

the probability of ruin before time t. We discuss, however, only the probability of ruin over an infinite horizon, $\psi(u)$, which is more tractable mathematically. Of course, $\psi(u)$ is an upper bound for $\psi(u, t)$.

The ideas for this chapter can be used to provide an early warning system for the guidance of an insurance project. A model must necessarily be selected to represent the risk process. The probability of ruin, on the basis of that model, warns management of the project about some of the risks involved. Again, particular models developed in this chapter make simplifying assumptions to keep the mathematics tractable. The effects of interest, expenses, dividends, and experience rating are not included. Nevertheless, these models provide a means of analyzing the risk process. In practice, they would be supplemented by additional analyses.

Before we consider the continuous time model we turn to the *discrete time surplus process* defined by considering the values of $U(t)$ at only integer values of t. Traditionally, this sequence of random variables is denoted

$$\{U_n : n = 0, 1, 2, \ldots\}.$$

This can be viewed as examining the amount of surplus on a periodic basis, much as would be done by the managers of insurance enterprises who are required to submit financial reports on the operations on a yearly, semiannual, quarterly, or monthly basis.

13.2   A Discrete Time Model

Let U_n denote the insurer's surplus at time n, $n = 0, 1, 2, \ldots$. We assume that

$$U_n = u + nc - S_n \tag{13.2.1}$$

where u is the initial surplus, the amount of premiums received each period is constant and denoted by c, and S_n is the aggregate claims of the first n periods. Further we assume that

$$S_n = W_1 + W_2 + \cdots + W_n \tag{13.2.2}$$

where W_i is the sum of the claims in period i. At first we assume $W_1, W_2, \ldots$ are independent, identically distributed random variables with $\mu = E[W_i] < c$; later we will relax this constraint.

Thus, we can write U_n as

$$U_n = u + (c - W_1) + (c - W_2) + \cdots + (c - W_n). \tag{13.2.3}$$

Let

$$\tilde{T} = \min\{n : U_n < 0\} \tag{13.2.4}$$

denote the time of ruin (again with the understanding that $\tilde{T} = \infty$ if $U_n \geq 0$ for all n) and let

$$\tilde{\psi}(u) = \Pr(\tilde{T} < \infty) \tag{13.2.5}$$

denote the probability of ruin in this context.

There is an important connection between a quantity that we now define, the *adjustment coefficient,* and the probability of ruin. We define the adjustment coefficient $\tilde{R}$ as the positive solution of the equation

$$M_{W-c}(r) = E[e^{r(W-c)}] = e^{-rc} M_W(r) = 1 \tag{13.2.6}$$

or the equivalent equation

$$\log M_W(r) = rc \qquad (13.2.7)$$

where W denotes a random variable with the distribution of the annual claims, W_i.

The graph of $e^{-rc} M_W(r)$ (see Figure 13.2.1) can be traced by observing that

$$\frac{d}{dr} E[e^{r(W-c)}] = E[(W - c)e^{r(W-c)}]$$

and

$$\frac{d^2}{dr^2} E[e^{r(W-c)}] = E[(W - c)^2 e^{r(W-c)}].$$

FIGURE 13.2.1

Definition of $\tilde{R}$

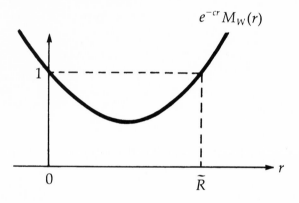

The first of these observations shows that the slope at $r = 0$ is $\mu - c$, a negative quantity, and the second shows that the graph is concave upward. Further, provided W has positive probability over values in excess of c, the first derivative, for some large enough r, becomes positive and remains so. Thus, $E[e^{r(W-c)}]$ has a minimum as indicated in Figure 13.2.1, and (13.2.6) will typically have a positive root as shown. This positive root is called the **adjustment coefficient.** Example 13.4.3 can be used to illustrate that $\tilde{R}$ does not exist for all distributions and values of c.

Example 13.2.1

Derive an expression for $\tilde{R}$ in the special case where the W_i's common distribution is $N(\mu, \sigma^2)$.

Solution:
   Here

$$\log[M_W(r)] = \mu\, r + \frac{\sigma^2 r^2}{2}.$$

Hence, the positive solution of (13.2.7) is

$$\tilde{R} = \frac{2(c - \mu)}{\sigma^2}$$

where, as assumed above, $\mu < c$. ▼

The connection between the adjustment coefficient and the probability of ruin is given in the following result.

Theorem 13.2.1

Let $U_n = u + nc - \sum_{i=1}^{n} W_i$ for $n = 1, 2, \ldots$, and $W_1, W_2, \ldots$ be mutually independent and identically distributed with $E[W_i] = \mu < c$. For $u > 0$,

$$\tilde{\psi}(u) = \frac{\exp(-\tilde{R}\, u)}{E[\exp(-\tilde{R}\, U_{\tilde{T}}) \mid \tilde{T} < \infty]}. \qquad (13.2.8)$$

Theorem 13.2.1 is a special case of Theorem 13.2.2 which is proved in the Appendix to this chapter.

Since $U_{\tilde{T}} < 0$ by definition, it follows from Theorem 13.2.1 that

$$\tilde{\psi}(u) < \exp(-\tilde{R}\, u). \qquad (13.2.9)$$

We now derive an approximation for $\tilde{R}$. In the discussion of Table 12.5.1 we saw that for a random variable X

$$\frac{d}{dt} \log M_X(t) \big|_{t=0} = E[X]$$

and

$$\frac{d^2}{dt^2} \log M_X(t) \big|_{t=0} = \text{Var}(X).$$

Hence, using the Maclaurin series expansion, we have

$$\log M_W(r) = \mu\, r + \frac{1}{2}\, \sigma^2\, r^2 + \cdots$$

where $\sigma^2 = \text{Var}(W)$. If we use only the first two terms of this expansion in (13.2.7), we obtain the approximation

$$\tilde{R} \cong \frac{2(c - \mu)}{\sigma^2}. \qquad (13.2.10)$$

Comparing this with Example 13.2.1, we observe that (13.2.10) is exact in the case where the W_i's common distribution is normal. Furthermore, if W has a compound distribution and the relative security loading θ is given by $c = (1 + \theta)\, \mu$, then (12.2.5) and (12.2.6) yield

---

Chapter 13   Collective Risk Models over an Extended Period   **403**

$$\tilde{R} \cong \frac{2\theta \, p_1 \, E[N]}{(p_2 - p_1^2)E[N] + p_1^2 \, \text{Var}(N)} \tag{13.2.11}$$

where N is a random variable distributed as the number of claims in a period.

Example 13.2.2

Approximate $\tilde{R}$ if
a. N has a Poisson distribution with parameter λ
b. N has a negative binomial distribution with parameters r and p.

Solution:

a. Here $E[N] = \text{Var}(N) = \lambda$, and (13.2.11) reduces to

$$\tilde{R} \cong \frac{2\theta \, p_1}{p_2}. \tag{13.2.12}$$

It follows from Exercise 13.6 that the right-hand side of (13.2.12) is actually an upper bound.
b. In this case,

$$E[N] = \frac{rq}{p},$$

$$\text{Var}(N) = \frac{rq}{p^2},$$

so it follows from (13.2.11) that

$$\tilde{R} \cong \frac{2\theta \, p_1}{p_2 + p_1^2[(1/p) - 1]}. \tag{13.2.13}$$

Note that for $p \to 1$, the result in (a) is obtained. ▼

It has been assumed that the total amounts of claims in different periods are independent random variables. In many cases, this assumption may be unrealistic. To investigate a situation of this type, we now consider an autoregressive model for the insurer's claim costs that generalizes the model previously considered and allows for correlation between the claims of successive periods.

We assume that W_i, the sum of claims in period i, is of the form

$$W_i = Y_i + a \, W_{i-1} \qquad i = 1, 2, \ldots. \tag{13.2.14}$$

Here $-1 < a < 1$, and $Y_1, Y_2, \ldots$ are independent and identically distributed random variables with $E[Y_i] < (1 - a) \, c$. The initial value $W_0 = w$ completes the description of this first-order autoregressive model for the W_i's.

The insurer's surplus U_n at time n is defined as in (13.2.1) and $\tilde{T}$, the time of ruin, as in (13.2.4). Note that the probability of ruin,

$$\tilde{\psi}(u, w) = \Pr(\tilde{T} < \infty), \tag{13.2.15}$$

is now a function of two variables. This generalizes the model considered previously, which corresponds to the special case $a = 0$.

We now use the iterative rule in (13.2.14) to obtain

$$W_i = Y_i + a\,Y_{i-1} + \cdots + a^{i-1}\,Y_1 + a^i\,w. \qquad (13.2.16)$$

Thus the total of the claims in the first n periods is

$$S_n = Y_n + (1 + a)\,Y_{n-1} + \cdots + (1 + a + \cdots + a^{n-1})\,Y_1$$
$$+ (a + a^2 + \cdots + a^n)\,w$$
$$= Y_n + \frac{1 - a^2}{1 - a}\,Y_{n-1} + \cdots + \frac{1 - a^n}{1 - a}\,Y_1 + a\,\frac{1 - a^n}{1 - a}\,w. \qquad (13.2.17)$$

This shows that Y_1 ultimately contributes $Y_1 / (1 - a)$ to the total claims. Hence, we assume that $c > E[Y_1] / (1 - a)$, and in analogy to (13.2.6), we define the adjustment coefficient as the positive solution of the equation

$$e^{-cr}\, M_{Y/(1-a)}\,(r) = 1. \qquad (13.2.18)$$

Thus $\tilde{R}$ is a positive number with the property that

$$\log E\left[\exp\left(\frac{\tilde{R}Y}{1 - a}\right)\right] - c\tilde{R} = 0. \qquad (13.2.19)$$

Note that $\tilde{R}$ depends on the common distribution of the Y_i's and on the values of a and c.

In the Appendix to this chapter, the following result will be derived.

Theorem 13.2.2

$$\tilde{\psi}(u, w) = \frac{\exp(-\tilde{R}\hat{u})}{E[\exp(-\tilde{R}\hat{U}_{\tilde{T}}) \mid \tilde{T} < \infty]}. \qquad (13.2.20)$$

Here we have used the notation

$$\hat{U}_n = U_n - \frac{a}{1 - a}\,W_n \qquad \hat{u} = \hat{U}_0. \qquad (13.2.21)$$

In a sense, $\hat{U}_n$ is a modified surplus. It is the actual surplus U_n adjusted by all future claims that are related to W_n. This interpretation of $\hat{U}_n$ is developed in Exercise 13.2.

If $a \geq 0$, it follows that $\hat{U}_{\tilde{T}} \leq U_{\tilde{T}} < 0$. Thus, in this case, the denominator of (13.2.20) is greater than 1, and we get a simplified upper bound for the probability of ruin.

Corollary 13.2.1

If $0 \leq a < 1$, then

$$\tilde{\psi}(u, w) \leq \exp(-\tilde{R}\hat{u}). \qquad (13.2.22)$$

Note that this generalizes (13.2.9).

13.3   A Continuous Time Model

We now formulate the ruin model using two continuous time random processes, the claim number process and the aggregate claim process. We usually model the first by a Poisson process and the second by a compound Poisson process.

For a certain portfolio of insurance, let $N(t)$ denote the number of claims and $S(t)$ the aggregate claims up to time t. We start the count at time 0; thus, $N(0) = 0$. Furthermore, $S(t) = 0$ as long as $N(t) = 0$. As in Chapter 12, we let X_i denote the amount of the i-th claim. Then

$$S(t) = X_1 + X_2 + X_3 + \cdots + X_{N(t)}. \tag{13.3.1}$$

The process $\{N(t), t \geq 0\}$ is called the **claim number process**, whereas $\{S(t), t \geq 0\}$ is called the **aggregate claim process.** These collections of random variables are called processes, and we are interested in the distributions simultaneously at all times $t \geq 0$. This is in contrast to Chapter 12 where we were interested in the number of claims and aggregate claims for a single period.

Let $t \geq 0$ and $h > 0$. From the definitions it follows that $N(t + h) - N(t)$ is the number of claims and $S(t + h) - S(t)$ is the aggregate amount of claims that occur in the time interval between t and $t + h$. Let T_i denote the time when the i-th claim occurs. Thus $T_1, T_2, \ldots$ are random variables such that $T_1 < T_2 < T_3 < \ldots$ to exclude the possibility that two or more claims occur at the same time. The time elapsed between successive claims is denoted by $V_1 = T_1$, and

$$V_i = T_i - T_{i-1} \qquad i > 1. \tag{13.3.2}$$

Typical outcomes of the claim number process and the aggregate claim process are depicted in Figures 13.3.1 and 13.3.2. Note that $N(t)$ and $S(t)$ are increasing step functions. The discontinuities are at times T_i when the claims occur, and the size of the steps at these times is 1 for $N(t)$ and the corresponding claim amount X_i for $S(t)$.

FIGURE 13.3.1

A Typical Outcome of the Claim Number Process

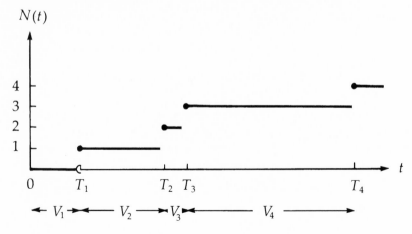

FIGURE 13.3.2

A Typical Outcome of the Aggregate Claim Process

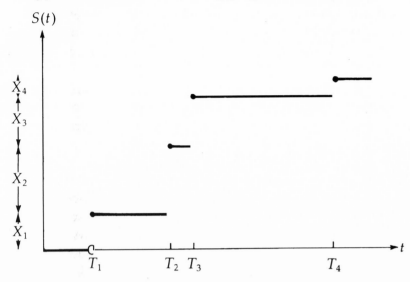

There are several ways to define the distribution of a claim number process. We examine two of them:

a. The **global method:** For all $t \geq 0$ and all $h > 0$ we specify the conditional distribution of $N(t + h) - N(t)$, given the values of $N(s)$ for $s \leq t$.

b. The **discrete method:** We specify the joint distribution of $V_1, V_2, V_3, \ldots$ or, equivalently, that of $T_1, T_2, T_3, \ldots$.

Example 13.3.1

Consider n people age x at time 0. Let $N(t)$ denote the number of deaths that have occurred by time t and T_i denote the time when the i-th death occurs ($i = 1, 2, \ldots, n$). We assume independence of the times-until-death. Specify the process $\{N(t), t \geq 0\}$ by each of the two methods above.

Solution:

a. The conditional distribution of $N(t + h) - N(t)$, given $N(t) = i$, is binomial with parameters $n - i$ and $_h q_{x+t}$, $i = 0, 1, 2, \ldots, n - 1$. Thus,

$$\Pr[N(t + h) - N(t) = k \mid N(t) = i]$$

$$= \binom{n-i}{k}(_h q_{x+t})^k (1 - {}_h q_{x+t})^{n-i-k} \qquad k = 0, 1, \ldots, n - i.$$

Note here that the conditional distribution depends on t and only on $N(s)$ at $s = t$.

b. We specify the joint distribution of $T_1, T_2, \ldots, T_n$ by iteration. First,

$$\Pr(T_1 > s) = (_s p_x)^n,$$

$$f_{T_1}(s) = n(_s p_x)^n \, \mu_x(s).$$

For $i = 1, 2, \ldots, n - 1$,

$$\Pr(T_{i+1} > t \mid T_i = s) = (_{t-s}p_{x+s})^{n-i}$$

and

$$f_{T_{i+1}|T_i}(t \mid s) = (n - i)(_{t-s}p_{x+s})^{n-i}\,\mu_x(t).$$

We observe that in this example the elapsed times between successive deaths are not mutually independent or identically distributed. ▼

We turn now to the Poisson process where the elapsed times between successive claims are mutually independent and identically distributed.

The **global method definition** of a **Poisson process** is as follows:

$$\Pr[N(t + h) - N(t) = k \mid N(s) \text{ for all } s \le t] = \frac{e^{-\lambda h}(\lambda h)^k}{k!}$$

$$k = 0, 1, 2, 3, \dots \text{ for all } t \ge 0 \text{ and } h > 0. \quad (13.3.3)$$

The following properties come from this definition of the Poisson process:

(i) The **increments are stationary;** that is, the distribution of $N(t + h) - N(t)$, which is Poisson with parameter λh, depends on the length of the interval but not on its location, t.

(ii) For any set of disjoint time intervals, the **increments are independent;** that is, for $t_1 < t_1 + h_1 < t_2 < t_2 + h_2 < t_3 \cdots < t_n + h_n$ the increments $N(t_1 + h_1) - N(t_1)$, $N(t_2 + h_2) - N(t_2)$, $\dots$, $N(t_n + h_n) - N(t_n)$ are mutually independent.

(iii) The **probability of simultaneous claims is zero:** that is,

$$\lim_{h \to 0} \frac{\Pr[N(t + h) - N(t) > 1]}{h} = \lim_{h \to 0} \frac{1 - e^{-\lambda h} - \lambda h e^{-\lambda h}}{h} = 0.$$

The **discrete method definition of the Poisson process** states that elapsed times V_1, V_2, V_3, $\dots$ are mutually independent and that each has the exponential distribution with parameter λ.

We now show the equivalence of these two definitions of the Poisson process. To see that the process defined by the global method implies the salient feature of the discrete method, we observe

$$\Pr(V_{i+1} > h \mid V_1, V_2, \dots, V_i) = \Pr\left[V_{i+1} > h \mid N(s) \text{ for all } s \le t = \sum_{j=1}^{i} V_j \right]$$

$$= \Pr[N(t + h) - N(t) = 0 \mid N(s), s \le t]$$

$$= e^{-\lambda h}, \quad (13.3.4)$$

the survival function of each V_i in the Poisson process.

To see that the process defined by the discrete method implies the salient feature of the global method, apply the definition of the $N(t)$'s, T_j's, and V_j's, the mutual independence and exponential distribution of the V_j's, to show that

$$\Pr[N(t + h) - N(t) = k \mid N(s) \text{ for } s \le t] = \Pr[T_k \le h \text{ and } T_k + V_{k+1} > h]. \quad (13.3.5)$$

Since $T_k = V_1 + V_2 + \cdots + V_k$, and the V_i's are independent and identically distributed with an exponential distribution with parameter λ, T_k has a gamma distribution with parameters k and λ. Then (13.3.5) is equal to

$$\int_0^h \Pr(T_k + V_{k+1} > h \mid T_k = u) f_{T_k}(u) \, du = \int_0^h \Pr(V_{k+1} > h - u) f_{T_k}(u) \, du$$

$$= \int_0^h e^{-\lambda(h-u)} \frac{\lambda^k u^{k-1} e^{-\lambda u}}{(k-1)!} \, du$$

$$= \frac{e^{-\lambda h} \lambda^k}{(k-1)!} \int_0^h u^{k-1} \, du = e^{-\lambda h} \frac{(\lambda h)^k}{k!},$$

the p.f. of the number of occurrences in a period of length h in a Poisson process.

We now define a compound Poisson process in this context. If for $S(t)$, defined in (13.3.1), the random variables X_1, X_2, X_3, ... are independent, identically distributed random variables with common d.f. $P(x)$, and if they are also independent of the process $\{N(t), t \geq 0\}$, assumed to be a Poisson process, the process $\{S(t), t \geq 0\}$ is said to be a *compound Poisson process.*

If the aggregate claims process is a compound Poisson process given by λ and $P(x)$, the following properties correspond to properties of the underlying claim number process:

a. If $t \geq 0$ and $h > 0$, the distribution of $S(t + h) - S(t)$ is compound Poisson with specifications λh and $P(x)$, that is,

$$\Pr[S(t+h) - S(t) \leq x \mid S(s) \text{ for } s \leq t] = \sum_{k=0}^{\infty} e^{-\lambda h} (\lambda h)^k \frac{P^{*k}(x)}{k!}$$

where $P^{*k}(x)$ is the k-fold convolution of the d.f. $P(x)$.

b. At any time t, the probability that the next claim occurs between $t + h$ and $t + h + dh$ and that the claim amount is less than or equal to x is $e^{-\lambda dh} (\lambda dh) P(x)$.

c. The process $\{S(t), t \geq 0\}$ has independent and stationary increments; that is, the aggregate claims of disjoint time intervals are independent random variables, and the distribution of each of these depends on only the length of the corresponding time interval and not on its location.

d. If $S(t)$ denotes a compound Poisson process and the value of t is fixed, $S(t)$ has a compound Poisson distribution with Poisson parameter λt. Formulas (12.3.2) and (12.3.3) give the mean and variance of $S(t)$:

$$E[S(t)] = \lambda t p_1, \tag{13.3.6}$$

$$\mathrm{Var}[S(t)] = \lambda t p_2. \tag{13.3.7}$$

13.4   Ruin Probabilities and the Claim Amount Distribution

The surplus process $\{U(t), t \geq 0\}$ can be studied by its relation, given in (13.1.1), to the claim process $S(t)$. For the remainder of the chapter, we assume that $S(t)$ is a compound Poisson process. With this assumption we can develop upper and lower bounds on $\psi(u)$. In the particular case of an exponential distribution of individual claims, there is an explicit form for $\psi(u)$.

First, we assume that the rate of premium collection c exceeds the expected claim payments per unit time, which is λp_1. Further, we define the relative security loading θ by the equation $c = (1 + \theta)\,\lambda p_1$ where θ is positive. We can see that $\theta = 0$ or $\theta < 0$ implies $\psi(u) = 1$; that is, ruin is certain.

Next, let $(-\infty, \gamma)$ denote the largest open interval for which the m.g.f. of $P(x)$ exists. We assume that γ is positive. In the case of the exponential distribution with parameter β, γ is equal to β, while for any bounded claim amount distribution, γ is $+\infty$. Furthermore, we assume that $M_X(r)$ tends to $+\infty$ as r tends to γ. That this assumption does not always hold for finite γ is demonstrated with an inverse Gaussian distribution in Example 13.4.3. A comparison of the figure that accompanies Example 13.4.3 with Figure 13.4.1 shows the importance of this assumption.

FIGURE 13.4.1

The Definition of R

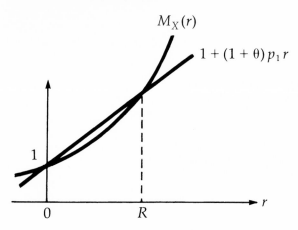

We now proceed by analogy with the definition of the adjustment coefficient in (13.2.6). The usefulness of this adjustment coefficient appears in the proof of Theorem 13.4.1.

Consider a period of length $t > 0$ where the amount of premiums collected is ct and the aggregate claim distribution is compound Poisson with expected number of claims λt. Then, by analogy with (13.2.6), we choose, for the adjustment coefficient, the smallest positive root of

$$M_{S(t)-ct}(r) = \mathrm{E}[e^{r(S(t)-ct)}] = e^{-rct}\,M_{S(t)}(r)$$

$$= e^{-rct}e^{\lambda t[M_X(r)-1]} = 1. \tag{13.4.1}$$

Thus,

$$\lambda[M_X(r) - 1] = cr. \tag{13.4.2}$$

Substituting $c = (1 + \theta)\lambda p_1$, we have the equivalent form

$$1 + (1 + \theta)p_1 r = M_X(r). \qquad (13.4.3)$$

The left-hand side of (13.4.3) is a linear function of r, whereas the right-hand side is a positive increasing function which by assumption tends to $+\infty$ as r tends to γ. Furthermore, the second derivative of the right-hand side is positive, so its graph is concave upward. The assumption that $c > \lambda p_1$ (equivalent to $\theta > 0$) means the slope, $(1 + \theta) p_1$, of the left-hand side of (13.4.3) exceeds the slope, $M_X'(0) = p_1$, of the right-hand side at $r = 0$. From Figure 13.4.1, we see that (13.4.3) has two solutions. Aside from the trivial solution $r = 0$, there is a positive solution $r = R$, which is defined to be the *adjustment coefficient.*

Example 13.4.1

Determine the adjustment coefficient if the claim amount distribution is exponential with parameter $\beta > 0$.

Solution:

The adjustment coefficient is obtained from (13.4.3) which is, for this example,

$$1 + \frac{(1 + \theta)r}{\beta} = \frac{\beta}{\beta - r}$$

or, as a quadratic equation in r,

$$(1 + \theta)r^2 - \theta\beta r = 0.$$

As expected, $r = 0$ is a solution, and the adjustment coefficient solution, the smallest positive root, is

$$R = \frac{\theta\beta}{1 + \theta}. \qquad \blacktriangledown$$

Example 13.4.2

Calculate the adjustment coefficient if all claims are of size 1.

Solution:

Formula (13.4.3) gives the adjustment coefficient as the positive root of

$$1 + (1 + \theta)r = e^r.$$

The results of numerical evaluation of the above equation for several values of θ are displayed below.

θ	R	θ	R
0.2	0.35420	1.0	1.25643
0.4	0.63903	1.2	1.41318
0.6	0.87640	1.4	1.55368
0.8	1.07941		$\blacktriangledown$

In general, the adjustment coefficient is an increasing function of the relative security loading, θ. This can be seen from Figure 13.4.1. As θ is increased, the slope of the straight line through the point (0, 1) is increased so that the point of intersection of the line and the curve moves to the right and upward.

Example 13.4.3

Assume that the claim amount distribution is inverse Gaussian with parameters α and β. For this assumption:
a. Determine the largest open interval $(-\infty, \gamma)$ for which $M_X(t)$ is defined.
b. Determine limit $M_X(t)$ as $t \to \gamma$.
c. Display the equation for the adjustment coefficient.
d. Display the graph corresponding to Figure 13.4.1 for the case when the limit in (b) is greater than $1 + (1 + \theta)(\alpha/\beta)\gamma$.
e. Display the graph corresponding to Figure 13.4.1 for the case when the limit in (b) is less than $1 + (1 + \theta)(\alpha/\beta)\gamma$.

Solution:

a. $M_X(t) = e^{\alpha[1 - \sqrt{(1 - 2t/\beta)}]}$, for $t < \beta/2$. So $\gamma = \beta/2$.

b. $\displaystyle\lim_{t \to \beta/2} M_X(t) = e^{\alpha}$.

c. $1 + (1 + \theta)(\alpha/\beta)r = e^{\alpha[1 - \sqrt{(1 - 2r/\beta)}]}$, for $r < \beta/2$.

d. If $e^{\alpha} > 1 + (1 + \theta)(\alpha/2)$, the graph is

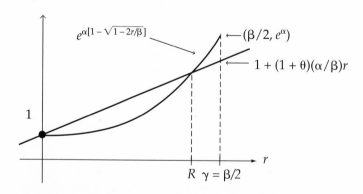

e. If $e^{\alpha} < 1 + (1 + \theta)(\alpha/2)$, the graph is

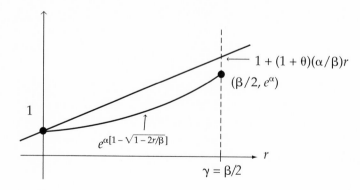

Observations:

1. We see in the graphs the possible failure of the definition of the adjustment coefficient when the limit of the claim distribution's m.g.f. is finite at the end of the open interval of its definition.
2. For a fixed expected claim size, α / β, the lines of the graphs are fixed for all β. As β increases the claim size's variance, α / β^2, decreases, and the point $(\beta / 2, e^\alpha)$ moves to the right and up, making the existence of R more likely. As β decreases the opposite is true.
3. An examination of the proof of Theorem 13.4.1 in the Appendix to this chapter reveals the use of the adjustment coefficient to set $-Rc + \lambda[M_X(R) - 1] = 0$ to obtain the equality of Theorem 13.4.1. For the situation in part (e) when the adjustment coefficient does not exist, this expression evaluated at γ is less than zero and the steps of the proof can be followed with R replaced by γ and the equalities replaced by inequalities. The resulting inequality is less useful than the equality obtained when the adjustment coefficient exists. ▼

An analog to Theorem 13.2.1 is the following result, which is proved in the Appendix to this chapter.

Theorem 13.4.1

If $U(t)$ is the surplus process based upon a compound Poisson aggregate claims process, $S(t)$, with $c > \lambda p_1$, that is, with positive relative security loading, then for $u \geq 0$,

$$\psi(u) = \frac{\exp(-Ru)}{E[\exp(-RU(T)) \mid T < \infty]} \qquad (13.4.4)$$

where R is the smallest positive root of (13.4.3).

The denominator is calculated with respect to the conditional distribution of the negative surplus, $U(T)$, given that ruin occurs: that is, $T < \infty$.

From Figure 13.4.1, we see that if $\theta \to 0$, the secant approaches the tangent to $M_X(r)$ at $r = 0$, which implies $R \to 0$. But then, from (13.4.4), $\psi(u) = 1$, or ruin is certain. Further, $U(t)$, $t > 0$, for the case where $\theta < 0$, will always be less than the corresponding $U(t)$ for $\theta \to 0$, and hence since ruin is certain for $\theta = 0$, ruin is also certain for $\theta < 0$. For these reasons, we remain with the assumption that $\theta > 0$.

In general, a closed form evaluation of the denominator of (13.4.4) is not possible. Exceptions are the case $u = 0$ (see Exercise 13.10), and the case where the claim amount distribution is exponential (see Example 13.4.4). However, the theorem can be used to derive inequalities. Since $U(T)$, given $T < \infty$, is necessarily negative, the denominator in (13.4.4) exceeds 1. It follows that

$$\psi(u) < e^{-Ru}. \qquad (13.4.5)$$

If the claim amount distribution is bounded so that $P(m) = 1$ for some finite m, it follows, given $T < \infty$, that $U(T) > -m$ since the surplus just before the claim must have been positive.

Thus,

$$\psi(u) > e^{-Ru}\, e^{-Rm} = e^{-R(u+m)}. \tag{13.4.6}$$

Some authors suggest the use of the approximation

$$\psi(u) \cong e^{-Ru}, \tag{13.4.7}$$

which, in view of (13.4.5), overstates the probability of ruin.

We now examine a special case where Theorem 13.4.1 can be applied to obtain an explicit expression for the ruin probability $\psi(u)$.

Example 13.4.4

Calculate the probability of ruin in the case that the claim amount distribution is exponential with parameter $\beta > 0$.

Solution:

Ruin, if it occurs, is assumed to take place at time T. Let $\hat{u}$ be the amount of surplus just prior to T. The event that $-U(T) > y$ can be restated as the event that X, the size of the claim causing ruin, exceeds $\hat{u} + y$, given that it exceeds $\hat{u}$. The conditional probability of this event is given by

$$\frac{\beta \int_{\hat{u}+y}^{\infty} e^{-\beta x}\, dx}{\beta \int_{\hat{u}}^{\infty} e^{-\beta x}\, dx} = e^{-\beta y},$$

so that the p.d.f. of $-U(T)$, given $T < \infty$, is

$$\frac{d}{dy}\left(1 - e^{-\beta y}\right) = \beta e^{-\beta y}.$$

Therefore,

$$E[\exp(-RU(T)) \mid T < \infty] = \beta \int_{0}^{\infty} e^{-\beta y} e^{Ry}\, dy$$

$$= \frac{\beta}{\beta - R}.$$

From Example 13.4.1, we know that the adjustment coefficient in this case is $R = \theta\beta/(1 + \theta)$. Combining this with (13.4.4) gives us

$$\psi(u) = \frac{(\beta - R)e^{-Ru}}{\beta}$$

$$= \frac{1}{1 + \theta} \exp\left(\frac{-\theta\beta u}{1 + \theta}\right)$$

$$= \frac{1}{1 + \theta} \exp\left[\frac{-\theta u}{(1 + \theta)p_1}\right]. \qquad (13.4.8)$$

▼

13.5   The First Surplus below the Initial Level

We continue with the continuous time model where the aggregate claim process, $S(t)$, is compound Poisson. Specifically, we consider the amount of the surplus at the time it first falls below the initial level (this, of course, may never happen). As an application, we find a simple expression for $\psi(0)$, the probability of ruin, if the initial surplus is 0.

The main theorem of this section, proved in the Appendix to this chapter, is the following.

Theorem 13.5.1

For a compound Poisson process, the probability that the surplus will ever fall below its initial level u, and will be between $u - y$ and $u - y - dy$ when it happens for the first time, is

$$\frac{\lambda}{c}[1 - P(y)]\,dy = \frac{1 - P(y)}{(1 + \theta)\,p_1}\,dy \qquad y > 0.$$

As an application of Theorem 13.5.1, we note that the probability that the surplus will ever fall below its original level is

$$\frac{1}{(1 + \theta)\,p_1}\int_0^\infty [1 - P(y)]\,dy = \frac{1}{1 + \theta} \qquad (13.5.1)$$

since

$$\int_0^\infty [1 - P(y)]\,dy = p_1.$$

In the special case of $u = 0$, (13.5.1) gives the probability that the surplus will even fall below zero, that is, its original level. Hence

$$\psi(0) = \frac{1}{1 + \theta}. \qquad (13.5.2)$$

It is remarkable that $\psi(0)$ depends only upon the relative security loading θ and not on the specific form of the claim amount distribution.

We note that

$$\frac{\lambda}{c}[1 - P(y)] = \frac{1 - P(y)}{(1 + \theta)\, p_1} \qquad y > 0$$

is not a p.d.f. since it does not integrate to 1. However, there is a related p.d.f. in the proper sense. Let L_1 be a random variable denoting the amount by which the surplus falls below the initial level for the first time, given that this ever happens. The p.d.f. for L_1 is obtained by dividing

$$\frac{1 - P(y)}{(1 + \theta)\, p_1}$$

by

$$\psi(0) = \frac{1}{1 + \theta}$$

and is

$$f_{L_1}(y) = \frac{1}{p_1}[1 - P(y)] \qquad y > 0. \tag{13.5.3}$$

The relationship between the m.g.f. of L_1 and that of the distribution of claim size X can be obtained by integration by parts:

$$
\begin{aligned}
M_{L_1}(r) &= \frac{1}{p_1} \int_0^\infty e^{ry}[1 - P(y)]\, dy \\
&= \frac{1}{p_1} \left\{ \left. \frac{e^{ry}}{r}[1 - P(y)] \right|_0^\infty + \frac{1}{r} \int_0^\infty e^{ry}\, p(y)\, dy \right\} \\
&= \frac{1}{p_1\, r}[M_X(r) - 1]. \tag{13.5.4}
\end{aligned}
$$

We illustrate further applications of Theorem 13.5.1 by means of the following examples.

Example 13.5.1

Write an expression for the distribution of the surplus level at the first time the surplus falls below the initial level u, given that it does fall below u, if all claims are of size 2.

Solution:

We have

$$1 - P(y) = \begin{cases} 1 & 0 \le y < 2 \\ 0 & y \ge 2. \end{cases}$$

Thus the p.d.f. for L_1 is

$$\frac{1}{p_1}[1 - P(y)] = \begin{cases} \dfrac{1}{2} & 0 \le y < 2 \\ 0 & \text{elsewhere.} \end{cases}$$

Therefore, L_1 is uniformly distributed between 0 and 2, so the surplus level after the first such drop is uniformly distributed between $u - 2$ and u. ▼

<hr/>

Example 13.5.2

Write an expression for the distribution of L_1 if the size of the individual claims has an exponential distribution with parameter β.

Solution:

Since $1 - P(y) = e^{-\beta y}$ for $y > 0$, the p.d.f. of L_1 is

$$\frac{1}{p_1}[1 - P(y)] = \beta e^{-\beta y} \qquad y > 0.$$

Hence, the distribution of L_1 is also exponential with parameter β. ▼

13.6 The Maximal Aggregate Loss

A new random variable, the *maximal aggregate loss*, is defined as

$$L = \max_{t \geq 0} \{S(t) - ct\}, \tag{13.6.1}$$

that is, as the maximal excess of aggregate claims over premiums received. Since $S(t) - ct = 0$ for $t = 0$, it follows that $L \geq 0$.

Theorem 13.5.1 is used in the proof of another theorem that gives an explicit formula for the m.g.f. of L. This can be used to provide information about $\psi(u)$. As an application, $\psi(u)$ is expressed for the case where the individual claim amount distribution is a weighted sum of exponential distributions.

To obtain the d.f. of the random variable L we consider, for $u \geq 0$, that

$$1 - \psi(u) = \Pr[U(t) \geq 0 \text{ for all } t]$$

$$= \Pr[u + ct - S(t) \geq 0 \text{ for all } t]$$

$$= \Pr[S(t) - ct \leq u \text{ for all } t].$$

But the right-hand side is equivalent to $\Pr(L \leq u)$, so we have

$$1 - \psi(u) = \Pr(L \leq u) \qquad u \geq 0. \tag{13.6.2}$$

It follows that $1 - \psi(u)$, the complement of the probability of ruin, can be interpreted as the d.f. of L. In particular, we have

$$1 - \psi(0) = \Pr(L \leq 0) = \Pr(L = 0) \tag{13.6.3}$$

since $L \geq 0$. In this case, the maximum loss is attained at time $t = 0$. Also, the distribution of L is of mixed type. There is a point mass of $1 - \psi(0)$ at the origin with the remaining probability distributed continuously over positive values of L.

The main result of this section is the following explicit formula for the m.g.f. of L, which, in view of (13.6.2), can be used to obtain information about $\psi(u)$.

<hr/>

$$M_L(r) = \frac{\theta \, p_1 \, r}{1 + (1 + \theta) \, p_1 \, r - M_X(r)}. \qquad (13.6.4)$$

An equivalent formula is

$$M_L(r) = \frac{\theta}{1 + \theta} + \frac{1}{1 + \theta} \frac{\theta[M_X(r) - 1]}{1 + (1 + \theta) \, p_1 \, r - M_X(r)}, \qquad (13.6.4A)$$

which reflects the point mass at the origin more directly, since the contribution to the m.g.f. of the probability at $L = 0$ is

$$1 - \psi(0) = \frac{\theta}{1 + \theta}$$

by (13.5.2). Notice that the equation used to define the adjustment coefficient is obtained by equating the denominator of (13.6.4) to 0.

Proof:

The proof of the theorem involves the consideration of the times when the aggregate loss process assumes new record highs. An outcome of the aggregate loss process is shown in Figure 13.6.1. In this outcome a new record high is established three times. After each record high there is a probability of $1 - \psi(0)$ that this record will not be broken and a probability of $\psi(0)$ that it will be broken. In making this statement we are relying on the fact that a compound Poisson process has stationary and independent increments.

FIGURE 13.6.1

A Typical Outcome of the Aggregate Loss Process

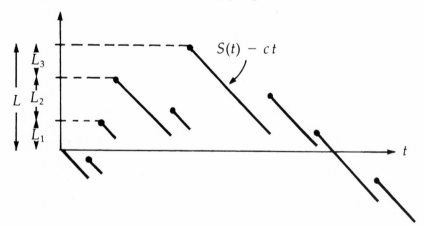

If the record is broken, the p.d.f. of the increase is that of L_1, which is given in (13.5.3). Figure 13.6.1 illustrates that we can represent L as a sum of a random number of random variables, thus

$$L = L_1 + L_2 + \cdots + L_N. \qquad (13.6.5)$$

Here N is the number of new record highs and has a geometric distribution with

$$\Pr(N = n) = [1 - \psi(0)][\psi(0)]^n$$

$$= \theta \left(\frac{1}{1 + \theta}\right)^{n+1} \qquad n = 0, 1, 2, \ldots, \tag{13.6.6}$$

and m.g.f.

$$M_N(r) = \frac{\theta}{1 + \theta - e^r}. \tag{13.6.7}$$

The random variables $N, L_1, L_2, \ldots$ are mutually independent, and the common p.d.f. of the L_i's is given by (13.5.3). According to (12.2.7), the m.g.f. of L is

$$M_L(r) = M_N [\log M_{L_1}(r)]$$

$$= \frac{\theta}{1 + \theta - M_{L_1}(r)}. \tag{13.6.8}$$

Formula (13.5.4) gives $M_{L_1}(r)$ in terms of $M_X(r)$ and thus

$$M_L(r) = \frac{\theta}{1 + \theta - [1/(p_1 r)][M_X(r) - 1]}$$

$$= \frac{\theta p_1 r}{1 + (1 + \theta) p_1 r - M_X(r)},$$

which was to be shown. The alternative formula (13.6.4A) can be verified by collecting terms over a common denominator. ∎

Observe that since $1 - \psi(u)$ is the d.f. of the random variable L—see (13.6.2)—where L has a point mass at the origin and a continuous density for positive values of u, we have

$$M_L(r) = 1 - \psi(0) + \int_0^\infty e^{ur} [-\psi'(u)] \, du$$

$$= \frac{\theta}{1 + \theta} + \int_0^\infty e^{ur} [-\psi'(u)] \, du.$$

Hence, (13.6.4A) states that

$$\int_0^\infty e^{ur} [-\psi'(u)] \, du = \frac{1}{1 + \theta} \frac{\theta[M_X(r) - 1]}{1 + (1 + \theta) p_1 r - M_X(r)}. \tag{13.6.9}$$

This formula can be used to find explicit expressions for $\psi(u)$ for certain families of claim amount distributions. One such family consists of mixtures of exponential distributions of the form

$$p(x) = \sum_{i=1}^n A_i \beta_i e^{-\beta_i x} \qquad x > 0,$$

$$\beta_i > 0, A_i > 0, A_1 + A_2 + \cdots + A_n = 1. \tag{13.6.10}$$

Then

$$M_X(r) = \sum_{i=1}^{n} A_i \frac{\beta_i}{\beta_i - r}. \qquad (13.6.11)$$

Originally, $M_X(r)$ is defined as an expectation and exists only for $r < \gamma = \min\{\beta_1, \ldots, \beta_n\}$. However, this function can be extended in a natural way to all $r \neq \beta_i$. For simplicity, we use the same symbol, $M_X(r)$, for this function.

We substitute (13.6.11) into (13.6.9) and recognize that the right-hand side of the result is a rational function of r, which, by applying the method of partial fractions, we can write in the following form:

$$\int_0^{\infty} e^{ur} [-\psi'(u)] \, du = \sum_{i=1}^{n} \frac{C_i \, r_i}{r_i - r}. \qquad (13.6.12)$$

The only function that satisfies this and $\psi(\infty) = 0$ is

$$\psi(u) = \sum_{i=1}^{n} C_i \, e^{-r_i u}. \qquad (13.6.13)$$

It follows that the probability of ruin is given by this expression. We illustrate this procedure with two examples.

Example 13.6.1

Derive an expression for $\psi(u)$ if the X_i's have an exponential claim amount distribution; that is, $n = 1$ in (13.6.10).

Solution:
Since

$$M_X(r) = \frac{\beta}{\beta - r} = \frac{1}{1 - p_1 \, r},$$

the right-hand side of (13.6.9) is

$$\left(\frac{1}{1 + \theta}\right) \left\{ \frac{\theta[1 / (1 - p_1 \, r) - 1]}{1 + (1 + \theta) p_1 \, r - 1 / (1 - p_1 \, r)} \right\} = \left(\frac{1}{1 + \theta}\right) \left[\frac{\theta}{\theta - (1 + \theta) p_1 \, r} \right]$$

$$= C_1 \frac{r_1}{r_1 - r}$$

where $C_1 = 1 / (1 + \theta)$ and $r_1 = \theta / [(1 + \theta) p_1]$. Then

$$\psi(u) = C_1 \, e^{-r_1 u}.$$

This formula was established previously in Example 13.4.4, formula (13.4.8). ▼

Example 13.6.2

Given that $\theta = 2/5$ and $p(x)$ is given by

$$p(x) = \frac{3}{2} e^{-3x} + \frac{7}{2} e^{-7x} \qquad x > 0,$$

calculate $\psi(u)$.

Solution:

From $p(x)$ we have

$$M_X(r) = \frac{3/2}{3 - r} + \frac{7/2}{7 - r}$$

and

$$p_1 = \left(\frac{1}{2}\right)\left(\frac{1}{3}\right) + \left(\frac{1}{2}\right)\left(\frac{1}{7}\right) = \frac{5}{21}.$$

We substitute these expressions into the right-hand side of (13.6.9), which, after some simplification, becomes

$$\left(\frac{6}{7}\right)\left(\frac{5 - r}{6 - 7r + r^2}\right).$$

The roots of the denominator are $r_1 = 1$ and $r_2 = 6$; hence this expression, rewritten in the form of (13.6.12), is

$$\frac{C_1}{1 - r} + \frac{6 C_2}{6 - r}.$$

The coefficients are determined to be

$$C_1 = \frac{24}{35},$$

$$C_2 = \frac{1}{35}.$$

Thus

$$\psi(u) = \frac{24}{35} e^{-u} + \frac{1}{35} e^{-6u} \qquad u \geq 0. \qquad \blacktriangledown$$

In Figure 13.6.2 a graph illustrates the points r_i satisfying the equation

$$1 + (1 + \theta) p_1 r = M_X(r) \tag{13.6.14}$$

where the distribution of X is a mixture of exponentials. The function $M_X(r)$ is given in (13.6.11) with $n = 3$.

FIGURE 13.6.2

The Solution of (13.6.14) for $n = 3$

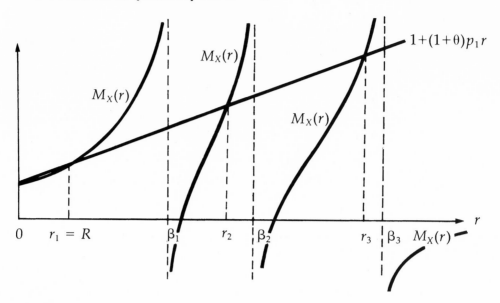

The right-hand side of (13.6.11) has discontinuities at $\beta_1, \beta_2, \ldots$, and at each of these arguments the value of the function shifts from $+\infty$ to $-\infty$. The figure illustrates that, in general, the r_i's will satisfy a condition of the form

$$r_1 = R < \beta_1 < r_2 < \beta_2 < \cdots < r_n < \beta_n. \tag{13.6.15}$$

Figure 13.4.1 illustrates that part of Figure 13.6.2 to the left of $\beta_1 = \gamma$.

Practical problems will necessitate consideration of claim distributions that are not mixtures of exponential distributions. For some distributions it may even be difficult to calculate the adjustment coefficient so as to be able to approximate ruin probabilities. The following method based on the first two moments of the claim amount distribution is easy to apply and seems to give satisfactory results for moderate values of u.

The first moment for the distribution of L is obtained in Exercise 13.13(b). The result is

$$E[L] = \frac{p_2}{2\,\theta\,p_1}. \tag{13.6.16}$$

Further, we know from (13.5.2) that $\psi(0) = 1/(1 + \theta)$, and from (13.4.5) that $\psi(u) < e^{-Ru}$. The approximation proposed here is that

$$1 - F_L(u) = \psi(u) \cong \frac{1}{1 + \theta} e^{-Ku} \qquad u > 0$$

where K is chosen so that the approximated value of $E[L]$ is equal to that given in (13.6.16). But

$$E[L] = \int_0^\infty [1 - F_L(u)]\, du \cong \frac{1}{1 + \theta} \frac{1}{K'},$$

so that

$$K = \frac{2\,\theta\, p_1}{(1 + \theta)\, p_2}$$

gives us the required equality. Thus our approximation is

$$\psi(u) \cong \frac{1}{1 + \theta} \exp\left[-\frac{2\,\theta\, p_1\, u}{(1 + \theta)\, p_2}\right] \qquad u > 0.$$

Note that if the claim distribution is exponential with mean p_1, so that $p_2 = 2\, p_1^2$, the result is exact; see (13.4.8). This method is extended in Exercise 13.19 to give an improved approximation.

13.7 Notes and References

The importance of the joint probability distribution of the time of ruin, T, and the surplus level immediately after ruin, $U(T)$, for a surplus process with aggregate claims following a compound Poisson process is indicated in the denominator of the expression for the probability of ruin in Theorem 13.4.1. The possibility of expressing ruin probabilities for such a surplus process in terms of the distribution of the claim amounts is demonstrated in Theorems 13.5.1 and 13.6.1. Several results in this area have been published since the publication of the first edition of *Actuarial Mathematics*. A recent paper by Gerber and Shiu (1998) provides a readable summary of these results. We quote their abstract:

This paper studies the joint distribution of the time of ruin, the surplus immediately before ruin, and the deficit at ruin. The classical model is generalized by discounting with respect to time of ruin. We show how to calculate an expected discounted penalty, which is due at ruin, and may depend on the deficit at ruin and the surplus immediately before ruin. The expected discounted penalty, considered as a function of the initial surplus, satisfies a certain renewal equation, which has a probabilistic interpretation. Explicit answers are obtained for zero and very large initial surplus, and for arbitrary surplus when the claim amount distribution is exponential. We generalize D. C. M. Dickson's formula, which expresses the joint distribution of the surplus immediately prior to and at ruin in terms of the probability of ultimate ruin. Explicit results are obtained when dividends are paid out to the stockholders according to a constant barrier strategy.

The reader of the proof of Theorem 13.5.1 will recognize the use of the penalty function in their paper.

General references are the texts by
- Beard, Pentikäinen, and Pesonen (1984)
- Beekman (1974)
- Bühlmann (1970)

- Gerber (1979)
- Panjer and Willmot (1992) and
- Seal (1969).

Ruin theory has been developed by the Scandinavian school (F. Lundberg, Cramér), and by the Italian school (DeFinetti); this development is accurately described in the text by Dubourdieu (1952).

We did not discuss the famous asymptotic formula for the probability of ruin,

$$\psi(u) \cong Ce^{-Ru} \qquad u \to \infty, \tag{13.7.1}$$

where C is some constant. In view of Theorem 13.4.1, this formula is quite plausible; it means that the denominator in (13.4.4) has a limit as $u \to \infty$ with the C in (13.7.1) as the reciprocal of this limit. In the case where the claim amount distribution is a mixture of exponential distributions, this asymptotic form is illustrated by (13.6.13).

The formula in Exercise 13.11 is called a defective renewal equation. Feller (1966) discussed the solutions of equations of this type; in particular, he proves (13.7.1). By the same technique, Gerber (1974) finds the limit of the conditional distribution of $-U(T)$, given $T < \infty$, for $u \to \infty$.

If we modify the model by assuming that the surplus earns interest at a constant force $\delta > 0$, we have to replace c by $c + \delta u$ in the integro-differential equation (13.A.12) in the Appendix to this chapter. In the case of exponential claim amounts, the resulting equation has an explicit solution in terms of the gamma function.

If the roles of premiums and claims are interchanged, with premiums representing payments by the insurer and claims representing payments to the insurer, so that

$$U(t) = u - ct + S(t)$$

where it is now assumed that $c < \lambda\, p_1$, then there is an explicit formula,

$$\psi(u) = e^{-Ru}.$$

To prove this, one establishes a result like Theorem 13.4.1 and observes that the surplus at the time of ruin is necessarily 0. It has been suggested that this model could be used for a portfolio of annuities where a death frees the reserve of the policyholder and leads to a negative claim.

Seal (1978b) discusses numerical methods for evaluating the probability of ruin in a finite time interval. Beekman and Bowers (1972) approximate $\psi(u, t)$ by matching moments. Gerber (1974) and DeVylder (1977) give upper bounds for $\psi(u, t)$ by martingale arguments.

Panjer and Willmot (1992, Chapter 11) discuss the ideas of this chapter using more advanced mathematical tools. Sections 11.4 and 11.5 are of particular interest because of the development of recursive methods for calculating the approximate probability of ultimate ruin.

Appendix

Proof of Theorem 13.2.2

The following calculation yields a simple recursion formula for the modified surplus:

$$\hat{U}_i = U_i - \frac{a}{1-a} W_i$$

$$= U_{i-1} + c - W_i - \frac{a}{1-a} W_i$$

$$= U_{i-1} + c - \frac{1}{1-a} W_i$$

$$= U_{i-1} + c - \frac{1}{1-a} (Y_i + a W_{i-1})$$

$$= \hat{U}_{i-1} + c - \frac{Y_i}{1-a} \qquad i = 1, 2, \dots . \qquad (13.A.1)$$

From (13.A.1), (13.2.18) and the independence of the Y_i's it follows that for any n,

$$E[\exp(-\tilde{R}[\hat{U}_n - \hat{U}_i])] = 1 \qquad i = 0, 1, \dots , n. \qquad (13.A.2)$$

Now consider the identity

$$E[\exp(-\tilde{R}\hat{U}_n)] = \sum_{i=1}^{n} E[\exp(-\tilde{R}\hat{U}_n) \mid \tilde{T} = i] \Pr(\tilde{T} = i)$$

$$+ E[\exp(-\tilde{R}\hat{U}_n) \mid \tilde{T} > n] \Pr(\tilde{T} > n). \qquad (13.A.3)$$

From (13.A.2) for $i = 0$, it follows that the expression on the left-hand side of (13.A.3) is $\exp(-\tilde{R}\hat{u})$. In the summation on the right-hand side we replace $\hat{U}_n$ by $\hat{U}_i + (\hat{U}_n - \hat{U}_i)$. The difference, $\hat{U}_n - \hat{U}_i$, is independent of $\hat{U}_1, \hat{U}_2, \dots , \hat{U}_i$. This can be confirmed by using (13.A.1) and the independence of the Y's. In particular, $(\hat{U}_n - \hat{U}_i)$ is independent of the event $\tilde{T} = i$. It follows from (13.A.2) that

$$E[\exp(-\tilde{R}\hat{U}_n) \mid \tilde{T} = i] = E[\exp(-\tilde{R}\hat{U}_i) \mid \tilde{T} = i].$$

Thus (13.A.3) can be written as

$$\exp(-\tilde{R}\hat{u}) = \sum_{i=1}^{n} E[\exp(-\tilde{R}\hat{U}_i) \mid \tilde{T} = i] \Pr(\tilde{T} = i)$$

$$+ E[\exp(-\tilde{R}\hat{U}_n) \mid \tilde{T} > n] \Pr(\tilde{T} > n), \qquad (13.A.4)$$

which is similar to (13.A.8) in the proof below of Theorem 13.4.1. Now we let $n \to \infty$. Then the first term on the right-hand side of (13.A.4) converges to

$$\sum_{i=1}^{\infty} E[\exp(-\tilde{R}\hat{U}_i) \mid \tilde{T} = i] \Pr(\tilde{T} = i) = E[\exp(-\tilde{R}\hat{U}_{\tilde{T}}) \mid \tilde{T} < \infty] \Pr(\tilde{T} < \infty).$$

Thus to complete the proof of Theorem 13.2.2 we have to show that the second term on the right-hand side of (13.A.4) vanishes for $n \to \infty$. We do this as follows.

From (13.2.17) it follows that

$$E[S_n] = n \frac{E[Y]}{1-a} - a \frac{1-a^n}{1-a} \left(\frac{E[Y]}{1-a} - w \right).$$

Since $c > E[Y]/(1-a)$, there is a positive number α such that $E[\hat{U}_n] > u + \alpha n$ if n is sufficiently large. Furthermore, it follows from (13.2.17) that there is a number β^2 such that $\mathrm{Var}(\hat{U}_n) < \beta^2 n$. Now the remainder of the proof that the second term on the right-hand side of (13.A.4) converges to 0 as $n \to \infty$ is similar to the proof that is shown in detail for the convergence of the second term on the right-hand side of (13.A.8) in the proof given below for Theorem 13.4.1. See Promislow (1991a) for a complete demonstration of this step. ■

Proof of Theorem 13.4.1

For $t > 0$ and $r > 0$, we consider

$$E[e^{-rU(t)}] = E[e^{-rU(t)} \mid T \le t]\, \mathrm{Pr}(T \le t)$$

$$+ E[e^{-rU(t)} \mid T > t]\, \mathrm{Pr}(T > t). \qquad (13.A.5)$$

Since $U(t) = u + ct - S(t)$, the term on the left-hand side is

$$\exp\{-ru - rct + \lambda t[M_X(r) - 1]\}. \qquad (13.A.6)$$

In the first term on the right-hand side, we write

$$U(t) = U(T) + [U(t) - U(T)]$$

$$= U(T) + c(t - T) - [S(t) - S(T)].$$

For a given T, the term in brackets is independent of $U(T)$ and has a compound Poisson distribution with Poisson parameter $\lambda (t - T)$. Hence the first term on the right-hand side of (13.A.5) can be written as

$$E[\exp(-r\, U(T))\exp\{-r\, c(t - T) + \lambda (t - T)[M_X(r) - 1]\} \mid T \le t]\, \mathrm{Pr}(T \le t).$$

$$(13.A.7)$$

Expressions (13.A.6) and (13.A.7) can be greatly simplified if we choose r such that

$$-rc + \lambda [M_X(r) - 1] = 0.$$

Two solutions exist (see Figure 13.4.1). The solution $r = 0$ gives a trivial identity when substituted into (13.A.5). The other solution, $r = R$, is the adjustment coefficient. If, with $r = R$, we substitute the simplified expressions into (13.A.5), we obtain

$$e^{-Ru} = E[e^{-RU(T)} \mid T \le t]\, \mathrm{Pr}(T \le t)$$

$$+ E[e^{-RU(t)} \mid T > t]\, \mathrm{Pr}(T > t). \qquad (13.A.8)$$

Now we let $t \to \infty$. The first term on the right-hand side converges to

$$E[e^{-RU(T)} \mid T < \infty]\, \psi(u).$$

Hence Theorem 13.4.1 follows if we can show that the second term on the right-hand side vanishes for $t \to \infty$. We shall show this as follows:

Let $\alpha = c - \lambda p_1$, $\beta^2 = \lambda p_2$. Thus, from (13.3.6) and (13.3.7),

$$E[U(t)] = E[u + ct - S(t)] = u + \alpha t,$$

and

$$\mathrm{Var}[U(t)] = \mathrm{Var}[S(t)] = \beta^2 t.$$

We consider $u + \alpha t - \beta t^{2/3}$, which is positive for t sufficiently large. Now we split the second term on the right-hand side of (13.A.8) by distinguishing whether $U(t)$ is less than or greater than $u + \alpha t - \beta t^{2/3}$. With this splitting, we have

$$E[e^{-RU(t)} \mid T > t, 0 \le U(t) \le u + \alpha t - \beta t^{2/3}]$$

$$\Pr[T > t, 0 \le U(t) \le u + \alpha t - \beta t^{2/3}]$$

$$+ E[e^{-RU(t)} \mid T > t, U(t) > u + \alpha t - \beta t^{2/3}]$$

$$\Pr[T > t, U(t) > u + \alpha t - \beta t^{2/3}]$$

$$\le \Pr[U(t) \le u + \alpha t - \beta t^{2/3}] + \exp[-R(u + \alpha t - \beta t^{2/3})]$$

$$\le t^{-1/3} + \exp[-R(u + \alpha t - \beta t^{2/3})]$$

by Chebychev's inequality. But with this upper bound, the second term on the right-hand side of (13.A.8) vanishes for $t \to \infty$. ∎

Proof of Theorem 13.5.1:

For this proof we introduce a new concept that is of interest in itself. Let $w(x)$, $x \le 0$, be a function with $w(x) \ge 0$. We define

$$\psi(u; w) = E[w(U(T)) \mid T < \infty]\, \psi(u), \tag{13.A.9}$$

considered as a function of the initial surplus, u. We may interpret $w(x)$ as a **penalty** if the surplus at the time of ruin is x. In this case $\psi(u; w)$ is the expected value of the penalty. Examples are

a. If $w(x) = e^{-Rx}$, then (13.4.4) shows that $\psi(u; w) = e^{-Ru}$

b. If $w(x) = 1$, then (13.A.9) shows that $\psi(u; w) = \psi(u)$

c. If

$$w_h(x) = \begin{cases} 1 & x < -h \\ 0 & -h \le x \le 0, \end{cases}$$

then

$$\psi(0; w_h) = \Pr[U(T) < -h \mid T < \infty]\, \psi(0).$$

We start the proof by showing that, for every bounded function $w(x)$, we have

$$\psi(0; w) = \frac{\lambda}{c} \int_0^\infty w(-y)[1 - P(y)]\, dy. \tag{13.A.10}$$

Using the law of total probability applied to the definition of the expected penalty (13.A.9) by conditioning on the number claims in the initial interval $(0, b)$, we have

$$\psi(u; w) = \Pr[N(b) = 0]\{\text{Conditional Expected Penalty given } N(b) = 0\}$$

$$+ \Pr[N(b) = 1]\{\text{Conditional Expected Penalty given } N(b) = 1\}$$

$$+ \Pr[N(b) > 1]\{\text{Conditional Expected Penalty given } N(b) > 1\}.$$

$$\tag{13.A.11}$$

From the properties of the Poisson counting process,

$$\Pr[N(b) = 0] = e^{-\lambda b},$$

$$\Pr[N(b) = 1] = \lambda b e^{-\lambda b},$$

$$\Pr[N(b) > 1] = b\,A(b), \text{ where the limit } A(b) \text{ is 0 as } b \text{ goes to 0.}$$

By the limitation of $w(x)$ to bounded non-negative functions, $0 \le w(x) \le M$ for some M. With this restriction, and the properties of the compound Poisson process, we proceed as follows:

For $N(b) = 0$, the conditional expected penalty is $\psi(u + cb; w)$. Since no claims have occurred and income has been received at the rate c, the surplus has advanced to $u + cb$ and the stationary independent increments place the process at a new starting point.

For $N(b) = 1$, we need to condition further on the amount, x, of the single claim:
- If $x \le u$, the surplus has remained positive, and as for the case of no claim, the conditional expected penalty is $\psi(u + cb - x; w)$.
- If $u < x \le u + cb$, it is sufficient to observe that the conditional expected penalty, say, $A(x, b)$, is less than or equal to the bound on $w(x)$, M.
- If $x > u + cb$, then the surplus became negative at the occurrence of the claim, and the conditional expected penalty is $w(u + \xi - x)$, where ξ is the amount of income received up to the time of claim.

Thus for $N(b) = 1$, the conditional expected penalty is

$$\int_0^u \psi(u + cb - x: w)\, p(x)dx + \int_u^{u+cb} A(x, b)p(x)\, dx + \int_{u+cb}^{\infty} w(u + \xi - x)p(x)\, dx.$$

For $N(b) > 1$, it is also sufficient to observe that the conditional expected penalty, say, $D(b)$, is less than or equal to the bound of $w(x)$, M.

Combining these three cases into (13.A.11), we obtain

$$\psi(u; w) = e^{-\lambda b}\,\psi(u + cb; w) + \lambda b e^{-\lambda b}\left[\int_0^u \psi(u + cb - x; w)p(x)\, dx\right.$$

$$\left. + \int_u^{u+cb} A(x, b)p(x)\, dx + \int_{u+cb}^{\infty} w(u + \xi - x)p(x)\, dx\right]$$

$$+ b\,A(b)\,D(b). \qquad (13.A.12)$$

Now subtract $\psi(u; w)$ from both sides of (13.A.12) and divide the result by cb to get

$$\frac{e^{-\lambda b}\psi(u + cb; w) - \psi(u; w)}{cb} + \frac{\lambda}{c}\,e^{-\lambda b}\left[\int_0^u \psi(u + cb - x; w)p(x)\, dx\right.$$

$$\left. + \int_u^{u+cb} A(x, b)p(x)\, dx + \int_{u+cb}^{\infty} w(u + \xi - x)p(x)\, dx\right] + \frac{A(b)D(b)}{c} = 0. \quad (13.A.13)$$

As b goes to 0, the limits of the three terms of (13.A.13) are

$$\frac{-\lambda\psi(u; w) + c\psi'(u; w)}{c},$$

$$\frac{\lambda}{c}\left[\int_0^u \psi(u - x; w)p(x)\,dx + \int_u^\infty w(u - x)p(x)\,dx\right],$$

and 0.

Thus,

$$\psi'(u; w) = \frac{\lambda}{c}\psi(u; w) - \frac{\lambda}{c}\int_0^u \psi(u - x; w)\,p(x)\,dx$$

$$- \frac{\lambda}{c}\int_u^\infty w(u - x)\,p(x)\,dx. \qquad (13.A.14)$$

We now integrate this equation over u from 0 to z. The resulting double integrals can be reduced to single integrals by a change in variables. For the first double integral we replace x and u by x and $y = u - x$. Then

$$\int_0^z \int_0^u \psi(u - x; w)\,p(x)\,dx\,du = \int_0^z \int_0^{z-y} \psi(y; w)\,p(x)\,dx\,dy$$

$$= \int_0^z \psi(y; w)\,P(z - y)\,dy.$$

In the second double integral we replace x and u by x and $y = x - u$. Then

$$\int_0^z \int_u^\infty w(u - x)\,p(x)\,dx\,du = \int_0^\infty \int_y^{y+z} w(-y)\,p(x)\,dx\,dy$$

$$= \int_0^\infty w(-y)\,[P(y + z) - P(y)]\,dy.$$

Thus (13.A.14), integrated from 0 to z, gives

$$\psi(z; w) - \psi(0; w) = \frac{\lambda}{c}\int_0^z \psi(y; w)[1 - P(z - y)]\,dy$$

$$- \frac{\lambda}{c}\int_0^\infty w(-y)\,[P(y + z) - P(y)]\,dy. \qquad (13.A.15)$$

For $z \to \infty$, the first terms on both sides vanish leaving

$$-\psi(0; w) = -\frac{\lambda}{c}\int_0^\infty w(-y)\,[1 - P(y)]\,dy.$$

Now let $w_h(x)$ be defined as in Example (c); that is,

$$w_h(x) = \begin{cases} 1 & x < -h \\ 0 & -h \le x \le 0. \end{cases}$$

Then

$$\Pr[U(T) < -h \mid T < \infty]\,\psi(0) = \psi(0; w_h) = \frac{\lambda}{c}\int_h^\infty [1 - P(y)]\,dy.$$

Hence, when $u = 0$, the probability that the surplus ever falls below 0, and will be between $-h$ and $-h - dh$ when it happens, is

$$\frac{\lambda}{c}\,[1 - P(h)]\;dh.$$

If $u > 0$, an event with equal probability is that the surplus will ever fall below u, and will be between $u - h$ and $u - h - dh$ when it happens. This proves Theorem 13.5.1. ∎

Exercises

Section 13.2

13.1. Suppose that W_i assumes only the value 0 and $+2$ and that $\Pr(W = 0) = p$, $\Pr(W = 2) = q$ where $p + q = 1$. Assume that $c = 1$, $p > 1/2$ and that u is an integer. For this case, determine
   a. $U(\tilde{T})$ b. $\tilde{\psi}(u)$ in terms of $\tilde{R}$
   c. $\tilde{R}$ in terms of p, q d. $\tilde{\psi}(u)$ in terms of p, q.

13.2. Consider the claims in periods $n + 1, n + 2, \ldots, n + m$ and denote their total by $S_{n,m}$; that is,

$$S_{n,m} = W_{n+1} + W_{n+2} + \cdots + W_{n+m}.$$

The claim amount for each period is generated by the stochastic process described in (13.2.14). Verify the following:

   a. $$S_{n,m} = \sum_{i=1}^{m} Y_{n+i} \sum_{j=0}^{m-i} a^j + W_n \sum_{j=1}^{m} a^j$$

$$= \sum_{i=1}^{m} \left(\frac{1 - a^{(m-i+1)}}{1 - a} \right) Y_{n+i} + \left(\frac{a - a^{m+1}}{1 - a} \right) W_n.$$

   b. As $m \to \infty$ the final term on the right-hand side of the expression in (a) converges to

$$\frac{a\,W_n}{1 - a}.$$

   c. $\mathrm{E}[S_{n,m} \mid W_1 = w_1, W_2 = w_2, \ldots, W_n = w_n]$

$$= \left[\frac{m\,(1 - a) - a + a^{m+1}}{(1 - a)^2} \right] \mu + \left(\frac{a - a^{m+1}}{1 - a} \right) w_n$$

   where $\mathrm{E}(Y_{n+i}) = \mu$.

Section 13.3

13.3. Suppose that $V_1, V_2, \ldots$ are independent, identically distributed random variables with common d.f. $F(x)$ and p.d.f. $f(x)$, $x \geq 0$. Given $N(t) = i$ and $T_i = s$ ($s < t$), what is the probability of the occurrence of a claim between times t and $t + dt$? (This generalization of the Poisson process is called a *renewal process.*)

13.4.   Let $\{N(t), t \geq 0\}$ be a Poisson process with parameter λ and $p_n(t) = \Pr[N(t) = n]$.

a. Show that

$$p_0'(t) = -\lambda\, p_0(t),$$

$$p_n'(t) = -\lambda\, p_n(t) + \lambda\, p_{n-1}(t) \qquad n \geq 1.$$

b. Interpret these formulas.

Section 13.4

13.5.   Calculate $\lim_{\theta \to 0} R$ and $\lim_{\theta \to \infty} R$.

13.6.   Use

$$e^{rx} > 1 + r\,x + \frac{1}{2}\,(rx)^2 \qquad r > 0, x > 0$$

to show that

$$R < \frac{2\,\theta\, p_1}{p_2}.$$

13.7.   Suppose that $\theta = 2/5$ and

$$p(x) = \frac{3}{2}\, e^{-3x} + \frac{7}{2}\, e^{-7x} \qquad x > 0,$$

calculate

a. γ b. R.

13.8.   Suppose that the claim amount distribution is discrete with $p(1) = 1/4$ and $p(2) = 3/4$. If $R = \log 2$, calculate θ.

13.9.   Show that the adjustment coefficient can also be obtained as the unique solution of the equation

$$\int_0^\infty e^{rx}\, [1 - P(x)]\, dx = \frac{c}{\lambda} \qquad r < \gamma.$$

Section 13.5

13.10. Use Theorem 13.5.1 to evaluate the denominator in (13.4.4) in the case $u = 0$. Is your result consistent with (13.5.2)?

13.11. a. Show by interpretation that $\psi(u)$, $u \geq 0$, satisfies

$$\psi(u) = \frac{\lambda}{c} \int_0^u [1 - P(y)] \, \psi(u - y) \, dy + \frac{\lambda}{c} \int_u^\infty [1 - P(y)] \, dy.$$

[Hint: Use Theorem 13.5.1.]

b. The equation shown in part (a) is called a **renewal equation.** [See Exercise 13.3.] It is an integral equation because it is a relationship between functions where the relationship involves an integral. One of the methods of seeking a solution for an integral equation is to convert it to an **integro-differential equation.** Show that

$$\psi'(u) = \frac{\lambda}{c} \left\{ \psi(u) - \int_0^u \psi(u - y) p(y) dy - [1 - P(u)] \right\}$$

13.12. Substitute

$$M_X(r) = 1 + p_1 \, r + p_2 \, \frac{r^2}{2} + p_3 \, \frac{r^3}{6} + \cdots$$

into (13.5.4) to derive expressions for
a. $E[L_1]$　　　b. $E[L_1^2]$　　　c. $\text{Var}(L_1)$.

Section 13.6

13.13. a. For N as in (13.6.5), show that

$$E[N] = \frac{1}{\theta}$$

and

$$\text{Var}(N) = \frac{1 + \theta}{\theta^2}.$$

b. Use the result of Exercise 13.12 to derive expressions for $E[L]$ and $\text{Var}(L)$. [Hint: Formulas (13.6.5), (12.2.5), and (12.2.6), with $p_1 = E[L_1]$, $\text{Var}(X) = \text{Var}(L_1)$, are helpful. For an alternative derivation, expand $M_L(r)$ in (13.6.4) in powers of r.]

13.14. Determine the m.g.f. of L if all claims are of size 2.

13.15. Under certain assumptions, the probability of ruin is

$$\psi(u) = (0.3) \, e^{-2u} + (0.2) \, e^{-4u} + (0.1) \, e^{-7u} \qquad u \geq 0.$$

Calculate
a. θ　　　　　b. R.

13.16. What is the expected claim size for a distribution of the form (13.6.10)?

13.17. Suppose that $\lambda = 3$, $c = 1$, and

$$p(x) = \frac{1}{3} e^{-3x} + \frac{16}{3} e^{-6x} \qquad x > 0.$$

Calculate or derive

a. p_1

b. θ

c. $M_X(r)$

d. Expressions for the right-hand sides of (13.6.9) and (13.6.12)

e. An explicit formula for $\psi(u)$.

13.18. Suppose that $\lambda = 1$, $c = 10$, and

$$p(x) = \frac{9x}{25} e^{-3x/5} \qquad x > 0.$$

Calculate or derive

a. p_1

b. θ

c. $M_X(r)$

d. Expressions for the right-hand sides of (13.6.9) and (13.6.12)

e. An explicit formula for $\psi(u)$.

13.19. Beekman (1969) and Bowers's discussion thereof suggested the following approximation for the d.f. of L:

$$\Pr(L \le u) \cong \xi I(u) + (1 - \xi) G(u\colon \alpha, \beta)$$

where $I(x)$ is the degenerate d.f. of the constant 0 and $G(x\colon \alpha, \beta)$ is the d.f. of the gamma distribution with parameters α and β.

a. Determine ξ, α and β to match the point mass at the origin and the first two moments of L; see Exercise 13.13(b).

b. What is the resulting approximation for $\psi(u)$, $u \ge 0$?

13.20. In a surplus process, (1) aggregate claims follow a compound Poisson process, and (2) the claim amount distribution is a mixture of n exponential distributions with p.d.f. given by (13.6.10).

a. Show that the conditional distribution of L_1, given that the surplus falls below its initial level, is a mixture of the same n exponential distributions.

b. Determine an expression for the n weights of this mixture in terms of the weights and parameters of the claim amount distribution.

c. Determine $E[L_1]$.

13.21. For the surplus process in Example 13.6.2, determine:

a. The p.d.f. of L_1

b. $E[L_1]$

c. $\text{Var}(L_1)$.

13.22. In the context of formula (13.2.1) let $G_i = U_i - U_{i-1}$ denote the insurer's gain between times $i - 1$ and i. Suppose that $G_1, G_2, \ldots$ are independent, identically distributed random variables. Suppose further that $u(x) = -e^{-\alpha x}$, $\alpha > 0$, is the insurer's utility function. Show that

$$\mathrm{E}[u(U_{n+1}) \mid U_n = x] \geq u(x)$$

if and only if $\alpha \leq \tilde{R}$, and interpret the result.

13.23. If we change the time units so that the new units are f times the old units (for some $f > 0$), and let $\tilde{c}$, $\tilde{\lambda}$, $\tilde{\psi}(u, t)$ denote parameters of the model in terms of the new units,
  a. what are these new parameters in terms of c, λ, and $\psi(u, t)$?
  b. For which value of f is $\tilde{\lambda} = 1$? (Some authors refer to these units as *operational time.*)

13.24. In a surplus process:
  1. Aggregate claims have a compound Poisson process
  2. Claim amounts are uniformly distributed over $(0, 10)$
  3. $\theta = 0.05$
  4. $u = 0.0$
  5. $U(T)$ is the negative surplus at ruin
  6. $U(T\text{-})$ is the surplus position immediately before ruin [Note: $U(T\text{-}) - X = U(T)$, where X is the claim amount at ruin.]
  Determine $\mathrm{E}[U(T\text{-})|T < \infty]$.
  [Hint: $U(T\text{-})$ and $|U(T)|$ are identically distributed in this exercise. To verify this fact, see Gerber and Shiu (1998), formula (3.7).]

Appendix

13.25. Suppose that all claims are of size 1.
  a. State the equation for $\psi(u)$ that corresponds to (13.A.14).
  b. Solve the equation if $0 \leq u \leq 1$.

APPLICATIONS OF RISK THEORY

14.1 Introduction

The collective risk model was developed in Chapters 12 and 13. This model is built on the assumptions that a collection of policies generates a random number of claims in each period and that each claim can be for a random amount. To apply the model, we need information about the distribution of the number of claims and the distribution of individual claim amounts. The selection of these distributions was discussed in Section 12.3, and only definitional remarks are added in this chapter for the distribution of the number of claims. Here, the distribution of individual claim amounts is illustrated in terms of four different lines of insurance: fire, automobile, short-term disability, and hospital.

We discuss two methods of approximating the individual risk theory model for a portfolio of insurances by a collective model. For short-term situations, this provides the means of substituting collective models for individual models.

The concept of stop-loss reinsurance for a portfolio of policies is explored in general. The methods of Chapter 12 for calculating the distribution of aggregate claims provide the means for the calculation of net stop-loss reinsurance premiums. Additionally, we discuss the interpretation of one form of a group insurance dividend formula as a stop-loss insurance.

We give illustrations of analyses of reinsurance agreements using tools from Chapters 12 and 13, as well as a comparison of the adjustment coefficient, which is related to the probability of ruin, with $E[L]$, which is related more to the depth of ruin.

The main purpose of this chapter is to indicate various ways of applying risk theory to insurance problems.

14.2 Claim Amount Distributions

To provide an idea of the broad range of applications of risk theory models, four specific but diverse applications are presented in this section. Here the discussion is of the individual claim amount distribution. This can then be combined with probabilities of individual claims occurring, to provide an individual risk model, or it can be compounded with a distribution for number of claims from a collection of insurances, to provide a collective risk model. The applications suggested in this section might be used by an insurance company in managing a line of business or block of similar policies, or by an industrial firm that uses modeling in its risk management program.

Fire Insurance:

In this line of insurance, the claim event is a fire in an insured structure that creates a loss. Because fires can cause heavy damage, adequate probability should be assigned to the higher claim amounts by the d.f. $P(x)$. In actuarial literature, some standard distributions have been suggested. Three of these distributions are listed in Table 14.2.1.

TABLE 14.2.1

Typical Claim Amount Distributions

Name	$p(x)$	Mean	Variance
Lognormal	$(x\sigma\sqrt{2\pi})^{-1} \exp\left[\dfrac{-(\log x - m)^2}{2\,\sigma^2}\right]$ $x > 0, \quad \sigma > 0$	$\exp(m + \sigma^2/2)$	$(e^{\sigma^2} - 1)\exp(2m + \sigma^2)$
Pareto	$\dfrac{\alpha\,x_0^\alpha}{x^{\alpha+1}}$ $x > x_0 > 0, \quad \alpha > 0$	$\dfrac{\alpha\,x_0}{\alpha - 1}$ $\alpha > 1$	$\dfrac{\alpha\,x_0^2}{(\alpha - 2)(\alpha - 1)^2}$ $\alpha > 2$
Mixture of exponentials	$p\,\alpha\,e^{-\alpha x} + q\,\beta\,e^{-\beta x}$ $x > 0, \quad 0 < p < 1, \quad q = 1 - p, \quad \alpha, \beta > 0$	$\dfrac{p}{\alpha} + \dfrac{q}{\beta}$	$\dfrac{p(1 + q)}{\alpha^2} + \dfrac{q(1 + p)}{\beta^2} - \dfrac{2pq}{\alpha\beta}$

An indication of the wide dispersion of probability in the case of the Pareto distribution is given by the mean's not existing unless $\alpha > 1$ and the variance's not existing unless $\alpha > 2$. Such distributions are said to have *heavy tails.*

To apply one of these standard distributions, the parameters of the distribution could be estimated from a sample of claim amounts.

Automobile Physical Damage:

In this line of insurance, a claim event is an incident causing damage to an insured automobile. The claim amount will not have the wide variability found in fire insurance. For this reason, the gamma distribution (12.3.17) has given reasonable fit to data and has been used on occasion for the claim amount distribution. Again, the parameters of the distribution could be estimated from a sample of claim amounts.

Disability Insurance:

This insurance provides income benefits to disabled lives. Usually there is a defined *elimination period,* seven days for example, following the occurrence of disability until benefits commence. There is also an upper limit on the payment period, as short as 13 weeks or as long as the period until retirement age. When issued to a group, the insurance is called *group weekly indemnity insurance* or *group long-term disability insurance,* depending on the length of the payment period.

The benefit is a fixed amount per period, and the amount of claim is this fixed amount times the number of periods the disability continues beyond the elimination period. Let the random variable, Y, represent this number of periods. From claims statistics, the distribution of Y can be estimated and tabulated in a form such as Table 14.2.2. Note the analogy between the function represented in the second column of Table 14.2.2 and the survival function discussed for life tables in Chapter 3. As used in this case, the function is referred to as a **continuance function.** It yields probabilities of continuance or survival of a disability claim for the indicated length of time. Similar to the way the survival function can be employed to provide various probabilities of survival and death, the continuance function can be employed to provide various probabilities of continuance and termination of disability.

In applying a collective risk model for a group disability insurance of the type illustrated in Table 14.2.2, $\Pr(N = n)$ should be interpreted as the probability that n disabilities, each of which continues at least seven days, occur during the insurance term among the group of insureds.

If the income benefit is an amount c per day, the claim amount distribution is given by

$$p(x) = \Pr\left(Y = \frac{x}{c}\right) \qquad x = c, 2c, 3c, \dots, 28c, 31c, \dots, 87c, 91c.$$

Interest is not considered for this short-term insurance.

For group disability insurance a Poisson distribution is often appropriate for the distribution of the number of disablements that occur and continue through the elimination period. The expected number of disablements for the distribution is often assumed to be proportional to the number of lives in the group. The following example illustrates how a compound Poisson distribution might be used to model the experience of a group disability contract with a medium length benefit period. The number of claims generated by the group within a period of fixed length and the lengths of the benefit periods of the claims that occur are assumed to be mutually independent.

Example 14.2.1

Consider a disability insurance contract covering a group of 200 females all age 32. The benefit is a set of monthly payments of 2,000 each that commence three

Illustrative Distribution of Y, the Length of Claim under Group Weekly Disability Income Insurance (13-Week Maximum Benefit, 7-Day Elimination Period)

Length of Claim (in Days) y	$\Pr(Y > y)$	$\Pr(Y = y)$
0	1.00000	—
1	0.96500	0.03500
2	0.93026	0.03474
3	0.89677	0.03349
4	0.86359	0.03318
5	0.83164	0.03195
6	0.80004	0.03160
7	0.76964	0.03040
8	0.73962	0.03002
9	0.71077	0.02885
10	0.68376	0.02701
11	0.65846	0.02530
12	0.63476	0.02370
13	0.61254	0.02222
14	0.59171	0.02083
15	0.57218	0.01953
16	0.55387	0.01831
17	0.53615	0.01772
18	0.51953	0.01662
19	0.50342	0.01611
20	0.48832	0.01510
21	0.47367	0.01465
22	0.45993	0.01374
23	0.44659	0.01334
24	0.43364	0.01295
25	0.42150	0.01214
26	0.40970	0.01180
27	0.39864	0.01106
28	0.38788	0.01076
31	—	0.06361*
35	0.32427	—
38	—	0.04832
42	0.27595	—
45	—	0.03753
49	0.23842	—
52	—	0.02980
56	0.20862	—
59	—	0.02399
63	0.18463	—
66	—	0.01939
70	0.16524	—
73	—	0.01586
77	0.14938	—
80	—	0.01300
84	0.13638	—
87	—	0.01077
91	0.00000	0.12561
		1.00000

*For convenience, claim terminations of a week from here on have been considered as terminations at the end of the third day of the week.

months following the date of disablement and continue as long as the disability up to a maximum of 21 payments. We assume that a compound Poisson distribution is appropriate for S, the total claims for the group.

For the rate of disablement and the claim amount distribution we make use of an excerpt of a continuance table shown below that is appropriate for a group of 1,000 females age 32 as published in the 1987 Commissioners Group Long-Term Disability (GLTD) table. The table was constructed in a deterministic context. For this example we make the reasonable interpretation that the data are appropriate for a compound Poisson distribution, and the column headings have been adapted with Y in Column (3) used as defined above. The constant of proportionality for the rate of disablement per life is denoted by λ_{32}.

Continuance in GLTD Table
Female, Three-Month Elimination Period
Age at Disablement 32

(1) Months from Disablement	(2) Number of Payments (y)	(3) $1,000\,\lambda_{32}\,\Pr(Y \geq y)$
3	1	2.6640
4	2	2.4008
5	3	2.1343
6	4	1.9277
7	5	1.7664
8	6	1.6431
9	7	1.5442
10	8	1.4614
11	9	1.3898
12	10	1.3288
13	11	1.2767
14	12	1.2320
15	13	1.1926
16	14	1.1575
17	15	1.1261
18	16	1.0983
19	17	1.0735
20	18	1.0512
21	19	1.0308
22	20	1.0125
23	21	0.9961
24	22	0.9815

This table continues to 25 years following disablement.

Determine the mean and variance of S.

Solution:

The benefit (claim) amount is denoted by $X = 2,000\,Y$, $Y = 1, 2, \ldots, 21$, and the p.f. of Y is denoted by $p(y)$. Note that this formulation ignores interest over the 21-month period. The expected number of disablements that continue beyond the elimination period for the group of 200 lives is $200\,\lambda_{32}$. In this setup,

$$E[S] = 200\,\lambda_{32}\,E[X] = (2{,}000)(200)\,\lambda_{32}\,E[Y], \qquad (14.2.1)$$

and

$$\text{Var}(S) = 200\,\lambda_{32}\,E[X^2] = (2{,}000^2)(200)\,\lambda_{32}\,E[Y^2]. \qquad (14.2.2)$$

To express the moments of S in terms of the values given in the continuance table we proceed as follows:

$$
\begin{aligned}
E[Y] &= \sum_{y=1}^{21} y\,p(y) + 21\sum_{y=22}^{\infty} p(y) \\[2mm]
&= \sum_{y=1}^{21}\left(\sum_{x=1}^{y} 1\right) p(y) + 21\sum_{y=22}^{\infty} p(y) \\[2mm]
&= \sum_{x=1}^{21}\left[\sum_{y=x}^{21} p(y)\right] + 21\sum_{y=22}^{\infty} p(y) \\[2mm]
&= \sum_{x=1}^{21}\left[\sum_{y=x}^{\infty} p(y) - \sum_{y=22}^{\infty} p(y)\right] + 21\sum_{y=22}^{\infty} p(y) \\[2mm]
&= \sum_{x=1}^{21}\sum_{y=x}^{\infty} p(y) = \sum_{x=1}^{21}\Pr(Y \geq x).
\end{aligned}
$$

Upon substituting this expression into (14.2.1), we have

$$E[S] = 200\,\lambda_{32}\,E[X] = (2{,}000)(200)\,\lambda_{32}\,E[Y]$$

$$= 400(2.6640 + 2.4008 + \cdots + 0.99610) = 12{,}203.12.$$

For the calculation of the variance for the total claims of the group of 200 lives, we need the second moment equivalent of the substitution $m = \Sigma_{x=1}^{m}(1)$. It can be verified that $m^2 = \Sigma_{x=1}^{m}(2x-1)$. Thus

$$
\begin{aligned}
E(Y^2) &= \sum_{y=1}^{21} y^2 p(y) + (21)^2 \sum_{y=22}^{\infty} p(y) \\[2mm]
&= \left\{\sum_{y=1}^{21}\left[\sum_{x=1}^{y}(2x-1)\right]p(y) + (21)^2\sum_{y=22}^{\infty} p(y)\right\} \\[2mm]
&= \left\{\sum_{x=1}^{21}(2x-1)\left[\sum_{y=x}^{\infty} p(y) - \sum_{y=22}^{\infty} p(y)\right] + (21)^2\sum_{y=22}^{\infty} p(y)\right\} \\[2mm]
&= \sum_{x=1}^{21}(2x-1)\sum_{y=x}^{\infty} p(y) = \sum_{x=1}^{21}(2x-1)\Pr(Y \geq x).
\end{aligned}
$$

Upon substituting this expression into (14.2.2), we have

$$\text{Var}(S) = (2{,}000)^2(200)\,\lambda_{32}\,E[Y^2]$$

$$= (800{,}000)1{,}000\,\lambda_{32}\sum_{x=1}^{21}(2x-1)\Pr(Y \geq x)$$

$$= 800{,}000[1(2.6640) + 3(2.4008) + \cdots + 41(0.9961)]$$

$$= 425.9808 \times 10^6. \qquad \blacktriangledown$$

Hospital Insurance:

Here we consider hospital insurance that provides a flat daily benefit during hospitalization. A hospitalization continuance table can be used to produce a p.f. for the length of stay in a hospital for each hospitalization. A graph of a hospitalization continuance function is given in Figure 14.2.1.

Continuance Function for Hospital Insurance

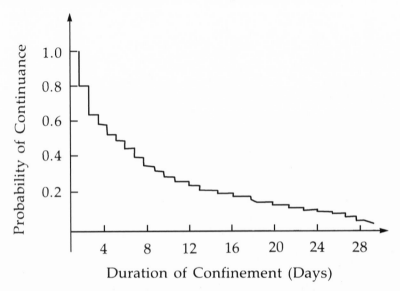

In applying a collective risk model to a hospital insurance of this type issued to a group of lives, $\Pr(N = n)$ should be interpreted as the probability that n hospitalizations, which meet the definition contained in the policy, occur during the period to members of the covered group. If the benefit amount is c per day, the p.f. of the claim amount is given by

$$p(x) = \Pr\left(Y = \frac{x}{c}\right) \qquad x = c, 2c, \ldots, mc$$

where the random variable Y represents the length of hospitalization in days and m is the maximum number of days for which benefits are paid.

The use of risk models in these applications permits us to estimate the required total pure premium. In addition, this estimate may be supplemented with statements about variability of losses.

14.3 Approximating the Individual Model

The individual and collective risk models are alternative constructions designed to capture key aspects of insurance systems. Each model leads to the development of a distribution of total claims for the modeled insurance system. In this section we develop two methods by which the compound Poisson distribution, usually

---

associated with the collective risk model, can be used to approximate the distribution of total claims in the individual model.

We consider the individual model developed in Chapter 2 for application to a group of n policies. The total claims in a policy period for the group is $S = X_1 + X_2 + \cdots + X_n$, where X_j is the claim that results from policy $j (j = 1, 2, \ldots, n)$. We distinguish between the occurrence of a claim and its amount, and we write

$$X_j = I_j B_j. \tag{14.3.1}$$

Here, I_j is 1 if policy j leads to a claim and 0 otherwise; B_j is the amount of such a claim, given that it occurs. On the assumption that I_j, B_j, $j = 1, 2, \ldots, n$, are mutually independent, it follows that

$$E[S] = \sum_{j=1}^{n} q_j \mu_j \tag{14.3.2}$$

and

$$\text{Var}(S) = \sum_{j=1}^{n} q_j(1 - q_j) \mu_j^2 + \sum_{j=1}^{n} q_j \sigma_j^2 \tag{14.3.3}$$

[see (2.2.25) and (2.2.26)], where q_j denotes the probability that policy j leads to a claim, $\mu_j = E[B_j]$, and $\sigma_j^2 = \text{Var}(B_j)$.

We denote the d.f. of B_j by $P_j(x)$. If a claim occurs, the probability that it comes from policy j is, by Bayes theorem, approximately $q_j / (q_1 + q_2 + \cdots + q_n)$. Then, by the law of total probability, the d.f. of the amount of a given claim is approximately

$$\sum_{j=1}^{n} \frac{q_j P_j(x)}{q_1 + \cdots + q_n}. \tag{14.3.4}$$

We next consider two methods of approximating the distribution of S by a compound Poisson distribution.

The first method uses the compound Poisson distribution with Poisson parameter

$$\lambda = q_1 + q_2 + \cdots + q_n \tag{14.3.5}$$

and d.f. of individual claim amounts

$$P(x) = \sum_{j=1}^{n} \frac{q_j}{\lambda} P_j(x). \tag{14.3.6}$$

The interpretation of (14.3.5) is that the expected number of claims in the compound Poisson model is the same as in the original individual risk model. Similarly, (14.3.6) means that the distribution of a claim, given that it has occurred, is the same in the two models, as can be seen from (14.3.4).

The compound Poisson distribution specified by (14.3.5) and (14.3.6) can also be explained as follows: In the individual model, the number of claims produced by policy j is a Bernoulli random variable. We approximate its distribution by the Poisson distribution with parameter q_j. Correspondingly, the distribution of X_j is approximated by the compound Poisson distribution given by q_j and $P_j(x)$. Then we use Theorem 12.4.1 to approximate the distribution of S by the compound Poisson distribution given by (14.3.5) and (14.3.6).

From (14.3.6), it follows that

$$p_k = \sum_{j=1}^{n} \frac{q_j}{\lambda} \, E[B_j^k] \qquad k = 1, 2, \ldots . \tag{14.3.7}$$

In particular,

$$p_1 = \sum_{j=1}^{n} \frac{q_j}{\lambda} \, \mu_i$$

and

$$p_2 = \sum_{j=1}^{n} \frac{q_j}{\lambda} \, (\mu_j^2 + \sigma_j^2).$$

Thus, the mean of the approximating compound Poisson distribution, λp_1, coincides with the mean of the total claims in the original individual model [see (14.3.2)]. On the other hand, the variance of the approximating compound Poisson distribution, λp_2, is

$$\sum_{j=1}^{n} q_j(\mu_j^2 + \sigma_j^2) \tag{14.3.8}$$

and exceeds the variance of total claims in the individual model [see (14.3.3)]. However, if the q_j's are small, the two variances are approximately the same.

Let us consider the special case where the claim amount for each policy is constant, $B_j = b_j$, so that $\mu_j = b_j$ and $\sigma_j = 0$. Then the p.f. of individual claim amounts according to (14.3.6) is

$$p(x) = \sum_{b_j=x} \frac{q_j}{\lambda} \tag{14.3.9}$$

where the sum is taken over the policies for which $b_j = x$. Furthermore, the ratio of the variance of total claims in the individual model [see (14.3.3)] to the variance of the approximating compound Poisson distribution [see (14.3.8)] is

$$\frac{\sum_{j=1}^{n} q_j b_j^2 (1 - q_j)}{\sum_{j=1}^{n} q_j b_j^2}. \tag{14.3.10}$$

This ratio can be interpreted as a weighted average of the probabilities of no claims, $1 - q_j$.

Example 14.3.1

In Example 2.5.1 we considered a portfolio of 1,800 policies. Approximate the distribution of aggregate claims by a compound Poisson distribution and discuss the resulting approximation for the variance of aggregate claims.

Solution:

According to (14.3.5),

$$\lambda = 500(0.02) + 500(0.02) + 300(0.1) + 500(0.1) = 100.$$

According to (14.3.9),

$$p(1) = \frac{500(0.02) + 300(0.1)}{100} = 0.4$$

$$p(2) = \frac{500(0.02) + 500(0.1)}{100} = 0.6.$$

Then $p_2 = p(1) + 4\,p(2) = 2.8$, and the variance of the compound Poisson approximation is $\lambda p_2 = 280$. As expected, this exceeds the variance of aggregate claims in the individual model, which was found to be 256 in Example 2.5.1. ▼

The second method to approximate the distribution of S uses the compound Poisson distribution with Poisson parameter

$$\tilde{\lambda} = \tilde{\lambda}_1 + \tilde{\lambda}_2 + \cdots + \tilde{\lambda}_n \tag{14.3.11}$$

where $\tilde{\lambda}_j = -\log(1 - q_j)$ and d.f. of individual claim amounts

$$\tilde{P}(x) = \sum_{j=1}^{n} \frac{\tilde{\lambda}_j}{\tilde{\lambda}} P_j(x). \tag{14.3.12}$$

The motivation for (14.3.11) and (14.3.12) is similar to that for (14.3.5) and (14.3.6). The key difference is that in (14.3.5) the expected numbers of claims in the two models are matched, whereas (14.3.11) implies

$$e^{-\tilde{\lambda}} = \prod_{j=1}^{n} (1 - q_j);$$

that is, the probabilities of no claims are the same in the two models.

Example 14.3.2

For the portfolio of 1,800 policies studied in Examples 2.5.1 and 14.3.1, calculate the compound Poisson approximation to the distribution of aggregate claims by the second method.

Solution:

$$\tilde{\lambda} = -500 \log(0.98) - 500 \log(0.98) - 300 \log(0.9)$$

$$-500 \log(0.9) = 104.5$$

$$\tilde{p}(1) = \frac{-500 \log{(0.98)} - 300 \log{(0.9)}}{104.5} = 0.399$$

$$\tilde{p}(2) = \frac{-500 \log{(0.98)} - 500 \log{(0.9)}}{104.5} = 0.601.$$

▼

In this section we have presented two methods for approximating the distribution of aggregate claims in the individual model by a compound Poisson distribution. If all the q_j's for the individual model are small (which could well be the case in connection with life insurance policies), the two methods produce very similar results since, in that case,

$$\tilde{\lambda}_j = -\log{(1 - q_j)} = q_j + \frac{1}{2} q_j^2 + \cdots \cong q_j.$$

14.4   Stop-Loss Reinsurance

The concept of an insurance with a deductible is discussed in Section 1.5. A definition is given in (1.5.1), and a property of optimality is established in Theorem 1.5.1. When such a coverage is written for a collection of insurance risks, it is called stop-loss reinsurance, the topic of this section. In a given application, S may denote the total claims in a given period for an insurance company, or for a block of business of a company, or for a life or health group insurance contract.

For a stop-loss contract with deductible d, the amount paid by the reinsurer to the ceding insurer is

$$I_d = \begin{cases} 0 & S \le d \\ S - d & S > d. \end{cases} \tag{14.4.1}$$

Sometimes this is written as $I_d = (S - d)_+$, where the plus subscript denotes the positive part of $S - d$.

Note that I_d, as a function of the aggregate claims S, is also a random variable. The amount of claims retained by the ceding insurer is

$$S - I_d = \begin{cases} S & S \le d \\ d & S > d. \end{cases} \tag{14.4.2}$$

Thus, the amount retained is bounded by d, which explains the name stop-loss contract.

We discuss methods to calculate $E[I_d]$, the expected claims paid by the reinsurance when the deductible is d. We denote the d.f. of S by $F_S(x)$ and first assume that S has a p.d.f. $f_S(x)$. Then,

$$E[I_d] = \int_d^\infty (x - d) f_S(x)\, dx. \tag{14.4.3}$$

Usually S cannot assume any negative values. We can extend the integral to $(0, \infty)$ and subtract the integral over $(0, d)$ to see that

$$E[I_d] = E[S] - d + \int_0^d (d - x) f_S(x)\, dx. \qquad (14.4.4)$$

If we set

$$f_S(x) = -\frac{d}{dx}\,[1 - F_S(x)]$$

in (14.4.3), integrate by parts and recall the implication following (3.5.1), we get

$$E[I_d] = \int_d^\infty [1 - F_S(x)]\, dx. \qquad (14.4.5)$$

Similarly, we obtain

$$E[I_d] = E[S] - \int_0^d [1 - F_S(x)]\, dx \qquad (14.4.6)$$

from (14.4.4).

Each of these four expressions for $E[I_d]$ has its own merit. If $E[S]$ is available, (14.4.4) and (14.4.6) are preferable where numerical integration is required, since the range of integration is finite. This reduces the possibilities of inaccurate approximation of $f_S(x)$ for large x. Formulas (14.4.5) and (14.4.6) hold for general distributions, including those of discrete or of mixed type. If the distribution of S is given in analytical form, for example, by a normal or gamma distribution, (14.4.3) might be the most tractable formula.

Example 14.4.1

If S has a gamma distribution, show that

$$E[I_d] = \frac{\alpha}{\beta}\,[1 - G(d{:}\alpha + 1, \beta)] - d\,[1 - G(d{:}\alpha, \beta)].$$

Solution:
From (14.4.3), we obtain

$$E[I_d] = \int_d^\infty x f_S(x)\, dx - d\,[1 - F_S(d)]$$

$$= \int_d^\infty \frac{\beta^\alpha}{\Gamma(\alpha)}\, x^\alpha\, e^{-\beta x}\, dx - d\,[1 - G(d{:}\alpha, \beta)].$$

Since $\alpha\Gamma(\alpha) = \Gamma(\alpha + 1)$, the integrand is α/β times the gamma p.d.f. with parameters $\alpha + 1$ and β. Hence the given formula follows. ▼

Example 14.4.2

Suppose that a, b are numbers with $\Pr(a < S < b) = 0$. Show that, for $a < d < b$, $E[I_d]$ can be obtained from $E[I_a]$ and $E[I_b]$ by linear interpolation.

Solution:

From the assumption, it follows that $F_S(x) = F_S(a)$ for $a \leq x < b$. We use this in (14.4.6) to see that

$$E[I_d] = E[I_a] - (d - a)[1 - F_S(a)];$$

that is, $E[I_d]$ is a linear function of d in the interval $[a, b]$.   ▼

We now consider the case where the possible values of S are non-negative integers and denote by $f_S(x)$ the p.f. of S ($x = 0, 1, 2, \ldots$). We assume that the deductible d is an integer. According to the preceding example, the expected stop-loss reinsurance claims for noninteger deductibles can be obtained by linear interpolation.

The formulas

$$E[I_d] = \sum_{x=d+1}^{\infty} (x - d)\, f_S(x) \tag{14.4.7}$$

and

$$E[I_d] = E[S] - d + \sum_{x=0}^{d-1} (d - x)\, f_S(x) \tag{14.4.8}$$

are the counterparts of (14.4.3) and (14.4.4). The integrals in (14.4.5) and (14.4.6) can be written as sums, since $F_S(x)$ is piecewise constant. We obtain

$$E[I_d] = \sum_{x=d}^{\infty} [1 - F_S(x)] \tag{14.4.9}$$

and

$$E[I_d] = E[S] - \sum_{x=0}^{d-1} [1 - F_S(x)]. \tag{14.4.10}$$

Example 14.4.3

For the aggregate claims distribution in Example 12.2.2 calculate, by two methods, the expected stop-loss reinsurance claims when the deductible is 7.

Solution:

According to (14.4.7),

$$E[I_7] = f_S(8) + 2\, f_S(9) = 0.0028.$$

Alternatively, according to (14.4.9),

$$E[I_7] = [1 - F_S(7)] + [1 - F_S(8)] = 0.0028.$$ ▼

Example 14.4.4

Calculate $E[I_6]$ for the compound Poisson distribution used in Example 12.4.2.

Solution:

Since the compound Poisson distribution has an infinite range, the use of (14.4.8) and (14.4.10) is more practical here. For example, using (14.4.8) we obtain

$$E[I_6] = E[S] - 6 + \sum_{x=0}^{5} (6 - x) f_S(x)$$

$$= 1.7 - 6 + 4.3547 = 0.0547. \qquad \blacktriangledown$$

In general, from (14.4.9), we obtain a recursive formula

$$E[I_{d+1}] = E[I_d] - [1 - F_S(d)] \qquad d = 0, 1, 2, \ldots . \qquad (14.4.11)$$

Thus $E[I_d]$ can be obtained recursively with starting value $E[I_0] = E[S]$.

This recursive approach is particularly convenient if S has a compound distribution that satisfies the conditions of Theorem 12.4.3. In this case, $f_S(x)$ also can be calculated recursively [see (12.4.16)–(12.4.18)]. As an example, for the compound Poisson distribution, we start with

$$f_S(0) = F_S(0) = e^{-\lambda}$$

and

$$E[I_0] = \lambda p_1,$$

and use the recursive formulas

$$f_S(x) = \frac{\lambda}{x} \sum_{j=1}^{\infty} j p(j) f_S(x - j),$$

$$F_S(x) = F_S(x - 1) + f_S(x),$$

$$E[I_x] = E[I_{x-1}] - [1 - F_S(x - 1)]$$

successively for $x = 1, 2, 3, \ldots .$

Example 14.4.5

Assume that S has a compound Poisson distribution with $\lambda = 1.5$, $p(1) = 2/3$, $p(2) = 1/3$. Calculate values of $f_S(x)$, $F_S(x)$, $E[I_x]$ for $x = 0, 1, 2, \ldots , 6$.

Solution:

First,

$$f_S(0) = F_S(0) = e^{-1.5} = 0.223$$

and

$$E[I_0] = \lambda\, p_1 = 1.5\,\frac{4}{3} = 2.$$

Then, since $\lambda\, j\, p(j) = 1$ for $j = 1, 2$,

$$f_S(x) = \frac{1}{x}\,[f_S(x-1) + f_S(x-2)] \qquad x = 1, 2, \ldots, 6.$$

Note that $f_S(1) = f_S(0)$.

The remaining steps and the results are displayed below.

x	$f_S(x) = (1/x)\,[f_S(x{-}1)$ $+ f_S(x{-}2)]$	$F_S(x) = F_S(x{-}1)$ $+ f_S(x)$	$E[I_x] = E[I_{x-1}]$ $+ F_S(x{-}1) - 1$
0	0.223	0.223	2.000
1	0.223	0.446	1.223
2	0.223	0.669	0.669
3	0.149	0.818	0.338
4	0.093	0.911	0.156
5	0.048	0.959	0.067
6	0.024	0.983	0.026

▼

Our discussion has focused on the calculation of $E[I_d]$, the expected stop-loss reinsurance claims. Typically, this is a lower bound for a stop-loss premium. The actual premium will contain a loading that reflects the variability of the reinsurer's payment, I_d. One measure of this variability is

$$\mathrm{Var}(I_d) = E[I_d^2] - E[I_d]^2.$$

In the discrete case, it is possible to compute $E[I_d^2]$ recursively (see Exercise 14.8).

We now turn to a dividend formula of group insurance because it is identical in concept to a stop-loss reinsurance. Recall that group insurance is the name used when an insurance covering many individuals is purchased in the form of a single contract by a sponsor such as an employer. Examples are given in the short-term disability illustration in Section 14.2 and Example 14.2.1. In this section we discuss one type of dividend formula that can be used in relation to group insurance.

We assume that for a premium of G the insurer will provide full coverage for total claims S in a given period. With the policyholder's knowledge, the premium contains a substantial loading $G - E[S] > 0$. Consequently, the policyholder anticipates a dividend D at the end of the period, which will be a function of S. Specifically, we assume that the dividend is of the form

$$D = \begin{cases} kG - S & S < kG \\ 0 & S \geq kG \end{cases} \qquad (14.4.12)$$

where $0 < k < 1$. Thus the policyholder pays G and in return receives S and D.

We now consider the expected value of D. For notational convenience, we assume that the distribution of S is continuous and denote the p.d.f. of S by $f_S(x)$; the discrete case is very similar, as shown in Example 14.4.6. From (14.4.12), we have

$$\mathrm{E}[D] = \int_0^{kG} (kG - x)\, f_S(x)\, dx. \tag{14.4.13}$$

Presumably, the insurer will set k small enough so that $\mathrm{E}[S] + \mathrm{E}[D] < G$.

Example 14.4.6

For a premium of five the insurer covers total claims S, having the compound Poisson distribution considered in Example 14.4.5. The insurer agrees to pay a dividend equal to the excess of 80% of the premium over the claims. Calculate $G - \mathrm{E}[S] - \mathrm{E}[D]$ (this is the expected value of the amount available to cover expenses, security loading, and so on).

Solution:

The dividend is of the form (14.4.12) with $k = 0.8$. Thus

$$\mathrm{E}[D] = 4\, f_S(0) + 3\, f_S(1) + 2\, f_S(2) + f_S(3) = 2.156.$$

Then,

$$G - \mathrm{E}[S] - \mathrm{E}[D] = 5 - 2 - 2.156 = 0.844. \qquad \blacktriangledown$$

We can rewrite the right-hand side of (14.4.13) as

$$\mathrm{E}[D] = \int_0^\infty (kG - x)\, f_S(x)\, dx + \int_{kG}^\infty (x - kG)\, f_S(x)\, dx.$$

Thus

$$\mathrm{E}[D] = kG - \mathrm{E}[S] + \mathrm{E}[I_{kG}] \tag{14.4.14}$$

where I_{kG} is the payment under a stop-loss contract with deductible kG. If the expected stop-loss claims $\mathrm{E}[I_d]$ have already been calculated for various deductibles, this is a convenient formula to obtain $\mathrm{E}[D]$.

Example 14.4.7

Use (14.4.14) to obtain $\mathrm{E}[D]$ in Example 14.4.6.

Solution:

Since $\mathrm{E}[I_4] = 0.156$,

$$\mathrm{E}[D] = 4 - 2 + 0.156 = 2.156. \qquad \blacktriangledown$$

There are more facets to the connection between a dividend formula of the type (14.4.12) and a stop-loss contract. We start with the identity

$$S + D = kG + I_{kG}. \tag{14.4.15}$$

This can be verified by distinguishing the cases: $S \leq kG$ where both sides equal kG, and $S > kG$ where both sides equal S. Subtracting G from both sides, we obtain

$$S + D - G = I_{kG} - (1 - k)G. \qquad (14.4.16)$$

We have the following interpretation: The balance of the claim payments and dividends received over the premium paid is the same as the corresponding balance for a stop-loss contract with deductible kG and stop-loss premium $(1 - k)G$.

This interpretation suggests that the insurer can regard the premium as split into two components,

$$G = kG + (1 - k)G. \qquad (14.4.17)$$

Claims are first paid from kG, and any remaining balance $kG - S$ (for $S < kG$) is paid as a dividend in accordance with (14.4.12). The second component, $(1 - k)G$, is used to provide a stop-loss reinsurance with deductible kG.

Formula (14.4.15) rearranged as

$$D = kG - S + I_{kG}$$

yields (14.4.14) again when expectations are taken on each side.

14.5 Analysis of Reinsurance Using Ruin Theory

Questions about type and amount of reinsurance to purchase can be answered in various ways. One approach is provided by the insurer adopting a utility function. From all available reinsurance arrangements, the insurer selects the one yielding the highest expected utility. This ideal approach, which is very simple in concept, is not commonly used in practice.

In preparation for a second approach, note that in Chapter 13 we considered the insurer's premium rate c to have a relative security loading θ such that $c = (1 + \theta) \lambda p_1$ [see (13.4.3)]. Here θ did not include any loading for expenses, and all of c was available for the risk process. For our further discussion of reinsurance, it is useful to define a reinsurance loading ξ by the formula

(reinsurance premium rate) $= (1 + \xi)$(expected rate of reinsurance payment).

$$(14.5.1)$$

The reinsurance premium rate, as determined by the reinsurer, will provide for reinsurance payments, expenses, security, and profit. The insurer can express the reinsurance premium rate in the format of the right-hand side of (14.5.1) to determine ξ. In particular, for expected stop-loss claims $E[I_d]$, given by (14.4.3), the loading ξ is 0.

The second approach recognizes that the purchase of reinsurance is necessarily a compromise between expected gain and security. Because of the loading contained in the reinsurance premium, the purchase of reinsurance will reduce the insurer's expected gain; on the other hand, a reasonable reinsurance arrangement will increase security in some sense. For this approach, a required standard of security is first defined, and then only reinsurance arrangements satisfying this standard are considered. From this set of admissible arrangements, the insurer selects the one that allows for the highest expected gain.

We consider two tools from ruin theory for evaluating reinsurance agreements. The first is the adjustment coefficient because it can be used to obtain information about the probability of ruin. As a second tool we examine the use of E[L], the expected value of the maximal aggregate loss. At this point the name *adjustment coefficient* reveals its meaning: If a certain reinsurance arrangement produces a value of R (or $\tilde{R}$) that is not large enough, the arrangement needs to be adjusted.

Example 14.5.1

An insurer has a portfolio producing annual aggregate claims that are independent and identically distributed; their common distribution is compound Poisson with $\lambda = 1.5$, $p(1) = 2/3$, $p(2) = 1/3$ (see Example 14.4.5). The annual premiums received are $c = 2.5$.
a. Calculate the adjustment coefficient that results from this portfolio.
b. Stop-loss coverage can be obtained for a reinsurance loading charge of 100%. Calculate the adjustment coefficient if a stop-loss contract is purchased with a deductible of

$$(i)\ 3 \quad (ii)\ 4 \quad (iii)\ 5.$$

Also, compare these alternatives from the point of view of expected gain.

Solution:

a. In this case, $R = \tilde{R}$, and we can obtain R from (13.2.6) or (13.4.2). The latter condition can be written

$$1.5 + 2.5r = e^r + (0.5)\,e^{2r}.$$

We obtain $R = \tilde{R} = 0.28$.
b. We consider case (i), $d = 3$, in detail. In Example 14.4.5 we computed $E[I_3] = 0.338$. The actual stop-loss premium is twice this amount, or 0.676. Thus the insurer's retained premium in year i is $2.5 - 0.676 = 1.824$, and retained claims are

$$\hat{W}_i = \begin{cases} W_i & W_i = 0, 1, 2, 3 \\ 3 & W_i > 3 \end{cases}$$

where W_i denotes the aggregate claims of year i. According to (13.2.6), $\tilde{R}$ is the positive solution of the equation

$$e^{-1.824r}\left\{ \sum_{x=0}^{2} f_W(x)\,e^{xr} + [1 - F_W(2)]\,e^{3r} \right\} = 1$$

(see Example 14.4.5). We calculate $\tilde{R} = 0.25$. The expected gain per year is

---

(the expected gain in the   − (the expected return of the reinsurer,   = 0.162.
absence of reinsurance,   which, because the reinsurer
$c - E[W_i] = 2.5 - 2 = 0.5$)   charges at rate 2 $E[I_3]$, is $E[I_3] = 0.338$)

The calculations for cases (ii) and (iii) are similar. The results are displayed below where $d = \infty$ represents the case of no reinsurance.

Stop-Loss Deductible, d	Adjustment Coefficient, $\tilde{R}$	Expected Gain
3	0.25	0.162
4	0.35	0.344
5	0.34	0.433
∞	0.28	0.500

With respect to security (as measured by the adjustment coefficient), a deductible of 4 is better than one of 5, which in turn is better than no reinsurance. With respect to expected gain, this order is reversed. Further, it can be observed that selecting a deductible of 3 would be an irrational decision. It is worse than no reinsurance with respect to both security and expected gain.   ▼

We next consider reinsurance arrangements where the reinsurer's payments depend on the individual claim amounts. In general, such a coverage is defined in terms of a function $h(x)$ with $0 \le h(x) \le x$ for all x. The interpretation is that $h(x)$ is the amount payable (by the reinsurer to the insurer) if a claim is of size x. A special case is *proportional reinsurance* where

$$h(x) = \alpha x \qquad 0 \le \alpha \le 1, \tag{14.5.2}$$

that is, where the reinsurer reimburses a constant percentage of the claim. A second case is *excess-of-loss reinsurance* where

$$h(x) = \begin{cases} 0 & x \le \beta \\ x - \beta & x > \beta \end{cases} \tag{14.5.3}$$

with $\beta \ge 0$ playing the role of a deductible. An excess-of-loss coverage is reminiscent of a stop-loss coverage [see (14.4.1)]. However, the excess-of-loss is applied to individual claims, while the stop-loss is applied to aggregate claims.

We assume the continuous time compound Poisson model of Chapter 13 and its notation. Correspondingly, we assume the reinsurance premiums are payable continuously at a rate c_h. Then the ceding insurer's adjustment coefficient, R_h, is the nontrivial solution of the equation

$$\lambda [M_{x-h(x)}(r) - 1] = (c - c_h) r. \tag{14.5.4}$$

This follows from (13.3.1) since the ceding insurer now receives income at a net rate of $c - c_h$ and pays $x - h(x)$ for a claim of size x.

Example 14.5.2

Consider a surplus process with (1) the aggregate claim process, $S(t)$, being compound Poisson where the claims have an exponential distribution with mean $= 1$, (2) the relative security loading is 25%, and (3) proportional reinsurance is available at a price 140% of the expected reinsured claims. Determine the proportion, α, of each claim reinsured that maximizes the adjustment coefficient, R, for the process with this reinsurance.

Solution:

By (14.5.4) R is the smallest positive root of

$$\lambda + (c - c_h)r = \lambda\, \text{E}[\exp\{r[X - h(X)]\}].$$

In this situation with $p_1 = 1$ and $h(x) = \alpha x$, we have $c = 1.25\,\lambda$ and $c_h = 1.4\,\alpha\,\lambda$. Further, for X with an exponential distribution,

$$\text{E}[\exp\{r[X - h(X)]\}] = \frac{1}{1 - (1 - \alpha)r}.$$

This leads to the equation for R as

$$1 + (1.25 - 1.4\alpha)r = \frac{1}{1 - (1 - \alpha)r},$$

and the solution for the adjustment coefficient is

$$R = \frac{(0.25 - 0.4\alpha)}{(1 - \alpha)(1.25 - 1.4\alpha)}.$$

The value of α that maximizes the value of the adjustment coefficient is

$$\alpha = \frac{5 - [3\,(35)^{1/2}/7]}{8} = 0.308067,$$

and this results in a value of the adjustment coefficient of

$$R = 0.223787. \qquad\qquad \blacktriangledown$$

This answer depends upon the relationship between the two loading rates in the example as explored in Exercise 14.16.

Example 14.5.3

Consider the same situation as described in Example 14.5.2. This time excess-of-loss reinsurance is available at a price of 140% of expected claims. Find the deductible amount, β, which maximizes the adjustment coefficient, R, for the process with this reinsurance.

Solution:

With excess-of-loss reinsurance, the claim size distribution is the exponential distribution truncated at β. Again we have

$c = 1.25\lambda$ but now $h(x) = x - \beta$ for $x > \beta$ and zero elsewhere, so

$$c_h = 1.4\lambda \int_\beta^\infty (x - \beta)\, e^{-x}\, dx = 1.4\lambda e^{-\beta}.$$

Further,

$$E[\exp\{r[X - h(X)]\}] = \int_0^\beta e^{rx}\, e^{-x}\, dx + \int_\beta^\infty e^{r\beta}\, e^{-x}\, dx$$

$$= \frac{1 - re^{-\beta(1-r)}}{(1 - r)}.$$

Thus, the nonlinear equation for R as a function of β is

$$1 + (1.25 - 1.4\, e^{-\beta})r - \frac{1 - re^{-\beta(1-r)}}{(1 - r)} = 0.$$

The following table shows the values of R corresponding to several different values of β.

E[h(X)]	β	R
0.00	infinite	0.2000
0.05	2.9957	0.2393
0.10	2.3026	0.2649
0.15	1.8971	0.2871
0.20	1.6094	0.3070
0.25	1.3863	0.3244
0.30	1.2040	0.3384
0.35	1.0498	0.3474
0.40	0.9163	0.3486
0.45	0.7985	0.3371
0.50	0.6931	0.3047
0.55	0.5978	0.2366
0.60	0.5108	0.1051

The value of $E[h(X)]$ that leads to the largest value of R requires additional work but can be determined to be 0.38167 corresponding to a value of the deductible, β, of 0.9632. This results in a value of R of 0.3493 which is considerably larger than that for the most favorable value available under proportional reinsurance examined in Example 14.5.2. ▼

Example 14.5.4

Compare the values of the adjustment coefficient, R, for the situations described in Examples 14.5.2 and 14.5.3 for pairs of α and β such that the reinsurer's expected payments, $E[h(X)]$, are the same, that is, if $\alpha = e^{-\beta}$.

Solution:

E[h(X)]	Proportional		Excess-of-Loss	
	α	R	β	R
0.00	0.00	0.2000	infinite	0.2000
0.05	0.05	0.2052	2.9957	0.2393
0.10	0.10	0.2102	2.3026	0.2649
0.15	0.15	0.2149	1.8971	0.2871
0.20	0.20	0.2191	1.6094	0.3070
0.25	0.25	0.2222	1.3863	0.3244
0.30	0.30	0.2238	1.2040	0.3384
0.35	0.35	0.2227	1.0498	0.3474
0.40	0.40	0.2174	0.9163	0.3486
0.45	0.45	0.2053	0.7985	0.3371
0.50	0.50	0.1818	0.6931	0.3047
0.55	0.55	0.1389	0.5978	0.2366
0.60	0.60	0.0610	0.5108	0.1051

For a given reinsurance loading, the excess-of-loss coverage consistently leads to a higher adjustment coefficient than that provided by the corresponding proportional coverage. We see below that this is not a coincidence. ▼

Somewhat similar to Theorem 1.5.1 is another theorem giving an optimality feature of excess-of-loss reinsurance. The proof of Theorem 14.5.1 is given in the Appendix to this chapter.

Theorem 14.5.1

Assume the compound Poisson model of Chapter 13. Let an arbitrary reinsurance be defined by $h(x)$, $0 \leq h(x) \leq x$, and c_h, its premium rate. Similarly, let an excess-of-loss reinsurance with deductible β be defined by $h_\beta(x)$ and c_β (simplified notation for c_{h_β}). Furthermore, let R_h and R_β denote the resulting adjustment coefficients, respectively. If $E[h(X)] = E[h_\beta(X)]$ and $c_h = c_\beta$, then $R_h \leq R_\beta$.

Since $c_h = (1 + \xi_h) \lambda E[h(X)]$ and $c_\beta = (1 + \xi_\beta) \lambda E[h_\beta(X)]$ where ξ_h and ξ_β are the loadings for the respective reinsurance coverages, the conditions of the theorem imply $\xi_h = \xi_\beta$. This limits the application of the theorem, as it may not be possible to secure excess-of-loss reinsurance with the same loading as for other reinsurances.

To illustrate this point, reconsider the situations of Examples 14.5.2 and 14.5.3. Assume that excess-of-loss reinsurance can be obtained only with a reinsurance loading of 75%, whereas the proportional reinsurance remains available with reinsurance loading of 40%. Proportional reinsurance with $\alpha = 0.25$, $\xi_h = 0.40$ has a premium rate of 1.4 $\alpha = 0.35$, and from Example 14.5.4 we see that $R = 0.2222$. The excess-of-loss reinsurance with the same expected cost has a deductible of $\beta = 1.3863$ and the premium rate would be 1.75 $e^{-\beta} = 0.4375$. Here, however, going through the process of Example 14.5.3 we obtain an R value of 0.1459. Thus the reinsurance premium rate would be higher than for proportional reinsurance, but the resulting adjustment coefficient would be lower and imply less protection against ruin.

We now shift attention to a second criterion for analyzing reinsurance arrangements. The criterion is to minimize the expected value of the maximal aggregate loss random variable, L. By its definition, $\Pr(L > u) = \psi(u)$. Since L is a non-negative random variable,

$$E[L] = \int_0^\infty \Pr(L > u)\, du = \int_0^\infty \psi(u)\, du, \qquad (14.5.5)$$

and minimizing $E[L]$ is related to the problem of reducing the probability of ruin. The two criteria are quite closely related since, by (13.4.5),

$$\psi(u) < e^{-Ru}$$

so that

$$E[L] = \int_0^\infty \psi(u)\, du < \frac{1}{R}.$$

Thus maximizing R is closely related to minimizing $E[L]$.

In the next two examples, we again determine a reinsurance arrangement of the proportional type and then of the excess-of-loss type, both of which minimize $E[L]$.

Example 14.5.5

Consider a surplus process where (1) the aggregate claim process, $S(t)$, is compound Poisson with claims having an exponential distribution with mean $= 1$, (2) the relative security loading is 25%, and (3) proportional reinsurance is available at a price 140% of the expected reinsured claims. Determine the proportion, α, of each claim reinsured that minimizes $E[L]$, the expected value of the maximal aggregate loss random variable.

Solution:

By (13.6.16) $E[L] = p_2 / (2p_1\theta)$. All numbers are in terms of premiums and claims retained by the original insurer, so $p_2 = E[(1 - \alpha)^2 X^2] = (1 - \alpha)^2\, E[X^2] = 2(1 - \alpha)^2$. The expression θp_1 is the net amount of loading collected and retained by the original insurer and is the difference $1.25 - 1.4\,\alpha - (1 - \alpha) = 0.25 - 0.4\,\alpha$. Thus $E[L] = (1 - \alpha)^2 / (0.25 - 0.4\,\alpha)$, and this is minimized at $\alpha = 0.25$. At this value of α, $E[L] = 3.75$. ▼

Example 14.5.6

Consider the same situation as described in Example 14.5.5. Find the deductible amount, β, which minimizes $E[L]$ if excess-of-loss reinsurance is available at a price of
a. 140% of the expected claims reinsured, and
b. 175% of the expected claims reinsured.

Solution:

With excess-of-loss reinsurance, the claim size distribution is the exponential distribution truncated at β. Here,

$$p_1 = \int_0^\beta x\, e^{-x}\, dx + \int_\beta^\infty \beta\, e^{-x}\, dx = 1 - e^{-\beta}$$

and

$$p_2 = \int_0^\beta x^2 e^{-x}\, dx + \int_\beta^\infty \beta^2\, e^{-x}\, dx = 2\,[1 - (\beta + 1)e^{-\beta}].$$

a. The net amount of loading collected and retained by the original insurer is the difference

$$1.25 - 1.4e^{-\beta} - (1 - e^{-\beta}) = 0.25 - 0.4e^{-\beta}.$$

Thus $E[L] = [1 - (\beta + 1)e^{-\beta}]/(0.25 - 0.4e^{-\beta})$. The value of β that minimizes this expression satisfies the equation

$$0.4 - 0.25\,\beta = 0.4\, e^{-\beta},$$

and the β that satisfies this is 1.02717. At this value of β, $E[L] = 2.56793$. This value of $E[L]$ is smaller than the one found in Example 14.5.5, suggesting that excess-of-loss reinsurance is also to be preferred over proportional reinsurance by this criterion.

b. By a similar process the value of β that minimizes $E[L]$ in part (b) satisfies the equation

$$0.75 - 0.25\,\beta = 0.75\, e^{-\beta},$$

and the β that satisfies this is 2.82143. At this value of β, $E[L] = 3.76192$. This value of $E[L]$ is slightly larger than the one found in Example 14.5.5 for proportional reinsurance. This suggests that excess-of-loss reinsurance, with higher loading, is not preferred over proportional reinsurance by the $E[L]$ criterion. ▼

Example 14.5.7

Compare the results of Examples 14.5.5 and 14.5.6 for pairs of α and β such that the reinsurer's expected payments, $E[h(X)]$, are the same, that is, if $\alpha = e^{-\beta}$.

Solution:

	Proportional 40% Loading		Excess-of-Loss 40% Loading		Excess-of-Loss 75% Loading	
E[h(X)]	α	E[L]	β	E[L]	β	E[L]
0.00	0.00	4.000	infinite	4.000	infinite	4.000
0.05	0.05	3.924	2.9957	3.479	2.9957	3.766
0.10	0.10	3.857	2.3026	3.189	2.3026	3.827
0.15	0.15	3.803	1.8971	2.976	1.8971	4.112
0.20	0.20	3.765	1.6094	2.812	1.6094	4.781
0.25	0.25	3.750	1.3863	2.690	1.3863	6.455
0.30	0.30	3.769	1.2040	2.606	1.2040	13.552
0.35	0.35	3.841	1.0498	2.569		
0.40	0.40	4.000	0.9163	2.594		
0.45	0.45	4.321	0.7985	2.724		
0.50	0.50	5.000	0.6931	3.069		
0.55	0.55	6.750	0.5978	4.040		
0.60	0.60	16.000	0.5108	9.350		

▼

Example 14.5.7 suggests that for the same loading levels, excess-of-loss reinsurance is to be preferred over proportional reinsurance. Exercise 14.24 illustrates the development of a result that formalizes this observation. At higher loading levels for excess-of-loss reinsurance the picture is mixed. For low amounts of reinsurance purchased, that is, low values of $E[h(X)]$, a superiority of excess-of-loss can still be observed. With higher amounts purchased, the proportional reinsurance with its smaller loading will be preferred.

14.6   Notes and References

A monograph by Hogg and Klugman (1984) demonstrates the use of claim statistics for selecting a claim amount distribution and estimating the parameters. Other references for this can be found in Seal (1969). The claim amount distribution for group weekly indemnity insurance was taken from papers by Miller (1951) and Bartlett (1965). The hospitalization continuance curve was derived from data in a paper by Gingery (1952).

The two methods for approximating the individual model by a collective model were suggested by Mereu (1972) and Wooddy (1973).

Calculating stop-loss premiums has been the subject of many papers. Bohman and Esscher (1963–64) reported on an extensive study of alternative methods of approximating the distribution of total claims and expected stop-loss claims. Bartlett (1965) discussed the use of the gamma distribution for the calculation of expected stop-loss claims. Bowers (1969) presented an upper bound, in terms of the mean and variance of aggregate claims, for expected stop-loss claims. This result has been generalized by Taylor (1977) and by Goovaerts and DeVylder (1980). In recent years several papers have developed methods for use with discrete claim distributions. These include Halmstad (1972), Mereu (1972), Gerber and Jones (1977), and Panjer (1980).

A link between the applications of risk theory and financial economics is established in Exercise 14.23. The result was obtained by Black and Scholes (1973), starting with assumptions about the operations of an efficient securities market. Their work is widely regarded as starting a new approach to many issues in financial economics.

The effect of reinsurance on the probability of ruin is discussed by Gerber (1980).

Appendix

Proof of Theorem 14.5.1:

We know that R_h is the positive root of

$$\lambda + (c - c_h)r = \lambda M_{X-h(X)}(r)$$

and R_β is the positive root of

$$\lambda + (c - c_\beta)r = \lambda M_{X-h_\beta(X)}(r).$$

Since $c_h = c_\beta$, we can see from Figure 14.A.1 that

$$M_{X-h(X)}(r) \geq M_{X-h_\beta(X)}(r) \qquad r > 0 \qquad\qquad (14.A.1)$$

implies $R_h \leq R_\beta$.

FIGURE 14.A.1

Proof of Theorem 14.5.1

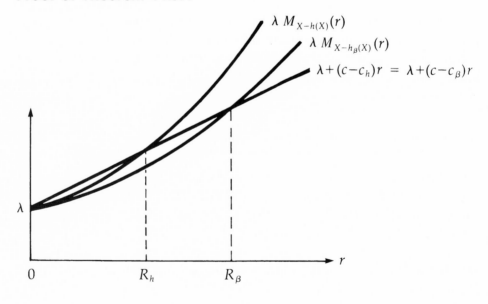

To establish (14.A.1), we first use the convexity of the exponential function to show that

$$\exp\{r[x - h(x)]\} \geq \exp\{r[x - h_\beta(x)]\}$$
$$+ r \exp\{r[x - h_\beta(x)]\} \, [h_\beta(x) - h(x)].$$

Since $x - h_\beta(x) \leq \beta$ and $x - h_\beta(x) = \beta$ whenever $h_\beta(x) - h(x) > 0$, it follows that

$$\exp\{r[x - h(x)]\} \geq \exp\{r[x - h_\beta(x)]\} + r \exp(r\beta)[h_\beta(x) - h(x)].$$

Then

$$E[\exp\{r[X - h(X)]\}] \geq E[\exp\{r[X - h_\beta(X)]\}]$$
$$+ r \exp(r\beta) \, E[h_\beta(X) - h(X)].$$

By the hypothesis of the theorem the last expectation is 0. This yields (14.A.1), from which the theorem follows. ∎

Exercises

Section 14.1

14.1. A term insurance provides the amount b if a claim occurs. The probability of a claim occurring is q.
   a. Consider the following loss random variable:

   $$L = \begin{cases} b - bq & \text{with probability } q \\ 0 - bq & \text{with probability } p = 1 - q. \end{cases}$$

   Verify that $E[L] = 0$.
   b. Calculate $\text{Var}(L)$.
   c. The security-loaded premium is taken as $bq + s\sqrt{\text{Var}(L)}$. If 100 identical policies of this type are sold and the loss random variables, as defined in part (a), for these policies are mutually independent, calculate the loading factor s such that the probability that the sum of these loss random variables exceeds the total security loading is less than 0.01.

Section 14.2

14.2. Verify the mean and variance entries in Table 14.2.1.

14.3. a. Calculate the mean of the distribution described in Table 14.2.2.
   b. By how much would the expected benefit per case of disability be reduced in the short-term disability insurance illustration if the 13-week maximum were replaced by a 10-week maximum?

14.4. Given that a disability has occurred, evaluate, on the basis of Table 14.2.2,
   a. $\text{Pr}(3 \leq Y \leq 6)$
   b. $\text{Pr}(10 \leq Y \leq 13)$
   c. $\text{Pr}(20 \leq Y \leq 23)$.

14.5. Consider a portfolio of 100 policies, each of which is for a 1-year term life insurance.

One-Year Mortality Rate	Amount Insured	
	1	4
0.01	10	20
0.02	30	40

The matrix entries give the number of policies in the portfolio for the indicated combination of amount insured and mortality rate.
a. If S represents the aggregate claims, calculate $E[S]$ and $Var(S)$.
b. What compound Poisson distribution would be used for approximating the individual model by the first method? What would be the resulting approximation for $Var(S)$?

14.6. Suppose that $B_j = b_j > 0$ for $j = 1, 2, \ldots, n$.
a. Write expressions for the mean and variance of the compound Poisson distribution chosen according to the second method.
b. Show that the values in (a) are higher than the corresponding values obtained by the first method. [Hint: First show that $\tilde{\lambda}_j > q_j$, $j = 1, 2, \ldots, n$.]
c. Compute the mean and variance of the compound Poisson distribution in Example 14.3.1 by the second method.

14.7. Calculate the probability that two claims that occur in the individual model are from policies i and j ($i \neq j$).

Section 14.4

14.8. Suppose that the possible claims are integers. Show that
$$E[I_d^2] = E[I_{d-1}^2] - 2 E[I_{d-1}] + 1 - F_S(d - 1).$$

14.9. Calculate $E[I_d]$ if S has the normal distribution with parameters μ and σ.

14.10. Suppose that the possible claims are integers. Express the following in terms of $F_S(x)$ and $f_S(x)$:
a. $\Delta E[I_x]$ b. $\Delta^2 E[I_x]$.

14.11. It is known that $E[I_d] = 1 - d - (1 - d^3)/3$ for $0 \leq d \leq 1$ and is equal to 0 for $d > 1$. Derive the p.d.f. of the underlying distribution of aggregate claims.

14.12. If S has a compound Poisson distribution given by $\lambda = 3$, $p(1) = 5/6$, $p(2) = 1/6$, calculate $f_S(x)$, $F_S(x)$, $E[I_x]$ for $x = 0, 1, 2$.

14.13. A dividend of the form (14.4.12) is to be used in Examples 14.4.6 and 14.4.7.

a. Calculate $G - E[S] - E[D]$ if $k = 0.9$.

b. Determine k such that $G - E[S] - E[D] = 0$.

14.14. A reinsurer will pay 80% of the excess of S over a deductible d, subject to a maximum payment of m. Express the expected claims under this coverage in terms of expected stop-loss claims.

14.15. In Example 14.4.5 determine d such that $E[I_d] = 0.2$.

Section 14.5

14.16. a. Repeat Example 14.5.2 with $\lambda = 1$, $c = 1 + \theta$, and $c_h = (1 + \xi)\alpha$.

b. Develop a relationship between θ and ξ so that the maximum of R occurs at $\alpha = 0$.

14.17. a. Repeat Example 14.5.5 with $\lambda = 1$, $c = 1 + \theta$, and $c_h = (1 + \xi)\alpha$.

b. Develop a relationship between θ and ξ so that the minimum of $E[L]$ occurs at $\alpha = 0$.

14.18. Reconsider the situation of Example 14.5.3, now with $\lambda = 1$, insurer's relative security loading θ, and excess-of-loss reinsurance available at a price of $1 + \xi$ times expected claims covered by the reinsurance.

a. Determine an expression for the ceding insurer's relative security loading after purchase of the reinsurance described.

b. Determine the equation from which the ceding insurer's adjustment coefficient can be obtained.

14.19. The annual claims, W_i, $i = 1, 2, \ldots$ for an insurance company are mutually independent and identically distributed, $N(10, 4)$. The company collects a relative security loading of 25%. A reinsurer is willing to accept the risk on any part, α, of the portfolio on a proportional basis for a reinsurance premium equal to 140% of the expected value of the claims reinsured.

a. Express the adjustment coefficient, $\tilde{R}$, for the portfolio with proportional reinsurance as a function of α.

b. Determine the value of α that maximizes the security of the insurance company by giving the largest value of $\tilde{R}$.

Miscellaneous

14.20. A reinsurer with wealth w and utility function $u(w)$ sets the stop-loss premium H_d corresponding to a deductible d so that $u(w) = E[u(w + H_d - I_d)]$ [see (1.3.6)]. Calculate H_d if $u(w) = -\alpha e^{-\alpha w}$ ($\alpha > 0$) and if S has the normal distribution with parameters μ and σ.

14.21. It is known that

$$E[I_d] = \left(\frac{\alpha}{\beta} - d\right)\left[1 - \Phi\left(-\frac{\alpha}{\sqrt{\beta d}} + \sqrt{\beta d}\right)\right]$$
$$+ \left(\frac{\alpha}{\beta} + d\right) e^{2\alpha} \Phi\left(-\frac{\alpha}{\sqrt{\beta d}} - \sqrt{\beta d}\right) \quad \text{for } d > 0.$$

Derive the p.d.f. of the underlying distribution of aggregate claims. Identify the distribution.

14.22. Let N have a Poisson distribution with parameter λ, a positive integer, and X have a degenerate distribution at $X = 1$.

a. Show that $E[I_\lambda] = \dfrac{\lambda^{\lambda+1}e^{-\lambda}}{\lambda!}$.

b. Use the result of Exercise 12.20 in which an approximation to the distribution of $(N - \lambda)/\sqrt{\lambda}$, when λ is large, is derived to confirm that

$$E[I_\lambda] \cong \frac{\sqrt{\lambda}}{\sqrt{2\pi}}.$$

c. Combine the results of parts (a) and (b) to derive the approximation

$$\lambda! \cong \lambda^{\lambda+1/2}e^{-\lambda}\sqrt{2\pi}.$$

(Historical Comment: This is known as Stirling's approximation for $\lambda!$, when λ is large. "In 1730 James Stirling, with help from De Moivre, derived this exponential approximation for factorials. De Moivre then showed in a paper of 1733 that the exponential error function gave a very good approximation of the distribution of possible outcomes for problems like the result of 1000 coin tosses" [*The Rise of Statistical Thinking*, T. M. Porter, Princeton University Press, 1986, p. 93]. In this exercise we have reversed the route followed by De Moivre and Stirling. We used the Central Limit Theorem to derive Stirling's approximation.)

14.23. a. If S has a lognormal distribution with parameters tm and $t\sigma^2$, $t > 0$, derive an expression for

$$E[e^{-\delta t}I_d], \text{ where } \delta > 0.$$

b. Determine the value of m such that the expectation of the discounted value of S is 1.

c. Rewrite your result of a. with this value of m.
[Remark: Your answer is the Black Scholes formula for a European call option, with exercise price d, on a stock with price 1 at $t = 0$ and price S at time t.]

14.24. For the compound Poisson process model of Chapter 13 with security loading θ, consider the excess-of-loss reinsurance contract $h_\beta(x)$ with loading ξ and the set of reinsurance contracts, $h(x)$, with $E[h(X)] = E[h_\beta(X)]$ and loading ξ. Assume that $\theta E[X] > \xi\, E[h(X)]$.

a. Verify that $E[L{:}h] = p_{2:h}/2\theta p_{1:h}$ where the h subscripts indicate the moments of the process of retained claims under reinsurance contract h.

b. Verify that under the hypothesis, the minimization of $E[L{:}h]$ over the set of possible reinsurance contracts with the specified premium and loading is equivalent to minimizing $p_{2:h}$.

c. Using the method of Exercise 1.21, confirm that $E[L{:}h_\beta] \leq E[L{:}h]$, thereby establishing another optimal property of excess-of-loss reinsurance.

INSURANCE MODELS INCLUDING EXPENSES

15.1 Introduction

The equivalence principle was introduced in Chapter 6 as a means for determining insurance premiums. In that chapter, the principle imposed the condition that the actuarial present values of benefits and benefit premiums be equal at the time the insurance is issued. In Chapters 7 and 8 this principle was applied to time periods beyond the initial date of contract. Benefit reserves were expressed as the actuarial present value of the difference between future benefit payments and future benefit premium income.

The foregoing chapters were devoted, in large part, to building a comprehensive model for insurance systems based on the equivalence principle. However, this model did not incorporate several aspects of insurance practice and economic reality. For example, an insurer has cash outflows other than claim payments. Expenditures of this general type include those for taxes and licenses as well as those for selling and servicing insurance policies. These expenses must be met from premium and investment income. In this chapter we incorporate expenses into the model for premiums and reserves.

The equivalence principle is extended to incorporate expense payments along with benefits as expenditures, and provisions for expenses are included in premiums and reserves. In this extension, it is assumed that the expenses incurred in connection with each policy are known with certainty. This extension is shown to provide a reasonable foundation for financial reporting for insurance enterprises.

Withdrawal benefits are common in life insurance, and they are required, and their amounts regulated, in many jurisdictions. In Section 15.3 a multiple decrement example is used to illustrate a comprehensive model involving death and withdrawal benefits and expenses. This model is used with the equivalence principle to derive premiums, reserves, and financial reports.

In the history of insurance practice and regulation, it has been convenient to approximate double decrement models incorporating expenses by using single-decrement-death-benefit-only models with suitably modified sets of benefit premiums. Some of these regulatory issues are discussed in Sections 16.2, 16.6, and 16.7.

15.2 Expense Augmented Models

The main ideas needed to incorporate expenses are first examined in an extended illustration. Tables 15.2.1A and 15.2.1B specify the salient features, selected for convenience and ease of calculation rather than for realism.

TABLE 15.2.1A

Specifications of Illustration: Description

1. Plan of insurance	3-year annual premium endowment insurance, issued to (x) with level benefits and premiums
2. Payment basis	Fully discrete
3. Mortality	$q_x = 0.1$, $q_{x+1} = 0.1111$, $q_{x+2} = 0.5$
4. Interest	Annual effective rate of $i = 0.15$
5. Amount of insurance	1,000
6. Expenses	
a. Timing	Paid at the beginning of each policy year
b. Amount	(as given in Table 15.2.1B)

TABLE 15.2.1B

Specifications of Illustration: Amount of Expenses

	First Year		Renewal Years	
Type of Expense	Percentage of Premium	Constant	Percentage of Premium	Constant
Sales commission	10%	—	2%	—
General expense	4	3	—	1
Taxes, licenses, and fees	2	—	2	—
Policy maintenance	2	1	2	1
Issue and classification	2	4	—	—
Total	20%	8	6%	2

15.2.1 Premiums and Reserves

Descriptive specifications 1 through 5 from Table 15.2.1A can be used with the equivalence principle to determine the level annual benefit premium for this insurance, $1,000\,P_{x:\overline{3}|} = 288.41$. Table 15.2.2 provides the details of the calculation of the corresponding benefit reserves.

TABLE 15.2.2
Benefit Reserve Calculations

(1) Curtate Future Lifetime	(2) Loss Variable	(3) Conditional Probability of Outcome	(4) (2) × (3)
At Issue ($_0L$)			
$K(x) = 0$	581.16	0.1	58.12
$K(x) = 1$	216.94	0.1	21.69
$K(x) \geq 2$	− 99.76	0.8	−79.81
		$1{,}000\ _0V_{x:\overline{3}|} = \mathrm{E}[_0L] =$	0.00
		$\sigma(_0L) =$	215.51
One Year after Issue ($_1L$)			
$K(x) = 1$	581.16	0.1111	64.57
$K(x) \geq 2$	216.94	0.8889	192.84
		$1{,}000\ _1V_{x:\overline{3}|} = \mathrm{E}[_1L] =$	257.41
		$\sigma(_1L) =$	114.46
Two Years after Issue ($_2L$)			
$K(x) \geq 2$	581.16	1.0	581.16
		$1{,}000\ _2V_{x:\overline{3}|} = \mathrm{E}[_2L] =$	581.16
		$\sigma(_2L) =$	0

As a final confirmation we can verify that $_3V_{x:\overline{3}|} = 1.0$:

$$1{,}000(_2V_{x:\overline{3}|} + P_{x:\overline{3}|})(1 + i) = 1{,}000$$

$$(581.16 + 288.41)(1.15) = 1{,}000$$

The expenses, as provided by Table 15.2.1B, are incorporated by modifying the loss variables. The present value of benefits is increased by the present value of expenses. This new total is then offset by the present value of level expense-loaded premiums, denoted by G. Table 15.2.3 is constructed using information from Table 15.2.1B.

TABLE 15.2.3
Expense Augmented Loss Variable ($_0L_e$)

Curtate Future Lifetime	Present Values		Probability of Outcome
	Benefits + Expenses	− Premiums	
$K(x) = 0$	$1{,}000v + (0.20G + 8)$	$- G\ddot{a}_{\overline{1}|}$	0.1
$K(x) = 1$	$1{,}000v^2 + (0.20G + 8) + (0.06G + 2)a_{\overline{1}|}$	$- G\ddot{a}_{\overline{2}|}$	0.1
$K(x) \geq 2$	$1{,}000v^3 + (0.20G + 8) + (0.06G + 2)a_{\overline{2}|}$	$- G\ddot{a}_{\overline{3}|}$	0.8
Expected Values	$688.58387 + (0.20G + 8) + (0.06G + 2)(1.3875236)$		
		$- G(2.3875236)$	

Implicit in the expense augmented loss variable ($_0L_e$) displayed in Table 15.2.3 is the decision to fund benefits and expenses with a level annual premium G. Other patterns for premiums are possible. In this case, the expense-loaded premium is determined by the equivalence principle; that is, the expected value of the expense augmented loss variable is 0. From Table 15.2.3,

$$688.58387 + (0.20G + 8) + (0.06G + 2)(1.3875236) - G(2.3875236) = 0.0.$$

This yields

$$G = 332.35,$$

which may be written

$$G = 1,000P_{x:\overline{3}|} + \text{level expense premium } (e)$$

$$= 288.41 + 43.94 = 332.35.$$

Table 15.2.4 exhibits the calculations of the expected values and standard deviations of the expense augmented loss variables at policy issue and at 1 and 2 years after issue. The total reserve is allocated into benefit and expense components. In each year, expected income from level benefit premium payments does not match expected benefit payments. This mismatching creates a non-negative benefit reserve. Likewise in each year, expected income from level expense loadings does not match expected payments for expenses. This mismatching creates a nonpositive expense reserve.

TABLE 15.2.4
Expected Values of Expense Augmented Loss Variables

Curtate Future Lifetime	$\left[\begin{array}{c}(\text{Present} \\ \text{Value of} \\ \text{Benefits})\end{array}\begin{array}{c}-(1{,}000 \times \\ P_{x:\overline{3}|} \times \\ \ddot{a}_{\overline{k+1}|})\end{array}\right]$	+	$\left[\begin{array}{c}(\text{Present} \\ \text{Value of} \\ \text{Expenses})\end{array} - e\,\ddot{a}_{\overline{k+1}|}\right]$	Conditional Probability of Outcome
At Issue ($_0L_e$)				
$K(x) = 0$	$(869.57 - 288.41)$	+	$(74.47 - 43.94)$	0.1
$K(x) = 1$	$(756.14 - 539.20)$	+	$(93.55 - 82.15)$	0.1
$K(x) \geq 2$	$(657.52 - 757.28)$	+	$(110.14 - 115.37)$	0.8

Expected Values: Benefit reserve + Expense reserve = Total reserve
                        0   +   0   =   0
                                              $\sigma(_0L_e) = 226.82$

One Year after Issue ($_1L_e$)				
$K(x) = 1$	$(869.57 - 288.41)$	+	$(21.94 - 43.94)$	0.1111
$K(x) \geq 2$	$(756.14 - 539.20)$	+	$(41.02 - 82.15)$	0.8889

Expected Values: Benefit reserve + Expense reserve = Total reserve
                     257.41   −   39.00   =   218.41
                                             $\sigma(_1L_e) =$ 120.47

Two Years after Issue ($_2L_e$)				
$K(x) \geq 2$	$(869.57 - 288.41)$	+	$(21.94 - 43.94)$	1.0

Expected Values: Benefit reserve + Expense reserve = Total reserve
                     581.16   −   22.00   =   559.16
                                             $\sigma(_2L_e) =$ 0

As a confirmation, the terminal total reserve (at the end of 3 years) is:

(total reserve at end of year 2 + loaded premium − expenses)(1 + i)
=(559.16   +   332.35   −   21.94   )(1.15) = 1,000

The following observations identify some of the key ideas in the illustration.

Observations:

1. Loss variables, as originally introduced, measure the present value of benefits less the present value of benefit premiums at the various times when benefits might be paid. These variables can be augmented to incorporate expenses and expense-loaded premiums.
2. The equivalence principle can be used to determine expense-loaded premiums and the associated total reserves (benefit reserves plus expense reserves).
3. The expense reserve is often negative in early policy years. This is a consequence of matching a decreasing stream of expense payments with a level stream of expense loadings.
4. Analysis and projection of expenses precede the determination of expense-loaded premiums.
5. The standard deviation of the expense augmented loss variable can be used to determine a contingency fund. This fund guards against inadequate balancing of premium and investment income with benefit and expense payments. Such a situation is possible due to the random nature of the time benefits are paid. Methods for this were illustrated in Chapter 8.

15.2.2   Accounting

In manufacturing enterprises, a product is usually built before it is sold. In most businesses that provide services, the service is performed before payment is received. An insurance operation is unusual in that premium income is received before the service of risk assumption is performed. It is this fact that motivates concerns by regulators and consumers about insurer solvency, and it also creates financial reporting issues.

Accounting is directed, in part, to matching the cost of providing a product or service with the revenue derived from selling it. The objective is to measure the economic gain or loss from engaging in these activities. Accounting in life insurance and annuity operations differs from that in many enterprises because income is received before costs are known. The reserve systems illustrated earlier, level benefit premium and expense-loaded premium, can be used to achieve an improved match between premium income and associated expenditures.

The illustration is continued in Tables 15.2.5 and 15.2.6, in which the following assumptions are made:
- The annual contract premium for each policy is 342.35, the expense-loaded premium plus an arbitrary amount of 10. The remainder, after paying the percent of premium expenses on the additional 10, is for profit and contingencies.

TABLE 15.2.5

Income Statements (10 Initial Insureds)

Income Statements	(a) Reporting Benefit Reserves as Liabilities	(b) Reporting Benefit Plus Expense Reserves as Liabilities
During First Year		
Income		
Premium (10)	3 423.50	3 423.50
Investment (15%)	548.82	548.82
	3 972.32	3 972.32
Charges to Income		
Expenses		
Percentage (20%)	684.70	684.70
Constant (8)	80.00	80.00
Claims (1)	1 000.00	1 000.00
Increase in reserves	2 316.69	1 965.69
	4 081.39	3 730.39
Net Income	−109.07	241.93
During Second Year		
Income		
Premium (9)	3 081.15	3 081.15
Investment (15%)	912.88	912.88
	3 994.03	3 994.03
Charges to Income		
Expenses		
Percentage (6%)	184.87	184.87
Constant (2)	18.00	18.00
Claims (1)	1 000.00	1 000.00
Increase in reserves	2 332.59	2 507.59
	3 535.46	3 710.46
Net Income	458.57	283.57
During Third Year		
Income		
Premium (8)	2 738.80	2 738.80
Investment (15%)	1 283.59	1 283.59
	4 022.39	4 022.39
Charges to Income		
Expenses		
Percentage (6%)	164.33	164.33
Constant (2)	16.00	16.00
Claims and maturities (8)	8 000.00	8 000.00
Increase in reserves	−4 649.28	−4 473.28
	3 531.05	3 707.05
Net income	491.34	315.34

Notes:
1. Investment income = (assets at end of prior year + premium income − expenses) (0.15).
2. Total net income = −109.07 + 458.57 + 491.34   Col. (a)
                 = 241.93 + 283.57 + 315.34   Col. (b)
                 = 840.84.
3. Alternative calculation (review specifications in Table 15.2.1B):
    total net income = (interest income on initial funds) + (accumulated value of net profit loadings)
                 $= 1{,}000[(1.15)^3 − 1] + 10[(10)(0.8)(1.15)^3 + 9(0.94)(1.15)^2 + (8)(0.94)(1.15)]$
                 = 840.91.
    The difference in results of these two calculations is attributed to rounding errors.

TABLE 15.2.6

Balance Sheets (10 Initial Insureds)

Balance Sheets	(a) Reporting Benefit Reserves as Liabilities	(b) Reporting Benefit Plus Expense Reserves as Liabilities
At End of First Year		
Assets	3 207.62	3 207.62
Liabilities (Reserves)	2 316.69	1 965.69
Surplus	890.93	1 241.93
	3 207.62	3 207.62
At End of Second Year		
Assets	5 998.78	5 998.78
Liabilities (Reserves)	4 649.28	4 473.28
Surplus	1 349.50	1 525.50
	5 998.78	5 998.78
At End of Third Year		
Assets	1 840.84	1 840.84
Liabilities (Reserves)	0	0
Surplus	1 840.84	1 840.84
	1 840.84	1 840.84

Notes:
1. Increase in surplus = total gains (see note 2 to Table 15.2.5). 1,840.84 − 1,000 = 840.84.
2. Surplus = (surplus at end of previous year + net income).
3. Assets = [assets at end of previous year + (net income + increase in reserves)]
   = [assets at end of previous year + (premiums + investment income − claims − expenses)].

- The accounting statements are derived using a deterministic survival group, initially consisting of 10 insureds. Each accounting entry can be divided by 10 to produce entries that can be interpreted as expected amounts for each initial insured.
- Expenses are paid and investment income is earned exactly as specified in Tables 15.2.1A and B.
- The hypothetical insurance operations start with an initial fund of 1,000.
- In the accounting statements in column (a), benefit reserves alone are reported as liabilities. In the accounting entries in column (b), benefit reserves plus expense reserves are reported as liabilities.

The set of accounting statements that use benefit reserves as liabilities is internally inconsistent in a sense. This is true because future expenses and provisions for these expenses in future premiums are not incorporated into liabilities.

The following observations indicate some additional key points in the accounting illustration.

Observations:

6. The amounts recognized as net income in the accounting statements are less variable when benefit plus expense reserves are reported as liabilities than in

the situation where benefit reserves alone are reported. Also, net income can be related to interest on surplus and the net profit loadings accumulated with interest.

7. Total gain over the 3-year period is not affected by the method selected for reporting liabilities.

8. In actual practice, expected results are not realized with the degree of certainty assumed in the illustration.

The practice and therefore the vocabulary of life insurance accounting are complicated by the fact that several groups of stakeholders, each with its own responsibilities and interests, rely on these statements. The ideas illustrated in column (a) of Tables 15.2.5 and 15.2.6 are related to those historically used in the United States for regulatory purposes. The ideas illustrated in column (b) are related to those used in financial statements intended for use by the capital markets.

15.3 Withdrawal Benefits

In Section 11.4 the idea of withdrawal benefits to be paid to terminating policyholders was introduced. The primary purpose of that section was the establishment of conditions under which premiums and reserves incorporating death and withdrawal benefits would be identical to those determined within a mortality-only model. This required that death and withdrawal be independent, and in Section 11.7 it was indicated that there are barriers to extending the result to the discrete model.

15.3.1 Premiums and Reserves

In this section the extended illustration constructed in Section 15.2 is expanded to a double decrement model with withdrawal benefits. The amounts of the withdrawal benefits are denoted by $b_{x+t}^{(2)}$, and they are determined in Example 15.3.1. This example is based on the principle incorporated into the law regulating minimum withdrawal benefits in the United States. It involves using a mortality-only benefit model, with an arbitrary provision for expenses. The principle is based on an extension of ideas introduced in Section 11.4; namely, that if withdrawal benefits in the double decrement model are approximately equal to the expense augmented reserves, benefit plus expense reserves, determined using an associated mortality-only model, then the effect on premiums and reserves of adding a withdrawal benefit will be small.

Example 15.3.1

The benefit premium determined by the equivalence principle and the assumptions listed in Table 15.2.1A is $1,000\ P_{x:\overline{3}|} = 288.41$. An arbitrary expense loading of $40 / \ddot{a}_{x:\overline{3}|} = 40 / 2.3875 = 16.75$ is added to the benefit premium to produce an expense-loaded premium of 305.16. Within regulations this is called an *adjusted premium* and is denoted in this example by 1,000 $P^A_{x:\overline{3}|}$. Determine withdrawal benefits with the assumptions listed in Table 15.2.1 using the following prospective reserve-type formula:

$$b^{(2)}_{x+t} = 1{,}000(A_{x+t:\overline{3-t}|} - P^A_{x:\overline{3}|}\, \ddot{a}_{x+t:\overline{3-t}|}).$$

Solution:

$$b^{(2)}_{x+1} = 1{,}000\, A_{x+1:\overline{2}|} - 305.16\, \ddot{a}_{x+1:\overline{2}|}$$

$$= 768.75 \qquad - 305.16(1.7729) = 227.73,$$

$$b^{(2)}_{x+2} = 1{,}000\, A_{x+2:\overline{1}|} - 305.16\, \ddot{a}_{x+2:\overline{1}|}$$

$$= 869.57 \qquad - 305.16 \qquad = 564.41. \qquad \blacktriangledown$$

The assumptions used to expand the illustration are shown in Table 15.3.1. Tables 15.3.2 and 15.3.3 are closely related to each other. In Table 15.3.2 the annual expense-loaded premium using the equivalence principle is determined. Table 15.3.3 corresponds to Table 15.2.4 and exhibits the calculation of benefit and expense reserves in the double decrement model. The observations following Table 15.2.4 remain valid.

TABLE 15.3.1

Specifications of Illustration Including Withdrawal Benefits

Withdrawal Benefits
  $b^{(2)}_{x+1} = 227.73$ $b^{(2)}_{x+2} = 564.41$

Multiple Decrement Probabilities
  $q^{(1)}_x = 0.1$ $q^{(1)}_{x+1} = 0.1111$

  $q^{(2)}_x = 0.1$ $q^{(2)}_{x+1} = 0.1111$

Deaths and withdrawals are assumed to be independent as described in Section 11.4. Withdrawals are assumed to occur only at the end of each year of age; that is, $_t p'^{(2)}_x$ is a step function as shown in Figure 10.6.2, the graph of $_t p'^{(3)}_x$. In this example, the value of $q^{(1)}_x = q_x$ and $q^{(1)}_{x+1} = q_{x+1}$.

Table 15.3.2 contains the data necessary to determine the (double decrement model) annual benefit premium, $P^2_{\overline{x}:\overline{3}|}$, annual expense loading, e, and the annual expense-loaded premium, G, by the equivalence principle. We have

$$621.0011 - P^2_{\overline{x}:\overline{3}|}\,(2.1661) = 0,$$

$$P^2_{\overline{x}:\overline{3}|} = 286.69,$$

$$621.0011 + (0.2G + 8) + (0.06G + 2)(1.1661) - G(2.1661) = 0,$$

$$G = 332.96,$$

TABLE 15.3.2

Expense Augmented Loss Variable, Double Decrement, at Issue

Curtate Future Lifetime $K(x)$	Outcome of Cause of Decrement $J(x)$	$\left(\begin{array}{c}\text{Present Value}\\\text{of Benefits}\end{array}\right)$	+	$\left(\begin{array}{c}\text{Present Value}\\\text{of Expenses}\end{array}\right)$	−	$\left(\begin{array}{c}\text{Present Value}\\\text{of Premiums}\end{array}\right)$	Probability of Outcome
0	1	$1{,}000.00v$	+	$(0.2G + 8.0)$	−	G	0.1
	2	$227.73v$	+	$(0.2G + 8.0)$	−	G	0.1
1	1	$1{,}000.00v^2$	+	$(0.2G + 8.0) + (0.06G + 2.0)a_{\overline{1}}$	−	$G\ddot{a}_{\overline{2}}$	0.0889
	2	$564.41v^2$	+	$(0.2G + 8.0) + (0.06G + 2.0)a_{\overline{1}}$	−	$G\ddot{a}_{\overline{2}}$	0.0889
≥2	1 or 2	$1{,}000.00v^3$	+	$(0.2G + 8.0) + (0.06G + 2.0)a_{\overline{2}}$	−	$G\ddot{a}_{\overline{3}}$	0.6222
Expected Values		621.011	+	$(0.2G + 8.0) + (0.06G + 2.0)(1.1661)$	−	$(1{,}000P^2_{x:\overline{3}} + e)(2.1661)$	

$\sigma({}_0L^2_e) = 224.25$

TABLE 15.3.3

Expense Augmented Loss Variable, Double Decrement

Outcome of — Curtate Future Lifetime $K(x)$	Cause of Decrement $J(x)$	$\left(\begin{array}{c}\text{Present}\\\text{Value of}\\\text{Benefits}\end{array}\right)$	$-$	$\left(\begin{array}{c}\text{Present Value}\\\text{of Benefit}\\\text{Premiums}\end{array}\right)$	$+$	$\left(\begin{array}{c}\text{Present}\\\text{Value of}\\\text{Expenses}\end{array}\right)$	$-$	$\left(\begin{array}{c}\text{Present}\\\text{Value of}\\\text{Loadings}\end{array}\right)$	Probability of Outcome
At Duration 1									
1	1	$1{,}000.00v$	$-$	$1{,}000P^2_{x:\overline{3}|}$	$+$	$(0.06G + 2.0)$	$-$	e	0.1111
1	2	$564.41v$	$-$	$1{,}000P^2_{x:\overline{3}|}$	$+$	$(0.06G + 2.0)$	$-$	e	0.1111
≥ 2	1 or 2	$1{,}000.00v^2$	$-$	$1{,}000P^2_{x:\overline{3}|}\ddot{a}_{\overline{2}|}$	$+$	$(0.06G + 2.0)\ddot{a}_{\overline{2}|}$	$-$	$e\ddot{a}_{\overline{2}|}$	0.7778
Expected Values		Benefit reserve 258.67			$+$	Expense reserve (-40.73)		$=$ Total reserve $= 217.94$	
$\sigma(_2L^2_e) = 120.44$									
At Duration 2									
≥ 2	1 or 2	$1{,}000.00v$	$-$	$1{,}000P^2_{x:\overline{3}|}$	$+$	$[0.06G + 2.0]$	$-$	e	1.0000
Expected Values		Benefit reserve 582.88			$+$	Expense reserve (-24.29)		$=$ Total reserve $= 558.59$	
$\sigma(_2L^2_e) = 0$									

As a confirmation of the terminal total reserve at end of year 3:
(Total reserve + loaded premium − expenses, all at duration 2)$(1 + i) = (558.59 + 332.96 − 21.98)(1.15) = 1{,}000.$

$$(0.2G + 8) + (0.06G + 2)(1.1661) - e(2.1661) = 0$$

$$e = 46.27.$$

As a confirmation, we have

$$G = P^2_{\bar{x}:\overline{3}|} + e,$$

$$332.96 = 286.69 + 46.27.$$

15.3.2 Accounting

As indicated in Section 15.1, the equivalence principle provides a conceptual framework for financial reporting of an insurance enterprise. In this section the financial reporting illustration of Section 15.2.2 will be extended to the double decrement model.

- The annual contract premium will be the annual level expense-loaded premium plus an arbitrary amount of 10 for profits and contingencies (less the percent of premium expenses on the 10).
- The accounting statements are derived using expected values for death and withdrawal benefit payments and for number of survivals. There are 10 initial insureds.
- Expenses are paid and investment income is earned as specified in Tables 15.2.1A and B.
- The hypothetical insurance operation starts with an initial fund of 1,000.
- In the accounting statements in column (a), benefit reserves, mortality-only model, are reported as liabilities, and in column (b) benefit and expenses reserves are reported as liabilities.

The financial statements in column (a) can be viewed as internally inconsistent because of the failure to incorporate future expenses and withdrawal benefits and provisions for these expenditures in future premiums into liabilities. Column (a) is displayed because of its historic role in regulation.

A comparison of Tables 15.2.5 and 15.2.6 with Tables 15.3.4 and 15.3.5 confirms the increased realism of financial statements using a double decrement model that incorporates expenses. The leveling effect on reported net income of the more comprehensive reserve system is also apparent. If the withdrawal benefits had not been selected to reduce their impact on premiums and reserves in the change from the single decrement model to the double decrement model, the difference in financial results between the two models would have been more pronounced.

15.4 Types of Expenses

The accounting system of an insurance enterprise is designed to record, classify, and summarize financial transactions. The same system, though, will furnish data on activity levels: the number and amount of sales, the number of claims paid, the number of premiums billed, and so on. After collecting this information, analysis

TABLE 15.3.4

Income Statements (10 Initial Insureds)

	(a) Reporting Single Decrement Benefit Reserves as Liabilities	(b) Reporting Double Decrement Benefit and Expense Reserves as Liabilities
During First Year		
Income		
Premiums (10)	3 429.60	3 429.60
Investment (15%)	549.55	549.55
	3 979.15	3 979.15
Charges to income		
Expenses		
Percentage (20%)	685.92	685.92
Constant (8)	80.00	80.00
Death benefits (1)	1 000.00	1 000.00
Withdrawal benefits (1)	227.73	227.73
Increase in reserve	2 059.28	1 743.52
	4 052.93	3 737.17
Net income	−73.78	241.98
During Second Year		
Income		
Premium (8)	2 743.68	2 743.68
Investment (15%)	832.28	832.28
	3 575.96	3 575.96
Charges to income		
Expenses		
Percentage (6%)	164.62	164.62
Constant (2)	16.00	16.00
Death benefits (0.8889)	888.90	888.90
Withdrawal benefits (0.8889)	501.70	501.70
Increase in reserves	1 556.83	1 732.15
	3 128.05	3 303.37
Net income	447.91	272.59
During Third Year		
Income		
Premium (6.2222)	2 133.97	2 133.97
Investment (15%)	1 047.56	1 047.56
	3 181.53	3 181.53
Charges to income		
Expenses		
Percentage (6%)	128.04	128.04
Constant (2)	12.44	12.44
Benefits (6.2222)	6 222.22	6 222.22
Increase in reserves	−3 616.11	−3 475.67
	2 746.59	2 887.03
Net income	434.94	294.50

TABLE 15.3.5

Balance Sheets (10 Initial Insureds)

	(a)	(b)
At end of first year		
Assets	2 985.50	2 985.50
Liabilities (Reserves)	2 059.29	1 743.52
Surplus	926.22	1 241.68
	2 985.50	2 985.20
At end of second year		
Assets	4 990.24	4 990.24
Liabilities (Reserves)	3 616.11	3 475.67
Surplus	1 374.13	1 514.57
	4 990.24	4 990.24
At end of third year		
Assets	1 809.07	1 809.07
Liabilities (Reserves)	0	0
Surplus	1 809.07	1 809.07

Notes on Tables 15.3.4 and 15.3.5

1. Total net income $= -73.78 + 447.91 + 434.94$

$\qquad\qquad = 809.07 \qquad\qquad$ Col. (a)

$\qquad\qquad = 241.98 + 272.59 + 294.50$

$\qquad\qquad = 809.07 \qquad\qquad$ Col. (b)

2. Alternative calculation of total income

(Interest income on initial funds) + (Accumulated value of profit loadings) =

$1{,}000[(1.15)^3 - 1] + 10[10(0.8)(1.15)^3 + 8(0.94)(1.15)^2 + (6.2222)(0.94)(1.15)] = 809.26$

The difference in the results of these two calculations is attributed to accumulated rounding errors that started with the use of a contract premium rounded to two decimal places.

can be performed with the goal of relating major expense items to the activities they support. These allocations will guide the determination of expense loading on premiums for insurance policies sold in the future. If the equivalence principle is applied, the actuarial present value of expense loadings will equal the actuarial present value of expenses charged to the policy.

Classification and allocation of the expenses of an insurance organization are perplexing tasks. An example is given in Table 15.4.1. Here a tentative classification system is adopted and the results traced.

In the determination of expense-loaded premiums, attention is concentrated on the insurance expenses. However, investment expenses are typically viewed as an offset to investment income and reflected in premiums through a reduction in the assumed interest rate.

In some instances practice indicates a natural relationship between expense items and activity levels. For example, it is common to compensate sales agents by a commission structure of percentages applied to first-year and renewal premiums. In Section 15.2 the commission paid was 10% of the premium in the first year and

TABLE 15.4.1

Classification Scheme for the Expenses of an Insurance Organization

Expense Classification	Components
Investment	(a) Analysis
	(b) Costs of buying, selling, and servicing
Insurance	
1. Acquisition	(a) Selling expense, including agents' commissions and advertising
	(b) Risk classification, including health examinations
	(c) Preparing new policies and records
2. Maintenance	(a) Premium collection and accounting
	(b) Beneficiary change and settlement option preparation
	(c) Policyholder correspondence
3. General	(a) Research
	(b) Actuarial and general legal services
	(c) General accounting and administration
	(d) Taxes, licenses, and fees
4. Settlement	(a) Claim investigation and legal defense
	(b) Costs of disbursing benefit payments

2% in the second and third years. Taxes on insurance organizations, especially those levied by the states, are often a percentage of the premium collected within the taxing jurisdiction. In Section 15.2, 2% of premiums were allocated to taxes, licenses, and fees.

The allocation of other items of expense is less clear-cut, and a combination of statistical analysis and judgment is often used. It is common practice to allocate acquisition expenses to the first policy year in premium-loading formulas because marketing and risk classification expenses are incurred for the purpose of generating and selling new insurance business. Some of these acquisition expenses vary with the size of the premium, commissions, for instance. Some vary with the amount of insurance, such as risk classification expense. Some expenses, like the creation of records, are incurred for each policy issued, independent of the size of the policy or premium.

The classification and allocation of expenses is an important management tool for controlling the operation of an insurance system. However, in the determination of premiums, the view of expenses is prospective rather than retrospective. The goal is to match future expenses with future premium loadings. Therefore, expense trends with expectations for inflation or deflation and future economies attributable to automation are built into expense loadings.

The provision within expense-loaded premiums for expenses classified in Table 15.4.1 as Insurance, General (a), (b), and (c) and for the expenses incurred in creating an insurance distribution system remain controversial. These expenses do not relate directly to activity associated with an individual policy. Some of these issues are discussed in Section 16.4.

Table 15.4.2 provides an illustration of the classification system in Table 15.4.1 for insurance expenses and associated loading factors.

TABLE 15.4.2
Illustration of the Allocation of Future Insurance Expenses

Classification	First Year Per Policy	First Year Per 1,000 Insurance	First Year Percent of Premium	Renewal Years Per Policy	Renewal Years Per 1,000 Insurance	Percent of Premium by Policy Year 2–9	Percent of Premium by Policy Year 10–15	Percent of Premium by Policy Year 16 over
1. Acquisition								
a. Sales expenses								
Commission	—	—	60%	—	—	7.0%	5.0%	3%
Sales offices	—	—	25	—	—	2.5	1.5	1
Other sales related	12.50	4.00	—	—	—	—	—	—
b. Classification	18.00	0.50	—	—	—	—	—	—
c. Issue and records	4.00	—	—	—	—	—	—	—
2. Maintenance	2.00	0.25	—	2.00	0.25	—	—	—
3. General								
a, b, c	4.00	0.25	—	4.00	0.25	—	—	—
d. Taxes	—	—	2	—	—	2.0	2.0	2
Total (1, 2, 3)	40.50	5.00	87%	6.00	0.50	11.5%	8.5%	6%
4. Settlement	18.00 per policy plus 0.10 per 1,000 insurance							

Example 15.4.1

Using the equivalence principle, develop a formula for the expense-loaded annual premium on a whole life policy, semicontinuous basis, issued to (x) for an amount $1,000b$. The expenses are those listed in Table 15.4.2. Use a single decrement model, or assume that withdrawal benefits will be determined so as to have no effect on premiums determined using the single decrement, mortality-only, model. A 15-year select life will be used under the assumption that expenditures for risk classification will result in select mortality.

Solution:

Let $G(b)$ denote the expense-loaded premium for a policy with a death benefit of b thousand. Then, using the equivalence principle,

(actuarial present value of expense-loaded premium) = (actuarial present value of claim and claim settlement expense plus other expenses);

$$G(b)\ddot{a}_{[x]} = 1,000b\,\bar{A}_{[x]} + [40.50 + 5.00b + 0.87G(b)]$$

$$+ (6.00a_{[x]} + 0.50ba_{[x]})$$

$$+ [(0.115a_{[x]:\overline{8}|} + 0.085_{9|6}\ddot{a}_{[x]} + 0.06_{15|}\ddot{a}_{[x]})\,G(b)]$$

$$+ (18.00 + 0.10b)\bar{A}_{[x]}\,;$$

$$G(b)(\ddot{a}_{[x]} - 0.87 - 0.115a_{[x]:\overline{8}|} - 0.085_{9|6}\ddot{a}_{[x]} - 0.06_{15|}\ddot{a}_{[x]})$$

$$= (1{,}000.1\,\bar{A}_{[x]} + 5.00 + 0.50a_{[x]})b + 40.50 + 6.00a_{[x]} + 18.00\bar{A}_{[x]}\,.$$

The level expense-loaded annual premium rate for death benefit $1{,}000b$ is

$$G(b) = \frac{(1{,}000.1\,\bar{A}_{[x]} + 5.00 + 0.50a_{[x]})b + 40.50 + 6.00a_{[x]} + 18.00\bar{A}_{[x]}}{0.94\ddot{a}_{[x]} - 0.755 - 0.03\ddot{a}_{[x]:\overline{9}|} - 0.025\ddot{a}_{[x]:\overline{15}|}}\,.$$

The level expense-loaded annual premium for each death benefit amount of b, measured in units of $1{,}000$, is

$$\frac{G(b)}{b} = \frac{1{,}000.1\,\bar{A}_{[x]} + 5.00 + 0.50a_{[x]} + (40.50 + 6.00a_{[x]} + 18.00\,\bar{A}_{[x]})/b}{0.94\ddot{a}_{[x]} - 0.755 - 0.03\ddot{a}_{[x]:\overline{9}|} - 0.025\ddot{a}_{[x]:\overline{15}|}}\,. \qquad \blacktriangledown$$

In practice, premiums are usually stated as a rate per unit of insurance. For life insurance, these rates have typically been per $1{,}000$ of initial death benefit. For immediate life annuities, the rates have typically been stated per unit of monthly income.

In Example 15.4.1, because of expenses that do not vary directly with b, the expense-loaded premium rate $G(b)$ depends on b. Provision for these per policy expenses can be made by special methods. One method is to replace b with an expected policy amount. A second method would be to separate the per policy expenses from those expense elements that vary directly with policy size and to balance these per policy expenses with a separate policy fee, independent of policy size. In Example 15.4.1 the annual policy fee would be

$$\frac{40.50 + 6.00a_{[x]} + 18.00\bar{A}_{[x]}}{0.94\ddot{a}_{[x]} - 0.755 - 0.03\ddot{a}_{[x]:\overline{9}|} - 0.025\ddot{a}_{[x]:\overline{15}|}}\,.$$

Often the policy fees are averaged over issue age so the policy fee is constant with respect to issue age.

15.5 Algebraic Foundations of Accounting: Single Decrement Model

In this section many of the ideas illustrated in Section 15.2.2 will be made more precise. Frequent reference to Tables 15.2.5 and 15.2.6 can help the reader follow the arguments.

One of the objectives of financial accounting is the determination, at periodic intervals, of the elements of the balance sheet equation

$$A(h) = L(h) + U(h). \qquad (15.5.1)$$

In (15.5.1), $A(h)$ denotes the amount of assets, $L(h)$ the amount of liabilities, and $U(h)$ the amount of owner's equity (surplus in the terminology of insurance accounting) at the end of accounting period h. Changes in surplus can be represented by

$$\Delta U(h) = \Delta A(h) - \Delta L(h) = \text{net income in period } h + 1. \qquad (15.5.2)$$

We illustrate this basic model using an algebraic development under idealized conditions as stated in Table 15.5.1.

TABLE 15.5.1

Specifications of Accounting Illustration

Level Benefit, Level Premium Insurance	
1. Plan of insurance	Whole life, unit amount
2. Payment basis	Fully discrete
3. Age and time of issue	Issued to (x) at the beginning of the first accounting period
4. Expenses	No expenses or expense loadings
5. Experience	Investment experience conforms to that assumed
	Accounting entries will be in terms of expected values at policy issue for each initial insured

---

The mathematics of the illustration build on the reserve recursion formula (8.3.10) with $b_h = 1$, $\pi_{h-1} = P_x$, and $_hV = {}_hV_x$. Multiplying by $_{h-1}p_x (1 + i)$ we have

$$_{h-1}p_x \left({}_{h-1}V_x + P_x \right)(1 + i) - {}_{h-1}p_x\, q_{x+h-1} = {}_hp_x\, {}_hV_x \qquad h = 1, 2, \ldots. \qquad (15.5.3)$$

Under the restrictive assumptions that have been made, (15.5.3) can be interpreted as the expected progress of insurance assets and liabilities for each member of an initial group of insureds. The left-hand side can be interpreted as the expected cash flows affecting assets. The right-hand side is the measure of the expected liabilities for each member of an initial group of insureds.

We illustrate by examining the first accounting period. During this period the expected assets per initial insured change as follows:

Increase	Premium income	$= P_x$
	Interest income	$= P_x\, i$
Decrease	Death claims	$= q_x$

If there are no initial funds,

$$A(1) = A(0) + [A(1) - A(0)] = 0 + [P_x(1 + i) - q_x],$$

and using (15.5.3) with $h = 1$, we have

$$A(1) = p_x\, V_x = L(1).$$

In this illustration, $A(1) - L(1) = U(1) = 0$.

Formula (15.5.3) can also be used to study the progress of accounting statements in a recursive fashion for all policy years. Suppose that at the end of accounting period h

---

$$A(h) = L(h)$$

and that we start the process during accounting period $h + 1$:

$$\Delta A(h) = \left\{ \begin{array}{l} \text{premium income} \\ + \text{ interest income} \\ - \text{ death claims} \end{array} \right\} = \left\{ \begin{array}{l} {}_hp_x \, P_x \\ + \, {}_hp_x \, ({}_hV_x + P_x)i \\ - \, {}_hp_x \, q_{x+h}. \end{array} \right\}$$

Then,

$$A(h + 1) = A(h) + \Delta A(h)$$

$$= {}_hp_x \, {}_hV_x + \{{}_hp_x \, [P_x + ({}_hV_x + P_x)i] - {}_hp_x \, q_{x+h}\}$$

$$= {}_hp_x \, [(P_x + {}_hV_x)(1 + i)] - {}_hp_x \, q_{x+h}$$

$$= {}_{h+1}p_x \, {}_{h+1}V_x = L(h + 1). \tag{15.5.4}$$

In this illustration, with no initial funds, profit, or contingency loadings, tracing expected results yields $A(h) - L(h) = U(h) = 0$, $h = 0, 1, 2, 3, \ldots$.

We now modify the assumptions of Table 15.5.1 by assuming that the benefit premium is loaded by the positive constant c and that the expenses for each surviving policy, paid at the beginning of accounting period h, are e_{h-1}. The loading constant may contain a component for profit; that is, the actuarial present value of the loadings c may be greater than the actuarial present value of the set of e_{h-1}, $h = 1, 2, \ldots$.

The augmented version of (15.5.3), incorporating loaded premiums and expenses, is

$${}_{h-1}p_x \, \{[{}_{h-1}V_x + \underline{u(h - 1)}] + (P_x + \underline{c}) - \underline{e_{h-1}}\} (1 + i) - {}_{h-1}p_x \, q_{x+h-1}$$

$$= {}_hp_x \, [{}_hV_x + \underline{u(h)}] \qquad h = 1, 2, 3, \ldots. \tag{15.5.5}$$

The elements introduced into the augmented version of (15.5.3) are underlined. In (15.5.5), $u(h)$ denotes the anticipated surplus for each surviving insured at the end of accounting period h.

Subtracting the unloaded version, (15.5.3), from (15.5.5) yields

$${}_{h-1}p_x \, [u(h - 1) + (c - e_{h-1})] (1 + i) = {}_hp_x \, u(h) \qquad h = 1, 2, 3, \ldots. \tag{15.5.6}$$

Multiplying difference equation (15.5.6) by v^h and rearranging terms yields

$$v^{h-1} \, {}_{h-1}p_x \, [u(h - 1) + (c - e_{h-1})] = v^h \, {}_hp_x \, u(h),$$

$$\Delta[v^{h-1} \, {}_{h-1}p_x \, u(h - 1)] = v^{h-1} \, {}_{h-1}p_x \, (c - e_{h-1}). \tag{15.5.7}$$

Imposing the initial condition $u(0) = 0$, we obtain from (15.5.7)

$$\sum_{j=1}^{h} \Delta[v^{j-1} \,_{j-1}p_x \, u(j-1)] = \sum_{j=1}^{h} v^{j-1} \,_{j-1}p_x \, (c - e_{j-1}),$$

$$v^h \,_hp_x \, u(h) = \sum_{j=1}^{h} v^{j-1} \,_{j-1}p_x \, (c - e_{j-1}),$$

$$_hp_x \, u(h) = \sum_{j=1}^{h} (1+i)^{h-j+1} \,_{j-1}p_x \, (c - e_{j-1}). \qquad (15.5.8)$$

That is, the expected surplus at the end of h accounting periods for each initial insured is the accumulated value of the expected contributions to surplus in each earlier accounting period. This result should be compared with Table 15.2.5, footnote 3.

If benefit reserves are reported as the measure of liabilities, the expected entries for each initial insured in the accounting statements of our idealized insurance system at the end of the accounting period h are as follows.

Balance Sheet (at end of accounting period h)

$$A(h) = L(h) + U(h)$$

$$= \,_hp_x \,_hV_x + \,_hp_x \, u(h)$$

$$= \,_hp_x \,_hV_x + \sum_{1}^{h} (1+i)^{h-j+1} \,_{j-1}p_x \, (c - e_{j-1})$$

Income Statement (h-th accounting period)

Income
    Premium income $_{h-1}p_x \, (P_x + c)$
    Investment income $_{h-1}p_x \, [_{h-1}V_x + u(h-1) + P_x + c - e_{h-1}] \, i$

       Total $_{h-1}p_x \, \{(P_x + c)(1+i) + [_{h-1}V_x + u(h-1) - e_{h-1}]i\}$

Charges to Income
    Death claims $_{h-1}p_x \, q_{x+h-1}$
    Expenses $_{h-1}p_x \, e_{h-1}$
    Changes in reserve liability $_hp_x \,_hV_x - \,_{h-1}p_x \,_{h-1}V_x$

       Total $_hp_x \,_hV_x - \,_{h-1}p_x \, (_{h-1}V_x - e_{h-1}) + \,_{h-1}p_x \, q_{x+h-1}$
  Net income (change in surplus) $_{h-1}p_x \, [u(h-1)i + (c - e_{h-1})(1+i)]$ (15.5.9)

In completing the accounting statements we have made use of (15.5.8) and (15.5.3). The left-hand columns of Tables 15.2.5 and 15.2.6 provide numerical illustrations of this display. The tables are in terms of a deterministic survivorship group rather than expected entries for each initial insured. Thus the expected surplus at the end of h accounting periods for each initial insured is

$$_hp_x \, u(h) = \,_{h-1}p_x \, u(h-1) + \,_{h-1}p_x \, [u(h-1)i + (c - e_{h-1})(1+i)]. \qquad (15.5.10)$$

Formula (15.5.10) is identical to (15.5.6); however, it was derived from an accounting viewpoint. Multiplying by v^h and rearranging yields

$$\Delta[v^{h-1}\,_{h-1}p_x\,u(h-1)] = v^{h-1}\,_{h-1}p_x\,(c - e_{h-1}),$$

which is (15.5.7) rederived with accounting interpretations.

Earlier in this chapter the point was made that, in practice, expenses tend to decrease as duration increases. Thus the expected surplus,

$$_hp_x\,u(h) = \sum_{j=1}^{h} (1 + i)^{h-j+1}\,_{j-1}p_x\,(c - e_{j-1}),$$

will typically be negative for small values of h and positive for larger values. This observation is made with respect to an accounting model in which benefit reserves are reported as the measure of liabilities, loadings are level, and expenses decrease with time following policy issue.

To avoid the situation in which assets are less than liabilities, in the early durations, several actions are possible:

- The insurance organization may obtain additional capital for the initial surplus, $u(0)$, to keep

$$u(0)(1 + i)^h + \sum_{j=1}^{h} (1 + i)^{h-j+1}\,_{j-1}p_x\,(c - e_{j-1})$$

  positive for $h = 0, 1, 2, 3, \ldots$.
- Loadings may depend on duration so that $c_{h-1} - e_{h-1} \geq 0$, $h = 1, 2, 3, \ldots$.
- The liabilities of the insurance organization could be based on a reserve principle that would reduce reported liabilities in early policy years. The reserve principle of reporting benefit plus expense reserves used in column (b) of Tables 15.2.5 and 15.2.6 is an example of such an action. (This last alternative is the subject of Sections 16.6 and 16.7.)

15.6 Asset Shares

To provide an algebraic foundation for accounting within a double decrement model, using the equivalence principle, it is necessary to develop a set of recursion relations. These recursion relations have many applications, and some of these applications are developed in Sections 16.4.2 and 16.5. The basic variable in these recursion equations has been given different names, depending on the application. In this section we call it *asset share*, a term laden with a long history. In other sections, depending on the application, different operational meanings are attached.

15.6.1 Recursion Relations

A life insurance policy is a long-term contract involving income to the insurer from premiums and investments and outgo as a result of death and withdrawal benefit payments and expenses. Contract premiums actually charged for a unit of insurance are influenced by competition, and withdrawal values are influenced by law and competition. There is a need for a calculation of the balance, in the sense of actuarial present values, between the various elements of the price-benefit structure. The asset share calculation, outlined in this section, is designed to fill this need. It is not a historic summary of past results, but a prospective calculation of some complexity attempting to capture most elements that influence the expected financial progress of a group of policies.

We will start with an extension of (15.5.5) for a unit of insurance,

$$_h p_x^{(\tau)} \, (_h AS) = {_{h-1} p_x^{(\tau)}} \{ [_{h-1} AS + G(1 - c_{h-1}) - e_{h-1}](1 + i)$$

$$- q_{x+h-1}^{(1)} - q_{x+h-1}^{(2)} \, _h CV \} \qquad h = 1, 2, 3, \dots . \qquad (15.6.1)$$

Multiplying (15.6.1) by $1/{_{h-1} p_x^{(\tau)}}$ yields

$$p_{x+h-1}^{(\tau)} \, (_h AS) = [_{h-1} AS + G(1 - c_{h-1}) - e_{h-1}] \, (1 + i)$$

$$- q_{x+h-1}^{(1)} - q_{x+h-1}^{(2)} \, _h CV \qquad h = 1, 2, 3, \dots . \qquad (15.6.2)$$

In (15.6.1) and (15.6.2),

$_h AS$ denotes the expected asset share h years following policy issue, immediately before the start of policy year $h + 1$

G denotes the level contract premium

c_h denotes the fraction of the contract premium paid at time h for expenses

e_h denotes the amount of per policy expenses paid at time h

$q_{x+h}^{(1)}$ denotes the probability of decrement by death, before the attainment of age $x + h + 1$, for an insured now age $x + h$

$q_{x+h}^{(2)}$ denotes the probability of decrement by withdrawal, before the attainment of age $x + h + 1$, for an insured now age $x + h$

$_h CV$ denotes the amount of the withdrawal benefit paid at time h. This is also called a *cash value*.

Formula (15.6.1) is based on the assumptions of a fully discrete payment basis, unit death claims paid at the end of the year of death, and $_h CV$ paid at the end of the year of withdrawal.

Formula (15.6.1) is a generalization of the recursion relationship connecting successive terminal reserves. It will be rewritten in several ways that are reminiscent of similar manipulations with reserve equations. Multiplying (15.6.2) by $v^h l_{x+h-1}^{(\tau)}$ and rearranging the terms yields

$$\Delta(l_{x+h-1}^{(\tau)} \, v^{h-1} \, _{h-1} AS) = [G(1 - c_{h-1}) - e_{h-1}] l_{x+h-1}^{(\tau)} \, v^{h-1}$$

$$- (d_{x+h-1}^{(1)} + d_{x+h-1}^{(2)} \, _h CV) \, v^h \qquad h = 1, 2, 3, \dots . \qquad (15.6.3)$$

The sum of the left-hand side over $h = 1, 2, \dots , n$ telescopes to

$$l^{(\tau)}_{x+n} \, v^n \, _nAS - l^{(\tau)}_x \, _0AS = \sum_{h=1}^{n} \{[G(1 - c_{h-1}) - e_{h-1}]l^{(\tau)}_{x+h-1} \, v^{h-1}$$

$$- (d^{(1)}_{x+h-1} + d^{(2)}_{x+h-1} \, _hCV) \, v^h\}. \tag{15.6.4}$$

If $_0AS = 0$, we have $_nAS$ equal to

$$\sum_{h=1}^{n} \frac{\{[G(1 - c_{h-1}) - e_{h-1}]l^{(\tau)}_{x+h-1}(1 + i) - (d^{(1)}_{x+h-1} + d^{(2)}_{x+h-1} \, _hCV)\}(1 + i)^{n-h}}{l^{(\tau)}_{x+n}}. \tag{15.6.5}$$

For a whole life insurance, we set $n = \omega - x$ in (15.6.4). Then, recognizing that ultimately the expected asset share is zero, we rearrange (15.6.5) to obtain

$$G\ddot{a}^{(\tau)}_x = A^{(1)}_x + \sum_{h=1}^{\omega-x} (Gc_{h-1} + e_{h-1}) \, v^{h-1} \, _{h-1}p^{(\tau)}_x + \sum_{h=1}^{\omega-x} {}_{h-1}p^{(\tau)}_x \, q^{(2)}_{x+h-1} \, v^h \, _hCV. \tag{15.6.6}$$

Formula (15.6.6) can be interpreted as a general formula for an expense-loaded premium using the equivalence principle. Appropriate modifications can alter the formula from a whole life to an endowment or term policy.

Making the substitution

$$p^{(\tau)}_{x+h-1} = 1 - q^{(1)}_{x+h-1} - q^{(2)}_{x+h-1}$$

allows us to rewrite (15.6.2) as

$$_hAS = [_{h-1}AS + G(1 - c_{h-1}) - e_{h-1}] \, (1 + i)$$

$$- q^{(1)}_{x+h-1} \, (1 - {}_hAS) - q^{(2)}_{x+h-1} \, (_hCV - {}_hAS). \tag{15.6.7}$$

This form emphasizes the importance of the difference, $_hCV - {}_hAS$, on the progression of asset shares.

Asset share calculations can be viewed as tracing the expected progress of the assets, per surviving policy, of a block of similar policies. The calculations for fixed contract premiums, expense commitments, and cash values can be made to check the balance between the various components of the price-benefit structure. The objective of the calculations might be to determine if $_kAS \geq {}_kV$, for all but the very early policy years.

15.6.2 Accounting

Let $_hAS = {}_hV + u(h)$, where $_hV$ is the reserve liability and $u(h)$ the anticipated surplus for each surviving insured at the end of accounting period h. The values for $u(h)$ may be negative, especially during early policy years. Assume that reserve liabilities are generated by the recursion relation

$$_hV \, p^{(\tau)}_{x+h-1} = (_{h-1}V + P) \, (1 + i)$$

$$- q^{(1)}_{x+h-1} - q^{(2)}_{x+h-1} \, _hCV \qquad h = 1, 2, 3, \ldots. \tag{15.6.8}$$

Formula (15.6.8) is a recursion relation that determines benefit reserves within the double decrement model. These correspond to the benefit reserves calculated in Table 15.3.3.

Multiply (15.6.2) and (15.6.8) by $_{h-1}p_x^{(\tau)}$ and subtract to obtain

$$u(h) \,_h p_x^{(\tau)} = [u(h-1) + G(1 - c_{h-1}) - e_{h-1} - P](1+i) \,_{h-1}p_x^{(\tau)}$$

$$h = 1, 2, \ldots . \tag{15.6.9}$$

Let $G = P + c$ and $Gc_{h-1} + e_{h-1} = E_{h-1}$ (total expenses), and (15.6.9) becomes

$$u(h) \,_h p_x^{(\tau)} = [u(h-1) + c - E_{h-1}] (1+i) \,_{h-1}p_x^{(\tau)} \tag{15.6.10}$$

which is a double decrement version of (15.5.10). Multiplying recursion relation (15.6.10) by v^h and rearranging terms yields

$$\Delta v^{h-1} \,_{h-1}p_x^{(\tau)} \, u(h-1) = v^{h-1} \,_{h-1}p_x^{(\tau)} \, (c - E_{h-1}).$$

Following exactly the same steps as in Section 15.5 to obtain (15.5.8), we obtain

$$_h p_x^{(\tau)} \, u(h) = \sum_{j=1}^{h} (1+i)^{h-j+1} \,_{j-1}p_x^{(\tau)} \, (c - E_{j-1}). \tag{15.6.11}$$

The remaining developments in Section (15.5) follow in identical fashion with the substitution of corresponding multiple decrement for single decrement probabilities and the addition of expected withdrawal benefits $_{h-1}p_x^{(\tau)} \, q_{x+h-1}^{(2)} \,_{h-1}CV$. The illustration in Tables 15.3.4 and 15.3.5, column (b), provides a worked example of these ideas.

Example 15.6.1

Consider again the illustration that was started in Table 15.2.1 and expanded to include withdrawal benefits in Table 15.3.1. Assume, as in Tables 15.3.4 and 15.3.5, that $G = 342.96$. Calculate a set of asset shares.

Solution:

We use (15.6.2) to guide our calculation.

Period

h $\{[_{h-1}AS + G(1 - c_{h-1}) - e_{h-1}](1+i) - 1{,}000 \, q_{x+h-1}^{(1)} - \,_h CV \, q_{x+h-1}^{(2)}\} / p_{x+h-1}^{(\tau)} = \,_h AS$

1 $\{[0 + 342.96 (1 - 0.20) - 8.0](1.15) - 1{,}000(0.1) - 227.73(0.1)\} / 0.8 = 229.44$

2 $\{[229.44 + 342.96(1 - 0.06) - 2.0](1.15) - 1{,}000(0.1111) - 564.41(0.1111)\} / 0.7778 = 589.46$

3 $\{[589.46 + 342.96(1 - 0.06) - 2.0](1.15) - 1{,}000\} / 1.0 = 46.32$

The motivation for calling $_h AS$ an asset share can be appreciated by a comparison of the solution to this example and the final assets reported at the end of the third year in Table 15.3.5:

(Asset Share) (Expected number of insureds = Total Expected Assets
                      receiving death, maturity, or
                      withdrawal benefits at the
                      end of policy year three)

$$(46.32)[(10)(0.6222)] = 288.22,$$

(Expected assets at the end   − (Assets accumulated
  of the third policy year)   from the initial fund)

$$1,809.07 − 1,000 \, (1.15)^3 = 288.20.$$

The difference is due to rounding in each computation.   ▼

15.7   Expenses, Reserves, and General Insurances

A number of new ideas, using two simple illustrations, are developed in Sections 15.2 and 15.3. In Section 8.2 reserves for a general life insurance, single decrement model, ignoring expenses, were displayed. The development started with the following loss variable for $T(x) > t$:

$$_tL = b_{T(x)} \, v^{T(x)-t} − \int_t^{T(x)} \pi_u \, v^{u-t} \, du.$$

Our goal is to extend this model to incorporate features of recent sections. First we will add a benefit associated with withdrawal,

$$_tL^2 = \begin{cases} b_{T(x)}^{(1)} \, v^{T(x)-t} − \displaystyle\int_t^{T(x)} \pi_u^2 \, v^{u-t} \, du, & \text{decrement by death} \\[2mm] b_{T(x)}^{(2)} \, v^{T(x)-t} − \displaystyle\int_t^{T(x)} \pi_u^2 \, v^{u-t} \, du, & \text{decrement by withdrawal.} \end{cases}$$

The superscript ^{2} has been added to the loss variable and premium rate symbols to denote that a withdrawal benefit has been added to the initial model.

Second, we add expenses at rate E_t at time t, measured from issue. This corresponds to what was done in (15.6.10). The subscript e is joined to the loss variable symbol and the premium rate symbol to denote that expenses have been added to the model. It is assumed that $_e\pi_u^2$ has been determined by the equivalence principle:

$$_tL_e^2 = \begin{cases} b_{T(x)}^{(1)} \, v^{T(x)-t} − \displaystyle\int_t^{T(x)} (_e\pi_u^2 − E_u)v^{u-t} \, du, & \text{decrement by death} \\[2mm] b_{T(x)}^{(2)} \, v^{T(x)-t} − \displaystyle\int_t^{T(x)} (_e\pi_u^2 − E_u)v^{u-t} \, du, & \text{decrement by withdrawal.} \end{cases}$$

Then, changing the integration variable to $s = u − t$, we can write the conditional expectation of $_tL_e^2$, given $T(x) > t$,

---

$$E[_tL_{\bar{e}}^2] = \int_t^\infty \left[b_y^{(1)}\, v^{y-t} - \int_0^{y-t} (_e\pi_{\bar{t}+s}^2 - E_{t+s})v^s\, ds \right]_{y-t}p_{x+t}^{(\tau)}\, \mu_{x+t}^{(1)}(y-t)\, dy$$

$$+ \int_t^\infty \left[b_y^{(2)}\, v^{y-t} - \int_0^{y-t} (_e\pi_{\bar{t}+s}^2 - E_{t+s})v^s\, ds \right]_{y-t}p_{x+t}^{(\tau)}\, \mu_{x+t}^{(2)}(y-t)\, dy. \quad (15.7.1)$$

Now change the outer integration variable to $u = y - t$ and collect terms as

$$E[_tL_{\bar{e}}^2] = \int_0^\infty \left[\sum_{j=1}^2 b_{t+u}^{(j)}\, \mu_{x+t}^{(j)}(u)v^u - \int_0^u (_e\pi_{\bar{t}+s}^2 - E_{t+s})v^s\, ds\, \mu_{x+t}^{(\tau)}(u) \right]\, _up_{x+t}^{(\tau)}\, du.$$

Using integration by parts on the second term yields

$$E[_tL_{\bar{e}}^2] = \int_0^\infty v^u \left\{ \left[\sum_{j=1}^2 b_{t+u}^{(j)}\, \mu_{x+t}^{(j)}(u) - _e\pi_{\bar{t}+u}^2 + E_{t+u} \right]\, _up_{x+t}^{(\tau)} \right\}\, du$$

$$= \int_0^\infty v^u [f(u{:}t)]\, du. \quad (15.7.2)$$

Formula (15.7.2) is of interest because the function

$$f(u{:}t) = [E_{t+u} + \sum_{j=1}^2 b_{t+u}^{(j)}\, \mu_{x+t}^{(j)}(u) - _e\pi_{\bar{t}+u}^2]\, _up_{x+t}^{(\tau)} \quad (15.7.3)$$

can be interpreted as the **expected cash flow** at time $t + u$ arising from the insurance policy, given survival to time t.

Because positive values of $f(u{:}t)$ are associated with expected cash outflows from the insurance enterprise, some actuaries prefer to consider the function $g(u{:}t) = -f(u{:}t)$ in which expected cash inflow would have positive values. Formula (15.7.3) also provides yet another interpretation of reserves. Reserves become the present values of future expected net cash outflows. Formula (8.6.1) provides the same interpretation in a less comprehensive model.

In Sections 15.2.2 and 15.3.2 it is illustrated that reserves can differ in their degree of comprehensiveness in accordance with the purpose of the valuation. In this section a very general insurance was introduced. For regulatory purposes reserves might be based on formula (8.2.4) under the assumption that to ignore expenses would be conservative in the sense that typically reserves are decreased by including expenses. The withdrawal benefit might also be omitted under the assumption that a properly determined withdrawal benefit will have only a small effect on reserves. For financial accounting to be used by the capital markets, (15.7.2) would usually be the basis of reserves.

In the financial management of life insurance companies, the rate of change in reserve liabilities with respect to changes in the valuation interest rate is of considerable concern. Using (15.7.2) and viewing the premium rate set at time 0 to be independent of future valuation interest rates, and assuming that the valuation interest rate is independent of the probabilities of death and withdrawal, we have

$$\frac{d}{d\delta}\, \mathrm{E}[_tL_{\bar{e}}^2] = -\int_0^\infty uv^u\, f(u{:}t)du.\qquad (15.7.4)$$

Example 15.7.1

Exhibit the expected cash flow function $f(u{:}t)$ for a fully continuous whole life policy, ignoring expenses, and display $d\,\mathrm{E}[_tL_{\bar{e}}^1]/d\delta$ in actuarial present-value functions. Remember that the premium was set at time 0 and is not a function of the current valuation interest rate.

Solution:

Modifying formulas (15.7.3) and (15.7.4) we have

$$f(u{:}t) = [\mu_{x+t}(u) - \bar{P}(\bar{A}_x)]_u p_{x+t}$$

and

$$\frac{d}{d\delta}\, \mathrm{E}[_tL_{\bar{e}}^1] = -\int_0^\infty uv^u\, [\mu_{x+t}(u) - \bar{P}(\bar{A}_x)]_u p_{x+t}\, du$$

$$= -(\bar{I}\bar{A})_{x+t} + \bar{P}(\bar{A}_x)(\bar{I}\bar{a})_{x+t}\,,$$

where $(\bar{I}\bar{A})_{x+t}$ and $(\bar{I}\bar{a})_{x+t}$ are calculated at the valuation interest rate. ▼

Typically, $g(0{:}0) < 0$ and there exists a u_0 such that $g(u{:}0) > 0$ for $u > u_0$. The time u_0 that expected cash flows cross from negative to positive may be useful in financial planning.

Example 15.7.2

Display the equation that would be used to determine the number u_0 for the policy described in Example 15.7.1.

Solution:

$$f(u{:}0) = [\mu_x(u) - \bar{P}(\bar{A}_x)]_u p_x = 0$$

or

$$\mu_x(u) = \bar{P}(\bar{A}_x). \qquad ▼$$

15.8 Notes and References

In this chapter we have used the clumsy term "expense-loaded premiums" for what some would call gross premiums. The use of the longer term is intended as a warning that the subject of premiums contains many topics other than the benefit premiums discussed in previous chapters and the expense loadings introduced here. These topics include competitive considerations, profit loadings in nonparticipating insurance, expected dividends in participating insurance, risk factors, and the impact of withdrawal benefits. Guertin (1965) discusses many of these topics. Chalke (1991) has criticized the traditional cost-plus determination of premiums. The criticisms are built on a foundation of classical microeconomics.

Fassel (1956) discusses the issues involved in estimating and allocating per policy expenses. Until the time of Fassel's paper, most per policy expenses were included in the loading for expenses that vary with the amount of insurance (assuming an average size policy). In fact, the use of either policy fees or the band system was viewed for many years as an inequitable allocation of expense charges.

Brenner et al. (1988) is a treatise on life insurance accounting. Horn (1971) studies the impact of various reserve systems on the time incidence of reported net income. Asset share calculations have a long history. Huffman (1978) discusses refinements in asset share calculations.

Exercises

Section 15.2

15.1. a. A gambling enterprise collects 0.55 from each of 1,000 customers on July 1 of year Z. It immediately invests the funds in a savings account earning 3% interest each 6 months. On July 1 of year $Z + 1$, 1,000 coins will be tossed, each assigned to a specific customer. If the customer's coin comes up heads, the customer receives a prize of 1. If the coin comes up tails, the prize is 0. Supply the figures for the balance sheet and income statement for the gambling enterprise on December 31 of year Z. Use actuarial present values for liabilities.

Balance Sheet	
Assets	Liabilities
Savings account	Reserves
	Surplus

Income Statement
Premium income
Interest income
Increase in revenues

  b. The random variable Y is the amount of the payments made on July 1 of year $Z + 1$ and has a binomial distribution. Using a normal approximation, evaluate

$$\Pr[Y(1.03)^{-1} - A > 0]$$

where A represents the assets as of December 31 of year Z.
  c. If the enterprise had only one customer, the scale of the operation would be 0.001 of that in part (a). Show that the probability displayed in (b) is equal to $1/2$ for the reduced enterprise.

15.2. An expense augmented loss variable for use with a whole life policy, fully continuous model, is given by

$$L_e = L + X$$

where

$$L = v^T - \bar{P}(\bar{A}_x)\, \ddot{a}_{\overline{T}|}$$

and

$$X = c_0 + (g - e)\, \ddot{a}_{\overline{T}|}.$$

In these expressions, L is interpreted as the loss variable associated with the benefit portion of the policy and X with the expenses. The symbol c_0 denotes nonrandom initial expenses, g the rate of continuous maintenance expense, and e the expense loading in the premium. The equivalence principle has been adopted and $E[L] = E[X] = 0$. Show that

a. $X = c_0 L$

b. $\text{Var}(L_e) = (1 + c_0)^2\, \text{Var}(L)$

c. $\text{Cov}(L, X) = c_0[{}^2\bar{A}_x - (\bar{A}_x)^2]/(\delta \ddot{a}_x)^2.$

15.3. A merchant has accounts receivable at the end of each annual accounting period. Experience has indicated that there is a probability of 0.25 that no payment will be received and 0.75 that full payment will be received at time T. The p.d.f. of T is given by $f(t) = 4 - 8t,\ 0 < t < 0.5$, where t is measured in years. At the end of a year, the merchant has 100 accounts receivable, each of amount 100. The random variable R_i is the present value at the end of the year of account i.

a. Verify that

$$R_i = 0 \text{ with probability } 0.25,$$

$$= 100\, v^T \text{ with probability } 0.75.$$

b. If $R_j,\ j = 1, 2, 3, \ldots, 100$ are independent random variables, calculate

(i) $\text{E}[\sum_1^{100} R_i]$, (ii) $\text{Var}(\sum_1^{100} R_i)$, when $\delta = 0.06$.

c. Repeat (b) if δ is 0.

d. The merchant elects to report an actuarial present value as the value of the accounts receivable. The results of part (a) are used. What is the reported value of accounts receivable?

e. As an alternative, the merchant might use the results of part (c) as the reported value of accounts receivable. What amount would be reported?

f. Another method for reporting accounts receivable would be to use the results of (c), $\delta = 0.00$, and to report

$$E\left[\sum_1^{100} R_i\right] - k\sqrt{\text{Var}\left(\sum_1^{100} R_i\right)}.$$

For what value of k is the amount reported in part (f) the same as in part (d)?

15.4. a. In the illustration in Table 15.3.1 assume that $b_{x+1}^{(2)} = 257.41$ and $b_{x+2}^{(2)} = 581.16$, the benefit reserves for the single decrement model, and determine $P_{x:\overline{3}|}^2$ using the equivalence principle.

b. Assume that $b_{x+1}^{(2)} = 218.41$ and $b_{x+2}^{(2)} = 559.16$, the total reserves for the single decrement model, and determine G, the expense-loaded premium, using the equivalence principle.

Section 15.4

15.5. The expense-loaded annual premium for a 1,000 endowment-at-age-65 life insurance with level annual premiums issued at age 40 is calculated using the following assumptions:
- Selling commission is 40% of the expense-loaded premium in the first year
- Renewal commissions are 5% of the expense-loaded premium for policy years 2 through 10
- Premium tax is 2% of the expense-loaded premium each year
- Maintenance expense is 12.50 per 1,000 of insurance in the first year and 4.00 per 1,000 of insurance thereafter
- The benefit premium is to provide for the immediate payment of death claims with no premium adjustment on death
- A 15-year select-and-ultimate mortality table is to be used.

Write an expression for the expense-loaded premium.

15.6. The expense-loaded premium for a single premium n-year endowment insurance is determined using the following assumptions:
- Taxes are 2-1/2% of the expense-loaded premium
- Commission is 4% of the expense-loaded premium
- Other expenses are 5 in the first year and 2.50 in each renewal year per 1,000 of insurance.

Claims are paid at the moment of death and expenses are incurred at the start of each policy year. Develop a formula for the expense-loaded premium issued to (x) for an insurance of 1,000.

15.7. For a fully discrete whole life policy of amount 1, the level expense-loaded premium is based on the following schedule of expenses:
- An initial expense of e_0
- Each policy year, including the first, an expense of $e_1 + e_2 P_x$
- The cost of claims settlement, paid along with the claim, of e_3 per unit of insurance.

If $G = a P_x + c$, determine a and c.

15.8. There are two random variables in this exercise. The random variable $T(x)$ is interpreted as time-until-death of a life age x at issue. The random variable

B is interpreted as the death benefit chosen by a randomly selected applicant for a whole life policy that uses a continuous model. The expense augmented loss variable associated with this policy is

$$L(T(x), B)_e = 0 \qquad\qquad T < 0$$

$$= Bv^T + \alpha B\bar{a}_{\overline{T}|} + \theta\bar{a}_{\overline{T}|}$$

$$+ \rho(B\pi + f)\bar{a}_{\overline{T}|} - (B\pi + f)\bar{a}_{\overline{T}|} \qquad 0 < T.$$

In this loss variable:

αB = rate of expense payments that are proportional to the death benefit, paid continuously during the lifetime of (x)

θ = rate of expense payments that are independent of benefit and premium amounts, paid continuously during the lifetime of (x)

$\rho(B\pi + f)$ = rate of expense payments that are proportional to premium payments, paid continuously during the lifetime of (x)

π = portion of continuously paid premium proportional to the death benefit

f = rate of policy fee paid continuously during the lifetime of (x).

Assume that $T(x)$ and B are independent.

a. Use a conditional equivalence principle, that is,

$$E[L(T(x), B)_e|B = b] = 0,$$

and exhibit a formula for the premium rate per unit of insurance; that is, derive a formula for $\pi + f/b$.

b. Use the unconditional equivalence principle

$$E[L(T(x), B)_e] = 0$$

and exhibit a formula for the constant premium rate per unit of insurance.

15.9. The p.d.f. of the amount of insurance issued on an individual policy for a particular plan of insurance is given by

$$f(b) = kb^{-3} \qquad b > 10$$

where b is measured in thousands. Calculate

a. The normalizing constant k

b. The expected policy amount

c. The median of the distribution of amounts of insurance.

15.10. A type of whole life policy, issued on a semicontinuous basis, has the following expense allocations.

	Percentage of Expense-Loaded Premium	Per 1,000 Insurance	Per Policy
First-year	30%	3.00	10.00
Renewal	5%	0.50	2.50

a. Write formulas for the expense-loaded first-year and renewal premiums assuming that per policy expenses are matched separately by first-year and renewal policy fees.

b. Write the formula for the policy fee to be paid in each year if per policy expenses are not matched separately by first-year and renewal policy fees.

Section 15.5

15.11. The continuous analogue of (15.5.5) is the differential equation

$$\frac{d}{dt} \, {}_tp_x \, [{}_t\bar{V}(\bar{A}_x) + \bar{u}(t)] = {}_tp_x \, [\bar{P}(\bar{A}_x) + \delta_t \, \bar{V}(\bar{A}_x)$$

$$+ \bar{c} - \bar{e}(t) + \delta\bar{u}(t) - \mu_x(t)].$$

Using this equation, and (8.6.4) rearranged, to express

$$\frac{d}{dt} \, [{}_tp_x \, {}_t\bar{V}(\bar{A}_x)],$$

show that

$$_tp_x \, \bar{u}(t) = \int_0^t e^{\delta(t-y)} \, {}_yp_x \, [\bar{c} - \bar{e}(y)] \, dy.$$

Section 15.6

15.12. If, in relation to (15.6.7), ${}_{10}AS_1$ is the asset share at the end of 10 years based on G_1 and ${}_{10}AS_2$ is the corresponding quantity based on G_2, write a formula for ${}_{10}AS_2 - {}_{10}AS_1$.

15.13. The continuous analogue of the difference equation (recursion relationship) in (15.6.3) is

$$\frac{d}{dt} \, {}_tp_x^{(\tau)} \, v^t \, {}_t\overline{AS} = [\bar{G}(1 - \bar{c}(t) - \bar{e}(t)]_t p_x^{(\tau)} \, v^t$$

$$- {}_tp_x^{(\tau)} \, [\mu_x^{(1)}(t) + \mu_x^{(2)}(t) \, {}_t\overline{CV}] \, v^t.$$

In this differential equation bars have been added to payment rate symbols to denote continuous payments.

a. Solve this differential equation and use the initial condition ${}_0\overline{AS} = 0$ to obtain the continuous version of (15.6.5):

$$_t\overline{AS} = \left\{ \int_0^t [\bar{G}(1 - \bar{c}(s)) - \bar{e}(s)] \, {}_sp_x^{(\tau)} \, v^s \, ds \right.$$

$$\left. - \int_0^t {}_sp_x^{(\tau)} \, [\mu_x^{(1)}(s) + \mu_x^{(2)}(s) \, {}_s\overline{CV}] \, v^s \, ds \right\} \Big/ (v^t \, {}_tp_x^{(\tau)}).$$

b. If the policy is a continuous model whole life policy, ${}_0\overline{AS} = {}_{\omega-x}\overline{AS} = 0$, show that

$$G\bar{a}_x^{(\tau)} = \bar{A}_x^{(1)} + \int_0^\infty [\bar{G}\bar{c}(s) + \bar{e}(s) + \mu_x^{(2)}(s) \, {}_s\overline{CV}] \, {}_sp_x^{(\tau)} \, v^s \, ds.$$

15.14. a. Start with (8.2.7) and derive the single decrement, without provision for expenses, version of (15.7.2):

$$_t\bar{V} = \int_0^\infty v^u \left\{ b_{t+u}\,\mu_x(t + u) - \pi_{t+u}] \;_u p_{x+t} \right\} du$$

$$= \int_0^\infty v^u f(u{:}t)\, du = \int_0^t (1 + i)^{t-\mu}\, g(u{:}\, 0)\, \frac{du}{_t p_x}.$$

In solving this exercise the assumption should be made that an aggregate mortality table is used as it was in Sections 7.2 and 7.3.

b. At time t the future force of interest changes from δ to δ'. No change in the distribution of time to death is expected because of this change in interest rates, and the insurance contract prohibits a change in π_{t+u}. The symbol $_t\bar{V}'$ denotes a reserve valued at rate δ'. Exhibit a formula for

$$_t\bar{V}' - {}_t\bar{V}.$$

[If the change from δ to δ' is related to observed changes in capital market interest rates, the difference $_t\bar{V}' - {}_t\bar{V}$ might be used to estimate the change in the market value of the reserve liability.]

BUSINESS AND REGULATORY CONSIDERATIONS

16.1 Introduction

In Chapter 15 a major step is taken toward bringing the models for life insurance developed in earlier chapters into accordance with business reality. Operating expenses and withdrawal benefits are introduced, and the implications of these new elements for premiums, reserves, and financial reports are illustrated.

Several topics are presented in this chapter that extend the theme of Chapter 15. Two basic ideas provide a thread that connects them.

The first idea is the development of single decrement models that approximate the results of more comprehensive multiple decrement models with expenses to a sufficient degree of accuracy for a particular purpose. For example, in many jurisdictions such approximate models are used in defining regulations. The motivation for these approximations comes from the perceived conceptual and computational complexity of multiple decrement models that incorporate expenses. With current computing capabilities, this motivation is reduced.

The second of these basic ideas comes from economics. Those who supply the capital to start and stabilize insurance enterprises expect to be rewarded for their investment. Contract premiums need to have an expected profit component that is related to the risk assumed by the investors. If the insurance organization developed from a mutual or cooperative endeavor, the corresponding issue is how to return favorable financial experience in an equitable fashion to the members. To address these issues, ideas must be drawn from economics.

16.2 Cash Values

Sections 11.4 and 15.3 are devoted to benefits paid on withdrawal and the premium and financial reporting consequences of these benefits. Withdrawal benefits are also called *nonforfeiture benefits*, because they cannot be lost as a result of the premature cessation of premium payments.

The determination of premiums and reserves has as a prerequisite the adoption of a principle. Likewise, in the determination of nonforfeiture benefits, a guiding principle is required. In this section we adopt a simple operational principle that is close to the one adopted in United States insurance regulation. The principle is that the withdrawing insured receives a value such that the benefit, premium, and reserve structure based on the single decrement model remains appropriate in the multiple decrement context. Adoption of this principle also permits the use of a less complex model for regulatory purposes.

This principle is motivated by a particular concept of equity involving the treatment of the two classes of policyholders, those who terminate before the basic insurance contract is fulfilled and those who continue. Clearly several concepts of what constitutes equity are possible, ranging from the view that terminating policyholders have not fulfilled the contract and are therefore not entitled to nonforfeiture benefits, to the view that a terminating policyholder should be returned to his original position by the return of the accumulated value of all premiums, perhaps less an insurance charge. The concept of equity, illustrated in this section, is an intermediate one; that is, withdrawing life insurance policyholders are entitled to nonforfeiture benefits, but these benefits should not force a change in the price-benefit structure for continuing policyholders.

The development in Section 11.4 does not include consideration of expenses and corresponding premium loadings. Therefore, if the general principle stated in that section is adopted for determining the value, at the time of premium default, of nonforfeiture benefits, some allowance needs to be made for these missing factors. An approximate method for adjusting benefit reserves for initial expenses not yet recovered from premium loadings, and for the risk of withdrawal at a financially inopportune time for the insurer, is to define

$$_kCV = {}_kV - {}_kSC. \tag{16.2.1}$$

In (16.2.1), $_kCV$ is the *cash value* of nonforfeiture benefits, $_kV$ is the terminal reserve, and $_kSC$ is the *surrender charge*, all at time $k = 1, 2, 3, \ldots$ following policy issue. Because of the difficulty of collecting additional funds from a withdrawing policyholder, $_kCV \geq 0$.

The cash values defined in (16.2.1) are the basis of what are called withdrawal benefits in Sections 11.4 and 15.3. In the earlier sections, these were denoted by $B^{(2)}_{x+t}$. These nonforfeiture benefits need not be paid in cash but are the basis for actuarially equivalent insurance benefits as described in Section 16.3.

A continuing theme in the regulation of the cash value of nonforfeiture benefits has been the need for direct recognition of the amount and incidence of expenses. One idea, in accord with this theme, is to define a minimum cash value for a unit insurance as

$$_kCV = A(k) - P^a\,\ddot{a}(k)$$

$$= {_k}V - (P^a - P)\,\ddot{a}(k). \tag{16.2.2}$$

Here $A(k)$ and $\ddot{a}(k)$ are, respectively, actuarial present-value insurance and annuity symbols appropriate for time k, $k = 1, 2, 3, \ldots$ following policy issue, $_kV$ denotes a terminal reserve at the same time, P is an annual benefit premium, and P^a is called an ***adjusted premium.*** The symbols $A(0)$ and $\ddot{a}(0)$ will be abbreviated to A and $\ddot{a}$, respectively. The regulatory problem becomes that of defining adjusted premiums.

The 1975 report of the Society of Actuaries committee studying nonforfeiture benefits and related matters contained consideration of two types of expenses in defining adjusted premiums. First is a level amount per unit of insurance, denoted by E, incurred each year throughout the premium paying period. Second is an additional expense for the first year of amount E_0. The contract premium rate G is assumed to be composed of an adjusted premium and the level annual expense component E. The first-year expense component E_0 is assumed to be provided by the adjusted premium. That is,

$$G = P^a + E, \tag{16.2.3A}$$

$$G\ddot{a} = (P^a + E)\ddot{a} = A + E_0 + E\,\ddot{a}. \tag{16.2.3B}$$

From (16.2.3B) we obtain

$$P^a = \frac{A + E_0}{\ddot{a}}. \tag{16.2.4}$$

Formula (16.2.4) can be rewritten, by substituting $\ddot{a} = a + 1$, as

$$P^a - E_0 + P^a\, a = A. \tag{16.2.5}$$

Example 16.2.1

The 1980 National Association of Insurance Commissioners (NAIC) Standard Nonforfeiture Law adopted (16.2.2) and (16.2.4) to define minimum cash values. The law specified that for policies with level benefits and contract premiums $E_0 = 1.25\min(P, 0.04) + 0.01$, where P denotes the benefit premium rate per unit of death benefit for the policy. Exhibit the provision for first-year expenses E_0 and the corresponding adjusted premium if (a) $P < 0.04$ and (b) $P \geq 0.04$.

Solution:

	E_0	P^a
a. $P < 0.04$	$1.25P + 0.01$	$\dfrac{A + 1.25P + 0.01}{\ddot{a}}$
b. $P \geq 0.04$	0.06	$\dfrac{A + 0.06}{\ddot{a}}.$

Example 15.3.1 can be interpreted as using (16.2.2) and (16.2.4) to determine cash values with $E_0 = 0.04$. ▼

In this section we have discussed the framework for defining minimum cash values used in many jurisdictions. The method is another example of a single decrement model, with somewhat arbitrary assumptions about the amount and time incidence of expenses, being used as an approximation to a more comprehensive double decrement model. In the history of nonforfeiture value regulation, changes in the general framework have been infrequent.

For a jurisdiction to complete the definition of minimum cash values, the interest rate and the life table to be used must be specified. Legislative changes to update the interest and mortality bases of minimum cash values have occurred more frequently than have changes to the general framework. The 1980 NAIC law provides for revisions of the maximum interest rate according to a formula based, in part, on an index of average interest rates prevailing during a period of time before policy issue.

Some of the modifications required when contract premiums or benefits are not level are discussed in Section 16.9. These modifications are covered with the closely related modifications required to adapt regulatory reserve liability standards to nonlevel contract premiums or benefits.

Because the original contract was one of insurance, there is a view that at least one of the nonforfeiture benefits should also be insurance. In this view, the cash value is a device to define the new insurance benefit. These insurance options are discussed in Section 16.3. Also, cash values form the basis of another important policy provision, the policy loan clause. This provision provides that the insurer will grant, on the security of the policy's cash value, a loan not greater than the cash value. At one time the interest rate on such loans was stated in the policy. In response to volatile interest rates, however, there has been a move to link policy loan interest rates to some market interest rate appropriate at the time the loan is made. Upon settlement of the policy on death, maturity, or surrender for cash, the outstanding indebtedness is subtracted from the proceeds.

16.3   Insurance Options

Cash values are available as a lump sum or as an insurance benefit of equal actuarial present value. Three common insurance benefits are discussed here.

16.3.1   Paid-up Insurance

The equivalence principle is used to determine the reduced amount of paid-up insurance according to the benefit provision in the policy. If premium default occurs at time k, as measured from policy issue, the general equation for the amount of paid-up insurance available, denoted by b_k, is

$$_kCV = b_k A(k),$$

$$b_k = \frac{_kCV}{A(k)} \qquad (16.3.1)$$

where $_kCV$ is the cash value available and $A(k)$ is the actuarial present value for a unit of future benefits under the policy at time k. In practice, various elaborations on the symbol $A(k)$ indicate, if appropriate, that continuous payment of claims and various term and endowment benefits are required.

For a unit of insurance and in the special case when $_kCV = {}_kV$, where $_kV$ is a benefit reserve, (16.3.1) may be rewritten to provide additional insight. Some of these ideas were developed in connection with (7.3.2) and (7.4.6). In this special case, the symbol $_kW = b_k = {}_kV / A(k)$ is used to denote the amount of paid-up insurance. In Table 16.3.1 some of the relationships between $_kW$ and other actuarial quantities are listed. Additional relationships of this type are called for in Exercises 16.7 and 16.8.

There is a general reasoning argument that leads to the results in Table 16.3.1. At age $x + k$ the benefit premium for a whole life insurance of 1 is P_{x+k}. Thus an annual premium of P_x, payable commencing at age $x + k$, would be sufficient to provide insurance of only P_x / P_{x+k}. Since P_x is the benefit premium actually paid for a unit of insurance, the difference at time k, $1 - P_x / P_{x+k}$, must be provided by the reserve. This reasoning can be applied to the other insurances.

TABLE 16.3.1
Amounts of Reduced Paid-up Insurance

Special Case $b_k = {}_kW = {}_kV/A(k)$

Fully Continuous Basis	Fully Discrete

Whole Life

$$_k\bar{W}(\bar{A}_x) = \frac{\bar{A}_{x+k} - \bar{P}(\bar{A}_x)\,\bar{a}_{x+k}}{\bar{A}_{x+k}} \qquad\qquad {}_kW_x = \frac{A_{x+k} - P_x\,\ddot{a}_{x+k}}{A_{x+k}}$$

$$= 1 - \frac{\bar{P}(\bar{A}_x)}{\bar{P}(\bar{A}_{x+k})} \qquad\qquad\qquad\qquad = 1 - \frac{P_x}{P_{x+k}}$$

n-Payment Life ($k < n$)

$$_k^n\bar{W}(\bar{A}_x) = \frac{\bar{A}_{x+k} - {}_n\bar{P}(\bar{A}_x)\,\ddot{a}_{x+k:\overline{n-k}|}}{\bar{A}_{x+k}} \qquad\qquad {}_k^nW_x = \frac{A_{x+k} - {}_nP_x\,\ddot{a}_{x+k:\overline{n-k}|}}{A_{x+k}}$$

$$= 1 - \frac{{}_n\bar{P}(\bar{A}_x)}{{}_{n-k}\bar{P}(\bar{A}_{x+k})} \qquad\qquad\qquad\qquad = 1 - \frac{{}_nP_x}{{}_{n-k}P_{x+k}}$$

n-Year Endowment ($k < n$)

$$_k\bar{W}(\bar{A}_{x:\overline{n}|}) = \frac{\bar{A}_{x+k:\overline{n-k}|} - \bar{P}(\bar{A}_{x:\overline{n}|})\,\bar{a}_{x+k:\overline{n-k}|}}{\bar{A}_{x+k:\overline{n-k}|}} \qquad\qquad {}_kW_{x:\overline{n}|} = \frac{A_{x+k:\overline{n-k}|} - P_{x:\overline{n}|}\,\ddot{a}_{x+k:\overline{n-k}|}}{A_{x+k:\overline{n-k}|}}$$

$$= 1 - \frac{\bar{P}(\bar{A}_{x:\overline{n}|})}{\bar{P}(\bar{A}_{x+k:\overline{n-k}|})} \qquad\qquad\qquad\qquad = 1 - \frac{P_{x:\overline{n}|}}{P_{x+k:\overline{n-k}|}}$$

16.3.2   Extended Term

The equivalence principle is used to determine the length of a paid-up term insurance for the full amount of the policy. The equation to be solved for s, in connection with an insurance with unit amount, is

$$_kCV = \bar{A}^{\,1}_{x+k:\overline{s}|}. \tag{16.3.2}$$

In the case of an endowment insurance, it may be that $s > n - k$, the remaining time to maturity. In that case the amount of cash value not used to purchase paid-up term insurance is used to buy a pure endowment of amount

$$\frac{_kCV - \bar{A}^{\,1}_{x+k:\overline{n-k}|}}{A_{x+k:\overline{n-k}|}^{\;\;1}}. \tag{16.3.3}$$

If a policy of amount b is subject to an outstanding policy loan of amount L at the time of premium default, life insurance policies usually provide that the extended-term insurance will be for amount $b - L$. Without this provision a policyholder with a policy loan of amount L and current death benefit of $b - L$ could, by the act of premium default, increase the amount of insurance to b. In the case of a policy loan of amount L, (16.3.2) is modified to

$$b \; _kCV - L = (b - L)\, \bar{A}^{\,1}_{x+k:\overline{s}|}.$$

If the terminating insured can elect either a reduced paid-up or an extended-term insurance equivalent, the insurer has granted an option to the terminating insured. Those in good health tend to elect reduced paid-up insurance, and those in impaired health extended term. To compensate for the cost of this option, some insurers use a life table with higher mortality in determining $A^{\,1}_{x+k:\overline{s}|}$ in (16.3.2) than is used in determining $A(k)$ in (16.3.1).

The basic idea is that the transition of a policyholder from one status defined in the policy to another is information that should be used in determining the conditional distribution of time until death following the transition. This idea also appears in the discussion of accelerated benefits in Section 17.7 and of last-survivor insurance in Section 18.7.

Example 16.3.1

A semicontinuous whole life insurance with a 100,000 death benefit is issued to (40). On the basis of the Illustrative Life Table with uniform distribution of deaths over each year of age and $i = 0.06$, determine the following as of duration 10:
a. The minimum nonforfeiture value according to the 1980 NAIC law.
b. If the policy cash value is 8,700, the length of the extended term insurance period.
c. Repeat part (b) with a policy loan of 5,000 outstanding.

Solution:

[The following calculations are done on the Illustrative Life Table spreadsheet constructed for the computing exercises.] Use of the Illustrative Life Table for *both* the original pricing and the determination of the length of the period extended term insurance available at termination may not be realistic, as the future lifetime of an insured electing the extended term option may be governed by higher mortality rates than the future lifetime of a newly insured life.

a. $P(\bar{A}_{40}) = \bar{A}_{40}/\ddot{a}_{40} = (i/\delta)A_{40}/\ddot{a}_{40} = 0.0112\ 11537$

  $E_0 = 1.25\ \mathrm{Min}[P(\bar{A}_{40}), 0.04] + 0.01 = 0.0240\ 14421$

  $P^a = P(\bar{A}_{40}) + E_0/\ddot{a}_{40} = 0.0128\ 32315$

  Min Cash Value @ 10 = 8,620.2247

  Benefit Reserve @ 10 = 10,770.4823.

b. From (16.3.2) we seek an s such that

$$8{,}700 = 100{,}000\bar{A}^1_{50:\overline{s}|}$$

  or

$$0.08700 = \bar{A}^1_{50:\overline{s}|}.$$

To accommodate the assumption of a uniform distribution of deaths within each year of age, we start by searching for the integer $\lfloor s \rfloor$ such that

$$\bar{A}^1_{50:\overline{\lfloor s \rfloor}|} < 0.08700 < \bar{A}^1_{50:\overline{\lfloor s \rfloor+1}|}.$$

From the Illustrative Life Table we have

$$\bar{A}^1_{50:\overline{13}|} = 0.083094960$$

  and

$$\bar{A}^1_{50:\overline{14}|} = 0.090194845.$$

[Hint: See (b), page 119.]

Thus,

$$0.087 = \bar{A}^1_{50:\overline{s}|} = 0.083094960 + v^{13}\ {}_{13}p_{50} \int_0^{s-13} q_{63}\, v^t\, dt \text{ and}$$

$$\frac{0.003905040(1.06)^{13}}{{}_{13}p_{50}\, q_{63}} = \frac{1 - v^{s-13}}{\log(1.06)},$$

$$v^{s-13} = 0.968948162 \text{ and}$$

$$s = 13 + 0.541355012.$$

This would probably be rounded up to 13 years and 198 days.

c. We now seek an s such that

$$(8{,}700 - 5{,}000) = (100{,}000 - 5{,}000)\bar{A}^1_{50:\overline{s}|}$$

  or

$$0.038947368 = \bar{A}^1_{50:\overline{s}|}.$$

Proceeding as in part (b), $s = 6.444084519$, which rounds up to 6 years and 163 days. ▼

16.3.3 Automatic Premium Loan

Another policy provision, one that is not classified as a nonforfeiture benefit by all actuaries, is the automatic premium loan. This provision keeps the policy in full force, if premium default occurs, for as long as the cash value is greater than the balance of the policy loan, which will be increasing because of interest and unpaid premiums added to the balance. The option to restore the policy to full force without a loan is available unilaterally to the insured under this option. Because the restoration to full force under the other nonforfeiture options typically requires the payment of accumulated due contract premiums and, often, evidence of insurability, there is lack of agreement on the classification of this benefit.

For default at time k, on a policy with a continuous payment basis for unit amount, the maximum length of the premium loan period would be determined by solving

$$G\,\bar{s}_{\overline{t}|i} = {}_{k+t}CV \tag{16.3.4}$$

for t. In (16.3.4),
- G is the contract premium per unit of insurance
- ${}_{k+t}CV$ is the cash value per unit of insurance and
- i is the policy loan interest rate.

In practice, t is sometimes taken as an integer such that

$$G\,\ddot{s}_{\overline{t}|i} \le {}_{k+t}CV$$

and

$$G\,\ddot{s}_{\overline{t+1}|i} > {}_{k+t+1}CV.$$

The remaining cash value, ${}_{k+t}CV - G\,\ddot{s}_{\overline{t}|i}$, is used to buy extended-term insurance.

Example 16.3.2

A fully continuous whole life insurance for unit amount issued to (x) is changed to a nonforfeiture benefit at the end of k years.
a. If ${}_kCV = {}_k\bar{V}(\bar{A}_x)$, express the ratio of the variance of the future loss associated with the changed insurance, immediately after the change, to the variance of the future loss at duration k on the original insurance if the nonforfeiture benefit is
  (i) Paid-up insurance
  (ii) Extended-term insurance.
b. If $x = 35$ and $k = 10$, calculate the ratios in parts [a-(i)] and [a-(ii)] on the basis of the Illustrative Life Table with interest at 6%. (See Exercise 6.10 and Exercise 7.23.)

Solution:

a. (i) By (7.2.5), the variance before the change is

$$\left[1 + \frac{\bar{P}(\bar{A}_x)}{\delta}\right]^2 [^2\bar{A}_{x+k} - (\bar{A}_{x+k})^2] = \frac{^2\bar{A}_{x+k} - (\bar{A}_{x+k})^2}{(1 - \bar{A}_x)^2}.$$

For the paid-up insurance the loss variable is

$$_k\bar{W}(\bar{A}_x)\, v^{T(x)-k} - \,_k\bar{V}(\bar{A}_x),$$

which has variance

$$[_k\bar{W}(\bar{A}_x)]^2 \, [^2\bar{A}_{x+k} - (\bar{A}_{x+k})^2].$$

The ratio of this to the variance before the change is

$$[_k\bar{W}(\bar{A}_x)]^2 \, (1 - \bar{A}_x)^2,$$

which is less than 1.

(ii) In the case of extended-term insurance, we have from (16.3.2) and (4.2.5) that the variance after the change is

$$^2\bar{A}^{\,1}_{\overline{x+k:s|}} - (\bar{A}^{\,1}_{\overline{x+k:s|}})^2.$$

The ratio of the variances is

$$\frac{[^2\bar{A}^{\,1}_{\overline{x+k:s|}} - (\bar{A}^{\,1}_{\overline{x+k:s|}})^2] \, (1 - \bar{A}_x)^2}{^2\bar{A}_{x+k} - (\bar{A}_{x+k})^2}.$$

b. (i) $_{10}\bar{W}(\bar{A}_{35}) = \,_{10}\bar{V}(\bar{A}_{35}) / \bar{A}_{45} = 0.08604 / 0.20718 = 0.41529$

$\bar{A}_{35} = 0.13254$

$[0.41529\,(1 - 0.13254)]^2 = 0.13.$

The variance of the loss on the paid-up insurance is 13% of the variance of the loss at duration ten on the original insurance.

(ii) $_{10}\bar{V}(\bar{A}_{35}) = 0.08604\, A^{\,1}_{\overline{45:s|}}$

yields a value of s between 19 and 20. With $s = 19$,

$$\frac{^2\bar{A}^{\,1}_{\overline{45:19|}} - (\bar{A}^{\,1}_{\overline{45:19|}})^2}{^2\bar{A}_{45} - (\bar{A}_{45})^2} \, (1 - \bar{A}_{35})^2 = \frac{0.04308}{0.02922} \, (0.86746)^2 = 1.11.$$

Since s is between 19 and 20, the variance has increased to approximately 111% of what it was before the cessation of premium payments. ▼

16.4 Premiums and Economic Considerations

Sections 15.2.1 and 15.3.1 develop ideas about introducing expected expenses into premium formulas by applying the equivalence principle. The resulting premiums are described as expense-loaded premiums, but they also could be called expected-cost premiums. In Sections 15.2.2 and 15.3.2 a provision for contingencies and profits is introduced by adding a flat extra amount to the expense-loaded premium. The formulation of profit objectives and the inclusion of these objectives into the premium determination process are not discussed.

In this section four premium determination methods, which can be stated in terms of the models that incorporate expenses, are reviewed. The four methods are studied in an order related to increasing economic sophistication of the profit objective.

16.4.1 Natural Premiums

In determining the contract premium, a method called *the natural premium and reserve method* can be used to fix premiums and cash values in one coordinated process. The method starts with the calculation of a set of expense-loaded premiums and reserves using the single decrement model as is done in Table 15.2.4. The withdrawal benefits are then set equal to the total reserves, benefit plus expense reserves, and a profit component is added to the expense-loaded premium to produce a contract premium. The method relies on the fact that withdrawal benefits determined in this fashion will have a small impact on premiums and reserves determined within a double decrement model recognizing expenses. Of course, the resulting withdrawal benefits must be checked to confirm that they satisfy regulatory minimum values. The terms natural premiums and natural reserves have been used with a different meaning in some actuarial applications. Section 15.3 provides insights into this method.

16.4.2 Fund Objective

Formula (15.6.6) is described there as a general formula for an expense-loaded premium determined by the equivalence principle. The developments of Section 15.6.1 can be extended to provide a method for introducing an expected profit objective component to produce a contract premium.

In this extension, management sets an asset share goal, $K > {}_{20}V$, for instance. If expected expense and cash value obligations are known, (15.6.5) can be used to determine G, the contract premium, using the following development. Let a trial value of the contract premium, denoted by H, be selected arbitrarily, and let ${}_{20}AS$ be the result of using (15.6.5) with this H and $n = 20$:

$$
{}_{20}AS = \left\{ \sum_{h=1}^{20} [H(1 - c_{h-1}) - e_{h-1}]\, l_{x+h-1}^{(\tau)} (1 + i)^{21-h} \right.
$$

$$
\left. - (d_{x+h-1}^{(1)} + d_{x+h-1}^{(2)}\, {}_h CV) (1 + i)^{20-h} \right\} \Big/ l_{x+20}^{(\tau)}. \qquad (16.4.1)
$$

The fund goal is K, which should be the result of applying (16.4.1) with G replacing H. Then by subtraction,

$$
K - {}_{20}AS = \sum_{h=1}^{20} \frac{(G - H)(1 - c_{h-1}) l_{x+h-1}^{(\tau)}(1 + i)^{21-h}}{l_{x+20}^{(\tau)}},
$$

and the desired contract premium is given by

$$G = H + \frac{(K - {}_{20}AS)\ {}_{20}p_x^{(\tau)}\ v^{20}}{\sum\limits_{h=1}^{20} (1 - c_{h-1})\ {}_{h-1}p_x^{(\tau)}\ v^{h-1}}. \tag{16.4.2}$$

The effect of the second term in (16.4.2) is to produce a correction to the initial premium H that will cause the fund goal K to be reached in an actuarial present-value sense. The denominator of the second term can be interpreted as the actuarial present value of the increase in profit of a unit increase in the contract premiums.

16.4.3   Rate of Return Objective

Profit objectives in business are often stated in terms of a rate of return on the investment in the business. One view is that the principal investment made in creating an insurance enterprise is in developing a distribution system. An expected rate of return on the investment in the distribution system, in this view, can be expressed as a fraction of the actuarial present values of the sales commissions generated by the distribution system. In addition, this view also recognizes that because of the time incidence of expenses, the insurance enterprise must finance the acquisition expenses when a policy is issued, with the expectation that the policy will yield a future stream of returns.

To incorporate these ideas into a pricing method we start with the asset share model developed in Section 15.6. One necessary change is to separate the percentage expense term, $c_h = g_h + t_h$, where g_h is the commission rate paid and t_h combines other percentage expenses such as premium taxes.

In Table 15.3.4 the financial operations of a very small life insurance enterprise are traced assuming no deviations from expected results. The recursion relationship used to generate Tables 15.3.4 and 15.3.5 is closely related to asset share formula (15.6.7). We rewrite (15.6.7) assuming that after each year the difference ${}_hAS' - {}_hV$ is recognized as book profit or loss, to be denoted by ${}_hBP$, and the initial asset share for policy year $h + 1$ will be set as ${}_hV$. The symbol ${}_hV$ denotes a reserve liability fixed in advance. The prime has been added to the asset share symbol as a reminder that ${}_hBP$ is extracted from the expected fund progress as a profit.

Because ${}_hBP$ is measured at the end of the policy year for each insured who entered the year, we have

$$\begin{aligned}
{}_hBP = {}_hAS' - {}_hV = &\{[{}_{h-1}V + H(1 - g_{h-1} - t_{h-1}) - e_{h-1}](1 + i) \\
&- q_{x+h-1}^{(1)}(1 - {}_hV) - q_{x+h-1}^{(2)}({}_hCV - {}_hV)\} - {}_hV.
\end{aligned}$$

The book profits (${}_hBP$) are computed using an arbitrary initial premium H, which could be taken as the benefit premium; ${}_hBP$ can be negative. This is likely especially in early policy years.

The actuarial present values of book profits at the time of issue are given by

$$v_j^h\ {}_{h-1}p_x^{(\tau)}\ {}_hBP = v_j\ {}_{h-1}E_x^*\ {}_hBP \quad h = 1, 2, 3, \ldots$$

where v_j is valued at rate of interest j, the rate of return desired on the investment in new business. The asterisk has been added to the pure endowment symbol as a reminder that it is valued using a double decrement model and interest rate j.

For the initial choice of premium H, the actuarial present value at issue of book profits to the investor in the insurance enterprise is

$$Z = \sum_1^\infty v_{j\ h-1} E_x^* \ {}_h BP.$$

The actuarial present value at issue of future sales commissions based on the initial choice of premiums is

$$X = H \sum_{h=1}^\infty g_{h-1\ h-1} E_x^*,$$

and the actuarial present value at issue of increased book profits to the investor for each unit increase in premium H is

$$Y = \sum_{h=1}^\infty (1 - g_{h-1} - t_{h-1})(1 + i)v_{j\ h-1} E_x^*.$$

The quantity Y is closely related to the denominator in (16.4.2). The difference is that Y measures the impact of a unit change in premium over the entire policy period, while in (16.4.2), the impact is measured only for 20 years, at the end of which time a fund objective is to be met.

We let G, as before, denote the contract premium that meets the economic goal and assume that $G > H$. Two modified values are introduced. Let

$$Z' = Z + (G - H)Y \tag{16.4.3}$$

denote a modified value of the actuarial present value of book profits to the investor and

$$X' = \frac{G}{H} X \tag{16.4.4}$$

denote a modified value of the actuarial present value of future sales commissions.

The economic goal can be described as

$$Z' = bX' \tag{16.4.5}$$

where b is the required profit rate on the investment in the distribution system. Then, from (16.4.3)

$$(G - H)Y = Z' - Z$$

and using (16.4.4) and (16.4.5), we have

$$Z + (G - H)Y = bX' = b\frac{G}{H} X. \tag{16.4.6}$$

Formula (16.4.6) has an economic interpretation. The right-hand side of the equation states the economic goal. The left-hand side has two terms. The first term (Z)

is the actuarial present value of book profits with the initial choice of contract premium H. The second term, $(G - H)Y$, is the increase in the actuarial present value of book profits from increasing the contract premium by $G - H$.

Solving (16.4.6) for G yields

$$G = \frac{H^2Y - HZ}{HY - bX},$$

which will meet the rate of return requirement j on investment in new business and the profit rate on commissions b, which is related to the investment in the distribution system.

16.4.4 Risk-Based Objectives

Another justification of profit loadings is that the investor should be compensated directly for accepting risks. As in Section 15.3, let $_0L_e$ denote the expense augmented loss variable at issue associated with an insurance policy in a double decrement model. Then $\text{Var}(_0L_e)$ and $\sqrt{\text{Var}(_0L_e)}$ would be possible measures of the risk associated with the policy. Let the expense-loaded premium determined by the equivalence principle be denoted by P'. The contract premium, with a risk-adjusted profit loading, might be

$$P' + c\,\text{Var}(_0L_e) \qquad c > 0 \qquad\qquad (16.4.7)$$

or

$$P' + k\,\sqrt{\text{Var}(_0L_e)} \qquad k > 0. \qquad\qquad (16.4.8)$$

The premium in (16.4.7) involves the **variance premium principle,** and (16.4.8) involves the **standard deviation premium principle.**

$\text{Var}(_0L_e)$ measures the risk resulting from the uncertainty of the time and the cause of decrement. Because of the importance of investment rate risk in long-term insurances, some actuaries would either limit the application of the variance or standard deviation premium principles to short-term policies or incorporate random interest into the loss variables.

If c and k are both constant, then the standard deviation premium principle has the appeal that both the expense-loaded premium and the contract premium are in the same monetary units. If, however, c is a function of the risk in terms of (monetary unit)$^{-1}$, then the expense-loaded premium and the contract premium are both in the same monetary units under the variance premium principle.

An appealing property of the variance premium principle can be demonstrated by considering two independent expense-augmented loss variables, denoted by $_0L_e(1)$ and $_0L_e(2)$. Then,

$$c\,\text{Var}[_0L_e(1) + _0L_e(2)] = c\,\text{Var}[_0L_e(1)] + c\,\text{Var}[_0L_e(2)]. \qquad (16.4.9)$$

On the other hand,

$$k \sqrt{\text{Var}[_0L_e(1)] + \text{Var}[_0L_e(2)]} < k \sqrt{\text{Var}[_0L_e(1)]} + k \sqrt{\text{Var}[_0L_e(2)]}.$$

The relationship in (16.4.9) is called the **additive property** of the variance premium principle. The additive property means that the premium for a sum of independent risks is the sum of their individual premiums. The profit and contingencies loading for a collection of independent policies is the sum of the loadings for the individual policies. Exercise 16.11 shows that a simple proportional profit and contingencies loading also has the additive property.

Example 16.4.1

Use the results in Table 15.3.2 to determine contract premiums by (a) the variance principle with $c = 0.05$ and (b) the standard deviation principle with $k = 1.0$.

Solution:

a. $332.96 + 0.05(224.25) = 344.17$
b. $332.96 + 1.0 \sqrt{224.25} = 347.93$. ▼

16.5 Experience Adjustments

The set of asset shares as computed using (15.6.7), before a block of policies is issued, will almost certainly not equal the assets per surviving insured developed by experience. Nevertheless, the formulas of Section 15.6 can be used to gain insights into sources of financial gain or loss, measured with respect to expected results. Suppose that we trace the progress of $_kAS$ to $_{k+1}\widehat{AS}$ where the hat (circumflex) indicates that the $(k + 1)$-st asset share is derived from the expected k-th asset share using experience cost factors. A cost factor based on experience will have a hat added. In particular, $\hat{i}_{k+1}$ is the experience interest rate earned over the $(k + 1)$-st policy year. The experience asset share will be given by

$$_{k+1}\widehat{AS} = [_kAS + G(1 - \hat{c}_k) - \hat{e}_k](1 + \hat{i}_{k+1}) - \hat{q}^{(1)}_{x+k} (1 - {_{k+1}\widehat{AS}})$$

$$- \hat{q}^{(2)}_{x+k} (_{k+1}CV - {_{k+1}\widehat{AS}}). \qquad (16.5.1)$$

Subtracting (15.6.7), which traced the expected progress of the asset share, from (16.5.1) yields

a. $_{k+1}\widehat{AS} - {_{k+1}AS} = (_kAS + G)(\hat{i}_{k+1} - i)$

b. $\qquad\qquad + [(G\, c_k + e_k)(1 + i) - (G\, \hat{c}_k + \hat{e}_k)(1 + \hat{i}_{k+1})]$

c. $\qquad\qquad + [q^{(1)}_{x+k} (1 - {_{k+1}AS}) - \hat{q}^{(1)}_{x+k} (1 - {_{k+1}\widehat{AS}})]$

d. $\qquad\qquad + [q^{(2)}_{x+k} (_{k+1}CV - {_{k+1}AS}) - \hat{q}^{(2)}_{x+k} (_{k+1}CV - {_{k+1}\widehat{AS}})].$
$$(16.5.2)$$

In (16.5.2) the total deviation between the experience asset share and the expected asset share has been allocated into four components. Component (a) is associated with the deviation between the experience and the assumed interest rates. Component (b) is the difference between experience expenses and expected expenses, with an interest adjustment. Component (c) is the difference between assumed and experience mortality costs, and component (d) is the difference between assumed and experience withdrawal costs.

Participating life insurance is based on the principle that premiums are set at a level such that the probability is very low that premiums and associated investment income will be insufficient to fulfill the benefit and expense commitments implicit in the issuance of a block of policies. Under this principle, which can be viewed as an alternative to the equivalence principle, the expected value of a loss variable should be negative to generate financial margins to provide for deviations in experience unfavorable to the insurance system. As the uncertainty about experience is removed by the passage of time, the margins for adverse deviations built into the original price-benefit structure can be released and returned to the policyholders who, through higher premiums, carried the risks. These returns of funds not needed to match future risks are called *dividends*. A simplified version of (16.5.2) is used frequently in the analysis that leads to the determination of dividends.

For the simplified version, we start with a modification of (15.6.7). In this development $_kF$ will take the place of $_kAS$. The new symbol denotes a fund share that is no longer a consequence of the expected operation of the insurance system. Instead, the values of $_kF$ are amounts set in advance such that, with future premium and investment income, the block of policies under consideration has a high probability of meeting its benefit and expense obligations. Thus,

$$_{k+1}F = [_kF + G(1 - c_k) - e_k](1 + i) - q^{(1)}_{x+k}(1 - {}_{k+1}F)$$

$$- q^{(2)}_{x+k}({}_{k+1}CV - {}_{k+1}F). \qquad (16.5.3)$$

In (16.5.3), c_k, e_k, $q^{(1)}_{x+k}$, and $q^{(2)}_{x+k}$ are typically set at levels somewhat higher than expected, and i is set at a level somewhat lower than expected in order to provide margins to cover adverse deviations. These margins result in a small probability of a need for outside funds.

Formula (16.5.4) describes the fund share progress for a unit of insurance where experience cost factors are denoted with hats; that is,

$$_{k+1}F + {}_{k+1}D = [_kF + G(1 - \hat{c}_k) - \hat{e}_k](1 + \hat{i}_{k+1})$$

$$- \hat{q}^{(1)}_{x+k}(1 - {}_{k+1}F - {}_{k+1}D)$$

$$- \hat{q}^{(2)}_{x+k}({}_{k+1}CV - {}_{k+1}F - {}_{k+1}D). \qquad (16.5.4)$$

In (16.5.4) the dividend is denoted by $_{k+1}D$; it is the difference between the predetermined goal of $_{k+1}F$ and the fund share generated by experience. Subtracting (16.5.3) from (16.5.4) yields

a. $_{k+1}D = (_kF + G)(\hat{i}_{k+1} - i)$

b. $\quad + [(G c_k + e_k)(1 + i) - (G \hat{c}_k + \hat{e}_k)(1 + \hat{i}_{k+1})]$

c. $\quad + (1 - _{k+1}F)(q^{(1)}_{x+k} - \hat{q}^{(1)}_{x+k})$

d. $\quad + (_{k+1}CV - _{k+1}F)(q^{(2)}_{x+k} - \hat{q}^{(2)}_{x+k})$

e. $\quad + _{k+1}D \, (\hat{q}^{(1)}_{x+k} + \hat{q}^{(2)}_{x+k}).$ (16.5.5)

The components of (16.5.5) may be identified with experience factors that determine their size. Thus, (a) is associated with interest, (b) with expenses, (c) with mortality, (d) with voluntary terminations, and (e) with the payment of dividends only to survivors. If $_{k+1}CV = _{k+1}F$ and dividends are paid to insureds who die and to insureds who withdraw, and if $G c_k + e_k$ is denoted by E_k whereas $G \hat{c}_k + \hat{e}_k$ is denoted by $\hat{E}_k$, then (16.5.5) can be written in a three-term form,

$$_{k+1}D = (_kF + G)(\hat{i}_{k+1} - i)$$
$$+ [E_k(1 + i) - \hat{E}_k(1 + \hat{i}_{k+1})]$$
$$+ (1 - _{k+1}F)(q^{(1)}_{x+k} - \hat{q}^{(1)}_{x+k}).$$ (16.5.6)

Example 16.5.1

In Example 15.6.1 a set of asset shares was computed for the 3-year annual level premium endowment insurance. Recall that the example was designed for convenience and ease of calculation rather than realism. Make the following assumptions about experience:

$$_0F = _0AS = 0$$
$$_1F = _1AS = 229.44$$
$$_2F = _2AS = 589.47$$
$$\hat{i}_1 = 0.15, \; \hat{i}_2 = 0.16$$
$$\hat{q}^{(1)}_x = 0.085, \; \hat{q}^{(2)}_x = 0.200$$
$$\hat{q}^{(1)}_{x+1} = 0.090, \; \hat{q}^{(2)}_x = 0.100$$
$$c_k = \hat{c}_k, \quad \text{for } k = 0, 1, \text{ and } 2$$
$$\hat{e}_0 = 10, \; \hat{e}_1 = 1.$$

Calculate $_1D$ and $_2D$ using (16.5.5), assuming that dividends are paid to those who die or withdraw.

Solution:

	$_1D$	$_2D$
(a) Interest $({}_kF + G)(\hat{i} - i)$	$(0 + 342.96)(0)$	$(299.44 + 342.96)(0.01)$
	$+$	$+$
(b) Expenses $(G\, c_k + e_k)(1 + i) -$ $(G\, \hat{c}_k + \hat{e}_k)(1 + \hat{i}_{k+1})$	$[342.96(0.20) + 8](1.15)$ $- [342.96(0.20) + 10](1.15)$	$[342.96(0.06) + 2](1.15)$ $- [342.96(0.06) + 1](1.16)$
	$+$	$+$
(c) Mortality $[1,000 - {}_{k+1}F]$ $(q^{(1)}_{x+k} - \hat{q}^{(1)}_{x+k})$	$[1,000 - 229.44](0.015)$	$[1,000 - 589.47](0.0211)$
	$+$	$+$
(d) Withdrawal $[{}_{k+1}CV - {}_{k+1}F]$ $(q^{(2)}_{x+k} - \hat{q}^{(2)}_{x+k})$	$[227.73 - 229.44](-0.1)$	$[564.41 - 589.47]$ $\times (0.0111)$
(a)	0.0000	5.7240
(b)	−2.3000	0.9342
(c)	11.5584	8.6623
(d)	0.1708	−0.2781
Total	9.4292	15.0424

▼

16.6 Modified Reserve Methods

Two salient ideas about financial reporting for life insurance enterprises are indicated in the extended illustrations developed in Sections 15.2.2 and 15.3.2. The first of these ideas is that cash flows, and thus economic gains, are not affected by the method selected for reporting liabilities. The second is that using reserves derived from a multiple decrement model and incorporating expenses results in a more level stream of reported annual net income than when single decrement benefit reserves are used.

In Section 16.1 it was pointed out that single decrement approximations to more comprehensive multiple decrement models incorporating expenses are frequently used, especially for regulatory purposes. In this section the use of such an approximation for financial reporting will be developed.

A general fully discrete insurance on (x) is introduced by way of (8.2.1). Later in Chapter 8 it was shown that for a fixed schedule of death benefits, it is not necessary to determine a sequence of constant benefit premiums to define the corresponding benefit reserves by the equivalence principle. Nevertheless, regulatory or economic restrictions, such as ${}_kV \geq 0$, may make some sequences of nonconstant benefit premiums infeasible. Other examples of such restrictions might be the requirement that the benefit premium used for reserve purposes be less than or equal to the contract premium and, except for the first policy year, the benefit premium be a fixed proportion of the contract premium.

For insurance policies that provide for constant benefits and constant benefit premiums, a system of notation and nomenclature has been developed to define modified reserve systems with nonconstant benefit premiums that provide a more realistic matching of premium reserves and related expenses. These modified reserve systems are constructed using a single decrement model under the assumption that nonforfeiture values have been determined so as to minimize the gains and losses due to withdrawals.

A modified reserve method is one that does not use the actuarial present value of a set of level benefit premiums as a deduction from the actuarial present value of future benefits in defining reserves. Instead, a sequence of **step premiums** is defined. Usually no more than three different levels are involved, although the theory would permit more steps in the path. The three premium levels are denoted by α, the first-year benefit premium; β, the benefit premium for the next $j - 1$ years; and P, the level benefit premium assumed payable beyond the first j policy years. This set of premiums is constrained to have the same actuarial present value as the set of level benefit premiums so that

$$\alpha + \beta\,(\ddot{a}_{x:\overline{j}|} - 1) + P\,(\ddot{a}_{x:\overline{h}|} - \ddot{a}_{x:\overline{j}|}) = P\,\ddot{a}_{x:\overline{h}|},$$

$$\alpha + \beta\,a_{x:\overline{j-1}|} = P\,\ddot{a}_{x:\overline{j}|} \tag{16.6.1}$$

where h is the length of the premium paying period.

In the notation of Section 15.5 for level benefit premium reserves, amount c is expected to be available in the first policy year. This comes from a loaded premium of $P + c$ to offset first-year expenses. If $\alpha < P$, then $P + c - \alpha > c$ will be expected to be available, within the modified reserve accounting method, to match first-year expenses. If $\alpha < P$, a consequence is that $\beta > P$. This can be seen by rewriting (16.6.1) as

$$\alpha + \beta\,a_{x:\overline{j-1}|} = P(a_{x:\overline{j-1}|} + 1),$$

$$\beta = P + \frac{P - \alpha}{a_{x:\overline{j-1}|}}. \tag{16.6.2}$$

A second useful expression can be obtained from (16.6.1) as follows:

$$\beta(\ddot{a}_{x:\overline{j}|} - 1) = P\,\ddot{a}_{x:\overline{j}|} - \alpha,$$

$$\beta = P + \frac{\beta - \alpha}{\ddot{a}_{x:\overline{j}|}}. \tag{16.6.3}$$

Thus a modified reserve method for policies with constant benefits and premiums can be defined by specifying the length of the modification period j and either the first-year premium α, the renewal premium β, or the difference $\beta - \alpha$. Figure 16.6.1 provides a schematic diagram summarizing the relationship among the premiums making up a modified reserve method. The actuarial present value at issue of the premium components depicted by the shaded areas A and B are equal as can be seen from (16.6.1) rearranged as $P - \alpha = (\beta - P)a_{x:\overline{j-1}|}$.

FIGURE 16.6.1

Premiums in a Modified Reserve Method

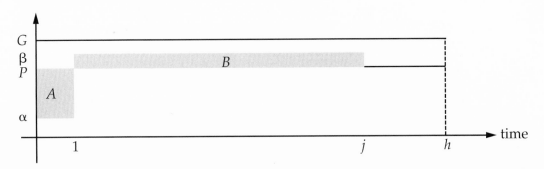

In (16.6.1) and (16.6.2) we use the symbols α and β to denote, respectively, the first-year and renewal benefit premiums for a j-year modified reserve method and P to denote the general symbol for the level benefit premium. In a similar fashion we use the symbol V^{Mod} to denote a terminal reserve computed by a modified method.

The following formula is used to calculate terminal reserves in the fully discrete case of an h-payment, n-year endowment insurance under a modified reserve method with a j-year modification period. During the modification period, $k < j$,

$$_k^h V_{x:\overline{n}|}^{Mod} = A_{x+k:\overline{n-k}|} - \beta \ddot{a}_{x+k:\overline{j-k}|} - {_hP}_{x:\overline{n}|} \, _{j-k|}\ddot{a}_{x+k:\overline{h-j}|}$$

$$= A_{x+k:\overline{n-k}|} - {_hP}_{x:\overline{n}|} \, \ddot{a}_{x+k:\overline{h-k}|} - (\beta - {_hP}_{x:\overline{n}|}) \ddot{a}_{x+k:\overline{j-k}|}$$

$$= {_k^h V}_{x:\overline{n}|} - (\beta - {_hP}_{x:\overline{n}|}) \ddot{a}_{x+k:\overline{j-k}|} \, .$$

The results of Chapter 8 for a general fully discrete insurance apply to a modified reserve system as described in this section. In (8.2.1), the correspondence is $b_{K(x)+1} = 1$, $\pi_0 = \alpha$, $\pi_h = \beta$, $h = 1, 2, \ldots$. This means that Theorem 8.5.1 holds for modified benefit reserves and can be used in risk management decisions.

After duration j, reserves under the modified reserve method are equal to those under the level benefit premium method.

Example 16.6.1

Whole life insurances, on a fully continuous basis, are to have reserves determined by a modified reserve method. Under this method, the first-year and renewal benefit premium rates are $\bar{\alpha}_x$ and $\bar{\beta}_x$, $\bar{\alpha}_x < \bar{P}(\bar{A}_x)$; the modification period is the entire policy period. Define the future loss variable and write equations that may be used to evaluate reserves.

Solution:

$$_tL^{Mod} = \begin{cases} v^{T(x)-t} - \bar{\alpha}_x \, \bar{a}_{\overline{T(x)-t}|} & 0 \le T(x) - t < 1 - t \\ v^{T(x)-t} - \bar{\alpha}_x \, \bar{a}_{\overline{1-t}|} - \bar{\beta}_x \,_{1-t|}\bar{a}_{\overline{(T(x)-t)-(1-t)}|} & T(x) - T \ge 1 - t \\ v^{T(x)-t} - \bar{\beta}_x \, \bar{a}_{\overline{T(x)-t}|} & \end{cases} \left.\begin{matrix} \\ \\ \\ \end{matrix}\right\} \begin{matrix} 0 \le t < 1 \\ \\ t \ge 1. \end{matrix}$$

By analogy with (7.2.3), the reserve is

$$_t\bar{V}(\bar{A}_x)^{Mod} = \begin{cases} \bar{A}_{x+t} - \bar{\alpha}_x \, \bar{a}_{x+t:\overline{1-t}|} - \bar{\beta}_x \,_{1-t|}\bar{a}_{x+t} & 0 \le t < 1 \\ \bar{A}_{x+t} - \bar{\beta}_x \, \bar{a}_{x+t} & t \ge 1. \end{cases}$$

In addition,

$$_t\bar{V}(\bar{A}_x) - _t\bar{V}(\bar{A}_x)^{Mod} = [\bar{\beta}_x - \bar{P}(\bar{A}_x)] \, \bar{a}_{x+t} \qquad t \ge 1.$$

Since we require that

$$\bar{\alpha}_x \, \bar{a}_{x:\overline{1}|} + \bar{\beta}_x \,_{1|}\bar{a}_x = \bar{P}(\bar{A}_x)(\bar{a}_{x:\overline{1}|} + _{1|}\bar{a}_x), \tag{16.6.4}$$

we have, similar to (16.6.2),

$$\bar{\beta}_x = \bar{P}(\bar{A}_x) + \frac{[\bar{P}(\bar{A}_x) - \bar{\alpha}_x] \, \bar{a}_{x:\overline{1}|}}{_{1|}\bar{a}_x}$$

and

$$\bar{\beta}_x > \bar{P}(\bar{A}_x).$$

Therefore,

$$_t\bar{V}(\bar{A}_x) - _t\bar{V}(\bar{A}_x)^{Mod} \ge 0 \qquad t \ge 1. \qquad \blacktriangledown$$

Example 16.6.2

Using the information given in Example 16.6.1, derive a retrospective formula for $_t\bar{V}(\bar{A}_x)^{Mod}$.

Solution:

Consider the case where $0 \le t < 1$ and recall that

$$\bar{A}_x = \bar{\alpha}_x \, \bar{a}_{x:\overline{1}|} + \bar{\beta}_x \,_{1|}\bar{a}_x$$

$$= \bar{\alpha}_x (\bar{a}_{x:\overline{t}|} + \bar{a}_{x+t:\overline{1-t}|} \,_tE_x) + \bar{\beta}_x (_{1-t|}\bar{a}_{x+t} \,_tE_x).$$

Then, using notation from Section 7.3, we have

$$_t\bar{V}(\bar{A}_x)^{Mod} = \bar{A}_{x+t} - \bar{\alpha}_x \, \bar{a}_{x+t:\overline{1-t}|} - \bar{\beta}_x \,_{1-t|}\bar{a}_{x+t}$$

$$= \bar{A}_{x+t} - \frac{\bar{A}_x - \bar{\alpha}_x \, \bar{a}_{x:\overline{t}|}}{_tE_x} \qquad 0 \le t < 1$$

$$= \bar{\alpha}_x \, \bar{s}_{x:\overline{t}|} - _t\bar{k}_x.$$

In addition,

$$_t\bar{V}(\bar{A}_x) - _t\bar{V}(\bar{A}_x)^{Mod} = [\bar{P}(\bar{A}_x) - \bar{\alpha}_x] \, \bar{s}_{x:\overline{t}|} \qquad 0 \le t < 1.$$

In the case $t \ge 1$, we recall that

$$\bar{A}_x = \bar{\alpha}_x \, \bar{a}_{x:\overline{1}|} + \bar{\beta}_x (_{1|}\bar{a}_{x:\overline{t-1}|} + \bar{a}_{x+t} \,_tE_x).$$

Then

$$_t\bar{V}(\bar{A}_x)^{Mod} = \bar{A}_{x+t} - \bar{\beta}_x\,\bar{a}_{x+t}$$

$$= \bar{A}_{x+t} - \frac{\bar{A}_x - \bar{\alpha}_x\,\bar{a}_{x:\bar{1}|} - \bar{\beta}_x\,{}_{1|}\bar{a}_{x:\overline{t-1}|}}{{}_tE_x}.$$

$$= \frac{\bar{\alpha}_x\,\bar{a}_{x:\bar{1}|}}{{}_tE_x} + \bar{\beta}_x\,\bar{s}_{x+1:\overline{t-1}|} - \bar{k}_x.$$

▼

16.7   Full Preliminary Term

In order to develop a reserve method that increases the effective expense loading, $G - \alpha$, in the first policy year to better match the large first-year expenses, α is usually constrained to be less than P. However, in accordance with certain regulatory principles, there is a practical lower bound on the value of α.

This lower bound is derived from the recognition that negative reserve liabilities are effectively accounting assets. Since the collection of future contract premiums is uncertain, some regulatory agencies have not permitted such negative reserves to be included in the balance sheet in statutory assessment of insurance company solvency. Thus a practical objective of the reserve method is to avoid a negative reserve at the end of the first policy year. This means that, for a level unit benefit policy, the smallest feasible value of α will be $A^1_{x:\bar{1}|}$ on the fully discrete basis. This requirement was applied in Example 8.2.1. The result may be seen as follows:

$$_1V \geq 0,$$

$$\alpha\,\ddot{s}_{x:\bar{1}|} - {}_1k_x \geq 0, \tag{16.7.1}$$

$$\alpha \geq A^1_{x:\bar{1}|}.$$

If α is set at the minimum level and the modification period, j, is the entire premium paying period, the resulting method is called the *full preliminary term (FPT)* method. Under the *FPT* method, the reserve at the end of the first policy year is 0.

For this fully discrete basis, the renewal valuation premium β may be obtained from (16.6.1) by substituting for a general h-payment level premium insurance with actuarial present value denoted by A; that is, let $A(1)$ denote the actuarial present value for an insurance issued at age $x + 1$ for the benefits remaining thereafter. Then

$$A^1_{x:\bar{1}|} + \beta\,{}_{1|}\ddot{a}_{x:\overline{h-1}|} = P\,\ddot{a}_{x:\bar{h}|}$$

$$= A$$

$$= A^1_{x:\bar{1}|} + {}_1E_x\,A(1) \tag{16.7.2}$$

or

$$\beta = \frac{{}_1E_x\,A(1)}{{}_{1|}\ddot{a}_{x:\overline{h-1}|}} = \frac{A(1)}{\ddot{a}_{x+1:\overline{h-1}|}}.$$

In words, β is the annual benefit premium for a similar insurance issued at an age 1 year older, with premiums paid for 1 less year in the case of a limited premium paying period, and maturing at the same age as the original insurance.

For a fully continuous basis, the smallest feasible value for the first-year premium rate, $\bar{\alpha}$, is $\bar{A}^1_{x:\overline{1}|}/\bar{a}_{x:\overline{1}|}$, again based on avoiding a negative terminal reserve at time 1. That is,

$$_1\bar{V}(\bar{A}_x) \geq 0,$$

$$\frac{\bar{\alpha}\,\bar{a}_{x:\overline{1}|}}{_1E_x} - {_1\bar{k}_x} \geq 0, \tag{16.7.3}$$

$$\bar{\alpha} \geq \frac{\bar{A}^1_{x:\overline{1}|}}{\bar{a}_{x:\overline{1}|}}.$$

The development for the renewal premium rate, $\bar{\beta}$, corresponds closely with the development of (16.7.2) above:

$$\bar{A}^1_{x:\overline{1}|} + \bar{\beta}_{1|}\bar{a}_{x:\overline{h-1}|} = \bar{P}(\bar{A})\,\bar{a}_{x:\overline{h}|}$$

$$= \bar{A}$$

$$= \bar{A}^1_{x:\overline{1}|} + {_1E_x}\,\bar{A}(1) \tag{16.7.4}$$

or

$$\bar{\beta} = \frac{_1E_x\,\bar{A}(1)}{_{1|}\bar{a}_{x:\overline{h-1}|}} = \frac{\bar{A}(1)}{\bar{a}_{x+1:\overline{h-1}|}}.$$

The effect of the *FPT* method on accounting statements can be demonstrated by modifying (15.5.5). We note that expense-loaded premiums under *FPT* are given by

$$P_x + c = A^1_{x:\overline{1}|} + c_0 = \beta_x + c_1$$

where c_0 is the loading in the first year and c_1 is the loading in renewal years. The analogue of (15.5.5) where, as before, $u(k)$ denotes the anticipated surplus for each expected surviving insured at end of accounting period k is, for $u(0) = 0$,

$$[(A^1_{x:\overline{1}|} + c_0) - e_0](1 + i) - q_x = p_x\,u(1)$$

$$(c_0 - e_0)(1 + i) = p_x\,u(1) \qquad k = 0, \tag{16.7.5A}$$

$$_kp_x\{[_kV^{FPT}_x + u(k)] + (\beta_x + c_1) - e_k\}\,(1 + i) - {_kp_x}\,q_{x+k}$$

$$= {_{k+1}p_x}\,[_{k+1}V^{FPT}_x + u(k + 1)] \qquad k = 1, 2, \ldots. \tag{16.7.5B}$$

Therefore, if

$$c_0 - e_0 = (P_x + c - A^1_{x:\overline{1}|} - e_0) > 0,$$

the first-year surplus in our idealized accounting illustration will be positive. In realistic situations,

$$c_0 = P_x + c - A^1_{x:\overline{1}|} > c$$

and $p_x\, u(1)$ will be greater than when liabilities are measured by level benefit premium reserves.

The recursion formulas, analogous to (8.3.10), are

$$A^1_{x:\overline{1}|}(1 + i) - q_x = 0 \tag{16.7.6A}$$

and

$$_kp_x({_kV^{FPT}_x} + \beta_x)(1 + i) - {_kp_x}\, q_{x+k} = {_{k+1}p_x}\, {_{k+1}V^{FPT}_x}. \tag{16.7.6B}$$

Subtracting (16.7.6B) from (16.7.5B) we obtain

$$_kp_x\, [u(k) + c_1 - e_k](1 + i) = {_{k+1}p_x}\, u(k + 1) \quad k = 1, 2, 3, \ldots. \tag{16.7.7}$$

Multiply (16.7.5A) and (16.7.7) by v^{k+1}, let $c'_k = c_0$ when $k = 0$ and $c'_k = c_1$ when $k = 1, 2, \ldots$, and we get

$$\Delta[v^k\, {_kp_x}\, u(k)] = v^k\, {_kp_x}\, (c'_k - e_k). \tag{16.7.8}$$

With $u(0) = 0$, difference equation (16.7.8) yields

$$\sum_{j=0}^{k-1} \Delta[v^j\, {_jp_x}\, u(j)] = \sum_{j=0}^{k-1} v^j\, {_jp_x}\, (c'_j - e_j), \tag{16.7.9}$$

$$_kp_x\, u(k) = \sum_{j=0}^{k-1} (1 + i)^{k-j}\, {_jp_x}\, (c'_j - e_j). \tag{16.7.10}$$

As in (15.5.8), the expected surplus for each initial insured in our idealized model is the accumulated value of the excess of loadings over expenses in each earlier year. The following comparisons of the annual expected contributions to surplus for each surviving insured in the cases of *FPT* reserves and of **level benefit premium (LBP)** reserves may be developed using (15.5.7) and (16.7.8).

FPT		LBP	
$c_0 - e_0$	$>$	$c - e_0$	
$c_1 - e_k$	$<$	$c - e_k$	$k = 1, 2, \ldots$	(16.7.11)

The inequalities displayed in (16.7.11) for the expected contributions to surplus are valid when $\alpha < P$ and $\beta > P$.

16.8   Modified Preliminary Term

If we adopt the principle that negative reserve liabilities are inappropriate on the balance sheet of an insurance enterprise, the *FPT* reserve method provides a minimum first-year terminal reserve and minimum first-year premium. According to (16.7.11), the annual surplus contributions in the first year under *FPT* and *LBP* are

$$\overset{FPT}{\overbrace{\qquad}}\quad\overset{LBP}{\overbrace{\qquad}}$$
$$P + c - A^1_{x:\overline{1}|} - e_0 = c_0 - e_0 > c - e_0.$$

A difficulty arises in that the magnitude of $P - A^1_{x:\overline{1}|}$ depends on the plan of insurance. Since $P_{x:\overline{n}|}$ is normally much greater than $P^1_{x:\overline{n}|}$, the expense margin to be used to offset first-year expenses will also be much greater for an n-year endowment insurance than for an n-year term insurance. One school of thought holds that if $P - A^1_{x:\overline{1}|}$ provides an acceptable expense margin for low-premium policies, it provides an excessive margin for high-premium policies. Under this line of reasoning, low-premium policies may be valued satisfactorily under the *FPT* method, but high-premium policies should use a modified reserve method that will produce a positive first-year terminal reserve.

A ***modified preliminary term reserve standard*** requires: (1) A decision rule by which policies are separated into low- and high-premium classes. (2) That for low-premium policies the *FPT* method, which specifies $\alpha = A^1_{x:\overline{1}|}$, is permitted. (3) A definition of a valuation method for high-premium policies by specifying β, $\beta - \alpha$, or an $\alpha > A^1_{x:\overline{1}|}$ and the length of the modification period.

An objective of government regulation is to reduce the threat to insureds that an insurance company cannot meet its obligations. In accordance with this objective, in some jurisdictions, an actuary is designated to have the responsibility to determine that reserves make adequate provision for future obligations for an insurance enterprise.

In other jurisdictions laws and regulations limit the choice of the methods and assumptions that may be used to estimate reserve liabilities for regulatory purposes. In some cases these laws and regulations define a modified reserve standard. Only one such standard remains of direct interest to actuaries practicing in the United States. The Standard Valuation Law defines the Commissioners Reserve Valuation Standard for life insurance. The elements of this standard are that
- High-premium policies are defined as those for which $\beta^{FPT} > {}_{19}P_{x+1}$, the *FPT* renewal benefit premium for a 20-payment life
- The *FPT* method is a minimum for low-premium policies
- A specific Commissioners Reserve Valuation Method (CRVM) be used for high-premium policies. Here the premium payment period is the modification period and

$$\beta^{CRVM} - \alpha^{CRVM} = {}_{19}P_{x+1} - A^1_{x:\overline{1}|}.$$

An application of (16.6.3) yields

$$\beta^{CRVM} = P + \frac{{}_{19}P_{x+1} - A^1_{x:\overline{1}|}}{\ddot{a}_{x:\overline{h}|}} \tag{16.8.1}$$

where h is the length of the premium paying period.

The decision flowchart implicit in a modified preliminary term standard, illustrated by the Commissioners Reserve Valuation Standard, is displayed in Figure 16.8.1.

FIGURE 16.8.1

Modified Preliminary Term Decision Flowchart

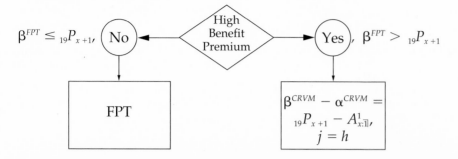

16.9 Nonlevel Premiums or Benefits

Section 16.2 covers the development of a single decrement model with arbitrary assumptions about the level of expenses and their time incidence for defining minimum cash values. In Section 16.8 a related development is done for the purposes of defining minimum reserves for financial reporting to regulators. In both of these sections the developments were limited to level premiums and benefits. The statutes supporting minimum reserve and minimum cash value regulation have typically contained specific provisions for level premium and benefit policies. Because of the limitless variation that can exist in schedules of premiums and benefits that are not level, the interpretations needed to apply the principles of the statutes have been left to regulators and professional judgment. The job is to take statutory and contractual language and to produce a mathematical model that is consistent with the intent of the language. This type of endeavor is typical of many actuarial assignments.

The main tool in adapting regulations designed for level death benefit and level contract premium policies to policies with nonlevel premiums or benefits is that of averaging. A sequence of nonlevel premiums or benefits will be replaced by a level sequence made up of weighted average premiums or benefits, respectively. The methods of adapting regulations for nonconstant premiums or benefits will differ by the weights used in the averaging.

16.9.1 Valuation

In Section 8.2 a general insurance, using a fully discrete basis, is discussed. This general insurance will be used to illustrate the problem. Recall that, under the insurance, a death benefit b_{j+1} is paid at the end of policy year $j + 1$ if death has occurred in that year. Annual premiums are payable, contingent on survival, at the beginning of each policy year during the premium period. The contract premium G_j is paid at time j, the beginning of policy year $j + 1$.

We describe here the interpretation by Menge (1946) for applying the Commissioners Reserve Valuation Standard to this general insurance. Formulas are given

---

for a term insurance with a description of the modifications for an endowment insurance. These rules are directly applicable to insurance policies with schedules of benefits and premiums. Policies providing for benefits or premiums that are tied to investment performance, or that can be changed at the election of the owner of the policy, require special consideration.

The first task is to determine the criterion for using *FPT*. As a first step, we calculate an ***equivalent level renewal amount (ELRA)***. For this insurance we have

$$ELRA = \frac{\sum_{j=0}^{n-2} b_{j+2}\, v^{j+1}\, {}_{j}p_{x+1}\, q_{x+1+j}}{A^{1}_{x+1:\overline{n-1}|}}. \tag{16.9.1}$$

The *ELRA* for an endowment insurance is calculated on the basis of the death benefits only and is thus also given by (16.9.1). *ELRA* can be interpreted as a weighted average benefit amount with weight

$$v^{j+1}\, \frac{{}_{j}p_{x+1}\, q_{x+1+j}}{A^{1}_{x+1:\overline{n-1}|}}.$$

In addition, the average ratio of renewal benefit premiums to renewal contract premiums is denoted by r_F and is determined by

$$r_F = \frac{\sum_{j=0}^{n-2} b_{j+2}\, v^{j+1}\, {}_{j}p_{x+1}\, q_{x+1+j}}{\sum_{j=0}^{h-2} G_{j+1}\, v^{j}\, {}_{j}p_{x+1}}. \tag{16.9.2}$$

The Menge interpretation depends on the assumption that the valuation premium is a constant fraction of the contract premium.

For endowment insurances, pure endowment benefits are included in the numerator for r_F.

Under the Menge interpretation, *FPT* is allowed if

$$r_F\, G_0 \le ELRA\, {}_{19}P_{x+1}. \tag{16.9.3}$$

If this condition is satisfied, *FPT* is interpreted as involving benefit premiums $\pi_0 = vb_1q_x$ and $\pi_j = r_F G_j$, $j = 1, 2, \ldots, h - 1$, where h is the length of the premium paying period. The modified reserve, for $k \ge 1$, is given by

$$_{k}V^{Mod} = \sum_{j=0}^{n-k-1} b_{k+j+1}\, v^{j+1}\, {}_{j}p_{x+k}\, q_{x+k+j} - r_F \sum_{j=0}^{h-k-1} G_{k+j}\, v^{j}\, {}_{j}p_{x+k}. \tag{16.9.4}$$

For endowment insurances, pure endowment benefits are added to the first term of (16.9.4).

In cases where (16.9.3) is not satisfied, the excess first-year expense allowance, comparable to $\beta - \alpha$, is given by

$$ELRA\, {}_{19}P_{x+1} - b_1\, A^{1}_{x:\overline{1}|}.$$

A modified average ratio of benefit premiums to contract premiums, denoted by r_C, is determined as

$$r_C = \frac{\displaystyle\sum_{j=0}^{n-1} b_{j+1}\, v^{j+1}\, {}_j p_x\, q_{x+j} + (ELRA\, {}_{19}P_{x+1} - b_1\, A^1_{x:\overline{1}|})}{\displaystyle\sum_{j=0}^{h-1} G_j\, v^j\, {}_j p_x}. \tag{16.9.5}$$

The modified reserve in this high-premium case is given by

$$_kV^{Mod} = \sum_{j=0}^{n-k-1} b_{k+j+1}\, v^{j+1}\, {}_j p_{x+k}\, q_{x+k+j} - r_C \sum_{j=0}^{h-k-1} G_{k+j}\, v^j\, {}_j p_{x+k}. \tag{16.9.6}$$

For endowment insurances, the numerator of r_C in (16.9.5) and the right-hand side of (16.9.6) are adjusted to include pure endowment benefits.

Example 16.9.1

Calculate the annual benefit premiums under the Commissioners Reserve Valuation Standard for a special 30-year endowment policy issued at age 35. The benefit is 150,000 for the first 20 years and 100,000 thereafter with a maturity benefit of 100,000. The contract premium is a level 2,500 for 10 years and thereafter is 1,250. Use the Illustrative Life Table with $i = 0.06$.

Solution:

The *ELRA* is based on the death benefit and is calculated as

$$ELRA = 50,000 \left(\frac{2A^1_{36:\overline{29}|} + A^1_{36:\overline{19}|}}{A^1_{36:\overline{29}|}} \right)$$

$$= 130,153.30.$$

The r_F factor is given by

$$r_F = \frac{50,000}{1,250} \left(\frac{2A_{36:\overline{29}|} + A^1_{36:\overline{19}|}}{\ddot{a}_{36:\overline{29}|} + \ddot{a}_{36:\overline{9}|}} \right)$$

$$= 0.91014604$$

and

$$_{19}P_{36} = 0.0116543.$$

For *FPT* to apply, (16.9.3) must be satisfied. However, since

$$r_F\, G_0 = (0.91014604)(2,500) = 2,275.37 > 1,516.85 = ELRA\, {}_{19}P_{36},$$

FPT is not allowed. The excess first-year expense allowance, corresponding to $\beta - \alpha$, is given by

$$ELRA\, {}_{19}P_{x+1} - b_1\, A^1_{x:\overline{1}|} = 1,516.8456 - 284.9395 = 1,231.9061$$

and

$$r_C = \frac{50{,}000(2A_{36:\overline{29}|} + A^1_{36:\overline{19}|}) + 1{,}231.9061}{1{,}250(\ddot{a}_{36:\overline{29}|} + \ddot{a}_{36:\overline{9}|})}$$

$$= 0.88223578.$$

Thus the renewal benefit premiums are

$$r_C(2{,}500) = 2{,}205.59, \quad \text{years } 2, 3, \ldots, 10$$

$$r_C(1{,}250) = 1{,}102.79, \quad \text{years } 11, 12, \ldots, 30,$$

and the first-year benefit premium

$$= r_C(2{,}500) - 1{,}231.9061$$

$$= 973.68. \qquad \blacktriangledown$$

An alternative interpretation of the Commissioners Reserve Valuation Standard as it applies to policies with nonlevel death benefits is contained in Actuarial Guideline XVII developed by the National Association of Insurance Commissioners. These guidelines do not have the force of law in most states but are designed to serve as guides in applying statutes to specific circumstances.

The guideline first requires the calculation of the average of the death benefits at the ends of policy years 2 through 10. Let M denote the average value; that is,

$$M = \frac{\sum_{i=0}^{8} b_{j+2}}{9}.$$

If

$$\frac{\sum_{j=0}^{n-2} b_{j+2}\, v^{j+1}\, {}_{j}p_{x+1}\, q_{x+1+j}}{\ddot{a}_{x+1:\overline{h-1}|}} > M\, {}_{19}P_{x+1},$$

then r_C is determined by (16.9.5) with M replacing $ELRA$. If the alternative inequality holds, then r_F is determined by (16.9.2). Reserve formulas (16.9.4) and (16.9.6) remain valid. The purpose of the guideline is to replace $ELRA$ with the simpler M.

16.9.2 Cash Values

The issues that arise with nonforfeiture benefits for such policies are similar, but there are differences. The 1980 NAIC law refers to an *average amount of insurance (AAI)* and indicates that this amount is based on benefit amounts at the ends of the first 10 policy years. Thus, in the notation of the general insurance of Section 8.2,

$$AAI = \frac{\sum\limits_{j=0}^{9} b_{j+1}}{10}$$

when $n \geq 10$. A level benefit premium is

$$P = \frac{\sum\limits_{j=0}^{n-1} b_{j+1}\, v^{j+1}\, {}_{j}p_x\, q_{x+j}}{\ddot{a}_{x:\overline{h}|}}. \tag{16.9.7}$$

An additional term is included in the numerator of (16.9.7) if pure endowment benefits are included. The formula for the first-year expense allowance depends on P and AAI and is defined as follows:

$$E_1 = \begin{cases} 1.25P + 0.01AAI & P < 0.04AAI \\ 0.06AAI & P \geq 0.04AAI. \end{cases} \tag{16.9.8}$$

The adjusted premium for any policy year is a multiple, r_N, of the corresponding contract premium for that policy year where

$$r_N = \frac{E_1 + \sum\limits_{j=0}^{n-1} b_{j+1}\, v^{j+1}\, {}_{j}p_x\, q_{x+j}}{\sum\limits_{j=0}^{h-1} G_j\, v^j\, {}_{j}p_x}. \tag{16.9.9}$$

The minimum cash value is given as

$${}_kCV = \sum\limits_{j=0}^{n-k-1} b_{k+j+1}\, v^{j+1}\, {}_{j}p_{x+k}\, q_{x+k+j} - r_N \sum\limits_{j=0}^{h-k-1} G_{k+j}\, v^j\, {}_{j}p_{x+k}. \tag{16.9.10}$$

Again, both (16.9.9) and (16.9.10) must be modified if pure endowment benefits are provided.

Example 16.9.2

Calculate the minimum cash values at durations 1, 2, 10, and 20 for the special 30-year endowment policy described in Example 16.9.1. Use (16.9.8), (16.9.9), and (16.9.10) with the Illustrative Life Table and 6% interest.

Solution:

The death benefit is 150,000 for the first 20 years and 100,000 thereafter. However, since the AAI is based on the first 10 policy years, $AAI = 150,000$. The level benefit premium for this policy is, at issue age 35,

$$P = \frac{50{,}000(2A_{35:\overline{30}|} + A^1_{35:\overline{20}|})}{\ddot{a}_{35:\overline{30}|}}$$

$$= 1622.9358.$$

Since

$$P = 1{,}622.94 \leq 6{,}000 = 0.04AAI,$$

then, according to (16.9.8),

$$E_1 = 1.25P + 0.01AAI$$

$$= 3{,}528.6698.$$

The contract premiums are 2,500 annually for 10 years and 1,250 annually for the remaining 20 years. The adjusted premium multiple, r_N, is

$$r_N = \frac{E_1 + 50{,}000(2A_{35:\overline{30}|} + A^1_{35:\overline{20}|})}{1{,}250(\ddot{a}_{35:\overline{30}|} + \ddot{a}_{35:\overline{10}|})}$$

$$= 0.9667466.$$

Formula (16.9.10) was used to obtain the following cash values for this contract.

k	$_kCV$
1	0.00
2	669.73
10	22 519.81
20	48 776.92

Formula (16.9.10) gives $-1{,}483.53$ for $_1CV$; however, negative values of CV cannot be collected from withdrawing policyholders, so it is arbitrarily set equal to zero.

▼

16.10   Notes and References

Cummins (1973) outlines the history of nonforfeiture values in the United States with emphasis on the pioneering work of Elizur Wright. Developments in other nations followed different paths. The 1941 NAIC report on nonforfeiture benefits provides an historical summary of United States regulation, a brief review of practices in other countries, discussion of the philosophic considerations regarding equity for withdrawing policyholders, and a development of the adjusted premium approach for defining minimum cash values. The 1975 Society of Actuaries committee report on nonforfeiture requirements is especially interesting for its discussions of problems in connection with policies that provide for variation in benefits after issue. Richardson (1977) supplemented this later report with an expense investigation for the purpose of defining the loading factors in adjusted premiums.

Shepherd (1940) developed the ideas on natural reserves and premiums. In two papers, one covering asset shares and nonforfeiture values (1939) and one covering gross premiums (1929), Hoskins developed many of the ideas in Section 16.4.2. The premium determination method that depends on a rate of return objective is a simplified version of work by Anderson (1959). Anderson also provides extensive background material on margins for contingencies and profits.

Dividends are discussed in detail by Jackson (1959) and by Maclean and Marshall (1937) in a monograph that also traces the history of surplus distribution. Cody (1981) expands earlier models to a more comprehensive model.

Full preliminary term reserves are also called Zillmerized reserves for the European actuary who developed the method. The Commissioners method and related recommendations were developed by two National Association of Insurance Commissioners (NAIC) committees with almost identical membership: the Committee to Study the Need for a New Mortality Table and Related Topics (1939) and the Committee to Study Nonforfeiture Benefits and Related Matters (1941). In recognition of their common chairman, these committees were popularly known as the Guertin Committees. Menge (1946) wrote a comprehensive paper on technical aspects of the Commissioners method. Tullis and Polkinghorn (1992) have written a monograph on the many issues that arise in valuing life insurance liabilities.

Exercises

Section 16.3

16.1. A company is planning to adopt a new life table. Indicate how you would determine the ages at policy issue, and times since issue, for which the reduced paid-up life insurance nonforfeiture benefits under whole life policies will be increased and for which they will be decreased. Use only a table of the annual benefit premiums for whole life policies computed on the bases of both the old and the new mortality tables. Assume that the cash values are calculated by applying the same percentage of the benefit reserve under the new table as was used under the old table.

16.2. An n-year, n-payment endowment insurance on a fully discrete payment basis, with unit amount of insurance, is issued to (x). In the event of default of premium payments, the insured has the option of
   • Reduced paid-up whole life insurance or
   • An extended term insurance, to the end of the endowment period, with a reduced pure endowment paid at age $x + n$.
   • The cash value at time t is ${}_tV_{x:\overline{n}|}$ and is sufficient to purchase paid-up whole life insurance of amount b or to purchase extended-term insurance of one together with a pure endowment at age $x + n$ of amount f. If $A_{x+t:\overline{n-t}|} = 2A_{x+t}$, express f in terms of b, $A^{1}_{x+t:\overline{n-t}|}$, and ${}_{n-t}E_{x+t}$.

16.3. A 20-year endowment insurance of unit amount on a fully continuous payment basis issued to (30) is lapsed at the end of 10 years when there is an indebtedness of amount L outstanding against the cash value ${}_{10}CV$. Express, in terms of actuarial present values,
   a. The amount of pure endowment, E, at the regular maturity date if extended term insurance for the amount of the policy less indebtedness, $1 - L$, can be continued to the maturity date;

---

b. The amount of the reserve on the extended-term insurance and the pure endowment 5 years after the date of lapse.

16.4. It has been suggested that the amount of reduced paid-up insurance should be in proportion to the number of annual premiums paid to the total number of premiums payable under the terms of the policy. Compare the amount of paid-up insurance under this suggested rule with ${}_{10}^{20}W_{40}$ and ${}_{10}W_{40:\overline{20}|}$ using the Illustrative Life Table and 6% interest.

16.5. Show that

$$\frac{d}{dt}[{}_t\bar{W}(\bar{A}_{x:\overline{n}|})] = \frac{\bar{P}(\bar{A}_{x:\overline{n}|}) - \mu_x(t)[1 - {}_t\bar{W}(\bar{A}_{x:\overline{n}|})]}{\bar{A}_{x+t:\overline{n-t}|}}$$

and interpret the equation. [Hint: Use (8.6.2) to write the derivatives of ${}_t\bar{V}(\bar{A}_{x:\overline{n}|})$ and $\bar{A}_{x+t:\overline{n-t}|}$.]

16.6. In the early years of life insurance, one company defined its cash values as

$$_kCV = h\,(G_{x+k} - G_x)\,\ddot{a}(k) \qquad k = 1, 2, \ldots$$

where the symbol G denotes a contract premium at the indicated age, and $\ddot{a}(k)$ denotes a life annuity due commencing at age $x + k$, continuing on survival to the end of the premium paying period. In practice h was set at $2/3$. If, by the 1980 NAIC law, the contract premiums for a whole life policy are taken as adjusted premiums, and if it is given that P_x and P_{x+k} are each less than 0.04 and $h = 0.9$, show that

$$_kCV = (0.909 + 1.125P_x)\,{}_kV_x + 1.125(P_{x+k} - P_x).$$

16.7. Let ${}_k\hat{W} = {}_kCV/A(k)$ where ${}_kCV = A(k) - P^a\,\ddot{a}(k)$, as in (16.2.2), and P^a is an adjusted premium. Construct a table for the three policies shown in Table 16.3.1 under a fully discrete model, relating ${}_k\hat{W}$ to adjusted and level benefit premiums.

16.8. If ${}_kW^{Mod} = {}_kV^{Mod}/A(k)$, where ${}_kV^{Mod}$ is the reserve at the end of the k-th policy year under the Commissioners Standard, as discussed in Section 16.8, construct a table for the three policies shown in Table 16.3.1, under a fully discrete model, relating ${}_kW^{Mod}$ to renewal and level benefit premiums. Assume the premium payment period in the limited payment plans is less than 20 years.

16.9. If ${}_{k+t}CV = {}_{k+t}\bar{V}(\bar{A}_x)$,
   a. Show that (16.3.4) for the length of the automatic premium loan period can be written as $H(t) = 0$ where $H(t) = \bar{a}_x\,G\,\bar{s}_{\overline{t}|i} + \bar{a}_{x+k+t} - \bar{a}_x$;
   b. Confirm that $H(0) < 0$ for survival functions where the force of mortality is increasing and, that as $t \to \infty$, $H(t)$ becomes positive and unbounded;
   c. Calculate $H'(t)$.

16.10. If, in relation to (16.4.1), $_{10}AS_1$ is the asset share at the end of 10 years based on G_1 and $_{10}AS_2$ is the corresponding quantity based on G_2, write a formula for $_{10}AS_2 - _{10}AS_1$.

16.11. Denote the expense-loaded premium determined by the equivalence principle by P' and the contract premium, loaded for profit and contingencies by G. If $G = P'(1 + \theta)$, $\theta > 0$, the contract premium has been determined by the *expected value premium principle.* This principle derives its name because the contract premium is proportional to the equivalence principle premium. Confirm that the expected value premium principle has the additive property. This can be done by working with two independent loss variables, $_0L_e^*(1)$ and $_0L_e^*(2)$, where the asterisk indicates that the premium included in the loss function is $(1 + \theta)$ times the expense loaded premium determined by the equivalence principle. Confirm that

$$E[_0L_e^*(1) + _0L_e^*(2)] = E[_0L_e^*(1)] + E[_0L_e^*(2)].$$

16.12. Suppose that there is an *experience premium,* denoted by $\hat{G}$, based on realistic mortality and expense assumptions such that

$$\hat{G} = v \,_{k+1}F - \,_kF + \hat{g} + v \hat{q}_{x+k}^{(1)} (1 - \,_{k+1}F)$$

where $\hat{g} = G\hat{c}_k + \hat{e}_k$, $k = 0, 1, 2, \ldots$. In addition, assume $_{k+1}CV = \,_{k+1}F$ for $k = 0, 1, 2, 3, \ldots$. Show that under these assumptions
a. $_{k+1}F = (_kF + \hat{G} - \hat{g})(1 + i) - \hat{q}_{x+k}^{(1)}(1 - \,_{k+1}F)$;
b. If dividends are paid to insureds who die or withdraw, (16.5.4) can be written as

$$_{k+1}F + \,_{k+1}D = [_kF + G - \hat{g}](1 + \hat{i}_{k+1}) - \hat{q}_{x+k}^{(1)} (1 - \,_{k+1}F)$$

and

$$_{k+1}D = (G - \hat{G})(1 + \hat{i}_{k+1}) + (_kF + \hat{G} - \hat{g})(\hat{i}_{k+1} - i).$$

This exercise outlines the *experience premium method* of dividend calculation.

16.13. The recursion relation between successive life annuity values is given by

$$(\ddot{a}_{x+h} - 1)(1 + i) = p_{x+h} \ddot{a}_{x+h+1} \qquad h = 0, 1, 2, \ldots .$$

a. If the actual experience interest rate is $\hat{i}_{h+1}$ and the experience survival probability is $\hat{p}_{x+h}$, the fund progress will be described by

$$(\ddot{a}_{x+h} - 1)(1 + \hat{i}_{h+1}) = \hat{p}_{x+h}(\ddot{a}_{x+h+1} + \Delta_{h+1})$$

where Δ_{h+1} is the survivor's share of deviations. Show that

$$\Delta_{h+1} = \frac{(\hat{i}_{h+1} - i)(\ddot{a}_{x+h} - 1) + (p_{x+h} - \hat{p}_{x+h}) \ddot{a}_{x+h+1}}{\hat{p}_{x+h}}$$

and interpret the result. [This formula is the basis of the two-factor contribution formula for annuity dividends.]

---

b. If the annuity income at the end of the year is adjusted to be r_{h+1} times the income as of the beginning of the year where

$$(\ddot{a}_{x+h} - 1)(1 + \hat{i}_{h+1}) = \hat{p}_{x+h}(r_{h+1})\,\ddot{a}_{x+h+1}\,,$$

express r_{h+1} in terms of i, $\hat{i}_{h+1}$, p_{x+h}, and $\hat{p}_{x+h}$.

Section 16.6

16.14. For a modified reserve method the period of modification is equal to the premium paying period. Show that

$$_k V^{Mod}_{x:\overline{n}|} = 1 - (\beta + d)\,\ddot{a}_{x+k:\overline{n-k}|}.$$

16.15. A modified reserve method for a whole life insurance, fully continuous basis, is defined by

$$\bar{\alpha}(t) = \frac{t}{m}\,\bar{\beta} \qquad 0 \le t < m$$

where $\bar{\beta}$ is the level premium for $t \ge m$.
a. Write a formula for $\bar{\beta}$.
b. Write a prospective formula for $_t\bar{V}(\bar{A}_x)^{Mod}$, $t < m$.

16.16. Calculate α_x^{Mod} and β_x^{Mod} in a modified reserve method for a fully discrete whole life insurance where $_1V_x^{Mod} = K$. The modification period is the premium paying period.

16.17. Under a modified reserve method for a fully discrete whole life insurance policy, the annual benefit premiums, P_x, are replaced (for reserve purposes) by annual premiums of α_x^{Mod} for the first n years and β_x^{Mod} thereafter. Show that

$$\frac{\beta_x^{Mod} - P_x}{P_x - \alpha_x^{Mod}} = \frac{\ddot{a}_x}{_n|\ddot{a}_x} - 1.$$

16.18. Show that

$$_kV - {_k}V^{Mod} = \left(\frac{\beta - \alpha}{\ddot{a}_{x:\overline{j}|}}\right)\ddot{a}_{x+k:\overline{j-k}|}$$

where j is the length of the modification period. Note that this difference can be interpreted as the unamortized portion of the extra first-year expense allowance.

16.19. Use the general symbols of (16.2.2) to define a modified reserve model for a level benefit, level premium policy:

$$_kV^{Mod} = A(k) - \beta\,\ddot{a}(k) \qquad k = 1, 2, 3, \ldots.$$

Confirm the following steps:

a.
$$_kV^{Mod} = vq_k + vp_k\, A(k+1) - \beta - \beta vp_k\, \ddot{a}(k+1)$$

$$= vq_k - \beta + vp_k\, _{k+1}V^{Mod}$$

$$(_kV^{Mod} + \beta)(1+i) = q_k(1 - {}_{k+1}V^{Mod}) + {}_{k+1}V^{Mod} \qquad k = 1, 2, \ldots.$$

b. If $_0V^{Mod}$ is defined as $(\alpha - \beta)$ the recursion relation in (a) can be extended to $k = 0$.

c. $\Delta v^k\, _kV^{Mod} = v^k\, \beta - q_k(1 - {}_{k+1}V^{Mod})\, v^{k+1}, \ k = 0, 1, 2, \ldots.$

d. Summing the expression in part (c) over $k = 0, 1, 2, \ldots, n-1$, confirm that

$$_nV^{Mod} = \beta \ddot{s}_{\overline{n}|} - (\beta - \alpha)(1+i)^n - \sum_{k=0}^{n-1} (1+i)^{n-k-1}\, q_k\, (1 - {}_{k+1}V^{Mod}).$$

Section 16.7

16.20. Show that

$$_kV^{FPT}_{x:\overline{n}|} = 1 - \frac{\ddot{a}_{x+k:\overline{n-k}|}}{\ddot{a}_{x+1:\overline{n-1}|}} \qquad k = 1, 2, \ldots, n.$$

16.21. A ***two-year preliminary term reserve method*** is defined with three valuation premiums:

First year:	$A^1_{x:\overline{1}|}$
Second year:	$A^1_{x+1:\overline{1}|}$
Thereafter:	Level benefit premium for age $x + 2$, no change in benefits or premium paying period.

Show that, for this method, the reserve on a whole life policy to (x) is given by

$$_1V^{Mod} = {}_2V^{Mod} = 0$$

$$_kV^{Mod} = {}_kV_x - (P_{x+2} - P_x)\, \ddot{a}_{x+k} \qquad k = 3, 4, 5, \ldots.$$

(This type of reserve system is common in health insurance.)

16.22. Consider a fully discrete whole life insurance on (x). Λ_h^{FPT} is defined as in (8.5.1) with $\pi_0 = A^1_{x:\overline{1}|}$, $\pi_h = P_{x+1}$, $h = 1, 2, \ldots$, and $_hV = {}_hV^{FPT}$. Show that, if $_1V_x > 0$,

$$\mathrm{Var}[\Lambda_0^{FPT}|K(x) = 0, 1, \ldots] = v^2\, p_x q_x > \mathrm{Var}[\Lambda_0|K(x) = 0, 1, \ldots].$$

Section 16.8

16.23. A proposed reserve valuation method has a first-year premium α and a renewal premium β applicable in all renewal years. The first-year premium is constrained to be at least equal to $A^1_{x:\overline{1}|}$. This provision allows the use of *FPT* for some policies and some ages. The excess of β over α cannot exceed 0.05. Assume that on a particular valuation basis $d = 0.03$, $\ddot{a}_x = 17$, $\ddot{a}_{x:\overline{12}|} = 9$, $A^1_{x:\overline{12}|} = 2/3$, and $A^1_{x:\overline{1}|} = 0.01$.

a. Calculate β for a whole life policy issued to (x).

b. Calculate $_{12}V_x^{Mod}$ for this method.

c. Assuming $\alpha = A_{x:\overline{1}|}^1 = 0.01$, calculate a test value for β for a 12-year endowment insurance on (x). Confirm that this value for β is inadmissible since $\beta - \alpha > 0.05$.

d. Using the result in (c), calculate β for a 12-year endowment insurance on (x).

e. Calculate $_1V_{x:\overline{12}|}^{Mod}$.

16.24. A modified preliminary term reserve standard is described as follows:

- Policies are divided into two classes: Class I, if the *FPT* renewal premium is greater than $_{19}P_{x+1}$; Class II, if the policy does not belong to Class I.
- For policies in Class I, the first-year premium is the same as that defined by the Commissioners Reserve Valuation Method. The renewal premium is such that the level benefit premium reserve is reached at the end of the premium paying period or 15 years, whichever comes first.
- For policies in Class II, the *FPT* method is prescribed.

For a fully discrete payment basis, 20-payment, 20-year endowment issued to (x), write an expression for α and β under this standard.

16.25. If $\beta^{FPT} > {}_{19}P_{x+1}$, the k-th terminal reserve by the Commissioners method on a fully discrete basis life insurance issued to (x) and paying level benefits may be written as

$$_kV^{CRVM} = \frac{A_{x:\overline{1}|}^1}{_kE_x} + {}_{19}P_{x+1}\,\ddot{s}_{x+1:\overline{k-1}|} + T\,\ddot{s}_{x:\overline{k}|} - \frac{A_{x:\overline{k}|}^1}{_kE_x}.$$

Derive an expression for T.

Section 16.9

16.26. Assume $\beta^{FPT} > {}_{19}P_{x+1}$ and

$$b_{j+1} = 1 \qquad\qquad j = 0, 1, \ldots, n - 1,$$

$$G_j = P(1 + \theta) \qquad j = 0, 1, \ldots, h - 1.$$

Show that (16.9.7) reduces to the formula for the k-th reserve by the Commissioners Standard.

SPECIAL ANNUITIES AND INSURANCES

17.1 Introduction

In this chapter we study a wide variety of policies that provide special annuity and insurance benefits; our aim is to determine actuarial present values, benefit and contract premiums, and benefit premium reserves. In Section 17.2 we examine a number of annuity contracts for a single life where the period during which payments are made may be longer than the future lifetime of the annuitant, or where there are benefits payable upon death. These contracts can arise from a settlement option under a life insurance policy, from the provisions of a pension plan, or from provisions of an individual annuity policy. Section 17.3 covers the closely related matter of the family income policy. Variable products, where benefit levels and reserves depend on investment results, are the subject of Section 17.4. These products become important when price inflation erodes the value of benefits stated in terms of fixed monetary units. In Section 17.5 types of policies that provide wide flexibility for changing benefit amounts and premium levels are examined. Some life insurance policies provide for benefit payments before death when the insured becomes terminally ill or has lost the ability to perform specified activities of daily living. These are called *accelerated benefits.* In Section 17.6 a multiple decrement model for such policies will be introduced. The model resembles the disability insurance models introduced in Chapter 11 in that both the time and amount of accelerated benefits payments may be random variables.

17.2 Special Types of Annuity Benefits

In this section we concentrate on calculating the actuarial present values of special forms of annuity benefits. The payment patterns depend on the contract premium collected. We determine the appropriate contract premium using the equivalence principle. We emphasize continuous payment annuities and justify the corresponding results for *m*-thly payment annuities by analogy.

Section 5.2 contained an analysis of n-year certain and life annuities. That type of life annuity provides for a guarantee of payments for at least n years. The annuities in this section can be viewed as special cases where the number n bears a relationship to the consideration paid for the annuity.

One illustration is the **installment refund annuity.** A sufficient number of payments is guaranteed so that the annuitant receives at least as much as the contract premium that was paid. Thus, for such a continuous annuity with contract premium G, the actuarial present value of benefits is

$$\bar{a}_{\overline{G|}} + {}_{G}E_x\, \bar{a}_{x+G}.$$

If the contract premium is to contain a loading of r times the premium, the equivalence principle requires that G satisfy

$$G(1 - r) = \bar{a}_{\overline{G|}} + {}_{G}E_x\, \bar{a}_{x+G}. \tag{17.2.1}$$

The difference between the left- and right-hand sides of the above expression could be evaluated for integer values of G. Then, an approximate value of G that equates the two sides is found by linear interpolation. Similar expressions hold for discrete versions, and G could be found for those in a similar manner.

A related annuity that contains some insurance features is the **cash refund annuity.** A death benefit is defined as the excess, if any, of the contract premium paid over the annuity payments received. If G is the single contract premium and T is the time of death, the present value of benefits on a continuous basis is

$$Z = \begin{cases} \bar{a}_{\overline{T|}} + (G - T)v^T & T \leq G \\ \bar{a}_{\overline{T|}} & T > G. \end{cases} \tag{17.2.2}$$

The actuarial present value of these benefits is given by

$$\mathrm{E}(Z) = \int_0^{\infty} \bar{a}_{\overline{t|}}\, {}_t p_x\, \mu_x(t)\, dt + \int_0^G (G - t)\, v^t\, {}_t p_x\, \mu_x(t)\, dt$$

$$= \bar{a}_x + G\, \bar{A}^1_{x:\overline{G|}} - (\bar{I}\bar{A})^1_{x:\overline{G|}}. \tag{17.2.3}$$

As for the installment refund annuity, the principle equivalence is used to determine G. If the loading is r times the contract premium, then

$$G(1 - r) = \bar{a}_x + G\, \bar{A}^1_{x:\overline{G|}} - (\bar{I}\bar{A})^1_{x:\overline{G|}}. \tag{17.2.4}$$

Linear interpolation can be used to approximate G after the difference between the left- and right-hand sides of (17.2.4) is evaluated for integer values of G.

Example 17.2.1

Consider a **partial cash refund annuity** with the present-value random variable defined as

$$Z = \begin{cases} \bar{a}_{\overline{T|}} + (\rho G - T)v^T & T < \rho G,\ 0 < \rho < 1 \\ \bar{a}_{\overline{T|}} & T \geq \rho G. \end{cases}$$

a. Show that (17.2.4) may be rewritten for a partial cash refund annuity as

$$G(1 - r) = \bar{a}_x + \rho G \bar{A}^{1}_{x:\overline{\rho G|}} - (\bar{I}\bar{A})^{1}_{x:\overline{\rho G|}}.$$

b. Form $H(G) = Gr + \bar{a}_x + \rho G \, \bar{A}^{1}_{x:\overline{\rho G|}} - (\bar{I}\bar{A})^{1}_{x:\overline{\rho G|}} = G$ for the purpose of determining G such that $H(G) = G$, by using an iterative solution method. The method will employ $H(G_i) = G_{i+1}$.
   (i) Display $H'(G)$ and $H''(G)$.
   (ii) Discuss the signs of $H'(G)$ and $H''(G)$ in the neighborhood of a root.

Solution:

a. Apply the equivalence principle to obtain

$$G(1 - r) = E[Z^*]$$

$$= \int_0^{\rho G} [\bar{a}_{\overline{t|}} + (\rho G - t)v^t] \, {}_tp_x \, \mu_x(t) \, dt$$

$$+ \int_{\rho G}^{\infty} \bar{a}_{\overline{t|}} \, {}_tp_x \, \mu_x(t) \, dt$$

$$= \bar{a}_x + \rho G \int_0^{\rho G} v^t \, {}_tp_x \, \mu_x(t) \, dt$$

$$- \int_0^{\rho G} t\,v^t \, {}_tp_x \, \mu_x(t) \, dt$$

$$= \bar{a}_x + \rho G \, \bar{A}^{1}_{x:\overline{\rho G|}} - (\bar{I}\bar{A})^{1}_{x:\overline{\rho G|}}.$$

b. (i) $H'(G) = r + \rho\bar{A}^{1}_{x:\overline{\rho G|}} + \rho[\rho G \, v^{\rho G} \, {}_{\rho G}p_x \, \mu_x(\rho G) - \rho G \, v^{\rho G} \, {}_{\rho G}p_x \, \mu_x(\rho G)]$

$$= r + \rho\bar{A}^{1}_{x:\overline{\rho G|}},$$

$H''(G) = \rho^2 \, v^{\rho G} \, {}_{\rho G}p_x \, \mu_x(\rho G) \geq 0.$

(ii) The rate of convergence of iterative methods for solving nonlinear equations depends on the magnitude of the first derivative $[H'(G)]$ in the neighborhood of the solution of the equation. Assume $H(G_i) = G_{i+1}$ is used to solve iteratively for G. We know that $H''(G) > 0$ and $H'(G) = r + \rho\bar{A}^{1}_{x:\overline{\rho G|}} = [G - \bar{a}_x + (\bar{I}\bar{A})^{1}_{x:\overline{\rho G|}}]/G$. But $G > \bar{a}_x > \bar{a}_x - (\bar{I}\bar{A})^{1}_{x:\overline{\rho G|}} > \bar{a}_x - (\bar{I}\bar{A})_x > 0$, so $0 < G - \bar{a}_x + (\bar{I}\bar{A})^{1}_{x:\overline{\rho G|}} < G$. Thus $0 < H'(G) < 1$ in the neighborhood of the value of G such that $H(G) = G$. The condition that $|H'(G)| < 1$ in the neighborhood of the solution is a sufficient condition for the iterative solution procedure, $H(G_i) = G_{i+1}$, to converge to G. ▼

17.3 Family Income Insurances

An *n-year family income insurance* provides an income from the date of death of the insured, continuing until n years have elapsed from the date of issue of the policy. It is typically paid for by premiums over the n-year period, or some period shorter than n years, to keep benefit reserves positive. Again, we start with a continuous annuity. If T is the time of death of the insured, the present value of benefits is

$$Z = \begin{cases} v^T \ \bar{a}_{\overline{n-T}|} & T \le n \\ 0 & t > n. \end{cases} \tag{17.3.1}$$

Usually, the interest rate involved in the annuity factor, $\bar{a}_{\overline{n-T}|}$, is the same as that in the present-value factor, v^T. A variation of this type of contract is the *mortgage protection policy* where the annuity factor in the benefit function represents the outstanding balance on a mortgage. The mortgage interest rate used in evaluating $\bar{a}_{\overline{n-T}|}$ may then be different from that used for evaluating v^T.

The actuarial present value for the family income benefit is given by

$$E[Z] = \int_0^n v^t \ \bar{a}_{\overline{n-t}|} \ _t p_x \ \mu_x(t) \ dt. \tag{17.3.2}$$

This integral can be converted to a current payment integral by integration by parts,

$$\bar{a}_{\overline{n}|} - \int_0^n v^t \ _t p_x \ dt = \int_0^n v^t \ (1 - \ _t p_x) \ dt = \bar{a}_{\overline{n}|} - \bar{a}_{x:\overline{n}|}. \tag{17.3.3}$$

The interpretation of the middle integral is that the annuity is payable at time t, for $t < n$, only if (x) is dead at that time, the probability of that event being $1 - \ _t p_x$. The first and third expressions in (17.3.3) can be interpreted as requiring a continuous payment, at a constant rate of 1 per year, until time n, but the payments must be returned if (x) is alive.

We conclude this section with an example combining aspects of a family income policy and a retirement annuity with a term certain.

Example 17.3.1

Calculate the actuarial present value of the benefits under a policy issued at age 40 providing the following annuity benefits payable continuously at a rate of 1 per year:
- In the event of death prior to age 65, a family income benefit ceasing at age 65 or 10 years after death, if later, and
- In the event of survival to age 65, a life annuity with 10 years certain.

Solution:

We prepare to write the current payment integral. The following table gives the conditions required for payments at time t and the corresponding probabilities.

Time	Condition	Probability
$0 < t \le 25$	(40) is dead	$1 - \ _t p_{40}$
$25 < t \le 35$	(40) was alive at $t - 10$	$_{t-10} p_{40}$
$t > 35$	(40) is alive	$_t p_{40}$

The actuarial present value is

$$\int_0^{25} v^t \left(1 - {}_tp_{40}\right) dt + \int_{25}^{35} v^t {}_{t-10}p_{40} \, dt + \int_{35}^{\infty} v^t {}_tp_{40} \, dt.$$

If we replace $t - 10$ by s in the middle integral, we obtain

$$\int_{15}^{25} v^{s+10} {}_sp_{40} \, ds = v^{10} \left(\bar{a}_{40:\overline{25|}} - \bar{a}_{40:\overline{15|}}\right).$$

Thus the actuarial present value of the benefit can be written as

$$\bar{a}_{\overline{25|}} - \bar{a}_{40:\overline{25|}} + v^{10} \left(\bar{a}_{40:\overline{25|}} - \bar{a}_{40:\overline{15|}}\right) + \bar{a}_{40} - \bar{a}_{40:\overline{35|}}. \qquad \blacktriangledown$$

17.4 Variable Products

We consider several products where the benefit levels and reserves depend upon the investment results. The investments associated with a product may be of any type. Typically, the particular investments are selected to be in accord with the announced objective of the insurance or annuity product. The original impetus for these products was to participate in the higher expected total returns (dividends, interest, and capital gains) available in equity investments and thus to provide some measure of protection against inflation. A typical contract provides guarantees concerning mortality and expense charges. Thus, the policyholder is not charged for adverse experience, nor does the policy benefit from favorable experience from these two sources. We examine the mechanisms for change in benefit level on an individual policy basis.

17.4.1 Variable Annuity

We consider here the *variable annuity*. During the premium-paying or *accumulation period*, a fund is accumulated from a single contribution, or from periodic deposits, at rates of return depending upon the investment performance of the fund. Typically, variable annuities make guarantees on maximum sales, administrative and investment expense charges, and the mortality basis in use. If we ignore gains and losses attributed to withdrawals and to death benefits at guaranteed levels, the expected growth of the fund share is given by

$$[F_k + \pi_k(1 - c_k) - e_k](1 + i'_{k+1}) = F_{k+1} + q_{x+k}(b_{k+1} - F_{k+1}); \qquad (17.4.1)$$

see (16.5.3). Here F_k is the fund share at time k; π_k is the size of the deposit at time k; c_k is the fraction of the premium, π_k, charged for those expenses at time k that are proportional to the premium paid at that time; e_k is the charge at time k for expenses not proportional to the premium; b_{k+1} is the benefit paid at time $k + 1$ for death between times k and $k + 1$; i'_{k+1} is the actual investment return, net of investment expenses, for the year following time k. The second term on the right-hand side of the equation is equal to 0 during the accumulation period, so we have the fund growing with interest only.

At retirement, the existing fund share is used to purchase a paid-up annuity, the purchase rates computed on a predetermined mortality basis and an ***assumed investment return (AIR)***. If the AIR is low, then the initial annuity payment will be low relative to the fund share, but the contract can be expected to provide an increasing payment pattern that offsets some of the effects of inflation. Let the AIR be denoted by i and, again, let the net actual investment return in the year following time k be i'_{k+1}. If the annuity benefit is paid only to those living at the beginning of each year, with the annuity payment level at time k equal to b_k, the reserve just before the payment is $b_k \ddot{a}_{x+k}$, with x the retirement age. The equation for the progress of the fund share would be

$$(b_k \ddot{a}_{x+k} - b_k)(1 + i'_{k+1}) = b_{k+1} p_{x+k} \ddot{a}_{x+k+1}. \qquad (17.4.2)$$

But from (5.3.4), we have

$$(\ddot{a}_{x+k} - 1)(1 + i) = p_{x+k} \ddot{a}_{x+k+1}. \qquad (17.4.3)$$

Dividing (17.4.2) by (17.4.3) gives

$$b_{k+1} = b_k \frac{1 + i'_{k+1}}{1 + i}. \qquad (17.4.4)$$

Thus, if $i'_{k+1} > i$, the benefit level will increase. Note that a high AIR can lead to a situation where the benefit amounts are frequently decreased.

The result, (17.4.4), holds for other payout options. This is indicated for the n-year certain and life annuity in Exercise 17.11. It also holds for m-thly payouts in slightly modified forms. First, let us consider adjusting the payout amount monthly. The formula connecting the annuity values for the first and second months of a contract year is

$$\left(\ddot{a}^{(12)}_{x+k} - \frac{1}{12} \right)\left(1 + \frac{i^{(12)}}{12} \right) = {}_{1/12}p_{x+k}\, \ddot{a}^{(12)}_{x+k+1/12},$$

while the progress of the fund share would be expressed by

$$\left(b_k \ddot{a}^{(12)}_{x+k} - \frac{b_k}{12} \right)\left(1 + \frac{i'^{(12)}_{k+1}}{12} \right) = {}_{1/12}p_{x+k}\, b_{k+1/12}\, \ddot{a}^{(12)}_{x+k+1/12}.$$

Division yields

$$b_{k+1/12} = \frac{b_k(1 + i'^{(12)}_{k+1}/12)}{1 + i^{(12)}/12}. \qquad (17.4.5)$$

Alternatively, we could adjust the payment size on an annual basis even though the payout is monthly. First, the formula for successive annual reserves for a monthly annuity is

$$(\ddot{a}^{(12)}_{x+k} - \ddot{a}^{(12)}_{x+k:\overline{1|}})(1 + i) = p_{x+k}\, \ddot{a}^{(12)}_{x+k+1}.$$

The equation for the growth of the fund share would be

$$(b_k \ddot{a}^{(12)}_{x+k} - b_k \ddot{a}^{(12)}_{x+k:\overline{1|}})(1 + i'_{k+1}) = p_{x+k}\, b_{k+1}\, \ddot{a}^{(12)}_{x+k+1}.$$

Thus we make a charge, $b_k \, \ddot{a}^{(12)}_{x+k:\overline{1}|}$, for the present year's annuity payments. Dividing the last two expressions gives (17.4.4) again,

$$b_{k+1} = b_k \, \frac{1 + i'_{k+1}}{1 + i}.$$

17.4.2 Fully Variable Life Insurance

There are a large number of possible designs for *variable life insurance*. We examine three distinct designs, all based on a whole life insurance. Each of these designs can be adapted to limited payment life insurances or to endowment insurances. Each is based on annual premiums with immediate payment of claims. Benefit amounts are changed at the beginning of each year.

The first design is what we call *fully variable life insurance*. Benefit amounts change with investment results, and premiums are kept proportional to benefit amounts. We start with a unit benefit amount and benefit premium $P(\bar{A}_x)$. The terminal reserve at time k is equal to the product of $_kV(\bar{A}_x)$ and b_k, the benefit amount to be paid in the year following time k. The benefit premium payable at time k is $b_k \, P(\bar{A}_x)$. Upon receipt of the benefit premium, term insurance for the benefit for the year is purchased, the cost being $b_k \, \bar{A}^{1}_{x+k:\overline{1}|}$. The equation that connects the expected fund size at the beginning and end of the year and is used to define the benefit for the subsequent year is

$$[b_k \, _kV(\bar{A}_x) + b_k \, P(\bar{A}_x) - b_k \, \bar{A}^{1}_{x+k:\overline{1}|}](1 + i'_{k+1}) = p_{x+k} \, b_{k+1} \, _{k+1}V(\bar{A}_x). \quad (17.4.6)$$

But we know

$$[_kV(\bar{A}_x) + P(\bar{A}_x) - \bar{A}^{1}_{x+k:\overline{1}|}](1 + i) = p_{x+k} \, _{k+1}V(\bar{A}_x). \quad (17.4.7)$$

Dividing (17.4.6) by (17.4.7), we obtain

$$b_{k+1} = b_k \, \frac{1 + i'_{k+1}}{1 + i}. \quad (17.4.8)$$

This is the same relationship that holds during the payout phase of a variable annuity, namely, (17.4.4).

17.4.3 Fixed Premium Variable Life Insurance

We next examine a *fixed premium variable life insurance*. The main difference from the fully variable design, as the name suggests, is that the benefit premium remains constant. Again we start with a unit benefit amount and write the equation connecting expected fund sizes,

$$[b'_k \, _kV(\bar{A}_x) + P(\bar{A}_x) - b_k \, \bar{A}^{1}_{x+k:\overline{1}|}](1 + i'_{k+1}) = p_{x+k} \, b_{k+1} \, _{k+1}V(\bar{A}_x). \quad (17.4.9)$$

Combining this with (17.4.7) gives us

$$b_{k+1} = b_k \left[\frac{_kV(\bar{A}_x) + P(\bar{A}_x) / b_k - \bar{A}^{1}_{x+k:\overline{1}|}}{_kV(\bar{A}_x) + P(\bar{A}_x) - \bar{A}^{1}_{x+k:\overline{1}|}} \right] \frac{1 + i'_{k+1}}{1 + i}. \quad (17.4.10)$$

The first factor on the left-hand side of (17.4.9) can be written as

$$(b_k - 1)\, {}_kV(\bar{A}_x) + {}_kV(\bar{A}_x) + P(\bar{A}_x) - b_k\, \bar{A}^{\,1}_{x+k:\overline{1}|}.$$

This shows that the fixed benefit premium supports both the initial face amount of 1 and the additional benefit, $b_k - 1$, generated by the actual investment returns.

17.4.4   Paid-up Insurance Increments

Here we consider an alternative used for the third design. We consider the changes in the benefit amount as paid-up and use the premium to support only the original benefit level. The equation connecting fund shares becomes

$$[(b_k - 1)\, \bar{A}_{x+k} + {}_kV(\bar{A}_x) + P(\bar{A}_x) - b_k\, \bar{A}^{\,1}_{x+k:\overline{1}|}](1 + i'_{k+1})$$
$$= p_{x+k}\,[(b_{k+1} - 1)\, \bar{A}_{x+k+1} + {}_{k+1}V(\bar{A}_x)]. \quad (17.4.11)$$

The left-hand side of (17.4.11) can be transformed as follows:

$$\{b_k\,(\bar{A}_{x+k} - \bar{A}^{\,1}_{x+k:\overline{1}|}) - [\bar{A}_{x+k} - {}_kV(\bar{A}_x) - P(\bar{A}_x)]\}(1 + i'_{k+1})$$
$$= [b_k\, {}_1E_{x+k}\, \bar{A}_{x+k+1} - P(\bar{A}_x)(\ddot{a}_{x+k} - 1)](1 + i'_{k+1})$$
$$= [b_k\, {}_1E_{x+k}\, \bar{A}_{x+k+1} - P(\bar{A}_x)({}_1E_{x+k}\, \ddot{a}_{x+k+1})](1 + i'_{k+1})$$
$$= p_{x+k}\, \bar{A}_{x+k+1}\left[b_k - \frac{P(\bar{A}_x)}{P(\bar{A}_{x+k+1})}\right]\frac{1 + i'_{k+1}}{1 + i}.$$

The right-hand side of (17.4.11) is most easily transformed by using the paid-up insurance formula for the reserve. It becomes

$$p_{x+k}\left\{(b_{k+1} - 1)\, \bar{A}_{x+k+1} + \bar{A}_{x+k+1}\left[1 - \frac{P(\bar{A}_x)}{P(\bar{A}_{x+k+1})}\right]\right\}$$
$$= p_{x+k}\, \bar{A}_{x+k+1}\left[b_{k+1} - \frac{P(\bar{A}_x)}{P(\bar{A}_{x+k+1})}\right].$$

Making these substitutions into (17.4.11), we find that the recursion formula for the benefit amount is

$$b_{k+1} - \frac{P(\bar{A}_x)}{P(\bar{A}_{x+k+1})} = \left[b_k - \frac{P(\bar{A}_x)}{P(\bar{A}_{x+k+1})}\right]\frac{1 + i'_{k+1}}{1 + i}. \quad (17.4.12)$$

This third design has the advantage that if, after a period of years with favorable investment returns resulting in $b_k > 1$, the investment returns level off at the AIR, then the benefit amounts will remain fixed. This is not true for the second design that led to (17.4.10).

The paid-up insurance increment design has been used most frequently in commercial practice. Exercise 17.14 explores another design.

17.5 Flexible Plan Products

In the early 1970s insurance companies began to offer several types of policies intended to provide the policyholder a broad range of options for changing benefit amounts, premiums, and plan of insurance. The companies typically allowed small increases in death benefit amounts without new evidence of insurability, but larger increases required such evidence. The insurance plans usually included all types of level premium, level benefit term plans, which as a limiting case include whole life. The more expensive plans offered were either all limited payment life plans or all endowment plans.

In Section 8.2 a model for life insurance policies with nonconstant benefits and premiums was developed. The schedule of premiums and benefits was assumed to have been determined when the policy is issued. In this section the option for changing benefits and premiums within bounds established by the contract is available to the insured. Both participating (with experience-based dividends) and nonparticipating versions were made available. A special dividend option was devised to allow the dividend to be added at net rates directly related to the cash value. This larger cash value was then used to extend the expiry date on term plans or to increase the benefit amounts on permanent plans. We refer to such products as *flexible plans* and illustrate a particularly simple version that shows some of the inherent complexities. We conclude the section by describing a second design that has less emphasis on the plan of insurance and some features in common with variable life plans, as described in the previous section.

17.5.1 Flexible Plan Illustration

Basic to the design of the type of flexible plan considered here is a formula used in reserve calculations relating the contract premium to the benefit premium. We use the following very simple relationship applied to both term and limited payment life plans, the latter being our choice for permanent coverage,

$$0.8G = P. \tag{17.5.1}$$

Here G is the contract premium and P is the benefit premium.

Another basic decision is to determine the form of the total expense charge and the related question of the adjustment of the reserves at times of plan change. We use full preliminary term reserves and nonforfeiture values in our illustration. It should be noted that the nonforfeiture and valuation laws may require higher minimum values, particularly for limited payment life plans. We define $_0V = -E_0$, where E_0 is the excess first-year expense allowance. This idea also appeared in Section 16.2. Then, from our adoption of full preliminary term reserves, we have $_1V = 0$ and, assuming a fully discrete basis,

$$_0V + P = vq_xb,$$

thus

$$E_0 = -_0V = P - vq_x b. \tag{17.5.2}$$

The equation connecting initial benefit amount, b, initial benefit premium, P, and initial plan of insurance with h, the premium payment term, is

$$_0V + P\ddot{a}_{x:\overline{h}|} = bA^1_{x:\overline{j}|}. \tag{17.5.3}$$

Here j equals either h (in case of a term plan) or $\omega - x$ (in case of limited payment life). Reserves are most easily determined by retrospective formulas since, as we will see, minor adjustments in benefits in the final year of a policy are usually required. Thus

$$_kV = \frac{_0V + P\ddot{a}_{x:\overline{k}|} - bA^1_{x:\overline{k}|}}{_kE_x}. \tag{17.5.4}$$

We illustrate the application of these formulas with the following example.

Example 17.5.1

Consider a policy issued at age 35 with an initial gross premium of 1,000 and an initial benefit amount of 120,000. Use the Illustrative Life Table with 6% interest to determine the excess first-year expense allowance, the fifth-year reserve, and the plan of insurance.

Solution:

From (17.5.1), we have $P = 800$. Therefore, the excess first-year expense allowance is

$$-_0V = P - 120,000vq_{35} = 572.05,$$

and the fifth-year reserve is given by

$$_5V = \frac{-572.05 + 800\ddot{a}_{35:\overline{5}|} - 120,000A^1_{35:\overline{5}|}}{_5E_{35}}$$

$$= 2,491.24.$$

The renewal benefit premium for 120,000 of whole life insurance at age 35 on a full preliminary basis is $120,000\, P_{36} = 1,057.37$. Since our benefit premium is only 800, the plan of insurance is one of the term plans. It can be verified that, by using retrospective formulas,

$$_{39}V = 3,375.72$$

and

$$_{40}V = -1,313.14.$$

Thus the plan of insurance is Term to Age 74. The reserve remaining at time 39 would typically be used to provide term insurance for a fraction of the following year. In our example, the number of days is given by

$$\frac{_{39}V}{120,000A^1_{74:\overline{1}|}} \, 365 = 230.$$

▼

At the time of change of benefit amount or premium, a new benefit premium is calculated along with any change in the reserve that might result from, for instance, a change in the assumed excess first-year expense allowance. For our simplified plan, the benefit premiums are a constant percentage of the contract premiums, and we assume that the revised reserve at the time of change, $_kV'$, is equal to the full preliminary term reserve on hand. The relationship between the revised reserve, new net premium, P', and new benefit amount, b', is of the same form as (17.5.3), namely,

$$_kV' + P'\ddot{a}_{x+k:\overline{h}|} = b'\, A^{\,1}_{x+k:\overline{j}|}. \tag{17.5.5}$$

Here j and h would, in general, change with the new relationship between premium and benefit amounts. Again, j equals either h or $\omega - x - k$, and it is most convenient to evaluate reserves by a retrospective formula. Thus, for $g = 1, 2, 3, \ldots$, we have

$$_{k+g}V' = \frac{_kV' + P'\ddot{a}_{x+k:\overline{g}|} - b'\, A^{\,1}_{x+k:\overline{g}|}}{_gE_{x+k}}. \tag{17.5.6}$$

We continue with three examples that are continuations of Example 17.5.1. These illustrate different types of change and show some characteristic calculations.

Example 17.5.2

The policyholder in Example 17.5.1 wishes, 5 years after issue, to change the contract premium of the policy to 2,000 and the benefit amount to 150,000. Determine the reserve 10 years after original issue and the new plan of insurance.

Solution:

$P' = 1,600$ and $_5V' = 2,491.24$ ($_5V' = {}_5V$ in Example 17.5.1). Thus, by (17.5.6),

$$_{10}V' = \frac{2,491.24 + 1,600\ddot{a}_{40:\overline{5}|} - 150,000A^{\,1}_{40:\overline{5}|}}{_5E_{40}}$$

$$= 10,319.89.$$

We know the plan of insurance is one of the limited payment life plans since $2,491.24 + 1,600\ddot{a}_{40}$ exceeds $150,000A_{40}$. It can be determined that the reserve at age 69 is the first one to exceed the actuarial present value of 150,000 of whole life insurance at the same age. Thus,

$$_{34}V' = \frac{2,491.24 + 1,600\ddot{a}_{40:\overline{29}|} - 150,000A^{\,1}_{40:\overline{29}|}}{_{29}E_{40}}$$

$$= 75,597.32,$$

while $150,000\, A_{69} = 74,954.44$. When the policyholder attains age 69, the policy will probably be changed to a paid-up life policy with face amount

$$\frac{75,597.32}{A_{69}} = 151,287. \qquad\qquad \blacktriangledown$$

Example 17.5.3

The policyholder in Example 17.5.1 wishes to change the policy after 5 years to Life Paid-up at Age 60 with a contract premium of 2,000. Determine the benefit level that results from these changes.

Solution:

$P = 0.8(2,000) = 1,600$, thus (17.5.5) gives us

$$2,491.24 + 1,600\ddot{a}_{40:\overline{20}|} = b' A_{40}.$$

Solving for b' gives $b' = 132,090$.   ▼

Example 17.5.4

After 5 years, the policyholder in Example 17.5.1 wishes to change his policy to Term to Age 65 with a coverage of 150,000. Determine the contract premium appropriate after the change.

Solution:

$P = 0.8G$; thus (17.5.5) gives us

$$2,491.24 + 0.8G\ddot{a}_{40:\overline{25}|} = 150,000A^1_{40:\overline{25}|}.$$

The solution of this equation is $G = 895.00$.   ▼

17.5.2   An Alternative Design

A second design combines aspects of variable life insurance with the preceding design of a flexible plan policy. The emphasis on the plan of insurance is not as strong in this design as it was in the first. Further, the emphasis is on the **risk amount** (previously referred to as the net amount at risk), rather than on the benefit amount. The risk amount can be determined at the beginning of policy year $k + 1$, and a fund growth equation can be written in terms of this factor, which we denote by r_k. Our analysis will be in terms of an annual model but, in practice, a monthly or even more frequent calculation is more common. The basic growth equation for the fund share, the analogue of (16.5.3) without allowance for withdrawals, is

$$({}_kF + G - E - r_k \, \bar{A}^1_{x+k:\overline{1}|})(1 + i'_{k+1}) = {}_{k+1}F. \tag{17.5.7}$$

Note that accumulation is under interest only, and, in case of death, the policyholder receives both the fund share, that is, the fund at the beginning of the year, ${}_kF + G - E - r_k \, \bar{A}^1_{x+k:\overline{1}|}$, and the risk amount adjusted for interest to the date of death. The risk amount might be selected to maintain an approximate level total benefit amount. The policyholder is given considerable flexibility in the choice of G, the contract premium, and r_k, the risk amount. The insurer typically makes a number of guarantees. Usually, i'_{k+1} is an investment return that must be at least equal to some minimum rate i. The risk charge is typically guaranteed to be no more than $r_k \, \bar{A}^1_{x+k:\overline{1}|}$, where the 1-year term insurance actuarial present value is calculated on the basis of interest rate i and a mortality table used in statutory reserve calculations.

The amount r_k typically must be equal to or greater than a lower bound established by tax regulations. The objective of these regulations is to prevent the favorable tax treatment given to life insurance contracts to be extended to contracts that are essentially savings programs.

Plans of insurance based on recursion relationship (17.5.7) have been called *universal life.* The encompassing title has been justified by the options granted to the insured to change the relative emphasis on death benefits and savings by changing the premium and death benefits. In some cases, the policy commits the insurer to use accumulation rates i_k that are based on a investments with a particular allocation. For example, i_k might be based on investments in common stocks. Such policies are called *variable universal life policies.*

Expense charges, E in (17.5.7), currently used are of several forms, including
- A constant percentage charge against all contract premiums
- Surrender charges such as a large but declining (with duration) percentage of the first-year premium or a transaction charge such as 25 for each withdrawal
- A flat amount per policy either in the first year only or a smaller amount for each policy year, and
- A first-year charge expressed as an amount per 1,000 of benefit.

The charges most subject to regulation are the excess first-year expense charges and the risk charges. Expenses are covered by the insurer, in addition to the stated formula charges, by a number of devices. Some of these are
- Reduced interest credits, limited to the guaranteed rate, for an initial corridor of policy cash values, for example, the first 1,000 of cash values
- An interest rate spread of 1 to 1 1/2% between the net investment yield and the rate applied to the cash values, and
- Recognizing that part of the risk charge actually contains some provision for expenses, just as do regular term insurance premiums.

As stated above, the emphasis on plan of insurance is not strong. At any time, a calculation parallel to that used in Examples 17.5.1 and 17.5.2 could be performed to determine the plan that is implicit in any specific pattern of premiums and benefits, current risk charges, expense charges, interest rates, and reserve.

17.6   Accelerated Benefits

Some life insurance contracts provide special benefits if the insured transfers to a state characterized by serious restrictions on daily activities and extraordinary care expenditures. Payment of those benefits reduces the basic death and withdrawal benefits. As a consequence, they are called *accelerated benefits.*

The word *state* is used to describe the two environments that characterize the distributions of time and cause of decrement because the word plays a similar role in the study of stochastic processes. Within insurance, the two states are labeled *active* and *disabled.*

Accelerated benefits can be divided into two classes. In one class a lump sum is paid, usually at the time of a confirmed diagnosis of the existence of a terminal illness. These are frequently called *dread disease benefits.* A second class involves income payments that commence when the insured has become unable to perform certain specified necessary activities of daily living. Some policies provide that the assistance needed to perform these activities must be provided in a long-term care institution. Other policies may permit the care to be provided at home or in a long-term care institution as long as that care is made necessary by the incapacity of the insured. This second class is often called *long-term care benefits.*

In presenting formulas for benefit premiums determined by the equivalence principle for such policies, we will use the multiple decrement model developed in Chapter 10. There is one important addition. As in Chapter 10, the symbol $_t p_x^{(\tau)} \, \mu_x^{(j)}(t)$ denotes the joint p.d.f. of the random variables time until decrement and cause of, or type of, decrement. The index $j = 1$ is associated with death, $j = 2$ with withdrawal, and $j = 3$ with transfer to a new state denoted by h. In our applications, h is a state such as being diagnosed as having a terminal illness, or being disabled to an extent that necessary daily services must be provided. For lives in state h, who entered that state at age $x + t$, the p.d.f. of time until decrement and cause, or type, of decrement is denoted by $_u(hp)_{x+t}^{(\tau)} \, (h\mu)_{x+t}^{(hj)} \, (u)$ for $u > 0$, where $(hj) = 1$ denotes decrement as a result of death, and $(hj) = 2$ denotes decrement due to withdrawal. This can be viewed as a conditional p.d.f. given transfer to state h at time t, measured from the time the policy was issued.

Our model does not provide for transfer from state h, the disabled state, back to the active state. Thus the three states to which an active life can transfer can be called *absorbing states.* References to models that permit returns to the active state are provided in Section 17.7.

Because of the known health impairment in state h, the distribution of time and cause of decrement in state h is undoubtedly different from that in the active state.

17.6.1 Lump Sum Benefits

This section consists of an extended example that employs the equivalence principle to determine the benefit premium rate for a life insurance policy that pays an accelerated benefit at the moment of transfer to state h. In practice h is typically the state of being diagnosed as having a terminal illness.

Example 17.6.1

The elements of the policy are given in Table 17.6.1.
a. Display the loss variable associated with the policy described in Table 17.6.1 for a life (x) to whom the policy is issued.
b. Use the equivalence principle to derive a formula for the annual benefit premium rate.

TABLE 17.6.1

Description of Immediate Benefit Policy

Death benefit:	1 paid at the moment of death while in the active state
	0.75 paid at the moment of death while in state h
Withdrawal benefit:	$_tCV$ paid at the moment of withdrawal from the active state
	$0.75 _{t+u}CV$ paid at the moment of withdrawal from state h at time $t + u$, where t is the time of transfer to state h
Accelerate benefit:	0.25 paid at the moment of transfer to state h
Premiums:	The premium is paid at a constant rate until death, withdrawal or transfer to state h

Solution:

a. The loss variable associated with this policy contains a new element. The symbol $B_{x+t}^{(3)}$ was introduced in Section 11.2. In this example it denotes the actuarial present value of benefits paid while the insured is in state h. The actuarial present value is determined as of the moment of transfer to state h.

Loss Variable	Domain	p.d.f.	Formula
$L = v^T - \pi\bar{a}_{\overline{T}}$	$0 \le T, J = 1$	$_tp_x^{(\tau)}\mu_x^{(1)}(t)$	17.6.1(a)
$\quad = v^T \,_TCV - \pi\bar{a}_{\overline{T}}$	$0 \le T, J = 2$	$_tp_x^{(\tau)}\mu_x^{(2)}(t)$	17.6.1(b)
$\quad = v^T B_{x+T}^{(3)} - \pi\bar{a}_{\overline{T}}$	$0 \le T, J = 3$	$_tp_x^{(\tau)}\mu_x^{(3)}(t)$	17.6.1(c)

$B_{x+t}^{(3)} = E_{U,HJ|T,J=3}[(b(U, HJ))]$ where

$$b(u, hj) = \begin{cases} 0.25 + 0.75\, v^u & 0 \le u, hj = 1 \quad _u(hp)_{x+t}^{(\tau)}\,(h\mu)_{x+t}^{(1)}(u) \\ 0.25 + 0.75\, v^u\,_{t+u}CV & 0 \le u, hj = 2 \quad _u(hp)_{x+t}^{(\tau)}(h\mu)_{x+t}^{(2)}(u) \end{cases} \quad \text{17.6.1(d)}$$

b. There are three components of $E_{T,J}[L]$. The components relate to (17.6.1[a]), (b), and (c), and they will be denoted, respectively by I_a, I_b, and I_c:

$$I_a = \int_0^\infty (v^t - \pi\bar{a}_{\overline{t}})\,_tp_x^{(\tau)}\,\mu_x^{(1)}(t)dt, \qquad \text{17.6.2(a)}$$

$$I_b = \int_0^\infty (v^t \,_tCV - \pi\bar{a}_{\overline{t}})\,_tp_x^{(\tau)}\,\mu_x^{(2)}(t)dt, \qquad \text{17.6.2(b)}$$

and

$$I_c = \int_0^\infty (v^t B_{x+t}^{(3)} - \pi\bar{a}_{\overline{t}})\,_tp_x^{(\tau)}\,\mu_x^{(3)}(t)dt. \qquad \text{17.6.2(c)}$$

In turn

$$B_{x+t}^{(3)} = \left[0.25 + 0.75 \int_0^\infty v^u\,_u(hp)_{x+t}^{(\tau)}\,(h\mu)_{x+t}^{(1)}(u)\,du \right.$$

$$\left. + 0.75 \int_0^\infty v^u\,_{t+u}CV\,_u(hp)_{x+t}^{(\tau)}\,(h\mu)_{x+t}^{(2)}(u)\,du \right]. \qquad \text{17.6.2(d)}$$

Using the equivalence principle and (2.2.10), we have

$$I_a + I_b + I_c = 0.$$

Solving for π, the benefit premium rate, we obtain

$$\pi = \frac{\left[\bar{A}_x^{(1)} + \int_0^\infty v^t \, {}_tCV \, {}_tp_x^{(\tau)}\mu_x^{(2)}(t)dt + \int_0^\infty v^t \, B_{x+t}^{(3)} \, {}_tp_x^{(\tau)}\mu_x^{(3)}(t)dt \right]}{\bar{a}_x^{(\tau)}}. \quad (17.6.3)$$

The methods illustrated in Section 11.2 can be used to evaluate integrals in (17.6.3). ▼

In Table 17.6.1 it was specified that an immediate payment of 0.25 be made at the moment of transfer to state h, and an additional payment of 0.75 is paid as a benefit on subsequent death. The table could have called for an amount b, $0 \leq b \leq 1$, to be paid on transfer to state h and $1 - b$ at the time of subsequent death.

17.6.2   Income Benefits

This section will consist of an extended example that will use the equivalence principle to determine the benefit premium rate for a life insurance policy that provides an accelerated benefit consisting of income payments that reduce the death benefit. The salient difference between Example 17.6.1 and Example 17.6.2 is in the definition of the conditional actuarial present-value function $B_{x+T}^{(3)}$.

Example 17.6.2

The policy under consideration has many of the feature of the policy described in Table 17.6.1. There is, however, no cash benefit at the moment of transferring to state h. While in state h, the death and withdrawal benefits are not reduced during a short elimination period of length e. For example, e might be 2 months. If the insured does not terminate in the elimination period, an income benefit at annual rate of 0.25 is paid for 2 years with a corresponding reduction in death and withdrawal benefits. Table 17.6.2 displays the definition of the benefit function from which $B_{x+t}^{(3)} = E_{U,HJ|T,J=3}[b(U, HJ)]$ is found. Apply the equivalence principle to determine the benefit premium rate.

Solution:
The solution follows the path of Example 17.6.1 except that $B_{x+t}^{(3)}$ is the conditional expected value of the function defined in Table 17.6.2 and replaces the corresponding function shown in 17.6.2(d). and (17.6.3). ▼

In Example 17.6.2 the income benefit was paid at an annual rate of 0.25 for 2 years; the annual income rate could have been b for n years where $0 \leq bn \leq 1$. Changes in b and n would change the relative emphasis on income and death benefits.

TABLE 17.6.2

Definition of Present Value of Benefits While in State h

P. V. Benefits $b(u, hj)$	Domain	p.d.f.
v^u	$0 \le u < e, hj = 1$	${}_u(hp)^{(\tau)}_{x+t} (h\mu)^{(1)}_{x+t}(u)$
$0.25\, v^e\, \bar{a}_{\overline{u-e}} + [1 - 0.25(u - e)]\, v^u$	$e \le u < e + 2, hj = 1$	
$0.25\, v^e\, \bar{a}_{\overline{2}} + 0.5\, v^u$	$e + 2 \le u, hj = 1$	
$v^u {}_{t+u}CV$	$0 \le u < e, hj = 2$	${}_u(hp)^{(\tau)}_{x+t} (h\mu)^{(2)}_{x+t}(u)$
$0.25\, v^e\, \bar{a}_{\overline{u-e}} + [1 - 0.25(u - e)]\, v^u {}_{t+u}CV$	$e \le u < e + 2, hj = 2$	
$0.25\, v^e\, \bar{a}_{\overline{2}} + 0.5\, v^u {}_{t+u}CV$	$e + 2 \le u, hj = 2$	

17.7   Notes and References

The foundations for variable annuities were built in a paper by Duncan (1952). Since 1969 there has been a flurry of activity on variable life insurance. The paper by Fraser, Miller, and Sternhell (1969), and its extensive discussion, is the basic reference. Miller (1971) provides a less formal introduction and some numerical illustrations. Papers by Biggs (1969) and Macarchuk (1969), and discussions of those, provide additional information on variable annuities.

It is difficult to discuss flexible plans of insurance in a book devoted to basic actuarial models. Issues related to these plans are primarily regulatory and administrative. The type of policy described in Section 17.5.1 is studied by Chapin (1976). The type of policy in Section 17.5.2 is the subject of a paper by Chalke and Davlin (1983).

Accelerated benefits, when issued as a rider to a basic policy, were discussed by Keller (1990). An appendix to the paper contains data on rates of transfer to a long-term care facility and the expected length of stay.

Jones (1994) provides an introduction to actuarial models in which transfers in both directions between the active and disabled states are possible.

Exercises

Section 17.2

17.1. The present value of a continuous annuity providing payments until n years after the death of an annuitant (x) is

$$Z = \bar{a}_{\overline{T+n}}.$$

Express the actuarial present value in current payment form.

17.2. Show that Var(Z), where Z is defined in Exercise 17.1, is

$$\frac{v^{2n}[{}^2\bar{A}_x - \bar{A}_x^2]}{\delta^2}.$$

17.3. Assume that $\delta > 0$ and $\mu_x(t) = \mu$, $0 \le t$. Use (17.2.1) to develop the formula

$$G(1 - r) = \frac{1 - e^{-\delta G}}{\delta} + \frac{e^{-(\mu+\delta)G}}{\mu + \delta}$$

to be solved for G.

17.4. Restate the formula of Exercise 17.3 for the case $\delta = 0$, $\mu > 0$, and $0 < r < 1$, and confirm that it does not have a positive solution.

Section 17.3

17.5. If Z is defined as in (17.3.1), show that

$$\text{Var}(Z) = \frac{{}^2\bar{A}_{x:\overline{n}|} - (\bar{A}_{x:\overline{n}|})^2}{\delta^2}.$$

17.6. Prove that the actuarial present value of an n-year continuous family income insurance with the annuity value calculated at a force of interest δ' is

$$\frac{\bar{A}^1_{x:\overline{n}|} - e^{-\delta'n}\,{}''\bar{A}^1_{x:\overline{n}|}}{\delta'}$$

where ${}''\bar{A}^1_{x:\overline{n}|}$ is evaluated at a force of interest $\delta'' = \delta - \delta'$.

17.7. A policy provides a continuous annuity-certain of 1 per annum beginning at the date of death of (x). If death occurs within 15 years of policy issue, the annuity is payable to the end of 20 years from policy issue. If death occurs between 15 and 20 years from policy issue, the annuity is payable for 5 years certain. Coverage ceases 20 years from policy issue. Write an exact expression for the actuarial present value.

17.8. A contract provides for the payment of 1,000 at the end of 20 years if the insured is then living or an income of 10 a month in the event of death before the 20th anniversary of the policy. The first income payment is due at the end of the policy month of death, but no payments are made after 20 years from the date of policy issue. Write the formula for the annual benefit premium at age x. Premiums are paid at the beginning of each policy year, and at most 20 payments are made.

17.9. Show that

$$\bar{a}_{\overline{n}|} - \bar{a}_{x:\overline{n}|} = \frac{\bar{A}^1_{x:\overline{n}|} - v^n \,{}_nq_x}{\delta}.$$

17.10. a. In relation to Example 17.3.1, construct the present value of benefits as a function of the time-until-death.
   b. Express the actuarial present value of benefits by the aggregate payment technique.
   c. Verify that integration by parts in the answer for (b) yields the expression obtained in Example 17.3.1.

17.11. a. Verify that

$$(\ddot{a}_{\overline{x:n}} - 1)(1 + i) = p_x \ddot{a}_{\overline{x+1:n-1}} + q_x \ddot{a}_{\overline{n-1}}.$$

b. Verify that (17.4.4) holds for a variable annuity with the payout made on an n-year certain and life basis.

17.12. a. Rearrange (17.4.10) to the following equivalent form:

$$b_{k+1} = \left[b_k - \frac{(b_k - 1)P(\bar{A}_x)}{{}_1E_{x+k} \, {}_{k+1}V(\bar{A}_x)} \right] \frac{1 + i'_{k+1}}{1 + i}.$$

b. If for the formula in part (a), $i'_{k+1} = i$, $k = 0, 1, 2, \ldots$, and $b_0 = 1$, show that $b_{k+1} = 1$, $k = 0, 1, 2, \ldots$.

c. If for the formula in part (a) $i'_{k+h} = i$ for some $k > 0$ and $h = 1, 2, \ldots$, show that the b_{k+h} will be constrained toward 1.

17.13. Rework Exercise 16.13(b), assuming $p'_{x+h} = p_{x+h}$ and show that $r_{h+1} = b_{h+1}/b_h$ as given in (17.4.4).

17.14. A fixed premium variable whole life insurance, discrete model, has death benefit b_{k+1} in year $k + 1$ equal to $F_{k+1} + (1 - {}_{k+1}V_x) = 1 + (F_{k+1} - {}_{k+1}V_x)$, where the fund share F_k satisfies the recursion equation

$$(F_k + P_x)(1 + i'_{k+1}) = q_{x+k} b_{k+1} + p_{x+k} F_{k+1}.$$

Here i'_{k+1} is the interest rate earned on the matching investments in year $k + 1$, and the premium P_x and reserve ${}_kV_x$ are based on the interest rate i.

a. Show that the recursion equation can be rearranged as

$$(F_k + P_x)(1 + i'_{k+1}) - q_{x+k}(1 - {}_{k+1}V_x) = F_{k+1}$$

and interpret this equation.

b. If $i'_{k+1} = i$, $k = 0, 1, 2, \ldots$, show that $F_{k+1} = {}_{k+1}V_x$ so that b_{k+1} is constant at 1.

c. Show that

$$b_{k+1} = b_k + (F_k + P_x)i'_{k+1} - ({}_kV_x + P_x)i.$$

[Note that in this design the death benefit for year $k + 1$ is b_{k+1} rather than b_k, as in (17.4.9). Further, the 1-year term insurance cost, as of the beginning of year $k + 1$, is here $b_{k+1} q_{x+k}/(1 + i'_{k+1})$ rather than $b_k q_{x+k}/(1 + i)$, as in (17.4.9): The administration of this design depends on the discrete model and the fact that death claims are paid at the end of the period.]

17.15. The policyholder in Example 17.5.1 wishes to change the policy after 5 years to Endowment Insurance to Age 65 with a annual contract premium of 5,000. Determine the benefit level that results from these changes.

17.16. a. The policyholder in Exercise 17.15 decides to elect only 160,000 of Endowment Insurance to Age 65, but will still pay a annual contract premium of 5,000 until a final, fractional premium is payable 1 year after the date of the last full premium. At what age is this fractional premium payable?

b. For the policy in part (a), what would be the reserve at the end of 10 years after the change to the endowment form?

Section 17.6

17.17. Use the results of Example 17.6.1 and the assumptions that $\mu_x^{(1)}(t) = \mu^{(1)}$, $\mu_x^{(2)}(t) = \mu^{(2)}$, $\mu_x^{(3)}(t) = \mu^{(3)}$, $(h\mu)_{x+t}^{(1)}(u) = (h\mu)^{(1)}$, $(h\mu)_{x+t}^{(2)}(u) = (h\mu)^{(2)}$, and $_tCV = 0$ and the force of interest $\delta > 0$ to show that

$$\pi = \mu^{(1)} + \mu^{(3)} \left[\frac{(hu)^{(1)} + (0.25)(hu)^{(2)} + 0.25\delta}{(hu)^{(1)} + (hu)^{(2)} + \delta} \right].$$

17.18. a. Rewrite the result in Exercise 17.17 as

$$\pi - \bar{P}(\bar{A}_x) = \mu^{(3)} \left[\frac{(h\mu)^{(1)} + 0.25(h\mu)^{(2)} + 0.25\delta}{(h\mu)^{(1)} + (h\mu)^{(2)} + \delta} \right].$$

b. This difference can be viewed as the extra benefit premium rate associated with the accelerated benefit. If $(h\mu)^{(2)} = 0$,

$$\pi - \bar{P}(\bar{A}_x) = \mu^{(3)} \left[\frac{(h\mu)^{(1)} + 0.25\delta}{(h\mu)^{(1)} + \delta} \right].$$

c. Observe the behavior of $\pi - \bar{P}(\bar{A}_x)$ as $\delta \to 0$ and as $\delta \to \infty$ in (b).

ADVANCED MULTIPLE
LIFE THEORY

18.1   Introduction

In Chapter 9 we defined the joint-life and last-survivor statuses, expressing their time-until-failure random variables in terms of those for the individual lives. We extended the concepts of Chapters 3–5 for this to obtain actuarial functions for the statuses of just two lives. On the assumption that the future lifetimes of the two lives were independent, the multiple-life actuarial functions were expressed in terms of the single-life functions, making it possible to calculate them using readily available life tables for single lives. Probabilities, annuities, and insurances, contingent on the order of the deaths of the two lives, were also discussed in Chapter 9.

In this chapter we extend these ideas to more than two lives. In fact, with more than two lives, the idea of a surviving status can be generalized. (See Sections 18.2 and 18.3.) With the ultimate goal of numerical evaluation of these functions, we use Theorem 18.2.1 to express the survival functions of these statuses in terms of only joint-life survival functions. Again, under the independent lifetimes assumptions, we evaluate these joint-life survival functions as products of individual life survival probabilities. Theorem 18.2.1 is a form of a general theorem of probability theory used in the so-called inclusion-exclusion method. A statement and proof of this more general theorem, designated as Theorem 18.2.2, is found in the Appendix to this chapter.

Contingent probabilities and functions and reversionary annuities are also generalized to more than two lives.

The annual benefit premium models of Chapters 6 and 7 are developed for the multiple-life statuses in Section 18.7, with some discussion of practical issues involved with one of the most common of these products, the second-to-die insurance policy.

18.2 More General Statuses

For m lives, (x_1), (x_2), $\ldots$, (x_m), the **k-survivor status**, denoted by

$$\left(\frac{k}{x_1 x_2 \cdots x_m}\right),$$

exists as long as at least k of the m lives survive and fails upon the $m-k+1$-st death among the m lives. This is a survival status as defined in Section 9.3. The previously defined joint-life status and the last-survivor status are, respectively, the m-survivor status and the 1-survivor status. When referring to either of these statuses, we will use its special symbol rather than the general k-survivor form. The future lifetime of the k-survivor status is the k-th largest of the set of m lifetimes $T(x_1)$, $T(x_2)$, $\ldots$, $T(x_m)$. Like the future lifetimes in Chapters 3 and 9, this one for the k-survivor status is the period of existence from a fixed initial time to a random termination time. With only a change in notation to display the status

$$\left(\frac{k}{x_1 x_2 \cdots x_m}\right),$$

the probability distribution and life table functions of Chapter 3 are applicable to the future lifetime of this status.

Annuity and insurance benefits are defined in terms of the future lifetime of a k-survivor status just as they were in Chapters 4 and 5 for (x). For a continuous annuity of 1 payable annually as long as at least k of the m lives survive, we have from (5.2.4) that the actuarial present value is

$$\bar{a}_{\frac{k}{x_1 x_2 \cdots x_m}} = \int_0^\infty v^t \, {}_tp_{\frac{k}{x_1 x_2 \cdots x_m}} \, dt. \tag{18.2.1}$$

The insurance paying a unit on the $m-k+1$-st death among the m lives would have the actuarial present value given by (4.2.6), that is,

$$\bar{A}_{\frac{k}{x_1 x_2 \cdots x_m}} = \int_0^\infty v^t \, {}_tp_{\frac{k}{x_1 x_2 \cdots x_m}} \, \mu_{\frac{k}{x_1 x_2 \cdots x_m}}(t) \, dt. \tag{18.2.2}$$

For the analysis and evaluation of probabilities and actuarial present values for these benefits (and other combinations of benefits) we will define a new type of status. For the m lives (x_1), (x_2), $\ldots$, (x_m), the $[k]$-**deferred survivor status** exists while exactly k of the m lives survive; that is, it comes into existence upon the $m-k$-th death and remains in existence until the next death. The notation for this status will be

$$\left(\frac{[k]}{x_1 x_2 \cdots x_m}\right).$$

For $k = m$, the $[m]$-deferred survivor status coincides with the m-survivor status. For $k = 0$, the $[0]$-deferred survivor status exists forever following the m-th death.

The status

$$\left(\frac{[k]}{x_1 x_2 \cdots x_m}\right)$$

is not a survival status as defined in Chapter 9. For instance, for $k < m$, $_tp\frac{[k]}{\overline{x_1 x_2 \cdots x_m}}$, which is the probability that exactly k of the m lives are surviving at time t, does not equal 1 at $t = 0$ and thus does not meet the requirements of a survival function as given in Table 3.2.1. In addition, as $t \to \infty$, $_tp\frac{[0]}{\overline{x_1 x_2 \cdots x_m}}$ goes to 1, which also violates those requirements. Moreover, for a [k]-deferred survivor status, the period of existence does not equal the time to failure. This means that annuity benefits must be carefully defined for this new status. The annuity with actuarial present value $\bar{a}\frac{[k]}{\overline{x_1 x_2 \cdots x_m}}$ is defined to be payable during the future lifetime of the [k]-deferred survivor status; hence it is a deferred annuity with a deferral period of random length. Since the time of failure of the [k]-deferred survivor status is equal to the time of failure of the k-survivor status, insurance benefits payable upon failure of the deferred status are essentially applications of the k-survivor status.

Example 18.2.1

A continuous annuity is payable as long as any of (w), (x), (y), and (z) are alive. At each death the annual rate of payment is reduced by 50%. Express the actuarial present value of such an annuity in terms of $\bar{a}\frac{[k]}{\overline{wxyz}}$, $k = 1, 2, 3, 4$. Assume a unit initial benefit rate.

Solution:

The actuarial present value is

$$\bar{a}\frac{[4]}{\overline{wxyz}} + \frac{1}{2}\,\bar{a}\frac{[3]}{\overline{wxyz}} + \frac{1}{4}\,\bar{a}\frac{[2]}{\overline{wxyz}} + \frac{1}{8}\,\bar{a}\frac{[1]}{\overline{wxyz}}.$$

The discussion of this annuity is continued (after Theorem 18.2.1) in Example 18.2.2.

▼

In Chapter 9 we expressed last-survivor probabilities and related actuarial present values in terms of those for single- and joint-life statuses. We shall use the following theorem to aid in obtaining the same results for the k-survivor statuses. A more general statement of the theorem for arbitrary events, as well as its proof, is given in the Appendix to this chapter. The basic symbols and operations of the calculus of finite differences, as used below in Theorem 18.2.1, are reviewed in Appendix 5.

Theorem 18.2.1

Let

$$_tD_j = \Sigma \; _tp_{x(1)x(2)\cdots x(j)}$$

where the sum is over all combinations of j out of the m lives. Then, for arbitrary numbers, $c_0, c_1, \ldots, c_m$,

$$\sum_{j=0}^{m} c_j \, _tp\frac{[j]}{\overline{x_1 x_2 \cdots x_m}} = c_0 + \sum_{j=1}^{m} \Delta^j c_0 \, _tD_j. \qquad (18.2.3)$$

Theorem 18.2.1 is applicable for lives with dependent future-lifetime variables. In most applications, however, we will assume mutually independent future lifetimes and calculate the terms of the ${}_tD_j'$s as products of individual survival probabilities.

An illustration of the algebra implicit in (18.2.3) is provided by

$$c_1 \, {}_tp_{\overline{xy}}^{[1]} + c_2 \, {}_tp_{\overline{xy}}^{[2]} = (\Delta c_0)({}_tp_x + {}_tp_y) + \Delta^2 c_0({}_tp_{xy})$$

$$= c_1({}_tp_x + {}_tp_y) + (c_2 - 2c_1){}_tp_{xy}.$$

Express the actuarial present value of the annuity described in Example 18.2.1 in terms of actuarial present values for annuities on single- and joint-life statuses.

Solution:

The actuarial present value is

$$\int_0^\infty v^t \left[\sum_{j=1}^4 \left(\frac{1}{2} \right)^{4-j} {}_tp_{\overline{wxyz}}^{[j]} \right] dt.$$

The coefficients and their differences are given below.

j	c_j	Δc_j	$\Delta^2 c_j$	$\Delta^3 c_j$	$\Delta^3 c_j$
0	0	$1/8$	0	$1/8$	0
1	$1/8$	$1/8$	$1/8$	$1/8$	—
2	$1/4$	$1/4$	$1/4$	—	—
3	$1/2$	$1/2$	—	—	—
4	1	—	—	—	—

Thus, the integral is equal to

$$\int_0^\infty v^t \left(\frac{1}{8} \, {}_tD_1 + \frac{1}{8} \, {}_tD_3 \right) dt = \frac{1}{8} (\bar{a}_w + \bar{a}_x + \bar{a}_y + \bar{a}_z) + \frac{1}{8} (\bar{a}_{wxy} + \bar{a}_{wxz} + \bar{a}_{wyz} + \bar{a}_{xyz}).$$

Such expressions can be examined for reasonableness by interpreting the final form in terms of a collection of annuities for which, at any outcome, the total of their rates of payment equals the rate of payment of the original annuity. For example, in this particular case the original annuity commences payment at rate 1, while the final form relates to a collection of four single-life and four joint-life annuities all paying at the rate $1/8$. At a time between the first and second deaths, the original annuity's rate would be $1/2$, while three of the single-life annuities and one of the joint-life annuities would still be in payment status, each with rate $1/8$. The rates at other times can be compared in a similar way. ▼

We have an expression for ${}_tp_{\overline{x_1 x_2 \cdots x_m}}^{[k]}$ as a special case of Theorem 18.2.1.

$$_tp\frac{[k]}{x_1 x_2 \cdots x_m} = \sum_{j=k}^{m} (-1)^{j-k} \binom{j}{k} {}_tD_j. \qquad (18.2.4)$$

Proof:

In Theorem 18.2.1, set $c_k = 1$ and $c_j = 0$ for $j \neq k$. For these c_j's, $\Delta^j c_0 = (E - 1)^j c_0 = (-1)^{j-k} \binom{j}{k}$, $j = k, k + 1, \ldots, m$. ∎

Example 18.2.3

Express the actuarial present value of a continuous annuity of 1 per annum while exactly three of five lives survive, in terms of actuarial present values of joint-life annuities.

Solution:

Using (5.2.4) and then (18.2.4), we have

$$\bar{a}\frac{[3]}{x_1 x_2 x_3 x_4 x_5} = \int_0^\infty v^t \, {}_tp\frac{[3]}{x_1 x_2 x_3 x_4 x_5} \, dt$$

$$= \int_0^\infty v^t \, ({}_tD_3 - 4 \, {}_tD_4 + 10 \, {}_tD_5) \, dt$$

$$= \bar{a}_{x_1 x_2 x_3} + \bar{a}_{x_1 x_2 x_4} + 8 \text{ more joint three-life annuity values}$$

$$- 4(a_{x_1 x_2 x_3 x_4} + \bar{a}_{x_1 x_2 x_3 x_5} + 3 \text{ more joint four-life annuity values})$$

$$+ 10\bar{a}_{x_1 x_2 x_3 x_4 x_5} \, . \qquad \blacktriangledown$$

From the relationship

$$_tp\frac{h}{x_1 x_2 \cdots x_m} = \sum_{j=h}^{m} {}_tp\frac{[j]}{x_1 x_2 \cdots x_m}, \qquad (18.2.5)$$

we have the following corollary to Theorem 18.2.1.

Corollary 18.2.2

For arbitrary numbers $d_0, d_1, d_m, \ldots, d_m$,

$$\sum_{j=0}^{m} d_j \, {}_tp\frac{j}{x_1 x_2 \cdots x_m} = d_0 + \sum_{j=1}^{m} \Delta^{j-1} d_1 \, {}_tD_j. \qquad (18.2.6)$$

Proof:

Using (18.2.5), we start with

$$\sum_{h=0}^{m} d_h \, {}_tp\frac{h}{x_1 x_2 \cdots x_m} = \sum_{h=0}^{m} \sum_{j=h}^{m} d_h \, {}_tp\frac{[j]}{x_1 x_2 \cdots x_m}.$$

Interchanging the summations, we can write

$$\sum_{j=0}^{m} d_j \, {}_tp\frac{j}{x_1 x_2 \cdots x_m} = \sum_{j=0}^{m} \left(\sum_{h=0}^{j} d_h \right) {}_tp\frac{[j]}{x_1 x_2 \cdots x_m},$$

---

which, by defining $c_j = \sum_{h=0}^{j} d_h$ for $j = 0, 1, \ldots, m$, is in the form of (18.2.3). For these c's, $c_0 = d_0$ and $\Delta c_j = d_{j+1}$ for $j = 0, 1, \ldots, m-1$, thus $\Delta^j c_0 = \Delta^{j-1}(\Delta c_0) = \Delta^{j-1} d_1$ for $j = 1, 2, \ldots, m$. Then we have, from the right-hand side of (18.2.3),

$$\sum_{j=0}^{m} d_j \, _tp_{\overline{x_1 x_2 \cdots x_m}}^{j} = d_0 + \sum_{j=1}^{m} \Delta^{j-1} d_1 \, _tD_j. \qquad \blacksquare$$

Corollary 18.2.1 can be used to express the survival function of the k-survivor status in terms of joint- and single-life survival functions.

Corollary 18.2.3

$$_tp_{\overline{x_1 x_2 \cdots x_m}}^{k} = \sum_{j=k}^{m} \left[(-1)^{j-k} \, \binom{j-1}{k-1} \right] \, _tD_j. \qquad (18.2.7)$$

Proof:

In Corollary 18.2.1, set $d_k = 1$ and $d_j = 0$, for $j \neq k$. For these d's, $\Delta^{j-1} d_1 = (E-1)^{j-1} d_1 = (-1)^{j-k} \binom{j-1}{k-1}$, $j = k, k+1, \ldots, m$. $\qquad \blacksquare$

From the expression for its survival function in (18.2.7) we can obtain, by differentiation, a parallel expression for the p.d.f. of the future lifetime of the k-survivor status, T, as

$$f_T(t) = \frac{d}{dt} \left(1 - \, _tp_{\overline{x_1 x_2 \cdots x_m}}^{k} \right) = \sum_{j=k}^{m} (-1)^{j-k} \binom{j-1}{k-1}(-\, _tD_j'). \qquad (18.2.8)$$

The actuarial present value and other characteristics of the probability distribution of the present value of a set of payments that depend on T can be determined using (18.2.7) or (18.2.8). In such determinations we use the fact that $-\, _tD_j'$ is the sum of the p.d.f.'s of the future lifetimes of the $\binom{m}{j}$ joint j-life statuses of the m lives.

Example 18.2.4

Let T denote the future lifetime of the last-survivor status of three lives. Exhibit in terms of joint- and single-life functions
a. The survival function
b. $E[v^T]$
c. $E[\bar{a}_{\overline{T}|}]$.

Solution:

a. By (18.2.7),

$$_tp_{\overline{x_1 x_2 x_3}} = \sum_{j=1}^{3} (-1)^{j-1} \binom{j-1}{0} \, _tD_j$$

$$= \, _tD_1 + (-1) \, _tD_2 + \, _tD_3$$

where

$$_tD_1 = {}_tp_{x_1} + {}_tp_{x_2} + {}_tp_{x_3},$$

$$_tD_2 = {}_tp_{x_1 x_2} + {}_tp_{x_1 x_3} + {}_tp_{x_2 x_3},$$

$$_tD_3 = {}_tp_{x_1 x_2 x_3}.$$

b. We denote $E[v^T]$ by $\bar{A}_{\overline{x_1 x_2 x_3}}$ and use (18.2.8) to obtain

$$\bar{A}_{\overline{x_1 x_2 x_3}} = \int_0^\infty v^t(-1)(_tD_1' - {}_tD_2' + {}_tD_3')\, dt$$

$$= \bar{A}_{x_1} + \bar{A}_{x_2} + \bar{A}_{x_3} - (\bar{A}_{x_1 x_2} + \bar{A}_{x_1 x_3} + \bar{A}_{x_2 x_3}) + \bar{A}_{x_1 x_2 x_3}.$$

c. Replacing v^T by $\bar{a}_{\overline{T}|}$ in part (b) and denoting $E[\bar{a}_{\overline{T}|}]$ by $\bar{a}_{\overline{x_1 x_2 x_3}}$, we have

$$\bar{a}_{\overline{x_1 x_2 x_3}} = \bar{a}_{x_1} + \bar{a}_{x_2} + \bar{a}_{x_3} - (\bar{a}_{x_1 x_2} + \bar{a}_{x_1 x_3} + \bar{a}_{x_2 x_3}) + \bar{a}_{x_1 x_2 x_3}.$$

For any survival status, $v^T + \delta \bar{a}_{\overline{T}|} = 1$, so we can calculate either of the expected values from the other using $\bar{A}_{\overline{x_1 x_2 x_3}} + \delta \bar{a}_{\overline{x_1 x_2 x_3}} = 1.$ ▼

By differentiating both sides of (18.2.6), we can extend the relationship to the corresponding p.d.f.'s. This can be used for insurances paying an amount upon each death among the m lives.

Example 18.2.5

Consider an insurance on (x), (y), and (z) paying 1 on the first death, 2 on the second death, and 3 on the third death. Express the actuarial present value for the insurance in terms of actuarial present values for unit amount insurances on single- and joint-life statuses.

Solution:

Let $f_j(t)$ be the p.d.f. for the future lifetime of the j-survivor status. The actuarial present value is

$$\int_0^\infty v^t[1 f_3(t) + 2 f_2(t) + 3 f_1(t)]\, dt.$$

In the notation of (18.2.6) we have the following:

j	d_j	Δd_j	$\Delta^2 d_j$	$\Delta^3 d_j$
0	0	3	-4	4
1	3	-1	0	—
2	2	-1	—	—
3	1	—	—	—

Hence the actuarial present value is

$$\int_0^\infty v^t(-1)(3\,{}_tD_1' - {}_tD_2')\, dt = 3\,(\bar{A}_x + \bar{A}_y + \bar{A}_z) - (\bar{A}_{xy} + \bar{A}_{xz} + \bar{A}_{yz}). \qquad ▼$$

18.3 Compound Statuses

In the previous section we defined statuses for several lives by means of the k-survivor status. Others statuses can be defined by compounding. A *compound status* is said to exist if the status is based on a combination of statuses, at least one of which is itself a status involving more than one life. We examine some possibilities in Example 18.3.1.

Example 18.3.1

Describe the conditions of payment for the annuities and insurances corresponding to the following actuarial present-value symbols:

a. $\bar{a}_{\overline{wx:yz}}$ b. $\bar{a}_{\overline{\overline{wx}:(yz)}}$ c. $\bar{a}_{(x:\overline{n}):(yz:\overline{m})}$

d. $\bar{A}_{\overline{wx:yz}}$ e. $\bar{A}_{\overline{(wx):(yz)}}$ f. $\bar{A}_{\overline{(wx):y:z}}$.

Solution:

a. The annuity is payable continuously at the rate of 1 per year while at least one of (w) and (x) and at least one of (y) and (z) survive. Thus the annuity is payable while three or four of the lives survive and while two survive if one is from the pair (w), (x) and the other from the pair (y), (z).

b. The annuity is payable continuously at the rate of 1 per year while at least two of the four lives survive and also while only one survives if that survivor is either (w) or (x).

c. The annuity is payable continuously at the rate of 1 per year while either (x) is alive and an n-year period has not elapsed, or while both (y) and (z) are alive and an m-year period has not elapsed.

d. A unit amount is payable at the moment of the first death if (y) or (z) dies first, and otherwise on the second death.

e. A unit amount is payable at the moment of the second death if two deaths consist of one from the (w), (x) group and the other from the (y), (z) group. If not, the payment is made at the time of the third death.

f. A unit amount is payable only after (y), (z), and one of (w) and (x) have died. In other words, it is payable at the moment of the third death if (w) or (x) remains alive, but otherwise at the moment of the fourth death. ▼

In applications, a numerical value for any one of these actuarial present values would most likely be obtained by first expressing it in terms of those for single- and joint-life statuses. The relationships in Section 9.4 among $T(xy)$, $T(\overline{xy})$, $T(x)$, and $T(y)$, and among $K(xy)$, $K(\overline{xy})$, $K(x)$, and $K(y)$, hold for survival statuses (u), (v). For example,

$$v^{T(uv)} + v^{T(\overline{uv})} = v^{T(u)} + v^{T(v)}. \tag{18.3.1}$$

Employing parts of Example 18.3.1, we will illustrate the process of using (18.3.1) and similar identities. First, we consider part (e):

$$\bar{A}_{\overline{(wx):(yz)}} = \bar{A}_{wx} + \bar{A}_{yz} - \bar{A}_{wxyz}.$$

Here, $(u) = (wx)$ and $(v) = (yz)$. To write $\bar{A}_{(wx):(yz)}$ as $\bar{A}_{wxyz}$ we have used

$$\min\{\min[T(w), T(x)], \min[T(y), T(z)]\} = \min[T(w), T(x), T(y), T(z)]. \quad (18.3.2)$$

For part (c) of Example 18.3.1, we have

$$\bar{a}_{\overline{(x:\overline{n}|)(yz:\overline{m}|)}} = \bar{a}_{x:\overline{n}|} + \bar{a}_{yz:\overline{m}|} - \bar{a}_{xyz:\overline{n}|}$$

where the last term is obtained from

$$\min[T(x), T(y), T(z), T(\overline{n}|), T(\overline{m}|)] = \min[T(x), T(y), T(z), T(\overline{n}|)]$$

for the case $n \le m$.

Other arrangements, as in parts (a), (b), (d), and (f) of Example 18.3.1, require the use of other relationships. For part (a), we want

$$\bar{a}_{\overline{wx}:\overline{yz}} = \mathrm{E}[\bar{a}_{\overline{T}|}] \quad (18.3.3)$$

where

$$T = \min[T(\overline{wx}), T(\overline{yz})]$$

$$= \min\{\max[T(w), T(x)], \max[T(y), T(z)]\}.$$

A simple answer, like (18.3.2), is not available for this random variable. To proceed, let us first assume that $T(\overline{wx})$ and $T(\overline{yz})$ are independent and look at $s(t)$, the survival function of T. Thus

$$s(t) = \Pr(T > t) = \Pr(\min[T(\overline{wx}), T(\overline{yz})] > t)$$

$$= \Pr[T(\overline{wx}) > t, T(\overline{yz}) > t]$$

$$= \Pr[T(\overline{wx}) > t] \Pr[T(\overline{yz}) > t]$$

$$= {}_t p_{\overline{wx}} \; {}_t p_{\overline{yz}}$$

$$= ({}_t p_w + {}_t p_x - {}_t p_{wx})({}_t p_y + {}_t p_z - {}_t p_{yz})$$

$$= {}_t p_{wy} + {}_t p_{wz} + {}_t p_{xy} + {}_t p_{xz} - {}_t p_{wyz} - {}_t p_{xyx}$$

$$- {}_t p_{wxy} - {}_t p_{wxz} + {}_t p_{wxyz} \quad (18.3.4)$$

for the independent case. Now, using (18.3.4), we obtain

$$\bar{a}_{\overline{wx}:\overline{yz}} = \int_0^\infty v^t \, s(t) \; dt$$

$$= \bar{a}_{wy} + \bar{a}_{wz} + \bar{a}_{xy} + \bar{a}_{xz} - \bar{a}_{wyz} - \bar{a}_{xyz} - \bar{a}_{wxy} - \bar{a}_{wxz} + \bar{a}_{wxyz}. \quad (18.3.5)$$

We return to (18.3.4) and show that a parallel relationship for the random variables holds, and then that (18.3.4) is true without the independence assumption. We start with the assertion that for all possible outcomes,

$$T(\overline{wx}:\overline{yz}) = T(wy) + T(wz) + T(xy) + T(xz) - T(wyz)$$

$$- T(xyz) - T(wxy) - T(wxz) + T(wxyz). \quad (18.3.6)$$

The outcomes can be collected into 24 mutually exclusive events according to the order of $T(w)$, $T(x)$, $T(y)$, and $T(z)$. Since the given assertion is symmetric in w and

---

x and symmetric in y and z, only six different outcomes require verification. As an example, consider $T(w) < T(x) < T(y) < T(z)$ for which the left-hand side of (18.3.6) is $T(\overline{wx:yz}) = T(x)$ and the right-hand side is, on a term-by-term basis,

$$T(w) + T(w) + T(x) + T(x) - T(w) - T(x) - T(w) - T(w) + T(w) = T(x)$$

as required. The other cases can be verified in the same way.

An expression in annuities that is parallel to (18.3.6) can be established by similar reasoning. Thus,

$$\bar{a}_{\overline{T(\overline{wx:yz})}} = \bar{a}_{\overline{T(wy)}} + \bar{a}_{\overline{T(wz)}} + \bar{a}_{\overline{T(xy)}} + \bar{a}_{\overline{T(xz)}}$$

$$- \bar{a}_{\overline{T(wyz)}} - \bar{a}_{\overline{T(xyz)}} - \bar{a}_{\overline{T(wxy)}} - \bar{a}_{\overline{T(wxz)}} + \bar{a}_{\overline{T(wxyz)}} . \qquad (18.3.7)$$

Taking expectations of both sides of this expression we have (18.3.5).

We emphasize two aspects of the independence assumption for this case. It would not be used to establish (18.3.7), nor is it required in the expectation calculation used to obtain (18.3.5) from (18.3.7). Again, however, to obtain joint-life status functions from single-life life tables, for convenience, we do assume that individual future lifetimes are independent.

18.4   Contingent Probabilities and Insurances

In this section we extend the notion of contingent functions (Section 9.9) to more than two lives. We start with an integral expression for the required probability, or actuarial present value, which can then be rewritten in terms of probabilities or actuarial present value defined on the first death. It is then possible to use some of the techniques of Section 9.10 to complete the evaluation. In any case, numerical integration methods can be used.

To obtain an integral expression for a probability, we use

$$\Pr(A) = \int_{-\infty}^{\infty} \Pr(A|T = t)\, f_T(t)\, dt \qquad (18.4.1)$$

where T will usually mean the time of death of an individual life.

Example 18.4.1

Express $_n q^2_{wxyz}$ in terms of functions contingent on the first death.

Solution:

Here A is the event that (y) is the second life among (w), (x), (y), and (z) to die and does so within n years. Since A is defined by $T(y)$, we use $T(y)$ as T in (18.4.1) to obtain

$$_n q^2_{wxyz} = \int_0^n \Pr(A|T(y) = t)\, _tp_y\, \mu_y(t)\, dt.$$

The integral's limits follow from

$$f_{T(y)}(t) = 0 \qquad t < 0$$

and

$$\Pr[A \,|\, T(y) = t] = 0 \qquad t > n.$$

Now, (y) will be the second to die if and only if there are exactly two of (w), (x), and (z) surviving at that time. If we assume that $T(y)$ is independent of $T(w)$, $T(x)$, and $T(z)$, then

$$\Pr[A \,|\, T(y) = t] = {}_t p^{[2]}_{\overline{wxz}} \qquad t < n$$

and

$$
\begin{aligned}
{}_n q^{\,2}_{wxyz} &= \int_0^n {}_t p^{[2]}_{\overline{wxz}} \; {}_t p_y \; \mu_y(t) \; dt \\[2mm]
&= \int_0^n ({}_t D_2 - 3 \, {}_t D_3) \; {}_t p_y \; \mu_y(t) \; dt \\[2mm]
&= {}_n q^{\,1}_{wxy} + {}_n q^{\,1}_{wyz} + {}_n q^{\,1}_{xyz} - 3 \, {}_n q^{\,1}_{wxyz}.
\end{aligned}
$$

(The second integral comes from applying Theorem 18.2.1.) ▼

The similarity of the final expression of Example 18.4.1 to previous results that did not require independence suggests the assumed independence was not necessary. Alternative derivations in Exercises 18.18 and 18.38 will verify that this is the case.

A contingent insurance can be analyzed by a similar procedure based on

$$\mathrm{E}[Z] = \int_{-\infty}^{\infty} \mathrm{E}[Z \,|\, T = t] \, f_T(t) \, dt. \tag{18.4.2}$$

Example 18.4.2

Express $\bar{A}^{\,2}_{wxy}$ in terms of actuarial present values for insurances contingent on the first death only.

Solution:

Let Z be the random variable representing the present value at issue of the insurance benefit. Since the insurance is payable on the death of (y), we choose $T(y)$ to play the role of T in the conditional expectation of (18.4.2):

$$\bar{A}^{\,2}_{wxy} = \mathrm{E}[Z] = \int_0^{\infty} \mathrm{E}[Z \,|\, T(y) = t] \; {}_t p_y \; \mu_y(t) \; dt.$$

If, at the death of (y) at duration t, there is exactly one of (w) and (x) surviving, the unit benefit will be paid; otherwise no benefit will be paid. Thus, we have

$$\mathrm{E}[Z \,|\, T(y) = t] = v^t \; {}_t p^{[1]}_{\overline{wx}}$$

and

$$\bar{A}_{\overline{wxy}}^{\;\;2} = \int_0^\infty v^t \; {}_tp_{\overline{wx}}^{[1]} \; {}_tp_y \; \mu_y(t) \; dt$$

$$= \int_0^\infty v^t({}_tD_1 - 2 \; {}_tD_2) \; {}_tp_y \; \mu_y(t) \; dt$$

$$= \bar{A}_{xy}^{\;1} + \bar{A}_{wy}^{\;1} - 2 \, \bar{A}_{\overline{wxy}}^{\;1}.$$

Because the benefit is 1, Var(Z) can be obtained by the rule of moments. ▼

18.5   Compound Contingent Functions

The functions in this section are distinguished from those in the previous section by specifications on the order of deaths prior to the death when the benefits are paid, or the event is defined. These specifications on the prior deaths are indicated by numbers placed below the symbols for the lives involved. We examine two such symbols and note the distinctions possible in the notation.

The symbols ${}_nq_{x\overset{2}{y}z}$ and ${}_nq_{x\overset{3}{y}z}$ both refer to events in which $T(x) < T(y) < T(z)$. They differ, though, in that the second death must occur before time n in the first event, while the third death must precede time n in the second event.

It is not always possible to express compound contingent functions completely in terms of functions depending only on the first death. On the other hand, the function can always be expressed as one or more multiple integrals of the joint p.d.f. of the future-lifetime random variables of the lives involved. The example of this general procedure (Example 18.5.1) is more complex than others in this section.

Example 18.5.1

Derive an expression for the probability that (w), (x), (y), and (z) die in that order with less than 10 years between the deaths of (w) and (z) and less than 5 years between the deaths of (x) and (y).

Solution:

We first define the event A for use in a multivariate version of (18.4.1):

$$A = \left\{ \begin{array}{c} T(w) < T(x) < T(y) < T(z) \\ T(z) - T(w) < 10 \\ T(y) - T(x) < 5 \end{array} \right\}. \tag{18.5.1}$$

We choose to condition on $T(w)$ and $T(x)$ because these are involved in both the upper and lower bounds for $T(y)$ and $T(z)$. That is,

$$\Pr(A) = \int_0^\infty \int_0^\infty \Pr(A \,|\, [T(w) = r] \cap [T(x) = s]) \; g_{T(w),T(x)}(r, s) \; ds \; dr \tag{18.5.2}$$

where $g_{T(w),T(x)}(r, s)$ is the joint p.d.f. of $T(w)$ and $T(x)$. Now, $\Pr[A|(T(w) = r) \cap (T(x) = s)]$ is equal to $\Pr(A^*)$ where

$$A^* = \left\{ \begin{array}{c} r < s < T(y) < T(z) < r + 10 \\ T(y) < s + 5 \end{array} \right\},$$

and the probability is calculated by the conditional distribution of $T(y)$ and $T(z)$, given $T(x) = s$ and $T(w) = r$. Thus, $\Pr(A^*)$ can be set up in the sample space of the random variables $T(y)$ and $T(z)$. Two cases are displayed in Figure 18.5.1.

FIGURE 18.5.1

Cases (A), $s < r + 5$, and (B), $r + 5 < s < r + 10$

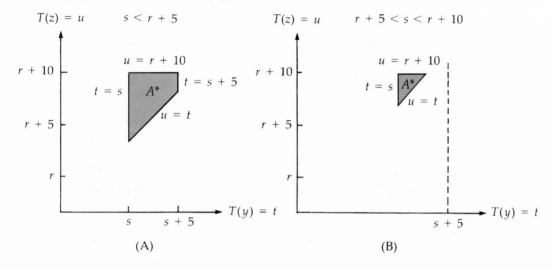

(A)

(B)

Using the abbreviated notation $h(t, u)$ for the conditional p.d.f. of $T(y)$ and $T(z)$ given $T(w) = r$ and $T(x) = s$, we have

$$\Pr(A^*) = \left\{ \begin{array}{ll} \int_s^{s+5} \int_t^{r+10} h(t, u)\, du\, dt & r < s < r + 5 \\[2ex] \int_s^{r+10} \int_t^{r+10} h(t, u)\, du\, dt & r + 5 < s < r + 10 \\[2ex] 0 & s > r + 10 \text{ or } s < r. \end{array} \right.$$

Substituting into (18.5.2), we have

$$\Pr(A) = \int_0^\infty \int_r^{r+5} \left[\int_s^{s+5} \int_t^{r+10} h(t, u) g_{T(w),T(x)}(r, s)\, du\, dt \right] ds\, dr$$

$$+ \int_0^\infty \int_{r+5}^{r+10} \left[\int_s^{r+10} \int_t^{r+10} h(t, u) g_{T(w),T(x)}(r, s)\, du\, dt \right] ds\, dr.$$

Under the assumption of mutually independent future lifetimes, the integrand can be replaced by

$$_r p_w\, \mu_w(r)\, _s p_x\, \mu_x(s)\, _t p_y\, \mu_y(t)\, _u p_z\, \mu_z(u). \qquad \blacktriangledown$$

We now examine some compound contingent probabilities that can be written in terms of single integrals. We will first obtain equivalent forms for a probability by applying (18.4.1).

Example 18.5.2

Write three different integrals for ${}_n q^3_{xy\overset{3}{z}}$ and reduce one of them to probability functions dependent on only the first death. Assume mutually independent future lifetimes.

Solution:

Here $A = \{T(x) < T(y) < T(z) < n\}$. We set three integrals by conditioning on each of the future lifetimes:

$$
{}_n q^3_{xy\overset{3}{z}} = \int_0^\infty \Pr[A \mid T(x) = t] \; {}_t p_x \; \mu_x(t) \, dt
$$

and

$$
\Pr[A \mid T(x) = t] = \begin{cases} 0 & t > n \\ {}_t p_{yz} \; {}_{n-t} q^2_{y+t:z+t} & t \le n; \end{cases}
$$

thus

$$
{}_n q^3_{xy\overset{3}{z}} = \int_0^n {}_t p_{yz} \; {}_{n-t} q^2_{y+t:z+t} \; {}_t p_x \; \mu_x(t) \, dt.
$$

Similarly,

$$
{}_n q^3_{xy\overset{3}{z}} = \int_0^\infty \Pr[A \mid T(y) = t] \; {}_t p_y \; \mu_y(t) \, dt
$$

$$
= \int_0^n {}_t q_x \; {}_t p_z \; {}_{n-t} q_{z+t} \; {}_t p_y \; \mu_y(t) \, dt
$$

and

$$
{}_n q^3_{xy\overset{3}{z}} = \int_0^\infty \Pr[A \mid T(z) = t] \; {}_t p_z \; \mu_z(t) \, dt
$$

$$
= \int_0^n {}_t q^2_{xy} \; {}_t p_z \; \mu_z(t) \, dt.
$$

The second of these integrals can be expressed in terms of first-death probabilities as follows:

$$
{}_n q^3_{xy\overset{3}{z}} = \int_0^n (1 - {}_t p_x)({}_t p_z - {}_n p_z) \; {}_t p_y \; \mu_y(t) \, dt
$$

$$
= {}_n q^1_{y\overset{1}{z}} - {}_n q^1_{xy\overset{1}{z}} - {}_n p_z \left({}_n q_y - {}_n q^1_{x\overset{1}{y}} \right). \qquad \blacktriangledown
$$

Example 18.5.3

Use (18.4.1) to write four different integral expressions for $_nq_{w\overset{3}{x}\overset{}{y}z}_{12}$ Assume mutually independent future lifetimes.

Solution:

Here $A = \{T(w) < T(x) < T(y) < T(z) \text{ and } T(y) < n\}$. Then

$$_nq_{w\overset{3}{x}\overset{}{y}z}_{12} = \int_0^n {}_tp_{xyz} \; {}_{n-t}q_{x+t:y+t:z+t}^{\;\;\;2}_{\;\;\;\;\;1} \; {}_tp_w \; \mu_w(t) \, dt$$

$$= \int_0^n {}_tq_w \; {}_tp_{yz} \; {}_{n-t}q_{y+t:z+t}^{\;\;\;1} \; {}_tp_x \; \mu_x(t) \, dt$$

$$= \int_0^n {}_tq_{wx}^{\;\;2} \; {}_tp_z \; {}_tp_y \; \mu_y(t) \, dt$$

$$= \int_0^n {}_tq_{w\overset{3}{x}\overset{}{y}}_1 \; {}_tp_z \; \mu_z(t) \, dt \; + \; _nq_{w\overset{3}{x}\overset{}{y}}_1 \; {}_np_z. \tag{18.5.3}$$

The last line, obtained by conditioning on $T(z)$, requires one expression for $T(z) < n$ and another for $T(z) > n$. ▼

In the application of (18.4.1) to the examples of this section we have used the assumption of independent future lifetimes in writing the $\Pr[A|T = t]$ factors of the integrands. We now consider the numerical evaluation of these probabilities when a single Gompertz mortality law is used for each life involved.

Example 18.5.4

Under a Gompertz law, show that

$$_{\infty}q_{w\overset{3}{x}\overset{}{y}z}_{12} = {}_{\infty}q_{wxyz}^{1} \; {}_{\infty}q_{xyz}^{1} \; {}_{\infty}q_{yz}^{1}.$$

Solution:

Letting $n \to \infty$ in (18.5.3), we have

$$_{\infty}q_{w\overset{3}{x}\overset{}{y}z}_{12} = \int_0^{\infty} {}_tq_w \; {}_tp_{yz} \; {}_{\infty}q_{y+t:z+t}^{\;\;\;1} \; {}_tp_x \; \mu_x(t) \, dt. \tag{18.5.4}$$

In Example 9.10.1(b) it was shown that, under the Gompertz mortality law,

$$_nq_{xy}^{1} = \frac{c^x}{c^w} \; {}_nq_w \tag{18.5.5}$$

where $c^w = c^x + c^y$. Adapting this and substituting it for $_{\infty}q_{y+t:z+t}^{1}$ in the integrand of (18.5.4), we obtain

$$\propto q_{\substack{wx\overset{3}{x}yz \\ 12}} = \int_0^\infty \frac{c^{y+t}}{c^{y+t} + c^{z+t}} \, {}_tq_w \, {}_tp_{yz} \, {}_tp_x \, \mu_x(t) \, dt$$

$$= \frac{c^y}{c^y + c^z} \left(\propto q_{xyz}^1 - \propto q_{wxyz}^1 \right).$$

Formula (18.5.5) can be extended to more than two lives and then used in this expression; therefore,

$$\propto q_{\substack{wx\overset{3}{y}z \\ 12}} = \frac{c^y}{c^y + c^z} \left(\frac{c^x}{c^x + c^y + c^z} - \frac{c^x}{c^w + c^x + c^y + c^z} \right)$$

$$= \left(\frac{c^w}{c^w + c^x + c^y + c^z} \right) \left(\frac{c^x}{c^x + c^y + c^z} \right) \left(\frac{c^y}{c^y + c^z} \right)$$

$$= \propto q_{wxyz}^1 \, \propto q_{xyz}^1 \, \propto q_{yz}^1.$$ ▼

18.6 More Reversionary Annuities

In Section 9.7 we examined a number of insurance and annuity contracts involving more than one life. Included in that discussion were the more common types of reversionary annuities, those involving only two lives and some examples with terms certain. We consider examples with terms certain measured from a date of death and examples with contingent events defining the start of the annuity payments. We also restrict our discussion to continuous annuities.

Let us examine two reversionary annuities with a term certain measured from the date of death. For a reversionary annuity paying an n-year temporary annuity to (y) after the death of (x), the term certain is a deferred status, so we go back to first principles. The present value at policy issue, Z, is

$$Z = \begin{cases} 0 & T(y) \leq T(x) \\ v^{T(x)} \, \bar{a}_{\overline{T(y) - T(x)}|} & T(x) < T(y) \leq T(x) + n \\ v^{T(x)} \, \bar{a}_{\overline{n}|} & T(x) + n \leq T(y). \end{cases}$$

Using (18.4.2) with conditioning on $T(x) = t$, we can write the actuarial present value as

$$E[Z] = \int_0^\infty E[Z \,|\, T(x) = t] \, {}_tp_x \, \mu_x(t) \, dt$$

$$= \int_0^\infty {}_tp_y \, v^t \, \bar{a}_{y+t:\overline{n}|} \, {}_tp_x \, \mu_x(t) \, dt. \tag{18.6.1}$$

By substituting

$$\bar{a}_{y+t:\overline{n}|} = \int_t^{t+n} v^{s-t} \, {}_{s-t}p_{y+t} \, ds$$

into (18.6.1) we obtain

$$E[Z] = \int_0^\infty \int_t^{t+n} v^s \, {}_sp_y \, {}_tp_x \, \mu_x(t) \, ds \, dt.$$

Next we interchange the order of integration so that

$$E[Z] = \int_0^n \int_0^s v^s \, {}_sp_y \, {}_tp_x \, \mu_x(t) \, dt \, ds + \int_n^\infty \int_{s-n}^s v^s \, {}_sp_y \, {}_tp_x \, \mu_x(t) \, dt \, ds$$

$$= \int_0^n v^s \, {}_sp_y \, (1 - {}_sp_x) \, ds + \int_n^\infty v^s \, {}_sp_y \, ({}_{s-n}p_x - {}_sp_x) \, ds$$

$$= \bar{a}_{y:\overline{n}|} - \bar{a}_{xy} + v^n \, {}_np_y \, \bar{a}_{x:y+n}. \tag{18.6.2}$$

The second display in (18.6.2) is the current payment form for this actuarial present value.

Another reversionary annuity of this type would be one where the annuity starts n years after the death of (x) and pays only as long as (y) remains alive. The present value at policy issue, Z, is

$$Z = \begin{cases} 0 & T(y) \le T(x) + n \\ (v^{T(x)+n})\bar{a}_{\overline{T(y)-T(x)-n}|} & T(x) + n < T(y). \end{cases}$$

Using (18.4.2) with conditioning on $T(x) = t$, we can write the actuarial present value as

$$E[Z] = \int_0^\infty E[Z|T(x) = t] \, {}_tp_x \, \mu_x(t) \, dt$$

$$= \int_0^\infty {}_{t+n}p_y \, v^{t+n} \, \bar{a}_{y+n+t} \, {}_tp_x \, \mu_x(t) \, dt. \tag{18.6.3}$$

By substituting

$${}_{t+n}p_y \, v^{t+n} \, \bar{a}_{y+n+t} = \int_{t+n}^\infty v^s \, {}_sp_y \, ds$$

into (18.6.3), we obtain

$$E[Z] = \int_0^\infty \int_{t+n}^\infty v^s \, {}_sp_y \, {}_tp_x \, \mu_x(t) \, ds \, dt.$$

Next we interchange the order of integration, so that

$$E[Z] = \int_n^\infty \int_0^{s-n} v^s \, {}_sp_y \, {}_tp_x \, \mu_x(t) \, dt \, ds$$

$$= \int_n^\infty v^s \, {}_sp_y \, (1 - {}_{s-n}p_x) \, ds$$

$$= v^n \, {}_np_y \, (\bar{a}_{y+n} - \bar{a}_{x:y+n}) = v^n \, {}_np_y \, \bar{a}_{x|y+n}. \tag{18.6.4}$$

Another class of reversionary annuities that we consider is of, perhaps, limited commercial interest: those where some contingent event must occur before payments start. We consider two such examples and proceed from first principles.

Example 18.6.1

Express the reversionary annuity's actuarial present value, which has symbol $\bar{a}^1_{xy|z}$, (a) by definition and (b) in the current payment form by interchanging the order of integration in your answer to (a).

Solution:

Using (18.4.2) and conditioning on $T(x) = t$,

$$\bar{a}^1_{xy|z} = \int_0^\infty v^t \, {}_tp_x \, \mu_x(t) \, {}_tp_y \, {}_tp_z \, \bar{a}_{z+t} \, dt$$

$$= \int_0^\infty {}_tp_x \, \mu_x(t) \, {}_tp_y \left(\int_t^\infty v^s \, {}_sp_z \, ds \right) dt$$

$$= \int_0^\infty v^s \, {}_sp_z \left[\int_0^s {}_tp_x \, \mu_x(t) \, {}_tp_y \, dt \right] ds$$

$$= \int_0^\infty v^s \, {}_sp_z \, {}_sq^1_{xy} \, ds. \qquad \blacktriangledown$$

This result can be considered as the current payment form of the actuarial present value. It shows that the general form for reversionary annuities can be interpreted quite broadly with the possibility that the failure of status (u) can involve a contingent probability. In general, we have

$$\bar{a}_{u|v} = \int_0^\infty v^t \, {}_tp_v \, {}_tq_u \, dt. \qquad (18.6.5)$$

Our next example shows a particularly simple case involving two lives where the actuarial present value can be reduced to a form not involving integrals.

Example 18.6.2

Express the actuarial present-value symbol $\bar{a}^1_{x:\overline{n}|\,y}$ in a form free of integrals.

Solution:

By (18.6.5),

$$\bar{a}^1_{x:\overline{n}|\,y} = \int_0^\infty v^t \, {}_tp_y \, {}_tq^1_{x:\overline{n}|} \, dt$$

$$= \int_0^n v^t \, {}_tp_y \left[\int_0^t {}_sp_x \, \mu_x(s) \, ds \right] dt + \int_n^\infty v^t \, {}_tp_y \left[\int_0^n {}_sp_x \, \mu_x(s) \, ds \right] dt$$

$$= \int_0^n v^t \, {}_tp_y \, (1 - {}_tp_x) \, dt + (1 - {}_np_x) \int_n^\infty v^t \, {}_tp_y \, dt$$

$$= \bar{a}_y - \bar{a}_{xy:\overline{n}|} - v^n \, {}_np_{xy} \, \bar{a}_{y+n}. \qquad \blacktriangledown$$

18.7 Benefit Premiums and Reserves

Here we examine benefit premiums and benefit reserves for the insurances of this chapter. As in Chapter 6, the benefit premium is defined by the equivalence principle. Following the development in Chapter 7, benefit reserves are defined prospectively as the conditional expectation of the future loss, given survival to the duration of the reserve.

The premium payment period must end no later than the time of claim payment and, in the case of contingent insurances, when it is clear that no claim payment can be made. The period may be shorter.

In the case of insurances payable on the first death, the premiums are payable only while all lives survive. Using the equivalence principle we have, for example, the following:

$$P_{xy}\, \ddot{a}_{xy} = A_{xy},$$

$$_{10}P^{\{4\}}(\bar{A}^{\ 1}_{xy:\overline{20|}})\, \ddot{a}^{\{4\}}_{xy:\overline{10|}} = \bar{A}^{\ 1}_{xy:\overline{20|}},$$

and

$$P(\bar{A}^{1}_{xyz})\ddot{a}_{xyz} = \bar{A}^{1}_{xyz}.$$

Insurances payable on the second or a later death give rise to more than one possible premium payment period. To minimize the benefit premium that can be charged for a particular insurance benefit, we use the longest period. The following example illustrates the process for a number of cases.

Example 18.7.1

Using the equivalence principle, write the equation for the following benefit premiums:

a. $P_{\overline{xy}}$ b. $P(\bar{A}^{\ 2}_{\overline{xyz}})$ c. $P(\bar{A}_{\overline{wx}:yz})$

d. $P(\bar{A}^{\ 2}_{xyz})$ e. $P(\bar{A}^{\ 2}_{\underset{1}{xyz}})$.

Solution:

a. $P_{\overline{xy}}\, \ddot{a}_{\overline{xy}} = A_{\overline{xy}}$

b. $P(\bar{A}^{\ 2}_{\overline{xyz}})\ddot{a}^{\ 2}_{\overline{xyz}} = \bar{A}^{\ 2}_{\overline{xyz}}$

c. $P(\bar{A}_{\overline{wx}:yz})\ddot{a}_{\overline{wx}:yz} = \bar{A}_{\overline{wx}:yz}$

d. As long as (y) and at least one of (x) and (z) are alive, payment of the benefit is still possible. Therefore,

$$P(\bar{A}^{\ 2}_{xyz})\, \ddot{a}_{y:\overline{xz}} = \bar{A}^{\ 2}_{xyz}.$$

e. In this case payment of the benefit is still possible if all are alive or if only (y) and (z) are alive. Thus the appropriate premium payment period is the lifetime

---

of (yz), and

$$P(\bar{A}_{\substack{\tilde{xyz} \\ 1}}^{2}) \, \ddot{a}_{yz} = \bar{A}_{\substack{\tilde{xyz} \\ 1}}^{2}.$$ ▼

As the conditional expectation of the future loss, the benefit reserve will depend on the condition of the status used in the calculation. The reserve is unique for an insurance payable on the first death because all lives must survive until termination of the insurance. We illustrate reserve formulas for two of these insurances:

$$_5V_{\substack{1 \\ \overline{xy}:\overline{10}}} = A_{\substack{1 \\ \overline{x+5:y+5}:\overline{5}}} - P_{\substack{1 \\ \overline{xy}:\overline{10}}} \, \ddot{a}_{x+5:y+5:\overline{5}}$$

where

$$P_{\substack{1 \\ \overline{xy}:\overline{10}}} \, \ddot{a}_{xy:\overline{10}} = A_{\substack{1 \\ \overline{xy}:\overline{10}}}$$

and

$$_5V^{1}_{xyz} = A^{1}_{x+5:y+5:z+5} - P^{1}_{xyz} \, \ddot{a}_{x+5:y+5:z+5} \,.$$

For an insurance payable on the second or later death, the benefit reserve can be calculated with the given condition of the expectation being either (a) which lives are surviving or (b) only that the insurance has not terminated through the last death.

Consider the simple case of a fully continuous unit insurance payable upon the failure of $(\overline{xy})$ with premiums payable until the second death. Let $_tL$ be the future loss at t. Given the information about which of x and y (or both) are surviving at t, we would have

$$\mathrm{E}[_tL \,|\, T(x) > t \cap T(y) > t] = \bar{A}_{\overline{x+t:y+t}} - \bar{P}(\bar{A}_{\overline{xy}}) \, \bar{a}_{\overline{x+t:y+t}}, \qquad (18.7.1)$$

$$\mathrm{E}[_tL \,|\, T(x) > t \cap T(y) \le t] = \bar{A}_{x+t} - \bar{P}(\bar{A}_{\overline{xy}}) \, \bar{a}_{x+t}, \qquad (18.7.2)$$

or

$$\mathrm{E}[_tL \,|\, T(x) \le t \cap T(y) > t] = \bar{A}_{y+t} - \bar{P}(\bar{A}_{\overline{xy}}) \, \bar{a}_{y+t}. \qquad (18.7.3)$$

On the other hand if the given information is only that the survival status $(\overline{xy})$ has not failed, the benefit reserve is

$$_t\bar{V}(\bar{A}_{\overline{xy}}) = \mathrm{E}[_tL \,|\, T(\overline{xy}) > t]$$

which we can calculate by the law of total probability as the sum

$$\mathrm{E}[_tL \,|\, T(x) > t \cap T(y) \le t] \, \mathrm{Pr}[T(x) > t \cap T(y) \le t]$$

$$+ \, \mathrm{E}[_tL \,|\, T(x) \le t \cap T(y) > t] \, \mathrm{Pr}[T(x) \le t \cap T(y) > t]$$

$$+ \, \mathrm{E}[_tL \,|\, T(x) > t \cap T(y) > t] \, \mathrm{Pr}[T(x) > t \cap T(y) > t]. \qquad (18.7.4)$$

In this expression the conditional expectations are given by (18.7.1)–(18.7.3). On the assumption of independent $T(x)$ and $T(y)$, the probabilities are of the form

$$\mathrm{Pr}[T(x) > t \cap T(y) \le t \,|\, T(\overline{xy}) > t] = \frac{_tp_x \, (1 - {_tp_y})}{_tp_x \, (1 - {_tp_y}) + {_tp_y} \, (1 - {_tp_x}) + {_tp_x} \, {_tp_y}}.$$

Combining these we have

$$
{}_t\bar{V}(\bar{A}_{\overline{xy}}) = \left[\frac{1}{{}_tp_x \, (1 - {}_tp_y) + {}_tp_y \, (1 - {}_tp_x) + {}_tp_x \, {}_tp_y} \right] \{ {}_tp_x(1 - {}_tp_y)[\bar{A}_{x+t} - \bar{P}(\bar{A}_{\overline{xy}})\bar{a}_{x+t}]
$$
$$
+ \, {}_tp_y(1 - {}_tp_x)[\bar{A}_{y+t} - \bar{P}(\bar{A}_{\overline{xy}})\bar{a}_{y+t}] + {}_tp_x \, {}_tp_y \, [\bar{A}_{\overline{x+t:y+t}} - \bar{P}(\bar{A}_{\overline{xy}})\bar{a}_{\overline{x+t:y+t}}] \}.
$$

$$(18.7.5)$$

We now use the results from Section 9.7,

$$
\bar{a}_{\overline{xy}} = \bar{a}_x + \bar{a}_y - \bar{a}_{xy}
$$

and

$$
\bar{A}_{\overline{xy}} = \bar{A}_x + \bar{A}_y - \bar{A}_{xy} \, ,
$$

in the final bracketed term of (18.7.5) to establish the equality

$$
{}_tp_x \, {}_tp_y[\bar{A}_{\overline{x+t:y+t}} - \bar{P}(\bar{A}_{\overline{xy}})\bar{a}_{\overline{x+t:y+t}}]
$$
$$
= \, {}_tp_x \, {}_tp_y[\bar{A}_{x+t} + \bar{A}_{y+t} - \bar{A}_{x+t:y+t} - \bar{P}(\bar{A}_{\overline{xy}})(\bar{a}_{x+t} + \bar{a}_{y+t} - \bar{a}_{x+t:y+t})].
$$

Substituting this into (18.7.5) we have

$$
{}_t\bar{V}(\bar{A}_{\overline{xy}}) = [({}_tp_x \, \bar{A}_{x+t} + {}_tp_y \, \bar{A}_{y+t} - {}_tp_x \, {}_tp_y \, \bar{A}_{x+t:y+t})
$$
$$
- \bar{P}(\bar{A}_{\overline{xy}})({}_tp_x \, \bar{a}_{x+t} + {}_tp_y \, \bar{a}_{y+t} - {}_tp_x \, {}_tp_y \, \bar{a}_{x+t:y+t})] / ({}_tp_x + {}_tp_y - {}_tp_{xy}) \quad (18.7.6)
$$

Because $(\overline{xy})$ is a survival status it has a proper conditional survival function, given that it has survived to t, which we will denote by ${}_up_{\overline{xy}+t}$. The benefit reserve for the insurance that was just discussed above can be calculated directly from the conditional survival function if it is first calculated. More precisely,

$$
{}_up_{\overline{xy}+t} = \Pr[T(xy) > u + t \mid T(xy) > t]
$$

$$
= \frac{{}_{t+u}p_x + {}_{t+u}p_y - {}_{t+u}p_{xy}}{{}_tp_x + {}_tp_y - {}_tp_{xy}}. \quad (18.7.7)
$$

We emphasize that only when $t = 0$ is it known that both (x) and (y) are alive. If we assume independence between the future lifetimes of (x) and (y), we have as the corresponding conditional p.d.f. for the last survivor status, given that it has survived to t,

$$
\frac{{}_{u+t}p_x \, \mu_x(t + u) + {}_{u+t}p_y \, \mu_y(t + u) - {}_{u+t}p_{xy}[\mu_x(t + u) + \mu_y(t + u)]}{{}_tp_x + {}_tp_y - {}_tp_{xy}}. \quad (18.7.8)
$$

If each of the ${}_{u+t}p$ factors in the numerators of (18.7.7) and (18.7.8) is factored as ${}_{u+t}p_x = {}_up_{x+t} \, {}_tp_x$, for example, then expressions in those equations will appear as weighted averages with the weights being the probabilities of survival to t.

When (18.7.8) is used to calculate $\mathrm{E}[v^{T(xy)-t} - \bar{P}(\bar{A}_{\overline{xy}}) \, \bar{a}_{\overline{T(xy)-t}} \mid T(xy) > t]$, then (18.7.6) is obtained again.

18.8 Notes and References

The practical applications of the ideas of this chapter have not been as numerous as those in some of the others. Nevertheless, extensive actuarial literature exists on various topics in multiple-life theory. Parts of Chapters 10, 11, 12, and 13 in Jordan (1967), and parts of Chapters 7 and 8 in Neill (1977) contain material on these topics.

Theorem 18.2.2 is a basic theorem of probability. It combines many of the ideas in Chapter 4 of Feller (1968). The technique used in proving results of this type is often called the *method of inclusion and exclusion.* The main results in the field are summarized and an extensive reference list provided by Takács (1967). Credit for the application of these algebraic methods in calculating life annuity values has been given to Waring. Earlier actuarial textbooks gave the results of Corollaries 18.2.1 and 18.2.3 by the so-called *Z method.* This was an algebraic mnemonic based on the observation that the coefficients of $_tD_j$ in $_tp_{\overline{x_1\cdots x_m}}^{[k]}$ and in $_tp_{\overline{x_1\cdots x_m}}^{k}$ are those in the expansions of $Z^k/(1 + Z)^{k+1}$ and $Z^k/(1 + Z)^k$, respectively.

An earlier version of Theorem 18.2.2 is contained in a discussion by Schuette and Nesbitt of a paper by White and Greville (1959). The use of these methods to determine the actuarial present value of a share in a share-and-share-alike last-survivor annuity is the subject of Exercise 18.36 and a paper by Rasor and Myers (1952). Another proof of Theorem 18.2.2 that avoids the use of ideas from probability is given by Buchta (1994).

Some of the issues regarding premiums and reserves on last-survivor insurances were discussed by Frasier in *The Actuary* (1978).

Life insurance policies with nonforfeiture values contain an embedded option. At each policy anniversary the insured has the option to take the nonforfeiture value and negotiate a new insurance contract, using health and market information available at that time, in an attempt to increase the actuarial present value of life insurance wealth. Reynolds (1994) discusses the cost implications of this option with respect to last survivor policies for which premiums, reserves, and nonforfeiture values are determined, using a conditional survival function as in (18.7.7). Reynolds develops the proposition that mortality antiselection, in the sense that those statuses exercising the withdrawal option will be in "better health," that is, the statuses will have a higher probability of long survival than those continuing, will be significant. Provision for the expected cost of this option should be built into the design of the policy. The argument depends on the observation that nonforfeiture values, like reserves, that are derived from conditional survival functions that assume only the survival of the status will tend to be larger than those that incorporate additional information about the survival of (x) and (y) as in (18.7.1), (18.7.2), and (18.7.3).

Appendix

Theorem 18.2.2

Let $A_1, A_2, \ldots, A_n$ represent the events of interest, and let $P_{[j]}$ denote the probability that exactly j of the n events take place. Further, let D_j be the sum, for all combinations of j events out of the n, of the probabilities that j specified events will occur, irrespective of the occurrence of the other $n - j$ events. Then, for any choice of numbers $c_0, c_1, \ldots, c_n$,

$$c_0 P_{[0]} + c_1 P_{[1]} + c_2 P_{[2]} + \cdots + c_n P_{[n]} = c_0 + D_1 \Delta c_0 + D_2 \Delta^2 c_0 + \cdots + D_n \Delta^n c_0.$$

Proof:

Let X_i denote the indicator for the event A_i, that is, $X_i = 1$ for sample points in A_i and $X_i = 0$ for sample points not in A_i. Let Y_j be the indicator such that $Y_j = 1$ for sample points in exactly j of the n events $A_1, A_2, \ldots, A_n$ and $Y_j = 0$ for the other sample points. We note that the expectation of Y_j is $P_{[j]}$. Finally, we define an operator, $\phi(E)$, a function of the shift operator, $E = 1 + \Delta$, by

$$\phi(E) = (X_1 E + 1 - X_1)(X_2 E + 1 - X_2) \cdots (X_n E + 1 - X_n).$$

We note that any factor equals E if the corresponding $X_i = 1$ and equals 1 if $X_i = 0$. After multiplying, we have for any single point

$$\phi(E) = Y_0 + Y_1 E + Y_2 E^2 + \cdots + Y_n E^n$$

since, in the expansion of the product, the power of E is equal to the number of the X_i equaling 1. Thus the exponent of E is equal to the number of the events $A_1, A_2, A_3, \ldots, A_n$ containing the sample point.

Since a power of the shift operator, E^j, applied to c_0 yields c_j, we obtain

$$\phi(E)c_0 = c_0 Y_0 + c_1 Y_1 + \cdots + c_n Y_n,$$

and then the expectation of $\phi(E)c_0$ is

$$c_0 P_{[0]} + c_1 P_{[1]} + \cdots + c_n P_{[n]}.$$

Since $E = 1 + \Delta$, we can also write $\phi(E)$ as

$$\phi(E) = (1 + X_1 \Delta)(1 + X_2 \Delta) \cdots (1 + X_n \Delta)$$

$$= 1 + \sum_{j=1}^{n} \left(\sum_{i_1, i_2, \ldots, i_j} X_{i_1} X_{i_2} \cdots X_{i_j} \right) \Delta^j,$$

which displays the coefficient of Δ^j as the sum of all possible products, $\binom{n}{j}$ in number, of the X_i taken j at a time. Since $X_{i_1} X_{i_2} \cdots X_{i_j} = 1$ only if the sample point is in $A_{i_1} A_{i_2} \cdots A_{i_j}$, the expectation of $X_{i_1} X_{i_2} \cdots X_{i_j}$ is $\Pr(A_{i_1} A_{i_2} \cdots A_{i_j})$ and the expectation of

$$\sum_{i_1, i_2, \ldots, i_j} X_{i_1} X_{i_2} \cdots X_{i_j}$$

is D_j. Hence the expectation of $\phi(E)c_0$ can also be written as

$$c_0 + D_1 \Delta c_0 + D_2 \Delta^2 c_0 + \cdots + D_n \Delta^n c_0.$$

Equating the two forms for the expectation of $\phi(E)c_0$ completes the proof of the theorem. ∎

The familiar inclusion-exclusion theorem of probability provides an example of applying Theorem 18.2.2. For $n = 4$,

$$\Pr(A_1 \cup A_2 \cup A_3 \cup A_4) = P_{[1]} + P_{[2]} + P_{[3]} + P_{[4]}.$$

Here $c_0 = 0$, and $c_1 = c_2 = c_3 = c_4 = 1$ in the first form of the expectation of $\phi(E)c_0$. From the table

i	c_i	Δc_i	$\Delta^2 c_i$	$\Delta^3 c_i$	$\Delta^4 c_i$
0	0	1	−1	1	−1
1	1	0	0	0	—
2	1	0	0	—	—
3	1	0	—	—	—
4	1	—	—	—	—

we see that the second form of the expectation is

$$\Pr(A_1 \cup A_2 \cup A_3 \cup A_4) = D_1 - D_2 + D_3 - D_4$$

$$= \sum_{i=1}^{4} \Pr(A_i) - \sum_{\substack{\text{all combinations} \\ \text{of two of} \\ 1,2,3,4}} \Pr(A_i A_j)$$

$$+ \sum_{\substack{\text{all combinations} \\ \text{of three of} \\ 1,2,3,4}} \Pr(A_i A_j A_k) - \Pr(A_1 A_2 A_3 A_4).$$

Exercises

Unless otherwise indicated, all lives are subject to the same table of mortality rates, and their time-until-death random variables are independent.

Section 18.2

18.1. Describe the events having probabilities given by the following expressions:

    a. $_tp_{wx} + {}_tp_{wy} + {}_tp_{wz} + {}_tp_{xy} + {}_tp_{xz} + {}_tp_{yz} - 3({}_tp_{wxy} + {}_tp_{wxz} + {}_tp_{wyz} + {}_tp_{xyz})$
        $+ 7\, {}_tp_{wxyz}$

    b. $_tp_w + {}_tp_x + {}_tp_y + {}_tp_z - 2({}_tp_{wx} + {}_tp_{wy} + {}_tp_{wz} + {}_tp_{xy} + {}_tp_{xz} + {}_tp_{yz})$
        $+ 4({}_tp_{wxy} + {}_tp_{wxz} + {}_tp_{wyz} + {}_tp_{xyz}) - 8\, {}_tp_{wxyz}\,.$

18.2. Use the corollaries of Section 18.2 to verify that $_tp_{\overline{x_1 x_2 \cdots x_m}}^{[0]} = 1 - {}_tp_{\overline{x_1 x_2 \cdots x_m}}^{1}.$

18.3. An extract from a table of joint-life annuities valued at 3-1/2% interest reads as follows.

Joint-Life Status	Actuarial Present Value of Joint-Life Annuity-Immediate
20:26:28	14.4
20:26:29	14.3
20:28:29	14.0
26:28:29	13.8
20:26:28:29	12.5

a. Calculate the actuarial present value of an annuity payable at the end of each year while exactly three of (20), (26), (28), and (29) are alive.

b. Calculate the actuarial present value for an insurance of 10,000 payable at the end of the year of death of the second life to fail out of (20), (26), (28), and (29).

18.4. Express $_tp_{\overline{wxyz}}^{\,2} - {}_tp_{\overline{wxyz}}^{\,[2]}$ in terms of $_tD_j$, $j = 1, 2, 3, 4$.

18.5. Express, in terms of annuity symbols, the actuarial present value of an annuity of 1 per year payable at the end of each year while (w) and at most one of (x), (y), and (z) are alive.

18.6. If $\mu_{40}(t) = 0.002$, $0 \le t \le 10$, and $\delta = 0.05$, calculate the value of $\bar{A}_{40:40:40:40:40:\overline{10}|}$.

18.7. A trust is set up to provide income to (x), (y), and (z). The fund is to provide a continuous income at the rate of 8 per year to each while all three are alive, at a rate of 10 per year to each while two are alive, and at a rate of 15 per year to a sole survivor. Calculate the actuarial present values of
a. All the payments to be made
b. All the payments to be made to (x).

18.8. An insurance provides a death benefit of 4 payable immediately upon the first death among four lives age x, a benefit of 3 payable upon the second death, a benefit of 2 payable upon the third death, and a benefit of 1 payable upon the last death. If $\bar{A}_x = 0.4$ and $\bar{A}_{xx} = 0.5$, evaluate the actuarial present value of this insurance.

Section 18.3

18.9. Develop an expression in terms of single- and joint-life annuity symbols for the actuarial present value of an annuity-immediate of 1,000 per month payable
a. While exactly one of (40) and (35) is surviving during the next 25 years
b. While at least one of (40) and (35) survives at an age less than age 65.

18.10. Express the following in terms of symbols of annuities certain and single- and joint-life annuities:

a. $\bar{a}_{\overline{x:y:\overline{n}|}}$

b. $\bar{a}_{\overline{(25:\overline{40}|):\overline{30}|}}$.

Section 18.4

18.11. If at each duration the force of mortality for (x) is $1/2$ that for (y) while the force of mortality for (z) is twice that for (y), what is the probability that of the three lives (x) will die

a. First

b. Second

c. Third.

18.12. Which of the following statements are true? Correct the others as necessary.

a. $\bar{A}_{\overline{wxyz}}^{\,1} = \bar{A}_{wxyz}^1 + \bar{A}_{wxyz}^{\ 1} + \bar{A}_{wxyz}^{\ \ 1} + \bar{A}_{wxyz}^{\ \ \ 1}$

b. $\bar{A}_{\overline{wxyz}}^{\,3} = \bar{A}_{wxyz}^2 + \bar{A}_{wxyz}^{\ 2} + \bar{A}_{wxyz}^{\ \ 2} + \bar{A}_{wxyz}^{\ \ \ 2}$

c. $\bar{A}_{wxyz}^{\ \ \ 3} = \bar{A}_{wz}^1 + \bar{A}_{xz}^1 + \bar{A}_{yz}^1 - (\bar{A}_{wxz}^{\ \ 1} + \bar{A}_{wyz}^{\ \ 1} + \bar{A}_{xyz}^{\ \ 1}) + \bar{A}_{wxyz}^{\ \ \ 1}$.

18.13. Write, as a definite integral, the actuarial present value for an insurance to be paid at the moment of death of (x) if (x) survives (y). The benefit amount is equal to the time elapsed between the issue of the policy and the date of death of (y).

18.14. If Gompertz's law applies with $\mu(40) = 0.003$ and $\mu(56) = 0.012$, calculate

a. $_{\infty}q_{40:\overset{2:3}{48}:56}$ b. $_{\infty}q_{40:\overset{2}{48}:56}$.

[Note: In part (a) the notation $2:3$ indicates the event that (48) dies second or third among the lives involved.]

18.15. An insurance of 1 issued on the lives (x), (y), and (z) is payable at the moment of death of (z) only if (x) has been dead at least 10 years and (y) has been dead less than 10 years. Express the actuarial present value of this insurance in terms of actuarial present values for insurances and pure endowments.

18.16. Develop an expression that does not involve integrals for the actuarial present value of an insurance of 1 payable 10 years after the death of (x), provided that either or both of (y) and (z) survive (x) and both are dead before the end of the 10-year period.

18.17. Obtain a formula for the single contract premium for a special contingent, unit insurance payable if (30) dies before (60), or within 5 years after the death of the latter, with return of the contract premium, without interest, 5 years after the death of (60) if no claim under the insurance arises by the death of (30). Assume the loading is $7\text{-}1/2\%$ of the benefit premium.

18.18. Without using the independence assumption, establish relations such as

$$_nq_{wxy}^{\ \ \ 1} = {}_nq_{wxyz}^{\ \ \ \ 1} + {}_nq_{xwxy\bar{z}}^{\ \ \ \ \ 2}{}_1,$$

and use them to obtain the result of Example 18.4.1.

18.19. Without using the independence assumption, establish the relations

$$\bar{A}_{xy}^{\ 1} = \bar{A}_{xyz}^{\ \ 1} + \bar{A}_{x\bar{y}z}^{\ \ 2}{}_1$$

$$\bar{A}_{yz}^{\ 1} = \bar{A}_{xyz}^{\ \ 1} + \bar{A}_{x\bar{y}z}^{\ \ 2}{}_1,$$

and use them to obtain the result of Example 18.4.2.

18.20. Express $_\infty q_{w\bar{x}yz}^{\ \ \ \ 2}{}_1$

a. As a definite integral
b. In terms of simple contingent probabilities.

18.21. Assuming that Gompertz's law applies, show that

a. $_tq_{xy}^{\ \ 2} = {}_tq_y - \dfrac{c^y}{c^x + c^y}\, {}_tq_{xy}$

b. $\bar{A}_{x y \bar{z}}^{\ \ \ 3}{}_1 = \dfrac{c^x}{c^x + c^y}\,\bar{A}_z - \dfrac{c^z}{c^y + c^z}\,\bar{A}_{yz} + \dfrac{c^y}{c^x + c^y}\dfrac{c^z}{c^x + c^y + c^z}\,\bar{A}_{xyz}.$

18.22. If $\mu(x) = 1/(100 - x)$ for $0 < x < 100$ applies for (20), (40), and (60), evaluate
a. $_\infty q_{20:\bar{40}:60}^{\ \ \ \ \ \ 2}{}_1$ b. $_\infty q_{20:40:60}^{\ \ \ \ \ \ 1}$ c. $_\infty q_{20:\bar{40}}^{\ \ \ \ 1}.$

This illustrates that $_\infty q_{x\bar{y}z}^{\ \ \ 2}{}_1 = {}_\infty q_{xyz}^{1}\, {}_\infty q_{yz}^{1}$, which holds on the basis of Gompertz's

law, does not hold in general.

18.23. On the basis of a mortality table following Gompertz's law (with $c^8 = 2$), $\bar{A}_{54} = 0.3$, $\bar{A}_{62} = 0.4$, and $\bar{A}_{70} = 0.52$. Determine $\bar{A}_{54:\bar{54}:62}^{\ \ \ \ \ \ \ 2}{}_1.$

18.24. Given $\bar{A}_w = 0.6$, $\bar{A}_{wx}^{\ 1} = 0.3$, $\bar{A}_{wxx}^{\ \ 1} = 0.2$, and $\bar{A}_{wxxx}^{\ \ \ 1} = 0.1$, evaluate
a. $\bar{A}_{wxxx}^{\ \ \ 2}$ b. $\bar{A}_{wxxx}^{\ \ \ 4}$ c. $\bar{A}_{wxxx}^{\ \ \ 4}{}_{122}.$

18.25. Express in integral form the probability that (x), (y), and (z) will die in that order within the next 25 years with at least 10 years separating the times of any pair of deaths.

18.26. Express in integral form the probability that (10), (20), and (30) will all die before attaining age 60 with (20) being the second to die.

18.27. Given $_\infty q^1_{xy} = 0.5537$, $_\infty q^1_{xz} = 0.6484$, $_\infty q^1_{xyz} = 0.5325$, and $_\infty q^2_{xyz} = {}_\infty q^3_{xyz}$, calculate $_\infty q^2_{xyz}$.

18.28. According to a certain mortality table, the probability that three lives age 70, 55, and 40 will die in that order at intervals of not less than 15 years is 0.048, and the probability that at least one of two lives now age 70 will be alive 15 years before the death of a life now age 55 is 0.8. Calculate the probability that neither of two lives now age 40 will survive to age 70.

18.29. Which of the following statements are true? Correct the others as necessary.

a. $\bar{A}{}^{\ \ 3}_{wx\overset{\smile}{y}z} = \int_0^\infty v^t \, {}_tq_w \, {}_tp_{xyz} \, \mu_x(t) \, \bar{A}_{y+t} \, dt$

b. $\int_0^{10} (1 - {}_{t+10}p_{50}) \, {}_tp_{60} \, \mu_{60}(t) \, dt + \int_{10}^\infty ({}_{t-10}p_{50} - {}_{t+10}p_{50}) \, {}_tp_{60} \, \mu_{60}(t) \, dt$

$$= \int_0^{10} (1 - {}_{t+10}p_{60}) \, {}_tp_{50} \, \mu_{50}(t) \, dt + \int_{10}^\infty ({}_{t-10}p_{60} - {}_{t+10}p_{60}) \, {}_tp_{50} \, \mu_{50}(t) \, dt$$

c. $_{30}q^1_{40:50:60} + {}_{30}q^2_{40:50:60} = {}_{30}q^1_{40:\overline{50:60}}$.

Section 18.6

18.30. Write an expression, free of integrals, for the actuarial present value of a continuous annuity payable at a rate of 1 per year
  a. During the lifetime of (y) and for 10 years following the death of (y) with no payments to be made while (x) is alive
  b. During the lifetime of (y) and for 10 years following the death of (y) with no payments to be made while (x) is alive or if (y) dies before (x).

18.31. Express in terms of annuity and insurance symbols the single contract premium to provide the following benefits with a loading of 8% of the contract premium:

A last-survivor annuity of 1 per annum on (x) and (y) deferred n years and reducing by $1/3$ on the first death: If the death of (x) occurs before the death of (y) and during the deferred period, the annuity on the reduced basis is commenced on the next anniversary. If the death of (x) occurs after the death of (y) and during the deferred period, the contract premium is to be refunded at the end of the year of death.

18.32. In Section 18.6, the reversionary annuities commenced payment if a status (u) was surviving upon the failure of a status (v). This idea can be extended to annuities with payment commencing upon the occurrence of two or more deaths in a prescribed order.
  a. Show that

$$a^2_{xy|z} = a_{y|z} - a^1_{xy|z}.$$

b. On the basis of a Gompertz mortality table, prove that

$$a_{\overline{xy}|z}^{2} = \frac{c^x}{c^x + c^y}\, a_z - a_{yz} + \frac{c^y}{c^x + c^y}\, a_{xyz}.$$

Section 18.7

18.33. Develop an expression for the annual benefit premium for a contingent pure endowment of 1 payable if (x) is alive n years after the death of (y).

18.34. What annuity actuarial present value should be used to obtain the annual benefit premium corresponding to the actuarial present value $A_{w\overset{2}{x}yz}^{}$?

Miscellaneous

18.35. An insurance on the event that (x) dies before age $x + n$ and (y) dies before age $y + m$, with $m < n$, pays 1 at the end of the year in which the second death occurs.

a. Show that the actuarial present value can be expressed as

$$A_{\overline{xy:m}|}^{1} + v^m\, {}_mp_x\, (1 - {}_mp_y)\, A_{\overline{x+m:n-m}|}^{1}.$$

b. What is the appropriate annuity actuarial present value to be used to obtain the annual benefit premium?

18.36. A collection of m lives are to share-and-share-alike in the income from a last-survivor annuity of 1 per annum payable continuously. The actuarial present value of (x_1)'s share is

$$\sum_{j=0}^{m-1} \frac{1}{j+1}\, \bar{a}_{x_1 : \overline{x_2 x_3 \cdots x_m}}^{[j]}.$$

Show that this actuarial present value can be expressed as

$$\bar{a}_{x_1} - \frac{1}{2}\left(\bar{a}_{x_1 x_2} + \cdots + \bar{a}_{x_1 x_m}\right)$$

$$+ \frac{1}{3}\left(\bar{a}_{x_1 x_2 x_3} + \cdots + \bar{a}_{x_1 x_{m-1} x_m}\right) - \cdots (-1)^{m-1}\frac{1}{m}\, \bar{a}_{x_1 x_2 \cdots x_m}.$$

$$\left[\text{Hint: Use Theorem 18.2.1 on } \sum_{j=0}^{m-1} \frac{1}{j+1}\, {}_tp_{\overline{x_2 \cdots x_m}}^{[j]}.\right]$$

18.37. State in words what is represented by

$$\int_0^\infty v^t\, {}_tq_x\, {}_tp_{yz}\, \mu_y(t)\, \bar{A}_{\overline{z+t:10}|}^{1}\, dt.$$

18.38. In the notation of Theorem 18.2.2 let

$$A_1 = \{T(y) < \min[n, T(x), T(z)]\},$$

$$A_2 = \{T(y) < \min[n, T(x), T(w)]\},$$

$$A_3 = \{T(y) < \min[n, T(w), T(z)]\}.$$

Show that the event A of Example 18.4.1 is the same as the event that occurs when exactly one of A_1, A_2, and A_3 occurs. Hence use Theorem 18.2.2 to establish the result of Example 18.4.1 without use of the independence assumption. [Hint: Argue that $\Pr(A_1) = {}_n q^1_{wxyz}$, $\Pr(A_1 A_2) = \Pr(A_1 A_3) = \Pr(A_2 A_3) = \Pr(A_1 A_2 A_3) = {}_n q^1_{wxyz}$, and $\Pr(A_1 [\text{not } A_2][\text{not } A_3]) = {}_n q^2_{wxyz}$.]

18.39. Consider a second-to-die whole life insurance with premiums payable for as long as at least one of (x) and (y) survive. Assume a fully discrete basis.

a. Show that ${}_k V_{\overline{xy}} = 1 - \dfrac{\ddot{a}_{\overline{xy}+k}}{\ddot{a}_{\overline{xy}}}$

where $\ddot{a}_{\overline{xy}+k} = \dfrac{{}_k p_x \, \ddot{a}_{x+k} + {}_k p_y \, \ddot{a}_{y+k} - {}_k p_x \, {}_k p_y \, \ddot{a}_{x+k:y+k}}{{}_k p_x + {}_k p_y - {}_k p_x \, {}_k p_y}.$

b. Show that $\ddot{a}_{\overline{xy}+k}$ can be evaluated by

$$\ddot{a}_{\overline{xy}+k} = \dfrac{\sum\limits_{j=k}^{\infty} v^j \, {}_j p_{\overline{xy}}}{v^k \, {}_k p_{\overline{xy}}}.$$

POPULATION THEORY

19.1   Introduction

Many of the ideas in Chapter 3 are building blocks in the construction of a mathematical theory of populations. For example, the survival function used to define the distribution of the random variable time-until-death, and to trace the progress of a survivorship group, plays a role in constructing models for populations.

The models developed in this chapter are general. They can be applied, with appropriate modifications, to the population of a political unit, a population of workers, or a wildlife population.

We are particularly interested in certain actuarial applications of population theory. In Section 19.5 a population model is used to study the progress of a system that provides life insurance benefits to a population. In Chapter 20 a population model is used as a component of a model for studying the progress of a system that provides retirement income benefits to a population.

19.2   The Lexis Diagram

In this section we introduce a convenient method of picturing the progress of a population. For example, the history of a workforce's participation can be represented by parallel line segments in a two-dimensional diagram called a *Lexis diagram.* (See Figure 19.2.1.) The pictured point of entry of an individual into the workforce population (with coordinates time of entry and age at entry) represents one end point of the line segment associated with that individual. The line segment then follows a diagonal path to the terminal end point representing exit from the workforce population (with coordinates time of exit and age at exit).

Figure 19.2.1 illustrates, for the population of workers depicted, that at time -25 measured from the present ($t = 0$) there were three active workers. At the present time there are two active workers. One might be interested in making statements

---

FIGURE 19.2.1

A Lexis Diagram

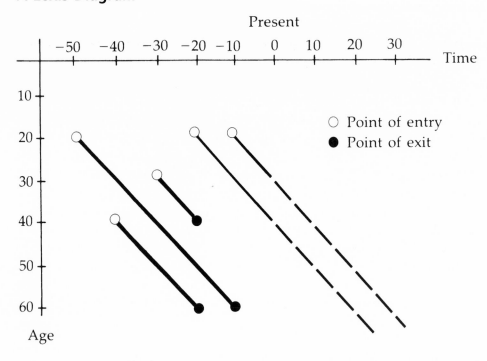

about their future working lifetimes. The dashed line segments in Figure 19.2.1 denote the prospective working lifetimes of the two currently active workers.

The following observations summarize features of a Lexis diagram.

Observations:

1. A fixed point in time is represented by a vertical line. The number of members of a population at that time is given by the number of parallel line segments (each representing an individual) that intersect the vertical line.
2. A fixed age is represented by a horizontal line. If a line segment associated with an individual intersects a horizontal line at age x_0, then that individual attained age x_0 while a member of the population.
3. If a member attains age x at time t, the member's time of birth is $u = t - x$. While x and t are used as coordinates in a Lexis diagram, we frequently use the variables x and u in our developments. One of the reasons for this is that while u is constant for each member of a population, it is not constant over the population.

There are many extensions of these ideas. For example, Lexis diagrams are used to picture the progress of cohorts of lives rather than of individuals. A cohort is a collection of individuals with a common birth period. In a model for a population of workers, several modes of exit may be recognized and entries can occur at different ages. These possibilities were discussed in Chapters 10 and 11.

The demographic models developed in the next two sections utilize only one mode of exit, interpreted as death. Likewise, only birth is considered as a mode of entry. A deterministic approach is taken.

19.3   A Continuous Model

For the remainder of this chapter we use a continuous model for populations rather than a discrete set of parallel line segments (each corresponding to a member) as was used for the illustration in Figure 19.2.1. This shift permits us to use calculus as well as many of the tools developed in earlier chapters. A parallel development based on a discrete model, and using tools from linear algebra, could have been used.

Again, we assume all entries are by birth and all exits are by death. Migration is excluded from the model. Births occur continuously, and $b(u)$ denotes the *density function for the number of births* at time u. That is, $b(u)\,du$ is the number of births between times u and $u + du$. We denote by $s(x, u)$ the survival function of those born at time u. This is called a *generation survival function.* We define

$$l(x, u) = b(u)\,s(x, u). \tag{19.3.1}$$

The function denoted by $l(x, u)$ is called a *population density function.*

The interpretation of the function $l(x, u)$ is facilitated by reference to a continuous version of a Lexis diagram. (See Figure 19.3.1.) This figure and the remaining figures in this section are two-dimensional. They are designed to aid in the interpretation of differential terms or to illustrate regions of integration. In each case, a three-dimensional figure, illustrating the function defined on the time-age plane, could have been drawn.

FIGURE 19.3.1

Interpretation of $l(x, u)$

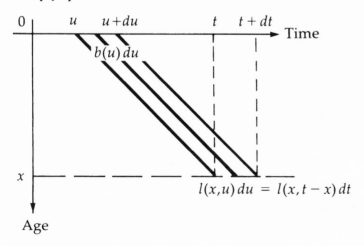

Of the $l(0, u)\, du = b(u)\, du$ births between times u and $u + du$, $l(x, u)\, du$ survive to age x. Let $t = x + u$, then $dt = du$, and this expression can be restated as

$$l(x, t - x)\, dt = \text{(number attaining age } x \text{ between}$$
$$\text{times } t \text{ and } t + dt). \tag{19.3.2}$$

From this it follows that the number attaining age x between times t_0 and t_1 is

$$\int_{t_0}^{t_1} l(x, t - x)\, dt. \tag{19.3.3}$$

Now we consider a different question. Let $x_0 < x_1$ be two ages and t_0 a given time. How many lives are there between ages x_0 and x_1 at time t_0? In posing this question the word "lives" has been attached to the values of an integral of the function $l(x, u)$ and, as in Chapter 3, no longer denotes a variable that must take on only integer values.

These lives would have attained age x_0 between times $t_0 - (x_1 - x_0)$ and t_0 and then survived to time t_0, as indicated in Figure 19.3.2. The diagonal dashed line traces a typical cohort of lives that will be between ages x_0 and x_1 at time t_0.

FIGURE 19.3.2

Number of Lives between Ages x_0 and x_1 at Time t_0

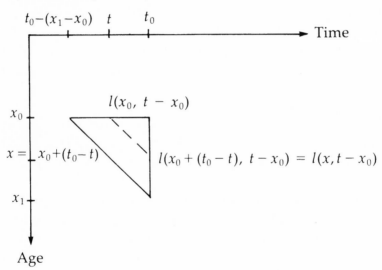

Thus the number we seek is

$$\int_{t_0 - (x_1 - x_0)}^{t_0} l(x_0, t - x_0) \frac{s(x_0 + t_0 - t, t - x_0)}{s(x_0, t - x_0)}\, dt. \tag{19.3.4}$$

In evaluating (19.3.4) we make use of (19.3.1) to write the integrand as $b(t - x_0) \times s(x_0 + t_0 - t, t - x_0) = l(x_0 + t_0 - t, t - x_0)$. If we let $x = x_0 + (t_0 - t)$, we can transform (19.3.4) into

$$-\int_{x_1}^{x_0} l(x, t_0 - x)\, dx = \int_{x_0}^{x_1} l(x, t_0 - x)\, dx. \qquad (19.3.5)$$

From (19.3.5) we can make the following statement:

$$l(x, t_0 - x)\, dx = (\text{number of lives between ages } x \text{ and } x + dx \text{ at time } t_0). \quad (19.3.6)$$

Therefore, the population density function has two interpretations. The first is given by (19.3.2) and (19.3.3) and relates to the number of lives attaining age x between times t and $t + dt$. The second is given by (19.3.5) and (19.3.6) and relates to the number of lives between ages x and $x + dx$ at time t_0. The two interpretations correspond to slicing a Lexis diagram for the population with the lines t and $t + dt$ in the first interpretation, and slicing the diagram with lines x and $x + dx$ in the second interpretation.

In order to incorporate deaths into our model we let

$$\mu(x, u) = -\frac{1}{s(x, u)}\frac{\partial}{\partial x} s(x, u) = -\frac{1}{l(x, u)}\frac{\partial}{\partial x} l(x, u) \qquad (19.3.7)$$

denote the **generation force of mortality** at age x for those born at time u. Figure 19.3.3 provides three interpretations following from this definition. These can be verified by making the indicated linear transformation to the bivariate population density function times the generation force of mortality and confirming that the Jacobian of the transformation is 1.

The total number of deaths in a given region of the time-age plane, as depicted in a Lexis diagram, is obtained by integrating one of the expressions in Figure 19.3.3 over the given region. The solution requires the calculation of a double integral.

There is an alternative method called the **in-and-out method,** which often provides an easy way to obtain the required number of deaths. This alternative method involves determining the numbers of lives entering and leaving the region. The difference between these two numbers is the number of deaths. In most situations, the in-and-out method requires evaluation of only two single integrals.

FIGURE 19.3.3

Interpretations of Population Density Times Generation Force of Mortality

A. $l(t - u, u)\mu(t - u, u)\, du\, dt$ = number of deaths between times t and $t + dt$ among those born between u and $u + du$.

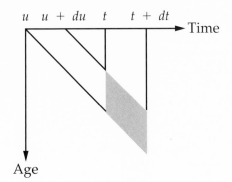

B. Substitute $u = t - x$, and we have $l(x, t - x)\mu(x, t - x)\, dt\, dx$ = number of deaths between ages x and $x + dx$ at times between t and $t + dt$.

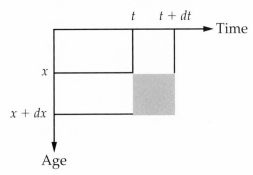

C. Substitute $x = t - u$, and we have $l(x, u)\,\mu(x, u)\, du\, dx$ = number of deaths between ages x and $x + dx$ of those born between u and $u + du$.

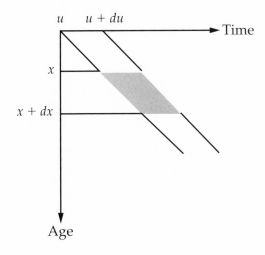

Example 19.3.1

How many lives will attain age x_0 between times t_0 and $t_0 + 1$ and die before time $t_0 + 3$?

Solution:

We must derive an expression for the number of deaths in the trapezoid illustrated in Figure 19.3.4.

FIGURE 19.3.4

Region Where Deaths Are Counted, Example 19.3.1

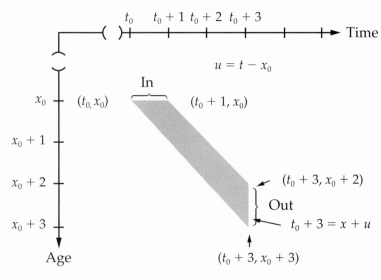

Double integral method: Using the interpretation of Figure 19.3.3C, we have for the required number of deaths

$$\int_{t_0-x_0}^{t_0+1-x_0} \int_{x_0}^{t_0+3-u} l(x,u)\,\mu(x,u)\,dx\,du.$$

Using (19.3.7), we have for the number of deaths

$$\int_{t_0-x_0}^{t_0+1-x_0} \int_{x_0}^{t_0+3-u} \left[-\frac{\partial l(x,u)}{\partial x} \right] dx\,du$$

$$= \int_{t_0-x_0}^{t_0+1-x_0} [l(x_0, u) - l(t_0 + 3 - u, u)]\,du$$

$$= \int_{t_0-x_0}^{t_0+1-x_0} l(x_0, u)\,du - \int_{t_0-x_0}^{t_0+1-x_0} l(t_0 + 3 - u, u)\,du.$$

We let $y = u + x_0$ in the first integral and $w = t_0 + 3 - u$ in the second to obtain for the number of deaths

$$\int_{t_0}^{t_0+1} l(x_0, y - x_0) \, dy - \int_{x_0+2}^{x_0+3} l(w, t_0 + 3 - w) \, dw.$$

In-and-out method: To obtain the required number of deaths we take the difference between the number of ins who attain age x_0 between times t_0 and $t_0 + 1$ and the number of outs who are alive between ages $x_0 + 2$ and $x_0 + 3$ at time $t_0 + 3$. Using (19.3.3) and (19.3.5), we have

$$\int_{t_0}^{t_0+1} l(x_0, y - x_0) \, dy - \int_{x_0+2}^{x_0+3} l(w, t_0 + 3 - w) \, dw,$$

which agrees with the result obtained using double integration. ▼

Example 19.3.2

Determine the number of those between ages 20 and 40 at time t_0 who will die before reaching age 70.

Solution:

We are asked to derive an expression for the number of deaths in the trapezoid illustrated in Figure 19.3.5.

FIGURE 19.3.5

Region Where Deaths Are Counted, Example 19.3.2

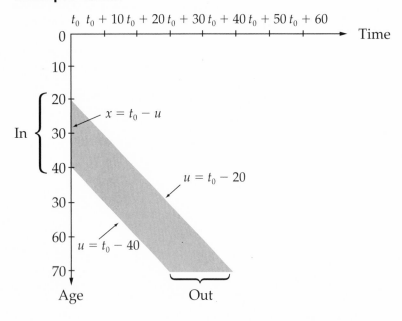

Double integral method: Using the interpretation in Figure 19.3.3C, the required number of deaths is given by

$$\int_{t_0-40}^{t_0-20} \int_{t_0-u}^{70} l(x,u)\, \mu(x,u)\, dx\, du$$

$$= \int_{t_0-40}^{t_0-20} \int_{t_0-u}^{70} \left[-\frac{\partial l(x,u)}{\partial x} \right] dx\, du$$

$$= \int_{t_0-40}^{t_0-20} [l(t_0-u,u) - l(70,u)]\, du$$

$$= \int_{t_0-40}^{t_0-20} l(t_0-u,u)\, du - \int_{t_0-400}^{t_0-20} l(70,u)\, du.$$

We let $y = t_0 - u$ in the first integral and $w = u + 70$ in the second integral to obtain the required number of deaths

$$\int_{20}^{40} l(y, t_0-y)\, dy - \int_{t_0+30}^{t_0+50} l(70, w-70)\, dw.$$

In-and-out method: We use (19.3.5) for the ins and (19.3.3) for the outs to obtain

$$\int_{20}^{40} l(x, t_0-x)\, dx - \int_{t_0+30}^{t_0+50} l(70, t-70)\, dt,$$

which agrees with the result using double integrals. ▼

19.4   Stationary and Stable Populations

Here we study two important special cases of the model described in Section 19.3. If $l(x,u)$ is independent of u, we call the result a *stationary population*. For a stationary population, (19.3.1) becomes

$$l(x,u) = b\, s(x) \tag{19.4.1}$$

where b is the constant density of births and $s(x)$ is a survival function that does not depend on the time of birth. For human populations, b is typically expressed as a number of births per year, and the age variable is measured in years. In accord with (3.3.1), we rewrite (19.4.1) as

$$l(x,u) = b\, s(x) = l_x \tag{19.4.2}$$

where b plays the role of the radix l_0.

For a stationary population we can write (19.3.5) as

$$\int_{x_0}^{x_1} l_x\, dx = T_{x_0} - T_{x_1}$$

and obtain the number of lives in the stationary population between ages x_0 and x_1 at any time t, expressed in terms of the function T_x introduced in (3.5.16) in connection with the analysis of a survivorship group. In addition, the interpretation of $l_x\, \mu(x)$ given by Figure 19.3.3B leads to

$$\int_{x_0}^{x_1} l_x \mu(x)\, dx = l_{x_0} - l_{x_1}$$

as the density of deaths between ages x_0 and x_1 at any time t. In particular, the density of deaths at age x_0 and greater equals the density of the number of lives attaining age x_0 at any time t, the interpretation provided by (19.3.2). These facts illustrate the aptness of the name stationary population.

If the population density function is of the form

$$l(x, u) = e^{Ru}\, b\, s(x) = e^{Ru}\, l_x \tag{19.4.3}$$

where $b > 0$ and R are constant and $s(x)$ is a survival function that is independent of the time of birth, the resulting population is called a **stable population**. The density of births at time u in a stable population is $e^{Ru} b = e^{Ru} l_0$. If $R = 0$, a stable population is a stationary population.

Using (19.3.5) we see that the total population at time t, denoted by $N(t)$, for a stable population is given by

$$N(t) = \int_0^\infty l(x, t - x)\, dx = e^{Rt} \int_0^\infty e^{-Rx} l_x\, dx. \tag{19.4.4}$$

Therefore, if $R > 0$, the population is growing exponentially, and if $R < 0$, the population is decreasing exponentially.

Again using (19.3.5) we see that the fraction of the total stable population that lies between ages x_0 and x_1 at time t is

$$\frac{\displaystyle\int_{x_0}^{x_1} l(x, t - x)\, dx}{\displaystyle\int_0^\infty l(x, t - x)\, dx} = \frac{\displaystyle\int_{x_0}^{x_1} e^{-Rx} l_x\, dx}{\displaystyle\int_0^\infty e^{-Rx} l_x\, dx}, \tag{19.4.5}$$

which is independent of t. Thus, while the size of a stable population may change over time, its relative age distribution is constant.

For a stable population, we can express the number of members between ages x_0 and x_1, using (19.3.5), as

$$\int_{x_0}^{x_1} l(x, t - x)\, dx = \int_{x_0}^{x_1} e^{R(t-x)} l_x\, dx$$

$$= e^{R(t-x_0)} l_{x_0} \bar{a}_{x_0:\overline{x_1 - x_0}|\delta = R}. \tag{19.4.6}$$

In the limit as $x_1 \to \infty$, the number of members alive above age x_0 at time t in a stable population may be written as $e^{R(t-x_0)} l_{x_0} \bar{a}_{x_0 @ \delta = R}$.

For a stable population, the force of mortality as given by (19.3.7) becomes, by reference to (19.4.3),

$$\mu(x, u) = -\frac{1}{l(x, u)} \frac{\partial}{\partial x} l(x, u) = \mu(x).$$

We can express the density of deaths at time t for a stable population between ages x_0 and x_1 as

$$\int_{x_0}^{x_1} e^{R(t-x)} l_x \, \mu(x) \, dx = l_{x_0} \, e^{R(t-x_0)} \bar{A}^1_{x_0:\overline{x_1-x_0}|\delta=R},$$ (19.4.7)

and the density of deaths at time t above age x_0 is $e^{R(t-x_0)} l_{x_0} \bar{A}_{x_0}$.

These facts about stable populations can be used, in connection with an identity from Chapter 5, to confirm a property of stable populations:

$$
\begin{pmatrix} \text{rate of population} \\ \text{change at time } t \\ \text{above age } x_0 \end{pmatrix}
= \dfrac{
\begin{pmatrix} \text{density of those} \\ \text{reaching age } x_0 \\ \text{at time } t \end{pmatrix}
- \begin{pmatrix} \text{density of deaths} \\ \text{above age } x_0 \\ \text{at time } t \end{pmatrix}
}{
\begin{pmatrix} \text{number above} \\ \text{age } x_0 \text{ at time } t \end{pmatrix}
}
$$

$$= \frac{e^{R(t-x_0)} l_{x_0} - R^{(t-x_0)} l_{x_0} \bar{A}_{x_0}}{e^{R(t-x_0)} l_{x_0} \bar{a}_{x_0}}$$

$$= \frac{1 - \bar{A}_{x_0}}{\bar{a}_{x_0}} = R.$$

The final step follows since the functions are calculated at force of interest R.

Example 19.4.1

For a stationary population the complete life expectancy at age 0, derived from the survival function, can be obtained by dividing the number in the population at time t by the birth density. That is,

$$\mathring{e}_0 = \int_0^\infty s(x) \, dx = \int_0^\infty \frac{l_x}{l_0} \, dx = \frac{T_0}{l_0}.$$

What is the result of performing a similar calculation with a stable population?

Solution:

$$\frac{N(t)}{e^{Rt} l_0} = \frac{\int_0^\infty l(x, t-x) \, dx}{e^{Rt} l_0} = \frac{\int_0^\infty e^{R(t-x)} l_x \, dx}{e^{Rt} l_0} = \bar{a}_0 \text{ at } \delta = R.$$

If $R > 0$, $\bar{a}_0 < \mathring{e}_0$, and if $R < 0$, $\bar{a}_0 > \mathring{e}_0$, and if $R = 0$, the stationary population result is obtained. This example demonstrates how the complete life expectancies cannot be observed directly from stable populations unless $R = 0$. ▼

19.5 Actuarial Applications

The conditions for a stable or stationary population are seldom realized because of changes in either the survival function or the density of births. However, these models are useful in studying alternative plans for funding life insurance or retirement income systems. By a funding plan we mean a budgeting plan for accumulating the funds necessary to provide the insurance or annuity benefits.

In this section and in Chapter 20 we depart from the models developed in Chapters 4 through 11, 15, and 16. These models were built by starting with a consideration of the operation of a single policy. In this section we study aggregate models for life insurance. In Chapter 20 similar models for pension systems are examined. The models considered are especially relevant to social and group insurance systems that provide benefits on death or retirement to broad groups or populations.

Example 19.5.1

Assume a population density function $l(x, u) = b(u) s(x)$ where the survival function is independent of u. Further, assume that in this population each member above age a is insured for a unit benefit under a fully continuous, whole life insurance with annual premiums payable from age a. The premium paid by each member is based on force of interest δ and survival function $s(x)$. Prove that

$$\bar{P}(\bar{A}_a) \int_a^\infty l(x, t - x)\, dx + \delta \int_a^\infty l(x, t - x)\, _{x-a}\bar{V}(\bar{A}_a)\, dx$$

$$= \int_a^\infty l(x, t - x)\mu(x)\, dx + \frac{d}{dt} \int_a^\infty l(x, t - x)\, _{x-a}\bar{V}(\bar{A}_a)\, dx. \qquad (19.5.1)$$

Solution:

General reasoning solution: Stated in words, (19.5.1) asserts

(rate of premium income at time t)

+ (rate of investment income at time t)

= (rate of benefit outgo at time t)

+ (rate of change in aggregate reserve at time t).

That is, (19.5.1) can be interpreted as an income allocation equation for a life insurance system covering a population aged a or greater. The left-hand side of (19.5.1) displays the sources of income, premiums, and interest, and the right-hand side displays the allocation of income to death benefits and changes in the aggregate reserve fund.

Analytic solution: We start with (8.6.4), implying for the present case

$$\frac{d}{dx}\, _{x-a}\bar{V}(\bar{A}_a) - \mu(x)\, _{x-a}\bar{V}(\bar{A}_a) + \mu(x) = \bar{P}(\bar{A}_a) + \delta\, _{x-a}\bar{V}(\bar{A}_a). \qquad (19.5.2)$$

We multiply (19.5.2) by $l(x, t - x)$ and integrate between a and the upper limit of survival. These operations yield

$$\int_a^\infty l(x, t - x)\, d[_{x-a}\bar{V}(\bar{A}_a)] - \int_a^\infty l(x, t - x)\mu(x)\, _{x-a}\bar{V}(\bar{A}_a)\, dx + \int_a^\infty l(x, t - x)\mu(x)\, dx$$

$$= \bar{P}(\bar{A}_a) \int_a^\infty l(x, t - x)\, dx + \delta \int_a^\infty l(x, t - x)\, _{x-a}\bar{V}(\bar{A}_a)\, dx. \qquad (19.5.3)$$

The first integral on the left-hand side of (19.5.3) is evaluated using integration by parts. We obtain

$$l(x, t - x) \,_{x-a}\bar{V}(\bar{A}_a) \bigg|_a^\infty + \int_a^\infty [b'(t - x) s(x) + l(x, t - x)\mu(x)] \,_{x-a}\bar{V}(\bar{A}_a) \, dx. \quad (19.5.4)$$

In completing the integration by parts it is important to recall that

$$\frac{d}{dx} l(x, t - x) = \frac{d}{dx} b(t - x) s(x)$$

$$= -b'(t - x) s(x) - b(t - x) s(x)\mu(x).$$

Substituting (19.5.4) into (19.5.3) and rearranging yields (19.5.1). ▼

Example 19.5.2

For the population life insurance system described in Example 19.5.1 assume that funding is on an assessment plan rather than on a whole life plan; that is, the annual assessment rate, denoted by π_t, per member at time t is equal to the rate of outgo per member at time t. Determine π_t.

Solution:

The assessment rate can be determined from

$$\pi_t \int_a^\infty l(x, t - x) \, dx = \int_a^\infty l(x, t - x)\mu(x) \, dx$$

or from

$$\pi_t = \frac{\displaystyle\int_a^\infty l(x, t - x)\mu(x) \, dx}{\displaystyle\int_a^\infty l(x, t - x) \, dx}. \quad (19.5.5)$$

▼

Example 19.5.3

Assume a stable population and rework
a. Example 19.5.1
b. Example 19.5.2.

Solution:

a. We start with (19.5.1), which has already been established for the more general population density function $l(x, u) = b(u) s(x)$. For this example, $l(x, u) = e^{Ru} b s(x)$, and the income allocation equation becomes

$$\bar{P}(\bar{A}_a) \int_a^\infty e^{R(t-x)} l_x \, dx + \delta \int_a^\infty e^{R(t-x)} l_x \,_{x-a}\bar{V}(\bar{A}_a) \, dx$$

$$= \int_a^\infty e^{R(t-x)} l_x \, \mu(x) \, dx + R \int_a^\infty e^{R(t-x)} l_x \,_{x-a}\bar{V}(\bar{A}_a) \, dx. \quad (19.5.6)$$

The factor e^{Rt} can be canceled from each term of (19.5.6). By an interpretation of (19.5.6) developed in the general reasoning solution of Example 19.5.1, the ratio of the rate of premium income to the rate of benefit outgo is

$$\frac{\bar{P}(\bar{A}_a) \int_a^\infty e^{-Rx} \, l_x \, dx}{\int_a^\infty e^{-Rx} \, l_x \, \mu(x) \, dx} = \frac{\bar{P}(\bar{A}_a)}{\bar{P}'(\bar{A}_a')}. \tag{19.5.7}$$

Here $\bar{P}'(\bar{A}_a')$ is computed at force of interest R.

If $R = 0$, the population is stationary, and the income allocation equation (19.5.6) becomes

$$\bar{P}(\bar{A}_a) \, T_a + \delta \int_a^\infty l_x \, {}_{x-a}\bar{V}(\bar{A}_a) \, dx = l_a, \tag{19.5.8}$$

and the ratio of the rate of premium income to the rate of benefit outgo, (19.5.7), becomes $\bar{P}(\bar{A}_a) \, \mathring{e}_a$.

b. In the stable population, the assessment rate determined in (19.5.5) becomes

$$\pi_t = \frac{\int_a^\infty e^{-Rx} \, l_x \, \mu(x) \, dx}{\int_a^\infty e^{-Rx} \, l_x \, dx} = \bar{P}'(\bar{A}_a'), \tag{19.5.9}$$

which is independent of t. If $R = 0$, that is, the population is stationary, then $\pi_t = 1/\mathring{e}_a$. ▼

Remark:

One aspect of Example 19.5.3 deserves special comment. The rate of premium payment required of each member of the stable population above age a under the whole life and assessment funding methods are, respectively, $\bar{P}(\bar{A}_a)$ and $\bar{P}'(\bar{A}_a')$. In Exercise 19.21 it is demonstrated that if the force of mortality is increasing, then

$$\bar{P}(\bar{A}_a) > \bar{P}'(\bar{A}_a') \text{ if } \delta < R$$
$$\bar{P}(\bar{A}_a) = \bar{P}'(\bar{A}_a') \text{ if } \delta = R$$
$$\bar{P}(\bar{A}_a) < \bar{P}'(\bar{A}_a') \text{ if } \delta > R.$$

That is, if the force of interest is less than the population growth rate, the required premium rate under the assessment funding method is less than under the whole life funding method. If the force of interest is greater than the population growth rate, the whole life funding method results in a smaller premium rate than does the assessment funding method.

Example 19.5.4

Provide a general reasoning interpretation of the stationary population income allocation equation (19.5.8) rearranged as

$$\int_a^\infty l_x \, _{x-a}\bar{V}(\bar{A}_a) \, dx = \frac{l_a - \bar{P}(\bar{A}_a)T_a}{\delta}.$$

Solution:

This rearranged form indicates that the aggregate reserve can be interpreted as the difference between the present values of two perpetuities:

$$\frac{l_a}{\delta} = \text{(the present value of a continuous perpetuity paying}$$
$$\text{death benefits at an annual rate of } l_a)$$

$$= \text{(the present value of death benefits to current members)}$$
$$+ \text{(the present value of death benefits to}$$
$$\text{future members);}$$

$$\frac{\bar{P}(\bar{A}_a)T_a}{\delta} = \text{(the present value of a continuous perpetuity paying}$$
$$\text{premiums at an annual rate of } \bar{P}(\bar{A}_a) \, T_a)$$

$$= \text{(the present value of premiums for current members)}$$
$$+ \text{(the present value of premiums for future members)}$$

Additional insights are obtained by noting that premiums at rate $\bar{P}(\bar{A}_a)$ will be payable from age a for future members. The present value of their premiums will be equal to the present value of their benefits. Hence, the second component of the interpretations of l_a/δ and $\bar{P}(\bar{A}_a)T_a/\delta$ are offsetting, and

$$\frac{l_a}{\delta} - \frac{\bar{P}(\bar{A}_a)T_a}{\delta} = \text{(the aggregate reserve for current members)}$$

$$= \text{(the present value of benefits for current members)}$$

$$- \text{(the present value of premiums for current members)}$$

$$= \int_a^\infty l_x \, _{x-a}\bar{V}(\bar{A}_a) \, dx.$$ ▼

Examples 19.5.1, 19.5.3, and 19.5.4 treat life insurance funding, or budgeting, methods for which a fund exists. In these examples the characteristics of the funds, after all members of the population above the entry age a are participants and have been since the entry age a, were examined. When all eligible members are participating and have participated since the entry age a, the system is said to be in a *mature state.* Until that time the total fund is subject to growth by a stream of new entrants. In our examples it will take $\omega - a$ years for the fund to reach a mature state.

19.6 Population Dynamics

In this section we return to an examination of the function $b(t)$, the density of births at time t. Our goal is to build a foundation under the development of the continuous model of Section 19.3. In addition, the conditions leading to stable or stationary populations, developed in Section 19.4, are explored.

In developing a mathematical model for the density of births we introduce the *force of birth function,* denoted by $\beta(x, u)$. Then, $\beta(x, t - x)\,dt$ represents the number of female children born between times t and $t + dt$ to a woman age x who was herself born at time $t - x$. The force of birth function is an age- and generation-specific instantaneous birthrate for female children.

The total number of female children born between t and $t + dt$ is

$$b_f(t)\,dt = \left[\int_0^\infty l_f(x, t - x)\,\beta(x, t - x)\,dx\right]dt. \tag{19.6.1}$$

In (19.6.1) the subscript f denotes that the function relates to female lives. Total births are obtained by multiplying a constant, (total births) / (female births), which is slightly greater than 2 for most human populations.

If we divide (19.6.1) by dt and substitute for $l_f(x, t - x)$ from (19.3.1), we see that the female birth density function satisfies the integral equation

$$b_f(t) = \int_0^\infty b_f(t - x)\,s_f(x, t - x)\,\beta(x, t - x)\,dx. \tag{19.6.2}$$

An integral equation is a statement about the relationship between functions where the relationship involves an integral. The problem is to find $b_f(t)$ given the functions $s_f(x, t - x)$ and $\beta(x, t - x)$. The function $s_f(x, t - x)\,\beta(x, t - x)$ is called the *net maternity function* and in (19.6.3) is denoted by $\phi(x, t - x)$.

For the remainder of this section we assume that the net maternity function does not depend on the year of birth of the mother. That is, $s_f(x, t - x)\beta(x, t - x) = \phi(x)$. With this assumption, the integral equation (19.6.2) becomes

$$b_f(t) = \int_0^\infty b_f(t - x)\,\phi(x)\,dx. \tag{19.6.3}$$

In this section we limit ourselves to verifying that a particular solution of (19.6.3) is

$$b_f(t) = b\,e^{Rt} \tag{19.6.4}$$

where b is a positive constant and R is the unique real solution of the equation

$$H(r) = 1 \tag{19.6.5}$$

where

$$H(r) = \int_0^\infty e^{-rx}\,\phi(x)\,dx.$$

Direct substitution of (19.6.4) into (19.6.3) yields

$$b\,e^{Rt} = \int_0^\infty b\,e^{R(t-x)}\,\phi(x)\,dx,$$

and upon the cancellation of constants this becomes

$$1 = \int_0^\infty e^{-Rx} \phi(x)\,dx = H(R).$$

We now show how the statement that $H(r) = 1$ yields a unique real solution can be verified.

Observations:

1. $H'(r) = -\int_0^\infty x e^{-rx} \phi(x)\,dx < 0$

2. $H(0) = \int_0^\infty \phi(x)\,dx > 0$

3. $\lim_{r \to \infty} H(r) = 0$

4. $\lim_{r \to -\infty} H(r) = \infty.$

These observations are summarized in Figure 19.6.1 together with the fact that

$$H''(r) = \int_0^\infty x^2\, e^{-rx}\, \phi(x)\,dx > 0.$$

FIGURE 19.6.1

Typical $H(r)$ Function, and Formula (19.6.5)

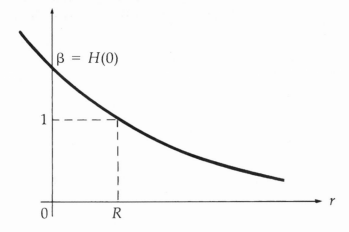

From Figure 19.6.1 we see that there is a unique real solution R (shown positive, but it could be negative), and the verification is complete.

If $b_f(t) = b e^{Rt}$, then $l_f(x, t - x) = b e^{R(t-x)} s_f(x)$, and the population of females is stable. In the special case where $R = 0$, the population of females is stationary.

To check whether R is positive, zero, or negative we examine the number β where

$$\beta = H(0) = \int_0^\infty \phi(x)\, dx.$$

By studying Figure 19.6.1 we can conclude
- If $\beta > 1$, R is positive, and the population is stable and increasing
- If $\beta = 1$, R is 0, and the population is stationary
- If $\beta < 1$, R is negative, and the population is stable and decreasing.

Since $H(0) = \beta$ can be interpreted as the number of female children produced by each female, it is called the **net reproduction rate.** The parameter R is called the **intrinsic rate of population growth.** ·

Remarks:

All populations are not stable, as might be inferred from this section. Several aspects of our model may not be in accord with actual experience. Our basic model, given by (19.6.2), is built on the assumption that the survival function and the force of birth do not change over time. In (19.6.3) we restrict it still further by assuming that the net maternity function depends on the age, but not the birth year, of mothers. Public health statistics disclose major changes in survival functions and in the forces of birth over time.

In addition, in solving integral equation (19.6.3), we obtained only the real solution to the equation $H(r) = 1$. Within the complex number field, an infinite number of solutions may be determined in addition to the single real solution. These additional roots of $H(r) = 1$ lead to general solutions of (19.6.3) of the form

$$\sum_j c_j b_f^{(j)}(t)$$

where each $b_f^{(j)}(t)$ is associated with a root of $H(r) = 1$. The complex roots, which occur in conjugate pairs, can serve to put a dampened wave structure into the birth density function.

Population theory is a collection of elegant mathematical ideas. However, there are also some very important statistical problems in estimating its key components, such as the survival function and the force of birth function, from available data. These functions have been observed to shift over time, reflecting the dynamic nature of human society.

As is true of all models of natural phenomena, the mathematical models of populations capture only a small part of the dynamic forces that shape the size and age distribution of real populations. Even if the stable population model is a satisfactory approximation at one time, it cannot be appropriate for the long term. The constant R cannot be greater than zero on a finite planet for a long time horizon. In a like manner, if R is negative for too long a period of time, the stable population faces extinction.

19.7 Notes and References

The foundations of population theory were built, in part, by Lotka who had experience answering life insurance questions. The basic theory is developed in a book by Keyfitz (1968), and applications are found in another book by Keyfitz (1977). Keyfitz and Beekman (1984) wrote a textbook directed toward helping students master demography through a graded set of exercises. Lexis diagrams are named for their originator Wilhelm Lexis (1837–1914), a German statistician, demographer, and economist. Charles Trowbridge (1952, 1955) promoted the use of stationary population models in the study of the characteristics of pension and life insurance funding methods.

Exercises

Section 19.2

19.1. Using the Lexis diagram of Figure 19.2.1 calculate
   a. The average age of employees at time -25
   b. The number of employees who have attained age 50 in the history of this workforce
   c. Of the employees at time -25, the number who have attained or will attain age 50 while in the workforce.

Section 19.3

19.2. Let

$$b(u) = 100 \left[1 + \cos \left(\frac{\pi u}{200} \right) \right] \qquad -\infty < u < \infty$$

$$s(x, u) = \cos \left(\frac{\pi x}{200} \right) \qquad 0 < x \leq 100.$$

   Calculate the number of individuals attaining age 50 between the times 50 and 100.

19.3. Let

$$b(u) = 100(1 - e^{-u/100}) \qquad u > 0$$

$$s(x) = e^{-x/100} \qquad x > 0.$$

   Calculate the number of individuals between ages 25 and 50 at time 100.

19.4. Calculate the number of lives who will attain age 25 between times 50 and 51 and die before time 53. Use the functions $b(u)$ and $s(x, u)$ specified in Exercise 19.3. (This is a numerical version of Example 19.3.1.)

19.5. Rework Example 19.3.2 assuming $s(x, u) = s(x)$ and $b(u) = l_0$.

19.6. Exhibit integrals for calculating the number of those between ages 20 and 50 at time 0 who will die at an age less than 80 and before time 50.

19.7.   a. Let $N(t)$ denote the number of members in a stable population at time t and show that $dN(t)/dt = R N(t)$.

   b. The birthrate at time t is defined as $b(t)/N(t)$. For a stable population show that the birthrate, denoted by $i(t)$, is

$$i(t) = \left[\int_0^\infty e^{-Rx} s(x) \, dx \right]^{-1}.$$

19.8.   If $\mu(x) = a x$, $a > 0$, and $b(u) = b e^{Ru}$, express the size of the total population at time t in terms of $\Phi(z)$, the d.f. for a $N(0,1)$ distribution.

19.9.   Assume a stable population and derive an expression for the average age of those between ages a and r at time t. Restate the expression assuming $R = 0$.

19.10. If $\tilde{\mu}(x) = \mu(x) + 0.05/\mathring{e}_x$, show that $\tilde{p}_x = p_x (T_{x+1}/T_x)^{0.05}$.

19.11. Confirm that $s^*(x) = e^{-Rx} s(x)$, $R \geq 0$, is a survival function. Then

   a. Exhibit the p.d.f. and d.f. associated with $s^*(x)$

   b. Show that the complete expectation of life at age x_0 associated with the survival function $s^*(x)$ is $\bar{a}_{x_0}$ and that the variance of the time-until-death is $2(\bar{I}\bar{a})_{x_0} - \bar{a}_{x_0}^2$. Here the annuity functions are calculated at force of interest R.

19.12. The crude death rate at time t is defined by

$$\frac{\int_0^\infty l(x, t - x) \mu(x, t - x) \, dx}{\int_0^\infty l(x, t - x) \, dx}.$$

If the population is stable, show that the crude death rate is equal to $i(t) - R$ where $i(t)$ is the birthrate defined in Exercise 19.7(b).

Section 19.5

19.13. Assume a stationary population with survival function $s(x)$ and that this same survival function is used in the evaluation of actuarial functions. Verify and interpret the equation

$$l_r \bar{a}_r + \delta \int_r^\infty l_x \bar{a}_x \, dx = T_r.$$

19.14. Assume a stable population with survival function $s(x)$ and that this same survival function is used in the evaluation of actuarial functions. Confirm and interpret the following identities:

---

a. $l(a, t - a) \bar{a}_{a:\overline{r-a}|} + \delta \int_a^r l(x, t - x) \bar{a}_{x:\overline{r-x}|} dx$

$$= \int_a^r l(x, t - x) dx + R \int_a^r l(x, t - x) \bar{a}_{x:\overline{r-x}|} dx.$$

[Hint: Evaluate the derivative of $l(x, t - x) \bar{a}_{x:\overline{r-x}|}$ using (5.2.27).]

b. $l(a, t - a) \bar{A}_a + \delta \int_a^\infty l(x, t - x) \bar{A}_x dx$

$$= \int_a^\infty l(x, t - x) \mu(x) dx + R \int_a^\infty l(x, t - x) \bar{A}_x dx.$$

19.15. If $b(u) = 100 e^{0.01u}$, age $a = 0$, and $s(x) = e^{-x/50}$, calculate the assessment rate, π_t, to fund a whole life insurance program as in Example 19.5.2.

19.16. The old age dependence ratio for a population at time t is

$$f(t) = \frac{\displaystyle\int_{65}^\infty l(x, t - x) dx}{\displaystyle\int_{20}^{65} l(x, t - x) dx}.$$

For a stable population show that

$$\frac{\partial}{\partial R} \log f(t) = \bar{x}_1 - \bar{x}_2$$

where $\bar{x}_1$ is the average age of those between ages 20 and 65 at time t and $\bar{x}_2$ is the average age of those above age 65 at time t.

Section 19.6

19.17. Given the net maternity function

$$\phi(x) = x^{\alpha-1} e^{-\beta x} \qquad \alpha > 0, \beta > 0$$

a. Calculate R
b. Is the population stable or stationary if $\alpha = 2$ and $\beta = 1$?

Miscellaneous

19.18. Assume that the number in a population at time t satisfies the differential equation

$$\frac{dN(t)}{dt} = \frac{c}{a} \{N(t)[a - N(t)]\} \qquad a > 0.$$

Note that as $N(t)$ approaches a, the rate of change in population size approaches 0. Such a model incorporates environmental limits on population growth.

a. Verify that the function $N(T) = a(1 + be^{-ct})^{-1}$, $b > 0$, satisfies the differential equation. This is called the **logistic function.**

---

b. If $c > 0$, calculate $\lim_{t \to \infty} N(t)$ and sketch the curve of $N(t)$.

c. Determine the abscissa of the point of inflection of $N(t)$.

19.19. If the force of mortality is strictly increasing, show in turn

a. $s(x) s(y) \geq s(x + y)$, $x \geq 0$, $y \geq 0$

b. $s(x) \int_0^\infty s(y)\, dy \geq \int_0^\infty s(x + y)\, dy$

c. $s(x) \int_0^\infty s(y)\, dy \geq \int_x^\infty s(w)\, dw$

d. $\int_0^\infty s(y)\, dy \geq \int_x^\infty \dfrac{s(w)}{s(x)}\, dw$

e. $\mathring{e}_0 \geq \mathring{e}_x$.

19.20. In Exercise 19.19, multiply by v^y and show that $\bar{a}_0 \geq \bar{a}_x$.

19.21. a. Show that $\bar{P}(\bar{A}_x)$ can be written as the weighted average of the force of mortality $\mu_x(t)$ where the weight function is

$$w(t, \delta) = \frac{v^t \,_t p_x}{\bar{a}_x}.$$

b. Verify that

(i) $\displaystyle\int_0^\infty w(t, \delta)\, dt = 1$

(ii) $\dfrac{\partial}{\partial t} w(t, \delta) \leq 0$

(iii) $\dfrac{\partial}{\partial \delta} w(t, \delta) = \dfrac{v^t \,_t p_x[-t\,\bar{a}_x + (\bar{I}\bar{a})_x]}{(\bar{a}_x)^2}.$

c. Verify the following:

(i) $\dfrac{\partial}{\partial \delta} w(0, \delta) > 0$

(ii) $\displaystyle\lim_{t \to \infty} \dfrac{\partial}{\partial \delta} w(t, \delta) = -\infty$

(iii) For a fixed δ, the only positive root of

$$\dfrac{\partial}{\partial \delta} w(t, \delta) = 0 \text{ is } \dfrac{(\bar{I}\bar{a})_x}{\bar{a}_x}.$$

d. If the force of mortality is strictly increasing, use results (b)(ii) and (b)(iii) to demonstrate that an increase in the force of interest increases the weight attached to small values of the force of mortality and decreases the weight attached to large values of the force of mortality. Therefore, if the force of mortality is strictly increasing, an increase in the force of interest will decrease $\bar{P}(\bar{A}_x)$.

THEORY OF PENSION FUNDING

20.1 Introduction

In Section 11.5 we studied the actuarial present values of benefits and contributions with respect to a participant in a pension plan. These actuarial present values for individual participants are necessary inputs into the process of determining the aggregate actuarial present values for the plan. If the pension plan is to provide security to the participants, these aggregated values of future benefits together with the current assets are balanced with the aggregate present values of future contributions. The pattern of aggregate contributions required to balance benefit payments is determined by an *actuarial cost* or *funding method.* In this chapter we define functions useful in summarizing the status of the funding of a pension plan. These functions are then used to define actuarial cost methods and to explore the properties of these methods.

For this we adopt some of the population theory of Chapter 19. Here the study is similar to that followed in Examples 19.5.1, 19.5.2, 19.5.3, and 19.5.4 for alternative funding or budgeting methods in the examination of a life insurance system for a population.

To integrate the ideas of this chapter with those developed earlier, the reader should keep in mind some basic limitations on the ideas presented here:
(1) To protect the interests of participants and to limit the amount of income on which taxes are deferred (because it is contributed to a pension plan), governments have chosen to regulate actuarial cost methods. These regulations are important in practice, but are not discussed here.
(2) Pension plans frequently provide many types of benefits. In addition to retirement income, death, disability, and withdrawal benefits are common. In many jurisdictions withdrawal benefits are required; these withdrawal benefits are called *vested benefits* in pension plans. The determination of the actuarial present value of some of these benefits was covered in Chapter 11. In this chapter, the model used provides only for retirement income benefits. This simplication is adopted so that attention can be focused on the properties of various actuarial cost methods. Although most pension plans provide retirement income at a

rate dependent in some way on income levels before retirement, the model used in this chapter specifies an initial pension benefit rate dependent only on the rate of income payment at retirement. Once again this simplification is made to permit concentration on the actuarial cost methods.

(3) A continuing theme in this work is that actuarial present values require the application of interest factors and probabilities to future contingent payments. In this chapter future payments may depend on a great many uncertain events. However, in accordance with our goal of studying actuarial cost methods, a deterministic view is adopted.

(4) Pension plan contributions are expenses for sponsoring organizations. To promote the comparability of income statements of organizations that sponsor pension plans, accounting practice restricts the actuarial cost methods that are acceptable for financial accounting. The restrictions are not discussed here.

20.2 The Model

We assume a population consisting of members entering at age a, retiring at age r and subject to a survival function, $s(x)$ with $s(a) = 1$. For $a < x < r$, decrement can occur for mortality or other causes, but for $x > r$ mortality is the only cause of decrement. The density of new entrants at age a at time u is given by $n(u)$ and the density of those attaining age x at time t by

$$n(u)\, s(x) \tag{20.2.1}$$

where $u = t - (x - a)$ is the time of entry into the plan. Formula (20.2.1) is related to (19.3.1), except that "births" occur at age a by becoming a plan participant. We assume the survival function does not depend on u.

We also assume that the salary rate for each member age x at time 0 is $w(x)$, $a < x < r$. The function $w(x)$ expresses the individual experience and merit components of salary change. Salary rates also change by a year-of-experience factor reflecting inflation and changes in the productivity of all participants. In this chapter the year-of-experience factor will be $e^{\tau t}$. This factor does not depend on the age of an individual. Thus, the annual salary rate expected at time t by a member age x is given by the formula

$$w(x)\, e^{\tau t} \qquad a < x < r. \tag{20.2.2}$$

This should be compared with the simpler model used in (11.5.1) where salary changes that are functions only of attained age are considered.

Comparing this with (19.3.5), we recognize that the total salary rate at time t for the $n(t - x + a)\, s(x)\, dx$ members between ages x and $x + dx$ is $n(t - x + a)\, s(x)\, w(x)\, \exp(\tau t)$, and the total annual salary rate at time t is

$$W_t = \int_a^r n(t - x + a)\, s(x)\, w(x)\, e^{\tau t}\, dx. \tag{20.2.3}$$

Formula (20.2.3) incorporates a notational convention used in this chapter. A subscripted symbol denotes a quantity for the entire group of covered workers. Thus W_t represents the total payroll payment rate at time t.

The model pension plan considered in this chapter provides retirement annuities payable only after attainment of retirement age r. The initial annual pension rate is a fraction f of the final salary rate. Thus for a member retiring at time t, the projected payment rate is

$$f\, w(r)\, e^{\tau t}. \tag{20.2.4}$$

For a retiree age x at time t, the annual rate of pension payment is projected as

$$f\, w(r)\, e^{\tau(t-x+r)}\, h(x) \qquad x \geq r$$

where $h(x)$ represents an adjustment factor applied to the initial pension payment rate of $f\, w(r)\, e^{\tau(t-x+r)}$ for those who retired $x - r$ years ago. We note that $h(r) = 1$. As an example, $h(x)$ may be the exponential function $\exp[\beta(x - r)]$ where β is a constant rate of increase (possibly related to the expected inflation rate).

The model plan that is at the center of our discussion of actuarial cost methods is a **defined-benefit plan.** The plan defines the benefits to be received by retiring participants, and we concentrate on describing actuarial cost methods that produce a stream of contributions and investment income to balance the benefit payments. In **defined-contribution plans** the starting point shifts. The contribution made on behalf of each participant is stated, perhaps as a constant or as a fraction of salary. The actuarial problem is then to calculate the benefit level that will produce an actuarial present value equal to the actuarial present value of the contributions. This may be determined at time of retirement by using the accumulated contributions to provide an equivalent retirement annuity, or on a year-by-year basis whereby a deferred retirement annuity is purchased by the contribution of each year.

20.3 Terminal Funding

Under the **terminal funding method** pensions are not funded by contributions during active membership. Instead, single contributions are made to the fund at the time of retirement. The required contribution rate, or **normal cost rate,** under the terminal funding method at time t, denoted by ${}^{T}P_t$, is the rate at which the actuarial present value of future pensions for members reaching age r is incurred at time t. To determine ${}^{T}P_t$ for the model plan, we assume interest is earned at an annual force of δ, and we denote by $\bar{a}_r^h$ the actuarial present value of a life annuity payable continuously to a life age r with income rate $h(x)$ per year when (r) attains age x. Therefore,

$$\bar{a}_r^h = \int_r^\infty e^{-\delta(x-r)}\, h(x)\, \frac{s(x)}{s(r)}\, dx. \tag{20.3.1}$$

From (19.3.2), we have $n(t - r + a) s(r) dt$ members attaining age r between times t and $t + dt$, and by (20.2.4) they will collect pensions at an average initial rate of $f w(r) \exp(\tau t)$. Therefore,

$$^T P_t = f w(r) e^{\tau t} n(t - r + a) s(r) \bar{a}_r^h. \tag{20.3.2}$$

We will see that $^T P_t$ is a basic building block for the various functions used to describe the funding operations for the model plan.

To illustrate the theory, we often refer to the *exponential case* having the following characteristics:

- $n(u) = n e^{Ru}$. Since we have assumed that the survival function is independent of time, we see from (19.4.3) and the form of $n(u)$ that the size of the population is changing exponentially at rate R, but with a stable age distribution within the population.
- $h(x) = e^{\beta(r-x)}$; that is, pensions are adjusted at a constant annual rate of β.

Before exploring the exponential case, we should understand its limitations. It is clear that conditions for exponential growth or decay cannot exist indefinitely. When the exponential case is approximately realized, the three key economic rates, interest δ, wages τ, and pension adjustment β, are interrelated. For example, if β is related to inflation, it is conventional to assume that $\delta > \beta$ even though there have been periods of unexpected inflation where the reverse holds. If $\beta > \tau$, the consequence would be an improvement in the economic position of retired lives relative to active lives, and therefore $\beta \leq \tau$ is usually assumed.

Example 20.3.1

In the exponential case, show that $^T P_{t+u} = e^{\rho u} \, {}^T P_t$ where $\rho = \tau + R$.

Solution:

From the definition of the exponential case we have

$$n(t + u - r + a) = n e^{R(t+u-r+a)}$$

and from (20.3.1)

$$\bar{a}_r^h = \int_r^\infty e^{-(\delta-\beta)(x-r)} \frac{s(x)}{s(r)} dx = \bar{a}_r'$$

where $\bar{a}_r'$ is valued at force of interest $\delta - \beta$. Then, using (20.3.2), we obtain

$$^T P_{t+u} = f w(r) e^{\tau(t+u)} n s(r) e^{R(t+u-r+a)} \bar{a}_r'$$

$$= e^{(\tau+R)u} f w(r) e^{\tau t} n s(r) e^{R(t-r+a)} \bar{a}_r' = e^{\rho u} \, {}^T P_t.$$

Several terms in this development can be interpreted independently. The rate $\rho = \tau + R$ can be interpreted as a rate of total economic growth or decay. The term $n s(r)$ can be interpreted as l_r the number of survivors at age r of n members in a survivorship group at age a governed by the multiple decrement survival function $s(x)$, $a \leq x \leq r$. ▼

20.4 Basic Functions for Retired Lives

In this section we discuss a number of basic functions defining several main concepts of pension funding as related to the retired group. A prefixed r is used in the notation to indicate the retired group.

20.4.1 Actuarial Present Value of Future Benefits, $(rA)_t$

The $n(t - x + a) s(x) dx$ members between ages x and $x + dx$ at time t retired $x - r$ years ago with pensions at an initial annual rate of $f w(r) e^{\tau(t-x+r)}$. For each unit of initial pension of a surviving retiree, there remains the actuarial present value

$$\bar{a}_x^h = \int_x^\infty e^{-\delta(y-x)} h(y) \frac{s(y)}{s(x)} dy \qquad (20.4.1)$$

where $s(y)$ is a single decrement survival function based only on mortality. Therefore, from (20.3.2),

$$(rA)_t = \int_r^\infty n(t - x + a) s(x) f w(r) e^{\tau(t-x+r)} \bar{a}_x^h dx. \qquad (20.4.2)$$

On substituting from (20.4.1), we can write a double integral form for $(rA)_t$; that is,

$$(rA)_t = \int_r^\infty n(t - x + a) f w(r) e^{\tau(t-x+r)} \left[\int_x^\infty e^{-\delta(y-x)} h(y) s(y) dy \right] dx. \qquad (20.4.3)$$

20.4.2 Benefit Payment Rate, B_t

For the retired members there is a new function to consider, B_t, the rate of benefit outgo at time t. In developing (20.4.2) for the actuarial present value of future benefits for retired lives, we saw that pensions for retirees now between ages x and $x + dx$ were paid at the initial rate of $n(t - x + a) s(x) f w(r) e^{\tau(t-x+r)} dx$. By age x, this rate has been adjusted by the factor $h(x)$. Hence,

$$B_t = \int_r^\infty n(t - x + a) s(x) f w(r) e^{\tau(t-x+r)} h(x) dx. \qquad (20.4.4)$$

First, we note that for all differentiable functions, g,

$$\frac{\partial}{\partial t} g(t - x + r) = -\frac{\partial}{\partial x} g(t - x + r).$$

Differentiation of B_t leads to

$$\frac{d}{dt} B_t = \int_r^\infty f w(r) s(x) h(x) \frac{\partial}{\partial t} [n(t - x + a) e^{\tau(t-x+r)}] dx$$

$$= -\int_r^\infty f w(r) s(x) h(x) \frac{\partial}{\partial x} [n(t - x + a) e^{\tau(t-x+r)}] dx$$

$$= -f \, w(r) \, s(x) \, h(x) \, n(t - x + a) \, e^{\tau(t-x+r)} \, \bigg|_{x=r}^{x=\infty}$$

$$+ \int_r^\infty f \, w(r) \, n(t - x + a) \, e^{\tau(t-x+r)} \, [s'(x) \, h(x) + s(x) \, h'(x)] \, dx$$

$$= \left[f \, w(r) \, n(t - r + a) \, s(r) \, e^{\tau t} \right.$$

$$\left. - \int_r^\infty f \, w(r) \, n(t - x + a) \, s(x) \, \mu(x) e^{\tau(t-x+r)} \, h(x) \, dx \right]$$

$$+ \int_r^\infty f \, w(r) \, n(t - x + a) \, s(x) \, e^{\tau(t-x+r)} \, h'(x) \, dx. \tag{20.4.5}$$

The terms within the brackets on the right-hand side of (20.4.5) measure the *replacement effect.* The first term is the rate at which the initial pensions for the newly retired members is increasing the benefit payment rate. The second term is the rate at which the benefit payment rate is being reduced by deaths at time t. The term outside the brackets is known as the *adjustment effect.* It measures the amount by which the benefit payment rate is being adjusted at time t.

20.4.3   The Allocation Equation

We are now in a position to state a basic formula for retired lives:

$$^T P_t + \delta(rA)_t = B_t + \frac{d}{dt} (rA)_t. \tag{20.4.6}$$

This equation can be argued from compound interest theory by considering $(rA)_t$ as a fund into which interest and terminal funding costs are paid and from which pensions are paid. The difference between the total rate of incomes and the rate of outgo determines the rate of change of the size of the fund.

The verification of (20.4.6) can be accomplished by differentiating $(rA)_t$ as given by (20.4.3). We have

$$\frac{d}{dt} (rA)_t = \int_r^\infty f \, w(r) \, \frac{\partial}{\partial t} [n(t - x + a) \, e^{\tau(t-x+r)}] \left[\int_x^\infty e^{-\delta(y-x)} \, h(y) \, s(y) \, dy \right] dx$$

$$= -f \, w(r) \int_r^\infty \left[\int_x^\infty e^{-\delta(y-x)} \, h(y) \, s(y) \, dy \right] \frac{\partial}{\partial x} [n(t - x + a) \, e^{\tau(t-x+r)}] \, dx$$

$$= -f \, w(r) \left\{ n(t - x + a) \, e^{\tau(t-x+r)} \int_x^\infty e^{-\delta(y-x)} \, h(y) \, s(y) \, dy \, \bigg|_{x=r}^{x=\infty} \right.$$

$$\left. - \int_r^\infty \left[\delta \int_x^\infty e^{-\delta(y-x)} \, h(y) \, s(y) \, dy - s(x) \, h(x) \right] n(t - x + a) \, e^{\tau(t-x+r)} \, dx \right\}$$

$$= {}^T P_t + \delta(rA)_t - B_t$$

where (20.4.4) is used to identify the B_t term.

Example 20.4.1

Show that for the exponential case,

a. $B_{t+u} = e^{\rho u} B_t, \rho = \tau + R$ (20.4.7)

b. $(rA)_{t+u} = e^{\rho u} (rA)_t$ (20.4.8)

c. $^T P_t + \theta(rA)_t = B_t, \theta = \delta - \rho$ (20.4.9)

d. $^T P_t < B_t$ if $\theta > 0$
    $^T P_t = B_t$ if $\theta = 0$
    $^T P_t > B_t$ if $\theta < 0$. (20.4.10)

Solution:

a. From (20.4.4),

$$B_{t+u} = \int_r^\infty n e^{R(t+u-x+a)} \, e^{\tau(t+u-x+r)} \, f \, w(r) \, s(x) \, e^{\beta(x-r)} \, dx$$

$$= e^{(R+\tau)u} \int_r^\infty n e^{R(t-x+a)} \, e^{\tau(t-x+r)} \, f \, w(r) \, s(x) \, e^{\beta(x-r)} \, dx$$

$$= e^{\rho u} \, B_t \, .$$

b. Substituting into (20.4.2) and following the pattern of the solution of part (a) yields the result.

c. Rewriting (20.4.8) as

$$\frac{(rA)_{t+u} - (rA)_t}{u} = \frac{e^{\rho u} - 1}{u} (rA)_t$$

and letting $u \to 0$, we obtain

$$\frac{d}{dt} (rA)_t = \rho \, (rA)_t \, . \tag{20.4.11}$$

Then substituting (20.4.11) into (20.4.6) yields the result for part (c).

d. The inequalities follow from (20.4.9). This example reveals the critical role played by $\theta = \delta - \tau - R$ in the exponential case. ▼

Example 20.4.2

For the model plan operating in a stationary population with fixed salaries and level pensions, develop and interpret the formula

$$(rA)_t = f \, w(r) \, \frac{T_r - l_r \bar{a}_r}{\delta}. \tag{20.4.12}$$

Solution:

Here $h(x) = 1, \tau = 0, \theta = \delta, B_t = f \, w(r) \, T_r, {}^T P_t = f \, w(r) \, l_r \, \bar{a}_r$, and (20.4.12) follows by substituting into (20.4.9). To interpret this result, we note that pensions of $f \, w(r)$ per year are payable continuously to all persons age r or older in the stationary population. This includes pensions for future new retirees who become eligible at the rate of l_r per year. These future pension payments form a perpetuity with present value equal to $f \, w(r) \, l_r \, \bar{a}_r / \delta$. The difference in the present values of these two

---

perpetuities is the present value of the future pensions to the closed group of participants now age r years or older, $(rA)_t$. ▼

20.5 Accrual of Actuarial Liability

Actuarial cost methods differ by the rate at which prospective pension obligations are recognized during the participants' working lifetimes. The terminal cost method described in Section 20.3 does not recognize the liability until the attainment of retirement age r. To express the accrual of actuarial liability for a pension commencing at age r, we define for a cost method an *accrual function* $M(x)$. Here $M(x)$ represents that fraction of the actuarial value of future pensions accrued as an actuarial liability at age x under the actuarial cost method. The function $M(x)$ is a nondecreasing, right-continuous function of the age variable with $0 \le M(x) \le 1$ for all $x \ge a$. Under *initial funding*, all the liability for the future pension is recognized when the participant enters at age a; thus $M(x) = 0$ for $x < a$ and $M(x) = 1$ for $x \ge a$. For other actuarial cost methods it will be assumed that $M(a) = 0$. For funding methods requiring accrual or recognition of the total liability by age r, $M(r) = 1$ for $x \ge r$.

The function $M(x)$ can also be defined in terms of a *pension accrual density function* denoted by $m(x)$ such that

$$M(x) = \int_a^x m(y)\,dy \qquad x \ge a. \tag{20.5.1}$$

Note the analogy between $M(x)$ and $m(x)$ and the d.f., $F_X(x)$, and p.d.f., $f_X(x)$. In general we assume that $m(x)$ is continuous for $a < x < r$, right continuous at a, and left continuous at r, and that $m(x) = 0$ for $x > r$. In this continuous case it follows from (20.5.1) that

$$m(x) = M'(x). \tag{20.5.2}$$

At points of discontinuity of $M'(x)$, the density $m(x)$ is not defined, and we can assign an arbitrary value to it, for example, the limit from the left or from the right.

The advantage of introducing the accrual function is that we can develop pension theory simultaneously for a whole family of actuarial cost methods rather than separately for each method.

Example 20.5.1

For $M(x) = \bar{a}_{a:\overline{x-a}} / \bar{a}_{a:\overline{r-a}}$, $a < x < r$, verify that

a. $M(x)$ has the properties of an accrual function.

b. $M(x) {}_{r-x|}\bar{a}_x$ is equal to the reserve at age x on a continuous annual premium deferred life annuity issued at age a and paying a continuous annuity of 1 per year commencing at age r.

Solution:

a.

$$M(x) = \frac{\int_a^x e^{-\delta(y-a)} s(y)\, dy}{\int_a^r e^{-\delta(y-a)} s(y)\, dy} \; ;$$

thus

$$M'(x) = m(x) = \frac{e^{-\delta(x-a)} s(x)}{\int_a^r e^{-\delta(y-a)} s(y)\, dy} . \tag{20.5.3}$$

$M(a) = 0$ and $M(r) = 1$ confirm that $M(x)$ has the properties of an accrual function.

b. A retrospective formula gives the reserve at age x as

$$\bar{P}(_{r-a|}\bar{a}_a)\, \bar{s}_{a:\overline{x-a|}} = \frac{_{r-a|}\bar{a}_a}{\bar{a}_{a:\overline{r-a|}}}\, \bar{s}_{a:\overline{x-a|}}$$

$$= \frac{_{x-a}E_a\; _{r-x|}\bar{a}_x\; \bar{a}_{a:\overline{x-a|}}}{\bar{a}_{a:\overline{r-a|}}\; _{x-a}E_a}$$

$$= _{r-x|}\bar{a}_x\, M(x). \qquad \blacktriangledown$$

20.6 Basic Functions for Active Lives

In this section we define a number of basic functions related to the funding of pension benefits in the model plan. The functions relate to the active group and are denoted in the symbols with a prefixed a.

20.6.1 Actuarial Present Value of Future Benefits, $(aA)_t$

The $n(t - x + a)\, s(x)$ members between ages x and $x + dx$ at time t will, at the end of $r - x$ years, incur the terminal funding cost of $^T P_{t+r-x}\, dx$. Hence,

$$(aA)_t = \int_a^r e^{-\delta(r-x)}\, ^T P_{t+r-x}\, dx. \tag{20.6.1}$$

Example 20.6.1

Show that

$$\frac{d}{dt}(aA)_t = e^{-\delta(r-a)}\, ^T P_{t+r-a} - {}^T P_t + \delta(aA)_t \tag{20.6.2}$$

and interpret the equation.

Solution:

Again, we note that

$$\frac{\partial}{\partial t}\, ^T P_{t+r-x} = -\frac{\partial}{\partial x}\, ^T P_{t+r-x}. \tag{20.6.3}$$

Thus

$$\frac{d}{dt}(aA)_t = \int_a^r e^{-\delta(r-x)} \frac{\partial}{\partial t} \, {}^T\!P_{t+r-x} \, dx$$

$$= -\int_a^r e^{-\delta(r-x)} \frac{\partial}{\partial x} \, {}^T\!P_{t+r-x} \, dx$$

$$= -e^{-\delta(r-x)} \, {}^T\!P_{t+r-x} \, \Big|_{x=a}^{x=r} + \delta \int_a^r {}^T\!P_{t+r-x} \, e^{-\delta(r-x)} \, dx$$

$$= {}^T\!P_{t+r-a} \, e^{-\delta(r-a)} - {}^T\!P_t + \delta(aA)_t.$$

The rate of change in the actuarial present value of future pensions equals the present value of the future terminal funding rate for new entrants (who will retire $r - a$ years later) less the terminal funding rate for active members retiring now plus the rate of interest income on the actuarial present value at time t. ▼

20.6.2 Normal Cost Rate, P_t

We assume that an actuarial cost method with accrual function $M(x)$ has been selected. We now want to express the normal cost rate for the model plan, that is, to display the function that, for our continuous model, allocates the actuarial present value of future pension benefits to the various times of valuation in a participant's active service.

As in (20.6.1) the future terminal funding cost for members between ages x and $x + dx$ at time t is ${}^T\!P_{t+r-x} \, dx$. In the normal cost function this liability is being recognized at an accrual rate $m(x)$. We have

$$P_t = \int_a^r e^{-\delta(r-x)} \, {}^T\!P_{t+r-x} \, m(x) \, dx$$

$$= e^{\tau t} f \, w(r) \, s(r) \, \bar{a}_r^h \int_a^r e^{-(\delta-\tau)(r-x)} \, n(t - x + a) \, m(x) \, dx. \qquad (20.6.4)$$

One can visualize how the normal cost rate, P_t, $u \le t \le u + r - a$, completely funds the pension benefit of a member who enters at age a at time u and retires $r - a$ years later. Consider the participants who enter between u and $u + du$. Their ultimate terminal funding cost rate will be ${}^T\!P_{u+r-a}$. At time t, the density of contributions of this group to the integral defining P_t is

$$e^{-\delta(r-x)} \, {}^T\!P_{t+r-x} \, m(x)$$

where $x = a + t - u$. In the $r - x$ years until retirement this will increase, because of interest earned, to

$${}^T\!P_{t+r-x} \, m(x), \qquad (20.6.5)$$

and this density in terms of u is ${}^T P_{u+r-a}\, m(a + t - u)$. Integrating these interest-accumulated contributions, we obtain

$$\int_u^{u+r-a} {}^T P_{u+r-a}\, m(a + t - u)\, dt = {}^T P_{u+r-a},$$

the required terminal funding cost rate.

Example 20.6.2

a. Show that in the exponential case

$$P_t = \exp\{-\delta[r - X(\theta)]\}\, {}^T P_{t+r-X(\theta)} \tag{20.6.6}$$

where

$$\theta = \delta - \rho = \delta - \tau - R$$

and

$$e^{\theta X(\theta)} = \int_a^r m(x)\, e^{\theta x}\, dx. \tag{20.6.7}$$

b. Interpret (20.6.6).

Solution:

a. From (20.6.4) and the solution of Example 20.3.1 we have

$$P_t = \int_a^r e^{-\delta(r-x)}\, {}^T P_{t+r-x}\, m(x)\, dx$$

$$= \int_a^r e^{-\delta(r-x)}\, {}^T P_{t+[X(\theta)-x]+r-X(\theta)}\, m(x)\, dx$$

$$= \int_a^r e^{-\delta(r-x)}\, e^{\rho[X(\theta)-x]}\, {}^T P_{t+r-X(\theta)}\, m(x)\, dx$$

$$= e^{[-\delta r + \rho X(\theta)]}\, {}^T P_{t+r-X(\theta)} \int_a^r e^{(\delta-\rho)x}\, m(x)\, dx.$$

Substitute $\delta - \theta$ for ρ; using (20.6.7), we have

$$P_t = e^{[-\delta r + (\delta-\theta)X(\theta)]}\, {}^T P_{t+r-X(\theta)}\, e^{\theta X(\theta)}$$

which reduces to (20.6.6).

b. The annual normal cost rate at time t is sufficient with interest to provide the terminal funding cost $r - X(\theta)$ years later. The number $X(\theta)$ has its existence assured by the mean value theorem for integrals and may be interpreted as an average age of normal cost payment associated with the accrual density function $m(x)$ in the exponential case with $\theta = \delta - \tau - R$. Hence, $X(\theta)$ depends on the interest rate and on salary and population change rates. ▼

20.6.3 Actuarial Accrued Liability, $(aV)_t$

We assume, as in Section 20.6.2, that an actuarial cost method with accrual function $M(x)$ has been chosen. By analogy with (20.6.4) we have that the *actuarial accrued liability* for active lives at time t is given by

$$(aV)_t = \int_a^r e^{-\delta(r-x)} \, {}^TP_{t+r-x} \, M(x) \, dx. \tag{20.6.8}$$

In the integral we are applying the concept that a fraction $M(x)$ of the actuarial present value of the future pension has accrued as an actuarial liability by age x.

If we rewrite (20.6.4) in the form

$$P_t = \int_a^r e^{-\delta(r-x)} \, {}^TP_{t+r-x} \, dM(x)$$

and integrate by parts, we obtain, by use of (20.6.3),

$$P_t = e^{-\delta(r-x)} \, {}^TP_{t+r-x} \, M(x) \, \Big|_{x=a}^{x=r} - \delta \int_a^r M(x) \, e^{-\delta(r-x)} \, {}^TP_{t+r-x} \, dx$$

$$+ \int_a^r M(x) \, e^{-\delta(r-x)} \, \frac{\partial}{\partial t} \, {}^TP_{t+r-x} \, dx$$

$$= {}^TP_t - \delta(aV)_t + \frac{d}{dt} \, (aV)_t$$

or

$$P_t + \delta(aV)_t = {}^TP_t + \frac{d}{dt} \, (aV)_t. \tag{20.6.9}$$

Equation (20.6.9) can be interpreted from the viewpoint of compound interest theory. We consider the actuarial accrued liability, $(aV)_t$, as a fund into which normal costs, at rate P_t, are paid and from which terminal funding costs, at rate ${}^TP_t$, are transferred when active members retire. The left-hand side of (20.6.9) is the income rate to the fund from normal costs and interest. The right-hand side represents the allocation of this income rate to the terminal funding rate and rate change in the fund size.

Example 20.6.3

Show that in the exponential case

a. $P_{t+u} = e^{\rho u} P_t, \ \rho = \tau + R$ (20.6.10)

b. $(aV)_{t+u} = e^{\rho u} (aV)_t$ (20.6.11)

c. $P_t + \theta(aV)_t = {}^TP_t, \ \theta = \delta - \rho$ (20.6.12)

d. $P_t < {}^TP_t \quad \text{if } \theta > 0$

    $P_t = {}^TP_t \quad \text{if } \theta = 0$

    $P_t > {}^TP_t \quad \text{if } \theta < 0.$ (20.6.13)

Solution:

a. In Example 20.3.1 we saw that ${}^{T}P_{t+u} = e^{\rho u}\,{}^{T}P_t$. Then, substituting into (20.6.4), we obtain

$$P_{t+u} = \int_a^r e^{-\delta(r-x)}\,{}^{T}P_{t+u+r-x}\,m(x)\,dx$$

$$= e^{\rho u}\int_a^r e^{-\delta(r-x)}\,{}^{T}P_{t+r-x}\,m(x)\,dx$$

$$= e^{\rho u}\,P_t.$$

b. The solution starts with the definition of $(aV)_t$ in (20.6.8) and follows the same steps as in part (a).

c. Rewriting (20.6.11) as

$$\frac{(aV)_{t+u} - (aV)_t}{u} = \frac{e^{\rho u} - 1}{u}(aV)_t$$

and letting $u \to 0$, we obtain

$$\frac{d}{dt}(aV)_t = \rho\,(aV)_t. \qquad (20.6.14)$$

Substituting (20.6.14) into (20.6.9) yields (20.6.12).

d. The inequalities follow from (20.6.12). Again, we see the critical role that $\theta = \delta - \tau - R$ plays in the exponential case. ▼

In line with our assumption that $M(x) = 1$ for $x \geq r$, there is no future normal cost in respect to the closed group of retirees at time t. Therefore, the actuarial accrued liability, $(rV)_t$, for retired members equals the actuarial present value of their future pensions; that is,

$$(rV)_t = (rA)_t. \qquad (20.6.15)$$

This has the further effect that we then have a differential equation for the actuarial accrued liability for retired lives, which is

$$^{T}P_t + \delta(rV)_t = B_t + \frac{d}{dt}(rV)_t. \qquad (20.6.16)$$

20.6.4 Actuarial Present Value of Future Normal Costs, $(Pa)_t$

In Section 20.6.1 we noted that $n(t - x + a)\,s(x)$ members between ages x and $x + dx$ at time t will have a terminal funding cost of ${}^{T}P_{t+r-x}\,dx$ when they retire $r - x$ years later. As these members pass from age y to $y + dy$, $x \leq y < r$, the normal cost $e^{-\delta(r-y)}\,{}^{T}P_{t+r-x}\,dx\,m(y)\,dy$ will be payable. The present value of this normal cost is

$$e^{-\delta(r-x)}\,{}^{T}P_{t+r-x}\,dx\,m(y)\,dy, \qquad (20.6.17)$$

and the present value of future normal costs, denoted by $(Pa)_t$, for all active members is

$$(Pa)_t = \int_a^r e^{-\delta(r-x)} \,^T P_{t+r-x} \int_x^r m(y) \, dy \, dx \qquad (20.6.18)$$

or

$$= e^{\tau t} f \, w(r) \, s(r) \, \bar{a}_r^h \int_a^r e^{-(\delta-\tau)(r-x)} \, n(t - x + a) \, [1 - M(x)] \, dx. \quad (20.6.19)$$

Figure 20.6.1 illustrates the ideas in the development of $(Pa)_t$. Expression (20.6.17) represents the present value at time t of the cost element in the shaded area. In (20.6.18), the inside integral represents the addition of elements along the diagonal, and the outer integral the present value of future normal costs at time t for all ages.

FIGURE 20.6.1
Formulation of $(Pa)_t$

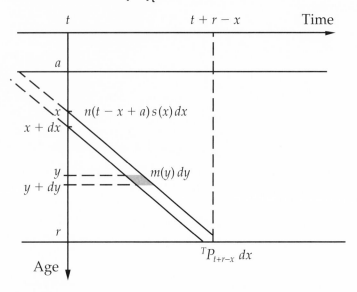

It follows from (20.6.18), (20.6.1), and (20.6.8) that

$$(Pa)_t = (aA)_t - (aV)_t$$

or

$$(aV)_t = (aA)_t - (Pa)_t. \qquad (20.6.20)$$

Formula (20.6.20) expresses the same concept as the prospective reserve formulas of Chapter 7 and is frequently used to define $(aV)_t$; that is,

(the actuarial liability at = (the actuarial present value of
time t for active members)   future pensions for active members)

− (the actuarial present value
of future normal costs).

By analogy with concepts from Chapter 7, $V = A - Pa$ or $A = V + Pa$, one can argue that the actuarial present value of future pensions for active lives is balanced by the actuarial accrued liability for active lives and the actuarial present value of future normal costs; that is,

---

$$(aA)_t = (aV)_t + (Pa)_t. \qquad (20.6.21)$$

The split between the two terms on the right-hand side of (20.6.21) is determined by the actuarial cost method selected as reflected in the accrual function $M(x)$.

<hr>

Example 20.6.4

a. Consider two accrual functions, $M_I(x)$ and $M_{II}(x)$. Show that if $D(x) = M_I(x) - M_{II}(x)$ is such that $D'(a) > 0$ and $D'(x) = 0$ has exactly one solution, $a < x < r$, then $(aV)_{It} > (aV)_{IIt}$.

b. If

$$M_I(x) = \frac{\bar{a}_{a:\overline{x-a}|}}{\bar{a}_{a:\overline{r-a}|}}$$

and

$$M_{II}(x) = \frac{x - a}{r - a},$$

show that

$$(aV)_{It} > (aV)_{IIt} .$$

Solution:

a. By properties of the accrual function, $D(a) = D(r) = 0$. We are given that $D'(a) > 0$ and $D'(x) = 0$ for exactly one value of x, $a < x < r$; hence, $D(x) > 0$ for $a < x < r$. Thus

$$(aV)_{It} - (aV)_{IIt} = \int_a^r e^{-\delta(r-x)} \, {}_TP_{t+r-x} \, D(x) \, dx$$

   is greater than 0, and the inequality follows.

b. We have

$$D'(x) = \frac{e^{-\delta(x-a)} s(x)}{\displaystyle\int_a^r e^{-\delta(y-a)} s(y) \, dy} - \frac{1}{r - a}.$$

Further, if $\delta > 1$, $e^{-\delta(y-a)} s(y) < 1$, and thus

$$\int_a^r e^{-\delta(y-a)} s(y) \, dy < \int_a^r dy = r - a.$$

Therefore

$$D'(a) = \frac{1}{\displaystyle\int_a^r e^{-\delta(y-a)} s(y) \, dy} - \frac{1}{r - a} > 0.$$

By a similar argument, $D'(r) < 0$. Since both $e^{-\delta(x-a)}$ and $s(x)$ are decreasing but positive functions of x, $D''(x) < 0$ and thus $D'(x) = 0$ for exactly one value of x, $a < x < r$. Then $(aV)_{It} > (aV)_{IIt}$ follows from part (a).

<hr>

In addition, by (20.6.21), we have

$$(aA)_t = (aV)_{It} + (Pa)_{It} = (aV)_{IIt} + (Pa)_{IIt}$$

so that

$$(Pa)_{IIt} > (Pa)_{It} . \qquad \blacktriangledown$$

20.7 Individual Actuarial Cost Methods

The general actuarial cost method defined by the accrual function $M(x)$ or its derivative, the accrual density function, is an individual cost method in the sense that $m(x)$ and $M(x)$ can be applied to yield the normal cost rate and the actuarial accrued liability for each participant. The total normal cost rate and actuarial accrued liability for active lives in the plan may be determined by adding the components attributed to each participant.

The individual pension funding functions, for an annuity starting at age r with a unit initial benefit rate for an active life age x, $a \le x \le r$, are defined as follows:

The actuarial present value of the benefit is given by

$$(aA)(x) = e^{-\delta(r-x)} \frac{s(r)}{s(x)} \bar{a}_r^h . \qquad (20.7.1)$$

The normal cost rate is given by

$$P(x) = (aA)(x) \, m(x), \qquad (20.7.2)$$

and the accrued actuarial liability is given by

$$(aV)(x) = (aA)(x) \, M(x). \qquad (20.7.3)$$

The actuarial present value of future normal costs is defined by

$$(Pa)(x) = (aA)(x) - (aV)(x) = (aA)(x) \, [1 - M(x)]. \qquad (20.7.4)$$

Note that these functions for a unit benefit for (x), instead of aggregate plan functions as of time t. Exercise 20.18 develops the details of the relations between these functions and the basic functions relating to the entire group studied in Section 20.6.

In *accrued benefit cost methods* $M(x)$ is directly related to the accrued benefit that a participant has acquired at age x under provisions of the plan. We look at two possibilities. If the projected benefit accrues uniformly during active service,

$$m(x) = \frac{1}{(r-a)} . \qquad (20.7.5)$$

If the accrual of the benefit is in proportion to total salary where there is an exponential time trend affecting all salaries,

$$m(x) = k\, w(x)\, e^{\tau x} = \frac{w(x)\, e^{\tau x}}{\displaystyle\int_a^r w(y)\, e^{\tau y}\, dy}. \tag{20.7.6}$$

As a special case if the accrual of benefits is in proportion to total salary with no time trend in salary, so that $\tau = 0$, then

$$m(x) = k\, w(x) = \frac{w(x)}{\displaystyle\int_a^r w(y)\, dy}. \tag{20.7.7}$$

For *entry-age actuarial cost methods,* the projected benefit is funded by a level contribution from entry age to retirement. Again, we look at two possibilities. If we define the normal cost rate, $P(x)$, given by (20.7.2) to be a constant, we have $P(x) = k = (aA)(x)\, m(x)$, so that

$$m(x) = \frac{k}{(aA)(x)} = \frac{k\, s(x)}{e^{-\delta(r-x)}\, s(r)\, \bar{a}_r^h} = k_1\, s(x)\, e^{-\delta x}.$$

Now, since $m(x)$ must integrate to 1 between a and r,

$$m(x) = \frac{s(x)\, e^{-\delta x}}{\displaystyle\int_a^r s(y)\, e^{-\delta y}\, dy}. \tag{20.7.8}$$

If, on the other hand, the contribution rate is a level fraction, π, of the salary where there is an exponential trend affecting all salaries, we have

$$P(x) = \pi\, w(x)\, e^{\tau x} = m(x)\, (aA)(x)$$

so

$$m(x) = \frac{e^{-\delta x}\, s(x)\, e^{\tau x}\, w(x)}{\displaystyle\int_a^r e^{-\delta y}\, s(y)\, e^{\tau y}\, w(y)\, dy}. \tag{20.7.9}$$

The actuarial accrued liability for an individual age x, that is, the difference between the actuarial present values of benefits and of future contributions, is

$$(aV)(x) = e^{-\delta(r-x)}\, \frac{s(r)}{s(x)}\, \bar{a}_r^h - \pi \int_x^r e^{-\delta(y-x)}\, \frac{s(y)}{s(x)}\, w(y)\, dy$$

$$= e^{-\delta(r-x)}\, \frac{s(r)}{s(x)}\, \bar{a}_r^h \left\{ 1 - \left[\frac{\displaystyle\int_x^r e^{-\delta y}\, s(y)\, w(y)\, dy}{\displaystyle\int_a^r e^{-\delta y}\, s(y)\, w(y)\, dy} \right] \right\}$$

$$= (aA)(x)\, M(x).$$

This confirms our choice of $m(x)$ function above in (20.7.9).

By a similar process it can be shown that if no exponential trend in salaries by time is assumed, the pension accrual density function is

$$m(x) = \frac{s(x)\ w(x)\ e^{-\delta x}}{\int_a^r s(y)\ w(y)\ e^{-\delta y}\ dy}. \tag{20.7.10}$$

Note that the fraction of projected benefits accrued as an actuarial liability in entry-age actuarial cost methods differs from the definition of the accrued benefits in most plans. A definition of accrued benefits is required for regulatory purposes and to communicate to participants about the benefits they are accruing. The distinction here is similar to the distinction between the reserve and the nonforfeiture benefit in ordinary insurance.

Also note that the contribution rate, paid by a plan sponsor that is following an individual actuarial cost method, will usually differ from the total normal cost rate specified by that method. There are two general reasons for this. First, at the inception of a plan or at times when a plan is amended, actuarial accrued liabilities for prior service may be changed. Second, the actuarial assumptions will not be realized exactly, thereby generating funding gains or losses. The decisions on how to adjust the contribution rate to fund these changes in the actuarial accrued liability, or to adjust for gains or losses, are important ones that are subject to regulation. The particular adjustments chosen are not compelled by the choice of individual actuarial cost method.

20.8   Group Actuarial Cost Methods

In this section we consider group or aggregate actuarial cost methods for which contributions are determined on a collective basis and not as a sum of contributions for individual participants. For the purpose of defining aggregate actuarial cost methods, we need three additional functions:
1. $(aF)_t$, the fund allocated to active members at time t
2. $(aC)_t$, the annual contribution rate at time t with respect to active participants
3. $(aU)_t$, the unfunded actuarial accrued liability with respect to active participants at time t.

Thus,

$$(aU)_t = (aV)_t - (aF)_t. \tag{20.8.1}$$

The fund for active members at time t can be described by the differential equation

$$\frac{d}{dt}(aF)_t = (aC)_t + \delta\ (aF)_t - {}^T P_t \tag{20.8.2}$$

with the initial value $(aF)_0$. The right-hand member of (20.8.2) indicates the two sources of income to the fund and the one source of outgo, that is, the transfer of the terminal funding cost to a fund for retired members.

In relation to an actuarial cost method, as determined by an accrual function, which implies a normal cost rate P_t [see (20.6.4)] and the unfunded accrued liability of active members $(aU)_t$ [see (20.6.8) and (20.8.1)], a natural form of contribution rate is

$$(aC)_t = P_t + \lambda(t)\,(aU)_t. \tag{20.8.3}$$

In (20.8.3) $\lambda(t)$ defines the process for amortizing $(aU)_t$.

Equation (20.8.3) points out a characteristic of aggregate actuarial cost methods not yet stated. These methods define a contribution rate, $(aC)_t$, that depends on the level of funding, that is, on the magnitude of $(aU)_t$. Here the adjustments required by plan changes or by gains and losses can be made automatically by following the actuarial cost method since the value of $(aU)_t$ will reflect such changes and gains and losses.

We consider one such amortization process, one in which

$$\lambda(t) = \frac{1}{\bar{a}_{P_t}} \tag{20.8.4}$$

where

$$\bar{a}_{P_t} = \frac{(Pa)_t}{P_t}. \tag{20.8.5}$$

Thus $(Pa)_t = P_t\,\bar{a}_{P_t}$, so $\bar{a}_{P_t}$ is the value of a unit temporary annuity such that this temporary annuity with a level income rate at the current normal cost rate, P_t, equals the actuarial present value of future normal costs for the current active members, $(Pa)_t$. In this case the notation has been selected to suggest the motivating idea.

Formula (20.8.3) can be rewritten for this particular choice of $\lambda(t)$ as

$$(aC)_t = P_t + \frac{(aV)_t - (aF)_t}{\bar{a}_{P_t}}$$

$$= \frac{(Pa)_t + (aV)_t - (aF)_t}{\bar{a}_{P_t}}$$

$$= \frac{(aA)_t - (aF)_t}{\bar{a}_{P_t}} \tag{20.8.6}$$

making use of (20.6.20). Thus, with $\lambda(t)$ given by (20.8.4), we have

$$(aC)_t\,\bar{a}_{P_t} = (aA)_t - (aF)_t. \tag{20.8.7}$$

The interpretation of (20.8.7) is that a temporary annuity at the rate of $(aC)_t$ is equivalent to the actuarial present value of future benefits for active members less the fund for them.

The formula governing the progress of the fund, (20.8.2), becomes, for $\lambda(t)$ given by (20.8.4),

$$\frac{d}{dt}(aF)_t = P_t + \frac{(aU)_t}{\bar{a}_{P_t}} + \delta\,(aF)_t - {}^TP_t. \tag{20.8.8}$$

We can write (20.6.9) as

$$\frac{d}{dt}(aV)_t = P_t + \delta\,(aV)_t - {}^TP_t{}'. \tag{20.8.9}$$

By subtracting (20.8.8) from (20.8.9), we get

$$\frac{d}{dt}(aU)_t = -\frac{(aU)_t}{\bar{a}_{P_t}} + \delta\,(aU)_t. \tag{20.8.10}$$

The differential equation (20.8.10) may be solved by replacing t by u, integrating with respect to u from 0 to t, and taking exponentials to obtain

$$(aU)_t = (aU)_0 \exp\left[-\int_0^t \left(\frac{1}{\bar{a}_{P_u}} - \delta\right) du\right]. \tag{20.8.11}$$

Upon substituting (20.8.1), we obtain

$$(aF)_t = (aV)_t - [(aV)_0 - (aF)_0] \exp\left[-\int_0^t \left(\frac{1}{\bar{a}_{P_u}} - \delta\right) du\right]. \tag{20.8.12}$$

Provided that $\bar{a}_{P_u}$ is smaller than $\bar{a}_{\overline{\infty}|} = 1/\delta$ so that $1/\bar{a}_{P_u} - \delta \geq \epsilon > 0$,

$$\exp\left[-\int_0^t \left(\frac{1}{\bar{a}_{P_u}} - \delta\right) du\right] \to 0$$

as $t \to \infty$, therefore $(aF)_t \to (aV)_t$.

Here the aggregate cost method with $\lambda(t) = 1/\bar{a}_{P_t}$ is asymptotically equivalent to the individual cost method defined by the accrual function used to evaluate $(aV)_t$ and P_t. There may be many accrual functions that produce functions such that $(Pa)_t/P_t$ is sufficiently small to assure the convergence of $(aF)_t$ to $(aV)_t$. Each of these accrual functions could produce a different pattern of contributions and a different ultimate fund. For completeness, when referring to an aggregate actuarial cost method, always specify the accrual function used. The aggregate cost method with entry-age accrual is particularly important in practice.

Clearly there are many possible choices for the function $\lambda(t)$ in determining the rate of amortization of $(aU)_0$. If the goal is the completion of amortization by the end of n years from some initial time 0, one choice for $\lambda(t)$ is

$$\lambda(t) = \frac{1}{\bar{a}_{\overline{n-t}|}} \qquad 0 < t < n.$$

Then, corresponding to (20.8.11), we obtain

$$(aU)_t = (aU)_0 \exp\left[-\int_0^t \left(\frac{1}{\bar{a}_{\overline{n-u}|}} - \delta\right) du\right]$$

$$= (aU)_0 \exp\left(-\int_0^t \frac{1}{\bar{s}_{\overline{n-u}|}}\, du\right). \tag{20.8.13}$$

It can be shown (Exercise 20.21) that

Section 20.8   Group Actuarial Cost Methods

$$-\int_0^t \frac{1}{\bar{s}_{\overline{n-u}|}} \, du = \log\left(\frac{\bar{s}_{\overline{n}|} - \bar{s}_{\overline{t}|}}{\bar{s}_{\overline{n}|}}\right).$$

Therefore (20.8.13) becomes

$$(aU)_t = (aU)_0 \frac{\bar{s}_{\overline{n}|} - \bar{s}_{\overline{t}|}}{\bar{s}_{\overline{n}|}},$$

and it can be shown that

$$(aC)_t = P_t + \frac{(aU)_0}{\bar{a}_{\overline{n}|}} \qquad 0 \le t \le n.$$

At time n, the funding goal will be achieved with $(aU)_n = 0$, and $(aC)_t$ will drop to P_t.

In practice, a common amortization pattern choice is to define $\lambda(t)$ as the reciprocal of an average annuity value for the future wages of the active lives. We define this to be $\bar{a}_{W_t} = (Wa)_t / W_t$, where $(Wa)_t$ is given by

$$(Wa)_t = \int_a^r n(t - x + a) \, s(x) \, w(x) \left[\int_x^r e^{-\delta(y-x)} \frac{s(y)}{s(x)} \frac{w(y)}{w(x)} e^{\tau(t+y-x)} \, dy \right] dx$$

$$= \int_a^r n(t - x + a) \left[\int_x^r e^{-\delta(y-x)} s(y) \, w(y) \, e^{\tau(t+y-x)} \, dy \right] dx. \qquad (20.8.14)$$

Combining (20.2.3) and (20.8.14), we have

$$\bar{a}_{W_t} = \frac{\int_a^r n(t - x + a) \int_x^r e^{-(\delta-\tau)(y-x)} s(y) \, w(y) \, dy \, dx}{\int_a^r n(t - x + a) \, s(x) \, w(x) \, dx}. \qquad (20.8.15)$$

You will be asked in Exercise 20.23 to verify that the above ratio is the same as $\bar{a}_{P_t}$ as defined by (20.8.5) for the entry-age actuarial cost method using a level percentage of salary as the normal cost pattern. Thus, the choice of $\lambda(t) = 1/\bar{a}_{W_t}$ yields a costing pattern that is asymptotically equivalent to the individual entry-age actuarial cost method with normal costs equal to a level percentage of salary using $m(x)$ given in (20.7.9).

Example 20.8.1

Assume a stationary population, that is, $n(a) = l_a$, $\tau = 0$, and $h(x) = 1$, with the accrual function associated with the level amount entry-age actuarial cost method, $M(x) = \bar{a}_{\overline{a:x-a}|} / \bar{a}_{\overline{a:r-a}|}$ (see Example 20.5.1).
a. Display λ.
b. Calculate $(aC)_0$ if $(aF)_0 = 0$.

Solution:

a. Formula (20.3.2) gives, for the stationary case,

$$^T P_t = f \, w(r) \, l_r \, \bar{a}_r$$

for all t. Thus from (20.6.19),

$$(Pa)_t = \int_a^r e^{-\delta(r-x)} f\, w(r)\, l_r\, \bar{a}_r \left(1 - \frac{\bar{a}_{a:\overline{x-a}}}{\bar{a}_{a:\overline{r-a}}}\right) dx.$$

Now, $M'(x) = m(x) = {}_{x-a}E_a / \bar{a}_{a:\overline{r-a}}$, so by (20.6.4)

$$P_t = \int_a^r e^{-\delta(r-x)} f\, w(r)\, l_r\, \bar{a}_r \, \frac{{}_{x-a}E_a}{\bar{a}_{a:\overline{r-a}}}\, dx.$$

Thus, (20.8.5) gives

$$\bar{a}_{P_t} = \frac{(Pa)_t}{P_t} = \frac{\displaystyle\int_a^r e^{\delta x}\, {}_{x-a}E_a\, \bar{a}_{x:\overline{r-x}}\, dx}{\displaystyle\int_a^r e^{\delta x}\, {}_{x-a}E_a\, dx}$$

$$= \frac{\displaystyle\int_a^r l_x\, \bar{a}_{x:\overline{r-x}}\, dx}{\displaystyle\int_a^r l_x\, dx},$$

and $\lambda = 1/\bar{a}_{P_t}$.

b. Substituting into (20.8.6) from (20.6.1),

$$(aC)_0 = \frac{\int_a^r e^{-\delta(r-x)} f\, w(r)\, l_r\, \bar{a}_r\, dx}{\bar{a}_{P_t}}$$

$$= \frac{f\, w(r)\, l_r\, \bar{a}_r\, \bar{a}_{\overline{r-a}} \displaystyle\int_a^r l_x\, dx}{\displaystyle\int_a^r l_x\, \bar{a}_{x:\overline{r-x}}\, dx}.$$

▼

20.9 Basic Functions for Active and Retired Members Combined

In Sections 20.4 and 20.6 we develop separate basic functions for retired and active members; this is a useful division for many purposes. The administrative system, the actuarial valuation problems, and even the investment policy may be different for the two groups. However, for other purposes it is useful to consider basic functions for the combined group of active and retired members.

The basic actuarial functions for the combined group are the sums of those for the retired members given in Section 20.4 and those for the active members given in Section 20.6. These are summarized in Table 20.9.1.

TABLE 20.9.1

Actuarial Functions for the Active, Retired, and Combined Member Groups of a Pension Plan

Function	Actives	Retireds	Combined
Actuarial present value at time t of future pensions[a,b]	$(aA)_t$	$(rA)_t$	$A_t = (aA)_t + (rA)_t$
Normal cost rate[c]	P_t	0	P_t
Actuarial accrued liability[d,e]	$(aV)_t$	$(rV)_t$	$V_t = (aV)_t + (rV)_t$
Actuarial present value of future normal costs[f]	$(Pa)_t$	0	$(Pa)_t$

[a] $(aA)_t$ is given in (20.6.1)
[b] $(rA)_t$ is given in (20.4.2)
[c] P_t is given in (20.6.4)
[d] $(aV)_t$ is given in (20.6.8)
[e] $(rV)_t$ is given in (20.6.15)
[f] $(Pa)_t$ is given in (20.6.18)

We can use the income allocation equations for active members (20.6.9) and for retired members (20.4.6) to obtain such an equation for the combined group. Thus,

$$P_t + \delta\, V_t = B_t + \frac{d}{dt}\, V_t. \tag{20.9.1}$$

In this equation normal cost and interest income into the fund are allocated to pension benefit payments and change in the actuarial accrued liability.

To obtain formulas for the combined group under aggregate funding we assume that pensions for retired members are fully funded so that $(rV)_t = (rF)_t$. Then, (20.8.1) may be rewritten as the unfunded actuarial liability for all members as

$$U_t = V_t - F_t$$

$$= (aV)_t + (rV)_t - (aV)_t - (rF)_t$$

$$= (aU)_t. \tag{20.9.2}$$

Further, since no contribution is required for the retired members, the contribution rate C_t for all members equals $(aC)_t$, the contribution rate for active members. In this case (20.8.3) may be rewritten as

$$C_t = P_t + \lambda(t)\, U_t. \tag{20.9.3}$$

If $\lambda(t) = 1/\bar{a}_{P_t}$, the contribution rate becomes

$$C_t = \frac{P_t\, \bar{a}_{P_t} + V_t - F_t}{\bar{a}_{P_t}}$$

$$= \frac{A_t - F_t}{\bar{a}_{P_t}}. \tag{20.9.4}$$

Thus when $(rF)_t = (rV)_t$, the results of the aggregate cost method defined for active members at t by (20.8.6) are equivalent to the results defined for all members by (20.9.4).

20.10   Notes and References

Many of the rudiments of the theory of pension funding appeared in a government publication known as the Bulletin on 23P. Charles Trowbridge (1952, 1963) did much to create a mathematical theory of pension funding. The more elaborate model used in this chapter was developed for a series of papers by Bowers, Hickman, and Nesbitt (1976, 1979). The stress on separate functions for active and retired lives is due to Kischuk (1976).

Several authors have studied the problems created for pension funding by inflationary influences on salaries, interest rates, and benefits. Papers by Allison and Winklevoss (1975) and Myers (1960) are in this class. John Trowbridge (1977) provides many observations on changes in pension funding in different nations in response to inflation.

Exercises

Section 20.2

20.1. In a stationary population with level salaries at rate w, what is the payroll function W_t?

Section 20.3

20.2. In the exponential case, what is the payroll function W_t?

20.3. Assume that the initial annual rate of retirement income for a life retiring at time t is given by

$$\frac{f}{b} \int_{t-b}^{t} w(r - t + y)\, e^{\tau y}\, dy \qquad 0 < b < r - a.$$

Other aspects of the model plan remain unchanged. For this benefit definition, based on a final average formula,
a. Show that the initial benefit rate at time t is given by

$$\frac{f}{b} \int_{0}^{b} w(r - z)\, e^{\tau (t-z)}\, dz$$

b. Display a formula for the terminal funding cost rate at time t
c. Rework Example 20.3.1.

20.4. The initial annual rate of retirement income for a life retiring at time t is given by $c(r - a)\, w\, e^{\tau t}$. Other aspects of the model plan remain unchanged.

For this initial benefit rate, based on the product of years of service and final salary level,

   a. Display a formula for the terminal funding cost rate at time t

   b. Rework Example 20.3.1.

20.5. If $s(x) = e^{-\mu(x-a)}$, $a \le x \le r$, display ${}^{T}P_{t}$ in the exponential case.

20.6. Consider an initially immature model with a stationary active population arising from the following assumptions:

   $a = 25$; $r = 65$; $n(t) = 0$ for $t < -40$ and $n(t) = 75$ for $t > -40$; $s(x) = (100 - x)/75$ for $25 < x < 100$; $\delta = 0.06$; $w(x) = 525/(100 - x)$; $\tau = 0.02$; $f = 0.6$; $h(x) = 1$.

   a. Find $\bar{a}_{x}^{h}$ and in particular $\bar{a}_{65}^{h}$.

   b. Find ${}^{T}P_{t}$.

Section 20.4

20.7. In the exponential case, show that $B_{t} = {}^{T}P_{t} \, (\bar{a}_{r}^{\prime h} / \bar{a}_{r}^{h})$ where

$$\bar{a}_{r}^{\prime h} = \int_{r}^{\infty} e^{-(\rho - \beta)(x-r)} \frac{s(x)}{s(r)} \, dx.$$

20.8. For the initially immature model with the stationary active population of Exercise 20.6:

   a. Find $(rA)_{t}$ by evaluating expression (20.4.3) for $t > 35$

   b. Find B_{t} for $t > 35$

   c. Verify the allocation equation (20.4.6) for $t > 35$.

Section 20.5

20.9. What is $M(x)$ in the case of terminal funding?

Section 20.6

20.10. Using the assumptions of Exercise 20.5 with $m(x) = 1/(r - a)$, determine P_{t}.

20.11. a. Show that

$$(aA)_{t} = \int_{t}^{t+r-a} e^{-\delta(y-t)} \, {}^{T}P_{y} \, dy.$$

   b. Differentiate the expression in part (a) to obtain an alternative solution to Example 20.6.1.

20.12. If

$$e^{\theta X(\theta)} = \int_{a}^{r} e^{\theta x} \, m(x) \, dx$$

   and

$$\mu = \int_a^r x\, m(x)\, dx,$$

show that
a. $X(\theta) > \mu$ if $\theta > 0$
b. $X(\theta) < \mu$ if $\theta < 0$
[Hint: Use Jensen's inequality (1.3.2) or (1.3.3)]
c. limit $X(\theta) = \mu$ as $\theta \to 0$.
[Hint: Think of $e^{\theta X(\theta)} = E[e^{\theta X}]$ as a m.g.f.]

20.13. In the exponential case, show that
a. $P_t = {}^T P_t \exp\{-\theta[r - X(\theta)]\}$
b. $(aV)_t = {}^T P_t\, \bar{a}_{\overline{r-X(\theta)}|\,\theta} = P_t\, \bar{s}_{\overline{r-X(\theta)}|\,\theta}.$

20.14. a. What do the formulas in Exercise 20.13 become if the model plan operates in a stationary population with $\tau = 0$?
b. What do the formulas in Exercise 20.13 become if $\theta = \delta - \rho = 0$?

20.15. a. Derive a normal cost rate to be applied to all salaries of those who enter at time u. Other aspects of the model plan are unchanged.
b. Using the result in (a), display the corresponding pension accrual density function for those who enter at time u.

20.16. a. For the model plan show that

$$P_t = f\, w(r)\, s(r)\, \bar{a}_r^h \int_a^r e^{-\delta(r-x)}\, e^{\tau(t+r-x)}\, n(t - x + a)\, m(x)\, dx.$$

b. If $\tau = 0$, $n(t) = l_a$, show that

$$P_t = f\, w(r) \int_a^r l_{x\ r-x} E_x\, \bar{a}_r^h\, m(x)\, dx$$

where $_{r-x}E_x$ is based on the survival function $s(x)$ and force of interest δ.

20.17. If $n(t) = l_a$ and

$$m(x) = \frac{w(x)\, e^{\tau x}}{\displaystyle\int_a^r w(y)\, e^{\tau y}\, dy}$$

show that

$$P_{t+u} = e^{\tau u}\, P_t.$$

Section 20.7

20.18. Assume that projected initial benefit rate at retirement for a life age x at time t is $f\, w(r)\, e^{\tau(t+r-x)}$ and the number of lives age x to $x + dx$ at time t is $n(t - x + a)\, s(x)\, dx$.

a. Verify that $(aA)_t$ as given by (20.6.1) is equal to

$$\int_a^r f\, w(r)\, e^{\tau(t+r-x)}\, n(t - x + a)\, s(x)\, (aA)(x)\, dx.$$

b. Verify that P_t as given by (20.6.4) is equal to

$$\int_a^r f\, w(r)\, e^{\tau(t+r-x)}\, n(t - x + a)\, s(x)\, P(x)\, dx.$$

c. Verify that $(aV)_t$ as given by (20.6.8) is equal to

$$\int_a^r f\, w(r)\, e^{\tau(t+r-x)}\, n(t - x + a)\, s(x)\, (aV)(x)\, dx.$$

d. Verify that $(Pa)_t$ as given by (20.6.18) is equal to

$$\int_a^r f\, w(r)\, e^{\tau(t+r-x)}\, n(t - x + a)\, s(x)\, (Pa)(x)\, dx.$$

20.19. Verify (20.7.9).

20.20. For the initially immature model with a stationary active population of Exercise 20.6,
 a. Find $(aA)_t$.
 b. Find $M(x)$ and $m(x)$ for the level accrual of benefits. For this actuarial cost method find
  i. $(aV)_t$ and
  ii. P_t.
  iii. Verify the allocation equation (20.6.9).
 c. Find $M(x)$ and $m(x)$ for costs as a level percentage of projected wages between ages 25 and 65. For this actuarial cost method find
  i. $(aV)_t$ and
  ii. P_t.
  iii. Verify the allocation equation (20.6.9).

Section 20.8

20.21. Verify that

 a.
$$-\int_0^t \frac{1}{\bar{s}_{\overline{n-y}|}}\, dy = \log\left(\frac{\bar{s}_{\overline{n}|} - \bar{s}_{\overline{t}|}}{\bar{s}_{\overline{n}|}}\right)$$

 b.
$$-\int_0^t \frac{1}{\bar{a}_{\overline{n-y}|}}\, dy = \log\left(\frac{\bar{a}_{\overline{n}|} - \bar{a}_{\overline{t}|}}{\bar{a}_{\overline{n}|}}\right).$$

20.22. a. Obtain a simplified formula for $\bar{a}_{P_t}$ in the exponential case.
 b. What does $\bar{a}_{P_t}$ become in the exponential case if $\theta = \delta - \rho = 0$?

20.23. Verify that the ratio $\bar{a}_{W_t}$, given by (20.8.15), is equal to the ratio $\bar{a}_{P_t}$, given by (20.8.5), when applied to the pension accrual density function given by (20.7.9).

20.24. For the initially immature model with the stationary active population of Exercise 20.6,
a. Find W_t
b. Find $(Wa)_t$, the present value of future projected wages for the active work force at time t
c. Verify that $\bar{a}_{W_t} = (Wa)_t / W_t$, the average annuity value for future wages, equals the average annuity value for entry-age normal costing (Exercise 20.20(c)) defined by

$$\bar{a}_{P_t} = \frac{(Pa)_t}{P_t} = \frac{(aA)_t - (aV)_t}{P_t}.$$

Miscellaneous Exercises

20.25. For the initially immature model with the stationary active population of Exercise 20.6, display and solve the differential equation for the size of the fund for active lives assuming a 15-year amortization of $(aV)_0$ using
a. The actuarial cost method of Exercise 20.20(b).
b. The actuarial cost method of Exercise 20.20(c).
[Hint: For $0 < t < 15$, modify (20.8.2) so that $(aC)_t$ equals the normal cost plus the amortization payment rate.]

INTEREST AS A RANDOM VARIABLE

21.1 Introduction

The developments in Chapters 3 through 11 and 15 through 18 were built on the basic assumptions that time until decrement and cause or type of decrement are random variables and their joint distribution is known. When interest earnings were introduced into the models for long-term financial operations, their effect was captured by interest rates that were assumed to be deterministic and usually constant. An examination of a set of observations of interest rates confirms that this assumption is unrealistic. Table 21.1.1 illustrates this point.

TABLE 21.1.1

Average Yield to Maturity for 30-Year U.S. Treasury Bonds in January of Year Indicated*

Year	Yield[†]	Year	Yield[†]
1978	8.18%	1987	7.39
1979	8.94	1988	8.83
1980	10.60	1989	8.93
1981	12.14	1990	8.26
1982	14.22	1991	8.27
1983	10.63	1992	7.58
1984	11.75	1993	7.34
1985	11.45	1994	6.29
1986	9.40	1995	7.85
		1996	6.05

*Source: "Economic Statistics for Employee Benefit Actuaries," April 1996, Schaumburg, Ill.: Society of Actuaries.
[†]Bond equivalent yield.

21.1.1   Incorporating Variability of Interest

There are several methods for incorporating the variability of interest rates into actuarial models.

1. Preset interest rate scenarios. These scenarios are sequences of future interest rates, indexed by time, that will be used with other assumptions and the equivalence principle in premium and reserve calculations. In more comprehensive models each scenario would specify other variables such as expenses and withdrawal rates in a way to be consistent with the corresponding interest rates. Furthermore, in these latter models, the interest rates themselves, both within a scenario as well as across scenarios, might be constructed to satisfy certain economic conditions.

   a. The scenarios can be specified without modeling of past data and designed simply to measure the adequacy of premiums and reserves over different paths of plausible future economic conditions. This would be a type of sensitivity analysis and is the subject of Section 21.2.1.

   b. The scenarios can be determined after a systematic review of alternative macroeconomic projections and a personal probability attached to each scenario by the actuary. This approach is the subject of Section 21.2.2.

2. Stochastic models most often based on an analysis of past data. This method is typically data centered, and both the selection of the model and the estimation of the model parameters are influenced by past observations. Data from some segments of the capital markets support the hypothesis that annual interest rates can be modeled as independent and identically distributed random variables. Other data may support models in which annual interest rates are dependent random variables. Each of these classes of models can be divided into those in which it is assumed that relevant economic information is captured in observed interest rates and those in which interest rates are modeled as depending on other economic variables that are incorporated into the model. These data-based stochastic models are studied in Sections 21.3 and 21.4.

3. Stochastic models that depend on assumed characteristics of capital markets. Within financial economics, elaborate theories of the operations of capital markets have been developed. A consequence of one of these theories is that a consensus forecast of future financial conditions is provided by current security prices and their relationships. For example, the relationship among yield rates and the corresponding maturity dates, a yield curve, contains information that can be used in building stochastic models for future interest rates and, perhaps, other economic variables. These ideas are introduced in Section 21.5.

In this chapter elements of each of these methods for making provision for the variability of interest rates are introduced. The application of these methods requires knowledge of macroeconomics, applied statistics, and financial economics, respectively. The three methods are developed in this chapter in the order in which they are listed, which is also the order in which they entered actuarial literature. Because of the diversity of the prerequisite ideas, the sections of this chapter cannot provide a complete background for any of the methods.

In earlier chapters, in which time and cause of decrement were assumed to be random variables, attention was devoted to risk management tools for moderating the unfortunate financial consequences of experience that deviated from that expected. These tools for an insurer included acquiring capital, buying reinsurance, increasing contingency loadings to premiums, and increasing the size of the insured group. In Section 21.6 some tools for managing interest rate risk are discussed.

21.1.2   Notation and Preliminaries

We use the symbol I_k to denote the random variable interpreted as the effective interest rate in the k-th transaction period; that is, I_k is the **one-period** interest rate for that k-th period: 1 at the end of the period has a present value of $1/(1 + I_k)$ at the beginning of the period. In most applications considered in this chapter, the transaction period will be a policy year. In most earlier developments it was assumed that I_k, $k = 1, 2, \ldots$, has a single point or degenerate distribution such that $\Pr(I_k = i) = 1$, $k = 1, 2, \ldots$.

An immediate consequence of assuming that the effective (one-period) interest rate is a random variable can be derived from Jensen's inequality, (1.3.3), where $u''(x) > 0$. The restated inequality is

$$E[u(X)] \geq u(E[X]).$$

If $u(x) = (1 + x)^{-1}$ and $X = I_k$, we have $u''(x) > 0$, $-1 < x$, and

$$E[(1 + I_k)^{-1}] \geq [1 + E(I_k)]^{-1}, \tag{21.1.1}$$

with equality holding only if I_k has a single point distribution.

Figure 21.1.1, a revision of Figure 1.3.1, is a graphical representation of the verification of (21.1.1).

FIGURE 21.1.1

Demonstration of Jensen's Inequality, $u'(x) < 0$, $u''(x) > 0$

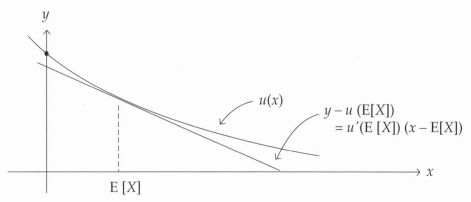

Inequality (21.1.1) can be converted to a statement about the effect of a random interest rate on the actuarial present value of 1 unit paid at the end of one period. The actuarial present value cannot be less than the present value of the payment at the expected interest rate.

21.2   Scenarios

A scenario is an outline of a projected sequence of events. In accordance with this definition, the determination of premiums and reserves in life insurance requires scenarios of future demographic and economic events. In previous chapters there has been a single scenario of future interest rates, and usually the rates have been identical. In this section, the idea of creating and using a number of scenarios of interest rates is developed.

21.2.1   Deterministic Scenarios

In this chapter a deterministic interest rate scenario is taken to be a sequence of future one-period interest rates $(i_1, i_2, i_3, \ldots)$ that has been determined by the actuary for use in an actuarial calculation. The elements of the sequence are selected as representing plausible prospective interest rates in accordance with the actuary's view of possible future economic environments. One scenario can be sufficient if the actuary is certain about future investment returns as a result of past investment decisions or special knowledge. As an alternative, several scenarios can be specified so that the sensitivity of actuarial present values to changes in the economic environment can be studied.

If several scenarios are used, we index the scenarios by $j = 1, 2, \ldots, m$, where m is the number of scenarios; that is, $({}_j i_1, {}_j i_2, {}_j i_3, \ldots)$ denotes interest scenario j. In addition, discount factors and annuity values that are specific to scenario j are denoted as follows:

$$_j v^0 = 1, \quad _j v^k = \prod_{r=1}^{k} (1 + {}_j i_r)^{-1}, \quad \text{and} \quad _j \ddot{a}_{\overline{n}|} = \sum_{k=0}^{n-1} {}_j v^k.$$

Using this notation, and ideas from Chapters 4, 5, and 6, it is natural to define

$$_j A_x = \mathrm{E}[{}_j v^{K+1}] = \sum_{k=0}^{\infty} {}_j v^{k+1} \, {}_k p_x \, q_{x+k}, \qquad (21.2.1a)$$

$$_j \ddot{a}_x = \mathrm{E}[{}_j \ddot{a}_{\overline{K+1}|}] = \sum_{k=0}^{\infty} {}_j \ddot{a}_{\overline{k+1}|} \, {}_k p_x \, q_{x+k}, \qquad (21.2.1b)$$

where K is the random variable defined as the number of complete future life years of a life age x. Applying the equivalence principle, we have

$$_j P_x = \frac{_j A_x}{_j \ddot{a}_x}. \qquad (21.2.1c)$$

The symbol $_j P_x$ used in (21.2.1c) is not part of IAN and runs the risk of being confused with the symbol used in Chapter 6 to denote the benefit premium for a limited payment life insurance. Despite the possible confusion, the symbol is used in this section to promote consistency with the symbols used to denote actuarial present values that are specific to scenario j.

Developing variances for the loss variables implicit in (21.2.1a, b, and c) requires care. The simplifications available with constant interest rates cannot be employed, and we must remember that the variances recognize only the random nature of time until death for a given interest rate scenario.

We have

$$\text{Var}(_jv^{K+1}) = \sum_{k=0}^{\infty} {}_jv^{2(k+1)} \, {}_kp_x \, q_{x+k} - (_jA_x)^2 = {}_j^2A_x - (_jA_x)^2,$$

$$\text{Var}(_j\ddot{a}_{\overline{K+1}}) = \sum_{k=0}^{\infty} (_j\ddot{a}_{\overline{k+1}})^2 \, {}_kp_x \, q_{x+k} - (_j\ddot{a}_x)^2$$

$$= \sum_{k=0}^{\infty} \left(\sum_{r=0}^{k} {}_jv^r \right)^2 \, {}_kp_x \, q_{x+k} - (_j\ddot{a}_x)^2,$$

and

$$\text{Var}(_jv^{K+1} - {}_jP_x \, {}_j\ddot{a}_{\overline{K+1}}) = \sum_{k=0}^{\infty} (_jv^{k+1} - {}_jP_x \, {}_j\ddot{a}_{\overline{k+1}})^2 \, {}_kp_x \, q_{x+k}.$$

Example 21.2.1

Four interest rate scenarios are defined.

j	$_ji_1$	$_ji_2$	$_ji_3$	$_ji_4$
1	0.06	0.06	0.06	0.06
2	0.06	0.03	0.03	0.03
3	0.06	0.09	0.09	0.09
4	0.06	0.03	0.09	0.03

The discrete distribution of the curtate future lifetime of (x) is given in the following table.

k	$_kp_x \, q_{x+k}$
0	0.1
1	0.2
2	0.3
3	0.4

Calculate $_jv^k$, $_j\ddot{a}_{\overline{k}}$ for $j = 1, 2, 3, 4$ and $k = 0, 1, 2, 3$, and $_jA_x$, $_j\ddot{a}_x$, $_jP_x$ for $j = 1, 2, 3, 4$.

Solution:

	$_jv^{k+1}$				$_j\ddot{a}_{\overline{k+1}\rceil}$			
j	$k=0$	$k=1$	$k=2$	$k=3$	$k=0$	$k=1$	$k=2$	$k=3$
1	0.9434	0.8900	0.8396	0.7921	1.0000	1.9434	2.8334	3.6730
2	0.9434	0.9159	0.8892	0.8633	1.0000	1.9434	2.8593	3.7486
3	0.9434	0.8655	0.7940	0.7285	1.0000	1.9434	2.8089	3.6029
4	0.9434	0.9159	0.8403	0.8158	1.0000	1.9434	2.8593	3.6996

j	$_jA_x$	$_j\ddot{a}_x$	$_jP_x$
1	0.8411	2.8079	0.2995
2	0.8896	2.8459	0.3126
3	0.7970	2.7725	0.2875
4	0.8559	2.8263	0.3028

▼

Example 21.2.2

Using the assumptions of Example 21.2.1, calculate $\sqrt{\mathrm{Var}(_jv^{K+1})}$ and $\sqrt{\mathrm{Var}(_j\ddot{a}_{\overline{K+1}\rceil})}$, $j=1, 2, 3, 4$.

Solution:

	$_jv^{2(k+1)}$				$(_j\ddot{a}_{\overline{k+1}\rceil})^2$			
j	$k=0$	$k=1$	$k=2$	$k=3$	$k=0$	$k=1$	$k=2$	$k=3$
1	0.8900	0.7921	0.7049	0.6274	1.0000	3.7768	8.0282	13.4910
2	0.8900	0.8389	0.7908	0.7454	1.0000	3.7768	8.1757	14.0517
3	0.8900	0.7491	0.6305	0.5307	1.0000	3.7768	7.8899	12.9811
4	0.8900	0.8389	0.7061	0.6656	1.0000	3.7768	8.1757	13.6871

$$\sqrt{\mathrm{Var}(_jv^{K+1})} = \qquad\qquad \sqrt{\mathrm{Var}(_j\ddot{a}_{\overline{K+1}\rceil})} =$$

$$\sqrt{\mathrm{E}[_jv^{2(K+1)}] - (\mathrm{E}[_jv^{K+1}])^2} \qquad \sqrt{\mathrm{E}[(_j\ddot{a}_{\overline{K+1}\rceil})^2] - (\mathrm{E}[_j\ddot{a}_{\overline{K+1}\rceil}])^2}$$

j		
1	$\sqrt{0.7099 - (0.8411)^2} = 0.0490$	$\sqrt{8.6602 - (2.8079)^2} = 0.8808$
2	$\sqrt{0.7921 - (0.8896)^2} = 0.0265$	$\sqrt{8.9286 - (2.8459)^2} = 0.9108$
3	$\sqrt{0.6402 - (0.7970)^2} = 0.0704$	$\sqrt{8.4147 - (2.7725)^2} = 0.8532$
4	$\sqrt{0.7348 - (0.8559)^2} = 0.0469$	$\sqrt{8.7828 - (2.8263)^2} = 0.8915$

▼

21.2.2 Random Scenarios: Deterministic Interest Rates

In building an interest rate model assume that the actuary has formulated m plausible interest scenarios. As a next step, a probability distribution on the m scenarios could be specified using methods for eliciting personal probabilities. The symbol $p(j)$ denotes the probability of scenario j. It is not the p.f. of claim amount as in Chapter 12.

The probability assignments should reflect the actuary's view of future investment returns. The probability elicitation process is closely related to the utility function elicitation process illustrated in Chapter 1.

Actuarial present values are defined using the joint distribution of the curtate future lifetime years (K) and interest scenario (J). The symbol J will be used in this chapter to denote the random variable interpreted as the index on the interest rate scenario. It is not the cause of decrement as in Chapter 10. We assume that K and J are independent. The asterisk presubscript has been added to actuarial present-value symbols to indicate that the expectation has been taken with respect to K and J:

$$_*A_x = \mathrm{E}_J \, \mathrm{E}_{K|J} \, [_jv^{K+1}] \ = \mathrm{E}_J \, [_jA_x]$$

$$= \sum_{j=1}^{m} {_jA_x} \, p(j), \tag{21.2.2a}$$

$$_*\ddot{a}_x = \mathrm{E}_J \, \mathrm{E}_{K|J} \, [_j\ddot{a}_{\overline{K+1}}] = \mathrm{E}_J \, [_j\ddot{a}_x]$$

$$= \sum_{j=1}^{m} {_j\ddot{a}_x} \, p(j). \tag{21.2.2b}$$

Continuing the same notational convention for the loss variable and premium for a fully discrete annual level premium whole life insurance, we have

$$L = {_jv^{K+1}} - {_*P_x} \, {_j\ddot{a}_{\overline{K+1}}}.$$

Using the equivalence principle, we have

$$\mathrm{E}_J \, \mathrm{E}_{K|J} \, [L] = 0,$$

or

$$_*P_x = \frac{_*A_x}{_*\ddot{a}_x},$$

and the variance of L is given by

$$\mathrm{Var}(L) = \sum_{j=1}^{m} \left[\sum_{k=0}^{\infty} ({_jv^{k+1}} - {_*P_x} \, {_j\ddot{a}_{\overline{k+1}}})^2 \, {_kp_x} \, q_{x+k} \right] p(j).$$

Example 21.2.3

Show that $_*A_x$, as given in (21.2.2a), can also be derived from $\mathrm{E}_K \, \mathrm{E}_{J|K} \, [_jv^{K+1}]$.

Solution:

Because of independence, levels of interest rates do not affect the distribution of mortality:

$$E_K \, E_{J|K} \left[{}_J v^{K+1} \right] = E_K \left[\sum_{j=1}^{m} {}_j v^{K+1} \, p(j) \right]$$

$$= \sum_{k=0}^{\infty} \left[\sum_{j=1}^{m} {}_j v^{k+1} \, p(j) \right] {}_k p_x \, q_{x+k}$$

$$= \sum_{j=1}^{m} {}_j A_x \, p(j) = {}_* A_x. \qquad \blacktriangledown$$

Now assume that there is a set of n lives each age x. Each member of the set has been issued an identical fully discrete annual level premium whole life insurance, and the curtate future lifetime random variables K_i, $i = 1, 2, \ldots$ are identically distributed. In addition K_i, $i = 1, 2, \ldots$, and J are mutually independent. The total loss random variable, if the benefit premium is determined by the equivalence principle, for the set of n insured is

$$\sum_{i=1}^{n} \left({}_J v^{K_i+1} - {}_* P_x \, {}_J \ddot{a}_{\overline{K_i+1|}} \right).$$

The variance of total losses is given by

$$\text{Var} \left[\sum_{i=1}^{n} \left({}_J v^{K_i+1} - {}_* P_x \, {}_J \ddot{a}_{\overline{K_i+1|}} \right) \right]$$

$$= \sum_{i=1}^{n} \text{Var}\left({}_J v^{K_i+1} - {}_* P_x \, {}_J \ddot{a}_{\overline{K_i+1|}} \right)$$

$$+ n(n-1)\text{Cov}\left({}_J v^{K_1+1} - {}_* P_x \, {}_J \ddot{a}_{\overline{K_1+1|}}, \, {}_J v^{K_2+1} - {}_* P_x \, {}_J \ddot{a}_{\overline{K_2+1|}} \right)$$

$$= n \, E\left[\left({}_J v^{K+1} - {}_* P_x \, {}_J \ddot{a}_{\overline{K+1|}} \right)^2 \right]$$

$$+ n(n-1) \, E\left[\left({}_J v^{K_1+1} - {}_* P_x \, {}_J \ddot{a}_{\overline{K_1+1|}} \right)\left({}_J v^{K_2+1} - {}_* P_x \, {}_J \ddot{a}_{\overline{K_2+1|}} \right) \right]$$

$$= n \, E_J \, E_{K|J} \left[\left({}_J v^{K+1} - {}_* P_x \, {}_J \ddot{a}_{\overline{K+1|}} \right)^2 \right]$$

$$+ n(n-1) \, E_J \, E_{K|J} \left[\left({}_J v^{K_1+1} - {}_* P_x \, {}_J \ddot{a}_{\overline{K_1+1|}} \right)\left({}_J v^{K_2+1} - {}_* P_x \, {}_J \ddot{a}_{\overline{K_2+1|}} \right) \right]$$

$$= n \, \text{Var}\left({}_J v^{K+1} - {}_* P_x \, {}_J \ddot{a}_{\overline{K+1|}} \right) + n(n-1) \left[\sum_{j=1}^{m} \left({}_j A_x - {}_* P_x \, {}_j \ddot{a}_x \right)^2 p(j) \right]$$

$$= n \sum_{j=1}^{m} \left[\sum_{k=0}^{\infty} \left({}_j v^{k+1} - {}_* P_x \, {}_j \ddot{a}_{\overline{k+1|}} \right)^2 {}_k p_x \, q_{x+k} + (n-1) \left({}_j A_x - {}_* P_x \, {}_j \ddot{a}_x \right)^2 \right] p(j).$$

If we are interested in the average loss, rather than total loss, in our risk portfolio of n identical policies, we have

$$\text{Var} \left[\frac{\sum_{i=1}^{n} \left({}_J v^{K_i+1} - {}_* P_x \, {}_J \ddot{a}_{\overline{K_i+1|}} \right)}{n} \right] =$$

$$\frac{\text{Var}(_jv^{K+1} - {}_*P_x \, _j\ddot{a}_{\overline{K+1}|})}{n} + \left(1 - \frac{1}{n}\right) \sum_{j=1}^{m} (_jA_x - {}_*P_x \, _j\ddot{a}_x)^2 \, p(j). \qquad (21.2.3)$$

As $n \to \infty$, the first term of (21.2.3) approaches zero, whereas the second term remains positive. The n components of the sum of loss variables that make up total losses are not independent. Increasing the number of independent insureds, in this more comprehensive model with its random interest scenarios, does not make the variance of average loss approach zero as it did when the future lifetime random variables were assumed to be mutually independent and the interest scenario was deterministic. This can be appreciated by observing that the summation in the second term of (21.2.3) becomes zero when there is a single deterministic interest scenario. The fact that all losses are subject to the same randomly determined interest scenario has recognized a risk management problem.

Example 21.2.4

Use the assumptions of Examples 21.2.1 and 21.2.2, assume that the actuary has made the following probability assignments to the interest rate scenarios, $p(1) = 0.5$, $p(2) = 0.2$, $p(3) = 0.2$, and $p(4) = 0.1$ and compute $_*P_x$ and $\text{Var}(_jv^{K+1} - {}_*P_x \, \ddot{a}_{\overline{K+1}|})$.

Solution:

Using the equivalence principle we have

$$E_J \, E_{K|J} \, [_jv^{K+1} - {}_*P_x \, _j\ddot{a}_{\overline{K+1}|}] = 0,$$

$$(_1A_x - {}_*P_x \, _1\ddot{a}_x)p(1) + (_2A_x - {}_*P_x \, _2\ddot{a}_x)p(2)$$

$$+ (_3A_x - {}_*P_x \, _3\ddot{a}_x)p(3) + (_4A_x - {}_*P_x \, _4\ddot{a}_x)p(4) = 0,$$

$$_*P_x = \frac{_*A_x}{_*\ddot{a}_x} = \frac{0.8435}{2.8103} = 0.3001,$$

and

$$\text{Var}(_jv^{K+1} - {}_*P_x \, _j\ddot{a}_{\overline{K+1}|}) = E_J \, E_{K|J} \, [(_jv^{K+1} - 0.3001 \, _j\ddot{a}_{\overline{K+1}|})^2]$$

$$= (0.0987)(0.5) + (0.0912)(0.2) + (0.1078)(0.2) + (0.0983)(0.1) = 0.0990. \qquad \blacktriangledown$$

21.3   Independent Interest Rates

In Section 21.2.2 random interest scenarios or paths were introduced. The probability assignments were made using the economic knowledge of the actuary. We consider now a stochastic model for interest rates in which the selection of the model and the estimates of the model parameters have been influenced by data. Suppose that the actuary has decided to model the forces of interest and has adopted the model

---

$$\log (1 + I_k) = \delta + \epsilon_k \quad k = 1, 2, 3, \ldots \qquad (21.3.1)$$

where δ is a non-negative constant and the ϵ_k are independent and identically distributed random variables with $N(0, \sigma^2)$ distributions. This model can be viewed as a long-term mean force of interest subject to random shocks. Because of the assumptions made about the distribution of the random shock terms, negative forces of interest are possible. Some actuaries view this possibility as invalidating the model in (21.3.1). Other actuaries adopt the model because it seems natural to model forces of interest, and negative values are observed in investment operations. Then the random variables $\log(1 + I_k)$ have identical $N(\delta, \sigma^2)$ distributions, and the $(1 + I_k)$ random variables have lognormal distributions.

The lognormal distribution was introduced in Table 14.2.1 as a claim amount distribution. From that table we recall that

$$E[1 + I_k] = \exp\left(\delta + \frac{\sigma^2}{2}\right) \geq 1$$

and

$$\text{Var}(1 + I_k) = (e^{\sigma^2} - 1) \exp(2\delta + \sigma^2) \geq 0.$$

The logarithm of the random variable version of the deterministic interest accumulation function $(1 + i)^n$ is the random variable

$$\log \prod_{k=1}^{n} (1 + I_k) = \sum_{k=1}^{n} \log (1 + I_k).$$

Using (21.3.1), this random variable has a $N(n\delta, n\sigma^2)$ distribution. As a consequence, the interest accumulation function has a lognormal distribution with

$$E\left[\prod_{k=1}^{n} (1 + I_k)\right] = e^{n(\delta + \sigma^2/2)}$$

and

$$\text{Var}\left[\prod_{k=1}^{n} (1 + I_k)\right] = (e^{\sigma^2} - 1)e^{n(2\delta + \sigma^2)}.$$

It is instructive to observe that if $\sigma^2 = 0$, the expected interest accumulation is $e^{n\delta}$, and its variance is zero.

The logarithm of the discount factor

$$\log(1 + I_k)^{-1} = -\log (1 + I_k) = -\delta - \epsilon_k$$

has a $N(-\delta, \sigma^2)$ distribution, and $(1 + I_k)^{-1}$ has a lognormal distribution with

$$E[(1 + I_k)^{-1}] = e^{-(\delta - \sigma^2/2)} > 0$$

and

$$\text{Var}[(1 + I_k)^{-1}] = (e^{\sigma^2} - 1)(e^{-2\delta + \sigma^2}) \geq 0.$$

We define the discount function as the random variable

$$\tilde{v}_n = \prod_{k=1}^{n} (1 + I_k)^{-1}$$

and

$$\tilde{v}_0 = 1.$$

The choice of the symbol $\tilde{v}_n$ is motivated by the use of v_n for the discount factor in Section 4.3. The tilde distinguishes a random variable, $\tilde{v}_n$. Then $\log \tilde{v}_n = -\Sigma_{k=1}^{n} \log (1 + I_k)$ has a $N(-n\delta, n\sigma^2)$ distribution, and $\tilde{v}_n$ has a lognormal distribution with

$$E[\tilde{v}_n] = e^{-n(\delta - \sigma^2/2)}$$

and

$$\text{Var}(\tilde{v}_n) = (e^{n\sigma^2} - 1)(e^{n(-2\delta + \sigma^2)}). \tag{21.3.2}$$

Once again, if $\sigma^2 = 0$, the deterministic results are recaptured.

We will assume that $I_k, k = 1, 2, 3, \ldots$ and K, curtate future lifetime, are mutually independent and consider comprehensive actuarial models. The actuarial present values of a unit benefit life insurance is

$$_*A_x = E[\tilde{v}_{K+1}]$$

$$= E_{\tilde{v}} \, E_{K|\tilde{v}} \, [\tilde{v}_{K+1}]$$

$$= E_{\tilde{v}} \left[\sum_{k=0}^{\infty} \tilde{v}_{k+1} \, {}_kp_x \, q_{x+k} \right]$$

$$= \sum_{k=0}^{\infty} e^{-(\delta - \sigma^2/2)(k+1)} \, {}_kp_x \, q_{x+k}. \tag{21.3.3}$$

The actuarial present value $_*A_x$ is calculated at deterministic force of interest $\delta - (\sigma^2/2)$. To measure risk, we determine

$$\text{Var}(\tilde{v}_{K+1}) = E[(\tilde{v}_{K+1})^2] - (_*A_x)^2$$

$$= E_{\tilde{v}} \, E_{K|\tilde{v}} \, [(\tilde{v}_{K+1})^2] - (_*A_x)^2$$

$$= E_{\tilde{v}} \left[\sum_{k=0}^{\infty} (\tilde{v}_{k+1})^2 \, {}_kp_x \, q_{x+k} \right] - (_*A_x)^2.$$

Since $\tilde{v}_{k+1}$ has a lognormal distribution with parameters $-(k+1)\delta$ and $(k+1)\sigma^2$, we can calculate $E[(\tilde{v}_{k+1})^2]$, the second moment about the origin, by

$$E[(\tilde{v}_{k+1})^2] = \text{Var}(\tilde{v}_{k+1}) + (E[\tilde{v}_{k+1}])^2$$

$$= (e^{(k+1)\sigma^2} - 1)(e^{(k+1)(-2\delta + \sigma^2)}) + e^{-2(k+1)(\delta - \sigma^2/2)}$$

$$= e^{-(k+1)[2(\delta - \sigma^2)]}, \tag{21.3.4}$$

and then

$$\mathrm{Var}(\tilde{v}_{K+1}) = \sum_{k=0}^{\infty} e^{-(k+1)[2(\delta-\sigma^2)]} \, {}_kp_x \, q_{x+k} - ({}_*A_x)^2.$$

We can see that when $\sigma^2 = 0$, the results of Chapter 4 are reproduced.

The formulas for the actuarial present values of annuities require more extensive developments. In the development, we continue to assume that I_k, $k = 1, 2, \ldots$, and K are mutually independent.

We define

$$\ddot{a}_{\overline{K}|\tilde{v}} = \sum_{s=0}^{K-1} \tilde{v}_s;$$

then

$$\mathrm{E}_{\tilde{v}|K} \left[\ddot{a}_{\overline{K+1}|\tilde{v}} \right] = \sum_{s=0}^{K} e^{s(-\delta+\sigma^2/2)}$$

$$= \ddot{a}_{\overline{K+1}|\delta-\sigma^2/2},$$

and

$$_*\ddot{a}_x = \mathrm{E}[\ddot{a}_{\overline{K+1}|\tilde{v}}] = \mathrm{E}_K \, \mathrm{E}_{\tilde{v}|K} \left[\ddot{a}_{\overline{K+1}|\tilde{v}} \right]$$

$$= \mathrm{E}_K \left[\ddot{a}_{\overline{K+1}|\delta-\sigma^2/2} \right]$$

$$= \sum_{k=0}^{\infty} (\ddot{a}_{\overline{k+1}|\delta-\sigma^2/2}) \, {}_kp_x \, q_{x+k}. \qquad (21.3.5)$$

To evaluate $\mathrm{Var}(\ddot{a}_{\overline{K+1}|\tilde{v}})$ we start with

$$\mathrm{E}_{\tilde{v}} \left[\left(\sum_{s=0}^{k} \tilde{v}_s \right)^2 \right] = \mathrm{E}_{\tilde{v}} \left[(1 + \tilde{v}_1 + \tilde{v}_2 + \cdots + \tilde{v}_k)^2 \right]$$

$$= \mathrm{E}_{\tilde{v}} \left[\sum_{s=0}^{k} (\tilde{v}_s)^2 + 2 \sum_{s=0}^{k-1} \sum_{r=s+1}^{k} \tilde{v}_s \, \tilde{v}_r \right]$$

$$= \sum_{s=0}^{k} e^{-s[2(\delta-\sigma^2)]} + 2 \sum_{s=0}^{k-1} \sum_{r=s+1}^{k} \mathrm{E}[\tilde{v}_s \, \tilde{v}_r].$$

Terms of the form $\mathrm{E}[(\tilde{v}_s)^2]$ were evaluated using (21.3.4).

We now examine the terms in the double summation and find that

$$\mathrm{E}[\tilde{v}_s \, \tilde{v}_r] = \mathrm{E}[(1 + I_1)^{-2} \cdots (1 + I_s)^{-2}(1 + I_{s+1})^{-1} \cdots (1 + I_r)^{-1}] \quad s < r$$

$$= e^{-s[2(\delta-\sigma^2)]-(r-s)(\delta-\sigma^2/2)}. \qquad (21.3.6)$$

The independence of the random variables I_k, $k = 1, 2, \ldots$ and (21.3.2) and (21.3.4) have been used to complete (21.3.6). As a result, we have

$$\mathrm{E}_{\tilde{v}} \left[\left(\sum_{s=0}^{k} \tilde{v}_s \right)^2 \right] = \sum_{s=0}^{k} e^{-s[(2(\delta-\sigma^2)]} + 2 \sum_{s=0}^{k-1} \sum_{r=s+1}^{k} e^{-s[2(\delta-\sigma^2)]-(r-s)(\delta-\sigma^2/2)}. \qquad (21.3.7)$$

The double summation in (21.3.7) can be simplified by interchanging the order of summation and using the formula for the summation of a geometric series. We have

$$2 \sum_{r=1}^{k} e^{-r(\delta - \sigma^2/2)} \sum_{s=0}^{r-1} e^{-s[\delta - (3\sigma^2/2)]} = 2 \sum_{r=1}^{k} e^{-r(\delta - \sigma^2/2)} \left(\frac{1 - e^{-r[\delta - (3\sigma^2/2)]}}{1 - e^{-[\delta - (3\sigma^2/2)]}} \right). \quad (21.3.8)$$

Note that the summation in (21.3.8) can start with $r = 0$ because the summand is then zero.

Combining the intermediate results in (21.3.7) and (21.3.8), we have

$$\mathrm{Var}(\ddot{a}_{\overline{K+1}|\tilde{v}}) = \mathrm{E}_K \, \mathrm{E}_{\tilde{v}|K} \, [(\ddot{a}_{\overline{K+1}|\tilde{v}})^2] - (_*\ddot{a}_x)^2$$

$$= \mathrm{E}_K \left[\sum_{s=0}^{K} e^{-s[2(\delta - \sigma^2)]} + 2 \sum_{r=0}^{K} \left(\frac{e^{-r(\delta - \sigma^2/2)} - e^{-r(2\delta - 2\sigma^2)}}{1 - e^{-[\delta - (3\sigma^2/2)]}} \right) \right] - (_*\ddot{a}_x)^2$$

$$= {}^\alpha\ddot{a}_x + 2 \frac{_*\ddot{a}_x - {}^\alpha\ddot{a}_x}{1 - e^{-[\delta - (3\sigma^2/2)]}} - (_*\ddot{a}_x)^2 \quad (21.3.9)$$

where ${}^\alpha\ddot{a}_x$ is evaluated at force of interest $2(\delta - \sigma^2)$.

If $\sigma^2 = 0$, (21.3.9) reduces to

$${}^2\ddot{a}_x + \frac{2(\ddot{a}_x - {}^2a_x)}{d} - (\ddot{a}_x)^2,$$

where ${}^2\ddot{a}_x$ is valued at force of interest 2δ and $\ddot{a}_x$ is valued at force of interest δ.

This result may be compared with (5.3.8) where

$$\mathrm{Var}(\ddot{a}_{\overline{K+1}|}) = \frac{{}^2A_x - (A_x)^2}{d^2}$$

$$= \frac{1 - (2d - d^2) \, {}^2\ddot{a}_x - 1 + 2 \, d\ddot{a}_x - d^2 \, \ddot{a}_x^2}{d^2}$$

$$= {}^2\ddot{a}_x + 2 \frac{(\ddot{a}_x - {}^2\ddot{a}_x)}{d} - (\ddot{a}_x)^2,$$

confirming again that when $\sigma^2 = 0$, deterministic interest results are recovered.

Example 21.3.1

Assume that $\log(1 + I_k) = \delta + \epsilon_k$, $k = 1, 2, 3 \ldots$ where $\delta = 0.06$, and the random shock terms have a $N(0, 0.0001)$ distribution. The curtate future lifetime random variable has the discrete distribution shown in Example 21.2.1. Calculate (a) $\mathrm{E}[\tilde{v}_{K+1}]$, (b) $\mathrm{Var}(\tilde{v}_{K+1})$, (c) $\mathrm{E}[\ddot{a}_{\overline{K+1}|\tilde{v}}]$, and (d) $\mathrm{Var}(\ddot{a}_{\overline{K+1}|\tilde{v}})$. Assume that K and I_k, $k = 1, 2, 3 \ldots$, are independent.

Solution:

Formula numbers refer to those displayed in this section.

---

a. $E[\tilde{v}_{K+1}] = \sum_{k=0}^{3} e^{-(0.06-0.00005)(k+1)}\ {}_kp_x\ q_{x+k}$

$\quad\quad = (0.9418)(0.1) + (0.8870)(0.2) + (0.8354)(0.3) + (0.7868)(0.4)$

$\quad\quad = 0.8369.$ by (21.3.3)

b. $Var(\tilde{v}_{K+1}) = \sum_{k=0}^{3} e^{-[2(0.06-0.0001)](k+1)}\ {}_kp_x\ q_{x+k} - ({}_*A_x)^2$

$\quad\quad = (0.8871)(0.1) + (0.7869)(0.2) + (0.6981)(0.3) + (0.6193)(0.4) - (0.8369)^2$

$\quad\quad = 0.0028.$ by (21.3.4)

c. $E[\ddot{a}_{\overline{K+1}|\tilde{v}}] = \sum_{k=0}^{3}\sum_{s=0}^{k} e^{-s(0.06-0.00005)}\ {}_kp_x\ q_{x+k}$

$\quad\quad = (1)(0.1) + (1.9418)(0.2) + (2.8288)(0.3) + (3.6642)(0.4)$

$\quad\quad = 2.8027.$

d. An input into the calculation of $Var(\ddot{a}_{\overline{K+1}|\tilde{v}})$ is ${}^\alpha\ddot{a}_x$, valued at force of interest $2(\delta - \sigma^2) = 0.1198$:

$${}^\alpha\ddot{a}_x = (1)(0.1) + (1.8871)(0.2) + (2.6740)(0.3) + (3.3721)(0.4)$$

$$= 2.6285,$$

$$Var(\ddot{a}_{\overline{K+1}|\tilde{v}}) = 2.6285 + 2\frac{(2.8027 - 2.6285)}{1 - e^{-0.05985}} - (2.8027)^2$$

$$= 8.6257 - 7.8551 = 0.7705.$$ by (21.3.9)

▼

Example 21.3.2

Adopt the assumptions about the distributions of $\log(1 + I_K)$ and K used in Example 21.3.1. Display the d.f. of $\tilde{v}_{K+1}$.

Solution:

$$Pr(\tilde{v}_{K+1} \le y) = E_K\ Pr(\tilde{v}_{K+1} \le y | K = k)$$

$$= \sum_{k=0}^{3} Pr(\tilde{v}_{k+1} \le y)\ {}_kp_x\ q_{x+k}.$$

We now use the fact that $\log \tilde{v}_n$ has a $N(-n\delta, n\sigma^2)$ distribution:

$$Pr(\tilde{v}_{K+1} \le y) = \sum_{k=0}^{3} Pr(\log \tilde{v}_{k+1} \le \log y)\ {}_kp_x\ q_{x+k}$$

$$= \sum_{k=0}^{3} Pr\left[\frac{\log \tilde{v}_{k+1} + (k+1)\delta}{\sqrt{(k+1)\sigma^2}} \le \frac{\log y + (k+1)\delta}{\sqrt{(k+1)\sigma^2}}\right]\ {}_kp_x\ q_{x+k}$$

$$= \sum_{k=0}^{3} \Phi \left[\frac{\log y + (k+1)\delta}{\sqrt{(k+1)\sigma^2}} \right] {}_kp_x \, q_{x+k}$$

$$= \sum_{k=0}^{3} \Phi \left[\frac{\log y + (k+1)(0.06)}{\sqrt{(k+1)(0.01)}} \right] {}_kp_x \, q_{x+k},$$

where $\Phi(w)$ is the d.f. of a random variable with a $N(0, 1)$ distribution. To illustrate, let $y = \mathrm{E}[\tilde{v}_{K+1}] = {}_*A_x = 0.8369$ and calculate $\Pr(\tilde{v}_{K+1} \leq 0.8369) = \Phi(-11.8051)(0.1) + \Phi(-4.1048)(0.2) + \Phi(0.1125)(0.3) + \Phi(3.0945)(0.4) = 0.5630$. Because the median of the distribution of $\tilde{v}_{K+1}$ is less than the mean, we have evidence that the distribution is skewed to the right. ▼

21.4 Dependent Interest Rates

Within financial economics there has been a continuing discussion about whether effective rates of interest within various classes of investments can be modeled as independent and identically distributed random variables. If the actuary accepts the evidence supporting the independent and identically distributed hypothesis, the methods developed in Section 21.3 are available. The actuary could alter these methods. For example, the distribution of the ϵ_k random shock terms might be assumed to be other than the $N(0, \sigma^2)$ distribution.

If the actuary rejects the hypothesis that effective rates are independent and identically distributed, two options are open. The first option is to develop a multivariate model that does not change as time passes. Such models are called stationary models. A simple model within this class will be developed in Section 21.4.1.

The second option is to adopt a model that incorporates the possibility of structural shifts in the investment environment. We do not discuss this type of model.

21.4.1 Moving Average Model

The developments of this section are limited to the model

$$\log(1 + I_k) = \delta + \epsilon_k - \theta\epsilon_{k-1} \quad k = 1, 2, 3, \ldots \tag{21.4.1}$$

where $\delta > 0$, and $\epsilon_k, k = 1, 2, \ldots$, are random variables that are mutually independent and each has a $N(0, \sigma^2)$ distribution. In addition, $|\theta| \leq 1$ and ϵ_0 is known. If $\theta = 0$, the model reduces to (21.3.1). This model is called a *moving average model of order one*, abbreviated MA(1).

The rationale for the model is that the force of interest has a long-term mean, denoted by δ, but random economic shocks create deviations from the mean. The shock for period k, ϵ_k, has a delayed and moderated impact on the force of interest in period $k + 1$ of size $-\theta\epsilon_k$.

We define $\tilde{v}_n$ as in Section 21.3:

$$\tilde{v}_n = \prod_{k=1}^{n} (1 + I_k)^{-1} = e^{-\Sigma_1^n(\delta + \epsilon_k - \theta\epsilon_{k-1})};$$

then

$$\log \tilde{v}_n = -\sum_{k=1}^{n} (\delta + \epsilon_k - \theta\epsilon_{k-1})$$

$$= -n\delta + \epsilon_n - \theta\epsilon_0 + (1 - \theta) \sum_{k=1}^{n-1} \epsilon_k,$$

and

$$E[\tilde{v}_n] = E[e^{-[n\delta + \epsilon_n - \theta\epsilon_0 + (1-\theta)\Sigma_{k=1}^{n-1} \epsilon_k]}].$$

We have assumed that the shock terms ϵ_k, $k = 1, 2, \ldots n$, are mutually independent and each has a $N(0, \sigma^2)$ distribution. Therefore, recalling the m.g.f. of a $N(0, \sigma^2)$ distribution, we have

$$E[e^{t\epsilon_k}] = e^{t^2\sigma^2/2} \quad k = 1, 2, 3, \ldots.$$

$$= M(t).$$

This result enables us to write

$$E[\tilde{v}_n] = e^{-n\delta} M(-1) e^{\theta\epsilon_0} M(\theta - 1)^{n-1}$$

$$= C_1 e^{-n\delta'} \quad n = 1, 2, 3, \ldots, \tag{21.4.2}$$

where $C_1 = M(-1) e^{\theta\epsilon_0} M(\theta - 1)^{-1}$ and $\delta' = \delta - \log M(\theta - 1)$. Note that, as in Section 21.3, we define $\tilde{v}_0 = 1$ and $E[\tilde{v}_0] = 1$, not C_1. If $\theta = 0$, then $\delta' = \delta - \log M(-1)$, $C_1 = 1$, and $E[\tilde{v}_n] = e^{-n[\delta - \log M(-1)]} = e^{-n(\delta - \sigma^2/2)}$, which agrees with (21.3.2), for the lognormal independent model.

With these preliminary results, we can calculate actuarial present values. The initial development will follow that used in (21.3.3):

$$_*A_x = E[\tilde{v}_{K+1}] = E_{\tilde{v}} \, E_{K|\tilde{v}} \, [\tilde{v}_{K+1}]$$

$$= E_{\tilde{v}} \left[\sum_{k=0}^{\infty} \tilde{v}_{k+1} \, _kp_x \, q_{x+k} \right]$$

$$= C_1 \sum_{k=0}^{\infty} e^{-(k+1)\delta'} \, _kp_x \, q_{x+k}. \tag{21.4.3}$$

Similarly,

$$_*\ddot{a}_x = E[\ddot{a}_{\overline{K+1}|\tilde{v}}] = E_{\tilde{v}} \, E_{K|\tilde{v}} \, [\ddot{a}_{\overline{K+1}|\tilde{v}}]$$

$$= E_{\tilde{v}} \left[\sum_{k=0}^{\infty} \left(1 + \sum_{s=1}^{k} \tilde{v}_s \right) \, _kp_x \, q_{x+k} \right]$$

$$= \sum_{k=0}^{\infty} \left(1 + \sum_{s=1}^{k} C_1 e^{-s\delta'}\right) {}_kp_x \, q_{x+k}$$

$$= \sum_{k=0}^{\infty} (1 + C_1 a_{\overline{k}|\delta'}) \, {}_kp_x \, q_{x+k}. \tag{21.4.4}$$

To continue the outline used in Section 21.3, we must develop formulas for $E[\tilde{v}_r \, \tilde{v}_s]$, $s < r$:

$$E[(\tilde{v}_n)^2] = E[e^{-2[n\delta + \epsilon_n - \theta\epsilon_0 + (1-\theta)\Sigma_{k=1}^{n-1}\epsilon_k]}]$$

$$= e^{-2n\delta} \, E[e^{-2\epsilon_n}] \, E[e^{2\theta\epsilon_0}] \, E[e^{-2(1-\theta)\epsilon}]^{n-1}$$

$$= e^{-2n\delta} \, M(-2) \, e^{2\theta\epsilon_0} \, M(2\theta - 2)^{n-1}.$$

We use abbreviated notation

$$E[(\tilde{v}_n)^2] = C_2 \, e^{-\delta''n}, \tag{21.4.5}$$

where $\delta'' = 2\delta - \log M(2\theta - 2)$ and

$$C_2 = \frac{M(-2) \, e^{2\theta\epsilon_0}}{M(2\theta - 2)}.$$

The term $E[\tilde{v}_r \, \tilde{v}_s]$ appears in expressions for $\mathrm{Var}(\ddot{a}_{\overline{K+1}|\tilde{v}})$. We note that $E[\tilde{v}_r \, \tilde{v}_0] = E[\tilde{v}_r]$. If $r > s \geq 1$, we have

$$E[\tilde{v}_r \, \tilde{v}_s] = E[e^{-[r\delta + \epsilon_r - \theta\epsilon_0 + (1-\theta)\Sigma_{j=1}^{r-1}\epsilon_j]} \times e^{-[s\delta + \epsilon_s - \theta\epsilon_0 + (1-\theta)\Sigma_{j=1}^{s-1}\epsilon_j]}]$$

$$= e^{-(r+s)\delta} \, E[e^{-\epsilon_r}]E[e^{(\theta-2)\epsilon_s}]E[e^{2\theta\epsilon_0}]E[e^{-2(1-\theta)\Sigma_{j=1}^{s-1}\epsilon_j}]E[e^{-(1-\theta)\Sigma_{j=s+1}^{r-1}\epsilon_j}]$$

$$= e^{-(r+s)\delta} \, M(-1)M(\theta - 2)e^{2\theta\epsilon_0}M[2(\theta - 1)]^{s-1}M(\theta - 1)^{r-s-1}$$

$$= C_3 \, e^{-\delta''s} \, e^{-\delta'(r-s)}$$

where δ' and δ'' are as defined previously and

$$C_3 = M(-1) \, M(\theta - 2)e^{2\theta\epsilon_0}\{M[2(\theta - 1)]^{-1} \, M(\theta - 1)^{-1}\}.$$

Using these building blocks, we turn to the development of formulas for the variances of present-value random variables in which the force of interest has a MA(1) model:

$$\mathrm{Var}(\tilde{v}_{K+1}) = E[(\tilde{v}_{K+1})^2] - ({}_*A_x)^2$$

$$= \sum_{k=0}^{\infty} C_2 e^{-\delta''(k+1)} \, {}_kp_x \, q_{x+k} - ({}_*A_x)^2, \tag{21.4.6}$$

where (21.4.3) and (21.4.5) have been used in the development.

For $\mathrm{Var}(\ddot{a}_{\overline{K+1}|\tilde{v}})$, we start with

$$E_{\tilde{v}}\left[\left(\sum_{s=0}^{k} \tilde{v}_s\right)^2\right] = E_{\tilde{v}}\left[\left(1 + \sum_{s=1}^{k} \tilde{v}_y^2\right) + 2\sum_{s=0}^{k-1}\sum_{r=s+1}^{k} \tilde{v}_r \, \tilde{v}_s\right]$$

$$= \left(1 + \sum_{s=1}^{k} C_2 \, e^{-\delta''s}\right) + 2\left(\sum_{r=1}^{k} C_1 e^{-r\delta'} + \sum_{s=1}^{k-1}\sum_{r=s+1}^{k} C_3 \, e^{-\delta''s - \delta'(r-s)}\right).$$

$$\tag{21.4.7}$$

Therefore,

$$\text{Var}(\ddot{a}_{\overline{K+1}|\tilde{v}}) = \sum_{k=0}^{\infty} \text{E}_{\tilde{v}}\left[\left(1 + \sum_{s=1}^{k} \tilde{v}_s\right)^2\right] {}_k p_x \, q_{x+k} - ({}_*\ddot{a}_x)^2, \qquad (21.4.8)$$

where components come from (21.4.7) and (21.4.4).

Example 21.4.1

Assume that $\log(1 + I_k)$ is given by (21.4.1) with $\delta = 0.06$, $\text{Var}(\epsilon_k) = 0.0001$, $\theta = -0.8$, and $\epsilon_0 = 0$. Calculate (a) δ', (b) C_1, (c) δ'', (d) C_2, and (e) C_3.

Solution:

a. $\delta' = \delta - \log M(\theta - 1)$

$\quad = 0.06 - \log(e^{(-0.8-1)^2(0.0001)/2})$

$\quad = 0.05984.$

b. $C_1 = \dfrac{M(-1)\, e^{\theta \epsilon_0}}{M(\theta - 1)} = e^{(0.0001)/2}\, e^{-(1.8)^2(0.0001)/2}$

$\quad = 0.99989.$

c. $\delta'' = 2\delta - \log M[2(\theta - 1)] = 0.12 - \log(e^{[2(-1.8)]^2(0.0001)/2]})$

$\quad = 0.119352.$

d. $C_2 = \dfrac{M(-2)e^{2\theta \epsilon_0}}{M(2\theta - 2)} = \dfrac{e^{(-2)^2(0.0001)/2}}{e^{(-3.6)^2(0.0001)/2}}$

$\quad = 0.99955.$

e. $C_3 = \dfrac{M(-1)\, M(\theta - 2)\, e^{2\theta \epsilon_0}}{M(2\theta - 2)\, M(\theta - 1)}$

$\quad = \dfrac{(e^{(0.0001)/2})(e^{(-2.8)^2(0.0001)/2})}{(e^{(-3.6)^2(0.0001)/2})(e^{(-1.8)^2(0.0001)/2})}$

$\quad = 0.99963.$ ▼

Example 21.4.2

Assume the interest rate model of Example 21.4.1 and the survival distribution of Example 21.2.1. Determine (a) $\text{E}[\tilde{v}_{K+1}]$, (b) $\text{Var}(\tilde{v}_{K+1})$, (c) $\text{E}[\ddot{a}_{\overline{K+1}|\tilde{v}}]$, and (d) $\text{Var}(\ddot{a}_{\overline{K+1}|\tilde{v}})$.

Solution:

Formula numbers refer to those displayed in this section.

a. $E[\tilde{v}_{K+1}] = E_K \, E_{\tilde{v}|K} \, [\tilde{v}_{K+1}]$ by (21.4.3)

$$= \sum_{k=0}^{\infty} C_1 \, e^{-(k+1)\delta'} \, {}_kp_x \, q_{x+k}$$

$$= (0.99989) \sum_{k=0}^{3} e^{-(k+1)(0.05984)} \, {}_kp_x \, q_{x+k}$$

$$= (0.99989)[(0.94192)(0.1) + (0.88720)(0.2) + (0.83567)(0.3)$$
$$+ (0.78713)(0.4)] = 0.83710.$$

b. $\mathrm{Var}(\tilde{v}_{K+1}) = \sum_{k=0}^{3} C_2 \, e^{-\delta''(k+1)} \, {}_kp_x \, q_{x+k} - ({}_*A_x)^2$ by (21.4.6)

$$= (0.99955)[(0.88721)(0.1) + (0.78714)(0.2)$$
$$+ (0.69836)(0.3) + (0.61959)(0.4)] - (0.83710)^2$$
$$= 0.0024.$$

c. $E[\ddot{a}_{\overline{K+1}|\tilde{v}}] = E_{\tilde{v}} \, E_{K|\tilde{v}} \, [\ddot{a}_{\overline{K+1}|\tilde{v}}]$ by (21.4.4)

$$= \sum_{k=0}^{3} \left(1 + \sum_{s=1}^{k} C_1 \, e^{-s\delta'} \right) \, {}_kp_x \, q_{x+k}$$

$$= (1)(0.1) + (1.94181)(0.2) + (2.82892)(0.3)$$
$$+ (3.66450)(0.4)$$
$$= 2.80284.$$

d. As a preliminary, we compute $E_{\tilde{v}} \, [(1 + \Sigma_{s=1}^{k} \, \tilde{v}_s)^2]$ for $k = 0, 1, 2, 3$ using (21.4.7).

The computations are summarized in the following table.

k	$E_{\tilde{v}} \, [(1 + \Sigma_{s=1}^{k} \, \tilde{v}_s)^2]$	
0	1	$= 1$
1	$[1 + C_2 \, e^{-\delta''} + 2C_1 \, e^{-\delta'}]$	$= 3.77043$
2	$[1 + C_2(e^{-\delta''} + e^{-2\delta''}) + 2(C_1 \, e^{-\delta'} + C_1 e^{-2\delta'}$ $+ C_3 \, e^{-\delta''-\delta'})]$	$= 8.00214$
3	$[1 + C_2(e^{-\delta''} + e^{-2\delta''} + e^{-3\delta''}) + 2 \, (C_1 e^{-\delta'} + e^{-2\delta'}$ $+ e^{-3\delta'}) + C_3(e^{-\delta''-\delta'} + e^{-\delta''-2\delta'}) + C_3(e^{-2\delta''-\delta''})]$	$= 13.42729$

$$\mathrm{Var}[\ddot{a}_{\overline{K+1}|\tilde{v}}] = (1)(0.1) + (3.77043)(0.2) + (8.00214)(0.3) + (13.42729)(0.4)$$
$$- (2.80284)^2 = 0.7699. \qquad \blacktriangledown$$

21.4.2   Implementation

Sections 21.3 and 21.4.1 illustrate that the development of formulas for the moments of present-value random variables, when interest rates are assumed to be random variables, can involve several steps. Other statistical models for $X_k = \log(1 + I_k)$, in the same class of models, such as

a. Autoregressive of order one AR(1)

$$(X_k - \delta) = \phi(X_{k-1} - \delta) + \epsilon_k \tag{21.4.9a}$$

b. AR(1) and MA(1)

$$(X_k - \delta) - \phi(X_{k-1} - \delta) = \epsilon_k - \theta\epsilon_{k-1} \tag{21.4.9b}$$

c. AR(1) on first differences

$$(X_k - X_{k-1}) - \phi(X_{k-1} - X_{k-2}) = \epsilon_k \tag{21.4.9c}$$

could be the subject of similar developments. The selection of an appropriate model for the force of interest and the estimation of the parameter are topics in statistics.

The problem of displaying the d.f. of present-value random variables remains. The technique used in Sections 4.2, 5.2, 6.2, and 7.2 are not feasible when K and $\tilde{v}_k$, the discrete future lifetime random variable and the discount factors, have a joint distribution.

In earlier chapters, where only future lifetimes were random variables, approximations were developed for the distribution of losses from a portfolio of risks. In these developments it was assumed that the future lifetime random variables are mutually independent. Typically these developments depended on a central limit theorem type of result to justify using an approximating normal distribution. When each of the component present-value random variables is a function of the same random interest process, the present-value random variables are no longer independent. This was illustrated in (21.2.3). Consequently, the distribution of total losses from a portfolio of present-value random variables cannot be routinely approximated using a normal distribution when interest rates are also random variables.

There are simulation-based approaches to the three problems of estimating the moments of present-value random variables, approximating the d.f. of a present value, and approximating the d.f. of the present value of losses from a portfolio of insurance risks. With a source of realizations of a random variable with a $N(0, \sigma^2)$ distribution, sample paths of $(I_1, I_2, \ldots)$ for models such as (21.3.1), (21.4.1), and (21.4.6a, b, and c) could be generated. If $\{I_k\}$, denoting the sequence of random future effective interest rates, and K, completed life years, are assumed to be independent, an empirical d.f. that would approximate the d.f. of an individual loss variable could be developed in a routine fashion.

To illustrate, suppose 100 sequences of future interest rates are generated using the MA(1) model of (21.4.1). For each of these sequences a realization of the random variable K, completed life years, using the survival function that has been assumed would be determined. These results could be used to compute 100 sample values of $\tilde{v}_{K+1}$. These values can be treated as a sample derived from the joint distribution of $\{I_k\}$ and K. The mean and variance of these 100 simulation sample values would be estimates of the mean and variance of the distribution of $\tilde{v}_{K+1}$. The empirical d.f. would estimate the d.f. of $\tilde{v}_{K+1}$.

The simulation process can also be used to approximate the d.f. of the present value of total losses from a portfolio with n individual risks. In this instance there is a set of completed life year random variables, $K_i: i = 1, 2, \ldots, n$. If these random variables are assumed to be independent, a set of realizations for each K_i random variable would be combined with a randomly generated interest scenario to produce a sample outcome of present value of total losses.

It should be clear why simulation, using computer-generated realizations of present-value random variables that may be functions of several random variables, has been widely used to construct empirical d.f.'s. These applications have made simulation an important tool in actuarial science.

If there is evidence that the random variables time-until-decrement and cause-of-decrement are not independent of $\{I_k\}$, then the generation of realizations of present-value random variables becomes more complicated. For example, the act and time of withdrawal from a life insurance or pension plan may not be independent of $\{I_k\}$.

21.5   Financial Economics Models

From the models developed in Section 21.3 and 21.4, one could be selected, and the parameters estimated, using data from the investment operations of the financial system being modeled. Critics of this procedure assert that it ignores important information available in current capital markets.

To illustrate the variability over time of yields to maturity of one type of security, the average yields to maturity of 30-year U.S. Treasury bonds were displayed in Figure 21.1.1. The changes in bond prices and yields reflect variations in the bond markets' assessment of future economic events. There are, of course, many other investments that might have displayed different patterns of yields over the same period. Economic news does not affect the yields of all securities in an identical fashion. Even Treasury securities with different maturities may exhibit various time series of yield rates.

21.5.1   Information in Prices and Maturities

To extract the information about the relationship between interest rates and maturities, free of confounding factors such as default and call (early maturity at the option of the borrower) risk, it is usual to analyze securities issued by central governments. In the United States this means Treasury obligations. Other bonds are analyzed by comparing them with Treasury bonds.

To illustrate the methods used in summarizing the relationship between interest rates and maturity dates, a review of basic ideas in the mathematics of finance is required. We consider *pure discount bonds* that pay 1 unit at maturity and are traded in a market with no transaction costs. These bonds are not subject to default risk. The number s denotes the current time, and discount bonds are available with maturities at times $s, s + 1 \ldots$. The prices of one bond at time s that matures t periods in the future is denoted by $P(s, s + t)$. We assume that

$$P(s, s) = 1,$$

$$\lim_{t \to \infty} P(s, t) = 0,$$

and if $u > t$,

$$P(s, t) > P(s, u).$$

The third assumption is equivalent to attaching a higher value to the earlier of two equal payments. The yield rate for t unit periods is denoted by $i(s, s + t)$ and is defined by

$$P(s, s + t) = [1 + i(s, s + t)]^{-t}. \tag{21.5.1}$$

The number $i(s, s + t)$ is called the t period *spot rate* at time s. The name derives from the fact that such rates can be determined from the current market and relate to a single payment at a particular future time. Spot rates $i(s, s + t)$ viewed as a function of t are called the *term structure* of interest rates at time s.

Forward rates are an alternative way of studying the relationship between time to maturity and interest rates. As the name suggests, forward rates are the interest rates that would be used for contracts concluded currently that cover transactions in future periods. It will be required that these rates be consistent with the set of spot rates observed in the current market. The consistency that will be required is that *no-arbitrage* opportunities will be present in the forward rates. An arbitrage opportunity exists in a capital market if there are two investment strategies available for the same investment period such that one strategy will result with certainty in greater wealth at the end of the period than the alternative strategy. To illustrate the no-arbitrage requirement, suppose an investor pays 1 for a discount bond maturing at time $s + u$ for amount $[1 + i(s, s + u)]^u$. Alternatively, the investor could buy a t period, $t < u$, bond and at time $s + t$ invest the maturity value in a second discount bond that will mature at time $s + u$ for amount

$$[1 + i(s, s + t)]^t [1 + j(s, s + t, s + u)]^{u-t},$$

where $j(s, s + t, s + u)$ is the forward rate at time s for a future transaction with cash flows at times $s + t$ and $s + u$. If no arbitrage opportunities exist, the two ultimate wealth amounts must be equal and

$$[1 + i(s, s + u)]^u = [1 + i(s, s + t)]^t [1 + j(s, s + t, s + u)]^{u-t} \quad (21.5.2)$$

or

$$[1 + j(s, s + t, s + u)]^{u-t} = \frac{[1 + i(s, s + u)]^u}{[1 + i(s, s + t)]^t} \quad 0 \le t \le u.$$

The special case when $u = t + 1$ yields

$$[1 + j(s, s + t, s + t + 1)] = \frac{[1 + i(s, s + t + 1)]^{t+1}}{[1 + i(s, s + t)]^t},$$

and when $t = 0$,

$$j(s, s, s + 1) = i(s, s + 1). \quad (21.5.3)$$

Repeated applications of (21.5.3) starting with $t = 0$ yield

$$[1 + i(s, s + t)]^t = [1 + j(s, s, s + 1)][1 + j(s, s + 1, s + 2)]$$

$$\cdots [1 + j(s, s + t - 1, s + t)]. \quad (21.5.4)$$

The current price of a bond paying coupons of amount c at the end of each of n periods and then paying a maturity value of F can be expressed in a consistent way using prices of discount bonds and spot or future rates as follows:

Using prices of discount bonds,

$$c \sum_{k=1}^{n} P(s, s + k) + F\, P(s, s + n). \quad (21.5.5a)$$

Using spot rates,

$$c \sum_{k=1}^{n} [1 + i(s, s + k)]^{-k} + F[1 + i(s, s + n)]^{-n}. \quad (21.5.5b)$$

Using forward rates,

$$c \sum_{k=1}^{n} \prod_{w=0}^{k-1} [1 + j(s, s + w, s + w + 1)]^{-1}$$

$$+ F \prod_{w=0}^{n-1} [1 + j(s, s + w, s + w + 1)]^{-1}. \quad (21.5.5c)$$

The equality of these three formulas for a bond price rests on the no-arbitrage assumption.

The time interval measuring the time of future coupon payments is not always 1 year. U.S. Treasury bonds typically have semiannual coupons. The bonds that were the subject of Table 21.1.1 would have $n = (30)(2) = 60$.

Yet another way of measuring the relationship between interest rates and time of maturity can be derived from (21.5.4b). The set of spot rates at time s, $i(s, s + k)$, $k = 0, 1, 2, \ldots$ is given, and the **par yield**, denoted by $y(s, s + m)$, is a set of artificial coupon payments determined from

$$1 = y(s, s + m) \sum_{k=1}^{m} [1 + i(s, s + k)]^{-k} + [1 + i(s, s + m)]^{-m} \quad m = 1, 2, \ldots, n.$$

$$(21.5.6)$$

The par yield can be described as the coupon rate on a bond trading at its maturity value in a market with a known set of spot rates and no-arbitrage opportunities. The graph of $y(s, s + n)$ as a function of n is the **yield curve** at time s. Par yields are most often expressed as **bond-equivalent yields**, that is, semiannual nominal rates.

FIGURE 21.5.1

Prototype Yield Curves

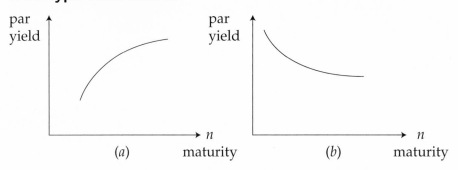

Figure 21.5.1(a) with its positive slope is a typical yield curve. Figure 21.5.1(b) with its negative slope is called an **inverted yield curve**. An inverted yield curve might result from the action of national monetary authorities to keep short-term interest rates high to retard price inflation. The capital markets' expectation is that inflation will be of short duration and long-term rates are not affected.

Example 21.5.1

Determine equivalent forward rates and par yield rates given the following set of spot rates.

t	$i(s, s + t)$
1	0.06
2	0.065
3	0.070

Solution:

Using (21.5.2),

$$1 + j(s, s + t, s + t + 1) = \frac{[1 + i(s, s + t + 1)]^{t+1}}{[1 + i(s, s + t)]^{t}}.$$

t	$j(s, s + t, s + t + 1)$
0	0.06
1	0.07002
2	0.08007

Using (21.5.5),

$$y(s, s + t) = \frac{1 - [1 + i(s, s + t)]^{-t}}{\sum_{k=1}^{t} [1 + i(s, s + k)]^{-k}}.$$

t	$y(s, s + t)$
1	0.06
2	0.06484
3	0.06955

Note that all three rates have a positive slope when viewed as a function of t.

▼

21.5.2   Stochastic Models

In this section we illustrate a method for generating sequences of future par yield rates. The randomly generated sequences can be inputs into simulations of the financial operations of a portfolio of insurance or pension contracts. In practice, par yield rates rather than spot or forward rates are modeled because investment experts are more familiar with them. It is therefore easier for these experts to select a model and specify the parameters.

We assume that the progress of the logarithm of par yield rates is determined by a modified autoregressive model of order one:

$$\log[Y(t, n)] = \lambda(t, n) + (1 - \phi_n) \log [Y(t - 1, n)] + \sigma_n \, \epsilon_{t,n}, \; t = 0, 1, 2, 3, \ldots.$$

$$(21.5.7)$$

The terms in (21.5.7) are defined as follows:

$Y(t, n) = $ the random par yield at time t for a bond maturing in n periods. It is assumed that the present time is $t = 0$.

$\lambda(t, n) = $ a drift parameter appropriate for period t for bonds with n periods until maturity. If $\lambda(t, n) = \lambda_n$ (21.5.7) would become a standard autoregressive model of order one [AR(1)]. The drift parameter $\lambda(t, n)$ can be adjusted for each t so that the no-arbitrage constraint or other constraint from financial economics can be satisfied.

$(1 - \phi_n)$ = an autoregressive parameter appropriate for bonds with maturity in n periods. The parameter ϕ_n determines the rate at which previous perturbations decay. For that reason, the parameter is called the rate of mean reversion in finance. In order to have a stationary time series model, $|1 - \phi_n| < 1$.

σ_n = the standard deviation of the random shocks.

$\epsilon_{t,n}$ = a random variable with a $N(0, 1)$ distribution for bonds with n periods to maturity for period t. The random variables ϵ_{t_1,n_1} and ϵ_{t_2,n_2} are independent if $t_1 \neq t_2$ and have correlation ρ_{n_1,n_2} if $t_1 = t_2$. If $n_1 = n_2$, $\rho_{n_1,n_2} = 1$. We are assuming that contemporaneous shocks are correlated.

Remark:

The model described by (21.5.7) is only one of a wide class of stochastic models that could be adopted. The selection of the model and estimation of the parameters would be influenced by the theory of financial economics and statistical data analysis. Formula (21.5.7) also illustrates another option in modeling interest rates. The models specified by (21.3.1), (21.4.1), and (21.4.6a, b, and c) were written for use with log $(1 + I_k)$, the random force of interest for period k. Formula (21.5.7) involves the logarithmic transformation of $Y(t, n)$. The transformation can be motivated as a device to stabilize the variance of the observations or to keep realizations of $Y(t, n)$ non-negative. This non-negative constraint is regarded by some actuaries as important. Exercise 21.9 illustrates the random walk model, which can be viewed as a special case of (21.5.7) with $1 - \phi = 1$ and $\lambda = 0$. The model developed in Exercise 21.9 for the rate of interest shares a property of (21.5.7) in that the random rate of interest is non-negative.

Models such as (21.5.7) can be used to estimate future yield curves. If (21.5.7) were adopted, the estimation of yield curves would require the selection of a set of maturity times, n, and corresponding parameter values λ_n, ϕ_n, σ_n for each value of n and correlation coefficients ρ_{n_1,n_2} for each pair of maturity times selected. The number of values of n would be kept small so that the number of parameters that would have to be specified would be manageable. Then using sets of randomly determined values of $\epsilon_{t,n}$, the outline of future yield curves at various values of t could be determined by simulating future values of $Y(t, n)$ using (21.5.7) for the selected key maturity times.

If the investment portfolio of interest to the actuary holds bonds with a constant maturity, (21.5.7) could be used directly to produce randomly generated sequences of future interest rates for use in simulation studies.

As yet, no adjustments have been made in the model parameters to conform to the actuary's judgment about the long-term mean rate or to force compliance with a market consistency requirement such as no-arbitrage. The parameter $\lambda(t, n)$ is available to incorporate such information.

For example, the following development provides a tool to the actuary for incorporating information about the long-term mean of the par yield rate for securities with fixed maturity n:

Let $\lambda(t, n) = \phi_n \log \mu_n$, which is independent of t; we can rewrite (21.5.7) as

$$\log[Y(t, n)] = \phi_n \log \mu_n + (1 - \phi_n) \log[Y(t - 1, n)] + \sigma_n \epsilon_{t,n}$$

$$t = 1, 2, 3, \ldots . \tag{21.5.8}$$

To facilitate subsequent steps, let

$$Z_t = \log[Y(t, n)],$$

$$\theta = \phi_n \log \mu_n,$$

$$\Psi = (1 - \phi_n) \quad 0 < \Psi < 1,$$

and (21.5.8) becomes

$$Z_t = \theta + \Psi Z_{t-1} + \sigma_n \epsilon_{t,n}, \tag{21.5.9}$$

a standard AR(1) model with drift parameter θ. Multiply successive equations for Z_{t-j} by Ψ^j to obtain

$$Z_t - \Psi Z_{t-1} = \theta + \sigma_n \epsilon_{t,n},$$

$$\Psi Z_{t-1} - \Psi^2 Z_{t-2} = \Psi \theta + \Psi \sigma_n \epsilon_{t-1,n},$$

$$\Psi^2 Z_{t-2} - \Psi^3 Z_{t-3} = \Psi^2 \theta + \Psi^2 \sigma_n \epsilon_{t-2,n},$$

$$\vdots \qquad\qquad \vdots$$

Adding this sequence of equations and assuming that t is large, we have

$$Z_t \doteq \frac{\theta}{1 - \Psi} + \sigma_n \sum_{j=0}^{t} \epsilon_{t-j,n} \Psi^j.$$

Exponentiating this approximation yields

$$e^{Z_t} \doteq \exp\left(\frac{\theta}{1 - \Psi} + \sigma_n \sum_{j=0}^{t} \epsilon_{t-j,n} \Psi^j\right),$$

$$Y(t, n) \doteq \mu_n \exp\left(\sigma_n \sum_{j=0}^{t} \epsilon_{t-j,n} \Psi^j\right).$$

The random variable $\sigma_n \sum_{j=0}^{t} \epsilon_{t-j,n} \Psi^j$ in the exponent has a normal distribution with mean zero and variance for large values of t that is approximately $\sigma_n^2 / (1 - \Psi^2)$.

Using these facts about the distribution of the random component, and recalling the m.g.f. for random variables with normal distributions, we have for large values of t

$$E[Y(t, n)] \doteq \mu_n \exp\left\{\frac{\sigma_n^2}{2[1 - (1 - \phi_n)^2]}\right\}. \tag{21.5.10}$$

If data or the actuary's judgment supports the existence of a long-term mean for the par yield on bonds that mature in n periods, the selected values of $\lambda(t, n) = \phi_n$, $\log \mu_n$, and σ_n^2 should be consistent with (21.5.10).

In addition to subjecting model parameters to consistency checks relative to estimates of the long-term mean, adjustments to the parameter $\lambda(t, n)$ can be made to be consistent with the no-arbitrage condition. In an efficient capital market, the observed rates $[i(0, n_1), i(0, n_2), \ldots, i(0, n_m)]$ for m different maturities would not present significant arbitrage opportunities. Such opportunities would present riskless strategies to increase wealth and would disappear as traders, seeking to exploit such opportunities, would reduce them. The estimated future yield curves determined by averaging many simulations may exhibit arbitrage opportunities. Such opportunities would constitute inconsistent behavior in the capital markets and to retain such opportunities in an estimated future yield curve would similarly be inconsistent.

To develop a method for adjusting an entire estimated yield curves to preclude arbitrage opportunities would involve several ideas beyond the scope of this development. Consequently, only bonds that mature in one period, $n = 1$, are considered. We adopt a simplification of (21.5.8) and assume that the goal is to produce interest scenarios each of length H periods; the model is

$$\log [Y(t, 1)] = \mu + \sigma_1 \epsilon_{t,1} \quad t = 1, 2, \ldots, H. \tag{21.5.11}$$

Generating m sequences of the form $(e_{1,1}, e_{2,1}, \ldots, e_{H,1})$ composed of realizations of the random variables $\epsilon_{t,1}$, would produce m sequences of possible future one-period rates $(e^{\mu + \sigma_1 e_{1,1}}, e^{\mu + \sigma_1 e_{2,1}}, \ldots, e^{\mu + \sigma_1 e_{H,1}})_j$, $j = 1, 2, \ldots, m$.

To minimize the opportunity for arbitrage at time 1, the value of the mean parameter μ in the model will be adjusted so that expected rates available at time 1 will not present such an opportunity. To achieve this objective each of the m values of $e^{\mu + \sigma_1 e_{1,1}}$ will be multiplied by $e^{\lambda_1 - \mu}$ where λ_1 is determined from

$$\sum_{j=1}^{m} \frac{[1 + y(0, 1)]^{-1} (1 + e^{\lambda_1 + \sigma_1 e_{1,1}})_j^{-1}}{m} = P(0, 2).$$

As before, $P(0, 2)$ is the observed price of a two-period discount bond. The symbol $(1 + e^{\lambda_1 + \sigma_1 e_{1,1}})_j^{-1}$ denotes that the variable $e_{1,1}$ comes from scenario j generated from (21.5.11).

The no-arbitrage adjustment for other years in the H-year planning period will be determined by solving successively for λ_{h-1}:

$$\sum_{j=1}^{m} \frac{[1 + y(0, 1)]^{-1}(1 + e^{\lambda_1 + \sigma_1 e_{1,1}})_j^{-1} \cdots (1 + e^{\lambda_{h-1} + \sigma_1 e_{h-1,1}})_j^{-1}}{m} = P(0, h),$$

where $h = 2, 3, \ldots, H$. The resulting m sequences of the form $[y(0, 1), e^{\lambda_1 + \sigma_1 e_{1,1}}, \ldots, e^{\lambda_{H-1} + \sigma_1 e_{H-1,1}}]_j$ can be used as stochastically generated scenarios of future interest rates where each scenario is assigned weight $1/m$.

Remark:

The no-arbitrage assumption about capital markets has been a theme in this section. Empirical investigations indicate that although arbitrage opportunities exist, they do not persist for long because of the activity of traders.

21.6 Management of Interest Risk

Constructing actuarial models for financial security systems provides a rational basis for pricing the promises made, for reporting on the financial status of the system, and for managing the risks inherent in the operations of these systems. Chapters 12 through 14 dealt in part with ideas for managing short-term risks. Chapters 4 through 11 dealt in part with managing the adverse consequences to financial security systems attributable to the random nature of time and cause of decrement.

In this section ideas for controlling the adverse consequences of changes in interest rates are discussed. In Section 21.6.1 special notation is introduced, and a simplified set of rules for managing interest rate risk within a deterministic environment is developed. In Section 21.6.2 a rather general set of conditions for the time and amount of asset cash flows to minimize interest rate risk within a random model is developed.

21.6.1 Immunization

Our model consists of the following:

$$\text{Reserve or Liabilities} = L(i) = n(A_{x+t} - P_x \, \ddot{a}_{x+t})$$

$$\text{Assets} = A(i) = \sum_{j=0}^{\infty} v^j \, a(j)$$

$$\text{Surplus} = S(i) = A(i) - L(i)$$

where

n = number of identical whole life policies in the model.

t = number of years since the n surviving policies were issued. Assets, liabilities, and surplus are measured at this time.

P_x = benefit premium at issue, but not necessarily appropriate at time t for a realistic appraisal of liabilities. This premium is used in cash flow calculations under the simplifying assumption that expense loadings match expenses.

$\{a(j)\}$ = a sequence of cash flows, coupons, dividends, and maturity values from existing assets, paid at the end of future policy years. In this deterministic environment these amounts are assumed to be certain, not subject to default.

i = valuation rate appropriate at time t. It is assumed, unrealistically, that i does not depend on the timing of future cash flows and that any immediate changes in i will not change the flat yield curve implicit in our assumptions about i.

Clearly this simplified single decrement model ignores withdrawal benefits, expenses, and their provision in contract premiums. Both asset and liability cash flows are assumed to be known and independent of the interest rate i. Some of these unrealistic features can be changed within a more comprehensive model. Other adjustments, such as making asset and liability cash flows depend in a realistic fashion on the valuation interest rate, are more complex.

Within our simple model, we might choose to think of the sequence of future asset cash flows $\{a(j)\}$ as a control variable. Management might elect to enter capital markets to achieve a $\{a(j)\}$ such that

$$\frac{dS(i)}{di} = \frac{d}{di}\,[A(i) - L(i)] = 0 \tag{21.6.1a}$$

and

$$\frac{dS^2(i)}{di^2} = \frac{d^2}{di^2}\,[A(i) - L(i)] > 0. \tag{21.6.1b}$$

These two conditions characterize a minimum value of $S(i)$. If a sequence of asset cash flows $\{a(j)\}$ could be found that would satisfy (21.6.1a) and (21.6.1b), any change in the valuation interest rate would lead to an increased surplus. The valuation interest rate is derived from current economic conditions at valuation time and is independent of the interest rate used at duration zero in calculating P_x.

From the first derivative (21.6.1a), we have

$$\frac{d}{di}\,S(i) = v\left\{-\sum_{j=1}^{\infty} v^j\,a(j) + n\left[\sum_{k=0}^{\infty}(k+1)v^{k+1}\,p_{x+t}\,q_{x+t+k} - P_x\sum_{k=1}^{\infty}k\,v^k\,{}_k p_{x+t}\right]\right\} = 0$$

or

$$\sum_{j=1}^{\infty} v^j\,a(j) = n[(IA)_{x+t} - P_x\,(Ia)_{x+t}]. \tag{21.6.2}$$

Combining the requirements on the first and second derivatives for a minimum value of $S(i)$, (21.6.1a) and (21.6.1b), we have

$$\sum_{j=1}^{\infty} j^2\,v^j\,a(j) > n\left[\sum_{k=0}^{\infty}(k+1)^2\,v_k^{k+1}\,p_{x+t}\,q_{x+k+t} - P_x\sum_{k=1}^{\infty}k^2\,{}_k p_x\right]. \tag{21.6.3}$$

The first derivative condition for the selection of $\{a(j)\}$ may be attainable. It is unlikely that the second derivative condition can be achieved in the capital markets.

If the second derivative condition could be realized and the assumptions of the model were valid, especially the flat yield curve used for pricing assets and valuing liabilities, it would constitute an arbitrage opportunity, for it would be an opportunity to increase surplus with no new investments or increase in risk on the basis of any change in valuation interest rate. In an efficient market such an opportunity would be nonexistent or fleeting.

The investment selection rules implicit in (21.6.2) and (21.6.3) have been called the immunization rules because their implementation would "immunize" or protect the value of $S(i)$ from changes in i.

21.6.2 General Stochastic Model

We now extend the ideas and their related symbols used in Section 21.6.1 to introduce stochastic elements. We have

$$S(\tilde{v}, \tilde{K}) = A(\tilde{v}) - L(\tilde{v}, \tilde{K}) \tag{21.6.4}$$

where $\tilde{v}$ is a sequence $\{\tilde{v}_j\}$ of random discount factors and $\tilde{K} = (K_1, K_2, \ldots, K_n)$ is a vector of n independent time-until-death random variables.

Unrealistically it will be assumed that the asset cash flow sequence $\{a(j)\}$ is deterministic. Callability and default, among other asset flow option-like characteristics, are not considered.

Using (2.2.11) we have

$$\text{Var}[S(\tilde{v}, \tilde{K})] = \text{Var}[\text{E}[S(\tilde{v}, \tilde{K})|\tilde{v}]] + \text{E}[\text{Var}[S(\tilde{v}, \tilde{K})|\tilde{v}]].$$

Because we assume that asset cash flows are deterministic in the whole life illustration of Section 21.6.1, we have

$$\text{E}[S(\tilde{v}, \tilde{K})|\tilde{v}] = \sum_{j=0}^{\infty} v_j\, a(j) - n \left[\sum_{k=0}^{\infty} (v_{k+1} - P_x\, \ddot{a}_{\overline{k+1}|\tilde{v}})\; {}_kp_x\, q_{x+k} \right]$$

and

$$\text{Var}[S(\tilde{v}, \tilde{K})|\tilde{v}] = \text{Var}[L(\tilde{v}, \tilde{K})|\tilde{v}].$$

Therefore,

$$\text{Var}[S(\tilde{v}, \tilde{K})] = \text{Var}_{\tilde{v}}\, [A(\tilde{v}) - \text{E}[L(\tilde{v}, \tilde{K})|\tilde{v}]]$$

$$+ \text{E}_{\tilde{v}}\, [\text{Var}[L(\tilde{v}, \tilde{K})|\tilde{v}]]. \tag{21.6.5}$$

We can rewrite (21.6.5) as

$$\text{Var}[S(\tilde{v}, \tilde{K})] = \text{Var}_{\tilde{v}}\, [A(\tilde{v})] + \text{Var}_{\tilde{v}}\, [\text{E}[L(\tilde{v}, \tilde{K}|\tilde{v}]$$

$$- 2\, \text{Cov}_{\tilde{v}}[A(\tilde{v}), \text{E}[L(\tilde{v}, \tilde{K})|\tilde{v}]] + \text{E}_{\tilde{v}}\, [\text{Var}[L(\tilde{v}, \tilde{K})|\tilde{v}]]. \tag{21.6.6}$$

The second and fourth terms of (21.6.6) can be combined to produce

$$\text{Var}[S(\tilde{v}, \tilde{K})] = \text{Var}_{\tilde{v}}\, [A(\tilde{v})] + \text{Var}[L(\tilde{v}, \tilde{K})]$$

$$- 2\, \text{Cov}_{\tilde{v}}[A(\tilde{v}), \text{E}[L(\tilde{v}, \tilde{K}|\tilde{v}]]. \tag{21.6.7}$$

We assume that the selection of $\{a(j)\}$, the sequence of asset cash flows, is under the control of the actuary and that the objective is to minimize $\text{Var}[S(\tilde{v}, \tilde{K})]$. Since the second term of (21.6.5) does not depend on the control variable $\{a(j)\}$, the minimization of $\text{Var}[S(\tilde{v}, \tilde{K})]$ can be achieved by minimizing the term

$$\text{Var}_{\tilde{v}}\,[A(\tilde{v}) - \text{E}[L(\tilde{v}, \tilde{K})|\tilde{v}]].$$

This variance will reach its minimum value of zero if $A(\tilde{v}) - \text{E}[L(\tilde{v}, \tilde{K}|\tilde{v}] = 0$ for each future year. If a sequence of asset cash flows satisfies

$$a(0) + {}_nP_x = 0,$$

$$a(j) - n[{}_{j-1}p_x q_{x+j-1} - P_x\,{}_jp_x] = 0, \quad j = 1, 2, \ldots \tag{21.6.8}$$

could be found, then

$$[a(0) + {}_nP_x] + \sum_{j=1}^{\infty} [a(j) - n({}_{j-1}p_x\,q_{x+j-1} - P_x\,{}_jp_x)]v_j = 0$$

and

$$\text{Var}_{\tilde{v}}[\tilde{A}(\tilde{v}) - \text{E}[L(\tilde{v}, \tilde{K})|\tilde{v}]] = 0.$$

In this very special case, we can substitute into (21.6.7) to obtain

$$\text{Var}[S(\tilde{v}, \tilde{K})] = \text{Var}[A(\tilde{v})] + \text{Var}[L(\tilde{v}, \tilde{K})] - 2\,\text{Cov}[A(\tilde{v}), A(\tilde{v})]$$

$$= \text{Var}[L(\tilde{v}, \tilde{K})] - \text{Var}[A(\tilde{v})].$$

The matching conditions in (21.6.8) resemble an equivalence principle. The matching requirement imposes stringent conditions on asset cash flows. For example, it is possible that the sequence of asset cash flows that will minimize $\text{Var}[S(\tilde{v}, \tilde{K})]$ will require investments $a(j) < 0$ for some j. Other economic and budget restrictions may influence the selection of the asset cash flow sequence.

21.7   Notes and References

The ideas developed in this chapter are built on ideas that are more diverse and of recent origin than are those in earlier chapters. As a consequence, these notes and references are important to an actuary seeking to apply or extend these ideas.

The integration of times series models for stochastic interest rates with random time and cause of decrement has been the subject of intense activity in recent years. Sections 21.3.1 and 21.4.1 follow Frees (1990). The portfolio interest rate risk management rules developed in Section 21.6.2 are also based on this work. More general developments, going beyond the MA(1) model, are by Bellhouse and Panjer (1980) and Giaccotti (1986).

The empirical analysis of interest rate data to determine the adequacy of various models has been a major endeavor in financial economics. Becker (1991) provides a good example of this work. Klein (1993) traces the implications of various distributions of the interest rates on insurance cash flow analysis. In particular, Klein examines the hypothesis that the distribution of random shock terms in interest rate random models may have heavy tails. The history of formulating and testing hypotheses about rates of return is summarized by Fama (1970).

Jetton (1988) classifies and illustrates methods for generating certain families of interest rate scenarios. Christiansen (1992) starts with Jetton's partial classification but expands the models considered and illustrates their applications. There is an emphasis on interest rate generators that produce rates that regress toward a mean after a perturbation and on shifts from among yield curves according to a matrix of transition probabilities. Tilley (1992) provides more background on the financial economics of interest rate scenario generators. A monograph by Boyle (1992), especially Chapters 2, 3, and 4, provides background for this chapter.

The immunization ideas of Section 21.6.1 have many roots. They were introduced into actuarial science by Redington (1952) and brought to the attention of North American actuaries by Vanderhoof (1972). The Vanderhoof paper contains a model for a life insurance company that is designed to replicate the characteristics of the U.S. life insurance industry in 1971.

In this chapter it is suggested that a stochastic model for generating simultaneously interest rate scenarios for several types of investments and certain other economic variables be constructed. The other economic variables might be an index of consumer prices, or the unemployment rate. The model would be constructed to include observed contemporaneous correlations among the variables, as well as autocorrelations across time. Such a comprehensive and consistent model would obviously be useful in simulating the future operations of a social security system, large pension plan, or insurance company. Since about 1980 a great deal of effort has been spent in constructing, testing, and using such models. A pioneering actuarial effort in this field was by Wilkie (1986). The model has been the subject of intense discussion by Geoghegan et al. (1992).

Exercises

Section 21.1

21.1. If I has a uniform distribution on the interval $(e^{0.03} - 1, e^{0.10} - 1)$ find $E[(1 + I)^{-1}] - (1 + E[I])^{-1}$.

21.2. The function $(1 + x)^{-1}$ can be written as the Taylor series expansion

$$(1 + x)^{-1} = 1 - x + x^2 - R(\theta) \qquad |x| < 1$$

where the remainder term

$$R(\theta) = \frac{x^3}{(1 + \theta)^2} \qquad |\theta| < |x| < 1.$$

If I has a uniform distribution on the internal $(0.02, 0.12)$ and the random variable $(1 + I)^{-1}$ is approximated by the first three terms of the Taylor series, evaluate

$$E[1 - I + I^2] - (1 + E[I])^{-1}.$$

21.3. The random variable I has a Pareto distribution with p.d.f.

$$f_I(x) = \frac{11}{(1 + x)^{12}} \quad 0 < x$$

$$= 0 \quad\quad \text{elsewhere.}$$

a. Find $E[I]$.
b. Find $E[(1 + I)^{-1}] - (1 + E[I])^{-1}$.

21.4. Adopt the model described by (21.3.1) and define the random variable $\tilde{v}_n$ as

$$\tilde{v}_n = \exp\left[-\sum_1^n \log(1 + I_k) \right].$$

a. Using the m.g.f. of $\log(1 + I_k)$ find $E[\tilde{v}_n]$.
b. Using the m.g.f. of $\log(1 + I_k)$ find $E[(\tilde{v}_n)^j]$, $j = 1, 2, 3, \ldots$.
c. Assume that the random variables $\tilde{v}$ and K, completed future life years, are independent and use the results of part b to determine
   (i) $E[(\tilde{v}_{K+1})^j]$ $j = 1, 2, 3, \ldots$
   (ii) $\text{Var}(\tilde{v}_{K+1})$.
d. Continue with the assumptions made in this exercise and confirm that

$$_*A_x + {}_*d \, _*\ddot{a}_x = 1,$$

where $_*d = 1 - e^{-(\delta - \sigma^2/2)}$.

21.5. Adopt the model described by (21.3.1) except that the random variables ϵ_k are independent, identically and uniformly distributed on the interval $(-0.05, 0.05)$, and $\delta = 0.05$. Let $Z = \Sigma_{k=1}^2 \log(1 + I_k)$ be the logarithm of the random two-period interest accumulation function.
a. Evaluate $E[Z]$ and $\text{Var}(Z)$.
b. Display the p.d.f. of Z.
c. Display the p.d.f. of $Y = e^Z$.

21.6. Adopt the assumptions of Exercise 21.5. Let $X_k = \log(1 + I_k)$ and $\bar{X} = \Sigma_1^n X_k / n$.
a. Provide a justification for the statement that

$$\frac{\bar{X} - 0.05}{\sqrt{0.01/12n}}$$

will have an approximate $N(0, 1)$ distribution as n becomes large.
b. Provide a justification for the statement that $\Sigma_1^n X_k$ has an approximate $N(0.5n, 0.01n/12)$ distribution.
c. Use the result in (b) and support the statement that $\Pi_1^n (1 + I_k)$, the random interest accumulation function, has an approximate lognormal distribution with parameters $\mu = 0.5n$ and $\sigma^2 = 0.01n/12$.

21.7. Adopt the model

$$\log(1 + I_k) = \log(1 + I_{k-1}) + \epsilon_k \quad k = 1, 2, 3, \ldots$$

$$= \delta \qquad\qquad k = 0$$

for annual interest rates. The assumptions about the random shock terms (ϵ_k) made in connection with (21.3.1) are also adopted. This is called a ***random walk*** model and has frequently been used in studies of rates of return in common stocks. Exhibit (a) $E[\log(1 + I_k)]$, (b) $Var[\log(1 + I_k)]$, and (c) the distribution of $\log(1 + I_k)$, $k = 1, 2, 3, \ldots$. [Hint: Confirm that

$$\log(1 + I_k) = \delta + \sum_1^k \epsilon_j.]$$

21.8. Using the model and assumptions of Exercise 21.7, (a) exhibit $E[\log \tilde{v}_n]$ and $Var(\log \tilde{v}_n)$, (b) state the distribution of $\log \tilde{v}_n$, and (c) answer (a) and (b) for $\tilde{v}_n$.

21.9. Another version of the random walk model is

$$\log I_k = \log I_{k-1} + \epsilon_k \qquad k = 1, 2, 3$$

$$= r \qquad\qquad k = 0,$$

where the random shock terms (ϵ_k) are mutually independent with $N(0, \sigma^2)$ distributions. Determine (a) $E[\log I_n]$, (b) $Var(\log I_n)$, and (c) the distribution of $\log I_n$.

21.10. This exercise is a continuation of Exercise 21.9. For the random variable I_n, state its distribution and find $E[I_n]$ and $Var(I_n)$.

Section 21.4

21.11. Confirm that (21.4.5) for $E[(\tilde{v}_n)^2]$ reduces to (21.3.4) if $\theta = 0$.

21.12. Confirm that (21.4.6) for $E[\tilde{v}_r \, \tilde{v}_s]$ reduces to (21.3.6) if $\theta = 0$.

21.13. Verify the entries under $Var(1 + I_k)$, $k = 1, 2, 3, \ldots$, in the following table:

Model	$Var(1 + I_k)$	Name
Formula (21.3.1)	$(e^{\sigma^2} - 1)e^{(2\delta + \sigma^2)}$	Lognormal
Formula (21.4.1)	$\sigma^2(1 + \theta^2)$	MA(1)
Exercise 21.7	$k\sigma^2$	Random walk

Note the increasing variance with the random walk, Exercise 21.7.

Section 21.5

21.14. Confirm that the model described in (21.5.7) is equivalent to

$$Y(t, n) = Y(t - 1, n)^{1 - \phi_n} \, e^{\lambda(t,n) + \sigma_n \epsilon_{t,n}}$$

---

and

$$\frac{Y(t, n)}{Y(t - 1, n)} = Y(t - 1, n)^{-\phi_n} e^{\lambda(t,n) + \sigma_n \epsilon_{t,n}}.$$

These formulas indicate why (21.5.7) is called a *multiplicative model*. Note that if the observed value $Y(0, n) = y(0, n) > 0$, $Y(t, n) > 0$.

21.15. If $\phi_n = 0$ and $\lambda(t, n) = \mu$ show that (21.5.7) becomes

$$\log Y(t, n) = \mu + \log Y(t - 1, n) + \sigma_n \epsilon_{t,n},$$

$$\Delta \log Y(t - 1, n) = \mu + \sigma_n \epsilon_{t,n},$$

$$\log Y(t, n) - \log Y(0, n) = t\mu + \sigma_n \sum_{s=1}^{t} \epsilon_{s,n},$$

$$E[\log Y(t,n)] = \log[y(0, n)] + t\mu,$$

and

$$\text{Var}[\log Y(t, n)] = t \, \sigma_n^2.$$

This is a random walk model with a drift term μ. Show that if $\mu = 0$, the results of Exercise 21.9 are replicated.

21.16. If $[1 + i(s, s + k)] = (1 + i)$, $k = 1, 2, 3, \ldots, n$, and the maturity value of a bond is 1, confirm that $y(s, s + n) = i$.

21.17. The spot rate at times are given in the following:

k	i(s, s + k)
1	0.050
2	0.055
3	0.060

Calculate the corresponding par yield rates $y(s, s + t)$ for bond maturities in $k = 1, 2, 3$ periods.

Section 21.6

21.18. Let $\bar{a}(t)$ denote the rate of cash flow from assets and $\bar{l}(t)$ denote the rate of cash flows from insurance operations. For example, $\bar{l}(t)$ would measure claims and expenses less premiums, at time t. These flows are assumed to be deterministic and independent of each other and the interest rate. Let $\bar{A}(\delta)$, $\bar{L}(\delta)$, and $\bar{S}(\delta) = \bar{A}(\delta) - \bar{L}(\delta)$ denote the current value of assets, liabilities, and surplus, respectively, valued at force of interest δ. We have

$$\bar{S}(\delta) = \bar{A}(\delta) - \bar{L}(\delta) = \int_0^\infty e^{-\delta t} [\bar{a}(t) - \bar{l}(t)] \, dt.$$

In addition, let $\bar{R}(\delta) = \bar{S}(\delta) / \bar{A}(\delta)$, which is interpreted as the surplus ratio.

Confirm that if $\bar{R}(\delta_0)$ is a minimum value of $\bar{R}(\delta)$, then

$$\frac{\bar{A}'(\delta_0)}{\bar{A}(\delta_0)} = \frac{\bar{L}'(\delta_0)}{\bar{L}(\delta_0)}$$

and

$$\frac{\bar{A}''(\delta_0)}{\bar{A}(\delta_0)} > \frac{\bar{L}''(\delta_0)}{\bar{L}(\delta_0)}.$$

21.19. The cash flow rate functions in this exercise will be related to the gamma density function; that is, both $\bar{a}(t)$ and $\bar{l}(t)$ of Exercise 21.18 will be of the form

$$f(t) = \frac{k\beta^\alpha t^{\alpha-1} e^{-\beta t}}{\Gamma(\alpha)} \quad k > 0.$$

a. Confirm the following result:

$$\int_0^\infty t^n e^{-\delta t} f(t)dt = \frac{k\beta^\alpha \Gamma(\alpha + n)}{(\beta + \delta)^{n+\alpha}\Gamma(\alpha)}$$

b. If the parameters of the asset cash flow are denoted by α_A, β_A, and k_A and of the liability cash flow by α_L, β_L, and k_L, confirm that the conditions for a minimum of $\bar{R}(\delta)$ as determined in Exercise 21.18 are

$$\frac{\beta_A^{\alpha_A} \alpha_A}{(\beta_A + \delta_0)^{\alpha_A+1}} = \frac{\beta_L^{\alpha_L} \alpha_L}{(\beta_L + \delta_0)^{\alpha_L+1}}$$

and

$$\frac{\alpha_A + 1}{\beta_A + \delta_0} > \frac{\alpha_L + 1}{\beta_L + \delta_0}.$$

21.20. Accept the results of Exercise 21.18. Verify that

$$\frac{\bar{A}'(\delta_0)}{\bar{A}(\delta_0)} = \frac{\bar{L}'(\delta_0)}{\bar{L}(\delta_0)}$$

is equivalent to

$$\frac{\displaystyle\int_0^\infty t\, e^{-\delta_0 t}\, \bar{a}(t)dt}{\displaystyle\int_0^\infty e^{-\delta_0 t}\, \bar{a}(t)dt} = \frac{\displaystyle\int_0^\infty t\, e^{-\delta_0 t}\, \bar{l}(t)dt}{\displaystyle\int_0^\infty e^{-\delta_0 t}\, \bar{l}(t)dt}.$$

This result leads to the interpretation that the ratio $\bar{A}'(\delta_0)/\bar{A}(\delta_0)$ is a weighted average of t, the time of asset cash flows with the weights provided by $e^{-\delta_0 t}\, \bar{a}(t)/\int_0^\infty e^{-\delta_0 t}\, \bar{a}(t)dt$. A similar interpretation can be made of $\bar{L}'(\delta_0)/\bar{L}(\delta_0)$. These weighted times of cash flows motivate calling $\bar{A}'(\delta_0)/\bar{A}(\delta_0)$ and $\bar{L}'(\delta_0)/\bar{L}(\delta_0)$ durations.

21.21. We adopt the second central moment of interia of the times of cash flows as a measure of dispersion of the times of cash flows. Confirm that the conditions developed in Exercise 21.18 are equivalent to the requirement that the dispersion of asset cash flows shall be equal to or greater than dispersion of liability cash flows.

[Hint: The second central moment of inertia for a mass with density at x of $m(x)$ is $\int_0^\infty (x - c)^2 m(x)dx$ where $c = \int_0^\infty xm(x)dx$.]

21.22. Adopt the symbols of Exercise 21.18 and build a model for a set of l_x fully continuous whole life policies. Make the following assumptions:

- The contract premium rate is $\bar{G} = \bar{P}(\bar{A}_x)(1 + \theta)$, $\theta > 0$.
- Expense payments are made at time t for survivors at a rate of ce^{-rt}, $r > 0$.
- Assumptions are realized.
  a. Confirm that $\bar{l}(t) = l_x[\mu_x(t) + ce^{-rt} - \bar{P}(\bar{A}_x)(1 + \theta)]_t p_x$.
  b. Express $\bar{L}(\delta)$ in actuarial present-value symbols.
  c. Express $\bar{L}'(\delta)$ in actuarial symbols.

Appendix 1

NORMAL DISTRIBUTION TABLE

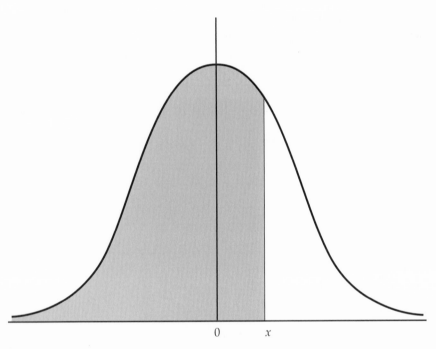

0   x

Normal Distribution

The table on page 674 gives the value of

$$\Phi(x) = \frac{1}{\sqrt{2\pi}} \int_{-\infty}^{x} e^{-w^2/2} \, dw$$

for certain values of x. The integer of x is given in the top row, and the first decimal place of x is given in the left column. Since the density function of x is symmetric, the value of the cumulative distribution function for negative x can be obtained by subtracting from unity the value of the cumulative distribution function for x.

x	0	1	2	3
0.0	0.5000	0.8413	0.9772	0.9987
0.1	0.5398	0.8643	0.9821	0.9990
0.2	0.5793	0.8849	0.9861	0.9993
0.3	0.6179	0.9032	0.9893	0.9995
0.4	0.6554	0.9192	0.9918	0.9997
0.5	0.6915	0.9332	0.9938	0.9998
0.6	0.7257	0.9452	0.9953	0.9998
0.7	0.7580	0.9554	0.9965	0.9999
0.8	0.7881	0.9641	0.9974	0.9999
0.9	0.8159	0.9713	0.9981	1.0000

Selected Points of the Normal Distribution

$\Phi(x)$	x
0.800	0.842
0.850	1.036
0.900	1.282
0.950	1.645
0.975	1.960
0.990	2.326
0.995	2.576

Appendix 2A

ILLUSTRATIVE LIFE TABLE

Illustrative Life Table: Basic Functions

Age	l_x	d_x	$1{,}000\ q_x$
0	100 000.00	2 042.1700	20.4217
1	97 957.83	131.5672	1.3431
2	97 826.26	119.7100	1.2237
3	97 706.55	109.8124	1.1239
4	97 596.74	101.7056	1.0421
5	97 495.03	95.2526	0.9770
6	97 399.78	90.2799	0.9269
7	97 309.50	86.6444	0.8904
8	97 222.86	84.1950	0.8660
9	97 138.66	82.7816	0.8522
10	97 055.88	82.2549	0.8475
11	96 973.63	82.4664	0.8504
12	96 891.16	83.2842	0.8594
13	96 807.88	84.5180	0.8730
14	96 723.36	86.0611	0.8898
15	96 637.30	87.7559	0.9081
16	96 549.54	89.6167	0.9282
17	96 459.92	91.6592	0.9502
18	96 368.27	93.9005	0.9744
19	96 274.36	96.3596	1.0009
20	96 178.01	99.0569	1.0299
21	96 078.95	102.0149	1.0618
22	95 976.93	105.2582	1.0967
23	95 871.68	108.8135	1.1350
24	95 762.86	112.7102	1.1770
25	95 650.15	116.9802	1.2330
26	95 533.17	121.6585	1.2735
27	95 411.51	126.7830	1.3288
28	95 284.73	132.3953	1.3895
29	95 152.33	138.5406	1.4560

Age	l_x	d_x	$1{,}000\ q_x$
30	95 013.79	145.2682	1.5289
31	94 868.53	152.6317	1.6089
32	94 715.89	160.6896	1.6965
33	94 555.20	169.5052	1.7927
34	94 385.70	179.1475	1.8980
35	94 206.55	189.6914	2.0136
36	94 016.86	201.2179	2.1402
37	93 815.64	213.8149	2.2791
38	93 601.83	227.5775	2.4313
39	93 374.25	242.6085	2.5982
40	93 131.64	259.0186	2.7812
41	92 872.62	276.9271	2.9818
42	92 595.70	296.4623	3.2017
43	92 299.23	317.7619	3.4427
44	91 981.47	340.9730	3.7070
45	91 640.50	366.2529	3.9966
46	91 274.25	393.7687	4.3141
47	90 880.48	423.6978	4.6621
48	90 456.78	456.2274	5.0436
49	90 000.55	491.5543	5.4617
50	89 509.00	529.8844	5.9199
51	88 979.11	571.4316	6.4221
52	88 407.68	616.4165	6.9724
53	87 791.26	665.0646	7.5755
54	87 126.20	717.6041	8.2364
55	86 408.60	774.2626	8.9605
56	85 634.33	835.2636	9.7538
57	84 799.07	900.8215	10.6230
58	83 898.25	971.1358	11.5752
59	82 927.11	1 046.3843	12.6181
60	81 880.73	1 126.7146	13.7604
61	80 754.01	1 212.2343	15.0114
62	79 541.78	1 302.9994	16.3813
63	78 238.78	1 399.0010	17.8812
64	76 839.78	1 500.1504	19.5231
65	75 339.63	1 606.2618	21.3203
66	73 733.37	1 717.0334	23.2871
67	72 016.33	1 832.0273	25.4391
68	70 184.31	1 950.6476	27.7932
69	68 233.66	2 072.1177	30.3680

Illustrative Life Table: Basic Functions

Age	l_x	d_x	$1,000\ q_x$
70	66 161.54	2 195.4578	33.1833
71	63 966.08	2 319.4639	36.2608
72	61 646.62	2 442.6884	39.6240
73	59 203.93	2 563.4258	43.2982
74	56 640.51	2 679.7050	47.3108
75	53 960.80	2 789.2905	51.6911
76	51 171.51	2 889.6965	56.4708
77	48 281.81	2 978.2164	61.6840
78	45 303.60	3 051.9717	67.3671
79	42 251.62	3 107.9833	73.5589
80	39 143.64	3 143.2679	80.3009
81	36 000.37	3 154.9603	87.6369
82	32 845.41	3 140.4624	95.6134
83	29 704.95	3 097.6146	104.2794
84	26 607.34	3 024.8830	113.6860
85	23 582.45	2 921.5530	123.8867
86	20 660.90	2 787.9129	134.9367
87	17 872.99	2 625.4088	146.8926
88	15 247.58	2 436.7474	159.8121
89	12 810.83	2 225.9244	173.7533
90	10 584.91	1 998.1533	188.7738
91	8 586.75	1 759.6818	204.9298
92	6 827.07	1 517.4869	222.2749
93	5 309.58	1 278.8606	240.8589
94	4 030.72	1 050.9136	260.7257
95	2 979.81	840.0452	281.9122
96	2 139.77	651.4422	304.4456
97	1 488.32	488.6776	328.3410
98	999.65	353.4741	353.5993
99	646.17	245.6772	380.2041
100	400.49	163.4494	408.1188
101	237.05	103.6560	437.2837
102	133.39	62.3746	467.6133
103	71.01	35.4358	498.9935
104	35.58	18.9023	531.2793
105	16.68	9.4105	564.2937
106	7.27	4.3438	597.8266
107	2.92	1.8458	631.6360
108	1.08	0.7163	665.4495
109	0.36	0.2517	698.9685
110	0.11	0.0793	731.8742

Age	$\ddot{a}_x$	1,000 A_x	1,000 (^2A_x)
0	16.80096	49.0025	25.9210
1	17.09819	32.1781	8.8845
2	17.08703	32.8097	8.6512
3	17.07314	33.5957	8.5072
4	17.05670	34.5264	8.4443
5	17.03786	35.5930	8.4547
6	17.01675	36.7875	8.5310
7	16.99351	38.1031	8.6666
8	16.96823	39.5341	8.8553
9	16.94100	41.0757	9.0917
10	16.91187	42.7245	9.3712
11	16.88089	44.4782	9.6902
12	16.84807	46.3359	10.0460
13	16.81340	48.2981	10.4373
14	16.77685	50.3669	10.8638
15	16.73836	52.5459	11.3268
16	16.69782	54.8404	11.8295
17	16.65515	57.2558	12.3749
18	16.61024	59.7977	12.9665
19	16.56299	62.4720	13.6080
20	16.51330	65.2848	14.3034
21	16.46105	68.2423	15.0569
22	16.40614	71.3508	15.8730
23	16.34843	74.6170	16.7566
24	16.28783	78.0476	17.7128
25	16.22419	81.6496	18.7472
26	16.15740	85.4300	19.8657
27	16.08733	89.3962	21.0744
28	16.01385	93.5555	22.3802
29	15.93683	97.9154	23.7900
30	15.85612	102.4835	25.3113
31	15.77161	107.2676	26.9520
32	15.68313	112.2754	28.7206
33	15.59057	117.5148	30.6259
34	15.49378	122.9935	32.6772
35	15.39262	128.7194	34.8843
36	15.28696	134.7002	37.2574
37	15.17666	140.9437	39.8074
38	15.06159	147.4572	42.5455
39	14.94161	154.2484	45.4833

Age	$\ddot{a}_x$	1,000 A_x	1,000 (^2A_x)
40	14.81661	161.3242	48.6332
41	14.68645	168.6916	52.0077
42	14.55102	176.3572	55.6199
43	14.41022	184.3271	59.4833
44	14.26394	192.6071	63.6117
45	14.11209	201.2024	68.0193
46	13.95459	210.1176	72.7205
47	13.79136	219.3569	77.7299
48	13.62235	228.9234	83.0624
49	13.44752	238.8198	88.7329
50	13.26683	249.0475	94.7561
51	13.08027	259.6073	101.1469
52	12.88785	270.4988	107.9196
53	12.68960	281.7206	115.0885
54	12.48556	293.2700	122.6672
55	12.27581	305.1431	130.6687
56	12.06042	317.3346	139.1053
57	11.83953	329.8381	147.9883
58	11.61327	342.6452	157.3280
59	11.38181	355.7466	167.1332
60	11.14535	369.1310	177.4113
61	10.90412	382.7858	188.1682
62	10.65836	396.6965	199.4077
63	10.40837	410.8471	211.1318
64	10.15444	425.2202	223.3401
65	9.89693	439.7965	236.0299
66	9.63619	454.5553	249.1958
67	9.37262	469.4742	262.8299
68	9.10664	484.5296	276.9212
69	8.83870	499.6963	291.4559
70	8.56925	514.9481	306.4172
71	8.29879	530.2574	321.7850
72	8.02781	545.5957	337.5361
73	7.75683	560.9339	353.6443
74	7.48639	576.2419	370.0803
75	7.21702	591.4895	386.8119
76	6.94925	606.6460	403.8038
77	6.68364	621.6808	421.0184
78	6.42071	636.5634	438.4155
79	6.16101	651.2639	455.9527

Age	$\ddot{a}_x$	1,000 A_x	1,000 (^2A_x)
80	5.90503	665.7528	473.5861
81	5.65330	680.0019	491.2698
82	5.40629	693.9837	508.9574
83	5.16446	707.6723	526.6012
84	4.92824	721.0431	544.1537
85	4.69803	734.0736	561.5675
86	4.47421	746.7428	578.7956
87	4.25710	759.0320	595.7923
88	4.04700	770.9244	612.5133
89	3.84417	782.4056	628.9163
90	3.64881	793.4636	644.9611
91	3.46110	804.0884	660.6105
92	3.28118	814.2726	675.8298
93	3.10914	824.0111	690.5878
94	2.94502	833.3007	704.8565
95	2.78885	842.1408	718.6115
96	2.64059	850.5325	731.8321
97	2.50020	858.4791	744.5010
98	2.36759	865.9853	756.6047
99	2.24265	873.0577	768.1330
100	2.12522	879.7043	779.0793
101	2.01517	885.9341	789.4400
102	1.91229	891.7573	799.2147
103	1.81639	897.1852	808.4054
104	1.72728	902.2295	817.0170
105	1.64472	906.9025	825.0563
106	1.56850	911.2170	832.5324
107	1.49838	915.1860	839.4558
108	1.43414	918.8224	845.8386
109	1.37553	922.1396	851.6944
110	1.32234	925.1507	857.0377

Age	$\ddot{a}_{xx}$	$1{,}000\, A_{xx}$	$1{,}000\, (^2A_{xx})$	$\ddot{a}_{x:x+10}$	$1{,}000\, A_{x:x+10}$	$1{,}000\, (^2A_{x:x+10})$
0	16.13448	86.7274	50.8875	16.28443	78.2400	34.7076
1	16.71842	53.6745	17.4565	16.55328	63.0218	18.1309
2	16.70637	54.3565	16.9753	16.52270	64.7527	18.2195
3	16.68957	55.3072	16.6683	16.48839	66.6947	18.4277
4	16.66839	56.5060	16.5191	16.45053	68.8378	18.7468
5	16.64317	57.9339	16.5121	16.40925	71.1745	19.1700
6	16.61421	59.5733	16.6324	16.36464	73.6996	19.6923
7	16.58178	61.4085	16.8664	16.31677	76.4091	20.3096
8	16.54614	63.4258	17.2017	16.26571	79.2997	21.0188
9	16.50749	65.6137	17.6271	16.21147	82.3696	21.8172
10	16.46599	67.9626	18.1330	16.15408	85.6181	22.7036
11	16.42178	70.4655	18.7116	16.09353	89.0457	23.6776
12	16.37492	73.1176	19.3572	16.02977	92.6543	24.7402
13	16.32547	75.9170	20.0661	15.96277	96.4469	25.8935
14	16.27340	78.8643	20.8373	15.89244	100.4282	27.1413
15	16.21865	81.9632	21.6726	15.81866	104.6042	28.4891
16	16.16111	85.2203	22.5769	15.74131	108.9826	29.9441
17	16.10065	88.6424	23.5556	15.66025	113.5710	31.5141
18	16.03715	92.2366	24.6142	15.57534	118.3771	33.2071
19	15.97049	96.0099	25.7588	15.48645	123.4087	35.0317
20	15.90053	99.9697	26.9958	15.39343	128.6737	36.9970
21	15.82715	104.1234	28.3320	15.29615	134.1800	39.1126
22	15.75021	108.4786	29.7746	15.19448	139.9353	41.3884
23	15.66958	113.0429	31.3311	15.08826	145.9474	43.8349
24	15.58511	117.8241	33.0098	14.97738	152.2240	46.4632
25	15.49667	122.8299	34.8192	14.86169	158.7725	49.2847
26	15.40413	128.0682	36.7681	14.74106	165.6003	52.3114
27	15.30734	133.5468	38.8662	14.61538	172.7144	55.5555
28	15.20617	139.2737	41.1234	14.48452	180.1217	59.0301
29	15.10047	145.2564	43.5502	14.34836	187.8286	62.7483
30	14.99012	151.5028	46.1574	14.20681	195.8411	66.7238
31	14.87498	158.0203	48.9566	14.05976	204.1648	70.9706
32	14.75491	164.8162	51.9595	13.90712	212.8047	75.5028
33	14.62981	171.8977	55.1785	13.74882	221.7652	80.3352
34	14.44953	179.2716	58.6264	13.58478	231.0501	85.4824
35	14.36398	186.9444	62.3164	13.41497	240.6623	90.9593
36	14.22304	194.9221	66.2622	13.23933	250.6040	96.7805
37	14.07662	203.2104	70.4777	13.05785	260.8765	102.9610
38	13.92461	211.8144	74.9770	12.87052	271.4799	109.5154
39	13.76695	220.7386	79.7749	12.67736	282.4136	116.4579

Age	$\ddot{a}_{xx}$	1,000 A_{xx}	1,000 $(^{2}A_{xx})$	$\ddot{a}_{x:x+10}$	1,000 $A_{x:x+10}$	1,000 $(^{2}A_{x:x+10})$
40	13.60357	229.9867	84.8858	12.47840	293.6755	123.8024
41	13.43441	239.5619	90.3247	12.27370	305.2625	131.5623
42	13.25943	249.4664	96.1064	12.06333	317.1700	139.7502
43	13.07861	259.7015	102.2457	11.84740	329.3924	148.3778
44	12.89194	270.2677	108.7571	11.62604	341.9222	157.4559
45	12.69943	281.1642	115.6552	11.39940	354.7507	166.9939
46	12.50112	292.3892	122.9537	11.16767	367.8678	177.0001
47	12.29706	303.9398	130.6661	10.93105	381.2615	187.4810
48	12.08733	315.8114	138.8051	10.68978	394.9184	198.4414
49	11.87202	327.9986	147.3826	10.44412	408.8233	209.8841
50	11.65127	340.4941	156.4093	10.19438	422.9597	221.8099
51	11.42522	353.2895	165.8951	9.94087	437.3092	234.2171
52	11.19405	366.3746	175.8482	9.68395	451.8518	247.1016
53	10.95797	379.7377	186.2752	9.42400	466.5661	260.4567
54	10.71721	393.3656	197.1814	9.16142	481.4292	274.2728
55	10.47203	407.2435	208.5696	8.89664	496.4168	288.5375
56	10.22273	421.3546	220.4410	8.63011	511.5030	303.2353
57	9.96964	435.6810	232.7940	8.36232	526.6612	318.3475
58	9.71308	450.2029	245.6250	8.09375	541.8633	333.8526
59	9.45345	464.8990	258.9275	7.82491	557.0805	349.7258
60	9.19114	479.7465	272.6922	7.55633	572.2833	365.9390
61	8.92659	494.7213	286.9070	7.28853	587.4417	382.4614
62	8.66024	509.7977	301.5568	7.02206	602.5251	399.2593
63	8.39257	524.9491	316.6234	6.75745	617.5030	416.2961
64	8.12406	540.1477	332.0853	6.49524	632.3449	433.5327
65	7.85522	555.3647	347.9183	6.23597	647.0206	450.9279
66	7.58658	570.5707	364.0947	5.98016	661.5006	468.4383
67	7.31867	585.7356	380.5839	5.72831	675.7560	486.0192
68	7.05202	600.8289	397.3525	5.48092	689.7590	503.6243
69	6.78718	615.8203	414.3642	5.23847	703.4830	521.2065
70	6.52467	630.6790	431.5803	5.00138	716.9030	538.7185
71	6.26504	645.3750	448.9598	4.77008	729.9954	556.1128
72	6.00881	659.8785	466.4595	4.54495	742.7386	573.3422
73	5.75650	674.1606	484.0346	4.32634	755.1127	590.3606
74	5.50858	688.1934	501.6393	4.11456	767.1002	607.1233
75	5.26555	701.9503	519.2266	3.90989	778.6857	623.5869
76	5.02783	715.4057	536.7489	3.71254	789.8559	639.7107
77	4.79586	728.5362	554.1588	3.52273	800.6001	655.4561
78	4.57002	741.3197	571.4091	3.34060	810.9096	670.7874
79	4.35066	753.7364	588.4536	3.16625	820.7782	685.6720

Illustrative Life Table: Joint Life Actuarial Functions, $i = 0.06$

Age	$\ddot{a}_{xx}$	$1,000\ A_{xx}$	$1,000\ (^2A_{xx})$	$\ddot{a}_{x:x+10}$	$1,000\ A_{x:x+10}$	$1,000\ (^2A_{x:x+10})$
80	4.13809	765.7683	605.2473	2.99977	830.2020	700.0806
81	3.93260	777.3999	621.7467	2.84117	839.1791	713.9874
82	3.73442	788.6175	637.9108	2.69046	847.7098	727.3701
83	3.54375	799.4102	653.7007	2.54760	855.7965	740.2101
84	3.36075	809.7690	669.0804	2.41251	863.4431	752.4921
85	3.18552	819.6876	684.0169	2.28509	870.6554	764.2049
86	3.01814	829.1617	698.4806	2.16521	877.4407	775.3401
87	2.85866	838.1892	712.4451	2.05273	883.8075	785.8931
88	2.70706	846.7701	725.8879	1.94748	889.7655	795.8619
89	2.56332	854.9067	738.7899	1.84925	895.3253	805.2478
90	2.42735	862.6027	751.1355	1.75786	900.4984	814.0543
91	2.29908	869.8636	762.9129	1.67309	905.2969	822.2875
92	2.17836	876.6967	774.1136	1.59471	909.7331	829.9554
93	2.06505	883.1102	784.7323	1.52251	913.8199	837.0680
94	1.95899	889.1137	794.7670	1.45626	917.5703	843.6367
95	1.85998	894.7179	804.2185	1.39571	920.9973	849.6744
96	1.76783	899.9341	813.0901	1.34065	924.1140	855.1951
97	1.68232	904.7742	821.3876	1.29084	926.9335	860.2140
98	1.60324	909.2506	829.1188	1.24605	929.4689	864.7475
99	1.53035	913.3762	836.2934	1.20604	931.7333	868.8126
100	1.46344	917.1638	842.9228	1.17060	933.7399	872.4279
101	1.40226	920.6266	849.0197	1.13946	935.5020	875.6129
102	1.34659	923.7777	854.5980	1.11241	937.0336	878.3888
103	1.29620	926.6301	859.6727	1.08917	938.3489	880.7785
104	1.25086	929.1969	864.2600	1.06949	939.4630	882.8066
105	1.21032	931.4911	868.3771	1.05308	940.3917	884.5002
106	1.17437	933.5261	872.0421	1.03965	941.1518	885.8881
107	1.14277	935.3151	875.2746	1.02889	941.7609	887.0017
108	1.11526	936.8720	878.0956	1.02047	942.2374	887.8735
109	1.09161	938.2110	880.5276	1.01406	942.6001	888.5376
110	1.07154	939.3470	882.5952	1.00934	942.8678	889.0280

Appendix 2B

ILLUSTRATIVE SERVICE TABLE

Age x	$l_x^{(\tau)}$	$d_x^{(d)}$	$d_x^{(w)}$	$d_x^{(i)}$	$d_x^{(r)}$	S_x
30	100 000	100	19 900	—	—	1.00
31	79 910	80	14 376	—	—	1.06
32	65 454	72	9 858	—	—	1.13
33	55 524	61	5 702	—	—	1.20
34	49 761	60	3 971	—	—	1.28
35	45 730	64	2 693	46	—	1.36
36	42 927	64	1 927	43	—	1.44
37	40 893	65	1 431	45	—	1.54
38	39 352	71	1 181	47	—	1.63
39	38 053	72	989	49	—	1.74
40	36 943	78	813	52	—	1.85
41	36 000	83	720	54	—	1.96
42	35 143	91	633	56	—	2.09
43	34 363	96	550	58	—	2.22
44	33 659	104	505	61	—	2.36
45	32 989	112	462	66	—	2.51
46	32 349	123	421	71	—	2.67
47	31 734	133	413	79	—	2.84
48	31 109	143	373	87	—	3.02
49	30 506	156	336	95	—	3.21
50	29 919	168	299	102	—	3.41
51	29 350	182	293	112	—	3.63
52	28 763	198	259	121	—	3.86
53	28 185	209	251	132	—	4.10
54	27 593	226	218	143	—	4.35
55	27 006	240	213	157	—	4.62
56	26 396	259	182	169	—	4.91
57	25 786	276	178	183	—	5.21
58	25 149	297	148	199	—	5.53
59	24 505	316	120	213	—	5.86

Age x	$l_x^{(\tau)}$	$d_x^{(d)}$	$d_x^{(w)}$	$d_x^{(i)}$	$d_x^{(r)}$	S_x
60	23 856	313	—	—	3 552	6.21
61	19 991	298	—	—	1 587	6.56
62	18 106	284	—	—	2 692	6.93
63	15 130	271	—	—	1 350	7.31
64	13 509	257	—	—	2 006	7.70
65	11 246	204	—	—	4 448	8.08
66	6 594	147	—	—	1 302	8.48
67	5 145	119	—	—	1 522	8.91
68	3 504	83	—	—	1 381	9.35
69	2 040	49	—	—	1 004	9.82
70	987	17	—	—	970	10.31

Appendix 3

SYMBOL INDEX

Symbol	Page		Symbol	Page
$A_{xy:\overline{n}}$	280		$\overset{\circ}{e}_x$	68
$\bar{A}^{1}_{xy:\overline{n}}$	283		$\hat{e}_k$	512
$^2A_{xy:\overline{n}}$	281		$\overset{\circ}{e}_{x:\overline{n}}$	71
$\bar{A}^{2}_{wxy}$	565		e_{xy}	272
$\bar{A}_{\overline{x_1x_2x_3}}$	561		$e_{\overline{xy}}$	272
$_kAS$	486		$\overset{\circ}{e}_{xy}$	272
$_k\hat{AS}$	512		$\overset{\circ}{e}_{\overline{xy}}$	272
$(AS)_{x+h}$	351		E	5, A5
(AAI)	526		E	501
			E_0	501
$b(u)$	587		$_nE_x$	101
b_j	230		$(ES)_{x+h+t}$	351
b_t	94		$ELRA$	525
$b_f(t)$	600			
B_t	611		f	609
$\hat{B}_{x+k}$	344		$f(u;t)$	490
$B^{(3)}_{x+t}$	549		$f_S(s)$	34
$B^{(j)}_{x+t}$	342		$F_X(x)$	28
$_hBP$	509		F_t	629
			$F^{(k)}$	35
c	410		$F_S(s)$	34
c_k	486		$_kF$	513
$\hat{c}_k$	512			
$c(t)$	399		G	4, 449, 467
C_1	651		$\hat{G}$	531
C_2	651		$G(b)$	407
C_3	651		$G(x:\alpha,\beta)$	387
C_h	234			
$_kCV$	486		$h(x)$	453, 609
			$H(r)$	600
$d^{(j)}_x$	316		$H(x:\alpha,\beta,x_0)$	387
$_nd_x$	59		$_u(hp)^{(\tau)}_{x+t}$	548
$_nd^{(j)}_x$	316		$(h\mu)^{(j)}_{x+t}(u)$	548
$_nd^{(\tau)}_x$	316			
$_tD_j$	557		i'_{k+1}	539
$_{k+1}D$	513		$\hat{i}_{k+1}$	512
$(DA)^1_{x:\overline{n}}$	117		$i(s,s+t)$	656
$(D\bar{A})^1_{x:\overline{n}}$	108		I_k	644
$_n\mathcal{D}_x$	59		I_d	445
$_n\mathcal{D}^{(j)}_x$	316		$I_d(x)$	17
$_n\mathcal{D}^{(\tau)}_x$	316		$_ji_k$	638
			$(IA)_x$	115
e	468		$(I\bar{A})_x$	106
e_{h-1}	483		$(\bar{I}\bar{A})_x$	106
e_x	69			

Symbol	Page		Symbol	Page
$_kW_x$	503		δ	96
$_kW_{x:\overline{n}|}$	503		δ_t	96
$_k^hW_x$	503			
$(Wa)_t$	627		θ	41, 617
$_k\bar{W}(\bar{A}_x)$	503			
$_k\bar{W}(\bar{A}_{x:\overline{n}|})$	503		$\lambda(t)$	625
$_k^h\bar{W}(\bar{A}_x)$	503		$\lambda(t,n)$	659
			Λ	373
(x)	52		Λ_h	242
$(x_1x_2\cdots x_m)$	263			
$\overline{(x_1x_2\cdots x_m)}$	268			
$\dfrac{k}{x_1x_2\cdots x_m}$	556		$\mu(x)$	55
			$\mu_x(t)$	79
$\dfrac{[k]}{x_1x_2\cdots x_m}$	556		$\mu_x^{(d)}$	351
			$\mu_x^{(i)}$	351
X_i	27, 367		$\mu_x^{(w)}$	351
$X(\theta)$	617		$\mu_x^{(j)}(t)$	311
			$\mu_x^{(\tau)}(t)$	311
Y	134		$\mu_{xy}(t)$	266
$y(s,s+m)$	657		$\mu_{\overline{xy}}(t)$	270
$Y(t,n)$	659		$\mu(x,u)$	589
z_t	94		π_h	230
Z	94		π_t	597
$_mZ_y$	352			
			ρ	610
α	294, 519			
$\alpha(m)$	152		τ	310, 608
$\bar{\alpha}$	520			
α^{CRVM}	522		$\phi(x)$	600
			$\phi(x,u)$	600
β	519, 610			
$\beta(m)$	152		$\psi(u)$	400
$\bar{\beta}$	520		$\tilde{\psi}(u)$	401
β^{CRVM}	522		$\psi(u,t)$	400
$\beta(x,u)$	600		$\psi(u;w)$	427
			$\tilde{\psi}(u,w)$	404
$\Gamma(\alpha)$	374			
			ω	63

Appendix 4

GENERAL RULES FOR SYMBOLS
OF ACTUARIAL FUNCTIONS

An actuarial function is represented by a principal symbol and a combination of auxiliary symbols such as letters, numerals, double dots, circles, hats, and horizontal and vertical bars. The principal symbol expresses the general definition of the function; choice and placement of the auxiliary symbols at the top and corners give precise meaning. We review the rules for selecting and placing the symbols and show one or more functional forms in common application areas.

This notation is based upon the system of International Actuarial Notation (IAN) that was originally adopted by the Second International Congress of Actuaries in London in 1898 and is modified periodically under the guidance of the Permanent Committee of Actuarial Notations of the International Actuarial Association. IAN is a basic system of principles that does not cover all areas of actuarial applications. In this text these principles have been followed, and sometimes extended, to construct consistent notation where needed.

This Appendix is meant to provide the reader with an overview of basic patterns for expressing the symbols appearing in this book. Although it is a good introduction to IAN, it is not exhaustive. Authoritative sources for further reference are:
- Actuarial Society of America, "International Actuarial Notation," *Transactions*, XLVIII, 1947: 166–176.
- Faculty of Actuaries, *Transactions*, XIX, 1950: 89.
- *Journal of the Institute of Actuaries*, LXXV, 1949: 121.

An actuarial symbol can be viewed as illustrated below. Box I represents the principal symbol, the others subscripts or superscripts. The roman numerals in the boxes correspond to the section designations of this Appendix.

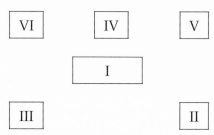

Section I.   Center

Principal Symbol	*Description*	*Topic*
i	Effective rate of interest for a time period, usually 1 year, or with a superscript in Position V, a nominal rate.	Interest
v	Present value of 1 due at the end of the effective interest period, usually 1 year.	
δ	Force of interest, usually stated as an annual rate.	
d	Effective rate of interest-in-advance, or discount rate, for a time period of usually 1 year, or with a superscript in Position V, a nominal rate. This symbol never has a subscript in Position II.	
l	Expected number, or number, of survivors at a given age.	Life Tables
d	Expected number, or number, of those dying within a given time period. This symbol always has a subscript in Position II.	
p	Probability of surviving for a given time period.	
q	Probability of dying within a given time period.	
μ	Force of mortality, usually stated on an annual basis.	
m	Central death rate for a given time period.	
L	Expected number, or number, of years lived within a time period by the survivors at the beginning of the period.	
T	Expected total, or total, future lifetime of the survivors at a given age. (The above are survivorship group definitions of the life table functions denoted by l, d, L, and T. For the alternative stationary population definitions, see Chapter 19.)	
A	Actuarial present value (net single premium) of an insurance or pure endowment of 1.	Life Insurance and Pure Endowments

Principal Symbol	Description	Topic
(IA)	Actuarial present value (net single premium) of an insurance with a benefit amount of 1 at the end of the first year, increasing linearly at a rate of 1 per year.	
(DA)	Actuarial present value (net single premium) of a term insurance with an initial benefit amount equal to the term and decreasing linearly at the rate of 1 per year.	
E	Actuarial present value of a pure endowment of 1.	
a	Actuarial present value of an annuity of 1 per time period, usually 1 year.	Annuities
s	Actuarial accumulated value of an annuity of 1 per time period, usually 1 year.	
(Ia)	Actuarial present value of an annuity payable at the rate of 1 per year at the end of the first year and increasing linearly at a rate of 1 per year.	
(Da)	Actuarial present value of a temporary annuity with an initial payment rate equal to the term and decreasing linearly at a rate of 1 per period.	
P	Level annual premium rate to cover only benefits, usually determined by the equivalence principle.	Premiums
V	Reserve to cover future benefits in excess of future benefit premiums.	Reserves
W	Face amount of a paid-up policy purchased with a cash value equal to the reserve. (Principle symbols for benefit premiums, reserves, and amounts of reduced paid-up insurance, P, V, and W, are combined with benefit symbols unless the benefit is a level unit insurance payable at the end of the year of death.)	[Examples: $\bar{P}_x$; $P(\bar{A}_x)$; $_{10}V^{(4)}(\bar{A}_{x:\overline{n}|})$; $P^{(12)}(_{30|}\ddot{a}_{35}^{(12)})]$
S	Salary scale function used to project salaries.	Pensions
Z	Average of a given number of salary scale function values, usually at unit intervals in the independent variable.	

Section II.   Lower Space to the Right

Auxiliary Symbol	Description	Examples
x; 10	A single letter or numeral is the individual's age at the commencement of the overall time period implied by the principal symbol.	a_x; $\bar{a}_{10}$ q_x; $_5q_{10}$ $\bar{A}_x$; A_{10}
$\overline{n\vert}$; $\overline{10\vert}$	A term certain is indicated by a single letter or numeral under an angle.	$A_{x:\overline{n\vert}}$; $\ddot{a}_{\overline{10\vert}}$
$[x]$; $[35]$ $[x] + t$; $[35 - n]$ $+ n$	Alphanumeric expressions enclosed by brackets indicate the age at which the life was selected. A term, representing duration since selection, may be added to the bracketed expression to express the attained age of the life.	$l_{[x]}$; $l_{[x]+10}$ $A_{[35]}$; $\ddot{a}^i_{[35-n]+n}$
xyz or $x{:}y{:}z$ $25{:}\overline{10\vert}$	Two or more alphanumeric characters indicate a joint status that survives until the first death or expiration of the indicated lives and terms certain.	l_{xyz}; $A_{x:y:z}$ $\ddot{a}_{25:\overline{10\vert}}$; $P_{25:\overline{10\vert}}$
$\frown$	This symbol emphasizes the joint status when ambiguity is possible.	$A_{\overset{\frown}{xy}:z}$
$\overset{1}{x}{:}\overline{10\vert}$; $\overset{2}{xyz}\!\!\!_{1}$	Numerals can be placed above or below the individual statuses of a collection of alphanumeric characters to show the order in which the units are to fail for an (insurable) event to occur. Benefits are payable upon the failure of the status with a numeral above it.	$\bar{A}^1_{x:\overline{n\vert}}$; $_\infty q^3_{\underset{12}{xyz}}$
$\overline{xyz}$; $\overline{65{:}60{:}10\vert}$	A horizontal bar over a collection of alphanumeric characters defines a status that survives until the last survivor of the individual statuses fails.	$a_{\overline{xyz}}$; $\bar{A}_{\overline{xy:n\vert}}$
$\dfrac{r}{\overline{xyz}}$; $\dfrac{[r]}{\overline{x{:}y{:}10}}$	A single alphanumeric character, say, r, above the right end of the bar over the set of alphanumeric characters defines a status that survives as long as at least r of the individual statuses survive. If the r is enclosed in brackets, the status exists only while exactly r of the individual statuses survive.	$\bar{a}^{[2]}_{\overline{xyz}}$; $\bar{A}^2_{\overline{xyz}}$

Auxiliary Symbol	Description	Examples
$y\|x$; $60\|55$ $\underset{1}{yz}\|x$	A vertical bar separating the alphanumeric characters indicates that the income or coverage of the principal symbol commences upon the failure, as specified, of the status before the bar and continues until the failure of the status following the bar, providing the statuses fail in that order.	$a_{y\|x}$ $a_{\underset{1}{wy\overset{3}{z}}\|x}$

Section III. Lower Space to the Left

Auxiliary Symbol	Description	Examples
n; 15	A single alphanumeric character shows the time for which the principal symbol is evaluated. For an annual premium, P, this position shows the maximum number of years for which the premiums are paid if this is less than the period of coverage of an insurance or the period of deferral for a deferred annuity.	${}_nP_x$; ${}_{15}E_{30}$ ${}_{20}P_{25}$; ${}_{20}V_{40:\overline{30}\|}$
$n\|m$; $n\|$	An alphanumeric pair separated by a vertical bar indicates a period of deferment (left of the bar) and a period following deferment (right of the bar). In some cases, when either is equal to 1 or infinity, it can be omitted.	${}_{n\|m}q_x$; ${}_{n\|}\bar{a}_x$

Section IV.   Top Center

Auxiliary Symbol	Description	Examples
..	The double dot (dieresis) on an annuity symbol indicates that the payments are at the beginning of the periods, that is, an annuity-due. Without the dieresis, the annuity is an annuity-immediate with payments at the ends of the periods.	$\ddot{a}_x$; $\ddot{s}_{\overline{40\vert}}$
—	A horizontal bar indicates that the frequency of events is infinite. For annuities the payments are considered to be made continuously, and for insurances the benefit is paid at the moment of failure.	$\bar{a}_x$; $\bar{A}_x$ $_3\bar{V}_x$; $\bar{P}(\bar{A}_x)$
∘	A circle (degree sign) means that the benefit or lifetime is complete, that is, credited up to the time of death.	$\mathring{a}_x$; $\mathring{e}_x$

Section V.   Upper Space to the Right

Auxiliary Symbol	Description	Examples
(m); (12)	An alphanumeric character in parentheses shows the number of annuity payments in an interest period, usually 1 year. For an insurance it is the number of periods in a year at the end of which the death benefit can be paid. On multiple decrement symbols it indicates the cause of decrement to be used or that the total of all decrements is to be used.	$s_{\overline{10\vert}}^{(12)}$; $A_x^{(m)}$ $q_x^{(2)}$; $_t p_x^{(\tau)}$
$\{m\}$; $\{12\}$	An alphanumeric character in braces shows the number of apportionable annuity-due payments in a time period, usually 1 year. On a principal symbol of a premium or a reserve, it shows that premiums are paid on this basis.	$\ddot{a}_{30:\overline{20\vert}}^{\{12\}}$; $P_{30}^{\{1\}}$ $_t V^{\{2\}}(\bar{A}_x)$
r; i	An alphabetic character indicates the special basis used for the actuarial present value.	$\ddot{a}_{65}^r$; $\ddot{a}_{\{x\}}^i$

Section VI.   Upper Space to the Left

Auxiliary Symbol	Description	Examples
h; 2	Alphanumeric character indicating the number of years during which premiums are paid if this is less than the coverage period of the insurance or the deferral period of the deferred annuity. This is used only on the principal symbols V or W where Position III is used for the time for which the function is evaluated.	${}_{5}^{h}V_{30}$
	In this text a new use for this position is to show that the actuarial present value of an annuity or an insurance is calculated at a multiple of the assumed force of interest.	${}^{2}\bar{A}_{x}$; ${}^{2}\ddot{a}_{20:\overline{10}|}$

Appendix 5

SOME MATHEMATICAL FORMULAS USEFUL IN ACTUARIAL MATHEMATICS

The purpose here is not to recall familiar standard formulas and techniques, but to indicate some that may be less familiar to actuarial students.

Calculus

If

$$F(t) = \int_{\alpha(t)}^{\beta(t)} f(x, t)\, dx,$$

then

$$\frac{dF(t)}{dt} = \int_{\alpha(t)}^{\beta(t)} \frac{\partial}{\partial t} f(x, t)\, dx + f(\beta(t), t)\, \frac{d}{dt}\, \beta(t)$$

$$- f(\alpha(t), t)\, \frac{d}{dt}\, \alpha(t).$$

Calculus of Finite Differences

Operators

a. Shift:

$$E[f(x)] = f(x + 1)$$

b. Difference:

$$\Delta f(x) = f(x + 1) - f(x) = (E - 1)f(x)$$

c. Repeated differences:

$$\Delta^n f(x) = \Delta[\Delta^{n-1} f(x)]$$

$$= (E - 1)^n f(x)$$

$$= \sum_{k=0}^{n} \binom{n}{k}(-1)^{n-k} f(x + k)$$

d. Difference of a product:

$$\Delta[f(x)\,g(x)] = f(x+1)\,\Delta g(x) + g(x)\,\Delta f(x)$$

e. Antidifference:

If

$$\Delta f(x) = g(x),$$

then

$$\Delta^{-1}\,g(x) = f(x) + w(x)$$

where

$$w(x) = w(x+1).$$

Applications

a. Representation of a polynomial (Newton's formula): Let $p_n(x)$ be a polynomial of degree n; then

$$p_n(x) = \sum_{k=0}^{n} \binom{x-a}{k} \Delta^k p_n(a).$$

b. Summation of series:

If

$$\Delta F(x) = f(x),$$

then

$$f(1) = F(2) - F(1)$$
$$f(2) = F(3) - F(2)$$

$$\cdot$$
$$\cdot$$
$$\cdot$$

$$f(n) = F(n+1) - F(n)$$

$$\sum_{x=1}^{n} f(x) = F(n+1) - F(1) = \Delta^{-1} f(x) \Big|_{1}^{n+1}.$$

c. Summation by parts:

$$\sum_{x=1}^{n} g(x)\,\Delta f(x) = f(x)\,g(x)\Big|_{1}^{n+1} - \Delta^{-1}[f(x+1)\,\Delta g(x)]\Big|_{1}^{n+1}$$

[Proof: Sum each side of the equation for $\Delta[f(x)g(x)]$ from $x = 1$ to $x = n$.]

Probability Distributions

Discrete Distributions	p.f.	Restrictions on Parameters	Moment Generating Function, $M(s)$	Moments Mean	Moments Variance
Binomial	$\binom{n}{x}p^x q^{n-x}$, $x = 0, 1, \ldots, n$	$0 < p < 1$ $q = 1 - p$	$(pe^s + q)^n$	np	npq
Bernoulli	Special case $n = 1$				
Negative Binomial	$\binom{r+x-1}{x}p^r q^x$, $x = 0, 1, 2, \ldots$	$0 < p < 1$ $q = 1 - p$ $r > 0$	$\left(\dfrac{p}{1 - qe^s}\right)^r$, $qe^s < 1$	$\dfrac{rq}{p}$	$\dfrac{rq}{p^2}$
Geometric	Special case $r = 1$				
Poisson	$\dfrac{e^{-\lambda}\lambda^x}{x!}$, $x = 0, 1, 2, \ldots$	$\lambda > 0$	$e^{\lambda(e^s - 1)}$	λ	λ
Uniform	$\dfrac{1}{n}$, $x = 1, \ldots, n$	n, a positive integer	$\dfrac{e^s(1 - e^{sn})}{n(1 - e^s)}$, $s \neq 0$ $\quad\quad 1, s = 0$	$\dfrac{n + 1}{2}$	$\dfrac{n^2 - 1}{12}$

Continuous Distributions	p.d.f.	Restrictions on Parameters	Moment Generating Function, $M(s)$	Moments	
				Mean	Variance
Uniform	$\dfrac{1}{b-a}, \ a < x < b$	—	$\dfrac{e^{bs} - e^{as}}{(b-a)s}, \ s \neq 0$ $1, \ s = 0$	$\dfrac{b+a}{2}$	$\dfrac{(b-a)^2}{12}$
Normal	$\dfrac{1}{\sigma\sqrt{2\pi}} \exp[-(x-\mu)^2/2\sigma^2],$ $-\infty < x < \infty$	$\sigma > 0$	$\exp(\mu s + \sigma^2 s^2/2)$	μ	σ^2
Gamma	$\dfrac{\beta^\alpha}{\Gamma(\alpha)} x^{\alpha-1} e^{-\beta x}, \ x > 0$	$\alpha > 0, \beta > 0$	$\left(\dfrac{\beta}{\beta - s}\right)^\alpha, \ s < \beta$	$\dfrac{\alpha}{\beta}$	$\dfrac{\alpha}{\beta^2}$
Exponential	Special case $\alpha = 1$				
Chi-square	Special case $\alpha = \dfrac{k}{2}, \ \beta = \dfrac{1}{2}$	k, a positive integer			
Inverse Gaussian	$\dfrac{\alpha}{\sqrt{2\pi\beta}} x^{-3/2} \exp\left[-\dfrac{(\beta x - \alpha)^2}{2\beta x}\right],$ $x > 0$	$\alpha > 0, \beta > 0$	$\exp\left[\alpha\left(1 - \sqrt{1 - \dfrac{2s}{\beta}}\right)\right],$ $s < \dfrac{\beta}{2}$	$\dfrac{\alpha}{\beta}$	$\dfrac{\alpha}{\beta^2}$
Pareto	$\alpha x_0^\alpha / x^{\alpha+1}, \ x > x_0$	$x_0 > 0, \alpha > 0$		$\dfrac{\alpha x_0}{\alpha - 1}$ $\alpha > 1$	$\dfrac{\alpha x_0^2}{(\alpha - 2)(\alpha - 1)^2}$ $\alpha > 2$
Lognormal	$\dfrac{1}{x\sigma\sqrt{2\pi}} \exp[-(\log x - m)^2/2\sigma^2],$ $x > 0$	$-\infty < m < \infty$ $\sigma > 0$		$e^{m+\sigma^2/2}$	$(e^{\sigma^2} - 1)e^{2m+\sigma^2}$

Appendix 6

BIBLIOGRAPHY

Actuarial Society of America. 1947. "International Actuarial Notation," *Transactions of the Actuarial Society of America* XLVIII:166–76.

Allen, J. M. 1907. "On the Relation between the Theories of Compound Interest and Life Contingencies," *Journal of the Institute of Actuaries* 41:305–37.

Allison, G. O., and Winklevoss, H. E. 1975. "The Interrelationship among Inflation Rates, Interest Rates, and Pension Costs," *Transactions of the Society of Actuaries* XXVII:197–210.

Anderson, J. C. H. 1959. "Gross Premium Calculations and Profit Measurement for Nonparticipating Insurance," *Transactions of the Society of Actuaries* XI:357–94.

Arrow, K. J. 1963. "Uncertainty and the Welfare of Medical Care," *American Economic Review* 53:941–73.

Balducci, G. 1921. Correspondence. *Journal of the Institute of Actuaries* 52:184.

Bartlett, D. K. 1965. "Excess Ratio Distributions in Risk Theory," *Transactions of the Society of Actuaries* XVII:435–63.

Batten, R. W. 1978. *Mortality Table Construction.* Englewood Cliffs, N.J.: Prentice Hall.

Beard, R. E., Pentikäinen, T., and Pesonen, E. 1984. *Risk Theory.* 3rd ed. New York: Chapman & Hall.

Becker, D. N. 1991. "Statistical Tests of the Lognormal Distribution as a Basis for Interest Rate Changes," *Transactions of the Society of Actuaries* XLIII:7–57.

Beekman, J. A. 1969. "A Ruin Function Approximation," *Transactions of the Society of Actuaries* XXI:41–48.

Beekman, J. A. 1974. *Two Stochastic Processes.* New York: Halsted Press.

Beekman, J. A., and Bowers, N. L. 1972. "An Approximation to the Finite Time Ruin Function," *Skandinavisk Aktuarietidskrift* 41–56, 128–37.

Bellhouse, D. R., and Panjer, H. H. 1980. "Stochastic Modelling of Interest Rates with Applications to Life Contingencies," *Journal of Risk and Insurance* 47:91–110.

Bellman, R. E., Kalaba, R. E., and Lockett, J. 1966. *Numerical Inversion of the Laplace Transform: Applications to Biology, Economics, Engineering, and Physics.* New York: American Elsevier.

Bicknell, W. S., and Nesbitt, C. J. 1956. "Premiums and Reserves in Multiple Decrement Theory," *Transactions of the Society of Actuaries* VIII:344–77.

Biggs, J. H. 1969. "Alternatives in Variable Annuity Benefit Design," *Transactions of the Society of Actuaries* XXI:495–517.

Black, F., and Scholes, M. 1973. "The Pricing of Options and Corporate Liabilities," *Journal of Political Economy* 81:637–59.

Boermeester, J. M. 1956. "Frequency Distribution of Mortality Costs," *Transactions of the Society of Actuaries* VIII:1–9.

Bohman, H., and Esscher F. 1963, 1964. "Studies in Risk Theory with Numerical Illustrations Concerning Distribution Functions and Stop-Loss Premiums," *Skandinavisk Aktuarietidskrift* 173–225, 1–40.

Borch, K. 1960. "An Attempt to Determine the Optimum Amount of Stop-Loss Reinsurance," *Transactions of the 16th International Congress of Actuaries* I:597–610.

Borch, K. 1974. *The Mathematical Theory of Insurance.* Lexington, Mass.: Lexington Books.

Bowers, N. L. 1966. "Expansions of Probability Density Functions as a Sum of Gamma Densities with Applications in Risk Theory," *Transactions of the Society of Actuaries* XVIII:125–37.

Bowers, N. L. 1967. "An Approximation to the Distribution of Annuity Costs," *Transactions of the Society of Actuaries* XIX:295–309.

Bowers, N. L. 1969. "An Upper Bound for the Net Stop-Loss Premium," *Transactions of the Society of Actuaries* XXI:211–18.

Bowers, N. L., Jr., Hickman, J. C., and Nesbitt, C. J. 1976. "Introduction to the Dynamics of Pension Funding," *Transactions of the Society of Actuaries* XXVIII: 177–203.

Bowers, N. L., Jr., Hickman, J. C., and Nesbitt, C. J. 1979. "The Dynamics of Pension Funding: Contribution Theory," *Transactions of the Society of Actuaries* XXXI: 93–119.

Boyle, P. P. 1992. *Options and the Management of Financial Risk.* Schaumburg, Ill.: Society of Actuaries.

Brenner, H. F., et al. 1988. *Life Insurance Accounting.* Durham, N.C.: Insurance Accounting and Systems Association.

Brillinger, D. R. 1961. "A Justification of Some Common Laws of Mortality," *Transactions of the Society of Actuaries* XIII:116–19.

Buchta, C. 1994. "An Elementary Proof of the Schuette-Nesbitt Formula," *Bulletin of the Swiss Association of Actuaries* 219–20.

Bühlmann, H. 1970. *Mathematical Methods in Risk Theory.* New York: Springer.

Carriere, J. F. 1994. "Dependent Decrement Theory," *Transactions of the Society of Actuaries* XLVI:45–65.

Chalke, S. A. 1991. "Macro Pricing: A Comprehensive Product Development Process," *Transactions of the Society of Actuaries* XLIII:137–94.

Chalke, S. A., and Davlin, M. F. 1983. "Universal Life Valuation and Nonforfeiture: A Generalized Model," *Transactions of the Society of Actuaries* XXXV:249–98.

Chamberlin, G. 1982. "The Proficient Instrument—a New Appraisal of the Commutation Function in the Context of Pension Fund Work," *Journal of the Institute of Actuaries Students' Society* 25:1–46.

Chapin, W. L. 1976. "Toward Adjustable Individual Life Policies," *Transactions of the Society of Actuaries* XXVIII:237–69.

Chiang, C. L. 1968. *Introduction to Stochastic Processes in Biostatistics.* New York: John Wiley and Sons.

Christiansen, S. L. 1992. "A Practical Guide to Interest Rate Generators for C-3 Risk," *Transactions of the Society of Actuaries* XLIV:101–34.

Cody, D. D. 1981. "An Expanded Financial Structure for Ordinary Dividends," *Transactions of the Society of Actuaries* XXXIII:313–38.

Committee on Ordinary Insurance and Annuities. 1982. "II. 1975–80 Basic Tables with Appendix of Age-Last Birthday Basic Tables," *TSA 1982 Reports* 56–81.

Cramér, H. 1930. *On the Mathematical Theory of Risk.* Stockholm: Centraltryckeriet.

Cummins, J. D. 1973. *Development of Life Insurance Surrender Values in the United States.* Homewood, Ill.: Richard D. Irwin.

DeGroot, M. H. 1970. *Optimal Statistical Decisions.* New York: McGraw-Hill.

DeGroot, M. H. 1986. *Probability and Statistics.* 2nd ed. Reading, Mass.: Addison-Wesley.

DeVylder, F. 1977. "Martingales and Ruin in a Dynamic Risk Process," *Scandinavian Actuarial Journal* 217–25.

Dropkin, L. B. 1959. "Some Considerations in Automobile Rating Systems Utilizing Individual Driving Records," *Proceedings of the Casualty Actuarial Society* XLVI: 165–76.

Dubourdieu, J. 1952. *Théorie Mathématique des Assurances.* Paris: Gauthier Villars.

Duncan, R. M. 1952. "A Retirement System Granting Unit Annuities and Investing in Equities," *Transactions of the Society of Actuaries* IV:317–44.

Elandt-Johnson, R. C., and Johnson, N. L. 1980. *Survival Models and Data Analysis.* New York: John Wiley and Sons.

Fama, E. F. 1970. "Efficient Capital Markets: A Review of Theory and Empirical Work," *Journal of Finance* 25:383–417.

Fassel, E. G. 1956. "Premium Rates Varying by Policy Size," *Transactions of the Society of Actuaries* VIII:390–419.

Feller, W. 1966. *An Introduction to Probability Theory and Its Applications.* Vol. II. New York: John Wiley and Sons.

Feller, W. 1968. *An Introduction to Probability Theory and Its Applications.* Vol. I. 3rd ed. New York: John Wiley and Sons.

Fraser, J. C., Miller, W. N., and Sternhell, C. M. 1969. "Analysis of Basic Actuarial Theory for Fixed Premium Variable Benefit Life Insurance," *Transactions of the Society of Actuaries* XXI:343–78, and discussions 379–457.

Frasier, W. M. 1978. "Second to Die Joint Life Cash Values and Reserves," *The Actuary* 12:3.

Frees, E. W. 1990. "Stochastic Life Contingencies with Solvency Considerations," *Transactions of the Society of Actuaries* XLII:91–129.

Frees, E. W., Carriere, J. F., and Valdez, E. 1996. "Annuity Valuation with Dependent Mortality," *Journal of Risk and Insurance* 63:229–61.

Fretwell, R. L., and Hickman, J. C. 1964. "Approximate Probability Statements about Life Annuity Costs," *Transactions of the Society of Actuaries* XVI:55–60.

Friedman, M., and Savage, L. J. 1948. "The Utility Analysis of Choices Involving Risk," *Journal of Political Economy* 56:279–304.

Genest, C. 1987. "Frank's Family of Bivariate Distributions," *Biometrika* CXXIV: 549–55.

Geoghegan, T. J., et al. 1992. "Report on the Wilkie Stochastic Investment Model," *Journal of the Institute of Actuaries* 119, Part II, No. 473:173–228.

Gerber, H. U. 1973. "Martingales in Risk Theory," *Mitteilungen der Vereinigung Schweizerischer Versicherungsmathematiker* LXXIII:205–16.

Gerber, H. U. 1974. "The Dilemma between Dividends and Safety and a Generalization of the Lundberg-Cramér Formulas," *Scandinavian Actuarial Journal* 46–57.

Gerber, H. U. 1976. "A Probabilistic Model for (Life) Contingencies and a Delta-Free Approach to Contingency Reserves," *Transactions of the Society of Actuaries* XXVIII:127–41.

Gerber, H. U. 1979. *An Introduction to Mathematical Risk Theory.* Huebner Foundation Monograph 8, distributed by Richard D. Irwin, Homewood, Ill.

Gerber, H. U. 1980. "Principles of Premium Calculation and Reinsurance," *Transactions of the 21st International Congress of Actuaries* I:137–42.

Gerber, H. U., and Jones, D. A. 1977. "Some Practical Considerations in Connection with the Calculation of Stop-Loss Premiums," *Transactions of the Society of Actuaries* XXVIII:215–32.

Gerber, H. U., and Shiu, E. S. 1998. "On the Time Value of Ruin," *North American Actuarial Journal* 2, no. 1 (January):48–78.

Giaccotto, C. 1986. "Stochastic Modelling of Interest Rates: Actuarial vs. Equilibrium Approach," *Journal of Risk and Insurance* 53:435–53.

Gingery, S. W. 1952. "Special Investigation of Group Hospital Expense Insurance Experience," *Transactions of the Society of Actuaries* IV:44–112.

Goovaerts, M. J., and DeVylder, F. 1980. "Upper Bounds on Stop-Loss Premiums under Constraints on Claim Size Distributions as Derived from Representation Theorems for Distribution Functions," *Scandinavian Actuarial Journal* 141–48.

Greenwood, M., and Yule, G. U. 1920. "An Inquiry into the Nature of Frequency Distributions Representative of Multiple Happenings with Particular Reference to the Occurrence of Multiple Attacks of Disease or Repeated Accidents," *Journal of the Royal Statistical Society* LXXXIII:255–79.

Greville, T. N. E. 1948. "Mortality Tables Analyzed by Cause of Death," *Record of the American Institute of Actuaries* XXXVII:283–94. Discussion in XXXVIII (1949): 77–79.

Greville, T. N. E. 1956. "Laws of Mortality Which Satisfy a Uniform Seniority Principle," *Journal of the Institute of Actuaries* 82:114–22.

Guertin, A. N. 1965. "Life Insurance Premiums," *Journal of Risk and Insurance* 32: 23–50.

Halmstad, D. G. 1972. "Underwriting the Catastrophe Accident Hazard," *Transactions of the Society of Actuaries* XXIV:D408–18.

Halmstad, D. G. 1976. "Exact Numerical Procedures in Discrete Risk Theory," *Transactions of the 20th International Congress of Actuaries* III:557–62.

Hattendorf, K. 1868. "The Risk with Life Assurance," E. A. Masius's *Rundschau der Versicherungen* (Review of Insurances), Leipzig; translated by Trevor Sibbett and reprinted in *Life Insurance Mathematics,* Vol. IV, Part 2 of *History of Actuarial Science,* edited by Steven Haberman and Trevor Sibbett. London: William Pickering, 1995.

Hickman, J. C. 1964. "A Statistical Approach to Premiums and Reserves in Multiple Decrement Theory," *Transactions of the Society of Actuaries* XVI:1–16.

Hoem, J. M. 1988. "The Versatility of the Markov Chain as a Tool in the Mathematics of Life Insurance," *Transactions of the 23rd International Congress of Actuaries,* Record of Proceedings 171–202.

Hogg, R. V., and Klugman, S. A. 1984. *Loss Distributions.* New York: John Wiley and Sons.

Hooker, P. F., and Longley-Cook, L. H. 1953. *Life and Other Contingencies.* Vol. I. Cambridge: Cambridge University Press.

Hooker, P. F., and Longley-Cook, L. H. 1957. *Life and Other Contingencies.* Vol. II. Cambridge: Cambridge University Press.

Horn, R. G. 1971. "Life Insurance Earnings and the Release from Risk Policy Reserve," *Transactions of the Society of Actuaries* XXIII:391–99.

Hoskins, J. E. 1929. "A New Method of Computing Non-Participating Premiums," *Transactions of the Actuarial Society of America* XXX:140–66.

Hoskins, J. E. 1939. "Asset Shares and Their Relation to Nonforfeiture Values," *Transactions of the Actuarial Society of America* XL:379–93.

Huffman, P. J. 1978. "Asset Share Mathematics," *Transactions of the Society of Actuaries* XXX:277–96.

Institute of Actuaries, Faculty of Actuaries, 1992, *Standard Tables of Mortality: The "80" Series.* Institute of Actuaries, Staple Inn Hall, High Holborn, London WCIV7QJ, U.K.; Faculty of Actuaries, 23 St. Andrew Square, Edinburgh EH21AQ, U.K.

Jackson, R. T. 1959. "Some Observations on Ordinary Dividends," *Transactions of the Society of Actuaries* XI:764–96.

Jenkins, W. A. 1943. "An Analysis of Self-Selection, among Annuitants, Including Comparisons with Selection among Insured Lives," *Transactions of the Actuarial Society of America* XLIV:227–39.

Jetton, M. F. 1988. "Interest Rate Scenarios," *Transactions of the Society of Actuaries* XL, Part I:423–37.

Jones, B. L. 1994. "Actuarial Calculations Using a Markov Model," *Transactions of the Society of Actuaries* XLVI:227–50.

Jordan, C. W. 1952. *Life Contingencies.* 2nd ed., 1967. Schaumburg, Ill.: Society of Actuaries.

Kahn, P. M. 1961. "Some Remarks on a Recent Paper by Borch," *ASTIN Bulletin* I:265–72.

Kahn, P. M. 1962. "An Introduction to Collective Risk Theory and Its Application to Stop-Loss Reinsurance," *Transactions of the Society of Actuaries* XIV:400–425.

Keller, J. B. 1990. "Pricing of Accelerated Benefit Plans," *Transactions of the Society of Actuaries* XLII:259–80.

Kendall, M., and Stuart, A. 1977. *The Advanced Theory of Statistics*. Vol. I. New York: Macmillan.

Keyfitz, N. 1968. *Introduction to the Mathematics of Population*. Reading, Mass.: Addison-Wesley.

Keyfitz, N. 1977. *Applied Mathematical Demography*. New York: John Wiley and Sons.

Keyfitz, N., and Beekman, J. 1984. *Demography through Problems*. New York: Springer.

King, G. 1887. *Institute of Actuaries' Textbook*. Part II. 2nd ed., 1902. London: Charles and Edwin Layton.

Kischuk, R. K. 1976. Discussion of "Fundamentals of Pension Funding," *Transactions of the Society of Actuaries* XXVIII:205–11.

Klein, G. E. 1993. "The Sensitivity of Cash-Flow Analysis to the Choice of Statistical Model for Interest Rate Changes," *Transactions of the Society of Actuaries* XLV: 79–124.

Kornya, P. S. 1983. "Distribution of Aggregate Claims in the Individual Risk Theory Model," *Transactions of the Society of Actuaries* XXXV:823–36.

Lauer, J. A. 1967. "Apportionable Basis for Net Premiums and Reserves," *Transactions of the Society of Actuaries* XIX:13–23.

Linton, M. A. 1919. "Analysis of the Endowment Premium," *Transactions of the Actuarial Society of America* XX:430–39.

London, D. 1988. *Survival Models and Their Estimation*. Winsted, Conn.: ACTEX Publications.

Lukacs, E. 1948. "On the Mathematical Theory of Risk," *Journal of the Institute of Actuaries Students' Society* 8:20–37.

Lundberg, O. 1940. *On Random Processes and Their Application to Sickness and Accident Statistics*. Uppsala: Almqvist and Wiksells.

Macarchuk, J. 1969. "Some Observations on the Actuarial Aspects of the Insured Variable Annuity," *Transactions of the Society of Actuaries* XXI:529–38.

Maclean, J. B., and Marshall, E. W. 1937. *Distribution of Surplus*. Schaumburg, Ill.: Society of Actuaries.

Makeham, W. M. 1874. "On the Application of the Theory of the Composition of Decremental Forces," *Journal of the Institute of Actuaries* 18:317–22.

Marshall, A. W., and Olkin, I. 1967, "A Multivariate Exponential Distribution," *Journal of the American Statistical Association* 62:30–44.

Marshall, A. W., and Olkin, I. 1988. "Families of Multivariate Distributions," *Journal of the American Statistical Association* 83:834–41.

McCrory, R. T. 1984. "Mortality Risk in Life Annuities," *Transactions of the Society of Actuaries* XXXVI:309–38.

Menge, W. O. 1932. "Forces of Decrement in a Multiple-Decrement Table," *Record of the American Institute of Actuaries* XXI:41–46.

Menge, W. O. 1946. "Commissioners Reserve Valuation Method," *Record of the American Institute of Actuaries* XXXV:258–300.

Mereu, J. A. 1961. "Some Observations on Actuarial Approximations," *Transactions of the Society of Actuaries* XIII:87–102.

Mereu, J. A. 1962. "Annuity Values Directly from Makeham Constants," *Transactions of the Society of Actuaries* XIV:269–86.

Mereu, J. A. 1972. "An Algorithm for Computing Expected Stop-Loss Claims under a Group Life Contract," *Transactions of the Society of Actuaries* XXIV:311–20.

Miller, M. D. 1951. "Group Weekly Indemnity Continuation Table Study," *Transactions of the Society of Actuaries* III:31–67.

Miller, W. N. 1971. "Variable Life Insurance Product Design," *Journal of Risk and Insurance* 38:527–42.

Mood, A. M., Graybill, F. A., and Boes, D. C. 1974. *Introduction to the Theory of Statistics*. New York: McGraw-Hill.

Myers, R. J. 1960. "Actuarial Analysis of Pension Plans under Inflationary Conditions," *Transactions of the 16th International Congress of Actuaries* I:301–15.

National Association of Insurance Commissioners. 1939. "Report of the Committee to Study the Need for a New Mortality Table and Related Topics." Kansas City: National Association of Insurance Commissioners.

National Association of Insurance Commissioners. 1941. "Report and Statements on Nonforfeiture Benefits and Related Matters." Kansas City: National Association of Insurance Commissioners.

Neill, A. 1977. *Life Contingencies*. London: Heinemann.

Nesbitt, C. J. 1964. Discussion of "A Statistical Approach to Premiums and Reserves in Multiple Decrement Theory," *Transactions of the Society of Actuaries* XV:149–53.

Nesbitt, C. J., and Van Eenam, M. L. 1948. "Rate Functions and Their Role in Actuarial Mathematics," *Record of the American Institute of Actuaries* XXXVII: 202–22.

Panjer, H. H. 1980. "The Aggregate Claims Distribution and Stop-Loss Reinsurance," *Transactions of the Society of Actuaries* XXXII:523–35.

Panjer, H. H., and Willmot, G. E. 1992. *Insurance Risk Models*. Schaumburg, Ill.: Society of Actuaries.

Pesonen, E. 1967. "On the Calculation of the Generalized Poisson Function," *ASTIN Bulletin* IV:120–28.

Pratt, J. W. 1964. "Risk Aversion in the Small and in the Large," *Econometrica* XXXII: 122–36.

Preston, S. H., Keyfitz, N., and Schoen, R. 1973. "Cause-of-Death Life Tables: Application of a New Technique to Worldwide Data," *Transactions of the Society of Actuaries* XXV:83–109.

Promislow, S. D. 1991a. "The Probability of Ruin in a Process with Dependent Increments," *Insurance: Mathematics and Economics* X:99–107.

Promislow, S. D. 1991b. "Select and Ultimate Models in Multiple Decrement Theory," *Transactions of the Society of Actuaries* XLIII:281–300.

Rasor, E. A., and Greville, T. N. E. 1952. "Complete Annuities," *Transactions of the Society of Actuaries* IV:574–82.

Rasor, E. A., and Myers, R. J. 1952. "Actuarial Note: Valuation of the Shares in a Share-and-Share-Alike Last Survivor Annuity," *Transactions of the Society of Actuaries* IV:128–30.

Redington, F. M. 1952. "A Review of the Principles of Life Office Valuation," *Journal of the Institute of Actuaries* LXXVII:286–340.

Renyi, A. 1962. *Wahrscheinlichkeitsrechnung*. Berlin: Deutscher Verlag der Wissenschaften.

Reynolds, Craig W. 1994. "Last Survivor Antiselection," *Product Development News*, Feb. Issue. Society of Actuaries.

Richardson, C. F. B. 1977. "Expense Formulas for Minimum Nonforfeiture Values," *Transactions of the Society of Actuaries* XXIX:222–29.

Robinson, J. M. 1984. Discussion of "Maximum Likelihood Alternatives to Actuarial Estimators of Mortality Rates," *Transactions of the Society of Actuaries* XXXVI: 125–38.

Scher, E. 1974. "Relationships among the Fully Continuous, the Discounted Continuous, and the Semicontinuous Reserve Bases for Ordinary Life Insurance," *Transactions of the Society of Actuaries* XXVI:597–606.

Seal, H. L. 1969. *Stochastic Theory of a Risk Business.* New York: John Wiley and Sons.

Seal, H. L. 1977. "Studies in the History of Probability and Statistics—Multiple Decrements or Competing Risks," *Biometrika* LXIV:429–39.

Seal, H. L. 1978a. "From Aggregate Claims Distribution to Probability of Ruin," *ASTIN Bulletin* X:47–53.

Seal, H. L. 1978b. *Survival Probabilities—The Goal of Risk Theory.* New York: John Wiley and Sons.

Shepherd, B. E. 1940. "Natural Reserves," *Transactions of the Actuarial Society of America* XLI:463–79.

Shiu, E. S. W. 1982. "Integer Functions and Life Contingencies," *Transactions of the Society of Actuaries* XXXIV:571–90.

Simon, L. J. 1960. "The Negative Binomial and the Poisson Distributions Compared," *Proceedings of the Casualty Actuarial Society* XLVII:20–24.

Society of Actuaries Committee on Actuarial Principles. 1992. "Principles of Actuarial Science," *Transactions of the Society of Actuaries* XLIV:565–91.

Special Committee on Valuation and Nonforfeiture Laws. 1975. "Report on Actuarial Principles and Practical Problems with Regard to Nonforfeiture Requirements," *Transactions of the Society of Actuaries* XXVII:549–633.

Spurgeon, E. F. 1922. 2nd ed., 1929. 3rd ed., 1932. *Life Contingencies.* Cambridge: Cambridge University Press.

Steffensen, J. F. 1929. "On Hattendorf's Theorem in the Theory of Risk," *Skandinavisk Aktuarietidskrift* 1–17.

Takács, L. 1967. *Combinatorial Methods in the Theory of Stochastic Processes.* New York: John Wiley and Sons.

Taylor, G. C. 1977. "Upper Bounds on Stop-Loss Premiums under Constraints on Claim Size Distributions," *Scandinavian Actuarial Journal* 94–105.

Taylor, R. H. 1952. "The Probability Distribution of Life Annuity Reserves and Its Application to a Pension System," *Proceedings of the Conference of Actuaries in Public Practice* II:100–150.

Tenenbein, A., and Vanderhoof, I. T. 1980. "New Mathematical Laws of Select and Ultimate Mortality," *Transactions of the Society of Actuaries* XXXII:119–58.

Thompson, J. S. 1934. "Select and Ultimate Mortality," *Transactions of the 10th International Congress of Actuaries* II:252–63.

Tilley, J. A. 1992. "An Actuarial Layman's Guide to Building Interest Rate Generators," *Transactions of the Society of Actuaries* XLIV:509–38.

Trowbridge, C. L. 1952. "Fundamentals of Pension-Funding," *Transactions of the Society of Actuaries* IV:17–43.

Trowbridge, C. L. 1955. "Funding of Group Life Insurance," *Transactions of the Society of Actuaries* VII:270–84.

Trowbridge, C. L. 1963. "The Unfunded Present Value Family of Pension Funding Methods," *Transactions of the Society of Actuaries* XV:151–69.

Trowbridge, J. R. 1977. "Assessmentism—An Alternative to Pensions Funding?" *Journal of the Institute of Actuaries* 104:173–204.

Tullis, M. A., and Polkinghorn, P, K. 1992. *Valuation of Life Insurance Liabilities.* 2nd ed. Winsted, Conn.: ACTEX Publications.

U.S. Department of Health and Welfare. Public Health Service. 1985. *United States Life Tables: 1979–81.* Washington, D.C.: Government Printing Office.

Vanderhoof, I. T. 1972. "The Interest Rate Assumption and the Maturity Structure of the Assets of a Life Insurance," *Transactions of the Society of Actuaries* XXIV: 157–92.

White, R. P., and Greville, T. N. E. 1959. "On Computing the Probability that Exactly k of n Independent Events Will Occur," *Transactions of the Society of Actuaries* XI:88–95.

Wilkie, A. D. 1986. "A Stochastic Investment Model for Actuarial Use," *Transactions of the Faculty of Actuaries* 39, Part 3:341–73.

Willett, A. H. 1951. *The Economic Theory of Risk and Insurance.* Philadelphia: University of Pennsylvania Press.

Williamson, W. R. 1942. "Selection," *Transactions of the Actuarial Society of America* XLIII:33–43.

Wittstein, T. 1873. "On Mathematical Statistics and Its Applications to Political Economy and Insurances," *Journal of the Institute of Actuaries and Assurance Magazine* XVII:178–89, 355–69, 417–35.

Wooddy, J. 1973. *Study Notes for Risk Theory.* Schaumburg, Ill.: Society of Actuaries.

Appendix 7

ANSWERS TO EXERCISES

Chapter 1

1.1. a. and b.

w	$u(w)$	$u(w_1,w_2)$	$u(w_1,w_2,w_3)$
0	-1.00	125×10^{-6}	-48×10^{-10}
4 000	-0.500	93×10^{-6}	-34×10^{-10}
6 700	-0.250	78×10^{-6}	-14×10^{-10}
8 300	-0.125	74×10^{-6}	—
10 000	0.000	—	—

1.2. b. 2, 2 d. 2 log 2

1.3. c. Var(X)

1.7. a. Yes, for all w b. $(90 < w < 100) \cup (w > 110)$

1.11. $-\dfrac{n}{2\alpha} \log (1 - 2\alpha)$

1.12. a. $G = 400 \log \dfrac{13}{12} = 32.02$ b. $G = 150 \log \dfrac{3}{2} = 60.82$

1.13. a. 30 b. 26

1.14. Complete insurance

1.17. a. $-[1 - F(d)]$

1.18. a. 10, 100

1.19. a. 50, $\dfrac{2,500}{3}$ b. $k = 0.25, d = 50$

     c. Var$[X - I_1(X)] = 468.75$, Var$[X - I_2(X)] = 260.42$

Chapter 2

2.1. $\dfrac{1}{2}, \dfrac{19}{4}$

2.2. $\dfrac{1}{2}, \dfrac{77}{12}$

2.3. $\dfrac{35}{4}, \dfrac{1{,}085}{48}$

2.4. $\dfrac{7}{4}, \dfrac{77}{48}$

2.5. $\dfrac{49}{4}, \dfrac{735}{16}$

2.6. $\dfrac{a}{100}$ and $a^2\left(\dfrac{197}{30{,}000}\right)$

2.7.

x	$F_S(x)$
0	0.2268
1	0.2916
2	0.4374
3	0.6210
4	0.7434
5	0.8586
6	0.9018
7	0.9582
8	0.9762
9	0.9918
10	0.9948
11	0.9988
12	0.9996
13	1.0000

2.8. c. $\dfrac{1}{48}, \dfrac{1}{6}, \dfrac{1}{2}$

2.9. $E[X] = \dfrac{\alpha}{\beta}, \ Var(X) = \dfrac{\alpha}{\beta^2}$

2.10. $E[X] = 1, Var(X) = \dfrac{1}{3}; E[Y] = \dfrac{3}{2}, Var(Y) = \dfrac{3}{4}; Pr(X + Y > 4) \cong 0.0748;$ $Pr(X + Y > 4) = 0.0833$

2.11. a. $b = -1, c = 1, d = a$ or $b = 1, c = 0, d = -a$
   b. 0.0228, 0.1587, 0.5000

2.12. a. 18, 36   b. 27.8713, 31.9607

2.13. a. 0.0041   b. 0.0045

2.14. 3.56; that is, 35,600

2.15. a. 6.4, 6.144   b. $7(10^4), 17.072(10^8)$ c. 1.37341

2.16. 0.0062

3.1.

s(x)	F(x)	f(x)	μ(x)
$\cos x$	$1 - \cos x$	$\sin x$	—
—	$1 - e^{-x}$	e^{-x}	1
$\dfrac{1}{1 + x}$	—	$\dfrac{1}{(1 + x)^2}$	$\dfrac{1}{1 + x}$

3.2.   a. $\exp\left[\dfrac{-B}{\log c}\,(c^x - 1)\right]$ b. $\exp(-ux^{n+1})$ $u = \dfrac{k}{n + 1}$

      c. $\left(1 + \dfrac{x}{b}\right)^{-a}$

3.3. $\mu(x) = \dfrac{x^2}{4},\ \ f(x) = \dfrac{x^2}{4}\,e^{-x^3/12},\ \ F(x) = 1 - e^{-x^3/12}$

3.4.   a. $\displaystyle\int_0^\infty \mu(x)\,dx < \infty$ b. $s'(x) > 0$ for some x including $x = 1, 2$

      c. $\displaystyle\int_0^\infty f_X(x)\,dx = 2^n\Gamma(n) > 1$ for $n \geq 1$

3.5.   a. $\dfrac{1}{100 - x}$ b. $\dfrac{x}{100}$ c. $\dfrac{1}{100}$ d. $\dfrac{3}{10}$

3.6.   a. $1 - \dfrac{t}{60}$ b. $\dfrac{1}{60 - t}$ c. $\dfrac{1}{60}$

3.7.   a. $\dfrac{8}{9}$ b. $\dfrac{1}{8}$ c. $\dfrac{1}{8}$ d. $\dfrac{1}{128}$ e. $\dfrac{128}{3}$

3.9.   0.001994

3.10. $f_X(x) = \binom{10}{x}(0.77107)^x(0.22893)^{10-x}$ $x = 0, 1, 2, \ldots, 10$

      $E[\mathcal{L}(x)] = 7.7107,\ \ \mathrm{Var}[\mathcal{L}(x)] = 1.765211$

3.11.   a. $\dfrac{9}{4}$ for each   b. $\dfrac{27}{16}$ for each   c. $-\dfrac{1}{3}$

3.12.   a. $_5q_0 = 0.01505$ is more than 10 times $_5q_5 = 0.001503$
      b. $_{55|5}q_{25} = 0.156729$

3.15.   1,436.19

3.18.   a. $\dfrac{1}{c}$ b. $\dfrac{1}{c^2}$ c. $\dfrac{1}{c}\log 2$ d. 0

3.19.   a. $te^{-t^2/2}$ b. $\sqrt{\dfrac{\pi}{2}}$

3.20.   a. $\dfrac{(100 - x)}{2}$ b. $\dfrac{(100 - x)^2}{12}$ c. $\dfrac{(100 - x)}{2}$

3.23. a. $\mathring{e}_x = \dfrac{10 - x}{2}$ $x = 0, 1, 2, \ldots, 9$

$e_x = \dfrac{9 - x}{2}$ $x = 0, 1, 2, \ldots, 9$

3.24. a. $u(0) = e^{-\lambda}$, $\quad -\dfrac{c(x)}{d(x)} = 0$, $\quad \dfrac{1}{d(x)} = \dfrac{\lambda}{x + 1}$

b. $u(0) = (1 - p)^n$, $\quad -\dfrac{c(x)}{d(x)} = 0$, $\quad \dfrac{1}{d(x)} = \dfrac{(n - x)p}{(x + 1)(1 - p)}$

3.25. a. $u(0) = 0 \quad -\dfrac{c(x)}{d(x)} = 1 \quad \dfrac{1}{d(x)} = v$

b. $u(0) = 0 \quad -\dfrac{c(x)}{d(x)} = 1 + i \quad \dfrac{1}{d(x)} = 1 + i$

3.28. Uniform distribution: 0.989709
Constant force: 0.989656
Balducci: 0.989602

3.29. a. 77.59 b. 29.11

3.30. a. 0.044 b. 0.04421

3.31.

	Uniform Distribution	Constant Force	Balducci
a.	0.012696	0.012616	0.012537
b.	0.013676	0.013770	0.013865
c.	0.013770	0.013770	0.013770

3.35. a. $\dfrac{\alpha}{\omega - x}$ b. $\dfrac{\omega - x}{\alpha + 1}$

3.36. a. 0.000877 b. 0.999189

3.37. a. 0.4076 b. 0.1786

3.39. 0.97920

3.40. $\log\left(1 - \dfrac{q_{[x]}}{2}\right) - \log(1 - q_{[x]})$

3.41. $q'_x < 2q_x$

3.43. a. $\left(\dfrac{1 + Bc^x}{1 + B}\right)^{-A/(B \log c)}$

3.44. a. $\dfrac{5^7}{4^{10}}$ b. 77.2105

3.45. b. $-\log(1 - q_x)$ c. $\dfrac{-q_x^2}{(1 - q_x)\log(1 - q_x)}$ d. $\dfrac{1}{45}$

3.49. $q_{40}^1 = 0.0055547$, $\quad q_{40} = 0.0027812$

3.50. Check value $e_{40} = 35.367$

3.51. $e_{20} = 46.038$, $\quad e_{40} = 28.366$, $\quad e_{60} = 13.264$, $\quad e_{80} = 3.889$, $\quad e_{100} = 0.503$

3.52. Check value $\overset{\circ}{e}_{40} = 35.867$

3.53. Starting value $e_{y:\overline{0}|} = 0$, Check value $e_{25:\overline{20}|} = 19.639$

3.54. Starting value $e_{\omega:\overline{10}|} = 0$, Check value $e_{40:\overline{10}|} = 9.809$

3.55. $e_{15:\overline{25}|} = 24.610$

Chapter 4

4.5. b. $\bar{A}^{1}_{x:\overline{n}|} = \dfrac{\mu_{x+n}}{\delta + \mu_{x+n}} A^{1}_{x:\overline{n}|}$ c. $-\dfrac{\mu_{x+n}}{\delta + \mu_{x+n}} (A^{1}_{x:\overline{n}|})^2$, where n satisfies (b)

   d. $n = \dfrac{\log 2}{\mu + \delta}$, $\min \mathrm{Cov}(Z_1, Z_2) = -\dfrac{\mu}{4(\mu + \delta)}$

4.6. a. 0.237832 b. 0.416667

4.7. a. 0.092099 b. 0.055321

4.8. a. $\dfrac{20}{3(100 - x)}\left[1 - \left(\dfrac{20}{120 - x}\right)^3\right]$,

   $\dfrac{20}{7(100 - x)}\left[1 - \left(\dfrac{20}{120 - x}\right)^7\right] - \left\{\dfrac{20}{3(100 - x)}\left[1 - \left(\dfrac{20}{120 - x}\right)^3\right]\right\}^2$

   b. $\dfrac{20}{3(100 - x)}\left[10 - 10\left(\dfrac{20}{120 - x}\right)^2 - (100 - x)\left(\dfrac{20}{120 - x}\right)^3\right]$

4.10. a. $\dfrac{\mu}{(\mu + \delta)^2}$ b. $\mu\left[\dfrac{2}{(\mu + 2\delta)^3} - \dfrac{\mu}{(\mu + \delta)^4}\right]$

4.11. a. $f_Z(z) = \begin{cases} 0.2\, z^{(-0.8)} & 0 < z < 1 \\ 0.0 & \text{elsewhere} \end{cases}$

   c. $1/6$, $25/396$.

4.12. $F_Z(z) = \begin{cases} 0.0 & z < v^n \\ 1.0 - F_T(\log z / \log v) & v^n \le z < 1 \\ 1.0 & 1 \le z \end{cases}$

4.13. a. $F_Z(z) = \begin{cases} 0.0 & z < e^{(-1.0)} \\ z^{0.2} & e^{(-1.0)} \le z < 1 \\ 1.0 & 1 \le z \end{cases}$

   c. $1/6 + (5/6)e^{(-1.2)}$

4.14. a. 0.407159 b. 5.554541

4.16. a. 0.5 b. 0.05

4.17. b. $(IA)_{x:\overline{m}|} = (IA)^{1}_{x:\overline{m}|} + mA^{1}_{x:\overline{m}|}$

4.19. a. $v^{[k+(j+1)/m]}$ b. $A^{(m)}_x = \displaystyle\sum_{k=0}^{\infty} v^{k+1}\, {}_kp_x \sum_{j=0}^{m-1} {}_{j/m|1/m}q_{x+k}\,(1 + i)^{[1-(j+1)/m]}$

4.23. $A_x + A^{1}_{x:\overline{65-x}|}$

4.24. 4,007.85

4.26. a. $\dfrac{9{,}100}{14 - k}$

   b. $1{,}000{,}000[^2A^{1}_{x:\overline{n}|} - (A^{1}_{x:\overline{n}|})^2] + (k\pi)^2[^2\bar{A}^{1}_{x:\overline{n}|} - (\bar{A}^{1}_{x:\overline{n}|})^2] - 2{,}000\, k\pi\, \bar{A}^{1}_{x:\overline{n}|}\, A^{1}_{x:\overline{n}|}$

   where π is the net single premium in (a)

4.27. a. 0.307215

4.34. a. $A^1_{20:\overline{20}|} = 0.01827$

   $^2A^1_{20:\overline{20}|} = 0.01143$

   b. 110,933,839

4.35. b. $A^1_{\omega:\overline{0}|} = 0.0$

4.36. a. 3.06569   b. $(I\bar{A})_x = (\bar{A}^1_{x:\overline{1}|} + vp_x\,\bar{A}_{x+1}) + vp_x\,(I\bar{A})_{x+1}$, $(I\bar{A})_\omega = 0$

   c. $(\bar{I}\bar{A})_x = [(\bar{I}\bar{A})^1_{x:\overline{1}|} + vp_x\,\bar{A}_{x+1}] + vp_x\,(\bar{I}\bar{A})_{x+1}$, $(\bar{I}\bar{A})_\omega = 0$

   d. $(I\bar{A})_x = (d/\delta)[q_x + p_x\,\bar{A}_{x+1}] + vp_x\,(I\bar{A})_{x+1}$,

   $$(\bar{I}\bar{A})_x = \frac{d}{\delta}\left[\left(\frac{i-\delta}{i\delta}\right)q_x + p_x\,\bar{A}_{x+1}\right] + vp_x\,(\bar{I}\bar{A})_{x+1}$$

4.38. b. $\bar{A}_{y:\overline{0}|} = 1$ c. $\bar{A}_{45:\overline{65-45}|} = 0.34743$

4.39. mean = 38,056.82, variance = 42,337,224.63

Chapter 5

5.1.   a. 16.008, 12.761, 5.397   b. 3.137, 10.230, 9.523

5.2.   a. 0.111, 0.251, 0.572   b. 0.0251

5.4. $-\mathrm{Var}(v^T) = -(^2\bar{A}_x - \bar{A}^2_x)$

5.6.   a. $F_y(y) = \begin{cases} 1 - (1 - \delta y)^{\mu/\delta} & 0 \le y < \dfrac{1}{\delta} \\ 1 & \dfrac{1}{\delta} \le y \end{cases}$

   b. $F_y(y) = \begin{cases} 1 - (1 - \delta y)^{\mu/\delta} & 0 \le y < \bar{a}_{\overline{n}|} \\ 1 & \bar{a}_{\overline{n}|} \le y \end{cases}$

   c. $F_y(y) = \begin{cases} 1 - (v^n - \delta y)^{\mu/\delta} & 0 \le y < \dfrac{v^n}{\delta} \\ 1 & \dfrac{v^n}{\delta} \le y \end{cases}$

   d. $F_y(y) = \begin{cases} 0 & 0 < y \le \bar{a}_{\overline{n}|} \\ 1 - (1 - \delta y)^{\mu/\delta} & \bar{a}_{\overline{n}|} < y < \dfrac{1}{\delta} \\ 1 & \dfrac{1}{\delta} \le y \end{cases}$

5.7. $\bar{a}_{x:\overline{n}|} = \bar{a}_{x:\overline{1}|} - v^n\,_np_x\,\bar{a}_{x+n:\overline{1}|} + vp_x\,\bar{a}_{x+1:\overline{n}|}$ $\begin{array}{l} n = 1, 2, \ldots \\ x = 0, 1, \ldots \end{array}$

   $\bar{a}_{\omega:\overline{n}|} = \bar{a}_{\omega:\overline{1}|}$ which equals $1/2$ by the trapezoidal rule

5.8. $_{n|}\bar{a}_x = v^n\,_np_x\,\bar{a}_{x+n:\overline{1}|} + vp_x\,_{n|}\bar{a}_{x+1}$ $\begin{array}{l} x = 0, 1, \ldots \\ n = 0, 1, 2, \ldots \end{array}$

   $_{n|}\bar{a}_\omega = 0$

5.9. $\bar{a}_{\overline{x:\overline{n}|}} = v^n\,_np_x\,\bar{a}_{x+n:\overline{1}|} + \bar{a}_{\overline{n}|}(1 - vp_x) + vp_x\,\bar{a}_{\overline{x+1:\overline{n}|}}$

   $\bar{a}_{\overline{\omega:\overline{n}|}} = \bar{a}_{\overline{n}|}$

5.14. $\dfrac{2}{i}\left(a_{x:\overline{n}|} - \,^2a_{x:\overline{n}|}\right) - \,^2a_{x:\overline{n}|} - (a_{x:\overline{n}|})^2$

5.15. $\dfrac{s_{\overline{1}|}^{(m)} - 1}{d^{(m)}} A_x$

5.16. a. $\dfrac{1}{m} \displaystyle\sum_{h=0}^{m-1} v^{h/m} \,_{h/m}p_x + \dfrac{1}{m} \displaystyle\sum_{h=m}^{(y-x)m-1} v^{h/m} \,_{h/m}p_x$

   b. $\alpha(m) - \beta(m)(1 - vp_x)$

   c. $c(x) = \alpha(m) - \beta(m)(1 - vp_x), \quad d(x) = vp_x, \quad \ddot{a}_{y:\overline{0}|}^{(m)} = 0$

5.17. $\ddot{a}_{x:\overline{n}|} - \dfrac{m-1}{2m}(1 - \,_nE_x), \quad \,_{n|}\ddot{a}_x - \dfrac{m-1}{2m}\,_nE_x$

5.22. a. $\alpha(m)\,\ddot{s}_{25:\overline{40}|} - \beta(m)\left(\dfrac{1}{\,_{40}E_{25}} - 1\right)$ b. (i) 15.038   (ii) 196.380

5.23. a. $Y = \begin{cases} (I\ddot{a})_{\overline{K+J+1/m}|}^{(m)} & K = 0, 1, \ldots, n-1, \quad J = 0, 1, \ldots, m-1 \\ (I\ddot{a})_{\overline{n}|}^{(m)} & K = n, n+1, \ldots \end{cases}$

5.24. a. $Y = \begin{cases} (D\ddot{a})_{\overline{K+J+1/m}|}^{(m)} & K = 0, 1, \ldots, n-1, \quad J = 0, 1, \ldots, m-1 \\ (D\ddot{a})_{\overline{n}|}^{(m)} & K = n, n+1, \ldots \end{cases}$

5.25. a. $Y = \begin{cases} (I\ddot{a})_{\overline{K+J+1/m}|}^{(m)} & K = 0, 1, \ldots, n-1, \quad J = 0, 1, \ldots, m-1 \\ n\,\ddot{a}_{\overline{K+J+1/m}|}^{(m)} & K = n, n+1, \ldots, \quad J = 0, 1, \ldots, m-1 \end{cases}$

5.31. a. $\ddot{a}_x + 0.03(Ia)_x$

   b. $\displaystyle\sum_{k=0}^{\infty} (1.03)^k v^k \,_kp_x = \ddot{a}_x'$ evaluated at interest rate $i' = \dfrac{i - 0.03}{1.03}$

5.32. $\displaystyle\int_0^n (n - t) v^t \,_tp_x \, dt$

5.33. $1{,}200\left(\dfrac{a_{30}^{(12)} + \,_{10|}a_{30}^{(12)} + 3\,_{20|}a_{30}^{(12)} + 5\,_{30|}a_{30}^{(12)} - 10\,_{40|}a_{30}^{(12)}}{\,_{40}E_{30}}\right)$

5.34. $\bar{a}_{35:\overline{25}|} - \,_{25}p_{35}\,\bar{a}_{\overline{25}|}$

5.35. $\ddot{a}_{x:\overline{n}|} - \,_np_x\,\ddot{a}_{\overline{n}|}$

5.36. $\dfrac{1}{12}\ddot{a}_{x:\overline{25}|} - \dfrac{25}{12}\,_{25}E_x$

5.38. $v^{2n}\,_np_x(1 - \,_np_x)\,\ddot{a}_{x+n}^2 + v^{2n}\,_np_x\,\dfrac{^2A_{x+n} - A_{x+n}^2}{d^2}$

5.41. a. $\alpha(m) = 1 + \dfrac{m^2 - 1}{12m^2}\delta^2 + \dfrac{2m^4 - 5m^2 + 3}{720m^4}\delta^4 + \cdots$

   $\beta(m) = \dfrac{m-1}{2m}\left[1 + \dfrac{m+1}{3m}\delta + \dfrac{m(m+1)}{12m^2}\delta^2 + \dfrac{(m+1)(6m^2 - 4)}{360m^3}\delta^3 + \cdots\right]$

   b. $\alpha(\infty) = 1 + \dfrac{1}{12}\delta^2 + \dfrac{1}{360}\delta^4 + \cdots$

   $\beta(\infty) = \dfrac{1}{2}\left[1 + \dfrac{1}{3}\delta + \dfrac{1}{12}\delta^2 + \dfrac{1}{60}\delta^3 + \cdots\right]$

5.44. $\dfrac{I}{\delta} + \left(J - \dfrac{I}{\delta}\right) v^T, \dfrac{I}{\delta} + \left(J - \dfrac{I}{\delta}\right) \bar{A}_x, \left(J - \dfrac{I}{\delta}\right)^2 ({}^2\bar{A}_x - \bar{A}_x^2)$

5.45. a. 14.353   b. 13.350   c. 1.002

5.51. a. 488.23   b. 700.48   c. 531.77

5.53. $\ddot{a}_{55:\overline{10|}} = 7.45735$

5.54. $\bar{a}_{55:\overline{10|}} = 7.19783$

5.56. $\bar{a}_{55:\overline{10|}} = 7.19783$

5.57. $\bar{a}_{60:\overline{10|}} = 6.46348, \quad \mathrm{Var}(X) = 1.82621$

5.58. $\ddot{a}_{65}^{(12)} = 10.13343, \quad \mathrm{Var}(Y) = 16.87662$

5.59. 10.41532

Chapter 6

6.1. $-0.43202, 0.39760$

6.3.   0.303598

6.4.   a. 0.02   b. 0.00857   c. 0.02885

6.6. $\dfrac{\mu}{\mu + 2\delta} = {}^2\bar{A}_x$

6.10.

| | **Annual Premiums for (35)** | | |
Insurance	**Fully Continuous**	**Semicontinuous**	**Fully Discrete**
10-Year endowment	0.075128	0.072885	0.072810
30-Year endowment	0.015371	0.014894	0.014751
60-Year endowment	0.008913	0.008621	0.008374
Whole life	0.008903	0.008611	0.008362
30-Year term	0.005117	0.004958	0.004815
10-Year term	0.002669	0.002589	0.002514

6.12. $A_x = \dfrac{1 - r}{1 + i - r}, P_x = \dfrac{1 - r}{1 + i},$

$\ddot{a}_x = \dfrac{1 + i}{1 + i - r},$

$\dfrac{{}^2A_x - A_x^2}{(d\ddot{a}_x)^2} = \dfrac{(1 - r)r}{1 + 2i + i^2 - r}$

6.13. 0.019139

6.15. 0.032868

6.16. 0.0413

6.17. With the common $(\bar{A}_{40:\overline{25|}})$ omitted from the premium symbols,
$P \le P^{(2)} \le P^{(4)} \le P^{(12)} \le \bar{P}$

6.18. $\dfrac{100}{99}$

6.19. 740.93

6.21. $P(A'^{1}_{45:\overline{20}|})$ where $A'^{1}_{45:\overline{20}|}$ is the actuarial present value of a 20-year term insurance on (45) under which $b_{k+1} = \ddot{s}_{\overline{k+1}|}$

6.22. a. 11.5451, 20.4106   b. 6.3099, 25.6458

6.24. $_{25}P_{40}$

6.25. b. $P^{(12)}(A^{(12)}_{\underset{65:\overline{10}|}{1}}) + d^{(12)}$

6.26. $\dfrac{100{,}000}{(1.1\ \ddot{s}_{\overline{30}|} - 0.1\ \ddot{s}_{35:\overline{30}|})}$

6.27. 0.008

6.28. $\dfrac{11{,}000\ A_x + 25\ \ddot{a}_{x:\overline{20}|}}{\ddot{a}_{x:\overline{20}|} - 1.1(I_{\overline{20}|}A)_x}$

6.29. $\dfrac{2\ A_{25} - A^{1}_{25:\overline{10}|}}{2\ \ddot{a}_{25:\overline{40}|} - \ddot{a}_{25:\overline{10}|}}$

6.30. $L_1 = v^T - \bar{P}(\bar{A}_x)\bar{a}_{\overline{T}|} \equiv 1 - \left(\dfrac{1}{\bar{a}_x}\right)\bar{a}_{\overline{T}|} = L_2$

6.31. a. -0.08 b. 0.1296   c. 0.1587

6.32. $\dfrac{\bar{A}_x}{2\ddot{a}_x - \ddot{a}_{x:\overline{5}|}}$

6.33. $_{20}P^{\{m\}}(\bar{A}_x) - {}_{20}P^{(m)}(\bar{A}_x) = {}_{20}\bar{P}(\bar{A}_x)\left(\dfrac{\bar{A}^{1}_{x:\overline{20}|} - A^{\overset{(m)}{1}}_{x:\overline{20}|}}{\delta \ddot{a}^{(m)}_{x:\overline{20}|}}\right)$

6.35. a. $f_L(u) = \begin{cases} \dfrac{\mu}{\delta u + \bar{P}}\left(\dfrac{\delta u + \bar{P}}{\delta + \bar{P}}\right)^{\mu/\delta} & -\dfrac{\bar{P}}{\delta} < u < 1 \\ 0 & \text{elsewhere} \end{cases}$

6.36. a. $\dfrac{1}{\sqrt{3}}$

   b. 0.02

Chapter 7

7.1. $_1V = 0.15111$ $_2V = 0.30809$ $_3V = 0.47118$ $_4V = 0.64067$

7.2. $_1V = 0.14925$ $_2V = 0.30492$ $_3V = 0.46741$ $_4V = 0.63712$

7.3. $_1V = 1.2871$ $_2V = 2.6996$ $_3V = 4.2553$ $_4V = 5.9748$

7.4. $_1V = 0.15064$ $_2V = 0.30730$ $_3V = 0.47025$ $_4V = 0.63980$

7.5. a. $1 = \dfrac{1}{5}\displaystyle\int_0^5 e^{0.1[1.06^{-t}(1+\bar{P}/\delta)-\bar{P}/\delta]}\,dt$ where $\delta = \log(1.06)$

   $_1\bar{V} = 10\log\left(\dfrac{1}{4}\displaystyle\int_0^4 e^{0.1[1.06^{-t}(1+\bar{P}/\delta)-\bar{P}/\delta]}\,dt\right)$ where $\bar{P}$ and δ are as in (a)

b. $\bar{P} = 0.388380$, $_1\bar{V} = 0.182825$

7.6. $_tL = \begin{cases} v^U - \bar{P}(\bar{A}_{x:\overline{n}|}) \, \bar{a}_{\overline{U}|} & U < n - t \\ v^{n-t} - \bar{P}(\bar{A}_{x:\overline{n}|}) \, \bar{a}_{\overline{n-t}|} & U \geq n - t \end{cases}$

7.7. $\mathrm{E}[_tL] = \bar{a}_{x+t:\overline{n-t}|}$, $\mathrm{Var}(_tL) = \dfrac{{}^2\bar{A}_{x+t:\overline{n-t}|} - \bar{A}^2_{x+t:\overline{n-t}|}}{\delta^2}$

7.8. a. $\bar{A}_{45:\overline{20}|} - {}_{20}\bar{P}(\bar{A}_{35:\overline{30}|}) \, \bar{a}_{45:\overline{10}|}$ b. $\bar{A}^1_{50:\overline{5}|}$

7.9. a. $u_0 = \dfrac{-\log(\bar{A}_x)}{\delta}$ b. 23.2476

7.10. 41.7524

7.11. $F_{_tL}(y) = 0 \hspace{5cm} y < v^{n-t} - \bar{P}(\bar{A}_{x:\overline{n}|}) \, \bar{a}_{\overline{n-t}|}$

$$F_{_tL}(y) = \dfrac{1 - F_{T(x)}\left(t - \dfrac{1}{\delta} \log \dfrac{\delta y + \bar{P}(\bar{A}_{x:\overline{n}|})}{\delta + \bar{P}(\bar{A}_{x:\overline{n}|})}\right)}{1 - F_{T(x)}(t)} \quad v^{n-t} - \bar{P}(\bar{A}_{x:\overline{n}|}) \, \bar{a}_{\overline{n-t}|} \leq y < 1$$

$F_{_tL}(y) = 1 \hspace{5cm} y \geq 1$

7.12. $F_{_tL}(y) = 0 \hspace{4cm} y < \bar{P}(\bar{A}^1_{x:\overline{n}|}) \, \bar{a}_{\overline{n-t}|}$

$$F_{_tL}(y) = \dfrac{1 - F_{T(x)}(n)}{1 - F_{T(x)}(t)} = \dfrac{{}_np_x}{{}_tp_x} \hspace{1.5cm} -\bar{P}(\bar{A}_{x:\overline{n}|}) \, \bar{a}_{\overline{n-t}|} \leq y < v^{n-t} - \bar{P}(\bar{A}^1_{x:\overline{n}|}) \, \bar{a}_{\overline{n-t}|}$$

$$F_{_tL}(y) = \dfrac{1 - F_{T(x)}\left(t - \dfrac{1}{\delta} \log \dfrac{\delta y + \bar{P}(\bar{A}^1_{x:\overline{n}|})}{\delta + \bar{P}(\bar{A}^1_{x:\overline{n}|})}\right)}{1 - F_{T(x)}(t)} \quad v^{n-t} - \bar{P}(\bar{A}^1_{x:\overline{n}|}) \leq y < 1$$

7.14. $\bar{A}_{50} - {}_{20}\bar{P}(\bar{A}_{40}) \, \bar{a}_{50:\overline{10}|}$, $[{}_{10}P(A_{50}) - {}_{20}P(A_{40})] \, \bar{a}_{50:\overline{10}|}$,

$\left[1 - \dfrac{{}_{20}\bar{P}(\bar{A}_{40})}{{}_{10}\bar{P}(\bar{A}_{50})}\right] \bar{A}_{50}$, ${}_{20}\bar{P}(\bar{A}_{40}) \, \bar{s}_{40:\overline{10}|} - {}_{10}\bar{k}_{40}$

7.15. $\bar{A}_{50:\overline{10}|} - \bar{P}(\bar{A}_{40:\overline{20}|}) \, \bar{a}_{50:\overline{10}|}$, $[\bar{P}(\bar{A}_{50:\overline{10}|}) - \bar{P}(\bar{A}_{40:\overline{20}|})] \, \bar{a}_{50:\overline{10}|}$,

$\left[1 - \dfrac{\bar{P}(\bar{A}_{40:\overline{20}|})}{\bar{P}(\bar{A}_{50:\overline{10}|})}\right] \bar{A}_{50:\overline{10}|}$, $\bar{P}(\bar{A}_{40:\overline{20}|}) \, \bar{s}_{40:\overline{10}|} - {}_{10}\bar{k}_{40}$,

$1 - \dfrac{\bar{a}_{50:\overline{10}|}}{\bar{a}_{40:\overline{20}|}}$, $\dfrac{\bar{P}(\bar{A}_{50:\overline{10}|}) - \bar{P}(\bar{A}_{40:\overline{20}|})}{\bar{P}(\bar{A}_{50:\overline{10}|}) + \delta}$, $\dfrac{\bar{A}_{50:\overline{10}|} - \bar{A}_{40:\overline{20}|}}{1 - \bar{A}_{40:\overline{20}|}}$

7.16. $\bar{P}({}_{30|}\bar{a}_{35}) \, \bar{s}_{35:\overline{20}|}$

7.18. (7.3.3)

7.19. $A_{50} - {}_{20}P_{40} \, \ddot{a}_{50:\overline{10}|}$, $({}_{10}P_{50} - {}_{20}P_{40}) \, \ddot{a}_{50:\overline{10}|}$, $\left(1 - \dfrac{{}_{20}P_{40}}{{}_{10}P_{50}}\right) A_{50}$,

${}_{20}P_{40} \, \ddot{s}_{40:\overline{10}|} - {}_{10}k_{40}$

7.20. $A_{50:\overline{10}|} - P_{40:\overline{20}|}\ \ddot{a}_{50:\overline{10}|}$, $(P_{50:\overline{10}|} - P_{40:\overline{20}|})\ \ddot{a}_{50:\overline{10}|}$,

$$\left(1 - \frac{P_{40:\overline{20}|}}{P_{50:\overline{10}|}}\right) A_{50:\overline{10}|},\ P_{40:\overline{20}|}\ \ddot{s}_{40:\overline{10}|} - {}_{10}k_{40},$$

$$1 - \frac{\ddot{a}_{50:\overline{10}|}}{\ddot{a}_{40:\overline{20}|}},\ \frac{P_{50:\overline{10}|} - P_{40:\overline{20}|}}{P_{50:\overline{10}|} + d},\ \frac{A_{50:\overline{10}|} - A_{40:\overline{20}|}}{1 - A_{40:\overline{20}|}}$$

7.22. $\dfrac{1}{5}$

7.23.

Insurance	Fully Continuous	Semicontinuous	Fully Discrete
30-Year endowment	0.17530	0.17504	0.17407
Whole life	0.08604	0.08566	0.08319
30-Year term	0.03379	0.03370	0.03273

7.24. (b) and (c)

7.26. All but (d)

7.27. All

7.29. 0.008

7.30. 0.240

7.31. a. 0.005527
      b. 0.051255
      c. 0.946122
      d. 0.132109

7.32. a. 0.0241821   b. 0.0189660

Chapter 8

8.1. a. $\dfrac{1 - r}{1 + i}$

     b. $\dfrac{(1 - r)(1 + i + r)}{(1 + i)(1 + i - r)}$

8.2. $\dfrac{\displaystyle\int_0^\infty b_t\ v^t\ {}_tp_x\ \mu_x(t)\ dt}{\displaystyle\int_0^\infty w(t)\ v^t\ {}_tp_x\ dt}$

8.3. a. $\dfrac{\mu}{\delta + \mu}$

     b. $\dfrac{\mu t}{\delta + \mu}$

8.5. a. $(P_{x+1} - vq_{x+h})\ {}_hp_x\ vq_x$
     b. $(P_{x+1} - vq_{x+h})\ {}_hp_x(v\ {}_jp_x\ q_{x+j} + {}_jq_x\ P_{x+1})$

c. If $P_{x+1} - vq_{x+n} < 0$, then $\text{Cov}(C_j, C_h) < 0$ for all $j < h$

8.6. If $1 - vq_{x+h}\, \ddot{s}_{\overline{h+1}|} < 0$, then $\text{Cov}(C_j, C_h) < 0$ for all $j < h$

8.13. $(\bar{A}_{x:\overline{40}|})$ is omitted from the reserve and premium symbols

   a. $\dfrac{1}{2}\,_{20}V + \dfrac{1}{2}\,_{21}V + \dfrac{1}{2}\,P$ b. $\dfrac{1}{2}\,_{20}\bar{V} + \dfrac{1}{2}\,_{21}\bar{V}$

   c. $\dfrac{1}{2}\,_{20}V^{(2)} + \dfrac{1}{2}\,_{21}V^{(2)}$ d. $\dfrac{1}{3}\,_{20}V^{(2)} + \dfrac{2}{3}\,_{21}V^{(2)} + \dfrac{1}{3}\,P^{(2)}$

   e. Same as (b) f. $\dfrac{1}{3}\,_{20}\bar{V} + \dfrac{2}{3}\,_{21}\bar{V} + \dfrac{1}{3}\,P^{\{2\}}$

8.14. 0.05448

8.17. b. $\text{Var}(L) = 0.076090$

8.18. a. 0.0067994 b. 0.1858077 c. 0.2012024
   d. 0.0275369 e. 0.0255406

8.21. $-\,_tp_x[\delta\,_t\bar{V}(\bar{A}_x) + \bar{P}(\bar{A}_x)]$

8.22. a. $_tp_x\,[\pi_t + \delta_t\bar{V} - b_t\,\mu_x(t)]$
   b. $v^t[\pi_t + \mu_x(t)\,_t\bar{V} - b_t\,\mu_x(t)]$
   c. $v^t\,_tp_x\,[\pi_t - b_t\,\mu_x(t)]$

8.26. a. and b. 1,491.03 c. 343.84 d. 0

8.27. a. 1,490,915
   b. 6,450,962; 1,495,093, which is 1.00280 times the reserve
   c. 5,311,375; supplement is 3,791, which is 0.00254 times the reserve
   d. For b.: 645,096,250; 149,133,281, which is 1.00028 times the reserve
      For c.: 531,137,500; supplement is 37,911, which is 0.00025 times the reserve

8.28. a. 1,104,260 is the reserve for these policies
   b. 6,450,962; 1,108,438, which is 1.00378 times the reserve
   c. 5,311,375; supplement is 3,791, which is 0.00343 times the reserve
   d. For b.: 645,096,250; 110,467,781, which is 1.00038 times the reserve
      For c.: 531,137,500; supplement is 37,911, which is 0.00034 times the reserve

8.29. $5,000[_{10}\bar{V}(\bar{A}_{30}) + P^{\{1\}}(\bar{A}_{30}) + {}_{11}\bar{V}(\bar{A}_{30})]$

8.30. a. 0.2 b. 0.25 c. 0.7584 d. 0.27

8.32. 0.081467

8.34. a. 355.6563
   b. 2,614.2511

8.35. a. $100,000\,\dfrac{A_{35:\overline{30}|}^{\,1}}{1 - A_{35:\overline{30}|}^{\,1}}$

   b. $100,000\,A_{35+k:\overline{30-k}|}^{\,1} + SA_{35+k:\overline{30-k}|}^{\,1}$

c. $\dfrac{S - SA_{35:\overline{k}|}^{1}}{A_{35:\overline{k}|}^{1}}$

d. $S = 18{,}575.08$, $\quad _{20}V = 53{,}962.62$

Chapter 9

9.1. a. $1 - \dfrac{1}{(1 + s)^{n-2}} - \dfrac{1}{(1 + t)^{n-2}} + \dfrac{1}{(1 + s + t)^{n-2}} \qquad s > 0,\, t > 0$

   b. $f_{T(x)}(s) = \dfrac{n - 2}{(1 + s)^{n-1}} \qquad s > 0$

   $F_{T(x)}(s) = 1 - \dfrac{1}{(1 + s)^{n-2}} \quad s > 0$

   $\mu(x + s) = \dfrac{n - 2}{1 + s} \qquad s > 0$

   c. $\mathrm{Cov}[T(x), T(y)] = \dfrac{1}{(n - 4)(n - 3)^2} \qquad \rho_{T(x)T(y)} = \dfrac{1}{n - 2}$

9.2. $\dfrac{1}{(1 + s + t)^{n-2}} \qquad s \geq 0,\, t \geq 0$

9.3. $F_{T(x)T(y)}(s, t) = \left[1 - \dfrac{1}{(1 + s)^{n-2}}\right]\left[1 - \dfrac{1}{(1 + t)^{n-2}}\right] \qquad s > 0,\, t > 0$

   $s_{T(x)T(y)}(s, t) = \dfrac{1}{(1 + s)^{n-2}} \dfrac{1}{(1 + t)^{n-2}} \qquad s \geq 0,\, t \geq 0$

9.4. a. $_{n}p_{x}\, _{n}p_{y}$

   b. $_{n}p_{x} + _{n}p_{y} - 2\, _{n}p_{x}\, _{n}p_{y}$

   c. $_{n}p_{x} + _{n}p_{y} - _{n}p_{x}\, _{n}p_{y}$

   d. $1 - _{n}p_{x}\, _{n}p_{y}$

   e. Same as for (d)

   f. $(1 - _{n}p_{x})(1 - _{n}p_{y}) = 1 - _{n}p_{x} - _{n}p_{y} + _{n}p_{x}\, _{n}p_{y}$

9.6. $_{n}q_{xx}$

9.7. $F_{T(xy)}(t) = 1 - \dfrac{1}{(1 + 2t)^{n-2}} \qquad t > 0$

   $s_{T(xy)}(t) = \dfrac{1}{(1 + 2t)^{n-2}} \qquad t \geq 0$

   $E[T(xy)] = \dfrac{1}{2(n - 3)}$

9.8. $f_{T(xy)}(t) = \begin{cases} \dfrac{(10 - t)^3}{2{,}500} & 0 < t < 10 \\[2mm] 0 & \text{elsewhere} \end{cases}$

9.10. $_{n|}q_{x} + _{n|}q_{y} - _{n|}q_{x}\, _{n|}q_{y}$

   No, since for $_{n|}q_{\overline{xy}}$ the second death must occur in year $n + 1$, and this is not the case for the requested probability.

9.11. a. $F_{T(\overline{xy})}(t) = 1 - \dfrac{2}{(1 + t)^{n-2}} + \dfrac{1}{(1 + 2t)^{n-2}}$ $\qquad t > 0$

$\qquad\qquad f_{T(\overline{xy})}(t) = 2(n - 2) \left[\dfrac{1}{(1 + t)^{n-1}} - \dfrac{1}{(1 + 2t)^{n-1}} \right] \qquad t > 0$

b. $E[T(\overline{xy})] = \dfrac{3}{2(n - 3)}$

c. $\mu_{\overline{xy}}(t) = \dfrac{2(n - 2)\, [1/(1 + t)^{n-1} - 1/(1 + 2t)^{n-1}]}{2/(1 + t)^{n-2} - 1/(1 + 2t)^{n-2}} \qquad t > 0$

9.12. $\dfrac{2}{9}$

9.13. a. $\dfrac{2}{3}$ b. $\dfrac{29}{30}$ c. 18.06 d. 36.94 e. 160.11 f. 182.33

g. 82.95 h. 0.49

9.14. $\mu_{xx}(0)\, \overset{\circ}{e}_{xx} - 1$

9.17. $\dfrac{531}{2,000}$

9.18. a. $\dfrac{1}{\alpha} \log \left[1 + \dfrac{(e^{\alpha t} - 1)^2}{e^{\alpha} - 1} \right]$ b. $\dfrac{(e^{\alpha t} - 1)(e^{\alpha} - 1)}{(e^{\alpha} - 1) + (e^{\alpha t} - 1)^2}$

9.19. $\dfrac{1}{\alpha} \log \left[1 + \dfrac{(e^{0.05\alpha} - 1)(e^{0.03\alpha} - 1)}{e^{\alpha} - 1} \right]$

9.20. a. 0.001500 b. 0.000266 c. 0.004232

9.21. An annuity of 1 payable at the end of each year for n years and for as long thereafter as (xy) exists.

9.22. An insurance of 1 payable on the death of (x), or at the end of n years, whichever is later.

9.24. $\bar{a}_{25:\overline{25}|} + \bar{a}_{30:\overline{20}|} - \bar{a}_{25:30:\overline{20}|}$

9.25. $_{20|}a_{30} + {}_{25|}a_{25} - {}_{25|}a_{25:30}$

9.26. $\dfrac{1}{6}\, \ddot{a}_{xy:\overline{n}|} + \dfrac{1}{2}\, \ddot{a}_{y:\overline{n}|} + \dfrac{1}{3}\, \ddot{a}_{x:\overline{n}|}$

9.27. $a_{x:\overline{n}|} + v^n\, {}_nP_x\, a_{x+n:y:\overline{m-n}|}$

9.28. $_{5|}\bar{a}_{55} + {}_{20|}\bar{a}_{40} - {}_{5|10}\bar{a}_{40:55} - {}_{20|}\bar{a}_{40:55}$

9.29. a. $[\ddot{a}_x^{(m)} + p(\ddot{a}_y^{(m)} - \ddot{a}_{xy}^{(m)})]$ b. $\dfrac{\ddot{a}_x^{(m)}}{\ddot{a}_x^{(m)} + p(\ddot{a}_y^{(m)} - \ddot{a}_{xy}^{(m)})}$

9.32. a. 7.0753 b. 7.0756

9.35. $w = \dfrac{3}{5}\, x + \dfrac{2}{5}\, y$

9.37. $\dfrac{1}{3}$

9.41. $_\infty q_{xy}^1 = {}_\infty q_{xy}^2$

9.44. $\bar{A}_{50} - \bar{A}^{\;\;1}_{50:\overline{20}|}$

9.45. $\bar{A}^1_{x:\overline{n}|} - \bar{A}^1_{xy} + {}_nE_x\,\bar{A}^{\;\;1}_{\overline{x+n}:y}$

9.46. $\dfrac{1}{12}$

9.47. a. 0.2755 b. $\dfrac{1}{4}\,\bar{A}_{40:50} + 0.0015\bar{a}_{40:50}$

9.48. $\dfrac{1}{3}$, 52.68

9.49. a. $\bar{a}_x + \bar{a}_{\overline{n}|} - \bar{a}_{x:\overline{n}|}$ b. $v^n\,{}_nq_x$

9.51. $\mu(x)\,\overset{\circ}{e}_{xy} - {}_\infty q^1_{xy}$

9.52. a. $(\mu_2 + \lambda)e^{-(\mu_2+\lambda)t}$ $t > 0$
   b. $e^{-(\mu_2+\lambda)t}$ $t \geq 0$
   c. $\dfrac{\lambda}{\mu_1 + \mu_2 + \lambda}$

Chapter 10

10.1.   a. $e^{-t\mu_x^{(\tau)}}\,\mu_x^{(j)}$ b. $\dfrac{\mu_x^{(j)}}{\mu_x^{(\tau)}}$ c. $e^{-t\mu_x^{(\tau)}}\,\mu_x^{(\tau)}$

10.2.   a. $\dfrac{j(50-t)^2}{50^3}$ b. $\dfrac{3(50-t)^2}{50^3}$ c. $\dfrac{j}{3}$ d. $\dfrac{j}{3}$

10.3.   a. $f_T(t) = p(u_1 + v_1)e^{-(u_1+v_1)t} + (1-p)(u_2+v_2)e^{-(u_2+v_2)t}$,

   $f_J(1) = \dfrac{pu_1}{u_1+v_1} + (1-p)\dfrac{u_2}{u_2+v_2}$, $f_J(2) = p\dfrac{v_1}{u_1+v_1} + (1-p)\dfrac{v_2}{u_2+v_2}$
   b. $s_T(t) = pe^{-(u_1+v_1)t} + (1-p)e^{-(u_2+v_2)t}$

10.4. ${}_3p_{65}^{(\tau)} = 0.75321$, ${}_{3|}q_{65}^{(1)} = 0.03766$, ${}_3q_{65}^{(2)} = 0.16504$

10.5.   a. 302.4 and 210.95 b. 231.0 and 177.64

10.6.   a. $h(1) = 0.231$, $h(2) = 0.4666$, $h(3) = 0.3024$
   b. $h(1|k=2) = 0.25$, $h(2|k=2) = 0.75$, $h(3|k=2) = 0$

10.7. $l_x^{(\tau)} = (a-x)e^{-x}$, $d_x^{(1)} = e^{-x}(1 - e^{-1})$,
   $d_x^{(2)} = (a - x - 1)e^{-x} - (a - x - 2)e^{-x-1}$

10.8. $1{,}000\left(\dfrac{a-x^2}{a}\right)e^{-cx}$

10.9.   a. ${}_tp_x^{(\tau)}\,(\mu_a^{(\tau)}(x+t-a) - \mu_a^{(\tau)}(x-a))$ b. ${}_tp_x^{(\tau)}\,\mu_a^{(j)}(x+t-a) + {}_tq_x^{(j)}\,\mu_a^{(\tau)}(x-a)$
   $- \mu_a^{(j)}(x-a)$ c. ${}_tp_x^{(\tau)}\,\mu_a^{(j)}(x+t-a)$

10.10.

k	$q_k'^{(1)} = 1 - (p_k^{(\tau)})^{q_k^{(1)}/q_k^{(\tau)}}$	$q_k'^{(2)} = 1 - (p_k^{(\tau)})^{q_k^{(2)}/q_k^{(\tau)}}$
0	0.17433	0.27332
1	0.11210	0.21163
2	0.05426	0.15410
3	0.00000	0.10000

10.11. a. $1 - e^{-c}$ b. c c. $c \int_0^1 {}_t p_x^{(\tau)} \, dt$

10.13. $m_x'^{(j)} \geq q_x'^{(j)} \geq q_x^{(j)}$

10.14. 0.0592

10.15. a. 0.0909   b. 0.0906

10.16.

k	$m_k^{(1)}$	$m_k^{(2)}$
0	0.18750	0.31250
1	0.11765	0.23529
2	0.05556	0.16667
3	0.00000	0.10526

10.17.

x	$p_x^{(\tau)}$	$q_x^{(1)}$	$q_x^{(2)}$	$q_x^{(3)}$
62	0.76048	0.01767	0.02665	0.19520
63	0.85027	0.02054	0.03193	0.09726
64	0.82115	0.02578	0.03705	0.11603

10.18.

x	$m_x^{(1)} = m_x'^{(1)}$	$m_x^{(2)} = m_x'^{(2)}$	$m_x^{(3)} = m_x'^{(3)}$	$m_x^{(\tau)}$	$q_x^{(1)}$	$q_x^{(2)}$	$q_x^{(3)}$
62	0.02020	0.03046	0.22222	0.27288	0.01777	0.02680	0.19554
63	0.02224	0.03459	0.10526	0.16209	0.02057	0.03200	0.09737
64	0.02840	0.04082	0.12766	0.19688	0.02585	0.03716	0.11622

10.20.

x	$m_x^{(1)}$	$m_x^{(2)}$	$m_x'^{(1)}$	$m_x'^{(2)}$
65	0.02073	0.05181	0.02073	0.05183
66	0.03141	0.06283	0.03144	0.06286
67	0.04233	0.07407	0.04237	0.07412
68	0.05348	0.08556	0.05355	0.08565
69	0.06486	0.09730	0.06499	0.09744

10.21. Revise (a) to $m_x^{(j)} \left/ \left(1 + \frac{1}{2} m_x^{(\tau)} \right) \right.$

10.22. c. i. ${}_t q_x^{(j)} = K_j \left(1 - e^{-[k/(n+1)]t^{n+1}} \right) = K_j \, {}_t q_x^{(\tau)}$

${}_t q_x'^{(j)} = 1 - e^{-[k/(n+1)]t^{n+1}} = 1 - ({}_t p_x^{(\tau)})^{K_j}$

ii. ${}_t q_x^{(j)} = K_j \left(1 - e^{(B/\log c)(c^t - 1)} \right) = K_j \, {}_t q_x^{(\tau)}$

${}_t q_x'^{(j)} = 1 - e^{K_t(B/\log c)(c^t - 1)} = 1 - ({}_t p_x^{(\tau)})^{K_j}$

10.25.

k	$q_k^{\prime(1)}$	$q_x^{\prime(2)}$
0	0.17143	0.27027
1	0.11111	0.21053
2	0.05405	0.15385
3	0.00000	0.10000

10.27. a. From $q_x^{(3)} = q_x^{\prime(3)} \left[1 - \frac{1}{2}(q_x^{\prime(1)} + q_x^{\prime(2)}) + \frac{1}{3} q_x^{\prime(1)} q_x^{\prime(2)} \right]$, obtain $q_x^{\prime(3)}$, then use

(9.6.3).

b. Obtain $q_x^{(1)}$ from a relation derived in Exercise 9.18,

$$q_x^{(1)} \cong q_x^{\prime(1)} \left[1 - \frac{1}{2}(q_x^{(2)} + q_x^{(3)}) \right]$$

10.28. $q_{69}^{(3)} = 0.94434$

10.29. $q_{50}^{\prime(1)} = 0.015$

10.30. $1 - \sum_{k=0}^{44} \frac{d_{20+k}^{(2)}}{l_{20}^{(\tau)}} = 1 - \frac{l_{20}^{(2)} - l_{65}^{(2)}}{l_{20}^{(\tau)}}$

10.31. a. Approximate $m_x^{(1)}$, $m_x^{(2)}$ from $q_x^{\prime(1)}$, $q_x^{\prime(2)}$, or approximate $q_x^{\prime(3)}$, $q_x^{\prime(4)}$ from $m_x^{(3)}$, $m_x^{(4)}$

b. $1 - \sum_{k=0}^{\infty} \frac{d_{y+k}^{(4)}}{l_y^{(\tau)}} = 1 - \frac{l_y^{(4)}}{l_y^{(\tau)}}$

10.32. (The probability of decrement = (the absolute rate
due to cause j when   of decrement
all causes are operating)   due to cause j)

                                    $-$ (the probability that decrement will
                                    occur due to causes k, $k \neq j$, and
                                    thereafter the event associated with j
                                    will occur prior to (x) attaining age $x + 1$)

10.34. a. $f_{T,J}(t, j) = \dfrac{\theta \beta^\alpha}{\Gamma(\alpha)} t^{\alpha-1} e^{-\beta t} \qquad j = 1, t \geq 0$

$= \dfrac{(1 - \theta)\beta^\alpha t^{\alpha-1} e^{-\beta t}}{\Gamma(\alpha)} \qquad j = 2, t \geq 0,$

$f_J(j) = \begin{cases} \theta & j = 1 \\ 1 - \theta & j = 2, \end{cases}$

$f_T(t) = \dfrac{\beta^\alpha t^{\alpha-1} e^{-\beta t}}{\Gamma(\alpha)}$

b. $E[T] = \dfrac{\alpha}{\beta}$, $Var(T) = \dfrac{\alpha}{\beta^2}$

Chapter 11

11.1. If 1 denotes death and 2 withdrawal for any other reason, the actuarial present value is

$$20{,}000 \int_0^{40} v^t \, {}_tp_{30}^{(\tau)} \, \mu_{30}^{(1)}(t) \, dt \;+\; 300 \int_0^{40} v^t \, {}_tp_{30}^{(\tau)} \, \mu_{30}^{(2)}(t) \; t \; {}_{40-t|}\bar{a}_{30+t} \; dt$$

$$+ \; 12{,}000 \, v^{40} \; {}_{40}p_{30}^{(\tau)} \, \bar{a}_{70}.$$

11.2. 0.31075, 0.19717

11.4. $S_x = \dfrac{x}{15} - \dfrac{1}{3} \qquad 20 \le x$

11.5. 2,250

11.6. a. Take $S_{30} = 1$. Then

$$S_{30+k} = \begin{cases} (1.05)^k & 0 \le k < 10 \\ (1.1)(1.05)^k & 10 \le k < 20 \\ (1.1)^2(1.05)^k & 20 \le k < 30 \\ (1.1)^3(1.05)^k & k \ge 30. \end{cases}$$

b. $1{,}200 \displaystyle\sum_{k=0}^{\omega-31} v^{k+1/2} \; {}_{k+1/2}p_{30}^{(\tau)} \, S_{30+k}$

11.7. $0.1 \displaystyle\sum_{k=0}^{\omega-36} v^{k+1/2} \; {}_{k+1/2}p_{35}^{(\tau)} \left[25{,}000\left(\dfrac{S_{35+k}}{S_{35}}\right) - 10{,}000(1.05)^k \right]$

11.8. a. $\displaystyle\sum_{k=5}^{\infty} v^{k+1/2} \; {}_kp_{50}^{(\tau)} \, q_{50+k}^{(r)} \left(20 + k + \dfrac{1}{2} \right) \left(\dfrac{{}_3Z_{50+k}}{S_{50}} \right) 640 \, \bar{a}_{50+k+1/2}^r$

$$+ \displaystyle\sum_{k=5}^{14} v^{k+1/2} \; {}_kp_{50}^{(\tau)} \, q_{50+k}^{(r)} \left(20 + k + \dfrac{1}{2} \right) \left(\dfrac{{}_3Z_{50+k}}{S_{50}} \right) 320 \, \bar{a}_{50+k+1/2:\overline{15-k-1/2|}}^r.$$

Since $q_{50+k}^{(r)} = 0$ for $k < 5$, these sums could be extended down to $k = 0$.

b. In the first sum, the terms for $k > 14$ are changed to

$$\displaystyle\sum_{k=15}^{\infty} v^{k+1/2} \; {}_kp_{50}^{(\tau)} \, q_{50+k}^{(r)} \left(\dfrac{{}_3Z_{50+k}}{S_{50}} \right)(22{,}400) \, \bar{a}_{50+k+1/2}^r.$$

c. In the answer to part (a), replace $(20 + k + 1/2)$ by 20.

11.9. a. $R(30, 20, 15) = 8{,}000 + 720 \displaystyle\sum_{j=0}^{14} \dfrac{S_{50+j}}{S_{50}}$

b. $R(30, 20, 15\text{-}1/2) = 8{,}000 + 720 \dfrac{\displaystyle\sum_{j=0}^{14} S_{50+j} + (1/2) \, S_{65}}{S_{50}}$

c. $8{,}000 \displaystyle\sum_{k=8}^{17} v^{k+1/2} \; {}_kp_{50}^{(\tau)} \, q_{50+k}^{(r)} \, \bar{a}_{50+k+1/2}^r$

d. $\displaystyle\sum_{k=0}^{17} v^{k+1/2} \; {}_kp_{50}^{(\tau)} \, q_{50+k}^{(r)} \, 720 \left[\dfrac{\displaystyle\sum_{j=0}^{k-1} S_{50+j} + (1/2)S_{50+k}}{S_{50}} \right] \bar{a}_{50+k+1/2}^r,$

which equals the sum with $k = 8$ to 17, or

$$\dfrac{720}{S_{50}} \left[\displaystyle\sum_{j=0}^{17} S_{50+j} \left(\dfrac{1}{2} v^{j+1/2} \; {}_jp_{50}^{(\tau)} \, q_{50+j}^{(r)} \, \bar{a}_{50+j+1/2}^r + \displaystyle\sum_{k=j+1}^{17} v^{k+1/2} \; {}_kp_{50}^{(\tau)} \, q_{50+k}^{(r)} \, \bar{a}_{50+k+1/2}^r \right) \right]$$

11.10. 1.0756

11.11. a. $20{,}000 \int_{15}^{\infty} v^t \, {}_tp_{40}^{(\tau)} \, \mu_{25}^{(r)}(15 + t) \, \dfrac{S_{40+t}}{S_{40}} \, \bar{a}_{40+t}^r \, dt$

b. $600 \int_{15}^{\infty} v^t \, {}_tp_{40}^{(\tau)} \, \mu_{25}^{(r)}(15 + t) \, \dfrac{S_{40+t}}{S_{40}} \, (15 + t) \, \bar{a}_{40+t}^r \, dt$

c. $600 \int_{0}^{15} v^t \, {}_tp_{40}^{(\tau)} \, \mu_{25}^{(w)}(15 + t) \, \dfrac{S_{40+t}}{S_{40}} \, (15 + t) \, {}_{15-t|}\bar{a}_{40+t}^w \, dt$

where the w superscript on the annuity symbol indicates that it is to be calculated using mortality rates appropriate for a life after withdrawal from employee status.

d. $1{,}000 \int_{15}^{\infty} v^t \, {}_tp_{40}^{(\tau)} \, \mu_{25}^{(r)}(15 + t) \left(8 + \int_{0}^{t} \dfrac{S_{40+u} \, du}{S_{40}} \right) \bar{a}_{40+t}^r \, dt$

Assuming S_x is a step function between integral ages,

$$1{,}000 \int_{15}^{\infty} v^t \, {}_tp_{40}^{(\tau)} \, \mu_{25}^{(r)}(15 + t) \left[8 + \dfrac{\left(\sum_{k=0}^{\lfloor t \rfloor - 1} S_{40+k} \right) + S_{40+\lfloor t \rfloor} (t - \lfloor t \rfloor)}{S_{40}} \right] \bar{a}_{40+t}^r \, dt$$

e. $1{,}000 \int_{0}^{15} v^t \, {}_tp_{40}^{(\tau)} \, \mu_{25}^{(w)}(15 + t) \left(8 + \dfrac{\int_{0}^{t} S_{40+u} \, du}{S_{40}} \right) {}_{15-t|}\bar{a}_{40+t}^w \, dt$

Assuming S_x is a step function between integral ages,

$$1{,}000 \int_{0}^{15} v^t \, {}_tp_{40}^{(\tau)} \, \mu_{25}^{(w)}(15 + t) \left[8 + \dfrac{\sum_{k=0}^{\lfloor t \rfloor - 1} S_{40+k} + S_{40+\lfloor t \rfloor} (t - \lfloor t \rfloor)}{S_{40}} \right] {}_{15-t|}\bar{a}_{40+t}^w \, dt$$

11.12. $\displaystyle\sum_{k=30}^{39} v^{k+1/2} \, {}_kp_{30}^{(\tau)} \, q_{30+k}^{(r)} \, (0.60)35{,}000 \, \dfrac{S_{30+k+1/2}}{S_{30}} \, \bar{a}_{30+k+1/2}^r$

$\displaystyle+ \sum_{k=40}^{\infty} v^{k+1/2} \, {}_kp_{30}^{(\tau)} \, q_{30+k}^{(r)} \, (0.60)35{,}000 \, \dfrac{S_{69+1/2}}{S_{30}} \, \bar{a}_{30+k+1/2}^r$

11.13. a. $24{,}000 \, \dfrac{\displaystyle\sum_{k=0}^{24} v^{k+1} \, {}_kp_{35}^{(\tau)} \, q_{35+k}^{(i)} \, \ddot{a}_{[36+k]:\overline{28-k|}}^{(12)i}}{\ddot{a}_{35:\overline{25|}}^{(\tau)}}$

b. $24{,}000 \, (_{15}^{20}\Pi_{45}^i - _{25}^{30}\Pi_{35}^i)\ddot{a}_{45:\overline{15|}}^{(\tau)}$ where $24{,}000 \, _{25}^{30}\Pi_{35}^i$ and $24{,}000 \, _{15}^{20}\Pi_{45}^i$ are the annual benefit premiums for the benefit for (35) and (45), respectively.

Chapter 12

12.1. $S = X_1 + X_2 + \cdots + X_N$ where N is the number of cars and X_i is the number of passengers in an i.

12.2. Let N denote the number of rainfalls and X_i the number of inches of rain in rainfall i.

12.3. a. npp_1 b. $npp_2 - np^2p_1^2$ c. $[p\,M_x(t) + 1 - p]^n$

12.4. a. 1.7 b. 0.81 c. 1.6 d. 0.44 e. 2.72 f. 2.8216

12.5. a. 2.72 b. 5.1

12.6. $e^{-2}, 0.2e^{-2}, 0.42e^{-2}, 0.681333e^{-2}, 1.008067e^{-2}$

12.8. $r = \dfrac{\lambda}{-\log(1-c)}$, $p = 1 - c$

12.9. $\dfrac{3^{24}\,x^{23}\,e^{-3x}}{23!}$

12.10. Poisson with parameter λp

12.12. Compound Poisson with $\lambda = 8$, $p(1) = 0.05$, $p(2) = 0.15$, $p(3) = 0.425$, $p(4) = 0.375$

12.13. Compound Poisson with $\lambda = 14$, $p(-2) = 1/14$, $p(1) = 4/14$, $p(3) = 9/14$

12.14. $\Pr(N = n + 1) = \lambda\,\dfrac{\Pr(N = n)}{n + 1}$

12.16. a. 0.425 b. 0.3984 c. 0.184; no: $\Pr(N_1 = 1, N_2 = 1) \neq \Pr(N_1 = 1)\,\Pr(N_2 = 1)$

12.17.

$x/f(x)$	Compound Poisson	Compound Negative Binomial	Compound Binomial
0	0.011109	0.044194	0.001953
1	0.034993	0.069606	0.012305
2	0.070112	0.096827	0.039727
3	0.105111	0.108230	0.085805
4	0.130100	0.110967	0.137767
5	0.138723	0.104988	0.173661
	$E(N) = 4.5$	$E(N) = 4.5$	$E(N) = 4.5$
	$\text{Var}(N) = 4.5$	$\text{Var}(N) = 9$	$\text{Var}(N) = 2.25$

12.25. a. $\Phi(2) = 0.9772$ b. $G\left(\dfrac{44}{3} : \dfrac{256}{9}, \dfrac{8}{3}\right)$

12.26. b. i. $\dfrac{p_2}{\lambda[p_1(1 + \theta)]^2}$ ii. $\dfrac{p_2 + (q/p)p_1^2}{(rq/p)(p_1(1 + \theta))^2}$

12.28. a. α, $\dfrac{\beta}{\pi_i}$

Chapter 13

13.1. a. -1 b. $e^{-\tilde{R}(u+1)}$ c. $\log \dfrac{p}{q}$ d. $\left(\dfrac{q}{p}\right)^{u+1}$

13.3. $\dfrac{f(t - s)}{1 - F(t - s)}\,dt$

13.5. 0; γ

13.7. a. 3   b. 1

13.8. $\dfrac{10}{7 \log 2} - 1$

13.12. a. $\left(\dfrac{1}{2}\right)\left(\dfrac{p_2}{p_1}\right)$ b. $\left(\dfrac{1}{3}\right)\left(\dfrac{p_3}{p_1}\right)$ c. $\left(\dfrac{1}{3}\right)\left(\dfrac{p_3}{p_1}\right) - \left(\dfrac{1}{4}\right)\left(\dfrac{p_2}{p_1}\right)^2$

13.13. b. $E[L] = \left(\dfrac{1}{2}\right)\left(\dfrac{p_2}{\theta p_1}\right)$, $\text{Var}(L) = \left(\dfrac{1}{3}\right)\left(\dfrac{p_3}{\theta p_1}\right) + \left(\dfrac{1}{4}\right)\left(\dfrac{p_2}{\theta p_1}\right)^2$

13.14. $\dfrac{2\theta r}{1 + (1 + \theta)2r - e^{2r}}$

13.15. a. $\dfrac{2}{3}$ b. 2

13.16. $p_1 = \displaystyle\sum_{i=1}^{n} \dfrac{A_i}{\beta_i}$

13.17. a. $\dfrac{5}{27}$ b. $\dfrac{4}{5}$ c. $\dfrac{-17r + 54}{3(3 - r)(6 - r)}$

  d. $\left(\dfrac{4}{9}\right)\left(\dfrac{10 - 3r}{8 - 6r + r^2}\right) = \left(\dfrac{4}{9}\right)\left(\dfrac{2}{2 - r}\right) + \left(\dfrac{1}{9}\right)\left(\dfrac{4}{4 - r}\right)$

  e. $\psi(u) = \dfrac{4}{9}e^{-2u} + \dfrac{1}{9}e^{-4u}$ Check: $\psi(0) = \dfrac{5}{9} = \dfrac{1}{1 + \theta}$

13.18. a. $\dfrac{10}{3}$ b. 2   c. $\dfrac{9}{(3 - 5r)^2}$

  d. $\left(\dfrac{2}{3}\right)\left(\dfrac{0.12 - 0.1r}{0.24 - 1.1r + r^2}\right) = \dfrac{0.4(0.3)}{0.3 - r} - \dfrac{0.067(0.8)}{0.8 - r}$

  e. $\psi(u) = 0.4e^{-0.3u} - 0.067e^{-0.8u}$

13.19. a. $\xi = \dfrac{\theta}{1 + \theta}$, $E[L] = \left(\dfrac{1}{1 + \theta}\right)\left(\dfrac{\alpha}{\beta}\right)$, $E[L^2] = \dfrac{1}{1 + \theta}\left(\dfrac{\alpha^2}{\beta^2} + \dfrac{\alpha}{\beta^2}\right)$

  b. $\psi(u) = \dfrac{1}{1 + \theta}\,[1 - G(u{:}\alpha,\beta)]$

13.20. a. $\displaystyle\sum_{i=1}^{n} \left[\dfrac{A_i/\beta_i}{\displaystyle\sum_{j=1}^{n} (A_j/\beta_j)}\right] \beta_i e^{-\beta_i x}$

  b. $\dfrac{A_i/\beta_i}{\left[\displaystyle\sum_{i=1}^{n} (A_i/\beta_i)\right]}$, $i = 1, 2, \ldots, n$

c. $\displaystyle\sum_{i=1}^{n} \left[\frac{A_i/\beta_i}{\displaystyle\sum_{j=1}^{n} (A_j/\beta_j)} \right] \frac{1}{\beta_i}$

13.21. a. $\dfrac{21}{10} (e^{-3x} + e^{-7x})$

b. $\dfrac{29}{105}$

c. $\dfrac{1,009}{11,025}$

13.23. a. $fc, f\lambda, \psi(u, ft)$ b. $\dfrac{1}{\lambda}$

13.24. $\dfrac{10}{3}$

13.25. a. $\psi'(u) = \begin{cases} \dfrac{\lambda}{c}\, \psi(u) - \dfrac{\lambda}{c} & 0 \le u \le 1 \\[3mm] \dfrac{\lambda}{c}\, \psi(u) - \dfrac{\lambda}{c}\, \psi(u - 1) & u > 1 \end{cases}$

b. $\psi(u) = 1 - \left(1 - \dfrac{\lambda}{c} \right) e^{(\lambda/c)u} \quad 0 \le u \le 1$

Chapter 14

14.1. b. $b^2\, pq$
       c. $s = 0.233$

14.3. a. 31.35 days   b. $2.99848\ c$

14.4. a. 0.13022   b. 0.09823   c. 0.05683

14.5. a. $E[S] = 4.7$, $\text{Var}(S) = 16.40$

       b. $\lambda = 1.7$, $p(1) = \dfrac{7}{17}$, $p(4) = \dfrac{10}{17}$, 16.7

14.6. a. $\displaystyle\sum_{j=1}^{n} b_j\, \tilde{\lambda}_j,\ \sum_{j=1}^{n} b_j^2\, \tilde{\lambda}_j$ c. 167, 293

14.7. $\dfrac{q_i q_j}{\displaystyle\sum\sum_{k<l} q_k q_l}$

14.9. $\sigma\phi\left(\dfrac{d - \mu}{\sigma}\right) - (d - \mu)\left[1 - \Phi\left(\dfrac{d - \mu}{\sigma}\right)\right]$

14.10. a. $-[1 - F_S(x)]$ b. $f_S(x + 1)$

14.11. $f_S(x) = 2x \quad 0 < x < 1$

14.12.

x	$f_S(x)$	$F_S(x)$	$E[I_x]$
0	0.050	0.050	3.500
1	0.124	0.174	2.550
2	0.180	0.354	1.724

14.13. a. 0.3885 b. 0.985

14.14. $0.8\, E[I_d] - 0.8\, E[I_l]$ where $l = d + \dfrac{m}{0.8}$

14.15. 3.758

14.16. a. $\alpha = \dfrac{\theta}{\xi} - \dfrac{|\xi - \theta|}{\xi\sqrt{1 + \xi}}$ b. $\theta < \xi$ and $(1 + \theta)^2 < 1 + \xi$

14.17. a. $\alpha = \dfrac{2\theta}{\xi} - 1$ b. $\xi > 2\theta$

14.18. $\dfrac{\theta - \xi e^{-\beta}}{1 - e^{-\beta}}$, $1 + [(1 + \theta) - (1 + \xi)e^{-\beta}]r = \dfrac{1 - re^{-\beta(1-r)}}{1 - r}$

14.19. $\tilde{R} = \dfrac{1.25 - 2\alpha}{(1 - \alpha)^2}$, $\alpha = 0.25$

14.20. $H_d = \dfrac{1}{\alpha} \log \left\{ \Phi\left(\dfrac{d - \mu}{\sigma}\right) \right.$

$$\left. + \left[1 - \Phi\left(\dfrac{d - \mu}{\sigma} - \alpha\sigma\right)\right] \exp\left[\alpha(\mu - d) + \dfrac{\alpha^2\sigma^2}{2}\right] \right\}$$

Note: The answer of Exercise 14.9 is the limit of H_d when $\alpha \to 0$.

14.21. Inverse Gaussian distribution with parameters α and β.

14.23. a. $e^{-\delta t}\left\{ e^{tm + t\sigma^2/2}\left[1 - \Phi\left(\dfrac{\log d - (tm + t\sigma^2)}{\sqrt{t}\,\sigma}\right)\right] - d\left[1 - \Phi\left(\dfrac{\log d - tm}{\sqrt{t}\,\sigma}\right)\right]\right\}$

b. $m = \delta - \sigma^2/2$

c. $\Phi\left(\dfrac{-\log d + t\delta + t\sigma^2/2}{\sigma\sqrt{t}}\right) - de^{-\delta t}\,\Phi\left(\dfrac{-\log d + t\delta - t\sigma^2/2}{\sigma\sqrt{t}}\right)$

Chapter 15

15.1. a.

Savings Account	566.50	Reserve	485.44
		Surplus	81.06
	566.50		566.50

Premium Income	550.00
Interest Income	16.50
	566.50
Increase in Reserves	485.44
Net Income	81.06

b. $1 - \Psi(5.28) = 0.00000$

15.3. b. i. 7,425.56   ii. 183,833

c. i. 7,500   ii. 187,500

d. 7,425.56   e. 7,500   f. 0.171914

15.4. a. 288.41   b. 332.35

15.5. $$\frac{1{,}000\,\bar{A}_{[40]:\overline{25}|} + 4\,\ddot{a}_{[40]:\overline{25}|} + 8.5}{0.93\,\ddot{a}_{[40]:\overline{25}|} + 0.05\,{}_{10}E_{[40]}\,\ddot{a}_{[40]+10:\overline{15}|} - 0.35}$$

15.6. $$\frac{1{,}000\,\bar{A}_{x:\overline{n}|} + 2.5\,\ddot{a}_{x:\overline{n}|} + 2.5}{0.935}$$

15.7. $a = 1 + e_0 + e_2 + e_3,\qquad c = e_1 + de_0$

15.8. a. $\dfrac{\bar{P}(\bar{A}_x) + \alpha}{1 - p} + \dfrac{\theta}{1 - p}\dfrac{1}{b} = \pi + \dfrac{f}{b}$

b. $\dfrac{\bar{P}(\bar{A}_x) + \alpha}{1 - p} + \dfrac{\theta}{1 - p}\dfrac{1}{\mathrm{E}[B]} = \pi + \dfrac{f}{\mathrm{E}[B]}$

15.9. a. 200   b. 20   c. $\sqrt{200}$

15.10. a. 1st Year $a'b + 14.29$ where $a' = \dfrac{1{,}000\bar{A}_x + 0.5\ddot{a}_x + 2.5}{0.95\bar{a}_x - 0.25}$

Renewal Years $a'b + 2.63$

b. All Years $a'b + \dfrac{2.5\ddot{a}_x - 7.5}{0.95\ddot{a}_x - 0.25}$

15.12. $(G_2 - G_1)\displaystyle\sum_{k=0}^{9}(1 - c_K)l_{x+k}^{(\tau)}\dfrac{(1 + i)^{10-k}}{l_{x+10}^{(\tau)}}$

15.14. b. $\displaystyle\int_0^\infty (e^{-\delta'u} - e^{-\delta u})[b_{t+u}\,\mu_x(t + u) - \pi_{t+u}]\,{}_u p_{x+t}\,du$

Chapter 16

16.1. ${}_tW'_x \gtreqqless {}_tW_x$ according as $\dfrac{P'_{x+t}}{P_{x+t}} \gtreqqless \dfrac{P'_x}{P_x}$

16.2. $\dfrac{b}{2} + \left(\dfrac{b}{2} - 1\right)\dfrac{A^{1}_{x+t:\overline{n-t}|}}{{}_{n-t}E_{x+t}}$

16.3. a. $\dfrac{{}_{10}CV - L - (1 - L)\,\bar{A}^{1}_{40:\overline{10}|}}{{}_{10}E_{40}}$ b. $(1 - L)\,\bar{A}^{1}_{45:\overline{5}|} + E\,{}_5E_{45}$

16.4. ${}_{10}^{20}W_{40} = 0.5829$, ${}_{10}W_{40:\overline{20}|} = 0.6232$, proportional amount $= 0.5$

16.7. Whole life: $1 - \dfrac{P^a_x}{P_{x+k}}$, *n*-Payment life: $1 - \dfrac{{}_nP^a_x}{{}_{n-k}P_{x+k}}$,

n-Year endowment: $\dfrac{1 - P^a_{x:\overline{n}|}}{P_{x+k:\overline{n-k}|}}$

16.8. Whole life: $1 - \dfrac{P_{x+1}}{P_{x+k}}$,

n-Payment life: $1 - \dfrac{\beta^{CRVM}}{{}_{n-k}P_{x+k}}$

$$\text{where } \beta^{CRVM} = {}_nP_x + \frac{{}_{19}P_{x+1} - A^1_{x:\overline{1}|}}{\ddot{a}_{x:\overline{n}|}},$$

$$n\text{-Year endowment: } 1 - \frac{\beta^{CRVM}}{P_{x+k:\overline{n-k}|}}$$

$$\text{where } \beta^{CRVM} = P_{x:\overline{n}|} + \frac{{}_{19}P_{x+1} - A^1_{x:\overline{1}|}}{\ddot{a}_{x:\overline{n}|}}$$

16.9. c. $\bar{a}_x \, G \, e^{\delta t} + \bar{a}_{x+k+t} \, (\mu_{x+k+t} + \delta) - 1$

16.10. $(G_2 - G_1) \sum_{k=0}^{9} (1 - c_k) \, l^{(\tau)}_{x+k} \dfrac{(1 + i)^{10-k}}{l^{(\tau)}_{x+10}}$

16.13. b. $\left(\dfrac{1 + \hat{i}_{h+1}}{1 + i} \right)\left(\dfrac{p_{x+h}}{p'_{x+h}} \right)$

16.15. $\bar{\beta} = \dfrac{\bar{A}_x}{(\bar{I}\bar{a})_{x:\overline{m}|}/m + {}_{m|}\bar{A}_x}$

16.16. $\alpha^{Mod}_x = A^1_{x:\overline{1}|} + K_1 E_x, \; \beta^{Mod}_x = P_{x+1} - \dfrac{K}{\ddot{a}_{x+1}}$

16.23. a. $\beta = 0.03, \; \alpha = 0.01, \; \beta - \alpha < 0.05$ b. 0.28 d. 0.0867 e. 0.0278

16.24. $\alpha = \beta^{CRVM}_{x:\overline{20}|} - ({}_{19}P_{x+1} - A^1_{x:\overline{1}|}), \; \beta = \dfrac{P_{x:\overline{20}|} \, \ddot{a}_{x:\overline{15}|} - \alpha}{a_{x:\overline{14}|}}$

16.25. $T = \beta^{CRVM} - {}_{19}P_{x+1}$

Chapter 17

17.1. $\bar{a}_{\overline{n}|} + \displaystyle\int_n^{\infty} v^s \, {}_{s-n}p_x \, ds$

17.7. $\dfrac{\bar{A}^1_{x:\overline{15}|} - v^{20} \, {}_{15}q_x}{\delta} + \bar{a}_{\overline{5}|}(\bar{A}^1_{x:\overline{20}|} - \bar{A}^1_{x:\overline{15}|}), \text{ or}$

$\bar{a}_{\overline{20}|} - \bar{a}_{x:\overline{20}|} + v^{20} \, {}_{15}p_x \, \bar{a}_{x+15:\overline{5}|} - v^{20} \, {}_{20}p_x \, \bar{a}_{\overline{5}|}$

17.8. $\dfrac{[1{,}000 \, A^1_{x:\overline{20}|} + 120(a^{(12)}_{\overline{20}|} - a^{(12)}_{x:\overline{20}|})]}{\ddot{a}_{x:\overline{20}|}}$

17.10. a.

$$Z = \begin{cases} v^T \, \bar{a}_{\overline{25-T}|} & T \le 15 \\ v^T \, \bar{a}_{\overline{10}|} & 15 < T \le 25 \\ v^{25} \, \bar{a}_{\overline{10}|} & 25 < T \le 35 \\ v^{25} \, \bar{a}_{\overline{T-25}|} & T > 35 \end{cases}$$

b. $\displaystyle\int_0^{15} v^t \, \bar{a}_{\overline{25-t}|} \, {}_tp_{40} \, \mu_{40}(t) \, dt + \bar{a}_{\overline{10}|} \int_{15}^{25} v^t \, {}_tp_{40} \, \mu_{40}(t) \, dt$

$\qquad + v^{25} \, \bar{a}_{\overline{10}|} \displaystyle\int_{25}^{35} {}_tp_{40} \, \mu_{40}(t) \, dt + v^{25} \int_{35}^{\infty} \bar{a}_{\overline{t-25}|} \, {}_tp_{40} \, \mu_{40}(t) \, dt$

17.15. 203,421

17.16. a. 55   b. 53,759.04

17.18. c. as $\delta \to 0 \quad \mu^{(3)}$
      as $\delta \to \infty \quad \mu^{(3)}/4$

Chapter 18

18.1. a. Either 2 or 4 of w, x, y, z survive to time t
       b. Either 1 or 3 of w, x, y, z survive to time t

18.3. a. 6.5   b. 3,236.71

18.4. ${}_tD_3 - 3\,{}_tD_4$ where ${}_tD_3 = {}_tp_{wxy} + {}_tp_{wxz} + {}_tp_{wyz} + {}_tp_{xyz}$ and ${}_tD_4 = {}_tp_{wxyz}$

18.5. $a_w - (a_{wxy} + a_{wxz} + a_{wyz}) + 2a_{wxyz}$

18.6. 0.624010

18.7. a. $15(\bar{a}_x + \bar{a}_y + \bar{a}_z) - 10(\bar{a}_{xy} + \bar{a}_{xz} + \bar{a}_{yz}) + 9\bar{a}_{xyz}$
       b. $15\bar{a}_x - 5(\bar{a}_{xy} + \bar{a}_{xz}) + 3\bar{a}_{xyz}$

18.8. 4.6

18.9. a. $12{,}000\,(a^{(12)}_{40:\overline{25}|} + a^{(12)}_{35:\overline{25}|} - 2a^{(12)}_{40:35:\overline{25}|})$
       b. $12{,}000\,(a^{(12)}_{40:\overline{25}|} + a^{(12)}_{35:\overline{30}|} - a^{(12)}_{40:35:\overline{25}|})$

18.10. a. $\bar{a}_x + \bar{a}_y + \bar{a}_{\overline{n}|} - \bar{a}_{y:\overline{n}|} - \bar{a}_{xy} - \bar{a}_{x:\overline{n}|} + \bar{a}_{xy:\overline{n}|}$
       b. $\bar{a}_{\overline{30}|} + \bar{a}_{25:\overline{40}|} - \bar{a}_{25:\overline{30}|}$

18.11. a. $\dfrac{1}{7}$ b. $\dfrac{26}{105}$ c. $\dfrac{64}{105}$

18.12. a. I is false. Change right-hand side to $\bar{A}^4_{wxyz} + \bar{A}_{w}{}^4_{xyz} + \bar{A}_{wx}{}^4_{yz} + \bar{A}_{wxy}{}^4_{z}$.
       b. II is true.
       c. III is false. Change right-hand side to $\bar{A}_{w}{}^1_{z} + \bar{A}_{x}{}^1_{z} + \bar{A}_{y}{}^1_{z} - 2(\bar{A}_{wx}{}^1_{z} + \bar{A}_{wy}{}^1_{z} + \bar{A}_{xy}{}^1_{z}) + 3\bar{A}_{wxy}{}^1_{z}$.

18.13. $\displaystyle\int_0^\infty v^t \,{}_tp_{xy}\,\mu_y(t)\,t\,\bar{A}_{x+t}\,dt$

18.14. a. $\dfrac{5}{7}$ b. $\dfrac{3}{7}$

18.15. $A_{z:\overline{10}|}^{\,1}\,(A_{y:z+10}^{\,1} - A_{xy:z+10}^{\,1}) - A_{yz:\overline{10}|}^{\,1}\,(A_{y+10:z+10}^{\,1} - A_{xy+10:z+10}^{\,1})$

18.16. $v^{10}(\bar{A}_{xy}^{1} + \bar{A}_{xz}^{1} - \bar{A}_{xyz}^{1}) - A_{y:\overline{10}|}^{1}\,\bar{A}_{x:y+10}^{1} - A_{z:\overline{10}|}^{1}\,\bar{A}_{x:z+10}^{1}$
       $+ A_{yz:\overline{10}|}^{1}\,\bar{A}_{x:y+10:z+10}^{1}$

18.17. $(\bar{A}_{30:\overline{5}|}^{1} + A_{30:\overline{5}|}^{\,1}\,\bar{A}_{35:60}^{1})\Big/\left(\dfrac{1}{1.075} - A_{30:\overline{5}|}^{\,1}\,\bar{A}_{35:60}^{1}\right)$

18.20. a. $\displaystyle\int_0^\infty (1 - {}_tp_w)\,{}_tp_x\,\mu_x(t)\,{}_tp_{yz}\,dt$ b. ${}_tq^1_{xyz} - {}_\infty q^1_{wxyz}$

18.22. a. $\dfrac{25}{72}$ b. $\dfrac{19}{36}$ c. $\dfrac{5}{8}$

18.23. 0.07

18.24. a. 0.3 b. 0.2 c. $\dfrac{1}{30}$

18.25. $\displaystyle\int_{10}^{15} (1 - {}_{t-10}p_x)\ {}_tp_y\ \mu_y(t)\ ({}_{t+10}p_z - {}_{25}p_z)\ dt$

18.26. $\displaystyle\int_{0}^{30} (1 - {}_tp_{10})\ {}_tp_{20}\ \mu_{20}(t)({}_tp_{30} - {}_{30}p_{30})\ dt$

$\displaystyle\qquad + \int_{0}^{30} (1 - {}_tp_{30})\ {}_tp_{20}\ \mu_{20}(t)\ ({}_tp_{10} - {}_{50}p_{10})\ dt$

$\displaystyle\qquad + \int_{30}^{40} (1 - {}_{30}p_{30})\ {}_tp_{20}\ \mu_{20}(t)({}_tp_{10} - {}_{50}p_{10})\ dt$

18.27. 0.2145

18.28. 0.2704

18.29. I. False. Insurance factor should be $\bar{A}^{\,1}_{y+t:z+t}$.
II True
III True

18.30. a. $\bar{a}_{\overline{10|}} - \bar{a}_{x:\overline{10|}} + v^{10}\ \bar{a}_y - v^{10}\ {}_{10}p_x\ \bar{a}_{x+10:y}$
b. $\bar{a}_{\overline{10|}}\ \bar{A}^1_{xy} + v^{10}\ \bar{a}_y - v^{10}\ \bar{a}_{xy}$

18.31. $G = \left[\dfrac{2}{3}\,(\ddot{a}_{x|y} + {}_{n|}\ddot{a}_x) + \dfrac{1}{3}\,{}_{n|}\ddot{a}_{xy} \right] \Big/ (0.92 - {}_nA^2_{xy})$

18.33. $\dfrac{\bar{A}_{x+n:\overset{1}{y}}}{\check{s}_{x:\overline{n|}} + \ddot{a}_{x:y+n}}$

18.34. $\ddot{a}_{xyz}$

18.35. b. $\ddot{a}_{\overline{xy}:\overline{m|}} + v^m\ {}_np_x\ (1 - {}_mp_y)\ \ddot{a}_{x+m:\overline{n-m|}}$

18.37. Insurance payable at the moment of z's death, if the deaths have occurred in the order x, y, z and only if the death of z is less than 10 years after the death of y.

Chapter 19

19.1. a. 45 b. 2 c. 2

19.2. $2{,}500\ \sqrt{2} + \dfrac{10{,}000}{\pi}$

19.3. $10{,}000 \left[e^{-1/4} - e^{-1/2} - \left(\dfrac{e^{-1}}{4} \right) \right]$

19.4. $100^2\ [e^{-51/100} - e^{-50/100} + e^{-28/100} - e^{-27/100}] + 100\ [e^{-1/4} + e^{-53/100}]$

19.5. $T_{20} - T_{40} - 20l_{70}$

19.6. $\displaystyle\int_{20}^{50} l(x, -x)\ dx - \int_{70}^{80} l(x, 50 - x)\ dx - \int_{30}^{50} l(80, t - 80)\ dt$

19.8. $b\,\dfrac{\sqrt{2\pi}}{\sqrt{a}} \left[1 - \Phi\left(\dfrac{R}{\sqrt{a}} \right) \right] \exp\left(Rt + \dfrac{R^2}{2a} \right)$

19.9. $a + \dfrac{(\bar{I}\bar{a})'_{a:\overline{r-a}|}}{\bar{a}'_{a:\overline{r-a}|}}$, $\displaystyle\int_a^r xl_x\,\dfrac{dx}{T_a - T_r}$

19.11. a. $e^{-Rx}\,s(x)(R + \mu_x)$, $1 - e^{-Rx}\,s(x)$

19.15. 0.02

19.17. a. $[\Gamma(\alpha)]^{1/a} - \beta$ b. stationary

19.18. b. a c. $\dfrac{\log b}{c}$

Chapter 20

20.1. $(T_a - T_r)w$

20.2. $ne^{R(t+a)+\tau t}\displaystyle\int_a^r e^{-Ry}\,s(y)\,w(y)\,dy$

20.3. b. $n(t - r + a)s(r)\,\bar{a}_r^h\left(\dfrac{f}{b}\right)\displaystyle\int_0^b w(r - y)e^{\tau(t-y)}\,dy$

   c. ${}^T P_{t+u} = ne^{R(t+u-r+a)}\,s(r)\,\bar{a}_r'\left(\dfrac{f}{b}\right)\displaystyle\int_0^b w(r - y)\,e^{\tau(t+u-y)}\,dy$

   $= e^{\rho u}\,{}^T P_t$

20.4. a. $c(r - a)w(r)\,e^{\tau t}\,n(t - r + a)s(r)\,\bar{a}_h^r$

   b. ${}^T P_{t+u} = c(r - a)\,w(r)\,e^{\tau(t+u)}\,n\,e^{R(t-r+a)}\,s(r)\,\bar{a}_r' = e^{\rho u}\,{}^T P_t$

20.5. $e^{\rho t}\,e^{-(R+\mu)(r-a)}\,fw(r)\,\bar{a}_r'$

20.6. a. $\dfrac{1}{0.06} - \dfrac{1 - e^{-6+0.06x}}{(100 - x)(0.06)^2}\qquad 25 < x < 100$
   $\bar{a}_{65}^h = 9.7020$

   b. $3{,}056.14\,e^{0.02t}\quad 0 \le t$
   $0 \qquad\qquad t < 0$

20.8. a. $34{,}175.71\,e^{0.02t}\qquad 0 \le t$
   b. $4{,}423.17\,e^{0.02t}\qquad 0 \le t$

20.9. $M(x) = \begin{cases} 0 & x < r \\ 1 & x \ge r \end{cases}$

20.10. $fw(r)\,\bar{a}_r'\,e^{-(R+\mu)(r-a)}\,e^{\rho t}\,\dfrac{\bar{a}_{\overline{r-a}|\theta}}{r - a}$ where $\theta = \delta - \rho$

20.14. a. $P_t = \exp(-\delta[r - X(\delta)])\,{}^T P_t$,
   $(aV)_t = {}^T P_t\,\bar{a}_{\overline{r-X(\delta)}|\delta} = P_t\,\bar{s}_{\overline{r-X(\delta)}|\delta}$

   b. $P_t = {}^T P_t\quad (aV)_t = {}^T P_t(r - \mu)$ where $\mu = \displaystyle\int_a^r xm(x)\,dx$

20.15. a. $\dfrac{fw(r)\,e^{(\tau-\delta)r}\,s(r)\,\bar{a}_r^h}{\displaystyle\int_a^r w(y)\,e^{(\tau-\delta)y}\,s(y)\,dy}$

   b. $\dfrac{e^{-(\delta-\tau)x}\,s(x)\,w(x)}{\displaystyle\int_a^r e^{-(\delta-\tau)y}\,s(y)\,w(y)\,dy}$

20.20. a. $60,977.92\ e^{0.02t}$

   b. $M(x) = \dfrac{x - 25}{40}$, $m(x) = \dfrac{1}{40}$

       i. $38,292.33\ e^{0.02t}$

       ii. $1,524.45\ e^{0.02t}$

   c. $M(x) = \dfrac{e^{-1} - e^{-0.04x}}{e^{-1} - e^{-2.6}}$, $\quad m(x) = \dfrac{0.04e^{-0.04x}}{e^{-1} - e^{-2.6}}$

       i. $45,479.00\ e^{0.02t}$

       ii. $1,236.88\ e^{0.02t}$

20.21. $\dfrac{d}{dt}\,(aF)_t = \left[\dfrac{(aV)_0}{\bar{a}_{\overline{15|}}} + P_t\right] + \delta(aF)_t - {}^{T}P_t \qquad 0 \le t < 15$

Initial condition $(aF)_0 = 0$

$$\dfrac{d}{dt}\,(aF)_t = P_t + \delta(aF)_t - {}^{T}P_t \qquad 15 \le t$$

Initial condition $(aF)_{15} = (aV)_{15}$

   a. $26,234.75\ e^{0.06t} + 38,292.33\ e^{0.02t} - 64,527.08 \qquad 0 \le t < 15,$
      $38,292.33\ e^{0.02t} \qquad 15 \le t$

   b. $31,158.47\ e^{0.06t} + 45,479.00\ e^{0.02t} - 76,637.48 \qquad 0 \le t < 15,$
      $45,479.00\ e^{0.02t} \qquad 15 \le t$

20.23. a. $\bar{a}_{\overline{X(\theta)-a|}\theta}$ b. $\mu - a$ where $\mu = \displaystyle\int_a^r x\,m(x)\,dx$

20.25. a. $21,000.00\ e^{0.02t}$

   b. $263,122.29\ e^{0.02t}$

Chapter 21

21.1.   0.000382

21.2.   0.001154

21.3.   a. $\dfrac{1}{10}$ b. $\dfrac{1}{132}$

21.4.   a. $e^{-n(\delta-\sigma^2/2)}$ b. $e^{-jn(\delta-j\sigma^2/2)}$

   c. i. $\displaystyle\sum_{k=0}^{\infty} e^{-j(k+1)(\delta-j\sigma^2/2)}\ {}_k p_x\ q_{x+k} = {}_*^{j}A_x$

       ii. ${}_*^{2}A_x - ({}_*A_x)^2$

21.5.   a. $0.10,\ \dfrac{2}{1,200}$ b. $f_z(z) = \begin{cases} 100\,z & 0 < z < 0.1 \\ 20 - 100\,z & 0.1 < z < 0.2 \\ 0 & \text{elsewhere} \end{cases}$

   c. $f_y(y) = \begin{cases} 100\,\log y/y & 1 < y < e^{0.1} \\ (20 - 100\,\log y)/y & e^{0.1} < y < e^{0.2} \\ 0 & \text{elsewhere} \end{cases}$

21.7.   a. δ b. $k\sigma^2$ c. $\log(1 + I_k) \sim N(\delta, k\sigma^2)$

21.8. a. $-n\delta, \dfrac{n(n+1)(2n+1)}{6}\sigma^2$ b. $\log(\tilde{v}_n) \sim N\left[-n\delta, \dfrac{n(n+1)(2n+1)}{6}\sigma^2\right]$

   c. $e^{-n(\delta-[(n+1)(2n+1)/12]\sigma^2)}$, $e^{-2n(\delta-[(n+1)(2n+1)/12]\sigma^2)}(e^{[n(n+1)(2n+1)/6]\sigma^2}-1)$

   d. $\tilde{v}_n \sim \text{lognormal}\left(-n\delta, \dfrac{n(n+1)(2n+1)}{6}\sigma^2\right)$

21.9. a. r b. $n\sigma^2$ c. $\log I_n \sim N(r, n\delta^2)$

21.10. $e^{r+(n\sigma^2/2)}$, $e^{2r+n\sigma^2}(e^{(n\sigma^2/2)}-1)$

21.17. 0.050000, 0.054866, 0.059611

21.22. b. $l_x(c^*\bar{a}_x - \theta\bar{A}_x)$

   c. $-l_x[(\bar{I}\bar{A})_x + c(I^*\bar{a})_x - \bar{P}(\bar{A}_x)(1+\theta)(\bar{I}\bar{a})_x]$

   where $^*\bar{a}_x$ is valued at $^*\delta = \delta + r$

Index

Interest rate
  bond equivalent yield, 658
  dependent, 649
  deterministic scenarios, 638
  forward rate, 656
  independent, 643
  inverted yield curve, 658
  one-period, 637
  par yield, 657
  random scenarios, 641
  spot rate, 656
  term structure, 656
  yield curve, 658
International Actuarial Notation (IAN), 53, A4
Interpolation
  exponential, 74
  harmonic, 74
  linear, 74, 239
Intrinsic rate of population growth, 602

Jensen's inequalities, 9, 21, 637

Law of mortality
  De Moivre, 78
  Gompertz, 78, 287, 295, 569
  Makeham, 78, 288, 296
  Weibull, 78
Law of uniform seniority, 302
Lexis diagram, 585
Life-age-x, 52
Life estate, 147
Life expectancy (see expectation of life)
Life table, 51
Life Table for the Total Population: United
  States, 1979–81, 60
Limited expected value function
  (see also expectation of life, temporary
  complete), 86
Limiting age, 63
Loading, 7, 536
Loss variable (see random variable, loss)

Maximal aggregate loss, 417, 447
  expected value, 422, 432, 452, 457
Method
  double integral, 590
  experience premium, 531
  in-and-out, 589
  modified reserve (see modified reserve)
  natural premiums and reserves, 508
  of inclusion and exclusion, 268, 576
Mode, 69
Model
  autoregressive, 659
  closed, 28
  collective risk, 367, 441
  dependent lifetimes, 274
  double decrement, 347, 512
  individual risk, 27
  moving average, 649
  multiple decrement, 341
  multiplicative, 670
  open, 28
  proportional hazard, 89
  random walk, 660, 669
  single decrement, 346

Modified reserve
  Commissioner's valuation method (CRVM),
    522
  full preliminary term (FPT), 519
  modified preliminary term, 522
  two-year preliminary term, 533
Mortality
  annual rate of, 67
  central rate of, 70, 321
  force of, 55
  n-year rate of, 67
Mortality table
  aggregate, 81
  select, 81
  select-and-ultimate, 81
  ultimate, 81
Multiple decrement table, 317
Multiplicative model, 670

National Association of Insurance
    Commissioners, 501, 529
  Actuarial Guideline XVII, 526
Net amount at risk, 236
Nonforfeiture benefit, 347, 500
  cash value, 486, 500
  extended insurance, 504
  minimum cash value, 526
  paid-up insurance, 502
Nonidentifiability, 265, 327
Normal cost rate, 609, 616
Normal power expansion, 46

Operational time, 434
Order statistic
  largest, 268
  smallest, 263

Penalty, 427
Pension plan
  benefits based on salary, 352
  defined benefit, 351, 354, 609
  defined contribution, 356, 609
  general model, 608
Policies, 7
Policy fee, 481
Policy loan clause, 502
Population
  stable, 594
  stationary, 593
Premium, 7
  adjusted, 472, 501
  annual, 180
  apportionable, 191
  benefit, 169, 573
  continuous, 170
  contract, 167, 536
  expense-loaded, 467, 508
  experience, 531
  exponential, 169
  natural, 508
  net, 7
  net stop-loss, 445
  percentile, 169, 174
  pure, 7